Free Online Access!

Plunkett's Retail Industry Almanac 2016

Your purchase includes access to Book Data and Exports online

As a book purchaser, you can register for free, 1-year, 1-seat online access to the latest data for your book's industry trends, statistics and company profiles. This includes tools to export company data. Simply send us this registration form, and we will send you a user name and password. In this manner, you will have access to our continual updates during the year. Certain restrictions apply.

_____ YES, please register me for free online access. I am the actual, original purchaser. (Proof of purchase may be required.)

Customer Name _____

Title_____

Organization _____

Address _____

City_____State_____Zip_____

Country (if other than USA) _____

Phone_____Fax _____

E-mail _____

Return to: ## Plunkett Research®, Ltd.

Attn: Registration
P.O. Drawer 541737, Houston, TX 77254-1737 USA
713.932.0000 · Fax 713.932.7080 · www.plunkettresearch.com
customersupport@plunkettresearch.com

* Purchasers of used books are not eligible to register. Use of online access is subject to the terms of the end user license agreement.

PLUNKETT'S RETAIL INDUSTRY ALMANAC 2016

The only comprehensive
guide to the retail industry

Jack W. Plunkett

Published by:
Plunkett Research®, Ltd., Houston, Texas
www.plunkettresearch.com

PLUNKETT'S RETAIL INDUSTRY ALMANAC 2016

Editor and Publisher:
Jack W. Plunkett

Executive Editor and Database Manager:
Martha Burgher Plunkett

Senior Editors and Researcher:
Isaac Snider

Editors, Researchers and Assistants:
Allan Butler
Anushree Gogate
Gina Sprenkel
Suzanne Zarosky
Shuang Zhou

E-Commerce & Enterprise Accounts Managers:
Jillian Claire Lim
Jessica Whipple

Information Technology Manager:
Seifelnaser Hamed

Video Production:
Zondra Victor

Special Thanks to:
U.S. Bureau of Economic Analysis
U.S. Bureau of Labor Statistics
U.S. Census Bureau
U.S. International Trade Administration

Plunkett Research®, Ltd.
P. O. Drawer 541737, Houston, Texas 77254 USA
Phone: 713.932.0000   Fax: 713.932.7080
www.plunkettresearch.com

Plunkett Research®, Ltd.
P. O. Drawer 541737
Houston, Texas 77254-1737
Phone: 713.932.0000, Fax: 713.932.7080 www.plunkettresearch.com

<u>ISBN13 #</u> 978-1-62831-382-6 (eBook Edition # 978-1-62831-701-5)

Business
Ref.
658.89
Plunkett
2016

Limited Warranty and Terms of Use:

PLUNKETT'S RETAIL INDUSTRY ALMANAC 2016

CONTENTS

Continued on next page

INTRODUCTION

PLUNKETT'S RETAIL INDUSTRY ALMANAC, the fifteenth edition of our guide to the retail field, is designed to be used as a general source for researchers of all types.

The data and areas of interest covered are intentionally broad, ranging from the various aspects of the retail industry, to emerging technology, to an in-depth look at the major firms (which we call "THE RETAIL 500") within the many segments that make up the retail system.

This reference book is designed to be a general source for researchers. It is especially intended to assist with market research, strategic planning, employment searches, contact or prospect list creation and financial research, and as a data resource for executives and students of all types.

PLUNKETT'S RETAIL INDUSTRY ALMANAC takes a rounded approach for the general reader. This book presents a complete overview of the retail field (see "How To Use This Book"). For example, the impact of the Internet upon retail sales is discussed in detail, along with easy to use tables on all facets of retail in general.

THE RETAIL 500 is our unique grouping of the biggest, most successful corporations in all segments of the retail industry. Tens of thousands of pieces of information, gathered from a wide variety of sources, have been researched and are presented in a unique form that can be easily understood. This section includes thorough indexes to THE RETAIL 500, by geography, industry, sales, brand names, subsidiary names and many other topics. (See Chapter 4.)

Especially helpful is the way in which PLUNKETT'S RETAIL INDUSTRY ALMANAC enables readers who have no business background to readily compare the financial records and growth plans of retail companies and major industry groups. You'll see the mid-term financial record of each firm, along with the impact of earnings, sales and strategic plans on each company's potential to fuel growth, serve new markets, and provide investment and employment opportunities.

No other source provides this book's easy-to-understand comparisons of growth, expenditures, technologies, corporations and many other items of great importance to people of all types who may be studying this, one of the largest industries in the world today.

By scanning the data groups and the unique indexes, you can find the best information to fit your personal research needs. The major companies in retail are profiled and then compared using several different groups of specific criteria. Which firms are the biggest employers? Which companies earn the most profits? These things and much more are easy to find.

In addition to individual company profiles, an overview of retail technology and trends is provided. This book's job is to help you sort through easy-to-understand summaries of today's trends in a quick and effective manner.

Whatever your purpose for researching the retail field, you'll find this book to be a valuable guide. Nonetheless, as is true with all resources, this volume has limitations that the reader should be aware of:

- Financial data and other corporate information can change quickly. A book of this type can be no more current than the data that was available as of the time of editing. Consequently, the financial picture, management and ownership of the firm(s) you are studying may have changed since the date of this book. For example, this almanac includes the most up-to-date sales figures and profits available to the editors as of late-2015. That means that we have typically used corporate financial data as of the end of 2014.

- Corporate mergers, acquisitions and downsizing are occurring at a very rapid rate. Such events may have created significant change, subsequent to the publishing of this book, within a company you are studying.

- Some of the companies in THE RETAIL 500 are so large in scope and in variety of business endeavors conducted within a parent organization, that we have been unable to completely list all subsidiaries, affiliations, divisions and activities within a firm's corporate structure.

- This volume is intended to be a general guide to a vast industry. That means that researchers should look to this book for an overview and, when conducting in-depth research, should contact the specific corporations or industry associations in question for the very latest changes and data. Where possible, we have listed contact names, toll-free telephone numbers and Internet site addresses for the companies, government agencies and industry associations involved so that the reader may get further details without unnecessary delay.

- Tables of industry data and statistics used in this book include the latest numbers available at the time of printing, generally through the end of 2014. In a few cases, the only complete data available was for earlier years.

- We have used exhaustive efforts to locate and fairly present accurate and complete data. However, when using this book or any other source for business and industry information, the reader should use caution and diligence by conducting further research where it seems appropriate. We wish you success in your endeavors, and we trust that your experience with this book will be both satisfactory and productive.

Jack W. Plunkett
Houston, Texas
December 2015

HOW TO USE THIS BOOK

The two primary sections of this book are devoted first to the retail industry as a whole and then to the "Individual Data Listings" for THE RETAIL 500. If time permits, you should begin your research in the front chapters of this book. Also, you will find lengthy indexes in Chapter 4 and in the back of the book.

📽 Video Tip
For our brief video introduction to the Retail industry, see www.plunkettresearch.com/video/retail.

THE RETAIL INDUSTRY

Chapter 1: Major Trends Affecting the Retail Industry.
This chapter presents an encapsulated view of the major trends that are creating rapid changes in the retail industry today.

Chapter 2: Retail Industry Statistics.
This chapter presents in-depth statistics ranging from an industry overview to e-commerce numbers to average household expenditures and much more.

Chapter 3: Important Retail Industry Contacts – Addresses, Telephone Numbers and Internet Sites.
This chapter covers contacts for important government agencies, retail organizations and trade groups. Included are numerous important Internet sites.

THE RETAIL 500

Chapter 4: THE RETAIL 500: Who They Are and How They Were Chosen.
The companies compared in this book (the actual count is 484) were carefully selected from the retail industry, largely in the United States. 135 of the firms are based outside the U.S. For a complete description, see THE RETAIL 500 indexes in this chapter.

Individual Data Listings:
Look at one of the companies in THE RETAIL 500's Individual Data Listings. You'll find the following information fields:

Company Name:
The company profiles are in alphabetical order by company name. If you don't find the company you are seeking, it may be a subsidiary or division of one of the firms covered in this book. Try looking it up in the Index by Subsidiaries, Brand Names and Selected Affiliations in the back of the book.

Industry Code:

Industry Group Code: An NAIC code used to group companies within like segments.

Types of Business:

A listing of the primary types of business specialties conducted by the firm.

Brands/Divisions/Affiliations:

Major brand names, operating divisions or subsidiaries of the firm, as well as major corporate affiliations—such as another firm that owns a significant portion of the company's stock. A complete Index by Subsidiaries, Brand Names and Selected Affiliations is in the back of the book.

Contacts:

The names and titles up to 27 top officers of the company are listed, including human resources contacts.

Growth Plans/ Special Features:

Listed here are observations regarding the firm's strategy, hiring plans, plans for growth and product development, along with general information regarding a company's business and prospects.

Financial Data:

Revenue (2015 or the latest fiscal year available to the editors, plus up to five previous years): This figure represents consolidated worldwide sales from all operations. These numbers may be estimates.

R&D Expense (2015 or the latest fiscal year available to the editors, plus up to five previous years): This figure represents expenses associated with the research and development of a company's goods or services. These numbers may be estimates.

Operating Income (2015 or the latest fiscal year available to the editors, plus up to five previous years): This figure represents the amount of profit realized from annual operations after deducting operating expenses including costs of goods sold, wages and depreciation. These numbers may be estimates.

Operating Margin % (2015 or the latest fiscal year available to the editors, plus up to five previous years): This figure is a ratio derived by dividing operating income by net revenues. It is a measurement of a firm's pricing strategy and operating efficiency. These numbers may be estimates.

SGA Expense (2015 or the latest fiscal year available to the editors, plus up to five previous years): This figure represents the sum of selling, general and administrative expenses of a company, including costs such as warranty, advertising,

interest, personnel, utilities, office space rent, etc. These numbers may be estimates.

Net Income (2015 or the latest fiscal year available to the editors, plus up to five previous years): This figure represents consolidated, after-tax net profit from all operations. These numbers may be estimates.

Operating Cash Flow (2015 or the latest fiscal year available to the editors, plus up to five previous years): This figure is a measure of the amount of cash generated by a firm's normal business operations. It is calculated as net income before depreciation and after income taxes, adjusted for working capital. It is a prime indicator of a company's ability to generate enough cash to pay its bills. These numbers may be estimates.

Capital Expenditure (2015 or the latest fiscal year available to the editors, plus up to five previous years): This figure represents funds used for investment in or improvement of physical assets such as offices, equipment or factories and the purchase or creation of new facilities and/or equipment. These numbers may be estimates.

EBITDA (2015 or the latest fiscal year available to the editors, plus up to five previous years): This figure is an acronym for earnings before interest, taxes, depreciation and amortization. It represents a company's financial performance calculated as revenue minus expenses (excluding taxes, depreciation and interest), and is a prime indicator of profitability. These numbers may be estimates.

Return on Assets % (2015 or the latest fiscal year available to the editors, plus up to five previous years): This figure is an indicator of the profitability of a company relative to its total assets. It is calculated by dividing annual net earnings by total assets. These numbers may be estimates.

Return on Equity % (2015 or the latest fiscal year available to the editors, plus up to five previous years): This figure is a measurement of net income as a percentage of shareholders' equity. It is also called the rate of return on the ownership interest. It is a vital indicator of the quality of a company's operations. These numbers may be estimates.

Debt to Equity (2015 or the latest fiscal year available to the editors, plus up to five previous years): A ratio of the company's long-term debt to its shareholders' equity. This is an indicator of the overall financial leverage of the firm. These numbers may be estimates.

Address:

The firm's full headquarters address, the headquarters telephone, plus toll-free and fax numbers where available. Also provided is the World Wide Web site address.

Stock Ticker, Exchange: When available, the unique stock market symbol used to identify this firm's common stock for trading and tracking purposes is indicated. Where appropriate, this field may contain "private" or "subsidiary" rather than a ticker symbol. If the firm is a publicly-held company headquartered outside of the U.S., its international ticker and exchange are given.

Total Number of Employees: The approximate total number of employees, worldwide, as of 2015 (or the latest data available to the editors).

Parent Company: If the firm is a subsidiary, its parent company is listed.

Salaries/Bonuses:

(The following descriptions generally apply to U.S. employers only.)

Highest Executive Salary: The highest executive salary paid, typically a 2015 amount (or the latest year available to the editors) and typically paid to the Chief Executive Officer.

Highest Executive Bonus: The apparent bonus, if any, paid to the above person.

Second Highest Executive Salary: The next-highest executive salary paid, typically a 2015 amount (or the latest year available to the editors) and typically paid to the President or Chief Operating Officer.

Second Highest Executive Bonus: The apparent bonus, if any, paid to the above person.

Other Thoughts:

Estimated Female Officers or Directors: It is difficult to obtain this information on an exact basis, and employers generally do not disclose the data in a public way. However, we have indicated what our best efforts reveal to be the apparent number of women who either are in the posts of corporate officers or sit on the board of directors. There is a wide variance from company to company.

Hot Spot for Advancement for Women/Minorities: A "Y" in appropriate fields indicates "Yes." These are firms that appear either to have posted a substantial number of women and/or minorities to high posts or that appear to have a good record of going out of their way to recruit, train, promote and retain women or minorities. (See the Index of Hot Spots For Women and Minorities in the back of the book.) This information may change frequently and can be difficult to obtain and verify. Consequently, the reader should use caution and conduct further investigation where appropriate.

Glossary: A short list of retail industry terms.

Chapter 1

MAJOR TRENDS AFFECTING THE RETAIL INDUSTRY

Major Trends Affecting the Retail Industry:

1) Introduction to the Retail Industry
2) Wal-Mart Still Dominates, but Faces Slowing Revenue Growth
3) Department Stores Reposition for Today's Consumer While Outlet Stores Proliferate
4) Warehouse Clubs and Discount Department Stores Battle for Market Share
5) Private Label Brands Grow in Share of Total Store Sales
6) Diverse Selling Techniques Boost Direct Marketers and Non-Store Sales
7) Apple Sets the Bar for Showcase Stores and Super-Merchandisers
8) For the Long-Term in the U.S., Consumers Increase Savings/Less Inclined to Use Debt
9) Bricks, Clicks and Catalogs Create Synergies While Online Sales Growth Surges
10) Retail Technologies Advance for Store Checkout and Restaurant Orders/Apps and Location-Based Ads Drive Sales
11) RFID Drives Inventory Management Evolution
12) Advanced Vending Machines Enable Retailers to Set up Mini-Stores at Airports
13) Smartphones and Financial Technology ("FinTech") Enable New Mobile Payment Methods
14) Near Field Communications (NFC) Changes Credit and Debit Cards
15) Self-Service Apparel Fitting Technologies Grow in Stores and Online
16) Retailers Look for Long-Term Growth in Emerging Markets, Including China, India and Brazil
17) Retail Center Occupancy Is High, with Sales Rising in Upscale Malls/Online Sales Hurt Stores
18) Entertainment-Based Retailing, including Power Towns
19) Malls Remodel to Boost Sales and Attract Shoppers/Store Visitor Counts Are Disappointing
20) Fast Fashion: Designers and Retailers Speed Up
21) Luxury Item Sales Growth Slows
22) LOHAS- Socially Conscious Consumers Create Challenges and Opportunities for Advertisers and Marketers
23) How to Interpret Reports of Retail Sales

1) Introduction to the Retail Industry

📹 Video Tip

For our brief video introduction to the Retail industry, see www.plunkettresearch.com/video/retail.

Retail, with nearly 15.7 million employees in America alone (more than one out of 10 workers), is one of the largest industries in the world. Retail sales in the U.S. totaled an estimated $5.318 trillion during 2015, according to Plunkett Research, up about 2% for the year, and up dramatically from only $4.0 trillion during 2009. Total sales were $5.208 trillion in 2014 according to the U.S Census Bureau. (Sales at stores selling general merchandise, apparel, furniture and specialty items, referred to as "GAFO," totaled $1.2 trillion in 2014. GAFO is an important distinction. In contrast, retail sales of all types are considered to include automobiles, gasoline and restaurants.)

Factors that will impact the retail sector during 2016 in the U.S., Europe and most Developed Nations:

- Surveys show that consumers are focused on increasing their savings and paying down debt. This means that a large number of consumers wait to purchase until they can pay cash. When consumers do borrow, today's low interest rates will be a great benefit.
- In the U.S., a significant improvement in the unemployment rate and an improving economy, as of late 2015, point to a reasonably good retail environment in 2016. Nonetheless, consumers will remain cautious.
- Consumers, as of late 2015, were less interested in buying clothing and more interested spending on travel, automobiles and home remodeling or repairs.
- Consumers will benefit greatly from reduced gasoline prices worldwide. For example, U.S. households that drive their cars substantial distances could enjoy reduced gasoline expenses of $500 to $1,500 or more yearly. At the same time, consumers in nations that rely greatly on oil exports will be hurt (e.g., Russia).

- High stock market values and recovering house prices had created a "wealth effect," as of late 2015, which improved consumer confidence.
- A continuing slow economy in much of Europe points to a tough time for retailers there. The former fast-growth markets of China, India and Brazil are likely to continue to face slower economic growth and difficult retail environments.
- Price-sensitive consumers will continue to be more conservative. When they do spend, they want to feel like they are buying merchandise that is fairly priced, if not a significant bargain.
- Retail purchases via e-commerce are growing at a very strong rate worldwide, as more consumers have access to fast Internet connections, and e-commerce firms enhance their product offerings and delivery options. Store-based retailers will face ever-greater competition from online sites, while traffic at retail malls will be disappointing.

Source: Plunkett Research, Ltd.

Competition among retailers has never been tougher. A retailer without a significant competitive advantage doesn't stand a chance. Superstores are battling each other on every major corner, while Internet marketers are stealing customers from stores. Some consumers are using stores as showrooms where they can touch and feel the merchandise, and then making their purchases at lower costs online at sites like Amazon.com. Online selling at deep discounts is even making inroads into major consumer purchases such as jewelry.

Growth in online shopping has been driven by two factors. First, the number of fast Internet connections in U.S. homes and businesses leapt to nearly 104 million by the end of 2015 (plus 266 million wireless Internet connections) which makes buying online faster and more interactive. Next, there's the savvy marketing of online giants like Amazon.com (with more than $89 billion in 2014 revenues, up from only $34 billion in 2010, one of the fastest growing companies in the world), as well as the e-commerce efforts of traditional retailers such as Home Depot and Wal-Mart. These fast Internet connections are extremely important, even at the office, since a large number of workers take time out to shop online from their desktops. Globally, the number of Internet users has passed 3.2 billion.

Analysts at eMarketer reported growth in American e-commerce sales from $304 billion in 2014 to $347 billion in 2015. (These figures do not include online travel sales or sales of tickets to events.) By 2018 sales are expected to be as high as $492 billion.

Today, both retailers and their customers are much more conservative than they were during the long-term economic boom that ended in late 2007. Retailers of all types have been seeking creative ways to cut operating expenses. Methods range from reducing the size of stores to lowering the employee count to reducing inventory exposure.

For affluent shoppers, sales of luxury items have made a good comeback at many stores in America. Until 2013, luxury sales had been surging in China, where high-end stores including Tiffany & Co., Hermes and Gucci have done very well. However, new leadership in the Chinese government is discouraging extravagance. While it was once very common for business people to present luxury gifts to officials, this practice has recently been curtailed, and conspicuous displays of wealth and luxury are discouraged.

Less affluent U.S. and European consumers are focused on seeking the best possible prices. This means that revenues have been strong at so-called "dollar stores" in America, and at other outlets that are known for exceptionally low prices. Elsewhere, many retailers, including department stores, are forced to offer special prices on a frequent basis.

Sales of private-label items are generally growing quickly. Overall, private-label sales (in supermarkets, drug stores and mass merchandisers) grew 2.5% to reach $115.3 billion in the U.S. in 2014, according to the Private Label Manufacturers Association.

Coupons have made a big comeback. Major factors in this growth include the financially challenged consumer and the use of advances in technology. Coupon distribution via cellphones has made a huge impact. Also, the fact that consumers now use the Internet to search for and print out coupons caused significant growth. Another boost to coupon redemption is web sites that push special offers to members, such as Groupon. The success of this business strategy has led to a massive wave of coupon site startups around the world. It remains to be seen whether they can continue to lure retailers and restaurants to offer immense discounts and then split those discounted receipts with the coupon firms.

Over the long-term, the most exciting markets for retail industry growth may be emerging nations such as South Africa, China, India and Brazil. In China, many of the world's leading retail chains have opened large numbers of stores and new malls have been developed at a rapid clip, even in remote cities. This retail trend in China includes middle-of-the-road chains such as Nike and Starbucks, automotive centers including car dealers and tire and accessory stores such as Goodyear, as well as the world's top luxury retailers, including Chanel, Louis Vuitton and Fendi. The government in India is taking small steps to open the Indian market to foreign retail chains, but it remains a difficult environment due to regulatory issues and supply chain problems.

In the U.S. and Europe, many businesses outside the luxury field have repositioned themselves as providers of high-value, reasonably-priced merchandise. Household product makers are emphasizing lower-priced soaps and detergents, or high-value larger packages. Even companies that were already known for reasonably-priced goods have changed strategy to some degree. Many fashion-conscious women have become more conservative about the amount they are willing to spend on clothing.

Personal spending has shifted toward goods and services offering quality, durability, affordability and lasting value, with less focus on the purchase of trendy items for fashion's sake. Going forward, consumers will spend their money more wisely while using debt more carefully. Successful manufacturers, home builders, services providers and retailers will embrace this trend.

Meanwhile, during 2012-15, a surge in house values and stock market indexes created a wealth effect throughout most of America, along with Canada and other developed nations. This has encouraged consumers to spend a bit more, often on big purchases that they had put off during the recent recession, including automobiles, home remodeling and appliances. When consumers spend, they want to do so with the confidence that they are using their money in a smart way, and they want to pay cash instead of using credit cards.

Plunkett's Four Keys to Successful Consumer Products:
- *High Perceived Value*: The product must convincingly offer a high level of value and durability for the price, and give consumers confidence that their money is well and wisely spent.

- *Quality and Utility as well as Fashion:* Fashion will remain important, but quality will come first in the minds of many consumers. Products that offer quality, utility *and* fashion will have tremendous competitive advantage.

- *High Brand Reputation above Style:* The brand must stand for a company that clearly puts customer satisfaction and high value above all else. If the brand also stands for a firm with great styling, high social values, such as eco-consciousness, or other ancillary attributes, that's even better.

- *Cheap Chic Still Has a Place:* If a company wants to win the hearts of fashion-conscious, as well as budget-conscious consumers, it must provide exciting style at a moderate price. If an entire business model is based on trendy merchandise with a short useful life, then the company must strive to offer very high value—for example, the affordable fashions of such retailers as Sweden's H&M, Spain's Inditex and Japan's Uniqlo, a company that has been so successful at selling bargain fashions that its founder is Japan's wealthiest business person.

Perfect examples: Apple's iPod and iPhone
- ✓ High perceived value at reasonable prices
- ✓ Quality, utility and style
- ✓ High brand reputation
- ✓ Absolutely chic

Next, let's look at how these values can be applied successfully to retail stores.

Plunkett's Four Keys to Successful Retailing:
- *A High Value-High Quality Product Selection:* Depth of selection is less important than a reasonably-sized offering of products that the merchandiser has chosen because they consistently offer high value and quality.

- *Very Competitive Prices:* The goal here is to give the consumer confidence that the store faithfully delivers everyday low prices—meanwhile, managing the firm so as to allow the owners a viable profit margin.

- *Superior Service:* In-store help, follow-up service, problem-solving, installation and repairs offered easily and quickly, along with the ability to make returns and exchanges must be part of the package, with an absolute minimum of inconvenience to the consumer.

- *Seamless Integration of Bricks and Clicks*: Successful firms integrate their online endeavors with their physical presence in a manner that provides the highest possible level of convenience to customers.

Great example: Costco
- ✓ Reasonable product selection, including quality store brands as well as name brands that have good reputations. Costco succeeds by carrying a vastly smaller merchandise selection than its competitor Wal-Mart.
- ✓ Consistent, everyday low prices.
- ✓ An easy-to-find, always-staffed customer service desk. Also, rules about returns are generous and clear-cut, "We guarantee your satisfaction on every product we sell with a full refund. The following must be returned within 90 days of purchase for a refund: televisions, projectors, computers, cameras, camcorders, iPod/MP3 players and cellular phones."
- ✓ An easy-to-use web site with in-depth customer service information. When desired, customers may order merchandise online but return it to a store. Large items, upon request, can be picked up at the customer's home for return.

Internet Research Tips:
- The National Retail Federation (www.nrf.com) offers a wealth of information regarding the U.S. retail industry.
- The International Council of Shopping Centers (www.icsc.org) offers the latest information on shopping centers, malls and retail trends.

---

2) Wal-Mart Still Dominates, but Faces Slowing Revenue Growth

Wal-Mart is the world's largest retailer, based on revenue ($485.7 billion during the fiscal year ending in January 2015, up from $469.2 billion in 2014 and $447.0 in 2013), and is the largest corporate employer in the U.S. (more than 2.2 million total employees worldwide). The company served over 200 million weekly customers in stores in 27 countries, under 71 different banners in late 2015. Outside of America, Wal-Mart has a strong presence in such nations as Mexico, Canada and the UK.

However, even companies the size and scope of Wal-Mart have their problems. By the first quarter in 2014, Wal-Mart faced falling U.S. same store sales for five consecutive quarters. Sales at the company's small-format stores (which are usually located within or closer to major cities) fared slightly better that the firm's giant supercenters. In late 2014, Wal-Mart announced plans to reduce the number of new supercenters slated for construction while it would complete 240 new small stores through 2015. As of late 2015, sales at stores open at least one year rose by 1.5%, while its smaller Neighborhood Markets' sales rose by 8% for the quarter ending September 30, 2015. The firm reported same-store sales growth for five consecutive quarters from mid-2014 through the third quarter of 2015, a significant improvement. Wal-Mart hopes to rack up global online sales of $35 billion by early 2018, compared to $10 billion in fiscal 2014. Wal-Mart also hopes to attract the growing numbers of consumers who prefer to shop online. The company has been investing heavily in its workforce to reduce turnover, including a pay raise for a large number of its 1.2 million U.S. employees.

China continues to be a major focus for growth, but at a slower pace than previously planned. Wal-Mart initially planned to open thousands of stores when it first entered China in 1996. Its latest goal is 115 new stores by 2017 (which will bring the total store count to 530), after suffering slowing sales growth in the U.S. and some other countries. The company is also expanding its online presence in China, where e-commerce is booming thanks to companies like Ali Baba and Tencent.

Meanwhile, Wal-Mart ended its joint venture with Bharti Enterprises Ltd. in India. Particularly problematic for Wal-Mart was the Indian requirement that foreign companies obtain 30% of their products and services from local small businesses. Instead of relying on retail business in India, Wal-Mart is growing through wholesaling, where restrictions are not as harsh. As of early 2015, Wal-Mart had 20 wholesale stores in India, and planned to open an additional 40 to 50 locations by 2018. These stores operate largely as wholesale distribution outlets to a wide variety of small businesses and shops. Meanwhile, Wal-Mart launched e-commerce operations in India in 2014. For the fiscal year ending in January 2015, sales at non-U.S. stores reached $136.2 billion, compared to $136.5 billion in 2014 and $134.7 billion in 2013.

Due to its sheer size and customer base, Wal-Mart is still the one to beat in the retail industry in the U.S. and abroad. Over the long-term, Wal-Mart achieved its astounding success through deep discounts, high volume purchasing and cutting-edge technology that raised the chain's distribution and inventory control systems to the pinnacle of efficiency. Costs are cut to the bone while customers flock to the stores in massive numbers seeking everyday low prices.

Wal-Mart has taken a significant departure from its giant 200,000-square-foot Supercenter size by opening dozens of 30,000- to 60,000-square-foot Neighborhood Market grocery stores in cities across the U.S. As of late 2014, there were about 500 Neighborhood Markets which collectively posted a 5.5% sales increase over 2013. In Mexico, it has gone even smaller with a 2,690 square foot mini-grocer format called Bodega Aurrera Express. By the end of 2014, the firm had almost 900 of the stores open and sales grew by 12% over 2013.

Meanwhile, in late 2012, Wal-Mart began testing delivery of goods ordered online. The service, originally called Wal-Mart To Go but later renamed Walmart Grocery, offers same day service (if orders are received by noon local time and the item is in stock) from stores in cities including Philadelphia, Northern Virginia, Minneapolis, San Jose, San Francisco, Houston and Denver. Cost for same day delivery is $10, regardless of the size of the order. (Amazon.com offers a similar concept in several U.S. cities). Wal-Mart expanded its delivery service starting in 2014 to allow consumers to shop online and pick up the merchandise at a nearby store at no extra charge.

As one of the world's largest in-store pharmacy operators, the firm has slashed health care costs for many customers by offering $4 prescriptions for hundreds of generic drugs, along with low-cost prescription eyeglasses. Since a 2009 launch, Wal-Mart also has in-store medical clinics in about 140 stores nationwide. The clinics, which are operated by outside contractors, offer quick and inexpensive visits (a flat $59 fee or $4 for company employees) for such needs as school physicals and treatment for minor infections. In the same way that grocery customers drive sales in other Wal-Mart departments, these health care customers are likely to make purchases elsewhere in the store as long as they are already in a Wal-Mart. The firm is considering partnering with outside companies to expand the range of treatments offered, perhaps including care for chronic diseases.

Wal-Mart has significant influence on food companies, the products they produce and the way in which they package and distribute those products. The firm has doubled the amount of food purchased from local farmers in the U.S.

Wal-Mart relies on its massive grocery departments in its Supercenters to bring in customers, and it is not impervious to the marketing efforts of competing grocery chains. Firms such as Kroger Co., HEB and SuperValu, Inc. have redesigned stores to offer shoppers more relaxed, neighborhood shopping experiences in addition to stocking higher-end breads, meats and wine not carried by Wal-Mart.

3) Department Stores Reposition for Today's Consumer While Outlet Stores Proliferate

In order to better understand what is happening in the department store sector, a bit of history is in order. Older consumers may remember Sears Roebuck's "Sears has everything" line? Others might recall going into Saks Fifth Avenue's flagship store in Manhattan and finding everything from *haute couture* to a travel agency to a restaurant, plus a hair salon, a toy department and a fine jewelry department—all at full price? Things are quite different today.

The department store industry has evolved and generally suffered in recent decades. Originally, the department store was developed and enhanced by retail pioneers in France and America from the 1850s through the early 1900s. The department store was envisioned as an antidote to shopping at endless blocks full of small, mom-and-pop specialty shops such as hat stores, furniture stores, hardware stores and shoe stores. Marshall Field in Chicago (operating ever-larger downtown stores beginning in 1865), John Wannamaker in Philadelphia (using advanced advertising techniques to launch a giant department store by 1878) and Aristide Boucicaut in Paris (his Bon Marche became the first true department store by 1852) figured out that housewives would prefer to find everything under one roof—in "departments" that varied from hardware to books to housewares to food items to furniture to clothing. These department stores were located in the heart of the downtown area within major cities. Shopping at them was an all-day affair, eagerly looked forward to by many consumers. A mid-day break for lunch or tea was often taken in the stores' restaurants. In 1902, R.H. Macy opened what was billed as "the largest store on Earth" in Manhattan. The store featured nine stories, 33 elevators and several escalators.

Through the decades, tastes and consumer needs evolved. Downtown shopping fell out of favor, starting in the 1960s. The growing popularity of life in the suburbs, encouraging the creation of the enclosed mall, dictated a new role for department stores as "anchors" of malls. Consumers became accustomed to shopping near where they lived, not at old-fashioned downtown stores. While malls sprang up like wildflowers in suburban fields, big box stores, discount stores and power centers began competing for consumers' dollars.

Today, most "department" stores are actually mall-based apparel, accessories and cosmetics stores, with a few also offering a reasonable depth of housewares. If they offer any other types of merchandise, such as furniture or electronics, they are often in small, under-stocked sections that don't compete well against big box specialty stores such as Best Buy. The highest volume in the store on a per square foot basis is typically done in the cosmetics department, and cosmetics generally aren't on sale. That's why the first thing you see when you walk in the door is cosmetics. Other very high volume/high profit departments include fine jewelry along with ladies shoes and handbags. Again, you will nearly always find these departments in very conspicuous locations on the ground floor.

The majority of the balance of the store is apparel—mostly women's and children's, along with relatively small men's departments. "Department store" is a misnomer at this point. As they evolved in recent years, department stores dug themselves a financial hole by encouraging shoppers to buy during frequent "sale" events. The newest merchandise and styles are priced at full amounts for a short time, and then prices decrease quickly through bigger and bigger markdowns. (Apparel manufacturers may cover some of the cost of these markdowns.) Shoppers have been trained to wait for items to go on sale. Department store execs have tried to fight back by making more and more of their merchandise private-label "house brands" (with higher profit margins) instead of designer brands. Regardless, consumers generally want things to be on sale.

Major department store chains went broke by the score in the 1980s. Surviving companies repositioned themselves and sought new financial resources in order to survive. (Some had to overcome financial pressure caused by excessive leverage or overly aggressive expansion). They needed to learn to utilize advanced information systems and inventory methods. In addition, they had to learn to offer better value.

Consumers complained that department stores were hard to access, since most are anchor tenants in large malls. In many cases, it's necessary for customers to park their cars in remote lots, walk a long way to enter the department store and then navigate even further to find the merchandise area they need. Once there, sales clerks are often hard to find and registers are decentralized, which can make paying for merchandise more complicated than it should be. Add to that the higher prices charged by department stores as opposed to discount stores, and the shopping experience becomes a chore instead of a pleasure. Meanwhile, customer traffic at most malls in the U.S. is on a downward trend, as consumers migrate online.

Several chain operators are attempting to address these problems. Nordstrom is perhaps the best example of a department store company that is stemming the retail tide of discount stores and membership clubs. At about 150,000 square feet, newer Nordstrom stores are smaller than Nordstrom's former average store of 190,000 square feet, and thus take smaller investments and reduced inventory risk. The company has concentrated on locations with easy-to-use parking and access that does not force people to go through malls. The smaller size should also make stores easier for consumers to navigate and less costly to operate.

Continuously successful department stores are those on the leading edge of modern retailing. Nordstrom, for example, offers the utmost in personal service combined with unique and high-quality merchandise that offers high value (much of the merchandise is store brand). Nordstrom sales personnel receive above-average commission rates, and top sales people can earn $100,000 or more yearly.

After facing grueling double-digit losses during the Great Recession of 2008-09 (especially at luxury stores), many department stores are seeing growth again. Revenues for Saks, Inc. (owner of Saks Fifth Avenue and Saks Off 5th stores and a subsidiary of Hudson's Bay Company since 2013) for the year ending January 31, 2014, rose to $3.2 billion from 2013's $3.15 billion and 2012's $3.01 billion.

For the fiscal year ending July 31, 2015, Neiman Marcus Group reported revenues rising to $5.095 billion, up from $4.84 billion in 2014 and $4.65 billion in 2013. For 2015, the firm reported $14.9 million in net profit, after a loss of $147.2 million in 2014 and a profit of $163.7 million in 2013. It is interesting to note that 25% of the firm's 2015 revenue came from online sales. In 2013, the firm's investor group agreed to sell the company to investment firm Ares Management LLC and the Canadian Pension Plan Investment Board for $6 billion. As of late 2015, Neiman Marcus was considering an IPO of its stock.

Nordstrom fared well, with fiscal 2015 revenues of $13.5 billion, up from $12.54 billion in 2014 and $12.12 billion in 2013. For 2015, profits were $720 million, down from $734 million in 2014 and $735 million in 2013.

At Macy's, the leading mainstream department store chain, for its fiscal year ending January 31, 2015, revenues rose to $28.11 billion, from $27.93 billion in 2014 and $27.69 billion in 2013. For 2015, profits were $1.53 billion, up from $1.34 billion in 2014 and $1.34 billion in 2013. However, the big news in retail later in 2015 was Macy's significant drop in sales. Sales at stores open at least one year dropped during all of the first three quarters of the fiscal year.

Analysts are concerned that Macy's surprising sales slide may be a harbinger of dire times for department stores. Between 2006 and 2013, department stores' share of general merchandise sales fell from 15% to 9% (about a $20 billion decline). Department stores are also losing customers in younger age groups, especially Millennials who tend to spend discretionary income on travel, dining out, gym memberships and smartphones, while spending less on clothes. 2015 saw rises in consumer spending overall on automobiles, housing and health care but not on clothing.

Often, budget-conscious consumers are buying what they need, when they need it, as opposed to making impulse purchases. It's a delicate balance for stores that are buying less inventory (to cut costs), but also need to have desired items in stock when necessary. Stores are working with suppliers to shorten the gap between orders and delivery to make that balance a little easier.

Many department stores are investing in off-price outlets. Outlet-only stock is priced about 30% to 70% below comparable goods in regular stores. In-store markdowns at regular stores can erode profit margins and clutter elegant floor space with sale racks. Outlets can move merchandise that isn't selling in regular stores, while operating at lower costs in less-desirable real estate. Outlets also afford department stores the ability to stock lower-priced, outlet-only merchandise not normally available in regular stores. Saks, Inc. had 79 Off 5th outlets throughout the U.S. in late 2014, with additional stores planned for 2015. Nordstrom, Inc. had 142 Nordstrom Rack outlets in 2014, up from 95 in 2011. Bloomingdale's (a subsidiary of Macy's) saw its first outlet open for business in August 2010, and had 13 open by the end of 2014. Macy's launched Macy's Backstage off-price stores in 2015. Likewise, Lord

& Taylor opened the first Find @ Lord & Taylor store in Paramus, New Jersey in a former Loehmann's location. Sales at off-price stores were expected to collectively reach $42 billion in 2015, up from $27 billion in 2009, according to Customer Growth Partners.

4) Warehouse Clubs and Discount Department Stores Battle for Market Share

Wal-Mart might as well be the first chain mentioned in this category. Since its founding in 1962, Wal-Mart has flourished to become the world's top retailer by far. How does the Wal-Mart method work? Primarily, it meets the simple needs of average consumers by using money-back guarantees, everyday low prices, merchandise that is rarely out of stock, ease of access and floor help trained to offer assistance. Interestingly, Wal-Mart was first conceptualized as a rural store—a modern general store if you will—located in smaller communities that lacked much in the way of local shopping facilities. However, once it had conquered hundreds of small towns, Wal-Mart branched out into major metro areas with astonishing success, and eventually took that winning formula into foreign markets. What Wal-Mart, Costco and other discount stores lack in profit margin, they gain exponentially in volume.

With the addition of substantial grocery departments, discount stores are taking customers, and therefore profits, from traditional department, grocery and specialty stores—today more than ever before. In general, discount stores are able to provide the convenience that mall-based department stores lack, while offering everyday low prices. Wal-Mart and its competitors have plenty of parking by the door, fast centralized checkout, easy returns and quality inventory that includes broad categories of name-brand merchandise as well as value-priced store brands of high quality.

Another interesting point is that discount stores attract a broad customer demographic. People of all ages and incomes are shopping there. It's become commonplace to see luxury vehicles in Wal-Mart, Target and Kohl's parking lots alongside practical compact cars and light trucks. Convenience, value and practicality are key motivators for shoppers. Discount stores are superbly positioned to fill these needs.

A trend in a number of these stores is the development of discount-priced designer apparel lines. Haute couture designer Isaac Mizrahi worked

exclusively with Target, creating an inexpensive line of sophisticated clothing for women as well as trendy home décor items such as furniture, bedding and dinnerware. Other designers have followed this trend, including Jaclyn Smith at K-Mart, Vera Wang at Kohl's and Missoni at Target. Costco has long enjoyed success selling high-end items at discount prices, such as fine diamond jewelry and fine wines.

Discount Store Giants
(With approximate store count at 1/1/2015)

Wal-Mart: (year ended 1/31/15)
Fiscal 2015 Revenues	$486.7 billion
Employees	2,200,000
Stores	11,453*

Costco: (year ended 8/31/15)
Fiscal 2015 Revenues	$116.2 billion
Employees	195,000
Stores	686

Target: (year ended 1/31/15)
Fiscal 2015 Revenues	$72.6 billion
Employees	347,000
Stores	1,934**

* Includes International and U.S. stores, Supercenters, Sam's Clubs and Marketside Neighborhood Markets.
** Includes Targets and SuperTargets.

---

5) Private Label Brands Grow in Share of Total Store Sales

Discount stores and a number of other retailers are offering more and more products that are private label. Instead of being limited to selling branded products from major manufacturers like Procter & Gamble, growing numbers of stores are contracting for the manufacture of store-branded merchandise. Such is the case with Wal-Mart and its Ol' Roy dog food, the George line of apparel or the Sam's Choice products found in its Sam's Club stores. One-half of the goods sold at Target and Kroger stores are now privately branded (Kroger owns and operates dozens of manufacturing facilities in the U.S.). Costco's Kirkland Signature brand is on everything from cookware to paper goods to food items. Although this method has long been used by department store chains and a handful of specialty store chains, few have picked it up with as much enthusiasm or effectiveness as the discount retailers.

Sales of private-label items are generally growing at a faster rate than those of name brands. Overall, private-label sales in the U.S. (in supermarkets, drug stores, mass merchandisers and club and dollar stores) reached $115.3 billion in 2014, up from $112 billion in 2013, according to the Private Label Manufacturers Association (PLMA).

In supermarkets alone, store brand sales rose by $1.1 billion to reach a record $62.1 billion in 2014. Private label supermarket product sales were up 1.8% compared to only 1.1% for national brands. A 2013 survey conducted by Market Force Information found that 96% of respondents bought private-label brands at least some of the time.

Many consumers have determined that store brands offer consistently high quality at much lower everyday prices. According to PLMA, American consumers who bought store branded food and non-grocery items saved an estimated $27 billion in 2014.

As an alternative to going through the painful process of establishing their own brand names, discount stores have also been picking up brands that have been left by the wayside. Taking brand names that were abandoned by their original manufacturers, or ones whose trademarks have expired, the retailer then releases the product afresh, relying on the memories of its customers to inspire renewed sales of the product. A prime, and somewhat ironic, example of this is White Cloud toilet paper, which was originally made by Procter & Gamble. After P&G dropped the brand, it was picked up by Wal-Mart. Taking advantage of a once well-recognized brand name, Wal-Mart put its White Cloud private brand toilet paper on all its shelves and saw sales skyrocket as customers remembered an old favorite. Sitting next to it on the shelves, at a slightly higher price, was Charmin, the toilet paper currently made by Procter & Gamble.

Even Amazon.com is getting into private labels. In 2014, Amazon launched a line of house brand items called Amazon Elements. Initial products included diapers and baby wipes. Diapers have long been a very high volume item for Amazon. The Elements line is designed to appeal to eco-conscious and quality-conscious consumers. The firm provides very deep product origin information, such as where and when each item was made and the sources of ingredients. Amazon has also developed a line of electronic accessories called AmazonBasics, which includes chargers.

6) Diverse Selling Techniques Boost Direct Marketers and Non-Store Sales

Several decades ago, non-store retailing consisted only of catalogs (such as those from Sears, Roebuck & Co.), mail-order ads in magazines or newspapers and door-to-door peddlers of such items as Watkin's Vanilla Extract, Fuller Brushes and Kirby Vacuums. Slowly, non-store retailing evolved. By the 1970s, upscale catalogs such as the Horchow Collection had emerged in large numbers, catering to the growing base of affluent households where women were holding demanding, well-paying jobs and had less time or inclination for traditional shopping. At the same time, multi-level marketing was booming, and scores of new companies copied the methods of leaders like Avon, Amway and Mary Kay in selling cosmetics and other personal-care items through legions of independent representatives. Business-to-business catalogs of such items as office supplies also saw rapid growth. By the late 1980s, mail-order sales of personal computers and related accessories soared, as early leaders like Gateway and Dell Computer found success via aggressive advertising in computer magazines. Television shopping became sophisticated as the advent of new, niche cable TV channels created additional sales venues.

Today, non-store selling (sometimes called "direct selling") is giving traditional retail selling a run for its money. It has steadily chipped away at the market share of stores. For the past several years, however, non-store selling has been migrating more and more to the Internet, while selling through traditional direct marketing, such as through the mail or by telemarketing, is of less and less importance. The Direct Marketing Association reported that in 2014, U.S. retail sales made through direct marketing reached $34.47 billion, up 5.5% from 2013. 18.2 million people were involved with the technique in 2014, up from 16.8 million in 2013.

Direct selling involves both old-fashioned methods and state-of-the-art technologies. The direct marketing and direct response industry includes thousands of companies offering unique niche catalogs; television home shopping programs; millions of independent sales representatives selling everything from lingerie to cookware through personal calls and party-like events in the home; telemarketers; Internet-based retail sites; and firms using additional, innovative non-store methods.

The non-store category of retailing is comprised of the following sectors:

- Catalogs, direct mail and mail-order advertising
- Television home shopping programs and infomercials, along with direct-sales offers broadcast by radio
- Merchandise or services offered via interactive television programming

- Internet-based retail sites, including related e-mail and video marketing
- Direct sales offers advertised online and via e-mail
- Door-to-door and "party" selling
- Telemarketing

Note: Many sophisticated non-store retailers use combinations of these methods

Extremely sophisticated database software now enables direct marketers to mail, e-mail or telephone their offerings to well-targeted groups. For example, matching such data as home value, occupation, credit rating and automobile type owned against a database of residents in a particular city may identify those most likely to purchase a particular item or line of merchandise.

It is important to note that there are several purposes for direct marketing. For example, in the case of a catalog mailed to the home by a seller that does not operate any stores at all, the intent is to close the sale through direct contact with the consumer. This is more precisely defined as the "direct-response advertising" segment of direct marketing.

More broadly, direct marketing can have other purposes, including the generation of sales leads or the creation of a level of interest in the consumer that will generate store traffic. In instances where a retailer has both stores and catalog operations, direct marketing serves multiple functions. Neiman-Marcus' marketing synergism, delivered by its stores, catalogs and online site, is a good example. Pottery Barn and Victoria's Secret also are leaders in this type of multi-faceted retail marketing. Consequently, modern retailing, advertising and marketing methods have blurred the distinctions between mass media marketing and direct marketing. For example, is a banner ad on a web site a direct marketing effort or is it mass media advertising? If you simply look at the banner without clicking on it, and the meaning of the ad or the name of the retailer registers with you, then the ad may be a mass media branding success. On the other hand, if you click on the ad, and eventually make an online purchase rather than go to a retailer's store, then the ad is a direct-response advertising success.

With regard to telephone orders, today's so-called "telephone centers" are staffed with well-trained order takers and customer service representatives at both traditional and non-store retailing firms. Many of these call centers are outsourced to foreign countries where labor is cheaper than in the U.S. Consumer calls are routed to these centers, where operators use the latest in database and telecommunications technology to expertly answer questions, take orders and suggest high-profit-margin upgrades to those orders. Special software in the call centers keeps track of a customer's questions, complaints, purchases and needs. In seconds, an operator can see a customer's complete, long-term history of purchases and other activities with a simple keystroke on the computer. This not only provides faster and more thorough customer service, it may also give the customer a false sense of a personal relationship.

Catalogs and Direct-Mail Offerings: Catalog retailing remains an immense business. Billions of print catalogs, direct-mail offerings via letters, brochures, flyers and postcards are mailed to U.S. households each year. Catalog shopping can offer great convenience and frequently offers better prices than shopping in stores. Catalogs also remain a popular venue for items we may not want our neighbors to see us buying in a store. However, the recent recession resulted in direct mail budgets being cut. Retailers are reducing printing expenses and analyzing their lists more carefully in an effort to drop addresses that are less likely to respond.

Television-Based Shopping, Cable Systems and Interactive TV: Television shopping shows were an instant hit. For example, QVC, Inc., a subsidiary of Liberty Interactive Corporation, is a televised shopping network based in West Chester, Pennsylvania that broadcasts internationally with locations in Germany, Japan, Italy and the United Kingdom. "QVC" stands for quality, value and convenience. In the U.S. market, it reaches the majority of U.S. homes with cable service. Worldwide, QVC reaches more than 153 million homes annually. The network broadcasts themed shopping programming 24-hours-a-day with operators continuously available to take calls and process orders. QVC's 2014 revenue totaled $8.8 billion. It is important to note that QVC utilizes a dual-marketing strategy that relies heavily on driving TV viewers to its web site. $3.5 billion of 2014's revenues were booked over the Internet.

Interactive television services are growing rapidly, leading to new opportunities for direct selling via TV. With interactive cable TV services, subscribers can order movies on demand and other unique services. They also have the ability to respond to direct sales offers via their cable systems. For example, viewers watching a pay-per-view music concert may be able to order souvenirs such as t-shirts via the cable system. Cable TV offers another unique advantage to direct sellers and other advertisers. Since the cable system knows the address of the cable subscriber, that address information can be matched against demographic databases to create a unique profile of the subscriber based on likely household income, value and size of the home and other data. Ads displayed by the cable system can then be custom tailored to match the viewer's profile.

Independent Representatives, Party-Based Selling and Other Personal Direct Selling Methods: While this type of non-store retailing has been with us for a long time, the growing struggle of middle-class families to become stable, two-income households has added greatly to the popularity of a sideline career as an "independent consultant" for companies like Mary Kay, Avon and Amway. In addition to firms that engage in direct selling as their primary line of business, many manufacturers and retailers have found great success with direct marketing, such as the Pampered Chef unit of Berkshire Hathaway.

Using individual reps as sales agents has grown very rapidly outside the United States. Avon, Amway and other direct sales firms are enjoying soaring business in emerging nations, including China.

Representative selling has often been looked on with scorn, mostly because of the so-called "pyramid schemes" that often left recruits indebted to the company, trying to sell goods that no one wanted. Today's practices are very different, especially in legitimate businesses that look for long-term returns and loyalty from both customers and recruits. Companies like Avon, which has been in business for more than 100 years, have taken great pains to develop a functional recruiting and selling structure, and have come up with multi-level pay packages that can yield marketers a satisfying return and encourage "group leaders" not only to sign up recruits, but also to teach these recruits how to sell. Payments to these group leaders are based on sales of those they have recruited, giving them a strong incentive to take responsibility for those under them in the hierarchy.

Despite Avon's lengthy history and revenues of nearly $9 billion for 2014, it has been in a long-term slump in the U.S. The company is looking for a buyer for its North American operations. Avon has had difficulty adapting its products and practices to e-commerce and changing consumer tastes. The firm posted a loss nearly $400 million in 2014. Avon's and Mary Kay's business models inspired many other companies to launch new brands and sales networks

offering a broad spectrum of products, across the U.S. and around the world.

Another direct selling option from the home is women's apparel. Companies such as Doncaster, Carlisle and Worth enable women who are independent representatives to show and sell clothes and accessories from their homes or company show rooms at trunk shows, usually held four times per year. It's a model similar to Tupperware parties. At Doncaster, for example, "associates" are trained by district sales leaders to learn the ropes of fashion display, merchandising and marketing, as well as the nuts and bolts of processing orders and collecting payments. Each quarter, associates send out advance marketing materials and invitations (professionally produced by Doncaster) to friends and acquaintances. Appointments are made by customers to see and try on pieces from the current line. Orders are placed, and then the apparel is delivered to the customers within several weeks. Prices range from $60 for accessories up to $1,000 or more for suits and outerwear. Annual sales for these private companies run between $30 million and $130 million. Average annual income for associates is about $40,000, with top sellers earning more than $100,000.

Telemarketing: Despite the fact that many consumers find telemarketing annoying, it does create sales. "Do not call" list regulation at the federal level places the future of this industry in doubt. As of early 2005, the Federal Trade Commission amended its Telemarketing Sales Rule to require that telemarketers purge their call lists of all names and numbers found on the National Do Not Call Registry (www.donotcall.gov). This registry, which opened in June 2003, contains more than 200 million registrants.

E-mail and Social Media: E-mail blasts have been a popular marketing tool for years, and e-mail messages containing links to an advertiser's web site, pages on video sites such as YouTube, or social media sites such as the phenomenonally successful Facebook, Twitter, Instagram and Pinterest, pack a double punch. "Buy Now" buttons are now an option for advertisements on most social media.

E-mail is a personal, inexpensive way to reach potential customers. However, keeping e-mail addresses up to date is an ongoing challenge, and high costs lie in purchasing lists of current e-mail addresses. The most successful retailers keep in touch with customers whether in person, online or by mail, and verify e-mail addresses in the process. When a sale is complete, many firms such as Victoria's Secret and Talbot's are sending personal e-mail thank you messages with special offers on future purchases.

Social media is a giant step forward for firms seeking to reach customers within a particular demographic. Media site users create networks of friends with similar tastes and interests. Businesses can create accounts and pages on sites such as Facebook, for example, where users can "like" a company online. Friends of the user see the listing when checking out the user's profile and are likely to click on the business' page to learn more.

A number of retailers run promotions via e-mail, offering chances to win merchandise. Interested customers click on the offer and end up on Facebook where, by clicking "like" on the retailer's page, they are entered to win. Further chances to win are often available if users send news of this "like" to their Facebook friends.

Pinterest is a social media app and web site where users create online bulletin boards. Subject matter is up to the user, but common boards include wedding planning, trip planning, home improvement ideas, fitness plans and hobbies. Users "pin" graphic images and text to create boards. Pinterest offers support for Twitter cards, which link tweets to view pins or user boards. Pinterest had more than 100 million monthly unique visitors in September 2015, and raised another $367 million in venture capital that year, bringing its funding total since its inception to $1.1 billion.

7) Apple Sets the Bar for Showcase Stores and Super-Merchandisers

A few unique retailers have created the category of "super-merchandisers." They invest huge amounts of money on the construction of unique and entertaining stores where they devote large portions of floor spaces to non-retail purposes, either for ambiance and style or for demonstrations and practice areas for their products. These types of stores typically offer very deep merchandise selections while they cater to customers who are very passionate about a particular interest, hobby or shopping need. The focus is on an immersive customer experience. A perfect example is Bass Pro's Outdoor World stores, which are vast complexes filled with exciting displays of the latest hunting, camping, fishing and outdoor merchandise.

"Showcase stores," on the other hand, feature only one brand of merchandise. Ralph Lauren's immense signature stores in New York City, as well as in the heart of Chicago and Paris, are great examples. So are Nike's massive stores on New York City's 5th Avenue and in other prime, very high visibility locations. Showcase stores began as anomalies, too opulent to be considered profitable, but guaranteed to be tremendous advertising; and public relations vehicles because of their uniqueness, massive scale and very high traffic locations. Nonetheless, despite massive investments and extremely high rent, many have proven immensely profitable.

Such stores are staffed with the most qualified people available, people who are knowledgeable about the products and the use of them. Apple may well run the ultimate showcase stores based on the long lines of customers waiting to get in at almost any hour of the day or night. At its retail units, Apple's average sales per square foot of store space per year (calculated as trailing twelve months or "TTM") were an astonishing $4,798 in late 2014, according eMarketer (compared, for example, to $3,132 for Tiffany & Co., $1,895 for Michael Kors Holdings and $1,675 for lululemon athletica, all stores that are noted for high revenues per square foot).

Apple reaps its amazing sales by offering shoppers a unique experience in a carefully designed environment. The sleek, high-tech look of Apple products such as iPads and Macs are echoed in hip, modern spaces that are free of clutter. Apple's New York City store on Fifth Avenue, for example, features a two-story glass cube at the entrance, from which customers go below ground into the store. The New York location is open 24/7 and typically has a very long line of people waiting to get in.

Products are displayed in ways that highlight usage and invite shoppers to experiment. Technical support is available at Apple's Genius Bars where highly trained technicians handle product demonstrations, troubleshooting and on-site repairs. One to One sessions help clients set up their new computers, phones or music players including transferring files from old equipment along with tutoring on device features. Free workshops are offered on everything from digital photos to music to video to business systems. Staff must go through rigorous interview and training programs to teach them to solve customers' problems instead of merely selling them merchandise. Positions are highly coveted and must be earned.

Apple store layouts are carefully designed. The "red zone" area closest to the door features the latest products and, during new product launches, staff members gather there to applaud and cheer customers leaving the store with their new purchases.

Children's play areas allow parents to shop elsewhere in the store without distraction while the kids are busy with games and educational software. Cash registers are being phased out and replaced with iPod Touches that staff use anywhere in the stores to read credit cards or remotely open hidden registers for a cash transaction. Apple had 450 stores by late 2014, with 265 in the U.S. The stores accounted for 12% of Apple's $183 billion in 2014 sales. The stores collectively draw 1 million visitors each day.

8) For the Long-Term in the U.S., Consumers Increase Savings/Less Inclined to Use Debt

Consumers in America have been paying down debt in general for several years, with three notable exceptions: 1) They have greatly increased their purchases of automobiles, and the total amount of car loans has been rising. This is due to the fact that consumers delayed car purchases during the recent recession. Also, low gasoline prices and low interest rates are encouraging new car purchases. 2) Total student debt rose significantly in recent years due to rising tuition costs and college fees, along with the fact that many young people returned to college or graduate school because they were discouraged by the difficult job market. 3) Mortgage debt, after a lengthy decline, rose sharply in the twelve months through June 2014, and then remained steady through the second quarter of 2015 as house prices rose and foreclosures declined.

The most telling change has been in consumer credit card use. During the first quarter of 2014, total credit card debt fell to its lowest levels in more than a decade, since 2002. By the same quarter of 2015, outstanding credit card balances had risen slightly to $700 billion, which was still down significantly compared to previous highs.

Credit card issuers have seen deep changes in consumer behavior. Industry-leader Visa announced that, for the quarter ending December 31, 2008, debit card spending in the United States surpassed credit card volume for the first time in the company's history. Visa's results show that consumers are using debit cards instead of credit cards, particularly when buying non-discretionary items like food, drugs and gasoline, to force themselves to use available funds rather than incur debt. The practice continued well into 2015.

In many parts of Western Europe, consumers are concerned about government debts, austerity measures and high unemployment, coupled with very low home values. Many households are budget-challenged.

In the United States, consumers face immense concerns over government debts and deficits, high, but improving, unemployment, along with lasting concerns over the effectiveness of national government. While their credit card balances have been declining, many consumers remain short on cash. (Fortunately, stock markets and home values had rebounded over the past few years, providing relief to some households. However, falling oil prices and a volatile stock market as of late 2015 were hurting consumers once again.) As of the second quarter in 2015, American households owed more than $3.24 trillion in non-housing outstanding consumer credit.

The drop in credit card and consumer debt has been much more dramatic. Balances on U.S. credit cards peaked in 2008 at $866 billion. By the second quarter of 2015, balances were $700 billion (which was up from $678.3 billion for the same quarter in 2014). The number of open credit card accounts has also fallen, from 496 million in 2008 to 313 million as of the first quarter of 2015, according to Argus Information & Advisory Services LLC.

During the last boom, growth in residential mortgages was extremely rapid. At the end of 2002, total mortgages outstanding in the U.S. for single-family homes and properties of up to four residential units totaled $6.4 trillion. By mid-2008, that amount had ballooned to $11.25 trillion, according to the Federal Reserve. This was more than four times the amount owed in 1990: $2.61 trillion.

Today, mortgages are more difficult to obtain than in the recent past, and households are being much more conservative in their real estate borrowing. Total residential mortgages owed were down to $10.03 trillion by the second quarter of 2012, both due to lower borrowing activity, and due to foreclosed mortgages being written off by lenders. By the second quarter of 2015, total residential mortgages for 1-4 family homes had fallen further to $9.90 trillion (although that was up slightly from 2014's $9.86 trillion for the same quarter).

A U.S. Bureau of Economic Analysis (BEA) report showed that the U.S. savings rate (that is, savings as a percent of after-tax disposable income) climbed from 0.6% for all of 2007, to 1.8% for 2008, further growing to 5.3% for 2010. (It was 4.6% in August 2015.) This savings rate may sound impressive, but it pales when compared to the 1980s average of 9.05%. (The 1990s savings rate averaged 5.83% for the decade, declining from 7.0% in 1990 to a meager 1.0% in 1999 as full-speed-ahead shoppers sailed into a sea of fiscal imprudence.)

Starting in late 2014, consumers are benefitting greatly from reduced gasoline prices worldwide. For example, U.S. households that drive their cars substantial amounts could enjoy reduced gasoline expenses of $500 to $1,500 or more yearly. Consumers will remain conservative, but this reduction in gasoline expenses will be of benefit to other types of businesses that rely on consumer purchases, including travel, entertainment, insurance, retailing and restaurants.

9) Bricks, Clicks and Catalogs Create Synergies While Online Sales Growth Surges

Analysts at eMarketer reported worldwide e-commerce sales of $1.316 trillion in 2014, expected to grow to $1.592 trillion in 2015. This figure includes online retail sales, but does not include digital downloads, sales of tickets to events or online gambling. The growth in e-commerce for 2014 was a sizzling 22.2%, compared to only 6.1% for retailing of all types, including retail stores. Global online sales have been supported by very strong results at Amazon.com, largely due to its competitive pricing, expansion of merchandise categories, free shipping for members of its "Prime" service and convenience of use. In 2015, Amazon will likely top $100 billion in revenues.

The recent year of 2013 can be marked as the date when in-store retailing truly began to suffer due to the continuous rapid growth of online shopping. Store traffic counts were down in the U.S. and many other nations, and retailers struggled to justify their inventory levels and operating budgets. This trend accelerated in 2014-2015. Generally speaking, a retailer without a successful online strategy doesn't have much of a future.

By 2015, Plunkett Research estimated that there were 104 million homes and businesses in the U.S. with broadband connections (plus 266 million wireless Internet access subscriptions for smartphones and tablets). Global Internet users topped 3.2 billion. Several factors will encourage consumers to do more of their shopping online, including today's wildly fluctuating gasoline costs, the fact that consumers feel pressed for time, the widespread adoption of high-speed Internet access, and the fact that the lowest prices can often be found online.

Online shopping often goes hand-in-hand with in-store shopping, or at least in-store browsing. A large number of shoppers browse web sites to gain information, later visiting a physical store to make a purchase. The reverse is also increasingly true—stores like Best Buy worry that shoppers come in to be able to touch and feel merchandise, and then go home to look for the best possible prices at online sites.

Many of the most successful companies among retail firms of all types will be those that take full advantage of the personal touch of traditional, store-based retailing and combine it with the growing popularity of catalog and Internet-based retailing. Such a strategy would entail:

- Seamless integration of store, catalog and Internet-based offerings to consumers, providing choices of 1) place and method of purchase, 2) method of pickup or shipment and 3) place or method of returns, repairs and additional services as needed.
- Communication of a seamless brand identity and level of service throughout catalogs, retail stores and web sites.
- Opportunities to offer personalized marketing and service through the use of customer profile data.

Few companies have reached this level of integration of traditional and non-traditional retailing. However, for good examples of companies that are evolving toward such "seamless" strategies, study Costco, Wal-Mart, REI, The Gap, Staples, Nordstrom and Victoria's Secret.

At lingerie giant Victoria's Secret, customers find enhanced flexibility and customer service thanks to the opportunity to shop via the web, Victoria's Secret catalogs or Victoria's Secret stores. In addition to the millions of catalogs that are mailed every week, stores hand out copies of the catalogs—which feature the web address of VictoriasSecret.com, as well as phone ordering options. The point is to create loyalty-inducing convenience for customers, giving them options for purchasing when, where and how they please.

Nordstrom began offering its customers the option to browse and buy online, and then pick up merchandise in stores as early as 2008. A year later, Nordstrom offered merchandise from all of its stores on its web site, effectively positioning each store as a warehouse for online shoppers. The response was immediately positive.

Wal-Mart offers "Pick Up Today," a program in which registered Wal-Mart shoppers order items online and then pick them up at their local store the same day. Best Buy has similar services, as do Bloomingdale's and Macy's. Although Wal-Mart was initially slow to embrace e-commerce, as of 2014 it became one of the largest U.S.-based online merchandisers, with more than $10 billion in global revenue.

These shop online but pickup in the store strategies were born because retailers were fighting a practice called "showrooming," in which shoppers browse for merchandise in stores but buy on rival retailers' web sites, especially Amazon.com. Amazon not only has a vast selection of items and free shipping for Prime members, its prices are also highly competitive.

One caveat in favor of brick and mortar stores is their ability to accept payments in cash. A sizeable number of Americans remain wary of online security and the possibility of identity theft, and they refuse to purchase items online via credit cards, even though they may comparison shop for prices. Also, there are a large number of consumers who are called "underbanked," that is, who are without bank accounts or credit cards. Wal-Mart offers customers the ability to order items online and then pick them up in stores using cash for payment.

Department stores are making a major shift in operations to support online orders. In yet another effort to compete with Amazon.com's success, Macy's converted many of its more than 800 stores to include expanded storerooms with cutting-edge technology to track inventory and generate shipping labels. Excess store inventory is shifted to highlighted positions on the company's web site, and merchandise that has sold out at the online distribution center may be found in stores, thereby remaining on the web site for sale and delivery by UPS. Online orders are being filled by stores closest to consumers, increasing efficiency and lowering costs.

Macy's is taking the technology a step further in select stores, where it is displaying merchandise with only one item of each style (instead of cramming the racks with every size available). Shoppers can look at the sample, and then use an app on their cell phones to let staff know what size and style they want to try on. Staff members collect the items from stockrooms and send them to fitting rooms via special hatches. Customers are alerted as to which fitting room is theirs via their phones. The practice allows Macy's to display more styles and avoid a cumbersome tangle of vast numbers of coat hangers.

Some brick and mortar retailers are opting to make selected merchandise available for online purchase only. Shoppers can browse samples in the stores and then place orders on their phones or at instore computer stations. Target tested the concept in 29 stores in 2015. Likewise, Bonobos (a clothing retailer) has samples in stores but all purchases are made online; and Blue Nile (diamond jewelry) has 500-square-foot "web rooms" where customers try on sample rings and then work with a stylist to pick a stone from a selection of 200,000 displayed on the firm's web site.

At the same time, a growing number of formerly online-only businesses are opening brick and mortar stores. For example, women's clothing site Boston Proper (a subsidiary of Chico's FAS) began opening boutiques in 2013 and had 14 open by early 2015. Rent the Runway, a dress and accessories rental site online, had four physical shops by late 2014. Online eyeglass retailer Warby Parker reported in late 2014 that its eight stores were collectively turning a profit and selling an average of $3,000 per square foot. The stores typically carry one-half to two-thirds of the styles and sizes available at such companies' web sites, and customers are encouraged to browse a computer station or use their phones to buy. Some retailers report that about 15% of their store purchases are made online at in-store kiosks.

As more and more people embrace online shopping, brick and mortar retailers must evolve to offer more convenience and speed. Shoppers are spending less time in stores as they prefer browsing on web sites and social media such as Facebook, Pinterest and Instagram. Chico's FAS reports that customers who once spent two hours in their stores now spend 45 minutes. Prices must transparently match those of competitors, or there is no sale.

SPOTLIGHT: Instant Smartphone Buying
A number of companies are implementing technology that allows shoppers to instantly purchase merchandise using their cellphones. ShopThis!, a partnership between MasterCard and Condé Nast, offers digital-edition magazine readers the ability to tap a shopping cart icon to buy items described in articles or featured in advertisements. Peapod, an online grocer that serves areas on the U.S. Northeast and Midwest, has a feature on its mobile app that affords users the ability to scan bar codes on grocery items at home or anywhere, automatically placing the item in the app's shopping cart, ready for purchase.

Another company, Paydiant, is working on technology that will allow TV watchers to scan quick response (QR) codes with their phones directly from their TV sets to buy desired items.

10) Retail Technologies Advance for Store Checkout and Restaurant Orders/Apps and Location-Based Ads Drive Sales

Retailers, especially grocery retailers, are investing heavily in new technology that will simplify transactions and increase customer service. Many shoppers have become used to the abundance of product information and the ease of finding it online. Brick and mortar retailers are having to find ways to offer similar information and convenience in stores. A host of advances, such as touch-screen information monitors, hand-held scanners, RFID tagging and fingerprint identification, are now in place at many stores worldwide.

Virtually all chain retailers are utilizing point-of-sale computer systems, in which bar code scanners immediately capture sales information at the cash register, adjust the inventory in the computer network and reorder merchandise automatically. The more advanced point-of-sale systems prompt cashiers with suggestions of additional merchandise that might go well with the items being purchased. This technology has helped companies like Wal-Mart and Nordstrom to become giants in their segments.

Checkout Technologies: Hand-held or shopping-cart mounted scanners can provide a "checkout-as-you-go" service. Shoppers pick up a scanning device and small computer monitor from a rack near the entrance (or grab a shopping cart with the device attached) and scan their store customer loyalty cards with a detachable barcode reader. Information about past purchases appears on the monitor as well as special offers dictated by personal preferences. As the shopper walks the aisles and scans items for purchase, the system keeps a running tally and suggests complementary items. Scan a jar of peanut butter, and the computer suggests buying jelly or offers an instant coupon on the brand of jelly purchased by that customer in the past. The system also beams signals to the store's central computer network regarding shoppers' locations in the store. The monitor displays information and special offers about nearby items, based on which aisle the customer happens to be in at a given time. An additional feature is the ability for shoppers to create online shopping lists at store web sites and have those lists beamed into the device and displayed on the monitor, complete with a map of the store indicating where each item can be found.

Ahold USA's Stop & Shop stores first had a shopping cart-mounted version of the system called the Shopping Buddy (made by IBM) in 20 of its stores in the northeastern U.S. In 2008, Stop & Shop switched to a smaller, hand-held device called easyShop which is made by Motorola and uses software developed by Modiv Media. The easyShop devices cost more than $500 each. As of 2012, Stop & Shop switched yet again to an even more powerful Motorola device called Scan It, which uploads a shopper's bill at self-checkout stations, and are in use in about 360 Ahold-owned Stop & Shop and Giant stores. Scan It apps are available for a variety of smartphones including Apple products and those on the Android operating system. Toshiba's TCxAmplify app enables shoppers to use their smartphones to scan items taken off shelves and placed in shopping baskets. When it's time to leave, users wave their phones in front of a computer, where a complete list of items is displayed and applicable loyalty program discounts applied. Payment can be made with credit cards or digital wallets such as Apple Pay. As of 2015, Shop-Rite groceries had the technology in many of its stores.

There are concerns that shoppers will attempt to leave stores without paying for their scanned merchandise. Video-surveillance is necessary as are random spot checks in which customers are required to pass through a traditional checkout stand where items are scanned all over again.

However, the efficiencies gained by shorter shopping times, customer convenience and personalized marketing may outweigh the growing pains. Watch for growing numbers of retailers to roll out versions of the personal scanning systems in the mid-term and beyond.

Paperless receipts are catching on as growing numbers of retailers offer digital transaction receipts that can be e-mailed to customers or posted to password-protected web sites. Participating retailers include Whole Foods Market, Gap, Inc., Sears and Kmart. Apple was a pioneer of the practice at its wildly popular stores. It also was among the first to offer checkout service from roving staff members with touch pad devices such as the iPod Touch, eliminating the need to wait in check-out lines.

Video Restaurant Menus and Ordering Kiosks: A number of restaurant chains, including Sonic Drive-Ins, are installing video menus that have point-of-purchase (POP) dynamic content. Customers place their orders using a touch screen, which are displayed complete with the total check amounts. Suggested additional items appear, some including special discount offers or promotions. The system is provided by MICROS Systems, a subsidiary of Oracle. The technology raises average check amounts, and also increases inventory efficiency, since it is connected with the restaurants' overall networks. If the POP is pushing a particular flavor of milkshake, for example, and customers respond, the system alerts owners to buy more ingredients. Installation and maintenance run about $135,000 per restaurant.

Meanwhile, Microsoft and CKE Restaurants, Inc. (which owns Hardee's and Carl's Jr.) were rolling out self-order kiosks in 2015. Using Dell Optiplex 3030 All-in-One devices, customers place their own orders and pay using credit cards or smartphone payment apps. Kiosks relay orders directly to kitchens, increasing speed and accuracy, and staff can easily update menus with seasonal offerings or promotions. The system also enables management to run sales and administrative reports, while employees can use the kiosks to clock in and out.

As of early 2015, TGI Fridays locations were equipping staff with rugged Windows 8.1 tablets, loaded with MICROS software, to use in collecting orders from customers and transmitting the orders to the kitchen. Leading restaurant chain Chili's has installed tabletop self-order devices made by Ziosk that can also receive orders, transmit them to the kitchen and handle credit card checkouts. In addition, the devices offer games and news feeds for a small additional fee. Chili's reported reliable increases in average checks, and the machines automatically suggest a 20% top for servers who deliver food and beverages. With U.S. restaurants under considerable pressure to raise employees' wages, many firms are keen to utilize advanced technologies that enable customers to enter and pay for their own orders, thus cutting down on the total number of staff members required to serve customers.

In-Store TV: Many retailers, including Kroger, Wal-Mart and Metro Group's Future Store in Rheinberg, Germany are installing large (up to 42 inch) plasma or high-definition LCD monitors throughout their stores. In the case of Wal-Mart, the monitors display a proprietary television network programmed with ads for a wide variety of merchandise. Each screen displays ads relating to nearby inventory. For example, a monitor near the bananas shows ads for produce, while another

monitor on the cereal aisle shows commercials for breakfast foods. Major food companies such as Kraft, Unilever and PepsiCo have bought airtime on the Wal-Mart network, which captures 130 million viewers every four weeks, making it the fifth-largest network in the U.S. (behind NBC, CBS, ABC and Fox). In addition to ads, in-store televisions often broadcast national and world news items and public service announcements.

Mobile Apps for Malls: Shopping mall owners including Simon Property Group, Westfield Group and Glimcher Realty Trust are experimenting with cellphone apps that do everything from helping shoppers remember where they parked, to providing mall maps, to alerting them to sales and promotions in nearby stores. Apps include Shopkick (which had 15 million users as of mid-2015, up from 8 million in 2014, and was acquired by SK Planet for $200 million), a rewards-based app that offers user points for visiting participating stores. The points can be converted into gift certificates or Facebook Credits.

Apple offers its iBeacon software on iOS7 mobile operating system that uses small signaling devices and works with apps such as Shopkick to alert customers to coupons or ads relating to nearby merchandise. For example, Hillshire Brands tested the software in 10 U.S. cities, finding that grocery shoppers were 20 times more likely to buy its brand of sausage when they received coupons and ads through the Epicurious recipe app. Major League Baseball placed beacons in 28 of 30 ballparks that transmit merchandise coupons and promote seat upgrades in addition to airing short location-specific videos about stadium history. Although only 3% of America's 3.6 million stores had adopted the use of iBeacon as of mid-2015, Apple hopes the software will catch on as usability becomes easier and cheaper. Google incorporated the software in its latest versions of Android, while GE Lighting is developing light bulbs that can track shoppers through iBeacon, meaning that retailers do not have to buy separate signaling hardware.

11) RFID Drives Inventory Management Evolution

The biggest technology breakthrough in inventory management is RFID (radio frequency identification)—the placement of microchips in product containers, cartons and packaging, combined with the use of special sensors in warehouses, hand-held scanners or store shelves that alert a central inventory management system as to shipment arrivals, product purchases and the need to restock inventory, communicating via wireless means. From loading docks to cash registers to parking lots, RFID readers have the potential to wirelessly track the movement of each and every item of inventory. Bar codes will be replaced by Electronic Product Codes (EPC), which are stored in RFID microchips. In retail stores, the chips could even eliminate the need to scan each item at checkout. Checkout stations will be equipped with receivers that automatically calculate purchases of an entire cart of merchandise at a time, rather than each individual item. These systems can lead to reductions in shoplifting and the elimination of costly manual inventory counts.

Leading suppliers of RFID equipment include:

Alien Technology, www.alientechnology.com
Avery Dennison, www.averydennison.com
Dust Networks,
www.linear.com/products/wireless_sensor_networks_-_dust_networks (a subsidiary of Linear Technology)
Intermec Technologies, www.intermec.com (a subsidiary of Honeywell International, Inc.)
Millennial Net, www.millennialnet.com
ODIN, www.odinrfid.com
Radiant RFID, www.radiantrfid.com
Savi, www.savi.com
SSE Technologies, www.ssetechnologies.com
Texas Instruments, www.ti.com
Thinfilm, www.thinfilm.no/

Another potential advantage of RFID is that manufacturers and distributors are able to reduce overall inventory, thanks to greater supply chain efficiency. Wal-Mart is heavily invested in this new technology. The greatest advantage of RFID implementation in stores such as Wal-Mart may be reduction of out-of-stock situations. The ability to keep popular items properly in stock means higher revenues.

At MIT, experts are endeavoring to enhance RFID systems by continuing work on a project originally called the Auto-ID Center. Now called EPCglobal, the initiative is backed by more than 50 companies including Wal-Mart, Procter & Gamble and Coca-Cola. (See www.gs1.org/epcglobal.) The project developed a common language for all RFID chips, thereby substantially reducing costs. It is estimated that costs must fall to between one and five cents per chip for this new wave of technology to be universally adopted. (As of 2015, costs in actual commercial RFID use were between 5 cents and 15

cents per tag for typical volume purchases, according to the RFID Journal.) EPCglobal has been at the forefront of design standards for all components of RFID systems, including electronic product codes for the tags and software to look after them.

Thinfilm is a Norway-based firm that uses printing to manufacture simple integrated electronics at a fraction of the cost of conventional electronics, in highly scalable processes compatible with high-volume, low-cost markets. Thinfilm has integrated sensing, data storage and display in a label format. Addition of a printed near-field communication (NFC) interface will allow Thinfilm's sensor labels to link sensor data to apps on mobile devices and/or cloud-based analytics. In early 2014, Thinfilm acquired U.S.-based NFC firm Kovio.

Yet another breakthrough in technology is the result of efforts made by Telmex Lab for Communications and Development, also at MIT. The lab has created a tiny dot called a Bokode that, while only 3 millimeters wide, can hold more than 10 megabytes of data. The data can be read by the camera installed in most smartphones.

The next step in RFID may be a nanoparticle-based covert barcode system that can be embedded in a wide variety of objects from polymers to drugs to inks to explosives. The nanoparticles are embedded during manufacturing and can be tracked by thermal analysis to follow the life of the object. Practical applications may include document authentication, manufacturer and/or vendor identification and location verification. Researchers at the Worcester Polytechnic Institute are studying the concept.

When fully implemented, advanced RFID and electronic sensor/monitor systems will be more than mere inventory management systems. They will be able to track virtually every item made, from the factory to the freight container to the shipping line to the warehouse to the store, even from the checkout lane to the home. They could even be used to sort recyclable items for reuse by the manufacturers, following the entire lifecycle of every product.

12) Advanced Vending Machines Enable Retailers to Set up Mini-Stores at Airports

A San Francisco startup company called Zoom Systems (www.zoomsystems.com) is placing extra-large vending machines, referred to as robotic retail store networks, in locations such as airports, hotels, office campuses and universities across the U.S. Instead of offering drinks and snacks, these machines typically offer up to 120 high-dollar items such as iPods, digital cameras, headphones and wireless laptop cards. Each machine is about 40 square feet in size. Users choose a product using a touch screen that displays detailed product information. A robotic arm retrieves a selected item and deposits it in a bin, at which time the user's credit card is charged. With hundreds of machines in place, Zoom is betting that consumers will have few problems with spending as much as $500 at a vending machine. Results are promising, as the machines generate between $60,000 and $240,000 in annual sales per location. Zoom had more than 1,500 ZoomShops in place as of 2015, in the U.S., Canada, Europe and Japan. Just as ZoomShops can be customized to locations, they can also be customized to brands. For example, a cosmetics company could customize a ZoomShop so that it carried the look and feel of the brand, and offered the best of its product line (Benefit Cosmetics LLC has pink vending machines that look like buses to sell its wares). Because the stores are located in high traffic consumer areas, these customized stores can provide branding opportunities as well.

Another widespread use for vending machines is DVD rentals. Customers charge the rental fees to credit cards. Redbox is a venture owned by Outerwall, Inc. (formerly called Coinstar, Inc.), that began with part ownership by a subsidiary of McDonald's Corporation. There were about 35,000 Redbox kiosks in the U.S. as of late 2015, in locations such as McDonald's restaurants, supermarkets, Wal-Marts and other high-traffic locations that offer a selection of about 120 to 200 movie titles each, for a modest daily rental fee. At their option, users may select DVDs online and then pick them up at a Redbox location. It costs the firm roughly $18,000 to install a kiosk. Redbox's revenues were $1.89 billion in 2014, $1.97 billion in 2013 and $1.91 billion in 2012. DVD rentals face daunting competition from online movie downloads, including the offerings of Netflix and Amazon.com.

13) Smartphones and Financial Technology ("FinTech") Enable New Mobile Payment Methods

A wide variety of services, technologies and strategies are now competing with conventional cash and credit cards for consumers' payment needs. Juniper Research expected global payments via mobile devices to rise 40% in 2014 over 2013, reaching $507 billion. However, in the U.S., consumers spent only about $50 billion in 2014 via mobile transactions, up from $37 billion in 2013.

Forrester Research forecasts that U.S. mobile-based payments will surge to $142 billion in 2019.

Smartphones as Credit Card Terminals: Smartphones are being used by merchants and service companies as credit cards, thanks to eBay's PayPal, Intuit and newer ventures including Square. Using a small scanner that plugs into a smartphone, users can process credit cards for a small fee. Square, for example, makes a device that plugs into the earphone jack of an iPhone or iPad (as well as some other smartphones). Related Square software is free and, once downloaded, users can ring up transactions for 15 cents each, plus 2.75% to 3.5% depending on the credit card company's rates. Likewise, PayPal has an iPhone app that is free, with transactions for bank accounts or PayPal accounts at no charge, or 30 cents plus 2.9% for credit card transactions. The technology is a boon for small businesses that previously worked only on a cash or check basis, since consumers increasingly rely on debit or credit cards.

SPOTLIGHT: Square

A frontrunner in mobile payment processing is Square (www.squareup.com), which offers an eponymous inch-square device called Square Reader that plugs into a smartphone. Credit or debit cards are swiped through a slot in the device and funds are deposited into the merchant's bank account less a transaction fee of at least 2.75%. Square accounts are set up through a free app called Square Register, and there is no credit check. The relatively low transaction fee and lack of credit testing is an attractive alternative to traditional bank-issued terminal systems. Square Reader is also capable of hands-free checkouts, in which mobile devices in customers' pockets or purses communicate automatically with nearby terminals. Receipts are transmitted after the transaction through the Square Register app. While Square was a pioneer in this technology, it now faces significant competition from a wide range of players, including Apple and Google.

Payments via Smartphones (Digital Wallets): To begin with, payment services have long been programmed into smartphones in much of Asia and in Scandinavia, which many users prefer over cash, credit cards or debit cards for small purchases. These phone-based payment accounts are typically pre-loaded with funds via a transfer from the user's bank account. Users are able to check the monetary balance on the smartphone's screen and then use phone-based online banking to transfer money from a checking or savings account to the chip. Virtually all mobile customers in Japan are using 3G and 4G mobile services, many of them utilizing smartphones that enable them to make payments. In South Korea, consumers receive offers from nearby stores and restaurants on their location-based smartphones and often pay their restaurant tabs and small purchases wirelessly.

Initially, the balance held in phone-based payment systems was typically no more than $200 or so, enough to make small, fast purchases. However, these services have evolved to enable consumers to make major debit and credit card charges.

The Google Wallet launched in 2011. It is an app that enables smartphones which are embedded with near field communication chips to pay for goods and services by waving the phones across readers at checkout counters. The related app is available on both the Apple App Store and Google play. Users with a Google Wallet account also are able to take advantage of Buy with Google icons on online shopping sites, and they can quickly book hotel rooms in Google's new hotel reservation service. Google Wallet account holders simply log into Google, and then do not have to enter shipping addresses or credit card numbers that are already stored in Google Wallet.

Payment via smartphone will be fostered by the fact that an increasing number of Americans are already interacting with their banks on their phones, keeping tabs on account balances and making transfers as needed. However, the difficulties of expanding America's smartphone-based financial activity into true mobile payments are many. Challenges include the facts that typical American smartphone users are wary of security issues, and there are already hundreds of millions of credit and debit cards in widespread use across the nation. U.S. households are very comfortable with using debit cards for day-to-day purchases, and it will be difficult for wireless payment firms to change their habits.

There are also questions about the fees generated by using mobile phones as payment devices. Every business involved in a transaction, from the credit card company to the smartphone service provider, wants a piece of the immense potential revenue. On the other side of the transactions, many retailers and restaurants are anxious to control mobile payments themselves and reduce their transaction costs.

Visa first announced the launch of Visa mobile services for Android-equipped phones back in 2008. T-Mobile and other carriers are marketing phones with Visa mobile software. Visa mobile customers

receive alerts of purchase activity based on customized card holder preferences. Consumers are able to personalize the types of alerts delivered to their mobile devices, such as the size of the transaction, or whether the transaction is in foreign currency. Because these alerts are triggered by the transaction as it passes through the Visa network, consumers will receive notifications almost immediately, a new way to combat fraud.

Customers holding the perk-loaded Visa Signature credit cards can download a special Visa Signature app via the Apple App Store and Google Play. The app enables them to connect to the card's concierge services, find nearby ATMs and access special offers, features and benefits.

In the U.S., consumers were barely aware of the payment by smartphone concept until 2014, when Apple announced Apple Pay. Users wave their iPhones over sales terminals and their credit card accounts are charged. Banks pay Apple 0.15% of every transaction made. The technology behind it, developed by Visa and MasterCard, replaces credit card information such as account numbers and expiration dates with unique series of numbers that validates the user's identity. Credit accounts may be linked to Apple Pay by taking a photo of a card or manually entering card information. Apple promises that credit card information will not be stored on iPhones or on the company's servers. The technology also works with the new Apple Watch, which launched in early 2015. Unfortunately, Apple was hit in early 2015 by a wave of fraudulent transactions using credit card data hacked from major retailers including Home Depot and Target. About 80% of the unauthorized purchases were made for high-priced merchandise at Apple stores.

By working with existing payment networks such as MasterCard, Apple is seamlessly entering the contactless (NFC) payment market. It doesn't need to invent a new network or new technology. It is simply adapting it into the iPhone and pushing it to its vast base of very enthusiastic Apple fans. According to MasterCard, there were already 2.5 million merchant locations worldwide equipped to handle NFC payments by 2014.

Apple is facing stiff competition from a group of more than 50 companies, including Wal-Mart, Best Buy, CVS, Lowe's and Gap, Inc., called Merchant Customer Exchange (MCX). MCX is working on CurrentC, a mobile wallet app that debits a customer's bank account instead of accessing credit card accounts. By bypassing credit cards, the merchants avoid the credit card transaction fees that currently cost them very significant amounts of money each year. Consumers use CurrentC by downloading a free app. MCX members by contractual agreement cannot accept competing mobile payments such as Apple Pay. Since the MCX consortium includes dozens of America's largest retailers (e.g., CVS is the nation's largest drug store chain), this is a major strategic offensive. However, by late 2015, MCX lost its exclusivity with its retail partners when the initial agreement expired, freeing the retailers to use alternative payment systems.

Digital wallets are also evolving to assist the rapidly growing number of consumers who make payments online. For example, MasterCard offers MasterPass. This service enables users to set up credit or debit card and shipping information in one secure electronic wallet. Once a user has filled out a shopping cart at a participating online store, he or she then clicks the "Buy With MasterPass" icon, logs in, and completes the purchase and payment. The intent is to increase convenience while reducing fraud.

Venmo, a hybrid of digital payment app and social media network, is gaining rapid market share among college students and urban professionals under age 30. The app enables money to be sent via smartphone between users who want to split bills at bars and restaurants or make or repay personal loans. The app, once downloaded to a user's smartphone, is linked to a bank account and often synced with social media contacts on sites such as Facebook. For the third quarter of 2014, the company reported that it processed $700 million in payments, up from $141 million for the same quarter in 2013. Venmo was acquired by Braintree, a Chicago-based mobile payment firm, of $26.2 million. PayPal bought Braintree for $800 million in 2014.

In China, where it is estimated that 650 million people use the Internet, the potential of the mobile payment market is staggering. iResearch expects the mobile payment market there to triple from $1 trillion in 2014 to $3 trillion in 2018. As of late 2015, social media giant Alibaba's Alipay mobile payment system held 80% of the market with about 350 million registered users. A number of other contenders are attempting to challenge Alipay's hold, notably major gaming and social media firm Tencent's Tenpay. Tencent's phenomenally popular social network, WeChat has 500 million users across China and more than 100 million accounts are linked to bank accounts.

14) Near Field Communications (NFC) Changes Credit and Debit Cards

As the world's leading credit card organization, Visa's very powerful brand could lead to rapid growth in mobile payments if it offers compelling services via near field technology (NFC). Visa's "payWave" technology enables card holders to pay at the cash register with a wave of a special credit card. Consumers are alerted to cash registers that use payWave by a unique logo at the register. They have the option of receiving a printed receipt, and enjoy Visa's zero consumer liability policy for unauthorized purchases if the card is lost or stolen.

NFC is similar to RFID, but can offer the advantage of two-way communications between devices. In the credit and debit card business, this is often referred to as contactless payment, waveable cards or tap and go. This means that consumers can simply wave the credit card past a reader—rather than rely on the swiping of a magnetic strip. The chip in each card uses encryption technology to deter theft and fraud. The idea is to speed up cash register lines and make things more convenient for consumers. For example, it is a practical technology for purchases at fast food counters, toll booths and vending machines. Signatures will not be required for small purchases made with these cards. Of course, ExxonMobil has been offering its contactless SpeedPass payment system at the gasoline pump for years, and millions of ExxonMobil card holders are enthusiastic users.

American Express offers "ExpressPay" contactless technology. Visa's system is called "Visa payWave". MasterCard has developed the "PayPass" NFC service in credit cards and debit cards. Generally, these technologies rely on an open software architecture that is easy for programmers to adopt.

NFC Sensors Will Revolutionize Monitoring of Goods and Patients

Oslo, Norway-based Thinfilm, a leader in printable thin electronic sensor and ID technology, suggests the following types of applications for NFC sensor monitoring:

- Temperature exposure of perishable goods such as food and pharmaceuticals can be verified.
- Disposable medical tests can be distributed to remote clinics and homes, with results communicated to medical records through a mobile device.

- Smart appliances can re-order supplies when quantities are getting low.
- Patients can be monitored with one-time use devices for blood-oxygen levels, pulse readings, and other vital signs. Data is gathered with the tap of a phone.

Another technology, called host card emulation (HCE), retrieves stored credit card information from the cloud, making extra security unnecessary. Visa and MasterCard have approved cards using HCE, and it is built into Android 4 and Android 5 (codenamed Lollipop and released in November 2014).

In March 2015, BMO Harris Bank, a unit of the Bank of Montreal, launched an NFC feature in which users enter a withdrawal amount on a cellphone app which generates a code called a QR code to the phone. The user then approaches an enabled ATM, presses a mobile cash button on the machine and places the phone with the QR code near a scanner to have the money dispensed. The bank promises transactions of 15 seconds compared to the usual 45 second average for a debit card withdrawal in addition to increased security.

15) Self-Service Apparel Fitting Technologies Grow in Stores and Online

Clothing Size Scanners: For those looking for better fit in a brick and mortar setting, there's the Virtual Fitting Room (VFR) by Intellifit, a private company outside of Philadelphia, Pennsylvania which was acquired by Unique Solutions in 2009. The VFR is a high-tech scanning booth that promises to scan customers for their exact measurements for use in making custom jeans. The process takes about 20 seconds, and is the result of technology developed by a U.S. Department of Energy research facility. Competitor Zugara, Inc. (www.zugara.com) offers three virtual dressing room products: WSS for Web, WSS for Kiosks and VSS for In-Store Retail. Using web cams and Kinect (Microsoft's motion-sensing device), Zugara's Webcam Social Shopper (WSS) system enables online and brick and mortar shoppers to view images of themselves wearing different items or against different backdrops and share those images with friends via Facebook and Twitter. WSS for Web is designed for e-commerce sites; WSS for Kiosks is for special event booths, in-store displays and out-of-home advertising; and VSS for In-Store Retail offers Virtual Style Sense technology that allows users to see themselves in various colors and

styles of store merchandise in fitting room mirrors. Zugara clients include Nordstrom, Ted Baker London, Barbie, Nokia, the Philadelphia Phillies and Major League Baseball.

Another initiative, True Fit, makes purchase suggestions to consumers from about 350 different brands based on favorite items already in shoppers' closets. True Fit was founded in Boston by statisticians interested in decreasing the 20% to 40% return rate for online clothing purchases. Rather than relying on measurements supplied by users, True Fit analyzes exact pattern measurements submitted by retailers. Shoppers enter information about their favorite clothes, including brand style and size. The system then matches those measurements with items available in participating stores and makes suggestions as to sizing. As of 2014, True Fit's retail partners included Macy's, Nordstrom, Lord & Taylor, Belk, Brooks Brothers and Gilt.com, and had surpassed 5 million users. In early 2015, the company raised $15 million in venture capital for expansion.

Interactive Mirrors & Windows: Mirrors that assist shoppers in matching styles or warn shoppers when items do not match use touch screens that allow shoppers to access information about apparel items such as available sizes or alternative item suggestions. Some mirrors utilize rear-projection that allows a shopper to stand in front of it while different outfits are projected onto the image (the shopper doesn't have to actually try an item on). Luxury Tec (which does business under the name Mirrus), a Winston Salem, North Carolina-based company, had about 3,000 of its interactive mirrors installed in clothing stores, airports, beauty salons and entertainment and sports venues around the world in 2012. However, the firm filed for bankruptcy in December 2013. A similar product, called Swivel, is made by FaceCake Marketing Technologies of Calabasas, California. Swivel uses Microsoft's Kinect Sensor to scan a shopper and display the shopper's image on a nearby monitor. The image can "model" selected apparel and accessories from every angle. Bloomingdale's New York City store and 19 other locations had installed Swivel as of mid-2012 and was continuing to add through 2014.

In a related technology, store windows have the ability to display selected items on an avatar via a touch screen. Shoppers can touch the window and use a menu to view a wide variety of items and combinations. Intel's smart mirror, which was in use in Neiman Marcus luxury department stores as of early 2015, can alter the color displayed in the image when a shopper makes a particular hand gesture, or display two looks side by side.

In December 2015, Neiman Marcus launched its new Memory Mirror, a giant video screen and camera that affords shoppers 360-degree views of outfits, the ability to compare clothing items side by side and reminders of what has been tried on. The technology, developed by MemoMi Labs, Inc., records eight-second videos that are password protected and can be emailed to friends and family. First tested at the store's San Francisco location, Memory Mirror was in 18 stores by late 2015.

Store Technologies for the Future: Intel, in partnership with a creative design firm in San Francisco, California called Frog Design, Inc. (www.frogdesign.com), worked on a prototype of an apparel kiosk that will serve as a virtual sales associate. To be used in department and other clothing stores, this kiosk enables shoppers to stand before a counter with two touch-screens, one at eye level and the other embedded in a waist-high counter. Wave a personal card (similar to shopping cards issued by grocery stores) before one of the screens and the system recognizes the shopper and has access to data regarding previous purchases. Wave the tag of a shirt from the store and the system displays information about coordinating pants, skirts, shorts or accessories for sale in the store; data regarding previous purchases that will complement the new shirt; and available discounts or sales prices that may apply. Intel hopes to outsource the building of these kiosks. Similar systems have been researched by other firms, including IBM's Virtual Mirror for assistance with cosmetics purchases (IBM worked with EZface on the project); and Microsoft, which also has worked on an apparel sales concept.

16) Retailers Look for Long-Term Growth in Emerging Markets, Including China, India and Brazil

The rise of vast numbers of low-income people to the middle class continues to create a massive global marketing opportunity. Wal-Mart already has roughly 260 million visitors to its stores worldwide in an average week, at 11,500 locations in 28 countries. How large will this number be on a global, long-term basis when the firm expands ever more deeply into Latin America, Asia and eventually Africa? 500 million? 1 billion? China is already a bigger market for GM's cars than its home nation of America. Amazon.com, Avon and McDonald's would not be the companies they are today without their immense

overseas customer bases, and they have barely scratched the surface of their potential growth.

Think of "middle class" as a condition that indicates, at the very least, that a family has a steady flow of a small amount of discretionary income that can be spent on luxuries or non-essential items. Solid entry into the middle class means that a household may own a scooter or a car (instead of walking, or riding a horse or a bicycle). A middle class family may own modern consumer electronics or be able to pay school tuition for its children.

Brazil was, until recently, an emerging economic powerhouse. Although Brazil's growth slowed in 2012-2015, there are numerous positive trends at work for the long-term. These include exceptional deep water offshore oil fields, an outstanding agriculture sector, along with other tremendous mineral resources, a young population and an entrepreneurial spirit. In 2015, the population of Brazil was only about 203.7 million, but it is growing, up from 194 million in 2009. By one government forecast, Brazil is expected to peak at a population of 219 million in 2037. Brazil faces a very long list of challenges, but nonetheless has tremendous potential.

Rising household income and a growing middle class in emerging nations offer lucrative expansion markets for retail firms headquartered elsewhere (such as leading retailers from Japan, Europe, the U.S. and Australia). However, multiple challenges face firms attempting to break into such markets. In addition to the need to understand local consumer tastes and requirements regarding packaging, displaying and advertising retail merchandise, there are daunting government regulations to overcome, and frequent encounters with difficulties in securing building permits and business licenses. Foreign retailers will eventually do well in these markets, but it is going to be a long haul requiring patience and significant investment. Another concern is that although economic growth continues in China, India that growth is slowing.

Chinese consumers are hungry for ever-widening varieties of products. These new shoppers seek the convenience, comfort and selection offered by Western-style stores. China's retail sector reached $4.10 trillion in 2014, up from $3.87 trillion in 2013, and only $2.86 trillion in 2011, according to the National Bureau of Statistics of China. The Chinese government has an official strategy of growing the importance of retail sales to the overall economy. The plan is for China to eventually be less reliant on exports and more reliant on domestic consumption.

Many of the world's largest general merchandise retailers are growing in China. Wal-Mart operated 415 stores in China as of late 2015, up from only189 in 2010, through a combination of joint ventures and minority-owned subsidiaries. German grocer Metro and, of course, Carrefour SA, the French discount giant, have all set up shop. Tesco Plc announced that it will have more than 200 hypermarkets in China by the end of 2015, up from a 105 stores in late 2011. The firm signed a 2014 store ownership joint venture with China Resources Enterprises. Carrefour has been opening hypermarkets at a rapid clip in China, expanding to 236 stores by late 2013. However, the company initially faced challenges at its new stores located in second- and third-tier cities.

New regulations, in accordance with China's 2001 entry into the World Trade Organization, took effect in December 2004 that allow foreign companies complete ownership of Chinese stores (foreigners were previously limited to a 65% stake and had to seek Chinese joint venture partners); require only local government approval instead of central-government okays; and allow stores to be located anywhere in China instead of only provincial capitals and selected large cities.

Although Chinese retailers of all kinds have the benefit of knowing the ins and outs of their local markets, they do not have the deep pockets, management expertise and scale of the foreign firms. The growing presence of Western retailers has created a healthy competitive atmosphere. In the mid-term, the new competition may drive forward the retail industry in China, as well as further develop the Chinese economy while it assists bottom lines in the U.S. and elsewhere.

Although China's economic growth is slowing, retail spending growth continues to increase. Industry analysts report that the country's retail sales in 2015 were expected to rise by 10.5% over 2014, well ahead of the estimated 6% to 7% in overall economic growth overall.

> **SPOTLIGHT: Dragon Mart**
>
> The Dragon Mart in Dubai is the largest Chinese shopping mall outside China. The mall is 0.75 miles long and has 3,950 shops offering everything from cheap furniture to fashion knock-offs to Chinese body products such as soaps, creams and lotions that claim to enhance beauty and health. The enormous facility, which attracts 65,000 visitors daily, is stocked by a logistics center next door which is operated by the China Ocean Shipping Company (COSCO), enabling goods to be delivered straight off the Dubai docks and wholesale purchases to be exported to any global destination. The Dubai Dragon Mart location is one of many spread out though the Middle East and Africa. The stores cater to emerging middle classes, which McKinsey estimates encompass 2 billion people who spend $6.9 trillion per year. In 2015, construction began on DragonMart2, a 2.9 million square foot expansion which will feature 500 new shops, Novo cinemas and another 4,500 parking spaces. A third phase is also planned with two residential towers, two 250-room hotels and 1.3 million square feet of leasable space.

India's retail sector had been largely closed to foreign companies. However, in September 2012, the Indian government opened the country's retail industry to foreign companies such as Ikea. The ruling allows foreign retailers to set up outlets through joint ventures, but stipulates that 30% of products sold must be sourced from small Indian firms. In 2013, India softened its position, allowing foreign firms five years to reach the 30% sourcing target. However, this ruling created significant controversy within India and led to strong protests from local firms that are concerned about attracting powerful foreign competition. A new government in 2014 reaffirmed limits on direct foreign investment in multi-brand retail ventures. Tesco secured government approval as of late 2014 for opening multi-brand stores through a 50-50 joint venture with Trent Hypermarket, Ltd., a unit of Tata Group.

Ikea has been sourcing products in India since 1987. The retailer hopes to invest $1.6 billion in India to open 25 stores over the next several years. In September 2014, the firm announced that it had signed agreements with the states of Karnataka and Telangana for the development of stores and distribution infrastructure. However, as of mid-2015, Ikea still did not have a store open, and the firm does not anticipate having one until 2017. Difficulties in compliance with local rules has delayed Ikea's plans.

Single brand retailers (e.g., Nike, Reebok, and Apple) are allowed a 51% stake in Indian wholesale outlets. Only a small percentage of India's retail business is conducted in chain stores so far. Most people shop at tiny "kirana" shops which are independently-owned microbusinesses that sell limited ranges of goods. While the middle class is smaller in India than in China, there remains exceptional long-term potential here for retailers.

Significant Indian retail enterprises exist, such as Pantaloon Retail (India) Ltd.'s Pantaloons department stores and Big Bazaar discount hypermarkets, Tata Group's Westside department stores and RPG Group's Spencer's. Pantaloon Retail had 116 large format stores in India in 2015, and 26 factory outlets.

Wal-Mart had hoped to open huge numbers of stores in India, in partnership with Bharti Enterprises, but dissolved the venture in 2013. This is a great disappointment to the giant American firm, as it has invested a vast amount of time and effort in India, including its six-year partnership with Bharti. Wal-Mart bought-out Bharti's stake in a separate wholesale partnership for the operation of cash and carry stores that sell at wholesale to businesses in India. As of mid-2015, the firm had 20 wholesale stores under the Best Price Cash & Carry name in India, and planned to open an additional 40 to 50 locations by 2018. Meanwhile, Wal-Mart launched e-commerce operations in India in 2014. Many firms find India too restrictive at present. Tough government regulations on top of difficulties in the supply chain (such as poor roads and subpar distribution systems) have pushed many companies to invest their time and money elsewhere.

India's consumers spend vastly less money per capita than China's. As of mid-2015, India had more than 300 malls, but most were struggling with high vacancy rates and poor sales. If regulations that inhibit foreign firms are eventually relaxed, India may see significant growth in retail.

17) Retail Center Occupancy Is High, with Sales Rising in Upscale Malls/Online Sales Hurt Stores

The largest enclosed shopping malls are sometimes referred to as "super-regional centers" (malls which include at least three department stores and at least 800,000 square feet of retail space.) Such malls often contain more than 1.2 million square feet. However, projects have become somewhat smaller since the recession of 2007-09, and it is much more difficult today for landlords to find multiple department store anchors.

Other types of shopping center properties, such as power centers and lifestyle centers, have been developing rapidly in recent years, in many cases robbing traffic from traditional malls. A "power center" is typically an open-air complex of category-dominant anchors such as category-killers, home improvement stores, discount stores and warehouse clubs. A "lifestyle center" is an open-air, highly landscaped configuration of approximately 50+ stores. Generally located near upscale neighborhoods, lifestyle centers offer leasable retail areas of 150,000 to 500,000 square feet, with at least 50,000 square feet of space typically dedicated to upscale national specialty stores such as Williams-Sonoma.

There are also hybrid centers, and value-oriented centers. Hybrids have some of the features of enclosed malls and lifestyle centers. That is, they have both open-air sections and enclosed sections. Value-oriented centers are built on formats that emphasize discounted prices. These include outlet malls. Many new value-oriented centers feature significant entertainment segments.

Cushman & Wakefield, a leading brokerage firm, reported shopping center completions in the U.S. in 2013 totaling 400 new centers and more than 129 million square feet, the first time shopping center completions rose since 2007. Up until then, so little retail space had been built that occupancy rates and rentals were improving in many markets. By the third quarter of 2015, analysts at Reis reported that the vacancy rate for regional malls was holding steady at 7.9%, down from a peak of 9.4% in the third quarter of 2011. For Neighborhood and Community malls (strip malls), the vacancy rate remained at 10.1%, down from the 11.1% peak in the third quarter of 2011.

Chain store executives are generally more cautious about opening new stores today. Many chains have significantly downsized their latest stores. While online sales have been soaring, retail store traffic and sales continued to be disappointing for some chains in 2014, including Wal-Mart's U.S. stores. National chain Coldwater Creek took bankruptcy in 2014, closing hundreds of stores. In 2015, American Apparel filed for Chapter 11 bankruptcy, as did Wet Seal and Quiksilver.

Analysts at eMarketer reported American e-commerce sales in 2014 of an estimated $430.2 billion (up significantly from $384.8 billion in 2013). This figure includes online retail sales, travel sales and digital downloads, but not sales of tickets to events or online gambling.

Shopping mall performance in recent years was sharply delineated by economic scale. Low-end malls showed weak sales per square foot while high-end malls were the most successful. Many malls that fit into the low-end category are old and outdated. CoStar Group, real estate information firm, reported in 2014 that about 80% of the 1,200 malls in the U.S. reported vacancy rates of less than 10% (down from 94% in 2006). However, approximately 3.4% of U.S. malls (typically on the low-end) were more than 40% empty.

Malls catering to wealthier customers cost more to build and operate, and are able to charge higher rental rates. Such malls have seen the best retail sales in recent years. For example, Taubman Centers, Inc., a luxury shopping center developer that owns malls in choice spots throughout the U.S., reported average sales per square foot of mall space of $809 in 2014, a figure much higher than typical malls. Average rent per square foot for 2014 was $60.58, up significantly from $57.33 in 2013 and $46.42 in 2012.

Simon Property Group, which owns, develops and manages major shopping centers throughout the U.S. and Puerto Rico, reported that regional mall sales per square foot improved slightly in 2014, reaching $619, up 0.2% from 2013. Base minimum rent per square foot reached $47.01 in 2014, up from $45.01 in 2013. These are rolling 12 month comparable sales per square foot for mall stores, less than 10,000 square feet in regional malls and all owned gross leasable area in premium outlets.

A number of retail chains, including Bloomingdale's and Nike, are experimenting with downsizing. Bloomingdale's store in Santa Monica, California, for example, is about one-eighth the size of its New York flagship store at only 105,000 square feet. The chain is gambling that shoppers are overwhelmed in larger stores that have greater volumes of merchandise from which to choose. Smaller spaces with few items could prove a cozier alternative, making shoppers more comfortable and therefore (hopefully) spending more. The Bloomingdale's store creatively utilizes its pared-down spaces by dropping dressing rooms when needed from recessed areas in the ceiling. The pod-like "rooms" look like Japanese lanterns. The 22,000-square-foot Nike store (compared to typical Nike-towns which are 50,000 square feet) in Santa Monica also uses flexible layout designs with cash registers mounted on moveable counters and interchangeable hardware fixtures that can be moved about at will.

As for post-recession power centers, 2013 began to see new tenants taking spaces formerly occupied by big box stores that have gone bankrupt. Spaces that previously held Circuit City, Borders or Mervyns are now home to discount retailers such as TJMaxx, Ross Dress for Less and Boot Barn. In the case of the latter, the western footwear retailer opened stores in spaces that were formerly Circuit Cities in 2012-13 in a number of U.S. markets.

SPOTLIGHT: Mall of America

The largest mall in the U.S. is the Mall of America (www.mallofamerica.com), located in Bloomington, Minnesota. First opened in 1992, it contains 4.2 million square feet of gross building area (2.5 million leasable) and is visited by an average of 110,000 people daily (or 40 million people per year). Entertainment is everywhere in this mall: 14 movie screens, a comedy club, night clubs, a 1.2-million gallon walk-through aquarium, a seven-acre amusement park, the Nickelodeon Universe theme park, LEGO building center, A.C.E.S. Flight Simulation and over 520 specialty shops.

Total employment in the center ranges from 11,000 in normal times and up to 13,000 during holiday and summer seasons. (Not everyone comes here just to shop: the Mall of America reports that more than 5,500 couples have exchanged wedding vows in the Mall's "Chapel of Love" wedding chapel, and the mall's mall-walking list, the "Walksport Mall Stars!" has registered more than 4,000 people.)

With the addition of a 306,000-square-foot Ikea home furnishings store, the mall enters its newest phase of construction. Shoppers from far and wide visit Bloomington and stay several days specifically to shop this mammoth mall. International visitors are common. Overall, visitors from outside the mall's 150-mile radius hover at around 35%.

The Ikea store, while not directly connected to the original mall, is part of a 42-acre new Phase II development just north of the original site. Tentative plans for new tenants include several hotels, an office building, a spa and entertainment attractions, which may include a performing arts theater. The Phase II mixed-use complex is zoned for up to 5.6 million square feet of new development.

18) Entertainment-Based Retailing, including Power Towns

Since the earliest days of the marketplace, merchants have realized that entertainment draws crowds of people who linger and shop. Even during the Dark Ages, jugglers, storytellers and other entertainers were an integral part of public markets, helping to draw throngs of people who might purchase goods.

For the foreseeable future, entertainment's value as a drawing card for retail customers will be of growing importance, especially for the retailing of goods beyond everyday staple items. In fact, the explosive growth of retailing over the Internet means that brick and mortar retailers must offer more than the mere availability of merchandise in order to lure shoppers out of their homes, away from their computer screens and web browsers and into the retail store. New shopping centers, especially those in urban areas, are devoting up to 40% of gross leasable area (GLA) to entertainment, restaurants and movie theaters.

Yet consumers still want the convenience found in neighborhood centers. Consequently, many new shopping center developments are including the most desirable elements of both power centers and lifestyle centers, including dominant anchor tenants in large formats, dotted with smaller specialty retailers and a plethora of entertainment and dining facilities, all set in a pleasant outdoor environment with sidewalks, trees, lawns and ponds. In many ways, they are the shopping center equivalent of the super-merchandiser stores.

These centers, sometimes called power towns, include Desert Ridge in Scottsdale, Arizona; the Burbank Empire Center in Burbank, California; and Avon Common in Avon, Ohio. They sprawl over 80 to 100 acres and contain 600,000 to 1,000,000 square feet of retail space. Builders spent 25% to 30% more on these areas than on a comparable power center, sparing no expense to make the stores and surrounding areas as pleasant and attractive as possible. Though the costs of power towns might be intimidating, they have impressive drawing power for customers. Desert Ridge, for example, brings in shoppers from a 15-mile radius, with many people driving past other shopping centers just to go there.

Beyond these initial projects, however, lies the potential for even more ambitious mixed-use projects. Developers are planning to make centers that not only provide entertainment but are also designed to be communities, with space for offices and residential areas. These projects may even include areas for post offices, day-care centers and community centers for performance theatres and galleries. An early form of this idea is found in the Easton Town Center, in Columbus, Ohio. Built for pedestrians instead of cars, the 1.7-million-square-foot retail center contains anchors such as Nordstrom, Barnes & Noble, a Trader Joe's and an AMC theatre, mixed in with a spa and fitness center, a comedy club and a mammography center. The retail center sits within a 1,300 acre, 12-million-square-foot mixed-use development overseen by The Georgetown Company and Limited Brands.

Canadian developer Triple Five Group (which owns the massive Mall of America in Minnesota) made headlines in early 2015 when it announced plans to build the largest enclosed mall in the U.S., to be located in Miami, Florida. The $4 billion American Dream Miami will feature a ski slope, a water park, a sea lion show, miniature golf, a bowling alley, a submarine ride, restaurants, a performing arts theater, a cinema, Ferris wheel, an ice rink and a roller coaster in addition to hotels and condominiums. Triple Five is hoping to capitalize on Miami's massive number of annual tourists, as well as explosive downtown population growth, which doubled from 40,466 in 2000 to 80,750 in 2014, and is expected to reach 92,519 by 2019.

Another ambitious project from the Triple Five Group is again on the drawing board in New Jersey. Originally called Xanadu, the rechristened American Dream Meadowlands was under construction on 21 acres as of late 2015. Anchor stores include Toys R Us (which is closing its Times Square flagship in 2016), Saks Fifth Avenue and Lord & Taylor. The complex will hold North America's largest indoor amusement park and the largest indoor water park, in addition to a ski slope, roller coaster and twin-body water slides. Completion is expected in 2017.

SPOTLIGHT: Dreamworks Animation Updates
Holiday Mall Visits

Starting in November 2014, eight U.S. malls
were featuring holiday tours through 2,000-square
foot Bavarian style cottages populated with
characters from Dreamworks' wildly popular *Shrek*
series, complete with simulated sleigh rides and visits
with live Santas. Parents make appointments
including online wish lists, negating waits in long
lines. LED screens in Santa's cottage feature pop-up
Shrek characters and hidden cameras take photos
while children visit Santa himself. The whole
structure can quickly change for other holidays
including Halloween by loading new LED images
and putting up different decorations. Each attraction
is called a Dreamworks DreamPlace.

19) Malls Remodel to Boost Sales and Attract Shoppers/Store Visitor Counts Are Disappointing

The face of retailing continues to evolve quickly.
Malls and their stores face daunting competition from
web sites, giant discount stores and wholesale clubs
such as Sam's. At the same time, many consumers
have lost enthusiasm for frivolous shopping and
needless credit card debt. Analysts at ShopperTrak
report that retail store traffic in general is down.
They further reported in 2014 that visits to first class
regional shopping malls are holding steady over the
past decade or so, but the number of stores that each
shopper enters has declined from 4.5 in 2007 to 3.0 in
2014. Malls are forced to adjust in order to stay in
business.

Mall owners and developers are finding that
investing in significant upgrades to existing malls can
yield exceptional financial rewards. General Growth
Properties invested $1.5 billion in redevelopment,
commencing work on 17 properties in 2012 and
acquired five interests in retail properties (totaling 1.3
million square feet) in 2014. Westfield Group spent
$3 billion between 2012 and 2015 (compared to the
$800 million it spent on redevelopment from 2008
through 2011).

Top malls typically bring in $700 per square foot
or more in annual sales, and have more than 1 million
square feet. Luxury anchor stores such as Neiman
Marcus, Nordstrom or Saks help ensure success, as
do smaller high-end retailers such as Tiffany, Prada
and Ralph Lauren. Shoppers also want cutting-edge
technology stores such as those operated by Apple,
Microsoft or Sony. Entertainment is an important
part of successful malls as well. Most

redevelopments include enhanced movie theaters
with full menus and lounge seating, children's play
areas and open pavilions for live entertainment.

One way to attract customers is to raise the
roof—literally tear off the connecting roofs between
stores to create an open-air environment. Parking
garages are coming down as well so shoppers can
park directly by the entrance of their favorite stores.
Typically built to have a single floor, the stand-alone
locations have plenty of close-in parking, and offer
shopping carts and centralized checkout stands for
convenience.

For example, Bella Terra in Huntington Beach,
California was an enclosed shopping mall built in
1966. Builder J.H. Snyder Company spent $170
million to tear off the roof and knock down walls,
transforming the mall into an open-air lifestyle center
with 74 shops and restaurants and a 4,000-seat, 20-
screen cinema megaplex. The rebuilt center features
Italian architecture and design accents. The Santa
Monica Place mall underwent a two-year, $265
million renovation, reopening in late 2010. The mall,
formerly an enclosed, three-story structure built in
the 1980s, now has roof-free spaces between stores
which converge on a central, open-air plaza. In 2012,
the Springfield Mall in Springfield, Virginia began a
multi-year, $200 million renovation that includes
building one centralized entrance, a state-of-the-art
movie theater complex and a food court in the initial
phase, as well as a 225-room hotel, pedestrian plazas,
recreational facilities and 2,000 residential units to be
part of later phases. In 2014, Houston's Galleria
began work on updating its Galleria III section,
moving anchor Saks Fifth Avenue to a larger 198,000
square foot space and closing one of the mall's two
Macy's stores. The project includes a standalone
structure in the current parking lot and a residential
tower.

Some operators of enclosed malls are scrambling
to find alternative tenants to fill empty spaces. Wal-
Mart, for example, opened a two-story store in a mall
in a suburb of New York City and a three-story
location in a Los Angeles mall formerly occupied by
a Macy's department store. The pluses for Wal-Mart
in these locations are access to mall shoppers without
having to acquire real estate that is scarce in
congested areas, as well as favorable leases with mall
owners who are anxious to fill large amounts of
space. On the other hand, Wal-Mart faces increased
security and logistics costs and the difficulty of
having to switch from a single-floor sprawl to multi-
story confusion. Costco is also experimenting with

former department-store spaces, opening three mall-based stores since 2010.

Tenants in marginal malls are morphing from strictly retail to include just about any entity that can pay the rent. Churches, government offices, schools, medical clinics and law firms are now often found in malls. Also, a number of cities are looking for cost-effective ways to use prime real estate that holds failing malls. Columbus, Ohio, for example, knocked down the City Center mall and built a park.

20) Fast Fashion: Designers and Retailers Speed Up

Several major retailers are based on a business model known as "fast fashion." Key players in this business include Sweden's Hennes & Mauritz (H&M); two Spain-based firms, Zara and Mango; the UK chain New Look; and Japan-based Uniqlo. For these retailers, success comes from designing trendy, inexpensive clothes that mimic high-end fashion and are delivered to consumers at lightning speed—two to four weeks from design to manufacturing to arrival in stores. This turnaround time is a far cry from the four to nine months that U.S. mass retailers typically require.

Fast fashion wasn't always part of New Look's business strategy. As the phenomenon began to heat up, New Look changed its business model to get a piece of the action. Originally a discount retailer, New Look has more than 800 stores, and ships merchandise to over 120 nations worldwide. New Look stocks new items every week in order to catch the attention of fashion-conscious shoppers.

Mango, which operated more than 2,415 stores in 107 countries as of early 2015, has developed a clever distribution system that keeps its products and its inventory current. Clothes are categorized according to basic style traits, such as dressy or casual, and then shipped to stores that are most successful at selling those specific categories of merchandise. This system has given it a competitive edge in the world of fast fashion and its products can hit the stores in just four weeks. Inditex, a massive apparel manufacturer and retailer headquartered in Spain, owns the Zara brand, which has more than 2,000 stores in 88 markets. Zara achieves one of the quickest turnaround times in the industry, as little as two weeks. Its efficiency should improve even further by the end of 2016 through the installation of RFID tag systems in all of its stores.

H&M is the largest player in the fast fashion market, both in terms of sales and stores. It operates over 3,500 stores worldwide, and posted $17.5 billion in fiscal 2014 sales. From design table to store rack, its lead time is three weeks. In keeping with the fast fashion model, H&M sometimes does not restock items—once they're gone, customers won't see them again.

H&M also faces competition from UK-based Primark Stores Limited, a brick and mortar only retailer with more than 250 stores in the UK, Ireland and Europe. With dresses selling for about $18, pants for less than $20 and boots for $25, Primark is sometimes even less expensive than H&M. During 2015, Primark planned to open seven locations in the northeastern U.S.

A practice related to fast fashion is "chasing," in which retailers order a small number of units for fast delivery to test the waters. Should the item(s) sell, retailers place a quick re-order. Teen-targeted retailer Aeropostale, Inc. is known for its chasing technique. The practice can be difficult for manufacturers, many of which were hard hit during the global recession, finding themselves with scaled-back orders or cancellations. Leery of ramping up production too quickly, some manufacturers are refusing late orders, leaving retailers short on merchandise to sell.

21) Luxury Item Sales Growth Slows

After falling off dramatically in the recession that began in late 2007, luxury goods sales began to rebound in 2010. Double digit growth was seen from 2010 through 2012. For 2015, Bain & Co. cut its forecast of global luxury spending from a rise of 2% to 4% to just 1%, or $280 billion, from 2014. High-end retailers such as Louis Vuitton and Burberry are facing tougher markets in China due to its slowing economy and the government's anti-extravagance and anti-corruption initiatives (luxury sales in China in 2015 are expected to fall for the second straight year). In the U.S., luxury good sales are being hurt by stock market volatility, along with a strong dollar that curbs purchases by tourists.

During the recession, luxury retailers began offering new merchandise at discounted prices in innovative and discreet ways. This practice continues, since even upscale shoppers demand competitive prices. Rather than post glaring "Sale" signs that may be perceived at odds with upscale images, retailers including Tiffany, Saks Fifth Avenue and Neiman Marcus are sometimes offering discounts at the time of purchase in innovative ways. For example, special discount offers may include something along the lines of a $100 store credit earned when making at least a $500 purchase. This is a practice long held at some chains for customers who purchase tens of thousands of dollars in merchandise at a given time. However, during the global recession, customers who made more modest purchases at a few national chains suddenly found themselves on favored customer lists.

For example, Neiman Marcus offers special promotions called "Midday Dash" sales in which e-mails are sent to preferred customers regarding one-day-only sale prices on specific merchandise. E-mails are sent early in the morning of the sale (which usually begins at 11:30 a.m. Eastern Standard Time). At the appointed hour, customers click on the link in the e-mail and view a limited access page on the Neiman Marcus site where around two dozen recently-stocked items are offered at as much as 50% off. A limited number of each item is available and are marked with "Sold Out" graphics on the web page once all have been purchased. Neiman Marcus also offers this kind of sale during evening hours.

Also, luxury brands have recently allowed e-commerce firms to offer last year's fashions at greatly reduced prices. Sites active in this market include Europe's yoox.com and gilt.com.

22) LOHAS- Socially Conscious Consumers Create Challenges and Opportunities for Advertisers and Marketers

LOHAS, an acronym for Lifestyles of Health and Sustainability, is a term used to describe the segment of consumers whose purchases are influenced by matters such as corporate social responsibility, recyclable materials, energy efficiency, organic contents, toxicity, allergens, environmental impact and alternative living styles. "Eco-friendly" products are important to them, but these consumers should not be confused with extreme "greens" or environmental fanatics.

LOHAS consumers typically prefer to buy organic or "natural" foods, dietary supplements and personal care products; they also often prefer alternative medicines and therapies in the form of acupuncture, massage and herbal remedies. Furthermore, these consumers tend to be strong advocates for renewable energy and seek out socially conscious products and companies.

LOHAS consumers are from all age groups and income levels. Although this group of people is far from homogeneous, it represents a significant and growing portion of the consumer market. Some of their issues have begun to gain popular momentum. In the face of growing levels of obesity, pervasive chemicals and hormones found in food, and the

world's massive fossil fuel consumption, concerns about personal health and sustainable energy have begun to affect consumer buying practices.

As a result, many more companies have begun to present themselves as environmentally and socially conscious entities. Many have taken steps to build green facilities, to place stricter controls on the working conditions at factories run by suppliers, or to ensure that fair wages are paid by suppliers. Many also contribute significant sums to charitable organizations. One example of this corporate trend is Gap Inc., which in 2004 released its first-ever "Social Responsibility Report." In an unusual move, the clothing retailer admitted problems with some suppliers regarding work and safety conditions, and revoked its approval of 136 factories. In the global business arena, social responsibility appears to be an important issue that companies must address.

Magazines as diverse as *Shape* and *Town and Country* have devoted entire issues to environmentally friendly topics. Advertisers jumped to provide eco-sensitive ads highlighting products that fall into "green" categories such as those using recycled packaging or non-animal tested. The trend has gathered strength, with regular columns and articles appearing every month in issues of a wide variety of publications.

Recent trends in high energy costs have combined with the global financial crisis to boost the LOHAS mentality. Consumers are now much more financially conservative, and they want items that are of lasting value. A "less is more" mentality will spread. For example, the continual growth in the size of the average new home built in the U.S. has stopped, and homes will be smaller, but smarter, going forward. The same is true in automobiles, as evidenced by the tremendous success of the small, but smart, cars like the Prius and the Mini. Health care costs and other considerations are boosting demand for products that promote a healthy lifestyle.

Discount giant Wal-Mart made news in mid-2009 when it informed its 100,000 suppliers that they must disclose full environmental costs of making their products. Wal-Mart will then compile a "sustainability index" based on the information and assign a grade to each supplier.

Internet Research Tip:

Wal-Mart, the world's largest retailer, has set dramatic goals for the application of the latest green technologies in packaging, energy and other areas. To see the results go to: http://corporate.walmart.com/global-responsibility/environmental-sustainability .

Savvy retailers, manufacturers and marketers will adopt the following practices in order to position themselves for the LOHAS market:

- Stress the utility and long-lasting value of products (as well as their inherent beauty and fashion)
- Stress an organization's sensitivity to environmental issues, energy concerns, personal health needs and restrained personal budgets
- Show consumers concrete examples of value, lowered environmental impact and/or reduced costs in products and services
- Cater to consumers' concerns about health issues by supporting appropriate causes and creating tie-ins to health education and issues
- Be aware that consumers will pay more for LOHAS-centric goods and services, but only when they see lasting value or reduced environmental impact. For example, surveys consistently show that many consumers will pay a bit more for electricity that is generated by renewable means. Another example: Each month, thousands of consumers pay a higher price for hybrid-equipped vehicles than they would have paid for traditional cars, despite the fact that it can take years and years to earn a return on that extra cost
- Day-to-day consumer products must be priced within reason, even if they have high LOHAS factors

23) How to Interpret Reports of Retail Sales

Because several different organizations publish monthly sales reports on America's retail sector, these reports can be tricky to interpret, depending on exactly which portion of retail you are trying to track.

Period Compared: At all times, you should be aware of the dates being compared. For example, a comparison of April 2015 sales over March 2015 (the previous month) will be quite different from a comparison of April 2015 sales over April 2014 (the previous year).

Same-Store Sales/Comparable Store Sales: You should also be aware of the difference in "Same-Store Sales" and "Total Sales." Same-Store Sales are results only for the stores in a retail chain that have been open for at least 12 months. This is a solid indicator of the consistency of sales through the chain. For example, in April 2004, Wal-Mart reported an increase in Total Sales of 11.7% over the previous year. However, Same-Store Sales were up only 4.4%. The difference accounted for the fact that Wal-Mart opened a large number of new stores over the previous 12 months. (Same-Store Sales may also be referred to as Comparable Store Sales.)

The following is a list of easy-to-use resources for retail sales trends.

A. U.S. Department of Commerce Reports—Retail Stores, Automobiles, Food Service

To begin with, the U.S. Department of Commerce (DOC) publishes its Monthly Retail Trade Survey, and a corresponding Annual Retail Trade Survey at www.census.gov/retail . When you see this bureau's retail trade figures in print, however, bear the following things in mind:

1) DOC includes all types of retail trade in its numbers, including new and used automobiles, gasoline and food service at restaurants.
2) Every month, the DOC surveys a few thousand stores and restaurants (out of a total U.S. base of about 3 million) to get its figures.
3) If you dig deeper into its reports, the DOC breaks down sales by category of store. Near the top of its reports, you will find "Total" (including autos and restaurants), "Total excluding automobiles and parts" and "GAFO." The GAFO figure represents General Merchandise stores only, including department stores, furnishings, electronics and appliances, clothing, books, sporting goods, office supplies and gifts.
4) Next, be aware that the DOC reports "Adjusted" and "Not Adjusted" sales. The Adjusted figures have been altered to allow for seasonal variations, such as the dates of major holidays.
5) The DOC publishes "Advance Monthly Sales" as an estimate for the previous month. For example, in mid-November, DOC

published advance estimates of October retail sales. A final, more conclusive report is published several weeks later. www.census.gov/retail

B. U.S. Department of Commerce—Retail E-Commerce Sales Reports

The DOC includes "Non Store Sales" in its monthly and annual reports. It also issues a very useful, separate report ("Retail E-Commerce Sales") that breaks out e-commerce sales and compares the market share of e-commerce to traditional sales. These reports track the growth of e-commerce sales over a period of several quarters and several years so that you can readily see the growth of Internet-based retailing. www.census.gov/retail

C. comScore E-Commerce Sales Reports

comScore Networks, Inc. (www.comscore.com) also tracks retail sales online on a continuing basis. Its figures can be very useful in tracking the growth of e-commerce, and they are published much faster than those of the DOC.

It's important to note that surveys of e-commerce sales can vary widely, depending on whether they include revenues from travel booked online (a huge category) and automobiles or other peripheral items sold online. The comScore reports are broken down to show the difference that adding in sales of travel would make.

D. Major Chain Store Sales and the International Council of Shopping Centers

An industry group that represents mall and shopping center owners, the International Council of Shopping Centers (ICSC, www.icsc.org), reports on sales at selected major national chains. While the reports are extremely useful in tracking general merchandise sales, it should not be confused with total retail sales at all types of stores.

ShopperTrak Weekly and Monthly Retail Reports: ShopperTrak (www.shoppertrak.com) promptly provides very useful retail sales reports. Its products include the respected National Retail Traffic Index (NRTI) and the National Retail Sales Estimate (NRSE).

National Retail Federation Monthly Reports: The National Retail Federation (NRF) is a massive trade organization representing firms involved in the retail industry. Its monthly reports on retail sales, which can be found at www.nrf.com, focus mainly on results at major chain stores, many of which are mall-based.

Chapter 2

RETAIL INDUSTRY STATISTICS

U.S. Retail Industry Overview

	Amount	Unit	Year	Source
Total Retail Sales in 2015[1]	5,318.2	Bil. US$	2015	PRE
Total Retail Sales in 2014[1]	5,208.4	Bil. US$	2014	Census
GAFO[2] sales in 2014	1,236.9	Bil. US$	2014	Census
Total e-Commerce Retail Sales in 2015[3]	347.3	Bil. US$	2015	eMarketer
Total e-Commerce Retail Sales in 2014[3]	304.1	Bil. US$	2014	eMarketer
Motor Vehicle & Parts Dealers	1,033.9	Bil. US$	2014	Census
Furniture & Home Furnishings	98.2	Bil. US$	2014	Census
Electronics & Appliance Stores	106.1	Bil. US$	2014	Census
Bldg. Materials & Garden Equip. & Supplies Dealers	318.7	Bil. US$	2014	Census
Food & Beverage Stores	662.9	Bil. US$	2014	Census
Health & Personal Care Stores	302.1	Bil. US$	2014	Census
Gasoline Stations	536.8	Bil. US$	2014	Census
Clothing & Accessories Stores	248.8	Bil. US$	2014	Census
Sporting Goods, Hobby, Book & Music Stores	83.9	Bil. US$	2014	Census
General Merchandise Stores	667.5	Bil. US$	2014	Census
Miscellaneous Store Retailers	115.3	Bil. US$	2014	Census
Nonstore Retailers	458.1	Bil. US$	2014	Census
Food Services & Drinking Places	576.2	Bil. US$	2014	Census
Annual Disposable Personal Income per Capita, 2013	39,123	Current US$	2013	BEA
Annual Disposable Personal Income per Capita, 2014	40,461	Current US$	2014	BEA
Total Exports of Goods	1,620.5	Bil. US$	2014	ITA
Total Imports of Goods	2,347.7	Bil. US$	2014	ITA
Employment in Retail Trade	15,692.5	Thou.	2015[4]	BLS
Number of U.S. Shopping Centers	113,400		2015	PRE

[1] Includes food services sales. [2] GAFO sales include general merchandise, apparel, furniture and miscellaneous specialty store segments within the retail industry. The term excludes automotive and food stores. [3] Does not include online travel or event ticket sales. [4] As of August 2015.

PRE = Plunkett Research estimate; Census = U.S. Census Bureau; eMarketer = eMarketer, Inc.; BEA = U.S. Bureau of Economic Analysis; ITA = International Trade Administration; BLS = U.S. Bureau of Labor Statistics

Source: Plunkett Research, Ltd. Copyright © 2015, All Rights Reserved
www.plunkettresearch.com

Annual Consumer Price Index, 1925-2015

U.S. City Average for All Urban Consumers, 1982-1984=100

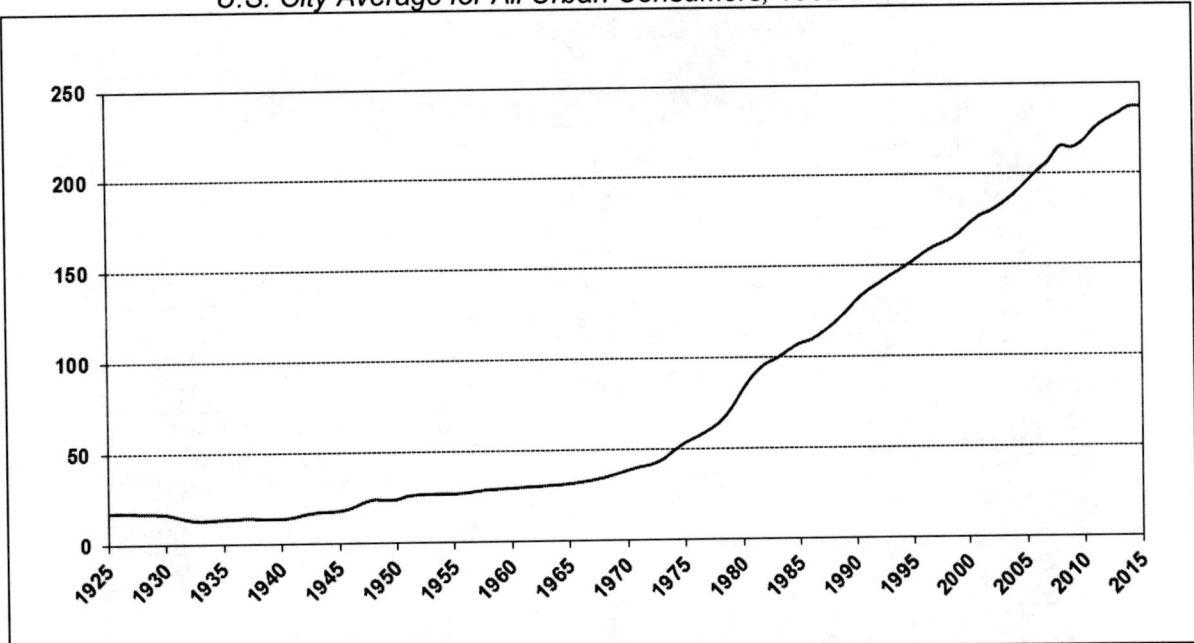

CPI Average Values and Percent Change

Year	CPI	% Change	Year	CPI	% Change	Year	CPI	% Change
1925	17.5	-12.50%	1965	31.5	6.42%	2005	195.3	13.41%
1930	16.7	-4.57%	1970	38.8	23.17%	2010	218.1	11.65%
1935	13.7	-17.96%	1975	53.8	38.66%	2011	224.9	3.16%
1940	14.0	2.19%	1980	82.4	53.16%	2012	229.6	2.07%
1945	18.0	28.57%	1985	107.6	30.58%	2013	233.0	1.46%
1950	24.1	33.89%	1990	130.7	21.47%	2014	236.7	1.62%
1955	26.8	11.20%	1995	152.4	16.60%	2015*	236.9	0.09%
1960	29.6	10.45%	2000	172.2	12.99%	Sept. 2015	237.945	1275.41%**

The Consumer Price Indexes (CPI) program produces monthly data on changes in the prices paid by urban consumers for a representative basket of goods and services.

* Value is a year-to-date average of January-September.

** Percent change from January 1925 to September 2015.

Source: Bureau of Labor Statistics

Plunkett Research, Ltd.

www.plunkettresearch.com

Exports, General Imports & Trade Balance in Goods, U.S.: 1989-2nd Quarter 2015

(In Billions of US$; Latest Year Available)

Year	Total goods[1]			Manufactured goods		
	Exports	Imports	Balance	Exports	Imports	Balance
1989	363.8	473.4	-109.6	285.7	398.3	-112.7
1990	393.0	495.3	-102.3	328.8	407.5	-78.7
1991	421.7	487.1	-65.4	362.2	406.8	-44.6
1992	448.2	532.7	-84.5	386.5	448.0	-61.6
1993	465.1	580.7	-115.6	405.2	492.2	-87.0
1994	512.6	663.3	-150.6	448.7	568.2	-119.6
1995	584.7	743.5	-158.8	508.1	638.2	-130.1
1996	625.1	795.3	-170.2	547.0	675.5	-128.5
1997	689.2	869.7	-180.5	614.3	743.4	-129.2
1998	682.1	911.9	-229.8	613.3	797.5	-184.2
1999	695.8	1,024.6	-328.8	629.2	886.3	-257.1
2000	781.9	1,218.0	-436.1	708.0	1,023.9	-315.9
2001	729.1	1,141.0	-411.9	655.8	960.7	-304.8
2002	693.1	1,161.4	-468.3	622.3	984.0	-361.7
2003	724.8	1,257.1	-532.4	646.7	1,048.2	-401.6
2004	814.9	1,469.7	-654.8	726.2	1,213.7	-487.5
2005	901.1	1,673.5	772.4	805.3	1,346.7	-541.4
2006	1,026.0	1,853.9	-828.0	914.4	1,481.7	-567.3
2007	1,148.2	1,957.0	-808.8	1,008.8	1,550.9	-542.1
2008	1,287.4	2,103.6	-816.2	1,112.3	1,577.5	-465.2
2009	1,056.0	1,559.6	-503.6	917.9	1,236.4	-318.5
2010	1,278.5	1,913.9	-635.4	1,101.4	1,513.1	-411.7
2011	1,482.5	2,208.0	-725.4	1,268.0	1,719.9	-451.9
2012	1,545.8	2,276.3	-730.4	1,341.4	1,809.1	-467.7
2013	1,578.4	2,268.4	-689.9	1,375.1	1,834.0	-458.9
2014	1,620.5	2,347.7	-727.2	1,402.3	1,927.0	-524.7
Q2 2015	760.7	1,109.9	-349.2	665.3	957.0	-291.7

[1] Includes non-monetary gold, military grant aid, special category shipments, trade between the U.S. Virgin Islands and foreign countries and undocumented exports to Canada. Adjustments were also made for carryover. Import values are based on transaction prices whenever possible.

Source: Foreign Trade Division, U.S. Census Bureau

Plunkett Research, Ltd.

www.plunkettresearch.com

Total U.S. Retail Sales & Annual Percent Change: 1992-2015

(Includes Retail Automobile, Gasoline & Food Services Sales)

Year	Total Retail Sales (In Billions of US$)	Percent Change (%)
1992	2,014.1	NA
1993	2,153.1	6.9%
1994	2,330.2	8.2%
1995	2,450.6	5.2%
1996	2,603.8	6.3%
1997	2,726.1	4.7%
1998	2,853.0	4.7%
1999	3,087.0	8.2%
2000	3,287.5	6.5%
2001	3,378.9	2.8%
2002	3,459.1	2.4%
2003	3,612.5	4.4%
2004	3,846.6	6.5%
2005	4,085.7	6.2%
2006	4,294.4	5.1%
2007	4,439.7	3.4%
2008	4,392.8	-1.1%
2009	4,066.8	-7.4%
2010	4,288.3	5.4%
2011	4,601.8	7.3%
2012	4,831.1	5.0%
2013	5,011.7	3.7%
2014	5,208.4	3.9%
2015*	5,318.3	2.1%

* Plunkett Research estimate.

NA = Not Available.

Source: U.S. Census Bureau; Plunkett Research, Ltd.

Plunkett Research, Ltd.

www.plunkettresearch.com

U.S. Retail Trade Corporation Statistics, 2nd Quarter 2015

(Data Not Seasonally Adjusted)

U.S. Retail Trade Corporations, Assets $50 Million and Over - Income Statement[1,2]	Q2 2015	Q1 2015	Q2 2014
	(In Millions US$)		
Net sales, receipts, and operating revenues	$669,959	$637,473	$655,373
Less: Depreciation, depletion, and amortization	13,242	13,311	12,511
Less: All other operating costs and expenses	622,859	592,683	611,116
Income (or loss) from operations	33,858	31,479	31,746
Interest expense	5,156	4,618	4,590
Net nonoperating income (expense)	4,016	2,965	3,573
Income (or loss) before income taxes	32,718	29,826	30,729
Less: Provision for current and deferred domestic income taxes	10,668	7,630	10,232
Income (or loss) after income taxes	22,050	22,196	20,497
Cash dividends charged to retained earnings in current quarter	6,217	13,400	5,870
Net income retained in business	15,833	8,796	14,627
Retained earnings at beginning of quarter	405,850	407,967	380,524
Other direct credits (or charges) to retained earnings (net)	(6,248)	(5,018)	(3,425)
Retained earnings at end of quarter	415,434	411,746	391,725

U.S. Retail Trade Corporations, Assets $50 Million and Over - Income Statement Ratios[1,2]	Q2 2015	Q1 2015	Q2 2014
	(In Cents Per US$ of Sales)		
Net sales, receipts, and operating revenues	100.00	100.00	100.00
Less: Depreciation, depletion, and amortization	1.98	2.09	1.91
Less: All other operating costs and expenses	92.97	92.97	93.25
Income (or loss) from operations	5.05	4.94	4.84
Interest expense	0.77	0.72	0.70
Net nonoperating income (expense)	0.60	0.47	0.55
Income (or loss) before income taxes	4.88	4.68	4.69
Less: Provision for current and deferred domestic income taxes	1.59	1.20	1.56
Income (or loss) after income taxes	3.29	3.48	3.13

U.S. Retail Trade Corporations, Assets $50 Million and Over - Operating Ratios[1,2]	Q2 2015	Q1 2015	Q2 2014
	(In Percentages)		
Annual rate of profit on stockholders' equity at end of period:			
Before income taxes	26.30	23.68	24.60
After income taxes	17.72	17.62	16.41
Annual rate of profit on total assets:			
Before income taxes	9.76	8.99	9.71
After income taxes	6.58	6.69	6.48

[1] Retail Trade data are the quarterly results of companies within the Retail Trade sector with total assets of $50 million and over at the time of sample selection.

[2] Complete Income Statement and Balance Sheet Financial Tables are available at the U.S. Census Quarterly Financial Report website.

Source: U.S. Census Bureau

Plunkett Research, Ltd.

www.plunkettresearch.com

Total Annual Sales of Merchant Wholesalers, U.S.: 2009-2014

(Figures In Millions of US$, Not Seasonally Adjusted)

NAICS Code	NAICS Description	2009	2010	2011	2012	2013	2014
42	Total Merchant Wholesalers, Except Manufacturers' Sales Branches and Offices	3,816,811	4,318,429	4,862,565	5,165,158	5,322,612	5,551,108
423	Durable Goods	1,739,701	1,990,944	2,220,613	2,379,057	2,452,714	2,588,460
4231	Motor Vehicle & Motor Vehicle Parts & Supplies	254,307	299,169	332,903	389,313	398,310	414,067
4232	Furniture & Home Furnishings	54,519	57,491	61,242	66,879	71,242	75,469
4233	Lumber & Other Construction Materials	85,389	85,264	87,051	92,491	103,531	109,832
4234	Professional & Commercial Equipment & Supplies	354,204	398,976	414,498	416,556	428,077	446,376
42343	Computer & Computer Peripheral Equipment & Software	182,010	219,945	222,876	219,188	223,806	233,911
4235	Metals & Minerals, Except Petroleum	109,910	133,784	167,091	174,323	168,878	186,033
4236	Electrical & Electronic Goods	341,603	395,082	433,693	481,739	517,144	556,435
4237	Hardware, & Plumbing & Heating Equipment & Supplies	90,113	95,675	103,179	111,017	116,225	121,559
4238	Machinery, Equipment, & Supplies	275,145	303,313	353,710	391,138	401,130	432,030
4239	Miscellaneous Durable Goods	174,511	222,190	267,246	255,601	248,177	246,659
424	Nondurable Goods	2,077,110	2,327,485	2,641,952	2,786,101	2,869,898	2,962,648
4241	Paper & Paper Products	81,667	84,032	85,810	86,642	88,325	92,808
4242	Drugs & Druggists' Sundries	390,818	413,828	440,448	457,058	482,837	544,387
4243	Apparel, Piece Goods, & Notions	126,523	137,225	144,191	149,103	155,380	169,112
4244	Grocery & Related Products	476,640	494,441	524,037	549,430	571,407	606,347
4245	Farm Product Raw Materials	165,342	183,914	227,987	246,510	260,275	254,179
4246	Chemicals & Allied Products	89,378	103,041	116,757	122,038	125,430	131,816
4247	Petroleum & Petroleum Products	433,416	587,092	756,431	806,488	810,124	786,989
4248	Beer, Wine, & Distilled Alcoholic Beverages	108,296	110,574	115,566	121,224	124,499	128,193
4249	Miscellaneous Nondurable Goods	205,030	213,338	230,725	247,608	251,621	248,817

Note: A merchant wholesaler is a business that sells to retailers, contractors, or other types of businesses (including farms), but not to the general public (or at least not in any significant amount). Estimates are based on data from the Monthly Wholesale Trade Survey, and have been benchmarked using the results of the Annual Wholesale Trade Survey.

Source: U.S. Census Bureau

Plunkett Research, Ltd.

www.plunkettresearch.com

Total Monthly Sales and Inventories of Merchant Wholesalers, U.S.: January-August 2015

(Estimates In Millions of US$, Not Seasonally Adjusted)

NAICS Code	NAICS Description	2015 Jan.	2015 Feb.	2015 March	2015 April	2015 May	2015 June	2015 July	2015 Aug.ᴾ
	Sales								
42	**Total Merchant Wholesalers, Except Manufacturers' Sales Branches and Offices**	**416,696**	**394,548**	**456,691**	**457,213**	**445,777**	**472,536**	**455,804**	**439,345**
423	**Durable Goods**	**202,133**	**186,690**	**223,768**	**219,485**	**209,412**	**229,025**	**218,802**	**213,316**
4231	Motor Vehicle & Motor Vehicle Parts & Supplies	32,556	31,880	38,326	37,463	36,738	37,882	37,250	35,894
4232	Furniture & Home Furnishings	6,091	5,680	6,564	6,727	6,349	6,931	6,821	6,936
4233	Lumber & Other Construction Materials	8,019	7,541	9,117	9,878	9,602	10,955	10,594	10,125
4234	Professional & Commercial Equipment & Supplies	34,398	31,063	38,877	36,644	33,488	40,721	38,323	34,832
42343	Computer & Computer Peripheral Equipment & Software	17,869	15,488	19,627	18,825	16,632	21,266	20,318	17,162
4235	Metals & Minerals, Except Petroleum	14,823	13,509	14,798	13,917	13,443	14,159	13,143	12,949
4236	Electrical & Electronic Goods	45,902	40,109	47,960	47,602	45,657	49,663	45,634	46,514
4237	Hardware, & Plumbing & Heating Equipment & Supplies	9,128	8,886	10,607	10,865	10,689	11,998	11,535	11,190
4238	Machinery, Equipment, & Supplies	32,920	30,590	38,055	37,785	35,322	37,297	36,544	36,066
4239	Miscellaneous Durable Goods	18,296	17,432	19,464	18,604	18,124	19,419	18,958	18,810
424	**Nondurable Goods**	**214,563**	**207,858**	**232,923**	**237,728**	**236,365**	**243,511**	**237,002**	**226,029**
4241	Paper & Paper Products	7,495	6,931	8,002	8,018	7,823	8,468	8,203	8,151
4242	Drugs & Druggists' Sundries	47,002	45,466	52,223	51,698	49,379	52,713	53,054	50,773
4243	Apparel, Piece Goods, & Notions	12,792	13,303	14,796	13,625	12,838	13,741	15,347	16,005
4244	Grocery & Related Products	48,303	45,945	51,754	51,357	51,807	50,810	52,138	51,501
4245	Farm Product Raw Materials	20,848	18,569	18,678	20,242	17,973	18,334	17,154	15,272
4246	Chemicals & Allied Products	10,573	10,051	11,048	11,045	10,486	11,337	11,256	10,617
4247	Petroleum & Petroleum Products	40,646	39,870	42,785	44,187	48,225	50,017	46,782	42,978
4248	Beer, Wine, & Distilled Alcoholic Beverages	8,410	9,061	10,691	11,059	11,451	12,824	11,791	11,202
4249	Miscellaneous Nondurable Goods	18,494	18,662	22,946	26,497	26,383	25,267	21,277	19,530

(Continued on Next Page)

Total Monthly Sales and Inventories of Merchant Wholesalers, U.S.: January-August 2015 (cont.)

(Estimates In Millions of US$, Not Seasonally Adjusted)

NAICS Code	NAICS Description	2015 Jan.	2015 Feb.	2015 March	2015 April	2015 May	2015 June	2015 July	2015 Aug.[P]
	Inventories								
42	Total Merchant Wholesalers, Except Manufacturers' Sales Branches and Offices	577,251	579,088	580,895	579,407	576,353	577,695	577,996	574,205
423	Durable Goods	352,832	356,407	356,857	358,753	359,762	359,614	361,532	359,503
4231	Motor Vehicle & Motor Vehicle Parts & Supplies	58,363	61,465	60,126	61,476	61,544	62,956	63,952	60,931
4232	Furniture & Home Furnishings	10,558	10,277	10,343	10,380	10,574	10,893	11,335	11,420
4233	Lumber & Other Construction Materials	13,839	14,130	14,385	14,905	15,028	14,967	14,919	14,772
4234	Professional & Commercial Equipment & Supplies	40,845	40,166	39,898	39,944	39,776	39,643	39,813	40,117
42343	Computer & Computer Peripheral Equipment & Software	15,996	15,336	15,628	15,770	15,979	15,903	15,844	16,052
4235	Metals & Minerals, Except Petroleum	32,622	32,332	32,223	31,576	31,419	30,937	30,461	29,734
4236	Electrical & Electronic Goods	46,303	46,611	47,037	47,258	47,920	47,558	48,301	49,479
4237	Hardware, & Plumbing & Heating Equipment & Supplies	21,641	21,901	22,527	22,963	23,011	22,730	22,941	22,989
4238	Machinery, Equipment, & Supplies	101,411	103,193	104,373	104,436	104,873	103,760	103,299	102,904
4239	Miscellaneous Durable Goods	27,250	26,332	25,945	25,815	25,617	26,170	26,511	27,157
424	Nondurable Goods	224,419	222,681	224,038	220,654	216,591	218,081	216,464	214,702
4241	Paper & Paper Products	7,835	7,667	7,598	7,895	7,750	7,768	7,787	7,576
4242	Drugs & Druggists' Sundries	53,823	52,495	54,821	54,031	56,712	55,674	55,481	54,808
4243	Apparel, Piece Goods, & Notions	27,356	26,875	26,239	27,026	27,753	29,872	31,411	32,128
4244	Grocery & Related Products	32,819	31,646	32,475	32,569	32,328	32,732	33,525	33,573
4245	Farm Product Raw Materials	27,089	26,230	24,567	20,514	16,606	16,955	15,478	14,150
4246	Chemicals & Allied Products	12,481	12,123	12,061	12,323	12,499	12,736	12,913	13,086
4247	Petroleum & Petroleum Products	18,388	19,172	18,454	19,234	19,146	20,395	18,884	17,965
4248	Beer, Wine, & Distilled Alcoholic Beverages	14,634	14,656	15,326	15,600	15,632	15,682	15,622	15,449
4249	Miscellaneous Nondurable Goods	29,994	31,817	32,497	31,462	28,165	26,267	25,363	25,967

Note: A merchant wholesaler is a business that sells to retailers, contractors, or other types of businesses (including farms), but not to the general public (or at least not in any significant amount). Estimates are based on data from the Monthly Wholesale Trade Survey, and have been benchmarked using the results of the Annual Wholesale Trade Survey.

[P] Preliminary estimates.

Source: U.S. Census Bureau

Plunkett Research, Ltd.

www.plunkettresearch.com

Retail & Food Services Sales by Kind of Business, U.S.:
Monthly, through August 2015

(In Millions of US$; Not Seasonally Adjusted)

Kind of Business	Jan.	Feb.	Mar.	Apr.	May	Jun.	Jul.	Aug.P	CY CUM	PY CUM
Retail & food services sales, Total	396,495	385,731	442,876	437,160	461,889	447,608	457,195	456,513	3,485,467	3,413,478
Retail sales & food services excl. motor vehicle & parts dealers	317,033	305,303	345,218	342,182	363,139	351,895	358,251	357,546	2,740,567	2,717,983
Retail sales, total	348,575	339,180	389,831	384,957	406,577	395,674	404,158	403,383	3,072,335	3,032,894
Retail sales, total (excl. motor vehicle & parts dealers)	269,113	258,752	292,173	289,979	307,827	299,961	305,214	304,416	2,327,435	2,337,399
GAFO[1]	89,902	89,530	100,225	96,255	105,020	99,657	101,980	107,860	790,429	778,449
Motor vehicle & parts dealers	79,462	80,428	97,658	94,978	98,750	95,713	98,944	98,967	744,900	695,495
Automobile & other motor vehicle dealers	72,978	73,890	90,187	87,561	91,388	87,987	91,112	91,481	686,584	637,608
Automobile dealers	69,448	69,859	83,862	80,756	84,166	80,929	84,603	85,661	639,284	594,344
New car dealers	62,426	61,314	75,100	72,374	76,213	73,192	76,847	77,943	575,409	533,847
Used car dealers	7,022	8,545	8,762	8,382	7,953	7,737	7,756	7,718	63,875	60,497
Automotive parts, acc. & tire stores	6,484	6,538	7,471	7,417	7,362	7,726	7,832	7,486	58,316	57,887
Furniture, home furnishings, electronic & appliance stores	15,965	15,355	16,564	15,356	16,448	16,369	16,838	17,095	129,990	127,610
Furniture & home furnishings stores	7,759	7,403	8,404	8,034	8,673	8,350	8,834	8,848	66,305	62,945
Furniture stores	4,371	4,221	4,696	4,314	4,820	4,591	4,745	4,830	36,588	34,452
Home furnishings stores	3,388	3,182	3,708	3,720	3,853	3,759	4,089	4,018	29,717	28,493
Electronics & appliance stores	8,206	7,952	8,160	7,322	7,775	8,019	8,004	8,247	63,685	64,665
Appliances, TV & other electronics stores	5,671	5,551	5,729	5,255	5,686	5,744	5,859	6,055	45,550	46,381
Household appliance stores	1,227	1,209	1,369	1,292	1,463	1,477	1,486	1,381	10,904	10,701
Radio, TV & other elect. stores	4,444	4,342	4,360	3,963	4,223	4,267	4,373	4,674	34,646	35,680
Computer & software stores	(S)	(S)	(S)	(S)	(S)	(S)	(S)	(S)	(S)	(S)
Building materials, garden equipment & supplies dealers	21,222	19,996	26,588	31,628	33,428	31,800	30,740	27,928	223,330	214,307
Building material & supplies dealers	18,857	17,695	23,021	25,840	27,170	26,903	26,957	24,703	191,146	182,521
Hardware stores	1,756	1,686	1,994	2,162	2,276	2,145	2,079	2,028	16,126	15,150
Food & beverage stores	55,954	51,402	56,081	55,070	58,679	56,275	58,724	57,372	449,557	436,225
Grocery stores	50,652	46,192	50,329	49,257	52,290	50,073	52,204	51,174	402,171	391,118
Supermarkets & other groc. (except conv.) stores	48,980	44,542	48,434	47,298	50,116	47,904	49,907	48,990	386,171	375,945
Beer, wine & liquor stores	3,578	3,519	3,882	3,867	4,371	4,243	4,526	4,251	32,237	30,950
Health & personal care stores	25,865	24,257	26,446	25,742	25,665	25,898	26,084	26,137	206,094	197,130
Pharmacies & drug stores	21,775	20,129	21,866	21,590	21,494	21,535	21,845	21,755	171,989	164,434

(Continued on next page)

Retail & Food Services Sales by Kind of Business, U.S.: Monthly, through August 2015 (cont.)

(In Millions of US$; Not Seasonally Adjusted)

Kind of Business	Jan.	Feb.	Mar.	Apr.	May	Jun.	Jul.	Aug.[P]	CY CUM	PY CUM
Gasoline stations	32,002	31,033	36,075	36,297	40,093	40,839	41,615	39,889	297,843	370,553
Clothing & clothing accessory stores	15,589	17,787	20,614	20,306	22,072	19,565	20,441	22,180	158,554	154,517
Clothing stores	11,543	12,541	15,465	15,120	16,198	14,574	15,178	16,134	116,753	112,384
Men's clothing stores	636	693	763	839	872	778	719	776	6,076	5,845
Women's clothing stores	2,806	3,094	3,968	3,873	4,200	3,623	3,565	3,799	28,928	28,904
Family clothing stores	5,813	6,297	7,874	7,774	8,355	7,586	8,207	8,520	60,426	57,503
Shoe stores	2,057	2,585	2,923	2,734	2,860	2,513	2,847	3,612	22,131	22,279
Jewelry stores	1,777	2,470	2,030	2,221	2,765	2,276	2,188	2,221	17,948	18,259
Sporting goods, hobby, book & music stores	6,365	5,606	6,710	6,414	6,839	6,924	7,026	8,169	54,053	51,132
Sporting goods stores	2,832	2,823	3,669	3,553	3,809	4,072	4,081	4,335	29,174	27,527
Book stores	1,426	683	660	658	764	699	717	1,550	7,157	7,169
General merchandise stores	49,475	48,413	53,890	51,667	57,034	54,286	54,941	57,309	427,015	424,641
Department stores (excl. LD)	10,855	11,237	13,197	12,390	13,714	12,712	12,691	13,724	100,520	102,580
Discount dept. stores	7,358	7,322	8,704	7,867	8,739	8,445	8,528	9,271	66,234	67,063
Department stores(excl. discount department stores)	3,497	3,915	4,493	4,523	4,975	4,267	4,163	4,453	34,286	35,517
Department stores (incl. LD)[2]	11,083	11,466	13,429	12,539	13,927	12,864	12,835	13,914	102,057	104,650
Discount dept. stores	7,460	7,424	8,787	7,867	8,775	8,445	8,528	9,316	66,602	68,005
Department stores(excl. discount department stores)	3,623	4,042	4,642	4,672	5,152	4,419	4,307	4,598	35,455	36,645
Other general merchandise stores	38,620	37,176	40,693	39,277	43,320	41,574	42,250	43,585	326,495	322,061
Warehouse clubs & superstores	33,847	32,142	35,074	33,835	37,421	35,963	36,643	38,066	282,991	280,692
All other general merchandise stores	4,773	5,034	5,619	5,442	5,899	5,611	5,607	5,519	43,504	41,369
Miscellaneous store retailers	8,635	8,571	9,329	9,480	10,656	10,469	10,464	10,581	78,185	74,465
Nonstore retailers	38,041	36,332	39,876	38,019	36,913	37,536	38,341	37,756	302,814	286,819
Electronic shopping & mail-order houses	30,633	28,819	32,840	32,270	31,908	32,509	33,383	33,102	255,464	229,476
Fuel dealers	4,389	4,542	3,623	2,173	1,577	1,456	1,449	1,386	20,595	28,219
Food services & drinking places	47,920	46,551	53,045	52,203	55,312	51,934	53,037	53,130	413,132	380,584
Full service restaurants	21,820	21,034	23,820	22,647	24,460	22,659	23,041	23,198	182,679	167,324
Limited service eating places	20,127	19,446	22,660	22,637	23,852	23,058	23,673	23,434	178,887	164,323
Drinking places	1,818	1,755	2,029	1,894	2,046	1,891	1,987	1,987	15,407	14,705

CY CUM = Current Year Cumulative. PY CUM = Previous Year Cumulative. LD = Leased Department Stores. P = Preliminary.

[1] GAFO represents stores classified in the following NAICS codes: 442, 443, 448, 451, 452, and 4532. NAICS code 4532 includes office supplies, stationery, and gift stores.

[2] Includes data for leased departments operated within department stores. Data for this line not included in any aggregate kind-of-business totals.

(S) Suppressed - Estimate does not meet publication standards because of high sampling variability (coefficient of variation is greater than 30%), poor response is less than 50%), or other concerns about the estimate's quality.

Source: U.S. Census Bureau

Plunkett Research, Ltd.

www.plunkettresearch.com

Retail & Food Services Sales by Kind of Business, U.S.:
2009-2014

(Estimates in Millions of US$; Not Seasonally Adjusted)

NAICS Code	Kind of Business	2009	2010	2011	2012	2013	2014
	Retail & food services sales, total	4,066,822	4,288,339	4,601,788	4,831,131	5,011,740	5,208,443
	Total (excl. motor vehicle & parts dealers)	3,394,907	3,545,172	3,787,200	3,943,141	4,049,759	4,174,533
	Retail sales, total	3,614,452	3,820,863	4,105,990	4,306,237	4,469,022	4,632,289
	Retail sales, total (excl. motor vehicle & parts dealers)	2,942,537	3,077,696	3,291,402	3,418,247	3,507,041	3,598,379
GAFO[1]		1,088,369	1,114,590	1,155,854	1,192,197	1,213,518	1,236,878
441	Motor vehicle & parts dealers	671,915	743,167	814,588	887,990	961,981	1,033,910
4411	Automobile dealers	552,200	621,471	686,336	754,579	822,075	888,261
44111	New car dealers	486,896	549,951	610,747	674,538	737,640	799,592
44112	Used car dealers	65,304	71,520	75,589	80,041	84,435	88,669
4413	Automotive parts, accessories & tire stores	74,409	78,218	83,183	84,349	85,094	86,162
442	Furniture & home furnishings	84,894	85,408	87,652	91,552	94,879	98,232
4421	Furniture stores	45,761	46,594	47,585	49,668	50,522	52,848
4422	Home furnishings stores	39,133	38,814	40,067	41,884	44,357	45,384
443	Electronics & appliance stores	95,533	97,642	100,287	102,644	103,744	106,081
44311	Appliance, T.V. & other electronics	72,907	71,580	72,287	73,080	73,365	75,282
443111	Household appliance stores	15,295	15,464	15,874	16,457	17,129	16,601
443112	Radio, T.V. & other electronics stores	57,612	56,116	56,413	56,623	56,236	58,681
44312	Computer & software stores	19,795	23,241	25,188	26,742	27,723	(S)
444	Building materials, garden equipment & supplies dealers	261,772	260,737	269,711	281,869	302,150	318,690
4441	Building materials & supplies dealers	227,663	225,961	232,958	242,616	260,310	273,871
44413	Hardware stores	18,697	18,749	20,099	20,821	21,091	22,968
445	Food & beverage stores	569,084	581,546	610,307	629,880	643,520	662,853
4451	Grocery stores	510,359	521,252	548,336	564,877	576,421	591,622
4453	Beer, wine & liquor stores	40,443	41,707	42,812	44,911	46,624	48,650
446	Health & personal care stores	253,278	261,204	272,707	275,799	283,761	302,144
44611	Pharmacies & drug stores	217,283	222,265	231,342	230,422	236,171	251,406
447	Gasoline stations	391,479	448,693	532,412	555,407	551,576	536,802
448	Clothing & accessories	204,192	212,847	227,984	238,773	244,548	248,848
4481	Clothing stores	151,155	157,924	167,615	175,342	178,517	181,773
44811	Men's clothing stores	7,550	7,565	8,240	8,757	9,209	9,492
44812	Women's clothing stores	36,857	38,881	41,678	43,896	43,948	46,479
44814	Family clothing stores	79,886	82,952	86,154	89,592	92,589	93,931
4482	Shoe stores	25,711	27,332	29,377	31,216	32,971	33,971
44831	Jewelry stores	25,567	25,725	28,795	29,760	30,305	30,514

(Continued on Next Page)

Retail & Food Services Sales by Kind of Business, U.S.: 2009-2014 (cont.)

(Estimates in Millions of US$)

NAICS Code	Kind of Business	2009	2010	2011	2012	2013	2014
451	**Sporting goods, hobby, book & music stores**	80,069	80,208	80,540	82,771	84,393	83,875
45111	Sporting goods stores	36,506	37,305	38,969	42,106	44,360	43,849
451211	Book stores	15,780	15,206	13,673	12,201	11,431	10,889
452	**General merchandise stores**	589,228	604,210	625,371	643,039	653,093	667,475
4521	Department stores (excl. L.D.)	186,799	185,062	183,764	177,794	171,749	168,896
452112	Discount department stores	123,212	119,808	117,564	114,279	110,600	108,232
4521	Department stores (incl. L.D.)	190,006	188,103	186,968	181,010	175,080	172,233
452112	Discount department stores	124,872	121,436	119,181	115,882	112,143	109,692
4529	Other general merchandise	402,429	419,148	441,607	465,245	481,344	498,579
45291	Warehouse clubs & superstores	354,566	368,050	386,423	406,414	419,581	433,568
45299	All other general merchandise stores	47,863	51,098	55,184	58,831	61,763	65,011
453	**Miscellaneous store retailers**	101,778	104,299	108,373	110,093	112,618	115,291
4532	Office supplies, stationery & gift stores	34,453	34,275	34,020	33,418	32,861	32,367
454	**Nonstore retailers**	311,230	340,902	376,058	406,420	432,759	458,088
4541	Electronic shopping & mail-order	235,352	262,912	293,582	325,817	348,126	374,556
722	**Food services & drinking places**	452,370	467,476	495,798	524,894	542,718	576,154
7221	Full service restaurants	193,985	198,908	214,081	227,559	234,778	252,097
7222	Limited service eating places	195,022	203,477	214,323	226,107	235,855	248,022
7224	Drinking places	19,990	20,236	20,623	21,466	21,507	22,208

[1] GAFO sales include general merchandise, apparel, furniture and miscellaneous specialty store segments within the retail industry. The term excludes automotive and food stores. GAFO represents stores classified in the following NAICS codes: 442, 443, 448, 451, 452, 4532.

L.D. = Leased Department Stores.

(S) Suppressed - Estimate does not meet publication standards because of high sampling variability (coefficient of variation is greater than 30%), poor response is less than 50%), or other concerns about the estimate's quality.

Source: U.S. Census Bureau

Plunkett Research, Ltd.
www.plunkettresearch.com

Estimated Quarterly U.S. Retail Sales, Total & E-Commerce:
1st Quarter 2006-2nd Quarter 2015
(In Millions of US$; Not Seasonally Adjusted, Holiday & Trading-Day Differences;
Does Not Include Food Services)

Quarter	Retail Sales in US$ Mil.		E-commerce as a % of Total Retail Sales	% Change Over Same Quarter Previous Year	
	Total	E-commerce*		Total Sales	E-commerce
2006 Q1	895,144	25,411	2.8	7.2	26.5
2006 Q2	985,254	25,734	2.6	5.8	23.3
2006 Q3	976,445	26,793	2.7	4.0	21.3
2006 Q4	1,017,242	35,056	3.4	3.3	25.0
2007 Q1	922,149	30,322	3.3	3.0	19.3
2007 Q2	1,014,251	31,493	3.1	2.9	22.4
2007 Q3	1,001,108	32,248	3.2	2.5	20.4
2007 Q4	1,061,748	42,063	4.0	4.4	20.0
2008 Q1	952,159	34,169	3.6	3.3	12.7
2008 Q2	1,030,586	34,170	3.3	1.6	8.5
2008 Q3	1,002,944	33,396	3.3	0.2	3.6
2008 Q4	960,717	39,498	4.1	-9.5	-6.1
2009 Q1	832,243	32,185	3.9	-12.6	-5.8
2009 Q2	910,007	32,789	3.6	-11.7	-4.0
2009 Q3	916,048	34,317	3.7	-8.7	2.8
2009 Q4	972,110	45,617	4.7	1.2	15.5
2010 Q1	880,879	36,842	4.2	5.8	14.5
2010 Q2	966,868	38,230	4.0	6.2	16.6
2010 Q3	956,616	39,809	4.2	4.4	16.0
2010 Q4	1,037,091	54,014	5.2	6.7	18.4
2011 Q1	950,321	43,841	4.6	7.9	19.0
2011 Q2	1,042,473	44,948	4.3	7.8	17.6
2011 Q3	1,034,463	45,545	4.4	8.1	14.4
2011 Q4	1,105,739	63,549	5.7	6.6	17.7
2012 Q1	1,023,847	50,589	4.9	7.7	15.4
2012 Q2	1,088,805	51,285	4.7	4.4	14.1
2012 Q3	1,077,244	52,643	4.9	4.1	15.6
2012 Q4	1,154,244	72,361	6.3	4.4	13.9
2013 Q1	1,055,389	58,215	5.5	3.1	15.1
2013 Q2	1,140,006	60,498	5.3	4.7	18.0
2013 Q3	1,135,418	61,857	5.4	5.4	17.5
2013 Q4	1,197,402	83,709	7.0	3.7	15.7
2014 Q1	1,077,723	66,938	6.2	2.1	15.0
2014 Q2	1,176,780	68,858	5.9	4.6	15.1
2014 Q3	1,168,187	70,351	6.0	4.2	15.7
2014 Q4	1,225,969	93,530	7.6	3.9	13.9
2015 Q1	1,077,586	74,920	7.0	1.5	14.4
2015 Q2[P]	1,187,172	78,750	6.6	0.9	14.4

[P] Preliminary Estimate.

* E-commerce sales are sales of goods and services over the Internet, an extranet, Electronic Data Interchange (EDI) or other online system. Payment may or may not be made online.

Source: U.S. Census Bureau
Plunkett Research, Ltd.
www.plunkettresearch.com

Total U.S. Disposable Income, Expenditures & Gross Domestic & National Product Per Capita: Selected Years, 1960-2014

(In US$; Per Capita Estimates)

Year	Disposable Personal Income		Personal Consumption Expenditures		Gross Domestic Product		Gross National Product		Population (In Thous.)
	Current US$	Chained (2009) US$	Current US$	Chained (2009) US$	Current US$	Chained (2009) US$	Current US$	Chained (2009) US$	
1960	2,083	11,877	1,834	10,461	3,006	17,182	3,023	17,318	180,760
1965	2,641	14,144	2,282	12,226	3,827	20,442	3,854	20,627	194,347
1970	3,713	16,643	3,158	14,155	5,246	23,003	5,277	23,183	205,089
1975	5,645	18,614	4,782	15,766	7,820	24,907	7,880	25,143	215,981
1980	8,861	20,159	7,705	17,528	12,570	28,295	12,720	28,676	227,726
1985	12,991	22,961	11,416	20,176	18,225	31,805	18,331	32,034	238,506
1990	17,235	25,556	15,291	22,675	23,901	35,756	24,040	35,986	250,181
1995	20,753	27,180	18,696	24,486	28,749	38,125	28,856	38,285	266,588
2000	26,206	31,524	24,053	28,933	36,419	44,475	36,550	44,649	282,398
2001	27,179	32,075	24,904	29,390	37,240	44,464	37,422	44,694	285,225
2002	28,127	32,754	25,643	29,862	38,122	44,829	38,291	45,041	287,955
2003	29,198	33,342	26,720	30,512	39,606	45,664	39,837	45,943	290,626
2004	30,697	34,221	28,166	31,399	41,857	46,967	42,160	47,321	293,262
2005	31,760	34,424	29,711	32,203	44,237	48,090	44,549	48,442	295,993
2006	33,589	35,458	31,136	32,868	46,369	48,905	46,595	49,156	298,818
2007	34,826	35,866	32,319	33,284	47,987	49,300	48,404	49,738	301,696
2008	36,101	36,078	32,881	32,860	48,330	48,697	48,895	49,270	304,543
2009	35,616	35,616	32,050	32,050	46,930	46,930	47,422	47,422	307,240
2010	36,274	35,684	32,931	32,395	48,302	47,719	48,967	48,323	309,808
2011	37,804	36,298	34,242	32,878	49,710	48,116	50,500	48,822	312,172
2012	39,440	37,165	35,137	33,111	51,368	48,822	52,124	49,482	314,499
2013	39,123	36,369	35,956	33,425	52,592	49,184	53,382	49,865	316,839
2014	40,461	37,084	37,177	34,075	54,353	50,010	55,178	50,715	319,173

Source: U.S. Bureau of Economic Analysis

Plunkett Research, Ltd.

www.plunkettresearch.com

Average Annual U.S. Household Expenditures: 2009-2014
(Latest Year Available)

Characteristic	2009	2010	2011	2012	2013	2014	% Change 13-14
Number of households (in thousands)	120,847	121,107	122,287	124,416	125,670	127,006	1.1%
Income before taxes	$62,857	$62,481	$63,685	$65,596	$63,784	$66,877	4.8%
General U.S. Household Characteristics							
Average age of head of household	49.4	49.4	49.7	50.0	50.1	50.3	0.4%
Average # of persons in household	2.5	2.5	2.5	2.5	2.5	2.5	0.0%
Average # of earners	1.3	1.3	1.3	1.3	1.3	1.3	0.0%
Average # of vehicles	2.0	1.9	1.9	1.9	1.9	1.9	0.0%
Percent homeowners	66	66	65	64	64	63	-1.6%
Average U.S. Household Expenditures (in US$)							
Average annual expenditures	49,067	48,109	49,705	51,442	51,100	53,495	4.7%
Food	6,372	6,129	6,458	6,599	6,602	6,759	2.4%
Food at home	3,753	3,624	3,838	3,921	3,977	3,971	-0.1%
Cereals & bakery products	506	502	531	538	544	519	-4.6%
Meats, poultry, fish & eggs	841	784	832	852	856	892	4.2%
Dairy products	406	380	407	419	414	423	2.2%
Fruits & vegetables	656	679	715	731	751	756	0.6%
Other food at home	1,343	1,278	1,353	1,380	1,412	1,382	-2.1%
Food away from home	2,619	2,505	2,620	2,678	2,625	2,787	6.2%
Alcoholic beverages	435	412	456	451	445	463	4.0%
Housing	16,895	16,557	16,803	16,887	17,148	17,798	3.8%
Shelter	10,075	9,812	9,825	9,891	10,080	10,491	4.1%
Utilities, fuels & public services	3,645	3,660	3,727	3,648	3,737	3,921	4.9%
Household operations	1,011	1,007	1,122	1,159	1,144	1,174	2.6%
Housekeeping supplies	659	612	615	610	645	632	-2.0%
House furnishings & equipment	1,506	1,467	1,514	1,580	1,542	1,581	2.5%
Apparel & services	1,725	1,700	1,740	1,736	1,604	1,786	11.3%
Transportation	7,658	7,677	8,293	8,998	9,004	9,073	0.8%
Vehicle purchases (net outlay)	2,657	2,588	2,669	3,210	3,271	3,301	0.9%
Gasoline & motor oil	1,986	2,132	2,655	2,756	2,611	2,468	-5.5%
Other vehicle expenses	2,536	2,464	2,454	2,490	2,584	2,723	5.4%
Public & other transportation	479	493	516	542	537	581	8.3%
Healthcare	3,126	3,157	3,313	3,556	3,631	4,290	18.2%
Entertainment	2,693	2,504	2,572	2,605	2,482	2,728	9.9%
Personal care products & services	596	582	634	628	608	645	6.1%
Reading	110	100	115	109	102	103	1.0%
Education	1,068	1,074	1,051	1,207	1,138	1,236	8.6%
Tobacco products & smoking supplies	380	362	351	332	330	319	-3.3%
Miscellaneous expenditures	816	849	775	829	645	782	21.2%
Cash contributions	1,723	1,633	1,721	1,913	1,834	1,788	-2.5%
Personal insurance & pensions	5,471	5,373	5,424	5,591	5,528	5,726	3.6%
Life & other personal insurance	309	318	317	353	319	327	2.6%
Pensions & Social Security	5,162	5,054	5,106	5,238	5,209	5,399	3.6%

Source: U.S. Bureau of Labor Statistics
Plunkett Research, Ltd.
www.plunkettresearch.com

Distribution of Total U.S. Annual Household Expenditures, by Major Category: 2014

(As Percentages of Total; For 2014, Average Total Spending = $53,495)

Expenditure Item	Percent Distribution
Housing	33.3%
Transportation	17.0%
Food	12.6%
Personal insurance & pensions*	10.7%
Healthcare	8.0%
Entertainment	5.1%
Cash contributions	3.3%
Apparel & services	3.3%
Education	2.3%
Miscellaneous	1.5%
Personal care products & services	1.2%
Alcoholic beverages	0.9%
Tobacco products & smoking supplies	0.6%
Reading	0.2%

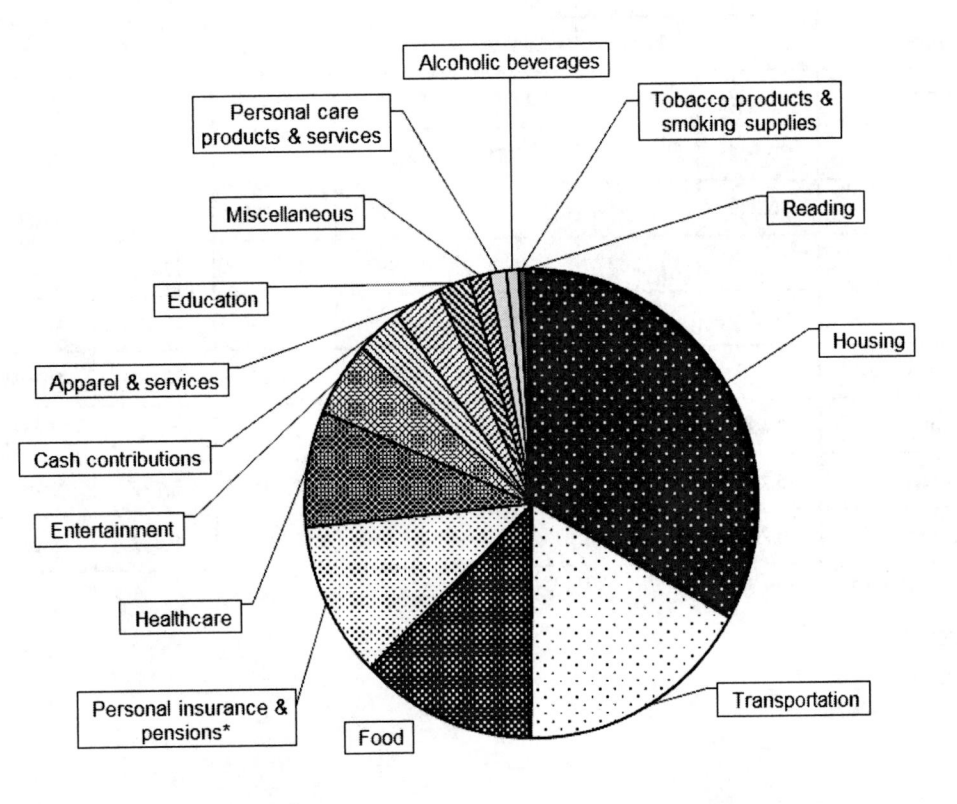

*Includes Social Security.

Source: Bureau of Labor Statistics; Plunkett Research, Ltd. Copyright © 2015, All Rights Reserved

www.plunkettresearch.com

Resident Population Estimates by Age, U.S.: 2007-2014

(In Thousands; Latest Year Available)

Characteristics	2007	2008	2009	2010	2011	2012	2013	2014
Summary Indicators								
Population, all ages	301,580	304,375	307,007	309,326	311,583	313,874	316,129	318,857
Median age	36.53	36.69	36.81	37.20	37.30	37.50	37.60	37.70
Five- & Ten-Year Age Groups								
Under 5 years	20,921	21,153	21,300	20,189	20,122	19,990	19,868	19,877
5 to 9 years	20,054	20,313	20,610	20,332	20,334	20,471	20,571	20,520
10 to 14 years	20,319	20,104	19,974	20,680	20,712	20,669	20,650	20,672
15 to 19 years	21,562	21,628	21,538	21,979	21,647	21,354	21,159	21,068
20 to 24 years	21,217	21,322	21,540	21,702	22,155	22,579	22,795	22,912
25 to 29 years	21,018	21,442	21,678	21,144	21,282	21,391	21,580	21,988
30 to 34 years	19,353	19,516	19,889	20,068	20,512	20,906	21,264	21,529
35 to 39 years	20,993	20,847	20,538	20,078	19,598	19,489	19,604	19,922
40 to 44 years	21,858	21,394	20,992	20,904	21,038	21,027	20,849	20,591
45 to 49 years	22,787	22,802	22,831	22,636	22,164	21,686	21,208	20,888
50 to 54 years	20,962	21,432	21,761	22,353	22,569	22,578	22,559	22,571
55 to 59 years	18,209	18,541	18,975	19,795	20,262	20,776	21,194	21,511
60 to 64 years	14,459	15,082	15,812	16,990	17,817	17,815	18,122	18,566
65 to 69 years	10,746	11,333	11,784	12,521	12,880	13,988	14,609	15,325
70 to 74 years	8,643	8,806	9,008	9,336	9,608	10,010	10,608	11,073
75 to 79 years	7,439	7,385	7,326	7,319	7,388	7,487	7,678	7,922
80 to 84 years	5,774	5,826	5,822	5,759	5,781	5,777	5,769	5,760
85 years & over	5,264	5,450	5,631	5,543	5,713	5,882	6,041	6,162

Census Bureau estimates; July 1 of year. Based on 2010 Census.

Source: U.S. Census Bureau

Plunkett Research, Ltd.

www.plunkettresearch.com

Employment in the Retail Industry, U.S.: 2008-August 2015

(Annual Estimates in Thousands of Employed Workers)

NAICS Code[1]	Industry Sector	2008	2009	2010	2011	2012	2013	2014	2015*
--	Retail Trade	15,283.0	14,522.3	14,440.4	14,667.8	14,840.8	15,078.8	15,364.3	15,692.5
441	Motor vehicle & parts dealers	1,831.2	1,637.5	1,629.2	1,691.2	1,737.0	1,793.1	1,861.4	1,955.1
4411	Automobile dealers	1,176.7	1,018.2	1,011.5	1,056.9	1,095.5	1,138.4	1,184.9	1,241.2
4412	Other motor vehicle dealers	162.4	135.8	128.6	127.5	129.8	133.8	139.9	153.1
4413	Auto parts, accessories & tire stores	492.1	483.4	489.2	506.8	511.8	520.9	536.5	560.8
442	Furniture & home furnishings stores	531.1	449.2	437.9	438.9	439.4	445.8	454.6	464.2
443	Electronics & appliance stores	569.6	515.7	522.3	527.4	507.4	496.7	491.2	495.3
443142	Electronics stores	502.4	456.2	464.8	469.4	448.2	437.7	432.2	434.6
444	Building material & garden supply stores	1,248.0	1,155.6	1,131.8	1,145.7	1,174.2	1,207.7	1,234.8	1,263.3
4441	Building material & supplies dealers	1,110.6	1,027.6	1,004.8	1,009.8	1,033.8	1,061.7	1,083.1	1,102.2
4442	Lawn & garden equipment & supplies stores	137.4	128.0	127.0	136.0	140.5	145.9	151.6	161.1
445	Food & beverage stores	2,862.0	2,830.0	2,808.2	2,822.8	2,861.3	2,929.7	2,993.9	3,056.4
4451	Grocery stores	2,502.8	2,479.0	2,460.5	2,471.7	2,502.3	2,563.0	2,620.9	2,672.1
4452	Specialty food stores	221.2	213.7	211.4	213.4	217.4	220.9	227.0	234.1
4453	Beer, wine & liquor stores	138.0	137.3	136.3	137.7	141.5	145.8	146.1	150.2
446	Health & personal care stores	1,002.8	986.0	980.5	980.9	997.9	1,015.8	1,021.0	1,025.0
44611	Pharmacies & drug stores	743.6	726.3	715.1	703.5	703.6	715.3	710.8	703.1
447	Gasoline stations	842.4	825.5	819.3	831.0	843.5	866.3	881.0	924.2
448	Clothing & clothing accessories stores	1,468.0	1,363.9	1,352.5	1,360.9	1,391.4	1,390.9	1,378.6	1,397.9
4481	Clothing stores	1,121.4	1,047.6	1,039.8	1,043.1	1,066.3	1,058.7	1,041.4	1,051.6
4482	Shoe stores	188.3	178.8	181.5	184.9	188.3	194.3	199.9	213.8
451	Sporting goods, hobby, book & music stores	621.9	589.2	579.1	577.9	582.2	602.5	612.9	590.9
4511	Sporting goods & musical instrument stores	477.5	460.3	459.2	474.4	488.8	510.6	522.9	503.5
4512	Book stores & news dealers	144.4	128.9	119.9	103.4	93.3	91.9	90.0	87.4
452	General merchandise stores	3,025.6	2,966.2	2,997.7	3,085.2	3,065.4	3,060.4	3,113.6	3,150.2
4521	Department stores	1,540.5	1,472.9	1,501.6	1,538.6	1,454.9	1,348.3	1,349.5	1,299.6
4529	Other general merchandise stores	1,485.1	1,493.3	1,496.1	1,546.6	1,610.6	1,712.1	1,764.1	1,850.6
453	Miscellaneous store retailers	842.5	782.4	761.5	772.4	794.0	802.5	817.8	835.5
4531	Florists	85.9	74.7	68.5	65.4	66.1	64.9	64.0	60.3
4532	Office supplies, stationery & gift stores	347.9	317.1	303.3	303.0	302.8	293.7	292.6	285.8
4533	Used merchandise stores	119.0	119.5	125.4	134.9	146.6	157.1	164.0	173.5
454	Nonstore retailers	438.0	421.1	420.6	433.5	447.1	467.4	503.5	534.5
4541	Electronic shopping & mail-order houses	252.0	244.4	247.1	262.0	278.4	298.4	328.8	353.9
4542	Vending machine operators	46.3	41.1	39.3	37.8	37.2	37.1	37.8	40.7
4543	Direct selling establishments	139.7	135.6	134.2	133.7	131.5	131.9	137.0	139.9

[1] For a full description of the NAICS codes used in this table, see www.census.gov/epcd/www/naics.html.

* Preliminary estimates as of August 2015.

Source: U.S. Bureau of Labor Statistics
Plunkett Research, Ltd.
www.plunkettresearch.com

Chapter 3

IMPORTANT RETAIL INDUSTRY CONTACTS

Addresses, Telephone Numbers and Internet Sites

Contents:

1) Advertising Resources
2) Advertising/Marketing Associations
3) Apparel Associations
4) Automotive Industry Associations
5) Booksellers Associations
6) Careers-First Time Jobs/New Grads
7) Careers-General Job Listings
8) Careers-Job Reference Tools
9) Computer & Electronics Industry Associations
10) Convenience Store Associations
11) Corporate Information Resources
12) Economic Data & Research
13) Entertainment Industry Associations
14) Floral Associations
15) Food Processor Industry Associations
16) Gardening and Plant Industry Associations
17) Gasoline Retailing Associations
18) Grocery Industry Associations
19) Industry Research/Market Research
20) Internet Usage Statistics
21) Liquor Industry Associations
22) Logistics & Supply Chain Associations
23) Manufacturing Associations-General
24) MBA Resources
25) Organic Food Industry Associations
26) Payment, E-Commerce and Data Interchange Technology
27) Privacy & Consumer Matters
28) Private Label (Generic) Manufacturing Associations
29) Real Estate Industry Associations
30) Real Estate Industry Resources
31) Restaurant Industry Associations
32) Retail Industry Associations
33) Retail Industry Resources
34) RFID Industry Associations
35) RFID Resources
36) Shopping Center Directories
37) Shopping Center Resources
38) Sporting Goods Industry Associations
39) Technology Transfer Associations
40) Textile & Fabric Associations
41) Textile & Fabric Resources
42) Toy Industry Associations
43) Trade Associations-General
44) Trade Associations-Global
45) U.S. Government Agencies
46) Watch Manufacturers Associations
47) Wholesale Distributors Associations

1) Advertising Resources

AdAsia
c/o BluePrint Media Pte Ltd.
102F Pasir Panjang Rd., 07-02 Citilink Complex
118530 Singapore
Phone: (65)6276-8831
E-mail Address: *editor@adasia.com.sg*

Web Address: www.adasiaonline.com

The AdAsia is a online magazine for the advertising, marketing and media community in Singapore and the Asia-Pacific region. The website includes news articles, events, jobs and general industry links and information.

2) Advertising/Marketing Associations

4A's (American Association of Advertising Agencies)
1065 Ave. of the Americas, Fl. 16
New York, NY 10018 USA
Phone: 212-682-2500
Web Address: www.aaaa.org
The 4A's (American Association of Advertising Agencies) is the national trade association representing the advertising agency industry in the U.S.

Advertising Research Foundation (ARF)
432 Park Ave. S., Fl. 6
New York, NY 10016-8013 USA
Phone: 212-751-5656
E-mail Address: Member-info@thearf.org
Web Address: www.thearf.org
The Advertising Research Foundation (ARF), a nonprofit corporate-membership association, is a leading professional organization in the fields of advertising, marketing and media research.

American Advertising Federation, Inc. (AAF)
1101 Vermont Ave. NW, Ste. 500
Washington, DC 20005-6306 USA
Phone: 202-898-0089
E-mail Address: addyinfo@aaf.org
Web Address: www.aaf.org
The American Advertising Federation, Inc. (AAF) protects and promotes the well-being of advertising through a nationally coordinated network of advertisers, agencies, media companies, local advertising clubs and college chapters.

Association of Coupon Professionals (ACP)
1051 Pontiac Rd.
Drexel Hill, PA 19026 USA
Phone: 610-789-1478
Fax: 610-789-5309
E-mail Address: John.Morgan@acp-hq.org
Web Address: www.couponpros.org
The Association of Coupon Professionals (ACP) is an association of professionals involved in the coupon industry, which offers education and insights to retailers and manufacturers on effective execution of coupon promotions.

Brand Activation Association (BAA)
650 First Ave., Ste. 2-SW
New York, NY 10016 USA
Phone: 212-420-1100
Fax: 212-533-7622
E-mail Address: cgoonan@baalink.org
Web Address: www.baalink.org
The Brand Activation Association (BAA), formerly the Promotion Marketing Association of America, Inc. (PMA), is a leading nonprofit trade association that represents the promotion marketing profession. The association operates as a division of Association of National Advertisers (ANA).

Canadian Marketing Association (CMA)
1 Concorde Gate, Ste. 607
Don Mills, ON M3C 3N6 Canada
Phone: 416-391-2362
Fax: 416-441-4062
Toll Free: 800-267-8805
E-mail Address: info@the-cma.org
Web Address: www.the-cma.org
The Canadian Marketing Association (CMA) is one of Canada's largest marketing associations representing corporate members from a variety of different sectors of the marketing industry.

Direct Marketing Association (DMA)
1120 Ave. of the Americas
New York, NY 10036-6700 USA
Phone: 212-768-7277
Web Address: thedma.org
The Direct Marketing Association (DMA) is the oldest and largest trade association for users and suppliers in the direct, database and interactive marketing fields.

Direct Selling Association (DSA)
1667 K St. NW, Ste. 1100
Washington, DC 20006-1660 USA
Phone: 202-452-8866
Fax: 202-452-9010
Web Address: www.dsa.org
The Direct Selling Association (DSA) is a trade organization for direct sellers.

eMarketing Association (eMA)
40 Blue Ridge Dr.
Charlestown, RI 02813 USA
Fax: 408-884-2461

Toll Free: 800-496-2950
E-mail Address: admin@emarketingassociation.com
Web Address: www.emarketingassociation.com
eMarketing Association (eMA) is the largest
international association of electronic marketing
professionals, with members in over 40 countries
worldwide. The organization provides a forum to
exchange knowledge and ideas and to make
professional contacts.

International Advertising Association (IAA)
747 Third Ave., Fl. 2
New York, NY 10017 USA
Phone: 646-722-2612
Fax: 646-722-2501
E-mail Address: iaa@iaaglobal.org
Web Address: www.iaaglobal.org
The International Advertising Association (IAA) is a
strategic partnership that champions the common
interests of disciplines across the full spectrum of the
marketing communications industry.

NEMOA (National Etailing & Mailing Organization of America)
P.O. Box 658
Scarborough, ME 04070 USA
Phone: 207-885-0090
Fax: 207-885-0097
E-mail Address: terri@nemoa.org
Web Address: www.nemoa.org
NEMOA offers direct marketing merchants of all
sizes, and the vendors that service them, an
affordable network to share knowledge, learn about
industry trends and connect with peers and experts in
a non-selling environment.

Outdoor Advertising Association of America, Inc. (OAAA)
1850 M St. NW, Ste. 1040
Washington, DC 20036 USA
Phone: 202-833-5566
Fax: 202-833-1522
Web Address: www.oaaa.org
The Outdoor Advertising Association of America,
Inc. (OAAA) is a leading trade association
representing the outdoor advertising industry.

Point-of-Purchase Advertising International (POPAI)
440 N. Wells St., Ste. 740
Chicago, IL 60654 USA
Phone: 312-863-2900
Fax: 312-229-1152

Web Address: www.popai.com
Point-of-Purchase Advertising International
(POPAI), formerly known as the Point-of-Purchase
Advertising Institute is an international nonprofit
trade association dedicated to serving the interests of
advertisers, retailers, producers and suppliers of
point-of-purchase products and services. POPAI has
over 1,400 member companies.

Promotional Products Association International (PPAI)
3125 Skyway Cir. N.
Irving, TX 75038-3526 USA
Phone: 972-252-0404
Fax: 972-258-3004
Toll Free: 888-426-7724
E-mail Address: kimt@ppai.org
Web Address: www.ppa.org
Promotional Products Association International
(PPAI) is an international trade association that
supports the promotional products industry.

3) Apparel Associations

American Apparel & Footwear Association (AAFA)
1601 N. Kent St., Ste. 12
Arlington, VA 22209 USA
Phone: 703-524-1864
Web Address: www.wewear.org
The American Apparel & Footwear Association,
formerly known as the American Apparel and
Footwear Manufacturing Association (AAFA) is the
national trade association for the apparel, footwear
and fashion industries and their suppliers.

British Footwear Association
3 Burystead Pl.
Wellingborough, NN8 1AH UK
Phone: 44-1933-229005
Fax: 44-1933-225009
E-mail Address:
info@britishfootwearassociation.co.uk
Web Address: www.britishfootwearassociation.co.uk
The British Footwear Association represents those in
all aspects of the footwear industry. The site serves as
a portal for the industry with links to member
companies, partners, trends and information.

China Chamber of Commerce for Import & Export of Textiles (CCCT)
Bldg. 12 S. Panjiayuan
Chaoyang District

Beijing, 100021 China
Phone: 86-10-6773-9246
Fax: 86-10-6771-9235
E-mail Address: info@ccct.org.cn
Web Address: www.ccct.org.cn/en/
The China Chamber of Commerce for Import and
Export of Textiles (CCCT), established in October
1988, is a leading national trade organization
representing exporters and importers of textiles and
clothing in China, with a membership of more than
12,000 companies.

Council of Fashion Designers of America (CFDA)
65 Bleeker, Fl. 11
New York, NY 10012 USA
E-mail Address: info@cfda.com
Web Address: www.cfda.com
The Council of Fashion Designers of America, Inc.
(CFDA) is a not-for-profit trade association of over
300 of America's foremost fashion and accessory
designers. Founded in 1962, the CFDA continues to
advance the status of fashion design as a branch of
American art and culture; to raise its artistic and
professional standards; to define a code of ethical
practices of mutual benefit in public and trade
relations; and, to promote appreciation of the fashion
arts through leadership in quality and aesthetic
discernment.

European Branded Clothing Alliance (EBCA)
c/o Hanover
Square De Meuus 35, Fl. 6
Brussels, B-1000 Belgium
Phone: 32-2-588-2616
E-mail Address: info@ebca-europe.org
Web Address: www.ebca-europe.org
The European Branded Clothing Alliance (EBCA) is
a coalition of over 60 European and global retail
clothing brands that employ over 150,000. The
EBCA acts as a collective voice for retail clothing
brands in items such as acting as an advisory board
for European Union policy-makers as they create
trade policy.

**Fashion Footwear Association of New York
(FFANY)**
274 Madison Ave., Ste. 1701
New York, NY 10016 USA
Phone: 212-751-6422
Fax: 212-751-6404
E-mail Address: info@ffany.org
Web Address: www.ffany.org

The Fashion Footwear Association of New York
(FFANY) includes 300 footwear manufacturers
representing 800 of the most well-known footwear
brands in the world.

Fashion Group International, Inc. (FGI)
8 W. 40th St., Fl. 7
New York, NY 10018 USA
Phone: 212-302-5511
Fax: 212-302-5533
E-mail Address: pmaffei@fgi.org
Web Address: www.fgi.org
The Fashion Group International, Inc. (FGI) is a
nonprofit association of professionals in all areas of
the fashion, apparel, accessories, beauty and home
industries.

**Garment Contractors Association of Southern
California, Inc. (GCA)**
110 E. 9th St., Ste. A701
Los Angeles, CA 90079 USA
Phone: 213-629-4422
Fax: 213-629-4517
E-mail Address:
information@garmentcontractors.org
Web Address: www.garmentcontractors.org
The Garment Contractors Association of Southern
California, Inc. (GCA) is a nonprofit association
representing the retail garment contracting businesses
in Southern California.

**Hong Kong Knitwear Exporters & Manufacturers
Association**
25 Kimberley Rd.
Rm 401-3 4/F Cheung Lee Comm. Bldg.
Kowloon, New Territories Hong Kong
Phone: 852-2-2755-2621
Fax: 852-2-2756-5672
Web Address:
www.textilecouncil.com/member_hkkema.html
Hong Kong Knitwear Exporters & Manufacturers
Association promotes manufacturing related to
knitwear products in Hong Kong.

**International Swimwear and Activewear Market
(ISAM)**
13351-D Riverside Dr., Ste. 658
Sherman Oaks, CA 91423 USA
Phone: 818-986-2152
Fax: 818-986-2637
E-mail Address: barbara@isamla.com
Web Address: www.isamla.com

The International Swimwear and Activewear Market (ISAM) is an association of retail swimwear and activewear manufacturers, related businesses and industries.

Textile & Fashion Federation, Singapore (TaFF)
No. 2 Leng Kee Rd.
02-10 Thye Hong Ctr.
Singapore, 159086 Singapore
Phone: 65-6735-8390
Web Address: www.taff.org.sg
The Textile & Fashion Federation, Singapore (TaFF) represents the textile and apparel industry in Singapore, which is one of the largest textile and apparel sourcing centers in the Asia-Pacific region.

4) Automotive Industry Associations

American International Automobile Dealers Association (AIADA)
500 Montgomery St., Ste. 800
Alexandria, VA 22314 USA
Fax: 703-519-7810
Toll Free: 800-462-4232
Web Address: www.aiada.org
American International Automobile Dealers Association (AIADA) is the lobbying and communications force in Washington, D.C. for the 10,000 American automobile dealerships that sell and service international nameplate brands.

Canadian Automobile Dealers Association (CADA)
85 Renfrew Dr.
Markham, ON L3R 0N9 Canada
Phone: 905-940-4959
Fax: 905-940-6870
Toll Free: 800-463-5289
Web Address: www.cada.ca
The Canadian Automobile Dealers Association (CADA) represents 3,200 automobile dealers across Canada.

National Automobile Dealers Association (NADA)
8400 Westpark Dr.
McLean, VA 22102 USA
Phone: 703-821-7000
Toll Free: 800-252-6232
Web Address: www.nada.org
The National Automobile Dealers Association (NADA) represents more than 17,000 new car and truck dealers, both import and domestic, operating more than 37,500 separate franchises.

5) Booksellers Associations

American Booksellers Association, Inc.
333 Westchester Ave., Ste. S202
White Plains, NY 10604 USA
Phone: 914-406-7500
Fax: 914-417-4013
Toll Free: 800-637-0037
E-mail Address: info@bookweb.org
Web Address: www.bookweb.org
The American Booksellers Association is a nonprofit association representing independent bookstores in the United States.

Christian Booksellers Association (CBA)
1365 Garden of the Gods Rd., Ste. 105
Colorado Springs, CO 80907 USA
Phone: 719-265-9895
Fax: 719-272-3510
Toll Free: 800-252-1950
E-mail Address: info@cbaonline.org
Web Address: www.cbaonline.org
The Christian Booksellers Association (CBA) is the international trade association of Christian book suppliers and retailers. It serves the interests and needs of member Christian stores and works with associate member book publishers, record companies, gift companies and other product suppliers.

National Association of College Stores (NACS)
500 E. Lorain St.
Oberlin, OH 44074 USA
Fax: 440-775-4769
Toll Free: 800-622-7498
E-mail Address: webteam@nacs.org
Web Address: www.nacs.org
The National Association of College Stores (NACS) is the professional trade association representing college retailers and associate members who supply books and other products to college stores.

6) Careers-First Time Jobs/New Grads

CollegeGrad.com, Inc.
950 Tower Ln., Fl. 6
Foster City, CA 94404 USA
E-mail Address: info@quinstreet.com
Web Address: www.collegegrad.com
CollegeGrad.com, Inc. offers in-depth resources for college students and recent grads seeking entry-level jobs.

MonsterCollege
799 Market St., Ste. 500
San Francisco, CA 94103 USA
E-mail Address: info@college.monster.com
Web Address: www.college.monster.com
MonsterCollege provides information about
internships and entry-level jobs, as well as career
advice and resume tips, to recent college graduates.

**National Association of Colleges and Employers
(NACE)**
62 Highland Ave.
Bethlehem, PA 18017-9085 USA
Phone: 610-868-1421
E-mail Address: customer_service@naceweb.org
Web Address: www.naceweb.org
The National Association of Colleges and Employers
(NACE) is a premier U.S. organization representing
college placement offices and corporate recruiters
who focus on hiring new grads.

---

7)   Careers-General Job Listings

CareerBuilder, Inc.
200 N La Salle St., Ste. 1100
Chicago, IL 60601 USA
Phone: 773-527-3600
Fax: 773-353-2452
Toll Free: 800-891-8880
Web Address: www.careerbuilder.com
CareerBuilder, Inc. focuses on the needs of
companies and also provides a database of job
openings. The site has over 1 million jobs posted by
300,000 employers, and receives an average 23
million unique visitors monthly. The company also
operates online career centers for 140 newspapers
and 9,000 online partners. Resumes are sent directly
to the company, and applicants can set up a special e-
mail account for job-seeking purposes. CareerBuilder
is primarily a joint venture between three newspaper
giants: The McClatchy Company, Gannett Co., Inc.
and Tribune Company.

CareerOneStop
Toll Free: 877-872-5627
E-mail Address: info@careeronestop.org
Web Address: www.careeronestop.org
CareerOneStop is operated by the employment
commissions of various state agencies. It contains job
listings in both the private and government sectors, as
well as a wide variety of useful career resources and
workforce information. CareerOneStop is sponsored
by the U.S. Department of Labor.

LaborMarketInfo (LMI)
Employment Development Dept.
800 Capitol Mall, MIC 83
Sacramento, CA 95814 USA
Phone: 916-262-2162
Fax: 916-262-2352
Web Address: www.labormarketinfo.edd.ca.gov
LaborMarketInfo (LMI) provides job seekers and
employers a wide range of resources, namely the
ability to find, access and use labor market
information and services. It provides statistics for
employment demographics on both a local and
regional level, as well as career searching tools for
California residents. The web site is sponsored by
California's Employment Development Office.

Recruiters Online Network
E-mail Address: rossi.tony@comcast.net
Web Address: www.recruitersonline.com
The Recruiters Online Network provides job postings
from thousands of recruiters, Careers Online
Magazine, a resume database, as well as other career
resources.

USAJOBS
1900 E St. NW, Ste. 6500
Washington, DC 20415-0001 USA
Web Address: www.usajobs.gov
USAJOBS, a program of the U.S. Office of Personnel
Management, is the official job site for the U.S.
Federal Government. It provides a comprehensive list
of U.S. government jobs, allowing users to search for
employment by location; agency; type of work; or by
senior executive positions. It also has special
employment sections for individuals with disabilities,
veterans and recent college graduates; an information
center, offering resume and interview tips and other
information; and allows users to create a profile and
post a resume.

---

8)   Careers-Job Reference Tools

Vault.com, Inc.
132 W. 31st St., Fl. 17
New York, NY 10001 USA
Fax: 212-366-6117
Toll Free: 800-535-2074
E-mail Address: customerservice@vault.com
Web Address: www.vault.com
Vault.com, Inc. is a comprehensive career web site
for employers and employees, with job postings and
valuable information on a wide variety of industries.

Its features and content are largely geared toward MBA degree holders.

9) Computer & Electronics Industry Associations

Business Technology Association (BTA)
12411 Wornall Rd., Ste. 200
Kansas City, MO 64145 USA
Phone: 816-941-3100
Fax: 816-941-4843
Toll Free: 800-826-6159
E-mail Address: brent@bta.org
Web Address: www.bta.org
The Business Technology Association (BTA) is an organization for resellers and dealers of business technology products. Its site offers buying groups, message boards, legal advice, news on industry trends and live chats.

Retail Solutions Providers Association (RSPA)
10130 Perimeter Pkwy., Ste. 420
Charlotte, NC 28216 USA
Phone: 704-357-3124
Fax: 704-357-3127
Toll Free: 800-782-2693
Web Address: www.gorspa.org
The Retail Solutions Providers Association (RSPA) is a trade association composed of businesses involved in the purchase, resale, enhancement, installation and maintenance of point-of-sale systems to and for end users.

10) Convenience Store Associations

Georgia Association of Convenience Stores (GACS)
168 N. Johnston St., Ste. 209
Dallas, GA 30132-4744 USA
Phone: 770-736-9723
Fax: 770-736-9725
Toll Free: 877-294-1885
Web Address: www.gacs.com
The Georgia Association of Convenience Stores (GACS) represents over 2,600 convenience stores in Georgia. Its web site provides industry links, membership information and government updates.

National Association of Convenience Stores (NACS)
1600 Duke St., Fl. 7
Alexandria, VA 22314 USA

Phone: 703-684-3600
Fax: 703-836-4564
Toll Free: 800-966-6227
Web Address: www.nacsonline.com
The National Association of Convenience Stores (NACS) is an international trade association representing 2,200 retail and 1,600 supplier company members in the convenience store industry.

New England Convenience Store Association (NECSA)
1044 Central St., Ste. 203
Stoughton, MA 02072 USA
Phone: 781-297-9600
Fax: 781-297-9601
Toll Free: 866-882-9090
E-mail Address: lisa@necsa.net
Web Address: www.necsa.net
The New England Convenience Store Association (NECSA) is a trade association representing the interests of convenience stores and their suppliers in the six New England states.

New York Association of Convenience Stores (NYACS)
130 Washington Ave., Ste. 300
Albany, NY 12210 USA
Phone: 518-432-1400
E-mail Address: info@nyacs.org
Web Address: www.nyacs.org
The New York Association of Convenience Stores (NYACS) is a nonprofit association composed of retail units and companies who supply services and products to the convenience store industry in New York.

South Carolina Association of Convenience Stores (SCACS)
P.O. Box 11405
Columbia, SC 29211 USA
Phone: 803-419-0804
Fax: 803-252-7799
E-mail Address: director@scacs.org
Web Address: www.scacs.org
The South Carolina Association of Convenience Stores (SCACS) is a non-profit trade association that represents and promotes the business interests of retailers and supplier members in South Carolina.

11) Corporate Information Resources

bizjournals.com
120 W. Morehead St., Ste. 400

Charlotte, NC 28202 USA
Web Address: www.bizjournals.com
Bizjournals.com is the online media division of
American City Business Journals, the publisher of
dozens of leading city business journals nationwide.
It provides access to research into the latest news
regarding companies both small and large. The
organization maintains 42 websites and 64 print
publications and sponsors over 700 annual industry
events.

Business Wire
101 California St., Fl. 20
San Francisco, CA 94111 USA
Phone: 415-986-4422
Fax: 415-788-5335
Toll Free: 800-227-0845
E-mail Address: info@businesswire.com
Web Address: www.businesswire.com
Business Wire offers news releases, industry- and
company-specific news, top headlines, conference
calls, IPOs on the Internet, media services and access
to tradeshownews.com and BW Connect On-line
through its informative and continuously updated
web site.

Edgar Online, Inc.
11200 Rockville Pike, Ste. 310
Rockville, MD 20852 USA
Phone: 301-287-0300
Fax: 301-287-0390
Toll Free: 888-870-2316
Web Address: www.edgar-online.com
Edgar Online, Inc. is a gateway and search tool for
viewing corporate documents, such as annual reports
on Form 10-K, filed with the U.S. Securities and
Exchange Commission.

PR Newswire Association LLC
350 Hudson St., Ste. 300
New York, NY 10014-4504 USA
Fax: 800-793-9313
Toll Free: 800-776-8090
E-mail Address: MediaInquiries@prnewswire.com
Web Address: www.prnewswire.com
PR Newswire Association LLC provides
comprehensive communications services for public
relations and investor relations professionals, ranging
from information distribution and market intelligence
to the creation of online multimedia content and
investor relations web sites. Users can also view
recent corporate press releases from companies

across the globe. The Association is owned by United
Business Media plc.

12) Economic Data & Research

**Centre for European Economic Research (The,
ZEW)**
L 7, 1
Mannheim, 68161 Germany
Phone: 49-621-1235-01
Fax: 49-621-1235-224
E-mail Address: info@zew.de
Web Address: www.zew.de/en
Zentrum fur Europaische Wirtschaftsforschung, The
Centre for European Economic Research (ZEW),
distinguishes itself in the analysis of internationally
comparative data in a European context and in the
creation of databases that serve as a basis for
scientific research. The institute maintains a special
library relevant to economic research and provides
external parties with selected data for the purpose of
scientific research. ZEW also offers public events
and seminars concentrating on banking, business and
other economic-political topics.

Economic and Social Research Council (ESRC)
Polaris House
North Star Ave.
Swindon, SN2 1UJ UK
Phone: 44-01793 413000
Fax: 44-01793 413001
E-mail Address: comms@esrc.ac.uk
Web Address: www.esrc.ac.uk
The Economic and Social Research Council (ESRC)
funds research and training in social and economic
issues. It is an independent organization, established
by Royal Charter. Current research areas include the
global economy; social diversity; environment and
energy; human behavior; and health and well-being.

Eurostat
5 Rue Alphonse Weicker
Joseph Bech Bldg.
Luxembourg, L-2721 Luxembourg
Phone: 352-4301-33444
Fax: 352-4301-35349
E-mail Address: eurostat-pressoffice@ec.europa.eu
Web Address: www.epp.eurostat.ec.europa.eu
Eurostat is the European Union's service that
publishes a wide variety of comprehensive statistics
on European industries, populations, trade,
agriculture, technology, environment and other
matters.

Federal Statistical Office of Germany
Gustav-Stresemann-Ring 11
Wiesbaden, D-65189 Germany
Phone: 49-611-75-1
Fax: 49-611-72-4000
Web Address: www.destatis.de
Federal Statistical Office of Germany publishes a
wide variety of nation and regional economic data of
interest to anyone who is studying Germany, one of
the world's leading economies. Data available
includes population, consumer prices, labor markets,
health care, industries and output.

India Brand Equity Foundation (IBEF)
Apparel House, Fl. 5
#519-22, Sector 44
Gurgaon, Haryana 122003 India
Phone: 91-124-4499600
Fax: 91-124-4499615
E-mail Address: info.brandindia@ibef.org
Web Address: www.ibef.org
India Brand Equity Foundation (IBEF) is a public-
private partnership between the Ministry of
Commerce and Industry, the Government of India
and the Confederation of Indian Industry. The
foundation's primary objective is to build positive
economic perceptions of India globally. It aims to
effectively present the India business perspective and
leverage business partnerships in a globalizing
marketplace.

National Bureau of Statistics (China)
57, Yuetan Nanjie, Sanlihe
Xicheng District
Beijing, 100826 China
Fax: 86-10-6878-2000
E-mail Address: info@gj.stats.cn
Web Address: www.stats.gov.cn/english
The National Bureau of Statistics (China) provides
statistics and economic data regarding China's
economy and society.

**Organization for Economic Co-operation and
Development (OECD)**
2 rue Andre Pascal
Cedex 16
Paris, 75775 France
Phone: 33-1-45-24-82-00
Fax: 33-1-45-24-85-00
Web Address: www.oecd.org
The Organization for Economic Co-operation and
Development (OECD) publishes detailed economic,
government, population, social and trade statistics on

a country-by-country basis for over 30 nations
representing the world's largest economies. Sectors
covered range from industry, labor, technology and
patents, to health care, environment and
globalization.

**Statistics Bureau, Director-General for Policy
Planning (Japan)**
19-1 Wakamatsu-cho
Shinjuku-ku
Tokyo, 162-8668 Japan
Phone: 81-3-5273-2020
E-mail Address: toukeisoudan@soumu.go.jp
Web Address: www.stat.go.jp/english
The Statistics Bureau, Director-General for Policy
Planning (Japan) and Statistical Research and
Training Institute, a part of the Japanese Ministry of
Internal Affairs and Communications, plays the
central role of producing and disseminating basic
official statistics and coordinating statistical work
under the Statistics Act and other legislation.

Statistics Canada
150 Tunney's Pasture Driveway
Ottawa, ON K1A 0T6 Canada
Phone: 514-283-8300
Fax: 877-287-4369
Toll Free: 800-263-1136
E-mail Address: infostats@statcan.gc.ca
Web Address: www.statcan.gc.ca
Statistics Canada provides a complete portal to
Canadian economic data and statistics. Its conducts
Canada's official census every five years, as well as
hundreds of surveys covering numerous aspects of
Canadian life.

13) Entertainment Industry Associations

Entertainment Merchants Association
16530 Ventura Blvd., Ste. 400
Encino, CA 91436-4551 USA
Phone: 818-385-1500
Fax: 818-933-0911
Web Address: www.entmerch.org
The Entertainment Merchants Association (EMA) is
the not-for-profit international trade association
dedicated to advancing the interests of the $35 billion
home entertainment industry. EMA was established
in April 2006 through the merger of the Video
Software Dealers Association (VSDA) and the
Interactive Entertainment Merchants Association
(IEMA).

14) Floral Associations

Society of American Florists (SAF)
1601 Duke St.
Alexandria, VA 22314 USA
Phone: 703-836-8700
Fax: 703-836-8705
Toll Free: 800-336-4743
E-mail Address: info@safnow.org
Web Address: www.safnow.org
The Society of American Florists (SAF) is the
networking organization for the retail floral industry.
It provides marketing, governmental advocacy,
industry intelligence and best practices information
for all participants in the U.S. floral industry.

15) Food Processor Industry Associations

Grocery Manufacturers Association (GMA)
1350 I St. NW, Ste. 300
Washington, DC 20005 USA
Phone: 202-639-5900
Fax: 202-639-5932
E-mail Address: info@gmaonline.org
Web Address: www.gmaonline.org
The Grocery Manufacturers Association (GMA),
formerly the National Food Products Association
(NFPA), is the voice of the food, beverage and
consumer products industry on scientific and public
policy issues involving food safety, food security,
nutrition, technical and regulatory matters and
consumer affairs.

Specialty Food Association, Inc.
136 Madison Ave., Fl. 12
New York, NY 10016 USA
Phone: 212-482-6440
Toll Free: 646-878-0301
Web Address: www.specialtyfood.com
The Specialty Food Association, Inc., formerly the
National Association for the Specialty Food Trade
(NASFT), is a not-for-profit trade association that
fosters trade, commerce and interest in the specialty
food industry.

16) Gardening and Plant Industry Associations

National Gardening Association (NGA)
237 Commerce St., Ste. 101
Williston, VT 05495 USA
Phone: 802-863-5251
Fax: 802-864-6889
Web Address: www.garden.org
The National Gardening Association (NGA) is a non-
profit organization that conduct market research,
promotes gardening activities and provides gardening
education. It is a leading provider of educational
materials about plants and gardens to students in the
K-12 grades.

17) Gasoline Retailing Associations

**Florida Petroleum Marketers and Convenience
Store Association (FPMA)**
227 S. Adams St.
Tallahassee, FL 32301 USA
Phone: 850-222-4028
Fax: 850-561-6625
E-mail Address: fpma@fpma.org
Web Address: www.fpma.org
The Florida Petroleum Marketers and Convenience
Store Association (FPMA) represents the petroleum
and convenience store industry in Florida. Its web
site includes Internet resources, government news,
general industry news and updated information.

**Indiana Petroleum Marketers and Convenience
Store Association (IPCA)**
115 W. Washington St., Ste. 1690
Indianapolis, IN 46204 USA
Phone: 317-633-4662
Fax: 317-630-1827
Toll Free: 800-732-1423
E-mail Address: kransdell@ipca.org
Web Address: www.ipca.org
The Indiana Petroleum Marketers and Convenience
Store Association (IPCA) represents Indiana's
petroleum marketers, lube oil dealers and
convenience store and truck stop operators.

**Kentucky Petroleum Marketers Association
(KPMA)**
2365 Harrodsburg Rd., Ste. A325
Lexington, KY 40504 USA
Phone: 859-219-3571
Fax: 859-406-1009
E-mail Address: kpma@kpma.org
Web Address: www.kpma.org
The Kentucky Petroleum Marketers Association
(KPMA) is a nonprofit trade association providing
information relevant to retail petroleum sales for all
segments of the petroleum industry in the state of
Kentucky.

Louisiana Oil Marketers and Convenience Stores Association (LOMCSA)
5647 Bankers Ave.
Baton Rouge, LA 70808 USA
Phone: 225-926-8300
Fax: 225-926-7722
E-mail Address: lomcsa@lomcsa.com
Web Address: www.lomcsa.com
The Louisiana Oil Marketers and Convenience Stores Association (LOMCSA) is a nonprofit organization that represents the business interests of independent distributors of petroleum products in Louisiana.

Maine Energy Marketers Association (MEMA)
25 Greenwood Rd.
P.O. Box 249
Brunswick, ME 04011-0249 USA
Phone: 207-729-5298
Fax: 207-721-9227
Toll Free: 888-863-3753
Web Address: www.maineenergymarketers.com
The Maine Energy Marketers Association (MEMA), formerly the Maine Oil Dealers Association, is a member organization that represents the petroleum industry and its customers in Maine.

Missouri Petroleum Marketers and Convenience Store Association (MPCA)
205 E. Capitol Ave., Ste. 200
Jefferson City, MO 65101 USA
Phone: 573-635-7117
Fax: 573-635-3575
E-mail Address: info@mpca.org
Web Address: www.mpca.org
The Missouri Petroleum Marketers and Convenience Store Association (MPCA) is dedicated to serving the interests of convenience stores across Missouri.

Ohio Petroleum Marketers & Convenience Store Association (OPMCA)
17 S. High St., Ste. 810
Columbus, OH 43215 USA
Phone: 614-947-8646
Fax: 614-947-8648
Web Address:
https://netforum.avectra.com/eWeb/StartPage.aspx?Site=OPMCA
The Ohio Petroleum Marketers & Convenience Store Association (OPMCA) is dedicated to serving the interests of retail petroleum marketers, independent refineries, truck stops, retail chains and convenience stores throughout Ohio.

Petroleum Marketers Association of America (PMAA)
1901 N. Ft. Myer Dr., Ste. 500
Arlington, VA 22209-1604 USA
Phone: 703-351-8000
Fax: 703-351-9160
E-mail Address: info@pmaa.org
Web Address: www.pmaa.org
The Petroleum Marketers Association of America (PMAA) is a federation of 47 state and regional trade associations comprised of approximately 8,000 independent petroleum marketers.

18) Grocery Industry Associations

Food Marketing Institute (FMI)
2345 Crystal Dr., Ste. 800
Arlington, VA 22202 USA
Phone: 202-452-8444
Fax: 202-429-4519
Web Address: www.fmi.org
The Food Marketing Institute (FMI) is a nonprofit association conducting programs in research, education, industry relations and public affairs on behalf of its 1,225 members.

International Dairy-Deli-Bakery Association (IDDBA)
636 Science Dr.
Madison, WI 53711-1073 USA
Phone: 608-310-5000
Fax: 608-238-6330
E-mail Address: iddba@iddba.org
Web Address: www.iddba.org
The International Dairy-Deli-Bakery Association (IDDBA) is a trade association that brings together retailers, manufacturers, brokers, distributors and interested industry professionals who provide dairy, deli and bakery products to consumers.

National Grocers Association (NGA)
1005 N. Glebe Rd., Ste. 250
Arlington, VA 22201-5758 USA
Phone: 703-516-0700
Fax: 703-516-0115
E-mail Address: feedback@nationalgrocers.org
Web Address: www.nationalgrocers.org
The National Grocers Association (NGA) is a national trade association representing retail and wholesale grocers that comprise the independent sector of the food distribution industry.

Neighborhood Market Association (NMA)
750 B St., Ste. 2340
San Diego, CA 92101 USA
Fax: 619-464-8440
Toll Free: 800-979-4427
E-mail Address: Info@neighborhoodmarket.org
Web Address: http://neighborhoodmarket.org/
The Neighborhood Market Association (NMA) is a
nonprofit membership organization dedicated to
supporting independent retailers in the food and
beverage industry throughout California, Nevada,
Arizona and the West Coast.

Pennsylvania Food Merchant Association (PFMA)
1029 Mumma Rd.
Wormleysburg, PA 17043 USA
Phone: 717-731-0600
Fax: 717-731-5472
Toll Free: 800-543-8207
E-mail Address: pfma@pfma.net
Web Address: www.pfma.org
The Pennsylvania Food Merchant Association
(PFMA) is a statewide trade association representing
retail food stores, wholesale distributors and
supermarkets in Pennsylvania.

19) Industry Research/Market Research

Forrester Research
60 Acorn Park Dr.
Cambridge, MA 02140 USA
Phone: 617-613-5730
E-mail Address: press@forrester.com
Web Address: www.forrester.com
Forrester Research is a publicly traded company that
identifies and analyzes emerging trends in technology
and their impact on business. Among the firm's
specialties are the financial services, retail, health
care, entertainment, automotive and information
technology industries.

Kantar Retail
24-28 Bloomsbury Way
London, WC1A 2PX SE1 2QY UK
Phone: 44-207-450-2627
Web Address: www.kantarretail.com
Kantar Retail, formed by the amalgamation of
Cannondale Associates, Glendinning Management
Consultants, Management Ventures Inc. and Retail
Forward, is a consulting business that provides in-
depth market research on retail. This firm's web site
contains press releases with forecasts and statistics
regarding retail activity and trends.

MarketResearch.com
11200 Rockville Pike, Ste. 504
Rockville, MD 20852 USA
Phone: 240-747-3093
Fax: 240-747-3004
Toll Free: 800-298-5699
E-mail Address:
customerservice@marketresearch.com
Web Address: www.marketresearch.com
MarketResearch.com is a leading broker for
professional market research and industry analysis.
Users are able to search the company's database of
research publications including data on global
industries, companies, products and trends.

NPD Group (The)
900 W. Shore Rd.
Port Washington, NY 11050 USA
Phone: 516-625-0700
Toll Free: 866-444-1411
Web Address: www.npd.com
The NPD Group is one of the world's leading market
research firms covering the retailing and related
sectors. NPD covers industries including automotive,
beauty, technology, entertainment, fashion, food &
beverage, home, software, toys and wireless.

Plunkett Research, Ltd.
P.O. Drawer 541737
Houston, TX 77254-1737 USA
Phone: 713-932-0000
Fax: 713-932-7080
E-mail Address:
customersupport@plunkettresearch.com
Web Address: www.plunkettresearch.com
Plunkett Research, Ltd. is a leading provider of
market research, industry trends analysis and
business statistics. Since 1985, it has served clients
worldwide, including corporations, universities,
libraries, consultants and government agencies. At
the firm's web site, visitors can view product
information and pricing and access a large amount of
basic market information on industries such as
financial services, InfoTech, e-commerce, health care
and biotech.

20) Internet Usage Statistics

ClickZ Network
55 Broad St., Fl. 22
New York, NY 10004 USA
Phone: 646-736-1842
Fax: 212-732-3857

Toll Free: 800-955-2719
Web Address: www.clickz.com
The ClickZ Network is a resource for interactive marketing news, information, commentary, advice and opinions. The web site seeks to provide valuable tools for marketers.

comScore, Inc.
11950 Democracy Dr., Ste. 600
Reston, VA 20190 USA
Phone: 703-438-2000
Fax: 703-438-2051
Toll Free: 866-276-6972
Web Address: www.comscore.com
comScore, Inc. provides excellent data on consumer behavior and audiences, particularly in terms of how consumers access and use online sites and digital data and entertainment. They are global leaders in Internet usage data.

eMarketer
11 Times Square
New York, NY 10036 USA
Toll Free: 800-405-0844
Web Address: www.emarketer.com
eMarketer is a comprehensive, objective and easy-to-use resource for any person or business interested in online marketing and emerging media. The firm offers news articles, market projections and analytical commentaries.

Nielsen
85 Broad St.
New York, NY 10004 USA
Toll Free: 800-864-1224
Web Address: www.nielsen.com
Nielsen offers detailed, real-time Internet, retail and media research and analysis.

21) Liquor Industry Associations

Distilled Spirits Council of the United States (DISCUS)
1250 Eye St. NW, Ste. 400
Washington, DC 20005 USA
Phone: 202-628-3544
Web Address: www.discus.org
The Distilled Spirits Council of the United States (DISCUS) is a national trade organization for the marketing and production of distilled spirits industry.

22) Logistics & Supply Chain Associations

American Association of Exporters and Importers (AAEI)
1717 K St. NW, Ste. 1120
Washington, DC 20006 USA
Phone: 202-857-8009
Fax: 202-857-7843
Web Address: www.aaei.org
The American Association of Exporters and Importers (AAEI) is the only national association dedicated exclusively to representing the interests of both United States importers and exporters.

China Federation of Logistics and Purchasing
25 Yuetan N. St.
Beijing, 100045 China
Phone: 86-10-6839-1462
Fax: 86-10-5856-6839-1462
Web Address: www.chinawuliu.com.cn
The China Federation of Logistics and Purchasing (CFLP) works in cooperation with other logistics and supply chain organizations internationally, especially throughout the Asia Pacific region, to advance the theory and practice of effective supply chain management.

Council of Supply Chain Management Professionals (CSCMP)
333 E. Butterfield Rd., Ste. 140
Lombard, IL 60148 USA
Phone: 630-574-0985
Fax: 630-574-0989
E-mail Address: membership@cscmp.org
Web Address: www.cscmp.org
The Council of Supply Chain Management Professionals (CSCMP) is a nonprofit organization of professionals interested in supply chain management. CSCMP provides educational, career development and networking opportunities to over 8,500 members.

GS1 Hong Kong
160 Gloucester Rd.
22/F, OTB Bldg.
Wanchai, Hong Kong Hong Kong
Phone: 852-2861-2819
E-mail Address: info@gs1hk.org
Web Address: www.gs1hk.org
GS1 Hong Kong, a new name of Hong Kong Article Numbering Association, is a not-for-profit, industry led organization to promote global standards, best practices and enabling technologies in the arena of global value and supply chain management.

GS1 Singapore
2985 Jalan Bukit Merah
Singapore, 159457 Singapore
Phone: 65-6826-3077
E-mail Address: contact@gs1.org.sg
Web Address:
http://www.gs1.org/countries/Singapore
GS1 Singapore is a nonprofit council appointed by
Singapore Trade Development Board to implement
and administer an international article numbering
system in Singapore. It is the sole representative of
EPCglobal Inc. in Singapore. GS1 Singapore also
provides the standards for GS1 XML, a business tool
for the automatic transmission of commercial data
from one computer system to another.

GS1 US
1009 Lenox Dr., Ste. 202
Lawrenceville, NJ 08648 USA
Phone: 609-620-0200
Fax: 609-620-1200
E-mail Address: info@gs1us.org
Web Address: www.gs1us.org
GS1 US, formerly known as the Uniform Code
Council, Inc., is a nonprofit organization created to
administer the Universal Product Code (UPC),
known as the GS1 System, in the United States. The
organization supports the implementation of
standardized identification numbers for use in bar
codes and e-commerce messaging standards such as
Electronic Data Interchange (EDI) and GS1
Extensible Markup Language (XML).

Hong Kong Logistics Development Council
21/F, E. Wing, Central Gov't Offices
2 Tim Mei Ave.
Tamar, Hong Kong Hong Kong
Phone: 852-3509-8252
Fax: 852-2523-0030
E-mail Address: logsuser@thb.gov.hk
Web Address: www.logisticshk.gov.hk
The Hong Kong Logistics Development Council
serves Hong Kong, a world-class logistics hub. Hong
Kong is one of the busiest container ports and
international air cargo handling centers in the world.
The association focuses on all logistics services; sea,
air and land transport and involves various policy
portfolios and services areas, including distribution,
supply chain management and information
technology.

**National Customs Brokers and Forwarders
Association of America, Inc. (NCBFAA)**
1200 18th St. NW, Ste. 901
Washington, DC 20036 USA
Phone: 202-466-0222
Fax: 202-466-0226
E-mail Address: comm@ncbfaa.org
Web Address: www.ncbfaa.org
The National Customs Brokers and Forwarders
Association of America, Inc. (NCBFAA) represents
the nation's leading freight forwarders, customs
brokers, NVOCCs and air cargo agents.

23) Manufacturing Associations-General

National Association of Manufacturers (NAM)
733 10th St. NW, Ste. 700
Washington, DC 20001 USA
Phone: 202-637-3000
Fax: 202-637-3182
Toll Free: 800-814-8468
E-mail Address: manufacturing@nam.org
Web Address: www.nam.org
The National Association of Manufacturers (NAM) is
one of the largest industrial trade associations in the
United States, representing manufacturers and
employees in every industrial sector. The association
lobbies Congress on behalf of its members and seeks
economic growth through the promotion of
manufacturing activities and legislation.

24) MBA Resources

MBA Depot
Web Address: www.mbadepot.com
MBA Depot is an online community and information
portal for MBAs, potential MBA program applicants
and business professionals.

25) Organic Food Industry Associations

Organic Trade Association
28 Vernon St., Ste. 413
Brattleboro, VT 05301 USA
Phone: 802-275-3800
Fax: 802-275-3801
Web Address: www.ota.com
The Organic Trade Association promotes organic
agriculture and products and maintains an interest in
public education and legislative policies.

26) Payment, E-Commerce and Data Interchange Technology

Data Interchange Standards Association (DISA)
8300 Greensboro Dr., Ste. 800
McLean, VA 22102 USA
Phone: 703-970-4480
Fax: 703-970-4488
E-mail Address: info@disa.org
Web Address: http://www.disa.org/about.cfm
The Data Interchange Standards Association (DISA)
is a leading nonprofit organization that supports the
development and use of electronic business
interchange standards in e-commerce.

27) Privacy & Consumer Matters

Consumer Data Industry Association (CDIA)
1090 Vermont Ave. NW, Ste. 200
Washington, DC 20005-4905 USA
Phone: 202-371-0910
Fax: 202-371-0134
E-mail Address: cdia@cdiaonline.org
Web Address: www.cdiaonline.org
The Consumer Data Industry Association (CDIA) is
an international trade association representing
consumer information companies that provide fraud
prevention and risk management products.

Electronic Privacy Information Center (EPIC)
1718 Connecticut Ave. NW, Ste. 200
Washington, DC 20009 USA
Phone: 202-483-1140
Fax: 202-483-1248
E-mail Address: info@epic.org
Web Address: www.epic.org
The Electronic Privacy Information Center (EPIC) is
public interest research center, established to focus
public attention on emerging civil liberties issues and
to protect privacy, the First Amendment and
constitutional values.

Get Safe Online
Clifton House
Four Elms Rd.
Cardiff, CF24 1LE UK
E-mail Address: info@getsafeonline.org
Web Address: www.getsafeonline.org
Get Safe Online is a joint initiative between the U.K.
government, law enforcement, leading businesses and
the public sector. Its aim is to provide computer users
and small businesses with free, independent, user-
friendly advice that will allow them to use the
internet confidently, safely and securely. It provides
videos and online advice about such subjects as
identify theft, computer security and safe purchasing
practices for products, services and travel.

Internet Crime Complaint Center (IC3)
Web Address: www.ic3.gov
The Internet Crime Complaint Center (IC3) is a joint
venture between the FBI and the National White
Collar Crime Center. It provides a central collection
point for Internet crime complaints, which are then
sent on to the appropriate government agency. At the
IC3 website, consumers may file a complaint online.
IC3 accepts Internet crime complaints either from the
person who believes they were defrauded, or from
third parties.

National Fraud Information Center (NFIC)
1701 K St. NW, Ste. 1200
c/o National Consumers League
Washington, DC 20006 USA
Phone: 202-835-3323
Fax: 202-835-0747
Toll Free: 800-876-7060
E-mail Address: info@nclnet.org
Web Address: www.fraud.org
The National Fraud Information Center (NFIC)
covers all types of fraud and provides information
about reporting fraud, as well as posting fraud alerts.

Privacy Times
P.O. Box 302
Cabin John, MD 20818 USA
Phone: 301-229-7002
Fax: 301-229-8011
E-mail Address: evan@privacytimes.com
Web Address: www.privacytimes.com
Privacy Times is a publication targeting attorneys and
professionals wishing to follow legislation and
developments in the information privacy arena,
including the Freedom of Information Act, direct
marketing, Caller ID and credit reports.

28) Private Label (Generic) Manufacturing Associations

Private Label Manufacturers Association (PLMA)
630 Third Ave.
New York, NY 10017 USA
Phone: 212-972-3131
Fax: 212-983-1382
E-mail Address: info@plma.com

Web Address: www.plma.com
The Private Label Manufacturers Association (PLMA) founded in 1979, represents more than 3,000 companies around the world and organizes trade shows, programs and services that are specifically designed for the industry. The private label sector includes makers of store branded and generic-labeled products in foods, consumer products and personal care items.

29) Real Estate Industry Associations

Institute of Real Estate Management (IREM)
430 N. Michigan Ave.
Chicago, IL 60611 USA
Fax: 800-338-4736
Toll Free: 800-837-0706
E-mail Address: getinfo@irem.org
Web Address: www.irem.org
The Institute of Real Estate Management (IREM) seeks to educate real estate managers, certify their competence and professionalism, serve as an advocate on issues affecting the real estate management industry and enhance its members' professional competence so they can better identify and meet the needs of those who use their services.

National Association of Real Estate Investment Trusts (NAREIT)
1875 I St. NW, Ste. 600
Washington, DC 20006 USA
Phone: 202-739-9400
Fax: 202-739-9401
Toll Free: 800-362-7348
Web Address: www.reit.com
The National Association of Real Estate Investment Trusts (NAREIT) is the representative to governmental policymakers for U.S. Real Estate Investment Trusts (REITs) and publicly traded real estate companies worldwide.

Property Management Association (PMA)
7508 Wisconsin Ave., Fl. 4
Bethesda, MD 20814 USA
Phone: 301-657-9200
Fax: 301-907-9326
E-mail Address: info@pma-dc.org
Web Address: www.pma-dc.org
The Property Management Association (PMA) is a real estate management organization that promotes the knowledge and practical education of the industry through monthly meetings, seminars and publications.

30) Real Estate Industry Resources

CoStar Group
1331 L St. NW
Washington, DC 20005 USA
Phone: 202-346-6500
Fax: 800-613-1301
Toll Free: 800-204-5960
E-mail Address: info@costargroup.com
Web Address: www.costar.com
CoStar Group operates a web site with extensive resources for brokers, owners and users of commercial real estate space. The group operates a listings database that allows users to analyze market trends, research property history and compare local rental rates for commercial real estate.

31) Restaurant Industry Associations

American Beverage Association
1101 16th St. NW
Washington, DC 20036 USA
Phone: 202-463-6732
Fax: 202-659-5349
E-mail Address: info@ameribev.org
Web Address: www.ameribev.org
The American Beverage Association (ABA) was founded in 1919 as the American Bottlers of Carbonated Beverages, and renamed the National Soft Drink Association in 1966. Today the ABA represents hundreds of beverage producers, distributors, franchise companies and support industries. They market hundreds of brands, flavors and packages, including regular and diet soft drinks, bottled water and water beverages, 100-percent juice and juice drinks, sports drinks, energy drinks and ready-to-drink teas.

National Association of Concessionaires (NAC)
180 N. Michigan Ave., Ste. 2215
Chicago, IL 60601 USA
Phone: 312-236-3858
Fax: 312-236-7809
E-mail Address: info@NAConline.org
Web Address: www.naconline.org
The National Association of Concessionaires (NAC) is the trade association for owners and operators of businesses in the recreation and leisure-time food and beverage concessions industry.

National Council of Chain Restaurants (NCCR)
1101 New York Ave. NW

Washington, DC 20005 USA
Phone: 202-783-7971
Fax: 202-737-2849
Toll Free: 800-673-4692
Web Address: www.nrf.com
The National Council of Chain Restaurants (NCCR), a division of the National Retail Federation (NRF), is an organization of 40 of the largest chain restaurant companies in the United States. It seeks to advance sound public policy that represents the best interests of the industry.

National Restaurant Association (NRA)
2055 L St. NW, Ste. 700
Washington, DC 20036 USA
Phone: 202-331-5900
Fax: 202-331-2429
Toll Free: 800-424-5156
Web Address: www.restaurant.org
The National Restaurant Association (NRA) is the leading business association for the restaurant industry. Its web site offers extensive industry information as well as government news, trends and membership perks.

32) Retail Industry Associations

Alabama Retail Association (ARA)
7265 Halcyon Summit Dr.
Montgomery, AL 36117-3502 USA
Phone: 334-263-5757
Fax: 334-262-3991
Toll Free: 800-239-5423
E-mail Address:
alabamaretailassociation@alabamaretail.org
Web Address: www.alabamaretail.org
The Alabama Retail Association (ARA) represents the retail industry in Alabama, with independent merchants and national companies as members.

American Association of Franchisees and Dealers (AAFD)
P.O. Box 10158
Palm Desert, CA 92255-1058 USA
Phone: 619-209-3775
Fax: 866-855-1988
Toll Free: 800-733-9858
Web Address: www.aafd.org
The American Association of Franchisees and Dealers (AAFD) is a national nonprofit trade association representing the rights and interests of franchisees and independent dealers throughout the United States.

Illinois Retail Merchants Association (IRMA)
19 S. LaSalle St., Ste. 300
Chicago, IL 60603 USA
Phone: 312-726-4600
Fax: 312-726-9570
Toll Free: 800-572-5044
E-mail Address: info@irma.org
Web Address: www.irma.org
The Illinois Retail Merchants Association (IRMA) is one of the largest state retail organizations and it represents more than 23,000 stores of all sizes and merchandise lines.

International Association of Airport Duty-Free Stores (IAADFS)
2025 M St. NW, Ste. 800
Washington, DC 20036-3309 USA
Phone: 202-367-1184
Fax: 202-429-5154
E-mail Address: iaadfs@iaadfs.org
Web Address: www.iaadfs.org
The International Association of Airport Duty-Free Stores (IAADFS) is an international trade association with 400 company members. Its purpose is to promote the airport duty-free industry as a segment of international business.

International Association of Department Stores (IADS)
11-13 Rue Guersant
Paris, 75017 France
Phone: 33-1-42-94-02-02
Fax: 33-1-42-94-02-04
E-mail Address: iads@iads.org
Web Address: www.iads.org
The International Association of Department Stores (IADS) is a worldwide association for department stores. Its members currently include traditional department stores from almost 20 countries.

International Premium Cigar & Pipe Retailers Association (IPCPR)
4 Bradley Park Ct., Ste. 2-H
Columbus, GA 31904-3637 USA
Phone: 706-494-1143
Fax: 706-494-1893
Web Address: www.ipcpr.org
The International Premium Cigar & Pipe Retailers Association (IPCPR), formerly the Retail Tobacco Dealers of America, is a trade association dedicated to serving retail tobacconists in the sale and promotion of legal tobacco products and related items.

Kentucky Retail Federation (KRF)
512 Capital Ave.
Frankfort, KY 40601 USA
Phone: 502-875-1444
E-mail Address: info@kyretail.com
Web Address: www.kyretail.com
The Kentucky Retail Federation (KRF) is Kentucky's
retail association, providing services such as public
relations information and business relations screening
as well as lists of important numbers.

Maryland Retailers Association (MRA)
171 Conduit St.
Annapolis, MD 21401 USA
Phone: 410-269-1440
Fax: 410-269-0325
Web Address: www.mdra.org
The Maryland Retailers Association (MRA) acts as
the retail industry's major statewide trade association
in Maryland, and consists of over 250 members at
approximately 1,400 locations.

Michigan Retailers Association (MRA)
603 S. Washington Ave.
Lansing, MI 48933 USA
Phone: 517-372-5656
Fax: 517-372-1303
Toll Free: 800-366-3699
E-mail Address: mra@retailers.com
Web Address: www.retailers.com
The Michigan Retailers Association (MRA) is the
state retail association in Michigan, providing
legislative representation, daily retail news, event
information and membership news.

Minnesota Retailers Association (MnRA)
400 Robert St. N., Ste. 1540
St. Paul, MN 55101 USA
Phone: 651-227-6631
Toll Free: 800-227-6762
E-mail Address: mnra@mnretail.org
Web Address: www.mnretail.org
The Minnesota Retailers Association (MnRA) is the
voice of retailing for the merchant community in
Minnesota, consisting of small independent retail
establishments as well as large national chains. The
association provides legislative services, money
saving programs and information services.

Museum Store Association (MSA)
3773 E. Cherry Creek N. Dr., Ste. 755
Denver, CO 80209-3804 USA
Phone: 303-504-9223

Fax: 303-504-9585
Web Address: www.museumdistrict.com
The Museum Store Association (MSA) is a nonprofit,
international organization representing cultural
commerce and museum store professionals.

Music Business Association (Music Biz)
1 Eves Dr., Ste. 138
Marlton, NJ 08053 USA
Phone: 856-596-2221
Fax: 856-596-3268
Web Address: musicbiz.org
The Music Business Association (Music Biz),
formerly the National Association of Recording
Merchandisers (NARM) and digitalmusic.org, is a
non-profit trade association that serves the music
retailing community in the areas of networking,
advocacy, education, information and promotion.

**National Automatic Merchandising Association
(NAMA)**
20 N. Wacker Dr., Ste. 3500
Chicago, IL 60606-3102 USA
Phone: 312-346-0370
Fax: 312-704-4140
E-mail Address: jbradshaw@vending.org
Web Address: www.vending.org
The National Automatic Merchandising Association
(NAMA) is a national trade association of the
merchandising, vending, office coffee service (OCS)
and contract food services management businesses.

**National Ice Cream Retailers Association
(NICRA)**
1028 W. Devon Ave.
Elk Grove Village, IL 60007 USA
Phone: 847-301-7500
Fax: 847-301-8402
Toll Free: 866-303-6960
Web Address: www.nicra.org
The National Ice Cream Retailers Association
(NICRA) is a trade organization representing ice
cream and frozen dessert retailers, wholesalers and
distributors, mainly in the U.S. and Canada.

National Retail Federation (NRF)
1101 New York Ave. NW
Washington, DC 20005 USA
Phone: 202-783-7971
Fax: 202-737-2849
Toll Free: 800-673-4692
Web Address: www.nrf.com

The National Retail Federation (NRF) is one of the world's largest retail trade organizations. Its membership includes the leading department, specialty, independent, discount and mass merchandise stores in the United States and 50 nations worldwide.

National Shoe Retailers Association (NSRA)
7386 N. La Cholla Blvd.
Tucson, AZ 85741 USA
Phone: 520-209-1710
Toll Free: 800-673-8446
Web Address: www.nsra.org
The National Shoe Retailers Association (NSRA) is a trade organization that provides practical information and business services. In addition, it serves as an advocate for the independent shoe retailing community, representing storeowners and operators within the broader retail industry.

New Hampshire Retail Association
48 Grandview Rd., Ste. 2
Bow, NH 03304 USA
Phone: 603-225-9748
Fax: 603-229-0060
E-mail Address: shop@retailnh.com
Web Address: www.retailnh.com
The New Hampshire Retail Association, formerly the Retail Merchants Association of New Hampshire (RMANH), is a statewide trade association representing over 900 businesses in New Hampshire. Its members range from small independent business owners to major corporations.

North American Retail Hardware Association Canada
528 Queen St. E.
Toronto, M5R 1V9 Canada
Phone: 416-489-3396
E-mail Address: mike@hardlines.ca
Web Address: www.nrha.org
The North American Retail Hardware Association Canada (NRHA Canada) advances the common interests of the Canadian retail hardlines industry.

North Carolina Retail Merchants Association (NCRMA)
209 Fayetteville St.
Raleigh, NC 27601 USA
Phone: 919-832-0811
E-mail Address: info@ncrma.org
Web Address: www.ncrma.org

The North Carolina Retail Merchants Association (NCRMA) is a nonprofit trade association for retailers in the state of North Carolina. On its web site, business owners and merchants can find links to the state government, as well as news and information on area retail trends.

North Dakota Retail Association (NDRA)
1014 E. Central Ave.
Bismarck, ND 58501 USA
Phone: 701-223-3370
Fax: 701-223-5004
Web Address: www.ndretail.org
The North Dakota Retail Association (NDRA) is a trade association composed of large and small retail businesses across North Dakota. Its site offers organization information and news affecting North Dakota merchants.

Pennsylvania Retailers Association (PRA)
224 Pine St.
Harrisburg, PA 17101 USA
Phone: 717-233-7976
Fax: 717-236-1234
Toll Free: 800-727-3824
E-mail Address: brian@paretailers.org
Web Address: www.paretailers.org
The Pennsylvania Retailers Association (PRA) is a membership organization that acts as the voice of the retailing industry in the Pennsylvania area.

Retail Council of Canada (RCC)
1881 Yonge St., Ste. 800
Toronto, ON M4S 3C4 Canada
Phone: 416-922-6678
Toll Free: 888-373-8245
E-mail Address: info@retailcouncil.org
Web Address: www.retailcouncil.org
The Retail Council of Canada (RCC) is a trade association for Canadian retailers, representing more than 45,000 stores.

Retail Industry Leaders Association (RILA)
1700 N. Moore St., Ste. 2250
Arlington, VA 22209 USA
Phone: 703-841-2300
Fax: 703-841-1184
E-mail Address: tripp.taylor@rila.org
Web Address: www.rila.org
The Retail Industry Leaders Association (RILA) is a world leading alliance of retailers and their product and service suppliers.

Retailers Association of India
111/112 Ascot Ctr., Next to Hotel ITC Maratha
Sahar Rd., Sahar, Andheri (E)
Mumbai, 400 099 India
Phone: 91-22-28269527
Fax: 91-22-28269536
E-mail Address: info@rai.net.in
Web Address: www.rai.net.in
The Retailers Association of India promotes and
supports retailers and the retail industry in India.

Singapore Retailers Association (SRA)
1 Coleman St.
05-11B The Adelphi
Singapore, 179803 Singapore
Phone: 65-6334-5223
E-mail Address: info@sra.org.sg
Web Address: www.retail.org.sg
Singapore Retailers Association (SRA) is a nonprofit,
independent, non-governmental retail trade body
funded entirely by the private sector. SRA seeks to
develop and promote the retail sector in Singapore.

South Dakota Retailers Association (SDRA)
320 E. Capitol Ave.
P.O. Box 638
Pierre, SD 57501 USA
Phone: 605-224-5050
Fax: 605-224-2059
Toll Free: 800-658-5545
Web Address: www.sdra.org
The South Dakota Retailers Association (SDRA) is
the statewide business organization representing
retailers in South Dakota. It provides its members
with legislative information, publications and links to
aid in business management.

Texas Retailers Association (TRA)
400 W. 15th St., Ste. 1405
Austin, TX 78701 USA
Phone: 512-472-8261
Fax: 512-474-5011
E-mail Address: txretailers@txretailers.org
Web Address: www.txretailers.org
The Texas Retailers Association (TRA) is composed
of small and large retailers throughout the state of
Texas. The association offers up-to-date industry
information and provides representation before the
Texas state legislature.

The Association of Resale Professionals (NARTS)
P.O. Box 190
St. Clair Shores, MI 48080 USA

Phone: 586-294-6700
Fax: 586-588-7018
Toll Free: 800-544-0751
E-mail Address: info@narts.org
Web Address: www.narts.org
The Association of Resale Professionals (NARTS),
formerly known as the National Association of
Resale and Thrift Shops is the only trade organization
representing the resale industry.

Vermont Retail Association (VRA)
148 State St.
Montpelier, VT 05602 USA
Phone: 802-839-1928
Fax: 802-839-1927
E-mail Address: info@vtrga.org
Web Address: www.vtretailers.com
The Vermont Retail Association (VRA) is a member
organization that represents Vermont retailers. It
offers various publications and advocacy services to
Vermont businesses.

Wyoming Retail Association (WRA)
1825 Carey Ave.
P.O. Box 1003
Cheyenne, WY 82001 USA
Phone: 307-634-8816
Fax: 307-632-0249
E-mail Address: info@wyoretail.org
Web Address: www.wyoretail.org/index2.cfm
The Wyoming Retail Association, formerly known as
the Wyoming Retail Merchants Association
(WRMA) represents large and small retailers and
allied businesses across Wyoming.

33) Retail Industry Resources

IndiaRetailing.com
S-21 Okhla Phase II
New Delhi, 110 020 India
Phone: 91-11-40525000
Fax: 91-11-40525001
E-mail Address: info@imagesgroup.in
Web Address: www.indiaretailing.com
An initiative of Images Group, IndiaRetailing.com is
a retail information interface portal with news related
to the industry and a glossary.

Luxury Marketing Council Worldwide
Phone: 212-517-4614
E-mail Address: gfurman@luxurycouncil.com
Web Address: www.luxurycouncil.com

The Luxury Marketing Council Worldwide is an invitation-only collaborative organization of approximately 5,000 retail CEOs and marketing executives representing more than 1000 major luxury goods and services on a global scale.

34) RFID Industry Associations

Association for Automatic Identification and Mobility (AIM)
20399 Rte. 19, Ste. 203
Cranberry Township, PA 16066 USA
Phone: 724-742-4470
E-mail Address: info@aimglobal.org
Web Address: www.aimglobal.org
The Association for Automatic Identification and Mobility (AIM) is a global trade organization dedicated to accelerating the growth and use of RFID and other automated identification and data capture/collection (AIDC) technologies and services. Its more than 900 members are manufacturers or service providers of RFID, bar code, card, biometrics and electronic article surveillance technologies.

EPCglobal Inc.
1009 Lenox Dr., Ste. 202
Lawrenceville, NJ 08648 U.S.
Phone: 609-620-0200
E-mail Address: info@gs1us.org
Web Address: www.gs1.org/epcglobal
EPCglobal Inc. is a global standards organization for the Electronic Product Code (EPC), which supports the use of RFID. It was initially developed by the Auto-ID Center, an academic research project at the Massachusetts Institute of Technology (MIT). Today, offices and affiliates of EPCglobal are based in nearly every nation of the world. The nonprofit organization is a joint venture between GS1, formerly known as EAN International, and GS1 US, formerly known as the Uniform Code Council.

35) RFID Resources

RFID.org
One Landmark N., 20399 Rte. 19, Ste. 203
Cranberry Township, PA 16066 USA
Phone: 724-742-4470
Fax: 724-742-4476
E-mail Address: info@aimglobal.org
Web Address: www.aimglobal.org/?RFID
RFID.org is a link to news, events, case studies and commentary relating to radio frequency identification

(RFID) technologies and applications. The site is sponsored by the global branch of the Association for Automatic Identification and Mobility (AIM GLOBAL).

36) Shopping Center Directories

Chain Store Guide (CSG)
10117 Princess Palm Ave., Ste. 375
Tampa, FL 33610 USA
Fax: 813-627-6888
Toll Free: 800-927-9292
E-mail Address: webmaster@chainstoreguide.com
Web Address: www.chainstoreguide.com
The Chain Store Guide (CSG) is a provider of comprehensive retail and foodservice intelligence. The CSG database contains over 700,000 retailers, foodservice operators, distributors and wholesalers in the U.S. and Canada.

Directory of Major Malls, Inc. (The)
P.O. Box 837
Nyack, NY 10960 USA
Phone: 845-348-7000
Toll Free: 800-898-6255
Web Address: www.shoppingcenters.com
The Directory of Major Malls, Inc. offers information on centers that have above 250,000 square feet of gross leaseable area (GLA). Information includes location, GLA, household income, area population and design of various centers.

Value Retail News
1221 Avenue of the Americas, Fl. 41
New York, NY 10020 USA
Phone: 646-728-3800
Fax: 732-694-1755
E-mail Address: icsc@icsc.org
Web Address: www.valueretailnews.com
Value Retail News, a division of the International Council of Shopping Centers, publishes several directories, including the Global Outlet Project Directory, a listing of factory outlet information; and the Value Retail Directory, which provides factory outlet tenant data.

37) Shopping Center Resources

ChainLinks Retail Advisors
300 Galleria Pkwy., Fl. 12
Atlanta, GA 30339 USA
Phone: 805-684-7767

Fax: 770-951-0054
Web Address: www.chainlinks.com
ChainLinks is a major retail-only, full-service real estate broker in the United States and Canada.

CoreNet Global
133 Peachtree St. NE, Ste. 3000
Atlanta, GA 30303 USA
Phone: 404-589-3200
Fax: 404-589-3201
Toll Free: 800-726-8111
E-mail Address: membership@corenetglobal.org
Web Address: www.corenetglobal.org
CoreNet Global is an organization for business leaders engaged in the strategic management of real estate for major corporations worldwide.

International Council of Shopping Centers (ICSC)
1221 Ave. of the Americas, Fl. 41
New York, NY 10020-1099 USA
Phone: 646-728-3800
Fax: 732-694-1690
E-mail Address: membership@icsc.org
Web Address: www.icsc.org
The International Council of Shopping Centers (ICSC) is the global trade association of the shopping center industry, and includes shopping center owners, developers, managers, marketing specialists, investors, lenders and retailers. ICSC's 70,000 members reach to over 100 countries and the organization links with more than 25 national and regional shopping center councils throughout the world.

38) Sporting Goods Industry Associations

Canadian Sporting Goods Association (CSGA)
Toll Free: 844-350-9902
E-mail Address: info@csga.ca
Web Address: www.csga.ca
The Canadian Sporting Goods Association (CSGA) represents the sporting goods industry in Canada.

National Ski and Snowboard Retailer Association (NSSRA)
1601 Feehanville Dr., Ste. 300
Mt. Prospect, IL 60056-6035 USA
Phone: 847-391-9825
Fax: 847-391-9827
Toll Free: 888-257-1168
E-mail Address: info@nssra.com
Web Address: www.nssra.com

The National Ski and Snowboard Retailer Association (NSSRA) provides ski and snowboard retailers across the U.S. with information and services. NSSRA also represents ski shops at the meetings of the American Society for Testing and Materials (ASTM) committee on snow skiing.

National Sporting Goods Association (NSGA)
1601 Feehanville Dr., Ste. 300
Mt. Prospect, IL 60056 USA
Fax: 847-391-9827
Toll Free: 800-815-5422
E-mail Address: info@nsga.org
Web Address: www.nsga.org
The National Sporting Goods Association (NSGA) is a trade association designed to help its members profit in a competitive marketplace. The group publishes excellent market research in addition to hosting a major annual conference.

World Federation of the Sporting Goods Industry (WFSGI)
Obere Zollgasse 75
P.O. Box 1664
Ostermundigen, Bern 3072 Switzerland
Phone: 41-31-939-60-61
Fax: 41-31-939-60-69
E-mail Address: info@wfsgi.org
Web Address: www.wfsgi.org
The World Federation of the Sporting Goods Industry (WFSGI) is a global, nonprofit, independent association of sporting goods industry suppliers, national sporting goods organizations and other industry-related businesses.

39) Technology Transfer Associations

Licensing Executives Society (USA and Canada), Inc.
1120 Route 73, Ste. 200
Mount Laurel, NJ 08054 USA
Phone: 856-437-4752
E-mail Address: info@les.org
Web Address: www.lesusacanada.org
Licensing Executives Society (USA and Canada), Inc., established in 1965, is a professional association composed of about 3,000 members who work in fields related to the development, use, transfer, manufacture and marketing of intellectual property. Members include executives, lawyers, licensing consultants, engineers, academic researchers, scientists and government officials. The society is part of the larger Licensing Executives Society

International, Inc. (same headquarters address), with a worldwide membership of some 12,000 members from approximately 80 countries.

40) Textile & Fabric Associations

Association of Suppliers to the British Clothing Industry (ASBCI)
25 Square Rd.
Halifax, Unit 5
West Yorkshire, HX1 1QG UK
Phone: 01-42-235-4666
Fax: 01-42-238-1184
E-mail Address: office@asbci.co.uk
Web Address: www.asbci.co.uk
The Association of Suppliers to the British Clothing Industry (ASBCI) represents members in all the key sectors connected with the industry. Examples of sectors are: fibers, fabrics, adhesives, dyers, threads, machinery, presses, garment processors, manufacturers, retailers, drycleaners, launderers, domestic detergent manufacturers, chemical suppliers, computer suppliers to the clothing industry, textile testing houses, research organizations.

Textile Clothing and Technology Corporation (TC2)
5651 Dillard Dr.
Cary, NC 27518 USA
Phone: 919-380-2156
Fax: 919-380-2181
Toll Free: 800-786-9889
Web Address: www.tc2.com
The Textile Clothing and Technology Corporation (TC2) is a nonprofit consortium of fiber producers, retailers, sewn products manufacturers, labor unions, academia and the federal government. The website provides access to other TC2 sites: Size USA; 3D Body Scanning; techexchange.com and inkdropprinting.com.

Textile Council of Hong Kong
25 Kimberley Rd., Cheung Lee Comm. Bldg.
Fl. 4, Rm 401-3, TST
Kowloon, New Territories China
Phone: 852-(2)-305-2893
Fax: 852-(2)-305-2493
E-mail Address: sec@textilecouncil.com
Web Address: www.textilecouncil.com.
The Textile Council of Hong Kong represents ten major textile associations and acts as a voice for the entire Hong Kong textile industry. Its affiliated associations' activities range from spinning, weaving, knitting, dyeing and finishing, garment making and the manufacture of textile goods.

41) Textile & Fabric Resources

National Textile Center (NTC)
2 Pastern Ln.
Blue Bell, PA 19422-2429 USA
Phone: 215-540-9840
Fax: 215-689-4835
E-mail Address: marty.ntcresearch@verizon.net
Web Address: www.ntcresearch.org
The National Textile Center (NTC) is a research consortium of eight universities that aims to enhance the knowledge base for the continuing viability of the U.S. fiber, textile, fabricated products and retail complex.

42) Toy Industry Associations

British Toy & Hobby Association (BTHA)
80 Camberwell Rd.
London, SE5 0EG UK
Phone: 44-20-7701-7271
Fax: 44-20-7708-2437
E-mail Address: admin@btha.co.uk
Web Address: www.btha.co.uk
British Toy & Hobby Association (BTHA) represents the interests of British toy manufacturers and has roughly 144 members that represent the toy, hobby and game market.

Toy Industry Association, Inc. (TIA)
1115 Broadway, Ste. 400
New York, NY 10010 USA
Phone: 212-675-1141
E-mail Address: info@toyassociation.org
Web Address: www.toyassociation.org
The Toy Industry Association, Inc. (TIA) is a leading organization for North American manufacturers, importers, designers, inventors and retailers of toys and games. It is the owner and manager of the annual PlayCon toy industry conference.

43) Trade Associations-General

Associated Chambers of Commerce and Industry of India (ASSOCHAM)
5, Sardar Patel Marg
Chanakyapuri
New Delhi, 110 021 India
Phone: 91-11-4655-0555

Fax: 91-11-2301-7008
E-mail Address: assocham@nic.in
Web Address: www.assocham.org
The Associated Chambers of Commerce and Industry
of India (ASSOCHAM) has a membership of more
than 300 chambers and trade associations and serves
members from all over India. It works with domestic
and international government agencies to advocate
for India's industry and trade activities.

BUSINESSEUROPE
168 Ave. de Cortenbergh
Brussels, 1000 Belgium
Phone: 32-2-237-65-11
Fax: 32-2-231-14-45
E-mail Address: main@businesseurope.eu
Web Address: www.businesseurope.eu
BUSINESSEUROPE is a major European trade
federation that operates in a manner similar to a
chamber of commerce. Its members are the central
national business federations of the 34 countries
throughout Europe from which they come.
Companies cannot become direct members of
BUSINESSEUROPE, though there is a support group
which offers the opportunity for firms to encourage
BUSINESSEUROPE objectives in various ways.

Fair Trade Federation (FTF)
100 W. 10th St., Ste. 604
Wilmington, DE 19801 USA
Phone: 302-655-5203
E-mail Address: info@fairtradefederation.org
Web Address: www.fairtradefederation.com
The Fair Trade Federation (FTF) is an association of
retailers, producers and wholesalers that seek to
provide fair wages and good working conditions for
artisans and farmers.

Franchising Association of India
15 Parsi Panchayat Rd., Andheri(E)
Champion Bldg., 3rd Fl.
Mumbai, 400 069 India
Phone: 91-22-2827-2490
E-mail Address: nanette.dsa@fai.co.in
Web Address: www.fai.co.in
The Franchising Association of India is a
membership organization to promote the business
environment of franchisors and franchising service
providers.

44) Trade Associations-Global

**United Nations Commission on International
Trade Law (UNCITL)**
Vienna Int'l Ctr.
P.O. Box 500
Vienna, A-1400 Austria
Phone: 43-1-26060-4060
Fax: 43-1-26060-5813
Web Address: www.uncitral.org
The United Nations Commission on International
Trade Law (UNCITL) is the core legal body within
the United Nations system in the field of international
trade law.

World Trade Organization (WTO)
Centre William Rappard
Rue de Lausanne 154
Geneva 21, CH-1211 Switzerland
Phone: 41-22-739-51-11
Fax: 41-22-731-42-06
E-mail Address: enquiries@wto.og
Web Address: www.wto.org
The World Trade Organization (WTO) is a global
organization dealing with the rules of trade between
nations. To become a member, nations must agree to
abide by certain guidelines. Membership increases a
nation's ability to import and export efficiently.

45) U.S. Government Agencies

Bureau of Economic Analysis (BEA)
1441 L St. NW
Washington, DC 20230 USA
Phone: 202-606-9900
E-mail Address: customerservice@bea.gov
Web Address: www.bea.gov
The Bureau of Economic Analysis (BEA), an agency
of the U.S. Department of Commerce, is the nation's
economic accountant, preparing estimates that
illuminate key national, international and regional
aspects of the U.S. economy.

Bureau of Labor Statistics (BLS)
2 Massachusetts Ave. NE
Postal Square Building
Washington, DC 20212-0001 USA
Phone: 202-691-5200
Fax: 202-691-7890
Toll Free: 800-877-8339
E-mail Address: blsdata_staff@bls.gov
Web Address: stats.bls.gov

The Bureau of Labor Statistics (BLS) is the principal fact-finding agency for the Federal Government in the field of labor economics and statistics. It is an independent national statistical agency that collects, processes, analyzes and disseminates statistical data to the American public, U.S. Congress, other federal agencies, state and local governments, business and labor. The BLS also serves as a statistical resource to the Department of Labor.

International Trade Administration (ITA)
1401 Constitution Ave. NW
U.S. Department of Commerce
Washington, DC 20230 USA
Toll Free: 800-872-8723
Web Address: www.trade.gov
The International Trade Administration (ITA) is a U.S. Government agency that provides a wealth of information regarding imports and exports. In addition, it publishes in-depth analyses and statistics on various industry sectors and provides assistance to U.S. firms that wish to increase their exports.

U.S. Census Bureau
4600 Silver Hill Rd.
Washington, DC 20233-8800 USA
Phone: 301-763-4636
Toll Free: 800-923-8282
Web Address: www.census.gov
The U.S. Census Bureau is the official collector of data about the people and economy of the U.S. Founded in 1790, it provides official social, demographic and economic information. In addition to the Population & Housing Census, which it conducts every 10 years, the U.S. Census Bureau numerous other surveys annually.

U.S. Department of Commerce (DOC)
1401 Constitution Ave. NW
Washington, DC 20230 USA
Phone: 202-482-2000
E-mail Address: TheSec@doc.gov
Web Address: www.commerce.gov
The U.S. Department of Commerce (DOC) regulates trade and provides valuable economic analysis of the economy.

U.S. Department of Labor (DOL)
200 Constitution Ave. NW
Frances Perkins Bldg.
Washington, DC 20210 USA
Toll Free: 866-487-2365
Web Address: www.dol.gov

The U.S. Department of Labor (DOL) is the government agency responsible for labor regulations.

U.S. Department of State
2201 C St. NW
Washington, DC 20520 USA
Phone: 202-647-4000
Toll Free: 800-877-8339
Web Address: www.state.gov
The Department of State is the head United States foreign affairs agency.

U.S. Securities and Exchange Commission (SEC)
100 F St. NE
Washington, DC 20549 USA
Phone: 202-942-8088
Web Address: www.sec.gov
The U.S. Securities and Exchange Commission (SEC) is a nonpartisan, quasi-judicial regulatory agency responsible for administering federal securities laws. These laws are designed to protect investors in securities markets and ensure that they have access to disclosure of all material information concerning publicly traded securities. Visitors to the web site can access the EDGAR database of corporate financial and business information.

U.S. Trade Representative (USTR)
600 17th St. NW
Washington, DC 20508 USA
Phone: 202-395-3230
Fax: 202-395-6121
E-mail Address: media@ustr.eop.gov
Web Address: www.ustr.gov
The U.S. Trade Representative (USTR) is the nation's chief trade negotiator and the principal trade policy advisor to the President.

46) Watch Manufacturers Associations

Hong Kong Watch Manufacturers Association (HKWMA)
10 Jubilee St.
Fu Hing Bldg., Fl. 2
Hong Kong, Hong Kong Hong Kong
Phone: 852-2522-5238
Fax: 852-2810-6614
E-mail Address: hkwma@netvigator.com
Web Address: www.hkwatchworld.com
The Hong Kong Watch Manufacturers Association (HKWMA) is an organization that seeks to consolidate the watch industry, promote manufacturers' interests and facilitate overseas

counterparts. The 600 member companies are all registered companies in Hong Kong.

47) Wholesale Distributors Associations

Convenience Distribution Association
11311 Sunset Hills Rd.
Reston, VA 20190 USA
Phone: 703-208-3358
E-mail Address: info@cdaweb.net
Web Address: https://cdaweb.net/
The Convenience Distribution Association, formerly known as the American Wholesale Marketers Association (AWMA) is an international trade organization that works on behalf of convenience products distributors in the U.S. It offers industry news, discussion forums and links to publications.

Global Market Development Center (GMDC)
1275 Lake Plaza Dr.
Colorado Springs, CO 80906-3583 USA
Phone: 719-576-4260
Fax: 719-576-2661
E-mail Address: info@gmdc.org
Web Address: www.gmdc.org
The Global Market Development Center (GMDC) is an international trade association serving the general merchandise, health and beauty care and pharmacy industries.

National Association of Wholesaler-Distributors (NAW)
1325 G St. NW, Ste. 1000
Washington, DC 20005 USA
Phone: 202-872-0885
Fax: 202-785-0586
E-mail Address: naw@naw.org
Web Address: www.naw.org
The National Association of Wholesaler-Distributors (NAW) represents the wholesale distribution industry. The association also operates the Wholesaler-Distributor Political Action Committee, the Distribution Research & Education Foundation and the NAW Service Corporation.

Chapter 4

THE RETAIL 500:
WHO THEY ARE AND HOW THEY WERE
CHOSEN

Includes Indexes by Company Name, Industry & Location

The companies chosen to be listed in PLUNKETT'S RETAIL INDUSTRY ALMANAC comprise a unique list. THE RETAIL 500 (the actual count is 484 companies) were chosen specifically for their dominance in the many facets of the retail industry in which they operate. Complete information about each firm can be found in the "Individual Profiles," beginning at the end of this chapter. These profiles are in alphabetical order by company name.

THE RETAIL 500 companies are from all parts of the United States, Canada, Europe, Asia and beyond. Essentially, the RETAIL 500 includes major chain store operators and franchisers, major non-store retailers, major automobile retailers and companies that make software and point of sale systems for retailing.

Note: Researchers seeking a comprehensive list of e-commerce companies should refer to PLUNKETT'S E-COMMERCE & INTERNET BUSINESS ALMANAC.

Simply stated, THE RETAIL 500 contains 484 of the largest, most successful, fastest growing firms in retail and related industries in the world. To be included in our list, the firms had to meet the following criteria:

1) Generally, these are corporations based in the U.S., however, the headquarters of 135 firms are located in other nations.

2) Prominence, or a significant presence, in retail and supporting fields. (See the following Industry Codes section for a complete list of types of businesses that are covered).

3) The companies in THE RETAIL 500 do not have to be exclusively in the retail field.

4) Financial data and vital statistics must have been available to the editors of this book, either directly from the company being written about or from outside sources deemed reliable and accurate by the editors. A small number of companies that we would like to have included are not listed because of a lack of sufficient, objective data.

INDEX OF COMPANIES WITHIN INDUSTRY GROUPS

The industry codes shown below are based on the 2012 NAIC code system (NAIC is used by many analysts as a replacement for older SIC codes because NAIC is more specific to today's industry sectors, see www.census.gov/NAICS). Companies are given a primary NAIC code, reflecting the main line of business of each firm.

Industry Group/Company	Industry Code	2014 Sales	2014 Profits
Apparel and Clothing Brands, Designers, Importers and Distributors			
Benetton Group SPA	424300	2,005,000,000	
Billabong International Ltd	424300	789,073,792	-164,481,664
Burberry Group plc	424300	3,588,337,664	496,711,680
Carters Inc	424300	2,893,868,032	194,670,000
Chanel SA	424300	5,000,000,000	
Christian Dior SA	424300	34,827,960,320	1,595,200,000
Coach Inc	424300	4,806,225,920	781,336,000
Diesel SpA	424300	2,000,000,000	
Dolce & Gabbana SpA (D&G)	424300	1,500,000,000	
Eileen Fisher Inc	424300	375,000,000	
Fila USA Inc	424300	279,200,000	
Filippa K	424300	115,000,000	
French Connection Group plc	424300	291,712,224	-9,395,167
Gianni Versace SpA	424300	595,900,000	28,602,180
G-III Apparel Group Ltd	424300	1,718,231,040	77,360,000
Giorgio Armani SpA	424300	2,725,740,000	
Haggar Corp	424300		
Hermes International SA	424300	4,615,867,392	962,488,896
Hugo Boss AG	424300	2,882,105,088	373,499,072
Jil Sander SpA	424300	155,000,000	
Kasper Group (The)	424300	450,000,000	
Kate Spade & Company Inc	424300	1,138,603,008	159,160,000
KERING SA	424300	11,249,396,736	592,757,760
Lacoste SA	424300	2,400,000,000	
Levi Strauss & Co	424300	4,754,000,000	104,300,000
Marc Ecko Enterprises	424300	1,100,000,000	
Max Mara Fashion Group SRL	424300	1,400,000,000	216,020,000
Michael Kors Holdings Ltd	424300	3,310,842,880	661,484,992
Nautica Enterprises Inc	424300		
OshKosh B'Gosh Inc	424300	408,341,000	9,000,000
Patagonia Inc	424300	600,000,000	
Prada SpA	424300	4,020,472,320	714,811,648
PVH Corp	424300	8,186,351,104	143,536,992
Quiksilver Inc	424300	1,570,398,976	-309,376,992
Ralph Lauren Corporation	424300	7,449,999,872	776,000,000
St John Knits International Inc	424300	335,000,000	
Stefanel SpA	424300	176,800,000	-8,900,000
Swank Inc	424300	155,000,000	
Tommy Hilfiger Corp	424300	3,582,000,000	504,000,000
Tory Burch LLC	424300	1,150,000,000	
Valentino Fashion Group SpA	424300	700,000,000	

Industry Group/Company	Industry Code	2014 Sales	2014 Profits
VF Corp	424300	12,282,161,152	1,047,505,024
Warnaco Swimwear Inc	424300		
Wolford AG	424300	174,692,624	-3,153,754
Zegna (Ermenegildo Zegna Holditalia SpA)	424300	1,384,482,000	81,238,200
Auctions			
Christies International plc	453998A	916,170,000	112,986,000
Sotheby's	453998A	938,052,992	117,795,000
Spectrum Group International Inc	453998A	7,304,597,000	
Automobile Parts and Accessories Stores			
Advance Auto Parts Inc	441310	9,843,861,504	493,824,992
AutoZone Inc	441310	9,475,312,640	1,069,744,000
Fisher Auto Parts Inc	441310		
O'Reilly Automotive Inc	441310	7,216,080,896	778,182,016
Pep Boys-Manny Moe & Jack (The)	441310	2,066,567,936	6,865,000
Boat Dealers			
MarineMax Inc	441222	624,691,968	11,272,000
West Marine Inc	441222	675,750,976	1,948,000
Book Stores			
Barnes & Noble College Booksellers Inc	451211	1,748,042,000	-12,951,432
Barnes & Noble Inc	451211	6,381,357,056	-47,268,000
Books A Million Inc	451211	470,300,992	-7,584,000
Hastings Entertainment Inc	451211	455,240,000	
LifeWay Christian Resources	451211		
Building Material Dealers			
84 Lumber Company	444190	2,300,000,000	110,000,000
Building Materials Holding Corp (BMC)	444190	2,250,000,000	
Ferguson Enterprises Inc	444190	11,660,000,000	418,051,240
Stock Building Supply Inc	444190	1,295,715,968	10,419,000
Business Associations			
CCA Global Partners	813910		
Children's and Infants' Clothing Stores			
Children's Place Retail Stores Inc (The)	448130	1,765,789,056	53,026,000
Gymboree Corp (The)	448130	1,230,000,000	-574,000,000
Tween Brands Inc	448130	1,349,000,000	
Chocolate and Confectionery Manufacturing			
Rocky Mountain Chocolate Factory Inc	311351	39,184,808	4,392,444
Clothing Accessories Stores			
Claire's Stores Inc	448150	1,513,177,000	-65,307,000
Clothing and Apparel Stores			
lululemon Athletica Inc	448100	1,591,187,968	279,547,008
Coffee Shops, Doughnut Shops, Ice Cream Parlors, Canteens and Snack Bars			
Starbucks Corporation	722515	16,447,800,320	2,068,099,968
Teavana Holdings Inc	722515	460,000,000	
Computer Software, Sales & Customer Relationship Management			
Shopify	511210K	105,018,000	-22,311,000

Industry Group/Company	Industry Code	2014 Sales	2014 Profits
Consulting Services, Administrative and General Management			
Franklin Covey Co	541611	205,164,992	18,067,000
Consumer Electronics and Appliances Rental			
Aaron's Inc	532210	2,725,239,040	78,233,000
Rent-A-Center Inc	532210	3,157,796,096	96,422,000
Consumer Goods Rental			
Bestway Inc	532299		
CORT Business Services Corporation	532299	420,000,000	
Convenience Stores			
FamilyMart Co Ltd	445120	2,877,890,560	206,988,144
Lawson Inc	445120	4,040,719,872	317,789,312
Seven & I Holdings Co Ltd	445120	46,897,049,600	1,565,905,280
Siam FamilyMart Co Ltd	445120		
UNY Co Ltd	445120	8,594,667,520	55,017,528
Convenience Stores with Gasoline			
7-Eleven Inc	447110	18,681,116,400	423,493,800
Alimentation Couche-Tard Inc	447110	37,956,599,808	811,200,000
Casey's General Stores Inc	447110	7,840,254,976	134,514,000
Cumberland Farms Inc	447110	10,150,000,000	
Love's Travel Stops & Country Stores LLC	447110	26,500,000,000	
Pantry Inc (The)	447110	7,545,664,000	13,224,000
Pilot Flying J	447110	32,100,000,000	
QuikTrip Corporation	447110	11,450,000,000	
RaceTrac Petroleum Inc	447110	8,430,000,000	
Stewart's Shops Corp	447110	1,545,000,000	
Wawa Inc	447110	9,330,000,000	
Cosmetics, Beauty Supplies and Perfume Stores			
A S Watson Group	446120	20,309,389,682	
Bare Escentuals Inc	446120	410,825,852	
Bath & Body Works LLC	446120	3,349,600,000	640,000,000
Body Shop International plc (The)	446120	1,657,942,140	981,976,440
Douglas Holding AG	446120	2,841,775,000	
Perfumania Holdings Inc	446120	575,857,024	-12,465,000
Ulta Salon Cosmetics & Fragrance Inc	446120	2,670,573,056	202,848,992
Crafts, Toys, Hobbies and Games (including Electronic Games) Stores			
A C Moore Arts & Crafts Inc	451120	465,000,000	
American Girl LLC	451120	645,300,000	113,600,000
Build-A-Bear Workshop Inc	451120	392,353,984	14,362,000
GameStop Corp	451120	9,039,500,288	354,200,000
Hobby Lobby Stores Inc	451120	3,350,000,000	
Michaels Stores Inc	451120	4,569,999,872	243,000,000
Toys R Us Inc	451120	11,500,000,000	-292,000,000
Department Stores (except Discount Department Stores)			
AEON Co Ltd	452111	53,253,353,472	691,936,832
Barney's New York Inc	452111	865,000,000	
Belk Inc	452111	4,038,117,888	158,532,992

Industry Group/Company	Industry Code	2014 Sales	2014 Profits
BHS Limited	452111		-32,184,600
BIM Birlesik Magazalar AS	452111	4,806,439,936	131,367,856
Bon-Ton Stores Inc (The)	452111	2,834,060,032	-3,556,000
Boscov's Inc	452111	1,000,000,000	
Dillard's Inc	452111	6,691,777,024	323,671,008
El Puerto de Liverpool SAB de CV	452111	4,816,736,256	461,507,008
Elder-Beerman Stores Corp (The)	452111		
Grupo Sanborns SA de CV	452111	2,449,322,496	173,700,192
H2O Retailing Corporation	452111	7,020,400,000	96,300,000
Hudson's Bay Company	452111	3,957,121,024	-195,530,304
Isetan Mitsukoshi Holdings Ltd	452111	11,004,437,504	180,482,816
J C Penney Company Inc	452111	11,859,000,320	-1,388,000,000
J Front Retailing Co	452111	9,545,578,496	288,269,536
John Lewis Partnership	452111	15,573,583,650	155,559,760
Lojas Americanas SA	452111	4,287,026,664	113,640,989
Lotte Shopping Co	452111	23,553,703,936	441,450,144
Macy's Inc	452111	27,931,000,832	1,486,000,000
Marks & Spencer Group plc	452111	15,878,909,952	808,292,416
Neiman Marcus Group Inc (The)	452111	4,839,331,000	-147,181,000
Nordstrom Inc	452111	12,540,000,256	734,000,000
Pick N Pay Stores Limited	452111	4,611,220,480	42,644,124
Saks Inc	452111	3,200,000,000	
Sears Canada Inc	452111	3,024,090,880	338,257,568
Sears Holdings Corporation	452111	36,188,000,256	-1,364,999,936
Stage Stores Inc	452111	1,633,555,968	16,642,000
Takashimaya Company Limited	452111	7,529,241,088	162,304,624
Viavarejo SA	452111	5,941,979,136	245,813,552
Diamond Mining			
De Beers SA	212399	1,400,000,000	
Direct Selling			
Alticor Inc (Amway)	454390	10,800,000,000	
Avon Products Inc	454390	8,851,399,680	-388,600,000
BeautiControl Inc	454390		
Mary Kay Inc	454390	3,200,000,000	
Tupperware Brands Corporation	454390	2,606,099,968	214,400,000
Discount Department Stores			
99 Cents Only Stores	452112	1,881,865,000	71,841,000
Army and Air Force Exchange Service (AAFES)	452112	9,200,000,000	373,000,000
Big Lots Inc	452112	5,301,912,064	125,295,000
Carrefour SA	452112	85,532,401,664	1,399,800,448
Distribuidora Internacional de Alimentacion SA	452112	9,096,143,872	368,979,104
Dollar General Corporation	452112	17,504,167,936	1,025,116,032
Dollar Tree Inc	452112	7,840,300,032	596,700,032
Family Dollar Stores Inc	452112	10,489,329,664	284,503,008
Five Below Inc	452112	535,401,984	32,142,000
Fred's Inc	452112	1,939,245,952	26,015,000
Groupe Auchan SA	452112	60,500,000,000	
Kmart Holding Corporation	452112	12,074,000,000	422,000,000
Kohl's Corp	452112	19,030,999,040	889,000,000

Industry Group/Company	Industry Code	2014 Sales	2014 Profits
Shopko Stores Operating Co LLC	452112	2,860,000,000	
Smart & Final Stores Inc	452112	3,534,244,096	33,118,000
Stein Mart Inc	452112	1,263,570,944	25,555,000
Sun Art Retail Group Ltd	452112	14,448,970,752	478,512,512
Tuesday Morning Corporation	452112	864,844,032	-10,176,000
Walmart de Mexico y Centroamerica	452112	26,214,912,000	1,808,697,472
Distributors of General Grocery Products (Groceries Wholesale Distribution, Excluding Meats, Frozen Foods and Vegetables)			
United Natural Foods Inc	424410	6,794,446,848	125,482,000
Electrical Appliance Manufacturing, Small			
NACCO Industries Inc	335210	896,782,016	-38,118,000
Fabric Stores			
Hancock Fabrics Inc	451130	283,144,000	-3,153,000
Jo Ann Stores Inc	451130	2,320,000,000	
Family Clothing Stores			
Abercrombie & Fitch Co	448140	4,116,897,024	54,628,000
American Eagle Outfitters Inc	448140	3,305,801,984	82,983,000
Buckle Inc (The)	448140	1,128,001,024	162,584,000
Burlington Stores Inc	448140	4,461,986,816	16,150,000
Cortefiel SA	448140		
Eddie Bauer LLC	448140	925,000,000	
Gap Inc (The)	448140	16,147,999,744	1,280,000,000
Gordmans Stores Inc	448140	627,387,008	8,013,000
Guess? Inc	448140	2,569,786,112	153,434,000
H&M (Hennes & Mauritz) AB	448140	18,022,508,544	2,377,625,344
Hot Topic Inc	448140	750,000,000	
J Crew Group Inc	448140	2,579,700,000	970,900,000
KiK Textilien & Non-Food GmbH	448140	2,500,000,000	
Lojas Renner SA	448140	1,367,127,040	123,540,968
Lord & Taylor LLC	448140	1,600,000,000	
NEXT plc	448140	5,760,315,392	852,033,792
Pacific Sunwear of California Inc	448140	797,792,000	-48,721,000
Ross Stores Inc	448140	10,230,352,896	837,304,000
SuperGroup PLC	448140	663,668,416	42,201,240
Tilly's Inc	448140	495,836,992	18,137,000
TJX Companies Inc (The)	448140	27,422,695,424	2,137,395,968
Tommy Bahama Group Inc	448140		
True Religion Apparel Inc	448140	510,000,000	
Uniqlo Co Ltd (Fast Retailing Co Ltd)	448140	11,515,917,312	660,651,648
Urban Outfitters Inc	448140	3,086,607,872	282,360,000
Zara International Inc	448140		
Food Service Contractors			
HMSHost Corp	722310	2,704,700,000	86,500,000
Freight Transportation Arrangement			
Li & Fung Limited	488510	19,288,498,176	469,646,016
Furniture Stores			
At Home Stores LLC	442110		
Cost Plus Inc	442110	2,023,479,447	115,886,000

Plunkett Research, Ltd.

Industry Group/Company	Industry Code	2014 Sales	2014 Profits
Ethan Allen Interiors Inc	442110	746,659,008	42,931,000
Haverty Furniture Companies Inc	442110	768,707,008	8,589,000
IKEA (Inter IKEA Systems BV)	442110	39,000,000,000	4,500,000,000
Jennifer Convertibles Inc	442110	62,800,000	
Kirklands Inc	442110	460,563,008	14,530,000
Mattress Firm Holding Corp	442110	1,222,429,056	52,924,000
Nebraska Furniture Mart Inc	442110	1,250,000,000	
Pier 1 Imports Inc	442110	1,771,742,976	107,531,000
Restoration Hardware Holdings Inc (RH)	442110	1,550,961,024	18,195,000
Rooms To Go Inc	442110	2,615,000,000	
Ryohin Keikaku Co Ltd (Muji)	442110	1,837,129,088	143,293,728
Sleepy's LLC	442110	860,000,000	
Gift, Novelty and Souvenir Stores			
Party City Inc	453220	2,271,257,088	56,123,000
Yankee Candle Company Inc	453220	994,452,000	
Greeting Card Publishers			
Hallmark Cards Inc	511191	3,800,000,000	
Hair, Nail and Skin Care Salons, Beauty Shops and Spas			
Ratner Companies	812110	200,000,000	
Regis Corporation	812110	1,892,436,992	-135,727,008
Hardware Stores			
Ace Hardware Corporation	444130	4,700,000,000	120,000,000
Barbeques Galore Inc	444130		
Do It Best Corp	444130	2,873,108,000	376,000
Leslie's Poolmart Inc	444130	660,000,000	
Tractor Supply Company	444130	5,711,714,816	370,884,992
True Value Company	444130	2,014,840,000	52,515,000
Health Foods, Vitamins and Nutritional Supplement Stores			
GNC Holdings Inc	446191	2,613,154,048	255,872,000
Herbalife Ltd	446191	4,958,600,192	308,700,000
Natural Health Trends Corp	446191	124,590,000	20,370,000
Nature's Sunshine Products Inc	446191	366,367,008	10,019,000
RBC Life Sciences Inc	446191	28,270,448	-602,811
Vitamin Shoppe Inc	446191	1,213,046,016	61,241,000
Home Centers, Building Materials			
B&Q plc	444110	5,667,445,000	286,437,250
Boral Limited	444110	3,135,407,104	121,964,952
Groupe Adeo	444110	21,500,000,000	
Home Depot Inc	444110	78,811,996,160	5,384,999,936
Home Retail Group plc	444110	8,722,103,296	83,170,328
Kingfisher plc	444110	17,134,628,864	1,091,995,648
Lowe's Companies Inc	444110	53,417,000,960	2,286,000,128
Menard Inc	444110	7,920,000,000	
RONA Inc	444110	3,103,299,328	59,278,028
Sears Hometown & Outlet Stores Inc	444110	2,421,562,112	35,550,000
Household Appliance Stores			
GOME Electrical Appliance	443141	9,494,720,512	160,159,808

Industry Group/Company	Industry Code	2014 Sales	2014 Profits
Yamada Denki Co	443141	15,771,394,048	166,218,384
Housewares, including Linen, Bath, Kitchen and Cookware			
At Home Group Inc	442299		
Bed Bath & Beyond Inc	442299	11,503,963,136	1,022,289,984
Container Store (The)	442299	748,537,984	8,166,000
Sur La Table	442299	1,958,000,000	
Thomas Kinkade Company	442299		
Williams Sonoma Inc	442299	4,387,889,152	278,902,016
Jewelry and Silverware Manufacturing			
Beauty Gems Holdings Co Ltd	339910		
Trendy Group International Holding Ltd (TGI)	339910		
Jewelry Stores			
Birks Group Inc	448310	281,164,992	-5,801,000
Bulgari SpA	448310		
Charming Charlie	448310	450,000,000	
Chow Tai Fook Jewellery Group Ltd	448310	9,986,813,952	961,071,744
Little Switzerland Inc	448310		
Piercing Pagoda Inc	448310	146,900,000	-6,300,000
Reeds Jewelers Inc	448310		
Richemont (Compagnie Financiere Richemont SA)	448310	11,934,728,192	2,322,167,040
Samuels Jewelers Inc	448310	123,362,335	3,706,619
Signet Jewelers Limited (Zale, Kay & Sterling Jewelers)	448310	4,209,200,128	368,000,000
Sterling Jewelers Inc	448310		
Tamara G Designs	448310		
Tiffany & Co	448310	4,031,130,112	181,368,992
Liquor Manufacturing (Distilleries)			
LVMH Moet Hennessy Louis Vuitton SA	312140	34,337,138,688	6,329,922,560
Luggage and Other Leather Goods Manufacturing			
Samsonite International SA	316998	2,350,706,944	186,256,000
Mail Order, Catalogs and other Direct Marketing, and TV Shopping			
Blair Corporation	454113		
Bluestem Brands Inc	454113	1,050,000,000	
EVINE Live Inc	454113	640,489,024	-2,515,000
Frontgate Marketing Inc	454113		
Hanover Direct Inc	454113		
Harry & David Holdings Inc	454113	386,601,000	9,084,000
HSN Inc (Home Shopping Network)	454113	3,587,994,880	172,984,000
L L Bean Inc	454113	1,610,000,000	650,000,000
Lands End Inc	454113	1,562,876,032	78,847,000
Lillian Vernon Corporation	454113		
Otto GmbH & Co KG (Otto Group)	454113	13,709,411,850	-222,861,800
QVC Inc	454113	8,801,000,000	1,279,000,000
Sculptz Inc	454113		
Spiegel Brands Inc	454113		
Men's Clothing Stores			
Destination XL Group Inc	448110	387,983,008	-59,786,000
Jos A Bank Clothiers Inc	448110	1,100,000,000	

Industry Group/Company	Industry Code	2014 Sales	2014 Profits
Men's Wearhouse Inc (The)	448110	2,473,232,896	83,791,000
Mortgage Brokers and Loan Brokers			
Bluestem Group Inc	522310		
Movie (Motion Pictures) Theaters			
Dalian Wanda Group Co Ltd	512131		
Musical Instrument and Supplies Stores			
Guitar Center Inc	451140	2,400,000,000	
New Automobile Parts and Supplies Distributors (Wholesale Distribution)			
CARQUEST Corp	423120	3,000,000,000	
Genuine Parts Company	423120	15,341,646,848	711,286,016
Nursery, Garden Center and Farm Supply Stores			
Calloway's Nursery Inc	444220	53,515,000	8,340,000
Office Supplies and Stationery Stores			
Office Depot Inc	453210	16,096,000,000	-354,000,000
Staples Inc	453210	23,114,262,528	620,068,992
Online Shopping, B2B and B2C Sales on the Internet (Ecommerce)			
dELiA*s Inc	454111	136,650,000	-58,511,000
Fanatics Inc	454111	1,150,000,000	
Honest Company (The)	454111	150,000,000	
PetMed Express Inc	454111	233,391,008	17,972,000
Raise Marketplace Inc	454111		
Teespring Inc	454111		
Vente Privee	454111	1,945,225,000	
Zulily Inc	454111	1,200,078,976	14,892,000
Optical Goods Stores			
Emerging Vision Inc	446130	78,500,000	
National Vision Inc	446130	695,000,000	
Optical Goods Stores			
Warby Parker	446130	40,000,000	
Optical Instrument and Lens (including Medical Devices) Manufacturing			
Luxottica Group SpA	333314	8,576,234,496	720,181,056
Paints and Coatings Manufacturing			
Sherwin Williams Company (The)	325510	11,129,533,440	865,886,976
Pawn Shops and Specialty Short-Term Financing			
Cash America International Inc	522298	1,094,695,936	98,638,000
EZcorp Inc	522298	988,531,968	-45,740,000
First Cash Financial Services Inc	522298	712,876,992	85,166,000
Personal Care Products; Cosmetics and Makeup; Fragrances and Perfumes; and Hair Care Products Manufacturing			
Estee Lauder Companies Inc (The)	325620	10,968,800,256	1,204,099,968
Pet and Pet Supplies Stores			
Petco Animal Supplies Inc	453910	3,925,000,000	75,000,000
PetSmart Inc	453910	6,916,626,944	419,520,000
Wild Birds Unlimited Inc	453910		

Industry Group/Company	Industry Code	2014 Sales	2014 Profits
Petroleum (Oil, Gasoline, LPG) Products Wholesale Distribution (except Bulk Station and Terminals)			
Parkland Fuel Corporation	424720	5,702,755,840	37,784,092
Pharmacies and Drug Stores			
CVS Health	446110	139,367,006,208	4,643,999,744
Duane Reade Inc	446110		
Jean Coutu Group Inc (The)	446110	2,070,681,728	331,060,608
Medicine Shoppe International Inc	446110		
RaiaDrogasil SA	446110	1,937,044,608	58,016,716
Rite Aid Corporation	446110	25,526,413,312	249,414,000
Shoppers Drug Mart Inc	446110	11,057,659,000	601,685,000
Walgreens Boots Alliance, Inc.	446110	76,391,997,440	1,932,000,000
Radio, Television and Other Electronics Stores			
Abt Electronics Inc	443142	385,000,000	
Best Buy Co Inc	443142	42,410,000,384	532,000,000
Brookstone Inc	443142		
Conn's Inc	443142	1,193,768,960	93,449,000
Dixons Carphone PLC	443142	39,675,328	73,929,184
Fry's Electronics Inc	443142	2,200,000,000	
Grupo Elektra SA de CV	443142	4,403,846,144	449,125,504
Hhgregg Inc	443142	2,338,569,984	228,000
Interbond Corporation of America (BrandsMart)	443142		
PC Richard & Son LLC	443142		
Trans World Entertainment Corp	443142	393,659,008	8,277,000
Shoe and Footwear Brands, Designers, Importers and Distributors			
Allen-Edmonds Shoe Corp	424340	130,000,000	
ECCO Sko A/S	424340	1,271,607,087	147,774,891
Genesco Inc	424340	2,624,972,032	92,653,000
Kenneth Cole Productions Inc	424340	565,000,000	
Nike Inc	424340	27,798,999,040	2,692,999,936
PUMA SE	424340	3,330,830,336	71,839,240
Red Wing Shoe Company Inc	424340	700,000,000	
Reebok International Ltd	424340	2,600,000,000	230,000,000
Salvatore Ferragamo SpA	424340	1,492,622,080	175,468,176
Saucony Inc	424340		
Skechers USA Inc	424340	2,386,668,032	138,811,008
Steven Madden Ltd	424340	1,334,951,040	111,880,000
Timberland Co	424340	1,700,000,000	
Weyco Group Inc	424340	320,488,000	19,020,000
Wolverine World Wide Inc	424340	2,761,100,032	133,100,000
Shoe Stores			
AeroGroup International Inc	448210		
Aldo Group Inc	448210		
Caleres Inc	448210	2,513,113,088	38,073,000
DSW Inc	448210	2,368,667,904	151,302,000
Finish Line Inc (The)	448210	1,670,409,984	76,903,000
Foot Locker Inc	448210	6,504,999,936	429,000,000
Hat World Inc	448210		

Industry Group/Company	Industry Code	2014 Sales	2014 Profits
Payless ShoeSource Inc	448210	2,800,000,000	
Rack Room Shoes Inc	448210		
Shoe Carnival Inc	448210	884,785,024	26,871,000
Vans Inc	448210		
Walking Company Holdings Inc (The)	448210	238,500,000	
Sporting Goods Stores			
Academy Sports & Outdoors Ltd	451110	3,900,000,000	
Bass Pro Shops Inc	451110	4,350,000,000	
Big 5 Sporting Goods Corporation	451110	977,859,968	14,876,000
Cabela's Inc	451110	3,647,650,048	201,715,008
Dick's Sporting Goods Inc	451110	6,213,173,248	337,598,016
Eastern Mountain Sports Inc	451110		
Hibbett Sports Inc	451110	851,964,992	70,877,000
Orvis Company Inc (The)	451110	310,000,000	
Oxylane Group (Decathlon)	451110	9,560,000,000	
Recreational Equipment Inc (REI)	451110	2,217,130,000	44,183,000
Sport Chalet Inc	451110	365,000,000	-2,900,000
Sports Authority Inc (The)	451110	2,865,000,000	
Sportsman's Guide Inc (The)	451110		
Sporting Goods, Athletic Products and Recreational Items Manufacturing			
Nautilus Inc	339920	274,447,008	18,795,000
Supermarkets and Other Grocery (except Convenience) Stores			
A&P (The Great Atlantic & Pacific Tea Co.)	445110	6,000,000,000	
Ahold USA Inc	445110	36,693,605,499	665,039,411
Albertson's Company Inc	445110	4,300,000,000	
ALDI Group	445110	77,125,000,000	
Arcs Company Limited	445110	5,031,742,976	
Associated Wholesale Grocers Inc	445110	8,550,000,000	
Axfood AB	445110	4,580,523,520	130,331,392
Carr-Gottstein Foods Co	445110		
Coles Group Ltd	445110	57,698,000,000	1,605,000,000
Companhia Brasileira de Distribuicao SA (CBD)	445110	17,171,569,664	332,817,920
Delhaize Group	445110	23,940,063,232	99,745,592
Demoulas Super Markets Inc	445110	3,700,000,000	
Federation of Migros Cooperatives	445110	5,794,289,574	72,412,365
Fresh Market Inc (The)	445110	1,511,656,960	50,807,000
George Weston Limited	445110	33,271,212,032	95,454,544
Giant Eagle Inc	445110	9,700,000,000	
Golub Corporation	445110	3,630,000,000	
Gristede's Foods Inc	445110		
Groupe Casino (Casino Guichard Perrachon SA)	445110	54,347,894,784	281,304,992
Harris Teeter Supermarkets Inc	445110	5,109,000,000	
HEB (HE Butt Grocery Company)	445110	21,000,000,000	
Hy-Vee Inc	445110	8,000,000,000	
Ingles Markets Inc	445110	3,835,985,920	51,426,456
Ito-Yokado Co Ltd	445110	10,897,143,300	10,605,998,250
J Sainsbury plc	445110	36,886,040,576	1,102,776,960

Industry Group/Company	Industry Code	2014 Sales	2014 Profits
Jeronimo Martins SGPS SA	445110	14,211,184,640	338,138,688
Koninklijke Ahold NV	445110	42,000,000,000	
Kroger Co (The)	445110	98,375,000,064	1,519,000,064
Lianhua Supermarket Holdings Co Ltd	445110	4,585,737,728	19,016,076
Lidl Stiftung & Co. KG	445110	74,824,800,000	
Loblaw Companies Limited	445110	32,281,059,328	40,151,516
Marsh Supermarkets Inc	445110	1,430,000,000	
Meijer Inc	445110	15,000,000,000	
METRO AG	445110	70,645,653,504	142,333,600
Metro Inc	445110	8,780,606,464	338,712,128
Nugget Markets	445110	315,000,000	
Organizacion Soriana SAB de CV	445110	6,053,318,656	220,167,568
Pathmark Stores Inc	445110	3,000,000,000	
Piggly Wiggly Midwest LLC	445110	1,575,000,000	
Publix Super Markets Inc	445110	30,802,466,816	1,735,308,032
Raley's Family of Fine Stores	445110	3,420,000,000	
REWE Group AG	445110	58,117,181,000	531,821,670
Roundy's Inc	445110	3,855,155,968	-309,867,008
Safeway Inc	445110	36,330,000,000	111,600,000
Saker ShopRites Inc	445110	1,780,000,000	
Save Mart Supermarkets	445110	4,500,000,000	
Schnuck Markets Inc	445110	2,675,000,000	
Southeastern Grocers LLC	445110	11,500,000,000	
SpartanNash Company	445110	7,916,062,208	58,596,000
Sprouts Farmers Market LLC	445110	2,967,424,000	107,692,000
Stater Bros Markets	445110	3,950,000,000	
Stew Leonard's	445110	420,000,000	
Supervalu Inc	445110	17,155,000,320	182,000,000
Tesco plc	445110	97,889,943,552	1,500,146,304
Trader Joe's Company Inc	445110	12,000,000,000	
United Supermarkets LLC	445110	1,250,000,000	
Village Super Market Inc	445110	1,518,636,032	5,045,000
Wegman's Food Markets Inc	445110	6,900,000,000	
Weis Markets Inc	445110	2,776,683,008	55,167,000
Western Beef Inc	445110		
Whole Foods Market Inc	445110	14,193,999,872	579,000,000
Wm Morrison Supermarkets PLC	445110	27,230,580,736	-366,565,536
Tire Dealers			
Canadian Tire Corp Ltd	441320	9,441,591,296	457,575,744
Discount Tire Co	441320	3,550,000,000	
Les Schwab Tire Centers	441320	1,660,000,000	
TBC Corporation	441320	3,500,000,000	
Tobacco and Tobacco Product Wholesale Distribution			
AMCON Distributing Co	424940	1,236,755,328	4,959,528
Upholstered Home Furniture Manufacturing			
Ashley Furniture Industries Inc	337121	4,050,000,000	
La-Z-Boy Incorporated	337121	1,357,318,016	55,056,000

Industry Group/Company	Industry Code	2014 Sales	2014 Profits
Vending Machine Operators			
Outerwall Inc	454210	2,303,002,880	106,618,000
Video Rental			
Redbox Automated Retail LLC	532230	1,893,135,000	236,769,000
Warehouse Clubs and Supercenters			
BJ's Wholesale Club Inc	452910	11,500,000,000	
Brazilian Distribution Company	452910	17,171,569,664	332,817,920
Cost U Less Inc	452910		
Costco Wholesale Corp	452910	112,640,000,000	2,058,000,000
Massmart Holdings Ltd	452910	5,711,200,768	78,888,352
PriceSmart Inc	452910	2,517,566,976	92,886,000
Sam's Club	452910	57,157,000,000	1,975,000,000
Shoprite Holdings Limited	452910	7,466,849,792	272,507,424
Target Corporation	452910	72,595,996,672	1,971,000,064
Wal-Mart Stores Inc	452910	476,293,988,352	16,021,999,616
Watches and Parts (except Crystals) Manufacturing			
Fossil Group Inc	334519A	3,509,690,880	376,707,008
Wireless Communications and Radio and TV Broadcasting Equipment Manufacturing, including Cellphones (Handsets)			
Apple Inc	334220	182,794,993,664	39,509,999,616
Women's Clothing Stores			
Aeropostale Inc	448120	2,090,902,016	-141,831,008
American Apparel Inc	448120	608,891,008	-68,817,000
Ann Inc	448120	2,493,490,944	102,430,000
Arcadia Group Limited	448120	4,124,046,560	218,041,925
Ascena Retail Group Inc	448120	4,790,600,192	133,400,000
Bebe Stores Inc	448120	425,116,992	-73,382,000
Brooks Brothers Group Inc	448120	850,000,000	
Cato Corp (The)	448120	920,033,024	54,322,000
Charlotte Russe Holding Inc	448120		
Chico's FAS Inc	448120	2,586,036,992	65,883,000
Christopher & Banks Corp	448120	435,753,984	8,690,000
Destination Maternity Corp	448120	516,959,008	10,497,000
Diane von Furstenberg Studio LP	448120	210,000,000	
Esprit Holdings Ltd	448120	3,125,689,344	27,093,522
Etam Developpement	448120	1,442,720,000	23,378,880
Express Inc	448120	2,219,124,992	116,539,000
FJ Benjamin Holdings	448120	259,881,424	-15,599,943
Forever 21 Inc	448120	3,850,000,000	
Francesca's Holdings Corp	448120	340,324,992	44,839,000
Frederick's of Hollywood Group Inc	448120	75,000,000	
Inditex (Industria de Diseno Textil SA)	448120	18,743,697,408	2,664,083,712
J Jill Group Inc (The)	448120	430,000,000	
L Brands Inc	448120	10,773,000,192	903,000,000
Limited Stores LLC	448120		
MadeWell	448120		
Mango/MNG Holding SL	448120	2,240,000,000	140,000,000
Moncler SpA	448120	789,083,256	148,109,404

Industry Group/Company	Industry Code	2014 Sales	2014 Profits
New Look Group plc	448120	2,348,695,440	-82,345,680
New York & Company Inc	448120	939,163,008	2,394,000
Rue21 Inc	448120	965,000,000	
Talbots Inc (The)	448120	1,100,000,000	
Victoria's Secret	448120	7,207,600,000	1,042,000,000
Wet Seal LLC (The)	448120	530,134,016	-38,383,000

ALPHABETICAL INDEX

De Beers SA
Delhaize Group
dELiA*s Inc
Demoulas Super Markets Inc
Destination Maternity Corp
Destination XL Group Inc
Diane von Furstenberg Studio LP
Dick's Sporting Goods Inc
Diesel SpA
Dillard's Inc
Discount Tire Co
Distribuidora Internacional de Alimentacion SA
Dixons Carphone PLC
Do It Best Corp
Dolce & Gabbana SpA (D&G)
Dollar General Corporation
Dollar Tree Inc
Douglas Holding AG
DSW Inc
Duane Reade Inc
Eastern Mountain Sports Inc
ECCO Sko A/S
Eddie Bauer LLC
Eileen Fisher Inc
El Puerto de Liverpool SAB de CV
Elder-Beerman Stores Corp (The)
Emerging Vision Inc
Esprit Holdings Ltd
Estee Lauder Companies Inc (The)
Etam Developpement
Ethan Allen Interiors Inc
EVINE Live Inc
Express Inc
EZcorp Inc
Family Dollar Stores Inc
FamilyMart Co Ltd
Fanatics Inc
Federation of Migros Cooperatives
Ferguson Enterprises Inc
Fila USA Inc
Filippa K
Finish Line Inc (The)
First Cash Financial Services Inc
Fisher Auto Parts Inc
Five Below Inc
FJ Benjamin Holdings
Foot Locker Inc
Forever 21 Inc
Fossil Group Inc
Francesca's Holdings Corp
Franklin Covey Co
Frederick's of Hollywood Group Inc
Fred's Inc
French Connection Group plc
Fresh Market Inc (The)
Frontgate Marketing Inc
Fry's Electronics Inc
GameStop Corp

Gap Inc (The)
Genesco Inc
Genuine Parts Company
George Weston Limited
Gianni Versace SpA
Giant Eagle Inc
G-III Apparel Group Ltd
Giorgio Armani SpA
GNC Holdings Inc
Golub Corporation
GOME Electrical Appliance
Gordmans Stores Inc
Gristede's Foods Inc
Groupe Adeo
Groupe Auchan SA
Groupe Casino (Casino Guichard Perrachon SA)
Grupo Elektra SA de CV
Grupo Sanborns SA de CV
Guess? Inc
Guitar Center Inc
Gymboree Corp (The)
H&M (Hennes & Mauritz) AB
H2O Retailing Corporation
Haggar Corp
Hallmark Cards Inc
Hancock Fabrics Inc
Hanover Direct Inc
Harris Teeter Supermarkets Inc
Harry & David Holdings Inc
Hastings Entertainment Inc
Hat World Inc
Haverty Furniture Companies Inc
HEB (HE Butt Grocery Company)
Herbalife Ltd
Hermes International SA
Hhgregg Inc
Hibbett Sports Inc
HMSHost Corp
Hobby Lobby Stores Inc
Home Depot Inc
Home Retail Group plc
Honest Company (The)
Hot Topic Inc
HSN Inc (Home Shopping Network)
Hudson's Bay Company
Hugo Boss AG
Hy-Vee Inc
IKEA (Inter IKEA Systems BV)
Inditex (Industria de Diseno Textil SA)
Ingles Markets Inc
Interbond Corporation of America (BrandsMart)
Isetan Mitsukoshi Holdings Ltd
Ito-Yokado Co Ltd
J C Penney Company Inc
J Crew Group Inc
J Front Retailing Co
J Jill Group Inc (The)
J Sainsbury plc

Jean Coutu Group Inc (The)
Jennifer Convertibles Inc
Jeronimo Martins SGPS SA
Jil Sander SpA
Jo Ann Stores Inc
John Lewis Partnership
Jos A Bank Clothiers Inc
Kasper Group (The)
Kate Spade & Company Inc
Kenneth Cole Productions Inc
KERING SA
KiK Textilien & Non-Food GmbH
Kingfisher plc
Kirklands Inc
Kmart Holding Corporation
Kohl's Corp
Koninklijke Ahold NV
Kroger Co (The)
L Brands Inc
L L Bean Inc
Lacoste SA
Lands End Inc
Lawson Inc
La-Z-Boy Incorporated
Les Schwab Tire Centers
Leslie's Poolmart Inc
Levi Strauss & Co
Li & Fung Limited
Lianhua Supermarket Holdings Co Ltd
Lidl Stiftung & Co. KG
LifeWay Christian Resources
Lillian Vernon Corporation
Limited Stores LLC
Little Switzerland Inc
Loblaw Companies Limited
Lojas Americanas SA
Lojas Renner SA
Lord & Taylor LLC
Lotte Shopping Co
Love's Travel Stops & Country Stores LLC
Lowe's Companies Inc
lululemon Athletica Inc
Luxottica Group SpA
LVMH Moet Hennessy Louis Vuitton SA
Macy's Inc
MadeWell
Mango/MNG Holding SL
Marc Ecko Enterprises
MarineMax Inc
Marks & Spencer Group plc
Marsh Supermarkets Inc
Mary Kay Inc
Massmart Holdings Ltd
Mattress Firm Holding Corp
Max Mara Fashion Group SRL
Medicine Shoppe International Inc
Meijer Inc
Menard Inc

Men's Wearhouse Inc (The)
METRO AG
Metro Inc
Michael Kors Holdings Ltd
Michaels Stores Inc
Moncler SpA
NACCO Industries Inc
National Vision Inc
Natural Health Trends Corp
Nature's Sunshine Products Inc
Nautica Enterprises Inc
Nautilus Inc
Nebraska Furniture Mart Inc
Neiman Marcus Group Inc (The)
New Look Group plc
New York & Company Inc
NEXT plc
Nike Inc
Nordstrom Inc
Nugget Markets
Office Depot Inc
O'Reilly Automotive Inc
Organizacion Soriana SAB de CV
Orvis Company Inc (The)
OshKosh B'Gosh Inc
Otto GmbH & Co KG (Otto Group)
Outerwall Inc
Oxylane Group (Decathlon)
Pacific Sunwear of California Inc
Pantry Inc (The)
Parkland Fuel Corporation
Party City Inc
Patagonia Inc
Pathmark Stores Inc
Payless ShoeSource Inc
PC Richard & Son LLC
Pep Boys-Manny Moe & Jack (The)
Perfumania Holdings Inc
Petco Animal Supplies Inc
PetMed Express Inc
PetSmart Inc
Pick N Pay Stores Limited
Pier 1 Imports Inc
Piercing Pagoda Inc
Piggly Wiggly Midwest LLC
Pilot Flying J
Prada SpA
PriceSmart Inc
Publix Super Markets Inc
PUMA SE
PVH Corp
Quiksilver Inc
QuikTrip Corporation
QVC Inc
RaceTrac Petroleum Inc
Rack Room Shoes Inc
RaiaDrogasil SA
Raise Marketplace Inc

Raley's Family of Fine Stores
Ralph Lauren Corporation
Ratner Companies
RBC Life Sciences Inc
Recreational Equipment Inc (REI)
Red Wing Shoe Company Inc
Redbox Automated Retail LLC
Reebok International Ltd
Reeds Jewelers Inc
Regis Corporation
Rent-A-Center Inc
Restoration Hardware Holdings Inc (RH)
REWE Group AG
Richemont (Compagnie Financiere Richemont SA)
Rite Aid Corporation
Rocky Mountain Chocolate Factory Inc
RONA Inc
Rooms To Go Inc
Ross Stores Inc
Roundy's Inc
Rue21 Inc
Ryohin Keikaku Co Ltd (Muji)
Safeway Inc
Saker ShopRites Inc
Saks Inc
Salvatore Ferragamo SpA
Sam's Club
Samsonite International SA
Samuels Jewelers Inc
Saucony Inc
Save Mart Supermarkets
Schnuck Markets Inc
Sculptz Inc
Sears Canada Inc
Sears Holdings Corporation
Sears Hometown & Outlet Stores Inc
Seven & I Holdings Co Ltd
Sherwin Williams Company (The)
Shoe Carnival Inc
Shopify
Shopko Stores Operating Co LLC
Shoppers Drug Mart Inc
Shoprite Holdings Limited
Siam FamilyMart Co Ltd
Signet Jewelers Limited (Zale, Kay & Sterling Jewelers)
Skechers USA Inc
Sleepy's LLC
Smart & Final Stores Inc
Sotheby's
Southeastern Grocers LLC
SpartanNash Company
Spectrum Group International Inc
Spiegel Brands Inc
Sport Chalet Inc
Sports Authority Inc (The)
Sportsman's Guide Inc (The)
Sprouts Farmers Market LLC
St John Knits International Inc

Stage Stores Inc
Staples Inc
Starbucks Corporation
Stater Bros Markets
Stefanel SpA
Stein Mart Inc
Sterling Jewelers Inc
Steven Madden Ltd
Stew Leonard's
Stewart's Shops Corp
Stock Building Supply Inc
Sun Art Retail Group Ltd
SuperGroup PLC
Supervalu Inc
Sur La Table
Swank Inc
Takashimaya Company Limited
Talbots Inc (The)
Tamara G Designs
Target Corporation
TBC Corporation
Teavana Holdings Inc
Teespring Inc
Tesco plc
Thomas Kinkade Company
Tiffany & Co
Tilly's Inc
Timberland Co
TJX Companies Inc (The)
Tommy Bahama Group Inc
Tommy Hilfiger Corp
Tory Burch LLC
Toys R Us Inc
Tractor Supply Company
Trader Joe's Company Inc
Trans World Entertainment Corp
Trendy Group International Holding Ltd (TGI)
True Religion Apparel Inc
True Value Company
Tuesday Morning Corporation
Tupperware Brands Corporation
Tween Brands Inc
Ulta Salon Cosmetics & Fragrance Inc
Uniqlo Co Ltd (Fast Retailing Co Ltd)
United Natural Foods Inc
United Supermarkets LLC
UNY Co Ltd
Urban Outfitters Inc
Valentino Fashion Group SpA
Vans Inc
Vente Privee
VF Corp
Viavarejo SA
Victoria's Secret
Village Super Market Inc
Vitamin Shoppe Inc
Walgreens Boots Alliance, Inc.
Walking Company Holdings Inc (The)

Walmart de Mexico y Centroamerica
Wal-Mart Stores Inc
Warby Parker
Warnaco Swimwear Inc
Wawa Inc
Wegman's Food Markets Inc
Weis Markets Inc
West Marine Inc
Western Beef Inc
Wet Seal LLC (The)
Weyco Group Inc
Whole Foods Market Inc
Wild Birds Unlimited Inc
Williams Sonoma Inc
Wm Morrison Supermarkets PLC
Wolford AG
Wolverine World Wide Inc
Yamada Denki Co
Yankee Candle Company Inc
Zara International Inc
Zegna (Ermenegildo Zegna Holditalia SpA)
Zulily Inc

INDEX OF U.S. HEADQUARTERS LOCATION BY STATE

To help you locate members of the firms geographically, the city and state of the headquarters of each company are in the following index.

ALABAMA
Books A Million Inc; Birmingham
Hibbett Sports Inc; Birmingham

ALASKA
Carr-Gottstein Foods Co; Anchorage

ARIZONA
Discount Tire Co; Scottsdale
Leslie's Poolmart Inc; Phoenix
PetSmart Inc; Phoenix
Sprouts Farmers Market LLC; Phoenix

ARKANSAS
Dillard's Inc; Little Rock
Sam's Club; Bentonville
Wal-Mart Stores Inc; Bentonville

CALIFORNIA
99 Cents Only Stores; City of Commerce
American Apparel Inc; Los Angeles
Apple Inc; Cupertino
Barbeques Galore Inc; Irvine
Bare Escentuals Inc; San Francisco
Bebe Stores Inc; Brisbane
Big 5 Sporting Goods Corporation; El Segundo
Charlotte Russe Holding Inc; San Diego
Cost Plus Inc; Oakland
Forever 21 Inc; Los Angeles
Frederick's of Hollywood Group Inc; Los Angeles
Fry's Electronics Inc; San Jose
Gap Inc (The); San Francisco
Guess? Inc; Los Angeles
Guitar Center Inc; Westlake Village
Gymboree Corp (The); San Francisco
Honest Company (The); Santa Monica
Hot Topic Inc; City of Industry
Levi Strauss & Co; San Francisco
Nugget Markets; Woodland
Pacific Sunwear of California Inc; Anaheim
Patagonia Inc; Ventura
Petco Animal Supplies Inc; San Diego
PriceSmart Inc; San Diego
Quiksilver Inc; Huntington Beach
Raley's Family of Fine Stores; West Sacramento
Restoration Hardware Holdings Inc (RH); Corte Madera
Ross Stores Inc; Dublin
Safeway Inc; Pleasanton
Save Mart Supermarkets; Modesto

Skechers USA Inc; Manhattan Beach
Smart & Final Stores Inc; Commerce
Spectrum Group International Inc; Irvine
Sport Chalet Inc; La Canada
St John Knits International Inc; Irvine
Stater Bros Markets; San Bernardino
Tamara G Designs; Pacific Grove
Teespring Inc; San Francisco
Thomas Kinkade Company; Morgan Hill
Tilly's Inc; Irvine
Trader Joe's Company Inc; Monrovia
True Religion Apparel Inc; Vernon
Vans Inc; Cypress
Walking Company Holdings Inc (The); Santa Barbara
Warnaco Swimwear Inc; Los Angeles
West Marine Inc; Watsonville
Wet Seal LLC (The); Foothill Ranch
Williams Sonoma Inc; San Francisco

COLORADO

Lillian Vernon Corporation; Colorado Springs
Rocky Mountain Chocolate Factory Inc; Durango
Sports Authority Inc (The); Englewood

CONNECTICUT

Brooks Brothers Group Inc; Enfield
Ethan Allen Interiors Inc; Danbury
Stew Leonard's; Norwalk

FLORIDA

Chico's FAS Inc; Fort Myers
Claire's Stores Inc; Pembroke Pines
Fanatics Inc; Jacksonville
HSN Inc (Home Shopping Network); St. Petersburg
Interbond Corporation of America (BrandsMart);
Hollywood
Little Switzerland Inc; Boca Raton
MarineMax Inc; Clearwater
Office Depot Inc; Boca Raton
PetMed Express Inc; Pompano Beach
Publix Super Markets Inc; Lakeland
Rooms To Go Inc; Seffner
Southeastern Grocers LLC; Jacksonville
Stein Mart Inc; Jacksonville
TBC Corporation; Palm Beach Gardens
Tupperware Brands Corporation; Orlando

GEORGIA

Aaron's Inc; Atlanta
Carters Inc; Atlanta
Genuine Parts Company; Atlanta
Haverty Furniture Companies Inc; Atlanta
Home Depot Inc; Atlanta
National Vision Inc; Duluth
RaceTrac Petroleum Inc; Atlanta
Teavana Holdings Inc; Atlanta

IDAHO

Albertson's Company Inc; Boise
Building Materials Holding Corp (BMC); Boise

ILLINOIS

Abt Electronics Inc; Glenview
Ace Hardware Corporation; Oak Brook
Kmart Holding Corporation; Hoffman Estates
Raise Marketplace Inc; Chicago
Redbox Automated Retail LLC; Oakbrook Terrace
Sears Holdings Corporation; Hoffman Estates
Sears Hometown & Outlet Stores Inc; Hoffman Estates
True Value Company; Chicago
Ulta Salon Cosmetics & Fragrance Inc; Bolingbrook
Walgreens Boots Alliance, Inc.; Deerfield

INDIANA

Do It Best Corp; Fort Wayne
Finish Line Inc (The); Indianapolis
Hat World Inc; Indianapolis
Hhgregg Inc; Indianapolis
Marsh Supermarkets Inc; Indianapolis
Shoe Carnival Inc; Evansville
Wild Birds Unlimited Inc; Carmel

IOWA

Casey's General Stores Inc; Ankeny
Hy-Vee Inc; West Des Moines

KANSAS

Associated Wholesale Grocers Inc; Kansas City
Payless ShoeSource Inc; Topeka

MAINE

L L Bean Inc; Freeport

MARYLAND

HMSHost Corp; Bethesda
Jos A Bank Clothiers Inc; Hampstead

MASSACHUSETTS

BJ's Wholesale Club Inc; Westborough
Cumberland Farms Inc; Framingham
Demoulas Super Markets Inc; Tewksbury
Destination XL Group Inc; Canton
J Jill Group Inc (The); Quincy
Reebok International Ltd; Canton
Samsonite International SA; Mansfield
Saucony Inc; Lexington
Staples Inc; Framingham
Talbots Inc (The); Hingham
TJX Companies Inc (The); Framingham
Yankee Candle Company Inc; South Deerfield

MICHIGAN

Alticor Inc (Amway); Ada

La-Z-Boy Incorporated; Monroe
Meijer Inc; Grand Rapids
SpartanNash Company; Grand Rapids
Wolverine World Wide Inc; Rockford

MINNESOTA
Best Buy Co Inc; Richfield
Bluestem Brands Inc; Eden Prairie
Bluestem Group Inc; Eden Praire
Christopher & Banks Corp; Plymouth
EVINE Live Inc; Eden Prairie
Red Wing Shoe Company Inc; Red Wing
Regis Corporation; Minneapolis
Sportsman's Guide Inc (The); St. Paul
Supervalu Inc; Eden Prairie
Target Corporation; Minneapolis

MISSISSIPPI
Hancock Fabrics Inc; Baldwyn

MISSOURI
Bass Pro Shops Inc; Springfield
Build-A-Bear Workshop Inc; St. Louis
Caleres Inc; St. Louis
CCA Global Partners; St. Louis
Hallmark Cards Inc; Kansas City
Medicine Shoppe International Inc; St. Louis
O'Reilly Automotive Inc; Springfield
Schnuck Markets Inc; St. Louis

NEBRASKA
AMCON Distributing Co; Omaha
Buckle Inc (The); Kearney
Cabela's Inc; Sidney
Gordmans Stores Inc; Omaha
Nebraska Furniture Mart Inc; Omaha

NEW HAMPSHIRE
Brookstone Inc; Merrimack
Eastern Mountain Sports Inc; Peterborough
Timberland Co; Stratham

NEW JERSEY
A C Moore Arts & Crafts Inc; Berlin
A&P (The Great Atlantic & Pacific Tea Co.); Montvale
AeroGroup International Inc; Edison
Barnes & Noble College Booksellers Inc; Basking Ridge
Bed Bath & Beyond Inc; Union
Burlington Stores Inc; Burlington
Children's Place Retail Stores Inc (The); Secaucus
Hanover Direct Inc; Weehawken
Party City Inc; Elmsford
Pathmark Stores Inc; Montvale
Saker ShopRites Inc; Freehold
Toys R Us Inc; Wayne
Village Super Market Inc; Springfield
Vitamin Shoppe Inc; North Bergen

NEW YORK
Aeropostale Inc; New York
Ann Inc; New York
Ascena Retail Group Inc; Suffern
Avon Products Inc; New York
Barnes & Noble Inc; New York
Barney's New York Inc; New York
Coach Inc; New York
dELiA*s Inc; New York
Diane von Furstenberg Studio LP; New York
Duane Reade Inc; New York
Eileen Fisher Inc; Irvington
Emerging Vision Inc; New York
Estee Lauder Companies Inc (The); New York
Fila USA Inc; New York
Foot Locker Inc; New York
G-III Apparel Group Ltd; New York
Golub Corporation; Schenectady
Gristede's Foods Inc; New York
J Crew Group Inc; New York
Jennifer Convertibles Inc; Woodbury
Kasper Group (The); New York
Kate Spade & Company Inc; New York
Kenneth Cole Productions Inc; New York
Lord & Taylor LLC; New York
Marc Ecko Enterprises; New York
Nautica Enterprises Inc; New York
New York & Company Inc; New York
PC Richard & Son LLC; Farmingdale
Perfumania Holdings Inc; Bellport
PVH Corp; New York
Ralph Lauren Corporation; New York
Saks Inc; New York
Sleepy's LLC; Hicksville
Sotheby's; New York
Spiegel Brands Inc; New York
Steven Madden Ltd; Long Island City
Stewart's Shops Corp; Saratoga Springs
Swank Inc; New York
Tiffany & Co; New York
Tory Burch LLC; New York
Trans World Entertainment Corp; Albany
Warby Parker; New York
Wegman's Food Markets Inc; Rochester
Western Beef Inc; Ridgewood

NORTH CAROLINA
Belk Inc; Charlotte
CARQUEST Corp; Raleigh
Cato Corp (The); Charlotte
Family Dollar Stores Inc; Charlotte
Fresh Market Inc (The); Greensboro
Harris Teeter Supermarkets Inc; Matthews
Ingles Markets Inc; Black Mountain
Lowe's Companies Inc; Mooresville
Pantry Inc (The); Cary
Rack Room Shoes Inc; Charlotte
Reeds Jewelers Inc; Wilmington

Stock Building Supply Inc; Raleigh
VF Corp; Greensboro

OHIO
Abercrombie & Fitch Co; New Albany
Bath & Body Works LLC; Reynoldsburg
Big Lots Inc; Columbus
DSW Inc; Columbus
Express Inc; Columbus
Frontgate Marketing Inc; West Chester
Jo Ann Stores Inc; Hudson
Kroger Co (The); Cincinnati
L Brands Inc; Columbus
Limited Stores LLC; New Albany
Macy's Inc; Cincinnati
NACCO Industries Inc; Cleveland
Sherwin Williams Company (The); Cleveland
Signet Jewelers Limited (Zale, Kay & Sterling Jewelers);
Akron
Sterling Jewelers Inc; Fairlawn
Tween Brands Inc; New Albany
Victoria's Secret; Reynoldsburg

OKLAHOMA
Hobby Lobby Stores Inc; Oklahoma City
Love's Travel Stops & Country Stores LLC; Oklahoma
City
QuikTrip Corporation; Tulsa

OREGON
Harry & David Holdings Inc; Medford
Les Schwab Tire Centers; Bend
Nike Inc; Beaverton

PENNSYLVANIA
84 Lumber Company; Eighty Four
Ahold USA Inc; Carlisle
American Eagle Outfitters Inc; Pittsburgh
Blair Corporation; Warren
Bon-Ton Stores Inc (The); York
Boscov's Inc; Reading
Destination Maternity Corp; Philadelphia
Dick's Sporting Goods Inc; Coraopolis
Elder-Beerman Stores Corp (The); York
Five Below Inc; Philadelphia
Giant Eagle Inc; Pittsburgh
GNC Holdings Inc; Pittsburgh
Pep Boys-Manny Moe & Jack (The); Philadelphia
QVC Inc; West Chester
Rite Aid Corporation; Camp Hill
Rue21 Inc; Warrendale
Sculptz Inc; Trevose
Urban Outfitters Inc; Philadelphia
Wawa Inc; Wawa
Weis Markets Inc; Sunbury

RHODE ISLAND
CVS Health; Woonsocket
United Natural Foods Inc; Providence

TENNESSEE
AutoZone Inc; Memphis
Dollar General Corporation; Goodlettsville
Fred's Inc; Memphis
Genesco Inc; Nashville
Kirklands Inc; Brentwood
LifeWay Christian Resources; Nashville
Pilot Flying J; Knoxville
Tractor Supply Company; Brentwood

TEXAS
7-Eleven Inc; Dallas
Academy Sports & Outdoors Ltd; Katy
Army and Air Force Exchange Service (AAFES); Dallas
At Home Group Inc; Plano
At Home Stores LLC; Plano
BeautiControl Inc; Carrollton
Bestway Inc; Dallas
Calloway's Nursery Inc; Fort Worth
Cash America International Inc; Fort Worth
Charming Charlie; Houston
Conn's Inc; The Woodlands
Container Store (The); Coppell
EZcorp Inc; Austin
First Cash Financial Services Inc; Arlington
Fossil Group Inc; Richardson
Francesca's Holdings Corp; Houston
GameStop Corp; Grapevine
Haggar Corp; Dallas
Hastings Entertainment Inc; Amarillo
HEB (HE Butt Grocery Company); San Antonio
J C Penney Company Inc; Plano
Mary Kay Inc; Dallas
Mattress Firm Holding Corp; Houston
Men's Wearhouse Inc (The); Houston
Michaels Stores Inc; Irving
Natural Health Trends Corp; Dallas
Neiman Marcus Group Inc (The); Dallas
Pier 1 Imports Inc; Fort Worth
Piercing Pagoda Inc; Irving
RBC Life Sciences Inc; Irving
Rent-A-Center Inc; Plano
Samuels Jewelers Inc; Austin
Stage Stores Inc; Houston
Tuesday Morning Corporation; Dallas
United Supermarkets LLC; Lubbock
Whole Foods Market Inc; Austin

UTAH
Franklin Covey Co; Salt Lake City
Nature's Sunshine Products Inc; Provo

VERMONT
Orvis Company Inc (The); Sunderland

VIRGINIA
Advance Auto Parts Inc; Roanoke
CORT Business Services Corporation; Chantilly
Dollar Tree Inc; Chesapeake
Ferguson Enterprises Inc; Newport News
Fisher Auto Parts Inc; Staunton
MadeWell; Lynchburg
Ratner Companies; Vienna

WASHINGTON
Cost U Less Inc; Bellevue
Costco Wholesale Corp; Issaquah
Eddie Bauer LLC; Bellevue
Nautilus Inc; Vancouver
Nordstrom Inc; Seattle
Outerwall Inc; Bellevue
Recreational Equipment Inc (REI); Kent
Starbucks Corporation; Seattle
Sur La Table; Seattle
Tommy Bahama Group Inc; Seattle
Zulily Inc; Seattle

WISCONSIN
Allen-Edmonds Shoe Corp; Port Washington
American Girl LLC; Middleton
Ashley Furniture Industries Inc; Arcadia
Kohl's Corp; Menomonee Falls
Lands End Inc; Dodgeville
Menard Inc; Eau Claire
OshKosh B'Gosh Inc; Oshkosh
Piggly Wiggly Midwest LLC; Dodgeville
Roundy's Inc; Milwaukee
Shopko Stores Operating Co LLC; Green Bay
Weyco Group Inc; Milwaukee

INDEX OF NON-U.S. HEADQUARTERS LOCATION BY COUNTRY

AUSTRALIA
Billabong International Ltd; Burleigh Heads
Boral Limited; Sydney
Coles Group Ltd; Tooronga

AUSTRIA
Wolford AG; Bregenz

BELGIUM
Delhaize Group; Brussels

BRAZIL
Brazilian Distribution Company; Sao Paulo
Companhia Brasileira de Distribuicao SA (CBD); Sao Paulo
Lojas Americanas SA; Rio de Janeiro
Lojas Renner SA; Porto Alegre
RaiaDrogasil SA; Sao Paulo
Viavarejo SA; Rio De Janeiro

CANADA
Aldo Group Inc; Montreal
Alimentation Couche-Tard Inc; Laval
Birks Group Inc; Montreal
Canadian Tire Corp Ltd; Toronto
George Weston Limited; Toronto
Hudson's Bay Company; Toronto
Jean Coutu Group Inc (The); Longueuil
Loblaw Companies Limited; Brampton
lululemon Athletica Inc; Vancouver
Metro Inc; Montreal
Parkland Fuel Corporation; Red Deer
RONA Inc; Boucherville
Sears Canada Inc; Toronto
Shopify; Ottawa
Shoppers Drug Mart Inc; Toronto

CAYMAN ISLANDS
Herbalife Ltd; Grand Cayman

CHINA
Dalian Wanda Group Co Ltd; Beijing
GOME Electrical Appliance; Beijing

DENMARK
ECCO Sko A/S; Bredebro

FRANCE
Carrefour SA; Paris
Chanel SA; Neuilly-sur-Seine
Christian Dior SA; Paris
Etam Developpement; Paris

Groupe Adeo; Lille Cedex
Groupe Auchan SA; Croix Cedex
Groupe Casino (Casino Guichard Perrachon SA); Saint-Etienne
Hermes International SA; Paris
KERING SA; Paris
Lacoste SA; Paris
LVMH Moet Hennessy Louis Vuitton SA; Paris
Oxylane Group (Decathlon); Villeneuve d'Ascq
Vente Privee; Paris

GERMANY
ALDI Group; Essen
Douglas Holding AG; Hagen
Hugo Boss AG; Metzingen
KiK Textilien & Non-Food GmbH; Bonen
Lidl Stiftung & Co. KG; Neckarsulm
METRO AG; Düsseldorf
Otto GmbH & Co KG (Otto Group); Hamburg
PUMA SE; Herzogenaurach
REWE Group AG; Cologne

HONG KONG
A S Watson Group; Hong Kong
Chow Tai Fook Jewellery Group Ltd; Central
Esprit Holdings Ltd; Kowloon
Li & Fung Limited; Hong Kong
Lianhua Supermarket Holdings Co Ltd; Wanchai
Sun Art Retail Group Ltd; Hong Kong
Tommy Hilfiger Corp; Hong Kong
Trendy Group International Holding Ltd (TGI); Hunghom

ITALY
Benetton Group SPA; Ponzano
Bulgari SpA; Roma
Diesel SpA; Vicenza
Dolce & Gabbana SpA (D&G); Milan
Gianni Versace SpA; Milan
Giorgio Armani SpA; Milan
Jil Sander SpA; Milan
Luxottica Group SpA; Milan
Max Mara Fashion Group SRL; Reggio Emilia
Moncler SpA; Milan
Prada SpA; Milano
Salvatore Ferragamo SpA; Florence
Stefanel SpA; Ponte di Piave
Valentino Fashion Group SpA; Milan
Zegna (Ermenegildo Zegna Holditalia SpA); Trivero, Bl

JAPAN
AEON Co Ltd; Chiba
Arcs Company Limited; Sapporo
FamilyMart Co Ltd; Tokyo
H2O Retailing Corporation; Osaka
Isetan Mitsukoshi Holdings Ltd; Tokyo
Ito-Yokado Co Ltd; Tokyo
J Front Retailing Co; Tokyo

Lawson Inc; Tokyo
Ryohin Keikaku Co Ltd (Muji); Tokyo
Seven & I Holdings Co Ltd; Tokyo
Takashimaya Company Limited; Osaka
Uniqlo Co Ltd (Fast Retailing Co Ltd); Yamaguchi City
UNY Co Ltd; Inazawa
Yamada Denki Co; Tokyo

KOREA
Lotte Shopping Co; Seoul

MEXICO
El Puerto de Liverpool SAB de CV; Mexico DF
Grupo Elektra SA de CV; Mexico DF
Grupo Sanborns SA de CV; Mexico DF
Organizacion Soriana SAB de CV; Monterrey
Walmart de Mexico y Centroamerica; Mexico DF

PORTUGAL
Jeronimo Martins SGPS SA; Lisbon

SINGAPORE
FJ Benjamin Holdings; Singapore

SOUTH AFRICA
De Beers SA; Johannesburg
Massmart Holdings Ltd; Sandton
Pick N Pay Stores Limited; Cape Town
Shoprite Holdings Limited; Brackenfell, Western Cape

SPAIN
Cortefiel SA; Madrid
Distribuidora Internacional de Alimentacion SA; Madrid
Inditex (Industria de Diseno Textil SA); Arteixo
Mango/MNG Holding SL; Barcelona
Zara International Inc; Arteixo

SWEDEN
Axfood AB; Stockholm
Filippa K; Stockholm
H&M (Hennes & Mauritz) AB; Stockholm
IKEA (Inter IKEA Systems BV); Delft

SWITZERLAND
Federation of Migros Cooperatives; Zurich
Richemont (Compagnie Financiere Richemont SA); Geneva

THAILAND
Beauty Gems Holdings Co Ltd; Bangkok
Siam FamilyMart Co Ltd; Bangkok

THE NETHERLANDS
Koninklijke Ahold NV; Amsterdam

TURKEY
BIM Birlesik Magazalar AS; Sancaktepe

UNITED KINGDOM
Arcadia Group Limited; London
B&Q plc; Eastleigh
BHS Limited; London
Body Shop International plc (The); Littlehampton
Burberry Group plc; London
Christies International plc; London
Dixons Carphone PLC; London
French Connection Group plc; London
Home Retail Group plc; Milton Keynes
J Sainsbury plc; London
John Lewis Partnership; London
Kingfisher plc; London
Marks & Spencer Group plc; London
Michael Kors Holdings Ltd; London
New Look Group plc; Weymouth
NEXT plc; Leicestershire
SuperGroup PLC; Gloucestershire
Tesco plc; Hertfordshire
Wm Morrison Supermarkets PLC; Bradford

Individual Profiles
On Each Of
THE RETAIL 500

7-Eleven Inc

NAIC Code: 447110

www.7-eleven.com

TYPES OF BUSINESS:

Convenience Stores
Gas Stations
Wine

BRANDS/DIVISIONS/AFFILIATES:

Seven & I Holdings Co Ltd
Southwest Convenience Stores
Garb-Ko Inc
Handee Marts Inc
Resort Retailers
Tony Horton Kitchen
Seven-Eleven Japan Co Ltd

CONTACTS: Note: Officers with more than one job title may be intentionally listed here more than once.

Joseph DePinto, CEO
Joseph DePinto, Pres.
Stanley Reynolds, CFO
Jesus Delgado-Jenkins, CMO
Scott Hintz, Sr. VP-Human Resources
Jesus Delgado-Jenkins, Exec. VP-Merch.
Rankin Gasaway, General Counsel
Jesus Delgado-Jenkins, Exec. VP-Logistics & Innovation
Chris Tanaco, Exec. VP-Int'l

GROWTH PLANS/SPECIAL FEATURES:

7-Eleven, Inc. is a wholly-owned subsidiary of Seven-Eleven Japan Co. Ltd., which in turn is a subsidiary of Seven & I Holdings Co. Ltd. The firm franchises and licenses over 8,700 7-Eleven convenience stores throughout the U.S. and Canada and over 56,000 stores in 18 countries including Thailand, Taiwan, Japan, Malaysia, Sweden and Norway. Stores have extended hours and offer approximately 2,500 products and services including beverages, candy, fresh take-out foods, groceries, tobacco items, beer, wine, self-serve gasoline, magazines, specialty items, lottery tickets and certain financial services. Recently, the company launched a new line of healthy and nutritious foods and cold-pressed juices under the Tony Horton Kitchen label in 104 Los Angeles-area stores. 7-Eleven operates a number of additional store chains, including Garb-Ko, Inc. in Michigan, Indiana and Ohio; Handee Marts, Inc. in Pennsylvania and Ohio; Resort Retailers in Utah; Southwest Convenience Stores in West Texas and New Mexico; and Prima Marketing in West Virginia. The company continues to focus on its point-of-sale (POS) automated retail information system, the first of its kind in use in a major convenience store chain. It also offers free ATM access to Citibank customers in most of its stores. In 2014, the firm signed a master franchise agreement with Seven Emirates Investment LCC to develop and operate 7-Eleven stores in the UAE, which will be the firm's first entry into the Middle East region.

7-Eleven offers employees medical, dental, life, disability and AD&D insurance; a 401(k) plan; a profit sharing plan; paid time off; an employee assistance program; domestic partner benefits; and adoption assistance.

FINANCIAL DATA: Note: Data for latest year may not have been available at press time.

In U.S. $	2015	2014	2013	2012	2011	2010
Revenue		18,681,116,400	12,858,582,000	12,331,670,516	14,806,900,000	19,081,923,000
R&D Expense						
Operating Income						
Operating Margin %						
SGA Expense						
Net Income		423,493,800	230,699,000	221,246,692	261,646,000	246,618,000
Operating Cash Flow						
Capital Expenditure						
EBITDA						
Return on Assets %						
Return on Equity %						
Debt to Equity						

CONTACT INFORMATION:

Phone: 214-828-7011   Fax: 214-828-7848
Toll-Free:
Address: 1722 Routh St., 1 Arts Plz., Ste. 1000, Dallas, TX 75201 United States

STOCK TICKER/OTHER:

Stock Ticker: Subsidiary   Exchange:
Employees: 20,000   Fiscal Year Ends: 12/31
Parent Company: SEVEN & I HOLDINGS CO LTD

SALARIES/BONUSES:

Top Exec. Salary: $ Bonus: $
Second Exec. Salary: $ Bonus: $

OTHER THOUGHTS:

Estimated Female Officers or Directors: 1
Hot Spot for Advancement for Women/Minorities:

84 Lumber Company

www.84lumber.com

NAIC Code: 444190

TYPES OF BUSINESS:

Hardware Stores
Building Materials
Construction Financing
Builder's Insurance
Travel Agency

BRANDS/DIVISIONS/AFFILIATES:

84 Lumber Travel
84 National Sales
Affordable Collection
Oaks Collection
Maggie's Management LLC

CONTACTS: Note: Officers with more than one job title may be intentionally listed here more than once.

Joe Hardy, CEO
Maggie Hardy Magerko, Pres.

GROWTH PLANS/SPECIAL FEATURES:

84 Lumber Company is a supplier of building materials, equipment and expertise to professional homebuilders, commercial contractors, remodelers and individuals. The company operates over 250 locations in 30 states including door shops, installation centers, engineered wood product shops and component manufacturing facilities, which offer lumber, plywood, insulation, trim, molding, flooring, siding, drywall, trusses, roofing, skylights, engineered lumber, hardware, doors and windows. 84 Lumber also offers a variety of services, such as turn-key installation and onsite management services. The company's manufacturing division builds metal plate connected roof and floor trusses and wall panels. 84 Lumber Travel is a full-service accredited travel agency offering no-fee service to professional contractors and other 84 Lumber customers. Through a team of professionals, the firm's 84 National Sales provides national homebuilders, who construct multi-family and single-family units for commercial sales, with geographic information and quotes. The firm offers builder's risk, general liability, workers compensation, commercial auto and personal insurance through Maggie's Management, LLC. 84 Lumber's installation services include framing, roofing, insulation, windows, doors, trip and siding. The firm sells entire home packages such as the Affordable Collection, which contains plans for easy-to-build homes from 500 square feet up to 2,851 square feet; and the Oaks Collection, which includes more elaborate designs in sizes up to 4,963 square feet. In addition, 84 Lumber has an affiliation with Nelson Design Group, an online provider of over 900 house plans.

The company offers its employees life, disability, medical, mental and dental insurance; a 401(k) plan; a profit sharing plan; and training and development programs.

FINANCIAL DATA: Note: Data for latest year may not have been available at press time.

In U.S. $	2015	2014	2013	2012	2011	2010
Revenue		2,300,000,000	2,100,000,000	1,875,000,000	1,400,000,000	1,350,000,000
R&D Expense						
Operating Income						
Operating Margin %						
SGA Expense						
Net Income		110,000,000	101,000,000	90,000,000		
Operating Cash Flow						
Capital Expenditure						
EBITDA						
Return on Assets %						
Return on Equity %						
Debt to Equity						

CONTACT INFORMATION:

Phone: 724-228-8820   Fax: 724-228-8058
Toll-Free:
Address: 1019 Rte. 519, Eighty Four, PA 15330 United States

STOCK TICKER/OTHER:

Stock Ticker: Private
Employees: 3,600
Parent Company:

Exchange:
Fiscal Year Ends: 12/31

SALARIES/BONUSES:

Top Exec. Salary: $ Bonus: $
Second Exec. Salary: $ Bonus: $

OTHER THOUGHTS:

Estimated Female Officers or Directors: 1
Hot Spot for Advancement for Women/Minorities:

99 Cents Only Stores

NAIC Code: 452112

TYPES OF BUSINESS:

Dollar Stores
Wholesale Distribution
Discount General Merchandise

BRANDS/DIVISIONS/AFFILIATES:

Ares Management LLC

CONTACTS: Note: Officers with more than one job title may be intentionally listed here more than once.

Geoffrey Covert, CEO
Mike Kvitko, Chief Merchandising Officer
Michael Fung, Interim Chief Admin. Officer
Russell Wolpert, Chief Legal Officer
Andrew Giancamilli, Chmn.

GROWTH PLANS/SPECIAL FEATURES:

99 Cents Only Stores, owned by Ares Management, LLC, is general merchandise retailer that markets value priced primarily consumable goods at a 99 cents or less price point for most items. The company's 350 stores sell a wide variety of name brand products, with an average store size approximately 21,000 square feet. The firm has locations in the four U.S. states of California, Texas, Arizona and Nevada. It two distribution centers are located in California and Texas Stores are located in a variety of areas including shopping centers, freestanding buildings or in central downtown locations. The company's plethora of merchandise include staple food items such as produce, deli, alcoholic and non alcoholic beverages and refrigerated and frozen food products In addition, its stores offer health and beauty items, household products and cleaning supplies, house wares and kitchen items, pet products, gardening and outdoor items, hardware stationary, party goods and seasonal items and electronics and entertainment products. The company also offers consumer quality closeout merchandise at a substantial retail discount The majority of product offerings are recognizable name brand merchandise, including items from 3M, Colgate-Palmolive Frito-Lay, Dole, General Mills, Hershey Foods, Energizer Battery, Johnson & Johnson and Kraft. Moreover, 99 Cents Only Stores sell merchandise through its Bargain Wholesale division at prices generally below normal wholesale levels to local, regional and national discount, drug and grocery store chains. The merchandise is sold to independent retailers distributors and exporters. The wholesale division allows the company to purchase products in larger volumes at more favorable prices.

99 Cents Only Stores employee benefits include a weekly pay cycle; merchandise discounts; 401(k) savings and retirement plans; flexible spending accounts; and medical, life, AD&D long-term disability, dental and vision plans.

FINANCIAL DATA: Note: Data for latest year may not have been available at press time.

In U.S. $	2015	2014	2013	2012	2011	2010
Revenue		1,881,865,000	1,788,958,000	1,531,696,000	1,423,878,000	1,355,170,000
R&D Expense						
Operating Income						
Operating Margin %						
SGA Expense						
Net Income		71,841,000	23,209,000	22,029,000	74,308,000	60,447,000
Operating Cash Flow						
Capital Expenditure						
EBITDA						
Return on Assets %						
Return on Equity %						
Debt to Equity						

CONTACT INFORMATION:

Phone: 323-980-8145   Fax:
Toll-Free:
Address: 4000 Union Pacific Ave., City of Commerce, CA 90023 United States

STOCK TICKER/OTHER:

Stock Ticker: Private
Employees: 13,000
Parent Company: ARES MANAGEMENT LLC

Exchange:
Fiscal Year Ends: 03/31

SALARIES/BONUSES:

Top Exec. Salary: $ Bonus: $
Second Exec. Salary: $ Bonus: $

OTHER THOUGHTS:

Estimated Female Officers or Directors:
Hot Spot for Advancement for Women/Minorities:

A C Moore Arts & Crafts Inc

www.acmoore.com

NAIC Code: 451120

TYPES OF BUSINESS:

Arts & Crafts, Retail
In-Store Classes
E-Commerce

BRANDS/DIVISIONS/AFFILIATES:

AC Moore Rewards
Sbar's Inc

CONTACTS: *Note: Officers with more than one job title may be intentionally listed here more than once.*

Joseph A. Jeffries, CEO
David Abelman, Chief Mktg. Officer
David Abelman, Chief Merch. Officer
David Stern, Chief Admin. Officer
Michael J. Metheny, Sr. VP-Supply Chain

GROWTH PLANS/SPECIAL FEATURES:

A.C. Moore Arts & Crafts, Inc., a subsidiary of Sbar's Inc., is a specialty retailer of arts, crafts and floral merchandise. The company operates a chain of approximately 140 stores in 17 states in the eastern U.S., from Maine to Florida. A.C. Moore sells more than 60,000 different items, with roughly 40,000 available in each store at a given time. Items cover a range of merchandise categories: art and scrapbooking, traditional crafts, floral and floral accessories, fashion crafts, home decor and frames and seasonal items. The company gives particular emphasis to the fall and winter holiday seasons, during which the greatest amount of seasonal merchandise is sold. Custom framing is available in a majority of A.C. Moore stores. The firm also offers in-store arts and crafts classes and programs for adults and children. The company's web site offers ideas for projects as well as instructional how-to videos. The firm additionally offers A.C. Moore Rewards, a customer loyalty program.

A.C. Moore offers employees medical, dental and life insurance; a 401(k) plan; yearly bonuses; flexible hours; and employee discounts.

FINANCIAL DATA: *Note: Data for latest year may not have been available at press time.*

In U.S. $	2015	2014	2013	2012	2011	2010
Revenue		465,000,000	468,900,000	460,000,000	450,000,000	448,058,000
R&D Expense						
Operating Income						
Operating Margin %						
SGA Expense						
Net Income						
Operating Cash Flow						
Capital Expenditure						
EBITDA						
Return on Assets %						
Return on Equity %						
Debt to Equity						

CONTACT INFORMATION:

Phone: 856-768-4930   Fax: 856-753-4723
Toll-Free: 888-226-6673
Address: 130 A.C. Moore Dr., Berlin, NJ 08009 United States

STOCK TICKER/OTHER:

Stock Ticker: Subsidiary
Employees: 1,449
Parent Company: Sbar's Inc

Exchange:
Fiscal Year Ends: 12/31

SALARIES/BONUSES:

Top Exec. Salary: $ Bonus: $
Second Exec. Salary: $ Bonus: $

OTHER THOUGHTS:

Estimated Female Officers or Directors:
Hot Spot for Advancement for Women/Minorities: Y

A S Watson Group

NAIC Code: 446120

TYPES OF BUSINESS:

Health & Beauty Stores
Beverages, Manufacturing & Distribution
Grocery Stores & Supermarkets
Liquor Stores
Electrical, Audio & Appliance Stores
Airport Retail Stores

BRANDS/DIVISIONS/AFFILIATES:

Hutchison Whampoa Limited
ICI PARIS XL
Perfume Shop (The)
Watsons Your Personal Store
Nuance-Watsons
FORTRESS
Watson's Wine Cellar
PARKnSHOP

CONTACTS: Note: Officers with more than one job title may be intentionally listed here more than once.

Kai Ming Lai, Group Managing Dir.

GROWTH PLANS/SPECIAL FEATURES:

A.S. Watson Group. (ASW) is the retail and manufacturing subsidiary of Hutchison Whampoa Limited., a Hong Kong trading conglomerate. The company has operations in 24 markets across Asia and Europe. Its subsidiaries operate through two business segments: retailing and manufacturing. The retailing segment has a portfolio of more than 12,000 stores operating 20 brands that involve several different product lines, including health and beauty, luxury perfumeries and cosmetics, food, electronics, fine wine and airport retail. ASW's health and beauty division is largely composed of health and beauty store chains in Asia and Europe. The A.S. Watson Luxury Division Europe consists of three brands: ICI PARIS XL, one of Benelux's market leaders, and The Perfume Shop, a leading specialty perfumery chain in the U.K. Its Asian retail chains include Watsons Your Personal Store and Nuance-Watsons (an airport duty-free chain) in Asia. Its European retail chains include Kruidvat, Trekpleister, Rossmann, Drogas, Superdrug, Savers and ICI PARIS XL. The firm's food, electronics and general merchandising division includes three Asian supermarket chains (PARKnSHOP, TASTE and Great Food Halls), one Asian electrical products chain (FORTRESS), one Asian wine store chain (Watson's Wine Cellar) and Badaracco SA, a Swiss-based wine wholesaler and distributor. ASW's manufacturing segment is a major producer and distributor of beverages throughout the Asia-Pacific region. Its products include bottled water (Watsons Water and Shanghai Sparkling Drinking Water), fruit juices (Mr. Juicy, MJ Sugar Cane Juice and MJ Plum Juice), soft drinks (Sunkist and Sarsae), tea drinks (Crystal Spring) and tonic and soda water (Watson's Mixer).

FINANCIAL DATA: Note: Data for latest year may not have been available at press time.

In U.S. $	2015	2014	2013	2012	2011	2010
Revenue		20,309,389,682	20,208,134,000	19,171,694,445	18,478,700,000	15,500,000,000
R&D Expense						
Operating Income						
Operating Margin %						
SGA Expense						
Net Income			1,366,103,000	1,296,114,545	1,200,900,000	1,010,640,000
Operating Cash Flow						
Capital Expenditure						
EBITDA						
Return on Assets %						
Return on Equity %						
Debt to Equity						

CONTACT INFORMATION:

Phone: 852-2606-8833   Fax: 852-2695-3664
Toll-Free:
Address: 1-5 Wo Liu Hang Rd., 11/F Watson House, Fo Tan, Hong Kong, 999077 Hong Kong

STOCK TICKER/OTHER:

Stock Ticker: Subsidiary
Employees: 105,500
Parent Company: HUTCHISON WHAMPOA LIMITED

Exchange:
Fiscal Year Ends: 12/31

SALARIES/BONUSES:

Top Exec. Salary: $ Bonus: $
Second Exec. Salary: $ Bonus: $

OTHER THOUGHTS:

Estimated Female Officers or Directors:
Hot Spot for Advancement for Women/Minorities:

A&P (The Great Atlantic & Pacific Tea Co.)   www.aptea.com

NAIC Code: 445110

TYPES OF BUSINESS:

Grocery Stores
Liquor Stores
Private Label Foods

BRANDS/DIVISIONS/AFFILIATES:

A&P
Waldbaums
Pathmark Stores Inc
Food Emporium (The)
Best Cellar at A&P
Food Basics
SuperFresh
Hartford Reserve

CONTACTS: Note: Officers with more than one job title may be intentionally listed here more than once.

Sam Martin, Pres.
Paul Hertz, Exec. VP-Oper.
Melissa Sungela, Chief Acct. Officer
Greg Mays, Chmn.

GROWTH PLANS/SPECIAL FEATURES:

The Great Atlantic & Pacific Tea Company (A&P) is a leading food retailer that operates more than 300 grocery stores in the northeast U.S. The company operates stores in six states under the brand names A&P, Waldbaum's, The Food Emporium, SuperFresh, Pathmark and Food Basics. A&P's stores sell groceries, meats, fresh produce and other items commonly offered in supermarkets. Most stores also feature bakeries, delicatessens, pharmacies, floral departments, fresh fish and cheese departments and onsite banking. The firm also sells private-label products under names such as America's Choice, Hartford Reserve, Two Forks Bakery, H Deli Food Emporium Trading Company, Green Way, Via Roma and Live Better. A&P has developed several alternative store types, and operates its stores with merchandise and pricing tailored to appeal to different segments of the market, including buyers seeking gourmet and diet restricted foods, premium quality private label goods and health and beauty products along with more traditional grocery products. It also maintains several value-priced wine, beer and spirits stores under the Best Cellar at A&P name adjacent to or adjoining several of its grocery stores. The company filed for bankruptcy in mid-2015, with plans to sell a large number of stores. There is some possibility that, eventually, all stores might be sold or closed.

FINANCIAL DATA: Note: Data for latest year may not have been available at press time.

In U.S. $	2015	2014	2013	2012	2011	2010
Revenue		6,000,000,000	6,400,000,000	6,700,000,000	8,078,450,000	8,813,470,000
R&D Expense						
Operating Income						
Operating Margin %						
SGA Expense						
Net Income						
Operating Cash Flow						
Capital Expenditure						
EBITDA						
Return on Assets %						
Return on Equity %						
Debt to Equity						

CONTACT INFORMATION:

Phone: 201-573-9700   Fax: 201-571-8719
Toll-Free:
Address: 2 Paragon Dr., Montvale, NJ 07645 United States

SALARIES/BONUSES:

Top Exec. Salary: $ Bonus: $
Second Exec. Salary: $ Bonus: $

STOCK TICKER/OTHER:

Stock Ticker: Private   Exchange:
Employees: 40,000   Fiscal Year Ends: 02/28
Parent Company:

OTHER THOUGHTS:

Estimated Female Officers or Directors: 1
Hot Spot for Advancement for Women/Minorities: Y

Aaron's Inc

NAIC Code: 532210

www.aaronsinc.com

TYPES OF BUSINESS:

Furniture Stores, Rental
Home & Office Accessories Rental
Consumer Electronics Rental
Household Appliances Rental
Business Equipment Rental
Furniture Manufacturing
Rent-to-Own Contracts
Home Staging

BRANDS/DIVISIONS/AFFILIATES:

Woodhaven Furniture
HomeSmart
Progressive Finance Holdings LLC
Aaron's Sales & Lease Ownership

CONTACTS: Note: Officers with more than one job title may be intentionally listed here more than once.

Ryan Woodley, CEO, Subsidiary
Robert Sinclair, Chief Accounting Officer
John Trainor, Chief Information Officer
John Robinson, Director
Ray Robinson, Director
Gilbert Danielson, Executive VP
Robert Kamerschen, Executive VP
Garet Hayes, Other Corporate Officer
Steven Michaels, President
David Strickland, Senior VP, Divisional
Tristan Montanero, Senior VP, Divisional
Michael Ryan, Senior VP, Divisional
James Cates, Senior VP, Divisional
Sharon Lawrence, Vice President, Divisional
Scott Harvey, Vice President, Divisional

GROWTH PLANS/SPECIAL FEATURES:

Aaron's, Inc. operates in the lease ownership, rental an specialty retailing businesses. The firm has five maj operating divisions: sales & lease ownership, Progressiv HomeSmart, franchise and manufacturing. Aaron's sales lease ownership division has approximately 1,243 compan operated sales and lease ownership stores in 28 states. I primary customers are those that are underserved b traditional stores, due to their credit scores and income. Th division provides household goods such as furnitur household appliances, electronics and accessories f consumers with limited or no access to traditional cred sources. The Progressive segment operates in the virtu lease-to-own market. The segment partners with retailer primarily in the furniture, mattress, mobile phone, consume electronics, appliance and household accessory industries, t offer a lease-purchase option for customers to acquire good they might not otherwise have been able to obtain. Th HomeSmart segment serves customers who prefer th flexibility of weekly payments and renewals. The product provided in this division are similar to those in the Aaron's sale and lease ownership stores. There are 83 company-operate HomeSmart stores in 11 states. The franchise busines segment franchises Aaron's Sales & Lease Ownership an HomeSmart stores in markets where the company does no have immediate plans to enter; therefore, the franchise store do not compete with company-operated stores. Franchise fee range from $15,000 to $50,000 per store depending on marke size. The manufacturing segment operates throug Woodhaven Furniture Industries, a major furniture lease company in the U.S. that manufactures its own furniture. Thi division produces upholstered living-room furniture an bedding. Aaron's stores also carry brands such as Samsung Frigidaire, Hewlett-Packard, LG, Maytag, Simmons, JVC Sharp and Magnavox. In 2014, the company sold its RIMCO operations. In 2014, the firm acquired Progressive Finance Holdings, LLC, a merchandise lease-to-own company.

FINANCIAL DATA: Note: Data for latest year may not have been available at press time.

In U.S. $	2015	2014	2013	2012	2011	2010
Revenue		2,725,239,000	2,234,631,000	2,222,588,000	2,024,049,000	1,876,847,000
R&D Expense						
Operating Income		139,843,000	187,058,000	279,706,000	183,377,000	190,786,000
Operating Margin %		5.13%	8.37%	12.58%	9.05%	10.16%
SGA Expense		1,291,400,000	1,027,601,000	962,656,000	908,748,000	824,929,000
Net Income		78,233,000	120,666,000	173,043,000	113,767,000	118,376,000
Operating Cash Flow		-48,962,000	308,437,000	59,754,000	307,195,000	49,261,000
Capital Expenditure		47,565,000	58,145,000	65,073,000	78,211,000	87,636,000
EBITDA		1,159,153,000	875,678,000	944,680,000	791,650,000	743,414,000
Return on Assets %		3.65%	6.62%	9.75%	7.02%	8.38%
Return on Equity %		6.62%	10.60%	16.38%	11.63%	12.68%
Debt to Equity		0.49	0.12	0.12	0.15	0.04

CONTACT INFORMATION:

Phone: 404 231-0011   Fax:
Toll-Free: 877-607-9999
Address: 309 E. Paces Ferry Rd., NE, Atlanta, GA 30305 United States

STOCK TICKER/OTHER:

Stock Ticker: AAN
Employees: 12,400
Parent Company:

Exchange: NYS
Fiscal Year Ends: 12/31

SALARIES/BONUSES:

Top Exec. Salary: $850,000   Bonus: $
Second Exec. Salary: Bonus: $
$675,000

OTHER THOUGHTS:

Estimated Female Officers or Directors: 3
Hot Spot for Advancement for Women/Minorities: Y

Abercrombie & Fitch Co

www.abercrombie.com

NAIC Code: 448140

TYPES OF BUSINESS:

Casual Apparel-Young Adults, Retail
Catalog & Online Sales
Children's Apparel
Casual Adult Apparel, Retail
Lingerie Stores

BRANDS/DIVISIONS/AFFILIATES:

Abercrombie & Fitch
Gilly Hicks
Hollister Co
abercrombie kids

CONTACTS: *Note: Officers with more than one job title may be intentionally listed here more than once.*

Jonathan Ramsden, CEO
Joanne Crevoiserat, CFO
Arthur Martinez, Chairman of the Board
Amy Zehrer, Executive VP, Divisional
Diane Chang, Executive VP, Divisional
Robert Bostrom, General Counsel
Fran Horowitz-Bonadies, President, Divisional
Christos Angelides, President, Divisional

GROWTH PLANS/SPECIAL FEATURES:

Abercrombie & Fitch Co. retails upscale casual American clothing and accessories. The Abercrombie & Fitch brand was established in 1892, and the firm became well known as a supplier of rugged, high-quality outdoor gear, outfitting expeditions, including those of Theodore Roosevelt, Ernest Hemingway, Charles Lindbergh and Richard Byrd. However, to boost sales and focus on a high-growth market segment, the company shifted its focus from outdoor gear and accessories to fashion-oriented casual wear. Abercrombie & Fitch currently operates 869 stores in North America, Europe and Asia through four store concepts. Abercrombie & Fitch (279 locations), the company's main store, targets men and women, offering casual clothing, accessories and fragrances. The firm's 122 abercrombie kids stores offer A&F-style clothing for boys and girls. Hollister Co., with 568 stores, markets Southern California- and surfing-inspired clothing and accessories to teenagers. The Gilly Hicks brand, sold in Hollister stores, comprises women's lingerie, loungewear and personal care products. Abercrombie & Fitch also sells merchandise through a catalog and three web sites, one each for A&F, abercrombie kids and Hollister.

FINANCIAL DATA: *Note: Data for latest year may not have been available at press time.*

In U.S. $	2015	2014	2013	2012	2011	2010
Revenue	3,744,030,000	4,116,897,000	4,510,805,000	4,158,058,000	3,468,777,000	2,928,626,000
R&D Expense						
Operating Income	113,519,000	80,823,000	374,233,000	190,030,000	231,932,000	117,912,000
Operating Margin %	3.03%	1.96%	8.29%	4.57%	6.68%	4.02%
SGA Expense	2,161,871,000	2,389,471,000	2,461,809,000	2,325,368,000	1,990,305,000	1,779,219,000
Net Income	51,821,000	54,628,000	237,011,000	127,658,000	150,283,000	254,000
Operating Cash Flow	312,480,000	175,493,000	684,171,000	365,219,000	391,789,000	402,200,000
Capital Expenditure	174,624,000	163,924,000	339,862,000	318,598,000	160,935,000	175,472,000
EBITDA	339,940,000	316,063,000	601,678,000	427,286,000	465,523,000	364,862,000
Return on Assets %	1.93%	1.87%	7.85%	4.25%	5.20%	.01%
Return on Equity %	3.32%	3.07%	12.87%	6.80%	8.08%	
Debt to Equity	0.24	0.10	0.03	0.03	0.03	0.03

CONTACT INFORMATION:

Phone: 614 283-6500   Fax: 614 283-6710
Toll-Free:
Address: 6301 Fitch Path, New Albany, OH 43054 United States

SALARIES/BONUSES:

Top Exec. Salary: $1,303,846   Bonus: $
Second Exec. Salary: $267,885   Bonus: $912,000

STOCK TICKER/OTHER:

Stock Ticker: ANF   Exchange: NYS
Employees: 90,000   Fiscal Year Ends: 01/31
Parent Company:

OTHER THOUGHTS:

Estimated Female Officers or Directors: 2

Hot Spot for Advancement for Women/Minorities: Y

Abt Electronics Inc

www.abt.com

NAIC Code: 443142

TYPES OF BUSINESS:

Electronics Stores

BRANDS/DIVISIONS/AFFILIATES:

Abt.com

CONTACTS: Note: Officers with more than one job title may be intentionally listed here more than once.

Robert Abt, CEO
Michael Abt, Pres.
Jennifer Guzman, Dir.-Human Resources
Dave Ifflan, Admin.-Network & System
John Kustes, Exec. VP-Oper.
Ken Au, Dir.-eCommerce
Brigitte Lambert, Controller
Steve Tazic, Dir.-eCommerce Mktg.
Billy Abt, VP
Richard Abt, VP
Jonathan Abt, VP

GROWTH PLANS/SPECIAL FEATURES:

Abt Electronics, Inc. is one of the largest independent single store appliance and electronics retailers in the U.S., located in Glenview, Illinois. Situated on 37 acres known as Chicagoland, the store includes an 100,000 square foot showroom, a mini-mall including retailers such as Apple and Sony, a 7,500 gallon salt-water aquarium and an atrium with a fountain designed after the Bellagio Hotel in Las Vegas. Although the company has only one retail location, it has established a nationwide network of clients through its Abt.com website. Abt sells a large variety of goods, including home appliances, audio equipment, cameras, camcorders, portable electronic, homes phones, mobile phones and accessories, computers, navigations systems, furniture, kitchen appliances, gaming consoles, plumbing equipment and more. As an authorized dealer of brands such as Panasonic, Bose and Toshiba, the company offers a manufacturer's warranty for its products in addition to its own extended protection plans. Additional services include installation, customer support, low price guarantee, no sales tax and free shipping. The company deliveries its products to all 50 states, Washington, D.C. and Puerto Rico.

Employee benefits include medical, dental and prescription coverage; life insurance; long-term disability; short- and long-term critical illness plans; 401(k); flexible spending accounts; free onsite fitness center; and employee discounts.

FINANCIAL DATA: Note: Data for latest year may not have been available at press time.

In U.S. $	2015	2014	2013	2012	2011	2010
Revenue		385,000,000	375,000,000	360,000,000	345,000,000	320,000,000
R&D Expense						
Operating Income						
Operating Margin %						
SGA Expense						
Net Income						
Operating Cash Flow						
Capital Expenditure						
EBITDA						
Return on Assets %						
Return on Equity %						
Debt to Equity						

CONTACT INFORMATION:

Phone: 847-967-8830   Fax:
Toll-Free: 888-228-5800
Address: 1200 N. Milwaukee Ave., Glenview, IL 60025 United States

SALARIES/BONUSES:

Top Exec. Salary: $ Bonus: $
Second Exec. Salary: $ Bonus: $

STOCK TICKER/OTHER:

Stock Ticker: Private
Employees: 1,350
Parent Company:

Exchange:
Fiscal Year Ends:

OTHER THOUGHTS:

Estimated Female Officers or Directors: 3
Hot Spot for Advancement for Women/Minorities: Y

Academy Sports & Outdoors Ltd

www.academy.com

NAIC Code: 451110

TYPES OF BUSINESS:

Sporting Goods Stores
Apparel
Footwear
Outdoor Sports Gear
Hunting Licenses

BRANDS/DIVISIONS/AFFILIATES:

KKR & Co LP (Kohlberg Kravis Roberts & Co)

CONTACTS: Note: Officers with more than one job title may be intentionally listed here more than once.

Rodney Faldyn, CEO
Rodney Faldyn, Pres.
Beth Menuer, Exec. VP-Footwear
Robert Frennea, Exec. VP-Apparel
Kevin Chapman, Exec. VP-Stores

GROWTH PLANS/SPECIAL FEATURES:

Academy Sports & Outdoors, Ltd., owned by KKR & Co LP, is one of the largest sporting goods retailers in the U.S. The company operates over 185 stores throughout 13 states including Alabama, Florida, Georgia, Arkansas, Louisiana, Mississippi, Kansas, Missouri, Oklahoma, North Carolina, South Carolina, Tennessee and Texas. Its retail operations also include a full e-commerce retail store. Academy Sports offers a broad selection of sporting equipment, apparel and footwear. The stores, which range in size from 50,000 to 100,000 square feet, are laid out in a racetrack format with soft goods on the inside, including branded and private label athletic and casual apparel, and hard goods, such as camping, hunting, fishing, marine, footwear and fitness and sporting goods, on the outside. The company distributes merchandise to its stores from its distribution centers located in Katy, Texas and Twiggs County, Georgia. The center utilizes radio frequency identification devices (RFID), automated inventory and replenishment systems and a state-of-the-art warehouse management system to smoothly operate its large processing and inventory space. In 2014, the firm announced that it will begin construction on another distribution center in Cookeville, Tennessee, expected to be operational in early 2016.

The company offers its employees a 401(k) plan; medical, dental and vision insurance; life insurance; short- and long-term disability benefits; tuition reimbursement; merchandise discounts; bereavement leave; continuing education benefits; and business travel accident insurance.

FINANCIAL DATA: Note: Data for latest year may not have been available at press time.

In U.S. $	2015	2014	2013	2012	2011	2010
Revenue		3,900,000,000	3,700,000,000	3,254,000,000	2,700,000,000	2,400,000,000
R&D Expense						
Operating Income						
Operating Margin %						
SGA Expense						
Net Income						
Operating Cash Flow						
Capital Expenditure						
EBITDA						
Return on Assets %						
Return on Equity %						
Debt to Equity						

CONTACT INFORMATION:

Phone: 281-646-5200   Fax: 281-646-5000
Toll-Free: 888-922-2336
Address: 1800 N. Mason Rd., Katy, TX 77449 United States

SALARIES/BONUSES:

Top Exec. Salary: $ Bonus: $
Second Exec. Salary: $ Bonus: $

STOCK TICKER/OTHER:

Stock Ticker: Private   Exchange:
Employees: 22,000   Fiscal Year Ends: 02/28
Parent Company: KKR & CO LP (KOHLBERG KRAVIS ROBERTS & CO)

OTHER THOUGHTS:

Estimated Female Officers or Directors: 1
Hot Spot for Advancement for Women/Minorities:

Ace Hardware Corporation

www.acehardware.com

NAIC Code: 444130

TYPES OF BUSINESS:

Hardware Stores
Online Sales
Hardware Distribution
Paint Manufacturing

BRANDS/DIVISIONS/AFFILIATES:

AceHardware.com
Clark + Kensington
Ace Hardware
Emery-Waterhouse
Ace Hardware International Holdings Ltd

CONTACTS: Note: Officers with more than one job title may be intentionally listed here more than once.

John Venhuizen, CEO
John Venhuizen, Pres.
William M. Guzik, CFO

GROWTH PLANS/SPECIAL FEATURES:

Ace Hardware Corporation is a leading U.S. hardwar
cooperative. It acts as a buyer, marketer and wholesal
distributor for its hardware store owner/members. Eac
hardware store in the system owns shares in the Ace Hardwar
Corporation cooperative. The firm distributes its product
through a network of over 4,900 cooperative stores located i
all 50 states and 60 countries around the world. Subsidiary Ac
Hardware International Holdings, Ltd. oversees the over 55
international store locations. Ace stores stock about 65,00
items both from nationally recognized brands and the firm'
proprietary Ace Hardware brand. In addition, the compan
manufactures and distributes paint under the Ace Hardwar
and Clark + Kensington brands. Through an agreement wit
Sears, the firm sells Craftsman tools and Benjamin Moor
paints. The company also rents equipment, such as law
combers, tillers and posthole diggers, to users on an hourly
daily, weekly or monthly basis. In addition to its brick-and
mortar locations, the firm provides e-commerce service
through AceHardware.com. Ace maintains 14 distributio
centers throughout the U.S. as well as international facilities i
Shanghai, Dubai and Panama. In 2014, the company acquire
Emery-Waterhouse.

The company offers its employees a 401(k) plan; medica
dental and vision insurance; tuition assistance; life an
disability insurance; flexible spending accounts; an employee
assistance program; and a discount program.

FINANCIAL DATA: Note: Data for latest year may not have been available at press time.

In U.S. $	2015	2014	2013	2012	2011	2010
Revenue		4,700,000,000	4,154,200,000	3,840,900,000	3,709,203,000	3,530,731,000
R&D Expense						
Operating Income						
Operating Margin %						
SGA Expense						
Net Income		120,000,000	104,500,000	81,800,000	77,926,000	75,105,000
Operating Cash Flow						
Capital Expenditure						
EBITDA						
Return on Assets %						
Return on Equity %						
Debt to Equity						

CONTACT INFORMATION:

Phone: 630-990-6600   Fax: 630-990-6838
Toll-Free: 888-827-4223
Address: 2200 Kensington Ct., Oak Brook, IL 60523 United States

SALARIES/BONUSES:

Top Exec. Salary: $ Bonus: $
Second Exec. Salary: $ Bonus: $

STOCK TICKER/OTHER:

Stock Ticker: Cooperative
Employees: 80,000
Parent Company:

Exchange:
Fiscal Year Ends: 12/31

OTHER THOUGHTS:

Estimated Female Officers or Directors:
Hot Spot for Advancement for Women/Minorities: Y

Advance Auto Parts Inc

www.advanceautoparts.com

NAIC Code: 441310

TYPES OF BUSINESS:

Auto Parts & Accessories Stores
Online Sales

BRANDS/DIVISIONS/AFFILIATES:

Advance Auto Parts
Advance Discount Auto Parts
Carquest Auto Parts
General Parts International Inc

CONTACTS: Note: Officers with more than one job title may be intentionally listed here more than once.

Darren Jackson, CEO
Michael Norona, CFO
John Brouillard, Chairman of the Board
Jill Livesay, Chief Accounting Officer
Charles Tyson, Executive VP, Divisional
Tammy Finley, Executive VP, Divisional
George Sherman, President
William Carter, Senior VP, Divisional

GROWTH PLANS/SPECIAL FEATURES:

Advance Auto Parts, Inc. is a leading specialty retailer of automotive aftermarket parts, accessories, batteries and maintenance items. The firm primarily operates in the U.S. and serves both do-it-yourself (DIY) and do-it-for-me (commercial) customers. It operates in four segments: Advance Auto Parts, Autopart International, Carquest and Worldpac. The Advance Auto Parts segment operates roughly 3,888 stores within the U.S., Puerto Rico and the Virgin Islands. The Autopart International segment accounts for 210 stores operating primarily in the Northeastern, Mid-Atlanctic and Southeastern regions of U.S. Its stores serve the commercial market, with an emphasis on parts for imported cars. The Carquest brand name operates approximately 1,125 stores. The Worldpac segment operates about 111 branches. The stores' product categories consist of parts, which include alternators, batteries, clutches, engines and engine parts; accessories, including floor mats, mirrors, vent shades and seat and steering wheel covers; chemicals, including antifreeze, Freon, fuel additives and car washes and waxes; and oil and other petroleum products. Its stores also provide a variety of services, including battery charging, oil and battery recycling, battery and wiper installation and electrical system testing.

The firm offers employees medical, dental and vision coverage; a 401(k); stock purchase plans; life and AD&D insurance; short- and long-term disability; flexible spending accounts; employee discounts; an employee assistance program; and dependent scholarships.

FINANCIAL DATA: Note: Data for latest year may not have been available at press time.

In U.S. $	2015	2014	2013	2012	2011	2010
Revenue		9,843,862,000	6,493,814,000	6,205,003,000	6,170,462,000	5,925,203,000
R&D Expense						
Operating Income		851,710,000	660,318,000	657,315,000	664,642,000	584,933,000
Operating Margin %		8.65%	10.16%	10.59%	10.77%	9.87%
SGA Expense		3,601,903,000	2,591,828,000	2,440,721,000	2,404,648,000	2,376,382,000
Net Income		493,825,000	391,758,000	387,670,000	394,682,000	346,053,000
Operating Cash Flow		708,991,000	545,250,000	685,281,000	828,849,000	666,159,000
Capital Expenditure		228,446,000	195,757,000	271,182,000	268,129,000	199,585,000
EBITDA		1,139,495,000	870,811,000	847,459,000	840,134,000	748,353,000
Return on Assets %		7.30%	7.69%	9.37%	11.26%	10.76%
Return on Equity %		28.06%	28.73%	37.66%	41.82%	29.80%
Debt to Equity		0.81	0.69	0.49	0.48	0.28

CONTACT INFORMATION:

Phone: 540-362-4911   Fax:
Toll-Free: 877-238-2623
Address: 5008 Airport Rd., Roanoke, VA 24012 United States

SALARIES/BONUSES:

Top Exec. Salary: $930,288   Bonus: $
Second Exec. Salary: $560,570   Bonus: $150,000

STOCK TICKER/OTHER:

Stock Ticker: AAP   Exchange: NYS
Employees: 73,000   Fiscal Year Ends: 12/31
Parent Company:

OTHER THOUGHTS:

Estimated Female Officers or Directors: 3
Hot Spot for Advancement for Women/Minorities: Y

Sales, profits and employees may be estimates. Financial information, benefits and other data can change quickly and may vary from those stated here.

AEON Co Ltd

NAIC Code: 452111

www.aeon.info

TYPES OF BUSINESS:

Department Stores
Supermarkets
Drug Stores
Financial Services
Food Processing

BRANDS/DIVISIONS/AFFILIATES:

AEON Retail Co Ltd

GROWTH PLANS/SPECIAL FEATURES:

AEON Co., Ltd. (AEON) is a holding company for AEON Retail Co., Ltd. AEON Retail owns and operates a variety of general merchandise stores (GMS), supermarkets, discount stores, drugstores, convenience stores and specialty stores. The firm operates a total of 18,740 different stores in 13 countries, of which 618 are GMS, 2,030 are supermarkets, 4,683 are convenience stores, 3,932 are specialty stores and 3,347 are drugstores. Additionally, AEON offers food processing services, merchandise procurement services, financial services, information technology (IT) services and other services. The company divides its operations into several lines of business. The GMS segment accounts for approximately 45% of revenues. The supermarket business is the second largest line of business, contributing 29% of revenue. Other lines of business include strategic call size stores, specialty stores China operation, financial services, shopping center development and services. The firm operates through its more than 250 subsidiaries and equity-method affiliates.

CONTACTS: Note: Officers with more than one job title may be intentionally listed here more than once.

Nur Qamarina Chew Binti Abdullah, Managing Dir.
Chong Swee Ying, General Manager-Mktg.
Lim Suan Imm, General Manager-Human Resources
Kenji Hiramatsu, General Manager-IT
Hiroyoshi Ekinaga, General Manager-Merchandise Dev.
Isao Yamaguchi, Sr. General Manager-Admin.
Ng Wei Chyun, General Manager-Legal
Yoshihiro Kaya, General Manager-Bus. Dev.
Yaacob Bin Mahmud, General Manager-Safety & Security
Tai Yit Chan, Joint Sec.
Liew Irene, Joint Sec.
Poh Ying Loo, Exec. Dir.
Akihiro Ohyama, Sr. Exec. General Manager-Supply

FINANCIAL DATA: Note: Data for latest year may not have been available at press time.

In U.S. $	2015	2014	2013	2012	2011	2010
Revenue	57,443,860,000	51,897,670,000	46,137,200,000	42,248,640,000	41,359,530,000	41,017,270,000
R&D Expense						
Operating Income	1,147,225,000	1,391,200,000	1,549,990,000	1,588,058,000	1,398,731,000	1,056,538,000
Operating Margin %	1.99%	2.68%	3.35%	3.75%	3.38%	2.57%
SGA Expense	3,718,842,000	3,269,050,000	2,660,542,000	2,371,034,000	2,312,093,000	2,382,817,000
Net Income	644,368,900	674,322,000	882,541,100	734,285,000	745,021,300	252,568,400
Operating Cash Flow	3,233,514,000	3,917,720,000	1,154,699,000	1,650,480,000	2,119,131,000	2,930,355,000
Capital Expenditure						
EBITDA	2,996,859,000	2,793,777,000	2,886,314,000	2,300,172,000	2,415,708,000	2,105,554,000
Return on Assets %	.57%	.72%	1.52%	1.70%	1.57%	.82%
Return on Equity %	3.61%	4.22%	7.57%	7.31%	6.90%	3.70%
Debt to Equity	1.04	0.92	0.96	0.96	0.97	1.12

CONTACT INFORMATION:

Phone: 81-4321-26042   Fax: 81-43212-6849
Toll-Free:
Address: 1-5-1 Nakase, Mihama-ku, Chiba-shi, Chiba, 261-8515 Japan

STOCK TICKER/OTHER:

Stock Ticker: AONNY   Exchange: PINX
Employees: 74,925   Fiscal Year Ends: 02/28
Parent Company:

SALARIES/BONUSES:

Top Exec. Salary: $ Bonus: $
Second Exec. Salary: $ Bonus: $

OTHER THOUGHTS:

Estimated Female Officers or Directors:
Hot Spot for Advancement for Women/Minorities:

AeroGroup International Inc

www.aerosoles.com

NAIC Code: 448210

TYPES OF BUSINESS:

Shoes, Retail
Handbags
Online Sales
Catalogs

BRANDS/DIVISIONS/AFFILIATES:

Aerosoles
Aerology
What's What
A2

CONTACTS: Note: Officers with more than one job title may be intentionally listed here more than once.

Jules Schneider, CEO
Jules Schneider, Pres.
Richard Morris, CFO
Andrew Scott, VP-Oper.

GROWTH PLANS/SPECIAL FEATURES:

AeroGroup International, Inc. designs, distributes and markets the Aerosoles brand of women's shoes and accessories. The Aerosoles product line includes several sub brands, such as A2, What's What and Aerology. The firm's products include boots; low-heeled, mid-heeled and high-heeled shoes; mules; flats; mobs and loafers; slides; sport shoes; wedges; sandals; pumps; open-toed footwear; and handbags, shoe care products and gifts. The company markets its products through approximately 85 Aerosoles retail and outlet stores, the Aerosoles retail catalog, an online catalog, the firm's web site and in thousands of department and specialty stores (such as Boscov's). Through several international partners, AeroGroup markets its products in 15 countries including Canada, Israel, Spain, the Philippines, Portugal, Hong Kong, China and Turkey. The firm's primary customer base is middle-aged women, though the company has been trying to expand its market through advertising and product placement in television shows that attract a younger audience.

FINANCIAL DATA: Note: Data for latest year may not have been available at press time.

In U.S. $	2015	2014	2013	2012	2011	2010
Revenue						
R&D Expense						
Operating Income						
Operating Margin %						
SGA Expense						
Net Income						
Operating Cash Flow						
Capital Expenditure						
EBITDA						
Return on Assets %						
Return on Equity %						
Debt to Equity						

CONTACT INFORMATION:

Phone: 732-985-6900   Fax: 732-985-3697
Toll-Free: 800-798-9478
Address: 201 Meadow Rd., Edison, NJ 08817 United States

STOCK TICKER/OTHER:

Stock Ticker: Private
Employees:
Parent Company:

Exchange:
Fiscal Year Ends: 06/30

SALARIES/BONUSES:

Top Exec. Salary: $ Bonus: $
Second Exec. Salary: $ Bonus: $

OTHER THOUGHTS:

Estimated Female Officers or Directors:
Hot Spot for Advancement for Women/Minorities:

Sales, profits and employees may be estimates. Financial information, benefits and other data can change quickly and may vary from those stated here.

Aeropostale Inc

www.aeropostale.com

NAIC Code: 448120

TYPES OF BUSINESS:

Teen Apparel-Retail
Online Sales
Children's Apparel-Retail

BRANDS/DIVISIONS/AFFILIATES:

Aeropostale West Inc
Aeropostale.com
P.S. from Aeropostale
GoJane.com

CONTACTS: *Note: Officers with more than one job title may be intentionally listed here more than once.*

Karin Hirtler-Garvey, Chairman of the Board
Ross Citta, Chief Accounting Officer
Marc Miller, COO
Julian Geiger, Director
Mary Pile, Executive VP, Divisional
Marc Schuback, General Counsel
David Dick, Senior VP

GROWTH PLANS/SPECIAL FEATURES:

Aeropostale, Inc., together with its wholly-owned subsidiary Aeropostale West, Inc., is a mall-based specialty designer marketer and retailer of casual apparel and accessories principally targeting young men and women ages 14-17 Aeropostale maintains control over its proprietary brands by designing, sourcing, marketing and selling all of its own merchandise, both through retail locations and its online store Aeropostale.com. The company's name is derived from the first transatlantic airmail carrier, Compagnie Generale Aeropostale The firm operates over 860 stores in the U.S., Puerto Rico and Canada. It also operates 26 P.S. from Aeropostale stores in 13 states. Additionally, through a licensing agreement, there are 239 Aeropostale and P.S. from Aeropostale locations in the Middle East, Asia, Europe and Latin America. The P.S. from Aeropostale concept offers casual clothing and accessories targeting elementary school children between the ages of 4 and 12. The firm leases a 315,000 square foot distribution and warehouse center in South River, New Jersey and a second distribution facility with 360,000 square feet of space in Ontario California. The company also operates fashion footwear and apparel retailer GoJane.com. Based in Ontario, California, Go Jane focuses primarily on fashion footwear, with a select offering of contemporary apparel and other accessories. The firm has a 45,000 square foot facility in Ontario, California to warehouse and fulfill GoJane merchandise.

Aeropostale offers its employees medical, dental and vision insurance; fitness programs; tuition reimbursement; disability coverage; an employee assistance program; a 401(k); life insurance; and merchandise discounts.

FINANCIAL DATA: *Note: Data for latest year may not have been available at press time.*

In U.S. $	2015	2014	2013	2012	2011	2010
Revenue	1,838,663,000	2,090,902,000	2,386,178,000	2,342,260,000	2,400,434,000	2,230,105,000
R&D Expense						
Operating Income	-213,138,000	-185,206,000	59,511,000	113,515,000	386,794,000	382,685,000
Operating Margin %	-11.59%	-8.85%	2.49%	4.84%	16.11%	17.15%
SGA Expense	508,611,000	542,569,000	529,846,000	494,829,000	499,368,000	464,462,000
Net Income	-206,458,000	-141,831,000	34,923,000	69,515,000	231,339,000	229,457,000
Operating Cash Flow	-55,710,000	-38,373,000	144,811,000	129,301,000	263,731,000	334,440,000
Capital Expenditure	23,837,000	84,089,000	72,309,000	73,323,000	100,807,000	53,883,000
EBITDA	-162,451,000	-120,820,000	125,291,000	178,628,000	445,513,000	435,536,000
Return on Assets %	-35.60%	-20.42%	4.73%	9.21%	29.55%	31.64%
Return on Equity %	-110.33%	-41.04%	8.51%	16.51%	53.35%	58.12%
Debt to Equity	1.48			0.25		

CONTACT INFORMATION:

Phone: 646 485-5410   Fax: 646 485-5430
Toll-Free:
Address: 112 W. 34th St., 22nd Fl., New York, NY 10120 United States

STOCK TICKER/OTHER:

Stock Ticker: ARO
Employees: 21,007
Parent Company:

Exchange: NYS
Fiscal Year Ends: 01/31

SALARIES/BONUSES:

Top Exec. Salary: $700,000   Bonus: $
Second Exec. Salary: $663,462   Bonus: $

OTHER THOUGHTS:

Estimated Female Officers or Directors: 12
Hot Spot for Advancement for Women/Minorities: Y

Ahold USA Inc

www.ahold.com

NAIC Code: 445110

TYPES OF BUSINESS:

Grocery Stores, Retail
Wholesale Food Distribution
Online Grocery Sales & Delivery

BRANDS/DIVISIONS/AFFILIATES:

Koninklijke Ahold NV
Giant-Landover
Giant-Carlisle
Stop & Shop
Giant Food Stores
Martin's Food Market
PeaPod.com

CONTACTS: *Note: Officers with more than one job title may be intentionally listed here more than once.*

James McCann, COO
Mark McGowan, Exec. VP-Merch.
Tom Hippler, General Counsel
Bhavdeep Singh, Exec. VP-Oper.
Jan van Dam, Exec. VP-e-commerce
Paula Price, Exec. VP-Finance
Jan van Dam, Exec. VP-Supply Chain Mgmt.

GROWTH PLANS/SPECIAL FEATURES:

Ahold USA, Inc. is the U.S. subsidiary of the Netherlands based company Koninklijke Ahold NV, which is one of the world's largest grocery retailers. Ahold USA operates around 770 supermarkets in three chains. The largest is Stop & Shop, which is divided into New England and Metro New York divisions. The 398 stores average 55,000 to 75,000 square feet, and many include gas stations, full service pharmacies and photo developing. The Giant-Landover chain operates 170 stores located within the Washington, D.C. metropolitan area. The Giant-Carlisle chain operates 200 stores in Pennsylvania, Virginia, West Virginia and Maryland under the names Giant Food Stores and Martin's Food Markets. Most Giant-Carlisle stores offer gas stations, a pharmacy and a large selection of organic foods. Ahold USA also operates PeaPod.com, which provides Internet-based home shopping and grocery delivery services to customers located within the metropolitan areas of Chicago and Milwaukee.

FINANCIAL DATA: *Note: Data for latest year may not have been available at press time.*

In U.S. $	2015	2014	2013	2012	2011	2010
Revenue		36,693,605,499	40,228,869,356	40,307,179,432	37,341,679,669	36,427,597,391
R&D Expense						
Operating Income						
Operating Margin %						
SGA Expense						
Net Income		665,039,411	3,128,918,493	1,128,482,625	1,254,415,457	1,052,130,172
Operating Cash Flow						
Capital Expenditure						
EBITDA						
Return on Assets %						
Return on Equity %						
Debt to Equity						

CONTACT INFORMATION:

Phone: 717-249-4000   Fax:
Toll-Free:
Address: 1149 Harrisburg Pike, Carlisle, PA 17013 United States

STOCK TICKER/OTHER:

Stock Ticker: Subsidiary
Employees: 230,000
Parent Company: Koninklijke Ahold NV

Exchange:
Fiscal Year Ends: 01/31

SALARIES/BONUSES:

Top Exec. Salary: $ Bonus: $
Second Exec. Salary: $ Bonus: $

OTHER THOUGHTS:

Estimated Female Officers or Directors: 2
Hot Spot for Advancement for Women/Minorities:

Sales, profits and employees may be estimates. Financial information, benefits and other data can change quickly and may vary from those stated here.

Albertson's Company Inc

www.albertsonsmarket.com

NAIC Code: 445110

TYPES OF BUSINESS:

Grocery Stores/Supermarkets
Pharmacy
Fuel Centers
Home Delivery
Online Services

BRANDS/DIVISIONS/AFFILIATES:

Cerberus Capital Management
Albertsons
Safeway
Tom Thumb
Randalls
Acme
Star Market
Carrs

CONTACTS: *Note: Officers with more than one job title may be intentionally listed here more than once.*

Robert G. Miller, CEO
Wayne A. Denningham, COO
Robert B. Dimond, CFO
Shane Sampson, Chief Mktg. & Merchandising Officer
Andrew J. Scoggin, Exec. VP-Human Resources
Justin Dye, Chief Admin. Officer
Shane Dorcheus, Pres., Southwest Div.
Wayne Denningham, Pres., Southern
Dennis Bassler, Pres., Northwest Div.
Susan Morris, Pres., Intermountain Div.
Robert G. Miller, Chmn.

GROWTH PLANS/SPECIAL FEATURES:

Albertson's Company, Inc. is one of the largest U.S. based retailers of food and drugs. The firm operates 2,205 stores in 33 states under 18 well-known banners, including Albertsons, Safeway, Vons, Jewel-Osco, Shaw's, Acme, Tom Thumb, Randalls, United Supermarkets, Pavilions, Star Market and Carrs. Albertson's Company operates in 121 Metropolitan Statistical Areas in the U.S. and is ranked first or second in market share in 68% of them. Of the 2,205 stores, 1,698 contain pharmacies and 378 have an adjacent fuel center. The firm serves, on average, each week 33 million customers. The pharmacy services offered by Albertson's Company include health screenings, immunizations and a pharmacy products discount card as well as drug interaction information provided through its web site. The company also operates 30 strategically located distribution centers and 21 manufacturing facilities. Under the Albertson's banner, the firm operates 456 stores in 16 states across the Western and Southern U.S.; Safeway operates 1,247 stores in 19 states across the Western, Southern and Mid-Atlantic U.S.; Acme, Jewel-Osco, Shaw's and Star Market operate 446 stores in 12 states across the Mid-Atlantic, Midwest and Northeast U.S.; and United Supermarkets operates 54 stores in North and West Texas. The company is owned by a consortium led Cerberus Capital Management and includes Kimco Realty and grocery chain SUPERVALU. In June 2015, Albertson's completed its acquisition and merger with Safeway, Inc. The following July, the firm filed a registration statement for an initial public offering, an S-1, with the Internal Revenue Service of the U.S.

FINANCIAL DATA: *Note: Data for latest year may not have been available at press time.*

In U.S. $	2015	2014	2013	2012	2011	2010
Revenue		4,300,000,000	4,225,000,000	4,200,000,000	4,000,000,000	4,000,000,000
R&D Expense						
Operating Income						
Operating Margin %						
SGA Expense						
Net Income						
Operating Cash Flow						
Capital Expenditure						
EBITDA						
Return on Assets %						
Return on Equity %						
Debt to Equity						

CONTACT INFORMATION:

Phone: 208-395-6200   Fax: 208-395-6349
Toll-Free: 877-932-7948
Address: 250 Parkcenter Blvd., Boise, ID 83706 United States

SALARIES/BONUSES:

Top Exec. Salary: $ Bonus: $
Second Exec. Salary: $ Bonus: $

STOCK TICKER/OTHER:

Stock Ticker: Private   Exchange:
Employees: 265,000   Fiscal Year Ends: 01/31
Parent Company: Cerberus Capital Management

OTHER THOUGHTS:

Estimated Female Officers or Directors: 1
Hot Spot for Advancement for Women/Minorities:

ALDI Group

www.aldi.com

NAIC Code: 445110

TYPES OF BUSINESS:
Discount Grocery Stores

BRANDS/DIVISIONS/AFFILIATES:
ALDI Nord
ALDI Sud
Hofer
Trader Joe's Company Inc

CONTACTS: *Note: Officers with more than one job title may be intentionally listed here more than once.*
Mathew Barnes, Managing Director
Jason Hart, Co-Pres.
Roman Heini, Managing Director
Charles (Chuck) Youngstrom, Co-Pres.
Joan Kavanaugh, VP-Purchasing

GROWTH PLANS/SPECIAL FEATURES:
ALDI Group (which stands for Albrecht Discounts) operates a chain of over 9,000 discount grocery stores in Europe, Australia and the U.S. It specializes in a limited assortment of private-label merchandise, offering approximately 1,500 deeply discounted household and grocery items in each store, compared to the average 40,000 items offered by traditional grocers. ALDI maintains low prices through an aggressive cost-cutting program, foregoing lavish in-store displays, bagging clerks, preferred customer cards and free grocery bags. ALDI has over 1,300 locations in 32 states in the U.S. (primarily in the eastern part of the country). The firm also owns the highly successful American chain of Trader Joe's specialty supermarkets. Germany, however, is the company's primary focus, where it controls 40% of the grocery market through its 4,300 ALDI Nord and ALDI Sud stores. In Austria and Slovenia, stores operate under the Hofer name. The firm plans an accelerated growth strategy of opening 650 new stores in the U.S. between 2014 and 2018. ALDI expects to average 130 new stores per year as a result of this growth strategy. In the UK, it plans to open 450 new stores between 2015 and 2022.

The firm provides employees major medical and dental insurance as well as a 401(k) plan.

FINANCIAL DATA: *Note: Data for latest year may not have been available at press time.*

In U.S. $	2015	2014	2013	2012	2011	2010
Revenue		77,125,000,000	74,900,000,000	70,833,890,000	67,500,000,000	65,880,000,000
R&D Expense						
Operating Income						
Operating Margin %						
SGA Expense						
Net Income						
Operating Cash Flow						
Capital Expenditure						
EBITDA						
Return on Assets %						
Return on Equity %						
Debt to Equity						

CONTACT INFORMATION:
Phone: 49-201-85-93-0   Fax: 49-201-85-93-31-9
Toll-Free:
Address: Eckenbergstrasse 16, Postfach 13 01 110, Essen, 45307 Germany

STOCK TICKER/OTHER:
Stock Ticker: Private
Employees: 13,700
Parent Company:

Exchange:
Fiscal Year Ends: 12/31

SALARIES/BONUSES:
Top Exec. Salary: $ Bonus: $
Second Exec. Salary: $ Bonus: $

OTHER THOUGHTS:
Estimated Female Officers or Directors: 1
Hot Spot for Advancement for Women/Minorities:

Aldo Group Inc

www.aldoshoes.com

NAIC Code: 448210

TYPES OF BUSINESS:

Shoes, Retail
Jewelry & Accessories
Leather Goods

BRANDS/DIVISIONS/AFFILIATES:

Aldo
Spring
Globo
Call It Spring
Little Burgundy
Locale

CONTACTS: Note: Officers with more than one job title may be intentionally listed here more than once.

Patrik Frisk, CEO
David Bensadoun, Pres.
Norman Joskolka, VP-Corp. Planning
Robert Raven, VP-Finance
David Bensadoun, VP-Global Retail

GROWTH PLANS/SPECIAL FEATURES:

Aldo Group, Inc. is a retail shoe company that markets men
and women's name-brand and private-label dress and casu
shoes, boots, handbags and accessories. The company ha
over 1,900 retail stores in Canada, the U.S., the U.K. an
Ireland as well as franchises in 60 countries. It markets it
products through stores within the Aldo Group, including Ald
Call It Spring, Spring, Little Burgundy and Globo stores. Th
firm's shoes range in price from $30-$200. Aldo's handba
products range from $12-$108 and consist of women
handbags, tote bags, clutches and men's and women's bag
and wallets. The company also sells accessories, includin
jewelry such as necklaces, rings and earrings; sunglasses; ha
accessories; outerwear, such as belts, hats, scarves, glove
and legwear; watches; and shoe care products, including sho
shine, cleaner, insoles and waterproofing spray. The compan
is named after owner and founder Aldo Bensadoun. Recer
developments include the launch of the upscale Locale chai
and the creation of a wholesale division to supply shoes to U.S
retail chains. In addition, the firm recently partnered with JC
Penny to open 500 Call It Spring shop-in-shops across the U.S

FINANCIAL DATA: Note: Data for latest year may not have been available at press time.

In U.S. $	2015	2014	2013	2012	2011	2010
Revenue						
R&D Expense						
Operating Income						
Operating Margin %						
SGA Expense						
Net Income						
Operating Cash Flow						
Capital Expenditure						
EBITDA						
Return on Assets %						
Return on Equity %						
Debt to Equity						

CONTACT INFORMATION:

Phone: 514-747-2536   Fax: 514-747-7993
Toll-Free: 888-818-2536
Address: 2300 Emile-Belanger, Montreal, QC H4R 3J4 Canada

STOCK TICKER/OTHER:

Stock Ticker: Private
Employees:
Parent Company:

Exchange:
Fiscal Year Ends: 12/31

SALARIES/BONUSES:

Top Exec. Salary: $ Bonus: $
Second Exec. Salary: $ Bonus: $

OTHER THOUGHTS:

Estimated Female Officers or Directors:
Hot Spot for Advancement for Women/Minorities:

Alimentation Couche-Tard Inc

www.couche-tard.com

NAIC Code: 447110

TYPES OF BUSINESS:

Convenience Stores
Gas Stations

BRANDS/DIVISIONS/AFFILIATES:

Couche-Tard
Mac's
Circle K
Pantry Inc (The)

CONTACTS: *Note: Officers with more than one job title may be intentionally listed here more than once.*

Brian Hannasch, CEO
Raymond Pare, CFO
Alain Bouchard, Chairman of the Board
Richard Fortin, Co-Founder
Jacques DAmours, Co-Founder
Hans-Olav Hoidahl, Executive VP, Divisional
Jorn Madsen, Executive VP, Divisional
Jacob Schram, President, Divisional
Jean Bernier, President, Divisional
Dennis Tewell, Senior VP, Divisional
Geoffrey Haxel, Senior VP, Divisional
Darrell Davis, Senior VP, Divisional

GROWTH PLANS/SPECIAL FEATURES:

Alimentation Couche-Tard, Inc. (ACT), based in Canada, is one of the largest owners and operators of convenience stores in North America. Its network of stores, which operate as Couche-Tard, Mac's and Circle K, includes more than 7,848 locations in North America, including 6,404 stores with motor fuel dispensing. In Europe, Alimentation Couche-Tard operates a broad retail network of 2,230 stores, most of which provide fuel, across Scandinavia, Poland, the Baltics and Russia. The firm's sites offer a variety of products and services, including petroleum, tobacco products, beer and wine, frozen beverages, candy and snacks, coffee, dairy items, fresh food and foodservice, ATMs, lottery tickets, cell phones, prepaid phone cards and financial services. Stores are operated by 13 business units located in four geographic markets across Canada (East, Central and West) and in nine major markets across 40 U.S. states and Washington, D.C. In addition, under licensing agreements, more than 4,700 stores operate under the Circle K brand in 12 other countries, including Japan, Hong Kong, China, Indonesia, Guam, Macau, Vietnam, Mexico and the UAE. In 2015, Alimentation Couche-Tard acquired The Pantry, Inc., a 1,152 store convenience store chain in Southeastern U.S.; 21 stores, 151 dealer fuel supply agreements and five developmental properties from Cinco J, Inc. and Tiger Tote Food Stores; and Shell's Denmark Retail, Commercial and Aviation businesses.

FINANCIAL DATA: *Note: Data for latest year may not have been available at press time.*

In U.S. $	2015	2014	2013	2012	2011	2010
Revenue	34,529,900,000	37,956,600,000	35,543,400,000	22,997,500,000	18,965,900,000	16,439,600,000
R&D Expense						
Operating Income	1,323,200,000	1,034,300,000	838,700,000	577,600,000	518,500,000	442,100,000
Operating Margin %	3.83%	2.72%	2.35%	2.51%	2.73%	2.68%
SGA Expense	3,376,900,000	3,423,100,000	3,235,200,000	2,151,700,000	2,050,400,000	1,906,700,000
Net Income	932,800,000	811,200,000	572,800,000	457,600,000	370,100,000	302,900,000
Operating Cash Flow	1,714,500,000	1,429,300,000	1,161,400,000	763,800,000	618,900,000	490,800,000
Capital Expenditure	634,500,000	529,400,000	537,300,000	316,600,000	224,800,000	230,900,000
EBITDA	1,857,100,000	1,635,000,000	1,262,700,000	855,700,000	736,400,000	649,800,000
Return on Assets %	8.72%	7.69%	7.63%	10.82%	9.61%	8.71%
Return on Equity %	23.75%	22.59%	21.24%	22.26%	20.84%	20.60%
Debt to Equity	0.78	0.65	0.92	0.08	0.26	0.45

CONTACT INFORMATION:

Phone: 450 662-6632   Fax: 450 662-6666
Toll-Free: 800-361-2612
Address: 4204 Industrial Blvd., Laval, QC H7L 0E3 Canada

STOCK TICKER/OTHER:

Stock Ticker: ATD.A   Exchange: TSE
Employees: 80,000   Fiscal Year Ends: 04/30
Parent Company:

SALARIES/BONUSES:

Top Exec. Salary: $ Bonus: $
Second Exec. Salary: $ Bonus: $

OTHER THOUGHTS:

Estimated Female Officers or Directors: 2
Hot Spot for Advancement for Women/Minorities: Y

Allen-Edmonds Shoe Corp

www.allenedmonds.com

NAIC Code: 424340

TYPES OF BUSINESS:

Footwear Distribution
Footwear, Retail
Accessories

BRANDS/DIVISIONS/AFFILIATES:

Goldner Hawn Johnson & Morrison Inc
Woodlore
Casual Comfort Collection
AllenEdmonds.com

CONTACTS: Note: Officers with more than one job title may be intentionally listed here more than once.

Paul Grangaard, CEO
Paul Grangaard, Pres.
Mark McNeill, Dir.-Merch.
Castillo Rosendo, Dir.-Quality
Al Dittrich, Sr. VP-Retail
Colin Hall, Gen. Mgr.-Int'l Bus.

GROWTH PLANS/SPECIAL FEATURES:

Allen-Edmonds Shoe Corp., owned by private investment firm Goldner Hawn Johnson & Morrison, Inc., manufactures and markets premium men's footwear, accessories and cedar products. The company makes its shoes from high-grade leather and full-leather linings. It crafts each pair of shoes by hand in a production process that includes over 212 production steps. Allen-Edmonds' 360-degree welt stitching binds the upper, insole and sole of a shoe all the way around. Because the method connects parts of the shoe subject to the most stress, it makes the firm's shoes last longer than other footwear and eliminates the need for a metal shank. The unique construction of Allen-Edmonds shoes allows it to offer a proprietary re-crafting service. Allen-Edmonds has two manufacturing facilities exclusively in the U.S. In order to ensure quality, the firm refuses to outsource overseas, despite the pressures of increased costs. In addition to having agents and distributors in countries around the world, Allen-Edmonds operates approximately 53 retail stores in the U.S. as well as leased departments and independent distributors in international markets and an e-commerce site at AllenEdmonds.com. Wholly-owned subsidiary Woodlore manufactures and distributes cedar shoetrees, storage chests and coat hangers as well as shoe care products. The Casual Comfort Collection, consisting of shoes made from calfskin and rubber soles, is marketed toward younger customers who may not be ready to own a more formal pair of Allen-Edmonds shoes.

FINANCIAL DATA: Note: Data for latest year may not have been available at press time.

In U.S. $	2015	2014	2013	2012	2011	2010
Revenue		130,000,000	126,000,000	120,000,000	100,000,000	80,000,000
R&D Expense						
Operating Income						
Operating Margin %						
SGA Expense						
Net Income						
Operating Cash Flow						
Capital Expenditure						
EBITDA						
Return on Assets %						
Return on Equity %						
Debt to Equity						

CONTACT INFORMATION:

Phone: 262-235-6000   Fax: 262-235-7427
Toll-Free:
Address: 201 E. Seven Hills Rd., Port Washington, WI 53074 United States

STOCK TICKER/OTHER:

Stock Ticker: Private   Exchange:
Employees: 1,000   Fiscal Year Ends: 12/31
Parent Company: Goldner Hawn Johnson & Morrison Inc

SALARIES/BONUSES:

Top Exec. Salary: $ Bonus: $
Second Exec. Salary: $ Bonus: $

OTHER THOUGHTS:

Estimated Female Officers or Directors:
Hot Spot for Advancement for Women/Minorities:

Alticor Inc (Amway)

www.alticor.com

NAIC Code: 454390

TYPES OF BUSINESS:

Assorted Merchandise, Direct Selling
Home Care Products
Development, Manufacturing & Logistics Services
Vitamins/Nutrition Products
Cosmetics
Personal Care Products
Commercial Products
Online Sales

BRANDS/DIVISIONS/AFFILIATES:

Amway Corporation
Access Business Group LLC
Amway Hotel Corporation
iCook
eSpring
Interleukin Genetics
Gurwitch Products
Alticor Corporate Enterprises

CONTACTS: Note: Officers with more than one job title may be intentionally listed here more than once.

Doug DeVos, Pres.
Candace S. Matthews, Chief Mktg. Officer
George David Calvert, Head-R&D
Bill Payne, Chief of Staff
Michael Mohr, General Counsel
Robin Horder-Koop, VP-Corp. Rel.
Michael Cazer, Head-Worldwide Financial Functions
Gan Chee Eng, Pres., Amway China, Hong Kong & Taiwan
John Parker, Chief Sales Officer
Steve Van Andel, Chmn.
Samir Behl, Pres., Amway Europe, Africa & India
George David Calvert, Head-Global Supply Chain

GROWTH PLANS/SPECIAL FEATURES:

Alticor, Inc. is the parent company of Amway Corporation, Access Business Group and Alticor Corporate Enterprises. Amway, Alticor's largest source of revenue, is a direct marketer of nearly 450 personal care, nutrition and commercial products through 3 million distributors worldwide in 100 countries. Amway's main products include Artistry cosmetics, Nutrilite vitamins and dietary supplements, eSpring water purification systems, Queen/iCook cookware, Legacy of Clean home cleaning products, Santinique hair styling products and Atmosphere air purifier systems. Access Business Group serves the business-to-business (B2B) market with services such as product development and formulation and manufacturing and logistics services, with a 256-acre manufacturing facility in Michigan. Alticor Corporate Enterprises is in charge of the firm's indirect selling companies, which include Gurwitch Products, a cosmetics and skin care company that develops, manufactures and markets cosmetics under the brand names Laura Mercier and ReVive; Interleukin Genetics, a publicly-listed creator of genetic health tests; and the Amway Hotel Corporation, which owns and operates the Amway Grand Plaza Hotel, JW Marriott and Courtyard by Marriott, all in Grand Rapids, Michigan. Alticor owns or manages manufacturing and distribution facilities throughout the world, including facilities in the U.S., China, India and Vietnam; organically certified farms for growing food supplements in the U.S., Mexico and Brazil; and distribution facilities in North America, Europe and the Far East.

The firm offers employees medical, dental and vision insurance as well as wellness programs.

FINANCIAL DATA: Note: Data for latest year may not have been available at press time.

In U.S. $	2015	2014	2013	2012	2011	2010
Revenue		10,800,000,000	11,800,000,000	11,300,000,000	10,900,000,000	9,200,000,000
R&D Expense						
Operating Income						
Operating Margin %						
SGA Expense						
Net Income						
Operating Cash Flow						
Capital Expenditure						
EBITDA						
Return on Assets %						
Return on Equity %						
Debt to Equity						

CONTACT INFORMATION:

Phone: 616-787-1000   Fax: 800-762-6308
Toll-Free: 800-253-6500
Address: 7575 Fulton St. E., Ada, MI 49355 United States

STOCK TICKER/OTHER:

Stock Ticker: Private
Employees: 14,000
Parent Company:

Exchange:
Fiscal Year Ends: 12/31

SALARIES/BONUSES:

Top Exec. Salary: $ Bonus: $
Second Exec. Salary: $ Bonus: $

OTHER THOUGHTS:

Estimated Female Officers or Directors: 5
Hot Spot for Advancement for Women/Minorities: Y

AMCON Distributing Co

www.amcon.com

NAIC Code: 424940

TYPES OF BUSINESS:

Tobacco and Tobacco Product, Distribution
Health Food Products, Retail
Cigarette Sales

BRANDS/DIVISIONS/AFFILIATES:

Chamberlin's Market & Cafe
Akin's Natural Foods Market

CONTACTS: Note: Officers with more than one job title may be intentionally listed here more than once.

Christopher Atayan, CEO
Andrew Plummer, CFO
Kathleen Evans, Director
Eric Hinkefent, President, Subsidiary

GROWTH PLANS/SPECIAL FEATURES:

AMCON Distributing Co. (ADC) is a leading wholesal
distributor and specialty retailer of consumer products. Th
company is divided into two segments: wholesale and retai
The wholesale segment services approximately 4,500 reta
outlets, including convenience stores, grocery stores, liqu
stores, drug stores and tobacco shops. The segment currentl
distributes over 16,000 different consumer products, includin
cigarettes and tobacco products, candy and othe
confectionery, beverages, groceries, paper products, healt
and beauty care products, frozen and chilled products an
institutional food service products. Other products includ
private label lines of snuff, water, candy products, batteries an
film. The segment also operates six distribution centers locate
in Illinois, Missouri, Nebraska, North Dakota, South Dakota an
Tennessee. The retail segment operates 16 health food store
in and around Orlando, Florida under the name Chamberlin'
Market & Cafe and Akin's Natural Foods Market stores i
Oklahoma, Nebraska, Missouri and Kansas. These store
carry more than 32,000 different national and regionall
branded and private label products, including natural, organi
and specialty foods, consisting of produce, baked goods
frozen foods, nutritional supplements, personal care items an
general merchandise. While the company sells a diversifie
product line, it remains dependent on cigarette sales, whic
represent 72% of its revenue. ADC's principal suppliers includ
Altria, RJ Reynolds, Commonwealth Brands, Lorillard
Hershey, Kelloggs, Kraft and Mars.

The firm offers employees medical and life insurance as we
as a 401(k) plan.

FINANCIAL DATA: Note: Data for latest year may not have been available at press time.

In U.S. $	2015	2014	2013	2012	2011	2010
Revenue	1,281,856,000	1,236,755,000	1,211,053,000	1,174,168,000	1,041,632,000	1,010,538,000
R&D Expense						
Operating Income	11,534,960	9,396,369	11,064,600	13,419,090	15,554,610	15,525,830
Operating Margin %	.89%	.75%	.91%	1.14%	1.49%	1.53%
SGA Expense	62,769,440	64,723,820	63,880,110	63,250,680	56,374,610	54,445,190
Net Income	6,361,278	4,959,528	5,858,672	7,367,562	8,064,036	8,965,812
Operating Cash Flow	-2,560,285	7,662,454	5,732,890	9,898,888	16,005,750	10,385,360
Capital Expenditure	1,018,391	2,796,326	2,113,426	1,480,782	1,988,139	1,920,655
EBITDA	13,868,200	11,913,290	13,754,430	16,152,220	18,014,640	17,348,530
Return on Assets %	5.38%	4.43%	5.32%	6.65%	7.79%	9.62%
Return on Equity %	10.82%	9.30%	11.50%	15.74%	20.88%	30.66%
Debt to Equity	0.39	0.35	0.37	0.40	0.64	0.73

CONTACT INFORMATION:

Phone: 402 331-3727   Fax: 402 331-4834
Toll-Free:
Address: 7405 Irvington Rd., Omaha, NE 68122 United States

STOCK TICKER/OTHER:

Stock Ticker: DIT
Employees: 840
Parent Company:

Exchange: ASE
Fiscal Year Ends: 09/30

SALARIES/BONUSES:

Top Exec. Salary: $521,760   Bonus: $652,088
Second Exec. Salary: Bonus: $137,917
$397,840

OTHER THOUGHTS:

Estimated Female Officers or Directors: 1
Hot Spot for Advancement for Women/Minorities:

American Apparel Inc

www.americanapparel.net

NAIC Code: 448120

TYPES OF BUSINESS:

Casual Apparel Manufacturing
Apparel Stores
Apparel Wholesale
E-commerce

BRANDS/DIVISIONS/AFFILIATES:

American Apparel (USA) LLC
American Apparel Dyeing and Finishing Inc
American Apparel Retail Inc
American Apparel Canada Wholesale Inc
American Apparel Canada Retail Inc

CONTACTS: *Note: Officers with more than one job title may be intentionally listed here more than once.*

Paula Schneider, CEO
Hassan Natha, CFO
Colleen Brown, Chairman of the Board
Chelsea Grayson, Executive VP
Martin Bailey, Other Executive Officer

GROWTH PLANS/SPECIAL FEATURES:

American Apparel, Inc. is a vertically-integrated manufacturer, distributor and retailer of branded fashion basic apparel. The company does not outsource its production, conducting all of its manufacturing in the Los Angeles metropolitan area. Its primary apparel manufacturing operations are conducted from an 800,000 square foot facility in downtown Los Angeles. Its retail operations principally target fashion-conscious young adults aged 20-32, with products including basic women's and men's apparel and accessories, along with product lines for children and pets. American Apparel operates approximately 239 stores in 20 countries, including the U.S., Canada, Mexico, Brazil, the U.K., Ireland, Austria, Belgium, Germany, France, Italy, Netherlands, Spain, Sweden, Switzerland, Israel, Australia, Japan, South Korea and China. Stores are located primarily in large metropolitan areas, emerging neighborhoods and university communities. In addition to its retail stores, American Apparel conducts an e-commerce website with 12 different localized online stores in seven languages that serves customers from 30 countries worldwide. The firm also operates a wholesale business, supplying t-shirts and other casual wear to distributors and screen printers. American Apparel operates in four business segments: U.S. Retail, U.S. Wholesale, Canada and International. Its domestic subsidiaries include American Apparel (USA), LLC; American Apparel Retail, Inc.; and American Apparel Dyeing and Finishing, Inc. It conducts business internationally through various direct and indirect subsidiaries, including American Apparel Canada Wholesale, Inc. and American Apparel Canada Retail, Inc. In October 2015, the New York Stock Exchange suspended trading of the firm's common stock and the company filed for bankruptcy protection.

FINANCIAL DATA: *Note: Data for latest year may not have been available at press time.*

In U.S. $	2015	2014	2013	2012	2011	2010
Revenue		608,891,000	633,941,000	617,310,000	547,336,000	532,989,000
R&D Expense						
Operating Income		-27,583,000	-29,295,000	962,000	-23,293,000	-50,053,000
Operating Margin %		-4.52%	-4.62%	.15%	-4.25%	-9.39%
SGA Expense		333,980,000	348,640,000	324,774,000	313,926,000	321,365,000
Net Income		-68,817,000	-106,298,000	-37,272,000	-39,314,000	-86,315,000
Operating Cash Flow		-5,212,000	-12,723,000	23,589,000	2,305,000	-32,370,000
Capital Expenditure		9,818,000	27,054,000	21,607,000	11,070,000	15,701,000
EBITDA		-908,000	-39,165,000	31,089,000	20,554,000	-22,269,000
Return on Assets %		-21.91%	-32.11%	-11.41%	-12.04%	-26.33%
Return on Equity %				-106.16%	-63.84%	-74.29%
Debt to Equity				5.11	2.05	0.07

CONTACT INFORMATION:

Phone: 213 488-0226   Fax:
Toll-Free:
Address: 747 Warehouse St., Los Angeles, CA 90021-1106 United States

STOCK TICKER/OTHER:

Stock Ticker: APPCQ
Employees: 10,000
Parent Company:

Exchange: PINX
Fiscal Year Ends: 12/31

SALARIES/BONUSES:

Top Exec. Salary: $230,201   Bonus: $418,275
Second Exec. Salary: $339,780   Bonus: $90,989

OTHER THOUGHTS:

Estimated Female Officers or Directors:
Hot Spot for Advancement for Women/Minorities:

Sales, profits and employees may be estimates. Financial information, benefits and other data can change quickly and may vary from those stated here.

American Eagle Outfitters Inc

NAIC Code: 448140

www.ae.com

TYPES OF BUSINESS:

Casual Apparel, Retail
Online Sales
Intimates Apparel
Children's Apparel

BRANDS/DIVISIONS/AFFILIATES:

American Eagle Outfitters
aerie by American Eagle
ae.com
aerie.com

CONTACTS: Note: Officers with more than one job title may be intentionally listed here more than once.

Jay Schottenstein, CEO
Mary Boland, CFO
Scott Hurd, Chief Accounting Officer
Michael Rempell, COO
Roger Markfield, Director
Simon Nankervis, Executive VP, Divisional
Charles Sandel, General Counsel
Jennifer Foyle, President, Divisional
Charles Kessler, President, Subsidiary
Jennifer Stoecklein, Secretary

GROWTH PLANS/SPECIAL FEATURES:

American Eagle Outfitters, Inc. (AE) designs, markets and retails casual clothing primarily targeted at teenagers and young adults. Denim is the cornerstone, and is complemented by a variety of other fashion conscious clothing, such as graphic tees, sweaters, and accessories. The firm sells merchandise under the American Eagle Outfitters and aerie by American Eagle (aerie) brand. AE's aerie collection includes bras, underwear, camis, hoodies, robes, boxers, sweats, leggings, fitness apparel and personal care products for teen girls and young adults. AE operates over 1,000 American Eagle Outfitters stores and 101 aerie stand-alone stores in the U.S., Puerto Rico and Canada. The firm also operates ae.com and aerie.com, e-commerce sites that feature an expanded offering of sizes, colors and styles of its merchandise. It ships its products to 81 countries through its e-commerce business. The firm offers a Visa co-branded credit card as well as a private label card issued by a third-party bank. Through several franchise agreements, AE has 101 company-operated stores in Canada, 18 in Mexico, five in Hong Kong, nine in China and six in Puerto Rico.

The company offers employees medical, dental and vision insurance; life insurance; pet insurance; adoption assistance; new dependant leave; tuition reimbursement; disability coverage; merchandise discounts; a 401(k) plan; athletic club reimbursement; and an employee stock purchase plan.

FINANCIAL DATA: Note: Data for latest year may not have been available at press time.

In U.S. $	2015	2014	2013	2012	2011	2010
Revenue	3,282,867,000	3,305,802,000	3,475,802,000	3,159,818,000	2,967,559,000	2,990,520,000
R&D Expense						
Operating Income	155,765,000	141,055,000	394,606,000	231,136,000	317,261,000	238,393,000
Operating Margin %	4.74%	4.26%	11.35%	7.31%	10.69%	7.97%
SGA Expense	806,498,000	796,505,000	834,601,000	735,828,000	713,197,000	756,256,000
Net Income	80,322,000	82,983,000	232,108,000	151,705,000	140,647,000	169,022,000
Operating Cash Flow	338,426,000	229,856,000	475,055,000	239,256,000	381,160,000	386,462,000
Capital Expenditure	246,266,000	285,334,000	95,064,000	134,322,000	84,259,000	127,419,000
EBITDA	298,116,000	275,102,000	523,003,000	374,292,000	462,809,000	385,876,000
Return on Assets %	4.73%	4.81%	12.52%	7.92%	7.00%	8.24%
Return on Equity %	6.96%	6.95%	17.59%	10.96%	9.60%	11.31%
Debt to Equity						

CONTACT INFORMATION:

Phone: 412 432-3300   Fax:
Toll-Free: 888-232-4535
Address: 77 Hot Metal St., Pittsburgh, PA 15203 United States

SALARIES/BONUSES:

Top Exec. Salary: $700,000   Bonus: $500,000
Second Exec. Salary: $1,188,000   Bonus: $

STOCK TICKER/OTHER:

Stock Ticker: AEO
Employees: 38,000
Parent Company:

Exchange: NYS
Fiscal Year Ends: 01/31

OTHER THOUGHTS:

Estimated Female Officers or Directors: 4
Hot Spot for Advancement for Women/Minorities: Y

American Girl LLC

www.americangirl.com

NAIC Code: 451120

TYPES OF BUSINESS:

Toys, Retail
Publishing, Books
Publishing, Magazines
Books, Retail

BRANDS/DIVISIONS/AFFILIATES:

Mattel Inc
Girl of the Year
My American Girl
Bitty Baby
American Girl Place
American Girl Boutique and Bistro
Innerstar University

CONTACTS: Note: Officers with more than one job title may be intentionally listed here more than once.

Jean Ann McKenzie, Pres.
Bryan Stockton, CEO-Mattel, Inc.

GROWTH PLANS/SPECIAL FEATURES:

American Girl, LLC, a subsidiary of Mattel, Inc., is a direct marketer, children's publisher/retailer of books, toys and magazines for girls ages 3-12. The company's American Girl characters include historical characters, which are designed to depict historical periods and convey life lessons through a series of books, and a line of 18-inch dolls. Additionally, the firm offers contemporary Girl of the Year characters, which also feature a series of books and a line of dolls. My American Girl dolls feature various combinations of skin tone, facial features, hair color, eye color, clothing and accessories as well access to the online community Innerstar University, where children can engage in games quizzes and challenges and interact with other players through their doll's avatar. The company's Bitty Baby line of dolls, storybooks, outfits and accessories are designed to encourage nurturing play and appeal to younger girls. The American Girl magazine, created for girls ages eight and up, is designed to affirm self-esteem, celebrate achievements and foster creativity. It has a circulation of over 400,000 issues. American Girl Place, the company's retail and entertainment site, has locations in Chicago, Denver, Kansas City, New York and Los Angeles. The American Girl Boutique and Bistro is another American Girl retail concept, offering the company's line of dolls and books and meal options in its Bistro. Located in shopping centers in Dallas, Houston, Washington D.C., Miami, Seattle, Atlanta, Boston and Minneapolis, the Boutique and Bistros are designed as birthday and other special occasion celebration locations, and feature separate party rooms as well as providing organized games and activities, special food and cake and party favors.

FINANCIAL DATA: Note: Data for latest year may not have been available at press time.

In U.S. $	2015	2014	2013	2012	2011	2010
Revenue		645,300,000	658,768,000	596,298,000	542,387,000	486,644,000
R&D Expense						
Operating Income						
Operating Margin %						
SGA Expense						
Net Income		113,600,000	138,029,000	121,642,000	111,104,000	112,923,000
Operating Cash Flow						
Capital Expenditure						
EBITDA						
Return on Assets %						
Return on Equity %						
Debt to Equity						

CONTACT INFORMATION:

Phone: 608-836-4848   Fax: 608-836-1999
Toll-Free:
Address: 8400 Fairway Place, Middleton, WI 53562 United States

STOCK TICKER/OTHER:

Stock Ticker: Subsidiary
Employees: 30,000
Parent Company: MATTEL INC

Exchange:
Fiscal Year Ends: 12/31

SALARIES/BONUSES:

Top Exec. Salary: $ Bonus: $
Second Exec. Salary: $ Bonus: $

OTHER THOUGHTS:

Estimated Female Officers or Directors: 1
Hot Spot for Advancement for Women/Minorities:

Ann Inc
NAIC Code: 448120

TYPES OF BUSINESS:
Women's Apparel, Retail
Clothing & Accessories
Shoes
Online & Catalog Sales

BRANDS/DIVISIONS/AFFILIATES:
Ann Taylor
LOFT
Lou & Grey
Ascena Retail Group Inc

CONTACTS: Note: Officers with more than one job title may be intentionally listed here more than once.
Katherine Krill, CEO
Michael Nicholson, CFO
Ronald Hovsepian, Chairman of the Board
Katherine Ramundo, Executive VP
Gary Muto, President, Divisional

GROWTH PLANS/SPECIAL FEATURES:

Ann, Inc. is one of the leading national specialty retailers of high-quality women's apparel, shoes and accessories. It stores offer a full range of career and casual separates dresses, tops, weekend wear, shoes and accessories coordinated as part of a total wardrobe strategy. The firm operates stores under the Ann Taylor, LOFT and Lou & Grey names, where Ann Taylor caters to affluent career women LOFT targets a value conscious woman, while remaining upscale, seeking a more casual wardrobe and Lou & Grey features everyday lounge collections. Merchandise is marketed in more than 1,000 stores throughout the U.S., Washington D.C., Puerto Rico and Canada. Ann Taylor operates 242 full price and 122 outlet stores; LOFT operates 650 full-price and outlet stores; and Lou & Grey operates stores in Connecticut and Massachusetts, with plans to open more. The stores are located primarily in regional malls and upscale specialty retail centers, and average 5,000 to 6,000 square feet in size. The overall trend for Ann Taylor stores is to seek a smaller footprint be it through remodeling/downsizing or new openings. The company's merchandise is predominately developed and designed by in-house design teams exclusively for its own stores, with a small portion bought through branded vendors In 2015, the firm was acquired by Ascena Retail Group, Inc. the owner of Dressbarn and Lane Bryant, for $2 billion. Ann operates as its wholly-owned subsidiary.

The firm offers employees medical, dental and vision insurance; flexible spending accounts; adoption assistance; life insurance; a transportation reimbursement program, discounted merchandise; a stock purchase plan; and a 401(k).

FINANCIAL DATA: Note: Data for latest year may not have been available at press time.

In U.S. $	2015	2014	2013	2012	2011	2010
Revenue		2,493,490,944	2,375,508,992	2,212,493,056	1,980,194,944	1,828,523,008
R&D Expense						
Operating Income						
Operating Margin %						
SGA Expense						
Net Income		102,430,000	102,585,000	86,566,000	73,397,000	-18,208,000
Operating Cash Flow						
Capital Expenditure						
EBITDA						
Return on Assets %						
Return on Equity %						
Debt to Equity						

CONTACT INFORMATION:
Phone: 212 541-3300   Fax: 212 541-3379
Toll-Free: 800-677-6788
Address: 7 Times Square, 15th Fl., New York, NY 10036 United States

STOCK TICKER/OTHER:
Stock Ticker: Subsidiary
Employees: 18,800
Parent Company: Ascena Retail Group Inc

Exchange:
Fiscal Year Ends: 01/31

SALARIES/BONUSES:
Top Exec. Salary: $ Bonus: $
Second Exec. Salary: $ Bonus: $

OTHER THOUGHTS:
Estimated Female Officers or Directors: 3
Hot Spot for Advancement for Women/Minorities: Y

Apple Inc

NAIC Code: 334220

www.apple.com

TYPES OF BUSINESS:
Electronics Design and Manufacturing
Software
Computers and Tablets
Retail Stores
Smartphones
Online Music Store
Apps Store
Home Entertainment Software & Systems

BRANDS/DIVISIONS/AFFILIATES:
Apple TV
iPad
iTunes
iOS
Mac
iPod
iPhone
iCloud

CONTACTS: *Note: Officers with more than one job title may be intentionally listed here more than once.*
Timothy Cook, CEO
Luca Maestri, CFO
Arthur Levinson, Chairman of the Board
Chris Kondo, Chief Accounting Officer
D. Sewell, General Counsel
Angela Ahrendts, Senior VP, Divisional
Jeffery Williams, Senior VP, Divisional
Eduardo Cue, Senior VP, Divisional
Daniel Riccio, Senior VP, Divisional
Craig Federighi, Senior VP, Divisional
Philip Schiller, Senior VP, Divisional

GROWTH PLANS/SPECIAL FEATURES:
Apple, Inc. designs, manufactures and markets personal computers, portable digital music players and mobile communication devices and sells a variety of related software, services, peripherals and networking applications. The company's products and services include iPhone, iPad, Mac, iPod, Apple TV, a portfolio of consumer and professional software applications, the iOS and OS X operating systems, iCloud and a variety of accessory, service and support offerings. The company also sells and delivers digital content and applications through the iTunes Store, App Store, iBookstore and Mac App Store. Peripheral products are sold directly to end-users through its retail and online stores and include printers, storage devices, computer memory, digital video and still camera and other computing products and supplies. Apple's retail stores have been a tremendous success. At its retail units, Apple's average sales per square foot of store space were an estimated $4,551 in 2014. Apple had 453 stores by mid-2015, up from 437 in 2014. Subsidiaries of the firm include Apple Sales International, Apple Operations International, Apples Operations Europe and Braeburn Capital, Inc. For 2014, Apple sold 169 million iPhones (accounting for 56% of revenues), 67 million iPads (17%), 18 million Macs (13%) and 14 million iPods (4%). iTunes, software and services provided 10% of revenues. In 2015, the firm released to market its MacBook consumer ultra-thin/ultra-portable notebook, its iPod Touch portable media player and its Apple Watch smartwatch.

Apple employee benefits include health and life insurance, long-term care insurance, an employee stock purchase plan, a 401(k), short- and long-term disability coverage, paid vacations and holidays, employee discounts, tuition assistance, wellness programs, personal and family counseling, financial education seminars and an onsite fitness center.

FINANCIAL DATA: *Note: Data for latest year may not have been available at press time.*

In U.S. $	2015	2014	2013	2012	2011	2010
Revenue	233,715,000,000	182,795,000,000	170,910,000,000	156,508,000,000	108,249,000,000	65,225,000,000
R&D Expense	8,067,000,000	6,041,000,000	4,475,000,000	3,381,000,000	2,429,000,000	1,782,000,000
Operating Income	71,230,000,000	52,503,000,000	48,999,000,000	55,241,000,000	33,790,000,000	18,385,000,000
Operating Margin %	30.47%	28.72%	28.66%	35.29%	31.21%	28.18%
SGA Expense	14,329,000,000	11,993,000,000	10,830,000,000	10,040,000,000	7,599,000,000	5,517,000,000
Net Income	53,394,000,000	39,510,000,000	37,037,000,000	41,733,000,000	25,922,000,000	14,013,000,000
Operating Cash Flow	81,266,000,000	59,713,000,000	53,666,000,000	50,856,000,000	37,529,000,000	18,595,000,000
Capital Expenditure	11,488,000,000	9,813,000,000	9,076,000,000	9,402,000,000	7,452,000,000	2,121,000,000
EBITDA	84,505,000,000	61,813,000,000	57,048,000,000	58,518,000,000	35,604,000,000	19,412,000,000
Return on Assets %	20.44%	18.00%	19.33%	28.54%	27.06%	22.84%
Return on Equity %	46.24%	33.61%	30.63%	42.84%	41.67%	35.28%
Debt to Equity	0.44	0.25	0.13			

CONTACT INFORMATION:
Phone: 408 996-1010   Fax: 408 974-2483
Toll-Free: 800-692-7753
Address: 1 Infinite Loop, Cupertino, CA 95014 United States

STOCK TICKER/OTHER:
Stock Ticker: AAPL
Employees: 92,600
Parent Company:

Exchange: NAS
Fiscal Year Ends: 09/30

SALARIES/BONUSES:
Top Exec. Salary: $1,748,462
Bonus: $

Second Exec. Salary: $947,596
Bonus: $

OTHER THOUGHTS:
Estimated Female Officers or Directors:

Hot Spot for Advancement for Women/Minorities:

Sales, profits and employees may be estimates. Financial information, benefits and other data can change quickly and may vary from those stated here.

Arcadia Group Limited

www.arcadiagroup.co.uk

NAIC Code: 448120

TYPES OF BUSINESS:

Apparel Stores-Men's & Women's

BRANDS/DIVISIONS/AFFILIATES:

Dorothy Perkins
Miss Selfridge
Wallis
TOPSHOP
Evans
Burton
Outfit
TOPMAN

CONTACTS: *Note: Officers with more than one job title may be intentionally listed here more than once.*

Ian Grabiner, CEO
Tania Foster-Brown, Dir.-Public Rel. & Comm.
Philip Green, Owner-Taveta Investments
Anthony Grabiner, Chmn.

GROWTH PLANS/SPECIAL FEATURES:

Arcadia Group Limited is one of the largest clothing retailers in the U.K. The firm operates several apparel chains with approximately 2,500 domestic stores. Arcadia also has more than 500 franchised stores in 35 countries, primarily in Europe, the Middle East and Asia. The company has nine brands: Dorothy Perkins, Miss Selfridge, Outfit, Wallis, TOPSHOP, Evans, Burton and TOPMAN. Dorothy Perkins, with 600 stores in the U.K. and over 120 outlets worldwide, targets female customers age 25-35, with tall, petite and maternity ranges available. Miss Selfridge markets fashion wear to young and trendy women ages 18-24. Outfit carries a mix of brands from TOPSHOP and TOPMAN to Oasis and Warehouse throughout the U.K., and claims to have something for everyone. Wallis, with over 400 standalone stores and concessions in the U.K. and Ireland, is an upscale brand that incorporates new trends and colors into its traditional glamour. TOPSHOP is a trendy, stylish and affordable brand for young women, with over 300 stores across the U.K and over 140 worldwide. TOPSHOP's flagship stores are located in London, Liverpool and Leeds, U.K.; Chicago, Illinois; Las Vegas, Nevada; and on Broadway in New York. Evans retails plus size classic clothing, footwear, lingerie and accessories for women ages 20-45 through stores in Ireland and the U.K. Burton is a mid-market menswear brand for ages 25-34 with stores in Ireland and the U.K. TOPMAN is a trendy, fashion-forward and affordable brand for young men. The firm is owned by one of the largest privately owned retail groups in Europe, Taveta Investments. In March 2015, Arcadia sold BHS Group Ltd. to Retail Acquisitions Ltd. for the nominal fee of $1.53, or £1.

The firm offers employees a pension plan, a bonus plan and a 25% discount on all Arcadia Group merchandise.

FINANCIAL DATA: *Note: Data for latest year may not have been available at press time.*

In U.S. $	2015	2014	2013	2012	2011	2010
Revenue		4,124,046,560	4,594,240,000	4,115,270,000	4,334,299,140	4,309,000,000
R&D Expense						
Operating Income						
Operating Margin %						
SGA Expense						
Net Income		218,041,925	281,850,000	280,328,000	307,658,740	
Operating Cash Flow						
Capital Expenditure						
EBITDA						
Return on Assets %						
Return on Equity %						
Debt to Equity						

CONTACT INFORMATION:

Phone: 44-20-7636-8040   Fax: 44-20-7927-0577
Toll-Free:
Address: 70 Berners St., Colegrave House, London, W1T 3NL United Kingdom

STOCK TICKER/OTHER:

Stock Ticker: Private   Exchange:
Employees: 44,000   Fiscal Year Ends: 08/31
Parent Company: TAVETA INVESTMENTS LTD

SALARIES/BONUSES:

Top Exec. Salary: $ Bonus: $
Second Exec. Salary: $ Bonus: $

OTHER THOUGHTS:

Estimated Female Officers or Directors: 1
Hot Spot for Advancement for Women/Minorities:

Arcs Company Limited

www.arcs-g.co.jp

NAIC Code: 445110

TYPES OF BUSINESS:
Supermarkets and Other Grocery (except Convenience) Stores

BRANDS/DIVISIONS/AFFILIATES:
Food Master Basic
Dinner Bell
Tokou
Western
Super Fuji
Fukuhara
Powers U
Universe

CONTACTS: Note: Officers with more than one job title may be intentionally listed here more than once.

Kiyoshi Yokoyama, CEO
Koichi Miura, Chmn.

GROWTH PLANS/SPECIAL FEATURES:
Arcs Company Limited operates supermarkets that mainly sell food products along with apparel and living related products. It is also engaged in the retail of alcohols and pharmaceuticals and the sale of cameras and photographic materials. Its stores include Super Arcs, a grocery chain averaging 10,764 to 15,069 square feet, and Big House, a chain targeting strip centers averaging 8,611 to 10,764 square feet. Ralse Marts are smaller scale stores for essential items, averaging 3,229 to 4,843 square feet. Ralse Stores are combination grocery and clothing stores averaging 4,300 to 6,458 square feet. Home Stores are neighborhood supermarkets of a similar scale to Ralse Marts. Universe stores are grocery stores averaging 6,458 square feet. Powers U discount supermarkets and liquor stores average 6,630 square feet. Fukuhara stores and supercenters offer groceries near major shopping centers and suburban areas. Super Fuji stores are a chain of moderate-sized community supermarkets ranging from 1,614 to 4,300 square feet. Western stores offer one stop food shopping and are generally located in shopping strips. Tokou stores offer groceries and clothing and are 1,600 to 10,764 square feet. Dinner Bell is a 24-hour supermarket. FoodMaster Basic is a grocery focused on prepared items and fresh fish products.

FINANCIAL DATA: Note: Data for latest year may not have been available at press time.

In U.S. $	2015	2014	2013	2012	2011	2010
Revenue		5,031,742,976	4,831,742,976	4,242,178,560	3,698,927,872	3,298,270,208
R&D Expense						
Operating Income						
Operating Margin %						
SGA Expense						
Net Income						
Operating Cash Flow						
Capital Expenditure						
EBITDA						
Return on Assets %						
Return on Equity %						
Debt to Equity						

CONTACT INFORMATION:
Phone: 81 118203773   Fax:
Toll-Free:
Address: 11-2-32, Minami 13-jo Nishi, Chuo-ku, Sapporo, 062-0931
Japan

STOCK TICKER/OTHER:
Stock Ticker: 9948
Employees: 4,746
Parent Company:

Exchange: Tokyo
Fiscal Year Ends:

SALARIES/BONUSES:
Top Exec. Salary: $ Bonus: $
Second Exec. Salary: $ Bonus: $

OTHER THOUGHTS:
Estimated Female Officers or Directors:
Hot Spot for Advancement for Women/Minorities:

Army and Air Force Exchange Service (AAFES)

www.shopmyexchange.com

NAIC Code: 452112

TYPES OF BUSINESS:

Department Stores
Apparel Stores, General
Convenience Stores
Fast Food Restaurants
Food Service

BRANDS/DIVISIONS/AFFILIATES:

Post Exchanges (PX)
Base Exchanges (BX)
ShopMyExchange.com

CONTACTS: *Note: Officers with more than one job title may be intentionally listed here more than once.*

Thomas C. Shull, CEO
Michael P. Howard, COO
Thomas P. Ockenfels, Chief of Staff
Judy Anstey, Media Contact
Anthony (Tony) Pearson, Sr. Enlisted Advisor

GROWTH PLANS/SPECIAL FEATURES:

Army and Air Force Exchange Service (AAFES) is
government agency under the Department of Defense (DOD
that operates more than 2,440 retail facilities in over 3
countries, all 50 U.S. states and five U.S. territories. AAFES
sells merchandise, food and services to approximately 2.
million authorized customers, which include active-duty militar
personnel, reservists, retirees and their family members. It
retail facilities include Post Exchanges (PX) on U.S. Army
bases, Base Exchanges (BX) on U.S. Air Force bases an
main stores at Marine installations. The company also currently
operates over 1,400 fast-food restaurants worldwide, including
Taco Bell, Burger King and Starbucks, as well as 3,37
concession operations. The firm operates 49 contingenc
locations in Afghanistan, Kuwait, Jordan, Oman, Qatar, UAE
Romania, Bosnia and Kosovo. The company's web site
ShopMyExchange.com, offers shoppers a catalog of over 18
million items. The firm operates food services in 76 cafeteria
for all DOD schools in 10 countries, providing roughly 4 million
meals annually. About 66.3% of AAFES's earnings go to the
Morale, Welfare and Recreation programs agency, which fund
libraries, sports programs, swimming pools, youth activities
golf courses, tickets and tour services, bowling centers, hobb
shops, music programs, outdoor facilities and other program
and facilities. Approximately 36% of the company's employee
are military family members or veterans.

The company offers employees benefits including health
dental and life insurance; a 401(k); a pension plan; flexible
spending accounts; and an assistance program.

FINANCIAL DATA: *Note: Data for latest year may not have been available at press time.*

In U.S. $	2015	2014	2013	2012	2011	2010
Revenue		9,200,000,000	8,300,000,000	10,281,200,000	9,902,800,000	9,792,600,000
R&D Expense						
Operating Income						
Operating Margin %						
SGA Expense						
Net Income		373,000,000	332,000,000	277,800,000	390,900,000	428,500,000
Operating Cash Flow						
Capital Expenditure						
EBITDA						
Return on Assets %						
Return on Equity %						
Debt to Equity						

CONTACT INFORMATION:

Phone: 214-312-2011   Fax: 800-455-0163
Toll-Free: 800-527-2345
Address: 3911 S. Walton Walker Blvd., Dallas, TX 75236 United States

STOCK TICKER/OTHER:

Stock Ticker: Government-Owned   Exchange:
Employees: 34,000   Fiscal Year Ends: 01/31
Parent Company:

SALARIES/BONUSES:

Top Exec. Salary: $ Bonus: $
Second Exec. Salary: $ Bonus: $

OTHER THOUGHTS:

Estimated Female Officers or Directors: 1
Hot Spot for Advancement for Women/Minorities:

Ascena Retail Group Inc

www.ascenaretail.com

NAIC Code: 448120

TYPES OF BUSINESS:

Women's Apparel, Retail
Teen Fashion Stores
Fashion Accessories
Private-Label Credit Cards

BRANDS/DIVISIONS/AFFILIATES:

dressbarn
maurices
Justice
Lane Bryant
Catherines
Ann Inc
The Dress Barn Inc

CONTACTS: Note: Officers with more than one job title may be intentionally listed here more than once.

Gary Muto, CEO, Subsidiary
David Jaffe, CEO
Robb Giammatteo, CFO
Elliot Jaffe, Co-Founder
Jonathan Pershing, Executive VP
Kevin Trolaro, Other Corporate Officer
Ernest Laporte, Senior VP

GROWTH PLANS/SPECIAL FEATURES:

Ascena Retail Group, Inc., formerly The Dress Barn, Inc., operates a national chain of value-priced specialty stores offering in-season, moderate to better quality apparel and accessories. The company has approximately 3,900 stores throughout the U.S., Puerto Rico and Canada. It now operates in following five segments based on a brand-oriented approach: Justice, Lane Bryant, maurices, dressbarn and Catherines. The Justice segment includes 997 specialty retail and outlet stores, e-commerce operations and licensed franchises internationally, offering fashionable apparel to girls ages 7-14, designed for an energetic lifestyle. Lane Bryant includes 771 specialty retail and outlet stores and e-commerce operations, and is a widely recognized brand name in plus-size fashion. The maurices segment includes 922 specialty retail and outlet stores and e-commerce operations, offering up-to-date fashion for women ages 20-35. The dressbarn segment includes 820 specialty retail and outlet stores and e-commerce operations, offering moderate-to-better quality career and casual fashion for working women ranging from their mid-30's to mid-50's. Catherines includes 386 specialty retail stores and e-commerce operations, and sells plus-size fashion to women 45 years and older who shop in the moderate price range and are concerned with comfort, fit and value. Ascena owns distribution centers for its various brands in Ohio, Iowa, Indiana, Maryland and Wisconsin. In August 2015, the firm acquired Ann, Inc., the parent of Ann Taylor and Loft.

FINANCIAL DATA: Note: Data for latest year may not have been available at press time.

In U.S. $	2015	2014	2013	2012	2011	2010
Revenue	4,802,900,000	4,790,600,000	4,714,900,000	3,353,300,000	2,914,000,000	2,374,571,000
R&D Expense						
Operating Income	-234,900,000	210,800,000	265,300,000	292,600,000	289,800,000	217,457,000
Operating Margin %	-4.89%	4.40%	5.62%	8.72%	9.94%	9.15%
SGA Expense	2,347,800,000	2,208,600,000	2,172,200,000	1,478,600,000	852,100,000	690,229,000
Net Income	-236,800,000	133,400,000	151,300,000	162,200,000	170,500,000	133,378,000
Operating Cash Flow	431,300,000	374,700,000	450,000,000	361,500,000	280,800,000	231,437,000
Capital Expenditure	312,500,000	477,500,000	290,900,000	150,400,000	102,100,000	65,179,000
EBITDA	-16,400,000	403,600,000	432,400,000	390,700,000	376,700,000	289,066,000
Return on Assets %	-7.84%	4.45%	5.32%	6.98%	9.76%	9.57%
Return on Equity %	-14.54%	8.09%	10.44%	12.98%	15.68%	16.24%
Debt to Equity	0.23	0.09	0.08	0.41	0.14	0.02

CONTACT INFORMATION:

Phone: 845 369-4500   Fax: 845 369-8001
Toll-Free: 800-373-7722
Address: 30 Dunnigan Dr., Suffern, NY 10901 United States

SALARIES/BONUSES:

Top Exec. Salary: Bonus: $
$1,000,000
Second Exec. Salary: Bonus: $147,766
$500,308

STOCK TICKER/OTHER:

Stock Ticker: ASNA   Exchange: NAS
Employees: 48,000   Fiscal Year Ends: 07/31
Parent Company:

OTHER THOUGHTS:

Estimated Female Officers or Directors: 2

Hot Spot for Advancement for Women/Minorities: Y

Ashley Furniture Industries Inc

NAIC Code: 337121

www.ashleyfurniture.com

TYPES OF BUSINESS:

Furniture Manufacturing & Distribution
Franchising of Furniture Stores
Mattresses

BRANDS/DIVISIONS/AFFILIATES:

Ashley Furniture HomeStores

CONTACTS: Note: Officers with more than one job title may be intentionally listed here more than once.

Todd R. Wanek, CEO
Todd Wanek, Pres.
Gino Mangione, Corp. Controller
Ronald G. Wanek, Chmn.

GROWTH PLANS/SPECIAL FEATURES:

Ashley Furniture Industries, Inc. is one of the nation's largest furniture manufacturers. The firm manufactures and imports upholstered, leather and hardwood furniture for living rooms, home offices and dining rooms as well as bedding and other furniture for bedrooms. Its products include stationary upholstered and leather furniture, recliners, sectionals, chairs, desks, dining room sets, entertainment centers, curios, lamps and tables. The firm is known for its glossy finish Millennium line of furniture as well as its Ashley Sleep brand mattresses. Ashley retails its furniture through licensed operating agreements with over 500 independently owned and operated Ashley Furniture HomeStores in addition to third-party furniture retailers. Ashley Furniture HomeStores market only Ashley products and maintain locations in 123 countries including U.S., Canada, Mexico, Costa Rica, Japan, Puerto Rico, Guatemala and Jordan. Ashley has plants and distribution centers in Wisconsin, Mississippi, North Carolina, Pennsylvania and California. More than one-half of its furniture is made in the United States, with the balance imported from Asia. While its sofa and chair frames are made in the U.S., the fabric is cut and sewn in Asia. The company operates its own fleet of more than 800 delivery trucks. Expansion plans include a goal of increasing its stores in Asia to 1,000 by 2025.

The company offers its employees medical, life, disability and dental insurance; a 401(k); tuition reimbursement; internal training programs; and a profit sharing plan.

FINANCIAL DATA: Note: Data for latest year may not have been available at press time.

In U.S. $	2015	2014	2013	2012	2011	2010
Revenue		4,050,000,000	3,825,000,000	3,500,000,000	3,510,000,000	3,000,000,000
R&D Expense						
Operating Income						
Operating Margin %						
SGA Expense						
Net Income						
Operating Cash Flow						
Capital Expenditure						
EBITDA						
Return on Assets %						
Return on Equity %						
Debt to Equity						

CONTACT INFORMATION:

Phone: 608-323-3377   Fax: 608-323-6008
Toll-Free:
Address: 1 Ashley Way, Arcadia, WI 54612 United States

STOCK TICKER/OTHER:

Stock Ticker: Private
Employees: 13,000
Parent Company:

Exchange:
Fiscal Year Ends: 12/31

SALARIES/BONUSES:

Top Exec. Salary: $ Bonus: $
Second Exec. Salary: $ Bonus: $

OTHER THOUGHTS:

Estimated Female Officers or Directors:
Hot Spot for Advancement for Women/Minorities:

Associated Wholesale Grocers Inc

www.awginc.com

NAIC Code: 445110

TYPES OF BUSINESS:

Grocery Stores, Retail
In-Store Pharmacies
Bakeries
Delis
Wholesale Grocery Distribution
Retail Support Services

BRANDS/DIVISIONS/AFFILIATES:

Country Mart
Price Chopper
Sun Fresh
Thriftway
Apple Market
Cash Saver
IGA
Valu Merchandisers Co

CONTACTS: Note: Officers with more than one job title may be intentionally listed here more than once.

Jerry Garland, CEO
Michael Rand, COO
Jerry Garland, Pres.
Robert C. Walker, CFO
Joe Busch, VP-Sales
Steve Dillard, VP-Corp. Sales Dev.
Bob Hufford, Chmn.

GROWTH PLANS/SPECIAL FEATURES:

Associated Wholesale Grocers, Inc. (AWG) is a grocery co-operative. The firm supplies more than 3,400 restores located in 30 states. AWG has developed several different store concepts depending on which market area the store is located. Country Mart is a warehouse-oriented, low-price store designed for small towns and rural areas. Price Chopper stores are among the company's most successful concepts, with large amounts of floor space, low prices, in-store pharmacies, salad bars, seafood and poultry departments, full-service bakeries and delis. Sun Fresh is an upscale store generally located in high-density residential areas and is focused on providing high-quality fresh foods. Thriftway is a convenient neighborhood store located in small and medium-sized market areas. Apple Market stores focus on providing high-quality perishables in a warm atmosphere and large store format. Cash Saver stores attempt to combine savings without sacrificing quality in small to medium-sized markets. Finally, IGA is the world's largest voluntary supermarket network. Valu Merchandisers Co., the company's wholesale distribution subsidiary, carries roughly 43,000 items, including 11,000 health and beauty care products, 7,000 specialty foods and dollar grocery items, 8,000 general merchandise items and 5,000 seasonal and promotional products. The subsidiary sells its products to over 3,400 stores in 30 states. The firm's services division offers programs focusing on advertising, training, print shop, store engineering, design and decor, electronic data exchange, real estate reclamation and retail systems support.

The company offers its employees a benefits package that includes health, dental, vision, life and disability insurance; flexible spending accounts; a 401(k) plan; tuition reimbursement; and an employee assistance program.

FINANCIAL DATA: Note: Data for latest year may not have been available at press time.

In U.S. $	2015	2014	2013	2012	2011	2010
Revenue		8,550,000,000	8,380,000,000	8,000,000,000	7,766,807,000	7,250,000,000
R&D Expense						
Operating Income						
Operating Margin %						
SGA Expense						
Net Income						
Operating Cash Flow						
Capital Expenditure						
EBITDA						
Return on Assets %						
Return on Equity %						
Debt to Equity						

CONTACT INFORMATION:

Phone: 913-288-1000   Fax: 913-288-1587
Toll-Free:
Address: 5000 Kansas Ave., Kansas City, KS 66106 United States

STOCK TICKER/OTHER:

Stock Ticker: Private
Employees: 21,000
Parent Company:

Exchange:
Fiscal Year Ends: 12/31

SALARIES/BONUSES:

Top Exec. Salary: $ Bonus: $
Second Exec. Salary: $ Bonus: $

OTHER THOUGHTS:

Estimated Female Officers or Directors:
Hot Spot for Advancement for Women/Minorities:

At Home Group Inc

NAIC Code: 442299

www.athome.com

TYPES OF BUSINESS:

Garden Supplies & Accessories
Home Accessories
Craft Items
Seasonal Merchandise

BRANDS/DIVISIONS/AFFILIATES:

At Home Stores LLC
At Home
Garden Ridge Corporation

CONTACTS: *Note: Officers with more than one job title may be intentionally listed here more than once.*

Lewis L. Bird, CEO
Judd Nystrom, CFO
Alissa M. Ahlman, CMO
Phyllis C. Hink, VP-Oper.

GROWTH PLANS/SPECIAL FEATURES:

At Home Group, Inc., formerly Garden Ridge Corporation, is a home decor products retailer. Through subsidiary At Hom Stores LLC, it offers patio furniture, home furnishings, wa decorations, decorative accents, rugs, housewares, garde products, home textiles, seasonal decorations, tabletop dec and wall decor. Home furniture includes sofas, chair barstools, dining tables, chairs, bedroom tables, cabinet shelving and racks. Outdoor products include pottery, lighting tables, chairs and umbrellas. Home textiles include beddinc window panels, pillows, cushions and kitchen/table linen: Housewares include dinnerware, drinkware, serveware cookware and bakeware. The company operates 90 At Hom brand stores throughout the U.S., and plans to open 200 mor by 2020. In 2014, Garden Ridge Corporation changed its nam to At Home Group, Inc. and moved its headquarters to Plano Texas.

FINANCIAL DATA: *Note: Data for latest year may not have been available at press time.*

In U.S. $	2015	2014	2013	2012	2011	2010
Revenue						
R&D Expense						
Operating Income						
Operating Margin %						
SGA Expense						
Net Income						
Operating Cash Flow						
Capital Expenditure						
EBITDA						
Return on Assets %						
Return on Equity %						
Debt to Equity						

CONTACT INFORMATION:

Phone: 281-578-2334   Fax:
Toll-Free:
Address: 1600 East Plano Parkway, Plano, TX 75074 United States

STOCK TICKER/OTHER:

Stock Ticker: Private
Employees:
Parent Company:

Exchange:
Fiscal Year Ends: 01/31

SALARIES/BONUSES:

Top Exec. Salary: $ Bonus: $
Second Exec. Salary: $ Bonus: $

OTHER THOUGHTS:

Estimated Female Officers or Directors: 1
Hot Spot for Advancement for Women/Minorities:

At Home Stores LLC

NAIC Code: 442110

TYPES OF BUSINESS:

Furniture Stores

BRANDS/DIVISIONS/AFFILIATES:

At Home Group Inc
At Home
Garden Ridge Corporation

GROWTH PLANS/SPECIAL FEATURES:

At Home Stores, LLC is a specialty retailer of home decor products. The company averages 120,000 square feet in size and offers approximately 50,000 unique items across broad product categories, including furniture, garden, home textiles, housewares, patio, rugs, seasonal decor, tabletop decor and wall decor. The firm currently operates 90 At Home locations throughout the U.S. AT Home was founded as Garden Ridge Pottery, was later renamed just Garden Ridge and rebranded as At Home in 2014. The company announced plans to open 200 At Home stores by 2020. In 2014, parent Garden Ridge Corporation moved its headquarters from Houston to Plano, and changed its corporate name to At Home Group, Inc.

CONTACTS: Note: Officers with more than one job title may be intentionally listed here more than once.

Lee Bird, CEO
Judd Nystrom, CFO
Alissa Ahlman, CMO
Valerie Davisson, Chief People Officer
Gary McClure, CIO

FINANCIAL DATA: Note: Data for latest year may not have been available at press time.

In U.S. $	2015	2014	2013	2012	2011	2010
Revenue						
R&D Expense						
Operating Income						
Operating Margin %						
SGA Expense						
Net Income						
Operating Cash Flow						
Capital Expenditure						
EBITDA						
Return on Assets %						
Return on Equity %						
Debt to Equity						

CONTACT INFORMATION:

Phone: 469-366-0863   Fax:
Toll-Free:
Address: 1600 E. Plano Pkwy., Plano, TX 75074 United States

STOCK TICKER/OTHER:

Stock Ticker: Subsidiary   Exchange:
Employees: Fiscal Year Ends:
Parent Company: At Home Group Inc

SALARIES/BONUSES:

Top Exec. Salary: $ Bonus: $
Second Exec. Salary: $ Bonus: $

OTHER THOUGHTS:

Estimated Female Officers or Directors: 6
Hot Spot for Advancement for Women/Minorities: Y

AutoZone Inc

www.autozone.com

NAIC Code: 441310

TYPES OF BUSINESS:
Auto Parts, Retail
Automotive Software
Online Sales
General Automotive Service

BRANDS/DIVISIONS/AFFILIATES:
Loan-a-Tool
ALLDATA LLC
ProElite
Econocraft
SureBuilt
Duralast

CONTACTS: Note: Officers with more than one job title may be intentionally listed here more than once.
William Rhodes, CEO
William Giles, CFO
Charlie Pleas, Chief Accounting Officer
Ronald Griffin, Chief Information Officer
Mark Finestone, Executive VP, Divisional
William Graves, Executive VP, Divisional
Thomas Newbern, Executive VP, Divisional
Larry Roesel, Senior VP, Divisional
Michael Womack, Senior VP, Divisional
Albert Saltiel, Senior VP, Divisional
Kristen Wright, Senior VP

GROWTH PLANS/SPECIAL FEATURES:

AutoZone, Inc. is a leading specialty retailer and distributor of automotive parts, chemicals and accessories, targeting do-it-yourself (DIY) customers. With 5,069 stores in the U.S. and Puerto Rico and 418 in Mexico, each AutoZone store carries an extensive product line for cars, sport utility vehicles (SUVs), vans and light trucks, including new and remanufactured automotive parts and maintenance items as well as non-automotive products. Many AutoZone stores have a commercial sales program that provides commercial credit and prompt delivery of parts and other products to local, regional and national repair garages, dealers and service stations. Although each of the company's stores carries the same basic product lines, the company tailors each store's parts inventory to the makes and models of the vehicles in their trade areas. Parts not kept in stock can be ordered and delivered to the store within a few days, or they can be ordered online. In-house brands such as Econocraft, Valucraft, ProElite, SureBuilt, and Duralast are offered at competitive value to customers. The company also has a Loan-a-Tool program, through which customers can borrow a specialty tool, such as a steering wheel puller, for which they would have little or no use other than for a single job. In addition, AutoZone provides other free services, including check engine light readings; collection of used oil for recycling; battery charging and installation assistance; and the testing of starters, alternators, batteries, sensors and actuators. Moreover, the company offers automotive diagnostic and repair software through its subsidiary ALLDATA LLC.

Employee benefits include a comprehensive wellness program; medical, dental and vision coverage; short- and long-term disability; life insurance; 401(k); a stock purchase plan; a credit union membership; an employee assistance program; employee discounts; adoption assistance; and tuition assistance.

FINANCIAL DATA: Note: Data for latest year may not have been available at press time.

In U.S. $	2015	2014	2013	2012	2011	2010
Revenue	10,187,340,000	9,475,313,000	9,147,530,000	8,603,863,000	8,072,973,000	7,362,618,000
R&D Expense						
Operating Income	1,953,051,000	1,830,223,000	1,773,098,000	1,628,891,000	1,494,803,000	1,319,414,000
Operating Margin %	19.17%	19.31%	19.38%	18.93%	18.51%	17.92%
SGA Expense	3,373,980,000	3,104,684,000	2,967,837,000	2,803,145,000	2,624,660,000	2,392,330,000
Net Income	1,160,241,000	1,069,744,000	1,016,480,000	930,373,000	848,974,000	738,311,000
Operating Cash Flow	1,525,123,000	1,341,234,000	1,415,011,000	1,223,981,000	1,291,538,000	1,196,252,000
Capital Expenditure	490,579,000	449,228,000	414,451,000	378,054,000	321,604,000	315,400,000
EBITDA	2,224,575,000	2,083,340,000	2,001,955,000	1,842,119,000	1,702,032,000	1,514,124,000
Return on Assets %	14.85%	14.84%	15.45%	15.33%	14.84%	13.55%
Return on Equity %						
Debt to Equity						

CONTACT INFORMATION:
Phone: 901 495-6500 Fax: 901 495-8300
Toll-Free: 800-288-6966
Address: 123 S. Front St., Memphis, TN 38103 United States

STOCK TICKER/OTHER:
Stock Ticker: AZO Exchange: NYS
Employees: 76,000 Fiscal Year Ends: 08/31
Parent Company:

SALARIES/BONUSES:
Top Exec. Salary: $1,000,000 Bonus: $
Second Exec. Salary: $560,539 Bonus: $

OTHER THOUGHTS:
Estimated Female Officers or Directors: 2

Hot Spot for Advancement for Women/Minorities: Y

Avon Products Inc

www.avoncompany.com

NAIC Code: 454390

TYPES OF BUSINESS:

Cosmetics & Beauty Supplies, Direct Selling
Fragrances & Toiletries
Gift & Decorative Items
Apparel & Accessories
Fashion Jewelry
Health & Fitness Products
Online Sales

BRANDS/DIVISIONS/AFFILIATES:

Avon Makeup Collection
Advance Techniques
ANEW
Avon Skin-So-Soft
Naturals
Mark
M-The Men's Catalog
Tiny Tillia

CONTACTS: *Note: Officers with more than one job title may be intentionally listed here more than once.*

Sherilyn McCoy, CEO
Karen Leu, Vice President
James Scully, CFO
Douglas Conant, Chairman of the Board
Robert Loughran, Chief Accounting Officer
Jeff Benjamin, General Counsel
Fernando Acosta, Other Corporate Officer
John Higson, Other Corporate Officer
Susan Ormiston, Other Executive Officer
Nilesh Patel, President, Geographical
David Legher, President, Geographical
Pablo Munoz, President, Geographical
David Powell, Senior VP, Divisional
Brian Salsberg, Senior VP, Divisional

GROWTH PLANS/SPECIAL FEATURES:

Avon Products, Inc. is a global manufacturer and marketer of beauty and related products. The firm groups these products into two categories: beauty, consisting of cosmetics, fragrances, skin care and toiletries, which accounts for roughly 73% of sales; and fashion & home, which consists of watches, apparel, footwear & accessories in the fashion line and decorative products, housewares, entertainment & leisure products in the home line, accounting for 27% of sales. The company sells makeup under the Avon Makeup Collection brand; skincare products under ANEW; bath and body products under Avon Skin-So-Soft, Naturals and Foot Works; hair care products under Advance Techniques; mom and baby products under the Tiny Tillia brand; and fragrance products under a variety of brands, including Crystal Aura, Derek Jeter Driven, U by Ungaro and Today, Tomorrow, Always. Additionally, Avon has launched a global business targeting teenage girls through the Mark brand name and a portfolio of products for men offered in a publication called M-The Men's Catalog. The company sells products primarily by direct selling and marketing through approximately 6 million independent representatives worldwide. The firm's international operations are conducted primarily through subsidiaries in 60 countries and territories outside of the U.S., and its products are distributed in 41 additional countries and territories through distributorships. In 2014, Avon and Coty, Inc. entered into a partnership in which Avon agreed to sell Coty products in Brazil. In July 2015, the firm sold its Liz Earle natural skincare brand.

Avon employees receive medical, dental, vision and life insurance coverage; adoption and child care benefits; tuition assistance; parental leave; subsidized gym memberships; product discounts; paid time off; employee assistance programs; flexible spending accounts; a 401(k); spouse and partner benefits; and a pension plan.

FINANCIAL DATA: *Note: Data for latest year may not have been available at press time.*

In U.S. $	2015	2014	2013	2012	2011	2010
Revenue		8,851,400,000	9,955,000,000	10,717,100,000	11,291,600,000	10,862,800,000
R&D Expense						
Operating Income		400,100,000	427,200,000	314,800,000	854,600,000	1,073,100,000
Operating Margin %		4.52%	4.29%	2.93%	7.56%	9.87%
SGA Expense		4,952,000,000	5,713,200,000	5,980,000,000	6,025,400,000	5,748,400,000
Net Income		-388,600,000	-56,400,000	-42,500,000	513,600,000	606,300,000
Operating Cash Flow		359,800,000	535,600,000	556,100,000	655,800,000	702,000,000
Capital Expenditure		131,100,000	197,300,000	228,800,000	276,700,000	331,200,000
EBITDA		467,900,000	507,800,000	552,500,000	1,075,100,000	1,227,300,000
Return on Assets %		-6.48%	-.81%	-.56%	6.58%	8.24%
Return on Equity %		-55.51%	-4.84%	-3.04%	31.83%	41.39%
Debt to Equity		8.50	2.32	2.15	1.56	1.53

CONTACT INFORMATION:

Phone: 212 282-5000   Fax:
Toll-Free:
Address: 777 Third Ave, New York, NY 10017 United States

STOCK TICKER/OTHER:

Stock Ticker: AVP
Employees: 33,200
Parent Company:

Exchange: NYS
Fiscal Year Ends: 12/31

SALARIES/BONUSES:

Top Exec. Salary: $ Bonus: $
Second Exec. Salary: $ Bonus: $

OTHER THOUGHTS:

Estimated Female Officers or Directors: 9
Hot Spot for Advancement for Women/Minorities: Y

Sales, profits and employees may be estimates. Financial information, benefits and other data can change quickly and may vary from those stated here.

Axfood AB

NAIC Code: 445110

TYPES OF BUSINESS:

Supermarkets

BRANDS/DIVISIONS/AFFILIATES:

Willys
Hemkop
Dagab
Axfood Snabbgross
Handlar'n
NetXtra
Axfood Narlivs
Tempo

CONTACTS: Note: Officers with more than one job title may be intentionally listed here more than once.

Anders Stralman, CEO
Anders Stralman, Pres.
Karin Hygrell-Jonsson, CFO
Louise Ring, Head-Human Resources
Jan Lindmark, Head-IT
Anders Quist, Head-Bus. Dev.
Anne Rhenman Eklund, Head-Corp. Comm.
Hans Holmstedt, Purchasing Dir.
Thomas Evertsson, Pres., Willys AB
Thomas Gareskog, Pres., Hemkop AB
Anders Agerberg, Div. Dir.-Dagab

GROWTH PLANS/SPECIAL FEATURES:

Axfood AB is a Swedish food retailing company. The reta
stores offer food and general goods, including hygier
products, seasonal products, CDs/DVDs, electronic device
and toys. The company own 258 stores conducted through th
wholly owned Hemkop and Willys chains. Hemkop offe
quality groceries and low prices. It offers a loyalty credit ca
which offers rewards for customers. Willys is a discount cha
and Willys Hemma is a smaller version of the larger store. I
addition, Axfood collaborates with a large number of proprieto
run stores that are tied to Axfood through agreements. Thes
include stores within the Hemkop chain as well as stores ru
under the Handlar'n and Tempo brands. It also operate
NetXtra, an online store. Axfood also wholesales groceries an
business to business sales. It operates those activities throug
the Dagab, Axfood Snabbgross and Axfood Narlivs store
Dagab repacks and stores goods in warehouses in order t
distribute to stores across Sweden. It ships to over 7,000 store
and customers from its two distribution centers. Axfood Narliv
operates convenience store wholesale. It sells to mini-mart
service stations and other convenience stores. Axfoo
Snabbgross focuses on restaurants, foodservices operator
and cafes.

FINANCIAL DATA: Note: Data for latest year may not have been available at press time.

In U.S. $	2015	2014	2013	2012	2011	2010
Revenue		4,431,777,000	4,320,994,000	4,180,961,000	4,006,956,000	3,945,346,000
R&D Expense						
Operating Income		166,635,000	149,936,900	137,269,500	143,948,700	139,227,200
Operating Margin %		3.75%	3.46%	3.28%	3.59%	3.52%
SGA Expense		483,897,900	477,218,700	454,071,700	450,617,000	424,360,700
Net Income		126,099,100	113,661,900	103,067,300	102,606,600	99,267,010
Operating Cash Flow		233,657,500	183,793,700	220,529,400	159,380,000	157,192,000
Capital Expenditure		64,489,010	82,108,330	82,799,280	102,721,800	90,399,780
EBITDA		244,367,300	223,984,100	208,668,000	209,819,600	200,952,400
Return on Assets %		11.76%	11.13%	10.48%	11.17%	11.61%
Return on Equity %		28.08%	27.25%	26.67%	28.70%	30.74%
Debt to Equity		0.01	0.01	0.01	0.01	0.01

CONTACT INFORMATION:

Phone: 46 855399000   Fax: 46 87302689
Toll-Free:
Address: Norra stationsgatan 80C, Stockholm, 107 69 Sweden

STOCK TICKER/OTHER:

Stock Ticker: AXFOF
Employees: 8,481
Parent Company:

Exchange: GREY
Fiscal Year Ends: 12/31

SALARIES/BONUSES:

Top Exec. Salary: $ Bonus: $
Second Exec. Salary: $ Bonus: $

OTHER THOUGHTS:

Estimated Female Officers or Directors: 8
Hot Spot for Advancement for Women/Minorities: Y

B&Q plc

NAIC Code: 444110

www.diy.com

TYPES OF BUSINESS:

Home Centers, Retail
Online Sales

BRANDS/DIVISIONS/AFFILIATES:

Kingfisher plc
B&Q Warehouse
B&Q Supercenter
B&Q Mini-Warehouse
B&Q Yangpu
B&Q Beijing

CONTACTS: Note: Officers with more than one job title may be intentionally listed here more than once.

Euan Sutherland, CEO
Vicky Garfitt, Mgr.-Digital Mktg.
Jacqueline Caston, Dir.-Comm.
Kevin O'Byrne, CEO-B&Q U.K. & Ireland
Ian Cheshire, Chmn.

GROWTH PLANS/SPECIAL FEATURES:

B&Q plc, a subsidiary of Kingfisher plc, is a U.K.-based chain of home and garden improvement stores. The company operates 350 retail locations in the U.K. and eight in Ireland that sell 40,000 home improvement products. It is one of the largest do-it-yourself (DIY) retailers in Europe and also operates internationally, with over 60 stores outside of the U.K., including B&Q Yangpu in Shanghai and B&Q Beijing. The firm operates three types of stores: B&Q Warehouses, which cater to dedicated DIY'ers through staff expertise and a wider range of products including garden, heavy end, decoration and furniture products; smaller B&Q Mini-Warehouses; and B&Q Supercenters, which are designed for everyday needs and carry around 16,000 products covering kitchen and bathroom equipment, lighting, floor coverings, tiles, gardening, hardware, decorating equipment and tools. B&Q's eco flagship store contains innovative developments such as 108 underground bore holes that are 100 meters deep, which heats and cools the store with energy from the earth, rainwater harvesting, solar thermal water heating panels and a green roof planted with sedum. The company also retails through its web site.

B&Q offers its employees paid holidays, pension plans and in-store discounts.

FINANCIAL DATA: Note: Data for latest year may not have been available at press time.

In U.S. $	2015	2014	2013	2012	2011	2010
Revenue		5,667,445,000	7,012,178,069	4,997,570,000	5,305,330,000	5,413,656,000
R&D Expense						
Operating Income						
Operating Margin %						
SGA Expense						
Net Income		286,437,250	308,535,835	313,006,000	292,473,000	298,505,000
Operating Cash Flow						
Capital Expenditure						
EBITDA						
Return on Assets %						
Return on Equity %						
Debt to Equity						

CONTACT INFORMATION:

Phone: 44-23-8025-6256   Fax: 44-23-8025-7480
Toll-Free:
Address: B&Q House, Chestnut Ave., Chandlers Ford, Eastleigh, Hampshire S053 3LE United Kingdom

STOCK TICKER/OTHER:

Stock Ticker: Subsidiary
Employees: 31,000
Parent Company: KINGFISHER PLC

Exchange:
Fiscal Year Ends: 01/31

SALARIES/BONUSES:

Top Exec. Salary: $ Bonus: $
Second Exec. Salary: $ Bonus: $

OTHER THOUGHTS:

Estimated Female Officers or Directors: 2
Hot Spot for Advancement for Women/Minorities:

Barbeques Galore Inc

www.bbqgalore.com

NAIC Code: 444130

TYPES OF BUSINESS:

Barbecue Grills & Accessories, Retail
Cooking Schools

BRANDS/DIVISIONS/AFFILIATES:

Grand Home Holdings Inc
Grand Hall Enterprise Co Ltd
Crossray
Barbeques Galore Outdoor Cooking School
Turbo
Grand Turbo

CONTACTS: Note: Officers with more than one job title may be intentionally listed here more than once.

Henrik Stepanyan, CEO
John Price, Head-Product Mgmt. & Dev.
Michael Lindblad, CEO-Barbeques Galore USA

GROWTH PLANS/SPECIAL FEATURES:

Barbeques Galore, Inc. is a U.S. retailer and manufacturer of barbecue equipment and outdoor living products. The firm is owned by Grand Home Holdings, Inc., a subsidiary of Taiwanese gas grill manufacturer Grand Hall Enterprise Co. Ltd. The company's stores carry a wide assortment of grills as well as a line of fireplace gas logs, outdoor heaters and related accessories. Products include gas grills, charcoal grills and Crossray grills (infrared grills); smokers; grill islands for kitchens; electric grills; grill parts; accessories, including grilling tools, grill toppers, cleaning and preparation equipment; and extra products such as spices, seasonings, salts and cooling oils and cookbooks. The company markets grills under its own featured brands, Turbo and Grand Turbo, along with grills from third-party manufacturers. The company has retail stores concentrated throughout California, Arizona and Texas. The firm also operates a culinary school, Barbeques Galore Outdoor Cooking School, in Irvine, California. Additionally, the company's web site features recipes and tips related to grilling and outdoor cooking.

FINANCIAL DATA: Note: Data for latest year may not have been available at press time.

In U.S. $	2015	2014	2013	2012	2011	2010
Revenue						
R&D Expense						
Operating Income						
Operating Margin %						
SGA Expense						
Net Income						
Operating Cash Flow						
Capital Expenditure						
EBITDA						
Return on Assets %						
Return on Equity %						
Debt to Equity						

CONTACT INFORMATION:

Phone: 949-597-2400   Fax:
Toll-Free: 800-752-3085
Address: 15041 Blake Pkwy., Irvine, CA 92602 United States

SALARIES/BONUSES:

Top Exec. Salary: $ Bonus: $
Second Exec. Salary: $ Bonus: $

STOCK TICKER/OTHER:

Stock Ticker: Subsidiary
Employees:
Parent Company: Grand Hall Enterprise Co Ltd

Exchange:
Fiscal Year Ends: 01/31

OTHER THOUGHTS:

Estimated Female Officers or Directors:
Hot Spot for Advancement for Women/Minorities: Y

Bare Escentuals Inc

www.bareescentuals.com

NAIC Code: 446120

TYPES OF BUSINESS:

Retail Cosmetics Sales
Direct Cosmetic Sales

BRANDS/DIVISIONS/AFFILIATES:

Shiseido Company
md formulations
Buxom
bareMinerals

CONTACTS: *Note: Officers with more than one job title may be intentionally listed here more than once.*

Simon Cowell, CEO
Leslie A. Blodgett, Chmn.

GROWTH PLANS/SPECIAL FEATURES:

Bare Escentuals, Inc. develops, markets and sells mineral-based cosmetics, skin care and body care products. The firm is a wholly-owned subsidiary of Shiseido Company, a Japan-based cosmetics and fine chemicals company. Bare Escentuals sells its products under the bareMinerals, Buxom and md formulations brands. The bareMinerals products include makeup for the face, such as foundation, concealer, blush and all-over-face color; eyes, including eye shadow, mascara and eyeliner; lipstick, lip gloss and lip balm; makeup primers; moisturizers; sun protection products; and makeup tools, including brushes, brush cleaners, travel and storage products and eyelash combs. Makeup products are made primarily from finely milled minerals and do not contain any chemical additives such as preservatives, talc, waxes, oils and other potential skin irritants. Lip gloss, eyeliner, eye shadow and mascara are also marketed under the Buxom brand. The md formulations brand includes a skincare product line that includes facial cleansers, moisturizers and creams, sunblock and lip balm. Bare Escentuals' products are marketed through Bare Escentuals Boutique retail locations in the U.S. as well as through Sephora, Ulta, Macy's, Dillards, Fine Salon & Spa and QVC. The company also sells products internationally.

FINANCIAL DATA: *Note: Data for latest year may not have been available at press time.*

In U.S. $	2015	2014	2013	2012	2011	2010
Revenue		410,825,852	366,808,796	369,371,771	363,099,854	348,727,011
R&D Expense						
Operating Income						
Operating Margin %						
SGA Expense						
Net Income						
Operating Cash Flow						
Capital Expenditure						
EBITDA						
Return on Assets %						
Return on Equity %						
Debt to Equity						

CONTACT INFORMATION:

Phone: 415-489-5000   Fax:
Toll-Free: 888-795-4747
Address: 71 Stevenson St., 22nd Fl., San Francisco, CA 94105 United States

STOCK TICKER/OTHER:

Stock Ticker: Subsidiary
Employees: 3,100
Parent Company: SHISEIDO COMPANY

Exchange:
Fiscal Year Ends: 12/31

SALARIES/BONUSES:

Top Exec. Salary: $ Bonus: $
Second Exec. Salary: $ Bonus: $

OTHER THOUGHTS:

Estimated Female Officers or Directors: 1
Hot Spot for Advancement for Women/Minorities:

Barnes & Noble College Booksellers Inc

www.bncollege.com

NAIC Code: 451211

TYPES OF BUSINESS:

Book Stores
Online Sales
Marketing Services
College Merchandise
Textbook Rentals
eTextbook Sales

BRANDS/DIVISIONS/AFFILIATES:

Barnes & Noble Inc
TextBooks.com
Barnes & Noble College Marketing Network
Nookstudy

CONTACTS: Note: Officers with more than one job title may be intentionally listed here more than once.

Max J. Roberts, CEO
Patrick Maloney, Pres.
Barry Brover, CFO
Lisa Malat, CMO
Joann Magill, VP-Human Resources
Stephen Culver, CIO
Bill Maloney, Exec. VP

GROWTH PLANS/SPECIAL FEATURES:

Barnes & Noble College Booksellers, Inc. (BNCB), a subsidia
of Barnes & Noble, Inc., is a leading college campus sto
operator for public and private universities. The compar
operates 724 campus stores and serves over 5.3 millic
students and faculty members. These stores provic
textbooks, trade books, school supplies, collegiate clothing ar
other merchandise. Colleges, universities and medical and la
schools hire BNCB to replace traditional campus cooperative
and receive a percentage of the sales. The academ
superstores, which are typically larger in size, provic
additional services besides traditional textbook sales and see
to engage the surrounding campus and local communities i
college activities and culture. The firm's college marketin
network division, B&N College Marketing Network, provide
on-campus marketing opportunities to businesses. In additio
the company operates Textbooks.com, an online retailer
new and used textbooks. The firm also offers an eTextboc
application, Nookstudy, which features a variety of importabl
format types as well as the ability to borrow eBooks ar
eTextbooks from other Nook and Nookstudy users. Parer
company Barnes & Noble announced in early 2015 that it plan
to spin off the college bookstore unit as a new publicly hel
company.

The company offers employees medical and dental insuranc
retirement savings plans, time off with pay, life and disabilit
plans, counseling resources and an employee assistanc
hotline.

FINANCIAL DATA: Note: Data for latest year may not have been available at press time.

In U.S. $	2015	2014	2013	2012	2011	2010
Revenue		1,748,042,000	1,763,248,000	1,743,662,000	1,778,159,000	833,648,000
R&D Expense						
Operating Income						
Operating Margin %						
SGA Expense						
Net Income		-12,951,432	-40,685,906	-15,858,590	-17,498,894	6,136,931
Operating Cash Flow						
Capital Expenditure						
EBITDA						
Return on Assets %						
Return on Equity %						
Debt to Equity						

CONTACT INFORMATION:

Phone: 908-991-2665   Fax: 908-991-2846
Toll-Free:
Address: 120 Mountain View Blvd., Basking Ridge, NJ 07920 United States

STOCK TICKER/OTHER:

Stock Ticker: Subsidiary
Employees: 5,300
Parent Company: BARNES & NOBLE INC

Exchange:
Fiscal Year Ends: 04/30

SALARIES/BONUSES:

Top Exec. Salary: $ Bonus: $
Second Exec. Salary: $ Bonus: $

OTHER THOUGHTS:

Estimated Female Officers or Directors:
Hot Spot for Advancement for Women/Minorities: Y

Barnes & Noble Inc

www.barnesandnobleinc.com

NAIC Code: 451211

TYPES OF BUSINESS:

Book Stores
Music & Software Sales
In-Store Cafes
Online Sales
Book Publishing
Book Distribution
eBooks and eBook Readers
College Book Stores

BRANDS/DIVISIONS/AFFILIATES:

Barnes & Noble College Bookstores
Barnes & Noble Classics
Sterling Publishing Co Inc
BarnesAndNoble.com
NOOK
Sterling
Sterling Children's Books

CONTACTS: Note: Officers with more than one job title may be intentionally listed here more than once.

Allen Lindstrom, CFO
Peter Herpich, Chief Accounting Officer
Ronald Boire, Chief Executive Officer
Christopher Grady-Troia, Chief Information Officer
Jaime Carey, COO
Leonard Riggio, Founder
Bradley Feuer, General Counsel
Frederic Argir, Other Executive Officer
Mahesh Veerina, President, Subsidiary
Mary Keating, Senior VP, Divisional
Michelle Smith, Vice President, Divisional
Andy Milevoj, Vice President, Divisional
David Deason, Vice President, Divisional
Mark Bottini, Vice President

GROWTH PLANS/SPECIAL FEATURES:

Barnes & Noble, Inc. (B&N) is one of the largest booksellers in the U.S., operating 1,372 total bookstores, 648 of which are retail bookstores, in all 50 states. Subsidiary Barnes & Noble College Booksellers, Inc., operating 724 campus bookstores, serves students and faculty members at colleges and universities nationwide, offering book textbook and course material for sale or rent. The online segment of B&N operates through BarnesAndNoble.com. The firm's retail segment includes the company's subsidiary publisher Sterling Publishing Co., Inc., offering series of books under the Sterling, Sterling Children's Books and Barnes & Noble Classics imprints. B&N's principal business is the sale of trade books (hardcover and paperback consumer titles); mass market paperbacks (mystery, romance, science fiction); children's books; eBooks; bargain books; magazines; gifts; toys; cafe products; music; movies; and NOOK, the company' branded e-reader and related accessories. Many B&N stores feature additional amenities, such as cafe areas serving sandwiches and Starbucks coffee; a children's area; and music, DVD, video and game sections, so as to compensate for dwindling traditional book sales. Typical stores stock between 21,000 and 170,000 titles within a variety of popular subject categories reflecting local interests, which are supplemented by new releases and bestsellers. NOOK Boutiques are now located in many stores, selling NOOK brand multimedia tablet products. In mid-2014, the firm announced that it will spin off Nook Media, its eBook reader business, as a free-standing, public company. Nook has been losing money for a long time. In July 2015, Barnes & Noble announced that its board had approved the spin-off of Barnes & Noble Education, Inc.

Employee benefits include medical and dental insurance, a flexible spending account, continuing education programs, merchandise discounts and a 401(k) savings plan.

FINANCIAL DATA: Note: Data for latest year may not have been available at press time.

In U.S. $	2015	2014	2013	2012	2011	2010
Revenue	6,069,497,000	6,381,357,000	6,839,005,000	7,129,199,000	6,998,565,000	5,810,564,000
R&D Expense						
Operating Income	133,173,000	34,192,000	-220,004,000	-61,303,000	-65,259,000	73,246,000
Operating Margin %	2.19%	.53%	-3.21%	-.85%	-.93%	1.26%
SGA Expense	1,545,152,000	1,606,936,000	1,675,376,000	1,739,452,000	1,629,465,000	1,395,725,000
Net Income	36,596,000	-47,268,000	-157,806,000	-68,867,000	-73,920,000	36,676,000
Operating Cash Flow	55,908,000	319,956,000	117,391,000	-24,112,000	199,072,000	128,226,000
Capital Expenditure	143,257,000	134,981,000	165,835,000	163,552,000	110,502,000	127,779,000
EBITDA	332,825,000	256,956,000	12,600,000	176,745,000	179,475,000	287,710,000
Return on Assets %	.37%	-1.30%	-4.20%	-1.87%	-2.02%	.98%
Return on Equity %	1.37%	-6.88%	-21.59%	-8.78%	-8.58%	4.06%
Debt to Equity			0.28	0.43	0.38	0.28

CONTACT INFORMATION:

Phone: 212 633-3300   Fax: 212 366-5186
Toll-Free:
Address: 122 5th Ave., New York, NY 10011 United States

SALARIES/BONUSES:

Top Exec. Salary: $1,200,000   Bonus: $
Second Exec. Salary: $1,064,080   Bonus: $

STOCK TICKER/OTHER:

Stock Ticker: BKS   Exchange: NYS
Employees: 28,000   Fiscal Year Ends: 04/30
Parent Company:

OTHER THOUGHTS:

Estimated Female Officers or Directors: 3

Hot Spot for Advancement for Women/Minorities: Y

Sales, profits and employees may be estimates. Financial information, benefits and other data can change quickly and may vary from those stated here.

Barney's New York Inc

www.barneys.com

NAIC Code: 452111

TYPES OF BUSINESS:

Department Stores
Apparel & Accessories
Home Furnishings
Cosmetics
Online Sales

BRANDS/DIVISIONS/AFFILIATES:

Perry Capital LLC
Barneys New York
Barneys CO-OP
Barneys Outlets
Barneys Greengrass
Completely Bare Hi-Tech Spa
Chantecaille Energy Spa
Fred's at Barneys New York

CONTACTS: Note: Officers with more than one job title may be intentionally listed here more than once.

Mark Lee, CEO
Vince Phelan, CFO
Abu Bakar, Sr. VP-IT
Dawn Brown, VP-Public Rel.

GROWTH PLANS/SPECIAL FEATURES:

Barneys New York, Inc., owned by Perry Capital LLC, is an upscale clothing retailer. It operates through three divisions, Barneys New York, with nine stores; Barneys CO-OP, 14 stores; and Barneys Outlets, approximately 25 stores. The Barneys New York stores are located in upscale markets and offer a variety of luxury services including a bridal/gift registry; a concierge service; Fred's at Barneys New York, a full service restaurant located in the Madison Avenue store; the Image Studio, which is a head to toe image consultation service; personal shopping; Studio Services, which is similar to the firm's personal shopping service but is catered to stylists, celebrities and costume designers; resident makeup artists; Completely Bare Hi-Tech Spa; Mrs. John L. Strong Stationary, which offers customized high end stationary; Barney Greengrass, a full service restaurant in the Beverly Hills store; a Barneys credit card, in which customers can earn points toward purchases; and the Chantecaille Energy Spa. Barneys New York sells clothing, jewelry, handbags, shoes, cosmetics, hair products, home products and accessories for dogs. Many items are available through the company's web site Barneys.com. Barneys CO-OP stores are located in fashion conscious areas on both coasts. The stores are centered on industrial-themed edgy, urban styles at slightly lower price points than Barneys New York stores. Barneys Outlet is the company's discount clearinghouse. Outlets are located primarily on the East and West coasts, with one location in Hawaii. In addition to the permanent outlet locations, four Barneys New York warehouse sales are held annually, one each spring and fall season in New York and Santa Monica.

FINANCIAL DATA: Note: Data for latest year may not have been available at press time.

In U.S. $	2015	2014	2013	2012	2011	2010
Revenue		865,000,000	848,000,000	800,000,000	750,000,000	710,000,000
R&D Expense						
Operating Income						
Operating Margin %						
SGA Expense						
Net Income						
Operating Cash Flow						
Capital Expenditure						
EBITDA						
Return on Assets %						
Return on Equity %						
Debt to Equity						

CONTACT INFORMATION:

Phone: 212-339-7300   Fax: 212-450-8489
Toll-Free: 800-926-5393
Address: 575 5th Ave., Fl. 11, New York, NY 10017 United States

STOCK TICKER/OTHER:

Stock Ticker: Private
Employees: 1,400   Exchange:
Parent Company: Perry Capital LLC   Fiscal Year Ends: 12/31

SALARIES/BONUSES:

Top Exec. Salary: $ Bonus: $
Second Exec. Salary: $ Bonus: $

OTHER THOUGHTS:

Estimated Female Officers or Directors: 1
Hot Spot for Advancement for Women/Minorities:

Bass Pro Shops Inc

www.basspro.com

NAIC Code: 451110

TYPES OF BUSINESS:
Sporting Goods, Retail
Sport Boats
Hunting & Fishing Equipment
Catalog & Online Sales
Outdoor Apparel
Resort Operations
Television Production

BRANDS/DIVISIONS/AFFILIATES:
Outdoor World
RedHead
American Rod & Gun
Big Cedar Lodge
Bass Pro Shop
Dogwood Canyon
Offshore Angler
White River Fly Shops

CONTACTS: Note: Officers with more than one job title may be intentionally listed here more than once.
James Hagale, CEO
James Hagale, COO
James Hagale, Pres.
Martin G. MacDonald, Dir.-Conservation
John L. Morris, Chmn.

GROWTH PLANS/SPECIAL FEATURES:

Bass Pro Shops, Inc. is a leader in sporting goods retail. The company markets its products through 87 retail stores in the U.S. and three in Canada, a mail-order catalog and its Internet sites. The firm is dedicated to providing outdoor recreational products, including specialty apparel, and also aims to inspire environmental conservation among its customers. The sporting goods superstores operate under the Bass Pro Shop and Outdoor World brand names. Products include boats and campers as well as fishing, hunting, camping, automobile and marine supplies. Many of these stores have a variety of unique features and attractions to draw more customers, including restaurants, snack bars, archery ranges, indoor fish tanks, waterfalls and video arcades. Aside from its stores, the company sells goods over the Internet and through catalogs/sales flyers under the Bass Pro Shops, RedHead, Offshore Angler and White River Fly Shops brand names. Its wholesale operations consist of Tracker Marine, a leader in sport boat manufacturing, and American Rod & Gun, one of the largest wholesale hunting and fishing distributors in the country. In addition to offering a variety of hunting and fishing trips and contests, Bass Pro runs the Wonders of Wildlife facility, a museum and conservation education center near its corporate headquarters, and Big Cedar Lodge, an outdoors-themed vacation spot in Missouri located near the company's own nature park, Dogwood Canyon. The company also produces a weekly television program on The Outdoor Channel and an international radio show.

FINANCIAL DATA: Note: Data for latest year may not have been available at press time.

In U.S. $	2015	2014	2013	2012	2011	2010
Revenue		4,350,000,000	4,200,000,000	4,150,000,000	4,000,000,000	3,830,000,000
R&D Expense						
Operating Income						
Operating Margin %						
SGA Expense						
Net Income						
Operating Cash Flow						
Capital Expenditure						
EBITDA						
Return on Assets %						
Return on Equity %						
Debt to Equity						

CONTACT INFORMATION:
Phone: 417-873-5000   Fax: 417-873-5060
Toll-Free: 800-227-7776
Address: 2500 E. Kearney St., Springfield, MO 65898 United States

STOCK TICKER/OTHER:
Stock Ticker: Private
Employees: 19,000
Parent Company:

Exchange:
Fiscal Year Ends: 12/31

SALARIES/BONUSES:
Top Exec. Salary: $ Bonus: $
Second Exec. Salary: $ Bonus: $

OTHER THOUGHTS:
Estimated Female Officers or Directors:
Hot Spot for Advancement for Women/Minorities:

Sales, profits and employees may be estimates. Financial information, benefits and other data can change quickly and may vary from those stated here.

Bath & Body Works LLC

NAIC Code: 446120

www.bathandbodyworks.com

TYPES OF BUSINESS:

Cosmetics, Retail
Candles
Body Care Products

BRANDS/DIVISIONS/AFFILIATES:

Bath & BodyWorks Outlets
CO Bigelow
L Brands Inc
Bath & Body Works
BathandBodyWorks.com
White Barn Candle Co

GROWTH PLANS/SPECIAL FEATURES:

Bath & Body Works, LLC (BBW) is a retailer selling person
care, beauty and home fragrance products marketed under th
Bath & Body Works, Bath & Body Works Outlets, C.O. Bigelo
and White Barn Candle Co. brand names in addition to thir
party brands. BBW is a wholly-owned subsidiary of L Brand
Inc. The company operates more than 1,600 stores in the U.
and Canada, located primarily in shopping malls, with th
average store size around 2,364 square feet. Bath & Boc
Works products are also available in 16 countries with 6
locations, and announced plans to open 40 BBW internation
stores in 2015. Its merchandise is sold through its retail stor
locations, catalogue and e-commerce site
BathAndBodyWorks.com. Merchandise includes body and ha
care products as well as personal care products, fragrance
accessories and aromatherapy products. The C.O. Bigelo
brand offers problem-solution formulas for skin and hair car
as well as shaving products for men. C.O. Bigelow products ar
available at all Bath & Body Works locations, and also at a stor
location in New York City. Some Bath & Body Works store
also offer massages and pedicures.

CONTACTS: Note: Officers with more than one job title may be intentionally listed here more than once.

Nicolas Coe, CEO
Andrew Meslow, COO
Camille McDonald, Pres., Brand Merch.
Leslie H. Wexner, Chmn.

FINANCIAL DATA: Note: Data for latest year may not have been available at press time.

In U.S. $	2015	2014	2013	2012	2011	2010
Revenue		3,349,600,000	3,117,900,000	2,902,000,000	2,674,000,000	2,515,000,000
R&D Expense						
Operating Income						
Operating Margin %						
SGA Expense						
Net Income		640,000,000	618,000,000	604,000,000	513,000,000	464,000,000
Operating Cash Flow						
Capital Expenditure						
EBITDA						
Return on Assets %						
Return on Equity %						
Debt to Equity						

CONTACT INFORMATION:

Phone: 614-856-6000   Fax: 614-856-6013
Toll-Free: 800-395-1001
Address: 7 Limited Pkwy E., Reynoldsburg, OH 43068 United States

STOCK TICKER/OTHER:

Stock Ticker: Subsidiary
Employees: 32,000
Parent Company: L BRANDS INC

Exchange:
Fiscal Year Ends: 02/02

SALARIES/BONUSES:

Top Exec. Salary: $ Bonus: $
Second Exec. Salary: $ Bonus: $

OTHER THOUGHTS:

Estimated Female Officers or Directors: 2
Hot Spot for Advancement for Women/Minorities:

BeautiControl Inc

www.beauticontrol.com

NAIC Code: 454390

TYPES OF BUSINESS:

Cosmetics & Beauty Supplies, Direct Selling
Jewelry

BRANDS/DIVISIONS/AFFILIATES:

Tupperware Brands Corporation
Spa ESCAPE
BeautiControl Research Institute
BeautiNet Plus
Skin Strategies

CONTACTS: *Note: Officers with more than one job title may be intentionally listed here more than once.*

Daisy S. Chin-Lor, Pres.
Timothy A. Kulhanek, CFO
Gary Jones, VP-Product Mktg. & Development
Amelia G. Spolec, CIO
James L. Montgomery, Sr. VP-Manufacturing Oper.

GROWTH PLANS/SPECIAL FEATURES:

BeautiControl, Inc., a subsidiary of Tupperware Brands Corporation, is one of the world's leading direct sellers of skin care and beauty products. The company manufactures a range of skin care products, cosmetics, bath and body care, toiletries, baby care, fragrances and jewelry. The firm sells its products directly through independent consultants who buy the products from BeautiControl as well as purchasing products online at the company web site, then selling them to consumers at home or in the workplace. The firm uses the party method of sales, designed to enable the purchaser to appreciate through demonstration the features and benefits of multiple products at once. Consultants provide free skin condition and color analysis through Spa ESCAPE sessions, which offer the services and products of a day spa using BeautiControl products. The company has over 140,000 independent skin care and image consultants who provide both product and image services to women across the U.S., Canada and Puerto Rico. BeautiControl also operates BeautiNet Plus, an online service that assists consultants in the management of their business; and The BeautiControl Research Institute, which focuses on research and development of new products. While most of the firm's consultants and target customers are women, BeautiControl does offer a line of products for men called Skin Strategies, which includes skin care and shaving supplies as well as five lines of cologne.

BeautiControl provides consultants with training, a BeautiControl sample product case and ongoing support including videos, advertising and marketing tools. Top consultants may earn recognition, vacations and diamond jewelry. The firm also offers a red Ford Mustang as part of its leadership program.

FINANCIAL DATA: *Note: Data for latest year may not have been available at press time.*

In U.S. $	2015	2014	2013	2012	2011	2010
Revenue						
R&D Expense						
Operating Income						
Operating Margin %						
SGA Expense						
Net Income						
Operating Cash Flow						
Capital Expenditure						
EBITDA						
Return on Assets %						
Return on Equity %						
Debt to Equity						

CONTACT INFORMATION:

Phone: 972-458-0601   Fax:
Toll-Free: 800-232-8841
Address: 2121 Midway Rd., Carrollton, TX 75006 United States

STOCK TICKER/OTHER:

Stock Ticker: Subsidiary
Employees:
Parent Company: TUPPERWARE BRANDS CORPORATION
Exchange:
Fiscal Year Ends: 12/31

SALARIES/BONUSES:

Top Exec. Salary: $ Bonus: $
Second Exec. Salary: $ Bonus: $

OTHER THOUGHTS:

Estimated Female Officers or Directors: 1
Hot Spot for Advancement for Women/Minorities:

Beauty Gems Holdings Co Ltd

NAIC Code: 339910

www.beautygems.com

TYPES OF BUSINESS:

Jewelry Manufacturing & Retailing
Jewelry Exporting

BRANDS/DIVISIONS/AFFILIATES:

Beauty Gems Group Co Ltd
Royal Diamond Polishing Works
Royal Diamond Cutting Co Ltd
Beauty Gems of U.S.A. Co Ltd
Beauty Diamond
Beauty Gems

CONTACTS: Note: Officers with more than one job title may be intentionally listed here more than once.

Suriyon Sriorathaikul, Managing Dir.
Surasit Sriorathaikul, Pres.
Pichait Palanugool, Vice Chmn.
Prayoon Sanguansin, Dir.-Advisory
Yupin Laiteerapong, VP
Sunee Sriorathaikul, Sr. Pres.

GROWTH PLANS/SPECIAL FEATURES:

Beauty Gems Holdings Co., Ltd., with operations dating back to 1964, is a Thailand-based jewelry maker and one of the leading exporters of gems and jewelry in Asia. Beauty Gems was formed to oversee the operations of a number of existing companies, including Beauty Gems Group Co., Ltd.; Royal Diamond Polishing Works; Royal Diamond Cutting Co., Ltd.; and Beauty Gems of U.S.A. Co., Ltd. The company and its affiliates specialize in diamond rings and other diamond jewelry, but also offer a full range of men's, women's, wedding and graduation gifts and birthstone jewelry in a variety of gemstones. These include sapphires, emeralds, pearls, mother of pearl, rubies, topazes, garnets, opals, turquoise, coral, aquamarine, citrine, amethysts, peridot, tourmaline, rhodolite, quartzes, moonstones, zircon, onyx and others. Jewelry is manufactured in gold, silver and platinum. Its workshops serve customers of various sizes, producing an assortment of products ranging from mass-market accessories manufactured in bulk to high-end, custom-designed jewelry pieces. Beauty Gems' manufacturing teams work under the guidance and supervision of master craftsmen and designers. In addition to its export and wholesale business, the firm also operates three retail outlets in Bangkok, under the Beauty Gems and Beauty Diamond brands, and sells its jewelry through in-store Beauty Diamond counters in Thai department stores. The company also works closely with the Bangkok Assay Office to ensure quality standards and remain in stride with technical advancements in the jewelry manufacturing field.

FINANCIAL DATA: Note: Data for latest year may not have been available at press time.

In U.S. $	2015	2014	2013	2012	2011	2010
Revenue						
R&D Expense						
Operating Income						
Operating Margin %						
SGA Expense						
Net Income						
Operating Cash Flow						
Capital Expenditure						
EBITDA						
Return on Assets %						
Return on Equity %						
Debt to Equity						

CONTACT INFORMATION:

Phone: 66-02234-604858   Fax: 66-02234-605960
Toll-Free:
Address: 10/18 N. Sathorn Rd., Bangrak, Bangkok, 10500 Thailand

STOCK TICKER/OTHER:

Stock Ticker: Private
Employees: 3,000
Parent Company:

Exchange:
Fiscal Year Ends:

SALARIES/BONUSES:

Top Exec. Salary: $ Bonus: $
Second Exec. Salary: $ Bonus: $

OTHER THOUGHTS:

Estimated Female Officers or Directors: 7
Hot Spot for Advancement for Women/Minorities: Y

Bebe Stores Inc

www.bebe.com

NAIC Code: 448120

TYPES OF BUSINESS:

Young Women's Apparel, Retail
Accessories
Shoes
Online Sales

BRANDS/DIVISIONS/AFFILIATES:

bebe
BEBE SPORT
Bebe.com

CONTACTS: Note: Officers with more than one job title may be intentionally listed here more than once.

Jim Wiggett, CEO
Liyuan Woo, CFO
Darren Horvath, Chief Accounting Officer
Brigitte Bogart, Executive VP, Divisional
Manny Mashouf, Founder
Gary Bosch, Vice President

GROWTH PLANS/SPECIAL FEATURES:

Bebe Stores, Inc. designs, develops and produces a line of contemporary women's apparel and accessories, marketed under the bebe and BEBE SPORT brand names. The company operates approximately 201 retail stores located in 34 states, Puerto Rico, Canada and online at www.bebe.com. These stores include 165 bebe stores and 36 bebe outlet stores. The bebe line of stores averages 4,000 square feet. Its stores are primarily located in regional shopping malls and freestanding street locations. In addition, the firm operates an online store at Bebe.com and has 89 international licensees in 20 countries. Bebe seeks to produce a distinctive fashion that fulfills the needs of the fashion conscious woman, be it every day wear to work, weekend or party attire. Offerings including suits, tops, skirts, dresses, pants, active wear, outerwear and handbags, shoes, jewelry and other accessories. Most of its merchandise is designed and developed in-house and manufactured in conjunction with third parties. Bebe maintains an eyewear license agreement with Altair Eyewear, Inc. to manufacture and distribute bebe-branded products to be sold at bebe stores and other retailers. The company has pursued growth through new store openings and the introduction of new product categories, including denim, leather, lingerie, swimwear and footwear. In 2014, the firm entered a licensing agreement with Zigi USA LLC to design, manufacture and distribute footwear to bebe stores, as well as to select major department stores and specialty retailers globally under the bebe trademarks. That same year, bebe discontinued its 2b operations.

Bebe offers its employees medical, dental and vision coverage; flexible spending accounts; life and disability insurance; a 401(k) plan; a stock purchase plan; an employee assistance program; and discounts on bebe merchandise.

FINANCIAL DATA: Note: Data for latest year may not have been available at press time.

In U.S. $	2015	2014	2013	2012	2011	2010
Revenue	427,997,000	425,117,000	484,686,000	530,831,000	493,274,000	508,968,000
R&D Expense						
Operating Income	-25,097,000	-59,669,000	-51,247,000	19,407,000	5,889,000	-11,105,000
Operating Margin %	-5.86%	-14.03%	-10.57%	3.65%	1.19%	-2.18%
SGA Expense	170,278,000	197,796,000	209,543,000	191,666,000	185,921,000	209,012,000
Net Income	-27,671,000	-73,382,000	-77,420,000	11,721,000	-1,779,000	-5,165,000
Operating Cash Flow	-25,040,000	-30,277,000	-8,370,000	32,740,000	21,860,000	37,556,000
Capital Expenditure	21,921,000	19,799,000	24,611,000	42,093,000	14,723,000	14,190,000
EBITDA	-7,250,000	-40,290,000	-29,687,000	39,686,000	27,961,000	15,213,000
Return on Assets %	-11.36%	-23.85%	-19.47%	2.62%	-.35%	-.91%
Return on Equity %	-16.43%	-33.00%	-24.90%	3.26%	-.49%	-1.24%
Debt to Equity						

CONTACT INFORMATION:

Phone: 415 715-3900   Fax:
Toll-Free: 877-232-3777
Address: 400 Valley Dr., Brisbane, CA 94005 United States

STOCK TICKER/OTHER:

Stock Ticker: BEBE
Employees: 3,254
Parent Company:

Exchange: NAS
Fiscal Year Ends: 07/31

SALARIES/BONUSES:

Top Exec. Salary: $500,000   Bonus: $
Second Exec. Salary: Bonus: $
$450,000

OTHER THOUGHTS:

Estimated Female Officers or Directors: 4
Hot Spot for Advancement for Women/Minorities: Y

Sales, profits and employees may be estimates. Financial information, benefits and other data can change quickly and may vary from those stated here.

Bed Bath & Beyond Inc

NAIC Code: 442299

www.bedbathandbeyond.com

TYPES OF BUSINESS:

Linens & Housewares, Retail
Small Appliances
Home Accessories
Health & Beauty Care
Baby & Toddler Merchandise

BRANDS/DIVISIONS/AFFILIATES:

Bed Bath & Beyond
Harmon
Christmas Tree Shops and That!
buybuy BABY Inc
World Market
Cost Plus Inc
Harmon Face Values
Harmon Stores Inc

CONTACTS: Note: Officers with more than one job title may be intentionally listed here more than once.

Steven Temares, CEO
Susan Lattmann, CFO
Warren Eisenberg, Co-Chairman
Leonard Feinstein, Co-Chairman
Eugene Castagna, COO
Arthur Stark, Other Executive Officer
Matthew Fiorilli, Senior VP, Divisional

GROWTH PLANS/SPECIAL FEATURES:

Bed Bath & Beyond, Inc. (BBB) is one of the nation's large
operators of domestic superstores, with approximately 1,51
stores in 50 states as well as Washington D.C., Canada an
Puerto Rico. BBB operates five retail entities: Bed Bath
Beyond; Harmon and Harmon Face Values; buybuy BABY
Christmas Tree Shops and That!; and World Market or Cos
Plus World Market. Bed Bath & Beyond stores offer a full lin
of domestic merchandise and home furnishings. The domesti
merchandise line includes items such as bed linens, bat
accessories and kitchen tiles, while its home furnishings lin
includes a variety of cookware, dinnerware and glassware
Harmon or Harmon Face Values sells beauty care products i
50 stores. Buybuy BABY is a retailer of infant and toddle
merchandise with 96 stores in 32 states. Christmas Tree Shop
and That! stores offer gifts, household items and furnishing
through 78 locations in 21 states. World Market or Cost Plu
World Market is a retailer selling a wide range of home
decorating items, furniture, holiday and other seasonal item
as well as specialty food and beverages with 270 stores in 3
states. The company also operates Linen Holdings, a provide
of a variety of textile products, amenities and other goods t
institutional customers in the hospitality, cruise line, foo
service, healthcare and other industries. Additionally, the firm
(through a joint venture) operates five stores in Mexico unde
the Bed Bath & Beyond name. BBB relies on paid advertising
and uses circulars and mailing pieces as its primary marketing
vehicles. In addition, the company has distribution facilities
which ship merchandise to stores or customers, totaling
approximately 6.0 million square feet. Moreover, the firm offers
a wide variety of products through its network of web sites
including www.buybuybaby.com, www.harmondiscount.com
www.worldmarket.com and www.bedbathandbeyond.com.

FINANCIAL DATA: Note: Data for latest year may not have been available at press time.

In U.S. $	2015	2014	2013	2012	2011	2010
Revenue	11,881,180,000	11,503,960,000	10,914,580,000	9,499,890,000	8,758,503,000	7,828,793,000
R&D Expense						
Operating Income	1,554,293,000	1,614,587,000	1,638,218,000	1,568,369,000	1,288,458,000	980,687,000
Operating Margin %	13.08%	14.03%	15.00%	16.50%	14.71%	12.52%
SGA Expense	3,065,486,000	2,950,995,000	2,750,537,000	2,362,564,000	2,334,471,000	2,227,432,000
Net Income	957,474,000	1,022,290,000	1,037,788,000	989,537,000	791,333,000	600,033,000
Operating Cash Flow	1,185,848,000	1,383,186,000	1,192,990,000	1,225,284,000	987,407,000	905,407,000
Capital Expenditure	330,637,000	317,180,000	354,682,000	243,374,000	183,474,000	153,680,000
EBITDA	1,793,486,000	1,833,396,000	1,832,946,000	1,752,242,000	1,472,278,000	1,164,919,000
Return on Assets %	14.60%	16.18%	17.29%	17.40%	14.65%	12.73%
Return on Equity %	28.64%	25.49%	25.93%	25.19%	20.86%	18.03%
Debt to Equity	0.54					

CONTACT INFORMATION:

Phone: 908 688-0888   Fax: 908 810-8813
Toll-Free: 800-462-3966
Address: 650 Liberty Ave., Union, NJ 07083 United States

SALARIES/BONUSES:

Top Exec. Salary: Bonus: $
$3,967,500
Second Exec. Salary: Bonus: $
$1,670,769

STOCK TICKER/OTHER:

Stock Ticker: BBBY
Employees: 60,000
Parent Company:

Exchange: NAS
Fiscal Year Ends: 02/28

OTHER THOUGHTS:

Estimated Female Officers or Directors: 1

Hot Spot for Advancement for Women/Minorities:

Belk Inc

NAIC Code: 452111

TYPES OF BUSINESS:

Department Stores
Women's Accessories & Cosmetics
Jewelry

BRANDS/DIVISIONS/AFFILIATES:

Belk
Carmen! Carmen! Prestige Salon and Spa at Belk
Richard Joseph Studio Salon/Spa at Belk
Belk Salon and Spa
Spa at Belk

CONTACTS: Note: Officers with more than one job title may be intentionally listed here more than once.

Thomas Belk, CEO
Adam Orvos, CFO
Rodney Samples, Chief Accounting Officer
John Belk, COO
Ralph Pitts, Executive VP
David Zant, Other Executive Officer

GROWTH PLANS/SPECIAL FEATURES:

Belk, Inc. is one of the largest department store businesses in the U.S., with 297 stores in 16 states, primarily in the southern U.S. The company has operated department stores since 1888. Belk stores offer national brands of apparel, shoes and accessories for men, women and children as well as cosmetics, home furnishings, house-wares, gifts and other types of merchandise. Its aim is to provide customers with the convenience of one stop shopping, all while maintaining a uniquely southern style and sensibility. Larger Belk stores include amenities such as hair salons, spas, restaurants and optical centers. The company operates 18 hair styling salons in various locations which offer spa services. The spas offer massage therapy, full skincare, nail and pedicure services and other specialized body treatments. Eight of the salons and spas operate under the name Carmen! Carmen! Prestige Salon and Spa at Belk, two under the name Richard Joseph Studio Salon/Spa at Belk and the remaining operating under the name Belk Salon and Spa. The firm's store range in size from 40,000 to 300,000 square feet, with an average size of approximately 92,000 square feet. Belk stores are typically anchor tenants in regional malls and shopping centers catering to medium and smaller markets.

The firm offers employees life, disability, auto, home, legal, medical, dental and vision insurance; an employee assistance program; merchandise discounts; flexible spending accounts; and a 401(k).

FINANCIAL DATA: Note: Data for latest year may not have been available at press time.

In U.S. $	2015	2014	2013	2012	2011	2010
Revenue	4,109,561,000	4,038,118,000	3,956,866,000	3,699,592,000	3,513,275,000	3,346,252,000
R&D Expense						
Operating Income	271,360,000	288,327,000	339,937,000	300,910,000	245,981,000	147,441,000
Operating Margin %	6.60%	7.14%	8.59%	8.13%	7.00%	4.40%
SGA Expense	1,064,348,000	1,023,266,000	985,225,000	938,008,000	914,078,000	888,982,000
Net Income	146,062,000	158,533,000	188,370,000	183,148,000	127,628,000	67,136,000
Operating Cash Flow	363,937,000	367,486,000	300,057,000	251,932,000	189,241,000	387,395,000
Capital Expenditure	231,324,000	224,228,000	182,773,000	143,844,000	82,409,000	42,326,000
EBITDA	426,406,000	425,550,000	462,607,000	423,077,000	386,789,000	306,899,000
Return on Assets %	5.59%	6.28%	7.54%	7.46%	5.13%	2.62%
Return on Equity %	10.73%	12.09%	15.07%	15.31%	11.34%	6.31%
Debt to Equity	0.23	0.28	0.30	0.33	0.46	0.62

CONTACT INFORMATION:

Phone: 704 357-1000   Fax: 704 357-1876
Toll-Free:
Address: 2801 W. Tyvola Rd., Charlotte, NC 28217 United States

SALARIES/BONUSES:

Top Exec. Salary: Bonus: $
$1,071,225
Second Exec. Salary: Bonus: $
$884,617

STOCK TICKER/OTHER:

Stock Ticker: BLKIB
Employees: 24,000
Parent Company:

Exchange: OTC
Fiscal Year Ends: 01/31

OTHER THOUGHTS:

Estimated Female Officers or Directors: 1

Hot Spot for Advancement for Women/Minorities: Y

Benetton Group SPA

NAIC Code: 424300

TYPES OF BUSINESS:

Apparel and Clothing Brands, Designers, Importers and Distributors
Retail Stores
Casual Clothing-Men's, Women's & Children's
Apparel Manufacturing
Arts Research Center
Magazine Publishing

BRANDS/DIVISIONS/AFFILIATES:

United Colors of Benetton
Sisley
Benetton International SA
COLORS
Fabrica
Undercolors of Benetton
Bencom Srl
Benetton USA Corp

CONTACTS: Note: Officers with more than one job title may be intentionally listed here more than once.

Biagio Chiarolanza, CEO
Lorenzo Zago, Head-Admin.

GROWTH PLANS/SPECIAL FEATURES:

Benetton Group SPA is a worldwide apparel retailer and manufacturer based in Italy. It manufactures over 150 million garments yearly at 21 factories and sells these in over 5,000 retail stores in 120 countries. Traditional western economies U.S., U.K., Europe, Australia and Japan, account for the majority of the company's sales, with developing and fast growth countries located in Asia, South America and Africa, accounting for the rest of the company's sales. The company markets apparel for men, women and children under various brands: United Colors of Benetton, Undercolors of Benetton, Sisley and Playlife. Benetton's stores are characterized by their large size and prominent positions in historic and commercial centers. The company recently introduced the megastore concept to its stores. Benetton also runs a series of communications projects, including Fabrica, an arts research center; COLORS magazine, which features stories reflecting a global consciousness; and support for sports, cinema, music and other media. The company operates numerous subsidiaries, including Bencom Srl, Benind SpA, Benetton International SA, Benetton Holding International NV SA and Benetton USA Corp. The Benetton Group plans to split into three units, separating its clothing, retailing and manufacturing businesses by 2015.

FINANCIAL DATA: Note: Data for latest year may not have been available at press time.

In U.S. $	2015	2014	2013	2012	2011	2010
Revenue		2,005,000,000	2,015,000,000	2,297,026,459	2,695,800,000	2,899,290,000
R&D Expense						
Operating Income						
Operating Margin %						
SGA Expense						
Net Income						
Operating Cash Flow						
Capital Expenditure						
EBITDA						
Return on Assets %						
Return on Equity %						
Debt to Equity						

CONTACT INFORMATION:

Phone: 39-0422-519036   Fax: 39-0422-519930
Toll-Free:
Address: Villa Minelli, Via Villa Minelli, 1, Ponzano, 31050 Italy

STOCK TICKER/OTHER:

Stock Ticker: Subsidiary
Employees: 8,000   Exchange:
Parent Company: Edizione S.r.L   Fiscal Year Ends: 12/31

SALARIES/BONUSES:

Top Exec. Salary: $ Bonus: $
Second Exec. Salary: $ Bonus: $

OTHER THOUGHTS:

Estimated Female Officers or Directors: 1
Hot Spot for Advancement for Women/Minorities:

Best Buy Co Inc

www.bestbuy.com

NAIC Code: 443142

TYPES OF BUSINESS:

Consumer Electronics Stores
Retail Music & Video Sales
Personal Computers
Office Supplies
Cell Phones and Accessories
Appliances
Cameras
Consumer Electronics Installation & Service

BRANDS/DIVISIONS/AFFILIATES:

Geek Squad
Best Buy Mobile
Best Buy Express
Magnolia Audio Video
Pacific Sales
Best Buy
Best Buy Canada

CONTACTS: Note: Officers with more than one job title may be intentionally listed here more than once.

Hubert Joly, CEO
Sharon Mccollam, CFO
Mathew Watson, Chief Accounting Officer
Greg Revelle, Chief Marketing Officer
Keith Nelsen, General Counsel
Matt Furman, Other Executive Officer
R. Mohan, Other Executive Officer
Shari Ballard, Other Executive Officer
Mary Kelley, President, Divisional

GROWTH PLANS/SPECIAL FEATURES:

Best Buy Co., Inc. is a leading retailer of name-brand consumer electronics, appliances and home office and entertainment products and services. The company conducts business in both the domestic and international markets. The domestic market includes all of the firm's U.S. businesses, operating under such brands as Best Buy; Best Buy Mobile; Geek Squad, which provides computer repair and installation services; Magnolia Audio Video; and Pacific Sales. The international segment, which is comprised of the firm's businesses in Canada and Mexico, operates under brand names such as Cell Shop, Best Buy, Best Buy Mobile and Geek Squad. The company's products include home office equipment, cameras, computer and audio/video equipment, computer upgrades and car audio and security system installation. The firm operates 1050 Best Buy stores in the U.S., 136 in Canada and 18 in Mexico; 367 U.S. Best Buy mobile stand-alone stores; 56 international Best Buy Mobile stores; four Magnolia Audio Video Stores; 30 Pacific Sales stores; and two Best Buy Express stores in Mexico. In February 2014, the company sold its mindSHIFT Technologies subsidiary as well as its Best Buy Europe subsidiary. In February 2015, the firm sold its Jiangsu Five Star Appliance Co Ltd company. That March, subsidiary Best Buy Canada announced it was consolidating its Future Shop chain by closing 66 Future Shop locations and transitioning an additional 65 Future Shop stores to the Best Buy Brand.

Employee benefits include medical, dental, vision, life, disability, health care and dependent care spending accounts. Wealth benefits include 401(k) accounts, an employee stock purchase plan and bonus/incentive programs.

FINANCIAL DATA: Note: Data for latest year may not have been available at press time.

In U.S. $	2015	2014	2013	2012	2011	2010
Revenue	40,339,000,000	42,410,000,000	45,085,000,000	50,705,000,000	50,272,000,000	49,694,000,000
R&D Expense						
Operating Income	1,450,000,000	1,140,000,000	-125,000,000	1,085,000,000	2,114,000,000	2,235,000,000
Operating Margin %	3.59%	2.68%		2.13%	4.20%	4.49%
SGA Expense	7,592,000,000	8,391,000,000	9,502,000,000	10,242,000,000	10,325,000,000	9,873,000,000
Net Income	1,233,000,000	532,000,000	-441,000,000	-1,231,000,000	1,277,000,000	1,317,000,000
Operating Cash Flow	1,935,000,000	1,094,000,000	1,454,000,000	3,293,000,000	1,190,000,000	2,206,000,000
Capital Expenditure	561,000,000	547,000,000	705,000,000	766,000,000	744,000,000	615,000,000
EBITDA	2,133,000,000	1,903,000,000	758,000,000	2,122,000,000	3,143,000,000	3,215,000,000
Return on Assets %	8.42%	3.79%		-7.27%	7.06%	7.71%
Return on Equity %	27.45%	13.34%		-23.79%	19.76%	24.02%
Debt to Equity	0.31	0.40		0.44	0.10	0.17

CONTACT INFORMATION:

Phone: 612 291-1000   Fax: 612 292-4001
Toll-Free:
Address: 7601 Penn Ave. S., Richfield, MN 55423 United States

STOCK TICKER/OTHER:

Stock Ticker: BBY
Employees: 125,000
Parent Company:

Exchange: NYS
Fiscal Year Ends: 02/28

SALARIES/BONUSES:

Top Exec. Salary: $1,175,000   Bonus: $
Second Exec. Salary: $925,000   Bonus: $

OTHER THOUGHTS:

Estimated Female Officers or Directors: 5

Hot Spot for Advancement for Women/Minorities: Y

Bestway Inc

NAIC Code: 532299

TYPES OF BUSINESS:

Rent-to-Own Stores
Furniture Rental
Electronics, Audio & Appliances Rental
Household Goods Rental
Lease & Purchase Plans

BRANDS/DIVISIONS/AFFILIATES:

Bestway Rent-To-Own
Bestway Rental Inc

CONTACTS: Note: Officers with more than one job title may be intentionally listed here more than once.

David A. Kraemer, CEO
David A. Kraemer, Pres.
Beth A. Durrett, CFO
Beth A. Durrett, Corp. Sec.

GROWTH PLANS/SPECIAL FEATURES:

Bestway, Inc. is a rent-to-own firm that owns and operates 8 rental-purchase stores in Alabama, Arkansas, Indian Kentucky, Mississippi, North Carolina, South Carolina, Texa and Tennessee. The Bestway Rent-To-Own stores a operated through the company's wholly-owned subsidiar Bestway Rental, Inc. The firm's rental program allow customers to rent products under a flexible rental-purchas agreement. The rental agreements typically have a 12-3 month term with weekly or monthly payment option Throughout the rental period, customers may elect to purchas the product rather than continuing to rent. Bestway offers wide variety of brands, styles and models of television set audio equipment, computers and DVD players. In addition, offers major home appliances such as washers, dryer refrigerators and freezers as well as furniture. It sells product under a full-service rental agreement, which requires th customer to pay the charge for each rental period in advance but requires no additional advance payments or securit deposits. The company also offers lease agreements tha include purchase options for customers. Bestway markets it products and services by selecting prominent store locations i retail shopping areas on main traffic thoroughfares, an advertises mainly through direct mail channels. The firm primarily serves customers in the low to middle income secto The firm offers brand name products by Ashley, Kenmore, LG Samsung, Dell and Compaq.

The company offers its employees medical, vision, life, long term disability and dental insurance; a 401(k) plan; a employee purchase program; and a comprehensive trainin program.

FINANCIAL DATA: Note: Data for latest year may not have been available at press time.

In U.S. $	2015	2014	2013	2012	2011	2010
Revenue						
R&D Expense						
Operating Income						
Operating Margin %						
SGA Expense						
Net Income						
Operating Cash Flow						
Capital Expenditure						
EBITDA						
Return on Assets %						
Return on Equity %						
Debt to Equity						

CONTACT INFORMATION:

Phone: 214-630-6655   Fax: 214-630-8404
Toll-Free: 800-530-1107
Address: 12400 Coit Rd, Ste. 950, Dallas, TX 75251 United States

SALARIES/BONUSES:

Top Exec. Salary: $ Bonus: $
Second Exec. Salary: $ Bonus: $

STOCK TICKER/OTHER:

Stock Ticker: Private
Employees: Exchange:
Parent Company: Fiscal Year Ends: 07/31

OTHER THOUGHTS:

Estimated Female Officers or Directors: 1
Hot Spot for Advancement for Women/Minorities:

BHS Limited

www.bhs.co.uk

NAIC Code: 452111

TYPES OF BUSINESS:

Department Stores
Women's Apparel
Men's Apparel
Children's Apparel
Home Furnishings
Credit Cards

BRANDS/DIVISIONS/AFFILIATES:

BHS
BHS Kids
Tammy
British Home Stores
Retail Acquisitions Ltd
BHS.co.uk

CONTACTS: *Note: Officers with more than one job title may be intentionally listed here more than once.*

Darren Topp, interim CEO
Ian Grabiner, CEO
Nigel P. Hall, Dir.-Finance, Arcadia

GROWTH PLANS/SPECIAL FEATURES:

BHS Limited, formerly British Home Stores, is a retailer operating 171 stores across the U.K. The company's products include items for women, men and children; wedding items; gifts; and home decor and furniture. Women's apparel and accessories include eveningwear, coats and jackets, trousers and jeans, swimwear and beachwear, shoes and boots, lingerie and sleepwear, knitwear, workwear and bags and accessories. Menswear includes casual and formal tops, t-shirts, trousers, suits, coats and jackets, sleepwear, footwear, socks and accessories. Items for children include a variety of casual and formal apparel, sleepwear, partywear and schoolwear under the BHS Kids brand. The firm's Tammy brand offers products for teen girls including accessories, gifts, jeans, dresses, jackets and coats, prom dresses, knitwear, leggings, shoes, skirts, shorts and pants. The wedding collection includes wedding dresses by popular designers, apparel for the entire wedding party, shoes, jewelry, sleepwear, eveningwear and personalized stationery. Gifts include wine, beer and spirits; children's toys; DVDs; Christmas cards and wrapping paper; and food items such as gourmet chocolates. BHS' home furnishing merchandise includes items for the entire house such as bedding, towels and bathmats, dining and cookware, mirrors, rugs, cushions, storage products, curtains, luggage, bathroom accessories, lighting and furniture. The firm has stores and boutiques across the U.K. and operations in Europe, Russia and the Middle East as well as an e-commerce site at BHS.co.uk. The company offers financial services via the BHS-branded MasterCard. In March 2015, the Arcadia Group sold BHS Limited to the consortium Retail Acquisitions Ltd. for the nominal price of $1.53, or one pound sterling.

FINANCIAL DATA: *Note: Data for latest year may not have been available at press time.*

In U.S. $	2015	2014	2013	2012	2011	2010
Revenue						
R&D Expense						
Operating Income						
Operating Margin %						
SGA Expense						
Net Income						
Operating Cash Flow						
Capital Expenditure						
EBITDA						
Return on Assets %						
Return on Equity %						
Debt to Equity						

CONTACT INFORMATION:

Phone: 44-845-196-0000   Fax: 44-207-723-1115
Toll-Free:
Address: 129-137 Marylebone Rd., London, NW15QD United Kingdom

STOCK TICKER/OTHER:

Stock Ticker: Subsidiary   Exchange:
Employees: Fiscal Year Ends:
Parent Company: Retail Acquisitions Ltd.

SALARIES/BONUSES:

Top Exec. Salary: $ Bonus: $
Second Exec. Salary: $ Bonus: $

OTHER THOUGHTS:

Estimated Female Officers or Directors: 3
Hot Spot for Advancement for Women/Minorities: Y

Big 5 Sporting Goods Corporation

NAIC Code: 451110

www.big5sportinggoods.com

TYPES OF BUSINESS:

Sporting Goods Stores

BRANDS/DIVISIONS/AFFILIATES:

Court Casuals
Golden Bear
Big 5 Services Corp
Pacifica
Rugged Exposure
Triple Nickel
Harsh

CONTACTS: Note: Officers with more than one job title may be intentionally listed here more than once.

Steven Miller, CEO
Barry Emerson, CFO
Richard Johnson, Executive VP
Boyd Clark, Senior VP, Divisional
Jeffrey Fraley, Senior VP, Divisional
Shane Starr, Senior VP, Divisional
Gary Meade, Senior VP

GROWTH PLANS/SPECIAL FEATURES:

Big 5 Sporting Goods Corporation is one of the leading sporting goods retailers in the U.S., with 439 locations in 12 states. The firm's in-store products include athletic shoes; apparel and accessories for team sports; fitness equipment; camping, hunting and fishing gear; tennis and golf equipment; winter sports gear; and in-line skates. Annually, its soft goods, such as apparel and footwear, generate 46.8% of total sales, while hard goods, including sporting equipment, generate 53.2%. Big 5 sells merchandise under company-owned trademark brands, such as Court Casuals, Golden Bear, Harsh, Pacifica, Rugged Exposure and Triple Nickel, as well as national third-party brands, such as adidas, Coleman, Easton, New Balance, Nike, Reebok, Spalding, Under Armour and Wilson. Stores average 11,000 square feet, which is significantly smaller than the average superstore format, allowing stores to cater to smaller markets. Store locations are normally freestanding or part of a multi-store shopping center and are chosen in collaboration with local real estate companies, mostly in markets close to those in which the company already has a presence. Big 5 owns a 953,000-square-foot distribution center in Riverside, California from which it operates all of its distribution activities. Through wholly-owned subsidiary Big 5 Services Corp., the firm manages its gift card operations.

FINANCIAL DATA: Note: Data for latest year may not have been available at press time.

In U.S. $	2015	2014	2013	2012	2011	2010
Revenue		977,860,000	993,323,000	940,490,000	902,134,000	896,813,000
R&D Expense						
Operating Income		25,175,000	47,427,000	25,972,000	19,167,000	34,224,000
Operating Margin %		2.57%	4.77%	2.76%	2.12%	3.81%
SGA Expense		288,274,000	281,313,000	276,797,000	272,436,000	263,488,000
Net Income		14,876,000	27,946,000	14,915,000	11,673,000	20,562,000
Operating Cash Flow		28,535,000	26,287,000	39,604,000	2,218,000	29,867,000
Capital Expenditure		22,565,000	22,035,000	12,901,000	12,990,000	15,628,000
EBITDA		46,680,000	67,619,000	44,867,000	37,711,000	52,851,000
Return on Assets %		3.31%	6.58%	3.72%	2.96%	5.42%
Return on Equity %		7.71%	15.73%	9.29%	7.59%	14.55%
Debt to Equity		0.34	0.23	0.30	0.42	0.33

CONTACT INFORMATION:

Phone: 310 536-0611   Fax:
Toll-Free: 800-898-2994
Address: 2525 E. El Segundo Blvd., El Segundo, CA 90245 United States

STOCK TICKER/OTHER:

Stock Ticker: BGFV   Exchange: NAS
Employees: 9,000   Fiscal Year Ends: 01/31
Parent Company:

SALARIES/BONUSES:

Top Exec. Salary: $507,692   Bonus: $200,000
Second Exec. Salary: Bonus: $120,000
$351,538

OTHER THOUGHTS:

Estimated Female Officers or Directors: 2
Hot Spot for Advancement for Women/Minorities:

Big Lots Inc

www.biglots.com

NAIC Code: 452112

TYPES OF BUSINESS:

Discount Stores, Closeout
Discounted Brand-Name Products
Wholesale Operations
Discount Furniture

BRANDS/DIVISIONS/AFFILIATES:

CONTACTS: Note: Officers with more than one job title may be intentionally listed here more than once.

David Campisi, CEO
Timothy Johnson, CFO
Philip Mallott, Chairman of the Board
Lisa Bachmann, COO
Michael Schlonsky, Executive VP, Divisional
Ronald Robins, General Counsel
Andrew Stein, Other Executive Officer

GROWTH PLANS/SPECIAL FEATURES:

Big Lots, Inc. is one of the nation's largest broad line closeout retailers. When a manufacturer has excess products due to overruns, packaging changes or discontinued items, Big Lots buys these items at a discount directly from that manufacturer. This allows the firm to provide name brand products at prices below traditional discount retailers. Big Lots supplements its closeout merchandise with everyday items sourced directly from domestic and international suppliers. The company purchases approximately 24% of its merchandise from overseas, with 20% coming from vendors within China. The company sells its merchandise under seven product categories: furniture, consumables, home, food, seasonal, electronics & others and hardlines & toys. Furniture products include upholstery, mattresses, ready-to-assemble products and case goods such as bedroom, dining room and living room furniture. Consumables include the food, health and beauty, plastics, papers, chemical and pet departments. The home category includes domestics, stationery and home decor products. The food category includes the food and specialty food departments. The seasonal category includes lawn and garden, Christmas, summer and other holiday goods. The electronics & other category includes the electronics, jewelry, infant accessories, and apparel departments as well as the results of certain large closeout deals. The Hardlines & toys category includes the toys, appliances, tools, paint and home maintenance departments. Big Lots operates 1,460 stores in 48 states, averaging approximately 30,900 square feet in size.

Big Lots offers associates medical, dental and vision insurance; life insurance; 401(k) with company match; disability coverage; paid sick days; bonus programs; educational assistance; and relocation assistance.

FINANCIAL DATA: Note: Data for latest year may not have been available at press time.

In U.S. $	2015	2014	2013	2012	2011	2010
Revenue	5,177,078,000	5,301,912,000	5,400,119,000	5,202,269,000	4,952,244,000	4,726,772,000
R&D Expense						
Operating Income	224,488,000	190,439,000	298,454,000	345,595,000	357,345,000	325,010,000
Operating Margin %	4.33%	3.59%	5.52%	6.64%	7.21%	6.87%
SGA Expense	1,699,764,000	1,759,745,000	1,712,910,000	1,634,532,000	1,576,500,000	1,532,356,000
Net Income	114,276,000	125,295,000	177,121,000	207,064,000	222,524,000	200,369,000
Operating Cash Flow	318,562,000	198,334,000	281,133,000	318,471,000	315,257,000	392,026,000
Capital Expenditure	93,460,000	104,786,000	131,273,000	131,293,000	107,563,000	78,708,000
EBITDA	344,190,000	304,348,000	404,791,000	435,702,000	436,563,000	400,089,000
Return on Assets %	6.77%	7.17%	10.43%	12.69%	13.53%	12.91%
Return on Equity %	13.51%	15.09%	22.40%	23.39%	22.84%	22.56%
Debt to Equity	0.07	0.08	0.22	0.08		

CONTACT INFORMATION:

Phone: 614 278-6800   Fax: 614 278-6666
Toll-Free:
Address: 300 Phillipi Rd., Columbus, OH 43228 United States

STOCK TICKER/OTHER:

Stock Ticker: BIG
Employees: 36,100
Parent Company:

Exchange: NYS
Fiscal Year Ends: 01/31

SALARIES/BONUSES:

Top Exec. Salary: $942,308   Bonus: $
Second Exec. Salary: $646,154   Bonus: $

OTHER THOUGHTS:

Estimated Female Officers or Directors: 1
Hot Spot for Advancement for Women/Minorities: Y

Billabong International Ltd

www.billabongbiz.com

NAIC Code: 424300

TYPES OF BUSINESS:

Apparel and Clothing Brands, Designers, Importers and Distributors
Surfboards, Skateboards & Paraphernalia
Retail Sales
Surf wear Apparel
Surfing Accessories

BRANDS/DIVISIONS/AFFILIATES:

Honolua Surf Company
Element
Von Zipper
RVCA
Sector 9
Kustom
Tigerlilly
Xcel

CONTACTS: *Note: Officers with more than one job title may be intentionally listed here more than once.*

Neil Fiske, CEO
Peter Myers, CFO
Maria Manning, Corp. Sec.
Ed Leasure, Pres., Americas
Shannan North, Gen. Mgr.-Asia Pacific
Ian Pollard, Chmn.
Jean-Louis Rodrigues, Gen. Mgr.-Europe

GROWTH PLANS/SPECIAL FEATURES:

Billabong International, Ltd. is a leading marketer, distributor
wholesaler and retailer of surfing, skateboarding and
snowboarding apparel, accessories, eyewear and wetsuits. I
markets products under the Billabong, Element, Von Zipper
Honolua Surf Company, Kustom, Palmers Surf, Xcel, Tigerlily
Sector 9, Tigerlilly and RVCA brand names. Billabong began in
1973 when two surfing devotees, Gordon and Rena Merchant
began producing surfing supplies that were formerly
completely unavailable to surfers, including triple-stitched
board shorts. The firm began exporting products internationally
in the 1980s, and now retails its products in more than 100
countries and approximately 10,000 stores across the globe
These venues include the company's wholly-owned stores in
Australia, North America, Europe, Japan, New Zealand, South
Africa and Brazil, which account for the majority of revenues
as well as licensed surf and sports dealers worldwide. Products
include a wide variety of board shorts, basic tees, slim fit tees
polos, wovens, fleece, walkshorts, pants, surf tees, wetsuits
rashvests, eyewear, bags and accessories. Billabong is
committed to sponsoring junior athlete development, and also
sponsors professional contests held on the Gold Coast o
Australia and the Jeffreys Bay in South Africa. In 2014, the firm
sold its 51% stake in SurfStich.com as well as its 100%
ownership of Swell.com.

FINANCIAL DATA: *Note: Data for latest year may not have been available at press time.*

In U.S. $	2015	2014	2013	2012	2011	2010
Revenue	768,142,800	818,808,800	979,661,800	1,051,704,000	1,229,683,000	1,083,057,000
R&D Expense						
Operating Income	-573,286	-49,601,260	-599,383,600	-375,034,700	113,431,700	158,210,000
Operating Margin %	-.07%	-6.05%	-61.18%	-35.65%	9.22%	14.60%
SGA Expense	456,704,100	489,275,500	358,603,600	387,162,800	644,026,100	508,445,900
Net Income	3,030,746	-170,679,900	-627,722,900	-201,306,500	87,007,220	106,615,100
Operating Cash Flow	-10,680,640	-55,954,860	8,716,132	57,612,650	17,772,580	136,746,500
Capital Expenditure	20,198,640	18,160,370	29,310,600	40,556,490	38,245,820	41,230,560
EBITDA	31,539,470	-12,786,830	-554,463,600	-319,226,600	150,674,800	192,629,100
Return on Assets %	.53%	-26.48%	-55.58%	-12.25%	5.14%	6.58%
Return on Equity %	1.50%	-86.26%	-132.19%	-24.81%	9.88%	12.19%
Debt to Equity	0.92	0.78	0.02	0.24	0.50	0.33

CONTACT INFORMATION:

Phone: 61 755899899   Fax: 61 755899654
Toll-Free:
Address: 1 Billabong Pl., Burleigh Heads, QLD 4220 Australia

SALARIES/BONUSES:

Top Exec. Salary: $ Bonus: $
Second Exec. Salary: $ Bonus: $

STOCK TICKER/OTHER:

Stock Ticker: BLLAF   Exchange: PINX
Employees: Fiscal Year Ends: 06/30
Parent Company:

OTHER THOUGHTS:

Estimated Female Officers or Directors: 3
Hot Spot for Advancement for Women/Minorities: Y

BIM Birlesik Magazalar AS

www.bim.com.tr

NAIC Code: 452111

TYPES OF BUSINESS:

Discount Department Stores

GROWTH PLANS/SPECIAL FEATURES:

BIM Birlesik Magazalar AS (BIM) operates a discount store chain in Turkey. Beginning with 21 stores in 1995, it currently maintains 4,502 store locations, and a distribution network of over 35 regional warehouses. BIM stores specialize in grocery and food products, including meat, breakfast and dairy items, beverages, bakery selections, legumes, snacks and sweets, fruits and vegetables, frozen food items and household cleaning supplies. Additionally, the stores maintain a limited selection of household merchandise such as electronics, toys, cookware, small appliances and other products on a weekly turnover basis. The majority of BIM's stock is private label merchandise produced exclusively for the company. It also operates BIM Stores SARL, a Moroccan-based subsidiary with 223 stores located in Morocco. The company also operates 81 stores in Egypt, with plans to open 54 more in the near future.

BRANDS/DIVISIONS/AFFILIATES:

BIM Stores SARL

CONTACTS:
Note: Officers with more than one job title may be intentionally listed here more than once.

Josef Wilhelmus Johannes Simons, Gen. Mgr.
Galip Aykac, COO
Haluk Dortluoglu, CFO
Mustafa Latif Topbas, Chmn.
Unsal Cetinkaya, Mgr.-Purchasing

FINANCIAL DATA:
Note: Data for latest year may not have been available at press time.

In U.S. $	2015	2014	2013	2012	2011	2010
Revenue		5,007,811,000	4,102,642,000	3,430,064,000	2,835,475,000	2,276,220,000
R&D Expense						
Operating Income		171,392,600	171,652,700	141,254,100	124,432,700	102,373,500
Operating Margin %		3.42%	4.18%	4.11%	4.38%	4.49%
SGA Expense		603,916,100	475,123,800	402,189,000	303,333,700	281,556,400
Net Income		136,871,700	142,995,100	114,719,400	103,497,100	85,052,460
Operating Cash Flow		196,991,500	194,714,500	150,582,000	159,450,900	118,003,900
Capital Expenditure		142,030,800	82,372,500	83,465,260	63,242,620	49,122,610
EBITDA		218,706,800	209,999,600	173,646,400	151,086,900	129,668,300
Return on Assets %		13.32%	17.09%	17.13%	19.25%	19.87%
Return on Equity %		36.79%	45.57%	46.36%	53.54%	84.22%
Debt to Equity						

CONTACT INFORMATION:

Phone: 90 2165640303   Fax: 90 2163117978
Toll-Free:
Address: Ebubekir Cad. No. 73, Sancaktepe, Istanbul 34887 Turkey

STOCK TICKER/OTHER:

Stock Ticker: BMBRF
Employees: 20,724
Parent Company:

Exchange: GREY
Fiscal Year Ends: 12/31

SALARIES/BONUSES:

Top Exec. Salary: $ Bonus: $
Second Exec. Salary: $ Bonus: $

OTHER THOUGHTS:

Estimated Female Officers or Directors:
Hot Spot for Advancement for Women/Minorities:

Birks Group Inc

NAIC Code: 448310

TYPES OF BUSINESS:

Jewelry, Retail Stores
Watches
Giftware
Jewelry Design Services
e-commerce

BRANDS/DIVISIONS/AFFILIATES:

Mayor's Jewelers Inc
Mayor's Jewelers of Florida Inc
Brinkhaus
Birks
Mayors

CONTACTS: Note: Officers with more than one job title may be intentionally listed here more than once.

Jean-Christophe Bedos, CEO
Pat Di Lillo, CFO
Lorenzo Montelera, Chairman of the Board
Helene Messier, Other Executive Officer
Miranda Melfi, Secretary
Albert Rahm, Vice President, Divisional
Marco Pasteris, Vice President, Divisional
Ian Dorais, Vice President, Divisional
Eva Hartling, Vice President, Divisional

GROWTH PLANS/SPECIAL FEATURES:

Birks Group Inc. is one of North America's leading luxury goods retailers. The company operates 47 stores throughout North America. In Canada, the firm operates 27 stores (including three large flagship locations) under the Birks brand name located in all of Canada's major retail districts. It has two additional stores in Vancouver and Calgary under the Brinkhaus brand name. Within the U.S., the company operates 17 stores under the Mayors brand, all of which are located in Florida and Georgia. Its U.S. stores are operated through two subsidiaries: Mayor's Jewelers, Inc. and Mayor's Jewelers of Florida, Inc. The firm also operates one store in Orlando, Florida under the Rolex name, which offers exclusively Rolex-branded timepieces. With a long-established reputation as a premier jeweler offering fine merchandise, it has been a continual destination for high end clientele. The firm specializes in designer jewelry; diamond, gemstone and precious metal jewelry; timepieces; and giftware, including writing instruments made by Cartier and Montblanc. Birks Group divides its sales into two principal product categories: timepieces (which accounted for 53% of its sales in fiscal 2015) and jewelry and other (47%), with the jewelry segment also including products such as giftware, repair and custom design services. Operations include traditional retail stores, a corporate sales division, e-commerce and wholesale activities, a design studio and manufacturing facilities. Its two manufacturing facilities, located in Montreal and Florida, produce stone set jewelry, silver and gold jewelry and one of a kind jewelry pieces.

FINANCIAL DATA: Note: Data for latest year may not have been available at press time.

In U.S. $	2015	2014	2013	2012	2011	2010
Revenue	301,637,000	281,165,000	292,759,000	302,317,000	270,948,000	255,057,000
R&D Expense						
Operating Income	5,296,000	3,729,000	10,805,000	10,442,000	3,597,000	-8,346,000
Operating Margin %	1.75%	1.32%	3.69%	3.45%	1.32%	-3.27%
SGA Expense	103,735,000	105,512,000	110,806,000	118,075,000	107,231,000	106,252,000
Net Income	-8,632,000	-5,801,000	1,513,000	219,000	-7,746,000	-19,471,000
Operating Cash Flow	10,600,000	-19,117,000	6,176,000	4,583,000	10,314,000	29,195,000
Capital Expenditure	6,277,000	6,595,000	6,254,000	4,511,000	2,567,000	1,725,000
EBITDA	8,644,000	9,252,000	15,576,000	15,434,000	9,385,000	-2,424,000
Return on Assets %	-4.65%	-3.13%	.82%	.11%	-4.11%	-9.78%
Return on Equity %	-104.98%	-38.70%	10.81%	1.90%	-52.11%	-72.98%
Debt to Equity	18.43	3.68	2.33	3.95	3.99	2.65

CONTACT INFORMATION:

Phone: 954 590-9462   Fax: 954 590-9062
Toll-Free:
Address: 1240 Phillips Sq., Montreal, QC H3B 3H4 Canada

STOCK TICKER/OTHER:

Stock Ticker: BGI
Employees: 633
Parent Company:

Exchange: ASE
Fiscal Year Ends: 03/31

SALARIES/BONUSES:

Top Exec. Salary:
$1,220,638
Second Exec. Salary:
$458,000

Bonus: $1,510,858

Bonus: $100,000

OTHER THOUGHTS:

Estimated Female Officers or Directors: 3

Hot Spot for Advancement for Women/Minorities: Y

BJ's Wholesale Club Inc

www.bjs.com

NAIC Code: 452910

TYPES OF BUSINESS:

Warehouse Clubs, Retail
Gas Stations
Optical Stores
Photo Labs
Travel Services
Pharmacies
Restaurant Supply

BRANDS/DIVISIONS/AFFILIATES:

Inner Circle
Executive Choice
Berkley and Jensen
Leonard Green & Partners lp
CVC Capital Partners
BJ's Gas
BJ's Optical
BJs.com

CONTACTS: Note: Officers with more than one job title may be intentionally listed here more than once.

Laura Sen, CEO
Laura Sen, Pres.
Robert Eddy, CFO
Peter Amalfi, CIO
Lon F. Povich, General Counsel
Thomas F. Gallagher, Exec. VP-Store Oper.

GROWTH PLANS/SPECIAL FEATURES:

BJ's Wholesale Club, Inc. introduced the warehouse club concept to New England in 1984 and has since expanded to become a leading warehouse club operator in the Eastern U.S. BJ's operates 205 warehouse clubs in 15 states and sells brand-name general merchandise items and food products. General merchandise items include office supplies, electronics, media, auto accessories, jewelry, books, apparel, toys, personal care items and seasonal items. Food categories include frozen foods, canned goods, fresh produce, dairy products, fresh meat and dry grocery items. The firm offers two types of membership, small business and individual household (also known as the Inner Circle), the latter of which targets home owners with above-average incomes. Both memberships are generally $50 per year, which include one free supplemental membership, with each additional supplemental membership costing $25. In addition to brand name merchandise, the company has its own private labels: Executive Choice for products marketed to business members, and Berkley and Jensen for products marketed to Inner Circle members. BJ's also offers its members a number of specialty services, including full-service optical stores; travel services, including member discounts on rental cars; food courts; a selection of garden sheds and gazebos; a propane tank filling service; and muffler and brake services. BJ's has gas stations under the BJ's Gas name, currently located at its various clubs. Additionally, it has optical departments under the BJ's Optical name, which offer eye examinations, eye glasses and contact lenses at its various clubs. The company also offers online shopping through BJs.com. The company is owned by private equity firms Leonard Green & Partners LP and CVC Capital Partners.

FINANCIAL DATA: Note: Data for latest year may not have been available at press time.

In U.S. $	2015	2014	2013	2012	2011	2010
Revenue		11,500,000,000	11,300,000,000	11,000,000,000	10,500,000,000	9,954,384,000
R&D Expense						
Operating Income						
Operating Margin %						
SGA Expense						
Net Income						
Operating Cash Flow						
Capital Expenditure						
EBITDA						
Return on Assets %						
Return on Equity %						
Debt to Equity						

CONTACT INFORMATION:

Phone: 508-651-7400   Fax: 508-651-6114
Toll-Free:
Address: 25 Research Dr., Westborough, MA 01581 United States

STOCK TICKER/OTHER:

Stock Ticker: Private
Employees: 25,000
Parent Company: Leonard Green & Partners LP

Exchange:
Fiscal Year Ends: 01/31

SALARIES/BONUSES:

Top Exec. Salary: $ Bonus: $
Second Exec. Salary: $ Bonus: $

OTHER THOUGHTS:

Estimated Female Officers or Directors: 1
Hot Spot for Advancement for Women/Minorities: Y

Sales, profits and employees may be estimates. Financial information, benefits and other data can change quickly and may vary from those stated here.

Blair Corporation

NAIC Code: 454113

TYPES OF BUSINESS:

Apparel, Catalog Sales
Online Sales
Retail & Outlet Stores
Home Products

BRANDS/DIVISIONS/AFFILIATES:

Bluestem Group Inc
Bluestem Brands Inc
Blair Warehouse Outlet

GROWTH PLANS/SPECIAL FEATURES:

Blair Corporation markets women's wear, men's wear an
home products through its catalogs and e-commerce site. Bla
merchandise is manufactured to its specifications b
independent suppliers, both domestic and foreign. Th
company is owned by Bluestem Group Inc., whose subsidiar
Bluestem Brands, Inc. owns 15 other catalog and e-commerc
brands, such as Willow Ridge, WinterSilks, Appleseed's an
Gold Violin. Low- to middle-income customers are the primar
demographic for Blair's merchandise. Women's wea
merchandise includes dresses, tops, pants, skirts, lingerie
sportswear, suits, jackets, outerwear and shoes. The men'
wear line includes shirts, suits, slacks, shoes and accessories
The home products line offers bedspread ensembles
draperies, furniture covers, area rugs, bath accessories
kitchenware, gifts, collectibles and personal care items
Additionally, Blair sells jewelry. In order to promote an
liquidate discontinued, overstocked and returned merchandise
the company sells its products through a retail store and the
Blair Warehouse Outlet store in Pennsylvania.

CONTACTS:
Note: Officers with more than one job title may be intentionally listed here more than once.

David Walde, CEO
David Walde, Pres.

FINANCIAL DATA:
Note: Data for latest year may not have been available at press time.

In U.S. $	2015	2014	2013	2012	2011	2010
Revenue						
R&D Expense						
Operating Income						
Operating Margin %						
SGA Expense						
Net Income						
Operating Cash Flow						
Capital Expenditure						
EBITDA						
Return on Assets %						
Return on Equity %						
Debt to Equity						

CONTACT INFORMATION:

Phone: 814-723-3600   Fax: 814-726-6376
Toll-Free: 800-458-6057
Address: 220 Hickory St., Warren, PA 16366 United States

STOCK TICKER/OTHER:

Stock Ticker: Subsidiary
Employees:
Parent Company: Bluestem Group Inc

Exchange:
Fiscal Year Ends: 12/31

SALARIES/BONUSES:

Top Exec. Salary: $ Bonus: $
Second Exec. Salary: $ Bonus: $

OTHER THOUGHTS:

Estimated Female Officers or Directors:
Hot Spot for Advancement for Women/Minorities:

Bluestem Brands Inc

www.bluestem.com

NAIC Code: 454113

TYPES OF BUSINESS:

Apparel, Direct Marketing
E-commerce

BRANDS/DIVISIONS/AFFILIATES:

Bluestem Group Inc
Appleseed's
Bedford Fair
Blair
Draper's & Damon's
Fingerhut
Gettington.com
Orchard Brands

CONTACTS: *Note: Officers with more than one job title may be intentionally listed here more than once.*

Steve Nave, CEO
Vince Jones, COO
Marc Sieger, Pres.
Mark Wagener, CFO
Chidam Chidambaram, CMO
Shawn Moren, Sr. VP-Human Resources

GROWTH PLANS/SPECIAL FEATURES:

Bluestem Brands, Inc., formerly Orchard Brands, is the parent company to 16 e-commerce retail brands. Its websites obtain more than 160 million visits annually. Bluestem boasts 2.61 million square feet of distribution space. Bluestem's brands are: Appleseed's, Bedford Fair, Blair, Draper's & Damon's, Fingerhut, Gettington.com, Gold Violin, Haband!, linensource, Norm Thompson, Old Pueblo Traders, PayCheck Direct, sahalie, Solutions, the TOG Shop and WinterSilks. Appleseed's offers apparel to women primarily over 60 years of age. Bedford Fair offers comfortable apparel and wardrobe staples at discount values. Blair offers women's and men's apparel and accessories, as well as dÃ©cor and furnishings for every room in the home. Draper's & Damon's offers ensembles, apparel separates and accessories for mature women. Fingerhut sells a variety of items such as electronics, furniture, bedding and wedding rings via brand names like Samsung, Keurig, Dyson, Seiko, Skechers and many more to customers across the U.S. Gettington.com sells a wide range of items by brands such as Reebok, Lucky, Dyson, La Prairie, Bandolino and Cuisinart. Gold Violin offers unique items and gifts designed to aid in independent, active living at any age. Haband! Offers fashion items for men and women, as well as home furnishings, gifts and gadgets. Linensource offers luxury bedding, sheets and home dÃ©cor. Norm Thompson features high-quality men's and women's apparel, shoes and accessories, as well as gifts and gourmet foods. Old Pueblo Traders offers apparel, accessories and footwear for women. PayCheck Direct is an employee purchase program that allows members to purchase brand name merchandise through payroll deduction. Sahalie offers apparels and accessories for men and women made from organically-produced fabrics and materials. Solutions provide home storage, organization, cooking, cleaning and gardening products. The TOG Shop offers a stylish terry cloth apparel line for women. WinterSilks offers apparel, sleepwear and intimate garments. In May 2015, Orchard Brands was acquired by Bluestem Group Inc., and emerged as Bluestem.

FINANCIAL DATA: *Note: Data for latest year may not have been available at press time.*

In U.S. $	2015	2014	2013	2012	2011	2010
Revenue		1,050,000,000	1,000,000,000	955,000,000	900,000,000	800,000,000
R&D Expense						
Operating Income						
Operating Margin %						
SGA Expense						
Net Income						
Operating Cash Flow						
Capital Expenditure						
EBITDA						
Return on Assets %						
Return on Equity %						
Debt to Equity						

CONTACT INFORMATION:

Phone: 952-656-3700   Fax:
Toll-Free:
Address: 6509 Flying Cloud Dr., Eden Prairie, MN 55344 United States

STOCK TICKER/OTHER:

Stock Ticker: Private   Exchange:
Employees: 1,300   Fiscal Year Ends:
Parent Company: Bluestem Group Inc.

SALARIES/BONUSES:

Top Exec. Salary: $ Bonus: $
Second Exec. Salary: $ Bonus: $

OTHER THOUGHTS:

Estimated Female Officers or Directors:
Hot Spot for Advancement for Women/Minorities:

Bluestem Group Inc

www.bluestem.com

NAIC Code: 522310

TYPES OF BUSINESS:

Commercial Real Estate & Construction Lending
Loan Services
Investments
Investment Research

BRANDS/DIVISIONS/AFFILIATES:

Appleseed's
Bedford Blair
Tog Shop (The)
WinterSilks
Norm Thompson
Haband
Orchard Brands Corporation
Capmark Financial Group Inc

CONTACTS: Note: Officers with more than one job title may be intentionally listed here more than once.

Steve Nave, CEO
Vince Jones, COO
William Gallagher, Pres.
Mark Wagener, CFO
Chidam Chidambaram, CMO
Shawn Moren, Sr.. VP-Human Resources
Linda A. Pickles, Chief Admin. Officer
Thomas L. Fairfield, General Counsel
Paul W. Kopsky, Jr., Principal Acct. Officer
Michael Lipson, Exec. VP

GROWTH PLANS/SPECIAL FEATURES:

Bluestem Group Inc., formerly Capmark Financial Group, Inc., is a holding company whose businesses include Bluestem Brands, Inc., a multi-brand, online retailer of a broad selection of name- brand and private label general merchandise serving low- to middle- income consumers in the U.S. Bluestem Brands is the parent to 16 e-commerce brands including: Appleseed's, providing apparel and modern updates to classic styles for women; Bedford Blair, an apparel value brand for women; Blair, offering men's and women's apparel and accessories; The Tog Shop, offering an assortment of stylish, classical apparel for mature women; WinterSilks, providing apparel, sleepwear & intimates and underlayers in luxurious fabrics; Norm Thompson, featuring high-quality men's and women's apparel, shoes and accessories, as well as one-of-a-kind gifts and gourmet foods; and Sahalie, offering apparel and accessories in high-performance fabrics, organically produced materials and sustainable product alternatives. Other brands Bluestem Brands is parent to include: Draper's & Damon's, Fingerhut, Gettington.com, Gold Violin, Haband, LinenSource, Old Pueblo Traders, PayCheck Direct and Solutions. Each brand is complemented by a large selection of merchandise with a variety of payment options to provide customers with the flexibility of paying over time. In July 2015, the Bluestem Group acquired Orchard Brands Corporation, a multi-brand family of 13 catalog and e-commerce brands serving the boomer and senior demographics.

FINANCIAL DATA: Note: Data for latest year may not have been available at press time.

In U.S. $	2015	2014	2013	2012	2011	2010
Revenue			151,445,000	245,016,000	22,800,000	
R&D Expense						
Operating Income						
Operating Margin %						
SGA Expense						
Net Income						
Operating Cash Flow						
Capital Expenditure						
EBITDA						
Return on Assets %						
Return on Equity %						
Debt to Equity						

CONTACT INFORMATION:

Phone: 952-656-3700   Fax:
Toll-Free:
Address: 6509 Flying Cloud Dr., Eden Praire, MN 55344 United States

STOCK TICKER/OTHER:

Stock Ticker: BGRP   Exchange: PINX
Employees: 35   Fiscal Year Ends: 12/31
Parent Company:

SALARIES/BONUSES:

Top Exec. Salary: $ Bonus: $
Second Exec. Salary: $ Bonus: $

OTHER THOUGHTS:

Estimated Female Officers or Directors: 1
Hot Spot for Advancement for Women/Minorities:

Body Shop International plc (The)

www.thebodyshop-usa.com

NAIC Code: 446120

TYPES OF BUSINESS:

Cosmetics, Retail
Direct Sales
Online Sales

BRANDS/DIVISIONS/AFFILIATES:

Loreal SA
Body Shop At Home (The)
Love Your Body
Community Trade Program

GROWTH PLANS/SPECIAL FEATURES:

The Body Shop International plc, a subsidiary of L'Oreal, is a skin and body care retailer. The firm operates in 60 worldwide markets, with over 3,000 stores. These products include body care, bath items, skin care, make-up, hair care, fragrances and candles and home fragrances. The Body Shop sells directly in the U.S., the U.K., Australia and Germany though its The Body Shop At Home division. It also offers e-commerce sites in the U.S., U.K., Japan, Australia and Canada. The Body Shop's Community Trade Program works to create sustainable trading relationships with disadvantaged communities around the world by sourcing raw materials and accessory items from over 25 suppliers in more than nine countries. As a customer loyalty incentive, the firm offers a Love Your Body membership card with special membership benefits. In recent years, The Body Shop became one of the first cosmetics and toiletries retailers to use sustainable palm oil.

CONTACTS: Note: Officers with more than one job title may be intentionally listed here more than once.

Sophie Gasperment, CEO
Adrian D. P. Bellamy, Chmn.

FINANCIAL DATA: Note: Data for latest year may not have been available at press time.

In U.S. $	2015	2014	2013	2012	2011	2010
Revenue		1,657,942,140	1,026,339,000	1,049,743,000	941,762,000	1,033,245,000
R&D Expense						
Operating Income						
Operating Margin %						
SGA Expense						
Net Income		981,976,440	173,106,000	172,780,840	152,438,570	89,377,000
Operating Cash Flow						
Capital Expenditure						
EBITDA						
Return on Assets %						
Return on Equity %						
Debt to Equity						

CONTACT INFORMATION:

Phone: 44-1-903-731-500   Fax: 44-1-903-726-250
Toll-Free: 800-092-9090
Address: Watersmead, Littlehampton, BN17 6LS United Kingdom

STOCK TICKER/OTHER:

Stock Ticker: Subsidiary
Employees: 2,820
Parent Company: LOREAL SA

Exchange:
Fiscal Year Ends: 12/31

SALARIES/BONUSES:

Top Exec. Salary: $ Bonus: $
Second Exec. Salary: $ Bonus: $

OTHER THOUGHTS:

Estimated Female Officers or Directors: 1
Hot Spot for Advancement for Women/Minorities:

Sales, profits and employees may be estimates. Financial information, benefits and other data can change quickly and may vary from those stated here.

Bon-Ton Stores Inc (The)

NAIC Code: 452111

TYPES OF BUSINESS:

Department Stores
Apparel, Accessories & Footwear
Home Furnishings
Private Brand Merchandise

BRANDS/DIVISIONS/AFFILIATES:

Herberger's
Boston Store
Carson's
Elder-Beerman
Bergner's
Younkers
Bon-Ton
Bonton.com

CONTACTS: Note: Officers with more than one job title may be intentionally listed here more than once.

Tim Grumbacher, Chairman of the Board
Michael Webb, Chief Accounting Officer
William Tracy, COO
Jimmy Mansker, Executive VP, Divisional
Stephen Byers, Executive VP, Divisional
Nancy Walsh, Executive VP
Luis Fernandez, Executive VP
Kathryn Bufano, President
Kim George, Vice President, Divisional
J. Yawman, Vice President

GROWTH PLANS/SPECIAL FEATURES:

The Bon-Ton Stores, Inc., founded in 1898, operates region
fashion department stores offering apparel, home furnishing
cosmetics, accessories and shoes. Currently, the compar
operates 270 stores in 26 states under the names Bon-To
Younkers, Carson's, Herberger's, Elder-Beerman, Bosto
Store and Bergner's. Its primary target customers are wome
aged 25-60 with annual household income between $55,00
and $125,000. In many of its markets, which desire but hav
limited access to branded merchandise, Bon-Ton is the primar
destination for fashion lines such as Anne Klein, Calvin Klei
Carters, Clinique, Coach, Clarks, Estee Lauder, Fossil, Fre
People, Frye, Jessica Simpson, Kenneth Cole, Keurig, Laurer
Polo, Jones New York, Nine West, Michael Kors, Stev
Madden, Lancome and Vince Camuto. The firm also offer
merchandise under private-branded labels, including Laur
Ashley, Ruff Hewn, Relativity, Studio Works, Breckenridge
Living Quarters, Paradise Collections, Kenneth Roberts
Cuddle Bear, John Bartlett, Casa by Victor Alfaro and Mambo
In addition to its brick-and-mortar stores, Bon-Ton operates e
commerce sites at Bonton.com as well as under its othe
operating banners. The company offers a proprietary credi
card and has over 3.8 million active card holders. Bon-To
owns a distribution center in Rockford, Illinois and lease
distribution centers in Allentown, Pennsylvania; Fairborn, Ohio
and Dayton, Ohio.

The firm offers employees medical, dental and visio
insurance; life insurance; long-term disability coverage; flexible
spending accounts; a 401(k); and group legal insurance.

FINANCIAL DATA: Note: Data for latest year may not have been available at press time.

In U.S. $	2015	2014	2013	2012	2011	2010
Revenue	2,822,896,000	2,834,060,000	2,978,836,000	2,953,530,000	3,046,485,000	3,034,937,000
R&D Expense						
Operating Income	56,534,000	69,380,000	69,999,000	66,631,000	135,148,000	86,722,000
Operating Margin %	2.00%	2.44%	2.34%	2.25%	4.43%	2.85%
SGA Expense	907,036,000	899,363,000	936,175,000	936,060,000	942,660,000	963,639,000
Net Income	-6,974,000	-3,556,000	-21,553,000	-12,128,000	21,494,000	-4,055,000
Operating Cash Flow	46,629,000	120,067,000	73,270,000	99,797,000	141,135,000	194,034,000
Capital Expenditure	90,707,000	77,336,000	73,770,000	67,235,000	46,268,000	32,346,000
EBITDA	146,503,000	150,827,000	149,843,000	170,172,000	237,694,000	198,357,000
Return on Assets %	-.43%	-.22%	-1.32%	-.74%	1.27%	-.22%
Return on Equity %	-6.46%	-2.98%	-17.79%	-7.70%	13.22%	-2.93%
Debt to Equity	10.22	6.66	7.42	6.61	5.00	7.17

CONTACT INFORMATION:

Phone: 717 757-7660   Fax: 717 751-3108
Toll-Free:
Address: 2801 E. Market St., York, PA 17402 United States

SALARIES/BONUSES:

Top Exec. Salary: Bonus: $
$1,000,000
Second Exec. Salary: Bonus: $350,000
$380,769

STOCK TICKER/OTHER:

Stock Ticker: BONT   Exchange: NAS
Employees: 25,200   Fiscal Year Ends: 01/31
Parent Company:

OTHER THOUGHTS:

Estimated Female Officers or Directors: 1

Hot Spot for Advancement for Women/Minorities: Y

Books A Million Inc

www.booksamillioninc.com

NAIC Code: 451211

TYPES OF BUSINESS:

Book Stores
Newsstands
Coffee Bars
Wholesale Distribution
Online Sales
Internet Development & Services

BRANDS/DIVISIONS/AFFILIATES:

Books and Co
Bookland
Joe Muggs
BAM!
NetCentral Inc
American Wholesale Book Company
Books-A-Million

CONTACTS: *Note: Officers with more than one job title may be intentionally listed here more than once.*

Terrance Finley, CEO
R. Noden, CFO
Clyde Anderson, Chairman of the Board
James Turner, Executive VP, Divisional

GROWTH PLANS/SPECIAL FEATURES:

Books-A-Million, Inc. is a leading retailer of books, magazines and related items in the southeastern U.S. It currently operates more than 250 stores in 32 states and Washington, D.C. The company has three business operating segments: retail trade, which consists of its retail stores; electronic commerce trade, which handles its online business; and real estate development and management, which develops and leases commercial retail real estate. The retail trade segment involves the company's traditional stores and superstores. Traditional stores are under names such as Bookland, Books-A-Million and BAM!, which are primarily located in enclosed malls and ranging in size from 2000 to 10,000 square feet. Superstores offer an extensive selection of books, magazines and general merchandise in a spacious, open environment in which customers can browse, read and shop. Books-A-Million superstores average in size from 8,000 to 39,000 square feet and operate under the names Books-A-Million, Books and Co., 2nd & Charles and BAM! Many of these superstores also feature Joe Muggs cafes, which serve a variety of coffees and pastries, or Yogurt Mountain, serving frozen yogurt with self-serve toppings. Both store formats offer a variety of bestsellers and other hardcover and paperback books, magazines and newspapers as well as other merchandise, such as gifts, collectibles, music and DVDs. The electronic commerce trade segment includes NetCentral, Inc., and is engaged in the retail sale of books and general merchandise over the Internet. The real estate development and management segment focuses on deriving revenues through developing and leasing commercial properties in order to earn rental income. Books-A-Million owns the distribution company American Wholesale Book Company, which markets primarily to other book retailers. In July 2015, the firm entered into an agreement with the Anderson Family where a newly organized entity owned by the Anderson Family would acquire the firm.

FINANCIAL DATA: *Note: Data for latest year may not have been available at press time.*

In U.S. $	2015	2014	2013	2012	2011	2010
Revenue	474,084,000	470,301,000	503,787,000	468,521,000	494,963,000	508,667,000
R&D Expense						
Operating Income	4,619,000	-1,479,000	6,911,000	-3,997,000	14,333,000	21,677,000
Operating Margin %	.97%	-.31%	1.37%	-.85%	2.89%	4.26%
SGA Expense	118,940,000	118,909,000	121,127,000	120,265,000	118,162,000	115,113,000
Net Income	3,538,000	-7,584,000	2,545,000	-2,823,000	8,939,000	13,836,000
Operating Cash Flow	24,738,000	4,443,000	15,114,000	28,437,000	29,703,000	31,985,000
Capital Expenditure	24,880,000	27,498,000	19,081,000	24,272,000	16,776,000	10,725,000
EBITDA	21,176,000	16,872,000	23,758,000	12,570,000	29,673,000	36,070,000
Return on Assets %	1.18%	-2.57%	.87%	-.98%	3.26%	5.00%
Return on Equity %	3.21%	-6.72%	2.20%	-2.43%	7.71%	12.62%
Debt to Equity	0.22	0.16	0.05	0.04		0.05

CONTACT INFORMATION:

Phone: 205 942-3737   Fax: 205 945-1772
Toll-Free: 800-201-3550
Address: 402 Industrial Ln., Birmingham, AL 35211 United States

STOCK TICKER/OTHER:

Stock Ticker: BAMM
Employees: 5,400
Parent Company:

Exchange: NAS
Fiscal Year Ends: 01/31

SALARIES/BONUSES:

Top Exec. Salary: $474,300   Bonus: $47,430
Second Exec. Salary: $408,447   Bonus: $40,845

OTHER THOUGHTS:

Estimated Female Officers or Directors:
Hot Spot for Advancement for Women/Minorities:

Sales, profits and employees may be estimates. Financial information, benefits and other data can change quickly and may vary from those stated here.

Boral Limited

NAIC Code: 444110

www.boral.com.au

TYPES OF BUSINESS:
Home Centers

BRANDS/DIVISIONS/AFFILIATES:
Dowell Windows
Boral USA
Boral Gypsum Asia

CONTACTS: Note: Officers with more than one job title may be intentionally listed here more than once.
Mike Kane, CEO
Rosaline Ng, CFO
Robert Gates, Chief Admin. Officer
Damien Sullivan, Group General Counsel
Matt Coren, Dir.-Group Strategy
Kylie FitzGerald, Manager-Group Communications
Kylie Fitzgerald, Manager-Investor Relations
Dominic Milligate, Company Secretary

GROWTH PLANS/SPECIAL FEATURES:
Boral Limited provides building and construction materials in Australia, the U.S. and Asia. The company operates through four divisions: Boral construction materials & cement, Boral building products, Boral USA and Boral gypsum. Boral construction materials & cement operates through 420 locations where it premixes concrete, producing either normal class standard concrete, special class concrete or decorative concrete. This division also operates 110 quarries, sands pits and gravel operations. Boral building products supplies bricks, stone, masonry, roof tiles, timber and windows. This division has six brick manufacturing sites in Victoria, New South Wales and Queensland; produces specialized cultured stone that weighs less than real stone with the same aesthetic appeal; operates three concrete roof tile plants and one clay roof tile plant; has nine hardwood manufacturing facilities; a softwood manufacturing facility; and sells windows under the brand Dowell Windows. In the U.S., the company operates through Boral USA, supplying bricks, concrete & clay roof tiles and manufactured stone veneer. It especially has a presence in Colorado and Denver, selling construction materials, and maintains a fly ash processing and distribution business on a national scale. In Asia, the company operates through Boral Gypsum Asia, supplying plasterboard and internal linings products. Countries of operation include South Korea, China, India, Thailand, Indonesia, Malaysia, Philippines, Singapore, Vietnam and the UAE.

FINANCIAL DATA: Note: Data for latest year may not have been available at press time.

In U.S. $	2015	2014	2013	2012	2011	2010
Revenue	3,138,538,000	3,253,560,000	3,804,425,000	3,444,241,000	3,430,950,000	3,287,154,000
R&D Expense						
Operating Income	135,762,800	103,045,400	-189,732,000	42,868,620	126,049,800	31,183,820
Operating Margin %	4.32%	3.16%	-4.98%	1.24%	3.67%	.94%
SGA Expense	1,449,281,000	771,270,000	894,471,600	1,632,440,000	1,597,897,000	1,117,432,000
Net Income	187,687,100	126,561,000	-154,896,700	128,971,000	122,471,300	-66,092,160
Operating Cash Flow	305,484,500	370,481,200	214,708,200	97,349,010	256,116,300	335,280,800
Capital Expenditure	182,502,000	195,866,500	261,228,400	302,636,400	252,537,800	131,381,000
EBITDA	448,258,200	324,399,300	65,507,920	395,019,300	365,734,300	233,038,800
Return on Assets %	4.49%	2.91%	-3.31%	2.90%	3.08%	-1.69%
Return on Equity %	7.47%	5.21%	-6.39%	5.48%	5.85%	-3.36%
Debt to Equity	0.37	0.26	0.46	0.47	0.29	0.50

CONTACT INFORMATION:
Phone: 61 292206300   Fax: 61 292336605
Toll-Free:
Address: Level 39, AMP Centre, Sydney, NSW 2000 Australia

STOCK TICKER/OTHER:
Stock Ticker: BOALY
Employees: 8,953
Parent Company:

Exchange: PINX
Fiscal Year Ends: 06/30

SALARIES/BONUSES:
Top Exec. Salary: $ Bonus: $
Second Exec. Salary: $ Bonus: $

OTHER THOUGHTS:
Estimated Female Officers or Directors: 2
Hot Spot for Advancement for Women/Minorities:

Boscov's Inc

www.boscovs.com

NAIC Code: 452111

TYPES OF BUSINESS:

Department Stores
Bridal Consulting
Beauty Salons
Travel Agencies
Hearing Evaluation Centers

BRANDS/DIVISIONS/AFFILIATES:

Boscov's Department Store LLC
Boscov's Travel
Boscov's Business Travel
BoscovsTravel.com
Boscovs.com
BoscovsBusinessTravel.com

CONTACTS: *Note: Officers with more than one job title may be intentionally listed here more than once.*

Albert Boscov, CEO
Sam Flamholz, Pres.-Boscov's Department Store, LLC
Toni Miller, CFO
Jon Holmquist, Sr. VP-Direct Mktg.
Ed Elko, Sr. VP-Human Resources
Ed McKeaney, Sr. Exec. VP-Merch. & Advertising
Toni Miller, Chief Admin. Officer
Larry Bergman, Sr. VP-Oper.
Russel C. Diehm, Chief Acct. Officer
Gary Boyer, Sr. VP
T.J. Javier, Sr. VP
John Young, Sr. VP
Brian Nugent, Sr. VP
Albert Boscov, Chmn.
Larry Bergman, Sr. VP-Supply Chain

GROWTH PLANS/SPECIAL FEATURES:

Boscov's, Inc., along with its operating partner, Boscov's Department Store, LLC, operates a string of 44 department stores in seven states, many of which anchor shopping malls. A majority of the company's stores are in Pennsylvania, where it was founded, with other locations in New York, New Jersey, Maryland, Ohio, Connecticut and Delaware. Stores feature a broad selection of products, from men's and women's apparel to electronics and appliances. Clothing brands offered include Liz Claiborne, Tommy Hilfiger, Calvin Klein, Champion and Jockey Classic. The company offers home appliances, kitchenware and decorations from brands such as Waterford Crystal, Lenox, Sauder, Whirlpool and Pfaltzgraff. Some of its newer brands, available in select stores, include Clinique, Estee Lauder and Lancome cosmetics. Shoppers also find home electronics, collectibles, sporting equipment, travel gear and gift cards. In many of its locations, the company has hearing evaluation and consultation centers, which sell digital hearing aids and offer free hearing tests. An affiliated travel agency, doing business as Boscov's Travel and Boscov's Business Travel, can be found at a number of Boscov's stores and through BoscovsTravel.com & BoscovsBusinessTravel.com. Besides its retail outlets, the firm also operates an e-commerce site, Boscovs.com, which offers the company's full line of products as well as a private label credit card that can be applied for and managed from the web site.

Boscov's offers employees an employee discount, an executive training program and summer internships.

FINANCIAL DATA: *Note: Data for latest year may not have been available at press time.*

In U.S. $	2015	2014	2013	2012	2011	2010
Revenue		1,000,000,000	1,030,000,000	1,000,000,000	960,000,000	925,000,000
R&D Expense						
Operating Income						
Operating Margin %						
SGA Expense						
Net Income						
Operating Cash Flow						
Capital Expenditure						
EBITDA						
Return on Assets %						
Return on Equity %						
Debt to Equity						

CONTACT INFORMATION:

Phone: 610-370-0507   Fax: 610-370-3495
Toll-Free: 800-284-8155
Address: 4500 Perkiomen Ave., Reading, PA 19606 United States

STOCK TICKER/OTHER:

Stock Ticker: Private
Employees: 8,000
Parent Company:

Exchange:
Fiscal Year Ends: 01/31

SALARIES/BONUSES:

Top Exec. Salary: $ Bonus: $
Second Exec. Salary: $ Bonus: $

OTHER THOUGHTS:

Estimated Female Officers or Directors: 1
Hot Spot for Advancement for Women/Minorities:

Brazilian Distribution Company

NAIC Code: 452910

www.grupopaodeacucar.com.br

TYPES OF BUSINESS:
Warehouse Clubs and Supercenters

BRANDS/DIVISIONS/AFFILIATES:
Casino Group
Extra Hiper
Minmercado Extra
Extra Supermercado
Pao de Aqucar
Assai
Pontofrio
Casasbahia.com.br

GROWTH PLANS/SPECIAL FEATURES:
Brazilian Distribution Company, a subsidiary of the Casin
Group, operates in the food and non-food retail busines
through its chain of hypermarkets and supermarkets.
operates through four business segments: food retail, sel
service wholesale, home appliances and e-commerce. Foo
retail covers supermarket sales of food and nonfood product
to consumers through the Pao de Aqucar, Extr
Supermercado, Extra Hiper and Minmercado Extra stores. Th
self-service wholesale segment sells food and non-foo
products to intermediate and retail consumers under the Assa
banner. The home appliances segment sells electronics, hom
appliances, furniture and other home items under the Cas
Bahia and Pontofrio brands. The e-commerce segmer
includes Extra.com.br; Pontofrio.com.br; CasasBahia.com.br
Barateiro.com.br; Partiuviagens.com.br; wholesale activities
and E-Hub, a marketplace e-commerce solution.

CONTACTS: Note: Officers with more than one job title may be intentionally listed here more than once.
Jean-Charles Naouri, Chmn.-Casino Group

FINANCIAL DATA: Note: Data for latest year may not have been available at press time.

In U.S. $	2015	2014	2013	2012	2011	2010
Revenue		17,098,090,000	15,064,130,000	13,288,220,000	12,158,360,000	8,373,998,000
R&D Expense						
Operating Income		1,016,622,000	756,968,100	745,867,500	548,636,000	418,000,900
Operating Margin %		5.94%	5.02%	5.61%	4.51%	4.99%
SGA Expense		3,075,698,000	2,782,857,000	2,639,139,000	2,510,175,000	1,508,790,000
Net Income		331,393,700	274,637,900	274,295,100	187,412,000	188,508,700
Operating Cash Flow		1,308,874,000	1,276,505,000	1,382,787,000	294,356,600	94,796,070
Capital Expenditure		495,003,000	482,637,600	363,592,100	379,478,400	389,629,700
EBITDA		1,259,557,000	982,792,000	963,519,700	501,630,100	356,155,600
Return on Assets %		3.04%	2.86%	3.03%	2.25%	3.01%
Return on Equity %		12.65%	11.70%	13.04%	9.75%	10.52%
Debt to Equity		0.29	0.45	0.73	0.81	0.78

CONTACT INFORMATION:
Phone: 55 1138860421   Fax: 55 1138842677
Toll-Free:
Address: Av. Brigadeiro Luiz Antonio 3142, Sao Paulo, SP 01402-901
Brazil

STOCK TICKER/OTHER:
Stock Ticker: CBDN
Employees: 159,829
Parent Company: Casino Group

Exchange: MEX
Fiscal Year Ends: 12/31

SALARIES/BONUSES:
Top Exec. Salary: $ Bonus: $
Second Exec. Salary: $ Bonus: $

OTHER THOUGHTS:
Estimated Female Officers or Directors: 1
Hot Spot for Advancement for Women/Minorities:

Brooks Brothers Group Inc

www.brooksbrothers.com

NAIC Code: 448120

TYPES OF BUSINESS:

Women's & Men's Apparel, Retail
Footwear
Accessories
Fragrances

BRANDS/DIVISIONS/AFFILIATES:

Luxottica Group

CONTACTS: *Note: Officers with more than one job title may be intentionally listed here more than once.*

Claudio Del Vecchio, CEO
Mauro Calderan, COO
Diane Ellis, Pres.
Brian Baumann, CFO
Vivien Kronengold, CMO
Sahal Laher, CIO
Claudio Del Vecchio, Chmn.

GROWTH PLANS/SPECIAL FEATURES:

Brooks Brothers Group, Inc. is a private company that owns several mostly mall-based retail stores. Brooks Brothers, the oldest surviving men's clothing store in the U.S., offers men's and women's professional and casual clothes and operates retail stores worldwide. The company also offers kids apparel, shoes and accessories for both boys and girls, as well as bedding, bath and home dÃ©cor. Products for men include dress shirts, sport shirts, ties, blazers, suits, outerwear, vests and sweaters, tuxedos, casual pants, polo shirts, t-shirts, shorts, underwear, socks and sleepwear. Products for women include non-iron dress shirts, dresses, sweaters, blouses, knits, tees, jackets, blazers, outwear, suits, pants, shorts, skirts and sleepwear. Shoes, belts, bags, scarves, jewelry, hats, fragrances, hats and music are also available for both men and women. The firm is owned by CEO Claudio del Vecchio, who acquired the company from his father's company, Luxottica Group. In October 2015, the firm partnered with Walton Brown Group to form a 50-50 joint venture that would expand its brand and products across the greater China region. The JV will take over the management of Brooks Brothers' existing retail network of 90 stores in the territory and activate a strategic plan to open more than 10 points of sale in its first two years of business, beginning in 2016. Points of sale areas include China, Hong Kong, Macau and Taiwan.

FINANCIAL DATA: *Note: Data for latest year may not have been available at press time.*

In U.S. $	2015	2014	2013	2012	2011	2010
Revenue		850,000,000	829,000,000	800,000,000	750,000,000	700,000,000
R&D Expense						
Operating Income						
Operating Margin %						
SGA Expense						
Net Income						
Operating Cash Flow						
Capital Expenditure						
EBITDA						
Return on Assets %						
Return on Equity %						
Debt to Equity						

CONTACT INFORMATION:

Phone: 860-741-0771   Fax: 860-745-9714
Toll-Free:
Address: 100 Phoenix Ave., Enfield, CT 06082 United States

SALARIES/BONUSES:

Top Exec. Salary: $ Bonus: $
Second Exec. Salary: $ Bonus: $

STOCK TICKER/OTHER:

Stock Ticker: Private   Exchange:
Employees: Fiscal Year Ends: 12/31
Parent Company:

OTHER THOUGHTS:

Estimated Female Officers or Directors: 1
Hot Spot for Advancement for Women/Minorities:

Brookstone Inc

www.brookstone.com

NAIC Code: 443142

TYPES OF BUSINESS:

Housewares & Gifts, Retail
Catalog & Online Sales
Leisure & Recreational Products
Specialty Tools
Airport Stores
Outlet Stores

BRANDS/DIVISIONS/AFFILIATES:

Brookstone.com
Brookstone
Sanpower Group Co Ltd
Brookstone Catalog

GROWTH PLANS/SPECIAL FEATURES:

Brookstone, Inc., a subsidiary of the Sanpower Group Co. Ltd., is a nationwide specialty retailer that develops proprietary branded products sold through retail stores, catalogs and the Internet. The Brookstone brand features an assortment of products divided into four categories: outdoor living, health and fitness, home and office and travel and auto. Products within these groups include bedding, personal care products, wine, massage items, audio/video equipment, lighting, kitchen items, travel items and tools. Brookstone operates approximately more than 200 stores throughout the U.S. and Puerto Rico, including airport-based stores, outlet stores and high-traffic shopping malls. On average, the firm opens roughly 10-15 stores each year. Brookstone's two busiest selling seasons occur prior to Christmas and Father's Day. Originally a direct mail company, the firm dedicates significant attention to its Brookstone Catalog. The company also sells online through Brookstone.com, one of its primary sales outlets and a direct marketing channel.

CONTACTS: Note: Officers with more than one job title may be intentionally listed here more than once.

Thomas Via, CEO
Frank Hu, VP-Oper.
James M. Speltz, Pres.
Valen Tong, CFO
Steven H. Schwartz, VP-Merch. & Prod. Dev.
Stephen A. Gould, General Counsel

FINANCIAL DATA: Note: Data for latest year may not have been available at press time.

In U.S. $	2015	2014	2013	2012	2011	2010
Revenue				519,613,000	496,766,000	468,191,000
R&D Expense						
Operating Income						
Operating Margin %						
SGA Expense						
Net Income						
Operating Cash Flow						
Capital Expenditure						
EBITDA						
Return on Assets %						
Return on Equity %						
Debt to Equity						

CONTACT INFORMATION:

Phone: 603-880-9500   Fax: 603-577-8004
Toll-Free: 866-576-7337
Address: 1 Innovation Way, Merrimack, NH 03054 United States

STOCK TICKER/OTHER:

Stock Ticker: Subsidiary   Exchange:
Employees: 1,191   Fiscal Year Ends: 01/31
Parent Company: Sanpower Group Co. Ltd.

SALARIES/BONUSES:

Top Exec. Salary: $ Bonus: $
Second Exec. Salary: $ Bonus: $

OTHER THOUGHTS:

Estimated Female Officers or Directors:
Hot Spot for Advancement for Women/Minorities:

Buckle Inc (The)

www.buckle.com

NAIC Code: 448140

TYPES OF BUSINESS:
Teen Apparel, Retail
Promotional Merchandise
Online Sales

BRANDS/DIVISIONS/AFFILIATES:
Buckle
Buckle [The]
Buckle Screenprinting
Buckle.com
BKE
Roxy
Big Star
Silver

CONTACTS: Note: Officers with more than one job title may be intentionally listed here more than once.
Dennis Nelson, CEO
Karen Rhoads, CFO
Daniel Hirschfeld, Chairman of the Board
Thomas Heacock, Controller
Kari Smith, Executive VP, Divisional
Kyle Hanson, General Counsel
Patricia Whisler, Senior VP, Divisional
Brett Milkie, Senior VP, Divisional
Robert Carlberg, Senior VP, Divisional
Michelle Hoffman, Vice President, Divisional
Kelli Molczyk, Vice President, Divisional
Diane Applegate, Vice President, Divisional

GROWTH PLANS/SPECIAL FEATURES:

The Buckle, Inc. is a retailer of medium- to better-priced casual apparel, footwear and accessories primarily for young men and women ages 15-30. The company operates roughly 464 stores in 44 states throughout the central, northwest, southwest and southeast U.S. These stores operate under the brand names Buckle and The Buckle. The majority of the stores are located in regional shopping malls, although some are located in strip centers, downtown areas and lifestyle centers. Buckle markets mostly brand-name casual apparel, including denim, tops, sportswear, outerwear, accessories and footwear. Brand name merchandise such as Rock Revival, Big Star Vintage, Silver, Miss Me, Affliction, Fossil, Bench, Billabong, Roxy, Sinful, American Fighter, 7 Diamonds, Obey and Savage constitute roughly 65% of total sales. The remaining merchandise consists of items manufactured to the company's specifications by private labels and merchandise marketed under its exclusive BKE label. The firm emphasizes personalized attention to its customers by providing free alterations, free gift-wrapping and a frequent shopper program. Buckle Screenprinting offers promotional merchandising to outside athletic teams, organizations, clubs and individuals. The company tailors individual store inventories to reflect differences in customer buying patterns by shipping new merchandise daily to most stores through its transfer program. This assures that popular merchandise is in stock and reduces the need to lower the price of low-selling merchandise at a particular location.

The firm offers employees medical and dental insurance, disability coverage, life insurance, performance bonuses, an employee assistance program, a 40% merchandise discount, a 401(k) plan and flexible spending accounts.

FINANCIAL DATA: Note: Data for latest year may not have been available at press time.

In U.S. $	2015	2014	2013	2012	2011	2010
Revenue	1,153,142,000	1,128,001,000	1,124,007,000	1,062,946,000	949,838,000	898,287,000
R&D Expense						
Operating Income	256,973,000	256,994,000	258,175,000	236,320,000	210,767,000	199,462,000
Operating Margin %	22.28%	22.78%	22.96%	22.23%	22.18%	22.20%
SGA Expense	250,359,000	242,151,000	241,140,000	232,335,000	208,362,000	201,157,000
Net Income	162,564,000	162,584,000	164,305,000	151,456,000	134,682,000	127,303,000
Operating Cash Flow	195,768,000	174,026,000	220,941,000	209,273,000	179,935,000	157,959,000
Capital Expenditure	45,454,000	28,811,000	30,297,000	36,627,000	54,945,000	50,561,000
EBITDA	288,652,000	289,625,000	292,009,000	269,089,000	240,548,000	224,597,000
Return on Assets %	29.84%	31.74%	32.55%	29.51%	27.38%	26.68%
Return on Equity %	45.33%	49.90%	50.33%	42.73%	38.48%	36.82%
Debt to Equity						

CONTACT INFORMATION:
Phone: 308 236-8491   Fax: 308 236-4493
Toll-Free: 800-626-1255
Address: 2407 W. 24th St., Kearney, NE 68845 United States

STOCK TICKER/OTHER:
Stock Ticker: BKE   Exchange: NYS
Employees: 8,900   Fiscal Year Ends: 01/31
Parent Company:

SALARIES/BONUSES:
Top Exec. Salary: $999,000   Bonus: $1,349,093
Second Exec. Salary: $410,000   Bonus: $286,682

OTHER THOUGHTS:
Estimated Female Officers or Directors: 3
Hot Spot for Advancement for Women/Minorities: Y

Sales, profits and employees may be estimates. Financial information, benefits and other data can change quickly and may vary from those stated here.

Build-A-Bear Workshop Inc

www.buildabear.com

NAIC Code: 451120

TYPES OF BUSINESS:

Retail-Stuffed Animals
Custom Stuffed Animal Making

BRANDS/DIVISIONS/AFFILIATES:

Ridemakerz LLC
Buildabear
www.buildabear.com
www.buildabear.com/play

CONTACTS: *Note: Officers with more than one job title may be intentionally listed here more than once.*

Sharon John, CEO
Vojin Todorovic, CFO
Mary Fiala, Chairman of the Board
Eric Fencl, Chief Administrative Officer
Gina Collins, Chief Marketing Officer
J. Hurt, COO
Barney Ebsworth, Director Emeritus
Maxine Clark, Director
Jennifer Kretchmar, Other Executive Officer

GROWTH PLANS/SPECIAL FEATURES:

Build-A-Bear Workshop, Inc. is a leading retail firm providing customers the opportunity to create and customize stuffed animals, providing an interactive shopping experience. The company has sold over 110 million stuffed animals since its inception in 1997. Customers choose from 30 styles of animals to customize, stuff and sew. The customer then accessorizes the stuffed animal with a wide variety of clothing, shoes and accessories. Build-A-Bear operates 324 stores primarily located in major malls, including 245 traditional and 20 non-traditional Build-A-Bear Workshop stores in the U.S. and Canada and 57 traditional Build-A-Bear Workshop stores in the U.K. and Ireland. Franchisees operated 71 Build-A-Bear Workshop stores in other international locations as well. In addition to the company's retail locations, Build-A-Bear markets its products through online channels www.buildabear.com. The company holds a minority interest in Ridemakerz, LLC, a company that allows children and families to build and customize their own personalized cars. In March 2015, the firm closed its Bearville game in order to launch a new Internet game called Buildabear at www.buildabear.com/play.

Build-A-Bear offers employees medical, life, AD&D, disability, dental, vision and prescription drug coverage; a wellness program; a 24/7 Nurse Line; paid time off for birthdays and holidays; a 401(k); flexible spending accounts; scholarship programs; and concierge services at the World Bearquarters.

FINANCIAL DATA: *Note: Data for latest year may not have been available at press time.*

In U.S. $	2015	2014	2013	2012	2011	2010
Revenue		392,354,000	379,069,000	380,941,000	394,375,000	401,452,000
R&D Expense						
Operating Income		16,077,000	-2,377,000	-48,429,000	-2,652,000	-2,472,000
Operating Margin %		4.09%	-.62%	-12.71%	-.67%	-.61%
SGA Expense		164,445,000	160,708,000	165,516,000	162,881,000	164,618,000
Net Income		14,362,000	-2,112,000	-49,295,000	-17,062,000	104,000
Operating Cash Flow		34,884,000	19,058,000	14,864,000	16,010,000	22,021,000
Capital Expenditure		10,890,000	19,362,000	17,268,000	12,248,000	14,649,000
EBITDA		34,205,000	16,839,000	-27,007,000	21,580,000	24,504,000
Return on Assets %		7.06%	-1.09%	-22.73%	-6.59%	.03%
Return on Equity %		15.78%	-2.52%	-46.42%	-11.89%	.06%
Debt to Equity						

CONTACT INFORMATION:

Phone: 314 423-8000   Fax:
Toll-Free: 877-789-2327
Address: 1954 Innerbelt Business Ctr. Dr., St. Louis, MO 63114 United States

STOCK TICKER/OTHER:

Stock Ticker: BBW
Employees: 4,300
Parent Company:

Exchange: NYS
Fiscal Year Ends: 12/31

SALARIES/BONUSES:

Top Exec. Salary: $656,250   Bonus: $
Second Exec. Salary: $376,223   Bonus: $

OTHER THOUGHTS:

Estimated Female Officers or Directors: 5
Hot Spot for Advancement for Women/Minorities: Y

Building Materials Holding Corp (BMC)

www.buildwithbmc.com

NAIC Code: 444190

TYPES OF BUSINESS:

Building Materials & Hardware Stores, Retail
Building & Construction Services

BRANDS/DIVISIONS/AFFILIATES:

BMC Design

CONTACTS: Note: Officers with more than one job title may be intentionally listed here more than once.

Jeffrey Rea, CEO
James Major, CFO
Andrew Freedman, Director
Lisa Hamblet, Executive VP, Divisional
Bryan Yeazel, Executive VP
Mark Necaise, Other Corporate Officer
Walter Randolph, President, Divisional
Duff Wakefield, President, Divisional
Steven Wilson, President, Divisional
C. Ball, Senior VP
Michael Farmer, Vice President, Divisional

GROWTH PLANS/SPECIAL FEATURES:

Building Materials Holding Corp. (BMHC) is a leading provider of building materials and services to residential, commercial and industrial contractors as well as professional repair and remodeling contractors and builders. The firm operates 38 lumber yards, 18 truss manufacturing facilities, 23 millwork operations and 8 showroom and design centers. Its principal products include lumber, panel products, engineered wood products, roofing materials, pre-hung doors and millwork, roof and floor trusses, pre-assembled windows, cabinets, hardware, paint and tools. BMHC also provides services such as pre-cutting lumber and pre-assembling windows to meet customer specifications. The firm's BMC Design subsidiary offers expert advice in millwork, windows and cabinetry selections. The company targets primarily professional contractors and builders engaged in residential construction and, to a lesser extent, light commercial and industrial construction. Additionally, the firm provides construction services to high-volume production homebuilders. Services include framing, concrete, plumbing, other construction trades, managing labor and construction schedules as well as sourcing materials. BMHC's primary growth plans consist of expansion through acquisitions, focusing on those that complement existing operations in growing building markets, and those that provide entry into fast-growing, attractive new markets. In June 2015, BMHC agreed to merge with Stock Building Supply Holdings, Inc. in order to expand the geographic reach of both companies across the U.S. That August, the firm agreed to acquire Robert Bowden Inc., a supplier of windows, doors, trim, millwork, siding and decking to professional customers.

BMHC offers its employees medical, dental and health insurance as well as a 401(k).

FINANCIAL DATA: Note: Data for latest year may not have been available at press time.

In U.S. $	2015	2014	2013	2012	2011	2010
Revenue		1,295,716,000	1,197,037,000	942,398,000	759,982,000	751,706,000
R&D Expense						
Operating Income		18,324,000	761,000	-18,907,000	-59,301,000	-122,834,000
Operating Margin %		1.41%	.06%	-2.00%	-7.80%	-16.34%
SGA Expense		279,717,000	254,935,000	221,192,000	213,036,000	246,338,000
Net Income		10,419,000	-4,635,000	-14,533,000	-42,133,000	-69,994,000
Operating Cash Flow		16,941,000	-40,264,000	-12,243,000	-7,001,000	-57,999,000
Capital Expenditure		43,306,000	7,448,000	2,741,000	1,339,000	2,506,000
EBITDA		32,454,000	13,694,000	-6,860,000	-44,707,000	-71,587,000
Return on Assets %		3.02%	-2.14%	-8.88%	-18.19%	
Return on Equity %		7.75%	-7.99%	-56.11%	-90.07%	
Debt to Equity		0.68	0.50	0.16	0.01	

CONTACT INFORMATION:

Phone: 208-331-4300   Fax: 208-331-4366
Toll-Free:
Address: 720 Park Blvd., Ste. 200, Raleigh, ID 27617 United States

STOCK TICKER/OTHER:

Stock Ticker: STCK
Employees: 5,000
Parent Company:

Exchange: NAS
Fiscal Year Ends: 12/31

SALARIES/BONUSES:

Top Exec. Salary: $600,000   Bonus: $
Second Exec. Salary: $310,000   Bonus: $200,000

OTHER THOUGHTS:

Estimated Female Officers or Directors: 2
Hot Spot for Advancement for Women/Minorities:

Bulgari SpA

NAIC Code: 448310

www.bulgari.com

TYPES OF BUSINESS:

Jewelry Retailing
Jewelry Design & Manufacturing
Hotel & Resort Operations
Restaurants

BRANDS/DIVISIONS/AFFILIATES:

Bulgari Hotels & Resorts
LB Diamonds Sarl
LVMH Moet Hennessy Louis Vuitton SA
Bulgari Qatar LLC
Bulgari Kuwait LLC
BVLGARI
Bulgari International Corporation NV
Omotesando

CONTACTS:
Note: Officers with more than one job title may be intentionally listed here more than once.

Francesco Trapani, CEO
Flavia Spena, CFO
Paolo Piantella, Dir.-External Rel.
Enrico Frizzi, Dir.-Finance
Silvio Ursini, Exec. VP-Bulgari Hotels & Resorts
Nicola Bulgari, VP
Paolo Bulgari, Chmn.

GROWTH PLANS/SPECIAL FEATURES:

Bulgari SpA, majority-owned by LVMH Moet Hennessy Louis Vuitton SA, is an Italian manufacturer and retailer of luxury items and fine jewelry. Bulgari's products include jewels and jewelry, watches, accessories, gifts and fragrances. Trademarked as BVLGARI, firm operates nearly 300 boutiques around the world. It also operates exclusive hotels and resorts in Milan and Bali as well as restaurants, Ginza and Omotesando, in downtown Tokyo and Bulgari il Cafe in Osaka. The resorts and restaurants are overseen by Bulgari Hotels & Resorts, a joint venture between Bulgari and Luxury Group, a division of Marriott International. The Bulgari Hotel in Milan offers luxury accommodations as well as a restaurant, a spa and an events facility. The Bulgari Resort in Bali comprises 58 traditional and contemporary villas overlooking the Indian Ocean and offers a restaurant, spa and an events facility. The company owns several regional operating subsidiaries, including Bulgari Ireland Ltd.; Bulgari Qatar LLC; Bulgari Kuwait WLL; and Bulgari International Corporation NV, which itself owns LB Diamonds Sarl.

FINANCIAL DATA:
Note: Data for latest year may not have been available at press time.

In U.S. $	2015	2014	2013	2012	2011	2010
Revenue			1,327,068,800	2,000,000,000	1,800,000,000	1,134,564,480
R&D Expense						
Operating Income						
Operating Margin %						
SGA Expense						
Net Income						
Operating Cash Flow						40,333,672
Capital Expenditure						
EBITDA						
Return on Assets %						
Return on Equity %						
Debt to Equity						

CONTACT INFORMATION:

Phone: 39-06-688-101   Fax: 39-06-688-10400
Toll-Free:
Address: Lungotevere Marzio, 11, Roma, 00187 Italy

STOCK TICKER/OTHER:

Stock Ticker: Subsidiary   Exchange:
Employees: 3,847   Fiscal Year Ends: 12/31
Parent Company: LVMH Moet Hennessy Louis Vuitton SA

SALARIES/BONUSES:

Top Exec. Salary: $ Bonus: $
Second Exec. Salary: $ Bonus: $

OTHER THOUGHTS:

Estimated Female Officers or Directors: 2
Hot Spot for Advancement for Women/Minorities:

Burberry Group plc

NAIC Code: 424300

www.burberryplc.com

TYPES OF BUSINESS:

Apparel and Clothing Brands, Designers, Importers and Distributors
Accessories
Licensing
Outerwear
Retail Stores
Manufacturing

BRANDS/DIVISIONS/AFFILIATES:

Burberry Prorsum
Burberry London
Burberry Brit
Burberry

CONTACTS: Note: Officers with more than one job title may be intentionally listed here more than once.

Angela Ahrendts, CEO
John Smith, COO
Carol Fairweather, CFO
John Peace, Chmn.

GROWTH PLANS/SPECIAL FEATURES:

Burberry Group plc is an English luxury brand that designs, sources, manufactures and distributes apparel and accessories through a network of retail, wholesale and licensing channels worldwide. Founded in 1856, the company's products today include apparel for women, men and children as well as accessories such as handbags, scarves, small leather goods, belts, shoes and jewelry. The firm manufactures a portion of its outerwear, with the majority of its projects sourced from third parties. It also has global licensing relationships in specialized product categories such as eyewear, fragrance and timepieces. In these arrangements, the company grants licenses for the design and manufacture of products bearing the Burberry name, while working with its partners to ensure consistency within its overall branding strategy. Burberry brands include Burberry Prorsum, the most fashion-forward collection and is inspired by runway shows; Burberry London, a tailored collection typically for customer work attire; and Burberry Brit, a casual collection. Burberry operates more than 500 directly operated stores and concessions in 50 countries. Its third-party distribution network includes worldwide franchise stores worldwide, as well as wholesale department and specialty stores in over 80 countries. Currently, retail/wholesale sales accounts for approximately 36% of company revenue, women's accounts for 30%, men's 23%, children 3% and beauty 8%. Burberry is responsible for the creation of gabardine fabric, the Burberry check pattern and its iconic trench coat, first worn by British officers during World War I. In October 2015, the firm launched its first Seoul, Korea flagship store.

FINANCIAL DATA: Note: Data for latest year may not have been available at press time.

In U.S. $	2015	2014	2013	2012	2011	2010
Revenue	3,771,938,000	3,482,823,000	2,987,862,000	2,776,333,000	2,244,297,000	1,771,609,000
R&D Expense						
Operating Income	658,205,500	665,829,500	516,937,200	563,428,700	451,610,000	323,646,400
Operating Margin %	17.45%	19.11%	17.30%	20.29%	20.12%	18.26%
SGA Expense	1,958,771,000	1,791,192,000		686,758,100	489,132,100	424,253,300
Net Income	502,735,700	482,106,000	380,153,700	393,607,800	311,537,700	121,685,100
Operating Cash Flow	680,031,100	635,632,500	635,184,000	554,608,800	393,458,300	550,423,000
Capital Expenditure	232,756,300	230,215,000	262,953,300	228,869,600	162,047,400	104,493,700
EBITDA	874,517,900	876,012,800	696,026,600	683,469,400	543,247,600	401,381,300
Return on Assets %	16.25%	17.37%	15.15%	17.70%	16.64%	7.18%
Return on Equity %	26.20%	29.55%	26.99%	33.31%	31.97%	14.41%
Debt to Equity						

CONTACT INFORMATION:

Phone: 44 2033673000   Fax: 44 2033674910
Toll-Free:
Address: Hourseferry Rd., Horseferry House, London,   SW1P 2AW
United Kingdom

STOCK TICKER/OTHER:

Stock Ticker: BBRYF
Employees: 10,851
Parent Company:

Exchange: PINX
Fiscal Year Ends: 03/31

SALARIES/BONUSES:

Top Exec. Salary: $ Bonus: $
Second Exec. Salary: $ Bonus: $

OTHER THOUGHTS:

Estimated Female Officers or Directors: 3
Hot Spot for Advancement for Women/Minorities: Y

Sales, profits and employees may be estimates. Financial information, benefits and other data can change quickly and may vary from those stated here.

Burlington Stores Inc

www.burlingtoninvestors.com

NAIC Code: 448140

TYPES OF BUSINESS:

Discount Apparel Stores
Linens/Housewares
Children's Furniture
Gifts
Online Sales
Children's Apparel
Maternity Apparel
Footwear

BRANDS/DIVISIONS/AFFILIATES:

Burlington Coat Factory Warehouse Corporation
MJM Designer Shoes
Cohoes Fashions
Super Baby Depot

CONTACTS: *Note: Officers with more than one job title may be intentionally listed here more than once.*

Thomas Kingsbury, CEO
John Crimmins, Chief Accounting Officer
Hobart Sichel, Chief Marketing Officer
Rick Seeger, Executive VP, Divisional
Fred Hand, Executive VP, Divisional
Mike Metheny, Executive VP, Divisional
Joyce Magrini, Executive VP, Divisional
Marc Katz, Executive VP
Jennifer Vecchio, Executive VP
Christopher Schaub, Vice President
Robert LaPenta, Vice President

GROWTH PLANS/SPECIAL FEATURES:

Burlington Stores, Inc. (formerly Burlington Coat Factory Warehouse Corporation), is a value priced retailer of branded apparel, baby furniture, home decor and gifts. Burlington operates 542 stores under the Burlington, MJM Designer Shoes, Cohoes Fashions stores and Super Baby Depot names throughout 44 states and Puerto Rico. Burlington Warehouse stores offer ladies sportswear, menswear, coats, family footwear, baby furniture, accessories, home decor and gifts. MJM Designer Shoes offers men's, women's and children's moderate- to higher-priced designer and fashion shoes, sandals, boots and sneakers as well as handbags, wallets, belts, socks, hosiery and novelty gifts. Cohoes Fashions offers designer label merchandise for men and women similar to that carried in Burlington stores as well as decorative gifts and home furnishings. Super Baby Depot sells brand name apparel, furniture and accessories for newborns, infants and toddlers. Burlington has two distribution centers in Edgewater Park, New Jersey and San Bernardino, California. The company also sells coats and baby products through its web site. Although irregular and discontinued products comprise a small portion of its merchandise, Burlington primarily sells items at below-traditional prices by maintaining inventory control and using a no-frills merchandising approach to business. All of Burlington's stores are located in shopping malls, strip malls or stand-alone locations, which are in close proximity to other department stores and population centers. Some stores contain departments licensed to unaffiliated parties for the sale of such items as lingerie, fragrances, shoes and jewelry.

The company offers its employees a 401(k) plan, a profit sharing plan, medical and dental insurance, life and disability insurance, an employee discount and training programs.

FINANCIAL DATA: *Note: Data for latest year may not have been available at press time.*

In U.S. $	2015	2014	2013	2012	2011	2010
Revenue	4,849,634,000	4,461,987,000	4,165,504,000	3,887,531,000	3,701,089,000	
R&D Expense						
Operating Income	260,306,000	203,876,000	29,165,000	-10,420,000	53,128,000	
Operating Margin %	5.36%	4.56%	.70%	-.26%	1.43%	
SGA Expense	1,520,929,000	1,391,788,000	1,312,682,000	1,215,774,000	1,153,573,000	
Net Income	65,955,000	16,150,000	25,301,000	-6,272,000	30,998,000	
Operating Cash Flow	302,335,000	289,351,000	452,509,000	249,983,000	208,704,000	
Capital Expenditure	220,980,000	168,267,000	166,721,000	153,373,000	132,131,000	
EBITDA	356,361,000	328,292,000	309,878,000	271,771,000	299,196,000	
Return on Assets %	2.51%	-3.73%	-4.88%	-5.17%		
Return on Equity %						
Debt to Equity						

CONTACT INFORMATION:

Phone: 609-387-7800　　Fax: 609-387-7071
Toll-Free:
Address: 1830 Route. 130 N., Burlington, NJ 08016 United States

STOCK TICKER/OTHER:

Stock Ticker: BURL
Employees: 34,000
Parent Company:

Exchange: NYS
Fiscal Year Ends: 01/28

SALARIES/BONUSES:

Top Exec. Salary: $1,071,203
Bonus: $225,000

Second Exec. Salary: $628,102
Bonus: $

OTHER THOUGHTS:

Estimated Female Officers or Directors: 1

Hot Spot for Advancement for Women/Minorities:

Cabela's Inc

www.cabelas.com

NAIC Code: 451110

TYPES OF BUSINESS:

Sporting Goods Stores
Hunting & Fishing Supplies
Camping Equipment
Outdoor Apparel
Catalog & Online Sales
Credit Card Programs

BRANDS/DIVISIONS/AFFILIATES:

World's Foremost Bank
Cabela's CLUB Visa
Cabela's Outpost Store

CONTACTS: *Note: Officers with more than one job title may be intentionally listed here more than once.*

Sean Baker, CEO, Subsidiary
Thomas Millner, CEO
Ralph Castner, CFO
James Cabela, Chairman of the Board
Charles Baldwin, Chief Administrative Officer
Scott Williams, Chief Marketing Officer
Michael Copeland, COO
Douglas Means, Executive VP
Brent LaSure, Secretary

GROWTH PLANS/SPECIAL FEATURES:

Cabela's, Inc. is a leading retailer of outdoor and hunting supply merchandise. Through its web site, mail-order catalogs and retail stores, the company supplies hunting, marine, automobile & ATV, fishing and camping equipment as well as brand-name casual clothing and home fashion accessories. It operates in three divisions: retail, direct and financial services. The retail division manages 50 retail stores in 26 states and four stores in Canada. The stores, which are considered tourist attractions, receive millions of visitors per year. They are designed to communicate an outdoor lifestyle environment characterized by the outdoor feel of the lighting, wood or tile flooring, cedar wood beams, open ceilings and lodge-style atmosphere. The retail-format stores range between 40,000 to 246,000 square feet, contain a mountain and pond with museum-quality taxidermy and native game fish, gun libraries featuring high-quality firearms, archery training systems, virtual shooting arcades, museums or educational centers and restaurants and banquet and meeting facilities. The direct segment of Cabela's is responsible for the company's catalog and Internet sales channel operations. Its Cabelas.com website is a cost-effective medium to offer a convenient, user-friendly and secure online shopping option for new and existing customers. Through its wholly-owned subsidiary World's Foremost Bank, the financial services division offers the Cabela's CLUB Visa credit card, a rewards-based program that allows customers to earn and redeem points by using their credit card. The firm currently has over 1.8 million active credit accounts.

FINANCIAL DATA: *Note: Data for latest year may not have been available at press time.*

In U.S. $	2015	2014	2013	2012	2011	2010
Revenue		3,647,650,000	3,599,577,000	3,112,682,000	2,811,166,000	2,663,242,000
R&D Expense						
Operating Income		335,395,000	361,361,000	275,699,000	231,548,000	186,762,000
Operating Margin %		9.19%	10.03%	8.85%	8.23%	7.01%
SGA Expense		1,251,325,000	1,201,519,000	1,046,861,000	954,125,000	895,405,000
Net Income		201,715,000	224,390,000	173,513,000	142,620,000	112,159,000
Operating Cash Flow		257,979,000	345,004,000	234,629,000	366,468,000	167,427,000
Capital Expenditure		440,891,000	333,009,000	214,267,000	126,740,000	75,349,000
EBITDA		453,434,000	458,824,000	361,106,000	310,237,000	264,034,000
Return on Assets %		2.86%	3.69%	3.18%	2.95%	3.19%
Return on Equity %		11.78%	15.04%	13.57%	12.93%	11.16%
Debt to Equity		1.68	1.72	1.56	1.11	1.20

CONTACT INFORMATION:

Phone: 308 254-5505   Fax: 308 254-4800
Toll-Free: 800-237-4444
Address: 1 Cabela Dr., Sidney, NE 69160 United States

SALARIES/BONUSES:

Top Exec. Salary: $989,000   Bonus: $
Second Exec. Salary: $503,846   Bonus: $

STOCK TICKER/OTHER:

Stock Ticker: CAB   Exchange: NYS
Employees: 19,300   Fiscal Year Ends: 12/31
Parent Company:

OTHER THOUGHTS:

Estimated Female Officers or Directors: 2
Hot Spot for Advancement for Women/Minorities:

Caleres Inc

NAIC Code: 448210

TYPES OF BUSINESS:

Shoes, Retail
Shoes, Wholesale
Online Sales

BRANDS/DIVISIONS/AFFILIATES:

Brown Shoe Company Inc
Famous Footwear
Naturalizer
Sam Edelman
Dr. Scholl's Shoes
Shoes.com Inc
Via Spiga
SamEdelman.com

CONTACTS: Note: Officers with more than one job title may be intentionally listed here more than once.

Diane Sullivan, CEO
Daniel Karpel, Chief Accounting Officer
Mark Schmitt, Chief Information Officer
Richard Ausick, President, Divisional
Daniel Friedman, President, Divisional
John Schmidt, President, Divisional
John Mazurk, President, Divisional
Kenneth Hannah, Senior VP
Douglas Koch, Senior VP
Michael Oberlander, Senior VP

GROWTH PLANS/SPECIAL FEATURES:

Caleres, Inc., formerly the Brown Shoe Company, Inc., is a global retailer and wholesaler of footwear for women and men. The firm operates more than 1,200 shoe stores in the U.S., Canada, Guam and China. These stores consist of 1,038 Famous Footwear stores and 179 specialty retail stores operating under the Naturalizer, Sam Edelman, Via Spiga and Dr. Scholl's Shoes names. Famous Footwear targets primarily female customers seeking to purchase brand-name shoes at value prices for themselves and their families. The majority of Famous Footwear stores are located in strip centers, with the remainder in outlet and regional malls. In addition to its brick-and-mortar locations, the firm maintains e-commerce sites for its brands, including FamousFootwear.com, DrSchollsShoes.com, SamEdelman.com and Naturalizer.com. Caleres also owns online shoe retailer Shoes.com, Inc. The firm's wholesale division designs, sources and markets branded and non-branded dress, casual and athletic footwear. The company's footwear is distributed to over 3,000 retailers, including department stores, mass merchandisers, national chains, independent retailers, catalogs and online retailers throughout the U.S. and Canada as well as in 60 other countries. During 2014, retail sales accounted for roughly 67% of its revenue, while wholesale sales accounted for the remaining 33%. In May 2015, the Brown Shoe Company, Inc. announced that it had changed its name to Caleres, Inc. in order to reflect the company's history and its passion for fit.

Brown Shoe Company offers its employees medical, dental and vision plans; life and disability insurance; a pension plan; a 401(k); and tuition assistance.

FINANCIAL DATA: Note: Data for latest year may not have been available at press time.

In U.S. $	2015	2014	2013	2012	2011	2010
Revenue	2,571,709,000	2,513,113,000	2,598,065,000	2,582,824,000	2,504,091,000	2,241,968,000
R&D Expense						
Operating Income	125,934,000	98,617,000	61,607,000	35,550,000	72,664,000	31,523,000
Operating Margin %	4.89%	3.92%	2.37%	1.37%	2.90%	1.40%
SGA Expense	910,682,000	909,749,000	918,957,000	937,419,000	922,976,000	859,693,000
Net Income	82,850,000	38,073,000	27,491,000	24,589,000	37,233,000	9,500,000
Operating Cash Flow	118,812,000	104,032,000	197,937,000	48,086,000	-2,312,000	118,078,000
Capital Expenditure	115,103,000	49,203,000	63,729,000	38,564,000	54,827,000	49,978,000
EBITDA	182,187,000	154,323,000	116,712,000	94,302,000	123,189,000	82,997,000
Return on Assets %	7.00%	3.28%	2.29%	2.07%	3.40%	.91%
Return on Equity %	16.28%	8.44%	6.56%	5.94%	9.11%	2.38%
Debt to Equity	0.36	0.41	0.46	0.48	0.36	0.37

CONTACT INFORMATION:

Phone: 314 854-4000   Fax: 314 854-4274
Toll-Free:
Address: 8300 Maryland Ave., St. Louis, MO 63105 United States

STOCK TICKER/OTHER:

Stock Ticker: CAL   Exchange: NYS
Employees: 11,000   Fiscal Year Ends: 01/31
Parent Company:

SALARIES/BONUSES:

Top Exec. Salary: Bonus: $
$1,000,000
Second Exec. Salary: Bonus: $
$625,000

OTHER THOUGHTS:

Estimated Female Officers or Directors: 4

Hot Spot for Advancement for Women/Minorities: Y

Calloway's Nursery Inc

www.calloways.com

NAIC Code: 444220

TYPES OF BUSINESS:

Garden Supplies & Plants, Retail

BRANDS/DIVISIONS/AFFILIATES:

Cornelius Nursery
Calloway's Nursery

CONTACTS: Note: Officers with more than one job title may be intentionally listed here more than once.

Jim Estill, Pres.
Daniel G. Reynolds, CFO
Kimberly Bird, Dir.-Retail Mktg.
Sam Weger, VP-Recruiting & Training
Marce E. Ward, VP-Merch.
John S. Peters, VP-Oper.
John T. Cosby, VP-Real Estate

GROWTH PLANS/SPECIAL FEATURES:

Calloway's Nursery, Inc. is a specialty retailer of lawn and garden products. The firm operates a 18-store chain of garden centers in two large metropolitan areas in Texas: Dallas-Fort Worth and Houston. The company selects the locations of its stores based on demographic data, traffic patterns and shopping habits. All of Calloway's retail locations are company-operated. Its retail garden centers operate as Calloway's Nursery in the Dallas-Fort Worth market and Cornelius Nursery in Houston. The firm specializes in offering quality and breadth of selection in bedding plants and nursery stock; its stores carry both organic and traditional garden solutions. Most of its sales consist of nursery plants. Related garden products such as soil amendments, flowers and fertilizers complement the live garden stock. Cornelius stores in the greater Houston area have developed a strong focus on Christmas items. The retail stores also offer expert advice to its customers by holding weekly educational gardening clinics which are led by Texas certified nursery professionals. Calloway's Nursery belongs to the Texas Nursery and Landscape Association (TNLA), and the majority of its full time employees are either Texas master certified nursery professionals or Texas certified nursery professionals.

The company provides employees with benefits including life insurance, flexible hours, a 401(k), paid time off and store discounts.

FINANCIAL DATA: Note: Data for latest year may not have been available at press time.

In U.S. $	2015	2014	2013	2012	2011	2010
Revenue		53,515,000	46,664,000	45,551,000	46,589,000	43,767,000
R&D Expense						
Operating Income						
Operating Margin %						
SGA Expense						
Net Income		8,340,000	827,000	609,000	1,295,000	1,004,000
Operating Cash Flow						
Capital Expenditure						
EBITDA						
Return on Assets %						
Return on Equity %						
Debt to Equity						

CONTACT INFORMATION:

Phone: 817-222-1122   Fax: 817-302-0031
Toll-Free:
Address: 4200 Airport Fwy., Ste. 200, Fort Worth, TX 76117 United States

STOCK TICKER/OTHER:

Stock Ticker: CLWY
Employees: 252
Parent Company:

Exchange: PINX
Fiscal Year Ends: 12/31

SALARIES/BONUSES:

Top Exec. Salary: $ Bonus: $
Second Exec. Salary: $ Bonus: $

OTHER THOUGHTS:

Estimated Female Officers or Directors: 1
Hot Spot for Advancement for Women/Minorities:

Canadian Tire Corp Ltd

NAIC Code: 441320

corp.canadiantire.ca

TYPES OF BUSINESS:

Retail-Auto Parts & Tires
Retail-Auto Accessories
Banking Services
Financial Services-Insurance & Loans
Roadside Assistance
Gas Stations
Convenience Stores
Retail-Sports & Work Apparel

BRANDS/DIVISIONS/AFFILIATES:

Canadian Tire Financial Services Ltd
PartSource
Canadian Tire Petroleum
Mark's Work Wearhouse Ltd
Canadian Tire Retail
L'Equipeur
Forzani Group Ltd (The)
Canadian Tire Jumpstart

CONTACTS: Note: Officers with more than one job title may be intentionally listed here more than once.

Mary Turner, CEO, Subsidiary
James Christie, Executive VP
Michael Medline, CEO
Gregory Craig, CFO, Subsidiary
Dean McCann, CFO
Maureen Sabia, Chairman of the Board
Eugene Roman, Chief Technology Officer
Allan MacDonald, COO
Rick White, COO, Subsidiary
Chad McKinnon, COO, Subsidiary
Stephen Wetmore, Deputy Chairman
Douglas Nathanson, General Counsel
Mahes Wickramasinghe, Other Executive Officer
Duncan Fulton, Other Executive Officer

GROWTH PLANS/SPECIAL FEATURES:

Canadian Tire Corp., Ltd. is a group of interrelated businesse
engaged in auto part and tire retail, financial services, appare
retail and convinience stores. It operates through six division:
Canadian Tire Retail (CTR); PartSource; Canadian Tir
Petroleum (CTP); Canadian Tire Bank (CTB); Mark's Wor
Wearhouse, Ltd. (Marks'); and The Forzani Group, Ltd. (FG
Sports). CTR offers branded products in the areas c
automotive parts, accessories and service; sports and leisur
products; home products; apparel; and tools and hardwar
through more than 490 stores. PartSource is an automotiv
parts specialty retail chain, targeting do-it-yourselfers an
commercial installers. CTP is one of Canada's larges
independent retailers of gasoline. It has nearly 301 agen
operated gas bars; 296 convenience stores and kiosks; and 8
car wash centers. CTB provides various financial products
including a range of branded credit, mostly backed b
MasterCard. CTB also offers high interest savings, tax fre
savings accounts; guaranteed investment certificates; and
insurance and warranty products. Mark's, called L'Equipeur i
Quebec, offers men's and women's casual clothing an
footwear for business-casual, recreational and industrial wor
environments. It operates through 386 stores across Canada
FGL Sports is one of Canada's largest retailers of sportin
goods, including footwear, apparel and equipment. It offer:
private-brand and brand-name products through 415 stores
across Canada. Canadian Tire Corp. also operates Canadia
Tire Jumpstart, which connects underprivileged children from
ages 4-18 with the opportunity and financial resources to
participate in community-based sport organizations.

FINANCIAL DATA: Note: Data for latest year may not have been available at press time.

In U.S. $	2015	2014	2013	2012	2011	2010
Revenue		9,336,974,000	8,829,554,000	8,561,047,000	7,781,823,000	6,728,249,000
R&D Expense						
Operating Income		752,253,100	667,071,200	601,892,400	570,951,200	447,261,400
Operating Margin %		8.05%	7.55%	7.03%	7.33%	6.64%
SGA Expense		2,013,500,000	1,489,223,000	1,423,819,000	1,514,021,000	24,722,990
Net Income		452,505,600	420,440,700	373,991,400	349,867,800	339,828,700
Operating Cash Flow		430,629,500	596,947,800	556,641,900	1,052,975,000	742,588,700
Capital Expenditure		515,961,300	382,232,400	214,715,400	269,255,800	230,598,100
EBITDA		1,027,502,000	937,301,000	866,503,400	810,015,000	709,924,400
Return on Assets %		4.28%	4.18%	3.91%	4.42%	5.16%
Return on Equity %		12.05%	11.30%	10.88%	11.01%	11.69%
Debt to Equity		0.43	0.45	0.49	0.53	0.26

CONTACT INFORMATION:

Phone: 416 480-3000   Fax: 416 544-7715
Toll-Free: 800-387-8803
Address: 2180 Yonge St., Toronto, ON M4P 2V8 Canada

STOCK TICKER/OTHER:

Stock Ticker: CTC
Employees: 28,272
Parent Company:

Exchange: TSE
Fiscal Year Ends: 12/31

SALARIES/BONUSES:

Top Exec. Salary: $ Bonus: $
Second Exec. Salary: $ Bonus: $

OTHER THOUGHTS:

Estimated Female Officers or Directors: 3
Hot Spot for Advancement for Women/Minorities: Y

CARQUEST Corp

www.carquest.com

NAIC Code: 423120

TYPES OF BUSINESS:

Auto Parts Distribution

BRANDS/DIVISIONS/AFFILIATES:

Advance Auto Parts Inc
TECH-NET Professional Auto Service
CARQUEST eServices
CARQUEST Technical Institute
Direct-Hit
WORLDPAC

CONTACTS: *Note: Officers with more than one job title may be intentionally listed here more than once.*

Randal Long, VP-Product Mgmt.
Mike DeSorbo, Dir.-Professional Markets
Jack Brouillard, Chmn.

GROWTH PLANS/SPECIAL FEATURES:

CARQUEST Auto Parts, a subsidiary of Advance Auto Parts, Inc., operates a chain of over 5,200 automotive parts stores, independently and distributor-owned, located throughout the U.S. and parts of Canada. Approximately 1,325 CARQUEST stores are independently owned. The group has 106 WORLDPAC branches. Items available in stores include temperature control and cooling products, steering and suspension products, engine and mechanical systems, brake systems, drivetrain systems, engine performance and emissions control systems, temperature control and cooling systems and electrical and vision systems. In addition, it provides parts, accessories, supplies and equipment for most models of light and heavy-weight trucks, recreational vehicles, agricultural equipment, buses and off-roading equipment. The firm also sells and distributes tools, equipment, chemicals, paint and accessories. CARQUEST's own branded line of products is sold to the distributor stores as well as to wholesalers for eventual resale to professional repair shops, service stations, dealerships and do-it-yourself (DIY) customers. CARQUEST owns TECH-NET Professional Auto Service, a network of independent automotive service facilities, and CARQUEST eServices, which provides professional customers with access to CARQUEST's inventory and catalog over the Internet at any time. Through the CARQUEST Technical Institute, the firm offers online and instructor-led training programs for professional technicians and automotive repair facility owners. CARQUEST also offers Direct-Hit, an online vehicle diagnostic service.

The company offers its employees medical, dental and vision insurance; a 401(k); paid vacation; life, AD&D and long-term disability insurance; an employee stock ownership plan; flexible spending accounts; an employee assistance program; and education reimbursement.

FINANCIAL DATA: *Note: Data for latest year may not have been available at press time.*

In U.S. $	2015	2014	2013	2012	2011	2010
Revenue		3,000,000,000	2,300,000,000	2,900,000,000	2,870,000,000	2,500,000,000
R&D Expense						
Operating Income						
Operating Margin %						
SGA Expense						
Net Income						
Operating Cash Flow						
Capital Expenditure						
EBITDA						
Return on Assets %						
Return on Equity %						
Debt to Equity						

CONTACT INFORMATION:

Phone: 919-573-3000   Fax: 919-573-2501
Toll-Free: 877-735-2233
Address: 2635 E. Millbrook Rd., Raleigh, NC 27604 United States

SALARIES/BONUSES:

Top Exec. Salary: $ Bonus: $
Second Exec. Salary: $ Bonus: $

STOCK TICKER/OTHER:

Stock Ticker: Subsidiary
Employees: 19,000
Parent Company: Advance Auto Parts Inc

Exchange:
Fiscal Year Ends: 12/31

OTHER THOUGHTS:

Estimated Female Officers or Directors:
Hot Spot for Advancement for Women/Minorities:

Carrefour SA

NAIC Code: 452112

www.carrefour.com

TYPES OF BUSINESS:

Hypermarkets
Supermarkets
Convenience Stores
Grocery Delivery & Distribution
Online Grocery Sales

BRANDS/DIVISIONS/AFFILIATES:

Carrefour Markets
Marche Plus
Shopi
8 a Huit
Marinopoulos
Di per Di
Promocash
PT Alfa Retailindo Tbk

CONTACTS: *Note: Officers with more than one job title may be intentionally listed here more than once.*

Georges Plassat, CEO
Pierre-Jean Sivignon, CFO
Jose Carlos Gonzalez-Hurtado, Group Chief Commercial Officer
Jean-Christophe Deslarzes, Chief Human Resources & Organization Officer
Eric Legros, Exec. Dir.-Group Merch.
Jerome Bedier, Gen. Sec.
Marie-Noelle Brouaux, Exec. Comm. Dir.
Eric Legros, Exec. Dir.-Group Merchandise
Georges Plassat, Chmn.

GROWTH PLANS/SPECIAL FEATURES:

Carrefour SA is a leading European retailer with about 10,860 stores in 33 countries worldwide. The firm directly owns slightly more than half of these stores, with the other 40% run by franchisees or partners. Its stores can be divided into four categories: hypermarkets, supermarkets, convenience stores and cash-and-carry stores. The Carrefour-branded hypermarkets (1,459 in number) carry an average of 40,000 to 80,000 food and non-food items and average approximately 90,400 square feet. Carrefour operates 3,115 supermarkets under the Carrefour, Carrefour Markets, GS and GB brand names. These stores feature competitively priced food items in spaces of 10,700 to 21,500 square feet. Its 6,111 convenience stores (Shopi, Marche Plus, 8 a Huit, Marinopoulos, Proxi and Di per Di) offer a neighborhood grocery feel with stores of 4,000 to 8,000 square feet. The 175 cash-and-carry stores, including Promocash, Docks Market and Gross IPer, cater mostly to hotels and restaurants with delivery of fresh groceries from centralized warehouses. In addition, Ooshop.com, the company's online supermarket, allows customers in France to order a variety of standard supermarket products and have them delivered to their homes. Through CarrefourOnline.com, it offers non-food retail items including leisure products such as DVDs, games, books and music as well as electronics. The company also holds a 60% stake in PT Alfa Retailindo Tbk, an Indonesian retailer.

FINANCIAL DATA: *Note: Data for latest year may not have been available at press time.*

In U.S. $	2015	2014	2013	2012	2011	2010
Revenue		80,996,350,000	81,375,230,000	80,793,650,000	85,386,950,000	97,122,820,000
R&D Expense						
Operating Income		2,729,666,000	2,528,018,000	1,521,905,000	-510,485,700	1,948,548,000
Operating Margin %		3.37%	3.10%	1.88%	-.59%	2.00%
SGA Expense		14,095,140,000	13,985,820,000	14,061,170,000	14,825,310,000	15,897,220,000
Net Income		1,325,565,000	1,340,423,000	1,308,584,000	393,742,600	602,818,800
Operating Cash Flow		2,768,934,000	1,777,679,000	2,093,946,000	2,247,835,000	2,903,719,000
Capital Expenditure		2,558,796,000	2,291,348,000	1,641,832,000	2,472,831,000	2,252,080,000
EBITDA		4,195,322,000	4,047,801,000	3,230,599,000	1,394,549,000	4,282,349,000
Return on Assets %		2.79%	2.82%	2.62%	.73%	.82%
Return on Equity %		14.66%	16.47%	17.48%	4.58%	4.35%
Debt to Equity		0.91	1.18	1.19	1.43	1.08

CONTACT INFORMATION:

Phone: 33 153701959   Fax:
Toll-Free:
Address: 26, quai Michelet, TSA 20016, Paris, 92695 France

STOCK TICKER/OTHER:

Stock Ticker: CRERF   Exchange: PINX
Employees: 381,227   Fiscal Year Ends: 12/31
Parent Company:

SALARIES/BONUSES:

Top Exec. Salary: $ Bonus: $
Second Exec. Salary: $ Bonus: $

OTHER THOUGHTS:

Estimated Female Officers or Directors: 1
Hot Spot for Advancement for Women/Minorities:

Carr-Gottstein Foods Co

www.carrsqc.com

NAIC Code: 445110

TYPES OF BUSINESS:

Grocery Stores, Retail
Wine & Liquor Stores
Tobacco Stores
Food Distribution
Freight Transportation

BRANDS/DIVISIONS/AFFILIATES:

Albertson's Company Inc
CarrsPlus Club

CONTACTS: Note: Officers with more than one job title may be intentionally listed here more than once.

Lawrence H. Hayward, Pres.
Donald J. Anderson, CFO
Steven A. Burd, CEO-Safeway Inc.
Jeffry L. Philipps, Sr. VP-Retail Div.

GROWTH PLANS/SPECIAL FEATURES:

Carr-Gottstein Foods Co. (Carrs), a subsidiary of Albertson's Company, Inc., is the leading food and drug retailer in Alaska, with 28 stores in several different formats. Founded in 1915 as J.B. Gottstein & Company, Carrs is the oldest company in Alaska. Although it has some small outlying stores, the majority of its stores are large supermarket/drug store combinations located in Fairbanks, Anchorage and the Kenai Peninsula. Carrs was the first supermarket chain in Alaska to offer such services as a 24-hour-a-day pharmacy, 59-minute photo processing, banking, a bakery, a service deli and a soup and salad bar. Carrs' freight transportation operations and full-line food warehouse and distribution center provide the company's retail locations with important merchandising benefits, cost advantages and operating efficiencies, enabling it to provide year-round grocery items. The firm also has a CarrsPlus Club card that offers discounts on items each week. In January 2015, Safeway, Inc. and Albertson's merged, making Carrs a subsidiary of Albertson's.

Carrs offers its employees flexible spending accounts; an employee assistance program; a 401(k) plan; a retirement plan; a stock purchase plan; and medical, dental, orthodontia, prescription and vision insurance.

FINANCIAL DATA: Note: Data for latest year may not have been available at press time.

In U.S. $	2015	2014	2013	2012	2011	2010
Revenue						
R&D Expense						
Operating Income						
Operating Margin %						
SGA Expense						
Net Income						
Operating Cash Flow						
Capital Expenditure						
EBITDA						
Return on Assets %						
Return on Equity %						
Debt to Equity						

CONTACT INFORMATION:

Phone: 907-561-1944   Fax: 925-467-3321
Toll-Free:
Address: 6401 A St., Anchorage, AK 99518 United States

STOCK TICKER/OTHER:

Stock Ticker: Subsidiary   Exchange:
Employees: 3,500   Fiscal Year Ends: 12/31
Parent Company: Albertson's Company Inc

SALARIES/BONUSES:

Top Exec. Salary: $ Bonus: $
Second Exec. Salary: $ Bonus: $

OTHER THOUGHTS:

Estimated Female Officers or Directors:
Hot Spot for Advancement for Women/Minorities:

Carters Inc

NAIC Code: 424300

www.carters.com

TYPES OF BUSINESS:

Apparel and Clothing Brands, Designers, Importers and Distributors
Retail Stores
Online Stores

BRANDS/DIVISIONS/AFFILIATES:

Just One You
Precious Firsts
Child of Mine
OshKosh B'gosh
Carter's
William Carter Company
OshKoshBgosh.com
Carters.com

CONTACTS: Note: Officers with more than one job title may be intentionally listed here more than once.

Michael Casey, CEO
Richard Westenberger, CFO
Kevin Corning, Executive VP, Divisional
Christopher Rork, Executive VP, Divisional
Lisa Evans, Executive VP
Michael Wu, General Counsel
Brian Lynch, President
Jill Wilson, Senior VP, Divisional
Greg Foglesong, Senior VP, Divisional
Jeffrey Williams, Senior VP, Divisional
Julie DEmilio, Senior VP, Divisional

GROWTH PLANS/SPECIAL FEATURES:

Carter's, Inc. is one of the largest branded marketers of appare
for babies and young children in the U.S. The company, which
operates through its William Carter Company subsidiary
designs, sources and markets clothing under two primar
brands: Carter's and OshKosh B'gosh. Its products are source
through contractual arrangements with manufacturers
worldwide for wholesale distribution to major domestic retailer
such as Toys R Us, Macy's, JCPenny, Costco, Kohl's, Walmar
and Target. Additionally, the company sells its products in
Carter's and OshKosh branded retail locations. There are
currently 531 Carter's stores and 200 OshKosh stores
throughout North America, situated predominately in strip and
outlet shopping centers. In addition, the company sells its
products at 124 company-operated stores in Canada, as well
as international wholesale, licensing and online channels
Merchandise is also available through the web sites
Carters.com and OshKoshBgosh.com. The retailer sells a wide
array of baby and toddler goods, including bodysuits, pajamas
undershirts, bibs, blankets and layettes. The company licenses
its name to other companies to create lifestyle merchandise
that appeals to older children or moms. Licensed merchandise
includes hosiery, underwear, bedding, toys, shoes, diaper
bags, room decor and accessories. The OshKosh division is a
specialty brand designed for sizes newborn to 12. It focuses on
the production of denim apparel and coordinating garments,
overalls and heavier fleece or woven pieces. In addition to its
two primary brands, the company produces clothing lines
exclusively available at select retailers, including Just One You
and Precious Firsts brands at Target and Child of Mine at
Walmart.

FINANCIAL DATA: Note: Data for latest year may not have been available at press time.

In U.S. $	2015	2014	2013	2012	2011	2010
Revenue		2,893,868,000	2,638,711,000	2,381,734,000	2,109,734,000	1,749,256,000
R&D Expense						
Operating Income		333,345,000	264,151,000	261,986,000	187,466,000	243,256,000
Operating Margin %		11.51%	10.01%	10.99%	8.88%	13.90%
SGA Expense		890,251,000	868,480,000	713,211,000	540,960,000	468,192,000
Net Income		194,670,000	160,407,000	161,150,000	114,016,000	146,472,000
Operating Cash Flow		282,397,000	209,696,000	278,619,000	81,074,000	85,821,000
Capital Expenditure		107,003,000	220,532,000	83,398,000	45,495,000	39,782,000
EBITDA		389,046,000	317,817,000	302,234,000	220,970,000	275,558,000
Return on Assets %		10.50%	9.31%	10.62%	8.57%	11.88%
Return on Equity %		26.17%	19.02%	17.99%	15.34%	23.70%
Debt to Equity		0.74	0.83	0.18	0.29	0.34

CONTACT INFORMATION:

Phone: 678-791-1000   Fax:
Toll-Free: 888-782-9548
Address: 3438 Peachtree Rd NE, Ste 1800, Atlanta, GA 30326 United States

STOCK TICKER/OTHER:

Stock Ticker: CRI
Employees: 11,565
Parent Company:

Exchange: NYS
Fiscal Year Ends: 12/31

SALARIES/BONUSES:

Top Exec. Salary: $953,308   Bonus: $
Second Exec. Salary: $688,846   Bonus: $

OTHER THOUGHTS:

Estimated Female Officers or Directors: 4
Hot Spot for Advancement for Women/Minorities: Y

Casey's General Stores Inc

www.caseys.com

NAIC Code: 447110

TYPES OF BUSINESS:

Convenience Stores
Franchising
Gas Stations

BRANDS/DIVISIONS/AFFILIATES:

Casey's General Store
CGS Sales Corp.
Casey's Services Company
Casey's Retail Company
Tobacco City Inc.
Casey's Marketing Company

CONTACTS: Note: Officers with more than one job title may be intentionally listed here more than once.

William Walljasper, CFO
Robert Myers, Chairman of the Board
Terry Handley, COO
Julia Jackowski, General Counsel
Brian Johnson, Secretary
John Soupene, Senior VP, Divisional
Sam Billmeyer, Senior VP, Divisional
Jay Soupene, Senior VP, Divisional
James Pistillo, Treasurer

GROWTH PLANS/SPECIAL FEATURES:

Casey's General Stores, Inc. has 1,878 stores in 14 Midwestern states, primarily Iowa, Missouri and Illinois, operating under the Casey's General Store banner. Casey's also operates one stand-alone pizza delivery and carry-out store. The firm's general stores carry more than 3,000 items, including a broad selection of food, beverages, tobacco products, health and beauty aids, automotive products and other non-food items. In addition, all but one location offers gasoline for sale on a self-service basis. During the firm's fiscal 2014-15 year, 45 stores were newly constructed and nine were closed down. Additionally, 36 stores were acquired, 32 opened and three were permanently closed. One is due to open in 2016. About 57% of the stores are located in markets with a population of less than 5,000, and approximately 18% of its stores are in communities with more than 20,000 persons. Casey's Distribution Center is adjacent to its corporate headquarters in Ankeny, Iowa. Casey's General Stores seek to meet the needs of residents of small towns by combining the features of a general store with a convenience store. Subsidiaries include Casey's Marketing Company, which oversees wholesale operations including the distribution center; Casey's Services Company, which provides store construction and transportation services; Casey's Retail Company, which holds the rights to the Casey's trademark; CGS Sales Corp., which operates one store in Iowa and one in Nebraska; and Tobacco City Inc., which operates one store in North Dakota.

Employees are offered medical, vision and dental; life insurance; short- and long-term disability; flexible spending accounts; a 401(k); a stock purchase plan; advancement opportunities; wellness programs; a scholarship program; accident insurance; critical illness insurance; and half-priced meals on the job.

FINANCIAL DATA: Note: Data for latest year may not have been available at press time.

In U.S. $	2015	2014	2013	2012	2011	2010
Revenue	7,767,216,000	7,840,255,000	7,250,840,000	6,987,804,000	5,635,240,000	4,637,087,000
R&D Expense						
Operating Income	323,250,000	245,802,000	210,177,000	218,707,000	191,084,000	192,515,000
Operating Margin %	4.16%	3.13%	2.89%	3.12%	3.39%	4.15%
SGA Expense	960,424,000	857,297,000	760,365,000	688,431,000	607,628,000	526,291,000
Net Income	180,628,000	134,514,000	110,625,000	116,791,000	94,623,000	116,962,000
Operating Cash Flow	341,682,000	314,160,000	286,328,000	294,879,000	261,443,000	214,068,000
Capital Expenditure	360,734,000	308,633,000	305,301,000	240,874,000	214,573,000	129,233,000
EBITDA	479,680,000	377,259,000	322,195,000	315,606,000	263,077,000	266,264,000
Return on Assets %	7.58%	6.28%	5.88%	6.89%	6.30%	8.82%
Return on Equity %	22.64%	20.34%	19.96%	25.67%	15.40%	15.13%
Debt to Equity	0.95	1.18	1.08	1.31	1.68	0.18

CONTACT INFORMATION:

Phone: 515 965-6100   Fax: 515 965-6205
Toll-Free:
Address: 1 Convenience Blvd., Ankeny, IA 50021 United States

STOCK TICKER/OTHER:

Stock Ticker: CASY
Employees: 29,749
Parent Company:

Exchange: NAS
Fiscal Year Ends: 04/30

SALARIES/BONUSES:

Top Exec. Salary: $1,050,000   Bonus: $
Second Exec. Salary: $700,000   Bonus: $

OTHER THOUGHTS:

Estimated Female Officers or Directors: 3

Hot Spot for Advancement for Women/Minorities: Y

Sales, profits and employees may be estimates. Financial information, benefits and other data can change quickly and may vary from those stated here.

Cash America International Inc

NAIC Code: 522298

www.cashamerica.com

TYPES OF BUSINESS:

Pawn Shops
Check Cashing
Payday Loans
Money Orders
Money Transfers
Stored Value Cards

BRANDS/DIVISIONS/AFFILIATES:

Mr. Payroll
Cash America Payday Advance
Cashland
Cash America SuperPawn
Enova International Inc

CONTACTS: Note: Officers with more than one job title may be intentionally listed here more than once.

Thomas Stuart, CEO
Thomas Bessant, CFO
Victor Pepe, Chief Information Officer
Daniel Feehan, Director
Jack Daugherty, Director
J. Linscott, Executive VP

GROWTH PLANS/SPECIAL FEATURES:

Cash America International, Inc. provides pawn lending, short-term cash advances, check cashing services and other specialty financial services. The company also sells merchandise in its pawnshops, primarily personal property that has been forfeited in connection with its pawn lending operations. The firm provides its specialty financial services in U.S. through over 900 locations in 22 states. The company offers secured non-recourse loans, commonly referred to as pawn loans, which are short-term loans (generally 30 to 90 days) made on the pledge of tangible personal property under the brand names Cash America Payday Advance, Cashland and Cash America SuperPawn. Cash America also offers short-term loans and secured and unsecured installment loans in some locations. Additionally, the firm offers check cashing and other ancillary products and services, including money orders, wire transfers, prepaid debit cards and auto insurance. Most of these ancillary products and services are provided through third-party vendors. Check-cashing services are provided through franchised and company-owned Mr. Payroll check cashing centers. In 2014, the company divested its pawn lending locations in Mexico and completed the spin-off of Enova International, Inc.

The company offers its employees health benefits as well as lifestyle benefits. Health benefits include medical, dental and vision coverage; life insurance; short- and long-term disability; health care and dependent care flexible spending; critical illness insurance; and accident insurance. Lifestyle benefits include a 401(k) program, merchandise discounts at the company's pawn locations, direct deposit, paid vacation and holidays, an employee assistance program, travel assistance and a group legal plan.

FINANCIAL DATA: Note: Data for latest year may not have been available at press time.

In U.S. $	2015	2014	2013	2012	2011	2010
Revenue		1,094,696,000	1,797,226,000	1,800,430,000	1,540,602,000	1,293,339,000
R&D Expense						
Operating Income		32,967,000	211,783,000	215,915,000	244,342,000	207,132,000
Operating Margin %		3.01%	11.78%	11.99%	15.86%	16.01%
SGA Expense		490,465,000	750,304,000	714,614,000	611,268,000	521,134,000
Net Income		98,638,000	142,528,000	107,470,000	135,963,000	115,538,000
Operating Cash Flow		521,149,000	586,430,000	518,281,000	448,856,000	351,306,000
Capital Expenditure		37,910,000	61,272,000	79,399,000	75,049,000	59,697,000
EBITDA		79,116,000	283,178,000	290,879,000	297,203,000	250,781,000
Return on Assets %		5.47%	7.30%	6.15%	8.76%	8.56%
Return on Equity %		8.90%	13.74%	11.34%	16.00%	15.68%
Debt to Equity		0.17	0.66	0.53	0.55	0.54

CONTACT INFORMATION:

Phone: 817 335-1100   Fax: 817 390-9333
Toll-Free: 800-223-8738
Address: 1600 W. 7th St., Fort Worth, TX 76102 United States

STOCK TICKER/OTHER:

Stock Ticker: CSH
Employees: 6,426
Parent Company:

Exchange: NYS
Fiscal Year Ends: 12/31

SALARIES/BONUSES:

Top Exec. Salary: $873,539   Bonus: $
Second Exec. Salary: $476,577   Bonus: $

OTHER THOUGHTS:

Estimated Female Officers or Directors:
Hot Spot for Advancement for Women/Minorities: Y

Cato Corp (The)

www.catofashions.com

NAIC Code: 448120

TYPES OF BUSINESS:

Women's Apparel, Retail
Children's Apparel
Junior's Apparel
Footwear
Accessories

BRANDS/DIVISIONS/AFFILIATES:

Cato Fashions
Cato Plus
It's Fashion
It's Fashion Metro
Versona Accessories
Cato

CONTACTS: Note: Officers with more than one job title may be intentionally listed here more than once.

Christin Reische, Assistant Secretary
John Cato, CEO
John Howe, CFO
Jeff Shock, Chief Accounting Officer
Sally Almason, Executive VP, Divisional
Gordon Smith, Executive VP
Michael Greer, Other Corporate Officer

GROWTH PLANS/SPECIAL FEATURES:

The Cato Corp. is a women's specialty fashion retailer. The firm operates under the names Cato, Cato Plus, Cato Fashions, It's Fashion, It's Fashion Metro and Versona Accessories. The company has 1,346 specialty stores in 32 states, primarily located in the southeastern U.S. The Cato Corp.'s stores feature a broad assortment of apparel and accessories, including dressy, career and casual sportswear; dresses; coats; and accessories such as shoes, lingerie, costume jewelry and handbags. Stores operating under the Cato brand primarily market products in junior or missy, plus sizes and girls sizes 7 to 16. The firm's It's Fashion stores market apparel, shoes and accessories for juniors, junior plus, young men, boys' sizes 8 to 20 and girls' sizes 7 to 16. The It's Fashion and It's Fashion Metro concepts offer fashion with a focus on the latest trendy styles for the entire family at low prices every day. The Versona Accessories concept offers quality fashion jewelry and accessories accented by key apparel items at exceptional values every day. A major portion of the company's merchandise is sold under its private labels and is produced by various vendors in accordance with the company's specifications. Most of its merchandise is purchased from about 100 primary vendors. The Cato Corp. offers its own credit card and layaway plan; these represent approximately 8% of the firm's retail sales. Most stores range in size from 2,000 to 19,000 square feet and are located primarily in strip shopping centers anchored by national discounters or market-dominant grocery stores. In determining store placement, the company uses site-selection and demographic criteria.

FINANCIAL DATA: Note: Data for latest year may not have been available at press time.

In U.S. $	2015	2014	2013	2012	2011	2010
Revenue	986,914,000	920,033,000	944,048,000	931,458,000	925,528,000	883,995,000
R&D Expense						
Operating Income	88,085,000	81,094,000	95,305,000	96,475,000	86,875,000	68,914,000
Operating Margin %	8.92%	8.81%	10.09%	10.35%	9.38%	7.79%
SGA Expense	276,234,000	245,868,000	244,327,000	238,982,000	251,121,000	245,483,000
Net Income	60,502,000	54,322,000	61,668,000	64,834,000	57,739,000	45,765,000
Operating Cash Flow	117,459,000	92,959,000	80,351,000	81,341,000	79,476,000	84,689,000
Capital Expenditure	28,901,000	31,542,000	45,175,000	35,890,000	19,559,000	9,960,000
EBITDA	113,556,000	106,186,000	121,542,000	122,117,000	112,668,000	90,809,000
Return on Assets %	10.04%	9.61%	11.38%	12.08%	11.51%	9.98%
Return on Equity %	15.68%	14.75%	17.32%	18.73%	18.71%	16.54%
Debt to Equity						

CONTACT INFORMATION:

Phone: 704 554-8510   Fax: 704 551-7200
Toll-Free:
Address: 8100 Denmark Rd., Charlotte, NC 28273 United States

STOCK TICKER/OTHER:

Stock Ticker: CATO
Employees: 10,000
Parent Company:

Exchange: NYS
Fiscal Year Ends: 01/31

SALARIES/BONUSES:

Top Exec. Salary: $1,147,388   Bonus: $

Second Exec. Salary: $419,375   Bonus: $

OTHER THOUGHTS:

Estimated Female Officers or Directors: 1

Hot Spot for Advancement for Women/Minorities:

Sales, profits and employees may be estimates. Financial information, benefits and other data can change quickly and may vary from those stated here.

CCA Global Partners

NAIC Code: 813910

www.ccaglobal.com

TYPES OF BUSINESS:

Retail Cooperative
Mortgages & Lending Services
Bicycle Shops
Formalwear Stores
Lighting Fixtures & Accessories, Retail
Flooring Materials Stores

BRANDS/DIVISIONS/AFFILIATES:

Carpet One
Flooring America
Lighting One
Bike Cooperative (The)
BizUnite
Lees
Healthier Living
International Design Guild

CONTACTS: *Note: Officers with more than one job title may be intentionally listed here more than once.*

Howard Brodsky, Co-CEO
Rick Bennet, Co-CEO
Jim Acker, CFO
Charlie Dilks, Chief Product Officer
Bob Wilson, Chief Administrative Officer
Charlie Dilks, Chief Prod. Officer
Bob Wilson, Chief Admin. Officer
Steve Pigman, Pres., Strategic Partners Group
Rick Bennet, Co-CEO
Howard Brodsky, Chmn.

GROWTH PLANS/SPECIAL FEATURES:

CCA Global Partners is a co-operative of entrepreneuri
storeowners. These persons own businesses in the floorin
mortgage, biking and light fixture industries. CCA promote
entrepreneurship by enabling smaller businesses to compet
with large, national corporations by increasing their collectiv
buying power and lowering their overall operating costs. Th
company also assists independent retailers through expe
marketing, merchandising programs and exclusive reta
brands. CCA provides each of its affiliates with a web site
inform customers of store locations and promotions as well a
an intranet site to facilitate communication betwee
participating companies. The firm also operates CCA Globa
University, an organization that offers training programs fro
management and leadership education to product, sales an
customer service training. CCA's affiliated companies includ
U.S. flooring companies Carpet One (1,000+ stores), Floorin
America, The Floor Trader, FEI Group, International Desig
Guild and ProSource. Flooring Canada is CCA's internationa
flooring company. The company's flooring stores offer an arra
of hardwood, carpet, laminate, ceramic, vinyl and rug product
the particular selection varying with the store brand. BizUnit
aims to aid organizations and their members in reducin
business costs. Lighting One offers commercial and residentia
lighting fixtures, ceiling fans and other accessories. The Bik
Cooperative is a chain of over 300 bicycle shops that sell
Giant-brand bicycles and various other high-quality bicycles
parts and accessories. The firm's exclusive brands includ
Healthier Living, Lees, Bedford Mills, Downs, Rustic River
Ilucio, Resista, Tigressa Softstyle Carpet and The Dabbier
Collection.

CCA offers its employees medical, dental, vision, disability an
life insurance; a dependant care spending account; a healt
care spending account; a 401(k) plan; and employee discounts

FINANCIAL DATA: *Note: Data for latest year may not have been available at press time.*

In U.S. $	2015	2014	2013	2012	2011	2010
Revenue						
R&D Expense						
Operating Income						
Operating Margin %						
SGA Expense						
Net Income						
Operating Cash Flow						
Capital Expenditure						
EBITDA						
Return on Assets %						
Return on Equity %						
Debt to Equity						

CONTACT INFORMATION:

Phone: 800-466-6984   Fax: 314-493-9671
Toll-Free: 800-466-6984
Address: 4301 Earth City Expressway, St. Louis, MO 63045 United States

STOCK TICKER/OTHER:

Stock Ticker: Private   Exchange:
Employees: Fiscal Year Ends: 09/30
Parent Company:

SALARIES/BONUSES:

Top Exec. Salary: $ Bonus: $
Second Exec. Salary: $ Bonus: $

OTHER THOUGHTS:

Estimated Female Officers or Directors: 2
Hot Spot for Advancement for Women/Minorities: Y

Chanel SA

NAIC Code: 424300

www.chanel.com

TYPES OF BUSINESS:

Apparel and Clothing Brands, Designers, Importers and Distributors
Retail-Fashion Boutiques
Fine Jewelry & Watches
Beachwear & Lingerie
Fragrances & Cosmetics

BRANDS/DIVISIONS/AFFILIATES:

Chanel Fragrance
Chanel Beauty
Chanel No. 5
Eres
CC
Paraffection
Robert Goossens

CONTACTS: *Note: Officers with more than one job title may be intentionally listed here more than once.*

Maureen Chiquet, CEO
Arie L. Kopelman, COO
Francoise Montenay, Pres.
Alain Wertheimer, Chmn.

GROWTH PLANS/SPECIAL FEATURES:

Chanel SA is an haute couture landmark in fashion, cosmetics and fragrances, with such memorable creations as the little black dress, Chanel No. 5, the tweed suit, the jersey dress, the chain belt and two-tone shoes. The company is also famous for its CC trademark, found on everything from cosmetic compacts to handbag closures. Founded in 1913 by stylist Gabrielle Chanel, known as Coco, the firm floundered for years until it was taken over by Karl Lagerfeld, who updated the style for a younger market. The house's style is known for its simplicity and pure lines as well as several recurrent themes, including the camellia, the star, the faceted rectangle (inspired by the gardens of the Place Vendome) and matelassee (the lozenge design quilted into racecourse jockey jackets). The company also creates watches and fine jewelry and has a single license with Luxxotica for eyewear. Chanel operates more than 300 boutiques worldwide, several of which are located in Japan. These boutiques are divided into watches and fine jewelry, fashion, eyewear and fragrance and beauty. Some locations carry only one or a selection of these product lines. The firm also owns Eres, a French swimwear and lingerie label with several boutiques in France, the U.S. and Italy. Other Chanel brands include Paraffection and Robert Goossens. In September 2015, the firm announced it would be opening its first store in the Nordic region in central Stockholm. The store will have more than 550 square feet of floor space.

FINANCIAL DATA: *Note: Data for latest year may not have been available at press time.*

In U.S. $	2015	2014	2013	2012	2011	2010
Revenue		5,000,000,000	4,700,000,000	4,250,000,000		
R&D Expense						
Operating Income						
Operating Margin %						
SGA Expense						
Net Income						
Operating Cash Flow						
Capital Expenditure						
EBITDA						
Return on Assets %						
Return on Equity %						
Debt to Equity						

CONTACT INFORMATION:

Phone: 33-1-46-43-40-00   Fax: 33-1-47-47-60-34
Toll-Free: 800-550-0005
Address: 135 Ave. Charles De Gaulle, Neuilly-sur-Seine, 92521 France

SALARIES/BONUSES:

Top Exec. Salary: $ Bonus: $
Second Exec. Salary: $ Bonus: $

STOCK TICKER/OTHER:

Stock Ticker: Private
Employees: 1,220
Parent Company:

Exchange:
Fiscal Year Ends: 12/31

OTHER THOUGHTS:

Estimated Female Officers or Directors: 1
Hot Spot for Advancement for Women/Minorities:

Charlotte Russe Holding Inc

www.charlotterusse.com

NAIC Code: 448120

TYPES OF BUSINESS:

Women's Apparel, Retail

BRANDS/DIVISIONS/AFFILIATES:

Charlotte Russe
Charlotte-Russe.com
Refuge
Advent International Corporation

CONTACTS: Note: Officers with more than one job title may be intentionally listed here more than once.

Jenny Ming, CEO
Jenny Ming, Pres.
Jennifer Mitchell, Sr. VP-Merch.
Frederick G. Silny, Treas.
Kara Stangl, Sr. VP-Merch.

GROWTH PLANS/SPECIAL FEATURES:

Charlotte Russe Holding, Inc., privately owned by Advent International Corporation, is a mall-based specialty retailer of fashionable, value-priced apparel and accessories targeting young women between ages 14-35. The stores offer a broad assortment of merchandise centered on styles that are affordable and feminine and reflect the latest fashion trends. There are over 500 Charlotte Russe stores located in 46 states and Puerto Rico. These stores reflect established fashion trends and rely on in-store graphics and window displays to convey a fashion-forward orientation. Charlotte Russe offers apparel, such as tops, dresses, shorts, pants and skirts, as well as seasonal items, such as prom dresses and outerwear. The majority of merchandise sold at Charlotte Russe stores is under the company's proprietary labels Charlotte Russe and Refuge. The company markets this merchandise to both younger career women and to teenagers, building brand awareness through a national print marketing campaign. Charlotte Russe stores are located predominantly in high-visibility, center court mall locations in spaces that average 7,100 square feet. Additionally, the firm offers online shopping at Charlotte-Russe.com. The company maintains a distribution center in Ontario, California.

FINANCIAL DATA: Note: Data for latest year may not have been available at press time.

In U.S. $	2015	2014	2013	2012	2011	2010
Revenue						
R&D Expense						
Operating Income						
Operating Margin %						
SGA Expense						
Net Income						
Operating Cash Flow						
Capital Expenditure						
EBITDA						
Return on Assets %						
Return on Equity %						
Debt to Equity						

CONTACT INFORMATION:

Phone: 858-587-1500 Fax: 858-587-0902
Toll-Free: 888-211-7271
Address: 5910 Pacific Ctr. Blvd., Ste. 120, San Diego, CA 92121 United States

STOCK TICKER/OTHER:

Stock Ticker: Private Exchange:
Employees: 2,271 Fiscal Year Ends: 09/30
Parent Company: Advent International Corporation

SALARIES/BONUSES:

Top Exec. Salary: $ Bonus: $
Second Exec. Salary: $ Bonus: $

OTHER THOUGHTS:

Estimated Female Officers or Directors: 4
Hot Spot for Advancement for Women/Minorities: Y

Charming Charlie

www.charmingcharlie.com

NAIC Code: 448310

TYPES OF BUSINESS:

Inexpensive Jewelry and Accessories Stores

BRANDS/DIVISIONS/AFFILIATES:

Charm Club

GROWTH PLANS/SPECIAL FEATURES:

Charming Charlie is a private retailer of women's accessories. The company sells thousands of fashion accessories including earrings, shoes, handbags, necklaces, rings, bracelets, scarves, wallets, pill boxes and cases for e-readers, cell phones and tablet computers, which are available at low prices. Instead of organizing its products traditionally by category, the company organizes its items by color. Repeat customers can earn points and receive discounts by enrolling in the Charm Club loyalty program, which rewards customers with a $5 certificate for every 1,000 points they accumulate. The firm was founded in 2004 and is headquartered in Houston, Texas. In June 2015, the firm opened its New York City flagship store on Fifth Avenue, featuring 16,000 square feet of floor space across three floors (two for retail and one for the brand's offices).

CONTACTS: Note: Officers with more than one job title may be intentionally listed here more than once.

Charlie Chanaratsopon, CEO

FINANCIAL DATA: Note: Data for latest year may not have been available at press time.

In U.S. $	2015	2014	2013	2012	2011	2010
Revenue		450,000,000	425,000,000	380,000,000		
R&D Expense						
Operating Income						
Operating Margin %						
SGA Expense						
Net Income						
Operating Cash Flow						
Capital Expenditure						
EBITDA						
Return on Assets %						
Return on Equity %						
Debt to Equity						

CONTACT INFORMATION:

Phone: 713-579-1936   Fax:
Toll-Free:
Address: 5999 Savoy Dr., Houston, TX 77036 United States

STOCK TICKER/OTHER:

Stock Ticker: Private
Employees: 3,500
Parent Company:

Exchange:
Fiscal Year Ends:

SALARIES/BONUSES:

Top Exec. Salary: $ Bonus: $
Second Exec. Salary: $ Bonus: $

OTHER THOUGHTS:

Estimated Female Officers or Directors:
Hot Spot for Advancement for Women/Minorities:

Sales, profits and employees may be estimates. Financial information, benefits and other data can change quickly and may vary from those stated here.

Chico's FAS Inc

NAIC Code: 448120

www.chicosfas.com

TYPES OF BUSINESS:

Women's Apparel, Retail
Online & Catalog Sales
Franchising

BRANDS/DIVISIONS/AFFILIATES:

Chico's
White House/Black Market
Soma Intimates
Boston Proper Inc
Passport Club

CONTACTS: Note: Officers with more than one job title may be intentionally listed here more than once.

Todd Vogensen, Assistant Secretary
David Dyer, CEO
David Oliver, Chief Accounting Officer
Eric Singleton, Chief Information Officer
Miki Berardelli, Chief Marketing Officer
Ross Roeder, Director
A. Rhodes, Executive VP
Sara Stensrud, Executive VP
Cynthia Murray, President, Divisional
Donna Colaco, President, Divisional
Laurie Van Brunt, President, Divisional
Sheryl Clark, President, Subsidiary
Sean McCartney, Senior VP, Divisional
Jennifer Adkins, Vice President, Divisional

GROWTH PLANS/SPECIAL FEATURES:

Chico's FAS, Inc. retails exclusively designed, private labe[
casual-to-formal clothing, complementary accessorie[
intimate apparel and gift items for women under the Chico'[
White House/Black Market, Soma Intimates and Boston Prope[
brands. Chico's currently operates 1,552 retail stores in 4[
states, Washington, D.C., the U.S. Virgin Islands and Puer[
Rico as well as e-commerce sites for all its brands. The fir[
also sells merchandise through franchise locations in Mexic[
Chico's primarily targets women aged 30 and over wit[
moderate to high income levels. Currently, there are more tha[
600 Chico's boutique stores and 100 Chico's outlet stores. Th[
majority of the firm's products are designed and developed b[
its Product Development Team, headquartered in Fort Myer[
Florida. The company offers Passport Club membership t[
women who have spent at least $500 over time, allowing ther[
perks such as a permanent 5% discount on future purchase[
Chico's also operates the White House/Black Market chain o[
more than 450 boutiques and over 60 outlet locations that focu[
on women aged 35 and older who lead active work and socia[
lives with moderate to high income levels. White House/Blac[
Market offers clothes predominately in shades of white an[
black, although the stores do offer clothing in other colors an[
a line of denim jeans as well. The Soma Intimates line current[
consists of 260 boutique-style stores and over 15 outle[
locations. Soma Intimates offers foundation products i[
intimate apparel, sleepwear, bodywear and active wear[
Boston Proper is an online- and catalog-based retailer o[
women's apparel and accessories, marketed to affluent womer[
between 35-55 years old. It also has 20 brick and mortar store[
in select U.S. markets.

FINANCIAL DATA: Note: Data for latest year may not have been available at press time.

In U.S. $	2015	2014	2013	2012	2011	2010
Revenue	2,675,211,000	2,586,037,000	2,581,057,000	2,196,360,000	1,904,954,000	1,713,150,000
R&D Expense						
Operating Income	116,343,000	141,183,000	287,538,000	222,377,000	177,082,000	108,153,000
Operating Margin %	4.34%	5.45%	11.14%	10.12%	9.29%	6.31%
SGA Expense	1,263,134,000	1,202,068,000	1,161,105,000	998,861,000	889,625,000	836,562,000
Net Income	64,641,000	65,883,000	180,219,000	140,874,000	115,394,000	69,646,000
Operating Cash Flow	282,483,000	236,682,000	368,273,000	255,181,000	239,626,000	215,370,000
Capital Expenditure	119,817,000	138,510,000	164,690,000	131,757,000	73,045,000	67,920,000
EBITDA	238,612,000	259,486,000	396,009,000	321,807,000	271,195,000	204,525,000
Return on Assets %	4.60%	4.46%	11.99%	9.91%	8.43%	5.47%
Return on Equity %	6.97%	6.58%	17.14%	13.58%	11.27%	7.39%
Debt to Equity						

CONTACT INFORMATION:

Phone: 239 277-6200   Fax: 239 277-5237
Toll-Free: 888-550-5559
Address: 11215 Metro Pkwy., Fort Myers, FL 33966 United States

SALARIES/BONUSES:

Top Exec. Salary: $950,000   Bonus: $
Second Exec. Salary: $338,462   Bonus: $400,000

STOCK TICKER/OTHER:

Stock Ticker: CHS
Employees: 23,800
Parent Company:

Exchange: NYS
Fiscal Year Ends: 01/31

OTHER THOUGHTS:

Estimated Female Officers or Directors: 11
Hot Spot for Advancement for Women/Minorities: Y

Children's Place Retail Stores Inc (The)   www.childrensplace.com

NAIC Code: 448130

TYPES OF BUSINESS:

Apparel-Children's, Retail
Online Sales

BRANDS/DIVISIONS/AFFILIATES:

ChildrensPlace.com

CONTACTS: Note: Officers with more than one job title may be intentionally listed here more than once.

Jane Elfers, CEO
Anurup Pruthi, CFO
Norman Matthews, Chairman of the Board
Michael Scarpa, COO
Bradley Cost, General Counsel
Kevin Low, Senior VP, Divisional
Lawrence McClure, Senior VP, Divisional
Gregory Poole, Senior VP, Divisional
Robert Vill, Vice President, Divisional

GROWTH PLANS/SPECIAL FEATURES:

The Children's Place Retail Stores, Inc. is a leading retailer of children's apparel and accessories. The firm designs, contracts to manufacture and sells high-quality, value-priced merchandise exclusively at its retail stores and on its web site, ChildrensPlace.com. The company sells clothes, shoes, socks, jewelry, belts, pajamas and various other seasonal items to boys and girls in three major size categories: 0 to 18 months, 6 months to 5T and 4 to 14. Currently, the firm operates 1,097 Children's Place stores in the U.S., Puerto Rico and Canada. The company stores are designed around four concepts in an effort to make the merchandise appealing to both parents and their children. The Apple-Maple store concept consists of light wood floors and trim, along with floor-to-ceiling glass windows that are ideal for displaying the company's colorful merchandise. The Technicolor concept store features bright colors within a boutique setting. The Tech2 (tech squared) stores have the brand aesthetics of a Technicolor store with the functionality of an Apple-Maple location and feature darker ceilings and floors, with white floor-wall fixtures. The company intends to use this format for new stores. Outlet stores are approximately 7,100 square feet and strategically located to allow for quick liquidation of overstocked merchandise.

FINANCIAL DATA: Note: Data for latest year may not have been available at press time.

In U.S. $	2015	2014	2013	2012	2011	2010
Revenue	1,761,324,000	1,765,789,000	1,809,486,000	1,715,862,000	1,673,999,000	1,643,587,000
R&D Expense						
Operating Income	80,043,000	76,283,000	89,715,000	110,007,000	136,336,000	130,072,000
Operating Margin %	4.54%	4.32%	4.95%	6.41%	8.14%	7.91%
SGA Expense	470,686,000	485,653,000	510,918,000	477,076,000	452,459,000	455,782,000
Net Income	56,888,000	53,026,000	63,243,000	77,225,000	83,124,000	88,354,000
Operating Cash Flow	161,410,000	173,470,000	205,042,000	156,103,000	174,511,000	155,177,000
Capital Expenditure	72,212,000	72,606,000	90,182,000	79,764,000	83,945,000	62,217,000
EBITDA	141,657,000	141,141,000	168,138,000	185,546,000	207,976,000	201,519,000
Return on Assets %	5.83%	5.54%	7.12%	9.05%	9.73%	9.85%
Return on Equity %	9.43%	8.56%	10.28%	12.69%	13.89%	15.54%
Debt to Equity						

CONTACT INFORMATION:

Phone: 201 558-2400   Fax: 201 227-0321
Toll-Free: 877-752-2387
Address: 500 Plaza Dr., Secaucus, NJ 07094 United States

STOCK TICKER/OTHER:

Stock Ticker: PLCE
Employees: 16,000
Parent Company:

Exchange: NAS
Fiscal Year Ends: 01/31

SALARIES/BONUSES:

Top Exec. Salary: Bonus: $
$1,100,000
Second Exec. Salary: Bonus: $
$768,269

OTHER THOUGHTS:

Estimated Female Officers or Directors: 4

Hot Spot for Advancement for Women/Minorities: Y

Chow Tai Fook Jewellery Group Ltd

www.chowtaifook.com

NAIC Code: 448310

TYPES OF BUSINESS:

Jewelry Stores
Watches
Jewelry Manufacturing

BRANDS/DIVISIONS/AFFILIATES:

Hearts On Fire

GROWTH PLANS/SPECIAL FEATURES:

Chow Tai Fook Jewellery Group Ltd., founded in 1938, is one of the world's largest jewelry retailers, with operations currently focused in Hong Kong, Macau and the People's Republic of China. The firm operates 2,286 points of sale (POS) in Mainland China and 122 watch locations. Chow Tai Fook also maintains an e-commerce segment to market and sell its jewelry. Principal products include gold products, gem-set jewelry, platinum/karat gold products and watches. In addition to retail operations, the firm is active in raw material procurement, design and production through two procurement departments, one dedicated to diamonds and one for gemstones, and factories located in Hong Kong, Shenzhen and Shunde. In 2015, mainland China jewelry accounted for 55.9% of sales revenue, mainland China watches accounted for 3% and Hong Kong, Macau and other markets accounted for 41.1%. In 2014, the company acquired U.S. luxury branded diamond company, Hearts On Fire, and opened its first Hearts On Fire store in Shanghai that same year.

CONTACTS:
Note: *Officers with more than one job title may be intentionally listed here more than once.*

Siu-Kee (Kent) Wong, Managing Dir.
Ping-Hei (Hamilton) Cheng, Group Finance Dir.
Chi-Kong (Adrian) Cheng, Exec. Dir.-Mktg. & Customer Relations Mgmt.
Chi-Heng (Conroy) Cheng, Exec. Dir.-Prod. Mgmt.
Chi-Keung (Peter) Suen, Exec. Dir.
Chi-Kong (Adrian) Cheng, Exec. Dir.-e-Commerce & Branding
Hiu-Sang (Albert) Chan, Exec. Dir.-Diamond Dept. Oper.
Kar-Shun (Henry) Cheng, Chmn.
Chan Sai-Cheong, Exec. Dir.-Mainland China & Overseas Oper.
Chi-Heng (Conroy) Cheng, Exec. Dir.-Procurement, Diamonds & Gemstones

FINANCIAL DATA:
Note: *Data for latest year may not have been available at press time.*

In U.S. $	2015	2014	2013	2012	2011	2010
Revenue	8,294,160,000	9,988,438,000	7,411,141,000	7,299,808,000	4,521,805,000	
R&D Expense						
Operating Income	926,620,100	1,199,638,000	958,040,800	1,100,563,000	609,922,800	
Operating Margin %	11.17%	12.01%	12.92%	15.07%	13.48%	
SGA Expense	1,592,894,000	1,575,190,000	1,184,696,000	1,036,754,000	685,616,300	
Net Income	714,327,200	961,228,000	732,728,000	847,894,100	473,891,100	
Operating Cash Flow	976,583,600	-699,320,100	1,294,287,000	-858,578,500	-337,085,300	
Capital Expenditure	258,514,200	153,361,400	118,314,700	111,901,500	99,217,120	
EBITDA	1,009,824,000	1,294,971,000	1,021,876,000	1,152,372,000	642,182,100	
Return on Assets %	8.87%	13.84%	12.14%	16.58%	12.17%	
Return on Equity %	14.24%	20.74%	17.78%	31.47%	31.28%	
Debt to Equity				0.11		

CONTACT INFORMATION:

Phone: 852 2524-3374   Fax:
Toll-Free:
Address: 42-46 QUEEN'S ROAD CENTRAL, Central, 999077 Hong Kong

STOCK TICKER/OTHER:

Stock Ticker: CJEWF   Exchange: PINX
Employees: 36,800   Fiscal Year Ends:
Parent Company:

SALARIES/BONUSES:

Top Exec. Salary: $ Bonus: $
Second Exec. Salary: $ Bonus: $

OTHER THOUGHTS:

Estimated Female Officers or Directors: 2
Hot Spot for Advancement for Women/Minorities:

Christian Dior SA

www.dior-finance.com/en-US/

NAIC Code: 424300

TYPES OF BUSINESS:

Apparel and Clothing Brands, Designers, Importers and Distributors
Leather Goods
Perfume & Cosmetics
Wines & Spirits
Watches & Jewelry
Online Sales
Cruise Lines

BRANDS/DIVISIONS/AFFILIATES:

Christian Dior Couture
Donna Karan International
LVMH Moet Hennessey Louis Vuitton SA
Dom Perignon
Veuve Clicquot
Moet Hennessy
Sephora
Fendi

CONTACTS: Note: Officers with more than one job title may be intentionally listed here more than once.

Sidney Toledano, Managing Dir.
Sidney Toledano, Group Managing Dir.
Bernard Arnault, Chmn.

GROWTH PLANS/SPECIAL FEATURES:

Christian Dior SA is a major international manufacturer and retailer of luxury goods. It owns the Dior fashion brand and has a 40.9% stake in LVMH Moet Hennessy Louis Vuitton SA. The company's business is divided into six segments: Christian Dior Couture, wines & spirits, fashion & leather goods, watches & jewelry, perfumes & cosmetics and selective retailing. The company operates more than 3,800 stores across these businesses. Christian Dior Couture creates individual haute couture clothing designs for celebrity clients as well as luxury ready-to-wear clothing and accessories that are sold both through other retailers and at the firm's international boutiques. In addition to Dior-branded fashions for men and women in its couture segment, the company owns a number of other fashion businesses, such as Givenchy, Donna Karan International, Fendi, Celine, Marc Jacobs and Kenzo. The wines & spirits segment produces brands such as Moet & Chandon, Veuve Clicquot, Dom Perignon and Moet Hennessy. The fashion & leather goods segment includes the Louis Vuitton, Celine, Loewe, Marc Jacobs, Pucci and Berluti brands, among others. The watches & jewelry segment includes the TAG Heuer, Bvlgari, Hublot, Chaumet and Zenith brands. Sephora, which is part of the firm's selective retailing and perfumes and cosmetics segments, operates over 360 stores across North America, as well as international stores and an online retail web site. The perfumes & cosmetics segment also includes BeneFit Cosmetics, an American brand that has expanded into the U.K., and carries Guerlain, Parfums Givenchy, Kenzo Parfums, Parfums Christian Dior and other lines. The selective retailing segment owns and operates Starboard Cruise Services in Miami, Florida.

FINANCIAL DATA: Note: Data for latest year may not have been available at press time.

In U.S. $	2015	2014	2013	2012	2011	2010
Revenue		34,827,960,320	32,024,400,000	30,200,800,000	27,683,418,112	23,743,578,112
R&D Expense						
Operating Income						
Operating Margin %						
SGA Expense						
Net Income		1,595,200,000	1,450,800,000	1,323,200,000	1,437,676,416	3,674,561,024
Operating Cash Flow						
Capital Expenditure						
EBITDA						
Return on Assets %						
Return on Equity %						
Debt to Equity						

CONTACT INFORMATION:

Phone: 33 140735444 Fax:
Toll-Free:
Address: 30 Ave. Montaigne, Paris, 75008 France

STOCK TICKER/OTHER:

Stock Ticker: CDI
Employees: 107,012
Parent Company:

Exchange: Paris
Fiscal Year Ends: 12/31

SALARIES/BONUSES:

Top Exec. Salary: $ Bonus: $
Second Exec. Salary: $ Bonus: $

OTHER THOUGHTS:

Estimated Female Officers or Directors: 2
Hot Spot for Advancement for Women/Minorities:

Christies International plc

NAIC Code: 453998A

www.christies.com

TYPES OF BUSINESS:

Auction Houses (General Merchandise)
Fine Art, Antiques & Luxury Items
Publishing
Fine Art Security
Real Estate
Mail Order Books
Art Education

BRANDS/DIVISIONS/AFFILIATES:

Artemis SA
Christie's International Real Estate Magazine
Christie's Publications
Christie's Magazine
Christie's Interiors
LotFinder
Christie's LIVE

CONTACTS: Note: Officers with more than one job title may be intentionally listed here more than once.

Patricia Barbizet, CEO
Francois de Ricqles, Pres.

GROWTH PLANS/SPECIAL FEATURES:

Christie's International plc is one of the world's largest and oldest auction houses. It is a subsidiary of Artemis SA, the holding company owned by Francois Pinault, French a collector and entrepreneur. The firm has 12 salesrooms i many of the world's major cities, including New York, Londo and Geneva. Christie's offers more than 450 sales per year i an excess of 80 categories. It operates 53 offices within 3. countries around the world, engaging in appraisal, preparatio and arrangement of the sale of some of the world's greates works of fine art as well as collectibles, antiquities, books manuscripts, furniture, decorative art, jewelry, watches, wine cigars, photographs, prints and automobiles. Christie' International Real Estate handles the global sale an advertisement of high-end properties. Christie's Publication: handles the company's print publications: Christie's Magazin and Christie's International Real Estate Magazine. Christie' web site contains information on the latest auctions and through LotFinder, enables clients to look up lot numbers and view auction catalog images two months in advance of a sale Customers are able to bid on items in person, through absentee bidding or through telephone bidding. In addition, the firm offers Christie's LIVE, a real-time, multi-media auction viewing and bidding site. Moreover, Christie's operates degree granting educational art programs in London and New York, a mail-order book service, an online art image library and ar security services. Christie's Interiors is the firm's global sales feature that offers home decor services.

FINANCIAL DATA: Note: Data for latest year may not have been available at press time.

In U.S. $	2015	2014	2013	2012	2011	2010
Revenue		916,170,000	817,333,300	1,020,000,000		
R&D Expense						
Operating Income						
Operating Margin %						
SGA Expense						
Net Income		112,986,000	122,600,000	153,000,000		
Operating Cash Flow						
Capital Expenditure						
EBITDA						
Return on Assets %						
Return on Equity %						
Debt to Equity						

CONTACT INFORMATION:

Phone: 44-20-7839-9060   Fax: 44-20-7839-1611
Toll-Free:
Address: 8 King St., St. James's, London, SW1Y 6QT United Kingdom

STOCK TICKER/OTHER:

Stock Ticker: Subsidiary
Employees: 1,851   Exchange:
Parent Company: ARTEMIS SA   Fiscal Year Ends: 12/31

SALARIES/BONUSES:

Top Exec. Salary: $ Bonus: $
Second Exec. Salary: $ Bonus: $

OTHER THOUGHTS:

Estimated Female Officers or Directors:
Hot Spot for Advancement for Women/Minorities: Y

Christopher & Banks Corp

www.christopherandbanks.com

NAIC Code: 448120

TYPES OF BUSINESS:

Women's Business Apparel, Retail
Private-Label Merchandise
Accessories

BRANDS/DIVISIONS/AFFILIATES:

C J Banks
ChristopherandBanks.com
CJBanks.com
Christopher & Banks

CONTACTS: *Note: Officers with more than one job title may be intentionally listed here more than once.*

Peter Michielutti, CFO
Paul Snyder, Chairman of the Board
Marc Ungerman, Controller
Luke Komarek, General Counsel
Lynn Derry, Other Corporate Officer
LuAnn Via, President
Monica Dahl, Senior VP, Divisional
Cindy Stemper, Senior VP, Divisional
Michelle Rice, Senior VP, Divisional

GROWTH PLANS/SPECIAL FEATURES:

Christopher & Banks Corp. (C&B) is a Minnesota-based specialty retailer of women's apparel. The company operates 535 stores in the U.S. under the names Christopher & Banks (314 stores), offering missy, petite and women sizes and 70 outlet stores. The stores are generally mall-based and located in small to mid-sized markets. Sportswear and sweaters account for the bulk of the company's sales, though the firm has been shifting merchandise focus away from sweaters and expanding its offering of novelty jackets and fashion-knit tops. The principal store concept, Christopher & Banks, emphasizes style, quality and value in casual sportswear and sweaters exclusively designed for working women ages 45-55. The company's plus size store concept, C.J. Banks, offers similar apparel in sizes 14-24 and is often paired with an existing Christopher & Banks store. It also offers petite sizes at most of its Christopher & Banks locations. In addition to its brick-and-mortar locations, C&B maintains e-commerce sites for both of its lines at ChristopherandBanks.com and CJBanks.com. To keep its fashions fresh, the company has begun testing new product categories, including sunglasses, scarves, handbags, swimwear and outerwear. The firm has also upgraded its customer service, offering merchandise on wooden hangers, receipts placed in envelopes and purchases wrapped in tissue and placed in drawstring bags.

FINANCIAL DATA: *Note: Data for latest year may not have been available at press time.*

In U.S. $	2015	2014	2013	2012	2011	2010
Revenue	418,584,000	435,754,000	430,302,000		448,130,000	455,402,000
R&D Expense						
Operating Income	9,415,000	8,876,000	-15,965,000		-14,559,000	-1,367,000
Operating Margin %	2.24%	2.03%	-3.71%		-3.24%	-.30%
SGA Expense	126,377,000	128,847,000	129,153,000		142,461,000	138,711,000
Net Income	47,126,000	8,690,000	-16,076,000		-22,167,000	158,000
Operating Cash Flow	19,001,000	25,054,000	-17,441,000		7,793,000	35,946,000
Capital Expenditure	20,270,000	8,544,000	3,623,000		8,428,000	5,969,000
EBITDA	21,201,000	22,106,000	2,749,000		10,177,000	24,618,000
Return on Assets %	27.31%	6.10%	-11.82%		-8.84%	.05%
Return on Equity %	42.29%	10.70%	-21.30%		-12.38%	.08%
Debt to Equity						

CONTACT INFORMATION:

Phone: 763 551-5000   Fax: 763 551-5198
Toll-Free:
Address: 2400 Xenium Ln. N., Plymouth, MN 55441 United States

STOCK TICKER/OTHER:

Stock Ticker: CBK
Employees: 4,605
Parent Company:

Exchange: NYS
Fiscal Year Ends: 01/31

SALARIES/BONUSES:

Top Exec. Salary: $842,308   Bonus: $
Second Exec. Salary: $436,923   Bonus: $

OTHER THOUGHTS:

Estimated Female Officers or Directors: 7
Hot Spot for Advancement for Women/Minorities: Y

Claire's Stores Inc

www.clairestores.com

NAIC Code: 448150

TYPES OF BUSINESS:

Teenage Apparel & Accessories, Retail
Jewelry
Novelty Items
Piercing Services
Franchising
Accessories
Seasonal Merchandise
Headwear

BRANDS/DIVISIONS/AFFILIATES:

Claire's
Icing
Apollo Advisors LP

CONTACTS: Note: Officers with more than one job title may be intentionally listed here more than once.

Beatrice Lafon, CEO
J. Per Brodin, CFO
Melanie Berry, Sr. VP-Mktg.
David DeVany, Sr. VP-IT
Rebecca Orand, General Counsel
Andrea Guthrie, Sr. VP-Strategic New Bus.
Michael R. Basler, Sr. VP-Finance
Holly Cohen, Sr. VP-Global Real Estate & Construction
William Hoeller, Exec. VP-Global Franchising

GROWTH PLANS/SPECIAL FEATURES:

Claire's Stores, Inc., owned by the private equity firm Apollo Advisors, LP, is a specialty retailer of value-priced costume jewelry and other fashion accessories. The company operates two store concepts: Claire's, which caters to fashion-conscious girls and teens age 3-18, and Icing, which caters to young women age 18-35. Claire's brand stores have a presence in 46 countries through the 2,610 company-operated Claire's stores in North America and Europe, 130 concession store-in-stores and 442 franchised stores in numerous other geographies. Icing operates 388 stores in the U.S., Canada and Puerto Rico. All stores share a similar format, with different store concepts and trade-names allowing for multiple store locations within a single mall. The company selects its merchandise from over 7,000 stock-keeping units (SKUs) and also provides ear-piercing services. Claire's stores are primarily located in shopping malls. The firm purchases merchandise, which is largely imported, from approximately 660 suppliers. The company's distributor is based in Hong Kong and is responsible for buying, merchandise development and overseas quality control.

Employee benefits include life and supplemental life insurance; medical, dental and AD&D coverage; income protection programs; several forms of paid time off; and a 401(k) plan.

FINANCIAL DATA: Note: Data for latest year may not have been available at press time.

In U.S. $	2015	2014	2013	2012	2011	2010
Revenue		1,513,177,000	1,557,020,000	1,495,900,000	1,426,397,000	1,342,389,000
R&D Expense						
Operating Income						
Operating Margin %						
SGA Expense						
Net Income		-65,307,000	1,282,000	11,632,000	4,323,000	-10,402,000
Operating Cash Flow						
Capital Expenditure						
EBITDA						
Return on Assets %						
Return on Equity %						
Debt to Equity						

CONTACT INFORMATION:

Phone: 954-433-3900   Fax: 954-433-3999
Toll-Free: 800-252-4737
Address: 3 SW 129th Ave., Pembroke Pines, FL 33027 United States

STOCK TICKER/OTHER:

Stock Ticker: Private
Employees: 18,000
Parent Company: APOLLO ADVISORS LP

Exchange:
Fiscal Year Ends: 01/31

SALARIES/BONUSES:

Top Exec. Salary: $ Bonus: $
Second Exec. Salary: $ Bonus: $

OTHER THOUGHTS:

Estimated Female Officers or Directors: 12
Hot Spot for Advancement for Women/Minorities: Y

Coach Inc

www.coach.com

NAIC Code: 424300

TYPES OF BUSINESS:

Apparel and Clothing Brands, Designers, Importers and Distributors
Online & Catalog Sales
Outlet Stores
Purses

BRANDS/DIVISIONS/AFFILIATES:

Coach.com
StuartWeitzman.com
Stuart Weitzman Intermediate LLC
Stuart Weitzman

CONTACTS: Note: Officers with more than one job title may be intentionally listed here more than once.

Jane Nielsen, CFO
Lew Frankfort, Chairman Emeritus
Jide Zeitlin, Chairman of the Board
Todd Kahn, Chief Administrative Officer
Victor Luis, Director
Christina Colone, Other Corporate Officer
Sarah Dunn, Other Corporate Officer
Ian Bickley, President, Divisional
David Duplantis, President, Divisional
Andre Cohen, President, Geographical
Gebhard Rainer, President

GROWTH PLANS/SPECIAL FEATURES:

Coach, Inc., founded in 1941, is a designer, producer and marketer of fine accessories and gifts for men and women, including handbags, women's and men's accessories, footwear, outerwear, business luggage and travel accessories, cases, eyewear, watches, jewelry and fragrance. The firm also licenses its name for watches, shoes and eyewear. The company divides its operations into three segments: North America (which accounts for 59% of total net sales in 2015), international (39%) and other (2%). Various Coach-brand products are available at 462 retail and outlet store locations in North America and 503 international store locations. The other segment comprises the Stuart Weitzman brand which is sold through department stores in North America and international distributors, including approximately 600 wholesale locations. The brand's most significant wholesale customers include Nordstrom, Saks and Neiman Marcus, and its products are also sold in freestanding flagship and retail stores, as well as e-commerce websites. Stuart Weitzman has 54 directly-operated stores with an average square footage of 1,687. Through the firm's Coach.com and stuartweitzman.com web sites, customers can shop for new products and locate a store nearest to them. Approximately 58% of the company's sales come from women's handbags, roughly 17% come from women's accessories (wristlets, cosmetic cases, money pieces, etc.), 16% from men's products, and the final 9% of sales derive from all other products (sunglasses, watches, fragrance, etc.). Over the last several years, Coach has successfully transformed itself from a manufacturer of classic leather products to a marketer of more modern, fashionable handbags and accessories, using a broader range of fabrics and materials. In May 2015, the firm acquired Stuart Weitzman Intermediate LLC, a designer and manufacturer of women's luxury footwear.

Coach employees receive medical, dental, life, short- and long-term disability, AD&D, vision and prescription drug insurance; flexible spending accounts; profit-sharing & employee stock plans; 401(k); paid holiday, vacation and sick leave; and a variety of related discounts.

FINANCIAL DATA: Note: Data for latest year may not have been available at press time.

In U.S. $	2015	2014	2013	2012	2011	2010
Revenue	4,191,600,000	4,806,226,000	5,075,390,000	4,763,180,000	4,158,507,000	3,607,636,000
R&D Expense						
Operating Income	618,000,000	1,120,074,000	1,524,541,000	1,511,989,000	1,304,924,000	1,150,171,000
Operating Margin %	14.74%	23.30%	30.03%	31.74%	31.37%	31.88%
SGA Expense	2,290,600,000	2,176,889,000	2,173,607,000	1,954,089,000	1,718,617,000	1,483,520,000
Net Income	402,400,000	781,336,000	1,034,420,000	1,038,910,000	880,800,000	734,940,000
Operating Cash Flow	937,400,000	985,410,000	1,413,974,000	1,221,689,000	1,033,271,000	990,877,000
Capital Expenditure	209,800,000	219,587,000	241,353,000	184,309,000	147,744,000	81,116,000
EBITDA	809,800,000	1,309,434,000	1,687,528,000	1,644,898,000	1,430,030,000	1,276,915,000
Return on Assets %	9.66%	21.71%	31.17%	36.20%	34.52%	29.21%
Return on Equity %	16.38%	32.35%	46.99%	57.62%	56.50%	45.91%
Debt to Equity	0.35				0.01	0.01

CONTACT INFORMATION:

Phone: 212 594-1850   Fax: 212 594-1682
Toll-Free: 888-262-6224
Address: 516 W. 34th St., New York, NY 10001 United States

STOCK TICKER/OTHER:

Stock Ticker: COH
Employees: 15,800
Parent Company:

Exchange: NYS
Fiscal Year Ends: 06/30

SALARIES/BONUSES:

Top Exec. Salary: $1,291,667   Bonus: $

Second Exec. Salary: $594,353   Bonus: $600,000

OTHER THOUGHTS:

Estimated Female Officers or Directors: 5

Hot Spot for Advancement for Women/Minorities: Y

Sales, profits and employees may be estimates. Financial information, benefits and other data can change quickly and may vary from those stated here.

Coles Group Ltd

NAIC Code: 445110

TYPES OF BUSINESS:

Grocery Stores, Retail
Convenience Stores
Hotels
Liquor Stores
Tire & Automotive Stores

BRANDS/DIVISIONS/AFFILIATES:

Coles Online
Coles Express
BI-LO
Vintage Cellars
Liquorland
1st Choice Liquor Superstores
Wesfarmers Ltd
Coles Life Insurance

CONTACTS: Note: Officers with more than one job title may be intentionally listed here more than once.

John Durkan, CEO
Sioned Rees-Thomas, Gen. Mgr.-Merch.
Paul Meadows, Group Gen. Counsel
Andy Coleman, Gen. Mgr.-Oper.
Stuart Machin, Dir.-Store Dev. & Oper.
Keith Louie, Gen. Mgr.-Coles Online
Robert Hadler, Gen. Mgr.-Corp. Affairs
Tony Buffin, Dir.-Finance
Richard Goyder, Managing Dir.-Wesfarmers Ltd.
Bob Every, Chmn.-Westfarmers Ltd.
Matt Swindells, Gen. Mgr.-Supply Chain Transformation

GROWTH PLANS/SPECIAL FEATURES:

Coles Group, Ltd., a subsidiary of Wesfarmers, Ltd., is one of Australia's largest retailers, operating more than 2,300 food, general merchandise and convenience stores throughout the country. The company's Coles and BI-LO supermarkets serve customers throughout Australia. Through Coles Online, an online supermarket, customers can order grocery items for delivery to areas in Queensland, New South Wales and Victoria, with service recently expanded to include cities in Western and South Australia. Coles Group also operates liquor stores under the names Liquorland, Vintage Cellars and 1st Choice Liquor Superstores as well as operating an online liquor distributor. Coles Group maintains a presence in the convenience store and fuel market through its Coles Express locations. It also retails apparel and home items through its licensing of U.S.-based Target stores all across Australia. In addition to Target, Coles Group operates licensed Kmart stores. The company also owns hotels under the Spirit Hotel name. In 2014, the firm launched Coles Life Insurance, offering affordable life insurance.

FINANCIAL DATA: Note: Data for latest year may not have been available at press time.

In U.S. $	2015	2014	2013	2012	2011	2010
Revenue		57,698,000,000	35,780,000,000	34,117,000,000	32,073,000,000	30,002,000,000
R&D Expense						
Operating Income						
Operating Margin %						
SGA Expense						
Net Income		1,605,000,000	1,533,000,000	1,356,000,000	1,166,000,000	962,000,000
Operating Cash Flow						
Capital Expenditure						
EBITDA						
Return on Assets %						
Return on Equity %						
Debt to Equity						

CONTACT INFORMATION:

Phone: 61-3-9829-3111   Fax: 61-3-9829-6787
Toll-Free:
Address: 800 Toorak Rd., Tooronga, VIC 3146 Australia

STOCK TICKER/OTHER:

Stock Ticker: Subsidiary
Employees: 98,000
Parent Company: WESFARMERS LTD

Exchange:
Fiscal Year Ends: 07/31

SALARIES/BONUSES:

Top Exec. Salary: $ Bonus: $
Second Exec. Salary: $ Bonus: $

OTHER THOUGHTS:

Estimated Female Officers or Directors: 1
Hot Spot for Advancement for Women/Minorities:

Companhia Brasileira de Distribuicao SA (CBD)

www.gpa-ri.com.br

NAIC Code: 445110

TYPES OF BUSINESS:

Grocery Stores
Consumer Electronics
Hypermarkets
Convenience Stores
Cash-and-Carry Stores

BRANDS/DIVISIONS/AFFILIATES:

Grupo Pao de Acucar
Pao de Acucar
Extra Supermercado
Extra Hipermercado
Minimercado Extra
Assai
Casas Bahia
Ponto Frio

CONTACTS: Note: Officers with more than one job title may be intentionally listed here more than once.

Ronaldo Iabrudi, CEO
Jean-Charles Naouri, Pres.
Christophe Hidalgo, CFO
Abilio dos Santos Diniz, Chmn.

GROWTH PLANS/SPECIAL FEATURES:

Companhia Brasileira de Distribuicao SA (CBD), also operating as Grupo Pao de Acucar, is a leading retailer in Brazil. It oversees 1,757 stores in 19 Brazilian states and the Federal District. The firm operates in three segments: retail, cash-and-carry and electronics and home appliances. The retail segment includes the operations of various food and non-food chain retailers within Brazil. Its retail chains include supermarkets Pao de Acucar, which is Brazil's largest high-end supermarket chain, with 168 locations, and Extra Supermercado, with 213 stores. It also operates a hypermarket format, Extra Hipermercado (138 locations), which offers a broad range of food and non-food products and services, and 164 Minimercado Extra convenience stores. The cash-and-carry segment of the company operates 61 Assai cash-and-carry stores. Electronics and home appliances are available through 602 Casas Bahia outlets and 397 Ponto Frio stores. CBD's distribution network consists of 58 distribution centers, the majority of which are located in and around Sao Paulo. Its e-commerce activities include food delivery, through Pao de Acucar Delivery, and non-food retail sites Extra.com.br and PontoFrio.com.br.

FINANCIAL DATA: Note: Data for latest year may not have been available at press time.

In U.S. $	2015	2014	2013	2012	2011	2010
Revenue		17,098,090,000	15,064,130,000	13,288,220,000	12,158,360,000	8,373,998,000
R&D Expense						
Operating Income		1,016,622,000	756,968,100	745,867,500	548,636,000	418,000,900
Operating Margin %		5.94%	5.02%	5.61%	4.51%	4.99%
SGA Expense		3,075,698,000	2,782,857,000	2,639,139,000	2,510,175,000	1,508,790,000
Net Income		331,393,700	274,637,900	274,295,100	187,412,000	188,508,700
Operating Cash Flow		1,308,874,000	1,276,505,000	1,382,787,000	294,356,600	94,796,070
Capital Expenditure		495,003,000	482,637,600	363,592,100	379,478,400	389,629,700
EBITDA		1,259,557,000	982,792,000	963,519,700	501,630,100	356,155,600
Return on Assets %		3.04%	2.86%	3.03%	2.25%	3.01%
Return on Equity %		12.65%	11.70%	13.04%	9.75%	10.52%
Debt to Equity		0.29	0.45	0.73	0.81	0.78

CONTACT INFORMATION:

Phone: 5511-3886-0421   Fax: 5511-3884-2677
Toll-Free:
Address: Ave. Brigadeiro Luis Antonio, 3,142, Sao Paulo, 01402901 Brazil

STOCK TICKER/OTHER:

Stock Ticker: CBD
Employees: 159,829
Parent Company:

Exchange: NYS
Fiscal Year Ends: 12/31

SALARIES/BONUSES:

Top Exec. Salary: $ Bonus: $
Second Exec. Salary: $ Bonus: $

OTHER THOUGHTS:

Estimated Female Officers or Directors: 1
Hot Spot for Advancement for Women/Minorities: Y

Conn's Inc

NAIC Code: 443142

TYPES OF BUSINESS:

Consumer Electronics Stores
Retail Sales
Online Sales
Consumer Credit

BRANDS/DIVISIONS/AFFILIATES:

Conn's

CONTACTS: *Note: Officers with more than one job title may be intentionally listed here more than once.*

Norman Miller, CEO
Thomas Moran, CFO
Theodore Wright, Chairman of the Board
Mark Haley, Chief Accounting Officer
Michael Poppe, COO
Robert Bell, General Counsel
Kim Canning, Other Corporate Officer
David Trahan, President, Divisional
Deana Moylan, Vice President, Divisional
Don Welch, Vice President, Divisional
Todd Renaud, Vice President
Jamie Piper, Vice President

GROWTH PLANS/SPECIAL FEATURES:

Conn's, Inc. is a specialty consumer electronics and home appliance retailer. The company currently operates 90 stores located in five states: Arizona (10), Colorado (6), Louisiana (5), Mississippi (1), Nevada (1), New Mexico (3), North Carolina (1), Oklahoma (3), South Carolina (2), Tennessee (3) and Texas (55). Each Conn's stores stocks on average over 2,900 products in four general categories: consumer electronics, home appliances, furniture and mattresses and home office. Consumer electronics include LCD, LED, 3-D and plasma televisions; Blu-ray players; home theater and video game products; camcorders; digital cameras; and portable audio equipment. Brands include Bose, Canon, Haier, Harmon/Kardon, LG, Microsoft, Monster, Nikon, Nintendo, Samsung, Sharp, Sony and Toshiba. Home appliances include refrigerators, freezers, washers, dryers, dishwashers, ranges and room air conditioners, representing such brands as Dyson, Electrolux, Eureka, Friedrich, General Electric, Haier, LG and Samsung. Furniture and mattresses include furniture and related accessories for the living room, dining room and bedroom as well as both traditional and specialty mattresses sold under the brands Bello, Elements, Franklin, Home Stretch, Jackson-Catnapper, Klaussner, Sealy, Serta, Steve Silver and Z-Line. Home office offers brands such as Acer, Asus, Dell, Hewlett-Packard, Microsoft, Samsung, Sony and Toshiba that sell computers, tablets, printers and accessories. Additionally, Conn's sells a number of seasonal items, including lawn and garden equipment. The company provides in-house credit arrangements to its customers, with 52% of its credit customers being repeat customers.

The company offers its employees medical and dental coverage, a prescription drug plan, a 401(k) plan, an employee stock purchase plan, tuition assistance, life and disability insurance and an employee discount plan.

FINANCIAL DATA: *Note: Data for latest year may not have been available at press time.*

In U.S. $	2015	2014	2013	2012	2011	2010
Revenue	1,485,218,000	1,193,769,000	865,032,000	792,302,000	790,524,000	836,675,000
R&D Expense						
Operating Income	119,867,000	161,852,000	100,512,000	29,701,000	28,585,000	17,783,000
Operating Margin %	8.07%	13.55%	11.61%	3.74%	3.61%	2.12%
SGA Expense	391,311,000	341,645,000	256,214,000	237,911,000	235,100,000	255,489,000
Net Income	58,513,000	93,449,000	52,612,000	-3,723,000	-1,009,000	7,722,000
Operating Cash Flow	-189,901,000	-210,262,000	-22,803,000	64,517,000	63,058,000	-31,868,000
Capital Expenditure	61,696,000	52,127,000	32,353,000	4,386,000	3,028,000	10,255,000
EBITDA	141,471,000	178,659,000	113,659,000	41,324,000	46,034,000	32,642,000
Return on Assets %	3.97%	8.46%	6.21%	-.45%	-.14%	1.44%
Return on Equity %	9.41%	17.56%	12.71%	-1.04%	-.28%	2.27%
Debt to Equity	1.18	0.90	0.55	0.90	1.04	0.30

CONTACT INFORMATION:

Phone: 409 832-1696   Fax: 409 832-4344
Toll-Free: 877-472-5422
Address: 4055 Technology Forest Blvd., Ste. 210, The Woodlands, TX 77381 United States

STOCK TICKER/OTHER:

Stock Ticker: CONN
Employees: 4,300
Parent Company:

Exchange: NAS
Fiscal Year Ends: 01/31

SALARIES/BONUSES:

Top Exec. Salary: $850,000   Bonus: $
Second Exec. Salary: $460,000   Bonus: $

OTHER THOUGHTS:

Estimated Female Officers or Directors: 1
Hot Spot for Advancement for Women/Minorities:

Container Store (The)

www.containerstore.com

NAIC Code: 442299

TYPES OF BUSINESS:

Home Organization Products, Retail
Luggage
Packing Materials
Specialty Boxes
Online Sales

BRANDS/DIVISIONS/AFFILIATES:

Elfa International AB
Leonard Green & Partners LP
Contained Home
Container Store (The)
Elfa

CONTACTS: Note: Officers with more than one job title may be intentionally listed here more than once.

Per von Mentzer, CEO, Subsidiary
William Tindell, CEO
Jodi Taylor, CFO
Melissa Reiff, COO
Sharon Tindell, Director
Peter Lodwick, General Counsel
Jeffrey Miller, Vice President

GROWTH PLANS/SPECIAL FEATURES:

The Container Store, owned by private equity firm Leonard Green & Partners LP, is a national retailer selling organizational and storage products. The company sells drawer and cabinet organizers, luggage, tool racks, packing materials, specialty and shipping boxes and locker organizers, among many other household objects designed to manage space efficiently. Store interiors have an open layout, which is divided into sections with brightly colored banners such as Closet, Kitchen and Laundry. The Container Store's operations are divided into two segments: The Container Store, made up of retail stores, website and call center; and Elfa, which designs and manufactures component-based shelving and drawer systems and made-to-measure sliding doors. The firm's stores average 25,000 square feet and carry more than 10,000 items. The majority of the company's approximately 70 stores are located in 24 states and Washington, D.C. The Container Store processes and ships its entire product line from its 725,000-square-foot distribution center in Coppell, Texas. The company's web site allows customers to view and order store products, plan organizational and storage projects and receive free customized assistance from in-store space planning experts. In 2014 this segment made up approximately 89% of the firm's total net sales. The firm is the exclusive distributor of Elfa International AB, a wholly owned Swedish subsidiary. Elfa has a total of four manufacturing facilities located in Sweden, Finland, and Poland. Business from The Container Store represented a total of 24% of Elfa's sales in 2014. Contained Home, the firm's new in-home, customized design and organization service where expert organizers go directly to customer homes is expected to be available late-2015.

The company offers its employees a benefits package that includes a 40% discount on merchandise; a 401(k) savings plan; paid vacation; an employee assistance program; domestic partner benefits; a corporate wellness program; transportation benefits; pet insurance; paid pregnancy disability leave; and medical, life, dental and vision insurance.

FINANCIAL DATA: Note: Data for latest year may not have been available at press time.

In U.S. $	2015	2014	2013	2012	2011	2010
Revenue	781,866,000	748,538,000	706,757,000	633,619,000	568,820,000	
R&D Expense						
Operating Income	46,971,000	31,027,000	24,142,000	-6,628,000	-14,918,000	
Operating Margin %	6.00%	4.14%	3.41%	-1.04%	-2.62%	
SGA Expense	382,439,000	376,080,000	338,942,000	298,868,000	271,221,000	
Net Income	22,673,000	8,166,000	-130,000	-30,671,000	-45,053,000	
Operating Cash Flow	64,625,000	50,762,000	45,186,000	42,470,000	48,764,000	
Capital Expenditure	48,740,000	48,565,000	48,559,000	41,220,000	18,175,000	
EBITDA	77,982,000	60,151,000	46,359,000	20,823,000	9,436,000	
Return on Assets %	2.92%	-6.71%	-12.06%	-14.63%		
Return on Equity %	11.36%	-23.96%	-38.80%	-46.88%		
Debt to Equity	1.61	1.66	1.18	1.25		

CONTACT INFORMATION:

Phone: 972-538-6900   Fax: 972-538-7623
Toll-Free: 800-733-3532
Address: 500 Freeport Pkwy., Coppell, TX 75019 United States

SALARIES/BONUSES:

Top Exec. Salary: $675,000   Bonus: $50,000
Second Exec. Salary: $625,000   Bonus: $75,000

STOCK TICKER/OTHER:

Stock Ticker: TCS   Exchange: NYS
Employees: 4,900   Fiscal Year Ends: 03/31
Parent Company: LEONARD GREEN & PARTNERS LP

OTHER THOUGHTS:

Estimated Female Officers or Directors: 5
Hot Spot for Advancement for Women/Minorities: Y

CORT Business Services Corporation

NAIC Code: 532299

www.cort.com

TYPES OF BUSINESS:

Furniture Stores, Rental
Residential Furniture Rental
Trade Show & Event Furniture Rental
Online Sales
Relocation Assistance Services
Office Furniture Rental

BRANDS/DIVISIONS/AFFILIATES:

Wesco Financial Corporation
Berkshire Hathaway Inc
CORT Trade Show & Event Furnishings
ApartmentSearch by CORT
Roomservice by CORT
AA Party Rentals

CONTACTS: Note: Officers with more than one job title may be intentionally listed here more than once.

Jeff Pederson, CEO
Lloyd Lenson, COO
Jeff Pederson, Pres.
Deborah Lansford, CFO
Lisa Woodworth, VP-Mktg.
Jeff Seidman, Corp. VP-Human Resources
Paula Newell, VP-Strategic Bus. Dev.
Kenneth S. Barron, Managing Dir.-Global Rel. & Customer Svcs.
Mike Davis, VP-CORT Trade Show & Events Furnishings

GROWTH PLANS/SPECIAL FEATURES:

CORT Business Services Corporation is a national furnitur rental company. The firm is a subsidiary of Wesco Financia Corporation, a Berkshire Hathaway company. Through its we site, customers can shop for a wide selection of furnitur encompassing different price ranges and styles. Hom furnishings include sofas, chairs, ottomans, media storage tables, sideboards, buffets, beds, dressers, mirrors nightstands, chests, TVs, DVD players, microwaves, desks lamps and accent pieces, such as artwork, rugs, plants an pillows. Office furnishings include bookcases, chairs, desks conference tables, reception sofas and file cabinets. Piece can be rented either individually or in package deals. Th company also provides both the sale of clearance furniture a well as rental services for housewares, including linens kitchenware and bath items. There are over 100 CORT showrooms in the U.S. The company also operates in the U.K as Roomservice by CORT and provides services in more tha 80 countries through a global business partner network. The CORT Trade Show & Event Furnishings division provide furniture for trade shows, meetings, special events, busines functions and parties. In addition to furniture rental, the firm offers a comprehensive relocation service throug ApartmentSearch by CORT, a free online apartment locato that also allows customers to search for single-family o townhome rental properties. The firm also provides destination services, including new city orientation and assistance setting up bank accounts or changing a driver's license. In addition the company offers hotel, car rental and utility setup resources In 2014, CORT acquired AA Party Rentals.

CORT offers its employees medical, dental and vision insurance; life insurance; long-term disability coverage; a 401(k) plan; a profit sharing plan; an employee assistance program; tuition reimbursement; and furniture rental & purchase discounts.

FINANCIAL DATA: Note: Data for latest year may not have been available at press time.

In U.S. $	2015	2014	2013	2012	2011	2010
Revenue		420,000,000				
R&D Expense						
Operating Income						
Operating Margin %						
SGA Expense						
Net Income						
Operating Cash Flow						
Capital Expenditure						
EBITDA						
Return on Assets %						
Return on Equity %						
Debt to Equity						

CONTACT INFORMATION:

Phone: 703-968-8500   Fax: 703-968-8502
Toll-Free: 888-360-2678
Address: 15000 Conference Center Dr., Ste. 440, Chantilly, VA 20151-3819 United States

STOCK TICKER/OTHER:

Stock Ticker: Subsidiary   Exchange:
Employees: Fiscal Year Ends: 12/31
Parent Company: BERKSHIRE HATHAWAY INC

SALARIES/BONUSES:

Top Exec. Salary: $ Bonus: $
Second Exec. Salary: $ Bonus: $

OTHER THOUGHTS:

Estimated Female Officers or Directors: 2
Hot Spot for Advancement for Women/Minorities:

Cortefiel SA

NAIC Code: 448140

TYPES OF BUSINESS:

Men's & Women's Apparel, Retail
Lingerie Stores
Perfume & Cosmetics
Online Sales

BRANDS/DIVISIONS/AFFILIATES:

Cortefiel
Springfield
Women'Secret
Pedro del Hierro
Fifty Factory
Antonio Miro Studio
WomenSecret.com
Cortefiel.com

CONTACTS: *Note: Officers with more than one job title may be intentionally listed here more than once.*

Juan Carlos Escribano Garcia, CEO
Ignacio Garcia, CFO
Joaquin G.Q. Rodriguez, Corp. Sec.
Ignacio Garcia, Dir.-Investor Rel.
Alex Cara, Managing Dir.-Global Franchise
Gonzalo H.F. de Angulo, Chmn.

GROWTH PLANS/SPECIAL FEATURES:

Cortefiel SA operates retail chains that specialize in clothing, perfume and lingerie. The company operates 2,056 points of sale in 83 countries, including 1462 direct operated stores and 594 franchises mostly under the Cortefiel, Pedro del Hierro, Springfield and Women'Secret brands. Cortefiel is a men and women's clothing brand with a modern fashionable look that is continually updated with in-store releases of new color proposals, combinations and styles every two weeks. Pedro del Hierro, or PdH, is a pret-a-porter (ready-to-wear) chain of independent stores and has locations within Cortefiel stores. Springfield is a women and men's fashion brand with a cosmopolitan, urban and youthful feel, targeted to young men and women ages 20-30. Women'Secret is a lingerie and casualwear chain targeted to women ages 18-35 that retails online at WomenSecret.com and worldwide through its franchised stores. In addition, the firm operates an outlet chain for all the Cortefiel brands under the name Fifty Factory. The firm produces its designs through the Antonio Miro Studio. Cortifiel owns six factories, including three in Morocco, two in Spain and one in Hungary. Cortefiel maintains Cortefiel.com, making all its stores and brands accessible online.

FINANCIAL DATA: *Note: Data for latest year may not have been available at press time.*

In U.S. $	2015	2014	2013	2012	2011	2010
Revenue						
R&D Expense						
Operating Income						
Operating Margin %						
SGA Expense						
Net Income						
Operating Cash Flow						
Capital Expenditure						
EBITDA						
Return on Assets %						
Return on Equity %						
Debt to Equity						

CONTACT INFORMATION:

Phone: 34-902-45-3545   Fax: 34-913-87-3874
Toll-Free:
Address: Ave. Del Llano Castellano, 51, Madrid, 28034 Spain

STOCK TICKER/OTHER:

Stock Ticker: Private
Employees: 9,904
Parent Company:

Exchange:
Fiscal Year Ends: 02/28

SALARIES/BONUSES:

Top Exec. Salary: $ Bonus: $
Second Exec. Salary: $ Bonus: $

OTHER THOUGHTS:

Estimated Female Officers or Directors:
Hot Spot for Advancement for Women/Minorities:

Cost Plus Inc

www.worldmarket.com

NAIC Code: 442110

TYPES OF BUSINESS:

Retail-Furniture
Housewares Retailer
Gourmet Foods Retailer
Wine Retailer

BRANDS/DIVISIONS/AFFILIATES:

Bed Bath & Beyond Inc
World Market
Cost Plus World Market

CONTACTS: Note: Officers with more than one job title may be intentionally listed here more than once.

Barry J. Feld, CEO
Barry J. Feld, Pres.
Jane L. Baughman, CFO
Elizabeth J.A. Allen, Sr. VP-Mktg.
Jeffrey A. Turner, CIO
Jane L. Baughman, Sec.
Jeffery A. Turner, Sr. VP-Oper.
Carrie F. Crooker, Sr. VP-Store Oper.
Matt Gee, VP-Consumables
Marilyn Incerty, VP-Home & Trend Dev.
Joseph H. Coulombe, Chmn.

GROWTH PLANS/SPECIAL FEATURES:

Cost Plus, Inc., a subsidiary of Bed, Bath & Beyond, Inc., is a retailer selling a wide range of home decorating items, furniture, gifts, holiday and other seasonal items and specialty food and beverages. The company's 270 World Market and Cost Plus World Market stores are located in 33 states and feature a selection good imported from more than 50 countries around the world. The firm's product offerings are designed to provide solutions to customers' casual living and home entertaining needs. Decorative items for the home include furniture, rugs, pillows, bath linens, lamps, window coverings, frames and baskets. In addition, Cost Plus sells a number of tabletop and kitchen items, including glassware, ceramics, textiles and cooking utensils; food and beverage items, such as wine, microbrewed and imported beer, coffee, tea and bottled water; and a variety of gift and decorative accessories, including collectibles, candles, framed art and holiday and other seasonal items.

Cost Plus offers its employees a flexible spending account; 401(k); employee assistance programs; medical, dental and vision plans; a prescription drug plan; and health and wellness programs.

FINANCIAL DATA: Note: Data for latest year may not have been available at press time.

In U.S. $	2015	2014	2013	2012	2011	2010
Revenue		2,023,479,447	1,958,837,800	2,089,489,800	963,833,000	916,564,000
R&D Expense						
Operating Income						
Operating Margin %						
SGA Expense						
Net Income		115,886,000	112,882,200	107,633,800	16,498,000	2,858,000
Operating Cash Flow						
Capital Expenditure						
EBITDA						
Return on Assets %						
Return on Equity %						
Debt to Equity						

CONTACT INFORMATION:

Phone: 510 893-7300   Fax: 510 893-3681
Toll-Free:
Address: 200 4th St., Oakland, CA 94607 United States

SALARIES/BONUSES:

Top Exec. Salary: $ Bonus: $
Second Exec. Salary: $ Bonus: $

STOCK TICKER/OTHER:

Stock Ticker: Subsidiary
Employees: 5,800
Parent Company: Bed Bath & Beyond Inc

Exchange:
Fiscal Year Ends: 01/31

OTHER THOUGHTS:

Estimated Female Officers or Directors: 4
Hot Spot for Advancement for Women/Minorities: Y

Cost U Less Inc

www.costuless.com

NAIC Code: 452910

TYPES OF BUSINESS:

Warehouse Clubs, Retail
Grocery Stores

BRANDS/DIVISIONS/AFFILIATES:

North West Company Inc

CONTACTS: Note: Officers with more than one job title may be intentionally listed here more than once.

Rex A. Wilhelm, Pres.
William W. Lofgren, VP-Information Systems
Tom Kallio, VP
J. Robert Cain, VP-Logistics

GROWTH PLANS/SPECIAL FEATURES:

Cost-U-Less, Inc., a subsidiary of Canadian firm North West Company, Inc., operates mid-sized warehouse club stores in island markets in the Caribbean and the Pacific. The company currently operates 13 retail stores, located in St. Thomas, St. Croix, Grand Cayman, Guam, Hawaii, California, American Samoa, Fiji, Netherlands Antilles and Barbados. These locations offer electronics, housewares, furniture, office products, personal care items, sporting goods, hardware, dry grocery goods, meat, produce, deli items and dairy goods. Cost-U-Less balances its product mix by providing popular U.S. brand names together with local ethnic items found in each island region. Although the firm employs many of the retailing methods of the larger participants in the warehouse club industry, it operates smaller stores that average 30,000 square feet, does not charge a membership fee and typically locates its stores in smaller geographic areas with less concentrated population centers. The company's business strategy is to enter small island markets ahead of large warehouse club competitors, select markets familiar with the warehouse club concept and offer U.S. goods where availability of such goods is minimal and significant demand exists. Cost-U-Less has refined a mid-sized building prototype that is designed to endure severe island weather conditions and incorporates low construction costs and easily replicated specifications.

FINANCIAL DATA: Note: Data for latest year may not have been available at press time.

In U.S. $	2015	2014	2013	2012	2011	2010
Revenue						
R&D Expense						
Operating Income						
Operating Margin %						
SGA Expense						
Net Income						
Operating Cash Flow						
Capital Expenditure						
EBITDA						
Return on Assets %						
Return on Equity %						
Debt to Equity						

CONTACT INFORMATION:

Phone: 425-945-0213   Fax: 425-945-0214
Toll-Free:
Address: 3633 136th Place SE, Ste. 110, Bellevue, WA 98006 United States

SALARIES/BONUSES:

Top Exec. Salary: $ Bonus: $
Second Exec. Salary: $ Bonus: $

STOCK TICKER/OTHER:

Stock Ticker: Subsidiary   Exchange:
Employees: Fiscal Year Ends: 12/31
Parent Company: NORTH WEST COMPANY INC

OTHER THOUGHTS:

Estimated Female Officers or Directors:
Hot Spot for Advancement for Women/Minorities:

Costco Wholesale Corp

NAIC Code: 452910

TYPES OF BUSINESS:

Warehouse Clubs, Retail
Food
Health & Beauty Products
Electronics
Furniture
Apparel
Automotive Supplies
Gasoline Sales

BRANDS/DIVISIONS/AFFILIATES:

Costco Wholesale Industries
Costco de Mexico
Kirkland Signature

CONTACTS: Note: Officers with more than one job title may be intentionally listed here more than once.

Jeffrey Brotman, Chairman of the Board
David Petterson, Senior VP
Douglas Schutt, COO, Divisional
Dennis Zook, COO, Divisional
Joseph Portera, COO, Divisional
John McKay, COO, Divisional
James Murphy, COO, Divisional
W. Jelinek, Director
Franz Lazarus, Executive VP, Divisional
Timothy Rose, Executive VP, Divisional
Richard Galanti, Executive VP
Paul Moulton, Executive VP
James Sinegal, Founder
John Sullivan, Secretary

GROWTH PLANS/SPECIAL FEATURES:

Costco Wholesale Corp. operates membership warehouse based on the concept that offering members very low prices o a limited selection of branded and private-label products w produce high sales volumes and rapid inventory turnover. Thi rapid turnover, combined with volume purchasing, efficien distribution and reduced handling of merchandise in self service warehouse facilities, allows the firm to operate a significantly lower margins than traditional discount retailers Costco buys the majority of its merchandise directly from manufacturers for shipment to warehouses or to consolidatio points, minimizing freight and handling costs. Products includ health and beauty aids, cleaning supplies, foods, alcohol appliances, electronics, tools, office supplies, furniture automotive supplies, apparel, cameras, house wares an books. Stores contain other features, including pharmacies print shops, photo labs and gas stations. Costco has three types of memberships: executive, business and gold star Memberships are designed to build customer loyalty and start at $55 per year. The firm operates 686 warehouses, including 480 in the U.S. and Puerto Rico, 27 in the U.K., 89 in Canada seven in Australia, 12 in Korea, 36 in Mexico, 11 in Taiwan, 2 in Japan and one in Spain. The stores average approximately 143,000 square feet and stock around distinct product including upscale items such as jewelry and wines. Costc Wholesale Industries, a division of the company, operate manufacturing businesses, including special food packaging optical laboratories, meat processing and jewelry distribution. The company also operates e-commerce web sites in the U.S. Canada, the U.K. and Mexico.

Costco offers its employees health care, dental, vision and prescription coverage; a 401(k) plan; employee assistance plans; a dependent care assistance plan; short- and long-term disability; life insurance; an employee stock purchase plan; health care reimbursement; and long-term care insurance.

FINANCIAL DATA: Note: Data for latest year may not have been available at press time.

In U.S. $	2015	2014	2013	2012	2011	2010
Revenue	116,199,000,000	112,640,000,000	105,156,000,000	99,137,000,000	88,915,000,000	77,946,000,000
R&D Expense						
Operating Income	3,624,000,000	3,220,000,000	3,053,000,000	2,759,000,000	2,439,000,000	2,077,000,000
Operating Margin %	3.11%	2.85%	2.90%	2.78%	2.74%	2.66%
SGA Expense	11,510,000,000	10,962,000,000	10,155,000,000	9,555,000,000	8,728,001,000	7,866,000,000
Net Income	2,377,000,000	2,058,000,000	2,039,000,000	1,709,000,000	1,462,000,000	1,303,000,000
Operating Cash Flow	4,285,000,000	3,984,000,000	3,437,000,000	3,057,000,000	3,198,000,000	2,780,000,000
Capital Expenditure	2,393,000,000	1,993,000,000	2,083,000,000	1,480,000,000	1,290,000,000	1,055,000,000
EBITDA	4,855,000,000	4,339,000,000	4,096,000,000	3,770,000,000	3,354,000,000	2,960,000,000
Return on Assets %	7.15%	6.50%	7.10%	6.34%	5.78%	5.69%
Return on Equity %	20.74%	17.79%	17.58%	14.02%	12.80%	12.50%
Debt to Equity	0.45	0.41	0.46	0.11	0.10	0.19

CONTACT INFORMATION:

Phone: 425 313-8100   Fax: 425 313-8103
Toll-Free: 800-774-2678
Address: 999 Lake Dr., Issaquah, WA 98027 United States

STOCK TICKER/OTHER:

Stock Ticker: COST
Employees: 195,000
Parent Company:

Exchange: NAS
Fiscal Year Ends: 08/31

SALARIES/BONUSES:

Top Exec. Salary: $650,000   Bonus: $90,400
Second Exec. Salary: $650,000   Bonus: $90,400

OTHER THOUGHTS:

Estimated Female Officers or Directors: 4
Hot Spot for Advancement for Women/Minorities: Y

Cumberland Farms Inc

www.cumberlandfarms.com

NAIC Code: 447110

TYPES OF BUSINESS:

Convenience Stores
Dairy Operations
Bakery Operations
Beverage Operations
Private-Label Foods
Gas Stations

BRANDS/DIVISIONS/AFFILIATES:

Gulf Oil LP

CONTACTS: Note: Officers with more than one job title may be intentionally listed here more than once.

Ari Haseotes, CEO
Ari N. Haseotes, Pres.
David Merriam, Sr. VP-Store Oper.
David Masuret, VP-Supply & Distribution

GROWTH PLANS/SPECIAL FEATURES:

Cumberland Farms, Inc. is one of the largest convenience stores and petroleum marketers in the Northeastern U.S. The company operates a network of nearly 600 convenience stores in 8 states. As part of its convenience store operations, Cumberland Farms conducts dairy, bakery and beverage operations, with two fluid milk processing facilities, a 120,000-square-foot bakery center and a 70,000-square-foot plastic and beverage facility. The firm also operates a grocery warehouse and distribution center in Massachusetts, which delivers groceries and other miscellaneous products to all of Cumberland Farms' convenience stores, except those in Florida. The company's private-label products include dairy products, bakery items, deli sandwiches, juices and beverages. Cumberland Farms also operates a distribution and wholesale petroleum subsidiary, Gulf Oil L.P., which includes approximately 2,000 branded filling stations in the Northeast. Other divisions include a real estate division, which focuses on the management of its commercial strip centers and retail sites. The firm is in the process of a multi-year re-branding strategy. As part of this strategy, Cumberland has introduced a new convenience store concept that features no-charge ATMs, prepared foods, frozen shake machines and more.

Cumberland Farms offers employees benefits including health, dental, vision, life and AD&D insurance; a 401(k); a fitness program; an assistance program; and paid time off.

FINANCIAL DATA: Note: Data for latest year may not have been available at press time.

In U.S. $	2015	2014	2013	2012	2011	2010
Revenue		10,150,000,000	10,000,000,000	9,800,000,000	8,020,000,000	6,570,000,000
R&D Expense						
Operating Income						
Operating Margin %						
SGA Expense						
Net Income						
Operating Cash Flow						
Capital Expenditure						
EBITDA						
Return on Assets %						
Return on Equity %						
Debt to Equity						

CONTACT INFORMATION:

Phone: 508-271-6624   Fax:
Toll-Free: 800-225-9702
Address: 100 Crossing Blvd., Framingham, MA 01702 United States

SALARIES/BONUSES:

Top Exec. Salary: $ Bonus: $
Second Exec. Salary: $ Bonus: $

STOCK TICKER/OTHER:

Stock Ticker: Private   Exchange:
Employees: 7,000   Fiscal Year Ends: 09/30
Parent Company:

OTHER THOUGHTS:

Estimated Female Officers or Directors: 8
Hot Spot for Advancement for Women/Minorities: Y

Sales, profits and employees may be estimates. Financial information, benefits and other data can change quickly and may vary from those stated here.

CVS Health

NAIC Code: 446110

TYPES OF BUSINESS:

Drug Stores
Pharmacy Benefits Management
Online Pharmacy Services

BRANDS/DIVISIONS/AFFILIATES:

MinuteClinic
SilverScript Insurance Company
CVS/pharmacy
Pennsylvania Life Insurance Company
Omnicare

CONTACTS: Note: Officers with more than one job title may be intentionally listed here more than once.

Larry Merlo, CEO
David Denton, CFO
David Dorman, Chairman of the Board
Eva Boratto, Chief Accounting Officer
Helena Foulkes, Chief Marketing Officer
Troyen Brennan, Chief Medical Officer
Per Lofberg, Executive VP
J. Joyner, Executive VP
Thomas Moriarty, Executive VP
Jonathan Roberts, Executive VP
Andrew Sussman, Other Executive Officer
Lisa Bisaccia, Other Executive Officer
Steven Gold, Other Executive Officer
Colleen McIntosh, Senior VP

GROWTH PLANS/SPECIAL FEATURES:

CVS Health Corporation is a leading provider of prescription and related health care services in the U.S. It operates in three segments: corporate, retail pharmacy and pharmacy services. The corporate segment provides management and administrative services to support the company's overall operations. The retail pharmacy segment includes over 7,800 retail drugstores, with 7,765 operating a pharmacy; online retail pharmacy web sites such as CVS.com, Navarro.com and Onofre.com.br; 17 onsite pharmacy stores; and retail health care clinics. The retail drugstores are located in 44 states, Puerto Rico, Washington, D.C. and Brazil operating under the CVS/pharmacy, CVS, Longs Drugs, Navarro Discount Pharmacy and Drogaria Onofre names. The division operates 971 retail health care clinics in 31 states under the MinuteClinic name, predominately located within CVS drugstores. The pharmacy services segment provides a full range of pharmacy benefit management services, including mail order pharmacy services, plan design and administration, formulary management, claims processing and health management programs. Through subsidiaries SilverScript Insurance Company and Pennsylvania Life Insurance Company, the division is a national provider of drug benefits to eligible beneficiaries under Medicare Part D. The segment operates a national retail pharmacy network with 27 retail specialty pharmacy stores; 11 specialty mail order pharmacies; four mail order dispensing services; and 86 branches with 70 ambulatory infusion suites. In June 2015, the firm agreed to buy Target's pharmacies and clinics for $1.9 billion. Target's 1,600 drugstores will be rebranded as CVS/pharmacy, while its 80 medical clinics will be rebranded as MinuteClinics. In August 2015, CVS health acquired Omnicare.

Employee benefits include medical, dental, vision and prescription coverage; free health screenings at MinuteClinic; a 401(k); employee stock purchase plan; short- and long-term disability; employee discounts; education reimbursement; an employee assistance program; and flexible spending accounts.

FINANCIAL DATA: Note: Data for latest year may not have been available at press time.

In U.S. $	2015	2014	2013	2012	2011	2010
Revenue		139,367,000,000	126,761,000,000	123,133,000,000	107,100,000,000	96,413,000,000
R&D Expense						
Operating Income		8,799,000,000	8,037,000,000	7,228,000,000	6,330,000,000	6,165,000,000
Operating Margin %		6.31%	6.34%	5.87%	5.91%	6.39%
SGA Expense		16,568,000,000	15,746,000,000	15,278,000,000	14,231,000,000	14,092,000,000
Net Income		4,644,000,000	4,592,000,000	3,877,000,000	3,461,000,000	3,427,000,000
Operating Cash Flow		8,137,000,000	5,783,000,000	6,671,000,000	5,856,000,000	4,779,000,000
Capital Expenditure		2,136,000,000	1,984,000,000	2,030,000,000	1,872,000,000	2,005,000,000
EBITDA		10,224,000,000	9,915,000,000	8,633,000,000	7,902,000,000	7,637,000,000
Return on Assets %		6.37%	6.68%	5.94%	5.46%	5.53%
Return on Equity %		12.23%	12.14%	10.23%	9.13%	9.32%
Debt to Equity		0.30	0.33	0.24	0.24	0.22

CONTACT INFORMATION:

Phone: 401 765-1500   Fax: 401 762-2137
Toll-Free: 888-746-7287
Address: 1 CVS Dr., Woonsocket, RI 02895 United States

STOCK TICKER/OTHER:

Stock Ticker: CVS   Exchange: NYS
Employees: 202,000   Fiscal Year Ends: 12/31
Parent Company:

SALARIES/BONUSES:

Top Exec. Salary: Bonus: $
$1,350,000
Second Exec. Salary: Bonus: $
$900,000

OTHER THOUGHTS:

Estimated Female Officers or Directors: 4

Hot Spot for Advancement for Women/Minorities: Y

Dalian Wanda Group Co Ltd

www.wanda-group.com

NAIC Code: 512131

TYPES OF BUSINESS:

Motion Picture Theaters (except Drive-Ins)
Motion Picture and Video Production
Motion Picture and Video Distribution
Performing Arts Companies
Amusement and Theme Parks
Hotels (except Casino Hotels) and Motels
Department Stores
Internet Publishing and Broadcasting and Web Search Portals

BRANDS/DIVISIONS/AFFILIATES:

Wanda Plazas
Qingdao Oriental Movie Metropolis
Continental Film Distribution
China Times
Popular Cinema
Wanda E-commerce
O2O e-commerce
99bill

CONTACTS:
Note: Officers with more than one job title may be intentionally listed here more than once.

Wang Jianlin, Chmn.

GROWTH PLANS/SPECIAL FEATURES:

Dalian Wanda Group Co. Ltd. is a private property developer with registered capital totaling $7 billion. The company operates in four major industries: commercial property, culture & tourism, e-commerce and department stores. Dalian Wanda's commercial property division is the largest commercial real estate company in the world, comprising 125 Wanda Plazas and 81 hotels with a total gross floor area of 70 million square feet (21.57 million square meters). Properties under construction include 70 Wanda Plazas and 69 hotels, with a combined gross floor area of 57 million square feet (17.47 million square meters). The culture & tourism division comprises cinemas, film production, film industry parks, performing arts, film technology entertainment, theme parks, entertainment franchises, print media, art investment and travel. This segment operates 187 theatres, with a total 1,657 screens (including 117 IMAX screens); the Qingdao Oriental Movie Metropolis film and television industrial park, which plans to open itself to the public in 2017; film technology entertainment includes Continental Film Distribution, a film distribution, marketing and planning company that plays a key role in Wanda's film industry operations; and print media operates weekly magazines China Times and Popular Cinema. The e-commerce division comprises Wanda E-commerce, a joint venture with Tencent and Baidu, which is developing its O2O e-commerce platform, spanning the areas of film, parenting, dining, shopping, entertainment, leisure, tourism, lifestyle and finance; and 99bill, an independent third-party payment platform. The department store division operates 99 department stores in major cities such as Beijing, Shanghai, Chengdu and Wuhan.

FINANCIAL DATA:
Note: Data for latest year may not have been available at press time.

In U.S. $	2015	2014	2013	2012	2011	2010
Revenue						
R&D Expense						
Operating Income						
Operating Margin %						
SGA Expense						
Net Income						
Operating Cash Flow						
Capital Expenditure						
EBITDA						
Return on Assets %						
Return on Equity %						
Debt to Equity						

CONTACT INFORMATION:

Phone: 86-10-85853888   Fax: 86-10-85853222
Toll-Free:
Address: Tower B, Wanda Plaza, No. 93, Jianguo Rd., Chaoyang District, Beijing, 100022 China

STOCK TICKER/OTHER:

Stock Ticker: Private
Employees:
Parent Company:

Exchange:
Fiscal Year Ends:

SALARIES/BONUSES:

Top Exec. Salary: $ Bonus: $
Second Exec. Salary: $ Bonus: $

OTHER THOUGHTS:

Estimated Female Officers or Directors:
Hot Spot for Advancement for Women/Minorities:

De Beers SA

NAIC Code: 212399

www.debeersgroup.com

TYPES OF BUSINESS:

Diamonds, Industrial, Mining and/or Beneficiating
Diamond Trading
Diamond Retailing
E-commerce

BRANDS/DIVISIONS/AFFILIATES:

Anglo American plc
DeBeers.com
De Beers Investments
De Beers Diamond Jewellers Ltd
Forevermark
Synova SA

GROWTH PLANS/SPECIAL FEATURES:

De Beers SA is one of the largest diamond miners in the world. Its operations include rough diamond exploration, mining and trading. The firm engages in open-pit, underground, marine and alluvial mining. Its major mining operations are located in Canada, South Africa, Botswana and Namibia. The firm's retail operations are handled by a joint venture with Moet Hennessy Louis Vuitton (LVMH). The venture is called De Beers Diamond Jewellers, Ltd. and operates stores worldwide as well as an e-commerce site at DeBeers.com. The firm's other brand is Forevermark. Forevermark diamonds are sold in over 1,400 retail stores across 34 markets worldwide. De Beers is owned by De Beers Investments, which is itself held by Anglo American plc (85%) and the government of Botswana (15%). In May 2015, the firm announced its intention to sell its Kimberley Mines Tailings asset, located in central South Africa and acquired a 33.4% stake in Synova SA, an owner and supplier of a patent laser micro jet technology.

CONTACTS:
Note: Officers with more than one job title may be intentionally listed here more than once.

Philippe Mellier, CEO
Bruce Cleaver, Dir.-Strategy & New Bus.
Varda Shine, CEO-Diamond Trading Company
Walter Huehn, CEO-Element Six
Tony Guthrie, CEO-De Beers Canada, Inc.
Mark Cutifani, Chmn.

FINANCIAL DATA:
Note: Data for latest year may not have been available at press time.

In U.S. $	2015	2014	2013	2012	2011	2010
Revenue						
R&D Expense						
Operating Income						
Operating Margin %						
SGA Expense						
Net Income						
Operating Cash Flow						
Capital Expenditure						
EBITDA						
Return on Assets %						
Return on Equity %						
Debt to Equity						

CONTACT INFORMATION:

Phone: 27-11-374-7000   Fax: 27-11-374-7700
Toll-Free:
Address: Cnr. Crownwood Rd & Diamond Dr., Private Bag X01, Johannesburg, 2193 South Africa

STOCK TICKER/OTHER:

Stock Ticker: Subsidiary
Employees: 20,000
Parent Company: Anglo American plc

Exchange:
Fiscal Year Ends: 12/31

SALARIES/BONUSES:

Top Exec. Salary: $ Bonus: $
Second Exec. Salary: $ Bonus: $

OTHER THOUGHTS:

Estimated Female Officers or Directors: 3
Hot Spot for Advancement for Women/Minorities: Y

Delhaize Group

www.delhaizegroup.com

NAIC Code: 445110

TYPES OF BUSINESS:

Grocery Stores
Convenience Stores

BRANDS/DIVISIONS/AFFILIATES:

Delhaize Le Lion
Food Lion
Bottom Dollar Food
Hannaford
Shop 'n Go
Red Market
Tom & Co
Proxy Delhaize

CONTACTS: *Note: Officers with more than one job title may be intentionally listed here more than once.*

Pierre-Olivier Beckers, CEO
Pierre-Olivier Beckers, Pres.
Pierre Bouchut, CFO
Nicolas Hollanders, Exec. VP-Human Resources
Nicolas Hollanders, Exec. VP-IT
Michael Waller, General Counsel
Kostas Macheras, CEO-Southeastern Europe
Stefan Descheemaeker, CEO-Delhaize Europe
Mats Jansson, Chmn.

GROWTH PLANS/SPECIAL FEATURES:

Delhaize Group is a Belgian international food retailer present in seven countries, with a total sales network of 3,468 stores. Delhaize's U.S. stores operate under the names Food Lion, Hannaford and Bottom Dollar Food. These markets sell a wide variety of groceries, including produce, meats, dairy products, seafood, frozen food, deli/bakery products and non-food items, such as health and beauty care, prescriptions and other household and personal products. The firm offers nationally and regionally advertised brand-name merchandise as well as products manufactured and packaged under the private label Food Lion. Food Lion stores are located in south east America, covering 10 states. Delhaize also owns and operates warehousing and distribution facilities in the U.S., including a transportation fleet spread throughout the eastern U.S. U.S. operations represent 63% of revenue. In Belgium and Luxembourg (24.7%), the firm operates over 836 Delhaize Le Lion, Ad Delhaize, Delhaize City, Proxy Delhaize, Shop -ˉn Go, Tom & Co and Red Market. In southeast Europe and Asia, the company maintains 1,105 total stores. In Greece the company operates 308 stores, including Romania, 410; Indonesia, 117; Serbia, 387; and Bosnia and Herzegovina, 39. In 2014, the company sold its Sweetbay, Harvey's and Reid's operations, as well as its Bulgarian operations. In June 2015, Delhaize Group agreed to merge with Ahold, a Dutch firm with that owns the Stop & Shop and Giant supermarkets in the U.S. The combined companies will be named Ahold Delhaize. It will have 6,500 total stores in America and Europe, along with 375,000 employees.

FINANCIAL DATA: *Note: Data for latest year may not have been available at press time.*

In U.S. $	2015	2014	2013	2012	2011	2010
Revenue		22,670,450,000	22,401,940,000	24,130,800,000	22,413,610,000	22,128,120,000
R&D Expense						
Operating Income		448,930,200	516,853,500	413,907,300	861,776,200	1,086,772,000
Operating Margin %		1.98%	2.30%	1.71%	3.84%	4.91%
SGA Expense		4,779,037,000	4,758,872,000	5,169,596,000	4,775,853,000	4,661,233,000
Net Income		94,455,770	189,972,800	111,436,600	504,117,900	609,186,600
Operating Cash Flow		1,217,312,000	1,257,641,000	1,494,311,000	1,173,799,000	1,397,733,000
Capital Expenditure		643,148,300	599,634,900	730,174,900	808,711,200	700,458,500
EBITDA		1,093,140,000	1,157,879,000	1,121,795,000	1,508,108,000	1,709,756,000
Return on Assets %		.75%	1.52%	.86%	4.10%	5.55%
Return on Equity %		1.69%	3.48%	1.97%	9.06%	12.13%
Debt to Equity		0.49	0.49	0.56	0.55	0.52

CONTACT INFORMATION:

Phone: 32 24122211   Fax: 32 24122222
Toll-Free:
Address: Rue Osseghemstraat 53, Brussels, 1080 Belgium

SALARIES/BONUSES:

Top Exec. Salary: Bonus: $435,133
$1,029,462
Second Exec. Salary: Bonus: $
$210,000

STOCK TICKER/OTHER:

Stock Ticker: DEG   Exchange: NYS
Employees: 152,000   Fiscal Year Ends: 12/31
Parent Company:

OTHER THOUGHTS:

Estimated Female Officers or Directors: 3

Hot Spot for Advancement for Women/Minorities: Y

dELiA*s Inc

www.delias.com

NAIC Code: 454111

TYPES OF BUSINESS:

Apparel Sales - Online Retailing
Cosmetics & Accessories
Young Women's Apparel

GROWTH PLANS/SPECIAL FEATURES:

dELiA*s, Inc. is an on-line retailer of apparel and fashion accessories primarily marketed toward teenage girls and young women. The company operates through its dELiA*s brand. Its catalogs feature a broad assortment of merchandise, including jeans, dresses, accessories, shoes and outerwear. The firm offers items from its own line as well as products from recognized and emerging brands. The company's only operation is its online store, Delias.com, which offers apparel, cosmetics, accessories, footwear and other products designed to complement the catalog merchandise. In 2014, dELiA*s entered into bankruptcy and announced it would be liquidating all of its 92 stores. In August 2015, it relaunched as an online-only store.

BRANDS/DIVISIONS/AFFILIATES:

dELiA*s
DELiAs.com

CONTACTS: Note: Officers with more than one job title may be intentionally listed here more than once.

Edward Brennan, CFO
Michael Zimmerman, Chairman of the Board
Ryan Schreiber, President
David Diamond, Vice President, Divisional

FINANCIAL DATA: Note: Data for latest year may not have been available at press time.

In U.S. $	2015	2014	2013	2012	2011	2010
Revenue		136,650,000	222,699,000	217,152,000	220,697,000	223,866,000
R&D Expense						
Operating Income		-52,596,000	-20,754,000	-22,942,000	-29,427,000	-15,867,000
Operating Margin %		-38.48%	-9.31%	-10.56%	-13.33%	-7.08%
SGA Expense		72,509,000	93,433,000	92,740,000	95,746,000	94,939,000
Net Income		-58,511,000	-21,554,000	-22,670,000	-21,643,000	-10,424,000
Operating Cash Flow		-60,735,000	-7,073,000	4,367,000	-7,765,000	-36,094,000
Capital Expenditure		2,783,000	4,541,000	4,015,000	5,819,000	12,571,000
EBITDA		-44,373,000	-11,846,000	-11,496,000	-18,758,000	-5,774,000
Return on Assets %		-70.97%	-20.54%	-17.77%	-14.00%	-5.57%
Return on Equity %		-187.79%	-41.70%	-31.02%	-22.79%	-9.42%
Debt to Equity						

CONTACT INFORMATION:

Phone: 212-590-6200   Fax:
Toll-Free: 866-293-3268
Address: 50 W. 23rd St., New York, NY 10010 United States

STOCK TICKER/OTHER:

Stock Ticker: DLIAQ   Exchange: PINX
Employees: 1,639   Fiscal Year Ends: 01/31
Parent Company:

SALARIES/BONUSES:

Top Exec. Salary: $264,281   Bonus: $235,000
Second Exec. Salary: Bonus: $
$400,577

OTHER THOUGHTS:

Estimated Female Officers or Directors: 1
Hot Spot for Advancement for Women/Minorities:

Demoulas Super Markets Inc

www.mydemoulas.net

NAIC Code: 445110

TYPES OF BUSINESS:

Grocery Stores
Real Estate

BRANDS/DIVISIONS/AFFILIATES:

Market Basket

GROWTH PLANS/SPECIAL FEATURES:

Demoulas Super Markets, Inc., founded in 1954, is a chain of over 71 grocery stores in Massachusetts, New Hampshire and Maine. All grocery stores operate under the Market Basket name. The company was founded by brothers George and Mike Demoulas, who purchased their parents' grocery store and extended it. In August 2014, due to continued controversy over ownership and leadership of the company, an agreement was reached to sell the 50.5% stake owned by the family of Arthur S. Demoulas to his cousin Arthur T. Demoulas. Most of the company's stores are located within shopping centers and other retail outlets. All other Market Baskets located elsewhere throughout the U.S. are not affiliated with Demoulas Super Markets.

CONTACTS: Note: Officers with more than one job title may be intentionally listed here more than once.

Arthur Demoulas, CEO
Donald Mulligan, VP-Finance
Julien Lacourse, Exec. VP-Mktg.
Joseph Rockwell, VP-Grocery Sales & Merchandising
David K. McLean, Mgr.-Oper.
Michael King, VP
Keith Cowan, Chmn.

FINANCIAL DATA: Note: Data for latest year may not have been available at press time.

In U.S. $	2015	2014	2013	2012	2011	2010
Revenue		3,700,000,000	3,500,000,000	3,400,000,000	3,350,000,000	3,200,000,000
R&D Expense						
Operating Income						
Operating Margin %						
SGA Expense						
Net Income						
Operating Cash Flow						
Capital Expenditure						
EBITDA						
Return on Assets %						
Return on Equity %						
Debt to Equity						

CONTACT INFORMATION:

Phone: 978-851-8000   Fax: 978-640-8390
Toll-Free:
Address: 875 East St., Tewksbury, MA 01876 United States

SALARIES/BONUSES:

Top Exec. Salary: $ Bonus: $
Second Exec. Salary: $ Bonus: $

STOCK TICKER/OTHER:

Stock Ticker: Private
Employees: 20,000
Parent Company:

Exchange:
Fiscal Year Ends: 12/31

OTHER THOUGHTS:

Estimated Female Officers or Directors:
Hot Spot for Advancement for Women/Minorities:

Destination Maternity Corp

www.destinationmaternity.com

NAIC Code: 448120

TYPES OF BUSINESS:

Women's Apparel, Retail
Maternity Apparel
Online Sales
Leased Maternity Departments
Spas

BRANDS/DIVISIONS/AFFILIATES:

Motherhood Maternity
Destination Maternity
A Pea in the Pod
Oh Baby by Motherhood
edamame
Two Hearts Maternity
Maternity Spa

CONTACTS: *Note: Officers with more than one job title may be intentionally listed here more than once.*

Anthony Romano, CEO
Judd Tirnauer, CFO
Arnaud Ajdler, Chairman of the Board
Ronald Masciantonio, Chief Administrative Officer
Christopher Daniel, President

GROWTH PLANS/SPECIAL FEATURES:

Destination Maternity Corp. is a leading designer, manufacturer and retailer of maternity apparel. It currently operates 568 stores under the Motherhood Maternity, A Pea in the Pod and Destination Maternity names as well as 1,320 leased maternity departments in department stores and baby specialty stores. The firm's stores, located throughout all 50 states, Canada and Puerto Rico, offer career, casual, exercise and special-occasion maternity apparel. Motherhood Maternity, serving the value-priced market, is the broadest of the firm's lines, featuring casual and career wear, formal attire, lingerie, sportswear and outerwear as well as accessories and plus sizes. The A Pea in the Pod brand features upscale maternity fashions, including career and casual merchandise as well as exclusive designer labels. Destination Maternity superstores typically carry the Motherhood and Pea brands and are located in regional malls and lifestyle centers. Four of its superstores also feature its edamame and Maternity Spa branded spas. The company's leased departments are located in stores such as Macy's, Sears, Boscov's, Gordman's and in select buybuy Baby stores. Additionally, its Oh Baby by Motherhood collection is offered exclusively at Kohl's stores and its Two Hearts Maternity collection is available only at Sears. In addition to brick-and-mortar locations, the firm markets its brands through direct marketing and several e-commerce sites. Additionally, the company has been expanding internationally through various franchise arrangements in Mexico, the Middle East and South Korea. Currently, its international presence consists of 78 franchised locations, including 59 shop-in-shop locations and 19 Destination Maternity branded stores.

Destination Maternity offers employees a health care plan, dental plan, an onsite fitness center, an employee assistance program, credit union membership, Relocation Resource Program, AD&D, short- and long-term disability coverage and life insurance.

FINANCIAL DATA: *Note: Data for latest year may not have been available at press time.*

In U.S. $	2015	2014	2013	2012	2011	2010
Revenue		516,959,000	540,259,000	541,476,000	545,394,000	531,192,000
R&D Expense						
Operating Income		14,507,000	37,494,000	33,105,000	38,244,000	31,433,000
Operating Margin %		2.80%	6.93%	6.11%	7.01%	5.91%
SGA Expense		250,253,000	252,026,000	255,623,000	257,421,000	251,653,000
Net Income		10,497,000	23,943,000	19,372,000	22,988,000	16,829,000
Operating Cash Flow		25,845,000	42,153,000	42,697,000	21,443,000	25,974,000
Capital Expenditure		42,135,000	16,022,000	9,521,000	12,583,000	10,741,000
EBITDA		29,718,000	49,934,000	45,569,000	51,009,000	44,329,000
Return on Assets %		4.78%	11.74%	9.72%	11.38%	8.39%
Return on Equity %		8.46%	21.03%	19.60%	27.98%	27.72%
Debt to Equity					0.30	0.54

CONTACT INFORMATION:

Phone: 215 873-2200   Fax:
Toll-Free:
Address: 456 N. 5th St., Philadelphia, PA 19123 United States

STOCK TICKER/OTHER:

Stock Ticker: DEST
Employees: 4,300
Parent Company:

Exchange: NAS
Fiscal Year Ends: 09/30

SALARIES/BONUSES:

Top Exec. Salary: $680,769   Bonus: $
Second Exec. Salary: Bonus: $
$533,333

OTHER THOUGHTS:

Estimated Female Officers or Directors: 1
Hot Spot for Advancement for Women/Minorities: Y

Destination XL Group Inc

www.destinationxl.com

NAIC Code: 448110

TYPES OF BUSINESS:

Men's Apparel-Retail
Big & Tall Apparel
Teen's Clothing & Accessories-Retail
Denim Products
Outlet Stores
Online Sales

BRANDS/DIVISIONS/AFFILIATES:

Destination XL
Casual Male XL
Casual Male XL Outlets
Rochester Clothing
DXL
Harbor Bay
Island Passport
DestinationXL.com

CONTACTS: Note: Officers with more than one job title may be intentionally listed here more than once.

David Levin, CEO
Peter Stratton, CFO
Seymour Holtzman, Chairman of the Board
John Cooney, Chief Accounting Officer
Derrick Walker, Chief Marketing Officer
Robert Molloy, General Counsel
Peter Schmitz, Other Executive Officer
Kenneth Ederle, Other Executive Officer
Francis Chane, Senior VP, Divisional
Walter Sprague, Senior VP, Divisional
Jack McKinney, Senior VP
Brian Reaves, Senior VP
Angela Chew, Senior VP

GROWTH PLANS/SPECIAL FEATURES:

Destination XL Group, Inc. is one of the largest specialty retailers of men's big and tall apparel, with retail operations in the U.S., Canada and Europe. The company operates 138 Destination XL stores, 157 Casual Male XL stores, 48 Casual Male XL Outlets stores, two DXL outlet stores and eight Rochester Clothing stores. Destination XL stores combine all of the firm's brands under one roof. The firm also has a direct business that includes several catalogs and e-commerce sites. The stores offer an extensive selection of quality sportswear, dress clothing and footwear for the big and tall customer at moderate prices. The majority of the company's merchandise is basic or fashion-neutral items, such as jeans, casual slacks, tee-shirts, polo shirts, dress shirts and suit separates from nationally-recognized brands such as Polo, Nautica, Dockers and Levi's and private label merchandise. Private label brands carried in the stores include Gold Series, Harbor Bay, Synrgy, True Nation, Oak Hill and Island Passport. The firm's clothing has features specifically designed for comfort, such as waist-relaxer pants, stretch belts, zipper ties, wide band socks, neck-relaxer shirts and clothing with comfort-stretch technology and reinforced stress points. The company recently redirected all its old web sites, ShoesXL.com, LivingXL.com, BTDirect.com, RochesterClothing.com and CasualMaleXL.com, to its new comprehensive site DestinationXL.com.

The firm offers employees medical, dental and vision insurance; a 401(k) plan; flexible spending accounts; tuition reimbursement; and product discounts.

FINANCIAL DATA: Note: Data for latest year may not have been available at press time.

In U.S. $	2015	2014	2013	2012	2011	2010
Revenue	414,020,000	387,983,000	399,640,000	397,655,000	393,642,000	395,168,000
R&D Expense						
Operating Income	-8,802,000	-13,079,000	13,924,000	-6,607,000	16,249,000	8,011,000
Operating Margin %	-2.12%	-3.37%	3.48%	-1.66%	4.12%	2.02%
SGA Expense	174,814,000	170,652,000	156,366,000	177,883,000	150,933,000	151,045,000
Net Income	-12,295,000	-59,786,000	6,126,000	42,663,000	15,371,000	6,110,000
Operating Cash Flow	13,805,000	24,898,000	29,895,000	23,426,000	19,022,000	30,774,000
Capital Expenditure	40,927,000	54,125,000	32,390,000	18,038,000	9,031,000	4,634,000
EBITDA	15,200,000	7,762,000	29,393,000	5,944,000	30,025,000	24,147,000
Return on Assets %	-4.93%	-24.73%	2.55%	20.49%	8.45%	3.19%
Return on Equity %	-12.45%	-44.92%	3.88%	32.11%	15.02%	7.40%
Debt to Equity	0.28	0.11				0.02

CONTACT INFORMATION:

Phone: 781 828-9300   Fax: 781 444-8999
Toll-Free: 800-767-0319
Address: 555 Turnpike St., Canton, MA 02021 United States

STOCK TICKER/OTHER:

Stock Ticker: DXLG
Employees: 2,435
Parent Company:

Exchange: NAS
Fiscal Year Ends: 01/31

SALARIES/BONUSES:

Top Exec. Salary: $811,200   Bonus: $
Second Exec. Salary: $343,269   Bonus: $

OTHER THOUGHTS:

Estimated Female Officers or Directors: 2
Hot Spot for Advancement for Women/Minorities:

Sales, profits and employees may be estimates. Financial information, benefits and other data can change quickly and may vary from those stated here.

Diane von Furstenberg Studio LP

NAIC Code: 448120

TYPES OF BUSINESS:

Fashion Apparel--Design & Retail
Jewelry
Home Furnishings
Handbags
Ready-to-wear Clothing
Footwear
Eyewear
Luggage

BRANDS/DIVISIONS/AFFILIATES:

CONTACTS: Note: Officers with more than one job title may be intentionally listed here more than once.

Paolo Riva, CEO
Paula Sutter, Pres.
Barry Diller, Chmn.

GROWTH PLANS/SPECIAL FEATURES:

Diane von Furstenberg Studio, LP (DVF) is a global luxury brand fashion house that retails complete lines of its ready-to-wear women's apparel. The company's eponymous apparel line started with the innovative wrap dress that is still sold in boutiques and retailers throughout the world. DVF is headquartered in New York City and markets its products towards women in need of versatile apparel. DVF retails collections of accessories, dresses, coats, tops, jackets, books, jewelry, sweaters, watches, shoes, luggage and handbags. In addition, the company retails sportswear, cosmetics, fragrances and home products. The DVF line is also sold in high end retail stores such as Henri Bendel, Bergdorf Goodman, Nordstrom, Barney's New York, Intermix and others. Additionally, the company operates a creative studio that serves as a lab for young budding artists to showcase and develop their work as interns. DVF distributes its products to a network of more than 55 countries and 1500 points of sale, including 132 DVF-owned and partnered stores throughout North and South America, Europe, the Middle East and Asia Pacific. DVF can also be found online at DVF.com. In May 2015, the firm signed a licensing deal with Brown Shoe Co., which will produce and distribute a women's shoe collection scheduled to launch in 2016.

FINANCIAL DATA: Note: Data for latest year may not have been available at press time.

In U.S. $	2015	2014	2013	2012	2011	2010
Revenue		210,000,000	205,000,000	200,000,000	200,000,000	180,000,000
R&D Expense						
Operating Income						
Operating Margin %						
SGA Expense						
Net Income						
Operating Cash Flow						
Capital Expenditure						
EBITDA						
Return on Assets %						
Return on Equity %						
Debt to Equity						

CONTACT INFORMATION:

Phone: 646-486-4800   Fax: 212-929-3971
Toll-Free: 888-472-2383
Address: 874 Washington St., New York, NY 10014 United States

STOCK TICKER/OTHER:

Stock Ticker: Private   Exchange:
Employees: Fiscal Year Ends:
Parent Company:

SALARIES/BONUSES:

Top Exec. Salary: $ Bonus: $
Second Exec. Salary: $ Bonus: $

OTHER THOUGHTS:

Estimated Female Officers or Directors: 3
Hot Spot for Advancement for Women/Minorities: Y

Dick's Sporting Goods Inc   www.dickssportinggoods.com

NAIC Code: 451110

TYPES OF BUSINESS:

Sporting Goods Stores
Outdoor Apparel
Footwear
Hunting & Fishing Supplies
Golf Supplies
Bicycles
Online Sales

BRANDS/DIVISIONS/AFFILIATES:

Dick's Sporting Goods
Golf Galaxy
Field & Stream
Maxfli
Ativa
Power Bolt
True Runner
Calia

CONTACTS: Note: Officers with more than one job title may be intentionally listed here more than once.

Edward Stack, CEO
Joseph Oliver, Chief Accounting Officer
Lauren Hobart, Chief Marketing Officer
William Colombo, Director
Lee Belitsky, Executive VP, Divisional
Michele Willoughby, Executive VP, Divisional
Teri List-Stoll, Executive VP
Andre Hawaux, Executive VP
Nathaniel Gilch, Other Corporate Officer
Deborah Victorelli, Senior VP, Divisional
John Hayes, Senior VP
Anne-Marie Megela, Vice President, Divisional

GROWTH PLANS/SPECIAL FEATURES:

Dick's Sporting Goods, Inc. (DSG) is a retail sporting goods chain that operates 558 Dick's Sporting Goods stores in 46 states as well as 79 Golf Galaxy stores in 29 states. The company offers a broad assortment of sporting goods equipment, footwear and apparel under national and private-label brands Aciscs, Callaway Golf, Columbia, Nike, Remington, TaylorMade-adidas Golf, The North Face and Under Armour. DSG also offers private brands and products through exclusive licenses such as adidas, DBX, Field & Stream, Fitness Gear, Maxfli, Nickent, Primed, Quest, Reebok, Slazenger, Top-Flite, Umbro and Walter Hagen. Each of the Dick's Sporting Goods locations typically contains six store-within-a-store specialty units: footwear, team sports, outdoor lodge, golf, fitness and athletic apparel. In addition to apparel and equipment sales, its stores offer a variety of services such as golf club fitting, repair and grip replacement; tennis and lacrosse racket stringing; ice skate sharpening; bicycle repair and servicing; scope mounting and bore sighting; and CO_2 tank filling for paintball. The Golf Galaxy stores are designed for serious golf enthusiasts and include artificial bent grass putting greens, golf simulators and private lessons. In addition to its retail locations, the firm maintains separate catalog and e-commerce sites for its chains. DGS recently opened two Field & Stream stores, a specialized outdoor concept, with plans to open eight additional locations; as well as one True Runner store, a specialized footwear concept. In 2014, the firm teamed with singer and actress Carrie Underwood to create an affordable collection of active wear labeled Calia.

FINANCIAL DATA: Note: Data for latest year may not have been available at press time.

In U.S. $	2015	2014	2013	2012	2011	2010
Revenue	6,814,479,000	6,213,173,000	5,836,119,000	5,211,802,000	4,871,492,000	4,412,835,000
R&D Expense						
Operating Income	554,059,000	536,812,000	523,674,000	432,020,000	309,249,000	225,571,000
Operating Margin %	8.13%	8.63%	8.97%	8.28%	6.34%	5.11%
SGA Expense	1,532,607,000	1,407,138,000	1,313,489,000	1,162,861,000	1,139,781,000	981,252,000
Net Income	344,198,000	337,598,000	290,709,000	263,906,000	182,077,000	135,359,000
Operating Cash Flow	605,978,000	403,870,000	438,284,000	410,421,000	389,967,000	401,329,000
Capital Expenditure	349,007,000	285,668,000	219,026,000	201,807,000	159,067,000	140,269,000
EBITDA	738,660,000	703,964,000	620,955,000	562,475,000	421,921,000	328,667,000
Return on Assets %	10.57%	11.33%	9.88%	9.43%	7.51%	6.42%
Return on Equity %	19.53%	20.58%	18.05%	17.61%	14.88%	13.68%
Debt to Equity				0.09	0.10	0.13

CONTACT INFORMATION:

Phone: 724 273-3400   Fax:
Toll-Free: 877-846-9997
Address: 345 Court St., Coraopolis, PA 15108 United States

STOCK TICKER/OTHER:

Stock Ticker: DKS   Exchange: NYS
Employees: 37,600   Fiscal Year Ends: 01/31
Parent Company:

SALARIES/BONUSES:

Top Exec. Salary: Bonus: $
$1,000,000
Second Exec. Salary: Bonus: $
$832,000

OTHER THOUGHTS:

Estimated Female Officers or Directors: 4

Hot Spot for Advancement for Women/Minorities: Y

Diesel SpA

NAIC Code: 424300

TYPES OF BUSINESS:

Apparel and Clothing Brands, Designers, Importers and Distributors
Retail Stores
Men's, Women's & Children's Casual Clothing
Accessories
Sportswear
Hotel Operation
Licensing
Wine

BRANDS/DIVISIONS/AFFILIATES:

Diesel
Diesel Black Gold
Diesel Kids
55DSL
Pelican Hotel (The)
Diesel Farm
Ducati Monster Diesel
Diesel.com

CONTACTS: *Note: Officers with more than one job title may be intentionally listed here more than once.*

Alessandro Bogliolo, CEO

GROWTH PLANS/SPECIAL FEATURES:

Diesel SpA designs and retails premium jeans and casua
clothing as well as sportswear and accessories for men
women and children. Diesel's main product lines are Diesel,
collection focused mainly on denim for men and women; Diese
Black Gold, a high-end collection pioneering in design, fabric
and product innovation; Diesel Kids, clothing for young peopl
with bright colors and modern lines; and 55DSL, a sportswea
collection for emerging extreme and action sports. Its product
are sold in over 80 countries through high-end departmen
stores and specialty retailers as well as company-owned store
(with approximately 50 located in the U.S.). These store
include four 'planet' stores (located in Milan, New York, Toky
and Hong Kong), which offer onsite tailoring, messenge
service, storewide Wi-Fi, e-commerce portals for shopping a
Diesel.com, wireless cash stations for purchases, a multilingua
staff and VIP services, along with its full clothing and accessor
lines. Diesel has licensing partnerships with leading companie
to develop watches and jewelry (Fossil), eyewear (Marcolin)
fragrances (L'Oreal), helmets (AGV), headphones (Monster)
bikes (Pinarello), strollers (Bugaboo) and a home collectio
(Foscarini, Moroso, Zucchi, Seletti and Scavolini). The firm als
markets its goods through catalogs and e-commerce sites
Additionally, Diesel owns and operates The Pelican Hotel, a
28-room, 1950s-style hotel on South Beach with rooms
designed to feel like movie sets; and Diesel Farm, a winery
Through a collaboration with Italian Motorcycle producer
Ducati, the firm produced limited edition motorcycle Ducat
Monster Diesel.

FINANCIAL DATA: *Note: Data for latest year may not have been available at press time.*

In U.S. $	2015	2014	2013	2012	2011	2010
Revenue		2,000,000,000	2,100,000,000	2,000,000,000	1,800,000,000	1,500,000,000
R&D Expense						
Operating Income						
Operating Margin %						
SGA Expense						
Net Income						
Operating Cash Flow						
Capital Expenditure						
EBITDA						
Return on Assets %						
Return on Equity %						
Debt to Equity						

CONTACT INFORMATION:

Phone: 39-0424-477555   Fax: 39-0424-708492
Toll-Free:
Address: Via dell Industria 7, Molvena, Vicenza, 36060 Italy

STOCK TICKER/OTHER:

Stock Ticker: Private
Employees:
Parent Company:

Exchange:
Fiscal Year Ends: 12/31

SALARIES/BONUSES:

Top Exec. Salary: $ Bonus: $
Second Exec. Salary: $ Bonus: $

OTHER THOUGHTS:

Estimated Female Officers or Directors:
Hot Spot for Advancement for Women/Minorities:

Dillard's Inc

www.dillards.com

NAIC Code: 452111

TYPES OF BUSINESS:

Department Stores
Online Sales
Catalogs
Construction & Remodeling
Real Estate Investment
Insurance

BRANDS/DIVISIONS/AFFILIATES:

Dillards.com
CDI Contractors LLC

CONTACTS: Note: Officers with more than one job title may be intentionally listed here more than once.

William Dillard, CEO
Chris Johnson, Co-CFO
Mike Dillard, Director
Drue Matheny, Director
Alex Dillard, Director
Phillip Watts, Senior VP
Denise Mahaffy, Vice President
Burt Squires, Vice President
Michael McNiff, Vice President
William Dillard, Vice President
Brant Musgrave, Vice President, Divisional
David Terry, Vice President, Divisional
Dean Worley, Vice President

GROWTH PLANS/SPECIAL FEATURES:

Dillard's, Inc. is one of the U.S.'s largest retail department stores, offering apparel, cosmetics and home furnishings. The firm operates 272 department stores, 25 clearance centers and an internet store, primarily in the southwestern and mid-western U.S. It sells name-brand and private-label merchandise including women's, petites, juniors, men's and children's apparel in addition to accessories, lingerie, cosmetics, furniture, electronics, shoes and other gifts and products. Most Dillard's stores are located in suburban shopping malls. The firm also sells merchandise through catalogs, various mail promotions and its web site, Dillards.com, which offers an online wedding, baby and gift registry service. Dillard's catalogs include the Men's, Women's, Shoes, Home and Entertainment, Handbags and Accessories and Gifts categories. Many stores also offer day spas as well as nail and hair care services. Dillard's also offers proprietary credit cards to its customers. The firm has six company owned distribution centers in Arkansas, Arizona, Georgia, Kansas, North Carolina and Texas. CDI Contractors, LLC is a full-service construction company based in Little Rock, Arkansas that construct stores for the company.

FINANCIAL DATA: Note: Data for latest year may not have been available at press time.

In U.S. $	2015	2014	2013	2012	2011	2010
Revenue	6,780,129,000	6,691,777,000	6,751,595,000	6,399,765,000	6,253,535,000	6,226,628,000
R&D Expense						
Operating Income	566,005,000	553,703,000	538,502,000	396,669,000	268,716,000	84,525,000
Operating Margin %	8.34%	8.27%	7.97%	6.19%	4.29%	1.35%
SGA Expense	1,690,836,000	1,658,869,000	1,706,364,000	1,679,017,000	1,676,838,000	1,702,454,000
Net Income	331,853,000	323,671,000	335,962,000	463,909,000	179,620,000	68,531,000
Operating Cash Flow	611,589,000	501,757,000	522,703,000	501,140,000	512,922,000	554,007,000
Capital Expenditure	151,888,000	94,923,000	136,632,000	115,651,000	98,184,000	75,089,000
EBITDA	821,485,000	810,940,000	810,918,000	728,195,000	605,903,000	423,291,000
Return on Assets %	8.07%	7.99%	8.04%	10.68%	4.00%	1.46%
Return on Equity %	16.54%	16.33%	16.70%	22.41%	8.18%	3.00%
Debt to Equity	0.40	0.41	0.41	0.40	0.43	0.42

CONTACT INFORMATION:

Phone: 501 376-5200   Fax: 501 376-5917
Toll-Free: 800-345-5273
Address: 1600 Cantrell Rd., Little Rock, AR 72201 United States

STOCK TICKER/OTHER:

Stock Ticker: DDS
Employees: 40,000
Parent Company:

Exchange: NYS
Fiscal Year Ends: 01/31

SALARIES/BONUSES:

Top Exec. Salary: $ Bonus: $
Second Exec. Salary: $ Bonus: $

OTHER THOUGHTS:

Estimated Female Officers or Directors:
Hot Spot for Advancement for Women/Minorities:

Discount Tire Co

www.discounttire.com

NAIC Code: 441320

TYPES OF BUSINESS:

Tire Stores
Mail-Order & Online Tire Sales
Roadside Assistance

BRANDS/DIVISIONS/AFFILIATES:

America's Tire Co
Discount Tire Direct
Discout Tire
CarCareONE
Road Hugger
Arizonian
MB Wheels
Pathfinder

CONTACTS: *Note: Officers with more than one job title may be intentionally listed here more than once.*

Michael Zuieback, CEO
Michael Zuieback, Pres.
Christian Roe, CFO
Bruce T. Halle, Chmn.

GROWTH PLANS/SPECIAL FEATURES:

Discount Tire Co., based in Arizona, is one of the largest independent tire dealers in the U.S. The firm operates over 900 stores in 28 states across the nation. These stores operate under the Discount Tire name as well as under the America's Tire Co. name in certain parts of California. Discount Tire carries leading tire brands such as BF Goodrich, Michelin, Goodyear, Pirelli and GT Radial as well in-house exclusive brands Road Hugger, Arizonian, MB Wheels and Pathfinder tires and wheels. The company also repairs tires, offers tire rotations and balancing and provides free air pressure checking to its customers. In addition, the firm sells and delivers tires through its mail-order/online division (Discount Tire Direct), which provides fast free shipping to a customer's door as well as through its web site. This web site also provides extensive information for its customers on all aspects of wheel and tire care. The firm offers a Discount Tire/America's Tire CarCareONE card, a credit card that also provides emergency roadside assistance. The CarCareONE card is underwritten by Synchrony Financial.

Discount Tires offers its employees benefits including flexible spending accounts; an employee assistance program; medical, vision, life and dental insurance; paid vacation; a 401(k) plan; and profit sharing plans. Part-time employees are eligible for medical insurance and a 401(k).

FINANCIAL DATA: *Note: Data for latest year may not have been available at press time.*

In U.S. $	2015	2014	2013	2012	2011	2010
Revenue		3,550,000,000	3,500,000,000	3,300,000,000	3,100,000,000	3,000,000,000
R&D Expense						
Operating Income						
Operating Margin %						
SGA Expense						
Net Income						
Operating Cash Flow						
Capital Expenditure						
EBITDA						
Return on Assets %						
Return on Equity %						
Debt to Equity						

CONTACT INFORMATION:

Phone: 480-606-6000   Fax: 480-951-8619
Toll-Free:
Address: 20225 N. Scottsdale Rd., Scottsdale, AZ 85254 United States

SALARIES/BONUSES:

Top Exec. Salary: $ Bonus: $
Second Exec. Salary: $ Bonus: $

STOCK TICKER/OTHER:

Stock Ticker: Private   Exchange:
Employees: 15,557   Fiscal Year Ends: 12/31
Parent Company:

OTHER THOUGHTS:

Estimated Female Officers or Directors:
Hot Spot for Advancement for Women/Minorities:

Distribuidora Internacional de Alimentacion SA   www.dia.es

NAIC Code: 452112

TYPES OF BUSINESS:
Discount Department Stores

BRANDS/DIVISIONS/AFFILIATES:
DIA Market
DIA Fresh and Fresh
DIA Maxi
La Plaza de DIA
Max Descuento
Clarel
El Arbol
Cada DIA

CONTACTS: Note: Officers with more than one job title may be intentionally listed here more than once.
Ricardo Curras de Don Pablos, CEO
Antonio Arnanz Martin, CFO
Juan Cubillo Jordan de Urries, Manager-Business & Merch.
Diego Cavestany de Dalmases, Sr. Manager-Spanish Operations
Antonio Coto Gutierrez, Sr. Manager-Latin America
Armando Sanchez Falcon, Chief Corp. Officer
Ana Maria Llopis, Chmn.
Javier La Calle Villalon, Sr. Manager-Portugal, Turkey & China

GROWTH PLANS/SPECIAL FEATURES:
Distribuidora Internacional De Alimentacion SA (DIA) owns and operates discount food stores in Spain, Brazil, Argentina and China. The company sells its own private label brands, of which its private-label catalogue runs 7,500 SKUs, including DIA, AS, bonte, BASIC cosmetics, BabySmile and JuniorSmile. These brands represent products such as personal care & hygiene, cosmetics, baby-related items and pet food. Stores marketed by the firm include DIA Market, a neighborhood store model that ranges from 1,300 to 2,300 square feet; DIA Fresh and Fresh, providing fruit, vegetables, meats and wines in stores approximately 500 square feet in size; DIA Maxi, the company's largest store format with square footage up to 3,200 sf and usually located on city outskirts; La Plaza de DIA, a daily concept family market that provides more than 5,000 daily types of needed products for consumers; Max Descuento, which provides products and services to professionals & self-employed workers in the hotel, catering and food industry such as telephone sales, orders by email and distribution to customers through a transport network; Clarel, a neighborhood store featuring health, beauty, household and personal care items; El Arbol, which provides fresh products such as meats and fish; Cada DIA, a small-town outlet concept primarily located in rural areas; Minipreco, of which DIA operates stores in towns and city centers of Portugal; and Mais Perto, another rural store concept. In Spain and Portugal, DIA operates 5,415 stores, 724 in Argentina, 799 in Brazil and 368 in China. In 2014, the firm acquired El Arbol Supermarket chain; and sold its entire business in France to Carrefour SA.

FINANCIAL DATA: Note: Data for latest year may not have been available at press time.

In U.S. $	2015	2014	2013	2012	2011	2010
Revenue		8,613,747,000	10,599,490,000	10,889,980,000	10,378,960,000	10,175,800,000
R&D Expense						
Operating Income		343,762,800	345,580,700	305,192,900	225,713,200	146,505,200
Operating Margin %		3.99%	3.26%	2.80%	2.17%	1.43%
SGA Expense					341,640,200	378,733,600
Net Income		349,411,000	222,086,700	155,359,600	100,159,200	124,059,700
Operating Cash Flow		408,777,000	496,543,400	449,696,400	498,225,500	574,555,300
Capital Expenditure		370,827,000	383,981,800	374,954,400	371,350,200	307,820,700
EBITDA		539,683,100	628,827,100	601,417,900	532,122,400	462,418,300
Return on Assets %		10.13%	6.17%	4.36%	3.00%	3.75%
Return on Equity %		117.31%	124.65%	116.70%	37.22%	28.38%
Debt to Equity		1.41	3.81	3.63	6.07	0.06

CONTACT INFORMATION:
Phone: 34 91398-5400   Fax:
Toll-Free:
Address: Parque Empresarial de las Roza 2A, Madrid, 28232 Spain

STOCK TICKER/OTHER:
Stock Ticker: DIDAF
Employees: 45,369
Parent Company:

Exchange: GREY
Fiscal Year Ends:

SALARIES/BONUSES:
Top Exec. Salary: $ Bonus: $
Second Exec. Salary: $ Bonus: $

OTHER THOUGHTS:
Estimated Female Officers or Directors: 1
Hot Spot for Advancement for Women/Minorities:

Dixons Carphone PLC

NAIC Code: 443142

www.dixonscarphone.com/

TYPES OF BUSINESS:

Radio, Television, and Other Electronics Stores

BRANDS/DIVISIONS/AFFILIATES:

Currys
PC World
Knowhow
Carphone Warehouse
Dixons Travel
Elkjop
Kotsovolos
PC City

CONTACTS: *Note: Officers with more than one job title may be intentionally listed here more than once.*

Sebastian James, CEO
Lord Kalms of Edgware, Pres.
Humphrey Singer, Dir.-Finance
Helen Grantham, Company Secretary & General Counsel
Andrew Lawley, Dir.-Group Strategy
Steve Ager, Dir.-Commercial
David Lloyd-Seed, Dir.-Investor Rel., Public Rel. & Corp. Affairs
Katie Bickerstaffe, CEO-U.K. & Ireland
Jaan Ivar Semlitsch, Managing Dir.-Northern Europe
Keith Hones, Interim Managing Dir.-Southern Europe
Phil Birbeck, Pres.

GROWTH PLANS/SPECIAL FEATURES:

Dixons Carphone PLC is a multi-channel retailer of hig
technology consumer electronics. With 3,000 locations in 1
countries, the company divides its operations into thre
segments: U.K. & Ireland, Northern Europe and Souther
Europe. The U.K. & Ireland segment comprises Carphon
Warehouse, a mobile phone retailer; Currys and Currys Digita
which both specialize in home electronics and househol
appliances; PC World, which is primarily combined with Curry
in dual-branded stores, provides computing service
Knowhow, a provider of after-sales services such as deliverie
installations and repairs; Dixons Travel, a retailer in majc
airports within the U.K. and Ireland; and Geek Squad, a
insurance, repairs and support provider for Carphon
Warehouse. The Norther Europe segment comprises E
Giganten, which sells home electronics and appliances i
Denmark and Sweden; Elkjop, which sells the same types c
products in Norway; Giganti, in Finland; and Dixons Trave
which operates in the Copenhagen Airport. The Souther
Europe segment comprises Kotsovolos, which sells hom
electronics in Greece; Phone House, a mobile phone retailer i
Spain and Portugal; and PC City, a chain of compute
superstores in Italy.

FINANCIAL DATA: *Note: Data for latest year may not have been available at press time.*

In U.S. $	2015	2014	2013	2012	2011	2010
Revenue	12,340,420,000	3,850,868,000	15,995,460	9,567,375	8,371,454	8,221,963
R&D Expense						
Operating Income	484,348,400	113,612,600	4,783,688	-80,276,260	94,627,320	56,806,290
Operating Margin %		2.95%	29.90%	-839.06%	1130.35%	690.90%
SGA Expense						
Net Income	145,005,500	71,755,310	6,278,590	1,139,863,000	98,065,590	327,084,600
Operating Cash Flow	64,280,800	660,746,900	37,223,070	-18,686,280	5,680,629	-4,185,727
Capital Expenditure	248,153,800	89,694,140	149,490	747,451	3,438,276	1,195,922
EBITDA	689,150,000	200,316,900	9,567,375	1,141,208,000	102,550,300	335,456,100
Return on Assets %		3.20%	.59%	100.62%	8.73%	28.33%
Return on Equity %		6.23%	.61%	104.02%	9.05%	39.61%
Debt to Equity		0.32				

CONTACT INFORMATION:

Phone: 44-208-8965000   Fax:
Toll-Free:
Address: 1 Portal Way, London, W3 6RS United Kingdom

STOCK TICKER/OTHER:

Stock Ticker: DSITF   Exchange: GREY
Employees: 18   Fiscal Year Ends: 04/30
Parent Company:

SALARIES/BONUSES:

Top Exec. Salary: $ Bonus: $
Second Exec. Salary: $ Bonus: $

OTHER THOUGHTS:

Estimated Female Officers or Directors: 2
Hot Spot for Advancement for Women/Minorities:

Do It Best Corp

www.doitbestcorp.com

NAIC Code: 444130

TYPES OF BUSINESS:

Hardware/Building Supply Cooperative
Marketing Support Services

BRANDS/DIVISIONS/AFFILIATES:

Do It Best
INCOM Distributor Supply Co
DoItBest.com
MyDoItBest.com
Adpak
Do It Best Paint Solutions
CORE

CONTACTS: *Note: Officers with more than one job title may be intentionally listed here more than once.*

Bob Taylor, CEO
Dan Starr, COO
Bob Taylor, Pres.
Doug Roth, CFO
Rich Lynch, VP-Mktg.
Gary Furst, VP-Human Resources & General Counsel
Mike Altendorf, VP-IT
Steve Markley, VP-Merch.
Gary Furst, General Counsel
Jay Brown, VP-Bus. Dev. & Sales
Doug Roth, VP-Finance
Quent Ondricek, VP-Lumber & Building Materials
Jim Lehrer, Chmn.
John Snider, VP-Retail Logistics

GROWTH PLANS/SPECIAL FEATURES:

Do It Best Corp., founded in 1945, is a member-owned cooperative with more than 3,800 associated hardware stores, home centers and lumberyards. The firm is one of the largest cooperatives in the U.S., with member stores in all 50 states and 53 countries around the world, and is the only U.S.-based full-line, full-service, member-owned distributor of lumber, hardware and building materials products. Do It Best stocks more than 67,000 hardware and building material products in its eight retail service centers located in Missouri, Illinois, South Carolina, Ohio, Nevada, New York, Texas and Oregon. The firm sells building materials and related products to its members at wholesale prices. Do It Best also operates an industrial/commercial division through INCOM Distributor Supply Co. The company provides low up-front prices and consistently high year-end rebates to help members grow and provide a second profit as well as offering numerous optional programs and services to help members build business. Programs include Do it Best gift cards; ADpak, a customizable advertising and merchandising program; CORE (College of Retail Education), a training program for new co-op members; DoItBest.com, an online retail site providing access to over 67,000 products; MyDoItBest.com, a member-exclusive site that allows members to check inventory and access other information; private brand flooring products, including carpet, hardwood, laminate, vinyl flooring and ceramic tile, through the Home Decor brand; painting offerings through Do It Best Paint Solutions; and rental center and store development programs.

Do It Best offers its employees a 401(k) plan; a profit sharing plan; tuition reimbursement; a product discount purchase program; a service award program; monthly staff member activities; and medical, dental, vision, prescription drug, life and disability income insurance.

FINANCIAL DATA: *Note: Data for latest year may not have been available at press time.*

In U.S. $	2015	2014	2013	2012	2011	2010
Revenue		2,873,108,000	2,799,515,000	2,682,198,000	2,411,791,000	2,381,977,000
R&D Expense						
Operating Income						
Operating Margin %						
SGA Expense						
Net Income		376,000	372,000	511,000	458,000	955,000
Operating Cash Flow						
Capital Expenditure						
EBITDA						
Return on Assets %						
Return on Equity %						
Debt to Equity						

CONTACT INFORMATION:

Phone: 260-748-5300   Fax: 260-748-5608
Toll-Free:
Address: 6502 Nelson Rd., Fort Wayne, IN 46803 United States

STOCK TICKER/OTHER:

Stock Ticker: Private
Employees: 1,432
Parent Company:

Exchange:
Fiscal Year Ends: 06/30

SALARIES/BONUSES:

Top Exec. Salary: $ Bonus: $
Second Exec. Salary: $ Bonus: $

OTHER THOUGHTS:

Estimated Female Officers or Directors: 1
Hot Spot for Advancement for Women/Minorities:

Sales, profits and employees may be estimates. Financial information, benefits and other data can change quickly and may vary from those stated here.

Dolce & Gabbana SpA (D&G)

www.dolcegabbana.com

NAIC Code: 424300

TYPES OF BUSINESS:

Apparel and Clothing Brands, Designers, Importers and Distributors
Designer Apparel
Retail Stores
Leather Goods
Accessories
Knitwear
Underwear
Beachwear

BRANDS/DIVISIONS/AFFILIATES:

Intenso
Alta Moda
One (The)
Gold
Light Blue

CONTACTS: Note: Officers with more than one job title may be intentionally listed here more than once.

Alfonso Dolce, CEO
Cristiana Ruella, COO
Stefano Gabbana, Pres.
Domenico Dolce, Chmn.

GROWTH PLANS/SPECIAL FEATURES:

Dolce & Gabbana SpA creates, markets and distributes high-end designer men's and women's collections of knitwear, leather goods, scarves, ties, shoes, underwear and beachwear. The Dolce & Gabbana brand has a cosmopolitan and elegant look that can be either distinctly masculine or feminine. Through various licensing agreements, the firm creates and distributes fragrances, eyewear and footwear for both of its brands. Its products are sold through 127 company-owned boutiques as well as high-end shops and department stores in over 40 countries around the world. The company has developed an anti-counterfeiting system, which includes a safety hologram produced by the Italian State Printing Works and Mint and found on the inside of every article of clothing. In addition to its clothing lines, the company has perfume and cologne lines called The One, Intenso and Light Blue; a line of cosmetics; and a restaurant in Milan called Gold. Recently, the company debuted its first couture line, Atla Moda, consisting of Sicilian inspired dresses.

FINANCIAL DATA: Note: Data for latest year may not have been available at press time.

In U.S. $	2015	2014	2013	2012	2011	2010
Revenue		1,500,000,000	1,560,000,000	1,500,000,000	1,480,000,000	1,392,371,226
R&D Expense						
Operating Income						
Operating Margin %						
SGA Expense						
Net Income						
Operating Cash Flow						
Capital Expenditure						
EBITDA						
Return on Assets %						
Return on Equity %						
Debt to Equity						

CONTACT INFORMATION:

Phone: 39-02-774271   Fax:
Toll-Free:
Address: Via Goldoni,10, Milan, 20129 Italy

STOCK TICKER/OTHER:

Stock Ticker: Private   Exchange:
Employees: 3,150   Fiscal Year Ends: 03/31
Parent Company:

SALARIES/BONUSES:

Top Exec. Salary: $ Bonus: $
Second Exec. Salary: $ Bonus: $

OTHER THOUGHTS:

Estimated Female Officers or Directors: 1
Hot Spot for Advancement for Women/Minorities:

Dollar General Corporation

www.dollargeneral.com

NAIC Code: 452112

TYPES OF BUSINESS:

Discount Stores

BRANDS/DIVISIONS/AFFILIATES:

Dollar General Literacy Foundation

CONTACTS: *Note: Officers with more than one job title may be intentionally listed here more than once.*

Todd Vasos, CEO
John Garratt, CFO
Richard Dreiling, Chairman of the Board
Anita Elliott, Chief Accounting Officer
Jeffery Owen, Executive VP, Divisional
John Flanigan, Executive VP, Divisional
Robert Ravener, Executive VP
Jim Thorpe, Executive VP
Rhonda Taylor, General Counsel
Christine Connolly, Secretary

GROWTH PLANS/SPECIAL FEATURES:

Dollar General Corporation operates 12,000 discount retail stores in 43 states, primarily in the southern, southwestern, midwestern and eastern United States. The firm runs conveniently sized stores offering a broad range of merchandise at low prices, including consumables, seasonal, home products and apparel. The company focuses on low and fixed income customers providing basic packaged and refrigerated food and dairy products, cleaning supplies, paper products, health and beauty care items, greeting cards, basic apparel, housewares, hardware and automotive supplies. The firm buys merchandise from a variety of suppliers including private and national brands such as Procter & Gamble, PepsiCo, Coca-Cola, Nestle, General Mills, Unilever, Kimberly Clark, Kellogg's and Nabisco. The company has 13 distribution facilities. Dollar General is affiliated with Dollar General Literacy Foundation committed to help adults and youth achieve educational goals.

The firm offers employees a 401(k) plan; a retirement plan; medical, dental, vision and prescription plans; flexible spending accounts; short- and long-term disability; wellness programs; business travel accident insurance; and rewards programs.

FINANCIAL DATA: *Note: Data for latest year may not have been available at press time.*

In U.S. $	2015	2014	2013	2012	2011	2010
Revenue	18,909,590,000	17,504,170,000	16,022,130,000	14,807,190,000	13,035,000,000	11,796,380,000
R&D Expense						
Operating Income	1,769,093,000	1,736,185,000	1,655,276,000	1,490,804,000	1,274,065,000	953,258,000
Operating Margin %	9.35%	9.91%	10.33%	10.06%	9.77%	8.08%
SGA Expense	4,033,414,000	3,699,557,000	3,430,125,000	3,207,106,000	2,902,491,000	2,736,613,000
Net Income	1,065,345,000	1,025,116,000	952,662,000	766,685,000	627,857,000	339,442,000
Operating Cash Flow	1,314,744,000	1,213,065,000	1,131,352,000	1,050,480,000	824,684,000	668,643,000
Capital Expenditure	373,967,000	538,444,000	571,596,000	514,861,000	420,395,000	250,747,000
EBITDA	2,111,446,000	2,050,151,000	1,928,231,000	1,705,688,000	1,514,111,000	1,154,631,000
Return on Assets %	9.64%	9.65%	9.49%	7.97%	6.82%	3.82%
Return on Equity %	19.17%	19.73%	19.73%	17.57%	16.86%	10.91%
Debt to Equity	0.46	0.50	0.55	0.56	0.81	1.00

CONTACT INFORMATION:

Phone: 615 855-4000   Fax: 615 855-5527
Toll-Free:
Address: 100 Mission Ridge, Goodlettsville, TN 37072 United States

STOCK TICKER/OTHER:

Stock Ticker: DG
Employees: 105,500
Parent Company:

Exchange: NYS
Fiscal Year Ends: 01/31

SALARIES/BONUSES:

Top Exec. Salary: $1,323,789   Bonus: $
Second Exec. Salary: $765,342   Bonus: $

OTHER THOUGHTS:

Estimated Female Officers or Directors: 4

Hot Spot for Advancement for Women/Minorities: Y

Dollar Tree Inc

www.dollartree.com

NAIC Code: 452112

TYPES OF BUSINESS:

Discount Stores
Dollar Stores

BRANDS/DIVISIONS/AFFILIATES:

Dollar Tree
Dollar Bills
Deal$
Dollar Giant
Family Dollar

CONTACTS: *Note: Officers with more than one job title may be intentionally listed here more than once.*

Bob Sasser, CEO
Kevin Wampler, CFO
J. Perry, Chairman Emeritus
Macon Brock, Chairman of the Board
Mike Matacunas, Chief Administrative Officer
Michael Witynski, COO
Gary Philbin, COO, Divisional
Howard Levine, Director
Stephen White, Other Executive Officer
Robert Rudman, Other Executive Officer
David Jacobs, Other Executive Officer
William Old, Other Executive Officer
Randy Guiler, Vice President, Divisional

GROWTH PLANS/SPECIAL FEATURES:

Dollar Tree, Inc. operates discount variety stores that offe
merchandise at the fixed price of $1.00 or less. The firm doe
business through more than 13,800 stores, primarily located i
shopping centers and malls throughout 48 states and fiv
Canadian provinces. Stores operate under the names Dolla
Tree, Dollar Tree Canada, Family Dollar, Dollar Giant, Dolla
Bill and Deals. Deals stores sell most items for $1.00 or les
but also sell products at higher prices. In addition, the compan
has 210 stores in Canada. These stores offer a wid
assortment of everyday general merchandise consisting o
consumable merchandise, including candy and food, healt
and beauty care and housewares; variety merchandise, whic
includes toys, durable housewares, gifts, party goods, greetin
cards and apparel; and seasonal goods, such as summer toys
lawn and garden merchandise and holiday merchandise. Th
firm operates 10 distribution centers located in Virginia
Mississippi, Illinois, California, Pennsylvania, Georgia
Oklahoma, Connecticut and Washington.

The firm offers employees medical, dental and vision
insurance; disability coverage; life insurance; health an
dependant care reimbursement accounts; a 401(k) plan; an
an employee stock purchase plan.

FINANCIAL DATA: *Note: Data for latest year may not have been available at press time.*

In U.S. $	2015	2014	2013	2012	2011	2010
Revenue	8,602,200,000	7,840,300,000	7,394,500,000	6,630,500,000	5,882,400,000	5,231,200,000
R&D Expense						
Operating Income	1,040,200,000	970,300,000	920,100,000	782,100,000	630,000,000	512,800,000
Operating Margin %	12.09%	12.37%	12.44%	11.79%	10.70%	9.80%
SGA Expense	1,993,800,000	1,819,500,000	1,732,600,000	1,596,200,000	1,457,600,000	1,344,000,000
Net Income	599,200,000	596,700,000	619,300,000	488,300,000	397,300,000	320,500,000
Operating Cash Flow	926,800,000	793,400,000	677,700,000	686,500,000	518,700,000	581,000,000
Capital Expenditure	325,600,000	330,400,000	312,200,000	250,100,000	178,900,000	164,800,000
EBITDA	1,246,100,000	1,160,800,000	1,157,000,000	946,300,000	789,700,000	672,500,000
Return on Assets %	18.90%	21.60%	24.37%	20.73%	17.01%	14.81%
Return on Equity %	40.54%	42.05%	41.12%	34.83%	27.51%	23.89%
Debt to Equity	0.42	0.64	0.15	0.18	0.17	0.17

CONTACT INFORMATION:

Phone: 757 321-5000   Fax: 757 857-6848
Toll-Free: 877-530-8733
Address: 500 Volvo Pkwy., Chesapeake, VA 23320 United States

STOCK TICKER/OTHER:

Stock Ticker: DLTR   Exchange: NAS
Employees: 90,000   Fiscal Year Ends: 01/31
Parent Company:

SALARIES/BONUSES:

Top Exec. Salary: Bonus: $
$1,505,769
Second Exec. Salary: Bonus: $
$830,769

OTHER THOUGHTS:

Estimated Female Officers or Directors: 1

Hot Spot for Advancement for Women/Minorities:

Douglas Holding AG

www.douglas-holding.com

NAIC Code: 446120

TYPES OF BUSINESS:

Cosmetics, Beauty Supplies, and Perfume Stores

BRANDS/DIVISIONS/AFFILIATES:

CVC Capital Partners
Kreke
Douglas Card
Nocibe

GROWTH PLANS/SPECIAL FEATURES:

Douglas Holding AG is a European perfumery chain with 1,700 specialty stores in 19 countries throughout Europe. The company's products comprise perfume, personal care, cosmetics and accessories. The firm operates its stores under the Douglas brand name. The Douglas Card is a loyalty program with more than 17 million members benefiting from the card's diverse advantages. In 2014, the company acquired French perfumerie chain Nocibe. In August 2015, Douglas Holding was acquired by CVC Capital Partners and the Kreke family, with CVC being the majority shareholder and the Kreke family holding a 15% stake.

CONTACTS: *Note: Officers with more than one job title may be intentionally listed here more than once.*

Henning Kreke, CEO
Erika Tertilt, CFO
Nicholas C. Denissen, Exec. VP-e-commerce

FINANCIAL DATA: *Note: Data for latest year may not have been available at press time.*

In U.S. $	2015	2014	2013	2012	2011	2010
Revenue		2,841,775,000	4,716,840,000	4,596,015,104	4,371,588,096	4,296,545,792
R&D Expense						
Operating Income						
Operating Margin %						
SGA Expense						
Net Income						
Operating Cash Flow						
Capital Expenditure						
EBITDA						
Return on Assets %						
Return on Equity %						
Debt to Equity						

CONTACT INFORMATION:

Phone: 49(0)2331690-0 Fax: 49(0)2331690-271
Toll-Free:
Address: Kabeler Straise 4, Hagen, 58099 Germany

STOCK TICKER/OTHER:

Stock Ticker: Subsidiary
Employees: 23,000
Parent Company: CVC Capital Partners
Exchange:
Fiscal Year Ends: 09/30

SALARIES/BONUSES:

Top Exec. Salary: $ Bonus: $
Second Exec. Salary: $ Bonus: $

OTHER THOUGHTS:

Estimated Female Officers or Directors:
Hot Spot for Advancement for Women/Minorities:

Sales, profits and employees may be estimates. Financial information, benefits and other data can change quickly and may vary from those stated here.

DSW Inc

NAIC Code: 448210

TYPES OF BUSINESS:

Discount Shoe Stores
Women's Merchandise
Men's Merchandise
Handbags
Luxury Designers
Accessories
Clearance Merchandise
Online Services

BRANDS/DIVISIONS/AFFILIATES:

DSW Rewards
Town Shoes
Shoe Company (The)
Shoe Warehouse
Townshoes.com

CONTACTS: Note: Officers with more than one job title may be intentionally listed here more than once.

Michael MacDonald, CEO
Mary Meixelsperger, CFO
Jay Schottenstein, Chairman of the Board
William Jordan, Chief Administrative Officer
Carrie McDermott, Executive VP
Harris Mustafa, Executive VP
Roger Rawlins, Executive VP
Christina Cheng, Other Corporate Officer
Deborah Ferree, Other Executive Officer

GROWTH PLANS/SPECIAL FEATURES:

DSW, Inc. is a leading retailer of specialty branded footwear in the U.S. DSW operates 431 stores in the U.S., Washington, D.C. and Puerto Rico. The stores offer a wide selection of brand name and designer shoes in dress, casual and athletic categories. Each store offers approximately 22,000 shoes in more than 2,000 styles. In addition, the retailer operates 370 leased shoe departments for Gordmans, Stein Mart and Frugal Fannies. The stores are largely self-service, allowing customers to try on shoes and check size availability without sales associates. New styles are located on the main floor, clearance in the rear and accessories and impulse buys in the front. The firm operates a 700,000-square-foot distribution center in Columbus, Ohio. The company maintains a loyalty program called DSW Rewards. The retailer uses this program to classify members by frequency, and uses direct mail and online communication to stimulate further sales and traffic. DSW also owns an equity interest in Town Shoes, a market leader in branded footwear in Canada. Town Shoes operates 182 locations primarily under The Shoe Company, Shoe Warehouse and Town Shoes banners, as well as the Townshoes.com online site.

DSW employees are offered competitive wages; comprehensive medical, vision, prescription, life, AD&D, disability and dental insurance; flexible spending accounts; an employee assistance plan; a 401(k) plan; an employee discount; and others.

FINANCIAL DATA: Note: Data for latest year may not have been available at press time.

In U.S. $	2015	2014	2013	2012	2011	2010
Revenue	2,496,092,000	2,368,668,000	2,257,778,000	2,024,329,000	1,822,376,000	1,602,605,000
R&D Expense						
Operating Income	242,132,000	241,388,000	236,802,000	151,450,000	173,583,000	93,455,000
Operating Margin %	9.70%	10.19%	10.48%	7.48%	9.52%	5.83%
SGA Expense	512,889,000	497,899,000	481,797,000		392,098,000	
Net Income	153,299,000	151,302,000	146,439,000	174,788,000	107,624,000	54,741,000
Operating Cash Flow	197,038,000	298,725,000	258,564,000	214,788,000	140,949,000	164,453,000
Capital Expenditure	98,126,000	86,412,000	134,477,000	74,707,000	46,735,000	23,080,000
EBITDA	313,660,000	308,705,000	299,308,000	205,310,000	226,140,000	139,565,000
Return on Assets %	10.72%	11.27%	11.85%	15.76%	11.57%	6.96%
Return on Equity %	15.25%	16.29%	17.80%	24.49%	18.46%	11.05%
Debt to Equity						

CONTACT INFORMATION:

Phone: 614 237-7100   Fax: 614 238-4200
Toll-Free: 866-379-7463
Address: 810 DSW Dr., Columbus, OH 43219 United States

STOCK TICKER/OTHER:

Stock Ticker: DSW   Exchange: NYS
Employees: 11,000   Fiscal Year Ends: 01/31
Parent Company:

SALARIES/BONUSES:

Top Exec. Salary: $1,050,000   Bonus: $

Second Exec. Salary: $1,000,000   Bonus: $

OTHER THOUGHTS:

Estimated Female Officers or Directors: 4

Hot Spot for Advancement for Women/Minorities: Y

Duane Reade Inc

www.duanereade.com

NAIC Code: 446110

TYPES OF BUSINESS:

Drug Stores
Retail Pharmacies
Nutraceuticals & Cosmetics
Photo Processing

BRANDS/DIVISIONS/AFFILIATES:

Walgreen Co
DuaneReade.com

CONTACTS: Note: Officers with more than one job title may be intentionally listed here more than once.

John K. Henry, CFO
Charles Newsom, VP-Store Operations
Joseph S. Iacko, VP-IT
Greg D. Wasson, CEO
John A. Lederer, Chmn.

GROWTH PLANS/SPECIAL FEATURES:

Duane Reade, Inc., owned by Walgreen Co., is one of the largest retail drug store chains in New York City. The drugstore chain operates more than 250 stores located throughout Manhattan's business and residential districts; New York's outer boroughs; and in the surrounding New York and New Jersey suburbs, including the Hudson River communities of northeastern New Jersey. Products and services offered include prescription and over-the-counter medications, vitamins, food and beverages, health aids, beauty products, greeting cards and photo processing. Duane Reade's extensive network of conveniently located pharmacies, strong local market position, pricing policies and reputation for high-quality health care products and services provide it with a competitive advantage in attracting pharmacy business from individual customers as well as managed care organizations, insurance companies and employers. The company's pharmacies employ computer systems that link all Duane Reade stores and enable them to provide customers with a broad range of services. The network profiles customer medical and other relevant information, supplies customers with information concerning their drug purchases for income tax and insurance purposes and prepares prescription labels and receipts. Duane Reade also has an interactive web site, DuaneReade.com, which customers may use to access company information, refill prescriptions and purchase over-the-counter medications as well as health and beauty care products and other non-pharmacy items.

FINANCIAL DATA: Note: Data for latest year may not have been available at press time.

In U.S. $	2015	2014	2013	2012	2011	2010
Revenue						
R&D Expense						
Operating Income						
Operating Margin %						
SGA Expense						
Net Income						
Operating Cash Flow						
Capital Expenditure						
EBITDA						
Return on Assets %						
Return on Equity %						
Debt to Equity						

CONTACT INFORMATION:

Phone: 212-273-5700   Fax: 212-244-6527
Toll-Free:
Address: 440 9th Ave., New York, NY 10001 United States

STOCK TICKER/OTHER:

Stock Ticker: Subsidiary
Employees: 7,000
Parent Company: WALGREEN CO

Exchange:
Fiscal Year Ends: 12/31

SALARIES/BONUSES:

Top Exec. Salary: $ Bonus: $
Second Exec. Salary: $ Bonus: $

OTHER THOUGHTS:

Estimated Female Officers or Directors:
Hot Spot for Advancement for Women/Minorities:

Eastern Mountain Sports Inc

NAIC Code: 451110

www.ems.com

TYPES OF BUSINESS:

Sporting Goods Stores
Outdoor Apparel
Outdoor Gear
Outdoor Sports Instruction

BRANDS/DIVISIONS/AFFILIATES:

EMS Climbing School
EMS Kayak School
EMS
Versa Capital Management Inc

CONTACTS: Note: Officers with more than one job title may be intentionally listed here more than once.

Mark Walsh, CEO
Robert Mayerson, Pres.
Ralph Lucarelli, Dir.-Visual Merch.
Ralph Lucarelli, Dir.-Store Planning
Joe Lentini, Dir.-Climbing & Adventure School

GROWTH PLANS/SPECIAL FEATURES:

Eastern Mountain Sports (EMS), owned by private equity investment firm Versa Capital Management, Inc., operates 6 outdoor specialty retail stores in the Northeast. The stores provide an extensive selection of clothing and gear for activities such as rock and ice climbing, mountaineering, kayaking and canoeing, camping, cycling and fitness. EMS stocks the most popular brand names in the outdoor industry, including Patagonia, Sierra Designs, Gregory, Kelty, Thule, The North Face, Marmot and Teva. In addition, the company designs and offers its own line of outdoor gear and clothing under the EMS name. The firm utilizes a large store format that includes comprehensive product offerings, allowing it to provide lower prices than those offered by local specialty outdoor retailers. EMS has a liberal return policy that allows customers to exchange, return or repair any item with a web invoice or original store receipt, even if the item has been damaged from use. Many of the firm's products are tested and demonstrated at its outdoor skills training schools. The EMS Climbing School in New Hampshire offers beginner, intermediate and advanced courses in rock climbing, ice climbing and mountaineering throughout the White Mountains. The EMS Kayak School in Massachusetts provides classes for every level through day and overnight trips throughout the Northeast.

FINANCIAL DATA: Note: Data for latest year may not have been available at press time.

In U.S. $	2015	2014	2013	2012	2011	2010
Revenue						
R&D Expense						
Operating Income						
Operating Margin %						
SGA Expense						
Net Income						
Operating Cash Flow						
Capital Expenditure						
EBITDA						
Return on Assets %						
Return on Equity %						
Debt to Equity						

CONTACT INFORMATION:

Phone: 603-924-9571   Fax: 603-924-9138
Toll-Free: 888-463-6367
Address: 1 Vose Farm Rd., Peterborough, NH 03458 United States

SALARIES/BONUSES:

Top Exec. Salary: $ Bonus: $
Second Exec. Salary: $ Bonus: $

STOCK TICKER/OTHER:

Stock Ticker: Private   Exchange:
Employees: 1,130   Fiscal Year Ends: 01/31
Parent Company: Versa Capital Management Inc

OTHER THOUGHTS:

Estimated Female Officers or Directors:
Hot Spot for Advancement for Women/Minorities:

ECCO Sko A/S

www.ecco.com

NAIC Code: 424340

TYPES OF BUSINESS:

Footwear Distribution
Retail Sales
Running Shoes
Golf Shoes
Walking Shoes
Outdoor Shoes
Leather Production

BRANDS/DIVISIONS/AFFILIATES:

ECCO Shoes International AG
ECCO Leather
Comfort Fibre System
Hydromax
Cambrelle
ECCO

CONTACTS: *Note: Officers with more than one job title may be intentionally listed here more than once.*

Dieter Kasprzak, Pres.
Steen Borgholm, CFO
Andreas Wortmann, Exec. VP-Prod. & Brand
Steen Borgholm, Exec. VP-Finance
Panagiotis Mytaros, Exec. VP-Production
Hanni T. Kasprzak, Chmn.
Michel Krol, Exec. VP-Global Sales

GROWTH PLANS/SPECIAL FEATURES:

ECCO Sko A/S is a Danish designer and manufacturer of footwear for men, women and children. Besides dress and casual shoes, the company produces athletic shoes, including shoes for golfing, running, walking and outdoor activities. ECCO's hallmark is its unique direct injection technology, wherein a polyurethane and thermoplastic urethane-based spray is applied directly onto the molded upper part of the shoe to form the sole. ECCO feels this special direct injection process helps provide its shoes with higher quality, flexibility and lightness than other shoes. It operates shoe factories in China, Indonesia, Portugal, Thailand and Slovakia as well as product development facilities in Denmark and Portugal. The firm also produces accessories through its Swiss subsidiary, ECCO Shoes International AG. The company's leather supply operations, managed by ECCO Leather, include tanneries in China, Thailand, Indonesia and the Netherlands, which supply ECCO's shoe factories and other shoe manufactures as well as manufacturers of gloves, bags and airplane and car seats. Annually, ECCO sells over 33% of its leather production to external customers. The company has invented numerous products, including the Comfort Fibre System vegetable tanned, metal-free insole; Hydromax leather treatment; and the Cambrelle removable, washable felt insole. ECCO manufactures over 20 million pairs of shoes each year, making it one of the largest shoe manufacturers in the world. The company's shoes are sold in 87 markets, including approximately 1,177 ECCO retail stores worldwide.

FINANCIAL DATA: *Note: Data for latest year may not have been available at press time.*

In U.S. $	2015	2014	2013	2012	2011	2010
Revenue		1,271,607,087	1,563,570,000	1,454,319,802	1,234,570,000	1,130,182,000
R&D Expense						
Operating Income						
Operating Margin %						
SGA Expense						
Net Income		147,774,891	147,080,770	123,413,885	96,594,000	75,826,000
Operating Cash Flow						
Capital Expenditure						
EBITDA						
Return on Assets %						
Return on Equity %						
Debt to Equity						

CONTACT INFORMATION:

Phone: 45-74-91-16-25   Fax: 45-74-71-03-60
Toll-Free:
Address: Industrivej 5, Bredebro, 6261 Denmark

SALARIES/BONUSES:

Top Exec. Salary: $ Bonus: $
Second Exec. Salary: $ Bonus: $

STOCK TICKER/OTHER:

Stock Ticker: Private   Exchange:
Employees: 21,000   Fiscal Year Ends: 12/31
Parent Company:

OTHER THOUGHTS:

Estimated Female Officers or Directors: 3
Hot Spot for Advancement for Women/Minorities: Y

Eddie Bauer LLC

NAIC Code: 448140

www.eddiebauer.com

TYPES OF BUSINESS:

Apparel Stores
Catalogs
Online Sales
Outlet Stores
Outdoor Wear
High-Performance Mountaineering Wear
Private Label Credit Cards

BRANDS/DIVISIONS/AFFILIATES:

Eddie Bauer Credit Cards
EddieBauer.com
Golden Gate Capital
Eddie Bauer Japan Inc
Eddie Bauer Holdings Inc
Eddie Bauer GmbH & Co Kg

CONTACTS: Note: Officers with more than one job title may be intentionally listed here more than once.

Michael Egeck, CEO
Michael R. Egeck, Pres.
Marvin Edward Toland, Sr. VP-Direct, e-Commerce & Catalog
William End, Chmn.

GROWTH PLANS/SPECIAL FEATURES:

Eddie Bauer, LLC, owned by Golden Gate Capital, is a leading multi-channel specialty retailer offering casual men's, women's and children's apparel as well as accessories and home furnishings. Founded in 1920, the company offers its apparel and related accessories through its Eddie Bauer apparel stores, outlet stores, mail-order catalogs and through its web site, EddieBauer.com. The company has approximately 370 stores in the U.S. and Canada. Eddie Bauer Japan, Inc., a joint venture between the company and Otto-Japan, Inc., develops Eddie Bauer stores and distributes catalogs in Japan. The firm's retail stores are generally located in upscale regional malls or in high-traffic metropolitan areas. Eddie Bauer's outlet stores are located predominately in outlet malls, value strip centers and other areas not serviced by its core specialty retail stores. The company also offers Eddie Bauer Credit Cards to its customers. Eddie Bauer partners with several companies and organizations that share the its spirit of adventure and love of the outdoors, such as Airstream, American Mountaineering Museum and the Leave No Trace Center for Outdoor Ethics. In November 2014, Eddie Bauer GmbH & Co. Kg was acquired by Eddie Bauer Holdings, Inc.

The company offers its corporate and full-time store employees medical, dental and vision coverage; prescription plans; life insurance; a 401(k) plan; flexible spending accounts; an employee assistance program; and discounts on Eddie Bauer merchandise.

FINANCIAL DATA: Note: Data for latest year may not have been available at press time.

In U.S. $	2015	2014	2013	2012	2011	2010
Revenue		925,000,000	890,000,000	870,000,000	850,000,000	825,000,000
R&D Expense						
Operating Income						
Operating Margin %						
SGA Expense						
Net Income						
Operating Cash Flow						
Capital Expenditure						
EBITDA						
Return on Assets %						
Return on Equity %						
Debt to Equity						

CONTACT INFORMATION:

Phone: 425-755-8100   Fax:
Toll-Free: 800-426-8020
Address: 10401 NE 8th Street, Ste 500, Bellevue, WA 98004 United States

STOCK TICKER/OTHER:

Stock Ticker: Subsidiary
Employees: 9,500
Parent Company: Golden Gate Capital

Exchange:
Fiscal Year Ends: 12/31

SALARIES/BONUSES:

Top Exec. Salary: $ Bonus: $
Second Exec. Salary: $ Bonus: $

OTHER THOUGHTS:

Estimated Female Officers or Directors:
Hot Spot for Advancement for Women/Minorities: Y

Eileen Fisher Inc

www.eileenfisher.com

NAIC Code: 424300

TYPES OF BUSINESS:

Apparel and Clothing Brands, Designers, Importers and Distributors
Retail Stores
Online Sales

BRANDS/DIVISIONS/AFFILIATES:

Eileen Fisher Home
Eco Collection
EileenFisher.com

CONTACTS: Note: Officers with more than one job title may be intentionally listed here more than once.

Eileen Fisher, Pres.
Kenneth Pollak, CFO
Ann Gilligan, Dir.-Mktg. Planning
Celeste Thompson, VP-Human Resources
Jim Gundell, VP-e-Commerce & Retail
Hayley Gluck, Controller
Karen Gray, Dir.-Stores
Amy Hall, Dir.-Social Consciousness
Ellie Thoren, Dir.-Visual Advertising

GROWTH PLANS/SPECIAL FEATURES:

Eileen Fisher, Inc. manufactures and retails women's business and casual clothing with an emphasis on comfort, versatility and style. Offerings include tanks and camis; tops and tees; sweaters and cardigans; jackets and vests; pants; skirts and dresses; sleepwear; outerwear; shoes; the Eco Collection; and accessories such as scarves, handbags and belts. Its products are sold through over 70 company-owned boutiques and outlets in 21 states. Eileen Fisher also distributes its products nationwide and in Canada through department and specialty stores, including Nordstrom, Saks Fifth Avenue and Neiman Marcus, and online, through EileenFisher.com. In addition to clothing, Eileen Fisher designs organic cotton and linen sheets and other home textiles out of natural fabrics for Garnet Hill. Through the Global Organic Textile Standard (GOTS) program, the firm buys fair-traded cotton from farmers and artisans in Peru.

The company offers employees medical and dental coverage, flexible spending accounts, life insurance, an employee assistance program, educational assistance, parental and partner leave, domestic partner coverage, adoption assistance, flexible work arrangements, a clothing allowance, sample sales and summer hours. Additionally, Eileen Fisher contributes to and supports programs that influence women's health, well-being, independence and empowerment. Wellness activities are offered at corporate offices and include massages, yoga classes and foot reflexology.

FINANCIAL DATA: Note: Data for latest year may not have been available at press time.

In U.S. $	2015	2014	2013	2012	2011	2010
Revenue		375,000,000	370,000,000	345,000,000	340,000,000	325,000,000
R&D Expense						
Operating Income						
Operating Margin %						
SGA Expense						
Net Income						
Operating Cash Flow						
Capital Expenditure						
EBITDA						
Return on Assets %						
Return on Equity %						
Debt to Equity						

CONTACT INFORMATION:

Phone: 914-591-5700   Fax: 914-591-8824
Toll-Free: 800-445-1603
Address: 2 Bridge St., Irvington, NY 10533-1527 United States

STOCK TICKER/OTHER:

Stock Ticker: Private
Employees: 985
Parent Company:

Exchange:
Fiscal Year Ends: 12/31

SALARIES/BONUSES:

Top Exec. Salary: $ Bonus: $
Second Exec. Salary: $ Bonus: $

OTHER THOUGHTS:

Estimated Female Officers or Directors: 8
Hot Spot for Advancement for Women/Minorities: Y

Sales, profits and employees may be estimates. Financial information, benefits and other data can change quickly and may vary from those stated here.

El Puerto de Liverpool SAB de CV

NAIC Code: 452111

www.liverpool.com.mx

TYPES OF BUSINESS:

Department Stores

BRANDS/DIVISIONS/AFFILIATES:

Liverpool
Fabricas de Francia
Galerias Fashion Card
Liverpool Premium Card
Fabricas de Francia Card

CONTACTS: Note: Officers with more than one job title may be intentionally listed here more than once.

Ignacio Pesqueria, Sec.
Max David, Chmn.

GROWTH PLANS/SPECIAL FEATURES:

El Puerto de Liverpool, SAB de CV is a Mexico-based company, operating stores across Mexico, for a total of 4.2 million square feet of sales floor. Its largest retail segment is its 99 department stores operating under the names Liverpool (in 70 locations), and Fabricas de Francia (23). The company's department stores sell a variety of products, including electronics, women's and men's apparel, children's merchandise, home goods, furniture and cosmetics. Additionally, the store operates six duty free locations in international points of entry, selling cosmetics, fragrances and accessories. Liverpool's real estate division operates 19 shopping centers, which house over 1,500 retail tenants. Additionally, the company is a non-bank credit card issuer, which accounts for a large portion of its revenue. Currently it offers three cards: the Liverpool and Fabricas de Francia Card, the Liverpool Premium Card (VISA) and the Galerias Fashion Card (available for use in the 19 shopping centers). The company currently has more than 3 million cardholders.

FINANCIAL DATA: Note: Data for latest year may not have been available at press time.

In U.S. $	2015	2014	2013	2012	2011	2010
Revenue		4,892,724,000	4,474,761,000	4,000,209,000	3,541,915,000	3,162,654,000
R&D Expense						
Operating Income		671,062,500	654,322,700	622,319,000	557,209,600	444,292,400
Operating Margin %		13.71%	14.62%	15.55%	15.73%	14.04%
SGA Expense		1,322,785,000	1,171,310,000	1,011,820,000	254,267,100	797,262,100
Net Income		468,787,600	465,071,000	434,623,800	395,147,600	311,258,900
Operating Cash Flow		703,805,600	392,884,300	387,324,800	291,884,000	318,317,300
Capital Expenditure		161,808,800	229,611,400	369,224,900	310,006,400	158,028,100
EBITDA		786,413,400	756,989,800	710,654,700	666,330,000	558,618,000
Return on Assets %		7.82%	8.55%	9.10%	9.26%	8.08%
Return on Equity %		13.21%	14.76%	15.51%	16.13%	14.48%
Debt to Equity		0.01	0.01	0.26	0.20	0.23

CONTACT INFORMATION:

Phone: 52 553286400   Fax: 52 552038855
Toll-Free:
Address: Av. Mariano Escobedo No. 425, Mexico DF, 11560 Mexico

STOCK TICKER/OTHER:

Stock Ticker: ELPQF   Exchange: GREY
Employees: Fiscal Year Ends: 12/31
Parent Company:

SALARIES/BONUSES:

Top Exec. Salary: $ Bonus: $
Second Exec. Salary: $ Bonus: $

OTHER THOUGHTS:

Estimated Female Officers or Directors:
Hot Spot for Advancement for Women/Minorities:

Elder-Beerman Stores Corp (The)   www.elder-beerman.com

NAIC Code: 452111

TYPES OF BUSINESS:

Department Stores
Furniture Stores

BRANDS/DIVISIONS/AFFILIATES:

Bon-Ton Stores Inc (The)
Elder-Beerman
Bergner's
Boston Store
Carson's
Bergerger's
Younkers

CONTACTS: *Note: Officers with more than one job title may be intentionally listed here more than once.*

Kathryn Bufano, CEO-The Bon-Ton Stores, Inc.
Brendan L. Hoffman, CEO
Tim Grumbacher, Chmn.
Tim Grumbacher, Chmn.-The Bon-Ton Stores, Inc.

GROWTH PLANS/SPECIAL FEATURES:

The Elder-Beerman Stores Corp. is a department store retailer, originally founded in Ohio in 1847. The firm is a wholly-owned subsidiary of The Bon-Ton Stores, Inc., which operates roughly 270 department stores in 26 states under the Bon-Ton, Elder-Beerman, Bergner's, Boston Store, Carson's, Herberger's and Younkers brand names. Stores under the Elder-Beerman name sell a wide range of moderate- to better-branded merchandise, including women's, men's and children's apparel and accessories; cosmetics; home furnishings; and other consumer goods. The firm maintains approximately 35 department stores principally located in the smaller Midwestern markets of Ohio, West Virginia, Indiana, Michigan and Kentucky. These stores typically feature services such as centralized customer service centers, bridal registry kiosks and self-select cosmetics.

The company offers employees benefits including medical, dental, vision and life insurance; long-term disability coverage; flexible spending accounts; and a 401(k) plan with company matching and retirement contribution.

FINANCIAL DATA: *Note: Data for latest year may not have been available at press time.*

In U.S. $	2015	2014	2013	2012	2011	2010
Revenue						
R&D Expense						
Operating Income						
Operating Margin %						
SGA Expense						
Net Income						
Operating Cash Flow						
Capital Expenditure						
EBITDA						
Return on Assets %						
Return on Equity %						
Debt to Equity						

CONTACT INFORMATION:

Phone: 717-757-7660   Fax: 717-751-3196
Toll-Free:
Address: 2801 E. Market St., York, PA 17402 United States

STOCK TICKER/OTHER:

Stock Ticker: Subsidiary   Exchange:
Employees: Fiscal Year Ends: 01/31
Parent Company: Bon-Ton Stores, Inc. (The)

SALARIES/BONUSES:

Top Exec. Salary: $ Bonus: $
Second Exec. Salary: $ Bonus: $

OTHER THOUGHTS:

Estimated Female Officers or Directors:
Hot Spot for Advancement for Women/Minorities: Y

Emerging Vision Inc

www.emergingvision.com

NAIC Code: 446130

TYPES OF BUSINESS:

Eyeglasses & Related Products, Retail
Franchise Operations
Group Vision Plan

BRANDS/DIVISIONS/AFFILIATES:

Sterling Optical
Site for Sore Eyes
Sterling VisionCare
VisionCare of California Inc
Combine Buying Group
Optical Group (The)
Eye Gallery (The)
Artful Eye

CONTACTS: *Note: Officers with more than one job title may be intentionally listed here more than once.*

Glenn Spina, CEO
Glenn Spina, Pres.
Brian P. Alessi, CFO
Brian P. Alessi, Corp. Sec.
Brian P. Alessi, Treas.
Alan Cohen, Chmn.

GROWTH PLANS/SPECIAL FEATURES:

Emerging Vision, Inc. is a leading operator of retail optical stores and one of the largest franchise optical chains in the U.S. It also operates optical purchasing groups in the U.S. and Canada. In total, Emerging Vision has nearly 125 stores in operation, consisting of both company-owned stores and franchised stores, located in 13 states, Washington, D.C. and the U.S. Virgin Islands. The company and its franchisees manage retail optical stores primarily under the trade name Sterling Optical; it also operates stores under the names Site for Sore Eyes and Sterling VisionCare. In addition, the firm operates VisionCare of California Inc., a specialized health care maintenance organization (HMO) that employs licensed optometrists to offer services in offices adjacent to or within most of Emerging Vision's California retail locations. Most of the company's stores offer eye care products and services such as prescription and non-prescription eyeglasses, eyeglass frames, ophthalmic lenses, contact lenses, sunglasses and a range of ancillary items. A majority of the locations also provide professional eye examinations by an onsite optometrist as well as unaffiliated practitioners. Additionally, the stores have an inventory of ophthalmic and contact lenses as well as lab equipment for cutting and edging lenses to fit into eyeglass frames. The storefronts are typically located in enclosed regional shopping malls and smaller strip centers. Through Combine Buying Group in the U.S. and The Optical Group in Canada, the company operates purchasing organizations that provide members with vendor discounts on optical products for resale. In 2014, the firm acquired The Eye Gallery and Artful Eye, which offer topline designer styles to customers in Atlanta and Northwest Florida.

FINANCIAL DATA: *Note: Data for latest year may not have been available at press time.*

In U.S. $	2015	2014	2013	2012	2011	2010
Revenue		78,500,000	77,500,000	73,000,000	70,000,000	67,587,000
R&D Expense						
Operating Income						
Operating Margin %						
SGA Expense						
Net Income						
Operating Cash Flow						
Capital Expenditure						
EBITDA						
Return on Assets %						
Return on Equity %						
Debt to Equity						

CONTACT INFORMATION:

Phone: 646-737-1500   Fax:
Toll-Free:
Address: 520 8th Ave., 23rd Fl., New York, NY 10018 United States

STOCK TICKER/OTHER:

Stock Ticker: Private   Exchange:
Employees: 88   Fiscal Year Ends: 12/31
Parent Company: EMVI ACQUISITION CORP

SALARIES/BONUSES:

Top Exec. Salary: $ Bonus: $
Second Exec. Salary: $ Bonus: $

OTHER THOUGHTS:

Estimated Female Officers or Directors:
Hot Spot for Advancement for Women/Minorities:

Esprit Holdings Ltd

www.esprit.com

NAIC Code: 448120

TYPES OF BUSINESS:

Apparel Stores
Footwear
Accessories
Women's Clothing
Men's Clothing
Children's Clothing
Home Furnishings

BRANDS/DIVISIONS/AFFILIATES:

Esprit
Red Earth

GROWTH PLANS/SPECIAL FEATURES:

Esprit Holdings Ltd. is a fashion retailer, selling clothing, footwear and accessories for men, women and children and retailing a home furnishings line. Headquartered in Hong Kong and Germany with an additional corporate office in New York, the firm operates over 900 stores and has over 7,800 wholesale outlets in 40 countries. Under the brand names Esprit and Red Earth, the company sells its products at freestanding stores, department store shop-in-shops and indoor boutiques. The retailer has several established product lines featuring women's wear, kid's wear and shoes and accessories. Esprit focuses on providing its customers with stylish and inexpensive clothing and accessories. Its Red Earth brand line features cosmetics and body care products.

CONTACTS: Note: Officers with more than one job title may be intentionally listed here more than once.

Jose Manuel Martinez Gutierrez, CEO
Thomas Tang Wing Yung, CFO
Ng Wai Yin Florence, Company Sec.

FINANCIAL DATA: Note: Data for latest year may not have been available at press time.

In U.S. $	2015	2014	2013	2012	2011	2010
Revenue	2,506,042,000	3,126,198,000	3,342,336,000	3,892,424,000	4,357,218,000	4,352,959,000
R&D Expense						
Operating Income	-475,246,000	46,582,630	-538,087,400	151,103,200	89,294,130	488,536,900
Operating Margin %	-18.96%	1.49%	-16.09%	3.88%	2.04%	11.22%
SGA Expense	648,801,800	734,741,000	800,808,300	882,231,200	884,811,800	770,484,400
Net Income	-476,923,500	27,097,930	-566,217,600	112,650,000	10,193,980	545,313,500
Operating Cash Flow	-9,290,718	182,975,500	-97,681,580	94,197,560	236,784,300	698,352,300
Capital Expenditure	45,034,180	48,389,160	118,585,700	183,233,600	185,298,200	194,718,000
EBITDA	-377,435,400	161,168,100	-411,501,400	250,591,300	209,815,400	824,938,400
Return on Assets %	-18.21%	.90%	-18.70%	3.44%	.30%	19.10%
Return on Equity %	-25.65%	1.25%	-27.25%	5.48%	.48%	27.72%
Debt to Equity				0.06	0.09	0.12

CONTACT INFORMATION:

Phone: 852 27654321   Fax: 852 23625576
Toll-Free:
Address: 39 Wang Chiu Rd., Enterprise Sq. 3, 43/F, Kowloon, Kowloon, Hong Kong 999077 Hong Kong

STOCK TICKER/OTHER:

Stock Ticker: ESHDF   Exchange: GREY
Employees: 9,626   Fiscal Year Ends: 06/30
Parent Company:

SALARIES/BONUSES:

Top Exec. Salary: $ Bonus: $
Second Exec. Salary: $ Bonus: $

OTHER THOUGHTS:

Estimated Female Officers or Directors:
Hot Spot for Advancement for Women/Minorities:

Estee Lauder Companies Inc (The)

NAIC Code: 325620

www.elcompanies.com

TYPES OF BUSINESS:

Cosmetics
Cosmetic & Fragrance Sales
Retail Cosmetics Stores
Hair Care Products

GROWTH PLANS/SPECIAL FEATURES:

The Estee Lauder Companies, Inc. is a global manufacture
and marketer of skin care, cosmetic, fragrance and hair car
products. The company's products are sold in over 15(
countries and territories under brand names such as Este
Lauder, Aramis, Clinique, Origins, M.A.C., Bobbi Brown, La
Mer and Aveda. The firm is also the global licensee fo
fragrances and cosmetics sold under the Tommy Hilfiger
Donna Karan, Michael Kors, Tom Ford, Tory Burch and Coach
brand names. Estee Lauder sells its products principally
through 30,000 points of sale, including upscale department
stores, specialty retailers, upscale perfumeries and
pharmacies and prestige salons and spas as well as
freestanding company-owned stores and spas, authorized
retailer web sites, stores on cruise ships, television direc
marketing, in-flight and duty-free shops and self-select outlets
The founding Lauder family still controls 86.7% of the
company's voting shares. The firm operates on a global basis
with over half of its sales generated outside the U.S. Skin care
products currently account for roughly 43% of the company's
sales; makeup products, 38%; fragrance products, 13%; and
hair care items, 5%. In 2015, the firm acquired Editions de
Parfums Frederic Malle, a fragrance brand; and GLAMGLOW
a skin care brand.

BRANDS/DIVISIONS/AFFILIATES:

Aveda
La Mer
Clinique
Estee Lauder
Bobbie Brown
Aramis
Origins
M.A.C.

CONTACTS: Note: Officers with more than one job title may be intentionally listed here more than once.

Fabrizio Freda, CEO
Cedric Prouve, President, Divisional
Tracey Travis, CFO
Leonard Lauder, Chairman Emeritus
William Lauder, Chairman of the Board
Ronald Lauder, Chairman, Divisional
Michael OHare, Executive VP, Divisional
Carl Haney, Executive VP, Divisional
Gregory Polcer, Executive VP, Divisional
Alexandra Trower, Executive VP, Divisional
Sara Moss, Executive VP
Spencer Smul, Other Corporate Officer
John Demsey, President, Divisional

FINANCIAL DATA: Note: Data for latest year may not have been available at press time.

In U.S. $	2015	2014	2013	2012	2011	2010
Revenue	10,780,400,000	10,968,800,000	10,181,700,000	9,713,601,000	8,810,000,000	7,795,800,000
R&D Expense						
Operating Income	1,606,300,000	1,827,600,000	1,526,000,000	1,311,700,000	1,089,400,000	789,900,000
Operating Margin %	14.90%	16.66%	14.98%	13.50%	12.36%	10.13%
SGA Expense	7,073,500,000	6,985,900,000	6,597,000,000	6,324,800,000	5,696,700,000	5,067,000,000
Net Income	1,088,900,000	1,204,100,000	1,019,800,000	856,900,000	700,800,000	478,300,000
Operating Cash Flow		1,535,200,000	1,226,300,000	1,126,700,000	1,027,000,000	956,700,000
Capital Expenditure		510,200,000	461,000,000	420,700,000	351,000,000	270,600,000
EBITDA	2,029,900,000	2,212,200,000	1,886,000,000	1,618,000,000	1,383,800,000	1,053,600,000
Return on Assets %	13.51%	16.03%	14.84%	13.31%	12.07%	9.09%
Return on Equity %	29.04%	33.71%	33.87%	31.95%	30.61%	26.65%
Debt to Equity		0.34	0.40	0.39	0.41	0.61

CONTACT INFORMATION:

Phone: 212 572-4200   Fax: 212 572-3941
Toll-Free:
Address: 767 5th Ave., New York, NY 10153 United States

STOCK TICKER/OTHER:

Stock Ticker: EL
Employees: 44,000
Parent Company:

Exchange: NYS
Fiscal Year Ends: 06/30

SALARIES/BONUSES:

Top Exec. Salary: Bonus: $
$1,800,000
Second Exec. Salary: Bonus: $
$1,500,000

OTHER THOUGHTS:

Estimated Female Officers or Directors: 10

Hot Spot for Advancement for Women/Minorities: Y

Etam Developpement

NAIC Code: 448120

TYPES OF BUSINESS:

Women's Apparel Stores
Retail Lingerie
Retail Accessories

BRANDS/DIVISIONS/AFFILIATES:

1.2.3
Undiz
Etam Lingerie

CONTACTS: *Note: Officers with more than one job title may be intentionally listed here more than once.*

Vanessa Michior, Managing General Partner
Pierre Milchior, Managing General Partner
Marie-Claire Tarica, Managing General Partner
Laurent Milchior, Managing General Partner

GROWTH PLANS/SPECIAL FEATURES:

Etam Developpement, headquartered in France, is an international group that focuses on women's fashions, including ready-to-wear, lingerie and accessories. The company has 4,122 outlets in 50 countries, including over 724 in France; more than 200 outlets in the rest of Europe; 2,935 in China; and about 244 franchised outlets in Eastern Europe, Asia-Oceania, Africa and the Middle East. The outlets operate under the Etam Lingerie, 1.2.3 and Undiz names. Its products cover much of the market in women's clothing, both in terms of age and price range. The company engages in the design and retailing of fashion products through three complementary brands: Etam, 1.2.3 and Undiz. Each brand has its own team of stylists, designers and product managers. Once each collection is designed, the company uses a global network of subcontractors and textile manufacturers for production, mainly in Asia, Southern and Eastern Europe and the Mediterranean basin. The Etam brand covers ready-to-wear, lingerie and accessories through three main categories: city wear, casual chic and weekend wear. Designers create a number of mini-collections each season, and retail stock is regularly rotated. The 1.2.3 brand aims to make upscale fashion available to a wider range of customers with broad, coordinated collections. The Undiz brand specializes in women's lingerie, offering a broad range of mix-and-match styles targeted at young urban women. The brand also offers a small collection of underwear basics for men.

FINANCIAL DATA: *Note: Data for latest year may not have been available at press time.*

In U.S. $	2015	2014	2013	2012	2011	2010
Revenue		1,442,720,000	1,681,673,000	1,614,161,015	1,533,230,000	1,493,580,000
R&D Expense						
Operating Income						
Operating Margin %						
SGA Expense						
Net Income		23,378,880	29,335,000	17,795,092	53,736,000	69,968,000
Operating Cash Flow						
Capital Expenditure						
EBITDA						
Return on Assets %						
Return on Equity %						
Debt to Equity						

CONTACT INFORMATION:

Phone: 33-3-08-38-29-35   Fax:
Toll-Free:
Address: 78, rue de Rivoli, Paris, 75004 France

STOCK TICKER/OTHER:

Stock Ticker: TAM
Employees: 21,000
Parent Company:

Exchange: Paris
Fiscal Year Ends: 12/31

SALARIES/BONUSES:

Top Exec. Salary: $ Bonus: $
Second Exec. Salary: $ Bonus: $

OTHER THOUGHTS:

Estimated Female Officers or Directors: 2
Hot Spot for Advancement for Women/Minorities:

Ethan Allen Interiors Inc

NAIC Code: 442110

www.ethanallen.com

TYPES OF BUSINESS:

Furniture-Retail
Furniture-Manufacturing & Distribution
Interior Design Services
Online Sales
Hotel Operation

BRANDS/DIVISIONS/AFFILIATES:

Ethan Allen Global Inc
Ethan Allen Hotel & Conference Center

CONTACTS: Note: Officers with more than one job title may be intentionally listed here more than once.

M. Kathwari, CEO
Corey Whitely, CFO
John Bedford, Chief Accounting Officer
Eric Koster, General Counsel
Daniel Grow, Senior VP, Divisional
Tracy Paccione, Vice President, Divisional

GROWTH PLANS/SPECIAL FEATURES:

Ethan Allen Interiors, Inc., the holding company for Ethan Allen Global, Inc., is a leading manufacturer, distributor and retailer of quality home furnishings and accessories. The company operates through two business segments: retail and wholesale. Retail sales account for 77% of net sales, while wholesale accounts for 23%. Through the operation of 29 service centers and eight manufacturing facilities in North America, including five manufacturing plants and one sawmill in the U.S. and two foreign manufacturing plants (one in Mexico and the other in Honduras), the retail segment distributes products to approximately 300 retail stores, which the firm refers to as design centers, primarily on a custom order, as-needed basis. Only 144 design centers are company-owned, while independent dealers operate the rest. Stores are typically located in urban settings as freestanding destination stores or as part of suburban strip malls and range in size from 15,000 to 25,000 square feet, averaging 16,000 square feet. Products include case good items, such as beds, dressers, tables, chairs and entertainment units; upholstery home furnishing items, such as recliners, sofas and loveseats; and home accessory items, such as window treatments, wall decor, lighting, bedding and area rugs. The wholesale division oversees the design, manufacture, sale and distribution of furnishing products. Through one national distribution center in the Southeast U.S., approximately 70% of its merchandise is manufactured in North America. The company owns the Ethan Allen Hotel and Conference Center, a 200-guestroom facility located near its corporate headquarters, used for both Ethan Allen functions and general public use.

FINANCIAL DATA: Note: Data for latest year may not have been available at press time.

In U.S. $	2015	2014	2013	2012	2011	2010
Revenue	754,600,000	746,659,000	729,083,000	729,373,000	678,960,000	590,054,000
R&D Expense						
Operating Income	65,934,000	69,636,000	60,437,000	49,697,000	31,933,000	-11,735,000
Operating Margin %	8.73%	9.32%	8.28%	6.81%	4.70%	-1.98%
SGA Expense	345,229,000	336,860,000	337,912,000	340,676,000	316,401,000	289,575,000
Net Income	37,142,000	42,931,000	32,478,000	49,694,000	29,250,000	-44,316,000
Operating Cash Flow	55,106,000	59,889,000	61,301,000	37,701,000	63,162,000	51,331,000
Capital Expenditure	19,787,000	19,305,000	19,005,000	22,884,000	9,094,000	9,922,000
EBITDA	85,076,000	87,842,000	78,445,000	68,840,000	58,313,000	22,535,000
Return on Assets %	5.88%	6.75%	5.14%	7.80%	4.64%	-6.93%
Return on Equity %	10.07%	12.24%	9.90%	16.47%	10.83%	-15.70%
Debt to Equity	0.20	0.35	0.39	0.47	0.58	0.77

CONTACT INFORMATION:

Phone: 203 743-8000   Fax: 203 743-8298
Toll-Free: 888-324-3571
Address: Ethan Allen Dr., Danbury, CT 06813-1966 United States

STOCK TICKER/OTHER:

Stock Ticker: ETH
Employees: 5,000
Parent Company:

Exchange: NYS
Fiscal Year Ends: 06/30

SALARIES/BONUSES:

Top Exec. Salary:
$1,150,050
Second Exec. Salary:
$386,539

Bonus: $

Bonus: $100,500

OTHER THOUGHTS:

Estimated Female Officers or Directors: 4

Hot Spot for Advancement for Women/Minorities: Y

EVINE Live Inc

NAIC Code: 454113

TYPES OF BUSINESS:
Television Shopping Programs
Online Sales

BRANDS/DIVISIONS/AFFILIATES:
EVINE Live
evine.com
ValueVision Media Inc
ShopHQ

CONTACTS: Note: Officers with more than one job title may be intentionally listed here more than once.
Tim Peterman, CFO
Nicholas Vassallo, Controller
Mark Bozek, Director
Robert Rosenblatt, Director
George Nuce, Executive VP
Michael Murray, Senior VP, Divisional
Jean-Guillaume Sabatier, Senior VP, Divisional
Penny Burnett, Senior VP
Beth McCartan, Vice President, Divisional
Ashish Akolkar, Vice President, Divisional

GROWTH PLANS/SPECIAL FEATURES:
EVINE Live, Inc., formerly ValueVision Media, Inc., is direct marketing company that markets, sells and distributes consumer products through multi-media channels, including TV, Internet, mobile and social media. The company's principal electronic media activity is its television home shopping network, which markets brand-name merchandise as well as proprietary and private-label consumer products. EVINE's live, 24-hour-a-day home shopping program EVINE Live (formerly ShopHQ) is broadcast through cable and satellite affiliations and a company-owned full power television station in Boston, Massachusetts to over 118 million homes throughout the U.S. Products sold on the network include jewelry, watches, computers and other electronics, housewares, apparel, cosmetics, seasonal items and other merchandise. The company complements its television home shopping business with the sale of merchandise through its e-commerce web site, evine.com, which also includes a live webcast feed of the television program, an archive of recent past programming, videos of individual products and links to clearance and auction sites. Watches and jewelry generate 42% of the firm's sales. The home and electronics division, representing everything from bed and bath textiles to GPS devises, generates 29% of the company's sales. Beauty, health and fitness accounts for 14%, while the fashion (apparel, outerwear and accessories) category generates the remaining 15%. In 2014, ValueVision Media changed its name to EVINE Live, Inc.

FINANCIAL DATA: Note: Data for latest year may not have been available at press time.

In U.S. $	2015	2014	2013	2012	2011	2010
Revenue	674,618,000	640,489,000	586,820,000	558,394,000	562,273,000	527,873,000
R&D Expense						
Operating Income	1,003,000	77,000	-23,297,000	-16,838,000	-15,466,000	-41,171,000
Operating Margin %	.14%	.01%	-3.97%	-3.01%	-2.75%	-7.79%
SGA Expense	235,600,000	217,627,000	211,334,000	208,355,000	200,707,000	198,320,000
Net Income	-1,378,000	-2,515,000	-27,676,000	-48,064,000	-25,868,000	-41,998,000
Operating Cash Flow	-1,315,000	13,953,000	-8,482,000	-12,949,000	327,000	-37,896,000
Capital Expenditure	25,178,000	11,077,000	10,157,000	11,096,000	7,584,000	7,578,000
EBITDA	9,885,000	12,680,000	-10,262,000	-29,626,000	-3,313,000	-22,841,000
Return on Assets %	-.56%	-1.12%	-12.85%	-21.04%	-11.90%	-6.71%
Return on Equity %	-1.69%	-3.23%	-30.94%	-52.03%	-30.17%	-15.65%
Debt to Equity	0.60	0.48	0.49	0.24	0.05	0.05

CONTACT INFORMATION:
Phone: 952 943-6000   Fax: 952 947-0188
Toll-Free: 800-676-5523
Address: 6740 Shady Oak Rd., Eden Prairie, MN 55344 United States

STOCK TICKER/OTHER:
Stock Ticker: EVLV   Exchange: NAS
Employees: 1,300   Fiscal Year Ends: 01/31
Parent Company:

SALARIES/BONUSES:
Top Exec. Salary: $404,983   Bonus: $506,849
Second Exec. Salary: $449,243   Bonus: $

OTHER THOUGHTS:
Estimated Female Officers or Directors: 4
Hot Spot for Advancement for Women/Minorities: Y

Express Inc

NAIC Code: 448120

TYPES OF BUSINESS:

Women's Apparel, Retail
Men's Apparel, Retail
Private Label Credit Cards

BRANDS/DIVISIONS/AFFILIATES:

Express

CONTACTS: Note: Officers with more than one job title may be intentionally listed here more than once.

David Kornberg, CEO
Periclis Pericleous, CFO
Michael Weiss, Chairman of the Board
Matthew Moellering, COO
Colin Campbell, Executive VP, Divisional
John Rafferty, Executive VP, Divisional
Jeanne St. Pierre, Executive VP, Divisional
Douglas Tilson, Executive VP, Divisional
Lacey Bundy, General Counsel
Marisa Jacobs, Vice President, Divisional

GROWTH PLANS/SPECIAL FEATURES:

Express, Inc. is a specialty retailer of women's and men'
private-label apparel, sportswear and accessories. I
internationally-inspired styles cater to fashion-consciou
casual, professional and urban women and men between th
ages of 20 and 30. Express' women's apparel includes tops
shirts, hoodies, jackets, suit jackets, outerwear, skirts, dresses
jeans, pants and accessories. Women's merchandise account
for 62% of its total sales. Men's apparel, which accounts for th
remaining 38%, includes shirts, graphic tees, crewnecks, trac
jackets, outerwear, jeans, pants and accessories. It currentl
operates 641 women's, men's and dual gender stores in th
U.S., Puerto Rico and Canada, each averaging about 8,80
gross square feet. Its in-house design studio, located on 5t
Avenue in New York City, is responsible for designin
substantially all of the firm's merchandise. The company's wel
site allows customers to browse and purchase its most up-to
date apparel styles and trends for the coming season as wel
as gain information about current and forthcoming storewid
sales. The web site also offers Internet-only product specials i
addition to a fashion blog featuring music playing in Express
retail stores. The entire catalog is available on Facebook a
well. The company also offers an Express credit card that gives
holders certain privileges including a rewards program
invitations to special events and other special offers.

The company offers employees benefits including medical
dental, vision and pharmacy programs; life insurance; short
and long-term disability benefits; flexible spending accounts; a
401(k) retirement plan; tuition reimbursement; adoptio
assistance; employee assistance programs; and merchandise
discounts.

FINANCIAL DATA: Note: Data for latest year may not have been available at press time.

In U.S. $	2015	2014	2013	2012	2011	2010
Revenue	2,165,481,000	2,219,125,000	2,148,069,000	2,073,355,000	1,905,814,000	1,721,066,000
R&D Expense						
Operating Income	136,597,000	214,259,000	251,563,000	270,946,000	199,251,000	126,837,000
Operating Margin %	6.30%	9.65%	11.71%	13.06%	10.45%	7.36%
SGA Expense	524,041,000	504,277,000	491,599,000	483,823,000	461,073,000	409,198,000
Net Income	68,325,000	116,539,000	139,267,000	140,697,000	127,388,000	75,307,000
Operating Cash Flow	156,570,000	195,075,000	269,364,000	212,609,000	219,958,000	200,721,000
Capital Expenditure	116,098,000	105,462,000	99,884,000	77,236,000	54,843,000	26,873,000
EBITDA	213,034,000	284,069,000	319,253,000	339,471,000	269,792,000	202,199,000
Return on Assets %	5.55%	10.58%	14.80%	16.31%	14.70%	8.70%
Return on Equity %	13.25%	27.55%	42.69%	68.41%	116.06%	80.77%
Debt to Equity	0.35	0.41	0.53	0.70	2.81	4.64

CONTACT INFORMATION:

Phone: 614 474-4001   Fax: 212 884-3221
Toll-Free: 888-397-1980
Address: 1 Express Dr., Columbus, OH 43230 United States

STOCK TICKER/OTHER:

Stock Ticker: EXPR
Employees: 18,000
Parent Company:

Exchange: NYS
Fiscal Year Ends: 01/31

SALARIES/BONUSES:

Top Exec. Salary: $1,500,000   Bonus: $

Second Exec. Salary: $750,000   Bonus: $

OTHER THOUGHTS:

Estimated Female Officers or Directors: 2

Hot Spot for Advancement for Women/Minorities: Y

Sales, profits and employees may be estimates. Financial information, benefits and other data can change quickly and may vary from those stated here.

EZcorp Inc

NAIC Code: 522298

www.ezcorp.com

TYPES OF BUSINESS:

Pawn Shops
Short-Term Loans
Auto Title Loans
Payday Loans

BRANDS/DIVISIONS/AFFILIATES:

EZPAWN
EZMONEY
Value Pawn & Jewelry
Grupo Finmat
Empeno Facil
Albermarle & Bond Holdings plc
Cash Converters International Limited
Prestaciones Finmart SAPI de CV

CONTACTS: Note: Officers with more than one job title may be intentionally listed here more than once.

Stuart Grimshaw, CEO
Mark Ashby, CFO
Lachlan Given, Chairman of the Board
Carl Spilker, Chief Risk Officer
Joseph Rotunda, Director
Thomas Welch, General Counsel
Jodie Maccarrone, Other Executive Officer
William Wood, Senior VP
Mark Trinske, Vice President, Divisional

GROWTH PLANS/SPECIAL FEATURES:

EZCorp, Inc. provides credit and other financial services to individuals who do not have cash resources or access to credit to meet their short-term financial needs. The company operates 497 U.S. pawn stores (operating as EZPAWN or Value Pawn & Jewelry), and 242 pawn stores in Mexico (operating as Empeno Facil); 501 U.S. financial services stores (operating primarily as EZMONEY), and 24 financial services stores in Canada (operating as CASHMAX); seven buy/sell stores in the U.S., 19 in Mexico and 15 in Canada (all operating as Cash Converters); and 53 Grupo Finmart locations in Mexico (operating as Crediamigo or Adex). At its pawn stores, the firm offers pawn loans (non-recourse loans collateralized by tangible personal property) and sells merchandise, primarily collateral forfeited from pawn lending operations. The firm also offers short-term non-collateralized loans, often called payday loans; auto title loans; and fee-based credit services at its EZMoney and CASHMAX stores. Typical items found at the stores include jewelry, electronics, tools, sporting goods and musical instruments, with jewelry accounting for approximately 53% of pawn loan collateral. Additionally, it owns approximately 32% of Cash Converters International Limited, an Australian company that franchises and operates a worldwide network of approximately 750 locations that provide financial services and buy and sell second-hand goods. In September 2015, the firm acquired 13 USA Pawn & Jewelry Company pawn stores located in Arizona and Oregon. That same year, it increased an additional 18% stake in Prestaciones Finmart SAPI de CV, owning a total 94% majority interest in the company. In 2014, the firm's joint venture, Albemarle & Bond plc entered bankruptcy reorganization in the U.K. and sold a majority of its business and assets.

FINANCIAL DATA: Note: Data for latest year may not have been available at press time.

In U.S. $	2015	2014	2013	2012	2011	2010
Revenue		988,532,000	1,010,307,000	992,467,000	869,317,000	733,045,000
R&D Expense						
Operating Income		96,617,000	138,991,000	201,440,000	173,963,000	141,886,000
Operating Margin %		9.77%	13.75%	20.29%	20.01%	19.35%
SGA Expense		482,169,000	466,699,000	397,521,000	342,322,000	289,404,000
Net Income		-45,740,000	34,077,000	143,708,000	122,159,000	97,294,000
Operating Cash Flow		89,244,000	126,473,000	150,448,000	148,441,000	124,725,000
Capital Expenditure		22,964,000	46,698,000	45,796,000	34,776,000	25,741,000
EBITDA		135,244,000	173,909,000	249,346,000	208,745,000	167,576,000
Return on Assets %		-3.32%	2.65%	14.55%	17.92%	17.70%
Return on Equity %		-5.11%	3.89%	19.17%	20.64%	20.80%
Debt to Equity		0.40	0.23	0.23	0.02	0.02

CONTACT INFORMATION:

Phone: 512 314-3400   Fax: 512 314-3404
Toll-Free: 800-873-7296
Address: 1901 Capital Pkwy., Austin, TX 78746 United States

STOCK TICKER/OTHER:

Stock Ticker: EZPW
Employees: 4,900
Parent Company:

Exchange: NAS
Fiscal Year Ends: 09/30

SALARIES/BONUSES:

Top Exec. Salary: $891,731   Bonus: $1,000,000
Second Exec. Salary: $807,692   Bonus: $1,000,000

OTHER THOUGHTS:

Estimated Female Officers or Directors: 1
Hot Spot for Advancement for Women/Minorities:

Family Dollar Stores Inc

www.familydollar.com

NAIC Code: 452112

TYPES OF BUSINESS:

Discount Stores
Dollar Stores

BRANDS/DIVISIONS/AFFILIATES:

Family Dollar
Dollar Tree Inc

CONTACTS: *Note: Officers with more than one job title may be intentionally listed here more than once.*

Gary M. Philbin, Pres.
Mary Winston, CFO
Barry Sullivan, Executive VP, Divisional
Jeffrey Macak, Executive VP, Divisional
James Snyder, General Counsel
Jason Reiser, Other Executive Officer
Bryan Venberg, Senior VP, Divisional

GROWTH PLANS/SPECIAL FEATURES:

Family Dollar Stores, Inc. operates a chain of roughly 8,100 general merchandise retail discount stores in the U.S., primarily serving low to lower-middle income consumers. These stores range in size from 7,500 to 9,500 square feet. The goods offered by Family Dollar generally have price points that range from under $1 to $10 and include apparel, food, cleaning products, paper products, home decor, beauty products, health aids, toys, pet products, automotive products, domestic items, seasonal goods and electronics. Substantially all of the firm's merchandise is purchased directly from the manufacturer. Family Dollar owns and operates 11 distribution centers. Nationally advertised brand name merchandise accounts for approximately 60% of Family Dollar's sales, with the rest accounting from the company's private label and closeout merchandise; consumables such as household chemicals, paper products, food, health & beauty items, hardware, automotive supplies and pet supplies; home products; seasonal and electronics.; and apparel and accessories. In July 2015, the firm was acquired by Dollar Tree, Inc.

Family Dollar Stores offers its employees medical, vision, dental and prescription drug benefits; life insurance; short- and long-term disability; flexible spending accounts; a 401(k) plan; and an employee stock purchase plan.

FINANCIAL DATA: *Note: Data for latest year may not have been available at press time.*

In U.S. $	2015	2014	2013	2012	2011	2010
Revenue		10,489,329,664	10,391,456,768	9,331,005,440	8,547,834,880	7,866,971,136
R&D Expense						
Operating Income						
Operating Margin %						
SGA Expense						
Net Income		284,503,008	443,575,008	422,240,000	388,444,992	358,135,008
Operating Cash Flow						
Capital Expenditure						
EBITDA						
Return on Assets %						
Return on Equity %						
Debt to Equity						

CONTACT INFORMATION:

Phone: 704 847-6961   Fax: 704 847-5534
Toll-Free:
Address: 10401 Old Monroe Rd., Charlotte, NC 28201 United States

STOCK TICKER/OTHER:

Stock Ticker: Subsidiary
Employees: 60,000
Parent Company: Dollar Tree Inc

Exchange:
Fiscal Year Ends: 08/31

SALARIES/BONUSES:

Top Exec. Salary: $ Bonus: $
Second Exec. Salary: $ Bonus: $

OTHER THOUGHTS:

Estimated Female Officers or Directors: 5
Hot Spot for Advancement for Women/Minorities: Y

FamilyMart Co Ltd

www.family.co.jp

NAIC Code: 445120

TYPES OF BUSINESS:
Convenience Stores

BRANDS/DIVISIONS/AFFILIATES:
FamilyMart
Okinawa FamilyMart Co Ltd
Minami Kyushu FamilyMart Co Ltd
Hokkaido FamilyMart Co Ltd
Taiwan FamilyMart Co Ltd
BGFretail Co Ltd
Famiport Multimedia Terminal
ViNa FamilyMart Co Ltd

CONTACTS: Note: Officers with more than one job title may be intentionally listed here more than once.
Junji Ueda, CEO
Isamu Nakayama, Pres.
Yoshiki Miyamoto, Sr. Managing Dir.
Akinori Wada, Managing Dir.
Toshio Kato, Managing Dir.

GROWTH PLANS/SPECIAL FEATURES:
FamilyMart Co., Ltd. is a Japan-based company that operates convenience stores. The company operates in two business segments: convenience stores and electronic commerce. The firm operates approximately 16,970 stores domestically and overseas in Taiwan, Thailand, China, Vietman, Indonesia and the Philippines under the FamilyMart brand name. The company conducts business through four Japanese franchisers, Okinawa FamilyMart Co., Ltd.; Minami Kyushu FamilyMart Co., Ltd.; Hokkaido FamilyMart Co., Ltd.; and JR Kyushu Retail, Inc., and nine franchisers, Taiwan FamilyMart Co., Ltd.; BGFretail Co., Ltd.; Siam FamilyMart Co., Ltd; Shanghai FamilyMart Co., Ltd.; Famima Corporation; Guangzhou FamilyMart Co., Ltd.; Suzhou FamilyMart Co., Ltd.; Dongguan FamilyMart Co., Ltd.; and Hangzhou FamilyMart Co., Ltd. FamilyMart's joint venture with ITOCHU Corporation, called ViNa FamilyMart Co. Ltd., operates the FamilyMart stores located in Vietnam. Its eight U.S. stores operate under the Famima!! Brand, with activities largely concentrated in Los Angeles, California. The firm's convenience stores offer four main products: fast food, which includes fried chicken, steamed meat buns and French fries; daily food, such as bento boxes, noodles, desserts and sandwiches; processed foods, including instant noodles, confectionary products, seasonings and alcoholic/nonalcoholic beverages; and nonfood items such as cigarettes and magazines. The stores also offer copying and express services. The electronic commerce segment, which operates through subsidiary Famiport Multimedia Terminal, is a provider of Internet shopping.

FINANCIAL DATA: Note: Data for latest year may not have been available at press time.

In U.S. $	2015	2014	2013	2012	2011	2010
Revenue	3,038,563,000	2,804,627,000	2,711,173,000	2,671,660,000	2,595,954,000	2,257,430,000
R&D Expense						
Operating Income	327,990,800	351,468,000	349,820,700	345,592,700	310,186,100	272,101,700
Operating Margin %	10.79%	12.53%	12.90%	12.93%	11.94%	12.05%
SGA Expense	173,689,000	166,028,300	164,275,400	166,344,800	172,918,000	163,715,500
Net Income	230,876,600	201,718,800	217,259,300	147,939,600	157,937,500	128,974,400
Operating Cash Flow	582,969,500	493,751,300	524,548,400	591,596,000	408,493,300	-53,349,130
Capital Expenditure	357,862,800	265,317,400	188,482,900	147,834,100	137,487,200	123,732,000
EBITDA	628,609,200	557,382,400	529,206,500	391,062,000	385,251,500	318,918,100
Return on Assets %	4.09%	4.05%	5.00%	3.64%	4.19%	3.67%
Return on Equity %	9.73%	9.15%	10.94%	7.75%	8.80%	7.73%
Debt to Equity	0.26	0.19	0.14	0.12	0.09	0.04

CONTACT INFORMATION:
Phone: 81-3-3989-6600   Fax:
Toll-Free:
Address: 3-1-1 Higashi-Ikebukuro, Sunshine 60 Bldg. 17/Fl, Tokyo, 170-6017 Japan

STOCK TICKER/OTHER:
Stock Ticker: FYRTF   Exchange: GREY
Employees: 7,500   Fiscal Year Ends:
Parent Company:

SALARIES/BONUSES:
Top Exec. Salary: $ Bonus: $
Second Exec. Salary: $ Bonus: $

OTHER THOUGHTS:
Estimated Female Officers or Directors:
Hot Spot for Advancement for Women/Minorities:

Sales, profits and employees may be estimates. Financial information, benefits and other data can change quickly and may vary from those stated here.

Fanatics Inc
NAIC Code: 454111

www.fanaticsinc.com

TYPES OF BUSINESS:
Electronic Shopping of Licensed Sports Merchandise

BRANDS/DIVISIONS/AFFILIATES:
Fanatics Authentic
Fanatics
FansEdge

GROWTH PLANS/SPECIAL FEATURES:
Fanatics, Inc. is an online retailer of licensed sport
merchandise. Customers can purchase merchandise throug
online sites through the Fanatics (Fanatics.com) an
FansEdge (FansEdge.com) brands. The firm also offers
collection of sports collectibles and memorabilia throug
Fanatics Authentic (FanaticsAuthentic.com). In addition to it
own sites, the firm also operates the sales sites of majo
professional sports leagues, including the NHL, NFL, MLB
NASCAR and PGA; major sport media brands, includin
ESPN, NBC and FOX Sports; and the sites of collegiate an
professional teams. Fanatics fulfills its orders from over 1.
million square feet of warehousing space.

CONTACTS: *Note: Officers with more than one job title may be intentionally listed here more than once.*
Doug Mack, CEO
Jamie Davis, Pres.
Thomas Baumlin, CFO
Chris Orton, CMO
Jack Boyle, Pres., Merch.
Mitch Trager, Chief Strategy Officer
Meier Raivich, VP-Branding
Gary Gertzog, Exec. VP-Bus. Affairs
Michael Rubin, Exec. Chmn.

FINANCIAL DATA: *Note: Data for latest year may not have been available at press time.*

In U.S. $	2015	2014	2013	2012	2011	2010
Revenue	1,200,000,000	1,150,000,000	1,000,000,000	800,000,000		
R&D Expense						
Operating Income						
Operating Margin %						
SGA Expense						
Net Income						
Operating Cash Flow						
Capital Expenditure						
EBITDA						
Return on Assets %						
Return on Equity %						
Debt to Equity						

CONTACT INFORMATION:
Phone: 904-421-1897   Fax:
Toll-Free: 877-833-7397
Address: 5245 Commonwealth Ave., Jacksonville, FL 32254 United States

STOCK TICKER/OTHER:
Stock Ticker: Private
Employees: 1,800
Parent Company:

Exchange:
Fiscal Year Ends:

SALARIES/BONUSES:
Top Exec. Salary: $ Bonus: $
Second Exec. Salary: $ Bonus: $

OTHER THOUGHTS:
Estimated Female Officers or Directors:
Hot Spot for Advancement for Women/Minorities:

Sales, profits and employees may be estimates. Financial information, benefits and other data can change quickly and may vary from those stated here.

Federation of Migros Cooperatives

www.migros.ch

NAIC Code: 445110

TYPES OF BUSINESS:

Grocery Stores
Department Stores
Furniture Stores
Sporting Goods Stores
Home & Garden Stores
Pharmaceutical Sales
Banking
Computers & Software

BRANDS/DIVISIONS/AFFILIATES:

Micasa
sportXX
Do It + Garden
Ex Libris
Migros Bank
Globus

CONTACTS: Note: Officers with more than one job title may be intentionally listed here more than once.

Herbert Bolliger, CEO
Herbert Bollinger, Pres.
Oskar Sager, Head-Mktg. Dept.
Gisele Girgis, Head-Human Resources
Andreas Munch, Head-IT
Annina Arpagaus, General Sec.
Muntwyler Raymond, Head-e-commerce
Monica Glisenti, Head-Corp. Comm.
Joerg Zulauf, VP
Walter Huber, Head-Industry Dept.
Claude Hauser, Chmn.
Andreas Munch, Head-Logistics Dept.

GROWTH PLANS/SPECIAL FEATURES:

Federation of Migros Cooperatives (Migros), founded in 1925, is one of Switzerland's largest retailers and private employers. The firm sells prescriptions and over-the-counter drugs, groceries, house and garden supplies, sports and wellness equipment, pet supplies, beauty and fashion products and electronics and operates travel agencies, gas stations, banks, catering services and hotels. It also offers meeting areas for local groups, travel services, books, movies and videos, computers and related software and a job exchange service for local communities. Migros owns and operates over 700 stores, including supermarkets, which average about 36,000 square feet of floor space; department stores; and specialized market stores. A large part of the company's products that are sold in the Migros supermarkets are produced by its own companies (20), 17 of which are in Switzerland, and produce more than 20,000 products. Subsidiaries include the furniture store line Micasa; the sporting goods line sportXX; Do It + Garden, a home improvement line for garden and other outdoor supplies; Ex Libris, a book and stationary store; and Globus, a gas station and convenience store. The company also offers banking services through Migros Bank. Migros is one of Switzerland's most famous and respected brand names. In other European countries, the firm offers importing and exporting services, including packing and shipping.

FINANCIAL DATA: Note: Data for latest year may not have been available at press time.

In U.S. $	2015	2014	2013	2012	2011	2010
Revenue		5,794,289,574	5,658,715,858			
R&D Expense						
Operating Income						
Operating Margin %						
SGA Expense						
Net Income		72,412,365	52,600,650			
Operating Cash Flow						
Capital Expenditure						
EBITDA						
Return on Assets %						
Return on Equity %						
Debt to Equity						

CONTACT INFORMATION:

Phone: 41-1-277-21-11   Fax: 41-1-277-25-25
Toll-Free:
Address: Limmatstrasse 152, Zurich, 8031 Switzerland

STOCK TICKER/OTHER:

Stock Ticker: Private
Employees:
Parent Company:

Exchange:
Fiscal Year Ends: 09/30

SALARIES/BONUSES:

Top Exec. Salary: $ Bonus: $
Second Exec. Salary: $ Bonus: $

OTHER THOUGHTS:

Estimated Female Officers or Directors: 4
Hot Spot for Advancement for Women/Minorities: Y

Ferguson Enterprises Inc

www.ferguson.com

NAIC Code: 444190

TYPES OF BUSINESS:

Plumbing Supplies, Retail
Wholesale Distribution
Construction Supplies, Retail
Waterworks Supplies
HVAC Equipment, Retail
PVF Supplies, Retail

BRANDS/DIVISIONS/AFFILIATES:

Wolseley plc
Ferguson Xpress
HP Products Corporation
Builders Appliance Center LLC
Ar-Jay Building Products Inc
Equarius Inc

CONTACTS: Note: Officers with more than one job title may be intentionally listed here more than once.

Frank W. Roach, CEO
Kevin Murphy, COO
Frank W. Roach, Pres.
Dave Keltner, CFO

GROWTH PLANS/SPECIAL FEATURES:

Ferguson Enterprises, Inc. is one of the largest wholesale distributors of plumbing supplies in the U.S. The company has been a subsidiary of Wolseley plc, one of largest distributors of plumbing and heating products in the world, since 1982. Ferguson has approximately 1,400 locations in all 50 U.S. states, Puerto Rico, the Caribbean and Mexico. Additionally, the firm operates Ferguson Xpress stores, largely self-service locations that market plumbing and light commercial products to contractors. In general, Ferguson's customers include homeowners, builders, contractors, engineers and other trade professionals. Ferguson operates in eight business groups: residential, heating and cooling equipment, industrial, commercial and mechanical, waterworks, hospitality, government and integrated services. The company's product offerings include plumbing supplies; pipes, valves and fittings; heating, ventilation and air conditioning (HVAC); waterworks; lighting; appliances; tools and safety equipment; gas fireplaces; and fire protection products. An internal delivery service moves products from distribution hubs to Ferguson branches, satellites and customers. Through other divisions, the company is involved in nuclear power provision, fire protection supply, valve assembly and testing and geosynthetic product supply to the mining industry. In 2015, the company acquired HP Products Corporation, a plumbing wholesale distributor; Builders Appliance Center, LLC; an appliance dealer; Ar-Jay Building Products, Inc., a cabinet, lighting and fireplace showroom; Equarius, Inc., a Neptune Meter distributor; Redlon & Johnson Supply, the plumbing distribution division of The Gage Company; and eight other companies.

Ferguson offers employees medical, dental and vision coverage; a 401(k) plan; short- and long-term disability; life insurance; flexible spending accounts; educational assistance; paid leave; onsite employee training courses; and a performance awards program.

FINANCIAL DATA: Note: Data for latest year may not have been available at press time.

In U.S. $	2015	2014	2013	2012	2011	2010
Revenue		11,660,000,000	10,600,000,000	10,815,862,000	10,927,063,684	10,640,992,102
R&D Expense						
Operating Income						
Operating Margin %						
SGA Expense						
Net Income		418,051,240	360,389,000	62,864,370	218,370,685	-274,026,747
Operating Cash Flow						
Capital Expenditure						
EBITDA						
Return on Assets %						
Return on Equity %						
Debt to Equity						

CONTACT INFORMATION:

Phone: 757-874-7795   Fax: 757-989-2501
Toll-Free:
Address: 12500 Jefferson Ave., Newport News, VA 23602 United States

STOCK TICKER/OTHER:

Stock Ticker: Subsidiary   Exchange:
Employees: 19,000   Fiscal Year Ends: 07/31
Parent Company: WOLSELEY PLC

SALARIES/BONUSES:

Top Exec. Salary: $ Bonus: $
Second Exec. Salary: $ Bonus: $

OTHER THOUGHTS:

Estimated Female Officers or Directors: 3
Hot Spot for Advancement for Women/Minorities: Y

Fila USA Inc

www.fila.com

NAIC Code: 424300

TYPES OF BUSINESS:
Apparel and Clothing Brands, Designers, Importers and Distributors
Footwear
Casual Wear

BRANDS/DIVISIONS/AFFILIATES:
Fila Korea Ltd
Essenza
Heritage
Baseline
Center Court
Collezione

CONTACTS: Note: Officers with more than one job title may be intentionally listed here more than once.
Jon Epstein, Pres.
Young-Chan Cho, CFO
Robert Erb, CMO
Sandy Hamilton, Dir.-IT
Jarita Bridges, Mgr.-Prod. Placement & Entertainment Mktg.
Kelly Macmanus Funke, Sr. Mgr.-e-commerce
Jarita Bridges, Head-Investor Rel.
Gene Yoon, CEO
Rob Baker, Dir.-Sportstyle Mktg.

GROWTH PLANS/SPECIAL FEATURES:
Fila USA, Inc., a subsidiary of Fila Korea Ltd., produces athletic footwear, apparel and accessories for men, women and children. Its products are segmented into categories based on sport applications, with specific lines tailored for basketball, tennis, soccer, yoga, fitness and training. These products are designed to complement athletes' movements. Its tennis line features a number of individual collections, from the classic Heritage collection to the updated Baseline, Center Court, Collezione and Essenza lines. The company has also introduced athletic apparel lines in collaboration with athletes including James Blake, Janko Tipsarevic and Dmitry Tursunov. In addition to athletic wear, Fila offers a line of lifestyle clothing designed for a younger, more style conscious shopper, featuring vintage styling and updated classics from Fila's history. The firm's original focus revolved around the textiles business before going on to specialize in knitwear production. The company entered the sports industry in 1973, after consolidating its expertise in the Italian textiles industry. Fila established itself in the tennis apparel industry with its innovative tubular manufacturing process that, until then, was only used for other products. It was also Fila that challenged the white-only tradition on tennis courts by creating a line of colored tennis apparel. The firm is committed to using cutting-edge technology and innovative materials.

The firm offers employees a health, dental and vision plan; short- and long-term disability; additional coverage through Aflac; a flexible spending account; a 401(k) savings plan; and an employee discount.

FINANCIAL DATA: Note: Data for latest year may not have been available at press time.

In U.S. $	2015	2014	2013	2012	2011	2010
Revenue		279,200,000	216,200,000	158,800,000		
R&D Expense						
Operating Income						
Operating Margin %						
SGA Expense						
Net Income						
Operating Cash Flow						
Capital Expenditure						
EBITDA						
Return on Assets %						
Return on Equity %						
Debt to Equity						

CONTACT INFORMATION:
Phone: 212-726-5900 Fax:
Toll-Free: 800-845-3452
Address: 340 Madison Ave, Fl. 3, New York, NY 10173 United States

STOCK TICKER/OTHER:
Stock Ticker: Subsidiary
Employees:
Parent Company: FILA KOREA LTD

Exchange:
Fiscal Year Ends: 12/31

SALARIES/BONUSES:
Top Exec. Salary: $ Bonus: $
Second Exec. Salary: $ Bonus: $

OTHER THOUGHTS:
Estimated Female Officers or Directors: 3
Hot Spot for Advancement for Women/Minorities: Y

Sales, profits and employees may be estimates. Financial information, benefits and other data can change quickly and may vary from those stated here.

Filippa K

NAIC Code: 424300

www.filippa-k.com

TYPES OF BUSINESS:
Apparel and Clothing Brands, Designers, Importers and Distributors
Apparel Stores

BRANDS/DIVISIONS/AFFILIATES:

GROWTH PLANS/SPECIAL FEATURES:

Filippa K is a Swedish company engaged in the design
manufacture and retailing of fashion apparel and accessorie
for men and women. The company's products include blouse
shirts, dresses, jackets, jeans, knits, outerwear, shoes, skirt
tights, trousers and accessories such as belts, wallet
handbags, hats, neckties, scarves and gloves. Filippa K
represented in 20 markets worldwide through 50 brand store
its own e-commerce business and more than 600 retailers suc
as Liberty, Bijenkorf, NK, Stockman and Illum. The compan
was founded in 1993 by Filippa Knutsson and Patrik Kihlborg
from a personal longing for sophisticated and clean fashio
The Filippa K brand is built on three core values: style
simplicity and quality. Filippa K operates offices in Austria
Belgium, Canada, Denmark, Finland, France, Germany, th
Netherlands, Norway, Spain, Sweden and the U.K.

CONTACTS: *Note: Officers with more than one job title may be intentionally listed here more than once.*
Amelie Soderberg, CEO
Magdalena Rodell Andersson, CFO
Eva Boding, Dir.-Mktg.
Birgitta Andersson, Mgr.-Human Resources
Susanna Liljeqvist, Mgr.-IT
Elin Larsson, Mgr.-Corp. Responsibility
Nina Bogstedt, Dir.-Range
Krister Nylund, Mgr.-Wholesale
Peter Cosmus, Mgr.-Int'l
Tomas Framberg, Mgr.-Supply Chain

FINANCIAL DATA: *Note: Data for latest year may not have been available at press time.*

In U.S. $	2015	2014	2013	2012	2011	2010
Revenue		115,000,000	110,000,000	100,000,000	81,521,380	62,332,536
R&D Expense						
Operating Income						
Operating Margin %						
SGA Expense						
Net Income						
Operating Cash Flow						
Capital Expenditure						
EBITDA						
Return on Assets %						
Return on Equity %						
Debt to Equity						

CONTACT INFORMATION:
Phone: 46-8-615-7000   Fax:
Toll-Free:
Address: Soder Malarstrand 65, 9tr, Stockholm, 118 25 Sweden

STOCK TICKER/OTHER:
Stock Ticker: Private
Employees: 200
Parent Company:

Exchange:
Fiscal Year Ends:

SALARIES/BONUSES:
Top Exec. Salary: $ Bonus: $
Second Exec. Salary: $ Bonus: $

OTHER THOUGHTS:
Estimated Female Officers or Directors: 10
Hot Spot for Advancement for Women/Minorities: Y

Finish Line Inc (The)

www.finishline.com

NAIC Code: 448210

TYPES OF BUSINESS:

Athletic Shoes, Retail
Activewear
Athletic Accessories

BRANDS/DIVISIONS/AFFILIATES:

Finish Line
FinishLine.com
M.FinishLine.com
Runnning Specialty

CONTACTS: *Note: Officers with more than one job title may be intentionally listed here more than once.*

Glenn Lyon, CEO
Edward Wilhelm, CFO
Daniel Marous, Executive VP, Divisional
Melissa Greenwell, Executive VP
Imran Jooma, Executive VP
Bill Kirkendall, Executive VP
Christopher Eck, General Counsel
Samuel Sato, President

GROWTH PLANS/SPECIAL FEATURES:

The Finish Line, Inc. is a mall-based specialty retailer of men's, women's and children's brand-name athletic, outdoor and casual footwear; activewear; and accessories in the U.S. The company owns and operates 634 Finish Line stores in 45 states, which average approximately 5,463 square feet. The firm attracts its core customers, typically males between 18 and 24, with a full range of leading athletic branded merchandise, including Nike, Brand Jordan, Reebok, adidas, Under Armour, Asics, Brooks, New Balance, Mizuno, The North Face and many others. Footwear products are categorized into sections by application, including basketball, running, sport style, fitness and outdoor. Most categories are available in men's, women's and children's styles. Footwear accounts for approximately 89% of the firm's net sales. The company purchases products from approximately 75 suppliers and manufacturers, the largest of which, Nike, represents around 73% of annual purchasing. Its stores also offer a range of softgoods products and licensed apparel, socks, athletic bags, backpacks, sunglasses, watches and shoe-care products, along with core basics apparel under a private label. The Finish Line maintains an e-commerce business through FinishLine.com and a mobile commerce site at M.FinishLine.com. In addition to Finish Line-branded locations, the firm operates 76 Running Specialty stores, a specialty running retailer of precision-fitted running shoes, apparel and accessories. Finish Line is the exclusive provider of athletic shoes, both in-store and online at Macy's, Inc., and manages the footwear and inventory for approximately 395 Macy's department stores in 37 U.S. states, District of Columbia and Puerto Rico.

The Finish Line offers its employees an education reimbursement plan; employee discounts; a stock purchase plan; a 401(k) savings plan; profit sharing; basic life insurance; and medical, dental, vision and prescription drug coverage plans.

FINANCIAL DATA: *Note: Data for latest year may not have been available at press time.*

In U.S. $	2015	2014	2013	2012	2011	2010
Revenue	1,820,586,000	1,670,410,000	1,443,365,000	1,369,259,000	1,229,002,000	1,172,415,000
R&D Expense						
Operating Income	120,430,000	120,105,000	112,297,000	134,335,000	109,633,000	72,058,000
Operating Margin %	6.61%	7.19%	7.78%	9.81%	8.92%	6.14%
SGA Expense	459,455,000	425,284,000	365,883,000	344,820,000	303,068,000	300,030,000
Net Income	81,993,000	76,903,000	71,473,000	84,804,000	68,834,000	35,672,000
Operating Cash Flow	101,802,000	118,984,000	81,493,000	94,740,000	108,574,000	157,458,000
Capital Expenditure	88,087,000	81,668,000	81,586,000	29,681,000	19,088,000	8,454,000
EBITDA	158,903,000	155,069,000	143,479,000	161,362,000	136,592,000	102,035,000
Return on Assets %	9.67%	10.04%	10.08%	12.32%	10.79%	5.90%
Return on Equity %	13.82%	13.89%	13.55%	16.63%	14.76%	8.23%
Debt to Equity						

CONTACT INFORMATION:

Phone: 317 899-1022   Fax: 317 895-2884
Toll-Free: 888-777-3949
Address: 3308 N. Mitthoeffer Rd., Indianapolis, IN 46235 United States

STOCK TICKER/OTHER:

Stock Ticker: FINL
Employees: 12,300
Parent Company:

Exchange: NAS
Fiscal Year Ends: 02/28

SALARIES/BONUSES:

Top Exec. Salary: $990,000   Bonus: $
Second Exec. Salary: $635,000   Bonus: $

OTHER THOUGHTS:

Estimated Female Officers or Directors: 3
Hot Spot for Advancement for Women/Minorities: Y

Sales, profits and employees may be estimates. Financial information, benefits and other data can change quickly and may vary from those stated here.

First Cash Financial Services Inc

www.firstcash.com

NAIC Code: 522298

TYPES OF BUSINESS:

Pawn Shops
Check Cashing
Cash Advance
Credit Services
Money Orders & Transfers
Credit Services Program

BRANDS/DIVISIONS/AFFILIATES:

Cash & Go Ltd
First Cash Advance

CONTACTS: Note: Officers with more than one job title may be intentionally listed here more than once.

Rick Wessel, CEO
R. Orr, CFO
Anna Alvarado, General Counsel
Peter Watson, Senior VP, Divisional
Raul Ramos, Senior VP, Divisional
Sean Moore, Senior VP, Divisional

GROWTH PLANS/SPECIAL FEATURES:

First Cash Financial Services, Inc. (FCFS) is a provider of pawn shops and specialty financial services. The company operates more than 1,000 locations across 13 U.S. states and 29 states in Mexico. The firm's pawn stores engage in both consumer finance and retail sales activities. They are a source for small consumer loans, advancing money against pledged tangible personal property such as jewelry, electronics, tools, sporting goods and music equipment. The pawn stores also retail previously-owned merchandise acquired through collateral forfeitures and over-the-counter purchases from customers. The firm also operates cash advance and consumer loan locations in Texas under the name First Cash Advance. These stores provide consumer financial services products including cash advances, title loans, credit services, check cashing, money orders, money transfers and prepaid card products. Additionally, FCFS is a 50% partner in Cash & Go, Ltd., a joint venture that currently owns and operates 37 check cashing and financial services kiosks located inside convenience stores in Texas. The company derives 60% of its revenues from retail merchandise sales, 28% from pawn loan fees, 5.2% from consumer loan & credit services fees and 6.8% from wholesale scrap jewelry. U.S. operations account for approximately 46% of the firm's revenues, while Mexico operations account for roughly 54%. In August 2014, the company acquired 47 pawn stores in 12 states in Mexico, 12 stores in South Carolina and 15 pawn stores in Southeastern U.S. In 2015, it acquired a 25-store chain of large format pawnshops, with 24 locations in North Carolina and one in Virginia, and acquired two pawn stores in Kentucky.

FINANCIAL DATA: Note: Data for latest year may not have been available at press time.

In U.S. $	2015	2014	2013	2012	2011	2010
Revenue		712,877,000	660,848,000	595,946,000	521,302,000	431,147,000
R&D Expense						
Operating Income		129,825,000	120,192,000	122,611,000	108,203,000	84,629,000
Operating Margin %		18.21%	18.18%	20.57%	20.75%	19.62%
SGA Expense		253,572,000	230,851,000	201,830,000	175,676,000	158,776,000
Net Income		85,166,000	83,846,000	80,359,000	77,782,000	57,658,000
Operating Cash Flow		97,679,000	106,718,000	88,792,000	80,375,000	73,645,000
Capital Expenditure		23,954,000	26,672,000	21,841,000	28,974,000	18,385,000
EBITDA		147,983,000	139,045,000	137,074,000	119,364,000	95,533,000
Return on Assets %		12.39%	14.37%	18.58%	22.23%	19.26%
Return on Equity %		19.73%	21.86%	24.06%	25.36%	22.59%
Debt to Equity		0.49	0.45	0.31		

CONTACT INFORMATION:

Phone: 817 460-3947   Fax: 817 461-7019
Toll-Free:
Address: 690 E. Lamar Blvd., Ste. 400, Arlington, TX 76011 United States

STOCK TICKER/OTHER:

Stock Ticker: FCFS
Employees: 7,900   Exchange: NAS
Parent Company: Fiscal Year Ends: 12/31

SALARIES/BONUSES:

Top Exec. Salary: $992,000   Bonus: $
Second Exec. Salary: Bonus: $400,000
$335,000

OTHER THOUGHTS:

Estimated Female Officers or Directors:
Hot Spot for Advancement for Women/Minorities:

Fisher Auto Parts Inc

www.fisherautoparts.com

NAIC Code: 441310

TYPES OF BUSINESS:

Auto Parts, Retail
Computer Systems

BRANDS/DIVISIONS/AFFILIATES:

Federated Auto Parts

CONTACTS: Note: Officers with more than one job title may be intentionally listed here more than once.

Bo Fisher, CEO
Arthur J. (Bo) Fisher, III, Pres.
Ken Cox, Treas.
Gregory Haan, Exec. VP
Mike Allen, VP

GROWTH PLANS/SPECIAL FEATURES:

Fisher Auto Parts, Inc., privately owned by the Fisher family, retails automotive parts to professional and amateur installers. The company operates through stores in 15 states and several distribution centers. Its products include parts related to brakes, chassis, exhaust systems, lighting, fuel systems, chemicals and oils, car paint and bodies, electrical components, heating and cooling components, tools and equipment, engines, ignitions and emissions. Suppliers of these products include companies such as Castrol; USA Industries; Dorman; Standard Motor Products, Inc.; World Wide Automotive; Anco; Wagner Lighting; Equus; Lisle; Schumacher Electric Corporation; Five Star Manufacturing; American Grease Stick, Co.; Amalie; Clean Rite; J-B Weld; Lubrimatic; Mobil; Pennzoil; Valvoline; WD-40; Bayco; Cardone Industries; 3M; BWD Automotive; and Campbell Hausfeld. In addition, the company offers business computer systems for the auto parts installer business in the form of parts ordering, point of sale (POS) and business management programs and electronic part and labor guides. The firm is a founding member of Federated Auto Parts, an auto parts distribution network of 100 corporations that serves more than 3,800 retail locations.

FINANCIAL DATA: Note: Data for latest year may not have been available at press time.

In U.S. $	2015	2014	2013	2012	2011	2010
Revenue						
R&D Expense						
Operating Income						
Operating Margin %						
SGA Expense						
Net Income						
Operating Cash Flow						
Capital Expenditure						
EBITDA						
Return on Assets %						
Return on Equity %						
Debt to Equity						

CONTACT INFORMATION:

Phone: 540-885-8901   Fax:
Toll-Free:
Address: 512 Greenville Ave., Staunton, VA 24401 United States

STOCK TICKER/OTHER:

Stock Ticker: Private
Employees: 5,100
Parent Company:

Exchange:
Fiscal Year Ends: 12/31

SALARIES/BONUSES:

Top Exec. Salary: $ Bonus: $
Second Exec. Salary: $ Bonus: $

OTHER THOUGHTS:

Estimated Female Officers or Directors:
Hot Spot for Advancement for Women/Minorities:

Sales, profits and employees may be estimates. Financial information, benefits and other data can change quickly and may vary from those stated here.

Five Below Inc

NAIC Code: 452112

TYPES OF BUSINESS:

Limited Price Variety Stores

BRANDS/DIVISIONS/AFFILIATES:

CONTACTS: Note: Officers with more than one job title may be intentionally listed here more than once.

Joel Anderson, CEO
Kenneth Bull, CFO
Thomas Vellios, Chairman of the Board
Eric Specter, Chief Administrative Officer
Michael Romanko, Executive VP, Divisional
Karen Procell, Secretary

GROWTH PLANS/SPECIAL FEATURES:

Five Below, Inc. is a specialty value retailer offering a broa
range of trend-right, high-quality merchandise targeted at tee
and pre-teen customers. It offers a dynamic, edited assortmer
of exciting products, all priced at $5 and below, including sele
brands and licensed merchandise across a number of
categories. The firm has over 366 stores located throughout 2
states. It organizes merchandise into the following categories
Style, which consists primarily of accessories such as novelt
socks, sunglasses, jewelry, scarves, gloves, hair accessorie
and attitude t-shirts; Room, which consists of items used to
complete and personalize its customer's living space, including
glitter lamps, posters, frames, fleece blankets, pillows, candles
incense and related items; Sports, including an assortment c
sport balls, team sports merchandise and fitness accessories
including hand weights, jump ropes and gym balls; Tech
consisting of a broad selection of accessories for PCs, ce
phones, MP3 players and tablet computers; Crafts, including a
wide assortment of craft activity kits, as well as arts and craft
supplies such as crayons, markers and stickers; and Seasona
(including the Party, Candy and Now categories), which
consists of seasonally-specific items used to celebrate and
decorate for events such as Christmas, Easter, Halloween and
St. Patrick's Day.

FINANCIAL DATA: Note: Data for latest year may not have been available at press time.

In U.S. $	2015	2014	2013	2012	2011	2010
Revenue	680,218,000	535,402,000	418,825,000	297,113,000	197,189,000	125,135,000
R&D Expense						
Operating Income	77,016,000	53,737,000	37,654,000	26,221,000	11,804,000	6,878,000
Operating Margin %	11.32%					
SGA Expense	160,775,000	134,279,000	112,182,000	78,640,000	54,339,000	33,217,000
Net Income	48,024,000	32,142,000	20,025,000	16,078,000	7,023,000	11,658,000
Operating Cash Flow	61,430,000	31,187,000	30,363,000	46,695,000	15,045,000	9,227,000
Capital Expenditure	32,322,000	25,931,000	22,890,000	18,558,000	14,883,000	7,285,000
EBITDA	94,218,000	67,206,000	47,253,000	33,292,000	16,609,000	10,538,000
Return on Assets %	18.22%	15.02%	-27.99%	13.41%	-1.06%	
Return on Equity %	32.97%	33.76%				
Debt to Equity			0.27			

CONTACT INFORMATION:

Phone: 215-546-7909   Fax:
Toll-Free:
Address: 1818 Market St., Ste. 1900, Philadelphia, PA 19103 United
States

STOCK TICKER/OTHER:

Stock Ticker: FIVE   Exchange: NAS
Employees: 6,700   Fiscal Year Ends: 01/31
Parent Company:

SALARIES/BONUSES:

Top Exec. Salary: $700,000   Bonus: $
Second Exec. Salary: Bonus: $
$378,650

OTHER THOUGHTS:

Estimated Female Officers or Directors:
Hot Spot for Advancement for Women/Minorities:

FJ Benjamin Holdings

www.fjbenjamin.com

NAIC Code: 448120

TYPES OF BUSINESS:

Apparel Stores
Clothing Distribution
Timepieces Retailing & Distribution

BRANDS/DIVISIONS/AFFILIATES:

FJ Benjamin (Taiwan) Ltd
FJ Benjamin Italy SRL
FJ Benjamin (Shanghai) Co Ltd
FJ Benjamin Fashions (US) Inc
Archangel Limited
RAOUL

CONTACTS: *Note: Officers with more than one job title may be intentionally listed here more than once.*

Eli Manasseh (Nash) Benjamin, CEO
Douglas Benjamin, COO
Karen Chong Mee Kang, CFO
Karen Chong Mee Kang, Corp. Sec.
Ian Lim, CEO-FJ Benjamin (Singapore) Pte Ltd.
Yeoh Oon Lai, CEO-Malaysia
David Nam, Gen. Mgr.-Shanghai
Frank Benjamin, Chmn.
Tony Fung, CEO-Hong Kong & Taiwan
Kim Tiong Quah, Dir.-Wholesale & Dist., Singapore

GROWTH PLANS/SPECIAL FEATURES:

FJ Benjamin Holdings is engaged in the retail and distribution of men's and women's clothing and accessories. The firm operates in four divisions: luxury and lifestyle fashion retailing and distribution, creative and design, timepiece distribution and investment. The luxury and lifestyle fashion division consolidates the firm's retail and distribution activities in Southeast Asia and Australia, offering such brands as Banana Republic, Catherine Deane, Celine, Gap, Givenchy, Goyard, GUESS, La Senza, RAOUL and Sheridan. The creative and design segment licenses the firm's in-house brand, RAOUL. The division also designs and manufactures merchandise. The timepiece distribution division distributes watches across Asia. Watch brands include Bell & Ross, ChronoSwiss, DeWitt, Girard-Perregaux, Gc, GUESS, Marc Ecko, Nautica, Victorinox Swiss Army, Rado and Sottomarino. The investment division consolidates FJ Benjamin's holdings in non-fashion ventures. FJ Benjamin controls more than 20 brands and operates 218 retail locations. Some of the firm's subsidiaries include F J Benjamin (Shanghai) Co., Ltd.; FJ Benjamin Fashions (U.S.), Inc.; FJ Benjamin (Taiwan) Ltd.; Archangel Limited; and FJ Benjamin Italy SRL.

FINANCIAL DATA: *Note: Data for latest year may not have been available at press time.*

In U.S. $	2015	2014	2013	2012	2011	2010
Revenue	207,852,800	260,836,900	264,522,800	278,573,400	250,719,400	204,982,300
R&D Expense						
Operating Income	-6,699,443	-8,474,012	5,813,221	14,392,790	13,002,180	3,637,690
Operating Margin %	-3.22%	-3.24%	2.19%	5.16%	5.18%	1.77%
SGA Expense	13,432,890	8,922,436	19,418,960	12,470,870	10,760,760	6,735,572
Net Income	-12,034,490	-15,657,300	3,150,304	9,592,593	9,046,408	5,851,475
Operating Cash Flow	-7,610,459	8,623,487	-6,568,387	-4,790,275	4,976,587	18,536,280
Capital Expenditure	3,181,474	11,729,160	7,584,957	6,017,952	5,556,068	3,645,483
EBITDA	-2,536,111	-4,527,455	13,004,300	20,815,240	17,766,240	13,183,530
Return on Assets %	-7.72%	-8.41%	1.62%	4.99%	4.80%	3.25%
Return on Equity %	-18.11%	-18.89%	3.35%	10.47%	9.65%	5.84%
Debt to Equity	0.07	0.03	0.05	0.01		

CONTACT INFORMATION:

Phone: 65 67370155   Fax: 65 67329616
Toll-Free:
Address: 10 Science Park Rd., 04-01 The Alpha, Singapore, 117684 Singapore

STOCK TICKER/OTHER:

Stock Ticker: FJBHF
Employees: 3,000
Parent Company:

Exchange: GREY
Fiscal Year Ends: 06/30

SALARIES/BONUSES:

Top Exec. Salary: $ Bonus: $
Second Exec. Salary: $ Bonus: $

OTHER THOUGHTS:

Estimated Female Officers or Directors: 7
Hot Spot for Advancement for Women/Minorities: Y

Foot Locker Inc

NAIC Code: 448210

www.footlocker-inc.com

TYPES OF BUSINESS:

Athletic Shoes, Retail
Athletic Apparel
Catalogs
Online Sales
Athletic Equipment

BRANDS/DIVISIONS/AFFILIATES:

Foot Locker
Lady Foot Locker
Kids Foot Locker
Champs Sports
Eastbay Inc
Footaction
SIX:02
final-score.com

CONTACTS: Note: Officers with more than one job title may be intentionally listed here more than once.

Lauren Peters, CFO
Giovanna Cipriano, Chief Accounting Officer
Peter Brown, Chief Information Officer
Nicholas Dipaolo, Director
Richard Johnson, Director
Robert Mchugh, Executive VP, Divisional
Paulette Alviti, Other Executive Officer
Jeffrey Berk, Senior VP, Divisional
Sheilagh Clarke, Senior VP
John Maurer, Treasurer

GROWTH PLANS/SPECIAL FEATURES:

Foot Locker, Inc. is one of the largest athletic footwear and apparel retailers in the world, operating approximately 3,423 stores in the U.S., Canada, Europe, Australia and New Zealand. The company operates several store formats, including Foot Locker, Lady Foot Locker, Kids Foot Locker, Champs Sports, Footaction and SIX:02. Foot Locker stores offer athletic-inspired performance products, manufactured primarily by the leading athletic brands. These stores offer products for activities such as running, basketball and cross-training. Lady Foot Locker is a U.S. retailer of athletic footwear, apparel and accessories for active women. Kids Foot Locker offers brand name athletic footwear, apparel and accessories for infants, boys and girls. Champs Sports is a mall-based retailer of specialty athletic footwear and apparel as well as an assortment of sporting equipment. Footaction stores offer athletic footwear and clothing with a street-inspired fashion style. The primary customers of Footaction are young males. SIX:02 is a fitness apparel brand and retailer marketed to women for any activity, style or body type. Retail locations also feature fitness zones, fitting lounge areas and a trained Fit Crew. In addition to its retail stores, the direct-to-customers segment, through affiliates such as Eastbay, Inc., sells merchandise through catalogs and web sites, including eastbay.com, final-score.com, eastbayteamsales.com, runnerspoint.com and sp24.com, as well as all Foot Locker web sites. In 2014, the CCS brand was transferred under the Eastbay banner.

FINANCIAL DATA: Note: Data for latest year may not have been available at press time.

In U.S. $	2015	2014	2013	2012	2011	2010
Revenue	7,151,000,000	6,505,000,000	6,182,000,000	5,623,000,000	5,049,000,000	4,854,000,000
R&D Expense						
Operating Income	809,000,000	666,000,000	610,000,000	437,000,000	262,000,000	70,000,000
Operating Margin %	11.31%	10.23%	9.86%	7.77%	5.18%	1.44%
SGA Expense	1,426,000,000	1,334,000,000	1,294,000,000	1,244,000,000	1,138,000,000	1,099,000,000
Net Income	520,000,000	429,000,000	397,000,000	278,000,000	169,000,000	48,000,000
Operating Cash Flow	712,000,000	530,000,000	416,000,000	497,000,000	326,000,000	345,000,000
Capital Expenditure	190,000,000	206,000,000	163,000,000	152,000,000	97,000,000	89,000,000
EBITDA	948,000,000	799,000,000	736,000,000	552,000,000	368,000,000	195,000,000
Return on Assets %	14.72%	12.51%	12.37%	9.35%	5.91%	1.68%
Return on Equity %	20.83%	17.60%	17.69%	13.44%	8.50%	2.47%
Debt to Equity	0.05	0.05	0.05	0.06	0.06	0.07

CONTACT INFORMATION:

Phone: 212 720-3700   Fax: 212 553-7026
Toll-Free: 800-991-6815
Address: 112 W. 34th St., New York, NY 10120 United States

STOCK TICKER/OTHER:

Stock Ticker: FL   Exchange: NYS
Employees: 44,568   Fiscal Year Ends: 01/31
Parent Company:

SALARIES/BONUSES:

Top Exec. Salary: $1,075,000   Bonus: $
Second Exec. Salary: $931,250   Bonus: $

OTHER THOUGHTS:

Estimated Female Officers or Directors: 3

Hot Spot for Advancement for Women/Minorities: Y

Forever 21 Inc

www.forever21.com

NAIC Code: 448120

TYPES OF BUSINESS:

Apparel-Women's & Men's, Retail
Accessories
Footwear
Cosmetics
Lingerie
Online Sales

BRANDS/DIVISIONS/AFFILIATES:

Forever XXI
F 21 Red
Forever 21 + Plus Size
Heritage 1981
Forever21.com

CONTACTS: Note: Officers with more than one job title may be intentionally listed here more than once.

Do Won Chang, CEO
Elizabeth Jain, CFO

GROWTH PLANS/SPECIAL FEATURES:

Forever 21, Inc. operates more than 730 largely mall-based clothing stores in 48 countries. Its retailers are located in the U.S., Australia, Brazil, Canada, China, France, Germany, Hong Kong, India, Israel, Japan, Korea, Latin America, Mexico, Philippines and the U.K. The company's business model is fast fashion, that is, to quickly imitate and manufacture the latest fashions and sell them at a low price. Traditional Forever 21 stores average 38,000 square feet in size, offering competitively priced trendy clothing, lingerie, cosmetics and accessories for women and junior girls. Forever XXI is the company's flagship store concept. Love 21 Contemporary is the firm's low priced sophisticated contemporary line. Forever 21 + Plus Size is the firm's plus size line. Heritage 1981 sells casual wear for girls and guys. F 21 Red offers lower prices than traditional Forever 21 stores, with deals like $1.80 camisoles, $3.80 t-shirts and $7.80 jeans. In addition to its retail locations, customers can buy clothing through the firm's online web site Forever21.com. Forever 21's goal is to become an $8 billion company by 2017 and open 600 new stores in the next three years.

FINANCIAL DATA: Note: Data for latest year may not have been available at press time.

In U.S. $	2015	2014	2013	2012	2011	2010
Revenue		3,850,000,000	3,700,000,000	3,400,000,000	2,600,000,000	2,500,000,000
R&D Expense						
Operating Income						
Operating Margin %						
SGA Expense						
Net Income						
Operating Cash Flow						
Capital Expenditure						
EBITDA						
Return on Assets %						
Return on Equity %						
Debt to Equity						

CONTACT INFORMATION:

Phone: 213-741-8257   Fax: 213-741-8995
Toll-Free:
Address: 3880 North Mission Road, Los Angeles, CA 90031 United States

STOCK TICKER/OTHER:

Stock Ticker: Private
Employees: 30,000
Parent Company:

Exchange:
Fiscal Year Ends: 02/28

SALARIES/BONUSES:

Top Exec. Salary: $ Bonus: $
Second Exec. Salary: $ Bonus: $

OTHER THOUGHTS:

Estimated Female Officers or Directors: 1
Hot Spot for Advancement for Women/Minorities:

Sales, profits and employees may be estimates. Financial information, benefits and other data can change quickly and may vary from those stated here.

Fossil Group Inc

www.fossil.com

NAIC Code: 334519A

TYPES OF BUSINESS:

Watches and Parts (except crystals) Manufacturing
Accessories
Online Sales
Leather Goods
Belts
Handbags
Jewelry
Retail Stores

BRANDS/DIVISIONS/AFFILIATES:

Fossil
Relic
Zodiac
Skagen

CONTACTS: *Note: Officers with more than one job title may be intentionally listed here more than once.*

Kosta Kartsotis, CEO
Dennis Secor, CFO
Darren Hart, Executive VP, Divisional
John White, Executive VP
Randy Hyne, General Counsel

GROWTH PLANS/SPECIAL FEATURES:

Fossil Group, Inc. designs, develops, markets and distribute
fashion accessories. The company's principal offerings includ
a line of men's and women's watches and jewelry sold unde
proprietary and licensed brands, handbags, leather good
sunglasses and apparel. In the watch and jewelry produ
category, Fossil has a diverse portfolio of globally recognize
brands such as Fossil, Relic, Skagen and Zodiac. Also, throug
license agreements, the company utilizes prestigious bran
names such as Burberry, DKNY, Michael Kors, Marc Jacob
Adidas and Emporio Armani. The company distribute
products through various channels including wholesale an
export as well as directly to the consumer. Domestically, th
company sells its products through a distribution network tha
includes Neiman Marcus, Nordstrom, Macy's, Dillard'
JCPenney, Kohl's, Saks Fifth Avenue, Wal-Mart and Targe
The firm also sells its products through a network of domesti
company-owned stores, which includes 153 retail and 14
outlet stores. Additionally, the company offers an extensiv
collection of Fossil brand products through its catalog and wel
site as well as proprietary and licensed watch and jewelr
brands through other managed and affiliate web sites
Internationally, products are sold to department stores an
specialty stores in over 150 countries through 25 company
owned foreign sales subsidiaries and through approximately 6
independent distributors. The firm's network of internationa
company-owned stores include 197 retail stores and 100 outle
stores. In 2014, the firm extended its partnership with Giorgi
Armani by ten years; and launched Tory Burch for watche
under an exclusive global licensing agreement.

FINANCIAL DATA: *Note: Data for latest year may not have been available at press time.*

In U.S. $	2015	2014	2013	2012	2011	2010
Revenue		3,509,691,000	3,259,971,000	2,857,508,000	2,567,302,000	2,030,690,000
R&D Expense						
Operating Income		566,536,000	561,596,000	488,840,000	471,991,000	376,414,000
Operating Margin %		16.14%	17.22%	17.10%	18.38%	18.53%
SGA Expense		1,434,636,000	1,300,090,000	1,117,703,000	967,195,000	778,750,000
Net Income		376,707,000	378,152,000	343,401,000	294,702,000	255,205,000
Operating Cash Flow		387,883,000	411,682,000	451,600,000	251,267,000	209,177,000
Capital Expenditure		104,182,000	110,052,000	122,804,000	131,496,000	46,812,000
EBITDA		669,907,000	652,951,000	562,918,000	505,875,000	425,889,000
Return on Assets %		16.97%	18.57%	19.70%	18.94%	18.60%
Return on Equity %		36.81%	32.85%	29.35%	27.41%	25.43%
Debt to Equity		0.62	0.46	0.06		

CONTACT INFORMATION:

Phone: 972 234-2525   Fax: 972 234-4669
Toll-Free: 800-449-3056
Address: 901 S. Central Expy., Richardson, TX 75080 United States

SALARIES/BONUSES:

Top Exec. Salary: $646,923   Bonus: $
Second Exec. Salary: Bonus: $
$626,923

STOCK TICKER/OTHER:

Stock Ticker: FOSL
Employees: 15,200
Parent Company:

Exchange: NAS
Fiscal Year Ends: 12/31

OTHER THOUGHTS:

Estimated Female Officers or Directors: 4
Hot Spot for Advancement for Women/Minorities: Y

Francesca's Holdings Corp

www.francescascollections.com

NAIC Code: 448120

TYPES OF BUSINESS:

Ladies Apparel Stores

GROWTH PLANS/SPECIAL FEATURES:

Francesca's Holdings Corp. operates a national chain of more than 600 retail stores in 47 states, designed and merchandised to feel like upscale, independently owned boutiques. The firm conducts its business through wholly-owned subsidiary Francesca's Collection, Inc. In addition to the retail stores, Francesca's also operates an e-commerce site at FrancescasCollections.com. Through its stores and e-commerce site, the company offers its customers a mix of fashion-forward women's apparel, jewelry, accessories and gift items. Keeping with its fashion-forward theme, the firm carries a broad selection of items in limited numbers and adds new items on a fairly regular basis to create a sense of scarcity and newness. Francesca's tailors its assortment of goods to appeal to its core target group, fashion conscious women between the ages of 18 and 35. Francesca's goal is to have 900 retail operations in the U.S over the next few years.

BRANDS/DIVISIONS/AFFILIATES:

Francesca's Collection Inc
FrancescasCollections.com

CONTACTS: *Note: Officers with more than one job title may be intentionally listed here more than once.*

Mark Vendetti, CFO
Michael Barnes, Chairman of the Board
Khalid Malik, Chief Administrative Officer
Cynthia Thomassee, Controller

FINANCIAL DATA: *Note: Data for latest year may not have been available at press time.*

In U.S. $	2015	2014	2013	2012	2011	2010
Revenue	377,497,000	340,325,000	296,373,000	204,158,000	135,176,000	79,367,000
R&D Expense						
Operating Income	52,774,000	74,270,000	77,940,000	43,531,000	29,643,000	17,482,000
Operating Margin %	13.97%	21.82%	26.29%	21.32%	21.92%	22.02%
SGA Expense	124,804,000	101,795,000	80,560,000	63,262,000	40,525,000	24,641,000
Net Income	32,108,000	44,839,000	47,061,000	22,501,000	16,895,000	10,604,000
Operating Cash Flow	54,444,000	50,142,000	56,999,000	46,471,000	21,020,000	13,277,000
Capital Expenditure	24,255,000	24,633,000	23,663,000	48,467,000	32,020,000	5,538,000
EBITDA	66,013,000	84,532,000	85,321,000	48,467,000	32,020,000	18,737,000
Return on Assets %	20.31%	34.07%	50.90%	34.23%	37.40%	-165.57%
Return on Equity %	34.28%	59.73%	105.80%			
Debt to Equity		0.32		1.30		

CONTACT INFORMATION:

Phone: 713 864-1358   Fax:
Toll-Free:
Address: 8760 Clay Road, Houston, TX 77080 United States

STOCK TICKER/OTHER:

Stock Ticker: FRAN   Exchange: NAS
Employees: 4,056   Fiscal Year Ends: 01/31
Parent Company:

SALARIES/BONUSES:

Top Exec. Salary: $546,154   Bonus: $
Second Exec. Salary: Bonus: $
$371,443

OTHER THOUGHTS:

Estimated Female Officers or Directors: 4
Hot Spot for Advancement for Women/Minorities: Y

Franklin Covey Co

NAIC Code: 541611

www.franklincovey.com

TYPES OF BUSINESS:

Organizational Consulting Services
Planning Aids
Training & Consulting
Seminars
Motivational Products
Online Sales

BRANDS/DIVISIONS/AFFILIATES:

FC Organizational Products LLC
7 Habits of Highly Effective People (The)
Winning Customer Loyalty

CONTACTS: Note: Officers with more than one job title may be intentionally listed here more than once.

Robert Whitman, CEO
Stephen Young, Controller
Shawn Moon, Executive VP, Divisional
Scott Miller, Executive VP, Divisional
Colleen Dom, Executive VP, Divisional
Michael Covey, Executive VP, Divisional
Clifton Davis, Executive VP

GROWTH PLANS/SPECIAL FEATURES:

Franklin Covey Co. provides consulting and training services on a global basis. It is involved in the business of marketing and sale of communication training programs and consulting services to clients such as government and educational institutions as well as for-profit enterprises. It specializes in offering seminars, workshops and educational materials designed to improve organizational effectiveness, written and oral business communication skills and personal effectiveness. Its programs, such as The 7 Habits of Highly Effective People and Winning Customer Loyalty, are divided into seven categories: leadership, productivity, trust, execution, sales performance, education and customer loyalty. Programs are delivered in a combination of methods, including onsite presentations by consultants, public workshops, books and publications, electronic tools and videos and online seminars. Its training seminars and programs are delivered through company-owned offices in the U.S., Australia, Japan and the U.K. as well as in over 165 other countries through licensee partners. Additionally, the firm licenses the Franklin Covey brand to FC Organizational Products LLC, which sells products such as day planners, software, binders, bags and cases, books, CDs and DVDs through retail stores, catalogs and its web site.

FINANCIAL DATA: Note: Data for latest year may not have been available at press time.

In U.S. $	2015	2014	2013	2012	2011	2010
Revenue	209,941,000	205,165,000	190,924,000	170,456,000	160,804,000	136,874,000
R&D Expense						
Operating Income	19,529,000	24,765,000	21,614,000	17,580,000	11,112,000	4,038,000
Operating Margin %	9.30%	12.07%	11.32%	10.31%	6.91%	2.95%
SGA Expense	108,802,000	106,164,000	101,176,000	89,462,000	85,255,000	77,604,000
Net Income	11,116,000	18,067,000	14,319,000	7,841,000	4,807,000	-518,000
Operating Cash Flow	26,190,000	18,124,000	15,528,000	15,562,000	15,643,000	7,024,000
Capital Expenditure	4,612,000	11,257,000	5,398,000	4,392,000	5,423,000	1,384,000
EBITDA	27,424,000	31,333,000	27,929,000	21,927,000	18,240,000	11,501,000
Return on Assets %	5.47%	9.15%	8.10%	4.97%	3.21%	-.35%
Return on Equity %	8.81%	15.49%	14.53%	9.23%	6.39%	-.73%
Debt to Equity	0.19	0.20	0.25	0.31	0.40	0.42

CONTACT INFORMATION:

Phone: 801 817-1776   Fax: 801 817-6085
Toll-Free: 800-827-1776
Address: 2200 W. Parkway Blvd., Salt Lake City, UT 84119 United States

STOCK TICKER/OTHER:

Stock Ticker: FC
Employees: 825
Parent Company:

Exchange: NYS
Fiscal Year Ends: 08/31

SALARIES/BONUSES:

Top Exec. Salary: $525,000   Bonus: $
Second Exec. Salary: $320,000   Bonus: $

OTHER THOUGHTS:

Estimated Female Officers or Directors: 4
Hot Spot for Advancement for Women/Minorities: Y

Frederick's of Hollywood Group Inc   www.fohgroup.com

NAIC Code: 448120

TYPES OF BUSINESS:

Lingerie & Sleepwear
Loungewear
Formal Apparel
Jewelry & Accessories
Shoes

BRANDS/DIVISIONS/AFFILIATES:

Seduction by Frederick's of Hollywood
Frederick's of Hollywood
Hollywood Exxtreme Cleavage
Get Cheeky
Harbinger Group Inc

CONTACTS: Note: Officers with more than one job title may be intentionally listed here more than once.

Thomas Lynch, CEO
Thomas Rende, CFO

GROWTH PLANS/SPECIAL FEATURES:

Frederick's of Hollywood Group, Inc. designs, manufactures, markets and sells an extensive line of ladies' intimate apparel. Its product line includes bras, panties, lingerie, corsets, hosiery, shape wear, sleepwear, dresses, tops, pants, shorts, skirts, formal wear, shoes, fragrances, personal care products, jewelry and bridal undergarments. The company operates in two divisions: retail and direct to consumer. The retail division manages mall-based Frederick's of Hollywood retail stores in 27 U.S. states (approximately one-third of these are located in California). These stores range in size from 900 square feet to 3,200, with its flagship store in Hollywood, California at 5,700 square feet. The direct to consumer business handles the company's e-commerce and catalog marketing operations. Some of its brands and trademarks include Hollywood Exxtreme Cleavage, Get Cheeky and Seduction by Frederick's of Hollywood. In addition to its intimate apparel, the firm has licensed the Frederick's of Hollywood brand to manufacturers of swimwear, Halloween costumes, jewelry and accessories. In February 2015, the company agreed to close a third (93) of its stores.

FINANCIAL DATA: Note: Data for latest year may not have been available at press time.

In U.S. $	2015	2014	2013	2012	2011	2010
Revenue		75,000,000	86,507,000	111,406,000	119,615,000	133,855,000
R&D Expense						
Operating Income						
Operating Margin %						
SGA Expense						
Net Income			-22,522,000	-6,432,000	-12,055,000	-21,164,000
Operating Cash Flow						
Capital Expenditure						
EBITDA						
Return on Assets %						
Return on Equity %						
Debt to Equity						

CONTACT INFORMATION:

Phone: 323 466-5151   Fax:
Toll-Free:
Address: 6255 Sunset Blvd, 6th Fl, Los Angeles, CA 90028 United States

STOCK TICKER/OTHER:

Stock Ticker: Private
Employees: 902
Parent Company: Harbinger Group Inc

Exchange:
Fiscal Year Ends: 07/31

SALARIES/BONUSES:

Top Exec. Salary: $ Bonus: $
Second Exec. Salary: $ Bonus: $

OTHER THOUGHTS:

Estimated Female Officers or Directors:
Hot Spot for Advancement for Women/Minorities: Y

Fred's Inc
NAIC Code: 452112

www.fredsinc.com

TYPES OF BUSINESS:
Discount Stores
Pharmacies
Photo Processing
General Merchandise

BRANDS/DIVISIONS/AFFILIATES:
Reeves-Sain Drug Store Inc
EntrustRx Specialty Pharmacy
EIRIS Health Services

CONTACTS: Note: Officers with more than one job title may be intentionally listed here more than once.
Jerry Shore, CEO
Michael Hayes, Chairman of the Board
W. Pugh, Chief Medical Officer
Rick Chambers, Executive VP, Divisional
Craig Barnes, Executive VP, Divisional
Michael Holligan, Executive VP, Divisional
Michael Bloom, President
Mark Dely, Secretary

GROWTH PLANS/SPECIAL FEATURES:
Fred's, Inc. operates 661 discount general merchandise an
three specialty pharmacy stores in 15 states in th
southeastern U.S. Fred's stores generally serve low, midd
and fixed income families located in small- to medium-size
towns. Approximately 85% of Fred's stores are in markets wi
populations of 15,000 or fewer people. Of these locations, 38
contain full-service pharmacies. Fred's also has a specialt
pharmacy facility, EIRIS Health Services, and provide
services to patients with chronic and serious medical condition
including Crohn's Disease, Hepatitis C, Psoriasis an
Rheumatoid Arthritis. The firm also markets goods an
services to 19 franchised Fred's stores. Fred's stores featur
over 12,000 items, including national brand names, off-brand
and Fred's private label. About half of Fred's store
merchandise is received through its distribution centers i
Georgia and Tennessee, while the remaining stock is shippe
directly from suppliers. The Fred's sales mix is divided into fou
categories: pharmaceuticals, which accounted for 41.9% o
sales in 2014; household goods and softlines, 25.3%
consumables 31.2%; and sales to franchised Fred's store
1.6%. The company's strategy for obtaining customers for ne
pharmacies is through the acquisition of prescription files fror
independent pharmacies. These acquisitions provide a
immediate sales benefit, and in many cases, the independer
pharmacist will move to Fred's. In April 2015, the firm acquire
Reeves-Sain Drug Store, Inc., a private specialty and reta
pharmacy company, including its EntrustRx specialt
pharmacy operation.

FINANCIAL DATA: Note: Data for latest year may not have been available at press time.

In U.S. $	2015	2014	2013	2012	2011	2010
Revenue	1,970,049,000	1,939,246,000	1,955,275,000	1,879,059,000	1,841,755,000	1,788,136,000
R&D Expense						
Operating Income	-48,412,000	39,198,000	39,078,000	51,155,000	46,718,000	38,494,000
Operating Margin %	-2.45%	2.02%	1.99%	2.72%	2.53%	2.15%
SGA Expense	511,142,000	480,596,000	487,713,000	453,195,000	451,064,000	434,356,000
Net Income	-28,904,000	26,015,000	29,629,000	33,428,000	29,587,000	23,615,000
Operating Cash Flow	63,703,000	58,861,000	46,198,000	76,565,000	42,057,000	64,249,000
Capital Expenditure	23,308,000	50,984,000	47,594,000	62,451,000	38,464,000	33,355,000
EBITDA	-7,349,000	80,245,000	78,619,000	85,501,000	76,188,000	65,070,000
Return on Assets %	-4.39%	3.96%	4.63%	5.44%	5.07%	4.23%
Return on Equity %	-6.66%	5.89%	6.93%	7.88%	7.17%	5.99%
Debt to Equity			0.02	0.01		0.01

CONTACT INFORMATION:
Phone: 901 365-8880   Fax: 901 365-8865
Toll-Free: 800-374-7417
Address: 4300 New Getwell Rd., Memphis, TN 38118 United States

STOCK TICKER/OTHER:
Stock Ticker: FRED   Exchange: NAS
Employees: 9,148   Fiscal Year Ends: 01/31
Parent Company:

SALARIES/BONUSES:
Top Exec. Salary: $700,000   Bonus: $
Second Exec. Salary: Bonus: $
$455,773

OTHER THOUGHTS:
Estimated Female Officers or Directors:
Hot Spot for Advancement for Women/Minorities:

French Connection Group plc

www.frenchconnection.com

NAIC Code: 424300

TYPES OF BUSINESS:

Apparel and Clothing Brands, Designers, Importers and Distributors
Accessories
Shoes
Cosmetics & Fragrances
Home Furnishings
Online & Mail Order Sales
Franchising
Retail Stores

BRANDS/DIVISIONS/AFFILIATES:

YMC
Great Plains
Toast
French Connection U.K.
fcuk

CONTACTS: *Note: Officers with more than one job title may be intentionally listed here more than once.*

Stephen Marks, CEO
Neil Williams, Dir.-Oper.
Roy Naismith, Dir.-Finance
Stephen Marks, Chmn.

GROWTH PLANS/SPECIAL FEATURES:

French Connection Group plc is a youth-oriented apparel company that retails and wholesales fashion clothing and accessories in more than 60 countries worldwide. Generally, the firm targets men and women ages 18-35. Its products are sold through its retail stores in the U.K., Europe, U.S., Australia, the Middle East and Canada; mail order service in the U.K. and U.S.; and on the Internet. The company has licensed French Connection operators in Australia, Asia and the Middle East. The firm also operates wholesale operations in London, Hong Kong, Paris, Toronto and New York. It owns four brands: French Connection, Great Plains, Toast and the menswear brand YMC. French Connection designs, produces and distributes its own brands of men's and women's products, including outerwear, dresses, skirts, jeans, footwear, casual wear, suits, denim, accessories and children's apparel, and is supported by unique advertising featuring the acronym for French Connection U.K., fcuk. Accessories such as hats, sunglasses, backpacks, fragrances and the company's new cosmetics line complement the brand's fashions. A range of homewares are also available through some of its stores. Fcuk is available worldwide. It is represented in the U.K., Europe, and the U.S. and through the firm's joint ventures in Asia. The Great Plains brand provides a range of fashionable mid-priced basic clothing for men and women and is available across the U.K. and in Europe. The Toast brand, represented only in the U.K., provides a range of garments and products that are available through mail order, online and at some retail locations.

FINANCIAL DATA: *Note: Data for latest year may not have been available at press time.*

In U.S. $	2015	2014	2013	2012	2011	2010
Revenue	266,840,100	283,134,500	294,944,200	322,002,000	319,610,100	317,666,800
R&D Expense						
Operating Income	-1,345,412	-6,577,571	-13,603,610	4,933,178	5,531,139	-4,484,707
Operating Margin %	-.50%	-2.32%	-4.61%	1.53%	1.73%	-1.41%
SGA Expense	135,737,100	151,583,100	162,794,900	147,995,300	153,377,000	157,861,700
Net Income	-2,242,354	-9,118,904	-15,397,490	7,922,983	-3,587,766	-37,223,070
Operating Cash Flow	-4,484,707	2,391,844	-6,278,590	-2,541,334	-1,644,393	1,943,373
Capital Expenditure	1,644,393	1,195,922	2,840,315	2,391,844	1,494,902	3,139,295
EBITDA	1,046,432	-3,737,256	-11,062,280	9,118,904	10,912,790	3,737,256
Return on Assets %	-1.52%	-5.82%	-8.86%	4.35%	-1.93%	-17.17%
Return on Equity %	-2.68%	-10.31%	-15.05%	7.32%	-3.38%	-29.15%
Debt to Equity						

CONTACT INFORMATION:

Phone: 44 2070367200   Fax: 44 2070367201
Toll-Free:
Address: 39 Camden St., Centro 1, London, NW1 0DX United Kingdom

SALARIES/BONUSES:

Top Exec. Salary: $ Bonus: $
Second Exec. Salary: $ Bonus: $

STOCK TICKER/OTHER:

Stock Ticker: FCOGF
Employees: 3,247
Parent Company:

Exchange: GREY
Fiscal Year Ends: 01/31

OTHER THOUGHTS:

Estimated Female Officers or Directors: 1
Hot Spot for Advancement for Women/Minorities:

Fresh Market Inc (The)

NAIC Code: 445110

www.thefreshmarket.com

TYPES OF BUSINESS:

Grocery Stores

BRANDS/DIVISIONS/AFFILIATES:

Fresh Market (The)

CONTACTS: Note: Officers with more than one job title may be intentionally listed here more than once.

Richard Anicetti, CEO
Jeffrey Ackerman, CFO
Ray Berry, Chairman of the Board
Jeff Short, Chief Accounting Officer
Scott Duggan, General Counsel
Matt Argano, Senior VP, Divisional
Randy Young, Senior VP, Divisional

GROWTH PLANS/SPECIAL FEATURES:

The Fresh Market, Inc. is a specialty grocery retailer offering high-quality food products and fresh produce. The firm, which was established in 1982, operates 169 stores in 27 states, primarily in the Southeast, Midwest, Mid-Atlantic and Northeast U.S. Florida, with 40 locations, is the company's largest market. The Fresh Market's stores average approximately 21,000 square feet, compared to the approximately 40,000 to 60,000 square foot stores operated by many conventional supermarkets. Within this relatively smaller size, the company focuses on higher-margin food. Its products include meat, seafood, produce, dairy, prepared foods, coffee, beer, wine, flowers, candles, cookbooks, kitchen items and seasonal/holiday gift baskets. Each Fresh Market location also has an in-house deli and bakery. The stores stock approximately 10,000 to 11,000 products at any one time. The firm sources its products from approximately 1,000 vendors and suppliers and uses separate providers for distribution.

The company offers employees medical, dental and vision insurance; a 20% discount on most store merchandise; an employee assistance program; annual bonus programs; a 401(k) plan; flexible spending accounts; disability coverage; and life insurance.

FINANCIAL DATA: Note: Data for latest year may not have been available at press time.

In U.S. $	2015	2014	2013	2012	2011	2010
Revenue	1,753,166,000	1,511,657,000	1,329,131,000	1,108,035,000		974,213,000
R&D Expense						
Operating Income	103,613,000	83,381,000	101,486,000	82,882,000		40,935,000
Operating Margin %	5.91%	5.51%	7.63%	7.48%		4.20%
SGA Expense	406,452,000	349,813,000	304,471,000	247,484,000		245,170,000
Net Income	63,025,000	50,807,000	64,133,000	51,395,000		22,915,000
Operating Cash Flow	143,025,000	140,372,000	91,914,000	108,511,000		111,438,000
Capital Expenditure	90,182,000	122,366,000	81,107,000	87,513,000		41,983,000
EBITDA	165,776,000	138,259,000	147,448,000	119,576,000		74,276,000
Return on Assets %	12.51%	11.88%	18.09%	17.65%		9.28%
Return on Equity %	21.54%	22.37%	39.49%	51.65%		33.32%
Debt to Equity	0.10	0.19	0.21	0.50		1.19

CONTACT INFORMATION:

Phone: 336 272-1338   Fax:
Toll-Free: 866-532-5989
Address: 628 Green Valley Rd., Ste. 500, Greensboro, NC 27408 United States

STOCK TICKER/OTHER:

Stock Ticker: TFM
Employees: 12,400
Parent Company:

Exchange: NAS
Fiscal Year Ends: 01/31

SALARIES/BONUSES:

Top Exec. Salary: $539,423   Bonus: $
Second Exec. Salary: $407,231   Bonus: $

OTHER THOUGHTS:

Estimated Female Officers or Directors: 1
Hot Spot for Advancement for Women/Minorities:

Frontgate Marketing Inc

www.frontgate.com/about-us/content

NAIC Code: 454113

TYPES OF BUSINESS:

High-End Gift and Home Furnishings Catalogs
Electronic Shopping

BRANDS/DIVISIONS/AFFILIATES:

HSN Inc
Grandin Road
Chasing Fireflies
Cornerstone Brands Inc
TravelSmith
Garnet Hill
Ballard Designs

GROWTH PLANS/SPECIAL FEATURES:

Frontgate Marketing, Inc., a subsidiary of HSN, Inc. is a retailer for high quality home goods. The firm sells its products through catalogues, three specialty books and through its digital presence. The firm is part of Cornerstone Brands, Inc., a group of direct marketing companies which includes Grandin Road, a seller of home accents; Ballard Designs, selling accents for home and garden; Chasing Fireflies, a children's brand; Garnet Hill, a seller of natural fiber home products; and TravelSmith, a luggage and travel products seller. Frontgate's products including outdoor furniture, outdoor decor, insect control products, grills, pool and beach equipment, home furniture, home decor, bedding, pet products, kitchen equipment, electronics and gifts. The firm's catalogs have a circulation of nearly 83 million households.

CONTACTS: Note: Officers with more than one job title may be intentionally listed here more than once.

H.R. Harvey, Pres.
Mindy Grossman, CEO-HSN, Inc.

FINANCIAL DATA: Note: Data for latest year may not have been available at press time.

In U.S. $	2015	2014	2013	2012	2011	2010
Revenue						
R&D Expense						
Operating Income						
Operating Margin %						
SGA Expense						
Net Income						
Operating Cash Flow						
Capital Expenditure						
EBITDA						
Return on Assets %						
Return on Equity %						
Debt to Equity						

CONTACT INFORMATION:

Phone: 856-868-8551   Fax:
Toll-Free: 888-263-9850
Address: 5566 West Chester Rd., West Chester, OH 45069 United States

STOCK TICKER/OTHER:

Stock Ticker: Subsidiary
Employees:
Parent Company: HSN, Inc.

Exchange:
Fiscal Year Ends:

SALARIES/BONUSES:

Top Exec. Salary: $ Bonus: $
Second Exec. Salary: $ Bonus: $

OTHER THOUGHTS:

Estimated Female Officers or Directors: 1
Hot Spot for Advancement for Women/Minorities:

Fry's Electronics Inc

NAIC Code: 443142

TYPES OF BUSINESS:

Electronics, Audio & Appliance Stores
Computer & Software Products
Online Sales
Product Support Services
ISP Administrator

BRANDS/DIVISIONS/AFFILIATES:

Frys.com
Fry's Electronics

CONTACTS: Note: Officers with more than one job title may be intentionally listed here more than once.

John Fry, CEO
William R. Fry, Pres.
David Fry, CFO
David Fry, CIO
Kathryn J. Kolder, Exec. VP

GROWTH PLANS/SPECIAL FEATURES:

Fry's Electronics, Inc. retails electronic items throug
warehouse-sized electronics superstores, with each stor
carrying over 50,000 electronic items. The stores are located i
Southern California, which has nine locations; Norther
California, eight; Texas, eight; Arizona and Georgia, with tw
stores each; and Illinois, Indiana, Nevada, Washington an
Oregon, with one store each. The stores range in size from
50,000 to over 180,000 square feet. While the company ha
grown since its inception in Silicon Valley in 1985, Fry's targe
customer continues to be the high-tech professional. In additio
to its stores, the firm sells electronics online through Frys.com
Fry's stores offer low prices, extensive inventory an
imaginatively themed stores, with each store having its ow
unique theme. For example, the Palo Alto store has a Wil
West theme; the Phoenix store has Aztec-themed decor; th
Houston store showcases the oil industry, replete with a field c
gushing oil derricks; and the Las Vegas store showcases the
history of the Las Vegas Strip. Every Fry's store offers service
and support for a variety of products. These products includ
computer hardware and software for both Microsoft and Appl
operating systems; technical manuals and other books; new
CDs, DVDs and Blu-ray discs; video games; audio, car audi
and video equipment such as flat screen TVs; and
communications equipment, such as blue tooth headsets and
answering machines. Other products include integrated
circuits, batteries and other electronic components and
accessories; appliances such as vacuums and microwaves
health and beauty products including air purifiers and electri
razors; and convenience and general merchandise items. In
addition to its retail arm, Fry's administers mobile and
broadband ISPs and other telecom services for business
clients.

FINANCIAL DATA: Note: Data for latest year may not have been available at press time.

In U.S. $	2015	2014	2013	2012	2011	2010
Revenue		2,200,000,000	2,150,000,000	2,000,000,000	2,100,000,000	2,400,000,000
R&D Expense						
Operating Income						
Operating Margin %						
SGA Expense						
Net Income						
Operating Cash Flow						
Capital Expenditure						
EBITDA						
Return on Assets %						
Return on Equity %						
Debt to Equity						

CONTACT INFORMATION:

Phone: 408-350-1484   Fax:
Toll-Free:
Address: 600 E. Brokaw Rd., San Jose, CA 95112 United States

STOCK TICKER/OTHER:

Stock Ticker: Private
Employees: 15,000
Parent Company:

Exchange:
Fiscal Year Ends: 12/31

SALARIES/BONUSES:

Top Exec. Salary: $ Bonus: $
Second Exec. Salary: $ Bonus: $

OTHER THOUGHTS:

Estimated Female Officers or Directors: 1
Hot Spot for Advancement for Women/Minorities:

GameStop Corp

www.gamestop.com

NAIC Code: 451120

TYPES OF BUSINESS:

Video Games-Retail
PC Software Sales
Game Accessories
Online Sales
Magazine Publication
Cellphone and Game Machine Refurbishing

BRANDS/DIVISIONS/AFFILIATES:

GameStop
Micromania
EB Games
Spring Mobile
Simply Mac
Geeknet Inc
ThinkGeek
Cricket

CONTACTS: *Note: Officers with more than one job title may be intentionally listed here more than once.*

J. Raines, CEO
Robert Lloyd, CFO
Daniel Dematteo, Chairman of the Board
Troy Crawford, Chief Accounting Officer
Tony Bartel, COO
Michael Hogan, Executive VP, Divisional
Michael Buskey, Executive VP
Michael Mauler, Executive VP

GROWTH PLANS/SPECIAL FEATURES:

GameStop Corp. is a retailer of video games and PC games. The company operates 6,690 company-operated stores worldwide, primarily in the U.S., Australia, Canada and Europe. GameStop divides its business into two segments: video game brands and technology brands. Video game brands comprises 6,206 stores, 4,138 of which are in the U.S., 331 are in Canada, 421 in Australia and 1,316 in Europe. All of the firm's retail operations engage in the sale of new and pre-owned video game systems, software and accessories. It sells various types of digital products, such as downloadable content, network point cards, prepaid digital/online timecards and digitally-downloadable software. Technology brands includes GameStop's Spring Mobile and Simply Mac businesses. Spring Mobile sells post-paid AT&T services and wireless products through its 361 AT&T-branded stores, as well as related products and accessories. Spring Mobile also sells pre-paid AT&T services, wireless devices and accessories through its 63 Cricket-branded stores. Simply Mac operates 60 stores which sell Apple products, including desktop computers, laptops, tablets and smart phones, as well as related products and accessories. Substantially all of GameStop's U.S. and European stores are operated under the GameStop name, except for Micromania in France. Canadian and Australian stores operate under the EB Games name. GameStop distributes its video game products to its U.S. stores through a 353,000 square foot distribution center in Grapevine, Texas; its Canadian products from distribution centers in Brampton, Ontario; its Australian products from its Brisbane distribution center; and its European operations are supported by five regionally-located centers in Italy, Germany, Sweden, Ireland and France. In July 2015, the firm acquired Geeknet, Inc., along with its ThinkGeek brand.

GameStop offers its employees medical, dental, vision and prescription drug coverage; paid holidays and vacation; flexible spending accounts; short- and long-term disability; a 401(k) plan; tuition reimbursement; and employee discounts.

FINANCIAL DATA: *Note: Data for latest year may not have been available at press time.*

In U.S. $	2015	2014	2013	2012	2011	2010
Revenue	9,296,000,000	9,039,500,000	8,886,700,000	9,550,500,000	9,473,700,000	9,077,997,000
R&D Expense						
Operating Income	618,300,000	573,500,000	-41,600,000	569,900,000	662,600,000	637,033,000
Operating Margin %	6.65%	6.34%	-.46%	5.96%	6.99%	7.01%
SGA Expense	2,001,000,000	1,892,400,000	1,835,900,000	1,842,100,000	1,700,300,000	1,635,124,000
Net Income	393,100,000	354,200,000	-269,700,000	339,900,000	408,000,000	377,265,000
Operating Cash Flow	480,500,000	762,700,000	632,400,000	624,700,000	591,200,000	644,173,000
Capital Expenditure	159,600,000	125,600,000	139,600,000	165,100,000	197,600,000	163,759,000
EBITDA	775,500,000	743,600,000	138,200,000	758,400,000	835,200,000	798,013,000
Return on Assets %	9.42%	8.61%	-6.00%	6.85%	8.14%	7.96%
Return on Equity %	18.20%	15.61%	-10.12%	11.44%	14.51%	15.02%
Debt to Equity	0.16				0.08	0.16

CONTACT INFORMATION:

Phone: 817 424-2000   Fax: 817 424-2062
Toll-Free: 800-883-8895
Address: 625 Westport Pkwy., Grapevine, TX 76051 United States

SALARIES/BONUSES:

Top Exec. Salary: $1,201,346   Bonus: $

Second Exec. Salary: $853,558   Bonus: $

STOCK TICKER/OTHER:

Stock Ticker: GME   Exchange: NYS
Employees: 18,000   Fiscal Year Ends: 01/31
Parent Company:

OTHER THOUGHTS:

Estimated Female Officers or Directors: 1

Hot Spot for Advancement for Women/Minorities:

Gap Inc (The)

NAIC Code: 448140

TYPES OF BUSINESS:

Casual Apparel Stores
Online Retailing
Shoes & Accessories
Personal Care Products
Children's Clothing
Babies' Clothing
Maternity Clothing
Exercise Clothing

BRANDS/DIVISIONS/AFFILIATES:

Athleta
GapKids
babyGap
Banana Republic
Old Navy
Gap Outlet
Intermix

CONTACTS: Note: Officers with more than one job title may be intentionally listed here more than once.

Sabrina Simmons, CFO
Arthur Peck, Director
Robert Fisher, Director
Solomon Goldfarb, Executive VP, Divisional
Sonia Syngal, Executive VP, Divisional
John Keiser, Executive VP, Divisional
Michelle Banks, Executive VP, Divisional
Stanton Jill, Executive VP, Divisional
Paul Adams, General Counsel
Jeff Kirwan, President, Divisional
Andi Owen, President, Geographical
Thomas Lima, Senior VP

GROWTH PLANS/SPECIAL FEATURES:

The Gap, Inc. (Gap) is a retailer of clothing, accessories and personal care products for adults, kids and babies. It has over 3,280 stores in the U.S., Canada, Mexico, the U.K., Japan, Germany, Ireland and France. It has more than 425 Gap and Banana Republic stores through franchise agreements in 90 countries throughout Asia, Europe, Latin America and the Middle East. The Gap brand includes GapKids, babyGap, GapBody and Gap Outlet as well as Banana Republic and Old Navy. Gap stores typically encompass all Gap-branded units such as Gap, babyGap and GapKids under one roof but segregate them into different areas, each with its own street/mall entrance. The firm also sells its products via Gap.com, BananaRepublic.com and OldNavy.com. Other brands of the firm include Athleta, which sells women's exercise and casual apparel, footwear and accessories; and Intermix, a fashion line which combines luxury and contemporary fashions. Old Navy operates stores in the U.S and Canada and offers a broad selection of apparel, shoes and accessories for adults, children and infants at more affordable prices. Banana Republic has locations in the U.S., Canada, the U.K. and Japan and sells men's and women's clothing, shoes, accessories, personal care products, intimate apparel and jewelry to a higher price-point market. In April 2015, the firm closed its subsidiary Piperlime operation in order to focus on other core brands. That May, The Gap opened a store in New Delhi, India; and that June, it announced plans to close a quarter of its Gap stores in North America, which will leave it with approximately 700 stores, down from 960.

Gap offers its employees benefits including medical, dental and vision insurance; life and disability insurance; adoption assistance; a 401(k) plan; an employee stock purchase plan; and merchandise discounts at all Gap-affiliated stores.

FINANCIAL DATA: Note: Data for latest year may not have been available at press time.

In U.S. $	2015	2014	2013	2012	2011	2010
Revenue	16,435,000,000	16,148,000,000	15,651,000,000	14,549,000,000	14,664,000,000	14,197,000,000
R&D Expense						
Operating Income	2,083,000,000	2,149,000,000	1,942,000,000	1,438,000,000	1,968,000,000	1,815,000,000
Operating Margin %	12.67%	13.30%	12.40%	9.88%	13.42%	12.78%
SGA Expense						
Net Income	1,262,000,000	1,280,000,000	1,135,000,000	833,000,000	1,204,000,000	1,102,000,000
Operating Cash Flow	2,129,000,000	1,705,000,000	1,936,000,000	1,363,000,000	1,744,000,000	1,928,000,000
Capital Expenditure	714,000,000	670,000,000	659,000,000	548,000,000	557,000,000	334,000,000
EBITDA	2,652,000,000	2,690,000,000	2,507,000,000	2,035,000,000	2,630,000,000	2,477,000,000
Return on Assets %	16.24%	16.71%	15.24%	11.50%	15.99%	14.17%
Return on Equity %	41.75%	42.98%	40.18%	24.37%	26.84%	23.75%
Debt to Equity	0.44	0.44	0.43	0.92	0.21	

CONTACT INFORMATION:

Phone: 650 952-4400   Fax: 650 952-4407
Toll-Free: 800-333-7899
Address: 2 Folsom St., San Francisco, CA 94105 United States

STOCK TICKER/OTHER:

Stock Ticker: GPS   Exchange: NYS
Employees: 141,000   Fiscal Year Ends: 01/31
Parent Company:

SALARIES/BONUSES:

Top Exec. Salary: $1,500,000   Bonus: $

Second Exec. Salary: $1,000,000   Bonus: $

OTHER THOUGHTS:

Estimated Female Officers or Directors: 6

Hot Spot for Advancement for Women/Minorities: Y

Genesco Inc

www.genesco.com

NAIC Code: 424340

TYPES OF BUSINESS:

Shoes, Retail
Retail Stores
Men's Accessories
Wholesale Operations
Hats, Retail
Catalog & Online Operations
Athletic Team Products

BRANDS/DIVISIONS/AFFILIATES:

Johnston & Murphy
Journeys
Underground by Journeys
Journeys Kidz
Schuh
JohnstonMurphy.com
Lids
Shi by Journeys

CONTACTS: *Note: Officers with more than one job title may be intentionally listed here more than once.*

Robert Dennis, CEO
Mimi Vaughn, CFO
Paul Williams, Chief Accounting Officer
Roger Sisson, Secretary
Jonathan Caplan, Senior VP
James Estepa, Senior VP
Kenneth Kocher, Senior VP
Parag Desai, Senior VP, Divisional
Matthew Johnson, Treasurer

GROWTH PLANS/SPECIAL FEATURES:

Genesco, Inc. is a leading specialty retailer of footwear, apparel and accessories through 3,128 retail stores worldwide. These include 2,824 footwear, headwear and sports apparel and accessory stores in the U.S. and Puerto Rico; 154 headwear and sports apparel and accessory stores and 42 footwear stores in Canada; and 108 footwear stores in the U.K. and Ireland. The company operates five business segments: Journeys group, Lids Sports group, Schuh group, Johnston & Murphy group and licensed brands. The Journey's group segment operates 1,182 stores, including Journeys, Journeys Kidz, Shi by Journeys and Underground by Journeys retail footwear chains, and markets products through a catalog and Journeys.com. Journeys stores target customers in the 13-22 year age group. Shi carries shoes targeted at women in their early 20s to mid-30s. Underground carries footwear, apparel and accessories for men and women. The Lids Sports group segment operates 1,364 stores, including Lids Locker Room, Lids Clubhouse, an e-commerce business and an athletic team dealer business operating as Lids Team Sports. The Schuh group segment operates 102 stores, comprised of the Schuh retail footwear chain, and e-commerce operations. Schuh stores targets men and women between 15 and 30 years of age, selling a broad range of branded casual and athletic footwear. The Johnston & Murphy group segment operates 170 retail and factory stores, as well as JohnstonMurphy.com, and sells footwear, luggage and accessories primarily targeting male business and professional customers. Retail prices for Johnston & Murphy footwear generally range from $100 to $275. The licensed brands segment is comprised primarily of Dockers footwear, marketed under a license from Levi Strauss & Company. This footwear is marketed to men ages 30 to 55 through many of the same national retail chains that carry Dockers slack and sportswear.

Employee benefits include medical, prescription, vision and dental coverage; 401(k) plan; stock purchase plan; life insurance; short- and long-term disability; employee discounts; flexible spending accounts; and adoption assistance.

FINANCIAL DATA: *Note: Data for latest year may not have been available at press time.*

In U.S. $	2015	2014	2013	2012	2011	2010
Revenue	2,859,844,000	2,624,972,000	2,604,817,000	2,291,987,000	1,789,839,000	1,574,352,000
R&D Expense						
Operating Income	167,266,000	163,435,000	167,970,000	143,870,000	86,083,000	60,422,000
Operating Margin %	5.84%	6.22%	6.44%	6.27%	4.80%	3.83%
SGA Expense	1,230,864,000	1,134,274,000	1,113,340,000	1,007,502,000	807,197,000	722,087,000
Net Income	97,725,000	92,653,000	110,536,000	81,959,000	53,211,000	28,813,000
Operating Cash Flow	189,764,000	139,999,000	123,210,000	144,960,000	102,608,000	142,096,000
Capital Expenditure	103,111,000	98,456,000	71,737,000	49,456,000	29,299,000	33,825,000
EBITDA	234,652,000	230,636,000	231,762,000	197,672,000	133,829,000	101,951,000
Return on Assets %	6.46%	6.68%	8.59%	7.45%	5.83%	3.42%
Return on Equity %	10.23%	10.77%	14.59%	12.32%	8.89%	5.65%
Debt to Equity	0.01	0.02	0.05	0.04		

CONTACT INFORMATION:

Phone: 615 367-7000   Fax: 615 367-8278
Toll-Free:
Address: 1415 Murfreesboro Rd., Nashville, TN 37217 United States

STOCK TICKER/OTHER:

Stock Ticker: GCO
Employees: 27,325
Parent Company:

Exchange: NYS
Fiscal Year Ends: 01/31

SALARIES/BONUSES:

Top Exec. Salary: $851,000   Bonus: $
Second Exec. Salary: $607,000   Bonus: $

OTHER THOUGHTS:

Estimated Female Officers or Directors: 2
Hot Spot for Advancement for Women/Minorities:

Sales, profits and employees may be estimates. Financial information, benefits and other data can change quickly and may vary from those stated here.

Genuine Parts Company

NAIC Code: 423120

www.genpt.com

TYPES OF BUSINESS:

Auto Parts, Distribution
Industrial Replacement Parts
Office Products Distribution
Electrical & Electronic Materials

BRANDS/DIVISIONS/AFFILIATES:

NAPA (National Automotive Parts Association)
UAP Inc
Motion Industries Inc
EIS Inc
S.P. Richards Company
Grupo Auto Todo
Covs Parts Pty Ltd.
Impact Products LLC

CONTACTS: *Note: Officers with more than one job title may be intentionally listed here more than once.*

Christopher Galla, Assistant General Counsel
Thomas Gallagher, CEO
Carol Yancey, CFO
Jean Douville, Chairman of the Board, Subsidiary
Paul Donahue, Director
Jerry Nix, Director
Timothy Breen, President, Subsidiary
James Neill, Senior VP, Divisional
Kirk Allan, Vice President, Divisional
Thomas Dunmon, Vice President, Divisional
Robert Swann, Vice President, Divisional
Sidney Jones, Vice President, Divisional
Vickie Smith, Vice President, Divisional

GROWTH PLANS/SPECIAL FEATURES:

Genuine Parts Company (GPC) distributes automotive an
industrial replacement parts, office products an
electrical/electronic materials. The company operates throug
four segments: The Automotive Parts Group; The Industria
Parts Group; The Electrical/Electronic Materials Group; an
The Office Products Group. The Automotive Parts Grou
distributes automotive replacement parts and accessory item
through the National Automotive Parts Association (NAPA),
voluntary trade association for the distribution of automotiv
parts. The group includes NAPA stores owned in the U.S. b
GPC. It provides over 450,000 automotive parts, accessor
and service items and operates 60 domestic NAPA automotiv
parts distribution centers in 40 states and approximately 1,10
NAPA Auto Parts stores in 45 states. In addition, UAP, Ind.,
wholly owned subsidiary, operates stores in Canada, as we
as stores and distribution centers in Mexico operated throug
wholly-owned subsidiary Grupo Auto Todo. GPC's Industria
Parts Group, operating through Motion Industries, Inc.
distributes industrial bearings and power transmissio
equipment replacement parts, including industrial automation
hydraulic and pneumatic components, industrial supplies an
material handling products. It operates 523 branches, 1
distribution centers and 39 service centers in North America
The Electrical/Electronic Materials Group, through EIS, Inc.
distributes process materials, production supplies, wire an
cable, insulating and conductive materials, assembly tools an
test equipment, to electrical and electronic manufacturers
throughout North America. Lastly, the Office Products Group
through S. P. Richards Company, is a wholesale distributor o
office and other business-related products for the daily
operation of businesses, schools, offices and institutions. From
a network of 44 distribution centers, it supplies more than
61,000 items to over 5,200 resellers throughout the U.S. and
Canada. In July 2015, GPC's Asia Pacific Unit acquired Covs
Parts Pty Ltd. From Automotive Holdings Group.

GPC offers employee benefits such as medical, dental, vision,
life, disability, and AD&D insurance. Additionally, employees
enjoy flexible spending accounts, 401(k) savings accounts, an
employee assistance program, tuition reimbursement,
employee discounts and a stock purchase plan.

FINANCIAL DATA: *Note: Data for latest year may not have been available at press time.*

In U.S. $	2015	2014	2013	2012	2011	2010
Revenue		15,341,650,000	14,077,840,000	13,013,870,000	12,458,880,000	11,207,590,000
R&D Expense						
Operating Income		1,124,226,000	1,058,236,000	1,023,231,000	909,484,000	786,348,000
Operating Margin %		7.32%	7.51%	7.86%	7.29%	7.01%
SGA Expense		3,314,030,000	3,019,036,000	2,648,430,000	2,594,372,000	2,366,667,000
Net Income		711,286,000	684,959,000	648,041,000	565,116,000	475,511,000
Operating Cash Flow		790,145,000	1,056,731,000	906,438,000	624,927,000	678,663,000
Capital Expenditure		107,681,000	124,063,000	101,987,000	103,469,000	85,379,000
EBITDA		1,291,140,000	1,205,232,000	1,137,797,000	1,006,778,000	879,176,000
Return on Assets %		8.93%	9.45%	10.21%	9.96%	9.08%
Return on Equity %		21.39%	21.58%	22.41%	20.26%	17.56%
Debt to Equity		0.15	0.14	0.08	0.17	0.08

CONTACT INFORMATION:

Phone: 770 953-1700   Fax: 770 956-2211
Toll-Free:
Address: 2999 Circle 75 Pkwy., Atlanta, GA 30339 United States

STOCK TICKER/OTHER:

Stock Ticker: GPC
Employees: 39,000
Parent Company:

Exchange: NYS
Fiscal Year Ends: 12/31

SALARIES/BONUSES:

Top Exec. Salary:
$1,091,750
Second Exec. Salary:
$612,000

Bonus: $

Bonus: $

OTHER THOUGHTS:

Estimated Female Officers or Directors: 2

Hot Spot for Advancement for Women/Minorities: Y

George Weston Limited

www.weston.ca

NAIC Code: 445110

TYPES OF BUSINESS:

Grocery Stores-Retail
Financial Services
Bakeries
Food Distribution

BRANDS/DIVISIONS/AFFILIATES:

Weston Foods
Loblaw Companies Limited
Weston Bakeries
Ready Bake Foods
Maplehurst Bakeries
Interbake Foods
President's Choice Financial
PC Blue Menu

CONTACTS: *Note: Officers with more than one job title may be intentionally listed here more than once.*

Kerry Rathbone, Assistant Secretary
Nadeem Mansour, Vice President, Divisional
W. Weston, CEO
Richard Dufresne, CFO
Allison Doner, Controller
Paviter Binning, Director
Rashid Wasti, Executive VP
Robert A. Balcom, Other Corporate Officer
Brian Bidulka, Other Executive Officer
Gordon A.M. Currie, Other Executive Officer
Khush Dadyburjor, Senior VP, Divisional
Geoffrey H. Wilson, Senior VP, Divisional
John Williams, Treasurer
Tamara Rebanks, Vice President, Divisional
Paul Barnicke, Vice President, Divisional
Ian Freedman, Vice President, Divisional
John Poos, Vice President, Divisional

GROWTH PLANS/SPECIAL FEATURES:

George Weston Limited (GWL), founded in 1882, is a major food processor and distributor throughout Canada and the U.S. The company is divided into two reportable segments: Weston Foods and Loblaw Companies Limited. Weston Foods, with over 40 locations, is primarily engaged in the fresh and frozen bakery industries in North America, with operations in biscuits and other bakery products. Its Canadian operations include Weston Bakeries, Ready Bake Foods, ACE Bakery and Colonial Cookies. Weston's U.S. operations consist of Maplehurst Bakeries, Interbake Foods and Norse Dairy Systems. Loblaw manages the company's food distribution units and is one of the largest food distributors in Canada. Moreover, the division is also a leading provider of general merchandise, drugstore and financial products and services. Loblaw owns and manages over 2,300 corporate, franchised and associated stores under multiple regional store names, including President's Choice, PC Blue Menu, PC Organics, PC Green Joe, Spendido, Farmer's Market, exact and no name. In addition, the firm makes available to consumers President's Choice Financial, whose services and products include daily banking services, mortgages, savings and investment products, mutual funds, loans and the PC MasterCard. The company also offers a loyalty program known as PC points.

GWL offers its employees an employee share ownership program and a group registered retirement savings plan, an onsite gym, a subsidized fitness membership, maternity and parental leave and paid personal leave.

FINANCIAL DATA: *Note: Data for latest year may not have been available at press time.*

In U.S. $	2015	2014	2013	2012	2011	2010
Revenue		32,902,550,000	25,159,010,000	24,529,700,000	24,255,500,000	23,979,800,000
R&D Expense						
Operating Income		728,953,600	1,214,423,000	1,042,861,000	1,205,433,000	1,111,036,000
Operating Margin %		2.21%	4.82%	4.25%	4.96%	4.63%
SGA Expense		7,655,137,000	5,000,786,000	4,982,057,000	4,754,306,000	4,558,020,000
Net Income		94,396,870	504,948,400	364,102,200	475,730,300	338,630,000
Operating Cash Flow		2,135,917,000	1,302,077,000	1,387,484,000	1,478,884,000	1,304,325,000
Capital Expenditure		909,506,400	740,191,400	863,806,200	769,409,400	976,932,700
EBITDA		1,918,654,000	1,940,380,000	1,672,173,000	1,913,410,000	1,648,199,000
Return on Assets %		.26%	2.90%	2.25%	3.01%	2.20%
Return on Equity %		1.28%	11.21%	8.71%	10.95%	6.91%
Debt to Equity		1.90	1.22	1.09	1.23	0.83

CONTACT INFORMATION:

Phone: 416 922-2500   Fax: 416 922-4395
Toll-Free:
Address: 22 St. Clair Ave. E., Toronto, ON M4T 2S7 Canada

SALARIES/BONUSES:

Top Exec. Salary: $ Bonus: $
Second Exec. Salary: $ Bonus: $

STOCK TICKER/OTHER:

Stock Ticker: WN
Employees: 5,800
Parent Company:

Exchange: TSE
Fiscal Year Ends: 12/31

OTHER THOUGHTS:

Estimated Female Officers or Directors: 6
Hot Spot for Advancement for Women/Minorities: Y

Gianni Versace SpA

NAIC Code: 424300

www.versace.com/en/the-group

TYPES OF BUSINESS:

Apparel and Clothing Brands, Designers, Importers and Distributors
Retail Boutiques
Accessories & Eyewear
Home Furnishings
Beauty Products & Fragrances
Hotels & Resorts

BRANDS/DIVISIONS/AFFILIATES:

Versace Collection
Versace Sport
Versus
Versace Jeans Couture
Palazzo Versace Dubai
Palazzo Versace Luxury Hotel and Resort
Blackstone Group LP (The)

CONTACTS: Note: Officers with more than one job title may be intentionally listed here more than once.

Gian Giacomo Ferraris, CEO
Donatella Versace, Dir.-Creative
Santo Versace, Chmn.

GROWTH PLANS/SPECIAL FEATURES:

Gianni Versace SpA, founded in 1978, is one of the world's leading international fashion houses. The company designs, manufactures, distributes and retails luxury fashion and lifestyle products, clothing, jewelry, accessories, fragrances, cosmetics and home furnishings under a variety of brand names. The company's portfolio of brands covers two primary segments of the market. The higher end is addressed by the Gianni Versace collection and includes apparel, jewelry, watches, accessories, fragrances, cosmetics and home furnishings, all of which are distributed through a world-wide retail network including free-standing boutiques in principal cities. The second segment is addressed towards a younger target consumer and includes the Versace Collection, Versace Sport, Versace Jeans Couture and Versus brands. These items are distributed through free-standing stores. The company's products are also sold through its 80 branded stores and approximately 1,800 corners in multi-brand/department stores. In partnership with Sunland Group Ltd., an Australian development company, the firm owns and operates the Palazzo Versace Luxury Hotel and Resort, a 205-room hotel located on the Gold Coast of Australia; and Palazzo Versace Dubai, located in the UAE. The firm is currently undergoing a complete restructuring of its brands and retail strategy. In 2014, The Blackstone Group, LP purchased a 20% stake in the company.

FINANCIAL DATA: Note: Data for latest year may not have been available at press time.

In U.S. $	2015	2014	2013	2012	2011	2010
Revenue		595,900,000	659,700,000	552,927,110	390,110,000	382,796,000
R&D Expense						
Operating Income						
Operating Margin %						
SGA Expense						
Net Income		28,602,180	15,000,000	11,700,000	9,500,000	
Operating Cash Flow						
Capital Expenditure						
EBITDA						
Return on Assets %						
Return on Equity %						
Debt to Equity						

CONTACT INFORMATION:

Phone: 39-02-76-09-31   Fax: 39-02-76-00-41-22
Toll-Free:
Address: Via Manzoni, 38, Milan, 20121 Italy

STOCK TICKER/OTHER:

Stock Ticker: Private
Employees:
Parent Company:

Exchange:
Fiscal Year Ends: 12/31

SALARIES/BONUSES:

Top Exec. Salary: $ Bonus: $
Second Exec. Salary: $ Bonus: $

OTHER THOUGHTS:

Estimated Female Officers or Directors: 1
Hot Spot for Advancement for Women/Minorities: Y

Giant Eagle Inc

www.gianteagle.com

NAIC Code: 445110

TYPES OF BUSINESS:

Grocery Stores
Video Rentals
Pharmacies
Gas Stations

BRANDS/DIVISIONS/AFFILIATES:

Giant Eagle
Market District
Giant Eagle Advantage Card

CONTACTS: *Note: Officers with more than one job title may be intentionally listed here more than once.*

Laura Shapira Karet, CEO
John Lucot, COO
David S. Shapira, Pres.
Ian Prisuta, Sr. VP-Grocery Merch.
Mark Minnaugh, Chief Admin. Officer
Brett L. Merrell, Sr. VP-Supermarket Strategy & Dev.

GROWTH PLANS/SPECIAL FEATURES:

Giant Eagle, Inc. operates nearly 218 corporate and independently owned grocery stores under the Giant Eagle name. These stores are primarily located in Ohio, Pennsylvania, West Virginia and Maryland. In addition to groceries, Giant Eagle stores offer video rentals, in-store banking, pharmacy services, floral shops, photo processing and ready-to-eat lunch/dinner dishes. Stores carry 20,000 to over 60,000 products, including more than 10,000 branded products. The company also operates seven stores under the name Market District. These stores carry primarily the same products as Giant Eagle stores, but include upscale amenities such as a kosher deli, international foods, a WiFi enabled cafe, cooking demonstrations and a focus on natural and organic foods. Over 4.6 million customers are enrolled in the Giant Eagle Advantage Card program, which provides special offers, lifestyle information and tips and electronic offers and discounts online. The company is active in its communities, aiding local food banks, community events, the United Way and other nonprofit organizations. It also recycles over 141 million pounds of material annually.

Employees of Giant Eagle receive health, dental and vision care; health savings accounts; flexible spending accounts; prescription discounts; a 401(k); a company-paid pension plan and life insurance; long- and short-term disability insurance; employee assistance plans; vacation packages; adoption benefits; and domestic partner benefits.

FINANCIAL DATA: *Note: Data for latest year may not have been available at press time.*

In U.S. $	2015	2014	2013	2012	2011	2010
Revenue		9,700,000,000	9,500,000,000	9,400,000,000	9,300,000,000	8,200,000,000
R&D Expense						
Operating Income						
Operating Margin %						
SGA Expense						
Net Income						
Operating Cash Flow						
Capital Expenditure						
EBITDA						
Return on Assets %						
Return on Equity %						
Debt to Equity						

CONTACT INFORMATION:

Phone: 412-963-6200   Fax: 412-968-1617
Toll-Free: 800-553-2324
Address: 101 Kappa Dr., Pittsburgh, PA 15238 United States

SALARIES/BONUSES:

Top Exec. Salary: $ Bonus: $
Second Exec. Salary: $ Bonus: $

STOCK TICKER/OTHER:

Stock Ticker: Private
Employees: 36,000
Parent Company:

Exchange:
Fiscal Year Ends: 06/30

OTHER THOUGHTS:

Estimated Female Officers or Directors: 2
Hot Spot for Advancement for Women/Minorities:

G-III Apparel Group Ltd

www.g-iii.com

NAIC Code: 424300

TYPES OF BUSINESS:

Apparel and Clothing Brands, Designers, Importers and Distributors
Outerwear & Sportswear
Handbags & Luggage
Leather Accessories

BRANDS/DIVISIONS/AFFILIATES:

Vilebrequin
Andrew Marc
Marc New York
Jessica Howard
Eliza J
Bass
Black Rivet

CONTACTS: *Note: Officers with more than one job title may be intentionally listed here more than once.*

Morris Goldfarb, CEO
Neal Nackman, CFO
Wayne Miller, COO
Sammy Aaron, Director

GROWTH PLANS/SPECIAL FEATURES:

G-III Apparel Group, Ltd. designs, manufactures, imports an
markets an extensive range of licensed and private-labe
branded outerwear and sportswear, including coats, jackets
pants, dresses and other sportswear items as well a
handbags and luggage. G-III operates in three segments
licensed products, non-licensed products and retail. Among it
many licensed brands are Calvin Klein, Kenneth Cole, Guess?
Cole Haan and Tommy Hilfiger. In the team sports business
the company has licenses with the National Football League
National Basketball Association, Major League Baseball
National Hockey League, Touch by Alyssa Milano and over 100
U.S. colleges and universities. The company-owned label
sold by the non-licensed apparel segment include Vilebrequin
Andrew Marc, Marc New York, Jessica Howard, Eliza J, Bass
and Black Rivet. The retail segment operates 185 Wilsons
Leather retail outlet stores, 156 G.H. Bass outlet stores and 7
Vilebrequin retail stores. G-III's products are generally sold by
department, specialty and mass merchant retail stores. The
firm imports its products from independent manufacturers
located primarily in China and, to a lesser extent, in Vietnam
Indonesia, Pakistan, India and Central and South America
Vilebrequin's products are manufactured in Bulgaria, Tunisia
Romania and Morocco. In June 2015, G-III (49%) formed a join
venture with Karl Lagerfeld Group BV (51%) for the
development of the Lagerfeld's brand in the North American
market.

FINANCIAL DATA: *Note: Data for latest year may not have been available at press time.*

In U.S. $	2015	2014	2013	2012	2011	2010
Revenue	2,116,855,000	1,718,231,000	1,399,719,000	1,231,201,000	1,063,404,000	800,864,000
R&D Expense						
Operating Income	164,895,000	131,451,000	100,488,000	86,224,000	96,932,000	56,207,000
Operating Margin %	7.78%	7.65%	7.17%	7.00%	9.11%	7.01%
SGA Expense	571,990,000	440,506,000	341,242,000	277,019,000	248,380,000	205,281,000
Net Income	110,361,000	77,360,000	56,875,000	49,620,000	56,682,000	31,718,000
Operating Cash Flow	81,600,000	84,593,000	54,494,000	6,776,000	-28,649,000	43,999,000
Capital Expenditure	42,566,000	29,283,000	11,615,000	17,410,000	19,407,000	1,477,000
EBITDA	185,269,000	145,127,000	109,710,000	92,426,000	102,665,000	61,587,000
Return on Assets %	11.75%	9.99%	9.00%	9.89%	14.37%	10.34%
Return on Equity %	17.18%	16.24%	14.44%	15.00%	21.16%	16.08%
Debt to Equity			0.03	0.04		

CONTACT INFORMATION:

Phone: 212 403-0500   Fax: 212 403-0551
Toll-Free:
Address: 512 7th Ave., New York, NY 10018 United States

SALARIES/BONUSES:

Top Exec. Salary:
$1,000,000
Second Exec. Salary:
$750,000

Bonus: $9,978,064

Bonus: $6,513,458

STOCK TICKER/OTHER:

Stock Ticker: GIII
Employees: 6,641
Parent Company:

Exchange: NAS
Fiscal Year Ends: 01/31

OTHER THOUGHTS:

Estimated Female Officers or Directors: 1

Hot Spot for Advancement for Women/Minorities:

Sales, profits and employees may be estimates. Financial information, benefits and other data can change quickly and may vary from those stated here.

Giorgio Armani SpA

www.giorgioarmani.com

NAIC Code: 424300

TYPES OF BUSINESS:

Apparel and Clothing Brands, Designers, Importers and Distributors
Men's & Women's Suits & Apparel
Children's Apparel
Home Furnishings & Accessories
Retail Apparel Stores
Jewelry, Cosmetics & Fragrances
Watches
Online Sales

BRANDS/DIVISIONS/AFFILIATES:

Giorgio Armani
Armani Collezioni
Emporio Armani
Armani Junior
A/X Armani Exchange
Armani Casa
Armani Dolci
Armani Hotels & Resorts

CONTACTS: Note: Officers with more than one job title may be intentionally listed here more than once.

Giorgio Armani, CEO
Giorgio Armani, Pres.
Bruno Laguardia, Head-Giorgio Armani Corp.
Livio Proli, Gen. Mgr.
Giorgio Armani, Chmn.

GROWTH PLANS/SPECIAL FEATURES:

Giorgio Armani SpA is one of the world's leading fashion and luxury goods groups, best known for its men's and women's suits. It designs, manufactures, distributes and retails fashion and lifestyle products, including apparel, accessories, glasses, watches, jewelry, home interiors, fragrances and cosmetics under a variety of brand names. The company also licenses its name for perfume, watches and accessories. The firm's brands include the men's and women's apparel collections Giorgio Armani, Armani Collezioni, Emporio Armani and A/X Armani Exchange; sportswear brand EA7; Armani Jeans; children's brand Armani Junior, which includes boy's, girl's and baby/toddler lines; and a home collection called Armani Casa, which includes furniture, home accessories, dishware and linens lines. Armani retails its products through various types of locations worldwide. Armani also owns a chain of chocolate stores, Armani Dolci throughout Europe, the Middle East and Asia. The company also owns manufacturing companies Intai Spa, Antinea Srl and Simint Spa. The company established Armani Hotels & Resorts through an agreement with Emaar Properties to develop, own and operate a collection of hotels, resorts and residences in major world cities and holiday destinations, including a luxury hotel in Dubai, in the Burj Khalifa; and a luxury hotel in Milan. In July 2015, the firm signed a luxury home project in Beijing, covering more than 700,000 square feet, the project consists of homes, offices, underground malls and a shopping street. The project is expected to be complete in 2017.

FINANCIAL DATA: Note: Data for latest year may not have been available at press time.

In U.S. $	2015	2014	2013	2012	2011	2010
Revenue		2,725,740,000	2,602,320,000	2,400,000,000	2,200,000,000	2,050,000,000
R&D Expense						
Operating Income						
Operating Margin %						
SGA Expense						
Net Income			434,500,000	351,945,000		
Operating Cash Flow						
Capital Expenditure						
EBITDA						
Return on Assets %						
Return on Equity %						
Debt to Equity						

CONTACT INFORMATION:

Phone: 39-02-723-18-1   Fax: 39-02-723-18-549
Toll-Free:
Address: Via Borgonuovo 11, Milan, 20121 Italy

STOCK TICKER/OTHER:

Stock Ticker: Private   Exchange:
Employees: 3,100   Fiscal Year Ends: 12/31
Parent Company:

SALARIES/BONUSES:

Top Exec. Salary: $ Bonus: $
Second Exec. Salary: $ Bonus: $

OTHER THOUGHTS:

Estimated Female Officers or Directors:
Hot Spot for Advancement for Women/Minorities:

GNC Holdings Inc

NAIC Code: 446191

www.gnc.com

TYPES OF BUSINESS:

Nutritional Supplements, Retail
Fitness Equipment
Online Sales
Nutritional Supplements, Manufacturing

BRANDS/DIVISIONS/AFFILIATES:

General Nutrition Centers Inc
GNC Live Well
GNC Puredge
Pro Performance
Ultra Mega
GNC.com
DiscountSupplements.co.uk
LuckyVitamin.com

CONTACTS: Note: Officers with more than one job title may be intentionally listed here more than once.

Michael Archbold, CEO
Tricia Tolivar, CFO
Jeffrey Hennion, Chief Marketing Officer
Patrick Fortune, Controller
Michael Hines, Director
Michael Dzura, Executive VP, Divisional
Daisy Vanderlinde, Other Executive Officer
James Sander, Other Executive Officer
Guru Ramanathan, Other Executive Officer
Greg Szabo, Senior VP, Divisional
Dennis Magulick, Vice President, Divisional

GROWTH PLANS/SPECIAL FEATURES:

GNC Holdings, Inc., the parent of General Nutrition Centers Inc. (GNC), is a leading specialty retailer of nutritional supplements in the U.S. The company operates more than 6,400 retail outlets throughout the U.S. and international markets. GNC Holdings operates in three segments: retail, accounting for 74% of revenue; franchise, 17%; and manufacturing/wholesale, 9%. The company's GNC Live Well store format offers a full range of supplements and expanded product lines, such as aromatherapy, bath and spa and a broad selection of self-care-related products. GNC's products are divided mainly into four groups: sports nutrition products, vitamins and minerals, diet products and other wellness products. Through a strategic alliance with Rite Aid Corporation, the firm manufactures Rite Aid private-label products and is present in 2,269 of the Rite Aid's total locations through a store-within-a-store model. The firm also sells its proprietary products to PetSmart and Sam's Club. Through a partnership with Drugstore.com, GNC has the exclusive online rights to sell GNC-brand products. The firm's products are sold under proprietary brands including Mega Men, Pro Performance AMP, Beyond Raw, GNC Puredge, GNC GenetixHD, Herbal Plus, Total Lean and Ultra Mega as well as under nationally recognized third party brands. The firm offers additional products through its online channels GNC.com, DiscountSupplements.co.uk and LuckyVitamin.com. GNC operates manufacturing facilities in South Carolina and distribution centers in Pennsylvania, Indiana, South Carolina and Arizona.

FINANCIAL DATA: Note: Data for latest year may not have been available at press time.

In U.S. $	2015	2014	2013	2012	2011	2010
Revenue		2,613,154,000	2,630,308,000	2,429,983,000	2,072,179,000	1,822,168,000
R&D Expense						
Operating Income		439,512,000	460,498,000	427,840,000	282,507,000	212,406,000
Operating Margin %		16.81%	17.50%	17.60%	13.63%	11.65%
SGA Expense		550,646,000	520,441,000	501,988,000	471,205,000	426,191,000
Net Income		255,872,000	265,021,000	240,196,000	132,333,000	111,947,000
Operating Cash Flow		303,785,000	238,104,000	221,216,000	174,674,000	141,500,000
Capital Expenditure		70,455,000	50,247,000	41,930,000	43,817,000	32,522,000
EBITDA		494,373,000	502,142,000	477,125,000	328,187,000	260,057,000
Return on Assets %		9.44%	10.01%	9.64%	5.25%	4.72%
Return on Equity %		32.56%	31.22%	25.82%	15.97%	19.40%
Debt to Equity		1.76	1.64	1.24	0.91	1.66

CONTACT INFORMATION:

Phone: 412 288-4600   Fax:
Toll-Free:
Address: 300 6th Ave., Pittsburgh, PA 15222 United States

STOCK TICKER/OTHER:

Stock Ticker: GNC
Employees: 16,500
Parent Company:

Exchange: NYS
Fiscal Year Ends: 12/31

SALARIES/BONUSES:

Top Exec. Salary: $365,385   Bonus: $545,833
Second Exec. Salary: $690,536   Bonus: $

OTHER THOUGHTS:

Estimated Female Officers or Directors:
Hot Spot for Advancement for Women/Minorities:

Golub Corporation

www.pricechopper.com

NAIC Code: 445110

TYPES OF BUSINESS:

Supermarkets
Online Sales & Delivery
Pharmacies

BRANDS/DIVISIONS/AFFILIATES:

Price Chopper
Ben and Bill's Deli
Central Market Classics
Price Chopper House Calls Pharmacy
Bella Roma Italian Specialties
Market 32
Fairway Pharmacy

CONTACTS: *Note: Officers with more than one job title may be intentionally listed here more than once.*

Jerel (Jerry) Gloub, CEO
Scott Grimmett, COO
Mona Golub, VP- PR, Consumer &Mktg. Services
Dick Bauer, CIO
Tony Farah, CTO
John J. Endres, Sr. VP-Finance
Neil M. Golub, Chmn.

GROWTH PLANS/SPECIAL FEATURES:

Golub Corporation, run by the Golub family since 1943, operates 135 Price Chopper Supermarkets and Market 32 grocery stores throughout New York, Vermont, Massachusetts, Connecticut, Pennsylvania and New Hampshire. In addition to the standard supermarket fare of meats, fresh produce and floral arrangements, Price Chopper stores offer proprietary-brand Central Market Classics appetizers, entrees, side dishes and desserts as well as freshly baked bagels, Bella Roma Italian Specialties, salad bars, artisan breads and deli meats. Several locations also contain a kosher section and Ben and Bill's Delis, designed to resemble traditional New York delicatessens. The Price Chopper web site allows online ordering of flowers, deli platters, fruit baskets, party cakes, lobster dinners and gift certificates. Pharmacies are located in 70 stores and at four separate Price Chopper House Calls Pharmacy locations. The company recently announced plans for growth through the year 2018. The plan includes new, expanded and replacement stores as well as new warehouses, major warehouse expansions and the construction of a new energy-efficient main office building. Golub is also continually introducing environmentally friendly technologies to its stores. In November 2014, the company announced a new banner for its store, Market 32. The rebranding was initiated in spring 2015. In August 2015, the firm's Price Chopper Supermarkets acquired Fairway Pharmacy in Montrose, PA.

The firm offers employees medical, vision and dental insurance; flexible spending accounts; life insurance; disability coverage; a 401(k) plan: a profit sharing plan: a pension program; tuition reimbursement; scholarships; and credit union membership. Employees own over 50% of the firm's privately held stock.

FINANCIAL DATA: *Note: Data for latest year may not have been available at press time.*

In U.S. $	2015	2014	2013	2012	2011	2010
Revenue		3,630,000,000	3,600,000,000	3,500,000,000	3,400,000,000	3,500,000,000
R&D Expense						
Operating Income						
Operating Margin %						
SGA Expense						
Net Income						
Operating Cash Flow						
Capital Expenditure						
EBITDA						
Return on Assets %						
Return on Equity %						
Debt to Equity						

CONTACT INFORMATION:

Phone: 518-355-5000   Fax: 518-379-3536
Toll-Free: 800-666-7667
Address: 461 Nott St., Schenectady, NY 12308 United States

STOCK TICKER/OTHER:

Stock Ticker: Private
Employees: 23,000
Parent Company:

Exchange:
Fiscal Year Ends: 04/30

SALARIES/BONUSES:

Top Exec. Salary: $ Bonus: $
Second Exec. Salary: $ Bonus: $

OTHER THOUGHTS:

Estimated Female Officers or Directors:
Hot Spot for Advancement for Women/Minorities: Y

Sales, profits and employees may be estimates. Financial information, benefits and other data can change quickly and may vary from those stated here.

GOME Electrical Appliance

NAIC Code: 443141

www.gome.com.hk

TYPES OF BUSINESS:

Household Appliance Stores

BRANDS/DIVISIONS/AFFILIATES:

GOME

GROWTH PLANS/SPECIAL FEATURES:

GOME Electrical Appliance is a specialty retail shop electrical appliances in China. The company's stores operat under the brand name GOME. In 2014, GOME owned 1,13: stores in 264 large and medium-sized cities nationwide. C these stores, 517 are non-listed GOME group stores, 256 are flagship stores, 335 are standard stores and 541 are specialized stores. Of 2014 revenue, 36% came from to brands from other retailers; Beijing, 17%; Guangzhou, 10% Shanghai, 9%; Shenzhen, 8%; Xian, 7%; Chengdu, 7%; and Chongqing, 6%.

CONTACTS: Note: Officers with more than one job title may be intentionally listed here more than once.

Jun Zhou Wang, CEO
Wei Fang, CFO
Xiao Chun Zou, Chmn.

FINANCIAL DATA: Note: Data for latest year may not have been available at press time.

In U.S. $	2015	2014	2013	2012	2011	2010
Revenue		9,447,759,000	8,828,052,000	7,492,371,000	9,363,384,000	7,968,655,000
R&D Expense						
Operating Income		207,273,500	158,796,500	-141,109,100	363,656,700	423,499,600
Operating Margin %		2.19%	1.79%	-1.88%	3.88%	5.31%
SGA Expense		1,444,345,000	1,364,405,000	1,287,718,000	1,271,294,000	982,882,700
Net Income		159,367,600	106,036,300	-126,783,000	281,953,700	307,045,800
Operating Cash Flow		134,817,200	312,273,300	647,581,100	59,991,080	606,245,100
Capital Expenditure		98,548,080	68,232,530	122,603,500	134,837,500	79,402,540
EBITDA		345,223,000	286,655,600	5,380,353	488,778,900	515,423,100
Return on Assets %		3.06%	2.35%	-1.62%	5.01%	5.45%
Return on Equity %		7.79%	5.74%	-3.83%	11.99%	14.78%
Debt to Equity						0.12

CONTACT INFORMATION:

Phone: 86-10-5928-8915   Fax: 86-10-5928-8925
Toll-Free:
Address: 18/F, Block B, Eagle Plaza, No.26 Xiaoyun Road, Beijing, 100016 China

STOCK TICKER/OTHER:

Stock Ticker: GMELY
Employees: 42,839
Parent Company:

Exchange: PINX
Fiscal Year Ends: 12/31

SALARIES/BONUSES:

Top Exec. Salary: $ Bonus: $
Second Exec. Salary: $ Bonus: $

OTHER THOUGHTS:

Estimated Female Officers or Directors: 3
Hot Spot for Advancement for Women/Minorities: Y

Gordmans Stores Inc

www.gordmans.com

NAIC Code: 448140

TYPES OF BUSINESS:

Apparel Stores
Off-Price Retail

BRANDS/DIVISIONS/AFFILIATES:

Gordmans

CONTACTS: *Note: Officers with more than one job title may be intentionally listed here more than once.*

Richard Heyman, Chief Information Officer
Michael Wirkkala, COO
T. King, Director
James Brown, Executive VP
Lisa Evans, Executive VP
Andrew Hall, Secretary
Geoffrey Ayoub, Senior VP, Divisional
Amy Myers, Senior VP, Divisional
Tracie Wickenhauser, Senior VP, Divisional
Roger Glenn, Senior VP, Divisional

GROWTH PLANS/SPECIAL FEATURES:

Gordmans Stores, Inc. is a discount apparel and accessories retailer operating throughout the Midwest and Southeast U.S. The firm currently operates 97 stores in 21 states, all under the Gordmans name. Its stores are located in a variety of shopping center developments, including regional enclosed shopping malls, lifestyle centers and power centers. The firm's merchandise assortment includes apparel for all ages, which accounted for 56.8% of its 2015 revenue; home fashions, 27.7%; and accessories, 15.5%. Additionally, the company maintains a licensing agreement with Destination Maternity Corporation to provide maternity products in each of its stores. It also has a similar arrangement with DSW, Inc. for its footwear departments. Gordmans is aligned in the off-price retail segment, offering nationally branded merchandise at prices below larger department store competitors. Unlike similar retailers in the off-price segment, Gordmans utilizes merchandising techniques, visual displays, a departmental floor layout, fixture systems, signing and graphics akin to those of department and specialty stores. The firm, through an agreement with Alliance Data Systems, offers a private label Gordmans credit card.

FINANCIAL DATA: *Note: Data for latest year may not have been available at press time.*

In U.S. $	2015	2014	2013	2012	2011	2010
Revenue	643,228,000	627,387,000	615,053,000	558,146,000	523,322,000	463,212,000
R&D Expense						
Operating Income	-931,000	14,793,000	38,131,000	40,895,000	25,960,000	26,193,000
Operating Margin %	- .14%	2.35%	6.19%	7.32%	4.96%	5.65%
SGA Expense	265,276,000	247,131,000	226,710,000	201,084,000	198,302,000	167,842,000
Net Income	-3,476,000	8,013,000	23,531,000	25,173,000	15,598,000	15,868,000
Operating Cash Flow	45,180,000	20,815,000	26,505,000	27,116,000	12,383,000	40,070,000
Capital Expenditure	42,862,000	60,133,000	34,237,000	31,164,000	8,959,000	3,865,000
EBITDA	12,767,000	24,634,000	45,109,000	45,202,000	28,595,000	27,950,000
Return on Assets %	-1.60%	4.02%	13.30%	17.49%	14.35%	18.67%
Return on Equity %	-8.65%	11.11%	26.12%	38.79%	39.99%	62.61%
Debt to Equity	0.74	1.06			0.01	0.02

CONTACT INFORMATION:

Phone: 402 691-4000   Fax: 402 691-4269
Toll-Free:
Address: 12100 W. Center Rd., Omaha, NE 68144 United States

STOCK TICKER/OTHER:

Stock Ticker: GMAN   Exchange: NAS
Employees: 550   Fiscal Year Ends: 01/31
Parent Company:

SALARIES/BONUSES:

Top Exec. Salary: $309,615   Bonus: $257,715
Second Exec. Salary: Bonus: $50,000
$291,346

OTHER THOUGHTS:

Estimated Female Officers or Directors: 1
Hot Spot for Advancement for Women/Minorities:

Gristede's Foods Inc

www.gristedes.com

NAIC Code: 445110

TYPES OF BUSINESS:
Grocery Stores
Pharmacies
Wholesale Groceries

BRANDS/DIVISIONS/AFFILIATES:
Red Apple Group Inc
City Produce Operating Corp.
Gristede's
Diamond Value Club

CONTACTS: Note: Officers with more than one job title may be intentionally listed here more than once.
John A. Catsimatidis, CEO
John A. Catsimatidis, Pres.
John A. Catsimatidis, Chmn.

GROWTH PLANS/SPECIAL FEATURES:

Gristede's Foods, Inc. operates supermarkets in the New York City area, mainly in Manhattan and Westchester County. Merchandise offered at the supermarkets includes fresh meats, produce, dry groceries, flowers, dairy products, fresh fruits/vegetables, poultry, fish, baked goods, frozen foods, gourmet foods, paper products and health/beauty aids. The company also provides a variety of customer services, including check cashing for qualified customers. In addition, four of the stores contain pharmacies. Most of the firm's supermarkets are relatively small due to the stores' typically urban environments and serve a predominantly affluent clientele. To supply the company's supermarkets, as well as third parties, Gristede's also operates a wholesale arm, City Produce Operating Corp. The company offers customers membership in the Diamond Value Club, a loyalty program that issues additional savings and purchase tracking through a Diamond Value Club card. The firm is wholly-owned by Red Apple Group, Inc., which has investments in oil refineries, convenience stores and real estate in New York, Pennsylvania and Ohio.

The company offers its employees benefits including medical, dental and vision coverage; and a 401(k) plan.

FINANCIAL DATA: Note: Data for latest year may not have been available at press time.

In U.S. $	2015	2014	2013	2012	2011	2010
Revenue						
R&D Expense						
Operating Income						
Operating Margin %						
SGA Expense						
Net Income						
Operating Cash Flow						
Capital Expenditure						
EBITDA						
Return on Assets %						
Return on Equity %						
Debt to Equity						

CONTACT INFORMATION:
Phone: 212-956-5803   Fax: 212-247-4509
Toll-Free:
Address: 823 11th Ave., New York, NY 10019 United States

STOCK TICKER/OTHER:
Stock Ticker: Subsidiary   Exchange:
Employees: 800   Fiscal Year Ends: 11/30
Parent Company: RED APPLE GROUP INC

SALARIES/BONUSES:
Top Exec. Salary: $ Bonus: $
Second Exec. Salary: $ Bonus: $

OTHER THOUGHTS:
Estimated Female Officers or Directors:
Hot Spot for Advancement for Women/Minorities:

Groupe Adeo

www.groupe-adeo.com

NAIC Code: 444110

TYPES OF BUSINESS:

Home Improvement Stores

BRANDS/DIVISIONS/AFFILIATES:

Leroy Merlin
www.kozikaza.com
AKI
decoclico.fr
zodio.fr
decoclico.fr
delamaison.fr
Bricoman

CONTACTS: Note: Officers with more than one job title may be intentionally listed here more than once.

Damien Deleplanque, CEO
Frank Lely, Dir.-Finance
Cristian Marinelli, Exec. VP-Human Resources
Regis Degelcke, Exec VP Warehouse Stores
Pascal Delfosse, Exec VP Multispecialist
Philippe Dailliez, Exec VP Strategy and Devel
Frank Lely, Exec. VP-Finance
Alain Ryckeboer, Managing Dir.-Leroy Merlin Brazil
Philippe Zimmerman, Managing Dir.-Leroy Merlin France
Matthieu Phanthala, Managing Dir.-Leroy Merlin China
Vincent Gentil, Managing Dir.-Leroy Merlin Russia
Pierre Cavarec, Managing Dir.-Leroy Merlin Ukraine
Felix Fernandez, Exec. VP-Supply Chain Management

GROWTH PLANS/SPECIAL FEATURES:

Groupe Adeo (ADEO), based in Lille, France, is one of Europe's largest retailers of home-improvement merchandise. The company is a combination of 30 autonomous companies in 12 countries dedicated to 15 retail chains. It is a leading supplier of consumer goods for household do-it-yourself and decorating projects, with a customer base of 300 million households. ADEO operates through five different business areas: multi-specialists, local chains, home decoration chains and warehouse/professional stores. The multi-specialist segment comprises 384 stores that range from 21,300 to 55,700 square feet and feature the Leroy Merlin and Kozikaza brands. Items within this division can also be found online at www.kozikaza.com. The local chains segment comprises 352 stores, of which 211 are franchises, which range from 3,200 to 13,000 square feet. Brands within this division include AKI, BRICO and Weldom. The specialist chain division comprises two Kbane stores in France. The home decoration chains division includes 14 ZODIO stores in Europe, five online sales referral websites and 1 Homes-Up showroom in Asia. The online sites include decoclico.fr, deco-smart.com, delamaison.fr, lightonline.fr and zodio.fr. The warehouse/professional stores segment comprises 72 Bricoman and Bricomart stores, as well as 165 DomPro outlets, all of which range from 16,400 to 32,800 square feet in size.

FINANCIAL DATA: Note: Data for latest year may not have been available at press time.

In U.S. $	2015	2014	2013	2012	2011	2010
Revenue		21,500,000,000	20,325,000,000	20,150,000,000	19,140,490,000	17,342,300,000
R&D Expense						
Operating Income						
Operating Margin %						
SGA Expense						
Net Income						
Operating Cash Flow						
Capital Expenditure						
EBITDA						
Return on Assets %						
Return on Equity %						
Debt to Equity						

CONTACT INFORMATION:

Phone: 33-359-31-5300   Fax: 33-328-880-8008
Toll-Free:
Address: 135 Rue Chanzy-Lezennes, Lille Cedex, 59712 France

STOCK TICKER/OTHER:

Stock Ticker: Private
Employees: 87,000
Parent Company:

Exchange:
Fiscal Year Ends:

SALARIES/BONUSES:

Top Exec. Salary: $ Bonus: $
Second Exec. Salary: $ Bonus: $

OTHER THOUGHTS:

Estimated Female Officers or Directors:
Hot Spot for Advancement for Women/Minorities:

Groupe Auchan SA

www.auchan.com

NAIC Code: 452112

TYPES OF BUSINESS:

Hypermarkets
Supermarkets
Shopping Centers
Consumer Banking
Real Estate
Housewares

BRANDS/DIVISIONS/AFFILIATES:

Les Halles d'Auchan
Pao de Acucar
Little Extra
A-tak
Auchandirect.fr
Oney Banque Accord
Immochan
Alinea

CONTACTS: *Note: Officers with more than one job title may be intentionally listed here more than once.*

Xavier de Mezerac, CFO
Philippe Gracia, Dir.-Human Resources
Patrick Bodin, Dir.-Planning & Mgmt.
Phillippe Baroukh, Gen. Mgr.-Hypermarkets
Jerome Guillemard, Chmn.-Banque Accord
Benoit Lheureux, Chmn.-Immochan
Philippe Saudo, Gen. Mgr.-Supermarkets
Vianney Mulliez, Chmn.

GROWTH PLANS/SPECIAL FEATURES:

Groupe Auchan SA is one of the largest retailers in the world The company operates 1,657 stores, consisting of 83 hypermarkets and 818 supermarkets in 16 countrie Hypermarkets typically stock between 30,000 and 100,00 food and non-food products in each store and serve 5,000 t 30,000 customers daily in 14 countries. They operate under th brand names of Auchan, Les Halles d'Auchan, Pao de Acuca Jumbo, Alcampo and RT Mart. Beyond general merchandise the hypermarkets also offer special areas and services including photo labs, jewelry shops and nurseries as well a opticians, travel services, insurance, telephony and financia products. The stores also feature gas stations. Auchan run supermarkets in Russia, Poland, Italy, Spain, France and Tunisia under the brand names A-tak, Simply Market and A2Pass. Supermarkets are present in eight countries and carr 7,000 to 13,000 products and serve 1,000 to 5,000 customer daily. The Auchan group also operates a wholly-owned banking subsidiary called Oney Banque Accord, with 7.6 millio customers in 11 countries. The bank in turn operates othe banking subsidiaries in countries across Europe as well as i Russia and China. Wholly-owned real estate subsidiar Immochan is the commercial property developer, promoter and investor for the group's real estate, managing 363 shopping centers in 12 countries. The firm's online presence include Auchandirect.fr, which offers home delivery; Auchan.fr, which offers food and non-food products for delivery or pickup GrosBill.com, which offers high-tech products; and AuchanDrive.fr and Chronodrive.com, where customers orde products that are then loaded into customer cars within minute at stores. In addition, the Auchan group owns Alinea, a furniture and interior design chain with 26 stores in France, and Little Extra, a household products retailer with 16 stores in France.

FINANCIAL DATA: *Note: Data for latest year may not have been available at press time.*

In U.S. $	2015	2014	2013	2012	2011	2010
Revenue		60,500,000,000	59,982,160,000	58,483,000,000	55,366,000,000	53,850,000,000
R&D Expense						
Operating Income						
Operating Margin %						
SGA Expense						
Net Income			956,425,000	818,012,000	101,005,000	1,024,810,000
Operating Cash Flow						
Capital Expenditure						
EBITDA						
Return on Assets %						
Return on Equity %						
Debt to Equity						

CONTACT INFORMATION:

Phone: 33-3-20-81-68-00   Fax: 33-3-20-81-69-09
Toll-Free:
Address: 40 Ave. de Flandre, BP 139, Croix Cedex, 59964 France

STOCK TICKER/OTHER:

Stock Ticker: Private
Employees: 300,000
Parent Company:

Exchange:
Fiscal Year Ends: 12/31

SALARIES/BONUSES:

Top Exec. Salary: $ Bonus: $
Second Exec. Salary: $ Bonus: $

OTHER THOUGHTS:

Estimated Female Officers or Directors:
Hot Spot for Advancement for Women/Minorities:

Groupe Casino (Casino Guichard Perrachon SA) www.groupe-casino.fr

NAIC Code: 445110

TYPES OF BUSINESS:

Supermarkets
Real Estate Development
E-Commerce
Financial Services

BRANDS/DIVISIONS/AFFILIATES:

Petit Casino
Leader Price Express
Casino Shop
Vival
Spar
Banque Casino
Groupe Rallye
Casino Bio

CONTACTS: Note: Officers with more than one job title may be intentionally listed here more than once.

Jean-Charles Naouri, CEO
Antoine Giscard-d'Estaing, CEO.-Corp. Financial
Yves Desjacques, Dir.-Human Resources
Herve Daudin, Dir.-Merch.
Arnaud Strasser, Exec. Dir.-Corp. Dev. & Holdings
Julien Lagubeau, Dir.-Strategic Planning
Tina Schuler, CEO-Leader Price
Jean-Paul Mochet, CEO-Franprix
Jean-Charles Naouri, Chmn.
Herve Daudin, Exec. Dir.-Supply Chain

GROWTH PLANS/SPECIAL FEATURES:

Groupe Casino (Casino Guichard Perrachon SA) is a French food retailer. The company operates a chain of 14,574 stores, more than 10,000 of which are located in France. Its brands include Casino Bio, Monoprix Bio, Leader Price Bio, Leader Price Kids, Casino Fair Trade Max Havelaar and Terre et Saveur. The firm operates 127 hypermarkets under the Casino Geant banner that primarily carry Groupe Casino's proprietary brands. It operates 444 Casino supermarkets. Groupe Casino's convenience stores operate under five banners: Petit Casino, Leader Price Express, Casino Shop, Vival and Spar. Petit Casino offers food products; Leader Price are discount markets with a selection of more than 4,000 products; Casino Shop are smaller stores located in urban areas; Vival stores used to be located in hub villages, but is now present in urban commercial areas; and Spar operates in urban and suburban areas, offering a range of convenience food products as well as photo development services and the selling of bus tickets. Groupe Casino's e-commerce site Cdiscount.com sells non-food items. The firm's subsidiary, Banque Casino, offers the Casino Mastercard credit card. Groupe Casino is roughly 49%-owned by Groupe Rallye.

FINANCIAL DATA: Note: Data for latest year may not have been available at press time.

In U.S. $	2015	2014	2013	2012	2011	2010
Revenue		51,465,650,000	51,626,980,000	44,543,850,000	36,467,360,000	30,860,500,000
R&D Expense						
Operating Income		1,842,418,000	2,785,914,000	2,524,835,000	1,476,269,000	1,394,549,000
Operating Margin %		3.57%	5.39%	5.66%	4.04%	4.51%
SGA Expense		11,069,370,000	11,043,900,000	9,725,761,000	1,478,392,000	6,830,532,000
Net Income		266,386,500	902,105,700	1,127,101,000	787,485,200	788,546,400
Operating Cash Flow		3,050,178,000	3,336,730,000	2,501,486,000	2,039,820,000	1,677,916,000
Capital Expenditure		1,622,729,000	1,701,265,000	1,479,453,000	1,308,584,000	994,438,800
EBITDA		2,915,393,000	4,011,717,000	3,712,430,000	2,604,432,000	1,859,399,000
Return on Assets %		.58%	1.98%	2.92%	2.04%	2.24%
Return on Equity %		3.26%	10.97%	14.86%	8.20%	8.18%
Debt to Equity		1.19	1.10	1.25	0.94	

CONTACT INFORMATION:

Phone: 33 477453131   Fax: 33 477453838
Toll-Free:
Address: 1, Esplanade de France B.P., 306 cedex 2, Saint-Etienne, 42008 France

STOCK TICKER/OTHER:

Stock Ticker: CGUIF
Employees: 335,436
Parent Company:

Exchange: GREY
Fiscal Year Ends: 12/31

SALARIES/BONUSES:

Top Exec. Salary: $ Bonus: $
Second Exec. Salary: $ Bonus: $

OTHER THOUGHTS:

Estimated Female Officers or Directors: 4
Hot Spot for Advancement for Women/Minorities: Y

Sales, profits and employees may be estimates. Financial information, benefits and other data can change quickly and may vary from those stated here.

Grupo Elektra SA de CV

NAIC Code: 443142

www.grupoelektra.com.mx

TYPES OF BUSINESS:

Electronics & Appliances, Retail
Furniture
Apparel
Online Sales
Financial Services
Consumer Credit
Insurance
Motorcycle Manufacturing

BRANDS/DIVISIONS/AFFILIATES:

Elektra
Salinas Y Rocha
Banco Azteca
Afore Azteca
Seguros Azteca
Punto Casa de Bolsa
Advance America

CONTACTS: *Note: Officers with more than one job title may be intentionally listed here more than once.*

Ricardo Benjamin Salinas Pliego, Pres.
Mauro Aguirre Regis, CFO
Ricardo B. Salinas Pliego, Chmn.

GROWTH PLANS/SPECIAL FEATURES:

Grupo Elektra SA de CV is a leading Latin American specialty retailer and consumer finance company, with operations in Mexico, Honduras, Brazil, El Salvador, Panama, Guatemala and Peru. Grupo Elektra operates through over 7,000 outlets. Through Elektra and Salinas Y Rocha stores, the company engages in the sale of household appliances, furniture and clothing. Elektra sells name-brand consumer electronics, small appliances and furniture, targeting low- and middle-income segments of the Mexican and Latin American population. The firm typically locates Elektra stores in Mexico's middle-class neighborhoods. Salinas Y Rocha stores offer a similar line of products but target a higher socioeconomic bracket. Banco Azteca, the group's financial services company, offers consumer credit and savings accounts from more than 4,300 points of sale (POS), including branches, retail stores and in stand-alone locations and other outlets. Grupo Elektra's bank services include Afore Azteca, a retirement fund manager; and Seguros Azteca, an insurance company. The firm also owns investment services company Punto Casa de Bolsa as well as Advance America, a financial services company which offers cash advances, title loans, bill payment and Visa prepaid cards. There are more than 2,400 branches of Advance America in the U.S.

FINANCIAL DATA: *Note: Data for latest year may not have been available at press time.*

In U.S. $	2015	2014	2013	2012	2011	2010
Revenue		4,473,320,000	4,271,053,000	4,218,602,000	3,141,092,000	2,781,843,000
R&D Expense						
Operating Income		349,554,000	406,128,200	551,588,500	394,002,400	285,174,800
Operating Margin %		7.81%	9.50%	13.07%	12.54%	10.25%
SGA Expense		1,923,396,000	1,914,926,000	1,702,473,000	1,173,644,000	984,301,100
Net Income		456,210,800	49,956,580	-1,160,821,000	1,816,216,000	29,741,750
Operating Cash Flow		1,522,590,000	911,821,900	-41,765,600	18,367,940	62,513,430
Capital Expenditure		144,555,100	209,958,300	205,616,300	141,632,400	106,139,000
EBITDA		820,489,500	307,369,300	-1,441,382,000	2,811,803,000	199,386,700
Return on Assets %		4.07%	.48%	-11.21%	20.19%	.38%
Return on Equity %		15.02%	1.81%	-34.27%	58.12%	1.25%
Debt to Equity		0.31	0.40	0.32	0.16	0.10

CONTACT INFORMATION:

Phone: 52 5585827000   Fax:
Toll-Free:
Address: Ave. Insurgentes Sur 3579, Mexico DF, 14000 Mexico

STOCK TICKER/OTHER:

Stock Ticker: ELEKTRA   Exchange: MEX
Employees: Fiscal Year Ends: 12/31
Parent Company:

SALARIES/BONUSES:

Top Exec. Salary: $ Bonus: $
Second Exec. Salary: $ Bonus: $

OTHER THOUGHTS:

Estimated Female Officers or Directors:
Hot Spot for Advancement for Women/Minorities:

Grupo Sanborns SA de CV

sanborns.com.mx

NAIC Code: 452111

TYPES OF BUSINESS:

Department Stores (except Discount Department Stores)

BRANDS/DIVISIONS/AFFILIATES:

Grupo Carso
Sanborns
Tower Records
Discolandia
Mixup
No Problem
Sanborns.com.mx

GROWTH PLANS/SPECIAL FEATURES:

Grupo Sanborns SA de CV is a retail company founded in Mexico City in 1903, by Walter and Frank Sanborn. The trademark of the franchise, the three owls, represent Frank and his sons, Francis and Jonathan, who manage the company. Sanborns is part of Grupo Carso. Sanborns operates nearly 50 Sears Mexico stores; approximately 125 Sanborns stores, a combination of restaurants, drugstores and book and gift shops; 34 Sanborns Cafes; and nearly 65 Discolandia, Mixup, No Problem and Tower Records music stores. The company also operates a web site, Sanborns.com.mx, that sells products such as electronics, computers, music, jewelry, watches, eyeglasses, perfume, makeup, books, toys and health and personal care items.

CONTACTS: Note: Officers with more than one job title may be intentionally listed here more than once.

Carlos Slim Domit, CEO

FINANCIAL DATA: Note: Data for latest year may not have been available at press time.

In U.S. $	2015	2014	2013	2012	2011	2010
Revenue		2,487,962,000	2,446,411,000	2,379,799,000	2,198,930,000	
R&D Expense						
Operating Income		279,983,100	317,466,500	275,683,100	259,761,300	
Operating Margin %		11.25%	12.97%	11.58%	11.81%	
SGA Expense		685,902,500	538,639,000	633,228,900	596,634,900	
Net Income		176,440,400	195,193,300	179,146,100	161,482,400	
Operating Cash Flow		181,570,900	171,722,800	206,404,200	198,528,800	
Capital Expenditure		153,748,100	101,155,500	45,220,810	73,988,080	
EBITDA		335,744,100	367,331,300	330,957,000	303,716,000	
Return on Assets %		7.39%	9.24%	9.70%	9.26%	
Return on Equity %		10.91%	16.09%	19.37%	17.21%	
Debt to Equity						

CONTACT INFORMATION:

Phone: 52 5553259990   Fax: 52 5553259974
Toll-Free:
Address: Avenida Calvario, No. 106, Mexico DF, 14000 Mexico

STOCK TICKER/OTHER:

Stock Ticker: GSANBORB-1   Exchange: MEX
Employees: Fiscal Year Ends:
Parent Company:

SALARIES/BONUSES:

Top Exec. Salary: $ Bonus: $
Second Exec. Salary: $ Bonus: $

OTHER THOUGHTS:

Estimated Female Officers or Directors:
Hot Spot for Advancement for Women/Minorities:

Sales, profits and employees may be estimates. Financial information, benefits and other data can change quickly and may vary from those stated here.

Guess? Inc

NAIC Code: 448140

TYPES OF BUSINESS:

Casual Clothing Stores
Accessories
Fragrances
Footwear
Online Sales
Jeans

BRANDS/DIVISIONS/AFFILIATES:

Baby GUESS
Guess Jeans
Triangle Design
Question Mark
YES
GUESS Kids
GUESS U.S.A.
G

CONTACTS: Note: Officers with more than one job title may be intentionally listed here more than once.

Sandeep Reddy, CFO
Paul Marciano, Chairman of the Board
Michael Relich, COO
Victor Amigo, Director
Maurice Marciano, Founder

GROWTH PLANS/SPECIAL FEATURES:

Guess?, Inc. designs, markets, distributes and licenses collections of contemporary apparel and accessories for men, women and children that reflect the American lifestyle and European fashion sensibilities. The company's apparel is marketed under trademarks including GUESS?, GUESS U.S.A., GUESS Jeans, Triangle Design, Question Mark, stylized G, GUESS Kids and Baby GUESS, YES. The lines include full collections of denim and cotton clothing, including jeans, pants, overalls, skirts, dresses, shorts, blouses, shirts, jackets and knitwear. The firm also grants licenses to manufactures and distributes a broad range of products that complement its apparel lines, including eyewear, watches, handbags, footwear, infants' and children's apparel, leather apparel, fragrance, jewelry and other fashion accessories. Guess products are sold through three primary distribution channels: its own stores in the U.S. and Canada, a network of wholesale accounts in the U.S. and via the Internet. The company operates 481 retail stores in the U.S. and Canada. The firm's licensees and distributors also operate an additional 1,187 stores outside the U.S. and Canada.

FINANCIAL DATA: Note: Data for latest year may not have been available at press time.

In U.S. $	2015	2014	2013	2012	2011	2010
Revenue	2,417,673,000	2,569,786,000	2,658,605,000	2,688,048,000	2,487,294,000	2,128,466,000
R&D Expense						
Operating Income	125,912,000	222,587,000	274,525,000	397,235,000	404,633,000	358,816,000
Operating Margin %	5.20%	8.66%	10.32%	14.77%	16.26%	16.85%
SGA Expense	741,973,000	741,105,000	792,598,000	747,587,000	680,311,000	577,963,000
Net Income	94,570,000	153,434,000	178,744,000	265,500,000	289,508,000	242,761,000
Operating Cash Flow	153,826,000	327,942,000	268,904,000	364,494,000	346,374,000	358,210,000
Capital Expenditure	71,498,000	75,438,000	99,591,000	124,870,000	123,065,000	82,286,000
EBITDA	230,438,000	323,251,000	371,952,000	480,629,000	490,082,000	428,479,000
Return on Assets %	5.61%	8.82%	10.04%	15.04%	18.00%	17.48%
Return on Equity %	8.48%	13.69%	15.79%	23.80%	27.90%	27.02%
Debt to Equity					0.01	0.01

CONTACT INFORMATION:

Phone: 213 765-3100   Fax: 213 744-7838
Toll-Free: 800-224-8377
Address: 1444 S. Alameda St., Los Angeles, CA 90021 United States

STOCK TICKER/OTHER:

Stock Ticker: GES
Employees: 13,700
Parent Company:

Exchange: NYS
Fiscal Year Ends: 01/31

SALARIES/BONUSES:

Top Exec. Salary: $1,500,000
Bonus: $

Second Exec. Salary: $405,179
Bonus: $337,500

OTHER THOUGHTS:

Estimated Female Officers or Directors: 2

Hot Spot for Advancement for Women/Minorities: Y

Guitar Center Inc

www.guitarcenter.com

NAIC Code: 451140

TYPES OF BUSINESS:

Musical Instruments, Retail
Audio & Recording Equipment
Catalog & Online Sales
Musical Instrument Rental

BRANDS/DIVISIONS/AFFILIATES:

Guitar Center
Music & Arts
Musician's Friend Inc
Music123 Inc
Fender Music Foundation

CONTACTS: *Note: Officers with more than one job title may be intentionally listed here more than once.*

Darrell Webb, CEO
Tim Martin, CFO
John Bagan, Exec. VP
Frank Hamlin, Exec. VP

GROWTH PLANS/SPECIAL FEATURES:

Guitar Center, Inc. is a leading U.S. retailer of musical instruments and equipment. It divides its operations into three segments: Guitar Center, Music & Arts and direct response. Guitar Center stores sell a wide range of instruments and equipment, including guitars, amplifiers, percussion instruments, keyboards and pro audio and recording equipment. Guitar Center stores range between 12,000 and 30,000 square feet of floor space and are organized into several departments, each focused on one product category, such as guitars, keyboards, drums and audio recording equipment. Customers are encouraged to play instruments in the store for a hands-on shopping experience and employees receive ongoing technical training in their department. The Music & Arts segment oversees Music & Arts retail locations in the U.S. These stores focus primarily on the beginning musician and on instrument rentals for school band and orchestra programs, offering a full range of brass and woodwind band instruments as well as stringed instruments and sheet music. A limited number of Music & Arts stores also provide in-store music lessons. The direct response segment offers direct response e-commerce and catalog sales of musical instruments and accessories through wholly-owned subsidiaries Musician's Friend, Inc. and Music123, Inc. Guitar Center also helps oversee the Fender Music Foundation, a nonprofit group that works to provide resources and financial assistance to support school and community-based music programs throughout the U.S.

Guitar Center offers its employees medical, dental and vision insurance; life insurance; a profit sharing plan; technical training related to products; and employee discounts on merchandise.

FINANCIAL DATA: *Note: Data for latest year may not have been available at press time.*

In U.S. $	2015	2014	2013	2012	2011	2010
Revenue		2,400,000,000	2,380,000,000	2,139,200,000	2,082,577,000	2,010,895,000
R&D Expense						
Operating Income						
Operating Margin %						
SGA Expense						
Net Income						
Operating Cash Flow						
Capital Expenditure						
EBITDA						
Return on Assets %						
Return on Equity %						
Debt to Equity						

CONTACT INFORMATION:

Phone: 818-735-8800   Fax: 866-498-7874
Toll-Free: 866-498-7882
Address: 5795 Lindero Canyon Rd., Westlake Village, CA 91362 United States

STOCK TICKER/OTHER:

Stock Ticker: Private
Employees: 10,500
Parent Company: BAIN CAPITAL LLC

Exchange:
Fiscal Year Ends: 12/31

SALARIES/BONUSES:

Top Exec. Salary: $ Bonus: $
Second Exec. Salary: $ Bonus: $

OTHER THOUGHTS:

Estimated Female Officers or Directors:
Hot Spot for Advancement for Women/Minorities:

Sales, profits and employees may be estimates. Financial information, benefits and other data can change quickly and may vary from those stated here.

Gymboree Corp (The)

NAIC Code: 448130

TYPES OF BUSINESS:

Apparel-Children's, Retail
Parent-Child Developmental Play Programs
Online Sales

BRANDS/DIVISIONS/AFFILIATES:

Gymboree
Gymboree Outlet
Janie & Jack
Crazy 8
Bain Capital LLC
Gymboree Play & Music
JanieAndJack.com
Gymboree.com

CONTACTS: Note: Officers with more than one job title may be intentionally listed here more than once.

Mark Breitbard, CEO
Evan Price, Pres.
Andy North, CFO
Lynda Gustafson, Corp. Controller

GROWTH PLANS/SPECIAL FEATURES:

The Gymboree Corp., owned by Bain Capital, LLC, is a specialty retailer of children's apparel and accessories. The company operates 633 retail stores in the U.S. and Canada under the Gymboree, Gymboree Outlet, Janie and Jack and Crazy 8 brands. Online shopping is provided to customers through Gymboree.com, JanieandJack.com and Crazy8.com. Stores are primarily located in regional shopping malls and in select suburban and urban locations. Gymboree apparel and accessories are characterized by bright colors, patterns, whimsical graphics and complex embellishments, and are designed for both functionality and durability for newborns to children age 12. The company operates 164 Gymboree Outlet stores selling similar merchandise at lower prices. The majority of this merchandise is developed and manufactured exclusively for the Gymboree Outlet stores. The Janie and Jack division, with 139 stores, offers higher-end clothing for newborn children through age eight. These stores are designed in an old-fashioned mercantile boutique style. The company's Crazy 8 division operates 383 stores, marketing towards children under fourteen. Gymboree Play & Music offers a variety of developmental classes, toys, books and music for children. The company operates directed parent-child developmental play programs at 708 franchised and company-operated Gymboree Play & Music centers throughout the U.S. and 40 countries.

Gymboree Corp offers its employees medical, dental, vision and life insurance; paid flex-time off; an employee assistance program; employee discounts; adoption assistance; and a 401(k) plan.

FINANCIAL DATA: Note: Data for latest year may not have been available at press time.

In U.S. $	2015	2014	2013	2012	2011	2010
Revenue		1,230,000,000	1,240,000,000	1,200,000,000	1,190,000,000	1,001,527,000
R&D Expense						
Operating Income						
Operating Margin %						
SGA Expense						
Net Income		-574,000,000	-203,000,000			
Operating Cash Flow						
Capital Expenditure						
EBITDA						
Return on Assets %						
Return on Equity %						
Debt to Equity						

CONTACT INFORMATION:

Phone: 415-278-7000   Fax: 707-678-1315
Toll-Free: 877-449-6932
Address: 500 Howard St., San Francisco, CA 94105 United States

STOCK TICKER/OTHER:

Stock Ticker: Private
Employees: 12,000   Exchange:
Parent Company: BAIN CAPITAL LLC   Fiscal Year Ends: 01/31

SALARIES/BONUSES:

Top Exec. Salary: $ Bonus: $
Second Exec. Salary: $ Bonus: $

OTHER THOUGHTS:

Estimated Female Officers or Directors: 1
Hot Spot for Advancement for Women/Minorities:

H&M (Hennes & Mauritz) AB

www.hm.com

NAIC Code: 448140

TYPES OF BUSINESS:

Apparel Stores, Moderately Priced
Cosmetics and Beauty Items
Men's & Women's Clothing
Accessories
Catalog & Online Sales

BRANDS/DIVISIONS/AFFILIATES:

H&M
Cheap Monday
H&M Rowells
COS (Collection of Style)
H&M Home
Weekday
Monki

CONTACTS: Note: Officers with more than one job title may be intentionally listed here more than once.

Karl-Johan Persson, CEO
Jyrki Tervonen, Dir.-Finance
Anna Tillberg Pantzar, Dir.-Mktg.
Sanna Lindberg, Dir.-Human Resources
Kjell-Olof Nilsson, Dir.-IT
Karl Gunnar Fagerlin, Dir.-Prod.
Bjorn Magnusson, Dir.-Bus. Dev.
Kristina Stenvinkel, Dir-Comm.
Nils Vinge, Dir-Investor Rel.
Anders Jonasson, Dir.-Accounts
Ann-Sofie Johansson, Dir.-Design
Daniel Erver, VP-Sales
Jonas Guldstrand, Dir.-Logistics
Pernilla Wohlfahrt, Dir.-New Bus.
Stefan Persson, Chmn.
Stina Westerstad, Dir.-Buying

GROWTH PLANS/SPECIAL FEATURES:

H&M (Hennes & Mauritz) AB is a Sweden-based fashion retailer that operates more than 3,600 stores in 59 countries, including the U.S. H&M's largest market exists in Sweden, Germany and the U.K. The company offers clothing for women, men, teenagers and children, concentrating predominately on customers aged 18-45. H&M also sells accessories and an in-house cosmetics line. Production takes place in Europe and Asia. In some regions, the firm also sells its products via catalogs and the Internet (which are operated by H&M Rowells). While H&M sees the Internet as an important factor in its growth, it foresees that the bulk of its revenue will be earned at its stores, with a growth target of increasing its stores by 10-15% per year. To that end, a key component of the company's success is the selection of superior store locations, primarily areas with high foot traffic. The firm's growth strategy is focused mainly on expanding into new markets and choosing attractive store locations. In addition to H&M's primary operations, the company operates several other brands, including the COS (Collection of Style) store chain, which is similar to H&M, but at higher price points; H&M Home, which offers textile fashions for the home through Internet and catalog sales and a showroom in Stockholm; Monki; Weekday; and Cheap Monday. H&M planned approximately 400 new stores for 2015, with an emphasis on China and the U.S. It opened 58 stores in American during 2014, including its 57,000 square foot flagship store on Fifth Avenue in New York City.

FINANCIAL DATA: Note: Data for latest year may not have been available at press time.

In U.S. $	2015	2014	2013	2012	2011	2010
Revenue		17,437,250,000	14,805,060,000	13,911,090,000	12,667,370,000	12,492,790,000
R&D Expense						
Operating Income		2,946,111,000	2,552,844,000	2,505,168,000	2,346,824,000	2,839,704,000
Operating Margin %		16.89%	17.24%	18.00%	18.52%	22.73%
SGA Expense		7,309,023,000	6,203,037,000	5,771,421,000	5,270,595,000	5,022,082,000
Net Income		2,300,415,000	1,975,206,000	1,942,386,000	1,821,930,000	2,151,284,000
Operating Cash Flow		2,781,779,000	2,745,389,000	2,176,504,000	2,006,069,000	2,514,841,000
Capital Expenditure		1,081,458,000	924,380,800	786,190,100	587,656,100	571,073,200
EBITDA		3,564,860,000	3,077,738,000	2,993,557,000	2,787,883,000	3,233,202,000
Return on Assets %		28.27%	27.25%	28.02%	26.50%	32.90%
Return on Equity %		41.27%	38.50%	38.36%	35.84%	44.17%
Debt to Equity						

CONTACT INFORMATION:

Phone: 46 87965500   Fax: 46 8208094
Toll-Free:
Address: Master Samuelsgatan 46A, Stockholm, 106 38 Sweden

STOCK TICKER/OTHER:

Stock Ticker: HMRZF   Exchange: PINX
Employees: 93,351   Fiscal Year Ends: 11/30
Parent Company:

SALARIES/BONUSES:

Top Exec. Salary: $ Bonus: $
Second Exec. Salary: $ Bonus: $

OTHER THOUGHTS:

Estimated Female Officers or Directors: 13
Hot Spot for Advancement for Women/Minorities: Y

H2O Retailing Corporation

www.h2o-retailing.co.jp

NAIC Code: 452111

TYPES OF BUSINESS:

Department Stores
Supermarkets
Life & Casualty Insurance
Pet Accessories
Furniture
Data Processing Services
Food Manufacturing
Real Estate Management

BRANDS/DIVISIONS/AFFILIATES:

Hankyu Hanshin Toho Group
Hanshoku Co Ltd
Hankyu Foods Inc
Hankyu Delica Inc
Oi Development Co Ltd
Hankyu Bakery Co Ltd
Hankyu Hanshin Department Stores Inc
Hankyu

CONTACTS: Note: Officers with more than one job title may be intentionally listed here more than once.

Atsushi Suzuki, Pres.
Tadatsugu Mori, Exec. Officer-Bus. Planning
Katsuhiro Hayashi, Exec. Officer

GROWTH PLANS/SPECIAL FEATURES:

H2O Retailing Corporation is a holding company operating through numerous Japanese subsidiaries. The company's primary divisions comprise the department store business, the supermarket business, the property management business and other businesses. The department store business operates primarily through subsidiary Hankyu Hanshin Department Stores, Inc., which controls 15 department stores throughout Japan, 11 under the Hankyu banner and 4 under the Hanshin banner. The supermarket business segment includes a number of subsidiaries, including Hanshoku Co. Ltd., which oversees a network of supermarkets; Hankyu Foods, Inc., which manufactures and sells laver seaweed and dried foods; Hankyu Delica, Inc., a manufacturer and retailer of prepared food and sushi; and Hankyu Bakery Co., Ltd., a commercial bakery. The property management business segment, overseen by subsidiary Oi Development Co., Ltd., is engaged in the management of commercial facilities, the operation and management of a hotel, the management of restaurants and cafes and pushcart vendor merchandising. This business segment's activities also include the sale of glasses and bread and the manufacture and sale of furniture and furnishings. The other businesses segment's operations include such varied activities as bookkeeping, security, consulting, web design, grocery home delivery, the sale of pet accessories, life and casualty insurance provision, organic farming, data processing and systems development. H2O Retailing is a member of the Hankyu Hanshin Toho Group, encompassing approximately 200 companies.

FINANCIAL DATA: Note: Data for latest year may not have been available at press time.

In U.S. $	2015	2014	2013	2012	2011	2010
Revenue		7,020,400,000	5,586,745,000	6,165,720,000	5,602,819,000	5,058,011,000
R&D Expense						
Operating Income						
Operating Margin %						
SGA Expense						
Net Income		96,300,000	65,968,000	12,890,000	37,470,000	32,441,000
Operating Cash Flow						
Capital Expenditure						
EBITDA						
Return on Assets %						
Return on Equity %						
Debt to Equity						

CONTACT INFORMATION:

Phone: 81-6-6365-8120   Fax: 81-6-6486-8320
Toll-Free:
Address: 8-7 Kakuda-cho, Kita-ku, Osaka, 530-8350 Japan

SALARIES/BONUSES:

Top Exec. Salary: $ Bonus: $
Second Exec. Salary: $ Bonus: $

STOCK TICKER/OTHER:

Stock Ticker: Subsidiary   Exchange:
Employees: 8,590   Fiscal Year Ends: 03/31
Parent Company: HANKYU HANSHIN TOHO GROUP

OTHER THOUGHTS:

Estimated Female Officers or Directors:
Hot Spot for Advancement for Women/Minorities:

Haggar Corp

www.haggar.com

NAIC Code: 424300

TYPES OF BUSINESS:

Apparel and Clothing Brands, Designers, Importers and Distributors
Retail Stores

BRANDS/DIVISIONS/AFFILIATES:

Haggar Clothing Co
Infinity Associates LLC
LK Life Khaki
Haggar Apparel Ltd
Haggar Canada Co

GROWTH PLANS/SPECIAL FEATURES:

Haggar Corp., along with its subsidiaries (including Haggar Clothing Co., its primary subsidiary), designs, manufactures, imports and markets casual and dress men's and women's apparel. The company is based in Dallas, Texas and markets clothing and accessories throughout the U.S., Canada, Mexico and the U.K. The firm is famous for first coining the term slacks in 1938 and for the introduction of wrinkle free cotton casual pants, pre-cuffed pants and expandable waist pants. Today, its products include pants, shorts, suits, sport coats, sweaters, shirts, dresses, skirts and vests. Recently, the company launched a new line of eco-friendly slacks called the LK Life Khaki brand. Hagar Clothing Co. is an official clothing partner of both the Pro Football Hall of Fame and the Hockey Hall of Fame. The company conducts foreign operations through Haggar Apparel, Ltd. and Haggar Canada Co. Haggar Corp. is owned by private equity group Infinity Associates LLC.

CONTACTS: Note: Officers with more than one job title may be intentionally listed here more than once.

Michael Stitt, CEO
Tim Lyons, Pres., Haggar Clothing Co.
Frank Brackenfd, Pres.

FINANCIAL DATA: Note: Data for latest year may not have been available at press time.

In U.S. $	2015	2014	2013	2012	2011	2010
Revenue						
R&D Expense						
Operating Income						
Operating Margin %						
SGA Expense						
Net Income						
Operating Cash Flow						
Capital Expenditure						
EBITDA						
Return on Assets %						
Return on Equity %						
Debt to Equity						

CONTACT INFORMATION:

Phone: 214-352-8481　　Fax: 214-956-4446
Toll-Free: 877-841-2219
Address: 11511 Luna Rd., Dallas, TX 75234 United States

STOCK TICKER/OTHER:

Stock Ticker: Private　　　　　　Exchange:
Employees:　　　　　　　　　　Fiscal Year Ends: 09/30
Parent Company: INFINITY ASSOCIATES LLC

SALARIES/BONUSES:

Top Exec. Salary: $　　Bonus: $
Second Exec. Salary: $　　Bonus: $

OTHER THOUGHTS:

Estimated Female Officers or Directors:
Hot Spot for Advancement for Women/Minorities:

Sales, profits and employees may be estimates. Financial information, benefits and other data can change quickly and may vary from those stated here.

Hallmark Cards Inc

NAIC Code: 511191

www.hallmark.com

TYPES OF BUSINESS:

Greeting Cards Publishing
Cable Television Broadcasting
Crayons & Art Products
Television Production & Distribution
Stationery

BRANDS/DIVISIONS/AFFILIATES:

Hallmark Gold Crown
Hallmark Marketing Corp
Hallmark Channel
Crown Media Holdings
Crown Center Redevelopment Corp
Crayola LLC
DaySpring Cards Inc
Silly Putty

CONTACTS: *Note: Officers with more than one job title may be intentionally listed here more than once.*

Donald J. Hall, Jr., CEO
Donald J. Hall, Jr., Pres.
Jim Shay, CFO
David E. Hall, Pres., North America Div.
Donald J. Hall, Chmn.

GROWTH PLANS/SPECIAL FEATURES:

Hallmark Cards, Inc. markets greeting cards and related products. The company operates wholesale and retail businesses for the sale of greeting and holiday cards, gifts, gift wrap, ornaments, memory-keeping products and stationery, with over 49,000 products available at any one time. The wholesale business distributes products to over 30,000 U.S. retailers and more than 100 countries, with products in approximately 30 languages. As a retailer, Hallmark distributes products in more than 2,250 Hallmark Gold Crown stores. The firm also operates through several subsidiaries. Crayola LLC produces Crayola crayons, art supplies and Silly Putty. Crown Media Holdings operates various cable television channels, including Hallmark Channel, which is viewed by almost 86 million subscribers worldwide. Crown Center Redevelopment Corp. is a commercial and residential complex near Hallmark's headquarters in Kansas City, Missouri. DaySpring Cards, Inc. produces Christian greeting cards and gifts available in over 2,000 Christian retail stores in the U.S. and over 60 countries. Hallmark Business Connections, the firm's business-to-business (B2B) division, supplies business greeting cards and operates employee recognition programs, sales programs and corporate health and wellness programs. Hallmark Baby, a wholly-owned subsidiary of Hallmark Marketing Corp. is a digital store offering baby and children's clothing online. FeeIn is the firm's subscription-based streaming video on demand service and film production company. Halls LLC operates Halls on Grand, a specialty department store in Kansas City's Crown Center.

The company offers its employees medical, dental and vision coverage; flexible spending plans; a 401(k) plan and profit sharing plan; child and elder care benefits; a fitness center; tuition reimbursement; and product discounts.

FINANCIAL DATA: *Note: Data for latest year may not have been available at press time.*

In U.S. $	2015	2014	2013	2012	2011	2010
Revenue		3,400,000,000	3,900,000,000	4,000,000,000	4,081,632,600	4,100,000,000
R&D Expense						
Operating Income						
Operating Margin %						
SGA Expense						
Net Income						
Operating Cash Flow						
Capital Expenditure						
EBITDA						
Return on Assets %						
Return on Equity %						
Debt to Equity						

CONTACT INFORMATION:

Phone: 816-274-5111   Fax:
Toll-Free: 800-425-5627
Address: 2501 McGee Trafficway, Kansas City, MO 64108 United States

SALARIES/BONUSES:

Top Exec. Salary: $ Bonus: $
Second Exec. Salary: $ Bonus: $

STOCK TICKER/OTHER:

Stock Ticker: Private   Exchange:
Employees: 30,300   Fiscal Year Ends: 12/31
Parent Company:

OTHER THOUGHTS:

Estimated Female Officers or Directors:
Hot Spot for Advancement for Women/Minorities:

Hancock Fabrics Inc

www.hancockfabrics.com

NAIC Code: 451130

TYPES OF BUSINESS:

Fabrics & Sewing Accessories, Retail
Wholesale Fabrics
Online Sales
Home Decorating Products

BRANDS/DIVISIONS/AFFILIATES:

HancockFabrics.com

CONTACTS: Note: Officers with more than one job title may be intentionally listed here more than once.

Steven R. Morgan, CEO
Steven R. Morgan, Pres.
James B. Brown, CFO
Susan van Benten, Sr. VP-Merch.
Dennis Lyons, Sr. VP-Store Oper.
Steven D. Scheiwe, Chmn.
William A. Sheffield, Sr. VP-Dist.

GROWTH PLANS/SPECIAL FEATURES:

Hancock Fabrics, Inc. is one of the largest fabric retailers in the U.S., operating 263 stores in 37 states. Hancock's stores offer a wide selection of apparel fabrics; home decorating products (drapery and upholstery fabrics and home accent pieces); quilting prints and kits; scrapbooking materials; and notions and accessories such as zippers, buttons, threads, sewing machines and patterns. Each of the retail stores maintains an inventory that includes staple fabrics, including cotton, fleece and decorator fabrics as well as seasonal and current fashion fabrics. The firm principally serves the sewing, needle arts and home decorating markets, which largely consist of women who are creative enthusiasts, making clothing and gifts for their families and friends and decorating their homes. Quilters and hobbyists also comprise a portion of the base of customers as do consumers of special occasion fabric. Hancock operates an e-commerce site, HancockFabrics.com, which offers all Hancock merchandise as well as a discussion forum for customers, project ideas, contests, sales flyers and sewing patterns. The company also has a 650,000-square-foot warehouse and distribution facility, a 28,000-square-foot manufacturing facility and an 80,000-square-foot corporate headquarters, all of which are based in Baldwyn, Mississippi.

FINANCIAL DATA: Note: Data for latest year may not have been available at press time.

In U.S. $	2015	2014	2013	2012	2011	2010
Revenue		283,144,000	277,989,000	271,993,000	275,465,000	274,058,000
R&D Expense						
Operating Income		2,736,000	-1,233,000	-6,462,000	-4,948,000	7,707,000
Operating Margin %		.96%	-.44%	-2.37%	-1.79%	2.81%
SGA Expense		114,172,000	109,653,000	115,047,000	115,098,000	109,681,000
Net Income		-3,153,000	-8,510,000	-11,298,000	-10,461,000	1,788,000
Operating Cash Flow		3,242,000	-11,278,000	-13,255,000	6,160,000	22,976,000
Capital Expenditure		5,412,000	2,698,000	4,934,000	5,392,000	3,084,000
EBITDA		7,687,000	4,119,000	-394,000	1,105,000	13,571,000
Return on Assets %		-2.05%	-5.73%	-7.86%	-7.22%	1.14%
Return on Equity %			-104.02%	-46.39%	-25.49%	3.78%
Debt to Equity			28.97	3.77	0.91	0.63

CONTACT INFORMATION:

Phone: 662 365-6000   Fax: 662-842-2834
Toll-Free: 877-322-7427
Address: One Fashion Way, Baldwyn, MS 38824 United States

SALARIES/BONUSES:

Top Exec. Salary: $ Bonus: $
Second Exec. Salary: $ Bonus: $

STOCK TICKER/OTHER:

Stock Ticker: HKFI   Exchange: PINX
Employees: 3,100   Fiscal Year Ends: 01/31
Parent Company:

OTHER THOUGHTS:

Estimated Female Officers or Directors: 1
Hot Spot for Advancement for Women/Minorities: Y

Hanover Direct Inc

NAIC Code: 454113

www.hanoverdirect.com

TYPES OF BUSINESS:

Apparel & General Merchandise, Catalogs
Gift Catalogs
Online Sales
E-Commerce Logistics Services
Bedding Manufacturing

BRANDS/DIVISIONS/AFFILIATES:

Company Kids
International Male
Scandia Home
Silhouettes
UnderGear
Company Store (The)

CONTACTS: *Note: Officers with more than one job title may be intentionally listed here more than once.*

Don Kelley, CEO
Don Kelley, Pres.
Jeffrey Rosenholtz, CIO
Missy Paxton, VP-Oper.
Suzanen Coccaro, VP-Planning
Suzanen Coccaro, VP-Finance

GROWTH PLANS/SPECIAL FEATURES:

Hanover Direct, Inc. is a direct marketer of brande merchandise through a portfolio of catalogs and web sites. I addition, Hanover provides telemarketing, informatio technology and e-commerce services to third-par businesses. The firm's direct marketing operations consist of portfolio of six catalogs and associated web sites: Th Company Store, Company Kids, Silhouettes, UnderGea International Male and Scandia Home. The Company Store i a home furnishings catalog that specializes in high qualit down/feather products and private labels. Company Kids sell many of the same items as The Company Store, but fo children. Silhouettes is a fashion catalog that carries women sizes 12W-34W. UnderGear is a direct-mail seller of men' underwear, swimwear, loungewear, workout wear an skincare. International Male, which offers online shoppin through UnderGear's web site, carries a full line of men' apparel, focusing on contemporary fashion at value prices an offering internationally recognized brand names. Hanove Direct also manufactures comforters and pillows that it sells i its catalogs under the name Scandia Home. Each of th company's specialty catalogs targets a different marke segment, offering a focused assortment of products designe to meet the needs and preferences of its customers.

The company offers employees health, life and disability insurance; tuition reimbursement; paid vacation and sick leave an employee referral program; a 401(k); and store discounts.

FINANCIAL DATA: *Note: Data for latest year may not have been available at press time.*

In U.S. $	2015	2014	2013	2012	2011	2010
Revenue						
R&D Expense						
Operating Income						
Operating Margin %						
SGA Expense						
Net Income						
Operating Cash Flow						
Capital Expenditure						
EBITDA						
Return on Assets %						
Return on Equity %						
Debt to Equity						

CONTACT INFORMATION:

Phone: 201-863-7300   Fax: 201-272-3465
Toll-Free:
Address: 1200 Harbor Blvd., Weehawken, NJ 07086 United States

SALARIES/BONUSES:

Top Exec. Salary: $ Bonus: $
Second Exec. Salary: $ Bonus: $

STOCK TICKER/OTHER:

Stock Ticker: Private   Exchange:
Employees: 1,840   Fiscal Year Ends: 12/31
Parent Company:

OTHER THOUGHTS:

Estimated Female Officers or Directors: 2
Hot Spot for Advancement for Women/Minorities:

Harris Teeter Supermarkets Inc

www.harristeeter.com

NAIC Code: 445110

TYPES OF BUSINESS:

Grocery Stores
Dairy Product Manufacturing
Pharmacies

BRANDS/DIVISIONS/AFFILIATES:

Harris Teeter Inc
Kroger Co (The)

CONTACTS: *Note: Officers with more than one job title may be intentionally listed here more than once.*

Frederick J. Morganthall, II, COO
Frederick J. Morganthall, II, Pres.
Chuck Corbeil, VP-Mktg.
Jim Clendenen, CIO
Douglas J. Yacenda, Sec.
Ronald H. Volger, Treas.
Rodney C. Antolock, Exec. VP
Jesse B. Libensperger, Assistant Treas.

GROWTH PLANS/SPECIAL FEATURES:

Harris Teeter Supermarkets, Inc. is a holding company that, through its wholly-owned subsidiary Harris Teeter, Inc. (Harris Teeter), operates a regional chain of 230 supermarkets throughout seven southeastern states and Washington, D.C. Harris Teeter stores carry a full assortment of groceries, produce, meat, seafood, delicatessen items, bakery items, wines and non-food products such as health, beauty care and floral items. Retail supermarket operations are supported by two company-owned distribution centers and one company-owned dairy production facility. Aside from the ice cream and dairy products which are produced by the company, all other items, including the stores' own branded product lines, are purchased either directly from manufacturers or from outside suppliers. More than 160 stores offer online pickup service and some markets also offer a home delivery option. In 2014, the firm was acquired by The Kroger Co.

Harris Teeter offers its employees medical, dental and vision benefits; life and AD&D insurance; flexible spending accounts for health care, dependent care and commuter expenses; a 401(k); educational assistance; and merchandise discounts.

FINANCIAL DATA: *Note: Data for latest year may not have been available at press time.*

In U.S. $	2015	2014	2013	2012	2011	2010
Revenue		5,109,000,000	4,709,866,000	4,535,414,000	4,285,565,000	4,099,353,000
R&D Expense						
Operating Income						
Operating Margin %						
SGA Expense						
Net Income			108,980,000	99,927,000	111,458,000	98,652,000
Operating Cash Flow						
Capital Expenditure						
EBITDA						
Return on Assets %						
Return on Equity %						
Debt to Equity						

CONTACT INFORMATION:

Phone: 704 844-3100   Fax:
Toll-Free:
Address: 701 Crestdale Rd., Matthews, NC 28105 United States

SALARIES/BONUSES:

Top Exec. Salary: $ Bonus: $
Second Exec. Salary: $ Bonus: $

STOCK TICKER/OTHER:

Stock Ticker: Subsidiary   Exchange:
Employees: 26,000   Fiscal Year Ends: 10/31
Parent Company: Kroger Co (The)

OTHER THOUGHTS:

Estimated Female Officers or Directors:
Hot Spot for Advancement for Women/Minorities:

Sales, profits and employees may be estimates. Financial information, benefits and other data can change quickly and may vary from those stated here.

Harry & David Holdings Inc

NAIC Code: 454113

www.harryanddavid.com/h/home

TYPES OF BUSINESS:

Fruit & Gifts-Direct Selling
Retail Fruit & Gift Stores
Catalog Sales
Online Sales

BRANDS/DIVISIONS/AFFILIATES:

Harry & David
Wolferman's
1-800-FLOWERS.COM Inc
Fruit-of-the-Month Club
Tower of Treats
Moose Munch
Royal Riviera
Cushman's Fruit Company

CONTACTS: Note: Officers with more than one job title may be intentionally listed here more than once.

Steve Lightman, Pres.
Michael Schwindle, CFO
Charles Hunsinger, CIO
Peter Kratz, Exec. VP-Oper.
Donald L. Cato, Sr. VP
Ross A. Klein, Chief Brand Officer

GROWTH PLANS/SPECIAL FEATURES:

Harry & David Holdings, Inc., a wholly-owned subsidiary of 1-800-FLOWERS.COM, Inc., is a retailer and producer of branded premium gift-quality fruit, gourmet food products and other gifts. The company markets its products through three brands: Harry & David, Cushman's Fruit Company and Wolferman's. The firm's Harry & David products include the flagship Royal Riviera pears, the Fruit-of-the-Month Club, the Tower of Treats gifts (stacked boxes filled with various products) and Moose Munch caramel and chocolate popcorn snacks. Harry & David Holdings is especially known for its direct marketing catalog and e-commerce operations; it also conducts business through phone, mail, business-to-business and wholesale distribution channels. The Harry & David Stores focus on products from the company's core gift product line, gift-ready packaging and selected tabletop, home decor accessory and entertainment products. The firm's Cushman's product line includes the Cushman HoneyBells Florida citrus line, while Wolferman's products include specialty English muffins and other breakfast products. In September 2014, the company was acquired by 1-800-FLOWERS.COM, Inc.

FINANCIAL DATA: Note: Data for latest year may not have been available at press time.

In U.S. $	2015	2014	2013	2012	2011	2010
Revenue		386,601,000	380,262,000	369,334,000	402,364,000	426,774,016
R&D Expense						
Operating Income						
Operating Margin %						
SGA Expense						
Net Income		9,084,000	12,958,000	180,208,000	-114,917,000	-39,228,000
Operating Cash Flow						
Capital Expenditure						
EBITDA						
Return on Assets %						
Return on Equity %						
Debt to Equity						

CONTACT INFORMATION:

Phone: 541 864-2362   Fax:
Toll-Free: 877-322-1200
Address: 2500 S. Pacific Hwy., Medford, OR 97501 United States

SALARIES/BONUSES:

Top Exec. Salary: $ Bonus: $
Second Exec. Salary: $ Bonus: $

STOCK TICKER/OTHER:

Stock Ticker: Subsidiary   Exchange:
Employees: 3,000   Fiscal Year Ends: 06/30
Parent Company: 1-800-FLOWERS.COM Inc

OTHER THOUGHTS:

Estimated Female Officers or Directors: 1
Hot Spot for Advancement for Women/Minorities:

Hastings Entertainment Inc

www.gohastings.com

NAIC Code: 451211

TYPES OF BUSINESS:

Book Stores
Video & DVD Rental
Music Sales
Video Game Sales
Used Books, Music & DVDs
Coffee Sales
Online Sales
Athletic Equipment Sales

BRANDS/DIVISIONS/AFFILIATES:

GoHastings.com
Hardback Cafe
goShip
Sun Adventure Sports
TRADESMART
Hastings
Draw Another Circle LLC

CONTACTS: Note: Officers with more than one job title may be intentionally listed here more than once.

John H. Marmaduke, CEO
John H. Marmaduke, Pres.
Dan Crow, CFO
Alan Van Ongevalle, Sr. VP-Merch.
Dan Crow, VP-Finance
Phil McConnell, VP
John H. Marmaduke, Chmn.

GROWTH PLANS/SPECIAL FEATURES:

Hastings Entertainment, Inc. is a multimedia entertainment retailer operating 126 superstores in 19 states, particularly in the Western and Midwestern U.S. The stores, which average 24,000 square feet of selling space, buy, sell, trade and rent books, music, periodicals, DVDs and Blu-Ray discs, video games, video game consoles and electronics. In addition to its brick-and-mortar locations, the firm operates goHastings.com, which offers a broad selection of books, music, software, video games and movies over the Internet; and sells products via the Amazon.com Marketplace. To support its e-commerce activities, Hastings developed the goShip program, which ships items sold online directly from store inventories. The target markets for Hastings' store locations are mid-sized towns with populations of less than 250,000. The company aims to achieve high levels of customer loyalty and repeat business. To this end, many of its stores offer such amenities as reading chairs, and 61 stores offer Hardback Cafe full-service coffee bars. Additionally, the company operates two Sun Adventure Sports locations in Texas. The firm's concept store, TRADESMART, in Littleton, Colorado, is a multimedia entertainment store offering primarily the same stock as Hastings stores, along with skateboards and paintball merchandise. In July 2014, the firm was acquired by Draw Another Circle, LLC.

FINANCIAL DATA: Note: Data for latest year may not have been available at press time.

In U.S. $	2015	2014	2013	2012	2011	2010
Revenue		455,240,000	435,962,000	462,501,000	496,387,000	521,055,000
R&D Expense						
Operating Income						
Operating Margin %						
SGA Expense						
Net Income			-10,183,000	-9,313,000	-17,579,000	1,705,000
Operating Cash Flow						
Capital Expenditure						
EBITDA						
Return on Assets %						
Return on Equity %						
Debt to Equity						

CONTACT INFORMATION:

Phone: 806 351-2300   Fax: 806 351-2424
Toll-Free: 877-427-8464
Address: 3601 Plains Blvd., Amarillo, TX 79102 United States

STOCK TICKER/OTHER:

Stock Ticker: Subsidiary   Exchange:
Employees: 4,400   Fiscal Year Ends: 01/31
Parent Company: Draw Another Circle, LLC

SALARIES/BONUSES:

Top Exec. Salary: $ Bonus: $
Second Exec. Salary: $ Bonus: $

OTHER THOUGHTS:

Estimated Female Officers or Directors: 1
Hot Spot for Advancement for Women/Minorities:

Hat World Inc

NAIC Code: 448210

TYPES OF BUSINESS:

Hats, Retail
Online Sales
Custom Embroidery

BRANDS/DIVISIONS/AFFILIATES:

Genesco Inc
Lids Kids
Lids
Hat World
Lids Locker Room
LIDS Club
Lids Team Sports
Head Quarters

CONTACTS: *Note: Officers with more than one job title may be intentionally listed here more than once.*

Griffin R. Taylor, Pres.
Scott Molander, COO
Robert J. Dennis, Chmn., Genesco, Inc.

GROWTH PLANS/SPECIAL FEATURES:

Hat World, Inc., a subsidiary of Genesco, Inc., is one of th largest licensed and branded headwear companies in the U.S It operates more than 1,000 factory outlet, airport, mall-base and street-level stores in the U.S., Puerto Rico and Canada specializing in baseball caps with professional and colleg sports teams' logos. Stores typically carry over 1,000 differe hats, including knit hats, straw hats and sports helmets. Lid Locker Room stores offer licensed sports apparel an sunglasses as well as custom embroidery. Although the firm mainly targets customers in their mid-teens to early 20 through the Hat World, Lids and Head Quarters retail brands, also markets the Lids Kids line of hats and apparel. Besides it retail locations, the company sells its products online a Lids.com, which also features a customizable hat option tha allows customers to select style, color and size as well a upload a custom graphic to be embroidered on the hat. Th firm's paid membership program, LIDS Club, provide members with a 20% discount on hat purchases and a 10% discount on accessory purchases in stores and online; prio notification on new and exclusive releases at LIDS Locke Room and Lids stores and online; and occasional special offer and discounts. The company also operates Lids Team Sports which offers sports team uniform and apparel services and sporting goods distribution.

FINANCIAL DATA: *Note: Data for latest year may not have been available at press time.*

In U.S. $	2015	2014	2013	2012	2011	2010
Revenue						
R&D Expense						
Operating Income						
Operating Margin %						
SGA Expense						
Net Income						
Operating Cash Flow						
Capital Expenditure						
EBITDA						
Return on Assets %						
Return on Equity %						
Debt to Equity						

CONTACT INFORMATION:

Phone: 317-334-9428   Fax: 317-337-1428
Toll-Free: 888-564-4287
Address: 7555 Woodland Dr., Indianapolis, IN 46278 United States

STOCK TICKER/OTHER:

Stock Ticker: Subsidiary   Exchange:
Employees: Fiscal Year Ends: 01/31
Parent Company: GENESCO INC

SALARIES/BONUSES:

Top Exec. Salary: $ Bonus: $
Second Exec. Salary: $ Bonus: $

OTHER THOUGHTS:

Estimated Female Officers or Directors:
Hot Spot for Advancement for Women/Minorities:

Haverty Furniture Companies Inc

www.havertys.com

NAIC Code: 442110

TYPES OF BUSINESS:

Furniture Stores
Home Accessory Sales
Mattress Sales

BRANDS/DIVISIONS/AFFILIATES:

Havertys

CONTACTS: Note: Officers with more than one job title may be intentionally listed here more than once.

Clarence Smith, CEO
Dennis Fink, CFO
J. Clary, Chief Information Officer
Steven Burdette, Executive VP, Divisional
Janet Taylor, General Counsel
Allan Deniro, Other Executive Officer
Jenny Parker, Secretary
Richard Gallagher, Senior VP, Divisional
Rawson Haverty, Senior VP, Divisional

GROWTH PLANS/SPECIAL FEATURES:

Haverty Furniture Companies, Inc. is a U.S. specialty furniture retailer. The firm operates approximately 119 retail furniture showrooms across 16 states in the Southern and Midwestern regions. Haverty Furniture sells a broad range of household furniture and accessories, including living room, bedroom and dining room furniture as well as bedding and lamps. Annually, bedroom furniture makes up 17.0% of the company's revenue; dining room furniture, 11.1%; occasional, 10.6%; upholstery, 39.9%; mattresses, 10.9%; and accessories, 10.5%. The company tailors its merchandise presentation to the needs and tastes of local markets and targets customers in the middle- and upper-middle-income segments. Although the majority of merchandise carried bears the Havertys name, its stores also offer many nationally recognized brands, including Sealy, Tempur-Pedic and Serta. The company offers financing through an internal revolving charge credit plan and a third-party finance company. The company's distribution system consists of three large distribution centers and several home delivery centers and local market cross-docks. Haverty Furniture's business strategies include convenient and appealing stores, complimentary advertising, helpful sales associates, merchandise selection and value, available and flexible financing options and timely home-delivery of purchases.

The company offers employees benefits including health, dental, vision, life, disability and accidental death insurance; a 401(k); tuition reimbursement; and flexible spending accounts for health care and dependent care.

FINANCIAL DATA: Note: Data for latest year may not have been available at press time.

In U.S. $	2015	2014	2013	2012	2011	2010
Revenue		768,707,000	746,410,000	670,366,000	621,363,000	620,331,000
R&D Expense						
Operating Income		26,130,000	53,097,000	23,516,000	4,603,000	7,956,000
Operating Margin %		3.39%	7.11%	3.50%	.74%	1.28%
SGA Expense		386,277,000	348,599,000	328,826,000	315,865,000	311,897,000
Net Income		8,589,000	32,265,000	14,911,000	15,463,000	8,444,000
Operating Cash Flow		55,454,000	55,889,000	52,168,000	19,072,000	24,201,000
Capital Expenditure		30,882,000	20,202,000	25,014,000	17,566,000	14,053,000
EBITDA		48,743,000	74,547,000	43,555,000	23,582,000	26,347,000
Return on Assets %		1.95%	7.86%	3.78%	4.09%	2.30%
Return on Equity %		2.90%	11.57%	5.71%	5.99%	3.39%
Debt to Equity		0.15	0.05	0.07	0.04	0.03

CONTACT INFORMATION:

Phone: 404 443-2900   Fax: 404 443-4180
Toll-Free:
Address: 780 Johnson Ferry Rd., Ste. 800, Atlanta, GA 30342 United States

STOCK TICKER/OTHER:

Stock Ticker: HVT
Employees: 3,388
Parent Company:

Exchange: NYS
Fiscal Year Ends: 12/31

SALARIES/BONUSES:

Top Exec. Salary: $625,000   Bonus: $
Second Exec. Salary: $380,000   Bonus: $

OTHER THOUGHTS:

Estimated Female Officers or Directors: 5
Hot Spot for Advancement for Women/Minorities: Y

Sales, profits and employees may be estimates. Financial information, benefits and other data can change quickly and may vary from those stated here.

HEB (HE Butt Grocery Company)

NAIC Code: 445110

TYPES OF BUSINESS:

Supermarkets
Grocery Stores
Gourmet Food Stores
Dairy Processing
Bakery
Pharmacy Services

BRANDS/DIVISIONS/AFFILIATES:

H-E-B
Central Market
H-E-B plus!
Joe V's Smart Shop
H-E-B Wireless
Temple Retail Support Center

CONTACTS: Note: Officers with more than one job title may be intentionally listed here more than once.

Charles C. Butt, CEO
Craig Boyan, COO
Craig Boyan, Pres.
Martin Otto, CFO
Martin Otto, Chief Merchant
Judy Lindquist, General Counsel
Lynette Padalecki, VP-Corp. Planning & Analysis
Winell Herron, VP-Public Affairs & Diversity
Scott McClelland, Pres., Houston Food & Drug Stores Div.
Suzanne Wade, Pres., San Antonio Food & Drug Stores Div.
William Fry, VP-Quality Assurance & Environmental Affairs
Roxanne Orsak, Exec. VP-Drug
Charles C. Butt, Chmn.
Mike Graham, Sr. VP-Logistics & Supply Chain

GROWTH PLANS/SPECIAL FEATURES:

H.E. Butt Grocery Company (HEB) is one of the largest regional food retailers in the southwestern U.S. and Mexico. It operates over 370 grocery stores in 150 communities in Texas and Mexico under the H-E-B brand name. The firm owns one of the largest milk plants in Texas as well as a large bread bakery, a meat plant, a pastry bakery, an ice cream plant, a chip plant and a photo processing lab. The stores carry a wide variety of merchandise, including a line of products under the H-E-B brand. H-E-B also operates nine Central Market stores, with locations in Houston, Dallas, Fort Worth, Plano, San Antonio, Southlake and Austin. Central Markets are gourmet specialty stores featuring large prepared foods-to-go areas, eat-in areas, comprehensive wine departments, specialty butcher and fish counters, a European bakery, a deli with meats, a large selection of cheeses from around the globe and a juice and ice cream bar. H-E-B plus! stores offer additional departments including Cook & Grill, Card & Party and a Tortilleria. H-E-B Wireless offers cell phone plans in partnership with providers such as Sprint and Nextel. The firm also owns a series of six discount stores in the Houston and Baytown, Texas area known as Joe V's Smart Shop. The company owns and operates a retail support center in Monterrey, Mexico as well as the Temple Retail Support Center, a 450,000 square foot warehouse and transportation facility in central Texas.

Employees of the firm are offered a variety of benefits, including discounts on groceries and a prescription plan. In 2015, the company launched a benefit whereby qualified employees receive an annual grant of shares of nonvoting stock equal to 3% of wages.

FINANCIAL DATA: Note: Data for latest year may not have been available at press time.

In U.S. $	2015	2014	2013	2012	2011	2010
Revenue	23,000,000,000	21,000,000,000	20,400,000,000	19,750,000,000	19,125,000,000	18,640,000,000
R&D Expense						
Operating Income						
Operating Margin %						
SGA Expense						
Net Income						
Operating Cash Flow						
Capital Expenditure						
EBITDA						
Return on Assets %						
Return on Equity %						
Debt to Equity						

CONTACT INFORMATION:

Phone: 210-938-8000   Fax: 210-938-8169
Toll-Free: 800-432-3113
Address: 646 S. Main Ave, San Antonio, TX 78204 United States

STOCK TICKER/OTHER:

Stock Ticker: Private   Exchange:
Employees: 86,000   Fiscal Year Ends: 10/31
Parent Company:

SALARIES/BONUSES:

Top Exec. Salary: $ Bonus: $
Second Exec. Salary: $ Bonus: $

OTHER THOUGHTS:

Estimated Female Officers or Directors: 5
Hot Spot for Advancement for Women/Minorities: Y

Herbalife Ltd

www.herbalife.com

NAIC Code: 446191

TYPES OF BUSINESS:

Nutritional Supplements, Direct Sales
Food & Dietary Supplements
Personal Care Products
Weight Management Products
Energy & Fitness Products

BRANDS/DIVISIONS/AFFILIATES:

Total Control
Formula 1
Liftoff
Herbalife24
NouriFusion
Best Defense
Garden 7
Skin Activator

CONTACTS: *Note: Officers with more than one job title may be intentionally listed here more than once.*

Michael O. Johnson, CEO
Richard P. Goudis, COO
Desmond Walsh, Pres.
John DeSimone, CFO
Brett R. Chapman, General Counsel
Michael O. Johnson, Chmn.

GROWTH PLANS/SPECIAL FEATURES:

Herbalife Ltd. is a marketing company that sells a wide range of weight management products, nutritional supplements and personal care products worldwide. The company conducts business in 91 countries through independent distributors. Products are marketed predominantly through Herbalife's network system, which enables independent distributors to earn profits by selling products to retail customers or other distributors. Herbalife currently markets 150 products. Its products are divided into five categories: weight management, which accounted for 64.1% of 2014 sales; targeted nutrition, 22.3%; energy, sports & fitness, 5.3%; outer nutrition, 3.6%; and literature, promotional & other products, 4.7%. Weight management products include meal replacement products, weight-loss enhancers and healthy snacks. Its products consist of the Formula 1 line of protein powders and meal replacements and Total Control protein bars and snacks. Targeted nutrition includes dietary and nutritional supplements containing herbs, vitamins, minerals and other natural ingredients. Products include Niteworks and Garden 7 phytonutrient supplements and Best Defense, designed for improved immune systems for children. Energy, sports and fitness includes products targeted toward people with active lifestyles such as the Liftoff energy drink and Herbalife24. The outer nutrition segment consists of personal care products such as skin cleansers, moisturizers, shampoos and conditioners. Other nutrition products include the Skin Activator anti-aging line and the NouriFusion skin care line. The literature, promotional and other products segment includes products geared toward distributors such as sale aids, informational audiotapes, CDs, DVDs and startup kits.

FINANCIAL DATA: *Note: Data for latest year may not have been available at press time.*

In U.S. $	2015	2014	2013	2012	2011	2010
Revenue		4,958,600,000	4,825,308,000	4,072,330,000	3,454,537,000	2,734,226,000
R&D Expense						
Operating Income		513,500,000	735,277,000	661,447,000	562,270,000	387,512,000
Operating Margin %		10.35%	15.23%	16.24%	16.27%	14.17%
SGA Expense		1,991,100,000	1,629,052,000	1,259,667,000	1,074,623,000	887,655,000
Net Income		308,700,000	527,525,000	477,190,000	412,578,000	290,533,000
Operating Cash Flow		511,400,000	772,875,000	567,784,000	509,331,000	380,402,000
Capital Expenditure		173,700,000	146,958,000	121,524,000	90,408,000	68,125,000
EBITDA		606,200,000	828,008,000	742,026,000	641,496,000	458,380,000
Return on Assets %		12.73%	25.25%	30.29%	30.80%	24.43%
Return on Equity %		284.45%	108.52%	97.29%	78.78%	68.64%
Debt to Equity			1.54	1.02	0.36	0.35

CONTACT INFORMATION:

Phone: 310 4109600   Fax: 310 2587019
Toll-Free:
Address: Ugland House, S. Church St., Grand Cayman, 90015 Cayman Islands

STOCK TICKER/OTHER:

Stock Ticker: HLF
Employees: 7,800
Parent Company:

Exchange: NYS
Fiscal Year Ends: 12/31

SALARIES/BONUSES:

Top Exec. Salary: $1,236,000   Bonus: $
Second Exec. Salary: $671,517   Bonus: $

OTHER THOUGHTS:

Estimated Female Officers or Directors: 1

Hot Spot for Advancement for Women/Minorities:

Sales, profits and employees may be estimates. Financial information, benefits and other data can change quickly and may vary from those stated here.

Hermes International SA

NAIC Code: 424300

www.hermes.com

TYPES OF BUSINESS:

Apparel and Clothing Brands, Designers, Importers and Distributors
Luxury Scarves & Ties
Accessories
Luxury Goods
Housewares
Retail Stores
Equestrian Gear
Apparel

BRANDS/DIVISIONS/AFFILIATES:

Joseph Erard Holding
Vaucher Manufacture Fleurier
Les Tissages Perrin

CONTACTS: Note: Officers with more than one job title may be intentionally listed here more than once.

Patrick Thomas, Exec. Chmn.
Mireille Maury, Managing Dir.-Finance
Beatriz Gonzales-Cristobal Poyo, Managing Dir.-Mktg.
Guillaume De Seynes, Managing Dir.-Mfg. Div.
Mireille Maury, Managing Dir.-Admin.
Patrick Albaladejo, Deputy Managing Dir.-Strategic Dev. & Corp. Image
Bertrand Puech, Chmn.-Emile Hermes SARL
Guillaume De Seynes, Managing Dir.-Equity Investments
Pierre-Alexis Dumas, Managing Dir.-Artistic
Eric de Seynes, Chmn.

GROWTH PLANS/SPECIAL FEATURES:

Hermes International SA, founded in 1837 as a leather good company that catered to equestrians, has since grown t include other articles of clothing. Current product lines includ leather goods, including handbags, luggage, diaries, sma leather goods and equestrian gear; perfumes; watches tableware; clothing and accessories, including men's wea women's wear, belts, hats, gloves, shoes and leather an enamel jewelry; and silk goods, such as scarves, ties and othe accoutrements. Leather goods and saddle equipment accoun for approximately 45% of the firm's revenue; ready-to-wea accessories, 23%; silks and textiles, 12%; other Hermes sectors, 7%; perfumes, 5%; other products, 5%; and watches 3%. Hermes distributes its products through 311 retail stores 207 of which are directly operated. The company also sells it products through a network of specialty stores located in airports and on board aircraft. Hermes owns a 25% stake ir Swiss watchmaker Vaucher Manufacture Fleurier, a 39.5% stake in Les Tissages Perrin and a 32.5% stake in Joseph Erard Holding. Customers for the most expensive Hermes handbags, costing $7,000 or more, may find themselves or waiting lists that last years until their turn arrives to receive one of these limited edition items.

FINANCIAL DATA: Note: Data for latest year may not have been available at press time.

In U.S. $	2015	2014	2013	2012	2011	2010
Revenue		4,371,073,000	3,984,972,000	3,697,678,000	3,015,368,000	2,547,971,000
R&D Expense						
Operating Income		1,378,948,000	1,292,664,000	1,187,171,000	939,463,400	709,161,200
Operating Margin %		31.54%	32.43%	32.10%	31.15%	27.83%
SGA Expense		1,370,882,000	1,289,693,000	1,200,119,000	1,003,672,000	851,375,500
Net Income		911,445,100	838,746,000	785,256,400	640,388,900	458,163,500
Operating Cash Flow		1,026,066,000	951,880,600	818,475,100	781,011,300	704,491,500
Capital Expenditure		295,996,800	224,146,700	279,122,100	196,552,900	146,777,900
EBITDA		1,533,792,000	1,436,895,000	1,311,449,000	1,057,374,000	812,213,400
Return on Assets %		19.72%	21.52%	22.23%	19.27%	15.73%
Return on Equity %		27.37%	30.57%	31.77%	26.63%	21.40%
Debt to Equity				0.01		

CONTACT INFORMATION:

Phone: 33 140174920   Fax: 33 140174921
Toll-Free:
Address: 24 rue du Faubourg Saint-Honore, Paris, 75008 France

STOCK TICKER/OTHER:

Stock Ticker: HESAF   Exchange: PINX
Employees: 11,718   Fiscal Year Ends: 12/31
Parent Company:

SALARIES/BONUSES:

Top Exec. Salary: $ Bonus: $
Second Exec. Salary: $ Bonus: $

OTHER THOUGHTS:

Estimated Female Officers or Directors: 4
Hot Spot for Advancement for Women/Minorities: Y

Hhgregg Inc

www.hhgregg.com

NAIC Code: 443142

TYPES OF BUSINESS:

Consumer Electronics Stores
Appliances
Furniture & Mattresses
e-commerce

BRANDS/DIVISIONS/AFFILIATES:

h.h.gregg
Fine Lines

CONTACTS: Note: Officers with more than one job title may be intentionally listed here more than once.

Dennis May, CEO
Robert Riesbeck, CFO
Catherine Langham, Chairman of the Board
Trent Taylor, Chief Information Officer
Keith Zimmerman, Other Executive Officer
Charles Young, Other Executive Officer

GROWTH PLANS/SPECIAL FEATURES:

Hhgregg, Inc. is a U.S.-based specialty retailer specializing in consumer electronics and home appliances. The company operates approximately 228 stores in 20 states under the h.h.gregg and Fine Lines names, primarily located in the Mid-West and along the eastern coast of the U.S. While average stores are 33,000 square feet in size, Hhgregg's newest store model ranges from 25,000 to 30,000 square feet. The firm's products fall into four categories: appliances, which accounted for 51% of sales in fiscal 2015; consumer electronics, 37%; computing and wireless, 7%; and home products, 5%. Appliances consist of refrigerators, cooking ranges, dishwashers, freezers, washers and dryers, sold under a variety of brand names including Amana, Bosch, Frigidaire, GE, Haier, KitchenAid, LG, Maytag, Samsung and Whirlpool. Consumer electrics consist of products such as LED televisions, audio systems, cameras and Blu-ray players, under brands such as Curtis, Haier, LG, Samsung, Seiki, Sharp, Sony and Toshiba. Computing and wireless products include notebook computers, tablets and mobile phones, and represent brands such as Apple, Asus, Curtis, Dell, Kindle, Lenovo, Hewlett Packard, Samsung, Sony and Toshiba. Home products include fitness equipment, furniture, mattresses and other home products, under the brands of Ashley, Pro-Form, Serta, Tech Craft and Tempur-Pedic. The firm also offers services including third-party premium service plans (PSPs), third-party in-home service and repair of the company's products, delivery and installation and in-home repair and maintenance.

FINANCIAL DATA: Note: Data for latest year may not have been available at press time.

In U.S. $	2015	2014	2013	2012	2011	2010
Revenue	2,129,374,000	2,338,570,000	2,474,759,000	2,493,392,000	2,077,651,000	1,534,253,000
R&D Expense						
Operating Income	-99,448,000	2,677,000	43,759,000	109,800,000	86,271,000	68,791,000
Operating Margin %	-4.67%	.11%	1.76%	4.40%	4.15%	4.48%
SGA Expense	617,217,000	618,129,000	633,188,000	616,023,000	517,163,000	380,990,000
Net Income	-132,746,000	228,000	25,369,000	81,373,000	48,208,000	39,198,000
Operating Cash Flow	12,763,000	82,651,000	66,053,000	117,037,000	58,997,000	107,880,000
Capital Expenditure	22,522,000	22,257,000	54,020,000	83,054,000	59,938,000	62,161,000
EBITDA	-59,185,000	45,807,000	83,903,000	143,575,000	111,658,000	86,852,000
Return on Assets %	-24.27%	.03%	3.84%	13.64%	8.34%	8.19%
Return on Equity %	-55.22%	.06%	7.18%	24.07%	16.91%	20.70%
Debt to Equity						0.34

CONTACT INFORMATION:

Phone: 317 848-8710   Fax: 317 848-8723
Toll-Free: 800-284-7344
Address: 4151 E. 96th St., Indianapolis, IN 46240 United States

SALARIES/BONUSES:

Top Exec. Salary: $657,200   Bonus: $
Second Exec. Salary: $360,385   Bonus: $

STOCK TICKER/OTHER:

Stock Ticker: HGG
Employees: 5,400
Parent Company:

Exchange: NYS
Fiscal Year Ends: 03/31

OTHER THOUGHTS:

Estimated Female Officers or Directors: 2
Hot Spot for Advancement for Women/Minorities:

Hibbett Sports Inc

www.hibbett.com

NAIC Code: 451110

TYPES OF BUSINESS:

Sporting Goods Stores
Sports Apparel
Athletic Shoes
Training Equipment

BRANDS/DIVISIONS/AFFILIATES:

Hibbett Sports
Hibbett Team Sales Inc
Sports Additions

CONTACTS: *Note: Officers with more than one job title may be intentionally listed here more than once.*

Jeffry Rosenthal, CEO
Scott Bowman, CFO
Michael Newsome, Chairman of the Board
Jared Briskin, Other Executive Officer
Elaine Rodgers, Secretary
Cathy Pryor, Senior VP, Divisional

GROWTH PLANS/SPECIAL FEATURES:

Hibbett Sports, Inc. is an operator of sporting goods stores in small to mid-sized markets predominantly in the Southeast, Southwest, Midwest and Mid-Atlantic U.S. Its stores offer a broad assortment of athletic equipment, footwear and apparel. The company's merchandise assortment features a broad selection of brand name merchandise emphasizing team sports complemented by localized apparel and accessories designed to appeal to a wide range of customers. Hibbett operates a total of 927 stores consisting of 910 Hibbett Sports stores and 17 smaller-format Sports Additions athletic shoe stores in 31 states. The firm's primary retail format is Hibbett Sports, a 5,000-square-foot store model located in strip centers frequently within in close proximity to Wal-Mart stores. Sports Additions stores are mall-based stores averaging 2,500 square feet with roughly 90% of merchandise consisting of athletic footwear and the remainder consisting of caps and a limited assortment of apparel. Sports Additions stores offer a broader assortment of athletic footwear, with a greater emphasis on fashion than the athletic footwear choices offered by traditional Hibbett Sports stores. Subsidiary Hibbett Team Sales, Inc. supplies customized athletic apparel, equipment and footwear to school, athletic and youth programs in Alabama, Georgia, Mississippi and Florida. It sells its merchandise directly to educational institutions and youth associations.

The firm offers employees life, disability, medical and dental insurance; a vision care plan; a stock purchase plan; a 401(k) plan; employee discounts; and a 529 college savings plan.

FINANCIAL DATA: *Note: Data for latest year may not have been available at press time.*

In U.S. $	2015	2014	2013	2012	2011	2010
Revenue	913,486,000	851,965,000	818,700,000	732,645,000	664,954,000	593,492,000
R&D Expense						
Operating Income	118,146,000	113,891,000	115,981,000	93,531,000	73,547,000	52,407,000
Operating Margin %	12.93%	13.36%	14.16%	12.76%	11.06%	8.83%
SGA Expense	192,648,000	181,527,000	169,872,000	155,672,000	143,232,000	129,888,000
Net Income	73,584,000	70,877,000	72,582,000	59,060,000	46,400,000	32,549,000
Operating Cash Flow	102,392,000	53,301,000	87,124,000	54,921,000	61,918,000	36,914,000
Capital Expenditure	22,873,000	50,507,000	21,970,000	12,997,000	10,476,000	9,605,000
EBITDA	134,158,000	127,749,000	129,024,000	106,761,000	87,212,000	66,372,000
Return on Assets %	16.94%	17.86%	21.00%	18.81%	15.70%	12.71%
Return on Equity %	23.40%	26.09%	32.77%	29.24%	24.73%	20.88%
Debt to Equity				0.01	0.01	

CONTACT INFORMATION:

Phone: 205 942-4292   Fax: 205 912-7290
Toll-Free:
Address: 2700 Milan Court, Birmingham, AL 35211 United States

STOCK TICKER/OTHER:

Stock Ticker: HIBB   Exchange: NAS
Employees: 8,700   Fiscal Year Ends: 01/31
Parent Company:

SALARIES/BONUSES:

Top Exec. Salary: $490,000   Bonus: $
Second Exec. Salary: $376,000   Bonus: $

OTHER THOUGHTS:

Estimated Female Officers or Directors: 3
Hot Spot for Advancement for Women/Minorities: Y

HMSHost Corp

www.hmshost.com

NAIC Code: 722310

TYPES OF BUSINESS:
Food Service Contractors
Food, Beverage & Retail Concessions
Travel Plazas
Food Courts

BRANDS/DIVISIONS/AFFILIATES:
Autogrill SpA
Ciao Gourmet Market
La Tapenade Mediterranean
Z Market
Wicker Park Seafood & Sushi Bar
Beaudevin
Jose Cuervo Tequileria

CONTACTS: Note: Officers with more than one job title may be intentionally listed here more than once.
Steve Johnson, CEO
Tom Fricke, Pres.

GROWTH PLANS/SPECIAL FEATURES:
HMSHost Corp., a wholly-owned subsidiary of Italy-based Autogrill SpA, is a leading provider of food and beverage concessions. The firm operates facilities in over 100 airports worldwide as well as 99 roadside travel plazas along major U.S. and Canada toll roads and turnpikes in the Northeast and Midwest. HMSHost also serves tourist destinations such as Space Center Houston and the Empire State Building. The company's international airport operations include food service outlets at major and regional airports in Canada, Australia, Singapore, Ireland, India, Denmark, Sweden, the Netherlands, the U.K., Malaysia, France, Finland, Russia, the Middle East, Vietnam, Indonesia and New Zealand. HMSHost is engaged in a range of national and local brand licensing and franchising relationships, providing its food service with well-known brands ranging from Wolfgang Puck, Quiznos Sub to Starbucks, Pizza Hut and the Chili's Too. The company also develops proprietary branded concepts including Ciao Gourmet Market, La Tapenade Mediterranean, Z Market, Wicker Park Seafood & Sushi Bar, Beaudevin and Jose Cuervo Tequileria.

FINANCIAL DATA: Note: Data for latest year may not have been available at press time.

In U.S. $	2015	2014	2013	2012	2011	2010
Revenue		2,704,700,000	2,759,400,000	2,700,000,000	2,679,000,000	2,546,400,000
R&D Expense						
Operating Income						
Operating Margin %						
SGA Expense						
Net Income		86,500,000	76,900,000			
Operating Cash Flow						
Capital Expenditure						
EBITDA						
Return on Assets %						
Return on Equity %						
Debt to Equity						

CONTACT INFORMATION:
Phone: 240-694-4100   Fax: 240-694-4790
Toll-Free:
Address: 6905 Rockledge Dr., Bethesda, MD 20817 United States

STOCK TICKER/OTHER:
Stock Ticker: Subsidiary
Employees: 34,480
Parent Company: AUTOGRILL SPA

Exchange:
Fiscal Year Ends: 12/31

SALARIES/BONUSES:
Top Exec. Salary: $ Bonus: $
Second Exec. Salary: $ Bonus: $

OTHER THOUGHTS:
Estimated Female Officers or Directors: 1
Hot Spot for Advancement for Women/Minorities:

Hobby Lobby Stores Inc

NAIC Code: 451120

www.hobbylobby.com

TYPES OF BUSINESS:

Arts & Crafts, Retail
Crafts
Fabrics
Furniture
Silk Flowers
Baskets
Home Accessories
Seasonal Merchandise

BRANDS/DIVISIONS/AFFILIATES:

Mardel
Hemispheres
Hobby Lobby

GROWTH PLANS/SPECIAL FEATURES:

Hobby Lobby Stores, Inc. operates a chain of arts and craf
supply stores, with 600 locations in 40 U.S. states. The firm
stores stock over 70,000 items, including fashion fabric
baskets, silk flowers, needlework, wearable art, picture framin
supplies, cards, party supplies, furniture and season
merchandise. In addition, many locations hold period
community crafts classes. Hobby Lobby's headquarters ar
located in a manufacturing, distribution and office complex i
Oklahoma City. The firm has two affiliated companies. Mard
is an independent retailer of Christian materials, education
products and office supplies with locations in seven U.S. state
Hemispheres is a retailer of home furnishings and accessorie
with six locations in Oklahoma and Texas. Hobby Lobby als
offers customers a Visa consumer card. Reward points ar
earned by shopping at a Hobby Lobby or using the car
anywhere Visa is accepted. Consumers receive a $25 reward
gift card for every 2,500 points earned through the card alon
with travel benefits and other convenient features.

CONTACTS:

Note: Officers with more than one job title may be intentionally listed here more than once.

David Green, CEO
Steven Green, Pres.
Jon Cargill, CFO
Ken Haywood, Sr. VP-Oper.

FINANCIAL DATA:

Note: Data for latest year may not have been available at press time.

In U.S. $	2015	2014	2013	2012	2011	2010
Revenue		3,350,000,000	3,300,000,000	3,000,000,000	2,280,000,000	2,300,000,000
R&D Expense						
Operating Income						
Operating Margin %						
SGA Expense						
Net Income						
Operating Cash Flow						
Capital Expenditure						
EBITDA						
Return on Assets %						
Return on Equity %						
Debt to Equity						

CONTACT INFORMATION:

Phone: 405-745-1100   Fax: 405-745-1636
Toll-Free:
Address: 7707 SW 44th St., Oklahoma City, OK 73179 United States

STOCK TICKER/OTHER:

Stock Ticker: Private
Employees: 23,000
Parent Company:

Exchange:
Fiscal Year Ends: 12/31

SALARIES/BONUSES:

Top Exec. Salary: $ Bonus: $
Second Exec. Salary: $ Bonus: $

OTHER THOUGHTS:

Estimated Female Officers or Directors:
Hot Spot for Advancement for Women/Minorities:

Home Depot Inc

NAIC Code: 444110

www.homedepot.com

TYPES OF BUSINESS:

Home Centers, Retail
Home Improvement Products
Building Materials
Lawn & Garden Products
Online & Catalog Sales
Tool & Truck Rental
Installation & Design Services

BRANDS/DIVISIONS/AFFILIATES:

Husky
Hampton Bay
Behr
RIDGID
Ryobi
Glacier Bay
Blinds.com
Interline Brands

CONTACTS: *Note: Officers with more than one job title may be intentionally listed here more than once.*

Carol Tome, CFO
Matt Carey, Chief Information Officer
Edward Decker, Executive VP, Divisional
Marc Powers, Executive VP, Divisional
Timothy Crow, Executive VP, Divisional
Mark Holifield, Executive VP, Divisional
Teresa Roseborough, Executive VP
Stephen Holmes, Other Corporate Officer
Craig Menear, President
Diane Dayhoff, Vice President, Divisional

GROWTH PLANS/SPECIAL FEATURES:

Home Depot, Inc. is one of the world's largest home improvement retailers. The company operates approximately 2,269 Home Depot stores throughout the U.S., Canada, Guam, Puerto Rico, the Virgin Islands and Mexico. A typical store encompasses 104,000 square feet of enclosed space with a 24,000 square foot outdoor garden center; these locations usually stock between 30,000 and 40,000 items. These stores sell an assortment of building materials, plumbing materials, electrical materials, kitchen products, hardware, seasonal items, paint, flooring and wall coverings. The firm's proprietary brands include Hampton Bay lighting, Husky hand tools, Behr Premium Plus paint, Vigoro lawn care products, RIDGID and Ryobi power tools and Glacier Bay bath fixtures. Home Depot markets its products primarily to three types of customers: professional customers, such as remodelers, contractors, repairmen and small business owners; do-it-for-me shoppers, who are homeowners that personally purchase Home Depot products but hire third-party individuals for installation and/or project completion; and do-it-yourself (DIY) customers, who are homeowners that both shop for and personally install and/or utilize the firm's materials. In 2014, Home Depot acquired Blinds.com. In July 2015, it acquired Interline Brands from P2 Capital Partners for $1.6 billion.

The company offers its employees medical, dental, vision, life, AD&D and disability insurance; a 401(k) plan; a stock purchase plan; adoption, education and relocation assistance; flexible spending accounts; a legal services plan; auto and homeowners insurance; and veterinary coverage.

FINANCIAL DATA: *Note: Data for latest year may not have been available at press time.*

In U.S. $	2015	2014	2013	2012	2011	2010
Revenue	83,176,000,000	78,812,000,000	74,754,000,000	70,395,000,000	67,997,000,000	66,176,000,000
R&D Expense						
Operating Income	10,469,000,000	9,166,000,000	7,766,000,000	6,661,000,000	5,839,000,000	4,803,000,000
Operating Margin %	12.58%	11.63%	10.38%	9.46%	8.58%	7.25%
SGA Expense	16,834,000,000	16,597,000,000	16,508,000,000	16,028,000,000	15,849,000,000	15,902,000,000
Net Income	6,345,000,000	5,385,000,000	4,535,000,000	3,883,000,000	3,338,000,000	2,661,000,000
Operating Cash Flow	8,242,000,000	7,628,000,000	6,975,000,000	6,651,000,000	4,585,000,000	5,125,000,000
Capital Expenditure	1,442,000,000	1,389,000,000	1,312,000,000	1,221,000,000	1,096,000,000	966,000,000
EBITDA	12,592,000,000	10,935,000,000	9,537,000,000	8,356,000,000	7,521,000,000	6,464,000,000
Return on Assets %	15.77%	13.19%	11.11%	9.63%	8.24%	6.48%
Return on Equity %	58.09%	35.54%	25.42%	21.11%	17.43%	14.31%
Debt to Equity	1.80	1.17	0.53	0.60	0.46	0.44

CONTACT INFORMATION:

Phone: 770 433-8211   Fax: 770 431-2707
Toll-Free: 800-553-3199
Address: 2455 Paces Ferry Rd. N.W., Atlanta, GA 30339 United States

STOCK TICKER/OTHER:

Stock Ticker: HD
Employees: 371
Parent Company:

Exchange: NYS
Fiscal Year Ends: 01/31

SALARIES/BONUSES:

Top Exec. Salary:
$1,019,231
Second Exec. Salary:
$991,104

Bonus: $

Bonus: $

OTHER THOUGHTS:

Estimated Female Officers or Directors: 7

Hot Spot for Advancement for Women/Minorities: Y

Home Retail Group plc

www.homeretailgroup.com

NAIC Code: 444110

TYPES OF BUSINESS:

General Merchandise, Retail
Home Centers, Retail
Direct Sales

BRANDS/DIVISIONS/AFFILIATES:

Argos
Homebase
www.argos.co.uk
www.homebase.co.uk

CONTACTS: *Note: Officers with more than one job title may be intentionally listed here more than once.*

John Walden, CEO
Richard Ashton, Dir.-Finance
Julie Elder, Dir.-Group HR
Gordon Bentley, Corp. Sec.
Don Davis, Dir.-Investor Rel.
Greg Ball, Managing Dir.-Financial Svcs. & Customer Service
Paul Loft, Managing Dir.-Homebase
Maria Thompson, Dir.-Commercial
John Walden, Managing Dir.-Argos
John Coombe, Chmn.

GROWTH PLANS/SPECIAL FEATURES:

Home Retail Group plc is a leading home and general merchandise retailer in the U.K. The company operates approximately 1,051 stores across the U.K. and Ireland. The firm sells products through two distinct and complementary retail brands: Argos and Homebase. Argos, through its 60 digital stores, offers over 40,000 general merchandise products via the Internet. Customers can purchase products over the phone and online. Home improvement retailer Homebase, with 296 stores, carries more than 50,000 products. These items include furniture, kitchen appliances, kitchenware, tableware, housewares, lighting, flooring and tiling products, decorating tools, bathroom accessories/sets, home electrical products, heating and cooling equipment, tools, hardware, building products, gardening supplies and outdoor lighting/heating equipment. Online purchasing is located at Home Retail's www.argos.co.uk and www.homebase.co.uk independent web sites. Home Retail Group also offers in-house financial services, which provide credit and insurance options to customers. Argos accounts for 72% of group sales, Homebase 26% and financial services accounts for the remainder.

FINANCIAL DATA: *Note: Data for latest year may not have been available at press time.*

In U.S. $	2015	2014	2013	2012	2011	2010
Revenue	8,536,490,000	8,465,632,000	8,185,189,000	8,345,741,000	8,748,019,000	9,003,349,000
R&D Expense						
Operating Income	152,330,500	104,643,200	205,399,600	147,546,900	385,684,800	440,248,700
Operating Margin %	1.78%	1.23%	2.50%	1.76%	4.40%	4.88%
SGA Expense	2,498,131,000	2,532,066,000	2,383,921,000	2,091,667,000	2,063,713,000	2,088,080,000
Net Income	107,035,000	80,724,730	140,520,800	108,828,900	285,376,900	313,630,500
Operating Cash Flow	285,077,900	214,369,000	442,491,100	310,491,200	399,886,400	528,747,000
Capital Expenditure	260,860,500	262,056,400	120,489,100	201,662,300	218,405,200	136,335,100
EBITDA	355,637,300	298,233,000	391,813,900	349,807,200	591,831,900	637,725,400
Return on Assets %	1.66%	1.27%	2.27%	1.78%	4.53%	4.95%
Return on Equity %	2.67%	1.99%	3.50%	2.71%	6.80%	7.45%
Debt to Equity						

CONTACT INFORMATION:

Phone: 44 1908600172   Fax: 44 1908692301
Toll-Free:
Address: 489-499 Avebury Blvd., Saxon Gate W., Milton Keynes, MK9 2NW United Kingdom

STOCK TICKER/OTHER:

Stock Ticker: HMRLF   Exchange: PINX
Employees: 46,589   Fiscal Year Ends: 03/31
Parent Company:

SALARIES/BONUSES:

Top Exec. Salary: $ Bonus: $
Second Exec. Salary: $ Bonus: $

OTHER THOUGHTS:

Estimated Female Officers or Directors: 4
Hot Spot for Advancement for Women/Minorities: Y

Honest Company (The)

www.honest.com

NAIC Code: 454111

TYPES OF BUSINESS:

Electronic Shopping
Sanitary Paper Product Manufacturing, Diapers & Wipes
Infant's Formulas Manufacturing
Baby Powder and Baby Oil Manufacturing

BRANDS/DIVISIONS/AFFILIATES:

Honest Beauty

CONTACTS: Note: Officers with more than one job title may be intentionally listed here more than once.

Brian Lee, CEO
Sean Kane, COO
Christopher Gavigan, Chief Product Officer

GROWTH PLANS/SPECIAL FEATURES:

The Honest Company, co-founded by actress Jessica Alba, is a consumer goods company that emphasis non-toxic household products. The company carries approximately 90 products, with its leading selling product being diapers. Products can be purchased separately or in bundles. Honest's Bundles deal allows consumers to have Honest eco-friendly diapers and products delivered to their homes every month, and by doing so can save up to 40%. The Diapers & Wipes bundle is $79.95 per month; the Essentials bundle of personal care & home cleaning items, of which customers can mix & match five items every month, is $35.95 per month; its Organic Formula Bundle, providing certified organic infant formula modeled after breastmilk, is $119.95 per month; and its Health & Wellness Bundle, which offers food-based supplements that can be mixed & matched, is $35.95 per month. Other products include training pants, swim diapers, wipes dispensers, ointments & lotions, powders, caddies, totes & bags, bottles, nursing items, shampoos & other toiletries, cleaning items for men, women and children, as well as baby carriers, towels and baby furnishings. In September 2015, the firm launched its Honest Beauty brand as a separate entity, with its own website (www.honestbeauty.com) and logo. Honest Beauty comprises 83 element product lines, including 17 skin-care products and a 66-piece makeup range. Its products are derived from botanicals free of parabens, phthalates, petrolatum, sulfates and chemical sunscreens.

FINANCIAL DATA: Note: Data for latest year may not have been available at press time.

In U.S. $	2015	2014	2013	2012	2011	2010
Revenue		150,000,000	50,000,000			
R&D Expense						
Operating Income						
Operating Margin %						
SGA Expense						
Net Income						
Operating Cash Flow						
Capital Expenditure						
EBITDA						
Return on Assets %						
Return on Equity %						
Debt to Equity						

CONTACT INFORMATION:

Phone: 888-862-8818   Fax:
Toll-Free: 888-862-8818
Address: 2700 Pennsylvania Ave., Ste. 1200, Santa Monica, CA 90404
United States

STOCK TICKER/OTHER:

Stock Ticker: Private
Employees: 275
Parent Company:

Exchange:
Fiscal Year Ends:

SALARIES/BONUSES:

Top Exec. Salary: $ Bonus: $
Second Exec. Salary: $ Bonus: $

OTHER THOUGHTS:

Estimated Female Officers or Directors:
Hot Spot for Advancement for Women/Minorities:

Hot Topic Inc
NAIC Code: 448140

www.hottopic.com

TYPES OF BUSINESS:
Music-Related Apparel Stores
Online Sales
Accessories
Cosmetics
Jewelry
Lingerie

BRANDS/DIVISIONS/AFFILIATES:
Hot Topic
Torrid
HotTopic.com
Torrid.com
Blackheart
BlackHeartLingerie.com
Sycamore Partners Management LLC

CONTACTS: Note: Officers with more than one job title may be intentionally listed here more than once.
Lisa Harper, CEO
Don Hendricks, COO
George Wehlitz, Jr, CFO
Kate Horton, VP
Mark Mizicko, Chief Planning Officer
Bruce Quinell, Chmn.

GROWTH PLANS/SPECIAL FEATURES:
Hot Topic, Inc. is a mall and Internet-based specialty retaile
that operates under the Hot Topic, Torrid and Blackhea
brands. The firm owns more than 600 Hot Topic stores, Torri
stores and Blackheart stores in the U.S., Puerto Rico an
Canada. Hot Topic stores are approximately 1,770 square fee
on average, while Torrid locations average roughly 2,49
square feet. The firm also sells merchandise similar to that i
its two stores through two distinct web sites: HotTopic.com an
Torrid.com. In recent years, the company introduced a nev
lingerie concept, Blackheart and launched its respective e
commerce site, BlackHeartLingerie.com. Hot Topic store
target males and females primarily between the ages of 12-22
selling a selection of licensed and non-licensed apparel
accessories and gift items that are influenced by popular musi
artists and pop culture trends. The stores also sell musi
CDs/vinyl LPs and DVDs. Torrid targets plus-size female
between the ages of 15-29, selling apparel, lingerie, shoes an
accessories. Blackheart targets women aged between 18 an
30 who consider lingerie to be a part of their fashion statement
The firm has developed a strategy focused on offering music
related merchandise in the mall environment. It track
alternative and rock music trends by visiting nightclubs
attending concerts and monitoring new music, music videos
and radio airplay. Hot Topic is owned by private equity firm
Sycamore Partners Management LLC. In September 2015, the
firm opened its first Hawaii store, and announced plans to ope
its first store in the Edmonton, Canada area, at Kingsway Mall

The firm offers employees medical, dental and vision
insurance; life insurance; disability coverage; a 401(k) plan; an
employee stock purchase plan; tuition assistance; and an
employee assistance program.

FINANCIAL DATA: Note: Data for latest year may not have been available at press time.

In U.S. $	2015	2014	2013	2012	2011	2010
Revenue		750,000,000	741,750,000	697,934,016	708,243,968	736,710,016
R&D Expense						
Operating Income						
Operating Margin %						
SGA Expense						
Net Income						
Operating Cash Flow						
Capital Expenditure						
EBITDA						
Return on Assets %						
Return on Equity %						
Debt to Equity						

CONTACT INFORMATION:
Phone: 626 839-4681   Fax: 626 839-4686
Toll-Free:
Address: 18305 E. San Jose Ave., City of Industry, CA 91748 United
States

STOCK TICKER/OTHER:
Stock Ticker: Private   Exchange:
Employees: 8,500   Fiscal Year Ends: 01/31
Parent Company: SYCAMORE PARTNERS MANAGEMENT LLC

SALARIES/BONUSES:
Top Exec. Salary: $ Bonus: $
Second Exec. Salary: $ Bonus: $

OTHER THOUGHTS:
Estimated Female Officers or Directors: 3
Hot Spot for Advancement for Women/Minorities: Y

HSN Inc (Home Shopping Network)

www.hsn.com

NAIC Code: 454113

TYPES OF BUSINESS:

Television Shopping
Direct Marketing
Online Sales
Cable & Broadcast Television
Catalog Sales
Retail Stores
Outlet Stores

BRANDS/DIVISIONS/AFFILIATES:

HSN
Cornerstone Brands Inc
Travelsmith
Grandin Road
Chasing Fireflies
Garnet Hill
Ballard Design

CONTACTS: Note: Officers with more than one job title may be intentionally listed here more than once.

Mindy Grossman, CEO
Judy Schmeling, CFO
Arthur Martinez, Chairman of the Board
William Brand, Chief Marketing Officer
Maria Martinez, Other Executive Officer
Gregory Henchel, Other Executive Officer
Jeffrey Kuster, President, Subsidiary

GROWTH PLANS/SPECIAL FEATURES:

HSN, Inc. (Home Shopping Network) is a multi-channel retailer offering shopping alternatives to more than 95 million U.S. households through its two operational segments, HSN and Cornerstone Brands. HSN offers home shopping experiences via television, online through HSN.com, in catalogs and in stores. The Home Shopping Network television program offers items ranging from 14-karat jewelry to cosmetics, home goods and apparel. In addition to its existing media platforms, HSN offers technological innovative services, such as Shop by Remote and Video on Demand. The segment also maintains a limited number of outlet stores. Cornerstone Brands distributes around 325 million catalogs annually, operates eight internet sites and runs 11 retail stores. The segment is comprised of home and apparel lifestyle brands, including Ballard Designs, Chasing Fireflies, Frontgate, Garnet Hill, Grandin Road, Improvements and TravelSmith, as well as corresponding e-commerce sites for each brand.

HSN offers employees medical, dental and vision insurance; life insurance; short- and long-term disability coverage; pet insurance; a retirement savings plan; wellness screenings; onsite car washing; dry cleaning services; and discounted home insurance, cell phones and fitness club memberships.

FINANCIAL DATA: Note: Data for latest year may not have been available at press time.

In U.S. $	2015	2014	2013	2012	2011	2010
Revenue		3,587,995,000	3,403,983,000	3,266,739,000	3,177,154,000	2,996,780,000
R&D Expense						
Operating Income		284,609,000	282,654,000	258,744,000	231,999,000	196,087,000
Operating Margin %		7.93%	8.30%	7.92%	7.30%	6.54%
SGA Expense		944,519,000	906,572,000	886,975,000	881,095,000	825,895,000
Net Income		172,984,000	178,449,000	130,675,000	123,070,000	98,523,000
Operating Cash Flow		138,690,000	231,754,000	142,052,000	166,253,000	133,616,000
Capital Expenditure		47,316,000	51,952,000	45,803,000	42,319,000	37,508,000
EBITDA		328,727,000	323,448,000	278,686,000	269,388,000	235,720,000
Return on Assets %		12.48%	13.36%	9.58%	8.98%	7.68%
Return on Equity %		30.57%	34.52%	23.88%	23.08%	24.01%
Debt to Equity		0.35	0.43	0.47	0.40	0.63

CONTACT INFORMATION:

Phone: 727 872-1000   Fax:
Toll-Free: 800-284-3100
Address: 1 HSN Dr., St. Petersburg, FL 33729 United States

SALARIES/BONUSES:

Top Exec. Salary: Bonus: $
$1,204,615
Second Exec. Salary: Bonus: $
$723,477

STOCK TICKER/OTHER:

Stock Ticker: HSNI   Exchange: NAS
Employees: 6,900   Fiscal Year Ends: 12/31
Parent Company:

OTHER THOUGHTS:

Estimated Female Officers or Directors: 9

Hot Spot for Advancement for Women/Minorities: Y

Hudson's Bay Company

NAIC Code: 452111

www.hbc.com

TYPES OF BUSINESS:

Department Stores
Apparel Retailing
Kitchen, Bed & Bath Stores
Discount & General Merchandise Stores

BRANDS/DIVISIONS/AFFILIATES:

Hudson's Bay
Lord & Taylor
Home Outfitters
Saks Fifth Avenue
NRDC Equity Partners LLC
Saks Fifth Avenue OFF 5TH
Galeria Kaufhof

CONTACTS: Note: Officers with more than one job title may be intentionally listed here more than once.

Gerald Storch, CEO
Bonnie Brooks, Vice Chairman
Paul Beesley, CFO
Todd Zator, Chief Accounting Officer
Jon Nordeen, Chief Information Officer
Richard Baker, Director
Stephen Cerrone, Executive VP
Ian Putnam, Executive VP
David Pickwoad, General Counsel
Marc Metrick, President, Divisional
Brian Pall, President, Divisional
Michael Burgess, President, Divisional
Donald Watros, President, Divisional
Jonathan Greller, President, Divisional
Elizabeth Rodbell, President, Subsidiary

GROWTH PLANS/SPECIAL FEATURES:

Hudson's Bay Company (HBC), founded in 1670, is one of Canada's oldest and largest department store retailers, with over 460 retail locations. HBC is owned by NRDC Equity Partners LLC. The company's leading retail banners are: Hudson's Bay, Lord & Taylor, Saks Fifth Avenue, Saks Fifth Avenue OFF 5TH and Home Outfitters. Hudson's Bay is a full-line department store chain that focuses on apparel, accessories and home merchandise in the mid-to-upper price range. Its stores are largely located in suburban and urban markets, including large downtown stores in most of Canada's major cities. Lord & Taylor is a fashion department store operating in the U.S. through more than 50 full-line store locations. Saks Fifth Avenue is a line of retail stores that strives to be synonymous with fashionable, gracious living by offering quality men's and women's fashions by European and American designers. Its merchandise and services are sold throughout its 38 stores servicing customers in 22 states. Saks Fifth Avenue OFF 5TH, with 77 stores, is a major national clearinghouse retailer that provides exceptional deals in stores and online. Over 800 brands by notable names in fashion allows customers to have access to high quality products at reduced prices. Home Outfitters focuses on product categories that include kitchen, bedroom and bathroom, with 67 large format stores across Canada. In September 2015, the firm acquired German department store chain Galeria Kaufhof from METRO AG for $2.73 billion.

FINANCIAL DATA: Note: Data for latest year may not have been available at press time.

In U.S. $	2015	2014	2013	2012	2011	2010
Revenue	6,120,063,000	3,913,275,000	3,054,413,000	2,884,049,000		
R&D Expense						
Operating Income	360,356,300	5,319,189	90,501,130	147,139,200		
Operating Margin %	5.88%	.13%	2.96%	5.10%		
SGA Expense	2,066,992,000	1,366,432,000	1,100,697,000	1,009,297,000		
Net Income	178,305,200	-193,363,700	-33,563,330	1,085,564,000		
Operating Cash Flow	409,802,300	88,778,010	264,910,600	51,543,690		
Capital Expenditure	319,151,300	218,386,400	152,008,900	127,510,700		
EBITDA	537,912,300	2,097,708	164,745,000	212,842,500		
Return on Assets %	2.80%	-4.61%	-1.23%	36.28%		
Return on Equity %	10.47%	-16.93%	-4.58%	151.58%		
Debt to Equity	1.14	1.42	0.71	0.94		

CONTACT INFORMATION:

Phone: 416-861-6112   Fax: 416-861-4720
Toll-Free: 800-521-2364
Address: 401 Bay St., Ste. 500, Toronto, ON M5H 2Y4 Canada

STOCK TICKER/OTHER:

Stock Ticker: HBC
Employees: 46,234
Parent Company: NRDC EQUITY PARTNERS LLC

Exchange: TSE
Fiscal Year Ends: 01/31

SALARIES/BONUSES:

Top Exec. Salary: $ Bonus: $
Second Exec. Salary: $ Bonus: $

OTHER THOUGHTS:

Estimated Female Officers or Directors: 6
Hot Spot for Advancement for Women/Minorities: Y

Hugo Boss AG

group.hugoboss.com

NAIC Code: 424300

TYPES OF BUSINESS:

Apparel and Clothing Brands, Designers, Importers and Distributors
Women's Apparel
Fragrances
Home Accessories
Leather Goods
Eyewear

BRANDS/DIVISIONS/AFFILIATES:

Hugo Boss
BOSS Black
BOSS Orange
BOSS Selection
BOSS Green
HUGO

CONTACTS: Note: Officers with more than one job title may be intentionally listed here more than once.

Claus-Dietrich Lahrs, CEO
Mark Langer, CFO
Claus-Dietrich Lahrs, Dir.-Sales
Mark Langer, Dir.-Human Resources & Labor Rel.
Mark Langer, Dir.-IT
Christoph Auhagen, Dir.-Mfg.
Mark Langer, Dir.-Legal Affairs
Hjordis Kettenbach, Head-Corp. Comm.
Dennis Weber, Dir.-Investor Rel.
Mark Langer, Head-Investor Rel.
Christoph Auhagen, Chief Brand Officer
Hellmut Albrecht, Chmn.
Mark Langer, Dir.-Logistics

GROWTH PLANS/SPECIAL FEATURES:

Hugo Boss AG is an international designer and licenser of clothes, accessories and fragrances. The firm's products are sold through approximately 1,000 company-owned stores and roughly 6,550 third-party retailers in 124 countries. The firm, which sells under the brands BOSS and HUGO, was formerly known for its men's wear, but has moved into women's wear, fragrances and other offerings, such as home accessories. BOSS comes in four labels: BOSS Black, BOSS Selection, BOSS Orange and BOSS Green. BOSS Black focuses on office, formal attire and leisurewear; the line includes shoes, bags, accessories, eyewear, watches and fragrances for men and women as well as bodywear and skincare for men. BOSS Selection is the premium tier of the company's menswear brands, featuring high-quality materials and expert tailoring. BOSS Orange is a more casual and unconventional leisurewear line for men and women with an urban sportswear theme. It includes men's and women's shoes, bags and accessories as well as men's bodywear and fragrances. BOSS Green is a men's collection designed for athletics and active outdoor performance, with an emphasis on golf. The HUGO brand includes business and leisurewear for young men and women with an emphasis on avant-garde yet appropriate style. HUGO brand products include shoes, bags, accessories, bodywear, eyewear and fragrances. The designing process for the company's new lines takes place at the Metzingen headquarters in Germany. The firm also has manufacturing facilities in Poland, the U.S., Turkey and Italy. It operates 11 online stores in Germany, Great Britain, France, Spain, Italy, the Netherlands, Belgium, Austria, Switzerland, the USA and China. More than 90% of the company's shares are free float on the Frankfurt Stock Exchange, Borse Frankfurt.

Hugo Boss offers apprenticeships, internships, traineeships and even dissertation writing as gateways to employment.

FINANCIAL DATA: Note: Data for latest year may not have been available at press time.

In U.S. $	2015	2014	2013	2012	2011	2010
Revenue		2,729,258,000	2,581,225,000	2,489,657,000	2,185,049,000	1,835,462,000
R&D Expense						
Operating Income		476,227,900	484,115,500	459,756,500	418,248,000	280,122,900
Operating Margin %		17.44%	18.75%	18.46%	19.14%	15.26%
SGA Expense		1,306,530,000	1,188,769,000	1,082,573,000	924,124,500	810,021,900
Net Income		353,691,200	349,130,800	326,237,500	308,803,500	197,290,500
Operating Cash Flow		419,667,000	441,860,900	416,456,500	320,194,400	327,235,100
Capital Expenditure		137,720,800	183,951,000	175,965,800	115,128,800	58,991,340
EBITDA		600,752,400	589,181,100	557,328,300	505,955,000	355,390,400
Return on Assets %		21.07%	21.32%	20.26%	20.28%	15.35%
Return on Equity %		42.76%	49.56%	55.25%	67.47%	68.07%
Debt to Equity		0.18	0.23			1.49

CONTACT INFORMATION:

Phone: 49 07123940   Fax: 49 07123942014
Toll-Free:
Address: Dieselstrasse 12, Metzingen, 72555 Germany

STOCK TICKER/OTHER:

Stock Ticker: BOSSY
Employees: 12,990
Parent Company:

Exchange: PINX
Fiscal Year Ends: 12/31

SALARIES/BONUSES:

Top Exec. Salary: $ Bonus: $
Second Exec. Salary: $ Bonus: $

OTHER THOUGHTS:

Estimated Female Officers or Directors:
Hot Spot for Advancement for Women/Minorities:

Hy-Vee Inc

NAIC Code: 445110

www.hy-vee.com

TYPES OF BUSINESS:

Grocery Stores/Supermarkets
Food Distribution
Florist Services
Construction Services
Specialty Foods
Banking & Wealth Management Services
Drug Stores

BRANDS/DIVISIONS/AFFILIATES:

Midwest Heritage Bank FSB
Midwest Country Fare
Full Circle
D & D Foods Inc
Florist Distributing Inc
Lomar Distributing Inc
Hy-Vee Weitz Construction

CONTACTS: Note: Officers with more than one job title may be intentionally listed here more than once.

Randall B. Edeker, CEO
Ron Taylor, Exec. VP-North Div.
Tom Watson, Exec. VP-East Div.
Randall B. Edeker, Chmn.

GROWTH PLANS/SPECIAL FEATURES:

Hy-Vee, Inc. is an employee-owned supermarket chain in the U.S., operating over 237 retail stores throughout Iowa, Illinois Missouri, Kansas, Nebraska, South Dakota, Wisconsin and Minnesota. The majority of its stores are located within Iowa The firm operates stores under the Hy-Vee, Hy-Vee Drugstore and Hy-Vee Pharmacy names. Hy-Vee's private label brands include Midwest Country Fare, Full Circle, World Classics Trading Company, Hy-Vee Mother's Choice, LeTechniq, D Lusso, Paws Premium and Hy-Vee HealthMarket. The company maintains two large distribution centers in Chariton and Cherokee, Iowa. Through its various subsidiaries, Hy-Vee has been able to establish a distribution system that enables the firm to remain a contender in a highly competitive market place. Its subsidiaries, which include D & D Foods, Inc.; Florist Distributing, Inc.; Lomar Distributing, Inc.; and Perishable Distributors of Iowa, Ltd., encompass a wide spectrum of distribution offerings including specialty foods, florist and plant supplies, as well as seafood and meat products. Additionally the firm operates the construction firm Hy-Vee Weitz Construction and Midwest Heritage Bank, FSB, a regional bank. The company's web site provides visitors with online shopping, gift cards, information on weekly specials, access to pharmacies and Internet banking. In March 2015, the firm's largest store opened in Bloomington, Illinois, boasting 108,000 square feet of retail space.

The firm offers its employees benefits such as medical and dental insurance, a prescription drug plan, life insurance, short-term disability, a 401(k) plan, a profit sharing trust, a wellness program, relocation assistance and discounted financial services through Midwest Heritage Bank.

FINANCIAL DATA: Note: Data for latest year may not have been available at press time.

In U.S. $	2015	2014	2013	2012	2011	2010
Revenue		8,000,000,000	7,850,000,000	7,700,000,000	7,300,000,000	6,900,000,000
R&D Expense						
Operating Income						
Operating Margin %						
SGA Expense						
Net Income						
Operating Cash Flow						
Capital Expenditure						
EBITDA						
Return on Assets %						
Return on Equity %						
Debt to Equity						

CONTACT INFORMATION:

Phone: 515-267-2800   Fax:
Toll-Free: 800-289-8343
Address: 5820 Westown Pkwy., West Des Moines, IA 50266 United States

STOCK TICKER/OTHER:

Stock Ticker: Private
Employees: 56,000
Parent Company:

Exchange:
Fiscal Year Ends: 09/30

SALARIES/BONUSES:

Top Exec. Salary: $ Bonus: $
Second Exec. Salary: $ Bonus: $

OTHER THOUGHTS:

Estimated Female Officers or Directors:
Hot Spot for Advancement for Women/Minorities:

IKEA (Inter IKEA Systems BV)

www.ikea.com

NAIC Code: 442110

TYPES OF BUSINESS:

Home Furnishings Retailer
Home Decorating Services
Online Sales
Catalog Sales

BRANDS/DIVISIONS/AFFILIATES:

Inter IKEA Holding SA
IKEA
Stichting Ingka

CONTACTS: *Note: Officers with more than one job title may be intentionally listed here more than once.*

Thomas Bergstrom, CEO
Mathia Kamprad, Chmn.

GROWTH PLANS/SPECIAL FEATURES:

IKEA (Inter IKEA Systems BV), owned by Inter IKEA Holding SA, is a multinational home furnishings company based in Sweden, with over 360 stores and offices in 27 countries and territories. The company designs and sells furniture products as well as various accessories for living and dining rooms, bathrooms, kitchens and offices, with a total product line of approximately 9,500 distinctive items. Flat packing and customers' willingness to assemble products allow IKEA to keep its prices low. Constantly cutting prices at its stores, the company strives to provide affordable yet trendy home furnishings. It has an extensive mail-order catalog, with more than 200 million total copies printed in 29 languages as well as a significant online presence. More than one billion unique customers visit the website annually compared to the 821 million visitors at physical locations. The firm continues to grow, with its fastest-growing areas being China, Russia and Poland. The company's vast supply chain includes more than 1,046 suppliers worldwide, with a significant amount of merchandise manufactured in China. In order to maintain its trendy and unique styles, an in-house design staff plus dozens of freelance consultants constantly design and reinterpret the merchandise. Each IKEA store contains a restaurant serving traditional Swedish food as well as hot dogs, drinks and local foods depending on the store location. The stores also contain a food market that sells prepared Swedish food items under the IKEA food label. The firm is organized as a non-profit under Sweden's laws, with control of the company concentrated within the founder's family. The parent company is owned by the Netherlands-based charitable foundation Stichting Ingka. IKEA plans to grow its sales to $50 billion Euros by 2020, with store expansion plans that would grow the chain to 500 units. Those plans include a $2 billion investment to open 10 stores in India by 2025. IKEA opened 12 stores in 10 nations, announced plans to open a store in Morocco during 2015, and five stores in Serbia during 2016.

FINANCIAL DATA: *Note: Data for latest year may not have been available at press time.*

In U.S. $	2015	2014	2013	2012	2011	2010
Revenue		39,000,000,000	37,000,000,000	35,000,000,000	33,000,000,000	31,000,000,000
R&D Expense						
Operating Income						
Operating Margin %						
SGA Expense						
Net Income		4,500,000,000				
Operating Cash Flow						
Capital Expenditure						
EBITDA						
Return on Assets %						
Return on Equity %						
Debt to Equity						

CONTACT INFORMATION:

Phone: 31-15-215-0750   Fax: 31-15-219-0533
Toll-Free:
Address: Olof Palmestraat 1, Delft, NL-2616 Sweden

STOCK TICKER/OTHER:

Stock Ticker: Private
Employees: 165,000
Parent Company: Inter IKEA Holding SA

Exchange:
Fiscal Year Ends: 08/31

SALARIES/BONUSES:

Top Exec. Salary: $ Bonus: $
Second Exec. Salary: $ Bonus: $

OTHER THOUGHTS:

Estimated Female Officers or Directors:
Hot Spot for Advancement for Women/Minorities:

Inditex (Industria de Diseno Textil SA)

www.inditex.com

NAIC Code: 448120

TYPES OF BUSINESS:

Fashion Apparel
Retail Stores
Textiles
Home Furnishings
Retail Stores

BRANDS/DIVISIONS/AFFILIATES:

Zara International Inc
Pull & Bear
Massimo Dutti
Bershka
Stradivarius
Oysho
Zara Home
Uterque

CONTACTS: Note: Officers with more than one job title may be intentionally listed here more than once.

Pablo Isla Alvarez de Tejera, CEO
Antonio A. Abadin, General Counsel
Pablo Isla Alvarez de Tejera, Chmn.

GROWTH PLANS/SPECIAL FEATURES:

Inditex (Industria de Diseno Textil SA) is a Spanish conglomerate of over 100 companies engaged in textile design, production, distribution and related businesses. As one of the world's largest fashion distribution companies, it owns or leases approximately 6,460 retail stores in 86 countries under the names Zara, Pull & Bear, Massimo Dutti, Bershka, Stradivarius, Oysho, Zara Home and Uterque. Zara is the firm's largest fashion brand, with 1,991 stores. Pull & Bear, which focuses on clothing for urban youth ages 14-28, has approximately 853 locations in 68 countries. Massimo Dutti, with 665 stores located in 63 countries, is designed to appeal to younger professionals. Bershka is aimed at a younger target market, with 954 stores open in 66 countries. Stradivarius boasts 858 stores in 56 countries, stocking more creative designs, fabrics and accessories. Oysho is a chain of stores focused primarily on women's lingerie and undergarments as well as casual outerwear and accessories; it currently has 549 locations in 39 countries. Zara Home is the Inditex Group's chain specializing in home furnishings, with a focus on textiles such as bed, table and bathroom linen, complemented with cutlery, glassware and decorative items. Zara Home currently features 394 locations in 45 countries. Uterque, the firm's newest store type, features fashion accessories and a select range of textile and leather garments all designed by an in-house creative team, with 76 store locations in 15 countries. The firm is famous for its lean inventory and fast-fashion strategy. It is able to obtain a new item of clothing from its design team, through its manufacturing plants and into its stores in as little as two weeks. Much of its manufacturing is done in Europe to reduce shipping time. For 2014, the company planned to open approximately 450 new stores worldwide. In January 2015, the firm acquired 47,360 square feet of commercial space on Broadway Avenue in New York to become a retail outlet for its Zara brand. That February, Inditex opened its first Australian store, showcasing its home decor Zara brand, including Zara Home Kids.

FINANCIAL DATA: Note: Data for latest year may not have been available at press time.

In U.S. $	2015	2014	2013	2012	2011	2010
Revenue	19,227,090,000	17,749,660,000	16,923,650,000	14,638,110,000	13,294,480,000	11,762,940,000
R&D Expense						
Operating Income	3,394,237,000	3,259,127,000	3,307,905,000	2,676,607,000	2,430,877,000	1,834,339,000
Operating Margin %	17.65%	18.36%	19.54%	18.28%	18.28%	15.59%
SGA Expense		6,365,962,000	5,948,361,000	5,220,886,000		
Net Income	2,653,833,000	2,522,799,000	2,505,475,000	2,050,739,000	1,848,022,000	1,403,185,000
Operating Cash Flow	3,446,580,000	3,000,586,000	3,310,146,000	2,556,314,000	2,712,911,000	2,463,117,000
Capital Expenditure	1,906,375,000	1,327,056,000	1,395,559,000	1,277,460,000	733,084,000	528,037,400
EBITDA	4,354,594,000	4,166,635,000	4,168,410,000	3,457,370,000	3,193,850,000	2,519,729,000
Return on Assets %	17.16%	17.84%	19.79%	18.59%	19.07%	16.31%
Return on Equity %	25.41%	26.87%	29.76%	28.00%	29.56%	26.15%
Debt to Equity						

CONTACT INFORMATION:

Phone: 34 981185400   Fax: 34 981185544
Toll-Free:
Address: Avenida Diputacion s/h, Arteixo, 15143 Spain

STOCK TICKER/OTHER:

Stock Ticker: IDEXF   Exchange: PINX
Employees: 120,314   Fiscal Year Ends:
Parent Company:

SALARIES/BONUSES:

Top Exec. Salary: $ Bonus: $
Second Exec. Salary: $ Bonus: $

OTHER THOUGHTS:

Estimated Female Officers or Directors: 2
Hot Spot for Advancement for Women/Minorities: Y

Ingles Markets Inc

www.ingles-markets.com

NAIC Code: 445110

TYPES OF BUSINESS:

Grocery Stores
Shopping Centers
Dairy Processing
Juices
Bottled Water
Gas Stations
Pharmacies

BRANDS/DIVISIONS/AFFILIATES:

Milkco Inc
Sav-Mor
Laura Lynn
Ingles

CONTACTS: Note: Officers with more than one job title may be intentionally listed here more than once.

Robert Ingle, CEO
Ronald Freeman, CFO
James Lanning, COO
L. Collins, Director
Pat Jackson, Secretary

GROWTH PLANS/SPECIAL FEATURES:

Ingles Markets, Inc. primarily operates supermarkets and shopping centers in the southeastern U.S. under the Ingles (193) and Sav-Mor (9) brand names. Headquartered in North Carolina, the company currently operates 202 supermarkets located in Georgia (71), North Carolina (71), South Carolina (36), Tennessee (21), Virginia (2) and Alabama (1). Ingles supermarkets offer a wide variety of nationally advertised food products, including fresh meat, dairy products, produce, frozen foods and non-food products such as health and beauty care items, general merchandise and private-label goods (under the Laura Lynn brand). In addition, Ingles focuses on selling high-growth, high-margin products to its customers through the development of book sections, media centers, floral departments, bakery departments and prepared foods. Ingles operates 96 pharmacies and 83 fuel stations. Almost all of the company's stores are located within 280 miles of its 919,000-square-foot warehouse and distribution facility in Asheville, North Carolina, from which the company distributes groceries, produce, meat and dairy products to all Ingles stores. The company operates a second 839,000-square-foot warehouse and distribution facility located adjacent to its existing distribution facility, which distributes frozen, health/beauty/cosmetic and general merchandise products previously distributed by third parties. The firm maintains its own fleet of tractor-trailer trucks for distribution purposes. Milkco, Inc., a fluid dairy processing subsidiary, provides most of the company's supermarkets with dairy products, citrus juices and bottled water products. Ingles owns 153 of its supermarkets, either free-standing or in shopping centers. In addition, the company owns 19 undeveloped sites which are suitable for a free-standing store or shopping center development.

The firm offers employees medical, dental and vision insurance; short-term disability coverage; flexible spending accounts; life insurance; medical leave; credit union membership; and a 401(k) plan.

FINANCIAL DATA: Note: Data for latest year may not have been available at press time.

In U.S. $	2015	2014	2013	2012	2011	2010
Revenue		3,835,986,000	3,738,541,000	3,709,434,000	3,559,921,000	3,390,052,000
R&D Expense						
Operating Income		123,345,200	125,574,200	123,846,800	118,516,800	110,964,600
Operating Margin %		3.21%	3.35%	3.33%	3.32%	3.27%
SGA Expense		722,644,200	706,497,500	697,603,000	677,889,200	653,674,000
Net Income		51,426,460	20,795,890	43,444,340	39,059,510	31,739,400
Operating Cash Flow		154,348,800	145,200,700	133,750,800	97,228,260	125,288,400
Capital Expenditure		108,338,400	101,453,000	180,628,800	97,506,370	92,025,300
EBITDA		224,009,900	180,274,400	217,904,900	208,084,400	200,119,800
Return on Assets %		3.09%	1.25%	2.66%	2.48%	2.08%
Return on Equity %		12.96%	4.79%	9.76%	9.23%	7.81%
Debt to Equity		2.41	2.17	1.71	1.90	1.75

CONTACT INFORMATION:

Phone: 828 669-2941   Fax: 828 669-3668
Toll-Free:
Address: 2913 U.S. Hwy. 70 W., Black Mountain, NC 28711 United States

STOCK TICKER/OTHER:

Stock Ticker: IMKTA
Employees: 23,000
Parent Company:

Exchange: NAS
Fiscal Year Ends: 09/30

SALARIES/BONUSES:

Top Exec. Salary: $611,923   Bonus: $350,000
Second Exec. Salary: $611,923   Bonus: $350,000

OTHER THOUGHTS:

Estimated Female Officers or Directors: 1
Hot Spot for Advancement for Women/Minorities:

Sales, profits and employees may be estimates. Financial information, benefits and other data can change quickly and may vary from those stated here.

Interbond Corporation of America (BrandsMart)

www.brandsmartusa.com

NAIC Code: 443142

TYPES OF BUSINESS:

Consumer Electronics Stores
Appliances
Furniture
Computers
Credit Cards

BRANDS/DIVISIONS/AFFILIATES:

BrandsMart USA
BrandsMart USA Credit Card
BrandsMart

GROWTH PLANS/SPECIAL FEATURES:

Interbond Corporation of America, which does business a
BrandsMart USA, is a retailer of discount electronics sales. Th
company operates nine multi-level stores in Florida an
Atlanta. The stores stock audiovisual equipment, cellula
phones, computers, furniture, televisions, appliances, hom
theater and satellite products and many associate
accessories. BrandsMart service centers employ technician
who are continually trained by the manufacturers of th
company's products. The company also provides custom
installation of audio/video systems. BrandsMart stores carr
more than 500 name brands and almost 50,000 items. The firm
offers a proprietary credit card, the BrandsMart USA Credi
Card, which provides preferred customer specials, charges n
annual fee and earns 1% from purchases made at BrandsMar
stores.

CONTACTS: *Note: Officers with more than one job title may be intentionally listed here more than once.*

Robert Perlman, CEO
Alan Rutner, Pres.
Eric Beazley, CFO
Larry Sinewitz, Exec. VP
Bobby Johnson, Sr. VP
Phil Lieberman, Gen. Mgr.
Robert Perlman, Chmn.

FINANCIAL DATA: *Note: Data for latest year may not have been available at press time.*

In U.S. $	2015	2014	2013	2012	2011	2010
Revenue						
R&D Expense						
Operating Income						
Operating Margin %						
SGA Expense						
Net Income						
Operating Cash Flow						
Capital Expenditure						
EBITDA						
Return on Assets %						
Return on Equity %						
Debt to Equity						

CONTACT INFORMATION:

Phone: 954-797-4000   Fax: 954-797-4061
Toll-Free: 800-432-8579
Address: 3200 SW 42nd St., Hollywood, FL 33312 United States

STOCK TICKER/OTHER:

Stock Ticker: Private   Exchange:
Employees: Fiscal Year Ends: 12/31
Parent Company:

SALARIES/BONUSES:

Top Exec. Salary: $ Bonus: $
Second Exec. Salary: $ Bonus: $

OTHER THOUGHTS:

Estimated Female Officers or Directors:
Hot Spot for Advancement for Women/Minorities:

Isetan Mitsukoshi Holdings Ltd

www.imhds.co.jp

NAIC Code: 452111

TYPES OF BUSINESS:

Department Stores
Supermarkets
Women's Apparel
Restaurants
Real Estate Management
Credit Cards
Supermarkets

BRANDS/DIVISIONS/AFFILIATES:

Isetan Co Ltd
Mitsukoshi Ltd
MICARD Co Ltd
Mammina Co Ltd

CONTACTS: *Note: Officers with more than one job title may be intentionally listed here more than once.*

Hiroshi Onishi, CEO
Hiroshi Onishi, Pres.
Shigeki Yamazaki, Gen. Mgr.-Finance & Acct. Division
Takaaki Muto, Managing Exec. Officer-Corp. Admin. Div.
Takuya Matsuo, Managing Exec. Officer-Oper.
Toshihiko Sugie, Managing Exec. Officer-Strategic Planning
Shigeki Yamazaki, Managing Exec. Officer-Finance & Acct. Div.
Toshinori Shirai, Exec. Officer-Strategic Planning Div.
Hideharu Wada, Gen. Mgr.-Bus. Coordination
Masakazu Nishida, Gen. Mgr.-Domestic Subsidiaries Div.
Kunio Ishizuka, Chmn.
Jun Yokoyama, Exec. Officer-Intl Bus. Div.

GROWTH PLANS/SPECIAL FEATURES:

Isetan Mitsukoshi Holdings Ltd. is a holding company operating through wholly-owned subsidiaries Isetan Co., Ltd. and Mitsukoshi, Ltd. Isetan Mitsukoshi's businesses are divided into department stores, other retail & specialty stores, credit & finance, real estate and other business. The department store business includes the operations of 29 subsidiary companies operating about 60 department stores. In Asia, the company operates in Thailand, Malaysia, China, Taiwan, Singapore and Japan. In the U.S., the firm has operations in Orlando, Florida. The other retail & specialty stores business consists of Mammina Co., Ltd., a women's apparel retailer. The credit & finance business operates through MICARD Co., Ltd., which provides credit cards, among other services. The real estate business operates through seven subsidiaries, which, in addition to building management, provide parking and interior design services. The operations of the other business segment include data processing, food, restaurants, logistics management, sports facility management, wholesale and import/export business, research, apparel, travel, staffing and other services, provided through 13 subsidiaries. In terms of net sales in 2014, department stores accounted for 84.6%; overseas department stores for 7.6%; and other retail and specialty stores, credit & finance, real estate business and other business for 7.8% combined.

FINANCIAL DATA: *Note: Data for latest year may not have been available at press time.*

In U.S. $	2015	2014	2013	2012	2011	2010
Revenue	10,323,550,000	10,724,290,000	10,033,050,000	10,062,170,000	9,906,773,000	10,481,690,000
R&D Expense						
Operating Income	268,474,200	281,158,200	216,180,000	193,417,000	89,210,070	33,897,070
Operating Margin %	2.60%	2.62%	2.15%	1.92%	.90%	.32%
SGA Expense	491,974,100	541,565,900	517,114,900	514,006,800	552,562,000	551,377,200
Net Income	242,164,800	175,888,200	210,207,300	483,753,400	27,567,230	-509,916,700
Operating Cash Flow	401,279,000	373,476,400	36,015,130	469,405,800	269,512,900	-29,247,070
Capital Expenditure	276,110,600	191,501,800	249,549,600	158,757,100	264,562,700	216,293,600
EBITDA	435,857,700	474,007,100	369,881,400	403,989,400	253,607,200	-123,220,800
Return on Assets %	2.32%	1.68%	2.06%	4.77%	.21%	-4.90%
Return on Equity %	5.49%	4.15%	5.32%	13.60%	.64%	-14.25%
Debt to Equity	0.17	0.17	0.16	0.27	0.28	0.17

CONTACT INFORMATION:

Phone: 81 358435115   Fax: 81 358436040
Toll-Free:
Address: 5-16-10, Shinjuku, Shinjuku-ku, Tokyo, 160-0022 Japan

STOCK TICKER/OTHER:

Stock Ticker: IMHDF   Exchange: GREY
Employees: 6,291   Fiscal Year Ends: 03/31
Parent Company:

SALARIES/BONUSES:

Top Exec. Salary: $ Bonus: $
Second Exec. Salary: $ Bonus: $

OTHER THOUGHTS:

Estimated Female Officers or Directors:
Hot Spot for Advancement for Women/Minorities:

Ito-Yokado Co Ltd

NAIC Code: 445110

TYPES OF BUSINESS:
Supermarkets
Malls
Superstores

BRANDS/DIVISIONS/AFFILIATES:
Seven & I Holdings Co Ltd
Ario
Chengdu Ito-Yokado
Hiroshi China Hall Sugar
Nanaco
POPPO

CONTACTS: Note: Officers with more than one job title may be intentionally listed here more than once.
Toshifumi Suzuki, CEO
Atsushi Kamei, Pres.
Toshifumi Suzuki, Chmn.

GROWTH PLANS/SPECIAL FEATURES:

Ito-Yokado Co., Ltd., a wholly-owned subsidiary of Seven & I Holdings Co., Ltd., operates approximately 200 supermarkets as well as nine distribution centers for perishable goods and two produce centers. The majority of the firm's stores are located in the Kanto region of Japan, with its remaining stores located in Chubu, Hokkaido, Tohoku, Kansai and Chugoku. The company's superstores provide apparel, household goods and food in Japan and China. In addition, superstore operations include food supermarkets in Japan and Beijing as well as the operation of specialty stores, which include drug and cosmetic stores and home centers. The firm is also focusing on the development of stores in China, which are operated in Sichuan Province by Chengdu Ito-Yokado and in Beijing by Hiroshi China Hall Sugar. Nanaco, Seven & I's prepaid electronic money service, is available in all Ito-Yokado stores, and many of the company's locations contain POPPO restaurants, a fast food chain owned by Seven & I, serving meals such as takoyaki (octopus dumpling), Chinese noodles and okonomiyaki (a type of pancake). The firm is developing private apparel brands as well as having brands developed exclusively for the company. It is also striving to increase the number of items it carries on consignment. Another growth area the firm is pursuing is the development of large-scale shopping centers with a mall format under the Ario name. In September 2015, the firm announced plans to close 40 unprofitable stores, or 20% of its stores.

FINANCIAL DATA: Note: Data for latest year may not have been available at press time.

In U.S. $	2015	2014	2013	2012	2011	2010
Revenue		10,897,143,300				
R&D Expense						
Operating Income						
Operating Margin %						
SGA Expense						
Net Income		10,605,998,250				
Operating Cash Flow						
Capital Expenditure						
EBITDA						
Return on Assets %						
Return on Equity %						
Debt to Equity						

CONTACT INFORMATION:
Phone: 81-3-6238-2111   Fax: 81-3-6238-3492
Toll-Free:
Address: 8-8, Nibancho, Chiyoda-ku, Tokyo, 105-8450 Japan

STOCK TICKER/OTHER:
Stock Ticker: Subsidiary   Exchange:
Employees: 15,633   Fiscal Year Ends: 02/28
Parent Company: SEVEN & I HOLDINGS CO LTD

SALARIES/BONUSES:
Top Exec. Salary: $ Bonus: $
Second Exec. Salary: $ Bonus: $

OTHER THOUGHTS:
Estimated Female Officers or Directors:
Hot Spot for Advancement for Women/Minorities:

J C Penney Company Inc

www.jcpenney.com

NAIC Code: 452111

TYPES OF BUSINESS:

Department Stores
Online & Catalog Sales
Optometry
Photography Services
Salons
Custom Decorating

BRANDS/DIVISIONS/AFFILIATES:

Original Arizona Jean Company (The)
JCPenney Optical Services
JCPenney Portraits
JCPenney Salon
JCPenney Custom Decorating
Ambrielle
Worthington
St. John's Bay

CONTACTS: *Note: Officers with more than one job title may be intentionally listed here more than once.*

Marvin Ellison, CEO
Andrew Drexler, Chief Accounting Officer
David Laverty, Chief Information Officer
Mary Stone West, Chief Marketing Officer
Myron Ullman, Director
Brynn Evanson, Executive VP, Divisional
Edward Record, Executive VP
Janet Link, Executive VP
Salil Virkar, Secretary
Kirk Waidelich, Senior VP, Divisional

GROWTH PLANS/SPECIAL FEATURES:

J.C. Penney Company, Inc. is a holding company for J.C. Penney Corp., Inc., a department store retailer. J.C. Penney provides merchandise and services through department stores, catalogs and the Internet. The company operates 1,020 JCPenney department stores in 49 U.S. states and Puerto Rico. The firm's major products include family apparel, jewelry, shoes, accessories and home furnishings. J.C. Penney's entire product offering is available online at JCPenny.com. Local stores receive revenue credit for online and catalog sales made within their regions. Company brands include Worthington, St. John's Bay, Okie Dokie, The Original Arizona Jean Company, Ambrielle, J. Ferrar, JCPenney Home Collection, Studio by JCPenney Home Collection, Decree, Xersion, Total Girl, monet, Liz Claiborne, Worthington, a.n.a. and Stafford. Other services offered by the company are JCPenney Optical Services, JCPenney Portraits, JCPenney Salon and JCPenney Custom Decorating, all of which can be found within JCPenney department stores. Additionally, the firm sells beauty products through Sephora stores at more than 500 JC Penney locations. J.C. Penney purchases its merchandise from more than 2,400 U.S.-based and international suppliers. The company has 14 facilities which includes merchandise distribution facilities, regional warehouses, furniture distribution centers and Internet/catalog order fulfillment centers.

FINANCIAL DATA: *Note: Data for latest year may not have been available at press time.*

In U.S. $	2015	2014	2013	2012	2011	2010
Revenue	12,257,000,000	11,859,000,000	12,985,000,000	17,260,000,000	17,759,000,000	17,556,000,000
R&D Expense						
Operating Income	-308,000,000	-1,420,000,000	-1,310,000,000	-2,000,000	832,000,000	663,000,000
Operating Margin %	-2.51%	-11.97%	-10.08%	-.01%	4.68%	3.77%
SGA Expense	3,999,000,000	4,251,000,000	4,859,000,000	5,230,000,000	5,613,000,000	5,747,000,000
Net Income	-771,000,000	-1,388,000,000	-985,000,000	-152,000,000	389,000,000	251,000,000
Operating Cash Flow	239,000,000	-1,814,000,000	-10,000,000	820,000,000	592,000,000	1,576,000,000
Capital Expenditure	252,000,000	951,000,000	810,000,000	634,000,000	499,000,000	600,000,000
EBITDA	323,000,000	-819,000,000	-767,000,000	516,000,000	1,343,000,000	1,158,000,000
Return on Assets %	-6.94%	-12.86%	-9.29%	-1.24%	3.03%	2.04%
Return on Equity %	-30.83%	-44.35%	-27.43%	-3.21%	7.59%	5.61%
Debt to Equity	2.80	1.58	0.93	0.71	0.56	0.62

CONTACT INFORMATION:

Phone: 972 431-1000   Fax: 972 591-9322
Toll-Free: 800-322-1189
Address: 6501 Legacy Dr., Plano, TX 75024 United States

STOCK TICKER/OTHER:

Stock Ticker: JCP
Employees: 114,000
Parent Company:

Exchange: NYS
Fiscal Year Ends: 01/31

SALARIES/BONUSES:

Top Exec. Salary: $325,000   Bonus: $4,140,000
Second Exec. Salary: $642,045   Bonus: $1,295,750

OTHER THOUGHTS:

Estimated Female Officers or Directors: 17
Hot Spot for Advancement for Women/Minorities: Y

Sales, profits and employees may be estimates. Financial information, benefits and other data can change quickly and may vary from those stated here.

J Crew Group Inc

www.jcrew.com

NAIC Code: 448140

TYPES OF BUSINESS:

Apparel, Retail
Catalog Sales
Online Sales
Outlet Stores
Private-Label Credit Card

BRANDS/DIVISIONS/AFFILIATES:

J.Crew
crewcuts
Madewell
Leonard Green & Partners LP
madewell.com
jcrew.com
jcrewfactory.com
TPG Capital

CONTACTS: *Note: Officers with more than one job title may be intentionally listed here more than once.*

Millard Drexler, CEO
James Scully, COO
Jenna Lyons, Pres.
Stuart Haselden, CFO
Lynda Markoe, Exec. VP-Human Resources
James S. Scully, Chief Admin. Officer
Jennifer L. O'Connor, General Counsel
Libby Wadle, Pres., J. Crew
Millard Drexler, Chmn.

GROWTH PLANS/SPECIAL FEATURES:

J.Crew Group, Inc., owned by TPG Capital and Leonard Green & Partners LP, is a multi-channel retailer of apparel an accessories for men, women and children. Its target custome base consists primarily of affluent, college-educated professional and fashion-conscious men and women. Men' offerings include sweaters, shirts, suits, ties, underwear, coats swimwear, belts, shoes and accessories; women's offering are similar, with the additions of dresses, skirts and sleepwear The firm's crewcuts brand features similar J.Crew style designed for the children's market, from toddler size 2 t children size 14. J Crew's operations are split into two primar sales channels: stores and direct. J.Crew's retail operation include 283 retail stores, 139 J. Crew factory stores and 9: Madewell stores throughout the U.S, Canada and the U.K Stores are generally located in regional malls, lifestyle centers shopping centers and street locations. In 2014, the J. Crew brand averaged 89.0% of the company's revenues; the Madewell brand, 9.5%; and other brands, 1.5%. The company's direct marketing division consists of its catalog and e-commerce operations. Its e-commerce business includes jcrew.com, madewell.com and jcrewfactory.com. Additionally the firm offers a private-label credit card through an agreemen with Comenity Bank. The company utilizes a 282,000-square foot distribution center in Asheville, North Carolina; and a 425,000 square foot facility and a 63,700 square foot facility in Lynchburg, Virginia, for J.Crew direct operations. Mos company merchandise is produced abroad, primarily in Asia J.Crew also sells women's merchandise under the Madewell brand, which focuses on vintage-inspired denim, apparel and accessories. After founding the Madewell subsidiary in 2006, i has enjoyed steady growth. The firm planned 15 new stores fo 2015, bringing the total to 100.

FINANCIAL DATA: *Note: Data for latest year may not have been available at press time.*

In U.S. $	2015	2014	2013	2012	2011	2010
Revenue		2,579,700,000	2,428,300,000	2,222,770,000	1,854,988,000	1,722,227,000
R&D Expense						
Operating Income						
Operating Margin %						
SGA Expense						
Net Income		970,900,000	1,006,100,000	96,100,000	51,514,000	121,505,000
Operating Cash Flow						
Capital Expenditure						
EBITDA						
Return on Assets %						
Return on Equity %						
Debt to Equity						

CONTACT INFORMATION:

Phone: 212-209-2500   Fax: 212-209-2666
Toll-Free: 800-562-0258
Address: 770 Broadway, New York, NY 10003 United States

SALARIES/BONUSES:

Top Exec. Salary: $ Bonus: $
Second Exec. Salary: $ Bonus: $

STOCK TICKER/OTHER:

Stock Ticker: Private   Exchange:
Employees: 14,000   Fiscal Year Ends: 01/31
Parent Company: TPG CAPITAL

OTHER THOUGHTS:

Estimated Female Officers or Directors: 4
Hot Spot for Advancement for Women/Minorities: Y

J Front Retailing Co

www.j-front-retailing.com

NAIC Code: 452111

TYPES OF BUSINESS:

Department Stores
Supermarkets
Restaurants
Construction Contracting
Direct Marketing
Credit Cards
Personnel Services

BRANDS/DIVISIONS/AFFILIATES:

Daimaru
Matsuzakaya
Parco

CONTACTS: Note: Officers with more than one job title may be intentionally listed here more than once.

Ryoichi Yamamoto, Pres.
Hiroyuki Tsutsumi, Sr. Gen. Mgr.-Finance
Takehiko Tadatsu, Group Organization Personnel Policy
Tomohiko Enomoto, Gen. Mgr.-IT Bus.
Toshiyasu Hayashi, Exec. Gen. Mgr.-Admin. Unit
Hiroto Tsukada, Exec. Gen. Mgr.-Mgmt. Strategy Unit
Hiroyuki Tsutsumi, Sr. Gen. Mgr.-Finance Div.
Shunichi Samura, Chmn.

GROWTH PLANS/SPECIAL FEATURES:

J. Front Retailing Co. is a Japanese holding company that owns retail store chains Daimaru and Matsuzakaya. J. Front was formed in 2007 through the merger of The Daimaru, Inc. and Matsuzakaya Co., Ltd. The company owns and operates approximately 19 department stores under the Daimaru and Matsuzakaya names. Additionally, J. Front operates the 25 Parco department stores. Matsuzakaya is one of the oldest department stores in Japan; it was established as a kimono shop in 1611 and was later converted to a Western-style department store during the 1900s. The company also maintains interests in construction works supervision and contracting, restaurants, wholesale import and export, direct marketing, credit cards, merchandise inspection and consulting, leasing and parking management and labor dispatch services. The department store business currently accounts for approximately 66% of J. Front's annual sales, while the Parco business accounts for 23.8%; the wholesale business, 4.4%; the credit business, 0.5%; and other businesses, 5.2%. The company maintains overseas offices in New York, Milan, Paris, London and Shanghai. For the past few years, J. Front has been undertaking the process of renewing and expanding many of its department stores in large cities.

FINANCIAL DATA: Note: Data for latest year may not have been available at press time.

In U.S. $	2015	2014	2013	2012	2011	2010
Revenue	9,328,624,000	9,302,574,000	8,867,901,000	7,639,743,000	7,710,240,000	7,973,423,000
R&D Expense						
Operating Income	341,575,600	339,344,000	250,409,800	175,239,000	164,924,600	150,812,300
Operating Margin %	3.66%	3.64%	2.82%	2.29%	2.13%	1.89%
SGA Expense	700,615,100	718,687,600	759,547,500	727,346,500	745,419,000	800,147,700
Net Income	186,584,000	280,931,000	111,575,500	157,369,400	74,359,300	71,648,840
Operating Cash Flow	362,342,400	304,578,600	211,197,300	197,726,100	172,609,700	186,616,500
Capital Expenditure	191,566,700	401,814,600	136,529,600	127,294,600	118,489,600	452,404,500
EBITDA	478,502,900	577,232,100	350,989,200	249,801,200	238,180,300	229,318,500
Return on Assets %	1.97%	3.14%	1.37%	2.43%	1.12%	1.03%
Return on Equity %	5.33%	8.87%	3.61%	5.77%	2.80%	2.62%
Debt to Equity	0.28	0.33	0.34	0.11	0.20	0.23

CONTACT INFORMATION:

Phone: 81-3-6895-0179   Fax:
Toll-Free:
Address: 1-1, Yaesu 2-Chome, Chuo-ku, Tokyo, 104-0061 Japan

STOCK TICKER/OTHER:

Stock Ticker: JFROF
Employees: 8,323
Parent Company:

Exchange: GREY
Fiscal Year Ends: 02/28

SALARIES/BONUSES:

Top Exec. Salary: $ Bonus: $
Second Exec. Salary: $ Bonus: $

OTHER THOUGHTS:

Estimated Female Officers or Directors:
Hot Spot for Advancement for Women/Minorities:

J Jill Group Inc (The)

NAIC Code: 448120

TYPES OF BUSINESS:

Women's Apparel, Retail
Online & Catalog Sales
Retail Stores
Accessories
Footwear
Credit Cards

BRANDS/DIVISIONS/AFFILIATES:

TowerBrook Capital Partners LP
J Jill
J Jill Compassion Fund
JJill.com

CONTACTS: Note: Officers with more than one job title may be intentionally listed here more than once.

Paula Bennett, CEO
Paula Bennett, Pres.
Mark Campton, VP-Visual Merch.
Mara D. Calame, General Counsel

GROWTH PLANS/SPECIAL FEATURES:

The J. Jill Group, Inc. (J. Jill) is a multi-channel specialty retailer of women's apparel, accessories and footwear, ranging from career to weekend wear, targeting a customer base of active, affluent women aged 35 and older. The firm operates approximately 225 retail locations including both department and outlet center locations throughout the U.S. Consumers have the option of making purchases through store locations, catalogues or online at JJill.com. J. Jill's products include sweaters, shirts, knit tees and tops, camisoles, pants, shorts, skirts, jackets, vests, dresses, shoes, jewelry, handbags and belts. In order to assure that all sizes and shapes of women are served, it carries sizes such as petites, misses, woman and tall. The brand also offers a private label credit card for direct and retail purchases. The merchandise, sold predominantly under the company's private label, is designed to be simple and comfortable with an emphasis on natural fibers, neutral colors and creative details. The firm gives back to the community through donations to the J. Jill Compassion Fund, which primarily funds organizations geared toward aiding women and their children. The company is headquartered in Quincy, Massachusetts and has a distribution center in Tilton, New Hampshire. In 2015, the firm was acquired by private equity firm, TowerBrook Capital Partners, LP.

The firm offers employees medical, dental, life and disability coverage; a 401(k); flexible spending accounts; service awards; paid time off; and employee assistance programs.

FINANCIAL DATA: Note: Data for latest year may not have been available at press time.

In U.S. $	2015	2014	2013	2012	2011	2010
Revenue		430,000,000	420,000,000	410,000,000	398,000,000	
R&D Expense						
Operating Income						
Operating Margin %						
SGA Expense						
Net Income						
Operating Cash Flow						
Capital Expenditure						
EBITDA						
Return on Assets %						
Return on Equity %						
Debt to Equity						

CONTACT INFORMATION:

Phone: 617-376-4300   Fax: 603-266-2802
Toll-Free: 800-343-5700
Address: 4 Batterymarch Park, Quincy, MA 02169 United States

STOCK TICKER/OTHER:

Stock Ticker: Private   Exchange:
Employees: 1,600   Fiscal Year Ends: 12/31
Parent Company: TowerBrook Capital Partners LP

SALARIES/BONUSES:

Top Exec. Salary: $ Bonus: $
Second Exec. Salary: $ Bonus: $

OTHER THOUGHTS:

Estimated Female Officers or Directors: 3
Hot Spot for Advancement for Women/Minorities: Y

J Sainsbury plc

www.j-sainsbury.co.uk

NAIC Code: 445110

TYPES OF BUSINESS:

Grocery Stores
Convenience Stores
Gas Stations
Clothing & Housewares
Real Estate Development
Banking
Online Media Downloads
Multi-Channel Marketing Services

BRANDS/DIVISIONS/AFFILIATES:

Sainsbury's Supermarket
Sainsbury's Bank
TU
Insight 2 Communication
eBooks by Sainsbury's

CONTACTS: Note: Officers with more than one job title may be intentionally listed here more than once.

Justin King, CEO
John Rogers, CFO
Sarah Warby, Dir.-Mktg.
Angie Risley, Group Human Resources Dir.
Rob Fraser, Dir.-IT
Roger Burnley, Managing Dir.-Merch. & Clothing
Tim Fallowfield, Sec.
Luke Jensen, Dir.-Group Dev.
Neil Sachdev, Dir.-Property
Helen Buck, Dir.-Retail
Mike Coupe, Dir.-Group Commercial
David Tyler, Chmn.
Roger Burnley, Managing Dir.-Logistics

GROWTH PLANS/SPECIAL FEATURES:

J. Sainsbury plc is a leading retailer operating supermarkets, convenience stores and a bank in the U.K. The company owns 598 Sainsbury's Supermarkets, which range from less than 15,000 to more than 40,000 square feet of retail space. These supermarkets process an average of 24 million transactions weekly. Besides a wide range of packaged food and grocery products, many stores offer bread baked on the premises, a delicatessen, meat and fish counters, pharmacies, coffee shops, restaurants and gas stations. The firm's Sainsbury's online service offers Internet-based home delivery services for groceries, wine, flowers, gifts and electronics. In addition, the company operates 714 convenience stores under the Sainsbury's name. Sainsbury sells a number of private-label products, including the Taste the Difference and by Sainsbury's lines. It also offers a proprietary clothing line under the TU label. Sainsbury's Bank, a joint venture between J. Sainsbury and Lloyds Banking Group, was the first supermarket-bank in the U.K. and now has over 1.6 million active customers. Additionally, the company operates pharmacies throughout its store network and manages outpatient pharmacies at several hospitals in the U.K. The firm's new business development initiatives include Insight 2 Communication (I2C), a joint venture company with Aimia that offers integrated multi-channel marketing services; MP3 download and video-on-demand services as part of its Sainsbury Entertainment platform; and majority ownership of eBooks by Sainsbury's, an e-book downloading service.

FINANCIAL DATA: Note: Data for latest year may not have been available at press time.

In U.S. $	2015	2014	2013	2012	2011	2010
Revenue	35,541,300,000	35,801,420,000	34,835,710,000	33,327,350,000	31,545,430,000	29,844,230,000
R&D Expense						
Operating Income	121,087,100	1,508,356,000	1,325,978,000	1,306,545,000	1,272,162,000	1,061,381,000
Operating Margin %	.34%	4.21%	3.80%	3.92%	4.03%	3.55%
SGA Expense	1,692,230,000	663,736,600	683,170,400			
Net Income	-248,153,800	1,070,350,000	917,870,100	893,951,600	956,737,500	874,517,900
Operating Cash Flow	1,361,856,000	1,403,713,000	1,466,499,000	1,587,586,000	1,270,667,000	1,499,387,000
Capital Expenditure	1,538,255,000	1,388,764,000	1,633,928,000	1,871,618,000	1,720,633,000	1,565,163,000
EBITDA	941,788,500	2,361,946,000	2,142,195,000	2,125,751,000	2,125,751,000	1,976,261,000
Return on Assets %	-1.00%	4.89%	4.90%	5.03%	5.75%	5.60%
Return on Equity %	-2.87%	12.20%	10.80%	10.82%	12.31%	12.52%
Debt to Equity	0.45	0.37	0.45	0.46	0.43	0.47

CONTACT INFORMATION:

Phone: 44 2076956000   Fax: 44 2076957610
Toll-Free:
Address: 33 Holborn, London, EC1N 2HT United Kingdom

STOCK TICKER/OTHER:

Stock Ticker: JSAIY   Exchange: PINX
Employees: 161,100   Fiscal Year Ends: 03/31
Parent Company:

SALARIES/BONUSES:

Top Exec. Salary: $ Bonus: $
Second Exec. Salary: $ Bonus: $

OTHER THOUGHTS:

Estimated Female Officers or Directors: 6
Hot Spot for Advancement for Women/Minorities: Y

Jean Coutu Group Inc (The)

www.jeancoutu.com

NAIC Code: 446110

TYPES OF BUSINESS:

Drug Stores
Generic Drug Manufacturing
Cosmetic Stores

BRANDS/DIVISIONS/AFFILIATES:

PJC Jean Coutu
PJC Clinique
PJC Sante
PJC Sante Beaute
Pro Doc Ltd

GROWTH PLANS/SPECIAL FEATURES:

The Jean Coutu Group, Inc. (JCG) is a leading Canadia
distributor and retailer of pharmaceuticals and over-the-counte
drugs. The firm's network consists of 416 PJC Jean Coutu, PJ
Clinique, PJC Sante and PJC Sante Beaute franchised reta
stores throughout Quebec, Ontario and New Brunswick
Canada. Through subsidiary Pro Doc Ltd., the fir
manufactures generic drugs, which are almost exclusively sol
in Quebec. The company maintains a portfolio of about 14
generic molecules and 315 different products.

The firm offers its employees a group insurance plan, weeken
work bonuses, yearly attendance bonuses, performanc
recognition programs and ongoing job training.

CONTACTS: *Note: Officers with more than one job title may be intentionally listed here more than once.*

Veronique Duval, Assistant Secretary
Helene Bisson, Vice President, Divisional
Francois Coutu, CEO
Andre Belzile, CFO
Jean Coutu, Chairman of the Board
Alain Boudreault, Chief Information Officer
Maxime Chamberland, Controller
Nicolle Forget, Director
Alain Lafortune, Executive VP, Divisional
Normand Messier, Executive VP, Divisional
Richard Mayrand, Executive VP, Divisional
Marcel Raymond, President, Subsidiary
Brigite Dufour, Secretary
Jean-Michel Coutu, Vice President, Divisional
Eric Laurence, Vice President, Divisional
Guy Franche, Vice President, Divisional
Louis Coutu, Vice President, Divisional

FINANCIAL DATA: *Note: Data for latest year may not have been available at press time.*

In U.S. $	2015	2014	2013	2012	2011	2010
Revenue	2,107,897,000	2,047,738,000	2,052,383,000	2,047,588,000	1,946,224,000	1,905,243,000
R&D Expense						
Operating Income	224,679,500	226,252,800	218,236,600	210,370,200	193,663,400	178,679,800
Operating Margin %	10.65%	11.04%	10.63%	10.27%	9.95%	9.37%
SGA Expense	213,366,900	195,761,100	185,422,400	178,005,500	172,386,700	163,396,500
Net Income	163,995,800	327,392,300	418,342,900	172,311,700	135,002,500	84,357,840
Operating Cash Flow	207,897,900	213,067,200	167,666,800	183,549,500	159,950,300	151,934,000
Capital Expenditure	71,696,670	37,309,240	27,719,720	35,661,040	32,889,070	35,136,610
EBITDA	249,402,500	411,300,600	502,625,900	251,874,800	219,510,200	206,549,300
Return on Assets %	17.45%	34.17%	45.29%	21.71%	17.75%	11.26%
Return on Equity %	22.34%	42.78%	63.45%	37.53%	33.18%	23.33%
Debt to Equity					0.32	0.39

CONTACT INFORMATION:

Phone: 450 646-9611   Fax: 450 646-2724
Toll-Free: 800-361-4607
Address: 530 Beriault St., Longueuil, QC J4G 1S8 Canada

SALARIES/BONUSES:

Top Exec. Salary: $ Bonus: $
Second Exec. Salary: $ Bonus: $

STOCK TICKER/OTHER:

Stock Ticker: PJC.A   Exchange: TSE
Employees: 1,074   Fiscal Year Ends: 03/31
Parent Company:

OTHER THOUGHTS:

Estimated Female Officers or Directors: 13
Hot Spot for Advancement for Women/Minorities: Y

Jennifer Convertibles Inc

www.jenniferfurniture.com

NAIC Code: 442110

TYPES OF BUSINESS:

Furniture Stores, Retail
Leather Furniture
Sofa Beds
Furniture Accessories

BRANDS/DIVISIONS/AFFILIATES:

Jennifer Convertibles
Jennifer Leather
Jennifer Clearance
Jennifer Home Furnishings
Haining Mengnu Group Co Ltd

GROWTH PLANS/SPECIAL FEATURES:

Jennifer Convertibles, Inc. is one of the largest sofa bed specialty retail store chains in the U.S. The firm owns and licenses the sofa bed specialty retail stores and operates as Jennifer Convertibles and Jennifer Leather. The company owns 65 Jennifer Convertibles stores, including Jennifer Clearance and Jennifer Home Furnishings, and eight Jennifer Leather stores located throughout the U.S. The Jennifer Convertibles stores specialize in the sale of a complete line of sofa beds as well as companion loveseats, recliners, chairs and ottomans. It is one of the largest dealers of Sealy and Simmons sofa beds in the U.S. The furniture ranges from high-end merchandise to relatively inexpensive models and is made by several manufacturers. Jennifer Leather stores offer leather living room furniture and accessories in a variety of styles and colors. The firm recently exited bankruptcy protection with one of its largest suppliers, Haining Mengnu Group Co. Ltd. of Haining, China, as the primary owner.

CONTACTS:
Note: Officers with more than one job title may be intentionally listed here more than once.

Gebing (Morris) Zou, CEO
Rami Abada, CFO
Gebing (Morris) Zou, Chmn.

FINANCIAL DATA:
Note: Data for latest year may not have been available at press time.

In U.S. $	2015	2014	2013	2012	2011	2010
Revenue		62,800,000	62,500,000	62,000,000	60,540,000	76,305,000
R&D Expense						
Operating Income						
Operating Margin %						
SGA Expense						
Net Income						
Operating Cash Flow						
Capital Expenditure						
EBITDA						
Return on Assets %						
Return on Equity %						
Debt to Equity						

CONTACT INFORMATION:

Phone: 516-496-1900   Fax: 516-496-0008
Toll-Free:
Address: 417 Crossways Park Dr., Woodbury, NY 11797 United States

STOCK TICKER/OTHER:

Stock Ticker: Private
Employees: 417
Parent Company:

Exchange:
Fiscal Year Ends: 08/31

SALARIES/BONUSES:

Top Exec. Salary: $ Bonus: $
Second Exec. Salary: $ Bonus: $

OTHER THOUGHTS:

Estimated Female Officers or Directors:
Hot Spot for Advancement for Women/Minorities:

Sales, profits and employees may be estimates. Financial information, benefits and other data can change quickly and may vary from those stated here.

Jeronimo Martins SGPS SA

www.jeronimomartins.pt

NAIC Code: 445110

TYPES OF BUSINESS:

Supermarkets and Other Grocery (except Convenience) Stores

BRANDS/DIVISIONS/AFFILIATES:

Pingo Doce
Recheio
ara
Biedronka
Unilever Jeronimo Martins
Gallo Worldwide
Hussel
Jeronymo

CONTACTS: Note: Officers with more than one job title may be intentionally listed here more than once.

Francisco Javier Van Engelen Sousa, CFO
Pedro Soares Dos Santos, Chmn.

GROWTH PLANS/SPECIAL FEATURES:

Jeronimo Martins SGPS SA is holding company principally engaged in retail and wholesale operations in Portugal and Poland. Currently, the company operates 3,435 stores across all segments. The company's business is structured in three segments: distribution, manufacturing and services. The distribution segment operates in Portugal, Poland and Colombia through the Pingo Doce, Recheio, ara and Biedronka brands. This segment specializes in food distribution, with the Pingo Doce brand as a leader in supermarket distribution. Operations are conducted through six distribution centers in Portugal, thirteen in Poland and one in Colombia. The manufacturing segment produces a variety of consumer goods in Portugal, with interest in Unilever Jeronimo Martins and Gallo Worldwide. Products manufactured include margarine, ice tea, ice cream and laundry detergent, which are sold to Portugal, Brazil, Angola and Venezuela. Gallo Worldwide is a spin-off of Unilever, manufacturing olive oil and vegetable oil, and whose products have a presence in 47 countries. The services segment represents and distributes international brands. Its operations are further divided into marketing & representation; restaurants & service; and Hussel. Marketing & representation consist of several food brands, in the categories of grocery, confectionery, beverages and milk and soy products. Restaurants & services operate three brands: Jeronymo, Ola and Jeronymo Food with Friends. Finally, Hussel is a specialty store which sells chocolates and candies; it is a joint venture between the firm and Douglas AG.

FINANCIAL DATA: Note: Data for latest year may not have been available at press time.

In U.S. $	2015	2014	2013	2012	2011	2010
Revenue		13,457,520,000	12,554,450,000	11,542,600,000	10,945,220,000	9,656,814,000
R&D Expense						
Operating Income		476,603,600	557,228,500	552,368,800	530,725,700	479,539,200
Operating Margin %		3.54%	4.43%	4.78%	4.84%	4.96%
SGA Expense		2,372,211,000	2,136,156,000	2,001,312,000	1,837,923,000	1,677,203,000
Net Income		320,206,100	405,688,600	382,490,700	379,262,200	318,148,300
Operating Cash Flow		776,185,500	727,112,000	717,192,000	789,494,200	
Capital Expenditure		526,582,400	550,183,600	524,269,800	409,182,400	419,773,100
EBITDA		770,314,400	821,789,600	791,127,600	752,809,300	479,539,200
Return on Assets %		5.87%	7.65%	7.68%	7.87%	7.03%
Return on Equity %		21.71%	29.47%	30.90%	34.61%	35.70%
Debt to Equity		0.26	0.26	0.47	0.34	0.75

CONTACT INFORMATION:

Phone: 351 217532000   Fax: 351 217526174
Toll-Free:
Address: Rua Actor Antonio Silva 7, Lisbon, 1649-033 Portugal

STOCK TICKER/OTHER:

Stock Ticker: JRONY   Exchange: PINX
Employees: 80,797   Fiscal Year Ends: 12/31
Parent Company:

SALARIES/BONUSES:

Top Exec. Salary: $ Bonus: $
Second Exec. Salary: $ Bonus: $

OTHER THOUGHTS:

Estimated Female Officers or Directors:
Hot Spot for Advancement for Women/Minorities:

Jil Sander SpA

NAIC Code: 424300

TYPES OF BUSINESS:

Apparel and Clothing Brands, Designers, Importers and Distributors
Women's & Men's Apparel
Eyewear
Accessories
Fragrances
Footwear
Jewelry
Small Leather Goods

BRANDS/DIVISIONS/AFFILIATES:

Onward Holdings Co Ltd
Jil Sander Navy
JilSander.com

CONTACTS: Note: Officers with more than one job title may be intentionally listed here more than once.

Alessandro Cremonesi, CEO
Jil Sander, Creative Dir.

GROWTH PLANS/SPECIAL FEATURES:

Jil Sander SpA is a fashion house that designs, manufactures and markets high-fashion men's and women's clothing lines. It is currently owned by Japanese apparel conglomerate Onward Holdings Co., Ltd. With foundations in Germany in the late 60s, the company is known for its finely tailored, minimalist approach to fashion design. Its products include men's and women's fashions, handbags, belts, jewelry, sunglasses, fragrances and footwear. The firm has recently launched a new line of women's wear, Jil Sander Navy, with a focus on more causal pieces and a more moderate price point than its flagship collection. In addition to its ready-to-wear collections, the firm provides sartorial, made-to-measure services for men's suiting and dress shirts. The company sells its products through flagship stores, freestanding stores and store-within-a-store concepts inside department stores. Additionally, the firm operates an e-commerce web site, JilSander.com. Jil Sander has a presence in Germany, France, the U.K., Switzerland, Italy, Austria, Russia, Taiwan, Thailand, Singapore, China, Hong Kong, South Korea, Japan and the U.S. Through strategic licenses with various manufacturers, the company sells jewelry, eyewear, underwear and beachwear.

FINANCIAL DATA: Note: Data for latest year may not have been available at press time.

In U.S. $	2015	2014	2013	2012	2011	2010
Revenue		155,000,000	145,000,000	140,000,000	135,263,438	120,000,000
R&D Expense						
Operating Income						
Operating Margin %						
SGA Expense						
Net Income						
Operating Cash Flow						
Capital Expenditure						
EBITDA						
Return on Assets %						
Return on Equity %						
Debt to Equity						

CONTACT INFORMATION:

Phone: 39-02-80-69-131   Fax: 39-02-80-69-13-364
Toll-Free:
Address: Foro Buonaparte, 71, Milan, 20121 Italy

STOCK TICKER/OTHER:

Stock Ticker: Subsidiary
Employees: 350
Parent Company: ONWARD HOLDINGS CO LTD
Exchange:
Fiscal Year Ends: 12/31

SALARIES/BONUSES:

Top Exec. Salary: $ Bonus: $
Second Exec. Salary: $ Bonus: $

OTHER THOUGHTS:

Estimated Female Officers or Directors: 1
Hot Spot for Advancement for Women/Minorities:

Jo Ann Stores Inc

www.joann.com

NAIC Code: 451130

TYPES OF BUSINESS:
Fabrics & Sewing Accessories, Retail
Crafts Equipment
Home Decorating Items
Seasonal Merchandise
Instructional Classes
Online Sales

BRANDS/DIVISIONS/AFFILIATES:
Jo-Ann Fabric and Craft
Leonard Green & Partners LP

CONTACTS: Note: Officers with more than one job title may be intentionally listed here more than once.
Jill Soltau, CEO
Travis Smith, Pres.
James Kerr, CFO
David Goldston, General Counsel
Kenneth Haverkost, Exec. VP-Store Oper.
Renee Jefferson, Treas.
Carolyn Tackett, Regional VP-California Region
Diana Young, Regional VP-Northeast Region
Roger Hawkins, Regional VP-Southeast Region
Edward Dann, Regional VP-Central Region
Scott Clark, VP-Supply Chain

GROWTH PLANS/SPECIAL FEATURES:

Jo-Ann Stores, Inc. owned by Leonard Green & Partners L.P is one of the largest fabric and craft retailers in the U.S. Th company's more than 850 retail locations operate under the Jc Ann Fabric and Craft name. The stores, located throughout 4 states, offer a wide variety of competitively priced item: including fashion, decorator, quilting and craft fabrics; notion: patterns; craft components; and silk and dried flowers. Large Jo-Ann's stores, offer an expanded and more comprehensiv product assortment, including such services as custom framin and educational programs. The company divides its produc in two categories: sewing, which consists of the firm's principa fabric business; and non-sewing components, which includ yarn and knitting accessories, paper crafting components brand name fine art materials such as painting supplies, flor: products, an assortment of craft related books, frames an framing equipment and home decor accessories. As a way t draw in new customers and maintain customer loyalty, th company also offers classes in sewing and other crafts. I addition to its retail stores, Jo-Ann operates a web site, whic features a community forum, craft projects and ideas an exclusive products only available online.

The company offers employees medical, dental and visior insurance; health care and dependant care spending account: an employee assistance program; disability coverage; life insurance; discounted home and auto insurance; family and medical leave; a 401(k) plan; and a college savings plan.

FINANCIAL DATA: Note: Data for latest year may not have been available at press time.

In U.S. $	2015	2014	2013	2012	2011	2010
Revenue		2,320,000,000	2,330,000,000	2,150,000,000	2,079,000,000	1,990,700,000
R&D Expense						
Operating Income						
Operating Margin %						
SGA Expense						
Net Income						
Operating Cash Flow						
Capital Expenditure						
EBITDA						
Return on Assets %						
Return on Equity %						
Debt to Equity						

CONTACT INFORMATION:
Phone: 330-656-2600   Fax: 330-463-6760
Toll-Free: 888-739-4120
Address: 5555 Darrow Rd., Hudson, OH 44236 United States

STOCK TICKER/OTHER:
Stock Ticker: Private   Exchange:
Employees: 23,000   Fiscal Year Ends: 01/29
Parent Company: LEONARD GREEN & PARTNERS LP

SALARIES/BONUSES:
Top Exec. Salary: $ Bonus: $
Second Exec. Salary: $ Bonus: $

OTHER THOUGHTS:
Estimated Female Officers or Directors:
Hot Spot for Advancement for Women/Minorities: Y

John Lewis Partnership

www.johnlewispartnership.co.uk

NAIC Code: 452111

TYPES OF BUSINESS:

Department Stores
Supermarkets
Online Retailing
Insurance

BRANDS/DIVISIONS/AFFILIATES:

John Lewis
Waitrose
JohnLewis.com
Waitrose.com
WaitroseCellar
Leckford Estate
Longstock Park Nursery
WaitrosePet

CONTACTS: *Note: Officers with more than one job title may be intentionally listed here more than once.*

Andy Street, Managing Dir.
Dino Rocos, Dir.-Oper
Berangere Michel, Dir.-Finance
Mark Lewis, Dir.-Retail
Harriet Hounsell, Dir.-Personnel
Paul Coby, Dir.-IT
Paula Nickolds, Dir.-Brand
Dino Rocos, Dir.-Oper.
Mark Lewis, Dir.-Online
Andrew Moys, Dir.-Comm.
Rachel Osdorne, Dir.-Financial
Harriet Hounsell, Divisional Registrar
Charlie Mayfield, Chmn.
Paula Nickolds, Dir.-Buying

GROWTH PLANS/SPECIAL FEATURES:

John Lewis Partnership is focused on the retail stores of John Lewis and Waitrose, owned by the firm's 85,500 partners. The company has 45 John Lewis stores located in the U.K., 32 of which are department stores and 11 of which are John Lewis at home stores. John Lewis stores feature 350,000 product lines, while the John Lewis e-commerce web site, JohnLewis.com, offers 280,000 product lines. The partnership has over 300 Waitrose supermarkets in the U.K. Waitrose offers 18,000 product lines and obtains most of its products from British producers. It offers online shopping through Waitrose.com as well as delivery services. Additionally, Waitrose offers a wide selection of wine, champagne and spirits as well as free delivery through WaitroseCellar and its online site WaitroseCellar.com. WaitroseFlorist, waitroseflorist.com, delivers hand tied bouquets and beautiful plants with directions on how to best care and display the flowers. Waitrose Gardens, waitrosegardens.com, offers nearly 6,000 gardening and floristry products including bulbs, seeds, flowers, plants, tools and garden care. WaitroseGifts, waitrosegifts.com, offers gift ideas including a range of exclusive products. The firm also operates WaitroseKitchen, waitrosekitchen.com, and WaitrosePet, waitrosepet.com, delivery everything needed for cooking at home and pet care. Waitrose also owns Longstock Park Nursery, housed in company-owned Leckford Estate in Hampshire in the U.K. Longstock sells a variety of flowers, shrubs, trees and aquatic plants. Additionally, the John Lewis brand offers several types of insurance, such as automobile, home, travel, pet, wedding, life and event insurance; three broadband packages; and a foreign currency exchange.

FINANCIAL DATA: *Note: Data for latest year may not have been available at press time.*

In U.S. $	2015	2014	2013	2012	2011	2010
Revenue		15,573,583,650	14,608,684,430			
R&D Expense						
Operating Income						
Operating Margin %						
SGA Expense						
Net Income		155,559,760	525,626,630			
Operating Cash Flow						
Capital Expenditure						
EBITDA						
Return on Assets %						
Return on Equity %						
Debt to Equity						

CONTACT INFORMATION:

Phone: 44-20-7828-1000   Fax:
Toll-Free:
Address: 171 Victoria St., London, SW1E 5NN United Kingdom

STOCK TICKER/OTHER:

Stock Ticker: Private   Exchange:
Employees: Fiscal Year Ends:
Parent Company:

OTHER THOUGHTS:

Estimated Female Officers or Directors: 10
Hot Spot for Advancement for Women/Minorities: Y

SALARIES/BONUSES:

Top Exec. Salary: $ Bonus: $
Second Exec. Salary: $ Bonus: $

Jos A Bank Clothiers Inc

www.josbank.com

NAIC Code: 448110

TYPES OF BUSINESS:

Business Apparel-Men's, Retail
Catalog Sales
Online Retail
Tailoring Services
Footwear
Casual Apparel
Accessories

BRANDS/DIVISIONS/AFFILIATES:

Jos. A. Bank Executive
Signature
Signature Gold
JosBankFormal.com
Men's Wearhouse Inc
Jos. A. Bank

CONTACTS: Note: Officers with more than one job title may be intentionally listed here more than once.

Douglas S. Ewert, CEO
R. Neal Black, Pres.
Jon W. Kimmins, CFO
James W. Thorne, Chief Merch. Officer
Charles D. Frazer, General Counsel
Gary M. Merry, Exec. VP-Store & Catalog Oper.
Robert B. Hensley, Exec. VP-Real Estate & Loss Prevention
Frank J. Barbarino, Sr. VP

GROWTH PLANS/SPECIAL FEATURES:

Jos. A. Bank Clothiers, Inc., established in 1905, is a leading retailer and direct marketer of men's tailored and casual clothing, footwear, golf apparel and accessories. The company sells all of its products under the Jos. A. Bank label, targeting the male career professional. Products are offered on three levels, which include the basic Jos. A. Bank Executive collection and the more refined Signature and Signature Gold collections. The company designs its own tailored products and selects, and sometimes purchases, raw materials, such as finished wool. Merchandise is manufactured by third-party domestic and international contract manufacturers to the firm's specifications. Jos. A. Bank has 600 stores nationwide. The company's newer stores operate under a format that integrates the firm's corporate casual and sportswear divisions with its other products. Most of the company's stores feature a tailor shop that provides a range of tailoring services. The firm also offers corporate customers the Corporate Card, which provides users with merchandise discounts. In addition to its retail stores, the firm operates a nationwide catalog, including four seasonal editions, and an e-commerce site. The company also operates JosBankFormal.com, a website for tuxedo rentals. The firm is a subsidiary of Men's Wearhouse, Inc.

The company offers its employees medical, dental and vision insurance; flexible spending accounts; prescription drug coverage; merchandise discounts; a 401(k); tuition reimbursement; an employee assistance program; and legal services.

FINANCIAL DATA: Note: Data for latest year may not have been available at press time.

In U.S. $	2015	2014	2013	2012	2011	2010
Revenue		1,100,000,000	1,049,313,024	979,852,032	858,128,000	770,316,032
R&D Expense						
Operating Income						
Operating Margin %						
SGA Expense						
Net Income			79,696,000	97,491,000	85,799,000	71,155,000
Operating Cash Flow						
Capital Expenditure						
EBITDA						
Return on Assets %						
Return on Equity %						
Debt to Equity						

CONTACT INFORMATION:

Phone: 410 239-2700   Fax: 410 239-5700
Toll-Free:
Address: 500 Hanover Pike, Hampstead, MD 21074 United States

STOCK TICKER/OTHER:

Stock Ticker: Subsidiary   Exchange:
Employees: 7,000   Fiscal Year Ends: 01/31
Parent Company: Men's Wearhouse Inc

SALARIES/BONUSES:

Top Exec. Salary: $ Bonus: $
Second Exec. Salary: $ Bonus: $

OTHER THOUGHTS:

Estimated Female Officers or Directors:
Hot Spot for Advancement for Women/Minorities:

Kasper Group (The)

www.kasper.com

NAIC Code: 424300

TYPES OF BUSINESS:

Apparel and Clothing Brands, Designers, Importers and Distributors
Outlet Stores

BRANDS/DIVISIONS/AFFILIATES:

Sycamore Partners
Kasper
Le Suit
Evan Picone
Albert Nipon

GROWTH PLANS/SPECIAL FEATURES:

The Kasper Group, formerly Kasper Ltd., is an international apparel and accessories company. The firm designs, markets, sources, manufactures and distributes women's suits, sportswear and evening wear. The Kasper line features two- and three-piece suiting and dresses. In the wholesale channel, the company sells products under brands such as Kasper, Le Suit, Evan Picone and Albert Nipon. Additionally, Kasper operates more than 40 Kasper branded outlets across the U.S., including Alabama, California, Florida, Georgia, Illinois, Indiana, Louisiana, Massachusetts, Maryland, Maine, Michigan, Mississippi, Missouri, North Carolina, New Jersey, New Hampshire, New York, Ohio, Pennsylvania, Tennessee, Texas and Virginia. Kasper is owned by private equity firm Sycamore Partners, and operates as an independent company. In 2014, Kasper's former parent, The Jones Group, was acquired by Sycamore Partners.

CONTACTS: Note: Officers with more than one job title may be intentionally listed here more than once.

Richard Dickson, CEO
Christopher R. Cade, Exec. VP

FINANCIAL DATA: Note: Data for latest year may not have been available at press time.

In U.S. $	2015	2014	2013	2012	2011	2010
Revenue		450,000,000	449,784,270	453,447,540	451,440,600	434,454,150
R&D Expense						
Operating Income						
Operating Margin %						
SGA Expense						
Net Income			-2,381,730	-6,649,500	6,226,350	6,576,960
Operating Cash Flow						
Capital Expenditure						
EBITDA						
Return on Assets %						
Return on Equity %						
Debt to Equity						

CONTACT INFORMATION:

Phone: 215-785-4000   Fax: 212-221-2708
Toll-Free: 800-223-7698
Address: 1412 Broadway, 5th Fl., New York, NY 10018 United States

STOCK TICKER/OTHER:

Stock Ticker: Private   Exchange:
Employees: 722   Fiscal Year Ends: 12/31
Parent Company: Sycamore Partners

SALARIES/BONUSES:

Top Exec. Salary: $ Bonus: $
Second Exec. Salary: $ Bonus: $

OTHER THOUGHTS:

Estimated Female Officers or Directors:
Hot Spot for Advancement for Women/Minorities:

Kate Spade & Company Inc

www.katespadeandcompany.com

NAIC Code: 424300

TYPES OF BUSINESS:

Apparel and Clothing Brands, Designers, Importers and Distributors
Apparel Marketing
Jewelry Design & Marketing

BRANDS/DIVISIONS/AFFILIATES:

kate spade new york
Jack Spade
Adelington Design Group
Globalluxe Kate Spade HK Limited
Fifth & Pacific Companies Inc
Kate Spade & Company

CONTACTS: Note: Officers with more than one job title may be intentionally listed here more than once.

Craig Leavitt, CEO
Thomas Linko, CFO
Nancy Karch, Director
Christopher DiNardo, General Counsel
Deborah Lloyd, Other Executive Officer
George Carrara, President
Linda Yanussi, Senior VP, Divisional
William Higley, Senior VP, Divisional
Priya Trivedi, Treasurer
Emily Garbaccio, Vice President, Divisional
Michael Rinaldo, Vice President

GROWTH PLANS/SPECIAL FEATURES:

Kate Spade & Company, Inc. designs and markets a portfolio of retail-based, premium accessories and apparel brands including kate spade new york and Jack Spade. Kate spade new york offers fashion products for women and children, as well as home products. These include handbags, small leather goods, fashion accessories, jewelry and fragrances, as well as footwear, swimwear, watches, optics, tabletop products, legwear, electronics cases, bedding and stationery. Jack Spade offers fashion products for men, including briefcases, travel bags, small leather goods, fashion accessories and apparel. The firm also owns the Adelington Design Group, a private jewelry design and development group, which markets brands through department stores and serves JCPenney via exclusive supplier agreements for the Liz Claiborne and Monet jewelry lines and Kohl's via an exclusive supplier agreement for Dana Buchman jewelry. In addition, the company has licenses for the Liz Claiborne New York brand, available at QVC and Lizwear, which is distributed through the club store channel. Kate Spade operates in North America, as well as internationally, including Japan, Southeast Asia, Europe and Latin America. In 2014, it sold its Lucky Brand Jeans business to an affiliate of Leonard Green & Partners, L.P. (LGP) for $225 million; and acquired the Kate Spade businesses in Hong Kong, Macau, Taiwan, Malaysia, Singapore, Indonesia and Thailand from Globalluxe Kate Spade HK Limited. That same year, parent Fifth & Pacific Companies, Inc. changed its name to Kate Spade & Company to reflect the company's brand portfolio. In 2015, Kate Spade discontinued its Kate Spade Saturday business and began to absorb its key offerings into the kate spade new york label; and closed its company-owned Jack Spade retail stores in order to reimagine the brand as an e-commerce label. That October, the firm introduced its comprehensive home furnishings collection of furniture, lighting, rugs and fabric.

FINANCIAL DATA: Note: Data for latest year may not have been available at press time.

In U.S. $	2015	2014	2013	2012	2011	2010
Revenue		1,138,603,000	1,264,935,000	1,505,094,000	1,518,721,000	2,500,072,000
R&D Expense						
Operating Income		33,472,000	-45,513,000	-34,451,000	-96,252,000	-179,514,000
Operating Margin %		2.93%	-3.59%	-2.28%	-6.33%	-7.18%
SGA Expense		645,266,000	766,103,000	877,426,000	904,619,000	1,415,441,000
Net Income		159,160,000	72,995,000	-74,505,000	-171,687,000	-251,467,000
Operating Cash Flow		14,364,000	-24,031,000	11,358,000	-17,028,000	150,641,000
Capital Expenditure		99,953,000	78,114,000	82,792,000	73,653,000	77,369,000
EBITDA		87,910,000	14,419,000	70,103,000	-10,283,000	-10,029,000
Return on Assets %		16.71%	7.76%	-8.04%	-15.55%	-17.56%
Return on Equity %		190.46%				-261.43%
Debt to Equity		2.00				

CONTACT INFORMATION:

Phone: 212-354-4900   Fax:
Toll-Free:
Address: 2 Park Ave., New York, NY 10016 United States

STOCK TICKER/OTHER:

Stock Ticker: KATE
Employees: 3,500
Parent Company: Kate Spade & Company

Exchange: NYS
Fiscal Year Ends: 12/31

SALARIES/BONUSES:

Top Exec. Salary: $1,752,048   Bonus: $1,625,000
Second Exec. Salary: $1,402,644   Bonus: $1,625,000

OTHER THOUGHTS:

Estimated Female Officers or Directors: 6

Hot Spot for Advancement for Women/Minorities: Y

Sales, profits and employees may be estimates. Financial information, benefits and other data can change quickly and may vary from those stated here.

Kenneth Cole Productions Inc

www.kennethcole.com

NAIC Code: 424340

TYPES OF BUSINESS:

Footwear Distribution
Footwear & Handbags
Men's & Women's Apparel
Retail Stores
Catalog & Online Sales

BRANDS/DIVISIONS/AFFILIATES:

Kenneth Cole New York
Kenneth Cole Reaction
Unlisted
Le Tigre
Gentle Souls
Kenneth Cole
Kenneth Cole Outlet
KCP Holdco Inc

CONTACTS: *Note: Officers with more than one job title may be intentionally listed here more than once.*

Marc Schneider, CEO
David P. Edelman, CFO
Kenneth D. Cole, Chief Creative Officer
Kenneth D. Cole, Chmn.

GROWTH PLANS/SPECIAL FEATURES:

Kenneth Cole Productions, Inc. (KCP), a private subsidiary of KCP Holdco, Inc., designs, sources, markets and licenses a broad range of fashion footwear, handbags, apparel and accessories under the Kenneth Cole New York, Kenneth Cole Reaction, Unlisted, Le Tigre and Gentle Souls brand names. The firm's products are targeted to appeal to modern, fashion-conscious consumers who seek accessible designer fashion that reflects a metropolitan lifestyle. Its operations are divided into three segments: wholesale, consumer direct and licensing. The wholesale segment includes sales to department stores, independent specialty stores, national chains and mass market retailers. Its products are currently distributed to U.S. retail shops as well as select locations in Canada, Europe, Australia, Malaysia and the Middle East. This segment also designs, develops and sources private label footwear and handbags for selected retailers. The consumer direct segment is responsible for the firm's full-priced retail stores and outlets as well as its e-commerce operations. The licensing segment handles the firm's relationships with its licensing partners. Though KCP maintains in-house design teams for the development of footwear, handbags and men's sportswear collections, all other product categories sold under its various brands are produced by licensee partners. Licensed product categories include men's tailored clothing, neckwear, belts, socks and jewelry; women's apparel, outerwear, jewelry and swimwear; children's apparel; and men's and women's watches, optical frames, sunglasses and fragrances.

FINANCIAL DATA: *Note: Data for latest year may not have been available at press time.*

In U.S. $	2015	2014	2013	2012	2011	2010
Revenue		565,000,000	550,000,000	500,000,000	478,900,000	411,652,000
R&D Expense						
Operating Income						
Operating Margin %						
SGA Expense						
Net Income						
Operating Cash Flow						
Capital Expenditure						
EBITDA						
Return on Assets %						
Return on Equity %						
Debt to Equity						

CONTACT INFORMATION:

Phone: 212-265-1500   Fax: 212-315-8279
Toll-Free:
Address: 603 W. 50th St., New York, NY 10019 United States

SALARIES/BONUSES:

Top Exec. Salary: $ Bonus: $
Second Exec. Salary: $ Bonus: $

STOCK TICKER/OTHER:

Stock Ticker: Private   Exchange:
Employees: Fiscal Year Ends: 12/31
Parent Company: KCP Holdco Inc

OTHER THOUGHTS:

Estimated Female Officers or Directors:
Hot Spot for Advancement for Women/Minorities: Y

KERING SA

NAIC Code: 424300

TYPES OF BUSINESS:

Apparel and Clothing Brands, Designers, Importers and Distributors
Luxury Goods & Fashions Manufacturing
Book, Software & Consumer Electronics Stores
Appliance & Furniture Stores
Watches & Jewelry
Lingerie, Shoes & Leather Goods

BRANDS/DIVISIONS/AFFILIATES:

Luxury Goods International SA
Ulysse Nardin
Gucci
Saint Laurent
Alexander McQueen
Bottega Veneta
Puma
Volcom

CONTACTS: Note: Officers with more than one job title may be intentionally listed here more than once.

Francois-Henri Pinault, CEO
Jean-Marc Duplaix, CFO
Belen Essioux Trujillo, Sr. VP-Human Resources
Louise Beveridge, Sr. VP-Comm.
Marie-Claire Daveu, Chief Sustainability Officer
Patrizio di Marco, CEO
Alexis Babeau, Managing Dir.-Luxury Goods
Jean-Francois Palus, Group Managing Dir.
Francois-Henri Pinault, Chmn.
Franz Koch, CEO-Puma SE

GROWTH PLANS/SPECIAL FEATURES:

Kering SA is a leading global retailer and manufacturer specializing in apparel and accessories. The company operates in two segments: luxury and sport & lifestyle. The luxury sector designs and manufactures premium leather goods, shoes, watches, jewelry, eyewear, perfume, scarves and ready-to-wear clothing under a variety of brand names such as Gucci, Bottega Veneta, Saint Laurent, Alexander McQueen, Balenciaga, Brioni, Christopher Kane, McQ, Stella McCartney, Tomas Maier, Sergio Rossi, Boucheron, Dodo, Girard-Perregaux, JEANRICHARD, Pomellato, Qeelin and Ulysse Nardin. This segment operates stores across its brand portfolio worldwide, reaching more than 120 countries. Subsidiary Luxury Goods International SA, based in Switzerland, operates Kering's international distribution and logistics business for its luxury brands. The sport & lifestyle segment, which includes the Puma, Volcom, Cobra and Electric brands, manufactures and retails footwear, sports apparel and accessories. In 2014, the firm acquired luxury watch manufacturer Ulysse Nardin.

FINANCIAL DATA: Note: Data for latest year may not have been available at press time.

In U.S. $	2015	2014	2013	2012	2011	2010
Revenue		10,652,810,000	10,345,980,000	10,333,140,000	12,976,740,000	15,500,400,000
R&D Expense						
Operating Income		1,647,033,000	1,387,757,000	1,874,576,000	1,638,967,000	1,419,384,000
Operating Margin %		15.46%	13.41%	18.14%	12.63%	9.15%
SGA Expense						
Net Income		561,322,000	52,640,520	1,112,455,000	1,109,590,000	1,077,539,000
Operating Cash Flow		1,338,619,000	1,618,377,000	1,449,737,000	1,315,588,000	1,460,562,000
Capital Expenditure		585,201,200	719,243,500	468,988,800	345,241,100	363,601,600
EBITDA		1,993,759,000	1,701,690,000	2,166,540,000	1,966,909,000	1,768,976,000
Return on Assets %		2.29%	.20%	4.17%	3.97%	3.92%
Return on Equity %		4.98%	.45%	9.38%	9.16%	9.38%
Debt to Equity		0.30	0.29	0.26	0.28	0.31

CONTACT INFORMATION:

Phone: 33-1-45-64-61-00   Fax: 33-1-45-64-60-00
Toll-Free:
Address: 10 Ave. Hoche, Paris, 75381 France

STOCK TICKER/OTHER:

Stock Ticker: PPRUY
Employees: 32,890
Parent Company:

Exchange: PINX
Fiscal Year Ends: 12/31

SALARIES/BONUSES:

Top Exec. Salary: $ Bonus: $
Second Exec. Salary: $ Bonus: $

OTHER THOUGHTS:

Estimated Female Officers or Directors: 5
Hot Spot for Advancement for Women/Minorities: Y

KiK Textilien & Non-Food GmbH

www.kik-textilien.com

NAIC Code: 448140

TYPES OF BUSINESS:

Clothing & Apparel Retail Stores
General Merchandise Stores

BRANDS/DIVISIONS/AFFILIATES:

Tengelmann Group
KiK

GROWTH PLANS/SPECIAL FEATURES:

KiK Textilien & Non-Food GmbH, a member of the Tengelmann Group, is a German discount retailer of general merchandise, operating more than 3,200 stores in Germany (2,600), Austria, the Czech Republic, Hungary, Slovakia, Slovenia and Croatia. KiK focuses primarily on inexpensive apparel for men, women and children, offering items including hats, blouses, sweaters, jackets, mittens, pants, skirts, socks and shoes. The firm's non-apparel merchandise is comprised of toys, kitchen items, jewelry and stationary as well as pet supplies, tools, perfumes and decorative pieces. The company averages 200 store openings per year and is pushing to reach 4,000 stores across Europe.

CONTACTS: Note: Officers with more than one job title may be intentionally listed here more than once.

Heinz Speet, CEO

FINANCIAL DATA: Note: Data for latest year may not have been available at press time.

In U.S. $	2015	2014	2013	2012	2011	2010
Revenue		2,500,000,000	2,400,000,000	2,309,370,000	1,583,570,000	1,509,670,000
R&D Expense						
Operating Income						
Operating Margin %						
SGA Expense						
Net Income						
Operating Cash Flow						
Capital Expenditure						
EBITDA						
Return on Assets %						
Return on Equity %						
Debt to Equity						

CONTACT INFORMATION:

Phone: 49-2383-95-4116   Fax:
Toll-Free:
Address: Siemensstrasse 21, Bonen, 59199 Germany

STOCK TICKER/OTHER:

Stock Ticker: Private
Employees: 20,000
Parent Company: Tengelmann Group

Exchange:
Fiscal Year Ends:

SALARIES/BONUSES:

Top Exec. Salary: $ Bonus: $
Second Exec. Salary: $ Bonus: $

OTHER THOUGHTS:

Estimated Female Officers or Directors:
Hot Spot for Advancement for Women/Minorities:

Sales, profits and employees may be estimates. Financial information, benefits and other data can change quickly and may vary from those stated here.

Kingfisher plc

NAIC Code: 444110

www.kingfisher.com

TYPES OF BUSINESS:

Building Materials & Garden Supplies Stores
Home Centers, Retail
Hardware Stores
Direct Hardware Sales
Do-it-Yourself Warehouse Stores

BRANDS/DIVISIONS/AFFILIATES:

B&Q
Castorama
Brico Depot
ScrewFix
Koctas
DIY.com
Mr Bricolage
B&Q China

CONTACTS: Note: Officers with more than one job title may be intentionally listed here more than once.

Veronique Laury, CEO
Karen Witts, CFO
Nick Folland, Dir.-Corp. Affairs
Ian Harding, Group Dir.-Comm.
Kevin OByrne, CEO-B&Q
Philippe Tible, CEO-Castorama & Brico Depot
Ian Playford, Group Dir.-Property
Daniel Bernard, Chmn.
Anthony Sutcliffe, Group Dir.-Sourcing

GROWTH PLANS/SPECIAL FEATURES:

Kingfisher plc is a leading home improvement retail firm wi
over 1,200 stores throughout Europe. Kingfisher's mai
subsidiary is B&Q plc, with 767 stores in the U.K. and Ireland
218 stores in France and 193 locations in other countries suc
as Poland, Spain, Russia, Romania, Germany, Turkey an
Portugal. In the U.K., B&Q stores stock over 40,000 DIY (do-i
yourself) garden and home improvement items. B&Q als
operates the e-commerce site DIY.com. Other brands includ
Castorama, with up to 50,000 products in each store; ScrewFi
with up to 18,000 products in each store; and Brico Depot, wit
10,500 DIY and renovation products available in larg
quantities in each store. Kingfisher also has a 50% interest i
Koctas, a joint venture business in Turkey. In 2014, th
company acquired Mr. Bricolage, a home improvement retailer
In April 2015, the firm sold a 70% stake in previously wholly
owned B&Q China to Wumei Holdings Group.

FINANCIAL DATA: Note: Data for latest year may not have been available at press time.

In U.S. $	2015	2014	2013	2012	2011	2010
Revenue	16,393,100,000	16,630,790,000	15,805,600,000	16,191,290,000	15,621,730,000	15,700,960,000
R&D Expense						
Operating Income	974,676,400	1,100,248,000	1,038,957,000	1,206,386,000	1,043,442,000	931,324,200
Operating Margin %	5.94%	6.61%	6.57%	7.45%	6.67%	5.93%
SGA Expense	5,139,474,000	5,129,010,000	4,957,096,000	4,103,507,000	4,055,670,000	4,054,175,000
Net Income	856,579,100	1,059,886,000	843,124,900	956,737,500	738,481,800	580,022,100
Operating Cash Flow	986,635,600	1,246,749,000	898,436,400	974,676,400	884,982,200	1,569,647,000
Capital Expenditure	411,098,100	454,450,300	472,389,200	672,706,000	463,419,700	382,695,000
EBITDA	1,373,815,000	1,539,750,000	1,430,622,000	1,589,081,000	1,423,147,000	1,339,433,000
Return on Assets %	5.86%	7.19%	5.77%	6.65%	5.07%	3.86%
Return on Equity %	9.14%	11.38%	9.50%	11.45%	9.50%	7.97%
Debt to Equity	0.03	0.03	0.05	0.06	0.10	0.17

CONTACT INFORMATION:

Phone: 44 2073728008   Fax: 44 2076441001
Toll-Free:
Address: 3 Sheldon Sq., Paddington, London, W2 6PX United Kingdom

STOCK TICKER/OTHER:

Stock Ticker: KGFHF
Employees: 79,415
Parent Company:

Exchange: PINX
Fiscal Year Ends: 02/28

SALARIES/BONUSES:

Top Exec. Salary: $ Bonus: $
Second Exec. Salary: $ Bonus: $

OTHER THOUGHTS:

Estimated Female Officers or Directors: 2
Hot Spot for Advancement for Women/Minorities: Y

Kirklands Inc

NAIC Code: 442110

TYPES OF BUSINESS:

Home Decor

BRANDS/DIVISIONS/AFFILIATES:

CONTACTS: Note: Officers with more than one job title may be intentionally listed here more than once.

R. Orr, Chairman of the Board
Adam Holland, Chief Accounting Officer
Carl Kirkland, Co-Founder
Michelle Graul, Executive VP, Divisional
W. Madden, President

GROWTH PLANS/SPECIAL FEATURES:

Kirkland's, Inc. is retail firm that specializes in home decor. Founded in 1966, the company operates approximately 344 stores in 35 states. These stores provide a wide array of distinctive merchandise, including garden accessories, framed art, decorative accessories, wall decor, candles, mirrors, lamps, accent furniture, textiles and artificial floral products. Kirkland's stores also offer an extensive assortment of holiday merchandise and products that are appropriate gifts for every occasion. The company aims to provide its customers, which are predominantly female, with a shopping experience characterized by a diverse, ever-changing merchandise selection at moderate prices. Nearly all of the firm's recently built locations are off-mall stores. Kirkland's sales are derived from art (14%), holiday items (12%), wall decor (11%), accent furniture (10%), decorative accessories (8%), fragrance items (8%), lamps (7%), mirrors (7%), textiles (7%) and personal accessories (4%). Though its stores carry some items that cost several hundred dollars, most of the firm's products are priced under $20. The company buys its merchandise from roughly 250 vendors. Due to its desire to differentiate its products from those of competitors, the firm repackages certain items offered by other companies. Approximately 273 of Kirkland's stores are located in outlet centers or freestanding buildings; these average roughly 8,000 square feet in size. The remaining stores are located in enclosed malls.

FINANCIAL DATA: Note: Data for latest year may not have been available at press time.

In U.S. $	2015	2014	2013	2012	2011	2010
Revenue	507,621,000	460,563,000	448,365,000	430,285,000	415,300,000	406,194,000
R&D Expense						
Operating Income	28,641,000	23,992,000	21,528,000	30,505,000	41,974,000	46,938,000
Operating Margin %	5.64%	5.20%	4.80%	7.08%	10.10%	11.55%
SGA Expense	94,738,000	86,620,000	83,181,000	78,892,000	74,799,000	71,300,000
Net Income	17,814,000	14,530,000	13,795,000	19,115,000	26,431,000	34,570,000
Operating Cash Flow	44,488,000	39,213,000	32,347,000	41,765,000	36,700,000	49,972,000
Capital Expenditure	29,647,000	17,954,000	31,373,000	26,652,000	22,633,000	10,313,000
EBITDA	47,734,000	40,180,000	34,956,000	43,081,000	55,122,000	61,699,000
Return on Assets %	7.18%	6.54%	6.71%	9.61%	14.65%	23.65%
Return on Equity %	12.44%	11.48%	11.71%	16.20%	25.56%	49.09%
Debt to Equity						

CONTACT INFORMATION:

Phone: 615 872-4800   Fax: 731 664-9345
Toll-Free:
Address: 5310 Maryland Way, Brentwood, TN 37027 United States

SALARIES/BONUSES:

Top Exec. Salary: $545,000   Bonus: $4,360
Second Exec. Salary: $364,230   Bonus: $2,220

STOCK TICKER/OTHER:

Stock Ticker: KIRK
Employees: 6,312
Parent Company:

Exchange: NAS
Fiscal Year Ends: 01/31

OTHER THOUGHTS:

Estimated Female Officers or Directors: 4
Hot Spot for Advancement for Women/Minorities: Y

Kmart Holding Corporation

NAIC Code: 452112

TYPES OF BUSINESS:

Discount Department Stores
Online Sales
Pharmacy Services
Grocery Sales
Video Rentals
Optical Shops

BRANDS/DIVISIONS/AFFILIATES:

Sears Holdings Corporation
Sears Auto Center
Kmart
Kmart Super Center

CONTACTS: Note: Officers with more than one job title may be intentionally listed here more than once.

Edward S. Lampert, CEO
Robert A. Schriesheim, CFO
Edward S. Lampert, CEO
Edward S. Lampert, Chmn.

GROWTH PLANS/SPECIAL FEATURES:

Kmart Holding Corporation, a subsidiary of Sears Holdings Corporation, is a mass merchandise retailer. The firm has 979 stores in 49 U.S. states, Guam, Puerto Rico and the U.S. Virgin Islands. This store count includes the traditional discount stores, averaging 94,000 square feet; and the Kmart Super Centers, which average 165,000 square feet. The traditional Kmart discount stores are one story, free standing units that carry a wide assortment of general merchandise and often include a pharmacy. The company sells certain proprietary Sears brand products, such as Kenmore, Craftsman and DieHard products, and offers services for these products within certain Kmart stores. The Super Centers feature a full line of general merchandise and groceries as well as a variety of ancillary services including video rentals, dry cleaning, hair care and optical and floral shops, and full grocery, deli and bakery operations, open 24 hours a day. In addition, there are seven Sears Auto Centers operating in certain Kmart stores. Sears Auto Centers offer a variety of professional automotive repair and maintenance services as well as a full assortment of automotive accessories.

FINANCIAL DATA: Note: Data for latest year may not have been available at press time.

In U.S. $	2015	2014	2013	2012	2011	2010
Revenue		12,074,000,000	13,194,000,000	15,285,000,000	15,593,000,000	15,743,000,000
R&D Expense						
Operating Income						
Operating Margin %						
SGA Expense						
Net Income		422,000,000	-351,000,000	-34,000,000	353,000,000	190,000,000
Operating Cash Flow						
Capital Expenditure						
EBITDA						
Return on Assets %						
Return on Equity %						
Debt to Equity						

CONTACT INFORMATION:

Phone: 847-286-2500   Fax: 847-286-5500
Toll-Free:
Address: 3333 Beverly Rd., Hoffman Estates, IL 60179 United States

STOCK TICKER/OTHER:

Stock Ticker: Subsidiary   Exchange:
Employees: 100,000   Fiscal Year Ends: 01/31
Parent Company: SEARS HOLDINGS CORPORATION

SALARIES/BONUSES:

Top Exec. Salary: $ Bonus: $
Second Exec. Salary: $ Bonus: $

OTHER THOUGHTS:

Estimated Female Officers or Directors:
Hot Spot for Advancement for Women/Minorities:

Kohl's Corp

www.kohls.com

NAIC Code: 452112

TYPES OF BUSINESS:

Discount Department Stores
Online Sales

BRANDS/DIVISIONS/AFFILIATES:

Kohls.com
Off-Aisle by Kohl

CONTACTS:
Note: Officers with more than one job title may be intentionally listed here more than once.

Wesley Mcdonald, CFO
Richard Schepp, Chief Administrative Officer
Sona Chawla, COO
Jason Kelroy, Executive VP
Michelle Gass, Other Executive Officer
Kevin Mansell, President

GROWTH PLANS/SPECIAL FEATURES:

Kohl's Corp. operates family-oriented specialty department stores. The company currently operates 1,162 stores in 49 states, with three store formats: prototype (approximately 88,000 square feet of retail space), small (approximately 68,000 square feet of retail space) and urban (approximately 125,000 square feet of retail space). Kohl's stores offer apparel, shoes and accessories for women, children and men; soft home products, such as sheets and pillows; and other home products, such as small electronics and luggage. The stores' brands include Dockers, Lee, Levi's, Jockey, Candie's, Nike, Dana Buchman, LC Lauren Conrad, Simply Vera Vera Wang, Dana Buchman Food Network and FILA Sport. Approximately 30% of Kohl's' merchandise is marketed towards women, 20% is marketed towards men, 18% is comprised of home furnishing products, 13% is designed for children, 10% is comprised of accessories and 9% is comprised of footwear. In addition to its physical retail locations, the company also markets its products through its e-commerce site, Kohls.com. The company maintains nine distribution centers located in Ohio, Texas, Virginia, Missouri, New York, California, Georgia and Illinois, and e-commerce fulfillment centers in Monroe, Ohio; Edgewood, Maryland; DeSoto, Texas; and San Bernardino, California. Kohl's has started an off-price format called Off-Aisle by Kohl, in which all sales are final.

The company offers its employees medical, dental and vision insurance; long-term disability and life insurance; a 401(k) plan; tuition reimbursement; onsite fitness classes, farmers market, child care, dry cleaning and food service; adoption assistance; parental leave; vacation; and merchandise discounts.

FINANCIAL DATA:
Note: Data for latest year may not have been available at press time.

In U.S. $	2015	2014	2013	2012	2011	2010
Revenue	19,023,000,000	19,031,000,000	19,279,000,000	18,804,000,000	18,391,000,000	17,178,000,000
R&D Expense						
Operating Income	1,689,000,000	1,742,000,000	1,890,000,000	2,158,000,000	1,914,000,000	1,712,000,000
Operating Margin %	8.87%	9.15%	9.80%	11.47%	10.40%	9.96%
SGA Expense	4,350,000,000	4,313,000,000	4,267,000,000	4,243,000,000	4,462,000,000	4,196,000,000
Net Income	867,000,000	889,000,000	986,000,000	1,167,000,000	1,114,000,000	991,000,000
Operating Cash Flow	2,024,000,000	1,884,000,000	1,265,000,000	2,143,000,000	1,676,000,000	2,234,000,000
Capital Expenditure	682,000,000	643,000,000	785,000,000	927,000,000	761,000,000	666,000,000
EBITDA	2,575,000,000	2,631,000,000	2,723,000,000	2,940,000,000	2,579,000,000	2,313,000,000
Return on Assets %	6.01%	6.28%	7.04%	8.43%	8.33%	8.09%
Return on Equity %	14.48%	14.78%	15.70%	15.97%	13.96%	13.58%
Debt to Equity	0.77	0.78	0.73	0.63	0.20	0.26

CONTACT INFORMATION:

Phone: 262 703-7000   Fax: 262 703-6373
Toll-Free:
Address: N56 W17000 Ridgewood Dr., Menomonee Falls, WI 53051 United States

STOCK TICKER/OTHER:

Stock Ticker: KSS
Employees: 137,000
Parent Company:

Exchange: NYS
Fiscal Year Ends: 01/31

SALARIES/BONUSES:

Top Exec. Salary: $1,352,700   Bonus: $
Second Exec. Salary: $932,600   Bonus: $

OTHER THOUGHTS:

Estimated Female Officers or Directors:

Hot Spot for Advancement for Women/Minorities: Y

Koninklijke Ahold NV

NAIC Code: 445110

www.ahold.com

TYPES OF BUSINESS:

Grocery Stores & Supermarkets
Food Distribution
Drugstores
Liquor Stores
Pharmacies
Online Groceries & Home Delivery
Convenience Stores

BRANDS/DIVISIONS/AFFILIATES:

Ahold USA
Stop & Shop New England
Giant-Landover
Giant-Carlisle
Gall & Gall
Peapod
Albert Heijn
Pingo Doce

CONTACTS: *Note: Officers with more than one job title may be intentionally listed here more than once.*

Dick Boer, CEO
Jeff Carr, CFO
Hanneke Faber, Chief Commercial Officer
Abbe Luersman, Chief Human Resources Officer
Lodewijk Hijmans van den Bergh, Chief Corp. Governance Counsel
James McCann, Chief Dev. Officer
Sander van der Laan, COO-Ahold Europe
Jan Hommen, Chmn.
James McCann, COO-Ahold U.S.

GROWTH PLANS/SPECIAL FEATURES:

Koninklijke Ahold NV (Ahold) is an international holdin
company for 3,206 local grocery store chains and foo
distribution companies in the U.S. and Europe that operat
under their own brand names. Ahold USA, the company's U.S
holding subsidiary, operates over 586 grocery stores and
handful of pharmacies, primarily on the eastern seaboar
through four retail operating subsidiaries: Stop & Shop Ne
England, Stop & Shop Metro New York, Giant-Landover an
Giant-Carlisle. Ahold also has a majority stake in Peapod, a
Internet-based grocery site that offers home delivery. Interne
sales account for an increasing amount of company revenue
It distributes national, private-label and signature brand foo
items and related products to customers, including restaurants
health care facilities, lodging establishments, cafeteria
schools and colleges. Ahold's Netherlands' operations includ
wholly-owned and majority-owned subsidiaries that operat
hypermarkets, supermarkets and convenience stores. In th
Netherlands, the company operates Albert Heijn, Etos (
drugstore chain), Gall & Gall (liquor stores) and bol.com, a
online shopping portal that sells general merchandise. Th
Czech Republic segment consists of Albert compact hype
markets and supermarkets and in Portugal, it operates Ping
Doce. The firm also holds a 49% interest in JMR - Gestao d
Empresas de Retalho, SGPS. S.A. (JMR). In June 2015
Delhaize Group, owner of the Food Lion and Giant stores i
America, agreed to merge with Ahold, The combine
companies will be named Ahold Delhaize and have 6,500 tota
stores in America and Europe, along with 375,000 employees

FINANCIAL DATA: *Note: Data for latest year may not have been available at press time.*

In U.S. $	2015	2014	2013	2012	2011	2010
Revenue		42,000,000,000	43,614,601,216	42,833,685,586	39,200,000,000	39,111,300,000
R&D Expense						
Operating Income						
Operating Margin %						
SGA Expense						
Net Income						
Operating Cash Flow						
Capital Expenditure						
EBITDA						
Return on Assets %						
Return on Equity %						
Debt to Equity						

CONTACT INFORMATION:

Phone: 31 886595100   Fax:
Toll-Free:
Address: Piet Heinkade 167-173, Amsterdam, 1019 GM Netherlands

STOCK TICKER/OTHER:

Stock Ticker: AHONY   Exchange: GREY
Employees: 230,000   Fiscal Year Ends: 12/31
Parent Company:

SALARIES/BONUSES:

Top Exec. Salary: $ Bonus: $
Second Exec. Salary: $ Bonus: $

OTHER THOUGHTS:

Estimated Female Officers or Directors: 3
Hot Spot for Advancement for Women/Minorities: Y

Kroger Co (The)

www.kroger.com

NAIC Code: 445110

TYPES OF BUSINESS:

Grocery Stores
Convenience Stores
Jewelry Stores
Pharmacies
Food Processing
Gas Stations
Department Stores

BRANDS/DIVISIONS/AFFILIATES:

Kroger
Fry's
Fred Meyer
QFC
Ralphs
Smith's
King Soopers
Quik Stop

CONTACTS: *Note: Officers with more than one job title may be intentionally listed here more than once.*

W. Mcmullen, CEO
Lynn Marmer, Vice President, Divisional
J. Schlotman, CFO
M. Van Oflen, Chief Accounting Officer
Christopher Hjelm, Chief Information Officer
Mark Tuffin, Senior VP
Geoffrey Covert, Senior VP
Kathleen Barclay, Senior VP, Divisional
M. Perry, Senior VP, Divisional
Alessandro Tosolini, Senior VP, Divisional
Michael Donnelly, Senior VP, Divisional
Todd Foley, Treasurer
Kevin Dougherty, Vice President, Divisional
Timothy Massa, Vice President, Divisional
Robert Clark, Vice President, Divisional
Erin Sharp, Vice President, Divisional
Christine Wheatley, Vice President, Divisional

GROWTH PLANS/SPECIAL FEATURES:

The Kroger Co. is one of the largest supermarket operators in the U.S. The company operates 2,625 supermarkets under a variety of names, such as Kroger, City Market, Dillons, Jay C, Food 4 Less, Fred Meyer, Fry's, Harris Teeter, King Soopers, QFC, Ralphs and Smith's. More than 1,300 of these stores have fuel centers. Kroger's supermarkets operate under one of four store formats: combination food and drug stores, multi-department stores, marketplace stores and price impact warehouses. The combo stores are the primary food store format and typically draw customers from a 2 to 2.5 mile radius; multi-department stores are larger in size than combos and sell merchandise such as apparel, home furnishings, dÃ©cor, outdoor living, electronics, automotive products, toys and fine jewelry; marketplace stores offer full-service grocery, pharmacy and beauty care departments, as well as general merchandise; and price impact warehouses offer low cost promotions for grocery, health and beauty items. Kroger's stores offer one-stop shopping including whole health sections, pharmacies, pet centers and world-class perishables, such as fresh seafood and organic produce. The firm also operates 782 convenience stores under the Quik Stop, Loaf N' Jug, Tom Thumb, Turkey Hill, Kwik Shop and Smith's Express names. Kroger's 326 fine jewelry stores operate under the Fred Meyer brand. Kroger manages a number of walk-in medical clinics located in its stores. The company operates 37 manufacturing plants, which supply approximately 40% of the corporate brand units sold in its retail outlets. These plants consist of 17 dairies, nine deli or bakery plants, five grocery product plants, two beverage plants, two meat plants and two cheese plants. In 2015, the firm agreed to acquire the 7-store Hillers Market chain in Southeast Michigan, which will operate under the Kroger banner.

The firm offers employees medical, dental, vision, prescription, life and personal accident insurance; disability coverage; flexible spending accounts; home owners and auto insurance; an employee assistance plan; credit union membership; a continuing education program; a stock purchase plan; and professional liability coverage.

FINANCIAL DATA: *Note: Data for latest year may not have been available at press time.*

In U.S. $	2015	2014	2013	2012	2011	2010
Revenue	108,465,000,000	98,375,000,000	96,751,000,000	90,374,000,000	82,189,000,000	76,733,000,000
R&D Expense						
Operating Income	3,137,000,000	2,725,000,000	2,764,000,000	1,278,000,000	2,182,000,000	1,091,000,000
Operating Margin %	2.89%	2.76%	2.85%	1.41%	2.65%	1.42%
SGA Expense	17,868,000,000	15,809,000,000	15,477,000,000	15,964,000,000	14,462,000,000	14,046,000,000
Net Income	1,728,000,000	1,519,000,000	1,497,000,000	602,000,000	1,116,000,000	70,000,000
Operating Cash Flow	4,163,000,000	3,380,000,000	2,833,000,000	2,658,000,000	3,366,000,000	2,922,000,000
Capital Expenditure	2,831,000,000	2,330,000,000	2,062,000,000	1,898,000,000	1,919,000,000	2,297,000,000
EBITDA	5,085,000,000	4,428,000,000	4,416,000,000	2,916,000,000	3,782,000,000	2,616,000,000
Return on Assets %	5.77%	5.63%	6.22%	2.56%	4.78%	.30%
Return on Equity %	32.01%	31.67%	36.56%	12.97%	22.03%	1.39%
Debt to Equity	1.80	1.79	1.46	1.72	1.37	1.54

CONTACT INFORMATION:

Phone: 513 762-4000   Fax: 513 762-1575
Toll-Free: 866-221-4141
Address: 1014 Vine St., Cincinnati, OH 45202 United States

STOCK TICKER/OTHER:

Stock Ticker: KR
Employees: 400,000
Parent Company:

Exchange: NYS
Fiscal Year Ends: 01/31

SALARIES/BONUSES:

Top Exec. Salary: $1,365,923   Bonus: $
Second Exec. Salary: $1,123,393   Bonus: $

OTHER THOUGHTS:

Estimated Female Officers or Directors: 5

Hot Spot for Advancement for Women/Minorities: Y

L Brands Inc

www.lb.com

NAIC Code: 448120

TYPES OF BUSINESS:

Apparel, Retail
Contract Manufacturing
Apparel Importing
Catalog & Online Sales
Lingerie
Cosmetics
Fragrances
Candles

BRANDS/DIVISIONS/AFFILIATES:

Victoria's Secret
Bath & Body Works
Victoria's Secret U.K.
White Barn Candle Company
C.O. Bigelow
La Senza
Henri Bendel
VictoriasSecret.com

CONTACTS: Note: Officers with more than one job title may be intentionally listed here more than once.

Charles McGuigan, CEO, Divisional
Nicholas Coe, CEO, Divisional
Sharen Turney, CEO, Subsidiary
Stuart Burgdoerfer, CFO
Leslie Wexner, Founder

GROWTH PLANS/SPECIAL FEATURES:

L Brands, Inc. is an apparel, lingerie, personal care products, accessories and fragrances retailer operating under various brand names, including Victoria's Secret and Bath & Body Works. The company operates approximately 2,969 retail stores. Victoria's Secret and Victoria's Secret U.K., with approximately 1,100 stores in the U.S., Canada and the U.K., are specialty retailers of women's intimate apparel, beauty products and related accessories. Victoria's Secret's direct marketing segment is in charge of the catalog. Bath & Body Works, with 1,600 stores in the U.S. and Canada, features personal care products and also operates White Barn Candle Company to supply its candle needs and C.O. Bigelow in Chicago for body products. L Brands also retains full ownership of the approximately 29 Henri Bendel women's personal care, apparel and accessory stores. In addition, the firm owns a 49% interest in Mast Global, a contract manufacturer and apparel importer, which supplies merchandise to Victoria's Secret, Express and Limited Stores. Finally, the company operates La Senza, a Canadian lingerie company with more than 140 stores in Canada. L Brands runs four e-commerce sites: VictoriasSecret.com, HenriBendel.com, LaSenza.com and BathandBodyWorks.com.

L Brands offers its employees medical, dental, prescription, life and vision insurance; short- and long-term disability coverage; an employee assistance program; flexible spending; a retirement plan; a 401(k); a stock purchase plan; product discounts; tuition assistance; paid time off; and adoption assistance.

FINANCIAL DATA: Note: Data for latest year may not have been available at press time.

In U.S. $	2015	2014	2013	2012	2011	2010
Revenue	11,454,000,000	10,773,000,000	10,459,000,000	10,364,000,000	9,613,000,000	8,632,001,000
R&D Expense						
Operating Income	1,953,000,000	1,743,000,000	1,573,000,000	1,238,000,000	1,284,000,000	868,000,000
Operating Margin %	17.05%	16.17%	15.03%	11.94%	13.35%	10.05%
SGA Expense	2,855,000,000	2,686,000,000	2,720,000,000	2,698,000,000	2,341,000,000	2,166,000,000
Net Income	1,042,000,000	903,000,000	753,000,000	850,000,000	805,000,000	448,000,000
Operating Cash Flow	1,786,000,000	1,248,000,000	1,351,000,000	1,266,000,000	1,284,000,000	1,174,000,000
Capital Expenditure	715,000,000	691,000,000	588,000,000	426,000,000	274,000,000	202,000,000
EBITDA	2,398,000,000	2,167,000,000	1,986,000,000	1,864,000,000	1,853,000,000	1,280,000,000
Return on Assets %	14.13%	13.66%	12.41%	13.53%	11.81%	6.33%
Return on Equity %				105.39%	44.00%	22.08%
Debt to Equity	264.72			25.40	1.69	1.24

CONTACT INFORMATION:

Phone: 614 415-7000   Fax: 614 479-7440
Toll-Free:
Address: 3 Limited Pkwy., Columbus, OH 43230 United States

STOCK TICKER/OTHER:

Stock Ticker: LB
Employees: 80,100
Parent Company:

Exchange: NYS
Fiscal Year Ends: 01/31

SALARIES/BONUSES:

Top Exec. Salary: $1,924,000
Bonus: $

Second Exec. Salary: $1,442,000
Bonus: $

OTHER THOUGHTS:

Estimated Female Officers or Directors: 1

Hot Spot for Advancement for Women/Minorities: Y

L L Bean Inc

www.llbean.com

NAIC Code: 454113

TYPES OF BUSINESS:

Outdoor Apparel, Catalogs
Camping & Fishing Equipment
Footwear
Housewares
Online Sales
Outdoor Activity Classes

BRANDS/DIVISIONS/AFFILIATES:

Bean Boots by L L Bean
L L Bean Outdoor Discovery Schools
L.L. Bean Outlet Store
L.L. Bean

CONTACTS: Note: Officers with more than one job title may be intentionally listed here more than once.

Christopher J. McCormick, CEO
Christopher J. McCormick, Pres.
Mark Fasold, CFO
Shawn Gorman, Chmn.

GROWTH PLANS/SPECIAL FEATURES:

L.L. Bean, Inc. is a retailer of more than 20,000 outdoor-related products, including apparel for men, women and children; footwear; luggage; housewares; and equipment for outdoor activities such as camping, hiking and fishing. With initial mail-order operations dating to 1912, the company now offers products through its retail stores, e-commerce sites and approximately 50 annual catalogs distributed to more than 170 countries. The company currently operates retail stores in the U.S., Japan and China, including its Freeport, Maine flagship store, a 200,000-square foot facility open 24-hours-a-day, year-round. U.S. locations outside of Maine include approximately 26 L.L. Bean stores and 10 L.L. Bean Outlet stores. Internationally, the company operates 21 stores in Japan. L.L. Bean's merchandise includes the Bean Boots by L. L. Bean, one of the company's signature products; boating gear; tote bags; and customized corporate and business items. The company manufactures its products at two facilities in Brunswick and Lewiston, Maine. In addition to retailing, the firm offers L. L. Bean Outdoor Discovery Schools, which provide adventures and programs that assist customers in discovering a variety of outdoor activities. In November 2015, the company opened its first Kansas store, becoming L. L. Bean's 26th U.S. store outside of Maine. It plans to open additional stores in the near future.

L.L. Bean offers employees benefits including health coverage; flexible spending accounts; an employee assistance program; life and disability insurance; a 401(k) plan and a company-paid pension plan; tuition reimbursement; employee discounts; onsite fitness programs and subsidies for gym memberships; the use of company vacation properties; and access to the Employee Use Room, which allows employees to borrow gear for outdoor activities.

FINANCIAL DATA: Note: Data for latest year may not have been available at press time.

In U.S. $	2015	2014	2013	2012	2011	2010
Revenue		1,610,000,000	1,521,000,000	1,520,000,000	1,450,000,000	1,400,000,000
R&D Expense						
Operating Income						
Operating Margin %						
SGA Expense						
Net Income		650,000,000	630,000,000	600,000,000		
Operating Cash Flow						
Capital Expenditure						
EBITDA						
Return on Assets %						
Return on Equity %						
Debt to Equity						

CONTACT INFORMATION:

Phone: 207-552-3028   Fax: 207-552-3080
Toll-Free: 800-441-5713
Address: 15 Casco St., Freeport, ME 04033 United States

STOCK TICKER/OTHER:

Stock Ticker: Private   Exchange:
Employees: 5,300   Fiscal Year Ends: 02/28
Parent Company:

SALARIES/BONUSES:

Top Exec. Salary: $ Bonus: $
Second Exec. Salary: $ Bonus: $

OTHER THOUGHTS:

Estimated Female Officers or Directors:
Hot Spot for Advancement for Women/Minorities:

Lacoste SA

www.lacoste.com

NAIC Code: 424300

TYPES OF BUSINESS:

Apparel and Clothing Brands, Designers, Importers and Distributors
Men's, Women's & Children's Apparel Stores
Apparel-Manufacturing
Apparel-Accessories
Home Textiles
Fragrances

BRANDS/DIVISIONS/AFFILIATES:

Lacoste Champions
Devanlay SA
Groupe Maus Freres SA

CONTACTS: *Note: Officers with more than one job title may be intentionally listed here more than once.*

Thierry Louis Joseph Guibert, CEO
Felipe Oliveira Baptista, Artistic Dir.
Marc Lumet, Sr. Exec. VP
Jean-Claude Fauvet, Sr. Exec. VP

GROWTH PLANS/SPECIAL FEATURES:

Lacoste SA is a manufacturer and retailer of fashionable spo
and street clothes for young men and women. Lacost
operates as a subsidiary of Groupe Maus Freres SA. Th
company revolutionized sportswear by placing Lacoste
trademark crocodile logo on its line of simple, lightweight cotto
polo shirts. Lacoste continues to market its clothing fo
amateurs and professionals of golf, tennis and yachting (it
traditional clientele), but it has also branched out into mor
general club and casual lines. In addition to a variety of appar
and shoes for casual, sport and club settings, Lacoste offers
kaleidoscope of accessories, including leather goods, belts
watches, footwear, key chains, linens, umbrellas, eyewear an
its own line of fragrances. Though some clothing i
manufactured in France, the firm owns several internationa
production facilities. Devanlay owns the exclusive rights to
manufacture Lacoste brand apparel; however, severa
companies were granted licensing agreements, such as the
Charment Group and Movado Group, which produce Lacoste
brand eyewear and watches. The company also granted the
manufacturing rights of its fragrance line to Proctor & Gamble
In addition, Lacoste offers sponsorships to the Lacoste
Champions, a group of professional golfers, yachters and
tennis players who endorse the company's clothing.

FINANCIAL DATA: *Note: Data for latest year may not have been available at press time.*

In U.S. $	2015	2014	2013	2012	2011	2010
Revenue		2,400,000,000	2,355,000,000	2,189,000,000	2,095,410,000	1,850,000,000
R&D Expense						
Operating Income						
Operating Margin %						
SGA Expense						
Net Income						
Operating Cash Flow						
Capital Expenditure						
EBITDA						
Return on Assets %						
Return on Equity %						
Debt to Equity						

CONTACT INFORMATION:

Phone: 33-8-99-868243   Fax: 33-1-42-611849
Toll-Free: 800-452-2678
Address: 6 Rue de la Chaussee D'Antin, Paris, 75009 France

STOCK TICKER/OTHER:

Stock Ticker: Subsidiary   Exchange:
Employees: 1,100   Fiscal Year Ends:
Parent Company: Groupe Maus Freres SA

SALARIES/BONUSES:

Top Exec. Salary: $ Bonus: $
Second Exec. Salary: $ Bonus: $

OTHER THOUGHTS:

Estimated Female Officers or Directors: 1
Hot Spot for Advancement for Women/Minorities:

Lands End Inc

www.landsend.com

NAIC Code: 454113

TYPES OF BUSINESS:

Casual Apparel, Catalogs
Retail & Outlet Stores
Online Sales
Luggage
Home Products

BRANDS/DIVISIONS/AFFILIATES:

Lands' End Canvas
LandsEnd.com
Lands' End

CONTACTS: *Note: Officers with more than one job title may be intentionally listed here more than once.*

Josephine Linden, Director
Federica Marchionni, Director
Michael Rosera, Executive VP
Kelly Ritchie, Senior VP, Divisional
Steven Rado, Senior VP
Dorian Williams, Senior VP
Bernard McCracken, Vice President

GROWTH PLANS/SPECIAL FEATURES:

Lands' End, Inc. is a leading direct retailer of traditionally-styled casual clothing for men, women and children as well as outerwear, swimwear, home products and wheeled and soft luggage. The company's products are offered through regular mailings of its primary and specialty catalogs, retail and outlet stores and via the Internet, at LandsEnd.com. The firm also operates several Inlet stores throughout the U.S. The firm additionally offers -¨not quite perfect' clothing and accessories at up to 70% off original catalog prices. A selection of Lands' End merchandise can also be found in Lands' End shops in select Sears retail locations. In addition, Lands' End has developed web sites for customers in the U.K., Japan, Austria, Germany, Canada and France as well as a business outfitters web site. The firm's Lands' End Canvas collection features updated designs and fits of classic casual apparel at higher price points than its regular collection. In April 2014, the firm was spun-off from Sears Holdings Corporation, and began trading publicly under the Nasdaq symbol LE.

Lands' End offers its employees health insurance, a retirement savings plan, employee discounts and emergency child care.

FINANCIAL DATA: *Note: Data for latest year may not have been available at press time.*

In U.S. $	2015	2014	2013	2012	2011	2010
Revenue	1,555,353,000	1,562,876,000	1,585,927,000	1,725,627,000		
R&D Expense						
Operating Income	139,643,000	128,341,000	82,003,000	121,808,000		
Operating Margin %	8.97%	8.21%	5.17%	7.05%		
SGA Expense	573,335,000	560,327,000	598,916,000	621,020,000		
Net Income	73,799,000	78,847,000	49,827,000	76,234,000		
Operating Cash Flow	211,121,000	114,919,000	96,248,000	14,510,000		
Capital Expenditure	16,608,000	9,887,000	14,993,000	15,119,000		
EBITDA	160,754,000	149,940,000	105,124,000	144,494,000		
Return on Assets %	5.79%	6.53%	4.09%			
Return on Equity %	12.33%	9.76%	6.05%			
Debt to Equity	1.25					

CONTACT INFORMATION:

Phone: 608-935-6170   Fax: 800-332-0103
Toll-Free: 800-963-4816
Address: 1 Lands' End Ln., Dodgeville, WI 53595 United States

SALARIES/BONUSES:

Top Exec. Salary: $833,654   Bonus: $150,000
Second Exec. Salary: $608,077   Bonus: $50,000

STOCK TICKER/OTHER:

Stock Ticker: LE
Employees: 6,000
Parent Company:

Exchange: NAS
Fiscal Year Ends: 12/31

OTHER THOUGHTS:

Estimated Female Officers or Directors: 4
Hot Spot for Advancement for Women/Minorities: Y

Lawson Inc

NAIC Code: 445120

TYPES OF BUSINESS:

Convenience Stores
ATM Operation
Entertainment Ticket Sales
E-commerce
International Franchising

BRANDS/DIVISIONS/AFFILIATES:

Lawson Mart Inc
Lawson ATM Networks Inc
Lawson HMV Entertainment Inc
Shanghai Hualian Lawson Inc
Lawson Okinawa Inc
Lawson
Lawson Store100
Natural Lawson

CONTACTS: Note: Officers with more than one job title may be intentionally listed here more than once.

Takeshi Niinami, CEO
Genichi Tamatsuka, COO
Takeshi Niinami, Pres.
Ichiro Kijima, Dir.-Mktg. Office
Tatsushi Satou, CIO
Masaharu Kamo, Group CEO-e-commerce
Kei Murayama, Dir.-Franchise Support

GROWTH PLANS/SPECIAL FEATURES:

Lawson, Inc. operates and franchises a chain of convenience stores located predominately in Japan. The company's 11,606 stores in Japan include three primary formats: conventional Lawson stores, Lawson Store100 and Natural Lawson. The conventional Lawson locations carry a variety of traditional convenience store items. These locations typically feature merchandise assortments based on the location, with an increasing number of these locations offering fresh food options. Lawson Store100 locations, typically situated in residential districts in metro Tokyo, stock an increased number of perishable items such as dairy, tofu and delicatessen products and cater largely to housewives and seniors. The Lawson Store100 brand is marketed and operated by Lawson Mart, Inc., a subsidiary of Lawson, Inc. Natural Lawson stores are geared more towards private products for health-conscious consumers and tend to be located in office and residential areas in major cities. Outside of Japan, the company operates or has franchised 411 stores in Shanghai, 110 stores in Chongqing, 39 stores in Dalian and 26 stores in Beijing. In addition to China, Lawson has 37 locations in Indonesia, 38 stores in Thailand and two stores in Hawaii. Beyond these stores, the company also offers a number of services through subsidiaries. Lawson ATM Networks, Inc. installs and services a network of roughly 8,614 ATMs across the country. Lawson HMV Entertainment, Inc. sells tickets to music, theater, sporting events and other attractions primarily through in-store Loppi and L Paca terminals. It also offers Internet merchandise sales and marketing businesses linked to Lawson stores. Other subsidiaries include Shanghai Hualian Lawson, Inc. and Lawson Okinawa, Inc.

FINANCIAL DATA: Note: Data for latest year may not have been available at press time.

In U.S. $	2015	2014	2013	2012	2011	2010
Revenue	4,040,649,000	3,937,854,000	3,955,691,000	3,886,810,000	3,581,030,000	3,791,335,000
R&D Expense						
Operating Income	571,973,400	552,854,100	537,597,600	501,266,000	450,716,600	407,990,200
Operating Margin %	14.15%	14.03%	13.59%	12.89%	12.58%	10.76%
SGA Expense		317,846,900	303,239,600	287,155,300	262,655,600	271,200,900
Net Income	268,774,400	309,699,300	271,809,500	208,097,300	212,544,400	102,519,000
Operating Cash Flow	897,270,000	661,410,800	691,315,100	700,793,700	585,996,400	330,246,900
Capital Expenditure	397,262,000	327,495,800	348,311,200	294,702,400	246,652,500	285,532,300
EBITDA	825,434,600	884,285,800	849,707,000	691,834,500	636,854,300	468,537,500
Return on Assets %	4.71%	6.32%	5.97%	4.94%	5.49%	2.84%
Return on Equity %	13.01%	16.06%	15.13%	11.97%	12.81%	6.47%
Debt to Equity	0.52	0.25	0.20	0.17	0.14	0.10

CONTACT INFORMATION:

Phone: 81-3-54352770   Fax:
Toll-Free:
Address: East Twr., Gate City Ohsaki, 11-2, Osaki 1-chome, Tokyo, 141-8643 Japan

STOCK TICKER/OTHER:

Stock Ticker: LWSOF
Employees: 5,700
Parent Company:

Exchange: GREY
Fiscal Year Ends:

SALARIES/BONUSES:

Top Exec. Salary: $ Bonus: $
Second Exec. Salary: $ Bonus: $

OTHER THOUGHTS:

Estimated Female Officers or Directors:
Hot Spot for Advancement for Women/Minorities:

La-Z-Boy Incorporated

www.la-z-boy.com

NAIC Code: 337121

TYPES OF BUSINESS:

Furniture Stores
Furniture Manufacturing

BRANDS/DIVISIONS/AFFILIATES:

La-Z-Boy Furniture Galleries
Comfort Studio
England Custom Comfort Center
American Drew
Hammary
Kincaid
La-Z-Boy

CONTACTS: Note: Officers with more than one job title may be intentionally listed here more than once.

Kurt Darrow, CEO
Louis Riccio, CFO
Margaret Mueller, Chief Accounting Officer
Otis Sawyer, President, Divisional
Steven Kincaid, President, Divisional
Mark Bacon, President, Divisional
James Klarr, Secretary
Darrell Edwards, Senior VP
J. Collier, Senior VP

GROWTH PLANS/SPECIAL FEATURES:

La-Z-Boy Incorporated manufactures, markets, imports, distributes and sells upholstered furniture and casegoods (wood) furniture for the home and office as well as for the hospitality, health care and assisted living industries. La-Z-Boy operates in three segments: upholstery, casegoods and retail. The upholstery segment manufactures, imports and exports upholstered furniture such as recliners & motion furniture, sofas, loveseats, chairs, sectionals, modular, ottomans and sleeper sofas, all under the La-Z-Boy brand. This division sells directly to La-Z-Boy Furniture Galleries stores, operators of Comfort Studio and England Custom Comfort Center locations, major dealers, as well as other independent retailers. The casegoods segment is an importer, marketer and distributor of casegoods (wood) furniture such as bedroom sets, dining room sets, entertainment centers and occasional pieces. This division all manufactures some coordinated upholstered furniture. Casegoods consists of three brands: American Drew, Hammary and Kincaid, and sells primarily to major dealers. The retail segment consists of 110 company-owned La-Z-Boy Furniture Galleries stores and primarily sells upholstered furniture to the end consumer through its retail network. In 2014, the firm sold its Bauhaus USA business unit; and closed its Lea Industries operations and liquidated its assets after being unable to sell the company.

FINANCIAL DATA: Note: Data for latest year may not have been available at press time.

In U.S. $	2015	2014	2013	2012	2011	2010
Revenue	1,425,395,000	1,357,318,000	1,332,525,000	1,231,676,000	1,187,143,000	1,179,212,000
R&D Expense						
Operating Income	103,165,000	89,296,000	67,627,000	49,631,000	25,909,000	41,943,000
Operating Margin %	7.23%	6.57%	5.07%	4.02%	2.18%	3.55%
SGA Expense	401,459,000	375,158,000	357,312,000	330,226,000	323,314,000	331,491,000
Net Income	70,773,000	55,056,000	46,389,000	87,966,000	24,047,000	32,538,000
Operating Cash Flow	86,751,000	90,832,000	68,440,000	82,848,000	27,846,000	89,659,000
Capital Expenditure	70,319,000	33,730,000	25,912,000	15,663,000	10,540,000	10,986,000
EBITDA	128,434,000	115,289,000	94,596,000	91,727,000	52,614,000	72,939,000
Return on Assets %	9.10%	7.38%	6.59%	13.75%	4.00%	5.60%
Return on Equity %	13.45%	10.93%	10.01%	21.90%	6.83%	10.04%
Debt to Equity			0.01	0.01	0.08	0.13

CONTACT INFORMATION:

Phone: 734 242-1444   Fax: 734 241-4422
Toll-Free: 800-375-6890
Address: One La-Z-Boy Drive, Monroe, MI 48162 United States

STOCK TICKER/OTHER:

Stock Ticker: LZB
Employees: 8,270
Parent Company:

Exchange: NYS
Fiscal Year Ends: 04/30

SALARIES/BONUSES:

Top Exec. Salary: $904,983   Bonus: $
Second Exec. Salary: $496,657   Bonus: $

OTHER THOUGHTS:

Estimated Female Officers or Directors: 1
Hot Spot for Advancement for Women/Minorities: Y

Les Schwab Tire Centers

NAIC Code: 441320

www.lesschwab.com

TYPES OF BUSINESS:

Tires, Retail
Alignments, Shock & Brake Service
Battery & Shock Retail

BRANDS/DIVISIONS/AFFILIATES:

Fleet Tire System

CONTACTS: *Note: Officers with more than one job title may be intentionally listed here more than once.*

Dick Borgman, CEO
Jack Cuniff, CFO
Dale Thompson, Chief Mktg. Officer
Scott Robins, Mgr.-Fleet Tire Systems
Brian Capp, VP-Mktg.
Dick Borgman, Chmn.
Ken Edwards, VP-Supply Chain Mgmt.

GROWTH PLANS/SPECIAL FEATURES:

Les Schwab Tire Centers independently operates a chain of stores that sell tires, wheels and batteries in addition to performing alignments, shock and brake services. Founder Les Schwab started the company in 1952 with the purchase of one tire store, and has expanded the group since to include over 450 company-owned stores and member dealer locations in the western U.S. Stores are located throughout California, Idaho, Montana, Nevada, Oregon, Utah, Colorado, Alaska and Washington. The company's corporate operations are in central Oregon, where it runs one of the largest retreading facilities in the U.S. and maintains a distribution center. The firm provides tires for passenger cars, light trucks, SUVs and farm vehicles as well as specialty tires such as ATV, motor home, boat and trailer, golf cart and lawn and garden tires. The firm's Fleet Tire System offers services to commercial accounts. Additionally, the company markets custom wheels and snow tires. Les Schwab Tire Centers also retails a variety of batteries for cars, buses, farm equipment, lawn and garden, aircraft and military, light trucks, motor homes, industrial equipment, RVs and boat trailers, golf carts, heavy trucks and equipment, motorcycles, ATVs and floor sweepers. Moreover, the firm retails a variety of shocks for light trucks, SUVs, lifted light trucks and passenger cars. Services include complete front-disc brake service, complete rear-drum brake services, performance suspension lifting and lowering solutions as well as standard, thrust and four-wheel alignment services.

Les Schwab Tire Centers offer its employees a benefits package that includes a retiree health plan; medical, dental, life and vision coverage; a retirement program; and vacation pay.

FINANCIAL DATA: *Note: Data for latest year may not have been available at press time.*

In U.S. $	2015	2014	2013	2012	2011	2010
Revenue		1,660,000,000	1,650,000,000	1,600,000,000	1,500,000,000	1,400,000,000
R&D Expense						
Operating Income						
Operating Margin %						
SGA Expense						
Net Income						
Operating Cash Flow						
Capital Expenditure						
EBITDA						
Return on Assets %						
Return on Equity %						
Debt to Equity						

CONTACT INFORMATION:

Phone: 541-447-4136　　　Fax: 541-416-5488
Toll-Free:
Address: 20900 Cooley Rd., Bend, OR 97701 United States

SALARIES/BONUSES:

Top Exec. Salary: $　　　　Bonus: $
Second Exec. Salary: $　　　Bonus: $

STOCK TICKER/OTHER:

Stock Ticker: Private
Employees: 7,900
Parent Company:

Exchange:
Fiscal Year Ends: 12/31

OTHER THOUGHTS:

Estimated Female Officers or Directors: 1
Hot Spot for Advancement for Women/Minorities:

Leslie's Poolmart Inc

www.lesliespool.com

NAIC Code: 444130

TYPES OF BUSINESS:

Swimming Pool Supplies, Retail
Catalog & Online Sales
Installation, Repair & Maintenance Services

BRANDS/DIVISIONS/AFFILIATES:

Leslie's Swimming Pool Supplies

CONTACTS: *Note: Officers with more than one job title may be intentionally listed here more than once.*

Lawrence H. Hayward, CEO
Michael L. Hatch, COO
Michael L. Hatch, Pres.
Steven L. Ortega, CFO
Craig A. Wright, Exec. VP-Sales
Stephen Blakeslee, CIO
Craig A. Wright, Exec. VP-Merch.
Kory Klecker, General Counsel
Brian Agnew, Sr. VP-Retail Oper.
Tony Gonzales, Sr. VP-Commercial & Service
Lawrence H. Hayward, Chmn.
Bradley S. Smith, Sr. VP-Supply Chain & Procurement

GROWTH PLANS/SPECIAL FEATURES:

Leslie's Poolmart, Inc. is a leading national specialty retailer of swimming pool supplies and related products. The company currently markets its products through more than 850 Leslie's Swimming Pool Supplies retail stores in 35 states, a mail-order catalog and an e-commerce site. Leslie's major product categories are pool chemicals; pool equipment; pool accessories; spas and hot tubs; above-ground pools in certain stores; floats, toys and games; and backyard and patio. Leslie's also manufactures chlorine tablets and repackages a variety of bulk chemicals into various containers suitable for retail sales. Additionally, the firm formulates a variety of specialty liquids, including water clarifiers, tile cleaners, algaecides and stain preventives. Leslie's focuses on customer service, with most stores supported by a service department that offers poolside equipment installation and repair, leak detection and repair and seasonal opening and closing services; totaling about 2,400 pool experts to serve customer's needs. The company's commercial clients, which include apartments, hotels, resorts, water parks and golf courses, are offered free delivery within 25 miles, certified pool operator training, onsite inspections and chemical automation programs. During 2014, the company opened 20 new stores.

The company offers its employee's medical, vision, dental and prescription drug coverage; life and disability insurance; a 401(k); paid time off; and an employee assistance program.

FINANCIAL DATA: *Note: Data for latest year may not have been available at press time.*

In U.S. $	2015	2014	2013	2012	2011	2010
Revenue		660,000,000	652,900,000	535,000,000	530,000,000	515,000,000
R&D Expense						
Operating Income						
Operating Margin %						
SGA Expense						
Net Income						
Operating Cash Flow						
Capital Expenditure						
EBITDA						
Return on Assets %						
Return on Equity %						
Debt to Equity						

CONTACT INFORMATION:

Phone: 602-366-3999   Fax: 602-366-3934
Toll-Free: 800-537-5437
Address: 3925 E. Broadway Rd., Ste. 100, Phoenix, AZ 85040 United States

STOCK TICKER/OTHER:

Stock Ticker: Private
Employees: 3,300
Parent Company: CVC Capital Partners

Exchange:
Fiscal Year Ends: 10/31

SALARIES/BONUSES:

Top Exec. Salary: $ Bonus: $
Second Exec. Salary: $ Bonus: $

OTHER THOUGHTS:

Estimated Female Officers or Directors:
Hot Spot for Advancement for Women/Minorities:

Levi Strauss & Co

NAIC Code: 424300

www.levistrauss.com

TYPES OF BUSINESS:

Apparel and Clothing Brands, Designers, Importers and Distributors
Footwear & Accessories
Retail Stores
COM Franchised Stores

BRANDS/DIVISIONS/AFFILIATES:

501 Original
Levi's
Dockers
Levi Strauss Signature
Levi's Workwear by Filson
Denizen

CONTACTS: Note: Officers with more than one job title may be intentionally listed here more than once.

Chip Bergh, CEO
Chip Bergh, Pres.
Harmit Singh, CFO
Craig Nomura, Pres., Global Retail
Seth Jaffe, Chief Counsel
Lisa Collier, Exec. VP
Aaron Boey, Exec. VP
James Curleigh, Exec. VP
Seth Ellison, Exec. VP
Roy Bagattini, Pres., Asia, Middle East & Africa
David Love, Chief Supply Chain Officer

GROWTH PLANS/SPECIAL FEATURES:

Levi Strauss & Co. is one of the world's largest and best-recognized name brands in the apparel industry, with retail outlets in over 110 countries. Best known for its trademark 501 Original jeans, the company has recently begun transforming its clothing line, expanding its core Levi's and Dockers brands and introducing its new Levi Strauss Signature brand for value-conscious consumers in North America, Europe and Asia. In addition to jeans, the company's product line includes an array of tops, footwear, outerwear and accessories. The firm is organized into three divisions: Levi Strauss Americas, based in the company's San Francisco main office; Levi Strauss Europe, based in Brussels; and the Asia Pacific Division, based in Singapore. The company's products are sold worldwide, including 2,600 locations that are company-owned or franchised. Levi Strauss was one of the first international corporations to establish a comprehensive ethical code of conduct for its manufacturing and finishing contractors, ensuring proper working conditions for its overseas workforce. Levi Strauss' Denizen brand is a line of jeans marketed for middle-class consumers. The firm's partnership with Filson, a Seattle-based outdoor clothing retailer, produces Levi's Workwear by Filson, a line of menswear.

Levi Strauss offers employees emergency financial assistance; apparel, technology and business discounts; and medical, dental, life and vision insurance.

FINANCIAL DATA: Note: Data for latest year may not have been available at press time.

In U.S. $	2015	2014	2013	2012	2011	2010
Revenue		4,754,000,000	4,681,700,000	4,610,000,000	4,762,000,000	4,410,000,000
R&D Expense						
Operating Income						
Operating Margin %						
SGA Expense						
Net Income		104,300,000	228,100,000	144,000,000	138,000,000	157,000,000
Operating Cash Flow						
Capital Expenditure						
EBITDA						
Return on Assets %						
Return on Equity %						
Debt to Equity						

CONTACT INFORMATION:

Phone: 415-501-6000   Fax: 415-501-7112
Toll-Free:
Address: 1155 Battery St., San Francisco, CA 94111 United States

STOCK TICKER/OTHER:

Stock Ticker: Private
Employees: 17,000
Parent Company:

Exchange:
Fiscal Year Ends: 11/30

SALARIES/BONUSES:

Top Exec. Salary: $ Bonus: $
Second Exec. Salary: $ Bonus: $

OTHER THOUGHTS:

Estimated Female Officers or Directors: 4
Hot Spot for Advancement for Women/Minorities: Y

Li & Fung Limited

www.funggroup.com

NAIC Code: 488510

TYPES OF BUSINESS:

Third Party Logistics (3PL)--Apparel
Supply Chain Management
Distribution & Warehousing
Ground Transport
Healthcare & Consumer Products, Manufacturing
Convenience Stores
Toys, Retail
Clothing, Distribution & Retail

BRANDS/DIVISIONS/AFFILIATES:

Li & Fung Ltd
Fung Retailing Limited
Circle K
Global Brands Group Holding Limited
Trinity Limited
Convenience Retail Asia Limited
Gieves & Hawkes
Saint Honore

CONTACTS: Note: Officers with more than one job title may be intentionally listed here more than once.

William K. Fung, Group Deputy Chmn.
Victor K. Fung, Chmn.

GROWTH PLANS/SPECIAL FEATURES:

Li & Fung Limited (Fung Group), through its subsidiaries, is engaged in logistics, trading, distribution and retailing. Li & Fung Ltd., the publicly traded export trading, logistics and distribution branch of the company, manages the logistics of producing and exporting an extensive range of private-label consumer goods. It operates through suppliers that deliver its goods in 40 countries around the world. Garments comprise the majority of Li & Fung's trading business, though it also deals in fashion accessories, home furnishings, toys, sporting goods and travel goods. Fung Group's distribution division is carried out by Global Brands Group Holding Limited, which operates in four segments: licensed brands, controlled brands, brand management and retail partnerships. The firm has over 350 iconic brands designed, licensed or under management, all of which are distributed from more than 50 offices and showrooms around the world. The firm's retail division is carried out through subsidiary Fung Retailing Limited, which operates roughly 600 retail outlets under the Circle K and Saint Honore brands in China through Convenience Retail Asia Limited. Through Trinity Limited, Fung Retailing offers high-end men's apparel at 441 locations under five international brands: Cerruti 1881, Gieves & Hawkes, D'urban, Intermezzo and Kent & Curwen. Branded Through Toys R US (Asia), Fung Retailing operates 150 Toys R Us Asia locations under license.

FINANCIAL DATA: Note: Data for latest year may not have been available at press time.

In U.S. $	2015	2014	2013	2012	2011	2010
Revenue		19,288,500,000	20,745,410,000	20,221,810,000	20,030,270,000	15,947,550,000
R&D Expense						
Operating Income		723,625,000	975,824,000	790,703,000	879,937,000	726,749,100
Operating Margin %		3.75%	4.70%	3.91%	4.39%	4.55%
SGA Expense		1,640,090,000	2,433,247,000	2,452,622,000	2,192,148,000	1,516,512,000
Net Income		469,646,000	755,287,000	622,564,000	681,404,000	549,985,200
Operating Cash Flow		637,939,000	942,773,000	586,121,000	924,223,000	747,008,400
Capital Expenditure		86,423,000	176,389,000	187,832,000	118,055,000	82,747,270
EBITDA		846,965,000	1,314,031,000	1,096,924,000	1,127,200,000	855,547,600
Return on Assets %		4.21%	5.92%	5.38%	6.66%	7.37%
Return on Equity %		11.55%	15.00%	14.41%	18.00%	18.55%
Debt to Equity		0.48	0.24	0.27	0.31	0.68

CONTACT INFORMATION:

Phone: 852 23002300   Fax: 852 23002000
Toll-Free:
Address: 888 Cheung Sha Wan Rd., LiFung Tower, 11th Fl., Hong Kong, Hong Kong 999077 Hong Kong

STOCK TICKER/OTHER:

Stock Ticker: LFUGY   Exchange: PINX
Employees: 25,000   Fiscal Year Ends: 12/31
Parent Company:

SALARIES/BONUSES:

Top Exec. Salary: $ Bonus: $
Second Exec. Salary: $ Bonus: $

OTHER THOUGHTS:

Estimated Female Officers or Directors:
Hot Spot for Advancement for Women/Minorities: Y

Lianhua Supermarket Holdings Co Ltd

lianhua.todayir.com/en/index.php

NAIC Code: 445110

TYPES OF BUSINESS:

Supermarkets
Convenience Stores

BRANDS/DIVISIONS/AFFILIATES:

Century Mart
Lianhua Supermarket
Lianhua Quick
Hualian Supermarket

GROWTH PLANS/SPECIAL FEATURES:

Lianhua Supermarket Holdings Co., Ltd. is a Shanghai-base
chain retail operator. The firm operates in three main reta
segments: hypermarkets, supermarkets and convenienc
stores. The company operates approximately 4,195 outlet
spanning 19 Chinese provinces and municipalities. The firm'
store brand names are Century Mart, Lianhua Supermarket
Hualian Supermarket and Lianhua Quick.

CONTACTS: Note: Officers with more than one job title may be intentionally listed here more than once.

Xu Ling-ling, CFO
Liang Wei, Vice Gen. Mgr.-Admin.
Cai Lan-ying, Deputy Gen. Mgr.-Oper.
Cai Lan-ying, Deputy Gen. Mgr.-Bus. Mgmt.
Hua Guo-ping, Deputy Chmn.
Tang Qi, Deputy Gen. Mgr.
Chen Jian-jun, Chmn.

FINANCIAL DATA: Note: Data for latest year may not have been available at press time.

In U.S. $	2015	2014	2013	2012	2011	2010
Revenue		4,563,056,000	4,755,731,000	4,537,244,000	4,702,524,000	4,052,002,000
R&D Expense						
Operating Income		37,872,370	39,643,750	80,216,470	129,816,700	121,372,900
Operating Margin %		.82%	.83%	1.76%	2.76%	2.99%
SGA Expense		1,074,106,000	1,082,396,000	1,033,441,000	965,898,400	879,774,700
Net Income		18,922,020	21,178,160	70,772,600	111,710,000	111,225,700
Operating Cash Flow		17,478,090	303,813,200	-978,901	124,071,800	349,827,400
Capital Expenditure		79,518,690	88,473,580	117,907,000	185,347,200	94,729,220
EBITDA		127,072,200	138,371,100	191,474,600	215,326,200	206,259,900
Return on Assets %		.15%	.25%	1.65%	3.23%	3.67%
Return on Equity %		.91%	1.56%	10.12%	20.19%	23.24%
Debt to Equity						

CONTACT INFORMATION:

Phone: 8621-5262-9922   Fax: 8621-5279-7976
Toll-Free:
Address: 26th-27th Floors, Harcourt Bldg, 39 Gloucester Road, Wanchai, 00980 Hong Kong

STOCK TICKER/OTHER:

Stock Ticker: LHUAF
Employees: 52,905
Parent Company:

Exchange: PINX
Fiscal Year Ends: 12/31

SALARIES/BONUSES:

Top Exec. Salary: $ Bonus: $
Second Exec. Salary: $ Bonus: $

OTHER THOUGHTS:

Estimated Female Officers or Directors: 2
Hot Spot for Advancement for Women/Minorities:

Lidl Stiftung & Co. KG

www.lidl-info.com

NAIC Code: 445110

TYPES OF BUSINESS:

Supermarkets

GROWTH PLANS/SPECIAL FEATURES:

Lidl Stiftung & Co. KG is one of Europe's leading grocers, with hundreds of stores spread throughout the continent and Great Britain. It is recognized as one of the world's leading retail brands, with a significant, long-term record of expansion. The company has stated plans to expand to the U.S., with its headquarters based in Arlington, Virginia. The U.S. debut is planned for the East Coast and could include 100 stores by 2018. Lidl stores are noted for very low retail prices. Lidl brand stores total nearly 10,000, with average sales of nearly $7.2 million per store per year. Lidl is a subsidiary of Schwarz Gruppe GmbH, a holding company that includes Lidl's sister company Kaufland.

BRANDS/DIVISIONS/AFFILIATES:

Kaufland
Schwarz Gruppe GmbH

CONTACTS: *Note: Officers with more than one job title may be intentionally listed here more than once.*

Sven Seidel, CEO-Lidl
Robin Goudsblom, Head of Purchasing-Lidl
Klaus Gehrig, Chmn.

FINANCIAL DATA: *Note: Data for latest year may not have been available at press time.*

In U.S. $	2015	2014	2013	2012	2011	2010
Revenue		74,824,800,000	72,330,600,000	70,000,000,000		
R&D Expense						
Operating Income						
Operating Margin %						
SGA Expense						
Net Income						
Operating Cash Flow						
Capital Expenditure						
EBITDA						
Return on Assets %						
Return on Equity %						
Debt to Equity						

CONTACT INFORMATION:

Phone: 49(0) 7132 94 20   Fax:
Toll-Free:
Address: StiftsbergstraÄŸe 1, Neckarsulm, 74167 Germany

STOCK TICKER/OTHER:

Stock Ticker: Subsidiary
Employees: 175,000
Parent Company: Schwarz Gruppe GmbH
Exchange:
Fiscal Year Ends:

SALARIES/BONUSES:

Top Exec. Salary: $ Bonus: $
Second Exec. Salary: $ Bonus: $

OTHER THOUGHTS:

Estimated Female Officers or Directors:
Hot Spot for Advancement for Women/Minorities:

Sales, profits and employees may be estimates. Financial information, benefits and other data can change quickly and may vary from those stated here.

LifeWay Christian Resources

NAIC Code: 451211

www.lifeway.com

TYPES OF BUSINESS:

Christian Books, Retail
Christian Book Publishing
Conference Centers
Online Sales
Church Supplies

BRANDS/DIVISIONS/AFFILIATES:

LifeWay Christian Stores
LifeWay Ridgecrest Conference Center
LifeWay Community Fund
B&H Publishing Group
Holman Christian Standard Bible
LifeWay.com
Ridgecrest
Crestridge

CONTACTS: *Note: Officers with more than one job title may be intentionally listed here more than once.*

Thom S. Rainer, CEO
Thom S. Rainer, Pres.
Jerry Rhyne, CFO
Ed Stetzer, VP-Insights Div.
Tim Hill, VP
Brad Waggoner, Exec. VP-Oper.
Jerry Rhyne, VP-Finance & Bus. Svcs.
Tim Vineyard, VP-LifeWay Christian Stores
Eric Geiger, VP-Church Resources Div.
Selma Wilson, VP-B&H Publishing Group

GROWTH PLANS/SPECIAL FEATURES:

LifeWay Christian Resources of the Southern Baptist Convention is a nonprofit organization. Founded in 1891, the company is one of the world's largest providers of Christian products and digital services. The firm sells Bibles; church literature; software; books; music; DVDs and videos; teaching recordings; and church supplies, such as furniture and signs. It operates 180 LifeWay Christian Stores across the U.S. These products are also available through an online channel, LifeWay.com. In addition, the organization owns and operates LifeWay Ridgecrest Conference Center in North Carolina. It also offers summer camp Ridgecrest for boys and summer camp Crestridge for girls on Ridgecrest's 1,300 acre campus. Through B&H Publishing Group, LifeWay produces a bible translation called the Holman Christian Standard Bible. The organization coordinates its activities and initiates retail operations through a 1.3-million-square-foot office space in Nashville, Tennessee. The LifeWay Community Fund supports 10 charities in middle Tennessee. LifeWay's web site includes resources such as links to counseling, Bible study courses and links to multimedia Bible stories for children. The firm's LifeWay Research division explores new ministry ventures.

Lifeway offers employees benefits including a 401(k); medical, dental, vision and life insurance; onsite credit union membership; vacation time; concierge services; discount programs; mission trips; free parking; and cafeteria access.

FINANCIAL DATA: *Note: Data for latest year may not have been available at press time.*

In U.S. $	2015	2014	2013	2012	2011	2010
Revenue						
R&D Expense						
Operating Income						
Operating Margin %						
SGA Expense						
Net Income						
Operating Cash Flow						
Capital Expenditure						
EBITDA						
Return on Assets %						
Return on Equity %						
Debt to Equity						

CONTACT INFORMATION:

Phone: 615-251-2000   Fax: 615-251-3899
Toll-Free:
Address: 1 LifeWay Plz., Nashville, TN 37234 United States

STOCK TICKER/OTHER:

Stock Ticker: Nonprofit   Exchange:
Employees: 4,000   Fiscal Year Ends: 09/30
Parent Company:

SALARIES/BONUSES:

Top Exec. Salary: $ Bonus: $
Second Exec. Salary: $ Bonus: $

OTHER THOUGHTS:

Estimated Female Officers or Directors: 1
Hot Spot for Advancement for Women/Minorities: Y

Lillian Vernon Corporation

www.lillianvernon.com

NAIC Code: 454113

TYPES OF BUSINESS:

Gifts & Housewares, Catalogs
Online Sales
Holiday Products
Children's Products
Garden Products
Personalized products

BRANDS/DIVISIONS/AFFILIATES:

Regent Equity Partners
Lilly's Kids
Big Sale
LillianVernon.com
SmartBuy Savings Club

CONTACTS: Note: Officers with more than one job title may be intentionally listed here more than once.

Richard Mather, CEO
Michael D. Muoio, Pres.
Ralph J. Thomann, Sr. VP-Oper.
Norman Foster, Sr. VP-Quality Assurance

GROWTH PLANS/SPECIAL FEATURES:

Lillian Vernon Corporation, privately-owned by Regent Equity Partners, is a national catalog and online retailer of gifts, housewares, gardening, season and children's products. Its products include dinnerware, blankets, pillows, cookware, tools, utensils, linens, tables, garden accents, statuaries, clocks, handbags and jewelry. The company mails more than 100 million catalogs and 4 million packages representing 6,000 different products. Lillian Vernon was founded by German immigrant Lillian Vernon in 1951. Personalization of gifts is always free of charge, and the company's products are 100% quality guaranteed within 60 days. SmartBuy Savings Club memberships include the silver member, which receives a membership card, 10% discount on every order, free personalized address labels and free holiday envelope seals; and the gold member, which receives the same as the silver as well as a premium holiday gift, member-only coupons, exclusive offers and sale previews. Silver annual membership costs $14.99 and gold membership costs $19.99. The firm's lillianvernon.com website includes the trademarked Lilly's Kids section, featuring toys, luggage, backpacks, lunch bags, totes, school supplies, beach towels, flip-flop sandals, water bottles, room organization items, sleeping bags, bathrobes and many other items. Most Lilly's Kids items can also be personalized. The website also features a Big Sale section with savings up to 80% off select items.

FINANCIAL DATA: Note: Data for latest year may not have been available at press time.

In U.S. $	2015	2014	2013	2012	2011	2010
Revenue						
R&D Expense						
Operating Income						
Operating Margin %						
SGA Expense						
Net Income						
Operating Cash Flow						
Capital Expenditure						
EBITDA						
Return on Assets %						
Return on Equity %						
Debt to Equity						

CONTACT INFORMATION:

Phone: 719-594-4100   Fax:
Toll-Free:
Address: 1005 E. Woodmen Rd, Colorado Springs, CO 80920 United States

STOCK TICKER/OTHER:

Stock Ticker: Private
Employees: 1,200
Parent Company: Regent Equity Partners

Exchange:
Fiscal Year Ends: 02/28

SALARIES/BONUSES:

Top Exec. Salary: $ Bonus: $
Second Exec. Salary: $ Bonus: $

OTHER THOUGHTS:

Estimated Female Officers or Directors: 1
Hot Spot for Advancement for Women/Minorities:

Limited Stores LLC

NAIC Code: 448120

www.thelimited.com

TYPES OF BUSINESS:

Women's Retail Apparel

BRANDS/DIVISIONS/AFFILIATES:

Sun Capital Partners Inc
The Limited
TheLimited.com

GROWTH PLANS/SPECIAL FEATURES:

Limited Stores LLC, owned by private equity firm Sun Capita
Partners, Inc., is a mall-based specialty store retailer focusing
on sportswear, leisurewear and professional apparel fo
women. The company operates The Limited, which offer
pants, tops, dresses, skirts, suits, jackets and outerwear
accessories and gift items. Currently, select stores feature the
Ranjana Khan limited-edition jewelry collection. The company'
e-commerce site, TheLimited.com, allows customers to shop
purchase and track their merchandise orders. The Limited
offers gift cards with amounts ranging from $10 to $1,000.
also offers a virtual gift card that can be e-mailed to its recipient

The company offers employees benefits including medical
dental, vision, disability and life insurance; employee
assistance programs; and 401(k) retirement plan.

CONTACTS: Note: Officers with more than one job title may be intentionally listed here more than once.

Diane Marie Ellis, CEO
Linda Heasley, Pres.

FINANCIAL DATA: Note: Data for latest year may not have been available at press time.

In U.S. $	2015	2014	2013	2012	2011	2010
Revenue						
R&D Expense						
Operating Income						
Operating Margin %						
SGA Expense						
Net Income						
Operating Cash Flow						
Capital Expenditure						
EBITDA						
Return on Assets %						
Return on Equity %						
Debt to Equity						

CONTACT INFORMATION:

Phone: 614289-2200   Fax:
Toll-Free: 877-583-1963
Address: 7775 Walton Pkwy., New Albany, OH 43054 United States

STOCK TICKER/OTHER:

Stock Ticker: Private   Exchange:
Employees: Fiscal Year Ends:
Parent Company: SUN CAPITAL PARTNERS INC

SALARIES/BONUSES:

Top Exec. Salary: $ Bonus: $
Second Exec. Salary: $ Bonus: $

OTHER THOUGHTS:

Estimated Female Officers or Directors: 1
Hot Spot for Advancement for Women/Minorities:

Little Switzerland Inc

www.littleswitzerland.com

NAIC Code: 448310

TYPES OF BUSINESS:

Luxury Items, Retail
Duty-Free Stores
Jewelry
China & Crystal
Gifts
Fragrances

BRANDS/DIVISIONS/AFFILIATES:

CI Group
NXP Corporation

CONTACTS: *Note: Officers with more than one job title may be intentionally listed here more than once.*

Robert L. Baumgardner, CEO
R. Christopher Cooper, Pres.
Patrick J. Hopper, CFO

GROWTH PLANS/SPECIAL FEATURES:

Little Switzerland, Inc. is a subsidiary of NXP Corporation, a jewelry retail chain providing fine jewelry, timepieces, sterling silver goods, china, crystal, stationery, fragrances and personal accessories. Little Switzerland is a duty-free specialty retailer of luxury items, such as watches, jewelry, crystal, china, fragrances and gifts. The company's 25 retail locations, located in nine Caribbean islands and Key West, Florida, primarily serve tourists from the U.S. The company's upscale merchandise is offered under a variety of brand names, including Breitling, Cartier, Movado, Pandora, TAG Heuer, David Yurman, Omega, John Hardy, Chopard, Tiffany & Co. and Roberto Coin. Additionally, Little Switzerland is the exclusive retailer of a number of brand-name products in the Caribbean islands. The firm's jewelry offerings include rings, earrings, bracelets, necklaces, pendants and charms, which range from impulse items under $100 to fine jewelry priced for several thousand. The company's distinctive stores are designed to be inviting, relaxing and otherwise conducive to shopping for luxury items. Stores are located in areas that are easily accessible to tourists, mainly in duty-free ports that are visited by cruise ships. Little Switzerland advertises its products in island-specific magazines as well as cruise line, travel and in-flight magazines. Additionally, the firm participates in the on-board promotional programs offered by all cruise lines operating in the Caribbean. Parent company NXP is owned by the CI Group of companies.

The firm offers employees benefits including health, dental, life and disability coverage; 401(k); paid vacation; employee discounts; flexible spending accounts; training; and an employee assistance program.

FINANCIAL DATA: *Note: Data for latest year may not have been available at press time.*

In U.S. $	2015	2014	2013	2012	2011	2010
Revenue						
R&D Expense						
Operating Income						
Operating Margin %						
SGA Expense						
Net Income						
Operating Cash Flow						
Capital Expenditure						
EBITDA						
Return on Assets %						
Return on Equity %						
Debt to Equity						

CONTACT INFORMATION:

Phone: 561-241-1115   Fax: 561-912-9138
Toll-Free: 800-524-2010
Address: 6800 Broken Sound Pkwy. NW, Boca Raton, FL 33487 United States

STOCK TICKER/OTHER:

Stock Ticker: Subsidiary
Employees:
Parent Company: NXP CORPORATION

Exchange:
Fiscal Year Ends: 05/31

SALARIES/BONUSES:

Top Exec. Salary: $ Bonus: $
Second Exec. Salary: $ Bonus: $

OTHER THOUGHTS:

Estimated Female Officers or Directors:
Hot Spot for Advancement for Women/Minorities:

Loblaw Companies Limited

www.loblaw.ca

NAIC Code: 445110

TYPES OF BUSINESS:

Grocery Stores/Supermarkets
Wholesale Supermarkets
Pharmacies
Banking Centers

BRANDS/DIVISIONS/AFFILIATES:

Extra Foods
Liquorstore
nofrills
Superstore
wholesale club
Loblaws
Shoppers Drug Mart Corp
Choice Properties Real Estate Investment Trust

CONTACTS: Note: Officers with more than one job title may be intentionally listed here more than once.

Galen Weston, CEO
Michael Motz, President, Divisional
Richard Dufresne, CFO
Sarah Davis, Chief Administrative Officer
Grant Froese, COO
Judy McCrie, Executive VP, Divisional
Mary-Alice Vuicic, Executive VP, Divisional
Mark Butler, Executive VP, Divisional
Gordon A.M. Currie, Executive VP
Andrew Iacobucci, President, Divisional
Garry Senecal, President, Divisional
Peter McLaughlin, President, Divisional
Mario Grauso, President, Divisional
Barry Columb, President, Subsidiary
Paviter Binning, President, Subsidiary
Robert Chant, Senior VP, Divisional

GROWTH PLANS/SPECIAL FEATURES:

Loblaw Companies Limited is one of Canada's largest food distributors and a leading provider of general merchandise products, drugstore products, pharmacy services and financial products and services. Although a publicly traded company, the majority of its shares are owned by former Chairman W. Galen Weston, and it is a subsidiary of his firm, George Weston Limited. The firm has approximately 2,300 corporate, franchised and associate-owned locations. The firm has approximately 570 company-owned and 496 franchised stores throughout Canada under multiple regional store names, including Extra Foods, Liquorstore, nofrills, Superstore, wholesale club, Shoppers Drug Mart, Loblaws, Zehrs, valu-mart, Fortinos', T&T Supermarket, provigo, maxi, club entrepot, Pharmaprix, SaveEasy and Atlantic Superstore. The average corporate store is approximately 64,800 square feet, while the average franchised store is 29,500 square feet. Loblaw has nine-owned warehouse locations across Canada. The firm owns several proprietary brands, including President's Choice, no name and Joe Fresh, and also runs banking centers in many of its stores under the name President's Choice Financial, with offerings including checking and savings accounts, home mortgages, mutual funds, personal loans and lines of credit. Through the PC Plus and Shoppers Optimum loyalty programs, shoppers are rewarded as consumers. Choice Properties Real Estate Investment Trust was recently created to optimize the value of Loblaw's real estate portfolio over time. In 2014, the firm acquired Shopper's Drug Mart Corp., one of Canada's largest retail pharmacy chains.

FINANCIAL DATA: Note: Data for latest year may not have been available at press time.

In U.S. $	2015	2014	2013	2012	2011	2010
Revenue		31,923,370,000	24,251,750,000	23,677,130,000	23,411,920,000	23,222,380,000
R&D Expense						
Operating Income		495,958,100	993,414,700	896,021,100	1,036,867,000	950,711,300
Operating Margin %		1.55%	4.09%	3.78%	4.42%	4.09%
SGA Expense		7,406,409,000	4,756,554,000	4,662,157,000	4,474,112,000	4,255,351,000
Net Income		39,706,620	471,984,400	486,968,000	576,120,600	510,192,600
Operating Cash Flow		1,924,647,000	1,117,030,000	1,226,410,000	1,359,015,000	1,194,195,000
Capital Expenditure		813,611,100	657,032,200	794,132,400	739,442,200	958,952,300
EBITDA		1,539,568,000	1,502,858,000	1,478,135,000	1,646,701,000	1,441,425,000
Return on Assets %		.19%	3.25%	3.67%	4.61%	4.40%
Return on Equity %		.53%	9.37%	10.46%	11.93%	10.35%
Debt to Equity		0.86	0.95	0.77	0.91	0.61

CONTACT INFORMATION:

Phone: 416 922-8500   Fax: 416 922-7791
Toll-Free: 888-495-5111
Address: 1 President's Choice Cir., Brampton, ON L6Y 5S5 Canada

SALARIES/BONUSES:

Top Exec. Salary: $ Bonus: $
Second Exec. Salary: $ Bonus: $

STOCK TICKER/OTHER:

Stock Ticker: L   Exchange: TSE
Employees: 195,000   Fiscal Year Ends: 12/31
Parent Company: GEORGE WESTON LIMITED

OTHER THOUGHTS:

Estimated Female Officers or Directors: 4
Hot Spot for Advancement for Women/Minorities: Y

Lojas Americanas SA

www.americanas.com.br

NAIC Code: 452111

TYPES OF BUSINESS:

Retail
Clothing
Food
Compact Discs
Perfume
Wine
Travel Services
Tickets

BRANDS/DIVISIONS/AFFILIATES:

www.americanas.com.br
Americanas.com

GROWTH PLANS/SPECIAL FEATURES:

Lojas Americanas SA (LASA) is a Brazil-based multi-channel online retail company. With more than 500,000 products, LASA serves 10 million customers via 20,000 Latin American participating companies. LASA delivers its products internationally, including books, CDs, DVDs, toys, games, computer-related items, photo-related items, phones/cell phones, electronics, home appliances, sporting goods, beauty & health products, fashion & accessories, housewares, bed & bath, as well as watches and gifts. The company's Internet channel is www.americanas.com.br, through which products can be searched by brand, title, price, age or author. In physical stores, LASA has erected Amereicanas.com Internet kiosks for shoppers to conveniently browse. The company also provides loyalty programs, incentive programs for its employees and a variety of business-to-consumer services.

CONTACTS: Note: Officers with more than one job title may be intentionally listed here more than once.

Miguel Gomes Pereira Sarmiento Gutierrez, CEO
Murilo dos Santos Correa, Dir.-Investor Rel.
Carlos Alberto Da Veiga Sicupira, Chmn.

FINANCIAL DATA: Note: Data for latest year may not have been available at press time.

In U.S. $	2015	2014	2013	2012	2011	2010
Revenue		4,287,026,664	5,249,600,000	4,439,900,000	3,908,800,000	3,677,800,000
R&D Expense						
Operating Income						
Operating Margin %						
SGA Expense						
Net Income		113,640,989	181,300,000	160,700,000	133,400,000	121,300,000
Operating Cash Flow						
Capital Expenditure						
EBITDA						
Return on Assets %						
Return on Equity %						
Debt to Equity						

CONTACT INFORMATION:

Phone: 55-21-2206-6613   Fax: 55-21-2206-6898
Toll-Free:
Address: 102 Rua Sacadura Cabral Saude, Rio de Janeiro, 20081-902 Brazil

STOCK TICKER/OTHER:

Stock Ticker: LAME4
Employees: 9,000
Parent Company:

Exchange: Sao Paulo
Fiscal Year Ends: 12/31

SALARIES/BONUSES:

Top Exec. Salary: $ Bonus: $
Second Exec. Salary: $ Bonus: $

OTHER THOUGHTS:

Estimated Female Officers or Directors:
Hot Spot for Advancement for Women/Minorities:

Lojas Renner SA

NAIC Code: 448140

TYPES OF BUSINESS:
Retail-Apparel
Retail-Accessories
Design & Manufacturing-Apparel
Insurance
Loans

BRANDS/DIVISIONS/AFFILIATES:
Renner Card
Lifestyle

CONTACTS: *Note: Officers with more than one job title may be intentionally listed here more than once.*
Jose Gallo, CEO
Paulo Soares, Dir.-Oper.
Jose Gallo, Pres.
Laurence Beltrao Gomes, CFO
Luciane Franciscone, Gen. Mgr.-Corp. Mktg.
Clarice M. Costa, Dir.-Human Resources
Emerson Silveira Kuze, Dir.-Tech.
Alessandra Shargorodsky, Gen. Mgr.-Eng. & Architecture
Adalberto Pereira dos Santos, Chief Admin. Officer
Emerson Silveira Kuze, Dir.-Bus. Mgmt.
Laurence Beltrao Gomes, Dir.-Investor Rel.
Mauricio Nemeth Paniquar, Gen. Mgr.-Logistics
Claudio Barone, Gen. Mgr.-Stores
Luis Alexandre Silva Ribeiro, Gen. Mgr.-Audit & Loss Prevention
Gabriela Cirne Lima, Gen. Mgr.-Style
Claudio T.L. Sonder, Chmn.
Haroldo L.R. Filho, Dir.-Procurement

GROWTH PLANS/SPECIAL FEATURES:
Lojas Renner SA is engaged in the design, development an
sale of women's, men's and children's apparel, footwea
underwear, cosmetics and other items through a network c
about 144 department stores throughout Brazil, locate
primarily in the South, Southeast, Midwest, North an
Northeast regions of the country. The firm markets it
merchandise under 16 brands, of which six represent it
Lifestyle concept. In addition to its proprietary brands an
additional branded products, the company imports about 6% c
its merchandise, consisting largely of synthetic fibers
embroidery, leather and knitwear as well as watches
sunglasses and costume jewelry. Lojas Renner's targe
customers are primarily women between 18 and 39 in middl
and upper-middle income levels. The company supplies it
stores through two distribution centers located in the states c
Santa Catarina and Sao Paulo. The firm also offers it
customers financial services, including personal loans
insurance, capitalization bonds and a store credit card, th
Renner Card. The Renner Card is responsible for about 60%
of the firm's total sales.

FINANCIAL DATA: *Note: Data for latest year may not have been available at press time.*

In U.S. $	2015	2014	2013	2012	2011	2010
Revenue		1,361,277,000	1,140,393,000	1,007,882,000	845,065,100	717,933,800
R&D Expense						
Operating Income		184,791,100	152,053,300	145,930,600	124,273,900	107,384,100
Operating Margin %		13.57%	13.33%	14.47%	14.70%	14.95%
SGA Expense		409,610,700	354,959,200	319,256,100	267,782,500	222,703,300
Net Income		123,012,300	106,308,000	92,738,300	87,912,480	80,376,790
Operating Cash Flow		154,243,600	99,472,630	116,392,200	71,519,710	146,034,000
Capital Expenditure		124,615,800	107,538,800	99,754,710	77,401,300	41,824,750
EBITDA		240,301,400	195,744,300	189,327,800	149,751,300	127,159,900
Return on Assets %		9.58%	9.83%	10.52%	12.38%	14.07%
Return on Equity %		28.15%	29.11%	28.88%	30.92%	38.91%
Debt to Equity		0.75	0.70	0.03	0.57	0.36

CONTACT INFORMATION:
Phone: 55-51-2121-7183   Fax: 55-51-3345-1481
Toll-Free:
Address: Av. Joaquim Porto Villanova 401, Porto Alegre, 91410400
Brazil

STOCK TICKER/OTHER:
Stock Ticker: LORPF
Employees: 16,870
Parent Company:

Exchange: GREY
Fiscal Year Ends: 12/31

SALARIES/BONUSES:
Top Exec. Salary: $ Bonus: $
Second Exec. Salary: $ Bonus: $

OTHER THOUGHTS:
Estimated Female Officers or Directors: 4
Hot Spot for Advancement for Women/Minorities: Y

Lord & Taylor LLC

www.lordandtaylor.com

NAIC Code: 448140

TYPES OF BUSINESS:

Department Stores

BRANDS/DIVISIONS/AFFILIATES:

Hudson's Bay Company
LordAndTaylor.com

CONTACTS: *Note: Officers with more than one job title may be intentionally listed here more than once.*

Liz Rodbell, Pres.
Michael Crotty, CMO
Don Watros, COO-Hudson's Bay Company
Russ Hardin, Chief Creative Officer
Bonnie Brooks, Vice Chmn.
Richard A. Baker, Chmn.

GROWTH PLANS/SPECIAL FEATURES:

Lord & Taylor LLC operates approximately 50 department stores in nine states in the northeastern U.S., ranging in size from 70,000 to 160,000 square feet. The firm also operates an e-commerce web site, LordAndTaylor.com. Brands sold by the company include Seven For All Mankind, Diesel, Iisli, Tracy Reese, Bryan by Bryan Bradley, Cole Haan, Lacoste and Kate Spade. Sportswear, denim, dresses and jewelry are some of the firm's best-performing categories. Additional products sold include shoes, handbags, fragrance, beauty products and accessories. The company's 650,000 square foot flagship store on Fifth Avenue in New York is famous for its annual Christmas window display. The Scarsdale branch in Westchester County is the chain's second-highest performing store with annual sales being more than $90 million. Lord & Taylor's biggest customers are suburban women in their mid-40s with roughly $125,000 in annual household income.

The firm offers employees medical, dental and vision benefits; a 401(k) plan; and store-wide discounts.

FINANCIAL DATA: *Note: Data for latest year may not have been available at press time.*

In U.S. $	2015	2014	2013	2012	2011	2010
Revenue		1,600,000,000				
R&D Expense						
Operating Income						
Operating Margin %						
SGA Expense						
Net Income						
Operating Cash Flow						
Capital Expenditure						
EBITDA						
Return on Assets %						
Return on Equity %						
Debt to Equity						

CONTACT INFORMATION:

Phone: 212-391-3344 Fax: 212-768-0743
Toll-Free: 800-223-7440
Address: 424 5th Ave., New York, NY 10018 United States

SALARIES/BONUSES:

Top Exec. Salary: $ Bonus: $
Second Exec. Salary: $ Bonus: $

STOCK TICKER/OTHER:

Stock Ticker: Subsidiary Exchange:
Employees: 7,500 Fiscal Year Ends:
Parent Company: HUDSON'S BAY COMPANY

OTHER THOUGHTS:

Estimated Female Officers or Directors: 2
Hot Spot for Advancement for Women/Minorities:

Lotte Shopping Co

NAIC Code: 452111

TYPES OF BUSINESS:
Retail Centers
Discount Outlets
Movie Theaters
Movie Distribution & Production

BRANDS/DIVISIONS/AFFILIATES:
Korea Seven
e-super
Lotte.com
Wiselect
Owolmokaga
Lotte Card Co Ltd
Lotte Home Shopping

CONTACTS: Note: Officers with more than one job title may be intentionally listed here more than once.
Shin Heon, CEO
Shin Youngja, Pres.
Lee Inwon, VP
Shin Dongbin, Chmn.

GROWTH PLANS/SPECIAL FEATURES:

Lotte Shopping Co. primarily operates department stores and discount stores across Korea, with overseas locations in Russia, China, Vietnam and Indonesia. Established in 1979, Lotte Shopping operates through the following four divisions: Lotte Department Store, Lotte Mart, Lotte Super and Lotte Cinema. The Lotte Department Store division operates 33 domestic department stores and eight overseas. The Lotte Mart division operates 114 discount outlets, with international locations in China, Vietnam and Indonesia. The division also operates an online store. The Lotte Super division, operating 1,280 supermarkets, carries some private brands, such as Owolmokaga and Wiselect, and generally offers a price 15% less than comparable brands. The division also operates e-super, an online shopping site. The Lotte Cinema division operates 103 theaters as well as engaging in movie distribution and production. Subsidiaries include Lotte Card Co., Ltd., a full service credit card company; and Lotte Home Shopping, which allows users to purchase items via TV, Internet or catalog. Lotte.com is one of Korea's first online shopping malls. Korea Seven, the Korean branch of the 7-Eleven chain of convenience stores, is also a subsidiary of the company.

FINANCIAL DATA: Note: Data for latest year may not have been available at press time.

In U.S. $	2015	2014	2013	2012	2011	2010
Revenue		24,207,900,000	24,304,510,000	21,575,240,000	19,171,140,000	16,383,870,000
R&D Expense						
Operating Income		1,023,794,000	1,279,559,000	1,264,230,000	1,432,595,000	1,376,455,000
Operating Margin %		4.22%	5.26%	5.85%	7.47%	8.40%
SGA Expense		2,813,008,000	2,762,127,000	2,530,291,000	726,808,600	595,550,100
Net Income		453,711,400	679,249,000	930,649,700	802,764,200	891,403,700
Operating Cash Flow		1,404,127,000	1,146,374,000	778,778,600	605,607,000	-43,540,100
Capital Expenditure		1,675,463,000	1,687,921,000	1,625,166,000	1,445,195,000	1,153,963,000
EBITDA		1,917,768,000	2,057,088,000	2,206,310,000	1,929,660,000	1,830,603,000
Return on Assets %		1.33%	2.07%	3.09%	2.99%	3.85%
Return on Equity %		3.19%	5.07%	7.49%	6.88%	8.13%
Debt to Equity		0.48	0.48	0.53	0.48	0.38

CONTACT INFORMATION:
Phone: 82 27712500   Fax:
Toll-Free:
Address: 81 Namdaemun-ro Jung-gu, Seoul, 100-801 South Korea

STOCK TICKER/OTHER:
Stock Ticker: LTSHY   Exchange: GREY
Employees: 25,313   Fiscal Year Ends: 12/31
Parent Company:

SALARIES/BONUSES:
Top Exec. Salary: $ Bonus: $
Second Exec. Salary: $ Bonus: $

OTHER THOUGHTS:
Estimated Female Officers or Directors:
Hot Spot for Advancement for Women/Minorities:

Love's Travel Stops & Country Stores LLC   www.loves.com

NAIC Code: 447110

TYPES OF BUSINESS:

Truck Stops
Fuel
Food Products
Restroom Facilities
Restaurant
I Love Rewards Program
Shower Facilities
Gift Cards

BRANDS/DIVISIONS/AFFILIATES:

Love's Country Stores
Love's Travel Stops
Gemini Motor Transport
Love's Truck Tire Care
Musket Corporation
I Love Rewards

CONTACTS: Note: Officers with more than one job title may be intentionally listed here more than once.

Greg Love, Co-CEO
Frank Love, Co-CEO
Frank Love, Pres.
Doug Stussi, CFO
Greg Love, Pres., Dev.
Jenny Love Meyer, VP-Comm.
Tom Love, Chmn.

GROWTH PLANS/SPECIAL FEATURES:

Love's Travel Stops & Country Stores LLC is one of the largest retail operators of truck stops, convenience stores and travel plazas in the U.S. The firm operates over 350 locations in 40 states under the brands Love's Country Stores, Love's Travel Stops, Gemini Motor Transport, Love's Truck Tire Care and Musket Corporation. These locations are primarily located near interstate highway exits and offer amenities such as ATMs, Internet kiosks, check cashing, money orders, showering facilities, laundry facilities, game rooms, public pay phones with data ports and audio book rentals. The firm's travel centers typically feature a restaurant, fueling facilities and retail merchandise. Country Stores are the firm's convenience stores, Travel Stops are interstate highway travel centers, Gemini haul petroleum fuel, Truck Tire Care provides roadside assistance and Musket is a trading & distribution firm. Love's includes approximately 120 franchised restaurants, such as Arby's, Carl's Jr., Chester's Fried Chicken, Godfather's Pizza, Hardee's and McDonalds. The firm's travel plazas sells candy, snacks and drinks; auto supplies like tires, oil, radar detectors and GPS units; and general merchandise such as children's toys, apparel and tools. The company's I Love Rewards program, available at all Love's locations, offers customers one cent toward their card for every gallon of gas purchased. The points expire one year after being put on the card. Once the balance reaches $5, the card can be used to purchase food or merchandise at any Love's. Program members can check their balance on the firm's web site. Love's celebrated its 50th anniversary in 2014.

Love's offers employees benefits including health, dental and life insurance; relocation assistance; a 401(k) plan with 4% matching and immediate vesting; and holiday pay.

FINANCIAL DATA: Note: Data for latest year may not have been available at press time.

In U.S. $	2015	2014	2013	2012	2011	2010
Revenue		26,500,000,000	26,090,000,000	22,040,000,000	24,400,000,000	17,000,000,000
R&D Expense						
Operating Income						
Operating Margin %						
SGA Expense						
Net Income						
Operating Cash Flow						
Capital Expenditure						
EBITDA						
Return on Assets %						
Return on Equity %						
Debt to Equity						

CONTACT INFORMATION:

Phone: 405-751-9000   Fax: 405-749-9110
Toll-Free: 800-388-0983
Address: 10601 N. Pennsylvania Ave., Oklahoma City, OK 73120 United States

STOCK TICKER/OTHER:

Stock Ticker: Private
Employees: 12,000
Parent Company:

Exchange:
Fiscal Year Ends: 12/30

SALARIES/BONUSES:

Top Exec. Salary: $ Bonus: $
Second Exec. Salary: $ Bonus: $

OTHER THOUGHTS:

Estimated Female Officers or Directors: 1
Hot Spot for Advancement for Women/Minorities:

Sales, profits and employees may be estimates. Financial information, benefits and other data can change quickly and may vary from those stated here.

Lowe's Companies Inc

www.lowes.com

NAIC Code: 444110

TYPES OF BUSINESS:

Home Centers, Retail
Home Improvement Products
Home Installation Services
Special Order Sales

BRANDS/DIVISIONS/AFFILIATES:

Orchard Supply Hardware
Iris
Kobalt
Blue Hawk
Utilitech
Aquasource
Lowes.com

CONTACTS: Note: Officers with more than one job title may be intentionally listed here more than once.

Robert Hull, CFO
Paul Ramsay, Chief Information Officer
Marshall Croom, Chief Risk Officer
Rick Damron, COO
Gaither Keener, Executive VP, Divisional
Ross Mccanless, General Counsel
N. Peace, Other Corporate Officer
Richard Maltsbarger, Other Corporate Officer
Michael Jones, Other Executive Officer
Maureen Ausura, Other Executive Officer
Robert Niblock, President
Matthew Hollifield, Senior VP

GROWTH PLANS/SPECIAL FEATURES:

Lowe's Companies, Inc. is one of the largest home improvement retailers in the world. The company owns roughly 1,840 stores in 50 states, Mexico and Canada, each carrying approximately 36,000 products and 201 million square feet of retail space. The company also operates 74 stores under the recently acquired Orchard Supply Hardware name in California and Oregon. Hundreds of thousands of items are also available through the firm's special order system. Lowe's stores chiefly serve do-it-yourself (DIY) homeowners and commercial business customers, including contractors, landscapers, electricians, painters and plumbers. Its home improvement product categories include building materials, lighting, cabinets and countertops, seasonal living, millwork, lumber, flooring, lawn and landscaping items, hardware, fashion and rough plumbing, appliances, paint, tools, plants and plant pots, outdoor power equipment, rough electrical, home environment and organization and windows and walls. Each Lowe's store carries a wide selection of national brand name merchandise such as Samsung, Whirlpool, Stainmaster, GE, Valspar, Sylvania, Dewalt, Owens Corning and Johns Manville; and exclusive brand names such as Kobalt, allen+roth, Blue Hawk, Utilitech and Aquasource. The company's Lowes.com web site facilitates customers researching, comparing and buying Lowe's products, and also allows customers to special order products not carried in its physical store locations. Lowe's entered the smarthome market with Iris, an affordable, cloud-based home management system, which allows users to interact and control their home's security cameras, thermostat, locks, lighting and appliances remotely from a smart phone or computer. In May 2015, the firm announced that it reached an agreement to lease 13 former Target Canada stores as well as an Ontario distribution center, expecting to generate 2,000 jobs in Canada.

Lowe's offers its employees life, short- and long-term disability, accident, auto, home, medical, dental and vision insurance; family assistance programs; stock purchase plan; tuition reimbursement; paid time off; 401(k); and flexible spending accounts.

FINANCIAL DATA: Note: Data for latest year may not have been available at press time.

In U.S. $	2015	2014	2013	2012	2011	2010
Revenue	56,223,000,000	53,417,000,000	50,521,000,000	50,208,000,000	48,815,000,000	47,220,000,000
R&D Expense						
Operating Income	4,792,000,000	4,149,000,000	3,560,000,000	3,277,000,000	3,560,000,000	3,112,000,000
Operating Margin %	8.52%	7.76%	7.04%	6.52%	7.29%	6.59%
SGA Expense	13,281,000,000	12,865,000,000	12,244,000,000	12,593,000,000	12,006,000,000	11,688,000,000
Net Income	2,698,000,000	2,286,000,000	1,959,000,000	1,839,000,000	2,010,000,000	1,783,000,000
Operating Cash Flow	4,929,000,000	4,111,000,000	3,762,000,000	4,349,000,000	3,852,000,000	4,054,000,000
Capital Expenditure	880,000,000	940,000,000	1,211,000,000	1,829,000,000	1,329,000,000	1,799,000,000
EBITDA	6,385,000,000	5,719,000,000	5,211,000,000	4,862,000,000	5,256,000,000	4,862,000,000
Return on Assets %	8.35%	6.99%	5.91%	5.46%	6.02%	5.42%
Return on Equity %	24.72%	17.78%	12.89%	10.61%	10.81%	9.60%
Debt to Equity	1.08	0.85	0.65	0.42	0.36	0.23

CONTACT INFORMATION:

Phone: 704 758-1000   Fax: 336 658-4766
Toll-Free: 800-445-6937
Address: 1000 Lowe's Blvd., Mooresville, NC 28117 United States

STOCK TICKER/OTHER:

Stock Ticker: LOW
Employees: 266,000
Parent Company:

Exchange: NYS
Fiscal Year Ends: 01/31

SALARIES/BONUSES:

Top Exec. Salary: $1,280,000   Bonus: $

Second Exec. Salary: $780,000   Bonus: $

OTHER THOUGHTS:

Estimated Female Officers or Directors: 3

Hot Spot for Advancement for Women/Minorities: Y

lululemon Athletica Inc

www.lululemon.com

NAIC Code: 448100

TYPES OF BUSINESS:

Athletic Apparel
Organic Products
Accessories

BRANDS/DIVISIONS/AFFILIATES:

lululemon athletica
luon
silverescent
luxtreme

CONTACTS: Note: Officers with more than one job title may be intentionally listed here more than once.

Laurent Potdevin, CEO
Stuart Haselden, CFO
Michael Casey, Co-Chairman
David Mussafer, Director
Scott Stump, Executive VP, Divisional
Lee Holman, Executive VP
Tara Poseley, Other Executive Officer
Tom Waller, Senior VP, Divisional

GROWTH PLANS/SPECIAL FEATURES:

lululemon athletica, Inc. is a designer and retailer of technical athletic apparel in North America, specializing in yoga-inspired apparel and accessories. The company offers a comprehensive line of performance apparel and accessories for both women and men. The apparel assortment, including items such as fitness pants, shorts, tops and jackets, is designed for healthy lifestyle activities such as yoga, dance, running and general fitness. Stores also host self-defense classes, yoga classes and goal-setting workshops led by community ambassadors. The firm's fitness-related accessories include an array of items such as bags, socks, hats, underwear, balance balls, yoga mats, yoga bricks, towels, water bottles and headbands. Lululemon's clothing line consists of several branded fabrics, including luon, made of nylon and lycra, which wicks away moisture, stretches in four directions and is designed to eliminate irritation; silverescent, which incorporates silver directly into the fabric as a way to reduce odors due to certain antibacterial properties of silver; and luxtreme, a silky and lightweight wicking fabric that is incorporated in the firm's running lines. The company also offers a line of casual, organic products made with organically grown, spun and dyed cotton as well as natural, sustainable and/or recycled materials, such as vitasea, derived from a seaweed compound. In addition, customers can bring in lululemon pants to any location for a complimentary hemming. Lululemon sells its products through 225 corporate-owned stores in North America, including 171 in the U.S. and 54 in Canada as well as its e-commerce site.

The company hires sales people who are fit, well educated and enthusiastic about exercise and healthy lifestyles. The stores attempt to develop deep relationships with customers through yoga classes, an engaging sales style and other special activities. Merchandise is typically sold at full price.

FINANCIAL DATA: Note: Data for latest year may not have been available at press time.

In U.S. $	2015	2014	2013	2012	2011	2010
Revenue	1,797,213,000	1,591,188,000	1,370,358,000	1,000,839,000	711,704,000	452,898,000
R&D Expense						
Operating Income	376,033,000	391,358,000	376,439,000	286,958,000	180,391,000	86,546,000
Operating Margin %	20.92%	24.59%	27.47%	28.67%	25.34%	19.10%
SGA Expense	538,147,000	448,718,000	386,387,000	282,312,000	212,784,000	136,161,000
Net Income	239,033,000	279,547,000	270,556,000	184,063,000	121,847,000	58,281,000
Operating Cash Flow	314,449,000	278,339,000	280,113,000	203,615,000	179,995,000	117,960,000
Capital Expenditure	119,733,000	106,408,000	93,229,000	122,311,000	42,839,000	16,307,000
EBITDA	434,397,000	440,426,000	419,439,000	317,217,000	205,005,000	107,378,000
Return on Assets %	18.77%	24.30%	30.30%	29.83%	30.21%	22.46%
Return on Equity %	21.86%	28.18%	36.34%	37.11%	39.08%	30.04%
Debt to Equity						

CONTACT INFORMATION:

Phone: 604 732-6124   Fax: 604 874-6124
Toll-Free: 877-263-9300
Address: 400-1818 Cornwall Ave., Vancouver, BC V6J 1C7 Canada

STOCK TICKER/OTHER:

Stock Ticker: LULU
Employees: 8,628
Parent Company:

Exchange: NAS
Fiscal Year Ends: 01/31

SALARIES/BONUSES:

Top Exec. Salary: $846,869   Bonus: $
Second Exec. Salary: $521,948   Bonus: $

OTHER THOUGHTS:

Estimated Female Officers or Directors: 5
Hot Spot for Advancement for Women/Minorities: Y

Sales, profits and employees may be estimates. Financial information, benefits and other data can change quickly and may vary from those stated here.

Luxottica Group SpA

www.luxottica.com

NAIC Code: 333314

TYPES OF BUSINESS:

Lens/Eyeglass Frame Manufacturing
Vision Plan Provider
Lens/Eyeglass Frame Retailer
Eye Care Services

BRANDS/DIVISIONS/AFFILIATES:

Ray-Ban
Oakley Inc
Luxottica Srl
LensCrafters Inc
EyeMed Vision Care LLC
Pearle Vision
Sunglass Hut Trading LLC
Luxottica Retail North America Inc

CONTACTS: *Note: Officers with more than one job title may be intentionally listed here more than once.*

Andrea Guerra, CEO
Enrico Cavatorta, CFO
Antonio Miyakawa, Dir.-Mktg., Style & Product
Nicola Pela, Dir.-Human Resources
Massimo Vian, Operations
Nicola Brandolese, Dir.-Bus. Dev.
Christina Parenti, Dir.-Corp. Comm.
Alessandra Senici, Dir.-Investor Rel.
Luca Fadda, Internal Audit
Susanna Zatta, Internal Communication
Paolo Pezzutto, Commercial Service Strategy & Planning
Paolo Alberti, Wholesale
Mark Weikel, Retail Optical, North America
Leonardo Del Vecchio, Chmn.

GROWTH PLANS/SPECIAL FEATURES:

Luxottica Group SpA is one of the world's largest manufacturers and retailers of prescription and fashion eyeglass frames and sunglasses. The firm's leading optical/sunglass retail brands include CHANEL, Oakley, LensCrafters, Pearle Vision, ILORI, The Optical Shop of Aspen and Sunglass Hut. Company-owned brands include Ray-Ban, Oakley, Vogue, Persol, Arnette, Oliver Peoples, Alain Mikli, Sferoflex and Luxottica. It licenses brands from Prada, Polo Ralph Lauren, Versace, Chanel, Donna Karan, Bvlgari, Dolce & Gabbana, Stella McCartney, Tory Burch and others. The firm operates through 50 subsidiaries, including Luxottica, Srl; Luxottica Retail North America, Inc.; Sunglass Hut Trading, LLC; and Arnette Optic Illusions, Inc. Luxottica distributes sunglasses in approximately 7,000 storefronts through its wholesale and retail networks in 130 countries worldwide. Luxottica is involved in the U.S. health care market through subsidiary EyeMed Vision Care, LLC. EyeMed offers members a vision plan including a network of optometrists, ophthalmologists and opticians as well as Luxottica eyeglass frames. The firm's manufacturing plants produce roughly 83 million units per year. The firm has 18 distribution centers worldwide. Approximately 44.3% of distributed frames are prescription and 55.7% of distributed frames are sunglasses.

FINANCIAL DATA: *Note: Data for latest year may not have been available at press time.*

In U.S. $	2015	2014	2013	2012	2011	2010
Revenue		8,121,410,000	7,760,880,000	7,520,528,000	6,603,926,000	6,153,459,000
R&D Expense						
Operating Income		1,228,576,000	1,120,388,000	1,042,249,000	856,618,200	755,814,800
Operating Margin %		15.12%	14.43%	13.85%	12.97%	12.28%
SGA Expense		4,160,319,000	3,961,763,000	3,953,344,000	3,446,339,000	3,285,439,000
Net Income		681,987,600	578,086,300	574,906,600	480,072,000	426,841,400
Operating Cash Flow		1,241,847,000	978,356,900	1,104,208,000	871,217,500	882,612,700
Capital Expenditure		445,031,000	398,199,000	401,726,800	356,895,300	244,479,100
EBITDA		1,641,840,000	1,512,514,000	1,435,704,000	1,210,126,000	1,098,005,000
Return on Assets %		7.27%	6.59%	6.34%	5.43%	5.31%
Return on Equity %		14.17%	13.40%	14.26%	13.16%	13.27%
Debt to Equity		0.34	0.41	0.51	0.62	0.74

CONTACT INFORMATION:

Phone: 39 2863341   Fax: 39 286334636
Toll-Free:
Address: Via C. Cantu, 2, Milan, 20123 Italy

STOCK TICKER/OTHER:

Stock Ticker: LUX   Exchange: NYS
Employees: 77,700   Fiscal Year Ends: 12/31
Parent Company:

SALARIES/BONUSES:

Top Exec. Salary: Bonus: $
$1,781,833
Second Exec. Salary: Bonus: $
$1,363,772

OTHER THOUGHTS:

Estimated Female Officers or Directors: 4

Hot Spot for Advancement for Women/Minorities: Y

LVMH Moet Hennessy Louis Vuitton SA

www.lvmh.com

NAIC Code: 312140

TYPES OF BUSINESS:

Luxury Goods, Manufacture & Retail
Wines & Spirits, Manufacturing
Fashion & Leather Goods, Manufacturing & Retail
Perfumes & Cosmetics, Manufacturing & Retail
Duty-Free Retail
Online Cosmetics & Apparel Retail
Watches & Jewelry, Manufacturing
Magazine Publishing & Advertising Services

BRANDS/DIVISIONS/AFFILIATES:

Dom Perignon
Aqua Di Parma
Benefit Cosmetics
Christian Dior SA
Le Bon Marche
Moet & Chandon
FRED
Louis Vuitton

CONTACTS: Note: Officers with more than one job title may be intentionally listed here more than once.

Bernard Arnault, CEO
Chantal Gaemperie, Dir.-Human Resources
Nicolas Bazire, Dir.-Dev. & Acquisitions
Jean-Jacques Guiony, Dir.-Finance
Antonio Belloni, Group Managing Dir.
Pierre-Yves Roussel, Dir.-Fashion Div.
Francesco Trapani, Dir.-Watches & Jewelry
Christophe Navarre, Dir.-Wines & Spirits
Bernard Arnault, Chmn.

GROWTH PLANS/SPECIAL FEATURES:

LVMH Moet Hennessy Louis Vuitton SA is a luxury goods company controlling a portfolio of approximately 70 luxury brands, operating in six sectors: wines & spirits, fashion & leather goods, watches & jewelry, perfumes & cosmetics, selective retailing and other activities. The company's wines & spirits brands include champagnes, such as Dom Perignon, Moet & Chandon, Krug, Mercier, Ruinart and Veuve Clicquot; several vineyards, including Chateau d'Yquem, Cloudy Bay and Cape Mentelle; Hennessy cognac; and several brands of whiskey, vodka, rum and sparkling wines. The firm's fashion & leather goods division includes the Donna Karan, Marc Jacobs, Givenchy, Kenzo, Berluti, Fendi and Louis Vuitton brands, while its watches & jewelry segment includes brands such as TAG Heuer, Zenith, Dior Watches, Chaumet, De Beers and FRED. The firm's perfumes include Aqua di Parma, Guerlain, Kenzo and Givenchy, and its cosmetics brands include Fresh, Make Up For Ever and Benefit Cosmetics. The company's selective retailing division operates several retail store brands, including Sephora cosmetics stores and Sephora.com; Le Bon Marche department stores; and Miami Cruiseline Services, which offers duty-free luxury shops aboard cruise ships; and DFS Galleria liquor, tobacco, cosmetics and fragrances duty-free stores, primarily located in the Asia-Pacific region. The other activities segment consists of businesses such as Royal Van Lent, which manufactures custom-designed yachts; La Samaritaine department store; and Groupe Les Echos, a French media conglomerate that focuses on financial news. Christian Dior SA owns a 42.4% stake in the firm. In 2014, the company formed a joint venture with designer Marco De Vincenzo for the development of his Marco De Vincenzo brand; the firm also acquired Clos des Lambrays, a prestigious vineyard in Burgundy.

FINANCIAL DATA: Note: Data for latest year may not have been available at press time.

In U.S. $	2015	2014	2013	2012	2011	2010
Revenue		32,516,130,000	30,935,860,000	29,825,730,000	25,109,310,000	21,565,630,000
R&D Expense						
Operating Income		5,763,924,000	6,255,307,000	6,090,805,000	5,469,944,000	4,424,563,000
Operating Margin %		17.72%	20.22%	20.42%	21.78%	20.51%
SGA Expense		14,982,380,000	13,874,380,000	13,016,850,000	10,935,640,000	9,355,365,000
Net Income		5,994,227,000	3,646,629,000	3,633,894,000	3,677,407,000	3,522,457,000
Operating Cash Flow		3,005,604,000	3,139,328,000	2,625,658,000	4,146,502,000	4,297,207,000
Capital Expenditure					1,856,215,000	1,063,423,000
EBITDA		7,775,090,000	7,798,438,000	7,469,435,000	6,433,605,000	6,070,640,000
Return on Assets %		10.35%	6.50%	7.05%	7.27%	8.75%
Return on Equity %		23.31%	13.40%	14.56%	15.46%	19.56%
Debt to Equity		0.23	0.15	0.15	0.18	0.19

CONTACT INFORMATION:

Phone: 33 144132222   Fax: 33 144132119
Toll-Free:
Address: 22 Ave. Montaigne, Paris, 75008 France

STOCK TICKER/OTHER:

Stock Ticker: LVMHF   Exchange: PINX
Employees: 114,635   Fiscal Year Ends: 12/31
Parent Company:

SALARIES/BONUSES:

Top Exec. Salary: $ Bonus: $
Second Exec. Salary: $ Bonus: $

OTHER THOUGHTS:

Estimated Female Officers or Directors: 4
Hot Spot for Advancement for Women/Minorities: Y

Sales, profits and employees may be estimates. Financial information, benefits and other data can change quickly and may vary from those stated here.

Macy's Inc

NAIC Code: 452111

www.macysinc.com

TYPES OF BUSINESS:

Department Stores
Bridal & Formalwear Stores
Direct Marketing
Online Sales
Catalogs
Wedding Planning & Bridal Registries
Credit Services
Furniture Stores

BRANDS/DIVISIONS/AFFILIATES:

FDS Bank
Macy's Backstage
Macy's Credit and Customer Service,
Macy's Logistics and Operations,
Macy's Systems and Technology Inc
Macy's Merchandising Group Inc
Bloomingdale's
Macys.com

CONTACTS: Note: Officers with more than one job title may be intentionally listed here more than once.

Linda Balicki, Assistant Secretary
Patti Ongman, Other Executive Officer
Terry Lundgren, CEO
Karen Hoguet, CFO
Jeffrey Kantor, Chairman, Divisional
Joel Belsky, Chief Accounting Officer
Dennis Broderick, Executive VP
Martine Reardon, Other Executive Officer
Robert Harrison, Other Executive Officer
Peter Sachse, Other Executive Officer
William Allen, Other Executive Officer
Timothy Baxter, Other Executive Officer
Molly Langenstein, Other Executive Officer
Jeffrey Gennette, President

GROWTH PLANS/SPECIAL FEATURES:

Macy's, Inc. is a U.S. operator of full-line department stores. The firm currently has approximately 840 stores in 45 states, Washington D.C., Guam and Puerto Rico. Macy's department stores, which operate under the brand names Macy's and Bloomingdale's, offer men's, women's and children's apparel and accessories; cosmetics; home furnishings; and other consumer goods. Through its stores, the firm conducts direct-to-customer catalog and e-commerce businesses via Bloomingdales.com and Macys.com. Additionally, the company offers online bridal registry and gift purchase facilities. The firm's owned brands include Charter Club, Alfani, Epic Threads, first impressions and Hotel Collection. It also licenses brands American Rag and Martha Stewart Collection from third parties. Feminine accessories, intimate apparel, shoes and cosmetics generate approximately 38% of Macy's revenues; feminine apparel accounts for 23%; men's and children's apparel derives 23%; and home and miscellaneous products account for 16%. The company conducts many of its support functions through direct/indirect subsidiary firms and divisions. These include FDS Bank and Macy's Credit and Customer Service, Inc., which both offer credit processing certain collections, customer service and credit marketing services; Macy's Systems and Technology, Inc., which offers operational electronic data processing and management information services; Macy's Merchandising Group, Inc., which designs, develops and markets the firm's private label brands; and Macy's Logistics and Operations, which operates warehouses and distribution services. In 2015, the firm opened off-price stores called Macy's Backstage in the New York City area; and it acquired Bluemercury Inc., a luxury beauty products and spa services retailer for $210 million. That September, it announced plans to close 35 to 40 stores in early 2016.

Macy's offers its employees medical and dental coverage; flexible spending accounts; wellness programs, including health screenings and Weight Watchers; disability protection; a 401(k) plan; an employee assistance program; tuition assistance; adoption assistance; paid vacation; leave of absence; life, AD&D and travel insurance; and a merchandise discount.

FINANCIAL DATA: Note: Data for latest year may not have been available at press time.

In U.S. $	2015	2014	2013	2012	2011	2010
Revenue	28,105,000,000	27,931,000,000	27,686,000,000	26,405,000,000	25,003,000,000	23,489,000,000
R&D Expense						
Operating Income	2,800,000,000	2,678,000,000	2,661,000,000	2,411,000,000	1,894,000,000	1,063,000,000
Operating Margin %	9.96%	9.58%	9.61%	9.13%	7.57%	4.52%
SGA Expense	8,355,000,000	8,440,000,000	8,482,000,000	8,281,000,000	8,260,000,000	8,062,000,000
Net Income	1,526,000,000	1,486,000,000	1,335,000,000	1,256,000,000	847,000,000	350,000,000
Operating Cash Flow	2,709,000,000	2,549,000,000	2,261,000,000	2,093,000,000	1,506,000,000	1,750,000,000
Capital Expenditure	1,068,000,000	863,000,000	942,000,000	764,000,000	505,000,000	460,000,000
EBITDA	3,821,000,000	3,700,000,000	3,588,000,000	3,500,000,000	3,049,000,000	2,279,000,000
Return on Assets %	7.08%	6.97%	6.19%	5.87%	4.03%	1.61%
Return on Equity %	26.24%	24.16%	22.27%	21.91%	16.55%	7.48%
Debt to Equity	1.35	1.07	1.12	1.12	1.26	1.79

CONTACT INFORMATION:

Phone: 513-579-7000   Fax:
Toll-Free: 800-261-5385
Address: 7 W. Seventh St., Cincinnati, OH 45202 United States

STOCK TICKER/OTHER:

Stock Ticker: M
Employees: 166,900
Parent Company:

Exchange: NYS
Fiscal Year Ends: 02/01

SALARIES/BONUSES:

Top Exec. Salary: $1,600,000   Bonus: $
Second Exec. Salary: $937,500   Bonus: $

OTHER THOUGHTS:

Estimated Female Officers or Directors: 5

Hot Spot for Advancement for Women/Minorities: Y

MadeWell

www.madewell.com

NAIC Code: 448120

TYPES OF BUSINESS:

Women's Clothing Stores

BRANDS/DIVISIONS/AFFILIATES:

J.Crew Group Inc
MadeWell Musings

CONTACTS: *Note: Officers with more than one job title may be intentionally listed here more than once.*

Millard Drexler, CEO
Michael J. Nicholson, Pres.
Michael J. Nicholson, CFO
Lynda Markoe, Exec. VP-Human Resources
Millard Drexler, Chmn.

GROWTH PLANS/SPECIAL FEATURES:

MadeWell, wholly-owned by J.Crew Group, Inc., is primarily a jeans-maker. The company also designs and manufactures things that go with denim, such as leather jackets, boots, t-shirts and totes. Its style is known as artful, cool, sexy, tomboyish, unexpected and effortless. Its www.madewell.com web site displays and sells new arrivals, gifts, denim, dresses, shirts, sweaters, coats, shoes and bags, and also has a link to items currently on sale. MadeWell Musings is a company blog located online at blog.madewell.com, with topics including style, denimmadewell, music, weeklyroundup, food, culture, noticed, howto, denimplus and everydaymadewell. Gift cards can be purchased over the Internet and received either by mail or by email. Additionally, MadeWell has a denim recycling program in which customers bring old jeans to a retail store. The jeans are sent to Blue Jeans Go Green and subsequently recycled into housing insulation. In return, customers receive $20 off a new pair of jeans.

FINANCIAL DATA: *Note: Data for latest year may not have been available at press time.*

In U.S. $	2015	2014	2013	2012	2011	2010
Revenue						
R&D Expense						
Operating Income						
Operating Margin %						
SGA Expense						
Net Income						
Operating Cash Flow						
Capital Expenditure						
EBITDA						
Return on Assets %						
Return on Equity %						
Debt to Equity						

CONTACT INFORMATION:

Phone: 434-385-5792   Fax: 434-385-5754
Toll-Free: 866-544-1937
Address: One Ivy Crescent, Lynchburg, VA 24513-1001 United States

STOCK TICKER/OTHER:

Stock Ticker: Subsidiary
Employees:
Parent Company: J Crew Group Inc

Exchange:
Fiscal Year Ends:

SALARIES/BONUSES:

Top Exec. Salary: $ Bonus: $
Second Exec. Salary: $ Bonus: $

OTHER THOUGHTS:

Estimated Female Officers or Directors:
Hot Spot for Advancement for Women/Minorities:

Mango/MNG Holding SL

NAIC Code: 448120

TYPES OF BUSINESS:

Women's Apparel, Retail
Apparel Manufacturing
Fast Fashion

BRANDS/DIVISIONS/AFFILIATES:

M by MNG
MngJEANS
MANGO
HE
MANGO Touch
Violeta by MANGO
MANGO MAN

CONTACTS: Note: Officers with more than one job title may be intentionally listed here more than once.

Isak Andic, Pres.
Toni Ruiz, CFO
Isak Andic, Chmn.

GROWTH PLANS/SPECIAL FEATURES:

Mango/MNG Holding SL is a multinational company engaged in the design, manufacture and marketing of clothing and accessories for young men and women. It has approximately 2,731 stores in 105 countries. The company specializes in fast fashion, a retail trend where stores continually fill their racks with a steady stream of new, trendy merchandise. Mango's clothing promotes a party-girl image and is famous for carrying clothing in an eclectic mix of body-hugging styles. The firm is also famous for its store atmosphere and layout. Mango mandates that store racks hang only one of each size of each garment, creating a sense of urgency in the customer. The company has several private-label brands including M by MNG and MngJEANS, over which it maintains tight control. Other brands include, MANGO MAN and Violeta by MANGO. Having manufacturing facilities in Europe allows Mango to make last-minute changes on pieces. The firm currently has stores under three names: MANGO, its main brand stores; HE, its men's clothing stores known for their black and gold decor; and MANGO TOUCH, stores with a feminine edge known for their mixture of classic and modern furnishings. Every Mango store also has its own set of traits dependent upon climate, shop location and whether large- or small-size clothing sells best at the store. The company's proprietary computer system matches the personality traits of its clothing to its stores, allowing the firm to dictate what pieces and styles should go to which stores. Mango hopes to grow to more than 3,500 stores and $6.8 billion in revenues by the end of 2017.

FINANCIAL DATA: Note: Data for latest year may not have been available at press time.

In U.S. $	2015	2014	2013	2012	2011	2010
Revenue		2,240,000,000	2,006,000,000	1,850,000,000		
R&D Expense						
Operating Income						
Operating Margin %						
SGA Expense						
Net Income		140,000,000	130,410,000	119,000,000		
Operating Cash Flow						
Capital Expenditure						
EBITDA						
Return on Assets %						
Return on Equity %						
Debt to Equity						

CONTACT INFORMATION:

Phone: 34-93-860-24-24   Fax: 34-93-860-22-07
Toll-Free:
Address: Mercaders 9-11, P.I. Riera de Caldes, Apt. 280, Barcelona, 08184 Spain

STOCK TICKER/OTHER:

Stock Ticker: Private
Employees: 12,200
Parent Company:

Exchange:
Fiscal Year Ends: 12/31

SALARIES/BONUSES:

Top Exec. Salary: $ Bonus: $
Second Exec. Salary: $ Bonus: $

OTHER THOUGHTS:

Estimated Female Officers or Directors:
Hot Spot for Advancement for Women/Minorities:

Marc Ecko Enterprises

www.marcecko.com

NAIC Code: 424300

TYPES OF BUSINESS:

Apparel and Clothing Brands, Designers, Importers and Distributors
Apparel Manufacturing-Women's
Apparel Retailing
Magazine Publishing
Video Games
Skateboards

BRANDS/DIVISIONS/AFFILIATES:

Ecko Unltd
Marc Ecko Cut & Sew
Ecko Red
Zoo York
Complex Magazine
Marc Echo Entertainment
Avirex
Complex Media Network

CONTACTS: Note: Officers with more than one job title may be intentionally listed here more than once.

Seth Gerszberg, CEO
Marc Ecko, Chief Creative Officer
Marc Ecko, Chmn.

GROWTH PLANS/SPECIAL FEATURES:

Marc Ecko Enterprises (MEE) is a private clothing designer, manufacturer and retailer focusing on urban, fashion forward customers. The company retails its products through department and specialty stores in the U.S. and through full price and outlet stores in over 100 international countries. MEE has eight primary brands: Ecko Unltd., a clothing line geared toward young men; Marc Ecko Cut & Sew, a menswear line; Zoo York, an action sports inspired clothing and accessories line as well as a line of skateboard and skate accessories; Complex Media, which includes Complex Magazine, which reaches more than 120 million unique users each month and the Complex Media Network, which consists of owned and partner web sites, as well as social and YouTube channels; Ecko Red, a juniors apparel line; Avirex, a sportswear line; Marc Ecko Entertainment, a videogame development and production firm; and ecko TV, an in-store and online video channel that showcases film projects from customers and independent film makers. MEE licensing agreements include footwear via the Skechers brand, watches through Callanen and kidswear through the Kids Headquarters line. Through the various MEE brands, the firm is able to offer a wide variety of merchandise including men's and women's apparel, formalwear, children's wear, outerwear, footwear, watches, eyewear, underwear, accessories and small leather goods. The company also developed a graffiti-themed video game with Atari, Inc. called Getting Up: Contents Under Pressure. The company maintains an e-commerce web site, Ecko.com, which has all MEE brands available.

FINANCIAL DATA: Note: Data for latest year may not have been available at press time.

In U.S. $	2015	2014	2013	2012	2011	2010
Revenue		1,100,000,000	1,050,000,000	1,000,000,000	950,000,000	900,000,000
R&D Expense						
Operating Income						
Operating Margin %						
SGA Expense						
Net Income						
Operating Cash Flow						
Capital Expenditure						
EBITDA						
Return on Assets %						
Return on Equity %						
Debt to Equity						

CONTACT INFORMATION:

Phone: 917-262-1002   Fax:
Toll-Free:
Address: 501 Tenth Ave, 7/Fl, New York, NY 10018 United States

STOCK TICKER/OTHER:

Stock Ticker: Private
Employees: 1,500
Parent Company:

Exchange:
Fiscal Year Ends:

SALARIES/BONUSES:

Top Exec. Salary: $ Bonus: $
Second Exec. Salary: $ Bonus: $

OTHER THOUGHTS:

Estimated Female Officers or Directors:
Hot Spot for Advancement for Women/Minorities: Y

MarineMax Inc

NAIC Code: 441222

TYPES OF BUSINESS:

Recreational Boats, Retail
Boat Parts & Accessories
Boat Repair & Maintenance
Boat Financing & Insurance
Slip & Storage Accommodations
Yacht Charter Services

BRANDS/DIVISIONS/AFFILIATES:

MarineMax Vacations

CONTACTS: Note: Officers with more than one job title may be intentionally listed here more than once.

Paulee Day, Assistant Secretary
William Mcgill, CEO
Michael Mclamb, CFO
Anthony Cassella, Chief Accounting Officer
Charles Cashman, Executive VP, Divisional
William McGill, Executive VP, Divisional

GROWTH PLANS/SPECIAL FEATURES:

MarineMax, Inc. is one of the largest recreational boat dealers in the U.S., marketing new and used sport boats, sport cruisers, yachts and fishing boats through 54 retail locations in 16 states. The company's product offerings include Sea Ray, Boston Whaler, Cabo, Hatteras and Meridian recreational boats and yachts, all of which are manufactured by Brunswick Corporation. Additionally, the firm is the exclusive dealer for Italy-based Azimut-Benetti Group's Azimut yachts, mega yachts and other recreational boats for the U.S. Sales of Brunswick products account for approximately 40% of the company's 2014 revenues. MarineMax also sells marine parts and accessories, including engines, propellers, oils, lubricants, steering and control systems, corrosion control products, engine service products, high-performance instruments and boating accessories, including life jackets, inflatables and water sports equipment. In addition, the company offers related boat financing, insurance and extended service contracts; repair and maintenance services; boat and yacht brokerage services; and, where available, storage accommodations, both at in-water slips and on land. The majority of the company's stores are located on waterfront properties. The waterfront retail locations are easily accessible to the boating populace, serve as in-water showrooms and enable the sales force to give the customer immediate in-water boat demonstrations. MarineMax's average selling price for a new boat is approximately $167,000. Besides its retail operations, the company owns a yacht charter business, MarineMax Vacations, located in Tortola, British Virgin Islands. Recently, the company expanded its third-party brand offerings with the addition of Ocean Alexander Yachts in all of its locations.

FINANCIAL DATA: Note: Data for latest year may not have been available at press time.

In U.S. $	2015	2014	2013	2012	2011	2010
Revenue		624,692,000	584,497,000	524,456,000	480,894,000	450,340,000
R&D Expense						
Operating Income		15,387,000	18,348,000	5,370,000	-8,402,000	-13,165,000
Operating Margin %		2.46%	3.13%	1.02%	-1.74%	-2.92%
SGA Expense		146,433,000	132,505,000	127,913,000	127,896,000	123,972,000
Net Income		11,272,000	15,024,000	1,099,000	-11,523,000	2,497,000
Operating Cash Flow		10,809,000	7,811,000	8,674,000	-14,680,000	40,216,000
Capital Expenditure		9,194,000	9,822,000	5,732,000	6,585,000	4,159,000
EBITDA		22,668,000	25,125,000	11,849,000	-1,787,000	-5,808,000
Return on Assets %		2.87%	4.02%	.30%	-3.29%	.68%
Return on Equity %		4.88%	7.10%	.55%	-5.80%	1.24%
Debt to Equity						

CONTACT INFORMATION:

Phone: 727 531-1700   Fax: 727 524-3954
Toll-Free:
Address: 18167 US Hwy. 19 N., Ste. 300, Clearwater, FL 33764 United States

STOCK TICKER/OTHER:

Stock Ticker: HZO
Employees: 1,228
Parent Company:

Exchange: NYS
Fiscal Year Ends: 09/30

SALARIES/BONUSES:

Top Exec. Salary: $550,000   Bonus: $
Second Exec. Salary: $315,000   Bonus: $

OTHER THOUGHTS:

Estimated Female Officers or Directors: 1
Hot Spot for Advancement for Women/Minorities:

Marks & Spencer Group plc

www.marksandspencer.com

NAIC Code: 452111

TYPES OF BUSINESS:

Department Stores
Grocery Stores
Food & Housewares
Financial Services
Food Courts
Franchising

BRANDS/DIVISIONS/AFFILIATES:

Marks & Spencer
Classic
Portfolio
Autograph
Indigo
Per Una
M&S.com

CONTACTS: Note: Officers with more than one job title may be intentionally listed here more than once.

Marc Bolland, CEO
Alan Stewart, CFO
Patrick Bousquet-Chavanne, Exec. Dir.-Mktg.
Tanith Dodge, Dir.-Human Resources
Darrell Stein, Dir.-IT
John Dixon, Exec. Dir.-Gen. Merch.
Amanda Mellor, Group Sec.
Steve Finlan, Dir.-Intl Oper.
Patrick Bousquet-Chavanne, Corp. Dir.- Bus. Dev.
Laura Wade-Gery, Exec. Dir.-Multi-Channel e-commerce
Dominic Fry, Dir-Comm.
Dominic Fry, Dir.-Investor Rel.
Steve Rowe, Exec. Dir.-Food
Clem Constantine, Dir.-Property
Andy Adcock, Trading Dir.-Food
Robert Swannel, Chmn.
Jan Heere, Dir.-Intl
Ddirk Lembregts, Dir.-Supply Chain

GROWTH PLANS/SPECIAL FEATURES:

Marks & Spencer Group plc serves as a holding company for the Marks & Spencer group of companies. Marks & Spencer is one of the leading mass merchandise retailers in the U.K., with an average of more than 33 million customers per week. The company has products sourced from more than 3,000 global suppliers. Marks & Spencer sells women's, men's and children's apparel as well as housewares and women's lingerie. The company's most notable apparel brands include Classic, Per Una, Limited Collection, Indigo and Autograph. The company also retails food products that include fresh produce, staple foods and ready-made meals. The firm has 852 stores throughout the U.K. In addition, the company has 480 international and franchised stores in roughly 59 countries throughout Europe, Asia and the Middle East. M&S.com is the company's e-commerce site, which includes its home catalogue and flower and wine delivery. In addition, the web site provides Christmas hamper delivery, which provides in-store food ordering services and lunchtime platter delivery services. In March 2015, the firm announced plans to invest and expand its China business, initially by entering the key cities of Beijing and Guangzhou during 2015 and 2016.

The company offers employees benefits including life assurance, a pension plan, a sharesave plan, subsidized health care and 20% employee discount.

FINANCIAL DATA: Note: Data for latest year may not have been available at press time.

In U.S. $	2015	2014	2013	2012	2011	2010
Revenue	15,414,540,000	15,411,990,000	14,989,090,000	14,850,810,000	14,560,800,000	14,256,290,000
R&D Expense						
Operating Income	1,048,375,000	1,038,210,000	1,130,146,000	1,115,945,000	1,251,084,000	1,273,657,000
Operating Margin %	6.80%	6.73%	7.53%	7.51%	8.59%	8.93%
SGA Expense	156,815,300	4,820,014,000				
Net Income	727,270,000	784,524,700	697,670,900	767,034,400	914,880,300	786,767,100
Operating Cash Flow	1,910,485,000	1,688,642,000	1,704,488,000	1,595,210,000	1,574,880,000	1,592,968,000
Capital Expenditure	1,046,133,000	959,129,300	1,240,321,000	1,077,376,000	678,386,700	642,060,500
EBITDA	1,868,478,000	1,803,151,000	1,729,602,000	1,903,459,000	2,075,971,000	1,893,742,000
Return on Assets %	6.04%	6.78%	6.28%	7.02%	8.44%	7.30%
Return on Equity %	16.47%	20.13%	17.62%	18.78%	25.27%	24.76%
Debt to Equity	0.54	0.61	0.68	0.69	0.71	1.05

CONTACT INFORMATION:

Phone: 44 2079354422   Fax: 44 2074872670
Toll-Free:
Address: 35 N. Wharf Rd., Waterside House, London, W2 1NW United Kingdom

STOCK TICKER/OTHER:

Stock Ticker: MAKSF   Exchange: PINX
Employees: 82,461   Fiscal Year Ends: 03/31
Parent Company:

SALARIES/BONUSES:

Top Exec. Salary: $ Bonus: $
Second Exec. Salary: $ Bonus: $

OTHER THOUGHTS:

Estimated Female Officers or Directors: 5
Hot Spot for Advancement for Women/Minorities: Y

Marsh Supermarkets Inc

NAIC Code: 445110

www.marsh.net

TYPES OF BUSINESS:

Grocery Stores
Convenience Stores
Catering Services
Cafeteria Management Services
Floral Shops
Online Grocery Sales & Delivery

BRANDS/DIVISIONS/AFFILIATES:

Marsh Supermarkets
O'Malia's Food Markets
Sun Capital Partners Inc
Marsh

GROWTH PLANS/SPECIAL FEATURES:

Marsh Supermarkets, Inc., owned by Sun Capital Partners, Inc., is a retail food chain headquartered in Indianapolis, Indiana. The company operates about 73 Marsh Supermarkets and two O'Malia's Food Markets in both Indiana and Ohio. Marsh is the largest pharmacy chain based in the state of Indiana, with 37 pharmacy locations. Overall, the company serves two million customers every week. Marsh's specialty offerings and services include grocery, pharmacy, meats, fresh produce, deli, bakery, spirits and floral. During 2014-15, the firm closed more than a dozen stores.

Marsh offers its employees benefits including medical, dental, life and disability coverage; prescription drug coverage; flexible spending accounts; and a 401(k) savings plan.

CONTACTS: Note: Officers with more than one job title may be intentionally listed here more than once.

Tom O'Boyle, CEO
David Kuncl, CMO
Jay Stanley, CIO
Bill Erickson, VP-Oper.
Connie Gardner, Sr. Dir.-Community Rel.

FINANCIAL DATA: Note: Data for latest year may not have been available at press time.

In U.S. $	2015	2014	2013	2012	2011	2010
Revenue		1,430,000,000	1,410,000,000	1,350,000,000	1,275,000,000	1,200,000,000
R&D Expense						
Operating Income						
Operating Margin %						
SGA Expense						
Net Income						
Operating Cash Flow						
Capital Expenditure						
EBITDA						
Return on Assets %						
Return on Equity %						
Debt to Equity						

CONTACT INFORMATION:

Phone: 317-594-2100   Fax: 317-594-2704
Toll-Free: 800-382-8798
Address: 9800 Crosspoint Blvd, Indianapolis, IN 46256 United States

STOCK TICKER/OTHER:

Stock Ticker: Private   Exchange:
Employees: 9,300   Fiscal Year Ends: 03/31
Parent Company: SUN CAPITAL PARTNERS INC

SALARIES/BONUSES:

Top Exec. Salary: $ Bonus: $
Second Exec. Salary: $ Bonus: $

OTHER THOUGHTS:

Estimated Female Officers or Directors: 1
Hot Spot for Advancement for Women/Minorities:

Mary Kay Inc

www.marykay.com

NAIC Code: 454390

TYPES OF BUSINESS:

Cosmetics & Beauty Supplies, Direct Selling
Online Retail
Fragrances
Over-the-Counter Drugs
Cosmetics & Beauty Supplies, Manufacturing

BRANDS/DIVISIONS/AFFILIATES:

Thinking of You
MK High Intensity
Belara
Domain
Velocity
Journey

CONTACTS:
Note: Officers with more than one job title may be intentionally listed here more than once.

David B. Holl, CEO
David B. Holl, Pres.
Deborah Gibbins, CFO
Sheryl Adkins-Green, Chief Mktg. Officer
Melinda Foster Sellers, Chief People Officer
Kregg Jodie, CIO
Nathan Moore, Chief Legal Officer
Darrell Overcash, Pres., North America Region
Tara Eustace, Pres., European Region
Jose Smeke, Pres., Latin American Region
Richard R. Rogers, Exec. Chmn.
K.K. Chua, Pres., Asia Pacific Region
Dennis Greaney, Chief Supply Chain Officer

GROWTH PLANS/SPECIAL FEATURES:

Mary Kay, Inc. is one of the largest direct sellers of skin care products in the U.S. The company's merchandise includes more than 200 products across several categories, including skin care, color cosmetics, spa and body care and fragrances. Skin care includes anti-aging creams; cleansers; moisturizers; basic skin care for different skin types; products for specific needs, such as acne treatment and oil control; and lip and eye care. Color cosmetics products include lip, eyes, cheeks, nails, foundations and powder color enhancers as well as travel sets and applicators. The Mary Kay fragrance line has specialty scents for both men and women, including Journey, Belara and Thinking of You for women, and Domain, MK High Intensity and Velocity for men. Mary Kay develops, tests, manufactures and packages the majority of its products at its own plants. Most inventory is manufactured at the Dallas site, where the company headquarters and the Mary Kay Museum are located. An additional manufacturing facility is located in China. With FDA approval, the company also manufactures and distributes certain products classified as over-the-counter drugs, such as sunscreens and acne treatment products. There are about 3.5 million Mary Kay independent beauty consultants serving customers in more than 35 countries worldwide. About 40% of new sales recruits are relatively young, aged 18 to 30. A new recruit pays $100 for a basic starter kit in order to begin selling Mary Kay products. Independent beauty consultants may eventually become independent sales directors and/or independent national sales directors.

FINANCIAL DATA:
Note: Data for latest year may not have been available at press time.

In U.S. $	2015	2014	2013	2012	2011	2010
Revenue		3,200,000,000	3,100,000,000	3,000,000,000	2,900,000,000	2,300,000,000
R&D Expense						
Operating Income						
Operating Margin %						
SGA Expense						
Net Income						
Operating Cash Flow						
Capital Expenditure						
EBITDA						
Return on Assets %						
Return on Equity %						
Debt to Equity						

CONTACT INFORMATION:

Phone: 972-687-6300   Fax: 972-687-1611
Toll-Free: 800-627-9529
Address: 16251 Dallas Pkwy., Dallas, TX 75001 United States

STOCK TICKER/OTHER:

Stock Ticker: Private   Exchange:
Employees: 5,000   Fiscal Year Ends: 12/31
Parent Company:

SALARIES/BONUSES:

Top Exec. Salary: $ Bonus: $
Second Exec. Salary: $ Bonus: $

OTHER THOUGHTS:

Estimated Female Officers or Directors: 3
Hot Spot for Advancement for Women/Minorities: Y

Sales, profits and employees may be estimates. Financial information, benefits and other data can change quickly and may vary from those stated here.

Massmart Holdings Ltd

NAIC Code: 452910

www.massmart.co.za

TYPES OF BUSINESS:
Warehouse Clubs and Supercenters

BRANDS/DIVISIONS/AFFILIATES:
Game
CBW Holdings
DionWired
Builders Warehouse
Makro
Shield
Builders Express
Builders Trade Depot

CONTACTS: *Note: Officers with more than one job title may be intentionally listed here more than once.*
Grant Pattison, CEO
Guy Harward, COO
Ilan Zwarensteign, Dir.-Finance
Pearl Maphoshe, Exec.-Human Resources
Michael Spivey, General Counsel
Llewellyn Walters, Div. CEO-Massbuild
Kevin Vyvyan-Day, Div. CEO-Cambridge Food
Robin Wright, Div. CEO-Massdiscounters
Doug Jones, Div. Managing Dir.-Masswarehouse
Mncane Mthunzi, Exec.-Supplier Dev.

GROWTH PLANS/SPECIAL FEATURES:
Massmart Holdings, Ltd. is a South African-based wholesale and retailer of branded consumer goods. The firm has nine wholesale and retail chains as well as a buying group, with 40 stores and 523 buying group members. The firm has operations in 13 countries throughout sub-Saharan Africa. operates in four divisions Massdiscounters, Masswarehouse Massbuild and MassCash. Massdiscounters operates two retail formats: Game and DionWired. Game is a discount retailer of general merchandise and non-perishable groceries for home, leisure and business use. Game operates throughout South Africa and in 14 major cities in sub-Saharan Africa DionWired is a South African electronics and appliance specialty store catering to the middle-to upper-end income consumer. Game and DionWired operate 153 stores between themselves. Masswarehouse sells food, liquor and general merchandise to retail and wholesale customers through 19 large format warehouse stores under the Makro and The Fruitspot brands. Massbuild operates four complementary brands: Builders Warehouse, which operates large DIY and home improvement stores in major urban areas; Builders Express, a chain of smaller neighborhood home and garden improvement stores; Builders Trade Depot, a chain of building contractor outlets; and Builders Superstore, which targets under-serviced areas. MassCash consists of wholesale food and cosmetics business interests as well as retail outlets, all of which target lower living standards measure (LSM) groups MassCash's wholesale division includes CBW Holdings Jumbo Cash & Carry, Trident and Shield, which sell food liquor, groceries and cosmetics in bulk to government franchise, small traders, general dealers and hawkers. Shield is the firm's buying group, with 523 members in the wholesale or retail food businesses. The firm's retail outlets operate under the Cambridge and Rhino Cash & Carry brand grocery chains

FINANCIAL DATA: *Note: Data for latest year may not have been available at press time.*

In U.S. $	2015	2014	2013	2012	2011	2010
Revenue		5,448,218,000	4,781,293,000	4,265,918,000	3,690,314,000	3,307,059,000
R&D Expense						
Operating Income		112,960,300	129,972,700	135,847,900	112,298,200	130,098,100
Operating Margin %		2.07%	2.71%	3.18%	3.04%	3.93%
SGA Expense			173,364,300	302,200,900	262,489,200	233,677,600
Net Income		75,255,780	81,869,760	82,211,260	64,035,020	84,455,420
Operating Cash Flow		51,963,980	24,483,570	78,259,600	7,910,290	87,368,630
Capital Expenditure						
EBITDA		171,963,400	178,758,600	182,055,100	148,504,400	160,233,900
Return on Assets %		3.92%		6.43%	5.31%	8.42%
Return on Equity %		20.55%		28.19%	22.55%	37.20%
Debt to Equity		0.40		0.19	0.25	0.11

CONTACT INFORMATION:
Phone: 27 115170000   Fax: 27 115170020
Toll-Free:
Address: Massmart House 16 Peltier Drive Sunninghill Ext 6, Sandton, 2157 South Africa

STOCK TICKER/OTHER:
Stock Ticker: MMRTY
Employees: 47,209
Parent Company:

Exchange: PINX
Fiscal Year Ends: 06/30

SALARIES/BONUSES:
Top Exec. Salary: $ Bonus: $
Second Exec. Salary: $ Bonus: $

OTHER THOUGHTS:
Estimated Female Officers or Directors: 1
Hot Spot for Advancement for Women/Minorities:

Mattress Firm Holding Corp

www.mattressfirm.com

NAIC Code: 442110

TYPES OF BUSINESS:

Mattress Stores
Mattress Discounters
1800mattress.com
mattress.com

BRANDS/DIVISIONS/AFFILIATES:

Mattress Firm
Sleep Train
Sleepy's

CONTACTS: *Note: Officers with more than one job title may be intentionally listed here more than once.*

R. Stagner, CEO
Scott McKinney, Vice President, Divisional
Alexander Weiss, CFO
William Watts, Chairman of the Board
Cathy Hauslein, Chief Accounting Officer
Michael Wilson, Chief Marketing Officer
Robert Killgore, COO
Dale Carlsen, Director
Stephen Fendrich, Executive VP, Divisional
Bruce Levy, Executive VP, Divisional
Karrie Forbes, Executive VP, Divisional
Kindel Elam, Executive VP
Kenneth Murphy, President
Brian Baxter, Senior VP, Divisional
Matthew Forbes, Senior VP, Divisional
Sam Woods, Senior VP, Divisional

GROWTH PLANS/SPECIAL FEATURES:

Mattress Firm Holding Corp. is a specialty retailer of mattresses and related products and accessories in the U.S. The firm currently has a presence in 105 markets across 40 states through its approximately 2,200 owned or franchised stores operating under the brand names of Mattress Firm and Sleep Train. Mattress sales account for about 90% of its $14 billion in total net sales. Key highlights that make them a preferred destination and that differentiate their brand and services include: extensive product selection; contemporary, easy-to-navigate store design utilizing its unique comfort by color merchandising approach that organizes mattresses by comfort style; price and comfort satisfaction guarantees; superior customer service by its well-trained and commissioned sales associates; mattress firm red carpet delivery service, which includes a three-hour delivery window; and highly visible and convenient store locations. Its competitive strengths are: distinctive retail format, economies of scale and strong market share positions in key markets, highly attractive new store economic model, efficient fulfillment model with lower working capital requirements & proven track record of managing through severe economic conditions. Its growth strategies are: expand its company-operated store base, Increase sales and profitability within its existing network of stores, selectively expand its franchise network & continue to expand its proprietary product offering and target additional channels of distribution. In late 2015, the company agreed to acquire Sleepy's, adding 1,050 stores to Mattress Firm's total, with the acquired stores being mainly in the Northeast and Mid-Atlantic states. This transaction would bring Mattress Firm's total store count to about 3,500, and gives it a presence in Massachusetts, Vermont, New Jersey, Maryland, Connecticut and Rhode Island.

FINANCIAL DATA: *Note: Data for latest year may not have been available at press time.*

In U.S. $	2015	2014	2013	2012	2011	2010
Revenue	1,810,613,000	1,222,429,000	1,012,733,000	708,607,000	497,310,000	434,350,000
R&D Expense						
Operating Income	97,698,000	96,946,000	75,816,000	60,541,000	32,252,000	21,024,000
Operating Margin %	5.39%	7.93%	7.48%	8.54%	6.48%	4.84%
SGA Expense	594,436,000	372,497,000	319,195,000	219,289,000	149,399,000	127,641,000
Net Income	44,251,000	52,924,000	39,871,000	34,351,000	349,000	-4,673,000
Operating Cash Flow	104,813,000	103,441,000	78,738,000	81,675,000	42,429,000	20,857,000
Capital Expenditure	79,897,000	55,546,000	68,604,000	34,356,000	27,330,000	10,863,000
EBITDA	139,438,000	126,444,000	99,334,000	72,296,000	47,706,000	40,144,000
Return on Assets %	3.69%	7.01%	5.95%	6.09%	.07%	-1.00%
Return on Equity %	11.58%	17.76%	16.21%	32.93%		
Debt to Equity	1.74	0.66	0.81	1.00		

CONTACT INFORMATION:

Phone: 713 923-1090   Fax:
Toll-Free:
Address: 5815 Gulf Freeway, Houston, TX 77023 United States

STOCK TICKER/OTHER:

Stock Ticker: MFRM   Exchange: NAS
Employees: 6,900   Fiscal Year Ends: 01/31
Parent Company:

SALARIES/BONUSES:

Top Exec. Salary: $600,000   Bonus: $
Second Exec. Salary: Bonus: $
$382,115

OTHER THOUGHTS:

Estimated Female Officers or Directors:
Hot Spot for Advancement for Women/Minorities:

Max Mara Fashion Group SRL

www.maxmarafashiongroup.com

NAIC Code: 424300

TYPES OF BUSINESS:

Apparel and Clothing Brands, Designers, Importers and Distributors
Apparel Manufacturing
Retail Stores
Perfume

BRANDS/DIVISIONS/AFFILIATES:

Max Mara
Sportmax
Pennyblack
Marella
Max&Co
Marina Renaldi
Max Mara Hosiery
Persona

CONTACTS: Note: Officers with more than one job title may be intentionally listed here more than once.

Ignazio Maramotti, Managing Dir.
Laura Lusuardi, Dir.-Design
Luigi Maramotti, Chmn.

GROWTH PLANS/SPECIAL FEATURES:

Max Mara Fashion Group SRL is one of the largest Italian clothing manufacturers and retailers of designer apparel for men and women. It has nine brands, including Max Mara, a collection of suits, coats and classic garments made from top quality fabrics; Sportmax, a collection designed to appeal to younger people; Pennyblack, which offers casual, elegant and romantic lines; Marella, a lower priced line; Persona, a collection of modern garments and accessories, which targets young women of all sizes; and Marina Rinaldi, a collection of plus-sized fashions. Other brands include Weekend MaxMara, Max&Co. and iBLUES. The family-owned and -operated company sells its clothing through high-end boutiques and in over 2,300 mono-brand and over 10,000 multi-brand stores in 105 countries under the names Max Mara, for luxury clothing, and Max&Co., for trendy clothing. The company's clothing is also sold through luxury retailers including Neiman Marcus, Saks Fifth Avenue and Barneys. All Max Mara clothing is produced at the company's production facility in Italy under heavy quality supervision. Max Mara also offers a perfume line and the Max Mara Hosiery brand.

FINANCIAL DATA: Note: Data for latest year may not have been available at press time.

In U.S. $	2015	2014	2013	2012	2011	2010
Revenue		1,400,000,000	1,425,000,000	1,400,000,000	1,630,000,000	1,525,000,000
R&D Expense						
Operating Income						
Operating Margin %						
SGA Expense						
Net Income		216,020,000				
Operating Cash Flow						
Capital Expenditure						
EBITDA						
Return on Assets %						
Return on Equity %						
Debt to Equity						

CONTACT INFORMATION:

Phone: 39-05-22-3991   Fax: 39-05-22-399-3254
Toll-Free:
Address: Via Giulia Maramotti 4, Reggio Emilia, 42124 Italy

STOCK TICKER/OTHER:

Stock Ticker: Private
Employees: 5,500
Parent Company:

Exchange:
Fiscal Year Ends: 12/31

SALARIES/BONUSES:

Top Exec. Salary: $ Bonus: $
Second Exec. Salary: $ Bonus: $

OTHER THOUGHTS:

Estimated Female Officers or Directors: 1
Hot Spot for Advancement for Women/Minorities:

Medicine Shoppe International Inc

www.medicineshoppe.com

NAIC Code: 446110

TYPES OF BUSINESS:

Pharmacies
Pharmaceuticals & Medical Supplies, Distribution

BRANDS/DIVISIONS/AFFILIATES:

Cardinal Health Inc
Medicine Shoppe
Medicap Pharmacy
MedicineShoppe.com

CONTACTS: Note: Officers with more than one job title may be intentionally listed here more than once.

Donald C. Schreiber, CFO
Kim Myers, General Counsel
Bill Rampy, Sr. VP-Franchise Oper.
Mike Meyer, VP-Franchise Dev.
John Fiacco, VP-Field Svcs.

GROWTH PLANS/SPECIAL FEATURES:

Medicine Shoppe International, Inc., a subsidiary of Cardinal Health, Inc., is one of the largest independent retail pharmacy franchisers and distributors of pharmaceuticals and medical supplies in the U.S. Medicine Shoppe currently operates over 500 Medicine Shoppe and Medicap Pharmacy locations across the U.S., and more than 200 international pharmacies. Locations include independently-situated pharmacies as well as others operating inside supermarkets. Its pharmacies specialize in prescriptions and offer health-related products, including certain non-prescription products under the Medicine Shoppe brand name. It also has pharmacies with the signification of Specialized Care Centers. These pharmacies each focus on a particular health concern, such as diabetes, long-term care or home medical supplies, and offer customers pharmacy staff that have special training and certifications in that particular area. The company's web site, MedicineShoppe.com, provides customers with information about Medicare as well as maintaining a Wellness Center, which includes information on vaccines, a wellness library of over 1,700 articles on common diseases and health conditions and information on drug prescriptions and their possible effects. In May 2015, the firm announced that all Medicine Shoppe and Medicap Pharmacy franchises will not sell tobacco or tobacco-related products.

FINANCIAL DATA: Note: Data for latest year may not have been available at press time.

In U.S. $	2015	2014	2013	2012	2011	2010
Revenue						
R&D Expense						
Operating Income						
Operating Margin %						
SGA Expense						
Net Income						
Operating Cash Flow						
Capital Expenditure						
EBITDA						
Return on Assets %						
Return on Equity %						
Debt to Equity						

CONTACT INFORMATION:

Phone: 314-993-6000   Fax: 314-872-5500
Toll-Free: 800-325-1397
Address: 1100 N. Lindbergh, St. Louis, MO 63132 United States

SALARIES/BONUSES:

Top Exec. Salary: $ Bonus: $
Second Exec. Salary: $ Bonus: $

STOCK TICKER/OTHER:

Stock Ticker: Subsidiary
Employees:
Parent Company: CARDINAL HEALTH INC

Exchange:
Fiscal Year Ends: 06/30

OTHER THOUGHTS:

Estimated Female Officers or Directors: 1
Hot Spot for Advancement for Women/Minorities:

Meijer Inc

NAIC Code: 445110

TYPES OF BUSINESS:

Grocery Stores
General Merchandise
Hardware
Photo Services
Pharmacies
In-Store Restaurants
Gasoline, Retail
Home Decor

BRANDS/DIVISIONS/AFFILIATES:

Meijer Real Estate
Purple Cow Creamery
Meijer
Meijer Gold
True Goodness by Meijer
True Goodness by Meijer Organics
Meijer Ecowise
Falls Creek

CONTACTS: *Note: Officers with more than one job title may be intentionally listed here more than once.*

Hendrik G. Meijer, Co-CEO
Mark A. Murray, Co-CEO
J.K. Symancyk, Pres.
Jim Walsh, CFO
Janet Emerson, VP-Retail Oper.
Stacie Behler, VP-Corp. Comm. & Public Rel.
Doug Meijer, Co-Chmn.

GROWTH PLANS/SPECIAL FEATURES:

Meijer, Inc. is a leading grocery retailer in the Midwest, wit over 213 superstores throughout Illinois, Indiana, Kentuck Michigan and Ohio. Each Meijer store carries brand-name an private-label products, including bulk foods, fresh produce frozen items, seafood and meat products. Most stores featur nearly 40 departments, such as electronics, hardware, toy garden, entertainment, jewelry, photo, banking, pharmacy books, apparel, automotive and furniture. Meijer Real Estat provides leasing and internal licenses on adjacent propertie former Meijer properties and in-store tenant space. Compan brands include Meijer, Meijer Gold, True Goodness by Meije True Goodness by Meijer Organics, Meijer Ecowise, Market of Meijer, At Home with Meijer, Falls Creek, MTA Sport, Sho Force, Fun Club, Studio M, Wave Zone, GFM, Bab Beginnings, Simple Pleasures and Lake & Trail. Th superstores also offer several in-store restaurants, includin delis and cafes. Meijer stores are open 24-hours-a-day an close only on Christmas. In addition to its retail stores, the firm operates a web site that features a baby club, wine guides contests, advertisements, pharmaceutical help and gardenin tips. The firm also owns the Purple Cow Creamery dair production facility in Ohio.

FINANCIAL DATA: *Note: Data for latest year may not have been available at press time.*

In U.S. $	2015	2014	2013	2012	2011	2010
Revenue		15,000,000,000	15,300,000,000	14,780,000,000	14,630,000,000	14,200,000,000
R&D Expense						
Operating Income						
Operating Margin %						
SGA Expense						
Net Income						
Operating Cash Flow						
Capital Expenditure						
EBITDA						
Return on Assets %						
Return on Equity %						
Debt to Equity						

CONTACT INFORMATION:

Phone: 616-453-6711   Fax: 616-791-2572
Toll-Free: 877-363-4537
Address: 2929 Walker Ave. NW, Grand Rapids, MI 49544 United States

STOCK TICKER/OTHER:

Stock Ticker: Private   Exchange:
Employees: 74,000   Fiscal Year Ends: 01/31
Parent Company:

SALARIES/BONUSES:

Top Exec. Salary: $ Bonus: $
Second Exec. Salary: $ Bonus: $

OTHER THOUGHTS:

Estimated Female Officers or Directors:
Hot Spot for Advancement for Women/Minorities: Y

Menard Inc

www.menards.com

NAIC Code: 444110

TYPES OF BUSINESS:

Home Improvement Stores
Lumber
Housing Materials
Building Materials Manufacturing
Prefabricated Houses

BRANDS/DIVISIONS/AFFILIATES:

Menards
Midwest Manufacturing
MasterForce
MasterCraft
Dakota
Grip Fast
Tuscany
Tool Shop

CONTACTS: Note: Officers with more than one job title may be intentionally listed here more than once.

John R. Menard, Jr., Pres.
Scott Collette, COO

GROWTH PLANS/SPECIAL FEATURES:

Menard, Inc. (Menards), is a family-owned company that began in 1960, is headquartered in Eau Claire, Wisconsin and has 280 home improvement stores. The company's stores are located throughout the Midwest in a 14-state region including: Illinois, Indiana, Iowa, Kansas, Kentucky, Michigan, Minnesota, Missouri, Nebraska, North Dakota, Ohio, South Dakota, Wisconsin and Wyoming. The firm's departments are: appliances; bath; building materials; doors, windows and millwork; electrical; flooring and rugs; grocery and pet; heating and cooling; home and dÃ©cor; kitchen; lighting and ceiling fans; maintenance, repair and operations; outdoors; paint; plumbing; home and patio; storage and organization; and tools and hardware. Menards provides a number of quality brands such as Midwest Manufacturing, Masterforce, Dakota, Mastercraft, Grip Fast, Tuscany, Tool Shop and Enchanted Garden/Enchanted Forest. The company's subsidiary, Midwest Manufacturing, operates a number of manufacturing facilities in Wisconsin, Illinois, Ohio, Nebraska, Iowa and Minnesota. Menard has four distribution centers in Plato, Illinois; Shelby, Iowa; Holiday City, Ohio; and Eau Claire, Wisconsin.

The company offers employees medical, dental and disability insurance; a profit sharing program; advancement opportunities; 401(k); store discounts; and bonuses.

FINANCIAL DATA: Note: Data for latest year may not have been available at press time.

In U.S. $	2015	2014	2013	2012	2011	2010
Revenue		7,920,000,000	7,775,000,000	7,600,000,000	7,475,000,000	7,170,000,000
R&D Expense						
Operating Income						
Operating Margin %						
SGA Expense						
Net Income						
Operating Cash Flow						
Capital Expenditure						
EBITDA						
Return on Assets %						
Return on Equity %						
Debt to Equity						

CONTACT INFORMATION:

Phone: 715-876-5911   Fax: 715-876-2868
Toll-Free:
Address: 4777 Menard Dr., Eau Claire, WI 54703 United States

STOCK TICKER/OTHER:

Stock Ticker: Private
Employees: 46,500
Parent Company:

Exchange:
Fiscal Year Ends: 01/31

SALARIES/BONUSES:

Top Exec. Salary: $ Bonus: $
Second Exec. Salary: $ Bonus: $

OTHER THOUGHTS:

Estimated Female Officers or Directors:
Hot Spot for Advancement for Women/Minorities:

Men's Wearhouse Inc (The)

www.menswearhouse.com

NAIC Code: 448110

TYPES OF BUSINESS:

Men's Apparel, Retail
Men's Suits
Shoes & Accessories
Business Casual Wear
Sportswear
Shoes & Accessories
Ladies' Career Apparel
Dry Cleaning & Laundry

BRANDS/DIVISIONS/AFFILIATES:

K&G
Moores
Men's Wearhouse and Tux
Jos A Bank
Men's Wearhouse
Twin Hill
Dimensions
Alexandra

CONTACTS: Note: Officers with more than one job title may be intentionally listed here more than once.

Jon Kimmins, CFO
William Sechrest, Chairman of the Board
Hyon Park, Chief Information Officer
Douglas Ewert, Director
James Bragg, Executive VP, Divisional
Mark Neutze, Executive VP, Divisional
Matthew Stringer, Executive VP, Divisional
Carole Souvenir, Executive VP, Divisional
Bruce Thorn, Executive VP
A. Rhodes, Executive VP
Mary Blake, President
Michael Conlon, Secretary
Kelly Dilts, Senior VP, Divisional
Brian Vaclavik, Senior VP
David Edwab, Vice Chairman of the Board

GROWTH PLANS/SPECIAL FEATURES:

The Men's Wearhouse, Inc. is a leading specialty retailer of men's suits and provider of tuxedo rental products in the U.S. and Canada, operating a total of 1,758 retail stores. The company conducts business through two segments: retail and corporate apparel. The retail segment comprises The Men's Wearhouse/Men's Wearhouse and Tux, Jos. A. Bank, Moores and K&G stores, as well as internet sites www.menswearhouse.com, www.josbank.com and www.josephabboud.com. The division operates 698 Men's Wearhouse retail apparel stores, as well as 210 Men's Wearhouse and Tux stores, which are referred to as rental stores and offer a full selection of tuxedo rental product and a limited selection of retail merchandise; Jos. A. Bank targets the male career professional with tailored and business casual clothing and accessories, and also offers tuxedo rentals at all of its stores (636); Moores is one of Canada's leading specialty retailers of men's apparel, with 123 retail stores in 10 provinces; and K&G stores offer a more value-oriented superstore approach with prices being up to 60% below regular prices, and offers both men's and ladies' apparel at its 91 stores in 27 U.S. states. The corporate apparel segment provides corporate clothing uniforms and workwear to workforces with operations conducted by Twin Hill in the U.S. and by the firm's U.K. holding company which operates under the Dimensions, Alexandra and Yaffy brand lines primarily in the U.K. In 2014, the firm acquired competitor Jos. A. Banks for $1.8 billion.

The Men's Wearhouse offers employees benefits including medical, dental, life and long-term disability insurance; a wellness program; 401(k) savings plan with company matching; employee stock discount program; tuition reimbursement; and merchandise discounts.

FINANCIAL DATA: Note: Data for latest year may not have been available at press time.

In U.S. $	2015	2014	2013	2012	2011	2010
Revenue	3,252,548,000	2,473,233,000	2,488,278,000	2,382,684,000	2,102,664,000	1,909,575,000
R&D Expense						
Operating Income	73,210,000	129,628,000	198,568,000	185,432,000	101,671,000	68,204,000
Operating Margin %	2.25%	5.24%	7.98%	7.78%	4.83%	3.57%
SGA Expense	1,285,404,000	947,665,000	909,098,000	861,453,000	790,908,000	710,049,000
Net Income	-387,000	83,791,000	131,716,000	120,601,000	67,697,000	45,508,000
Operating Cash Flow	94,764,000	188,930,000	225,730,000	162,797,000	169,947,000	163,155,000
Capital Expenditure	96,420,000	108,200,000	123,508,000	91,820,000	58,868,000	56,912,000
EBITDA	184,067,000	218,762,000	284,195,000	261,824,000	177,984,000	155,206,000
Return on Assets %	-.01%	5.49%	9.07%	8.84%	5.30%	3.76%
Return on Equity %	-.03%	7.95%	12.45%	12.12%	7.22%	5.21%
Debt to Equity	1.72	0.08				0.04

CONTACT INFORMATION:

Phone: 281 776-7000   Fax:
Toll-Free: 800-776-7848
Address: 6380 Rogerdale Rd., Houston, TX 77072 United States

STOCK TICKER/OTHER:

Stock Ticker: MW
Employees: 26,100
Parent Company:

Exchange: NYS
Fiscal Year Ends: 01/31

SALARIES/BONUSES:

Top Exec. Salary: $1,250,000
Bonus: $500,000

Second Exec. Salary: $484,615
Bonus: $300,000

OTHER THOUGHTS:

Estimated Female Officers or Directors: 1

Hot Spot for Advancement for Women/Minorities: Y

METRO AG

NAIC Code: 445110

www.metrogroup.de

TYPES OF BUSINESS:

Grocery Stores
Hypermarkets
Electronics, Audio & Appliance Stores
Home Centers
Department Stores
Restaurants
Athletic & Sporting Goods Stores

BRANDS/DIVISIONS/AFFILIATES:

Metro Cash & Carry International GmbH
MGA METRO Group Advertising GmbH
Real
Media-Saturn
Redcoon
MGL METRO Group Logistics
METRO Systems GmbH
METRO Properties

CONTACTS: Note: Officers with more than one job title may be intentionally listed here more than once.

Olaf Koch, CEO
Mark Frese, CFO
Heiko Hutmacher, Human Resources
Silvester Machio, CIO-Metro Group
Peter Wubben, Head-Corp. Comm.
Oliver Luckenbach, Head-IR
Pieter Haas, Member-Mgmt. Board
Franz Markus Haniel, Chmn.

GROWTH PLANS/SPECIAL FEATURES:

METRO AG is a German holding company for METRO Group. METRO Group, one of the world's largest retail companies, owns and operates approximately 2,200 retail locations in 31 European and Asian countries. These locations include wholesale stores, supermarkets, hypermarkets, department stores and specialty retailers. The company's four business units are: cash and carry, food retailing, nonfood specialty stores and department stores. The cash and carry unit, Metro Cash & Carry International GmbH, operates over 766 stores in 28 countries. The food retailing unit operates through Real, a chain of 311 hypermarkets under the Real brands of: Real Quality, Real Bio and Real Selection. Real Organic provides high quality, 100% organic produce or organic cultivation products that meet strict EU ecological guidelines. The nonfood specialty stores unit retails consumer electronics through Media-Saturn stores (986) in 15 countries. Media-Saturn holds a 100% stake in online retailer Redcoon. In addition to its retail operations, METRO owns companies involved in logistics (MGL METRO Group Logistics), information technology (METRO Systems GmbH), advertising (MGA METRO Group Advertising GmbH) and real estate (METRO Properties). In September 2015, the firm sold Galeria Kaufhof to Saks Fifth Avenue parent Hudson's Bay Company.

METRO AG offers its employees health insurance, a pension plan, group-run day care centers, holiday camps for employee's children and professional development & training.

FINANCIAL DATA: Note: Data for latest year may not have been available at press time.

In U.S. $	2015	2014	2013	2012	2011	2010
Revenue		66,899,090,000	49,160,510,000	70,830,150,000	70,790,880,000	71,380,970,000
R&D Expense						
Operating Income		752,462,200	746,094,400	1,476,269,000	2,242,529,000	2,346,536,000
Operating Margin %		1.12%		2.08%	3.16%	3.28%
SGA Expense		13,983,700,000	10,538,720,000	14,918,700,000	14,343,480,000	14,601,380,000
Net Income		134,785,200	-75,352,350	3,183,902	669,680,800	902,105,700
Operating Cash Flow		2,131,092,000	-1,876,380,000	2,483,444,000	2,277,551,000	2,668,110,000
Capital Expenditure		914,841,300	582,654,100	1,383,936,000	1,500,679,000	1,498,557,000
EBITDA		2,588,513,000	653,761,300	3,309,136,000	2,320,003,000	2,491,934,000
Return on Assets %		.45%			1.82%	2.47%
Return on Equity %		2.54%		.04%	9.95%	14.09%
Debt to Equity		0.89		1.11		

CONTACT INFORMATION:

Phone: 49-211-6886-0   Fax:
Toll-Free:
Address: Metro-strasse 1, DÃ¼sseldorf, 40235 Germany

SALARIES/BONUSES:

Top Exec. Salary: $ Bonus: $
Second Exec. Salary: $ Bonus: $

STOCK TICKER/OTHER:

Stock Ticker: MTAGF   Exchange: GREY
Employees: 250,000   Fiscal Year Ends: 12/31
Parent Company:

OTHER THOUGHTS:

Estimated Female Officers or Directors: 5
Hot Spot for Advancement for Women/Minorities: Y

Metro Inc

NAIC Code: 445110

TYPES OF BUSINESS:

Wholesale Merchandising
Supermarkets
Grocery Stores
Warehouses
Pharmaceutical distribution
Drug Stores
Discount Stores

BRANDS/DIVISIONS/AFFILIATES:

Metro Plus
Super C
Food Basics
Irresistibles
Selection
Marche AMI
Drug Basics
McMahon Distributeur Pharmaceutique Inc

CONTACTS: Note: Officers with more than one job title may be intentionally listed here more than once.

Eric La Fleche, CEO
Martin Allaire, Vice President, Divisional
Francois Thibault, CFO
Marc Giroux, Chief Marketing Officer
Simon Rivet, Secretary
Christian Bourbonniere, Senior VP, Divisional
Serge Boulanger, Senior VP, Divisional
Carmen Fortino, Senior VP
Roberto Sbrugnera, Vice President, Divisional
Genevieve Bich, Vice President, Divisional
Yves Vezina, Vice President, Divisional
Jacques Couture, Vice President, Divisional
Paul Denommee, Vice President
Paul Denommee, Vice President

GROWTH PLANS/SPECIAL FEATURES:

Metro, Inc. is a leader in the Canadian food industry. The company's operations are divided into two segments: food and pharmaceutical. The food segment comprises Metro's supermarkets, groceries, convenience stores, warehouses and its private brands. It holds leading positions in Canada's two largest markets, Quebec and Ontario, and operates a network of over 600 stores under the following banners: Metro, Metro Plus, Super C, Food Basics, Adonis and Premiere Moisson. At these stores, the firm sells groceries that include its private brands Irresistibles and Selection. Irresistibles, a healthy organic, allergy-free and fair trade food line, offers products with low fat, calories and salt; high fiber, vitamins and minerals and without hydrogenated oils, artificial flavors or artificial coloring. Selection is a low-cost food and pharmaceutical line including health and beauty products. The firm operates convenience stores through brands Marche Extra, Marche AMI, Service Servi Express and Depanneur Gem. Metro's warehouses are used to procure and store goods including meats and frozen foods, fruits and vegetables, dairy products and other general merchandise. The company runs 268 drugstores under the banners: Pharmacy and Drug Basics. Metro also operates drugstores through subsidiary McMahon Distributeur Pharmaceutique, Inc., under the Brunet and Clini-Plus banners, and sells pharmaceutical goods directly to authorized suppliers, independent/corporate drugstores and health care institutions.

Metro offers employees a retirement plan, collective insurance, personal holidays and education assistance.

FINANCIAL DATA: Note: Data for latest year may not have been available at press time.

In U.S. $	2015	2014	2013	2012	2011	2010
Revenue		8,683,313,000	8,542,767,000	8,998,269,000	8,563,594,000	8,497,891,000
R&D Expense						
Operating Income		453,779,200	450,707,600	532,218,600	433,176,700	438,870,500
Operating Margin %		5.22%	5.27%	5.91%	5.05%	5.16%
SGA Expense		828,519,900	516,485,700	814,585,000	15,133,470	
Net Income		334,959,000	534,091,500	360,955,600	289,408,800	293,529,300
Operating Cash Flow		323,871,200	424,636,100	409,128,000	406,955,400	410,401,600
Capital Expenditure		155,380,200	170,663,600	186,396,400	125,862,500	146,839,600
EBITDA		623,393,900	585,260,600	671,191,700	582,039,100	591,029,200
Return on Assets %		8.64%	13.96%	9.53%	7.89%	8.25%
Return on Equity %		16.33%	26.64%	18.84%	15.41%	16.64%
Debt to Equity		0.39	0.23	0.38	0.39	0.41

CONTACT INFORMATION:

Phone: 514 643-1000   Fax: 514 643-1030
Toll-Free: 800-561-8429
Address: 11011 Maurice-Duplessis Blvd. Maurice-Duplessis, Montreal, QC H1C 1V6 Canada

STOCK TICKER/OTHER:

Stock Ticker: MRU   Exchange: TSE
Employees: 65,000   Fiscal Year Ends: 09/30
Parent Company:

SALARIES/BONUSES:

Top Exec. Salary: $ Bonus: $
Second Exec. Salary: $ Bonus: $

OTHER THOUGHTS:

Estimated Female Officers or Directors: 3
Hot Spot for Advancement for Women/Minorities: Y

Michael Kors Holdings Ltd

www.michaelkors.com

NAIC Code: 424300

TYPES OF BUSINESS:

Apparel and Clothing Brands, Designers, Importers and Distributors
Designer Accessories
Retail Stores

BRANDS/DIVISIONS/AFFILIATES:

MichaelKors.com
Michael Kors
MICHAEL Michael Kors

CONTACTS: Note: Officers with more than one job title may be intentionally listed here more than once.

John D. Idol, CEO
Joseph B. Parsons, COO
Joseph B. Parsons, CFO
Lee S. Sporn, General Counsel
Brittton Russell, Sr. VP-Global Oper.
Lee S. Sporn, Sr. VP-Bus. Affairs
Joseph B. Parsons, Treas.
Michael Kors, Chief Creative Officer
John D. Idol, Chmn.

GROWTH PLANS/SPECIAL FEATURES:

Michael Kors Holdings, Ltd. is a designer, manufacturer and retailer of luxury American sportswear and accessories. The label was founded in 1981 by American fashion designer Michael Kors and has since expanded from a few boutiques offering women's ready-to-wear fashions to include full lines of handbags, shoes, accessories, beauty products and men's fashions. In total, Michael Kors Holdings operates approximately 343 stores in North America, and 183 international stores in Europe and Japan. It has a presence in 95 countries. The company sells its products wholesale in 4,038 locations: 2,541 North American department and specialty stores and 1,497 international department and specialty stores. The company operates a small number of Michael Kors collection boutiques that feature the designer's most luxurious collection of sportswear and accessories. More numerous are the Michael Kors lifestyle and outlet stores, which offer mainly shoe and handbag collections from the Michael Kors and MICHAEL Michael Kors collections and a limited selection of ready-to-wear pieces. These stores are located throughout the U.S., primarily in high-end malls and shopping centers. The firm also operates an e-commerce store at MichaelKors.com. Apart from the firm's owned boutiques and shops, the Michael Kors collections are sold in luxury department stores such as Neiman Marcus, Saks and Bloomingdale's. In addition to women's and men's fashion apparel and accessories, the company produces several lines of fragrances for men and women.

FINANCIAL DATA: Note: Data for latest year may not have been available at press time.

In U.S. $	2015	2014	2013	2012	2011	2010
Revenue	4,371,469,000	3,310,843,000	2,181,732,000	1,302,254,000	803,339,000	508,099,000
R&D Expense						
Operating Income	1,256,973,000	1,008,171,000	630,014,000	247,682,000	136,866,000	56,174,000
Operating Margin %	28.75%	30.45%	28.87%	19.01%	17.03%	11.05%
SGA Expense	1,251,431,000	926,913,000	621,536,000	464,568,000	279,822,000	191,717,000
Net Income	881,023,000	661,485,000	397,602,000	147,364,000	72,506,000	39,248,000
Operating Cash Flow	857,869,000	631,779,000	356,336,000	115,290,000	110,308,000	28,592,000
Capital Expenditure	385,433,000	213,560,000	129,867,000	88,187,000	57,830,000	32,175,000
EBITDA	1,395,398,000	1,087,825,000	684,305,000	285,236,000	162,409,000	75,017,000
Return on Assets %	35.89%	37.72%	40.48%	23.49%	14.23%	
Return on Equity %	43.53%	46.36%	52.89%	43.37%	45.38%	
Debt to Equity					0.81	

CONTACT INFORMATION:

Phone: 44-207-632-8600   Fax:
Toll-Free:
Address: 33 Kingsway, London, WC2B 6UF United Kingdom

SALARIES/BONUSES:

Top Exec. Salary: Bonus: $
$2,500,000
Second Exec. Salary: Bonus: $
$2,500,000

STOCK TICKER/OTHER:

Stock Ticker: KORS
Employees: 11,094
Parent Company:

Exchange: NYS
Fiscal Year Ends: 03/31

OTHER THOUGHTS:

Estimated Female Officers or Directors: 3

Hot Spot for Advancement for Women/Minorities: Y

Michaels Stores Inc

www.michaels.com

NAIC Code: 451120

TYPES OF BUSINESS:

Arts & Crafts Supplies, Retail
Custom Framing
Craft Classes
Online Sales
Decorating Supplies, Wholesale
Scrapbook Supplies

BRANDS/DIVISIONS/AFFILIATES:

Aaron Brothers
Artistree
Michaels

CONTACTS: Note: Officers with more than one job title may be intentionally listed here more than once.

Carl Rubin, CEO
Charles Sonsteby, CFO
Stephen Carlotti, Executive Vice President-Marketing
Theodore Bachmeier, Executive VP, Divisional
Philo Pappas, Executive VP, Divisional
Thomas DeCaro, Executive VP, Divisional
Michael Veitenheimer, General Counsel
Dennis Mullahy, Senior VP, Divisional
Lance Weibye, Senior VP, Divisional
Shawn Hearn, Senior VP, Divisional
Jennifer Robinson, Vice President, Divisional
James Sullivan, Vice President

GROWTH PLANS/SPECIAL FEATURES:

Michaels Stores, Inc. is a leading arts and crafts specialty retailer in North America, providing materials and education for creative activities in home decor, art and craft projects. The company's roughly 1,168 Michaels stores in 49 states and Canada offer approximately 36,000 items, including products for the do-it-yourself home decorator, such as wall decor, candles, containers, baskets, frames, mat boards, glass, backing materials, framed art, photo albums, silk flowers, dried flowers and artificial plants. Other merchandise includes hobby items, such as plastic model kits, cake decoration supplies and candy making supplies. General crafts account for 52% of sales; home decor and seasonal, 21%; framing, 17% and scrapbooking, 10%. The firm also offers in-store classes and demonstrations for adults and children alike. The majority of classes are offered free of charge or at a nominal price. Additionally, Michaels operates 120 Aaron Brothers stores located in Arizona, California, Colorado, Georgia, Idaho, Nevada, Oregon, Texas and Washington. Aaron Brothers offers approximately 7,100 items including photo frames, ready-made frames, custom framing and a wide selection of art supplies. Artistree is the company's non-retail frame manufacturer and handles Michaels custom frame orders. The firm also operates seven distribution facilities in California, Florida, Illinois, Pennsylvania, Texas and Washington. Michaels became a publically traded company in July 2014.

FINANCIAL DATA: Note: Data for latest year may not have been available at press time.

In U.S. $	2015	2014	2013	2012	2011	2010
Revenue	4,738,000,000	4,570,000,000	4,408,000,000	4,210,000,000	4,031,000,000	
R&D Expense						
Operating Income	627,000,000	610,000,000	592,000,000	538,000,000	488,000,000	
Operating Margin %	13.23%	13.34%	13.43%	12.77%	12.10%	
SGA Expense	1,239,000,000	1,193,000,000	1,147,000,000	1,123,000,000	1,059,000,000	
Net Income	217,000,000	243,000,000	200,000,000	157,000,000	103,000,000	
Operating Cash Flow	441,000,000	449,000,000	299,000,000	409,000,000	438,000,000	
Capital Expenditure	138,000,000	112,000,000	124,000,000	109,000,000	81,000,000	
EBITDA	661,000,000	700,000,000	657,000,000	612,000,000	528,000,000	
Return on Assets %	11.32%	14.43%	11.78%	8.54%		
Return on Equity %						
Debt to Equity						

CONTACT INFORMATION:

Phone: 972-409-1300   Fax: 972-409-1556
Toll-Free: 800-642-4235
Address: 8000 Bent Branch Dr., Irving, TX 75063 United States

STOCK TICKER/OTHER:

Stock Ticker: MIK   Exchange: NAS
Employees: 51,000   Fiscal Year Ends: 02/02
Parent Company:

SALARIES/BONUSES:

Top Exec. Salary: Bonus: $
$1,126,654
Second Exec. Salary: Bonus: $
$728,339

OTHER THOUGHTS:

Estimated Female Officers or Directors: 2

Hot Spot for Advancement for Women/Minorities:

Moncler SpA

NAIC Code: 448120

TYPES OF BUSINESS:

Women's Clothing Stores
Men's Clothing Stores

BRANDS/DIVISIONS/AFFILIATES:

GROWTH PLANS/SPECIAL FEATURES:

Moncler SpA is a fashion company specializing in luxury sportswear and down jackets. It designs and sells sportswear, predominately skiwear for men, women and children, as well as shoes and fashion accessories such as handbags, eyewear, hats, scarves, gloves and makeup bags. The firm's adult clothing includes pants, knitwear and outerwear. Children's clothing consists primarily of snow jackets and suits. Headquartered in Italy, the firm has 122 mono-brand stores throughout Europe, America and Asia/Japan. In 2014, the firm expanded its presence into Russia, with the opening of a boutique in Moscow.

CONTACTS: Note: Officers with more than one job title may be intentionally listed here more than once.

Remo Ruffini, Pres.
Remo Ruffini, Chmn.

FINANCIAL DATA: Note: Data for latest year may not have been available at press time.

In U.S. $	2015	2014	2013	2012	2011	2010
Revenue		789,083,256	714,653,000	602,137,000	447,672,000	347,724,000
R&D Expense						
Operating Income						
Operating Margin %						
SGA Expense						
Net Income		148,109,404	116,234,000	104,245,000	73,220,000	57,987,000
Operating Cash Flow						
Capital Expenditure						
EBITDA						
Return on Assets %						
Return on Equity %						
Debt to Equity						

CONTACT INFORMATION:

Phone: 39-02-422-041   Fax: 39-02-422-0441
Toll-Free:
Address: Via Stendhal 47, Milan, 20144 Italy

SALARIES/BONUSES:

Top Exec. Salary: $ Bonus: $
Second Exec. Salary: $ Bonus: $

STOCK TICKER/OTHER:

Stock Ticker: MONC
Employees: 1,376
Parent Company:

Exchange: Italy
Fiscal Year Ends:

OTHER THOUGHTS:

Estimated Female Officers or Directors: 3
Hot Spot for Advancement for Women/Minorities: Y

NACCO Industries Inc

NAIC Code: 335210

www.nacco.com

TYPES OF BUSINESS:

Kitchen Appliance Manufacturing
Coal/Lignite Mining
Kitchen Appliance Stores, Retail

BRANDS/DIVISIONS/AFFILIATES:

Hamilton Beach Brands Inc
Kitchen Collection LLC (The)
North American Coal Corporation (The)
Hamilton Beach
Proctor Silex
Kitchen Collection
Le Gourmet Chef
Weston Products LLC

CONTACTS: Note: Officers with more than one job title may be intentionally listed here more than once.

Mary Maloney, Assistant General Counsel
Gregory Salyers, Senior VP, Subsidiary
Miles Haberer, Assistant General Counsel
Jesse Adkins, Assistant Secretary
J.C. Butler, CEO, Subsidiary
Gregory Trepp, CEO, Subsidiary
Alfred Rankin, CEO
James Taylor, CFO, Subsidiary
Elizabeth Loveman, Chief Accounting Officer
John Pokorny, Controller, Subsidiary
Kathleen Diller, General Counsel, Subsidiary
John Neumann, General Counsel
Dana Sykes, Other Corporate Officer
Richard Moss, Other Corporate Officer
K. Grischow, Other Corporate Officer
Robert Strenski, President, Subsidiary
R. Tidey, Senior VP, Subsidiary
Michael Gregory, Vice President, Subsidiary
Keith Burns, Vice President, Subsidiary

GROWTH PLANS/SPECIAL FEATURES:

NACCO Industries, Inc. is a diversified holding company wi[
three primary subsidiaries: Hamilton Beach Brands, Inc. (HBB
The Kitchen Collection, LLC and The North American Co[
Corporation. Each of the company's subsidiaries operate
separately from the parent company. Through HBB, NACC[
Industries is a leading designer, marketer and distributor [
small electric household appliances as well as commerci[
products for restaurants, bars and hotels. HBB markets its reta[
products primarily in North America through mas[
merchandisers, national department stores, variety stor[
chains and independent retailers. HBB's brands includ[
Hamilton Beach and Proctor Silex. It also licensed the Jamb[
brand from Jamba Juice Company and sells Jamba brande[
blenders and juicing products. The Kitchen Collection LLC i[
the firm's specialty retailing subsidiary. It currently operate
248 stores under the Kitchen Collection and Le Gourmet Che[
brand names. Le Gourmet Chef stores are located primarily i[
outlet and traditional malls throughout the U.S. and featur[
gourmet foods and home entertainment products as well a[
brand name electric and non-electric kitchen items. The Nort[
American Coal Corporation, NACCO's mining subsidiary
mines and markets lignite coal primarily as fuel for powe[
generation and provides selected value-added mining service[
for other natural resources companies. In December 2014[
firm's subsidiary Hamilton Beach Brands, Inc. acquired Westo[
Products, LLC.

FINANCIAL DATA: Note: Data for latest year may not have been available at press time.

In U.S. $	2015	2014	2013	2012	2011	2010
Revenue		896,782,000	932,666,000	873,400,000	3,331,200,000	2,687,500,000
R&D Expense						
Operating Income		-66,309,000	61,336,000	67,500,000	174,100,000	140,300,000
Operating Margin %		-7.39%	6.57%	7.72%	5.22%	5.22%
SGA Expense		198,697,000	199,331,000	210,400,000	465,300,000	425,300,000
Net Income		-38,118,000	44,450,000	108,700,000	162,100,000	79,500,000
Operating Cash Flow		19,799,000	53,065,000	143,100,000	155,200,000	63,100,000
Capital Expenditure		57,500,000	57,449,000	44,700,000	36,700,000	26,300,000
EBITDA		-40,937,000	85,067,000	83,200,000	286,000,000	176,400,000
Return on Assets %		-4.82%	5.60%	8.43%	9.37%	5.05%
Return on Equity %		-14.97%	15.34%	25.34%	31.67%	18.83%
Debt to Equity		0.90	0.51	0.48	0.22	0.79

CONTACT INFORMATION:

Phone: 440 449-9600   Fax: 440 449-9607
Toll-Free: 800-531-3964
Address: 5875 Landerbrook Dr., Ste. 300, Cleveland, OH 44124 United States

STOCK TICKER/OTHER:

Stock Ticker: NC
Employees: 1,900
Parent Company:

Exchange: NYS
Fiscal Year Ends: 12/31

SALARIES/BONUSES:

Top Exec. Salary: $596,558   Bonus: $
Second Exec. Salary: $572,571   Bonus: $

OTHER THOUGHTS:

Estimated Female Officers or Directors:
Hot Spot for Advancement for Women/Minorities: Y

National Vision Inc

www.nationalvision.com

NAIC Code: 446130

TYPES OF BUSINESS:

Eyeglasses & Related Products, Retail
Optometrists

BRANDS/DIVISIONS/AFFILIATES:

Optical Center
Vision Center
Vista Optical

CONTACTS: Note: Officers with more than one job title may be intentionally listed here more than once.

Reade Fahs, CEO
J. Bruce Steffey, COO
J. Bruce Steffey, Pres.
Patrick R. Moore, CFO
Paul Gross, Sr. VP-Mktg.
Jeff Busbee, Chief Human Resources Officer
John Vaught, CIO
Desmond F. Taylor, Sr. VP-Merch.
Charlie Foell, Sr. VP-Mfg.
Mitchell Goodman, General Counsel
Sharon Pettit, Sr. VP-Retail Oper.
Robert W. Stein, Sr. VP-Professional & Managed Care Dev.
Chuck Criscillis, Treas.
Doug Olson, Sr. VP-Oper. & Organizational Dev.
Michael C. Thomas, Sr. VP-Retail Oper.
Debra Woyce, Sr. VP-Retail Oper.& Replenishment
Charlie Foell, Sr. VP-Dist.

GROWTH PLANS/SPECIAL FEATURES:

National Vision, Inc. operates more than 800 vision centers in 43 U.S. states, the District of Columbia and Puerto Rico. Most of these centers are located in host stores such as Walmart (under the Vision Center brand name) and Fred Meyer (under the Vista Optical brand name) or on military bases (under the Optical Center name). The Walmart locations account for the majority of the company's total revenues. The company's stores retail a wide range of optical products including eyeglasses, contact lenses and sunglasses. Eyeglass frames range from classic styles to designer names including Baby Phat and DKNY. Popular name-brand non-prescription sunglasses offered at the stores include Bolle, Ray Ban and Gargoyles. Some stores, including the Walmart Vision Center locations, staff a full-time optometrist and feature an in-store lab that can provide many eyeglasses and contact lenses within an hour. More complex prescriptions are processed individually at a state-of-the-art manufacturing facility owned and operated by the company. The company's lab network consists of two domestic locations (St. Cloud, MN and Lawrenceville, GA) and two international locations (China and Mexico). National Vision aims to open 75 new locations annually.

The company offers employees benefits including a comprehensive health care plan, dental insurance, a 401(k) plan with company matching, life insurance and short- and long-term disability coverage, flexible spending accounts, an employee assistance program, a scholarship program, access to a credit union and company discounts.

FINANCIAL DATA: Note: Data for latest year may not have been available at press time.

In U.S. $	2015	2014	2013	2012	2011	2010
Revenue		695,000,000	680,000,000	670,000,000	585,000,000	500,000,000
R&D Expense						
Operating Income						
Operating Margin %						
SGA Expense						
Net Income						
Operating Cash Flow						
Capital Expenditure						
EBITDA						
Return on Assets %						
Return on Equity %						
Debt to Equity						

CONTACT INFORMATION:

Phone: 770-822-3600   Fax: 770-822-3601
Toll-Free: 800-637-3597
Address: 2435 Commerce Ave, Bldg 2200, Duluth, GA 30096 United States

STOCK TICKER/OTHER:

Stock Ticker: Private
Employees: 1,913
Parent Company:

Exchange:
Fiscal Year Ends: 03/31

SALARIES/BONUSES:

Top Exec. Salary: $ Bonus: $
Second Exec. Salary: $ Bonus: $

OTHER THOUGHTS:

Estimated Female Officers or Directors: 2
Hot Spot for Advancement for Women/Minorities:

Natural Health Trends Corp

www.naturalhealthtrendscorp.com

NAIC Code: 446191

TYPES OF BUSINESS:
Food (Health) Supplement Stores
Personal Care Products
Cosmetics
Direct Selling
Online Retailing
Multi-Level Marketing

BRANDS/DIVISIONS/AFFILIATES:
NHT Global Inc
Alura
La Vie
Premium Noni Juice
Skindulgence
Triotein
Valura
TriFusion Max

CONTACTS: Note: Officers with more than one job title may be intentionally listed here more than once.
Timothy Davidson, CFO
Randall Mason, Director
Chris Sharng, President

GROWTH PLANS/SPECIAL FEATURES:

Natural Health Trends Corp. (NHTC) is a direct-selling company and e-commerce business headquartered in Dallas, Texas. Subsidiary NHT Global, Inc. sells personal care, wellness and quality of life products to a network of more than 20,000 independent distributors, who either use the products themselves or resell them to consumers. The firm has an active presence in the following markets: the U.S., Canada, Hong Kong, Taiwan, China, South Korea, Japan, Italy, Russia and Slovenia. The company offers an array of products in three primary categories: wellness, beauty and lifestyle. The wellness category includes a number of energy drinks and nutritional supplements. Key products include Premium Noni Juice, a fruit juice marketed as an energy beverage; Triotein, a lactose-free whey protein powder that provides the body with amino acids; Cluster X2, a product created for increased and more efficient cell hydration; FibeRich, a dietary supplement high in fiber; and TriFusion Max, a blended juice beverage rich in antioxidants. Beauty products include Skindulgence, a skin care system that claims to provide a 30-minute, non-surgical facelift; BioCell, a patented skincare treatment product; and 24K Renaissance Skin Rejuvenation Serum. Key items in the lifestyle category include Alura, an intimacy enhancing cream for women; Valura, a topical gel used to improve male sexual performance; and La Vie, an energy-boosting dietary supplement. Sales in the North American market represent only a small portion (roughly 3%) of its consolidated revenues, with Hong Kong representing the largest market at 85%. To become a distributor, the company requires an annual enrollment fee; after which, the salesperson can resell products to retail consumers or use them for personal consumption.

FINANCIAL DATA: Note: Data for latest year may not have been available at press time.

In U.S. $	2015	2014	2013	2012	2011	2010
Revenue		124,590,000	52,527,000	37,514,000	31,162,000	23,576,000
R&D Expense						
Operating Income		20,820,000	4,223,000	2,645,000	1,783,000	-3,079,000
Operating Margin %		16.71%	8.03%	7.05%	5.72%	-13.05%
SGA Expense		76,684,000	35,687,000	25,139,000	20,909,000	18,473,000
Net Income		20,370,000	4,089,000	2,630,000	2,305,000	-2,448,000
Operating Cash Flow		30,613,000	10,686,000	2,214,000	1,463,000	-292,000
Capital Expenditure		339,000	210,000	96,000	7,000	2,000
EBITDA		20,925,000	4,289,000	2,690,000	2,441,000	-1,265,000
Return on Assets %		56.26%	29.05%	36.43%	39.85%	-34.64%
Return on Equity %		125.61%	105.12%	613.38%		
Debt to Equity						

CONTACT INFORMATION:
Phone: 972 241-6525   Fax: 972 484-0688
Toll-Free:
Address: 4514 Cole Ave., Ste. 1400, Dallas, TX 75205 United States

STOCK TICKER/OTHER:
Stock Ticker: NHTC
Employees: 113
Parent Company:

Exchange: NAS
Fiscal Year Ends: 12/31

SALARIES/BONUSES:
Top Exec. Salary: $500,000   Bonus: $
Second Exec. Salary: $270,000   Bonus: $

OTHER THOUGHTS:
Estimated Female Officers or Directors:
Hot Spot for Advancement for Women/Minorities:

Nature's Sunshine Products Inc

www.naturessunshine.com

NAIC Code: 446191

TYPES OF BUSINESS:

Vitamin (Health) Supplement Stores
Herbal Products
Personal Care Products
Homeopathic Remedies

BRANDS/DIVISIONS/AFFILIATES:

Synergy Worldwide

CONTACTS: Note: Officers with more than one job title may be intentionally listed here more than once.

David Roberts, CEO, Subsidiary
Gregory Probert, CEO
Stephen Bunker, CFO
Matthew Tripp, Chief Scientific Officer
Susan Armstrong, COO
Kristine Hughes, Director
Richard Strulson, Executive VP
Paul Noack, President, Divisional

GROWTH PLANS/SPECIAL FEATURES:

Nature's Sunshine Products, Inc. (NSP) is a direct-selling company that manufactures and markets herbal products, vitamins & mineral supplements and personal care products. NSP is represented by more than 625,000 independent distributors worldwide that market over 700 products. In addition to the U.S., the firm markets its products to more than 45 countries, including Belarus, Canada, Colombia, Costa Rica, the Czech Republic, Denmark, the Dominican Republic, Ecuador, El Salvador, Finland, Germany, Guatemala, Honduras, Hong Kong and Iceland. NSP exports its products to Argentina, Australia, Chile, Israel, New Zealand and Norway. The company operates in four segments: Nature Sunshine Products (NSP) Americas; NSP Russia, Central and Eastern Europe; Synergy Worldwide; and China and New Markets, which offers a variation on the NSP formulas. Products sold in the U.S. are shipped directly from manufacturing and warehouse facilities located in Spanish Fork, Utah as well as from regional warehouses located in Ohio, Texas and Georgia. International distribution is supported through various local facilities. North America derived the majority of net sales in 2014 with 42.8%; and Russia, Central and Eastern Europe, 37.5%. The company's products consist of six categories: general health; Immune; digestive; cardiovascular; weight management; and personal care products, such as oils, lotions, and shampoo and skin cleansers. The products support a number of health and body-related functions, including weight management; daily health care; aromatherapy; personal and home care (water purification, cookware and cleaning products); and body system support, which aids in digestion, immune, respiratory, circulatory and nervous system functioning.

The firm offers employees service awards, paid time off, health insurance, a 401(k), education assistance, an employee assistance program, up to $750 in free product credit a year and adoption assistance.

FINANCIAL DATA: Note: Data for latest year may not have been available at press time.

In U.S. $	2015	2014	2013	2012	2011	2010
Revenue		366,367,000	378,096,000	367,468,000	367,813,000	349,918,000
R&D Expense						
Operating Income		19,048,000	24,057,000	34,016,000	20,165,000	11,263,000
Operating Margin %		5.19%	6.36%	9.25%	5.48%	3.21%
SGA Expense		255,735,000	259,225,000	240,128,000	278,238,000	269,615,000
Net Income		10,019,000	17,609,000	25,380,000	17,601,000	-1,233,000
Operating Cash Flow		14,182,000	29,378,000	26,651,000	3,908,000	16,150,000
Capital Expenditure		26,285,000	8,570,000	6,629,000	2,419,000	2,595,000
EBITDA		23,682,000	30,350,000	39,752,000	26,463,000	18,244,000
Return on Assets %		5.05%	8.94%	13.72%	10.50%	-.76%
Return on Equity %		8.69%	15.94%	24.99%	22.59%	-1.96%
Debt to Equity			0.09	0.11	0.06	

CONTACT INFORMATION:

Phone: 801 342-4300   Fax: 801 342-4305
Toll-Free: 800-223-8225
Address: 75 E. 1700 S., Provo, UT 84606 United States

SALARIES/BONUSES:

Top Exec. Salary: $525,000   Bonus: $
Second Exec. Salary: $415,000   Bonus: $

STOCK TICKER/OTHER:

Stock Ticker: NATR   Exchange: NAS
Employees: 964   Fiscal Year Ends: 12/31
Parent Company:

OTHER THOUGHTS:

Estimated Female Officers or Directors: 1
Hot Spot for Advancement for Women/Minorities: Y

Sales, profits and employees may be estimates. Financial information, benefits and other data can change quickly and may vary from those stated here.

Nautica Enterprises Inc

NAIC Code: 424300

TYPES OF BUSINESS:

Apparel and Clothing Brands, Designers, Importers and Distributors
Retail Stores
Retailing
Fragrances
Accessories
Home Furnishings

BRANDS/DIVISIONS/AFFILIATES:

VF Corp
Nautica
Nautica Jeans Company
Nautica Spa
Nautica Home Furniture

CONTACTS: Note: Officers with more than one job title may be intentionally listed here more than once.

Harvey Sanders, CEO
Eric C. Wiseman, CEO

GROWTH PLANS/SPECIAL FEATURES:

Nautica Enterprises, Inc., a subsidiary of VF Corp., is a designer, producer, distributor and retailer of men's, women' and children's fashion sportswear, denim bottoms, footwea and sleepwear. The company's target is men and wome between the ages of 25-44. Types of apparel for men, wome and children include Polo shirts, T-shirts, fleece an activewear, sweaters, pants and shorts, dresses, skirts, jeans outerwear and blazers, swimwear, underwear and sleepwear All fabric is preshrunk and seams are taped to preven abrasion. Recently, the company introduced a new line o women's sportswear. Additionally, the firm licenses Nautica brand home furnishings and accessories through the Nautica Home Furniture business segment. Each collection's product: include unique comforter sets, sheet collections an pillowcases, quilts, decorative pillows, towels and bath rugs Accessories include watches, fragrances, belts, scarves cufflinks, sunglasses, hats, socks, ties, wallets, umbrellas backpacks, towel bags and duffel bags. Company-owned brands include Nautica, Nautica Spa and Nautica Jeans Company. The Nautica Spa collection is only available fo individual in-store purchase. Nautica is the principal lifestyle brand in VF Corp.'s Sportswear Coalition business segment which operates Nautica retail outlet stores in outlet malls across the U.S. In addition to outlet stores, Nautica products are sold wholesale, primarily to leading department and specialty stores, and can be purchased by individuals at chain retail locations as well as online. Customers receive free shipping on all online purchases exceeding $100. Independent licensees also operate 265 Nautica-branded stores and over 3,000 Nautica-branded shop-in-shops worldwide. Nautica apparel is sold in over 75 countries.

Parent company VF Corp. offers its employees medical, life, disability, AD&D, dental and vision coverage; tuition assistance; an employee assistance program; flexible spending accounts; product discounts; wellness programs; and a 401(k) plan.

FINANCIAL DATA: Note: Data for latest year may not have been available at press time.

In U.S. $	2015	2014	2013	2012	2011	2010
Revenue						
R&D Expense						
Operating Income						
Operating Margin %						
SGA Expense						
Net Income						
Operating Cash Flow						
Capital Expenditure						
EBITDA						
Return on Assets %						
Return on Equity %						
Debt to Equity						

CONTACT INFORMATION:

Phone: 212-541-5757   Fax: 212-887-8136
Toll-Free: 866-376-4184
Address: 40 W. 57th St., New York, NY 10019 United States

STOCK TICKER/OTHER:

Stock Ticker: Subsidiary
Employees:
Parent Company: VF CORP

Exchange:
Fiscal Year Ends: 02/28

SALARIES/BONUSES:

Top Exec. Salary: $ Bonus: $
Second Exec. Salary: $ Bonus: $

OTHER THOUGHTS:

Estimated Female Officers or Directors:
Hot Spot for Advancement for Women/Minorities:

Nautilus Inc

www.nautilusinc.com

NAIC Code: 339920

TYPES OF BUSINESS:

Fitness Equipment
Online Retail
Retail Sales

BRANDS/DIVISIONS/AFFILIATES:

Bowflex
Nautilus
Airdyne
Schwinn Fitness
SelectTech
TreadClimber
Universal
DualTrack

CONTACTS: *Note: Officers with more than one job title may be intentionally listed here more than once.*

Bruce Cazenave, CEO
Sidharth Nayar, CFO
M. Johnson, Chairman of the Board
William Mcmahon, COO
Wayne Bolio, General Counsel
Robert Murdock, General Manager, Divisional
Jeffery Collins, Vice President, Divisional

GROWTH PLANS/SPECIAL FEATURES:

Nautilus, Inc. designs, develops and markets branded health and fitness products under four key brands: Nautilus, Schwinn Fitness, Universal and Bowflex. The Nautilus brand includes the Nautilus and DualTrack product lines; free weights and benches; and a complete line of cardio equipment, such as treadmills, ellipticals, bikes and the Nautilus T616 Treadmill. The Schwinn Fitness brand offers indoor cycling equipment, upright and recumbent exercise bikes, treadmills and ellipticals. The Schwinn brand includes its Airdyne stationery bikes. The Universal brand offers dumbbells, kettlebell sets and workout benches. To date, the company's principal and most successful product has been the Bowflex line of home fitness equipment. Bowflex offers both strength and cardio products, including all-in-one cardio machine, the Bowflex Max Trainer M3 and M5, Bowflex TreadClimber treadmill, SelectTech dumbbells, weight benches and treadmills. The firm markets directly to consumers through a variety of channels, including television commercials, infomercials, print media, response mailings and the Internet. Nautilus also distributes its products through a network of retail companies, such as sporting goods stores, Internet retailers, large-format and warehouse stores and smaller specialty retailers.

The firm offers employees medical, dental and vision coverage; dependent and domestic partner coverage; flexible spending accounts; disability insurance; life insurance; a 401(k); an employee assistance program; tuition reimbursement; product discounts; and access to an onsite fitness center.

FINANCIAL DATA: *Note: Data for latest year may not have been available at press time.*

In U.S. $	2015	2014	2013	2012	2011	2010
Revenue		274,447,000	218,803,000	193,926,000	180,412,000	168,450,000
R&D Expense		7,231,000	5,562,000	4,163,000	3,223,000	2,905,000
Operating Income		30,154,000	15,724,000	10,588,000	3,599,000	-9,569,000
Operating Margin %		10.98%	7.18%	5.45%	1.99%	-5.68%
SGA Expense		103,190,000	85,191,000	76,286,000	71,637,000	83,410,000
Net Income		18,795,000	47,954,000	16,883,000	1,420,000	-22,841,000
Operating Cash Flow		34,372,000	21,086,000	12,813,000	4,598,000	-10,659,000
Capital Expenditure		3,181,000	3,590,000	2,442,000	2,506,000	222,000
EBITDA		34,273,000	19,068,000	13,685,000	7,468,000	-2,463,000
Return on Assets %		11.77%	40.31%	19.06%	1.76%	-23.60%
Return on Equity %		18.55%	71.10%	44.85%	4.52%	-54.85%
Debt to Equity						

CONTACT INFORMATION:

Phone: 360 859-2900   Fax: 360 694-7755
Toll-Free:
Address: 16400 S.E. Nautilus Dr., Vancouver, WA 98683 United States

STOCK TICKER/OTHER:

Stock Ticker: NLS
Employees: 340
Parent Company:

Exchange: NYS
Fiscal Year Ends: 12/31

SALARIES/BONUSES:

Top Exec. Salary: $419,423   Bonus: $
Second Exec. Salary: $274,231   Bonus: $

OTHER THOUGHTS:

Estimated Female Officers or Directors: 1
Hot Spot for Advancement for Women/Minorities:

Nebraska Furniture Mart Inc

NAIC Code: 442110

www.nfm.com

TYPES OF BUSINESS:

Furniture Stores
Appliances
Flooring
Electronics
Mattresses
Home Décor
Fitness Equipment

BRANDS/DIVISIONS/AFFILIATES:

Berkshire Hathaway Inc

GROWTH PLANS/SPECIAL FEATURES:

Nebraska Furniture Mart, Inc., a subsidiary of Berkshire Hathaway, Inc., is a retailer of furniture, appliances, electronics, flooring, mattresses, home decor and fitness equipment. The company has four locations in Omaha, Nebraska; Kansas City, Kansas; Des Moines, Iowa; and The Colony, Texas. The Omaha and Kansas City locations each have over 450,000 square feet of retail space; the Des Moines store has 24,000 square feet; and the Texas store has 560,000 square feet. The Des Moines store sells appliances, electronics and flooring only. The Omaha and Des Moines stores average more than $400 million each in annual sales.

Employees of the firm receive benefits including health, dental and vision coverage; 401(k); an employee assistance program; paid time off; tuition reimbursement; a wellness program; flexible spending accounts; and an employee discount.

CONTACTS: *Note: Officers with more than one job title may be intentionally listed here more than once.*

Irvin Blumkin, CEO
Ron Blumkin, COO
Ron Blumkin, Pres.
Doug Hamlin, CFO
Mark Hamilton, Dir.-Mktg.
Megan Berry Barlow, Dir.-Human Resources
David Bash, Dir.-IT
Jeff Lind, Chief Strategy & Dev. Officer
Mark Hamilton, Dir.-e-commerce
Tony Boldt, Dir.-Kansas City Store
Elizabeth Barton, Dir.-Customer Rel.
Dale Brinks, Dir.-Warehouse Oper.
Steve Riley, Dir.-Furniture and Flooring
Irvin Blumkin, Chmn.

FINANCIAL DATA: *Note: Data for latest year may not have been available at press time.*

In U.S. $	2015	2014	2013	2012	2011	2010
Revenue		1,250,000,000	1,200,000,000	1,300,000,000	1,200,000,000	1,100,000,000
R&D Expense						
Operating Income						
Operating Margin %						
SGA Expense						
Net Income						
Operating Cash Flow						
Capital Expenditure						
EBITDA						
Return on Assets %						
Return on Equity %						
Debt to Equity						

CONTACT INFORMATION:

Phone: 402-397-6100 Fax:
Toll-Free: 800-336-9136
Address: 700 S. 72nd St., Omaha, NE 68114 United States

SALARIES/BONUSES:

Top Exec. Salary: $ Bonus: $
Second Exec. Salary: $ Bonus: $

STOCK TICKER/OTHER:

Stock Ticker: Subsidiary   Exchange:
Employees: 2,800   Fiscal Year Ends:
Parent Company: BERKSHIRE HATHAWAY INC

OTHER THOUGHTS:

Estimated Female Officers or Directors: 2
Hot Spot for Advancement for Women/Minorities:

Neiman Marcus Group Inc (The)

www.neimanmarcus.com

NAIC Code: 452111

TYPES OF BUSINESS:

Department Stores, Luxury
Online & Catalog Sales
Corporate Gifts
Fine Jewelry
Fine Apparel
Cosmetics
Housewares & Linens

BRANDS/DIVISIONS/AFFILIATES:

Ares Management LP
Leonard Green & Partners LP
Canada Pension Plan Investment Board
Neiman Marcus
Last Call
CUSP
Bergdorf Goodman
InCircle

CONTACTS: Note: Officers with more than one job title may be intentionally listed here more than once.

Karen W. Katz, CEO
Donald T. Grimes, COO
Karen W. Katz, Pres.
Donald T. Grimes, CFO
James Gold, CMO
Joseph Weber, Chief Human Resources Officer
Michael R. Kingston, CIO
Tracy Preston, General Counsel
Wayne Hussey, Sr. VP-Store Dev. & Properties
John Koryl, Pres., Neiman Marcus Direct
Dale Stapleton, Chief Acct. Officer
Stacie Shirley, Sr. VP-Finance
James Gold, Pres., Specialty Retail
Thomas Lind, Sr. VP-Program Mgmt.

GROWTH PLANS/SPECIAL FEATURES:

The Neiman Marcus Group, Inc. specializes in high-end retail sales. The company's 41 Neiman Marcus stores, 30 Last Call clearance stores, 12 Last Call studios, six CUSP stores and two Bergdorf Goodman stores. The firm also offers upscale merchandise such as fine jewelry, home decor, chocolates, perfumes and accessories. CUSP stores, which are smaller concept stores, are located in Virginia, Massachusetts, Illinois, California and Washington, D.C. and are designed to appeal to fashion-forward women aged 21-45. Neiman Marcus is well-known for its emphasis on maintaining its customer base through personal contact, including event invitations, thank-you notes, birthday greetings and personal correspondence alerting customers that new merchandise has arrived. The firm's rewards program, InCircle, helps drive sales, representing more than 50% of the group's yearly revenue. Along with its brick-and-mortar operations, the firm's Neiman Marcus direct division conducts online and catalog sales of fashion apparel, accessories and home furnishings through the Neiman Marcus brand; online and catalog sales of home furnishings and accessories through the Horchow brand; and online sales of fashion apparel and accessories through the Bergdorf Goodman brand. The company is owned by private investment funds affiliated with Ares Management, LP, Leonard Green & Partners, LP and Canada Pension Plan Investment Board. In 2014, NMG acquired mytheresa.com, a global online luxury fashion business.

Neiman Marcus offers its employees medical, dental, life, short- and long-term disability and AD&D insurance; paid holidays and vacations; federal credit union membership; education assistance; business travel insurance; same-sex domestic partner benefits; employee assistance program; adoption benefits; health care spending accounts; dependent care spending accounts; scholarship award program for dependent children; prenatal/well-baby care programs; discounts on store and catalog merchandise; computer purchase program; and a retirement savings plan.

FINANCIAL DATA: Note: Data for latest year may not have been available at press time.

In U.S. $	2015	2014	2013	2012	2011	2010
Revenue	5,095,000,000	4,839,331,000	4,650,000,000	4,345,374,000	4,000,000,000	3,690,000,000
R&D Expense						
Operating Income						
Operating Margin %						
SGA Expense						
Net Income	14,900,000	-147,181,000	163,700,000	140,086,000	31,600,000	-1,800,000,000
Operating Cash Flow						
Capital Expenditure						
EBITDA						
Return on Assets %						
Return on Equity %						
Debt to Equity						

CONTACT INFORMATION:

Phone: 214-741-6911   Fax: 214-573-5320
Toll-Free: 888-888-4757
Address: 1618 Main St., 1 Marcus Square, Dallas, TX 75201 United States

STOCK TICKER/OTHER:

Stock Ticker: Private
Employees: 16,000
Parent Company: Ares Management LP

Exchange:
Fiscal Year Ends: 07/31

SALARIES/BONUSES:

Top Exec. Salary: $ Bonus: $
Second Exec. Salary: $ Bonus: $

OTHER THOUGHTS:

Estimated Female Officers or Directors: 6
Hot Spot for Advancement for Women/Minorities: Y

New Look Group plc

www.newlook.com

NAIC Code: 448120

TYPES OF BUSINESS:

Women's & Children's Clothing-Retail
Lingerie Sales
Shoe Sales
Plus-Size Apparel
Men's Apparel

BRANDS/DIVISIONS/AFFILIATES:

Brave Soul
Label Lounge
New Look
Newlook.com
Brait SE

CONTACTS: Note: Officers with more than one job title may be intentionally listed here more than once.

Anders Kristiansen, CEO
Mike Iddon, CFO
Tom Singh, Dir.-Commercial

GROWTH PLANS/SPECIAL FEATURES:

New Look Group plc is a British retailer that sells women's, men's, teens' and kids' clothing, shoes and accessories. The firm operates over 569 New Look stores throughout the UK and the Republic of Ireland, and over 200 across Europe and Asia. The largest location is located in Newcastle upon Tyne with 30,000 square feet of retail space. The firm's web site, Newlook.com, ships to over 120 countries worldwide, generating 14% of revenues. The firm also has over 3.5 million email alert subscribers. New Look has an in-house design team of more than 30 designers who develop unique and exclusive fashion merchandise, allowing the company to limit its exposure to supply-driven trends. The company's brands include Label Lounge and Brave Soul. Additionally, New Look supplies other company brands, such as 18 & East, Rocket Dog and Lee. In September 2014, the company sold its French fashion business, Mim. In 2015, Brait SE acquired a 90% stake in the company.

FINANCIAL DATA: Note: Data for latest year may not have been available at press time.

In U.S. $	2015	2014	2013	2012	2011	2010
Revenue		2,348,695,440	2,497,270,000	2,250,000,000	2,332,189,000	2,336,104,000
R&D Expense						
Operating Income						
Operating Margin %						
SGA Expense						
Net Income		-82,345,680	194,053,000	105,343,000	-4,628,000	31,442,000
Operating Cash Flow						
Capital Expenditure						
EBITDA						
Return on Assets %						
Return on Equity %						
Debt to Equity						

CONTACT INFORMATION:

Phone: 44-1305-765-000   Fax:
Toll-Free:
Address: Mercery Rd., New Look House, Weymouth, DT3 5HJ United Kingdom

STOCK TICKER/OTHER:

Stock Ticker: Private
Employees: 30,000
Parent Company: Brait SE

Exchange:
Fiscal Year Ends: 03/31

SALARIES/BONUSES:

Top Exec. Salary: $ Bonus: $
Second Exec. Salary: $ Bonus: $

OTHER THOUGHTS:

Estimated Female Officers or Directors:
Hot Spot for Advancement for Women/Minorities:

New York & Company Inc

www.nyandcompany.com

NAIC Code: 448120

TYPES OF BUSINESS:
Apparel-Women's, Retail

BRANDS/DIVISIONS/AFFILIATES:
New York & Company
Lerner
Lerner New York
NY Style
Soho Jeans
City Style
NY&C
NYandCompany.com

CONTACTS: Note: Officers with more than one job title may be intentionally listed here more than once.

Gregory Scott, CEO
Sheamus Toal, CFO
Grace Nichols, Chairman of the Board
Faeth Bradley, Executive VP, Divisional
Kevin Finnegan, Executive VP, Divisional
John Worthington, President
Adam Ratner, Vice President

GROWTH PLANS/SPECIAL FEATURES:

New York & Company, Inc. is a specialty retailer of women's apparel that targets fashion-conscious women between the ages of 25 and 45. It designs and sources its proprietary branded merchandise sold exclusively through its national network of New York & Company retail stores and online. The company operates about 504 retail stores in 43 states. The stores are typically concentrated in large population centers of the U.S. and are located in shopping malls, lifestyle centers and off-mall locations, including urban street locations. The firm operates a web site, NYandCompany.com, through which customers can place and track orders, apply for the NY&C Rewards credit card and purchase New York & Company gift cards. New York & Company offers a merchandise assortment consisting of casual and wear-to-work apparel and accessories, including pants, jackets, knit tops, blouses, sweaters, denim, t-shirts, activewear, handbags and jewelry. New product lines are introduced in five major deliveries every year: spring, summer, fall, holiday and pre-spring; these deliveries are updated every four weeks to keep merchandise up to date with changing fashions. Brand names include New York & Company, Lerner, Lerner New York, NY Style, Soho Jeans, City Style and NY&C.

New York & Company offers its employees medical, dental, life, disability, vision and prescription drug coverage; medical reimbursement; flexible spending accounts; a 401(k) plan; a retirement plan; adoption assistance; tuition reimbursement; employee discounts; and commuter expense reimbursement.

FINANCIAL DATA: Note: Data for latest year may not have been available at press time.

In U.S. $	2015	2014	2013	2012	2011	2010
Revenue	923,332,000	939,163,000	966,434,000	956,456,000	1,021,699,000	1,006,675,000
R&D Expense						
Operating Income	-15,596,000	3,077,000	2,252,000	-35,570,000	-66,379,000	-23,926,000
Operating Margin %	-1.68%	.32%	.23%	-3.71%	-6.49%	-2.37%
SGA Expense	265,371,000	261,293,000	262,569,000	257,188,000	298,419,000	274,139,000
Net Income	-16,885,000	2,394,000	2,100,000	-38,937,000	-76,461,000	-13,481,000
Operating Cash Flow	12,000,000	27,888,000	27,380,000	-8,554,000	10,803,000	55,300,000
Capital Expenditure	26,781,000	18,836,000	18,144,000	12,158,000	15,695,000	13,285,000
EBITDA	11,724,000	35,804,000	37,178,000	2,704,000	-25,238,000	18,570,000
Return on Assets %	-5.71%	.82%	.71%	-11.93%	-19.31%	-3.01%
Return on Equity %	-15.88%	2.18%	2.03%	-33.28%	-44.71%	-6.26%
Debt to Equity	0.13					0.03

CONTACT INFORMATION:
Phone: 212 884-2000   Fax: 212 884-2396
Toll-Free: 800-961-9906
Address: 330 West 34th St., 9/Fl, New York, NY 10001 United States

SALARIES/BONUSES:
Top Exec. Salary: $867,308   Bonus: $
Second Exec. Salary: $500,000   Bonus: $

STOCK TICKER/OTHER:
Stock Ticker: NWY
Employees: 6,349
Parent Company:

Exchange: NYS
Fiscal Year Ends: 01/31

OTHER THOUGHTS:
Estimated Female Officers or Directors: 3
Hot Spot for Advancement for Women/Minorities: Y

NEXT plc
NAIC Code: 448140

TYPES OF BUSINESS:
Men's, Women's & Children's Clothing-Retail
Franchising
Catalog & Online Sales
Online Flower & Gift Sales
Call Center Services
Customer Support Services
Housewares

BRANDS/DIVISIONS/AFFILIATES:
NEXT Directory
NextElectric.co.uk
NEXT Sourcing Limited
Lipsy Limited
NEXT Manufacturing Pvt Limited

CONTACTS: Note: Officers with more than one job title may be intentionally listed here more than once.
Simon A. Wolfson, CEO
David W. Keens, Dir.-Finance
Jane Shields, Dir.-Mktg. & Sales
Christos E. Angelides, Dir.-Prod.
Michael Law, Dir.-Oper.
John O. Barton, Chmn.

GROWTH PLANS/SPECIAL FEATURES:
NEXT plc retails moderately priced clothing for men, women and children as well as housewares and furniture. Its three main retail channels are its more than 500 NEXT retail stores in the U.K. and Ireland, targeting 20-30 year-olds looking for trendy but affordable clothes; the NEXT international division, which operates nearly 200 locations overseas in 37 countries in Europe, Asia and the Middle East; and subsidiary NEXT Directory, which offers a mail catalog and an e-commerce web site, NextElectric.co.uk. Its other main business operations include NEXT Sourcing Limited, which buys, sources and designs products branded NEXT; and Lipsy Limited, which designs and sells young women's clothing through wholesale, retail and website channels. NEXT Manufacturing Pvt Limited provides sourcing operations occur in Hong Kong, Mainland China, Sri Lanka, India and the U.K. NEXT also owns garment manufacturing facilities in Sri Lanka.

NEXT offers its employees a retirement plan and an employee stock ownership plan.

FINANCIAL DATA: Note: Data for latest year may not have been available at press time.

In U.S. $	2015	2014	2013	2012	2011	2010
Revenue	5,979,311,000	5,590,935,000	5,326,039,000	5,144,109,000	4,929,740,000	5,092,385,000
R&D Expense						
Operating Income	1,214,010,000	1,080,515,000	1,039,107,000	899,632,300	847,310,700	791,999,300
Operating Margin %	20.30%	19.32%	19.50%	17.48%	17.18%	15.55%
SGA Expense	808,891,700	768,230,300	703,351,600	367,297,500	333,662,200	404,072,100
Net Income	949,113,500	826,980,000	760,456,800	709,929,200	599,605,300	544,294,000
Operating Cash Flow	1,111,011,000	919,066,000	985,140,700	750,441,000	643,406,000	806,350,300
Capital Expenditure	169,671,400	157,413,200	121,984,000	201,961,300	215,714,400	147,397,400
EBITDA	1,405,507,000	1,252,579,000	1,208,031,000	1,082,907,000	1,024,307,000	980,506,500
Return on Assets %	28.68%	27.39%	27.14%	26.04%	23.01%	21.08%
Return on Equity %	208.78%	193.46%	200.11%	208.74%	219.24%	265.57%
Debt to Equity	2.60	2.79	1.98	2.92	2.02	3.90

CONTACT INFORMATION:
Phone: 44 1162842429   Fax:
Toll-Free:
Address: Enderby Leicester, Leicestershire, LE19 4AT United Kingdom

STOCK TICKER/OTHER:
Stock Ticker: NXGPF
Employees: 47,562
Parent Company:

Exchange: GREY
Fiscal Year Ends: 01/31

SALARIES/BONUSES:
Top Exec. Salary: $ Bonus: $
Second Exec. Salary: $ Bonus: $

OTHER THOUGHTS:
Estimated Female Officers or Directors: 4
Hot Spot for Advancement for Women/Minorities: Y

Nike Inc

www.nike.com

NAIC Code: 424340

TYPES OF BUSINESS:

Footwear Distribution
Athletic Equipment
Sports Accessories
Retail Stores
Sports Apparel
Plastic Products
Hockey Products
Swimwear

BRANDS/DIVISIONS/AFFILIATES:

All Star
Chuck Taylor
Converse Inc
Hurley International LLC
One Star
Jordan
Star Chevron
Jack Purcell

CONTACTS: Note: Officers with more than one job title may be intentionally listed here more than once.

Mark Parker, CEO
Philip Knight, Chairman of the Board
Chris Abston, Chief Accounting Officer
Hilary Krane, Chief Administrative Officer
Eric Sprunk, COO
David Ayre, Executive VP, Divisional
John Slusher, Executive VP, Divisional
Andrew Campion, Executive VP
Trevor Edwards, President, Divisional
Jeanne Jackson, President, Divisional
John Coburn, Vice President

GROWTH PLANS/SPECIAL FEATURES:

Nike, Inc. designs, develops and markets footwear, apparel, equipment and accessories. It is one of the largest sellers of athletic footwear and athletic apparel in the world. The company's athletic footwear products are designed primarily for specific athletic use, although a large percentage of its products are worn for casual or leisure purposes. Running, training, basketball and soccer sport-inspired urban shoes and children's shoes are the firm's top-selling product categories. Nike also markets shoes designed for tennis, golf, baseball, football, lacrosse, walking, outdoor activities, skateboarding, bicycling, volleyball, wrestling, cheerleading, aquatic activities and other athletic and recreational uses. The firm maintains several wholly-owned subsidiaries: Converse, Inc., which distributes and licenses footwear, apparel and accessories through brand names Converse, All Star, One Star, Chuck Taylor, Star Chevron and Jack Purcell; Hurley International LLC, which is headquartered in the U.K. and designs/distributes a collection of action sports apparel sold under the Hurley brand; and Jordan, which sells a line of basketball shoes, clothing and gear for men. Nike sells its products to retail accounts, through Nike-owned retail stores and through a mix of independent distributors and licensees worldwide. Within the U.S. the firm operates 322 Nike Brand and subsidiary retail stores: 209 Nike locations, 84 Converse factory stores and 29 Hurley locations. In the international market, which includes countries within Europe, Asia, South America and Africa, the firm maintains 536 retail stores (530 Nike and six Converse). In March 2015, the sportswear giant announced it will launch partnerships with Garmin, TomTom, Wahoo Fitness and Netpulse in an effort to broaden its Nike+ running community.

FINANCIAL DATA: Note: Data for latest year may not have been available at press time.

In U.S. $	2015	2014	2013	2012	2011	2010
Revenue	30,601,000,000	27,799,000,000	25,313,000,000	24,128,000,000	20,862,000,000	19,014,000,000
R&D Expense						
Operating Income	4,175,000,000	3,680,000,000	3,254,000,000	3,040,000,000	2,815,000,000	2,474,000,000
Operating Margin %	13.64%	13.23%	12.85%	12.59%	13.49%	13.01%
SGA Expense	9,892,000,000	8,766,000,000	7,780,000,000	7,431,000,000	6,693,000,000	6,326,400,000
Net Income	3,273,000,000	2,693,000,000	2,485,000,000	2,223,000,000	2,133,000,000	1,906,700,000
Operating Cash Flow	4,680,000,000	3,003,000,000	3,027,000,000	1,899,000,000	1,812,000,000	3,164,200,000
Capital Expenditure	963,000,000	880,000,000	636,000,000	597,000,000	432,000,000	335,100,000
EBITDA	4,824,000,000	4,312,000,000	3,767,000,000	3,445,000,000	3,206,000,000	2,869,500,000
Return on Assets %	16.28%	14.88%	15.03%	14.59%	14.50%	13.78%
Return on Equity %	27.81%	24.50%	23.07%	21.98%	21.76%	20.67%
Debt to Equity	0.08	0.11	0.10	0.02	0.02	0.04

CONTACT INFORMATION:

Phone: 503 671-6453 Fax: 503 671-6300
Toll-Free: 800-344-6453
Address: 1 Bowerman Dr., Beaverton, OR 97005 United States

STOCK TICKER/OTHER:

Stock Ticker: NKE
Employees: 62,600
Parent Company:

Exchange: NYS
Fiscal Year Ends: 05/31

SALARIES/BONUSES:

Top Exec. Salary: $1,550,000 Bonus: $
Second Exec. Salary: $935,000 Bonus: $

OTHER THOUGHTS:

Estimated Female Officers or Directors: 2

Hot Spot for Advancement for Women/Minorities: Y

Sales, profits and employees may be estimates. Financial information, benefits and other data can change quickly and may vary from those stated here.

Nordstrom Inc
NAIC Code: 452111

TYPES OF BUSINESS:

Department Stores
Outlet Stores
Online Retailing
Catalog Sales
Financial Services
Federal Savings Bank

BRANDS/DIVISIONS/AFFILIATES:

Nordstrom fsb
Nordstrom Rack
Last Chance
Nordstrom.com
TrunkClub.com
Hautelook Inc
Nordstrom
Jeffrey

CONTACTS: Note: Officers with more than one job title may be intentionally listed here more than once.

Michael Koppel, CFO
Enrique Hernandez, Chairman of the Board
James Howell, Chief Accounting Officer
Daniel Little, Chief Information Officer
Peter Nordstrom, Director
Blake Nordstrom, Director
Erik Nordstrom, Director
Ken Worzel, Executive VP, Divisional
Brian Dennehy, Executive VP
Robert Sari, Executive VP
Geevy Thomas, Executive VP
James Nordstrom, Executive VP

GROWTH PLANS/SPECIAL FEATURES:

Nordstrom, Inc., founded in 1901, is an upscale fashion apparel and shoe retailer. Nordstrom operates a total of 290 stores in 38 states, as well as an e-commerce business through Nordstrom.com, HauteLook and TrunkClub.com. It sells a wide selection of apparel, shoes and accessories for women, men and children. The west and east coasts of the U.S. are the areas where the company has its largest presence. Nordstrom consists of two segments: retail and credit. The retail segment includes 115 Nordstrom branded full-line stores, 167 off-price Nordstrom Rack stores, two Canadian full-line stores, as well as other retail channels Trunk Club showrooms, Jeffrey boutiques and a clearance store that operates under the Last Chance name. The credit segment includes Nordstrom' wholly-owned federal savings bank, Nordstrom fsb, through which it offers a private label credit card, two Nordstrom VISA credit cards and a debit card. It generates income through finance charges and fees on these cards and saves on interchange fees that the retail segment would incur when its customers use third-party cards. In 2014, Nordstrom opened two Nordstrom Rack stores in California; 25 additional Nordstrom Rack stores throughout the U.S.; three full-line Nordstrom stores; and announced plans to close its full-line stores in Vancouver, Washington, and in Portland, Oregon at the Lloyd Center. In 2015, it closed its Mall of Georgia store and opened a store in Milwaukee, Wisconsin and in Ottawa, Canada; and plans to open another store in the Minneapolis Saint Paul region in the Fall 2015, and other Canadian stores in the Fall years of 2015, 2016 and Spring of 2017.

Nordstrom offers employees benefits including medical, dental, vision, AD&D, life and short- and long-term disability insurance; wellness programs; 401(k) plan & profit sharing; employee stock purchase plan; access to the company bank and credit union; employee assistance programs; adoption financial assistance; and merchandise discounts.

FINANCIAL DATA: Note: Data for latest year may not have been available at press time.

In U.S. $	2015	2014	2013	2012	2011	2010
Revenue	13,506,000,000	12,540,000,000	12,148,000,000	10,877,000,000	9,700,000,000	8,627,000,000
R&D Expense						
Operating Income	1,323,000,000	1,350,000,000	1,345,000,000	1,249,000,000	1,118,000,000	834,000,000
Operating Margin %	9.79%	10.76%	11.07%	11.48%	11.52%	9.66%
SGA Expense	3,777,000,000	3,453,000,000	3,371,000,000	3,036,000,000	2,685,000,000	2,465,000,000
Net Income	720,000,000	734,000,000	735,000,000	683,000,000	613,000,000	441,000,000
Operating Cash Flow	1,220,000,000	1,320,000,000	1,110,000,000	1,177,000,000	1,177,000,000	1,251,000,000
Capital Expenditure	861,000,000	803,000,000	513,000,000	511,000,000	399,000,000	360,000,000
EBITDA	1,832,000,000	1,805,000,000	1,713,000,000	1,576,000,000	1,451,000,000	1,115,000,000
Return on Assets %	8.08%	8.80%	8.86%	8.56%	8.73%	7.20%
Return on Equity %	31.85%	36.76%	37.99%	34.34%	34.12%	31.70%
Debt to Equity	1.27	1.49	1.63	1.60	1.37	1.43

CONTACT INFORMATION:

Phone: 206 628-2111   Fax: 206 628-1795
Toll-Free: 888-282-6060
Address: 1617 Sixth Avenue, Seattle, WA 98101 United States

STOCK TICKER/OTHER:

Stock Ticker: JWN
Employees: 67,000
Parent Company:

Exchange: NYS
Fiscal Year Ends: 01/31

SALARIES/BONUSES:

Top Exec. Salary: $742,000   Bonus: $
Second Exec. Salary: Bonus: $
$722,986

OTHER THOUGHTS:

Estimated Female Officers or Directors: 8
Hot Spot for Advancement for Women/Minorities: Y

Nugget Markets

www.nuggetmarket.com

NAIC Code: 445110

TYPES OF BUSINESS:

Supermarket

BRANDS/DIVISIONS/AFFILIATES:

FishWise
Price Survey
NuggetMarket.com
Nugget Markets
Food 4 Less

CONTACTS: *Note: Officers with more than one job title may be intentionally listed here more than once.*

Eric Stille, CEO
Chris Carpenter, COO
Eric Stille, Pres.
Dennis Lindsay, CFO
Kate Stille, Dir.-Mktg.
Stephanie Stille, Store Director
Kraig Brady, Dir.-Oper.
Eugene N. Stille, Chmn.
Barry Ashcraft, Dir.-Purchasing

GROWTH PLANS/SPECIAL FEATURES:

Nugget Markets is a family-owned chain of nine Nugget Markets full-service grocery stores in the Sacramento, California area. The stores offer conventional and organic produce, provided through local partner Nor-Cal Produce; meat and seafood, including natural Angus beef, free-range chicken and Nugget's own sausage; specialty grocery items; over 400 varieties of specialty cheese; bakery products; adult beverages; staple grocery products; eco-friendly bath, body and hair-care products; and vitamins, herbs and supplements. The company's FishWise system is a color-coded labeling program designed to make customers aware of the sustainability and population health of particular seafood items sold. The stores also maintain kitchens with different prepared meals inspired by Asian and other international cuisines as well as staples such as sandwiches and salads. Additionally, coffee and juice bars are located in each establishment. The company aims to offer the lowest prices in the area and provides a Price Survey for customers to compare Nugget prices to those of other stores. The number of people who believe Nugget provides the lowest prices are then posted above the front entrance. The firm provides recipes for entrees, appetizers, desserts, sides and condiments as well as a calendar of store events on NuggetMarket.com. Such events include wine tastings, sponsorship and seasonal events and talks with health professionals. In addition to the nine Nugget Markets, the firm also owns three Food 4 Less franchises in Northern California. Food 4 Less is a national warehouse store grocery chain that offers no frills, and customers bag their own groceries.

Employees look forward to the annual Bag-Off, a competition in which they race to stuff bags with groceries. The firm offers employees health, prescription, vision and dental coverage; a 401(k); a profit sharing plan; a flexible spending account; a flexible work schedule; and life insurance. Store employees and managers are paid at significantly higer rates than the industry's average. Employees who work at least 22 hours weekly may qualify for health insurance, and the company pays most or all of the premiums.

FINANCIAL DATA: *Note: Data for latest year may not have been available at press time.*

In U.S. $	2015	2014	2013	2012	2011	2010
Revenue		315,000,000	310,000,000	300,000,000	292,000,000	301,000,000
R&D Expense						
Operating Income						
Operating Margin %						
SGA Expense						
Net Income						
Operating Cash Flow						
Capital Expenditure						
EBITDA						
Return on Assets %						
Return on Equity %						
Debt to Equity						

CONTACT INFORMATION:

Phone: 530-669-3300   Fax: 530-662-0929
Toll-Free:
Address: 168 Court St., Woodland, CA 95695 United States

STOCK TICKER/OTHER:

Stock Ticker: Private
Employees: 1,150
Parent Company:

Exchange:
Fiscal Year Ends:

SALARIES/BONUSES:

Top Exec. Salary: $ Bonus: $
Second Exec. Salary: $ Bonus: $

OTHER THOUGHTS:

Estimated Female Officers or Directors: 1
Hot Spot for Advancement for Women/Minorities:

Office Depot Inc

NAIC Code: 453210

www.officedepot.com

TYPES OF BUSINESS:

Office Supplies, Retail
Office Design Services
Online Retailing
Copy Services
Direct Marketing
Office Furnishings

BRANDS/DIVISIONS/AFFILIATES:

Office Depot
OfficeMax
Office Depot Copy & Print Depot
OfficeMax ImPress

CONTACTS: Note: Officers with more than one job title may be intentionally listed here more than once.

Roland Smith, CEO
Stephen Hare, CFO
Kim Moehler, Chief Accounting Officer
Michael Allison, Executive VP
Juliet Johansson, Executive VP
Steven Schmidt, Executive VP
Elisa Garcia C., Executive VP
Mark Cosby, President, Geographical

GROWTH PLANS/SPECIAL FEATURES:

Office Depot, Inc. is a global supplier of office products and services to consumers and businesses of all sizes. In November 2013, the company merged with OfficeMax, Inc. Office Depot currently operates under the Office Depot and OfficeMax brands and utilizes other proprietary company and product brand names. The company operates through four business segments. The North American retail division sells a wide range products such as office supplies and paper; print and document services; technology products and solutions and office furniture through office supply stores in the U.S., Puerto Rico and the U.S. Virgin Islands. In 2014, this division operated 1,745 office supply stores. The North American business solutions division provides the company's nationally-branded office supplies, technology products, cleaning and break room supplies, office furniture, certain services and other solutions to customers through direct channel sales. The international division includes the company's businesses throughout Europe, Asia/Pacific and Latin America, operating in 27 countries. This division sells office products and services through direct mail catalogs, contract sales forces, Internet sites and retail stores. The trademarked Office Depot Copy & Print Depot and OfficeMax ImPress division provides printing, digital imaging, reproduction, mailing, as well as shipping through UPS, FedEx and the U.S. Postal Service. This division also offers personal computer support and network installation services throughout the U.S., providing customer support for in-home, in-office and in-store technology needs. In February 2015, Staples announced plans to acquire Office Depot for $6.3 billion. That October, the Federal Trade Commission agreed to issue its decision regarding the transaction by year's end.

Office Depot offers its employees medical/dental/vision/life insurance plans, spouse/dependent life insurance, retirement savings plan, stock options, short- and long-term disability and an employee assistance program.

FINANCIAL DATA: Note: Data for latest year may not have been available at press time.

In U.S. $	2015	2014	2013	2012	2011	2010
Revenue		16,096,000,000	11,242,000,000	10,695,650,000	11,489,530,000	11,633,090,000
R&D Expense						
Operating Income		-275,000,000	-205,000,000	-30,841,000	33,754,000	-37,291,000
Operating Margin %		-1.70%	-1.82%	-.28%	.29%	-.32%
SGA Expense		3,560,000,000	2,560,000,000	3,208,200,000	3,392,692,000	3,343,133,000
Net Income		-354,000,000	-20,000,000	-77,111,000	95,694,000	-44,623,000
Operating Cash Flow		156,000,000	-107,000,000	179,332,000	199,667,000	203,126,000
Capital Expenditure		123,000,000	137,000,000	120,260,000	130,317,000	169,452,000
EBITDA		62,000,000	405,000,000	196,703,000	277,252,000	210,142,000
Return on Assets %		-4.94%	-1.61%	-2.66%	1.36%	-1.72%
Return on Equity %		-19.21%	-6.82%	-15.71%	8.36%	-11.03%
Debt to Equity		0.93	0.75	0.73	0.87	0.94

CONTACT INFORMATION:

Phone: 561 438-4800   Fax: 561 265-4406
Toll-Free: 800-463-3768
Address: 6600 N. Military Rd., Boca Raton, FL 33496 United States

STOCK TICKER/OTHER:

Stock Ticker: ODP
Employees: 56,000
Parent Company:

Exchange: NAS
Fiscal Year Ends: 12/31

SALARIES/BONUSES:

Top Exec. Salary: $1,400,000
Bonus: $

Second Exec. Salary: $525,000
Bonus: $500,000

OTHER THOUGHTS:

Estimated Female Officers or Directors: 6

Hot Spot for Advancement for Women/Minorities: Y

O'Reilly Automotive Inc

www.oreillyauto.com

NAIC Code: 441310

TYPES OF BUSINESS:

Auto Parts, Retail
Tools
Auto Accessories

BRANDS/DIVISIONS/AFFILIATES:

O'Reilly Auto Parts
Power Torque
BrakeBest
Prestone
Master Pro
Omnispark
Super Start
Ultima

CONTACTS: Note: Officers with more than one job title may be intentionally listed here more than once.

Gregory Henslee, CEO
Thomas McFall, CFO
David OReilly, Chairman of the Board
Ted Wise, Executive VP, Divisional
Jeff Shaw, Executive VP, Divisional
Tricia Headley, Secretary
Brad Beckham, Senior VP, Divisional
Byron Childers, Senior VP, Divisional
Randy Johnson, Senior VP, Divisional
Gregory Johnson, Senior VP, Divisional
Larry Ellis, Senior VP, Divisional
Mike Swearengin, Senior VP, Divisional
Tony Bartholomew, Senior VP, Divisional
Stephen Jasinski, Senior VP, Divisional
Lawrence OReilly, Vice Chairman of the Board
Charles OReilly, Vice Chairman of the Board

GROWTH PLANS/SPECIAL FEATURES:

O'Reilly Automotive, Inc. is one of the largest specialty retailers of automotive aftermarket parts, tools, supplies, equipment and accessories in the U.S., selling products to both do-it-yourself (DIY) customers and professional installers. The company operates 4,366 stores under the O'Reilly Auto Parts name in 43 states across the U.S. Stores carry an average of 41,000 stock keeping units (SKUs) with an extensive product line consisting of new and remanufactured automotive hard parts, such as alternators, starters, brake system components, batteries, chassis parts and engine parts; maintenance items, such as oil, antifreeze, fluids, wiper blades, lighting, engine additives and appearance products; accessories, such as floor mats, truck accessories and seat covers; and a complete line of auto body paint and related materials, automotive tools and professional service equipment. Store merchandise generally consists of nationally recognized, well-advertised, name-brand products such as AC Delco, Armor All, Bosch, BWD, Cardone, Castrol, Gates Rubber, Monroe, Moog, Pennzoil, Prestone, Quaker State, STP, Turtle Wax, Valvoline, Wagner and Wix. In addition to name-brand products, stores carry a wide variety of high-quality private-label products under the BestTest, BrakeBest, Import Direct, Master Pro, Micro-Gard, Murray, Precision, Power Torque, Super Start, Ultima and Omnispark brands. O'Reilly operates 26 distribution centers and 283 hub stores, each equipped with highly automated material handling equipment that expedites the movement of products to loading areas for shipment to individual stores on a nightly basis.

O'Reilly offers its employees a benefits package that includes medical, dental, vision, pharmacy and life insurance; a credit union membership; a 401(k) plan with company match; a profit sharing plan; paid time off; a discount stock purchase plan; and an employee assistance program.

FINANCIAL DATA: Note: Data for latest year may not have been available at press time.

In U.S. $	2015	2014	2013	2012	2011	2010
Revenue		7,216,081,000	6,649,237,000	6,182,184,000	5,788,816,000	5,397,525,000
R&D Expense						
Operating Income		1,270,374,000	1,103,485,000	977,393,000	866,766,000	712,776,000
Operating Margin %		17.60%	16.59%	15.80%	14.97%	13.20%
SGA Expense		2,438,527,000	2,265,516,000	2,120,025,000	1,973,381,000	1,908,216,000
Net Income		778,182,000	670,292,000	585,746,000	507,673,000	419,373,000
Operating Cash Flow		1,190,430,000	908,026,000	1,251,555,000	1,118,991,000	703,687,000
Capital Expenditure		429,987,000	395,881,000	300,719,000	328,319,000	365,419,000
EBITDA		1,469,677,000	1,291,196,000	1,158,827,000	1,009,818,000	890,088,000
Return on Assets %		12.34%	11.34%	10.41%	9.62%	8.53%
Return on Equity %		39.05%	32.90%	23.65%	16.76%	14.22%
Debt to Equity		0.69	0.71	0.51	0.28	0.11

CONTACT INFORMATION:

Phone: 417 862-6708   Fax: 417 863-2242
Toll-Free: 800-755-6759
Address: 233 S. Patterson Ave., Springfield, MO 65802 United States

STOCK TICKER/OTHER:

Stock Ticker: ORLY
Employees: 67,926
Parent Company:

Exchange: NAS
Fiscal Year Ends: 12/31

SALARIES/BONUSES:

Top Exec. Salary: $1,087,500   Bonus: $
Second Exec. Salary: $633,269   Bonus: $

OTHER THOUGHTS:

Estimated Female Officers or Directors: 1

Hot Spot for Advancement for Women/Minorities: Y

Sales, profits and employees may be estimates. Financial information, benefits and other data can change quickly and may vary from those stated here.

Organizacion Soriana SAB de CV

NAIC Code: 445110

TYPES OF BUSINESS:
Supermarkets and Other Grocery (except Convenience) Stores

BRANDS/DIVISIONS/AFFILIATES:
Soriana Hiper
Soriana Super
Soriana Mercado
Soriana Express
City Club
Super City

GROWTH PLANS/SPECIAL FEATURES:
Organizacion Soriana, SAB de CV operates 674 supermarke
stores in Mexico under the names Soriana Hiper, Sorian
Super, Soriana Mercado, Soriana Express and City Clut
Some of the supermarkets' offerings include clothing, healt
care products, home goods and food. The firm also operate
convenience stores under the Super City brand name
Organizacion Soriana has stores in 261 municipalitie
throughout the 32 states of Mexico. Additionally, the compan
is engaged in the real estate industry. It offers rentals and i
also engaged in commercial development.

CONTACTS: Note: Officers with more than one job title may be intentionally listed here more than once.
Ricardo Martin Bringas, CEO
Francisco Javier Martin Bringas, Chmn.

FINANCIAL DATA: Note: Data for latest year may not have been available at press time.

In U.S. $	2015	2014	2013	2012	2011	2010
Revenue		6,148,814,000	6,341,963,000	6,316,784,000	5,933,460,000	5,657,961,000
R&D Expense						
Operating Income		300,522,800	335,619,300	326,650,500	298,822,200	308,188,600
Operating Margin %		4.88%	5.29%	5.17%	5.03%	5.44%
SGA Expense		1,057,545,000	1,006,635,000	974,730,000		
Net Income		223,640,900	188,227,600	214,810,000	184,787,600	197,960,400
Operating Cash Flow		410,841,000	315,345,900	376,133,200	386,204,500	345,888,200
Capital Expenditure		182,967,400	220,803,400	209,603,800	209,198,000	184,315,400
EBITDA		426,327,000	454,922,000	448,381,500	420,724,500	429,560,200
Return on Assets %		4.63%	4.06%	4.79%	4.27%	4.85%
Return on Equity %		8.24%	7.45%	9.09%	8.40%	10.25%
Debt to Equity		0.02	0.02	0.02	0.02	0.18

CONTACT INFORMATION:
Phone: 52 018183299000   Fax: 52 018183299127
Toll-Free:
Address: Alejandro De rodas 3102-A, Monterrey, 64610 Mexico

STOCK TICKER/OTHER:
Stock Ticker: ONZBF   Exchange: GREY
Employees: Fiscal Year Ends: 12/31
Parent Company:

SALARIES/BONUSES:
Top Exec. Salary: $ Bonus: $
Second Exec. Salary: $ Bonus: $

OTHER THOUGHTS:
Estimated Female Officers or Directors:
Hot Spot for Advancement for Women/Minorities:

Orvis Company Inc (The)

www.orvis.com

NAIC Code: 451110

TYPES OF BUSINESS:

Outdoor Apparel, Retail
Fly-Fishing & Hunting Equipment
Home Furnishings
Catalog & Online Sales
Luggage & Accessories
Guided Trips & Travel Services
Firearms
Log Home Design & Construction

BRANDS/DIVISIONS/AFFILIATES:

Orvis Travel
Orvis Log Homes
Orvis Shooting Grounds at Pursell Farms

CONTACTS: Note: Officers with more than one job title may be intentionally listed here more than once.

Leigh Perkins, Jr., CEO
Raymond G. McCready, Pres.
Robert J. Bean, CFO
Bill Eyre, CMO
Dave Finnegan, CIO
David Perkins, Vice Chmn.

GROWTH PLANS/SPECIAL FEATURES:

The Orvis Company, Inc. is a retailer of outdoor products. The firm markets fly fishing equipment, outdoor apparel and home products through retailers, outlets and authorized dealers in the U.S. and U.K. The company's outdoor apparel includes men's and women's clothing; outerwear; footwear; and accessories such as insect-repellent clothing, hats, luggage and wallets. Its fly-fishing products include waders/boots, lines, leaders, rods, reels, vests, packs and fly-fishing apparel. The firm's hunting products include shotguns, shotgun accessories and hunting apparel. In addition, Orvis runs fly-fishing and shooting schools and seminars; guided fishing and hunting trips through its series of lodges; and Orvis Travel helps customers plan international vacations with a focus on outdoor activities. The company's home furnishings include bedding, lighting, dining furniture, kitchen furniture, bedroom furniture, tables, chairs, desks, tableware, outdoor furniture and fireplace accessories. It also offers dog products including apparel, beds, crates and toys. The firm operates over 80 retail stores in the U.S. and U.K. Additionally, the company sells products through 500 authorized Orvis dealers, which primarily sell fly-fishing products and apparel. Orvis also markets products through catalogs and an e-commerce web site. Other activities include Orvis Log Homes, a division that offers six log home design packages and complete construction options through Rocky Mountain Log Homes Co. In September 2015, the firm, along with partner Pursell Farms LLC, opened its first Orvis Shooting Grounds at Pursell Farms, comprising 3,200 Alabama acres with sporting clays, wingshooting and fly-fishing schools.

FINANCIAL DATA: Note: Data for latest year may not have been available at press time.

In U.S. $	2015	2014	2013	2012	2011	2010
Revenue		310,000,000	305,000,000	340,000,000	285,000,000	
R&D Expense						
Operating Income						
Operating Margin %						
SGA Expense						
Net Income						
Operating Cash Flow						
Capital Expenditure						
EBITDA						
Return on Assets %						
Return on Equity %						
Debt to Equity						

CONTACT INFORMATION:

Phone: 802-362-1300   Fax: 802-362-0141
Toll-Free: 888-235-9763
Address: 178 Conservation Way, Sunderland, VT 05250 United States

SALARIES/BONUSES:

Top Exec. Salary: $ Bonus: $
Second Exec. Salary: $ Bonus: $

STOCK TICKER/OTHER:

Stock Ticker: Private
Employees: 2,500
Parent Company:

Exchange:
Fiscal Year Ends: 09/30

OTHER THOUGHTS:

Estimated Female Officers or Directors:
Hot Spot for Advancement for Women/Minorities:

Sales, profits and employees may be estimates. Financial information, benefits and other data can change quickly and may vary from those stated here.

OshKosh B'Gosh Inc

NAIC Code: 424300

www.oshkoshbgosh.com

TYPES OF BUSINESS:
Apparel and Clothing Brands, Designers, Importers and Distributors
Home Furnishings
Retail Stores

BRANDS/DIVISIONS/AFFILIATES:
Carters Inc
OshKosh Baby
OshKosh
Genuine Kids from OshKosh
www.oshkoshbgosh.com
www.oshkosh.com

CONTACTS: *Note: Officers with more than one job title may be intentionally listed here more than once.*
Michael D. Casey, CEO-Carter's Inc.
Jill A. Wilson, Sr. VP-HR & Talent Development, Carter's Inc.
Lisa A. Fitzgerald, Exec.VP-Brand
Michael D. Casey, Chmn.-Carter's Inc.

GROWTH PLANS/SPECIAL FEATURES:
OshKosh B'Gosh, Inc., a subsidiary of Carter's, Inc., manufactures and sells colorful, seasonal apparel for kids. Founded in 1895, the company was historically a local manufacturer of adult workwear, predominately denim bib overalls for railroad workers and farmers. The children's line was started as a youth version of the adult overalls as a novelty item for proud parents. Presently, the children's apparel line not only includes bib overalls, but also features pants, shorts, footwear, sleepwear, shoes, hosiery and accessories. The OshKosh brand comes in boys and girls sizes 2t to size 12 in addition to OshKosh Baby for infants, sizes 0-24 months. The company operates approximately 200 retails sores in the U.S., 152 of which are outlet stores and 48 are specialty stores. It also operates online channels www.oshkoshbgosh.com and www.oshkosh.com. It has six domestic licensees selling apparel and accessories within the U.S. and 25 licenses internationally across 35 countries. Its largest licensing agreement is with Target Corporation, through which Target sells products under the Genuine Kids from OshKosh brand.

FINANCIAL DATA: *Note: Data for latest year may not have been available at press time.*

In U.S. $	2015	2014	2013	2012	2011	2010
Revenue		408,341,000	363,875,000	363,095,000	362,788,000	340,371,000
R&D Expense						
Operating Income						
Operating Margin %						
SGA Expense						
Net Income		9,000,000	8,363,000	-3,666,000	-8,836,000	-10,959,000
Operating Cash Flow						
Capital Expenditure						
EBITDA						
Return on Assets %						
Return on Equity %						
Debt to Equity						

CONTACT INFORMATION:
Phone: 920-231-8800   Fax: 920-231-8621
Toll-Free: 800-692-4674
Address: 112 Otter Ave., Oshkosh, WI 54901 United States

STOCK TICKER/OTHER:
Stock Ticker: Subsidiary
Employees: 2,624
Parent Company: CARTERS INC

Exchange:
Fiscal Year Ends: 12/31

SALARIES/BONUSES:
Top Exec. Salary: $ Bonus: $
Second Exec. Salary: $ Bonus: $

OTHER THOUGHTS:
Estimated Female Officers or Directors: 1
Hot Spot for Advancement for Women/Minorities:

Otto GmbH & Co KG (Otto Group)

www.ottogroup.com

NAIC Code: 454113

TYPES OF BUSINESS:

Assorted Merchandise, Direct Selling
Catalog & Online Sales
Household Goods, Retail
Travel Agencies
Computer Equipment
Financial Services
Logistics Services
Wholesale Trading

BRANDS/DIVISIONS/AFFILIATES:

EOS
OTTO
About You
Otto Group Russia
OTTO Office
Hermes Group (The)
Baur
Argosyn

CONTACTS: *Note: Officers with more than one job title may be intentionally listed here more than once.*

Hans-Otto Schrader, CEO
Petra Scharner-Wolff, CFO
Rainer Hillebrand, Dir.-Corp. Strategy
Rainer Hillebrand, Dir.-e-commerce
Jurgen Schulte-Laggenbeck, Dir.-Finance
Timm Homann, Dir.-Retail
Hanjo Schneider, Dir.-Svcs.
Alexander Birken, Dir.-Multichannel Distance Selling
Hans-Otto Schrader, Chmn.

GROWTH PLANS/SPECIAL FEATURES:

Otto GmbH & Co. KG (Otto Group) is a world renowned e-commerce retailer. Otto Group's business activities comprise 123 companies, as well as access to more than 100 online company stores worldwide. The firm has more than 50 million active online customers worldwide, and derived more than $7.1 billion in 2014 online sales. Its subsidiary retail channels include About You, Ackermann, Alba Moda, Ambellis, baumarkt, Baur, Blancheporte, bon prix, CB2, cnouch, Collins, Crate&Barrel, Eddie Bauer, Edited, Ekinova, e-ventures, fgh, Frankonia, Heine, Jelmoli, Kuche & Co., The Land of Nod, Lascana, limango, Mania Factum, Mirapodo, myToys, HA OM, naturloft neckermann.de, OTTO, Otto Group Russia, Otto Japan, OTTO Office, Posthas, privilege, Project A Ventures, Quelle, Schlafwelt, Schwab, sheego, Shopping 24, smatch.com, SporScheck, 3Si Groupe, 3 Suisses, Unito, Universal, Venca and Witt-Gruppe. The group is known as the largest textiles retailer in Germany, and has shipped more than 530 million packages by Hermes throughout all of Europe. The Hermes Group, an affiliate of Otto Group companies, is responsible for the prompt and precise worldwide transport of goods of all weights. Its multichannel retail segment, which accounts for approximately 63% of the firm's net revenue, offers fashion & footwear products, lifestyle accessories, furniture and interior decorations, as well as technology, sport and leisure products. Its financial segment, which accounts for more than 26% of net revenue, provides consumer credit, liquidity management, payment, receivables management, banking & debt collection and information management services, as well as insurance services to corporate and private customers. Subsidiaries in this segment include Argosyn, Finnovato, Hanseatic Bank, Liquid Labs, RatePay, Risk Ident and Yapital. In 2015, the firm ceased its catalogue operations in order to become an online-only retailer.

FINANCIAL DATA: *Note: Data for latest year may not have been available at press time.*

In U.S. $	2015	2014	2013	2012	2011	2010
Revenue		13,709,411,850	15,863,035,696	15,610,856,917	15,546,882,000	14,599,700,000
R&D Expense						
Operating Income						
Operating Margin %						
SGA Expense						
Net Income		-222,861,800	193,872,855	30,965,803	246,745,000	270,540,000
Operating Cash Flow						
Capital Expenditure						
EBITDA						
Return on Assets %						
Return on Equity %						
Debt to Equity						

CONTACT INFORMATION:

Phone: 49-40-64-61-401   Fax: 49-40-64-61-449
Toll-Free:
Address: Wandsbeker Strasse 1-7, Hamburg, 22179 Germany

STOCK TICKER/OTHER:

Stock Ticker: Private
Employees: 54,000
Parent Company:

Exchange:
Fiscal Year Ends: 02/28

SALARIES/BONUSES:

Top Exec. Salary: $ Bonus: $
Second Exec. Salary: $ Bonus: $

OTHER THOUGHTS:

Estimated Female Officers or Directors: 1
Hot Spot for Advancement for Women/Minorities:

Sales, profits and employees may be estimates. Financial information, benefits and other data can change quickly and may vary from those stated here.

Outerwall Inc

NAIC Code: 454210

www.outerwall.com

TYPES OF BUSINESS:

Coin Exchange Machines
Vending Machines

BRANDS/DIVISIONS/AFFILIATES:

Redbox
Coinstar
ecoATM
SAMPLEit

CONTACTS: Note: Officers with more than one job title may be intentionally listed here more than once.

Erik Prusch, CEO
Galen Smith, CFO
Nelson Chan, Chairman of the Board
Peter Osvaldik, Chief Accounting Officer
Donald Rench, General Counsel
Art Pettigrue, Other Corporate Officer
Rosemary Moothart, Other Corporate Officer
Mark Horak, President, Subsidiary
James Gaherity, President, Subsidiary
Angie McCabe, Vice President, Divisional

GROWTH PLANS/SPECIAL FEATURES:

Outerwall, Inc. is a leading provider of automated reta
solutions. Core offerings in automated retail include th
Redbox business, where consumers can rent or purchas
movies and videogames from self-service kiosks; Coinsta
business, where consumers can convert their coin to cash o
stored value products at self-service coin counting kiosks; an
new ventures, focused on identifying, evaluating, building an
developing new self-service concepts. Within the Redbo
segment, the company operates more than 43,000 Redbo
kiosks in 36,140 locations, where consumers can rent o
purchase movies and video games and, in select markets
purchase tickets for events. Redbox kiosks are available i
every state, Puerto Rico and Canada, and are installe
primarily at leading grocery stores, mass retailers, drug stores
restaurants and convenience stores, including Walgreens
Walmart, Kroger and 7-Eleven. Within the Coinstar segmen
the company owns and operates approximately 21,340 coin
counting kiosks in 20,250 locations, where consumers fee
loose change into the kiosks, which count the change and the
dispense vouchers or, in some cases, issue stored valu
products, at the consumer's election. Coinstar kiosks ar
available across the U.S., where they provide a convenient an
trouble-free service to retailers such as Kroger and Walmar
and in Canada, Puerto Rico, Ireland and the U.K. Outerwall i
the only multi-national, fully automated network of self-servic
coin-counting kiosks in the U.S. market. Revenue is generate
through transaction fees from consumers and product partners
The new ventures segment identifies, evaluates, builds an
develops new self-service concepts in the automated retai
sector. This division is currently exploring its consumer produc
sampling concept, SAMPLEit, in the beauty and consume
packaged goods industry. Wholly-owned ecoATM, whic
operates more than 1,800 automated kiosks, buys back most
used consumer electronic mobile devices directly fron
customers.

The company offers employees medical, dental and life
insurance as well as a 401(k) plan.

FINANCIAL DATA: Note: Data for latest year may not have been available at press time.

In U.S. $	2015	2014	2013	2012	2011	2010
Revenue		2,303,003,000	2,306,601,000	2,202,043,000	1,845,372,000	1,436,421,000
R&D Expense		13,047,000	13,084,000	13,913,000	11,557,000	7,437,000
Operating Income		248,377,000	260,968,000	262,758,000	209,885,000	143,207,000
Operating Margin %		10.78%	11.31%	11.93%	11.37%	9.96%
SGA Expense		229,961,000	254,178,000	237,870,000	192,361,000	157,844,000
Net Income		106,618,000	174,792,000	150,230,000	103,883,000	51,008,000
Operating Cash Flow		338,351,000	324,091,000	463,906,000	416,194,000	306,095,000
Capital Expenditure		97,924,000	157,669,000	208,054,000	179,236,000	170,847,000
EBITDA		424,700,000	468,129,000	447,765,000	361,371,000	272,815,000
Return on Assets %		6.12%	10.10%	9.91%	7.55%	4.07%
Return on Equity %		34.61%	32.73%	27.81%	21.32%	11.92%
Debt to Equity		9.67	1.32	0.64	0.69	0.40

CONTACT INFORMATION:

Phone: 425 943-8000   Fax: 425 943-8030
Toll-Free: 800-928-2274
Address: 1800 114th Ave. S.E., Bellevue, WA 98004 United States

SALARIES/BONUSES:

Top Exec. Salary: $772,183   Bonus: $
Second Exec. Salary: $418,692   Bonus: $60,037

STOCK TICKER/OTHER:

Stock Ticker: OUTR   Exchange: NAS
Employees: 2,760   Fiscal Year Ends: 12/31
Parent Company:

OTHER THOUGHTS:

Estimated Female Officers or Directors: 4
Hot Spot for Advancement for Women/Minorities: Y

Oxylane Group (Decathlon)

www.oxylane.com

NAIC Code: 451110

TYPES OF BUSINESS:

Sporting Goods Stores
Ski Equipment Rental
E-Commerce
Professional Equipment Sales & Consulting

BRANDS/DIVISIONS/AFFILIATES:

Decathlon
Decathlon Pro
Naturum
Ozflip
Pecheur.com
RuedelaMer.com
Storck
Vieux Plongeur

CONTACTS: *Note: Officers with more than one job title may be intentionally listed here more than once.*

Yves Claude, CEO

GROWTH PLANS/SPECIAL FEATURES:

Oxylane Group (Decathlon) is a French sporting goods producer and chain. Decathlon's business activities comprise the research and retail of sports-related equipment and accessories for all levels of sports people. It conceptualizes, designs and produces its brands in order to develop technical, efficient and economical products which are sold exclusively at Decathlon branded stores. The company's brands include Domyos, BTWIN, KIPSTA, TRIBORD, nabaiji, Quenchua, Wed'ze, simond, Kalenji, newfeel, Artengo, Inesis, Geologic, Caperlan, Solognac, Fouganza, Oxelo, Aptonia, Geonaute and ORAO. Oxylane sells and distributes these brands through local and online retailers such as Decathlon, which provides equipment and apparel for up to 70 sports in each store. Its retail formats include Decathlon Pro, Naturum, Ozflip, Pecheur.com, RuedelaMer.com, Storck and Vieux Plongeur. Decathlon Pro sells sporting equipment to organizations and companies; Naturum is a fishing and outdoor sports e-commerce shop; Ozflip sells scooters online; Pecheur.com sells fishing products only; Rue de la Mer is a boat specialist; Storck sells German bicycles; and Vieux Plongeur is a diving, spearfishing and freediving company. Additionally, Decathlon provides various services such as its Alsolia funding solutions, Atelier repair services, developing hockey equipment, Decathlon Sports Insurance services, Jiwok MP3 personal coach application, Skimium ski renting services, Sowego active mobility solutions, Sporeka gift cards and Decathlon Villages that provide the ability to practice sports such as horse riding, hiking, skiing and football.

FINANCIAL DATA: *Note: Data for latest year may not have been available at press time.*

In U.S. $	2015	2014	2013	2012	2011	2010
Revenue		9,560,000,000	9,227,120,000	8,677,570,000	8,427,720,000	8,296,569,000
R&D Expense						
Operating Income						
Operating Margin %						
SGA Expense						
Net Income						
Operating Cash Flow						
Capital Expenditure						
EBITDA						
Return on Assets %						
Return on Equity %						
Debt to Equity						

CONTACT INFORMATION:

Phone: 3303-2033-5000   Fax: 330-81008-0808
Toll-Free:
Address: 4 Blvd. de Mons, Villeneuve d'Ascq, 59665 France

STOCK TICKER/OTHER:

Stock Ticker: Private
Employees: 329,418
Parent Company:

Exchange:
Fiscal Year Ends: 03/31

SALARIES/BONUSES:

Top Exec. Salary: $ Bonus: $
Second Exec. Salary: $ Bonus: $

OTHER THOUGHTS:

Estimated Female Officers or Directors:
Hot Spot for Advancement for Women/Minorities:

Pacific Sunwear of California Inc

www.pacsun.com

NAIC Code: 448140

TYPES OF BUSINESS:

Casual Apparel, Retail
Teen & Young Adult Apparel
Accessories
Footwear
Online Sales

BRANDS/DIVISIONS/AFFILIATES:

PacSun
Pacific Sunwear
PacSun.com
On the Byas
Bullhead
Reign+Storm
LA Hearts
Nollie

CONTACTS: Note: Officers with more than one job title may be intentionally listed here more than once.

Gary Schoenfeld, CEO
Peter Starrett, Chairman of the Board
Craig Gosselin, General Counsel
Jonathan Brewer, Senior VP, Divisional
Brieane Breuer, Senior VP, Divisional
Alfred Chang, Senior VP, Divisional
Amber Fredman-Tarshis, Senior VP
Ernie Sibal, Vice President, Divisional
Chris Tedford, Vice President

GROWTH PLANS/SPECIAL FEATURES:

Pacific Sunwear of California, Inc. is a leading specialty retailer of everyday casual apparel, accessories and footwear designed to meet the lifestyle needs of active teens and young adults. The company operates two nationwide primarily mall-based chains of retail stores under names PacSun and Pacific Sunwear, with approximately 605 stores in all 50 states and Puerto Rico. PacSun's typical customers are young people who prefer a casual, fun look. Much of the fashion influence at the PacSun stores comes from surfing, skateboarding and snowboarding as well as from brand names associated with these sports. A typical store offers accessories such as sunglasses and hats, footwear and casual apparel, such as shorts, jeans, swimwear and shirts under its heritage brand names including Billabong, Crooks and Castles, Diamond Supply Co., Fox Racing, Hurley, Neff, Nike, O'Neill, Roxy, RVCA, Vans, Volcom and Young and Reckless, among others. The company also offers merchandise under its proprietary labels Bullhead, LA Hearts, On the Byas, Nollie and Reign+Storm. In addition to its retail operations, Pacific Sunwear operates the e-commerce site PacSun.com. The company also allows many of its heritage brands to set up brand fixtures featuring brand-specific signage and merchandise within its stores, and some have even formed brand shops that create a store within a store experience. Pacific Sunwear operates a 450,000 square foot distribution center in Olathe, Kansas.

The company offers employees medical, dental, vision and life insurance; in-store discounts; and a 401(k). The corporate location offers an onsite fitness facility, PacSun Cafe, a wellness room, a new mother's room and a rewards program.

FINANCIAL DATA: Note: Data for latest year may not have been available at press time.

In U.S. $	2015	2014	2013	2012	2011	2010
Revenue	826,777,000	797,792,000	803,071,000	833,751,000	929,506,000	1,027,101,000
R&D Expense						
Operating Income	-15,141,000	-21,433,000	-38,019,000	-80,376,000	-95,144,000	-81,125,000
Operating Margin %	-1.83%	-2.68%	-4.73%	-9.64%	-10.23%	-7.89%
SGA Expense	238,374,000	220,677,000	238,999,000	261,169,000	300,530,000	339,728,000
Net Income	-29,355,000	-48,721,000	-52,074,000	-106,423,000	-96,648,000	-70,302,000
Operating Cash Flow	10,732,000	-7,724,000	6,444,000	-47,404,000	-40,885,000	87,451,000
Capital Expenditure	15,595,000	12,337,000	15,393,000	13,235,000	17,159,000	23,498,000
EBITDA	8,872,000	4,078,000	-7,733,000	-37,871,000	-39,497,000	-10,758,000
Return on Assets %	-11.18%	-16.61%	-15.56%	-28.13%	-22.00%	-13.43%
Return on Equity %	-672.35%	-118.09%	-58.68%	-65.00%	-37.10%	-20.71%
Debt to Equity		4.74	1.23	0.65	0.13	

CONTACT INFORMATION:

Phone: 714 414-4000   Fax: 714 414-4260
Toll-Free: 800-444-6770
Address: 3450 E. Miraloma Ave., Anaheim, CA 92806 United States

STOCK TICKER/OTHER:

Stock Ticker: PSUN
Employees: 8,777
Parent Company:

Exchange: NAS
Fiscal Year Ends: 01/31

SALARIES/BONUSES:

Top Exec. Salary: $1,050,000   Bonus: $1,400,700

Second Exec. Salary: $405,586   Bonus: $271,133

OTHER THOUGHTS:

Estimated Female Officers or Directors: 6

Hot Spot for Advancement for Women/Minorities: Y

Pantry Inc (The)

www.thepantry.com

NAIC Code: 447110

TYPES OF BUSINESS:

Convenience Stores
Gas Stations
Fast Food

BRANDS/DIVISIONS/AFFILIATES:

Kangaroo Express
Alimenation Couche-Tard Inc

CONTACTS: Note: Officers with more than one job title may be intentionally listed here more than once.

Berry Epley, Assistant Secretary
B. Preslar, CFO
Thomas Dickson, Chairman of the Board
David Zodikoff, Chief Information Officer
Dennis Hatchell, Director
Thomas Carney, General Counsel
Boris Zelmanovich, Other Executive Officer
Gordon Schmidt, Senior VP, Divisional
Keith Bell, Senior VP, Divisional
Keith Oreson, Senior VP, Divisional

GROWTH PLANS/SPECIAL FEATURES:

The Pantry, Inc. is a leading operator of convenience stores in the Southeast U.S. It operates over 1,500 convenience stores in 13 states under a variety of brand names, including its primary operating banner, Kangaroo Express. Many of these locations also include quick service restaurants from nationally branded food franchises as well as a variety of proprietary food service programs. Its stores generate revenue from two broad sales categories: fuel operations and merchandise operations. The company purchases gasoline from major oil companies and independent refiners and offers a mix of branded and private brand gasoline at its locations based on an evaluation of local market conditions. Approximately 44.4% of the firm's locations that sell gasoline are Marathon branded, 22.2% BP branded and 33.4% all others. The firm's merchandise includes numerous offerings, such as tobacco, packaged beverages, beer and wine, candy and snacks, newspapers and magazines and health and beauty products. Its services revenue is derived from sales of lottery tickets, prepaid products, money orders, public telephones, ATMs and amusement and video gaming service offerings. The firm was acquired by Alimenation Couche-Tard, Inc. in March 2015, and Kangaroo Express stores are expected to be rebranded under Circle K brand by beginning of 2016.

The firm offers employees medical, dental and vision insurance; an employee assistance plan; a 401(k) saving plan; and AD&D and family life insurance.

FINANCIAL DATA: Note: Data for latest year may not have been available at press time.

In U.S. $	2015	2014	2013	2012	2011	2010
Revenue		7,545,664,000	7,821,955,072	8,253,242,880	8,138,500,096	7,265,262,080
R&D Expense						
Operating Income						
Operating Margin %						
SGA Expense						
Net Income		13,224,000	-3,012,000	-2,547,000	9,815,000	-165,615,008
Operating Cash Flow						
Capital Expenditure						
EBITDA						
Return on Assets %						
Return on Equity %						
Debt to Equity						

CONTACT INFORMATION:

Phone: 919 774-6700   Fax: 919 774-3329
Toll-Free: 877-798-4792
Address: 305 Gregson Dr., Cary, NC 27511 United States

STOCK TICKER/OTHER:

Stock Ticker: Subsidiary
Employees: 14,903
Parent Company: Alimenation Couche-Tard Inc

Exchange:
Fiscal Year Ends: 09/30

SALARIES/BONUSES:

Top Exec. Salary: $ Bonus: $
Second Exec. Salary: $ Bonus: $

OTHER THOUGHTS:

Estimated Female Officers or Directors: 1
Hot Spot for Advancement for Women/Minorities:

Parkland Fuel Corporation

www.parkland.ca

NAIC Code: 424720

TYPES OF BUSINESS:
Gasoline and Fuel Distribution
Convenience Stores
Propane Sales

BRANDS/DIVISIONS/AFFILIATES:
Sparlings Propane Co Ltd
Bluewave Energy
Island Petroleum
Columbia Fuels
Farstad Oil Inc
Superpumper Inc
Elbow River Marketing Ltd
Pioneer Energy

CONTACTS: Note: Officers with more than one job title may be intentionally listed here more than once.
Robert Espey, CEO
Michael McMillan, CFO
James Pantelidis, Chairman of the Board
Donna Strating, Chief Information Officer
Kendall Waiting, General Counsel
Paul Lapensee, Vice President, Divisional
C. Kilty, Vice President, Divisional
Irfhan Rawji, Vice President, Divisional
Andrew Cruickshank, Vice President, Divisional
Jane Savage, Vice President, Divisional

GROWTH PLANS/SPECIAL FEATURES:
Parkland Fuel Corporation is a marketer and distributor of petroleum products. Parkland operates its business through seven subsidiaries: Sparlings Propane Co. Ltd., Bluewave Energy, Island Petroleum, Columbia Fuels, Farstad Oil, Inc. Superpumper, Inc., and Elbow River Marketing Ltd. Sparlings is Ontario's second largest propane company and the oldest propane company in Canada. Sparlings provides energy supply, appliances, equipment and technical support to diverse markets in Central Canada. Bluewave Energy is Shell's largest distributor of fuel and lubricant products in Canada, specializing in the delivery of furnace oil, propane, diesel fuel, gasoline, lubricants, marine gas oil and heavy fuel oil to homes and businesses such as farms, fishing vessels, trucking fleets, mines and oil and gas drilling rigs. Island Petroleum is a leading independent heating fuel supplier on Prince Edward Island. Columbia Fuels is a fuel distribution company that provides British Columbia with high quality fuel and lubricant products, innovative services and customer service. Farstad has a fleet of over 50 transports serving all of North Dakota and Montana along with portions of Minnesota, South Dakota and Wyoming. Farstad supplies and distributes approximately one billion liters of gasoline and distillates, 80 million liters of propane and 10 million liters of lubricants annually. Superpumper is a regional convenience store chain based in Minot, North Dakota, and presently has 14 store locations. Elbow River is a North American transporter, supplier and marketer of petroleum products including liquefied petroleum gases (butane, propane and condensate), crude oil, heavy fuel oil, and a growing portfolio of refined fuel and bio-fuel products. In 2014, Parkland acquired North Dakota-based SPF Energy, Inc., the holding company for Farstad Oil and Superpumper. During 2015, the firm acquired 11 Chevron-branded service stations in British Columbia; and Pioneer Energy, a North American fuels and lubricants marketer and distributor. It agreed to acquire two retail service stations in North Dakota that October.

FINANCIAL DATA: Note: Data for latest year may not have been available at press time.

In U.S. $	2015	2014	2013	2012	2011	2010
Revenue		5,639,567,000	4,242,931,000	3,096,844,000	2,982,100,000	2,182,680,000
R&D Expense						
Operating Income		65,377,320	120,392,700	112,307,600	60,291,880	30,324,620
Operating Margin %		1.15%	2.83%	3.62%	2.02%	1.38%
SGA Expense		281,428,500	226,155,400	174,144,200	194,431,300	176,049,400
Net Income		37,365,430	68,892,490	63,571,050	32,900,310	22,620,790
Operating Cash Flow		128,252,400	99,741,530	102,173,400	67,133,410	3,348,092
Capital Expenditure		37,587,180	42,311,520	37,013,310	34,289,290	30,620,550
EBITDA		127,728,700	148,421,100	147,965,600	117,572,800	79,554,830
Return on Assets %		3.57%	8.49%	9.28%	4.98%	4.59%
Return on Equity %		9.90%	23.29%	26.56%	18.36%	15.77%
Debt to Equity		0.76	0.61	0.82	1.27	1.93

CONTACT INFORMATION:
Phone: 403 357-6405   Fax: 403 352-0042
Toll-Free:
Address: Riverside Office Plz., 100, 4919 - 59th St., Red Deer, AB T4N 6C9 Canada

STOCK TICKER/OTHER:
Stock Ticker: PKI
Employees: 1,250
Parent Company:

Exchange: TSE
Fiscal Year Ends: 12/31

SALARIES/BONUSES:
Top Exec. Salary: $ Bonus: $
Second Exec. Salary: $ Bonus: $

OTHER THOUGHTS:
Estimated Female Officers or Directors:
Hot Spot for Advancement for Women/Minorities:

Party City Inc

www.partycity.com

NAIC Code: 453220

TYPES OF BUSINESS:
Party Supplies, Retail
Party Supplies Manufacturing and Distribution

BRANDS/DIVISIONS/AFFILIATES:
Amscam
Designware
Anagram
Costumes USA
PartyCity.com
Halloween City
U.S. Balloon Manufacturing Co Inc

CONTACTS: *Note: Officers with more than one job title may be intentionally listed here more than once.*
Michael Correale, CFO
Gerald Rittenberg, Chairman of the Board
James Harrison, Director
Gregg Melnick, President

GROWTH PLANS/SPECIAL FEATURES:
Party City, Inc. is one of the largest party goods suppliers in North America. Party City owns and operates more than 900 locations throughout the U.S. and Canada. The firm is also a leading global designer, manufacturer and distributor of decorated party supplies, with products found in over 40,000 retail outlets worldwide, including its own stores as well as independent retailers. Its operations consist of two segments: wholesale and retail. The wholesale segment generates approximately 71.5% of annual revenues globally through sales of Amscan, Designware, Anagram, Costumes USA and other party supplies to party goods retailers throughout the world. The retail segment generates 28.5% of revenues from the sale of merchandise to the end consumer through its chain of company-owned party goods stores, online through e-commerce web sites, including PartyCity.com, and through its chain of temporary Halloween City locations. In 2014, the firm acquired U.S. Balloon Manufacturing Co., Inc., a distributor of metallic balloons.

FINANCIAL DATA: *Note: Data for latest year may not have been available at press time.*

In U.S. $	2015	2014	2013	2012	2011	2010
Revenue		2,271,257,000	2,045,113,000		1,871,975,000	1,599,094,000
R&D Expense		19,390,000	19,311,000		16,636,000	14,923,000
Operating Income		243,142,000	161,602,000		201,370,000	127,436,000
Operating Margin %		10.70%	7.90%		10.75%	7.96%
SGA Expense		618,738,000	584,192,000		521,311,000	474,008,000
Net Income		56,123,000	4,019,000		76,275,000	49,319,000
Operating Cash Flow		136,387,000	135,818,000		161,264,000	61,168,000
Capital Expenditure		78,241,000	61,241,000		44,483,000	49,623,000
EBITDA		326,032,000	256,226,000		261,001,000	176,854,000
Return on Assets %		1.67%	.12%		4.35%	
Return on Equity %		11.89%	.87%		23.55%	
Debt to Equity		4.36	4.67		2.57	

CONTACT INFORMATION:
Phone: 914-345-2020   Fax:
Toll-Free:
Address: 80 Grasslands Rd., Elmsford, NJ 10523 United States

STOCK TICKER/OTHER:
Stock Ticker: PRTY
Employees: 14,627
Parent Company:

Exchange: NYS
Fiscal Year Ends: 12/31

SALARIES/BONUSES:
Top Exec. Salary: Bonus: $
$1,403,910
Second Exec. Salary: Bonus: $
$1,193,323

OTHER THOUGHTS:
Estimated Female Officers or Directors:

Hot Spot for Advancement for Women/Minorities:

Patagonia Inc

NAIC Code: 424300

www.patagonia.com

TYPES OF BUSINESS:

Apparel and Clothing Brands, Designers, Importers and Distributors
Outdoor Equipment
Catalog Sales
Surfing Apparel
Surfing Equipment

BRANDS/DIVISIONS/AFFILIATES:

Patagonia Works
Patagonia Music
Regulator
PCR Clothing
Capilene
Synchilla

CONTACTS: *Note: Officers with more than one job title may be intentionally listed here more than once.*

Rose Marcario, CEO
Casey Sheahan, Pres.
Dean Carter, VP-Human Resources
Rob BonDurant, VP-Merch.
Dmitri Siegel, VP-Global e-commerce
Jenn Rapp, Dir.-Comm. & Public Rel.
John Collins, VP-Sales, Americas & Asia Pacific

GROWTH PLANS/SPECIAL FEATURES:

Patagonia, Inc., a subsidiary of Patagonia Works, markets and sells outdoor clothing and equipment developed and designed for a broad range of extreme sports, such as rock climbing, mountaineering, white-water kayaking, mountain biking, surfing and skiing. Patagonia sells its products through company-owned retail outlets worldwide as well as through hundreds of other outdoor gear and clothing stores. Patagonia has pioneered many materials now considered essential for outdoor enthusiasts, such as polypropylene, Capilene and Synchilla, which are designed to retain warmth even when the material becomes moist from precipitation or sweat. The firm's Regulator system combines soft shells, insulation and moisture transition layers into jackets and pants to create an integrated clothing system designed to keep people warm and dry even in the most adverse weather conditions. The company also introduced t-shirts made from organically grown cotton, and PCR Clothing, a fleece product line made from recycled plastic soda bottles. The firm is committed to promoting and helping conserve nature and contributes its time, services and at least 1% of its sales to hundreds of global environmental initiatives. As of Fall 2014, Patagonia uses 100% traceable down to ensure that birds were not force-fed or live-plucked and that down is not blended with down from unknown sources. Through its Patagonia Music initiative, the firm features exclusive songs from world-class musicians on its website, which when purchased on iTunes go towards supporting nonprofit environmental groups.

Health insurance is provided to all employees who work at least 20 hours weekly. Eight weeks of leave is provided to new mothers and fathers. Tuition assistance is available.

FINANCIAL DATA: *Note: Data for latest year may not have been available at press time.*

In U.S. $	2015	2014	2013	2012	2011	2010
Revenue		600,000,000	572,000,000	543,000,000	400,000,000	330,000,000
R&D Expense						
Operating Income						
Operating Margin %						
SGA Expense						
Net Income						
Operating Cash Flow						
Capital Expenditure						
EBITDA						
Return on Assets %						
Return on Equity %						
Debt to Equity						

CONTACT INFORMATION:

Phone: 805-643-8616   Fax: 800-543-5522
Toll-Free: 800-638-6464
Address: 259 W. Santa Clara St., Ventura, CA 93001 United States

STOCK TICKER/OTHER:

Stock Ticker: Subsidiary
Employees: 2,000
Parent Company: Patagonia Works

Exchange:
Fiscal Year Ends: 04/30

SALARIES/BONUSES:

Top Exec. Salary: $ Bonus: $
Second Exec. Salary: $ Bonus: $

OTHER THOUGHTS:

Estimated Female Officers or Directors: 2
Hot Spot for Advancement for Women/Minorities:

Pathmark Stores Inc

www.pathmark.com

NAIC Code: 445110

TYPES OF BUSINESS:

Supermarkets
Pharmacies
Media Rental

BRANDS/DIVISIONS/AFFILIATES:

Great Atlantic & Pacific Tea Company Inc (The)
Pathmark PERKS
A&P
FoodBasics
The Food Emporium
Waldbaums
SuperFresh

GROWTH PLANS/SPECIAL FEATURES:

Pathmark Stores, Inc., a subsidiary of The Great Atlantic & Pacific Tea Company, Inc. (A&P), operates a full-service supermarket chain in four states: New York, New Jersey, Pennsylvania and Delaware. Pathmark's 81 store locations are designed to provide one-stop shopping in high-traffic urban and suburban locations, offering a wide assortment of foods and general merchandise. In addition to items from nationally recognized brands, the company provides a variety of private label products under the A&P, FoodBasics, The Food Emporium, Pathmark, Waldbaums and SuperFresh brand names. Other in-store conveniences include retail pharmacies at most locations as well as DVD rentals, full-service espresso bars and bank services. The Pathmark PERKS card allows customers to download manufacturer's coupons on it to use in Pathmark stores, instead of clipping or printing them. In June 2015, the firm's parent, A&P, filed for U.S. Chapter 11 bankruptcy protection.

CONTACTS: Note: Officers with more than one job title may be intentionally listed here more than once.

Paul Hertz, CEO
Frank G. Vitrano, Pres.
Mark C. Kramer, Exec. VP-Store Operations
John T. Derderian, Exec. VP-Strategy

FINANCIAL DATA: Note: Data for latest year may not have been available at press time.

In U.S. $	2015	2014	2013	2012	2011	2010
Revenue		3,000,000,000	2,691,800,000			
R&D Expense						
Operating Income						
Operating Margin %						
SGA Expense						
Net Income						
Operating Cash Flow						
Capital Expenditure						
EBITDA						
Return on Assets %						
Return on Equity %						
Debt to Equity						

CONTACT INFORMATION:

Phone: 201-573-9700   Fax: 201 505-3054
Toll-Free: 866-443-7374
Address: 2 Paragon Dr., Montvale, NJ 07645 United States

SALARIES/BONUSES:

Top Exec. Salary: $ Bonus: $
Second Exec. Salary: $ Bonus: $

STOCK TICKER/OTHER:

Stock Ticker: Subsidiary   Exchange:
Employees: 22,400   Fiscal Year Ends: 02/28
Parent Company: GREAT ATLANTIC & PACIFIC TEA CO INC

OTHER THOUGHTS:

Estimated Female Officers or Directors:
Hot Spot for Advancement for Women/Minorities:

Sales, profits and employees may be estimates. Financial information, benefits and other data can change quickly and may vary from those stated here.

Payless ShoeSource Inc

NAIC Code: 448210

TYPES OF BUSINESS:

Discount Shoe Stores
Online Retail
Shoe Dyeing
Beauty Products

BRANDS/DIVISIONS/AFFILIATES:

Payless Holdings
Airwalk
Payless.com
Dexflex Comfort
Dexter
Brash
SmartFit
Payless ShoeSource

CONTACTS: Note: Officers with more than one job title may be intentionally listed here more than once.

W. Paul Jones, CEO
Vincent DeSantis, CMO
Betty Click, VP-Human Resources
Bill Mcdonald, IT
Philip D. Vostrejs, Divisional Sr. VP-Merch. Planning
Michele A. Bergerac, Sr. VP-Women's & Accessories
Robert Bruennig, Sr. VP-Men's, Kids & Athletics

GROWTH PLANS/SPECIAL FEATURES:

Payless ShoeSource, Inc. is owned by Payless Holdings an
is one of the world's largest family footwear retailers. The firm'
core business, the Payless ShoeSource chain, feature
fashionable, quality footwear for women, men and children so
at affordable prices in a self-service shopping format. Th
Payless ShoeSource chain operates more than 4,000 store
throughout all 50 states and in St. Lucia, Australia, Barbados
Jamaica, the Philippines and Thailand. The firm also ha
roughly 300 franchised payless stores throughout Easter
Europe, the Middle East and Asia. Locations for Payles
ShoeSource stores include regional malls, shopping centers
central business districts and freestanding buildings. Payles
stores sell a broad assortment of quality footwear, includin
athletic, casual, dress, sandals, work and fashion boots
slippers and accessories, such as handbags, bath and beaut
products and hosiery. The firm's brand portfolio include
Airwalk, Brash, American Eagle, Champion, SmartFi
Christian Siriano, Dexflex Comfort and Dexter. Designe
collections have been created through the firm's relationshi
with New York-based fashion designers and include suc
brands as Alice + Olivia. In addition to its stores, the firm
operates Payless.com, which allows customers to shop online

Employees of the firm receive benefits including medical
dental, vision, life and disability coverage; flexible spending
accounts; an employee stock ownership plan; 401(k); tuition
reimbursement; adoption assistance; an employee assistance
program; and time off.

FINANCIAL DATA: Note: Data for latest year may not have been available at press time.

In U.S. $	2015	2014	2013	2012	2011	2010
Revenue		2,800,000,000	2,500,000,000	2,450,000,000	2,442,500,000	2,519,600,000
R&D Expense						
Operating Income						
Operating Margin %						
SGA Expense						
Net Income						
Operating Cash Flow						
Capital Expenditure						
EBITDA						
Return on Assets %						
Return on Equity %						
Debt to Equity						

CONTACT INFORMATION:

Phone: 785-233-5171   Fax: 785-368-7519
Toll-Free: 877-474-6379
Address: 3231 SE 6th Ave., Topeka, KS 66607 United States

STOCK TICKER/OTHER:

Stock Ticker: Subsidiary   Exchange:
Employees: 25,000   Fiscal Year Ends: 01/31
Parent Company: Collective Brands Inc

SALARIES/BONUSES:

Top Exec. Salary: $ Bonus: $
Second Exec. Salary: $ Bonus: $

OTHER THOUGHTS:

Estimated Female Officers or Directors: 1
Hot Spot for Advancement for Women/Minorities:

PC Richard & Son LLC

www.pcrichard.com

NAIC Code: 443142

TYPES OF BUSINESS:

Electronics, Audio & Appliance Stores
Online Sales
Audio Installation Services

BRANDS/DIVISIONS/AFFILIATES:

PCRichard.com
Nobody Beats The Wiz

CONTACTS: *Note: Officers with more than one job title may be intentionally listed here more than once.*

Gary Richard, CEO
Gregg Richard, Pres.
Gary Richard, Chmn.

GROWTH PLANS/SPECIAL FEATURES:

P.C. Richard & Son, LLC operates 66 electronics and appliance stores primarily in the New York metropolitan tri-state area. Founded by Peter Christian Richard, P.C. Richard began by selling hardware, but over the years it switched to the business of consumer appliances, electronics and computers. The company is still owned and operated by the Richard family. Its stores carry brands such as GE, Whirlpool, Kitchen-Aid, Frigidaire, Electrolux, Samsung, HP, Microsoft, Amana, Nintendo, LG, Maytag and Disney. In addition to the retail stores, P.C. Richard sells directly through its web site, PCRichard.com, offering a full line of appliances, televisions, housewares, telephones, computers, cameras, video games, video surveillance equipment and portable electronics. Additionally, the company offers audio installation services at 42 of its locations in the Bronx, Brooklyn, Westchester, Queens, Nassau and Suffolk counties; Pennsylvania; and New Jersey. The company also offers a buying card that allows subscribers to receive special promotional offers. One of the firm's competitive strategies is a Low Price Guarantee policy. If a customer finds a lower price offered by a company-approved competitor within 40 days of purchase, the firm will refund them the entire difference. P.C. Richard also owns the name Nobody Beats The Wiz as well as its customer lists and trademark.

P.C. Richard offers full-time employees (35 or more hours per week) benefits including medical, dental and life insurance; a 401(k) retirement savings plan with company matching; a flexible spending account; and employee discounts.

FINANCIAL DATA: *Note: Data for latest year may not have been available at press time.*

In U.S. $	2015	2014	2013	2012	2011	2010
Revenue						
R&D Expense						
Operating Income						
Operating Margin %						
SGA Expense						
Net Income						
Operating Cash Flow						
Capital Expenditure						
EBITDA						
Return on Assets %						
Return on Equity %						
Debt to Equity						

CONTACT INFORMATION:

Phone: 631-843-4300   Fax: 631-843-4309
Toll-Free: 877-727-1909
Address: 150 Price Pkwy., Farmingdale, NY 11735 United States

SALARIES/BONUSES:

Top Exec. Salary: $ Bonus: $
Second Exec. Salary: $ Bonus: $

STOCK TICKER/OTHER:

Stock Ticker: Private   Exchange:
Employees: 2,700   Fiscal Year Ends: 01/31
Parent Company:

OTHER THOUGHTS:

Estimated Female Officers or Directors:
Hot Spot for Advancement for Women/Minorities:

Pep Boys-Manny Moe & Jack (The)

www.pepboys.com

NAIC Code: 441310

TYPES OF BUSINESS:

Auto Parts, Retail
Automotive Services
Installation Services
Used Vehicle Inspections

BRANDS/DIVISIONS/AFFILIATES:

Pep Express
Pep Boys Supercenter
Pep Boys Service & Tire Center

CONTACTS: *Note: Officers with more than one job title may be intentionally listed here more than once.*

Scott Sider, CEO
David Stern, CFO
Robert Hotz, Chairman of the Board
Rodney Schriver, Chief Accounting Officer
Sanjay Sood, Controller
Brian Zuckerman, General Counsel
Thomas Carey, Other Executive Officer
James Flanagan, Other Executive Officer
Christopher Adams, Senior VP, Divisional
John Kelly, Senior VP, Divisional
Joseph Cirelli, Senior VP, Divisional

GROWTH PLANS/SPECIAL FEATURES:

The Pep Boys-Manny, Moe & Jack (Pep Boys) operates a leading automotive retail and service chain specializing in the sale, installation and servicing of automotive parts, tires and accessories. Pep Boys has over 806 locations throughout the U.S. and Puerto Rico, consisting of 563 Supercenters, six Pep Express stores and 237 Service & Tire centers. These locations total over 12.9 million square feet of retail space, including more than 7,500 service bays. Supercenters average approximately 20,000 square feet; and Service & Tire Centers, 6,000 square feet. Supercenters carry approximately 28,000 items and Service & Tire Centers, 2,000 items. These items include tires, batteries and new and remanufactured car parts; chemicals and maintenance items; fashion, electronic and performance accessories; personal transportation merchandise; and garage and repair shop products. The company sells products under national brand names and private labels, including Cornell, Futura, Definity, Proline, Prostart, Prosteer, Prostop and ValueGrade. Professional automotive services are available at Supercenters or Service & Tire locations, with the average Service & Tire location housing six service bays. Services cover oil changes, transmission flushes, brake services, tire alignments, suspension work, tune-ups and diagnostics, state inspections and emissions testing and air conditioning services. In late 2015, the firm agreed to be acquired by Japanese tire firm Bridgestone.

The firm offers employees medical, dental and vision insurance; flexible spending accounts; a 401(k) with company match; life and disability coverage; a paid time off program; tuition reimbursement; and merchandise discounts.

FINANCIAL DATA: *Note: Data for latest year may not have been available at press time.*

In U.S. $	2015	2014	2013	2012	2011	2010
Revenue	2,084,603,000	2,066,568,000	2,090,730,000	2,063,627,000	1,988,641,000	1,910,938,000
R&D Expense						
Operating Income	-18,857,000	22,298,000	11,654,000	65,570,000	82,580,000	57,059,000
Operating Margin %	-.90%	1.07%	.55%	3.17%	4.15%	2.98%
SGA Expense	484,182,000	464,852,000	481,169,000	443,986,000	442,239,000	430,261,000
Net Income	-27,293,000	6,865,000	12,810,000	28,903,000	36,631,000	23,036,000
Operating Cash Flow	27,444,000	59,404,000	88,491,000	73,650,000	117,195,000	87,223,000
Capital Expenditure	67,269,000	53,982,000	54,696,000	74,746,000	70,252,000	43,214,000
EBITDA	57,430,000	89,922,000	135,287,000	147,436,000	159,340,000	129,849,000
Return on Assets %	-1.73%	.42%	.79%	1.81%	2.39%	1.50%
Return on Equity %	-5.09%	1.26%	2.45%	5.88%	7.94%	5.31%
Debt to Equity	0.40	0.36	0.36	0.58	0.61	0.69

CONTACT INFORMATION:

Phone: 215 430-9000   Fax: 215 227-4067
Toll-Free: 800-737-2697
Address: 3111 W. Allegheny Ave., Philadelphia, PA 19132 United States

STOCK TICKER/OTHER:

Stock Ticker: PBY   Exchange: NYS
Employees: 18,914   Fiscal Year Ends: 01/31
Parent Company:

SALARIES/BONUSES:

Top Exec. Salary: $597,361   Bonus: $
Second Exec. Salary: Bonus: $
$404,615

OTHER THOUGHTS:

Estimated Female Officers or Directors: 1
Hot Spot for Advancement for Women/Minorities:

Perfumania Holdings Inc

NAIC Code: 446120

TYPES OF BUSINESS:

Fragrances, Online Retail
Fragrance Retail Stores
Wholesale Fragrances
Cosmetics
Accessories

BRANDS/DIVISIONS/AFFILIATES:

Perfumania Inc
Scents of Worth Inc
Perfumania.com Inc
Quality King Fragrance Inc
Parlux Fragrances LLC
Five Star Fragrance Company Inc
Tommy Bahama
Bijan

CONTACTS: Note: Officers with more than one job title may be intentionally listed here more than once.

Michael Katz, CEO
Donna Dellomo, CFO
Stephen Nussdorf, Chairman of the Board

GROWTH PLANS/SPECIAL FEATURES:

Perfumania Holdings, Inc. is a wholesale distributor and specialty retailer of perfumes and fragrances. The company operates its business through three subsidiaries: Perfumania, Inc., a specialty retailer of fragrances and related products; Scents of Worth, Inc. (SOW), which sells fragrances in retail stores and on a consignment basis; and Pefumania.com, Inc., an Internet retailer of fragrances and other specialty items. Perfumania Holdings separates its operations into two industry segments, wholesale and retail. The wholesale segment includes subsidiaries Quality King Fragrance, Inc. (QKF), Parlux Fragrances, LLC and Five Star Fragrance Company, Inc. QKF distributes fragrances to mass market retailers, drug stores, chain stores, retail wholesale clubs, traditional wholesalers and other distributors throughout the U.S. Parlux and Five Star own and license designer brands sold to national department stores, international distributors through QKF, SOW and Perfumania's retail stores. Parlux engages in the manufacture, distribution and sale of Kenneth Cole, Shawn Carter (Jay-Z), Paris Hilton, Jessica Simpson, Rihanna, Marc Ecko, Vince Camuto, Donald Trump and Ivanka Trump fragrances and beauty products on an exclusive basis as a licensee or sub-licensee. Five Star's owned and licensed brands include Tommy Bahama, Isaac Mizrahi, Bijan, Michael Jordan and many more. Five Star also handles the manufacturing of the Jerome Privee product line, which includes bath and body products sold exclusively in Perfumania stores. The retail segment retails and distributes fragrances, and operates 320 full service retail stores that specialize in the sale of fragrances and related products at discounted prices up to 75% below manufacturers' suggest retail prices. Each Perfumania retail store generally offers about 2,000 different fragrance items for women, men and children. Stores are located in the U.S., Puerto Rico and the U.S. Virgin Islands.

The firm offers employees a 401(k) plan, health insurance and paid vacation and sick leave.

FINANCIAL DATA: Note: Data for latest year may not have been available at press time.

In U.S. $	2015	2014	2013	2012	2011	2010
Revenue	583,955,000	575,857,000	534,779,000	493,507,000	484,800,000	510,922,000
R&D Expense						
Operating Income	12,538,000	-1,291,000	-48,209,000	12,673,000	6,782,000	2,563,000
Operating Margin %	2.14%	-.22%	-9.01%	2.56%	1.39%	.50%
SGA Expense	247,616,000	240,992,000	234,622,000	167,348,000	162,157,000	164,141,000
Net Income	2,647,000	-12,465,000	-56,013,000	4,131,000	-3,724,000	-15,828,000
Operating Cash Flow	44,518,000	-1,471,000	-7,368,000	33,922,000	-11,083,000	121,039,000
Capital Expenditure	12,392,000	5,500,000	7,088,000	4,044,000	2,978,000	4,821,000
EBITDA	22,864,000	10,682,000	-33,958,000	20,386,000	15,691,000	12,329,000
Return on Assets %	.65%	-2.95%	-15.85%	1.40%	-1.22%	-4.47%
Return on Equity %	2.83%	-12.82%	-66.71%	6.59%	-5.97%	-21.98%
Debt to Equity	1.73	2.15	1.84	0.48	0.98	0.03

CONTACT INFORMATION:

Phone: 631 866-4100   Fax:
Toll-Free:
Address: 35 Sawgrass Drive, Ste. 2, Bellport, NY 11713 United States

STOCK TICKER/OTHER:

Stock Ticker: PERF
Employees: 2,154
Parent Company:

Exchange: NAS
Fiscal Year Ends: 01/31

SALARIES/BONUSES:

Top Exec. Salary: $413,200   Bonus: $
Second Exec. Salary: $340,400   Bonus: $

OTHER THOUGHTS:

Estimated Female Officers or Directors: 2
Hot Spot for Advancement for Women/Minorities:

Petco Animal Supplies Inc

NAIC Code: 453910

www.petco.com

TYPES OF BUSINESS:

Pets & Pet Supplies, Retail
Online Sales
Pet Grooming
Veterinary Services
Obedience Training
Pet Photography

BRANDS/DIVISIONS/AFFILIATES:

Petco Foundation (The)
P.A.L.S.
Think Adoption First
Unleashed by Petco

CONTACTS: Note: Officers with more than one job title may be intentionally listed here more than once.

Jim Myers, CEO
Brad Weston, Pres.
Michael Nuzzo, CFO
Michael Zuna, Exec. VP-Mktg.
Charlie Piscitello, Exec. VP-Human Resources
Kelly Breitenbecher, Sr. VP
Thomas A. Farello, Sr. VP-Oper.
Lisa Epstein, Sr. Comm. Specialist
Jim Myers, Chmn.

GROWTH PLANS/SPECIAL FEATURES:

Petco Animal Supplies, Inc. is a leading specialty retailer of premium pet food, supplies and services. The company currently operates over 1,400 stores and more than 12 Unleashed by Petco neighborhood shops. Petco's superstores carry more than 10,000 products including premium pet food and treats; small animals such as fish, birds and reptiles as well as related supplies; collars and leashes; grooming products; toys; pet carriers; cat furniture; dog houses and beds; vitamins and veterinary supplies. Most stores also provide a variety of pet services, including professional grooming, veterinary clinics, vaccinations, obedience training and pet photography. Several services are performed in glass-walled stations in order to increase customer awareness and confidence in the services. In light of overpopulation problems, Petco chooses not to sell dogs and cats, though it does support adoption programs such as Petfinder.com through in-store Think Adoption First kiosks in many stores. The firm also operates the P.A.L.S. (Petco animal lovers save) customer loyalty program. Members receive special benefits and savings through the use of the P.A.L.S. card, which allows Petco to target customers and track shopping habits. In addition to its retail stores, the company operates an e-commerce site, which offers Petco merchandise, pet tips, a community forum, online specials and information about The Petco Foundation, an animal welfare and rights group. In late 2015, Petco agreed to be acquired by CVC Capital Partners, a private equity investment firm, and Canada Pension Plan Investment Board.

Petco offers its employees medical, dental, disability, vision, life and AD&D insurance plans; discounted pet insurance; a 401(k); flexible spending accounts; an employee assistance program; fitness discounts; paid time off; and merchandise discounts.

FINANCIAL DATA: Note: Data for latest year may not have been available at press time.

In U.S. $	2015	2014	2013	2012	2011	2010
Revenue		3,925,000,000	3,550,000,000	3,200,000,000	2,855,000,000	2,750,000,000
R&D Expense						
Operating Income						
Operating Margin %						
SGA Expense						
Net Income		75,000,000				
Operating Cash Flow						
Capital Expenditure						
EBITDA						
Return on Assets %						
Return on Equity %						
Debt to Equity						

CONTACT INFORMATION:

Phone: 858-453-7845   Fax:
Toll-Free:
Address: 9125 Rehco Rd., San Diego, CA 92121 United States

SALARIES/BONUSES:

Top Exec. Salary: $ Bonus: $
Second Exec. Salary: $ Bonus: $

STOCK TICKER/OTHER:

Stock Ticker: Private
Employees: 25,500
Parent Company: TPG CAPITAL

Exchange:
Fiscal Year Ends: 01/31

OTHER THOUGHTS:

Estimated Female Officers or Directors: 2
Hot Spot for Advancement for Women/Minorities:

PetMed Express Inc

www.1800petmeds.com

NAIC Code: 454111

TYPES OF BUSINESS:

Prescription & Non-Prescription Pet Drugs
Internet
Pet Care Products
Prescription Medications
Grooming

BRANDS/DIVISIONS/AFFILIATES:

1-800-PetMeds
PetHealth101.com

CONTACTS: *Note: Officers with more than one job title may be intentionally listed here more than once.*

Menderes Akdag, CEO
Bruce Rosenbloom, CFO
Robert Schweitzer, Director

GROWTH PLANS/SPECIAL FEATURES:

PetMed Express, Inc., doing business as 1-800-PetMeds, is a nationwide pet pharmacy that markets prescription/non-prescription pet medications and other health products for dogs, cats and horses. PetMed markets its products through national television, online, telephone and through direct mail/print and e-mail advertising campaigns. The 1-800-PetMeds catalog is a full-color catalog featuring the firm's most popular products and is produced by a combination of in-house writers, production artists and independent contractors. The firm offers roughly 3,000 products, including such brands as Frontline Plus, K9 Advantix, Advantage, Heartgard Plus, Sentinel, Revolution and Rimadyl. Non-prescription medications include flea and tick control products, bone and joint care products, vitamins and nutritional supplements and hygiene products. Prescription medications offered by the company include heartworm preventatives, thyroid and arthritis medications, antibiotics and other specialty medications as well as generic substitutes. In addition to pet medications, the firm also sells grooming tools, odor controllers, beds, bowls, leashes, training aids and treats. Sales of non-prescription medications generated 50% of PetMed's fiscal 2015 sales while prescription medications accounted for the remainder. The company's average retail purchase is approximately $77. The company attracts 30 million visitors to its web site annually, of whom roughly 9% place an order. Internet sales generate 80% of the firm's total sales. Approximately 50% of the firm's customers reside in California, Florida, Texas, New York, Pennsylvania, Virginia, North Carolina and New Jersey. PetMed additionally sponsors PetHealth101.com, which provides information regarding pet behavior, illness and natural and pharmaceutical remedies for pet problems.

PetMed offers employees medical, dental and vision plans; supplemental insurance; paid time off; 401(k); and a preferred legal plan.

FINANCIAL DATA: *Note: Data for latest year may not have been available at press time.*

In U.S. $	2015	2014	2013	2012	2011	2010
Revenue	229,395,000	233,391,000	227,829,000	238,250,000	231,642,000	238,266,000
R&D Expense						
Operating Income	27,613,000	28,218,000	27,005,000	26,022,000	33,024,000	40,542,000
Operating Margin %	12.03%	12.09%	11.85%	10.92%	14.25%	17.01%
SGA Expense	47,997,000	48,532,000	49,025,000	52,732,000	49,557,000	49,998,000
Net Income	17,453,000	17,972,000	17,165,000	16,659,000	20,871,000	26,002,000
Operating Cash Flow	32,043,000	13,506,000	13,290,000	20,391,000	30,106,000	27,685,000
Capital Expenditure	918,000	45,000	626,000	705,000	677,000	1,047,000
EBITDA	28,273,000	29,085,000	28,096,000	27,433,000	34,399,000	41,863,000
Return on Assets %	21.65%	23.71%	20.90%	16.88%	19.83%	27.93%
Return on Equity %	23.96%	26.78%	23.64%	18.70%	21.53%	30.26%
Debt to Equity						

CONTACT INFORMATION:

Phone: 954 979-5995   Fax: 954 971-0544
Toll-Free: 800-738-6337
Address: 1441 S.W. 29th Ave., Pompano Beach, FL 33069 United States

STOCK TICKER/OTHER:

Stock Ticker: PETS
Employees: 182
Parent Company:

Exchange: NAS
Fiscal Year Ends: 03/31

SALARIES/BONUSES:

Top Exec. Salary: $550,000   Bonus: $
Second Exec. Salary: $273,640   Bonus: $ 450

OTHER THOUGHTS:

Estimated Female Officers or Directors:
Hot Spot for Advancement for Women/Minorities:

PetSmart Inc

NAIC Code: 453910

TYPES OF BUSINESS:

Pets & Pet Supplies, Retail
Online & Catalog Sales
Pet Training
In-Store Adoption Centers
Veterinary Services
Pet Boarding
Pet Grooming

BRANDS/DIVISIONS/AFFILIATES:

BC Partners
PetSmart.com
PetsHotels
PetPerks
Medical Management International Inc
Banfield
Pet360

CONTACTS: *Note: Officers with more than one job title may be intentionally listed here more than once.*

Michael J. Massey, CEO
Gregg Scanlon, Sr. VP-Operations
David Lenhardt, CEO
Erick Goldberg, Sr. VP-Human Resources
Donald Beaver, Chief Information Officer
Michael Goodwin, Sr. VP-CIO
Paulette Dodson, General Counsel
Erick Goldberg, Senior VP, Divisional
Bruce Thorn, Senior VP, Divisional
Jaye Perricone, Senior VP, Divisional
Matthew McAdam, Senior VP, Divisional
Melvin Tucker, Senior VP, Divisional
Gene Burt, Senior VP, Divisional

GROWTH PLANS/SPECIAL FEATURES:

PetSmart, Inc. is a leading operator of superstores specializing in pet food, supplies and services. The company operates over 1,404 stores in the U.S., Puerto Rico and Canada, which offer an assortment of pet services and products. Its stores range in size from 12,000 to 27,500 square feet and carry roughly 11,000 distinct items in store and 9,000 additional items online through PetSmart.com. These items include nationally recognized brand names and a selection of proprietary or private label brands. PetSmart stores sell supplies for dogs, cats, fresh-water tropical fish, reptiles, birds and other small pets. The firm offers a PetPerks loyalty program to its customers. PetSmart stores also offer value-added pet services including grooming, training, boarding and day camp; and it operates full-service veterinary hospitals in 844 stores. Medical Management International, Inc., an operator of veterinary hospitals, operates 837 of PetSmart's hospitals under the name Banfield, The Pet Hospital. The remaining seven hospitals are located in Canada and operated by other third parties. PetSmart offers pet boarding in more than 200 stores through its PetSmart PetsHotels. PetsHotels provide boarding for dogs and cats, which includes 24-hour supervision by caregivers who are PetSmart-trained to provide personalized pet care, temperature controlled rooms and suites and play time as well as day camp for dogs. The company also actively supports pet adoption through its in-store adoption centers. In 2014, PetSmart announced the acquisition of Pet360, an online resource for pet parents; and opened a new distribution center in Berks County, Pennsylvania. In March 2015, PetSmart was acquired by private equity firm BC Partners for $8.3 billion.

PetSmart offers its employees medical, dental and vision insurance; life and AD&D insurance; short- and long-term disability; a 401(k) plan; an employee stock purchase plan; adoption assistance; associate discount; tuition assistance; flexible spending accounts; and a work/life balance program.

FINANCIAL DATA: *Note: Data for latest year may not have been available at press time.*

In U.S. $	2015	2014	2013	2012	2011	2010
Revenue		6,916,626,944	6,758,237,184	6,113,304,064	5,693,796,864	5,336,392,192
R&D Expense						
Operating Income						
Operating Margin %						
SGA Expense						
Net Income		419,520,000	389,528,992	290,243,008	239,867,008	198,324,992
Operating Cash Flow						
Capital Expenditure						
EBITDA						
Return on Assets %						
Return on Equity %						
Debt to Equity						

CONTACT INFORMATION:

Phone: 623 580-6100　　Fax:
Toll-Free: 800-738-1385
Address: 19601 N. 27th Ave., Phoenix, AZ 85027 United States

STOCK TICKER/OTHER:

Stock Ticker: Private
Employees: 53,000
Parent Company: BC Partners

Exchange:
Fiscal Year Ends: 01/31

SALARIES/BONUSES:

Top Exec. Salary: $　　　　Bonus: $
Second Exec. Salary: $　　　Bonus: $

OTHER THOUGHTS:

Estimated Female Officers or Directors: 3
Hot Spot for Advancement for Women/Minorities: Y

Pick N Pay Stores Limited

www.picknpay.co.za

NAIC Code: 452111

TYPES OF BUSINESS:

Department Stores (except Discount Department Stores)

BRANDS/DIVISIONS/AFFILIATES:

Pick N Pay
Boxer
Boxer Build
Boxer Super Liquors
Boxer Punch
Fresh Living Magazine
TM Supermarkets

CONTACTS: *Note: Officers with more than one job title may be intentionally listed here more than once.*

Richard Brasher, CEO
Aboubakar (Bakar) Jakoet, CFO
Jonathan Ackerman, Head-Mktg.
Debra Muller, Corp. Sec.
Richard van Rensburg, Deputy CEO

GROWTH PLANS/SPECIAL FEATURES:

Pick N Pay Stores Limited is a retailer of food, clothing and general merchandise. The company operates hypermarkets, supermarkets, liquor stores and clothing stores in South Africa, Namibia, Botswana, Zambia, Mozambique, Mauritius, Swaziland, Lesotho and Australia under the Pick N Pay and Boxer brands. In total, the firm owns 20 hypermarkets, 200 supermarkets, 152 liquor stores, four pharmacies and 88 clothing stores as Pick N Pay. An additional 277 supermarkets, 121 liquor stores and 14 clothing stores are also franchised under the Pick N Pay name. Under the Boxer brand, the company operates 123 Boxer supermarkets, 19 Boxer Build hardware stores, 21 Boxer Super Liquors and 16 Boxer Punch convenience stores. The company also owns a 49% interest in TM Supermarkets, which operates 53 TM Supermarket branded stores. A majority of stores also feature pharmacies and clinics. In addition to retail, the firm also allows customers to book flights, transfer money and manage store-to-door delivery. Pick N Pay also publishes the Fresh Living Magazine, which offers recipes, party tips and home living advice.

FINANCIAL DATA: *Note: Data for latest year may not have been available at press time.*

In U.S. $	2015	2014	2013	2012	2011	2010
Revenue	4,665,384,000	4,398,888,000	4,130,865,000	3,856,214,000	3,620,320,000	3,832,964,000
R&D Expense						
Operating Income	86,427,750	70,412,040	59,407,320	81,542,190	91,759,370	127,421,900
Operating Margin %	1.85%	1.60%	1.43%	2.11%	2.53%	3.32%
SGA Expense	263,994,600	250,202,100	247,372,500	59,923,060	135,018,500	61,560,870
Net Income	60,055,480	40,680,490	38,373,620	77,604,470	54,702,960	82,859,420
Operating Cash Flow	116,382,300	148,100,100	-5,694,015	85,612,340	1,212,679	66,084,020
Capital Expenditure	73,631,900	81,653,700	84,504,190	112,277,300	86,818,040	83,131,220
EBITDA	147,026,800	134,189,200	127,937,600	137,862,100	142,866,100	185,052,000
Return on Assets %	5.98%	4.30%	4.43%	9.71%	7.03%	10.91%
Return on Equity %	29.54%	22.80%	22.84%	48.80%	36.47%	75.44%
Debt to Equity	0.15	0.27	0.70	0.32	0.29	0.31

CONTACT INFORMATION:

Phone: 27 216581000   Fax: 27 217970314
Toll-Free:
Address: 101 Rosmead Avenue, Kenilworth, Cape Town, 7708 South Africa

STOCK TICKER/OTHER:

Stock Ticker: PKPYY
Employees: 48,700
Parent Company:

Exchange: PINX
Fiscal Year Ends: 02/28

SALARIES/BONUSES:

Top Exec. Salary: $ Bonus: $
Second Exec. Salary: $ Bonus: $

OTHER THOUGHTS:

Estimated Female Officers or Directors: 4
Hot Spot for Advancement for Women/Minorities: Y

Pier 1 Imports Inc

NAIC Code: 442110

www.pier1.com

TYPES OF BUSINESS:

Furniture & Housewares Stores
Kitchen Goods
Dining Goods & Accessories
Specialty & Novelty Ornaments

BRANDS/DIVISIONS/AFFILIATES:

Pier 1 Imports
Pier1.com

CONTACTS: Note: Officers with more than one job title may be intentionally listed here more than once.

Alexander Smith, CEO
Terry London, Chairman of the Board
Darla Ramirez, Chief Accounting Officer
Catherine David, Executive VP, Divisional
Gregory Humenesky, Executive VP, Divisional
Laura Coffey, Executive VP, Divisional
Sharon Leite, Executive VP, Divisional
Eric Hunter, Executive VP, Divisional
Michael Benkel, Executive VP, Divisional
Jeffrey Boyer, Executive VP
Michael Carter, Senior VP, Divisional
Andrew Laudato, Senior VP

GROWTH PLANS/SPECIAL FEATURES:

Pier 1 Imports, Inc. operates a chain of specialty retail stores
The firm operates approximately 1,065 Pier 1 Imports stores in
the U.S. and Canada. Pier 1 Imports stores average
approximately 9,900 square feet which includes an average o
approximately 7,900 square feet of retail selling space. These
stores sell a wide variety of furniture, decorative home
furnishings, dining and kitchen goods, bath and bedding
accessories and other items for the home. Products range from
housewares to seasonal items and are generally replaced by
new items every year. The company's merchandise is mostly
imported directly from foreign suppliers, with 59% of its sales
derived from merchandise produced in China, 14% produced
in India and approximately 18% collectively derived from
merchandise produced in Vietnam, Indonesia and the U.S. The
firm supplies merchandise and licenses the Pier 1 Imports
name to Grupo Sanborns SA de CV, which sells the firm's
merchandise to 68 store-within-a-store formats in Sears
Mexico stores as well as one in El Salvador. The agreements
with Grupo Sanborns will expire January 2017, unless renewed
and extended. In addition, Pier 1 Imports sells its products
online through Pier1.com. Approximately 65% of the firm's
sales are derived from decorative accessories, while furniture
sales account for the remaining 35%. Between January and
August 2015, the firm opened new stores in Georgia, Virginia,
Wisconsin, New Hampshire, Hawaii, Tennessee, Texas
Alaska, Ohio, Florida, Wyoming, Massachusetts and Utah.

FINANCIAL DATA: Note: Data for latest year may not have been available at press time.

In U.S. $	2015	2014	2013	2012	2011	2010
Revenue	1,865,782,000	1,771,743,000	1,704,885,000	1,533,611,000	1,396,470,000	1,290,852,000
R&D Expense						
Operating Income	127,271,000	175,500,000	198,986,000	154,760,000	103,748,000	-3,253,000
Operating Margin %	6.82%	9.90%	11.67%	10.09%	7.42%	- .25%
SGA Expense	576,131,000	531,190,000	513,085,000	475,162,000	431,900,000	421,179,000
Net Income	75,162,000	107,531,000	129,444,000	168,938,000	100,125,000	86,847,000
Operating Cash Flow	65,691,000	159,232,000	124,049,000	142,221,000	148,385,000	70,555,000
Capital Expenditure	81,859,000	80,306,000	80,363,000	62,316,000	31,049,000	5,246,000
EBITDA	184,961,000	223,024,000	240,174,000	198,143,000	142,718,000	89,112,000
Return on Assets %	8.77%	12.94%	15.40%	21.56%	14.44%	13.37%
Return on Equity %	19.10%	21.79%	25.11%	37.27%	27.96%	38.82%
Debt to Equity	0.60	0.02	0.01	0.01	0.02	0.06

CONTACT INFORMATION:

Phone: 817 252-8000   Fax: 817 334-0191
Toll-Free: 800-245-4595
Address: 100 Pier 1 Pl., Fort Worth, TX 76102 United States

SALARIES/BONUSES:

Top Exec. Salary: Bonus: $
$1,250,000
Second Exec. Salary: Bonus: $
$453,077

STOCK TICKER/OTHER:

Stock Ticker: PIR   Exchange: NYS
Employees: 24,000   Fiscal Year Ends: 02/28
Parent Company:

OTHER THOUGHTS:

Estimated Female Officers or Directors: 6

Hot Spot for Advancement for Women/Minorities: Y

Piercing Pagoda Inc

www.pagoda.com

NAIC Code: 448310

TYPES OF BUSINESS:

Jewelry, Retail
Piercing Services

BRANDS/DIVISIONS/AFFILIATES:

Signet Jewelers Ltd
Pagoda.com
Piercing Pagoda

GROWTH PLANS/SPECIAL FEATURES:

Piercing Pagoda, Inc., a subsidiary of Signet Jewelers Ltd., is a gold kiosk leader within shopping malls. The company is a leader in the ear-piercing business. Piercing Pagoda operates approximately 780 kiosks through the company's Signet Zale division, with kiosks averaging 190 square feet in size. The kiosks offer a wide selection of 10-karat and 14-karat gold jewelry, including chains, bracelets, rings, charms, body jewelry and earrings. Some locations also sell silver, stainless steel and diamond jewelry. The firm also offers no-cost layaway and gift certificates. Ear piercing services are complimentary with the purchase of earrings. The company's stores are generally located in high-traffic concourses of regional shopping malls. The company offers an e-commerce site, Pagoda.com.

CONTACTS: Note: Officers with more than one job title may be intentionally listed here more than once.

Theophlius Killion, CEO
John F. Eureyecko, Pres.
Theophlius Killion, CEO-Zale Corporation
Richard H. Penske, Chmn.

FINANCIAL DATA: Note: Data for latest year may not have been available at press time.

In U.S. $	2015	2014	2013	2012	2011	2010
Revenue		146,900,000	239,722,000	238,692,000	239,231,000	226,187,000
R&D Expense						
Operating Income						
Operating Margin %						
SGA Expense						
Net Income		-6,300,000	1,271,226	-3,491,753	-15,418,137	-93,672,000
Operating Cash Flow						
Capital Expenditure						
EBITDA						
Return on Assets %						
Return on Equity %						
Debt to Equity						

CONTACT INFORMATION:

Phone: 972-580-4000   Fax: 972-580-5266
Toll-Free: 800-866-9700
Address: 901 W. Walnut Hill Ln., Irving, TX 75038 United States

STOCK TICKER/OTHER:

Stock Ticker: Subsidiary
Employees: 1,510
Parent Company: Signet Jewelers Ltd.

Exchange:
Fiscal Year Ends: 03/31

SALARIES/BONUSES:

Top Exec. Salary: $ Bonus: $
Second Exec. Salary: $ Bonus: $

OTHER THOUGHTS:

Estimated Female Officers or Directors:
Hot Spot for Advancement for Women/Minorities:

Piggly Wiggly Midwest LLC

NAIC Code: 445110

www.shopthepig.com

TYPES OF BUSINESS:

Grocery Stores
Food Wholesaler

BRANDS/DIVISIONS/AFFILIATES:

Certifresh Holdings Inc
Certified Grocers Midwest Inc
Topco
Springtime
Pig Points
Piggly Wiggly Preferred Club Card

CONTACTS: *Note: Officers with more than one job title may be intentionally listed here more than once.*

Paul Butera, CEO
Gary Suokko, COO
Michael Isken, CFO

GROWTH PLANS/SPECIAL FEATURES:

Piggly Wiggly Midwest LLC is a wholesale distributor and retailer of groceries and other foods. The firm is a subsidiary of Certifresh Holdings, Inc., which is owned by Certified Grocers Midwest, Inc. The company also manages the Piggly Wiggly supermarket chain stores in Wisconsin and northern Illinois. The firm's supermarkets, primarily located in small and suburban communities, offer various products, including groceries, frozen foods, fresh produce and dairy products as well as non-food items. Select stores also offer wine and liquor, lottery tickets, photo processing services and in-store banking. The company's private-label products include Topco fresh meats and Springtime soft drinks, fruit drinks and bottled water. Its coordinated merchandising and advertising efforts include weekly newspaper ad inserts, billboards, television and radio spots and sponsorship of entertainment and charitable events. Piggly Wiggly's Pig Points is a fuel discount program that allows customers to pay as little as one cent per gallon of gas. Members earn fuel discounts by using Piggly Wiggle Preferred Club Cards when purchasing any of the thousands specially-marked Pig Points products throughout Piggly Wiggly stores. Fuel discounts can be redeemed at participating fuel partners.

FINANCIAL DATA: *Note: Data for latest year may not have been available at press time.*

In U.S. $	2015	2014	2013	2012	2011	2010
Revenue		1,575,000,000	1,550,000,000	1,500,000,000	1,400,000,000	1,300,000,000
R&D Expense						
Operating Income						
Operating Margin %						
SGA Expense						
Net Income						
Operating Cash Flow						
Capital Expenditure						
EBITDA						
Return on Assets %						
Return on Equity %						
Debt to Equity						

CONTACT INFORMATION:

Phone: 608-935-2366   Fax:
Toll-Free:
Address: 316 W. Spring Street #7, Dodgeville, WI 53533 United States

STOCK TICKER/OTHER:

Stock Ticker: Subsidiary   Exchange:
Employees: 750   Fiscal Year Ends: 12/31
Parent Company: Certified Grocers Midwest, Inc.

SALARIES/BONUSES:

Top Exec. Salary: $ Bonus: $
Second Exec. Salary: $ Bonus: $

OTHER THOUGHTS:

Estimated Female Officers or Directors:
Hot Spot for Advancement for Women/Minorities:

unkett Research, Ltd.

Pilot Flying J

www.pilotflyingj.com

NAIC Code: 447110

TYPES OF BUSINESS:

Truck Stops
Petroleum Product Distribution

BRANDS/DIVISIONS/AFFILIATES:

Pilot Travel Center
Flying J
Frequent Fueler Advantage
UNI-MAXX TRUCK CARE
Maxum Petroleum Inc

CONTACTS: Note: Officers with more than one job title may be intentionally listed here more than once.

Jimmy Haslam, CEO
Mark Hazelwood, Pres.

GROWTH PLANS/SPECIAL FEATURES:

Pilot Flying J (PFJ) is one of the largest retail operators of truck stops, convenience stores and travel plazas in the U.S. and Canada. The firm's more than 650 locations are primarily located near interstate highway exits and operate under the Pilot Travel Center and Flying J banners. These centers provide fueling facilities, restaurants (including Arby's, Dairy Queen, Subway and Wendy's) and retail merchandise. Some of the additional services and amenities offered include showers, ATMs, Internet kiosks, check cashing, money orders, laundry, audio book rentals, truck washes, truck service centers and CAT Scales. The firm also maintains a customer loyalty and rewards program, Frequent Fueler Advantage. Many of PFJ's travel centers offer truck maintenance and repair services through the UNI-MAXX TRUCK CARE network, an independent network of Goodyear dealers. Services include 24-hour-a-day road service, preventative maintenance, tire service, part replacement, oil changes and other light mechanical work. Subsidiary Maxum Petroleum, Inc. is an independent energy logistics company that sells and distributes refined petroleum products to commercial and industrial customers in the U.S. and Panama. The company is owned by the founding Haslam family. In October 2015, the Haslam family acquired CVC Capital Partner's remaining stake in Pilot Flying J.

PFJ offers its employees medical, dental and vision benefits; AD&D insurance; a 401(k); tuition reimbursement; adoption assistance; and short- and long-term disability insurance.

FINANCIAL DATA: Note: Data for latest year may not have been available at press time.

In U.S. $	2015	2014	2013	2012	2011	2010
Revenue		32,100,000,000	30,430,000,000	31,000,000,000	30,000,000,000	25,000,000,000
R&D Expense						
Operating Income						
Operating Margin %						
SGA Expense						
Net Income						
Operating Cash Flow						
Capital Expenditure						
EBITDA						
Return on Assets %						
Return on Equity %						
Debt to Equity						

CONTACT INFORMATION:

Phone: 865-588-7487   Fax: 865-450-2800
Toll-Free: 800-562-6210
Address: 5508 Lonas Dr., Knoxville, TN 37909 United States

SALARIES/BONUSES:

Top Exec. Salary: $ Bonus: $
Second Exec. Salary: $ Bonus: $

STOCK TICKER/OTHER:

Stock Ticker: Private   Exchange:
Employees: 25,000   Fiscal Year Ends:
Parent Company:

OTHER THOUGHTS:

Estimated Female Officers or Directors:
Hot Spot for Advancement for Women/Minorities:

Sales, profits and employees may be estimates. Financial information, benefits and other data can change quickly and may vary from those stated here.

Prada SpA

NAIC Code: 424300

TYPES OF BUSINESS:

Apparel and Clothing Brands, Designers, Importers and Distributors
Leather Goods
Retail Stores

BRANDS/DIVISIONS/AFFILIATES:

Church & Co.
Prada Donna
Car Shoe
Granello
Miu Miu
Tannerie Limoges
Prada
Pasticceria Marchesi

CONTACTS: *Note: Officers with more than one job title may be intentionally listed here more than once.*

Patrizio Bertelli, CEO
Donatello Galli, CFO
Carlo Mazzi, Chmn.

GROWTH PLANS/SPECIAL FEATURES:

Prada SpA Group manufactures and sells upscale apparel, shoes, accessories and fragrances for men and women. The company was originally created through the merger of leather goods businesses run by Miuccia Prada and her husband Patrizio Bertelli, who together continue to own approximately 95% of the business. Prada started out as a small family luggage business, based in a shop in the Galleria Emmanuele Vittorio in Italy. It is now a multi-label operation with approximately 594 directly-operated stores around the world in over 70 countries. Its original brand lines include Prada, Prada Donna, Granello and Miu Miu (a less expensive apparel line). The firm has also acquired luxury brands such as English shoe manufacturer Church & Co. The Prada store in New York was the first of a string of epicenters, or flagship retail stores. The company currently produces work under the brands Prada, Miu Miu, Church's and Car Shoe. Production takes place exclusively in Italy, with the exception of Church & Co. shoes for men which are made in the U.K. Prada also owns Marchesi 1824, an iconic cafe in Milan, Italy, founded in 1824, in the same location in which it operates today. In 2014, the firm acquired a 50% stake in French tannery Tannerie Megisserie Hervy (now named Tannerie Limoges SAS), a joint venture with the firm's long time industrial partner Conceria Superior SpA; and an 80% stake in the Pasticceria Marchesi, an Italian pastry shop.

FINANCIAL DATA: *Note: Data for latest year may not have been available at press time.*

In U.S. $	2015	2014	2013	2012	2011	2010
Revenue	3,980,516,864	4,020,472,320	3,695,315,200	2,864,162,048	2,293,757,440	1,749,737,088
R&D Expense						
Operating Income						
Operating Margin %						
SGA Expense						
Net Income	514,662,560	714,811,648	709,736,960	489,117,632	281,102,144	112,256,376
Operating Cash Flow						
Capital Expenditure						
EBITDA						
Return on Assets %						
Return on Equity %						
Debt to Equity						

CONTACT INFORMATION:

Phone: 39 2550281   Fax: 39 255028859
Toll-Free:
Address: Via Antonio Fogazzaro 28, Milano, 20135 Italy

STOCK TICKER/OTHER:

Stock Ticker: PRDSY   Exchange: PINX
Employees: 11,962   Fiscal Year Ends: 01/31
Parent Company:

SALARIES/BONUSES:

Top Exec. Salary: $ Bonus: $
Second Exec. Salary: $ Bonus: $

OTHER THOUGHTS:

Estimated Female Officers or Directors:
Hot Spot for Advancement for Women/Minorities:

PriceSmart Inc

www.pricesmart.com

NAIC Code: 452910

TYPES OF BUSINESS:

Warehouse Clubs, Retail
Merchandise
Warehouse Club Membership

BRANDS/DIVISIONS/AFFILIATES:

CONTACTS:
Note: Officers with more than one job title may be intentionally listed here more than once.

Jose Laparte, CEO
John Heffner, CFO
Robert Price, Chairman of the Board
William Naylon, COO
Rodrigo Calvo, Executive VP, Divisional
Brud Drachman, Executive VP, Divisional
John Hildebrandt, Executive VP, Divisional
Robert Gans, Executive VP
Thomas Martin, Executive VP

GROWTH PLANS/SPECIAL FEATURES:

PriceSmart, Inc. is one of the largest operators of warehouse membership clubs in Central America, the Caribbean and South America. The company serves over 2.3 million cardholders at 37 owned and operated warehouse clubs in 12 countries and one U.S. territory. PriceSmart's membership club model is similar to U.S. clubs like Costco and Sam's, with some differences: smaller store size, lower membership fees (average $30), and merchandise is tailored to local preferences as well as for retail and wholesale customers. PriceSmart warehouse clubs can be found in Colombia, 6; Costa Rica, 6; Panama, 5; Trinidad, 4; Guatemala, 3; Dominican Republic, 3; Honduras, 3; El Salvador, 2; and one each in Aruba, Barbados, Jamaica, Nicaragua and the U.S. Virgin Islands. Online shopping is available to its members in all countries. Merchandise departments include electronics, computers, baby, automotive, restaurant/institutional, sporting goods, outdoor, hardware, toys and games, appliances, housewares, bed and bath, luggage, health care, furniture, office and fashion accessories. In 2014, the company opened one new warehouse club in Honduras and two in Colombia. In July 2015, it opened another warehouse club in Panama.

FINANCIAL DATA:
Note: Data for latest year may not have been available at press time.

In U.S. $	2015	2014	2013	2012	2011	2010
Revenue	2,802,603,000	2,517,567,000	2,299,812,000	2,050,745,000	1,714,247,000	1,395,891,000
R&D Expense						
Operating Income	146,366,000	136,707,000	127,935,000	107,926,000	90,880,000	74,893,000
Operating Margin %	5.22%	5.43%	5.56%	5.26%	5.30%	5.36%
SGA Expense	301,393,000	265,751,000	242,449,000	224,039,000	192,663,000	160,716,000
Net Income	89,124,000	92,886,000	84,265,000	67,621,000	61,750,000	49,315,000
Operating Cash Flow	110,503,000	137,275,000	130,633,000	89,889,000	75,599,000	83,029,000
Capital Expenditure	89,185,000	118,101,000	69,927,000	52,705,000	47,033,000	50,207,000
EBITDA	177,481,000	167,019,000	151,871,000	132,644,000	114,426,000	90,223,000
Return on Assets %	9.10%	10.51%	10.79%	9.65%	9.98%	9.30%
Return on Equity %	15.78%	18.04%	18.72%	17.01%	17.34%	15.49%
Debt to Equity	0.12	0.14	0.12	0.17	0.16	0.16

CONTACT INFORMATION:

Phone: 858 404-8800   Fax: 858 404-8848
Toll-Free:
Address: 9740 Scranton Rd., San Diego, CA 92121 United States

STOCK TICKER/OTHER:

Stock Ticker: PSMT   Exchange: NAS
Employees: 6,772   Fiscal Year Ends: 08/31
Parent Company:

SALARIES/BONUSES:

Top Exec. Salary: $579,850   Bonus: $
Second Exec. Salary: $413,440 Bonus: $

OTHER THOUGHTS:

Estimated Female Officers or Directors: 4
Hot Spot for Advancement for Women/Minorities: Y

Publix Super Markets Inc

NAIC Code: 445110

www.publix.com

TYPES OF BUSINESS:

Grocery Stores
Dairy, Deli & Bakery Products
Convenience Stores
Liquor Stores
Restaurants

BRANDS/DIVISIONS/AFFILIATES:

CONTACTS: Note: Officers with more than one job title may be intentionally listed here more than once.

Sharon Miller, Assistant Secretary
David Bornmann, Vice President
William Crenshaw, CEO
David Phillips, CFO
Laurie Zeitlin, Chief Information Officer
Charles Jenkins, Director
Hoyt Barnett, Director
Randall Jones, President
John Hrabusa, Senior VP
John Attaway, Senior VP
Linda Hall, Vice President
Dale Myers, Vice President
David Duncan, Vice President
David Bridges, Vice President
Michael Smith, Vice President
Thomas Mclaughlin, Vice President
William Fauerbach, Vice President
Alfred Ottolino, Vice President
Mark Irby, Vice President
John Frazier, Vice President
Marc Salm, Vice President

GROWTH PLANS/SPECIAL FEATURES:

Publix Super Markets, Inc. is a leading operator of supermarkets, with 1,097 locations in Alabama, Florida, Georgia, South Carolina, North Carolina and Tennessee. The firm's supermarkets sell groceries, dairy products, produce, deli foods, bakery items, meat, seafood, housewares and health and beauty merchandise. Many stores also feature pharmacies, floral departments, photo labs, liquor stores and in-store banking areas. It also owns several pharmacy and convenience store locations under various names. Publix's lines of merchandise include a variety of nationally advertised and private label brands as well as some unbranded merchandise, such as produce, meat and seafood. In addition to its retail operations, Publix manufactures dairy, bakery and deli products through manufacturing facilities located in Lakeland, Miami, Jacksonville, Sarasota, Orlando, Deerfield Beach and Boynton Beach, Florida and Lawrenceville, Georgia. The firm is one of the largest employee-owned grocery stores in the U.S. In April 2015, the firm acquired two former Lowes Foods stores in North Carolina, expanding its presence into its most recent state.

Publix offers its employees health, dental and vision coverage; quarterly retail bonuses; an employee stock ownership plan; holiday bonuses; free hot lunches; prescription discounts; a 401(k) plan; a profit sharing plan; access to a credit union; tuition reimbursement; and an employee assistance plan.

FINANCIAL DATA: Note: Data for latest year may not have been available at press time.

In U.S. $	2015	2014	2013	2012	2011	2010
Revenue		30,802,470,000	29,147,520,000	27,706,770,000	27,178,760,000	25,328,050,000
R&D Expense						
Operating Income		2,400,861,000	2,319,738,000	2,165,251,000	2,134,925,000	1,921,324,000
Operating Margin %		7.79%	7.95%	7.81%	7.85%	7.58%
SGA Expense		6,168,955,000	5,890,461,000	5,630,537,000	5,523,469,000	5,295,287,000
Net Income		1,735,308,000	1,653,954,000	1,552,255,000	1,491,966,000	1,338,147,000
Operating Cash Flow		2,777,232,000	2,567,303,000	2,604,207,000	2,341,187,000	2,265,968,000
Capital Expenditure		1,374,124,000	668,485,000	697,112,000	602,952,000	468,530,000
EBITDA		2,914,254,000	2,821,427,000	2,795,833,000	2,627,564,000	2,428,665,000
Return on Assets %		12.12%	12.80%	13.18%	13.92%	13.96%
Return on Equity %		16.12%	17.13%	20.36%	22.23%	19.73%
Debt to Equity		0.01	0.01	0.01	0.01	0.01

CONTACT INFORMATION:

Phone: 863 688-1188   Fax: 863 688-5532
Toll-Free: 800-242-1227
Address: 3300 Publix Corporate Pkwy., Lakeland, FL 33811 United States

STOCK TICKER/OTHER:

Stock Ticker: PUSH
Employees: 175,000
Parent Company:

Exchange: PINX
Fiscal Year Ends: 12/31

SALARIES/BONUSES:

Top Exec. Salary: $777,400   Bonus: $
Second Exec. Salary: $622,193   Bonus: $

OTHER THOUGHTS:

Estimated Female Officers or Directors: 5
Hot Spot for Advancement for Women/Minorities: Y

Sales, profits and employees may be estimates. Financial information, benefits and other data can change quickly and may vary from those stated here.

PUMA SE

www.puma.com

NAIC Code: 424340

TYPES OF BUSINESS:

Footwear Distribution
Athletic Apparel
Sports Equipment
Retail Stores

BRANDS/DIVISIONS/AFFILIATES:

PUMA
Tretorn
Kering SA
Cobra Golf

CONTACTS: *Note: Officers with more than one job title may be intentionally listed here more than once.*

Bjorn Gulden, CEO
Lars Sorensen, COO
Michael Lammermann, CFO
Michael Lammermann, General Manager-Legal
Michael Lammermann, General Manager-Finance
Jean-Francois Palus, Chmn.

GROWTH PLANS/SPECIAL FEATURES:

PUMA SE (PUMA) is an international footwear, apparel and accessories company based in Germany. Luxury fashion conglomerate Kering owns an 84% controlling stake in the company. PUMA develops and markets footwear, t-shirts, shorts, pants, jackets, caps, swimwear, socks and head- and wristbands as well as a variety of athletic equipment under the PUMA, Tretorn and Cobra Golf brands. The firm designs products for multiple sports, including running, soccer, football, tennis, baseball, cricket and motocross and relies on celebrity endorsement as well as high-profile advertising campaigns to fulfill its marketing strategies. PUMA has provided apparel to the national soccer team of Cameroon, Belgium's Club Brugge, tennis star Serena Williams, baseball player Johnny Damon, motocross medalist Travis Pastrana and a variety of teams playing in the World Athletics Championships for the Jamaican Federation. The company has also partnered with fashion designers such as Rudolf Dassler, Alexander McQueen, Yasuhiro Mihara and Sergio Rossi. Products are distributed in more than 120 countries through sporting goods stores, department stores, online stores and PUMA sports boutiques located around the world.

FINANCIAL DATA: *Note: Data for latest year may not have been available at press time.*

In U.S. $	2015	2014	2013	2012	2011	2010
Revenue		3,154,186,000	3,168,301,000	3,471,196,000	3,193,454,000	2,872,304,000
R&D Expense		85,965,360	85,753,100		81,720,160	67,498,730
Operating Income		135,846,500	66,331,300	120,139,200	353,625,400	325,607,100
Operating Margin %		4.30%	2.09%	3.46%	11.07%	11.33%
SGA Expense		1,287,464,000	1,361,331,000		1,202,454,000	1,092,078,000
Net Income		68,029,380	5,624,894	74,503,310	244,523,700	214,595,000
Operating Cash Flow		134,148,400	116,000,200	166,305,800	134,572,900	179,784,400
Capital Expenditure		77,050,430	59,114,450	86,177,620	75,458,480	58,583,800
EBITDA		189,442,200	123,429,300	200,904,200	419,107,700	402,126,800
Return on Assets %		2.63%	.21%	2.74%	9.30%	9.23%
Return on Equity %		4.16%	.34%	4.39%	15.38%	15.40%
Debt to Equity						

CONTACT INFORMATION:

Phone: 49 09132810   Fax: 49 09132812246
Toll-Free:
Address: Puma-Way 1, Herzogenaurach, 91074 Germany

SALARIES/BONUSES:

Top Exec. Salary: $ Bonus: $
Second Exec. Salary: $ Bonus: $

STOCK TICKER/OTHER:

Stock Ticker: PMMAF
Employees: 10,830
Parent Company: Kering SA

Exchange: GREY
Fiscal Year Ends: 12/31

OTHER THOUGHTS:

Estimated Female Officers or Directors:
Hot Spot for Advancement for Women/Minorities:

PVH Corp

NAIC Code: 424300

TYPES OF BUSINESS:

Apparel and Clothing Brands, Designers, Importers and Distributors
Sportswear
Footwear
Outlet Stores
Neckwear
Jeans
Dress Shirts
Apparel Wholesale

BRANDS/DIVISIONS/AFFILIATES:

Calvin Klein
Van Heusen
Tommy Hilfiger
ARROW
Warner's
Olga
Warnaco Group Inc (The)
Izod

CONTACTS: *Note: Officers with more than one job title may be intentionally listed here more than once.*

Francis Duane, CEO, Geographical
Daniel Grieder, CEO, Subsidiary
Steven Shiffman, CEO, Subsidiary
Emanuel Chirico, CEO
James Holmes, Chief Accounting Officer
Michael Shaffer, COO
Fred Gehring, Director
Kozel David, Executive VP, Divisional
Mark Fischer, Executive VP
Dana Perlman, Senior VP, Divisional

GROWTH PLANS/SPECIAL FEATURES:

PVH Corp. manufactures, distributes and sells clothing an shoes for men, women and children. The firm operates unde several brand names, including owned brands such as Calvi Klein, Van Heusen, Tommy Hilfiger, ARROW, Warner's, Olga Eagle and IZOD as well as licensed brands such as Speed Geoffrey Beene, Kenneth Cole, Sean John, Michael Kor Chaps, Donald J. Trump, DKNY, Nautica, Ted Baker, J. Garcia Claiborne, Ike Behar, Jones New York and Ryan Seacres PVH distributes to department stores and other wholesal clients as well as selling through outlet stores operating unde the firm's brand names. It currently maintains retail location across its brand portfolio in the U.S., Canada, Europe and Japan. The company operates in three primary segments Tommy Hilfiger, which consists of Tommy Hilfiger Nort America and Tommy Hilfiger international; Calvin Klein, which includes Calvin Klein North America and Calvin Klei international; and Heritage Brands, which consists of th Heritage Brands' wholesale and retail segments. Wholly owned The Warnaco Group, Inc., enables PVH to have ful control over the Calvin Klein brand, as Warnaco held licensing rights for Calvin Klein jeans and underwear. In 2015, the firm announced plans to close its Izod retail division by year's end.

PVH offers employees medical, dental and life insurance; a employee assistance program; flexible spending accounts domestic partner benefits; a 401(k); a pension plan; a 529 college savings program; group auto and home owner's insurance; discounts on company merchandise; educatio assistance; and college scholarships for children of employees

FINANCIAL DATA: *Note: Data for latest year may not have been available at press time.*

In U.S. $	2015	2014	2013	2012	2011	2010
Revenue	8,241,200,000	8,186,351,000	6,042,999,000	5,890,624,000	4,636,848,000	2,398,731,000
R&D Expense						
Operating Income	613,100,000	513,462,000	654,915,000	559,653,000	203,395,000	243,812,000
Operating Margin %	7.43%	6.27%	10.83%	9.50%	4.38%	10.16%
SGA Expense	3,713,600,000	3,673,469,000	2,594,315,000	2,481,370,000	2,071,416,000	938,791,000
Net Income	439,000,000	143,537,000	433,840,000	317,881,000	53,805,000	161,910,000
Operating Cash Flow	789,100,000	411,859,000	569,537,000	490,721,000	352,227,000	214,452,000
Capital Expenditure	255,800,000	237,142,000	210,554,000	169,841,000	100,995,000	23,856,000
EBITDA	779,600,000	834,559,000	802,215,000	692,930,000	352,271,000	294,996,000
Return on Assets %	3.90%	1.48%	5.79%	4.71%	1.18%	7.13%
Return on Equity %	10.09%	3.78%	14.57%	13.29%	3.14%	14.94%
Debt to Equity	0.78	0.89	0.67	0.72	1.04	0.34

CONTACT INFORMATION:

Phone: 212 381-3500   Fax: 212 247-5309
Toll-Free: 866-214-6694
Address: 200 Madison Ave., New York, NY 10016 United States

STOCK TICKER/OTHER:

Stock Ticker: PVH
Employees: 34,100
Parent Company:

Exchange: NYS
Fiscal Year Ends: 01/31

SALARIES/BONUSES:

Top Exec. Salary: $1,350,000   Bonus: $

Second Exec. Salary: $1,090,517   Bonus: $

OTHER THOUGHTS:

Estimated Female Officers or Directors: 12

Hot Spot for Advancement for Women/Minorities: Y

Quiksilver Inc

NAIC Code: 424300

TYPES OF BUSINESS:

Apparel and Clothing Brands, Designers, Importers and Distributors
Snow & Surf Apparel & Equipment
Accessories
Swimwear
Retail Stores

BRANDS/DIVISIONS/AFFILIATES:

Quicksilver
Roxy
Roxy Girl
DC

CONTACTS: *Note: Officers with more than one job title may be intentionally listed here more than once.*

Pierre Agnes, CEO
Thomas Chambolle, CFO
Robert McKnight, Chairman of the Board
Alan Vickers, Executive VP, Divisional
Greg Healy, President

GROWTH PLANS/SPECIAL FEATURES:

Quiksilver, Inc. is an internationally diversified firm that designs, produces, retails and distributes branded apparel, footwear, accessories and related products. It operates in four segments: Americas, consisting of North, South and Central America with revenue generating primarily from the U.S., Canada, Brazil and Mexico; EMEA, consisting of Europe, the Middle East and Africa with primary revenue generating from the U.K., Europe, Russia and South Africa; Asia Pacific, comprising Australia, Japan, New Zealand, South Korea, Taiwan and Indonesia; and corporation operations, consisting primarily of its sourcing services to licensees. The company's brands are focused on different sports within the outdoor market. The Quiksilver and Roxy brands are rooted in the sport of surfing and are leading brands representing the boardriding lifestyle, which includes surfing, skateboarding and snowboarding. Quiksilver has grown to include shirts, shorts, t-shirts, pants, jackets, fleece, snowboard wear, footwear, hats, backpacks, wetsuits, watches, eyewear and other accessories. In addition, the brand has expanded its target market to include boys, toddlers and infants. The Roxy brand includes sportswear, footwear, backpacks, snowboard wear, swimwear, backpacks, snowboard boots, skis, fragrance, beauty care, bedroom furnishings and other accessories for young women. The brand also includes Roxy Girl for girls and infants. The firm's DC brand specializes in technical shoes made for skateboarding and snowboarding as well as sandals and general branded apparel. The company's products are sold in over 115 countries in its 935 owned or licensed stores as well as a wide range of other distribution channels, including surf shops, snowboard shops, skate shops and other specialty stores and select department stores. In 2014, apparel accounted for 75% of the firm's revenues and footwear accounted for 25%. In 2014, the firm sold subsidiary Hawk Designs, Inc. and its majority ownership in Surfdome. In September 2015, the firm announced that its U.S. business unit will enter bankruptcy. It appears that the unit intends to remain in business after obtaining new capital.

FINANCIAL DATA: *Note: Data for latest year may not have been available at press time.*

In U.S. $	2015	2014	2013	2012	2011	2010
Revenue		1,570,399,000	1,810,570,000	2,013,239,000	1,953,061,000	1,837,620,000
R&D Expense						
Operating Income		-253,471,000	2,547,000	56,968,000	41,512,000	123,525,000
Operating Margin %		-16.14%	.14%	2.82%	2.12%	6.72%
SGA Expense		827,181,000	857,557,000	916,144,000	895,949,000	832,066,000
Net Income		-309,377,000	-232,565,000	-10,756,000	-21,258,000	-9,684,000
Operating Cash Flow		-26,935,000	27,192,000	-13,539,000	54,149,000	203,482,000
Capital Expenditure		53,415,000	52,182,000	66,081,000	89,590,000	43,135,000
EBITDA		-201,533,000	52,505,000	111,869,000	96,771,000	183,303,000
Return on Assets %		-21.50%	-13.93%	-.61%	-1.22%	-.54%
Return on Equity %		-145.33%	-48.80%	-1.80%	-3.48%	-1.81%
Debt to Equity		14.15	2.18	1.23	1.18	1.14

CONTACT INFORMATION:

Phone: 714 889-2200   Fax: 714 645-0313
Toll-Free:
Address: 15202 Graham St., Huntington Beach, CA 92649 United States

STOCK TICKER/OTHER:

Stock Ticker: ZQKSQ   Exchange: PINX
Employees: 6,100   Fiscal Year Ends: 10/31
Parent Company:

SALARIES/BONUSES:

Top Exec. Salary: Bonus: $
$1,000,000
Second Exec. Salary: Bonus: $
$1,000,000

OTHER THOUGHTS:

Estimated Female Officers or Directors: 1

Hot Spot for Advancement for Women/Minorities:

QuikTrip Corporation

NAIC Code: 447110

TYPES OF BUSINESS:

Convenience Stores
Gas Stations
Truck Stops

BRANDS/DIVISIONS/AFFILIATES:

QT Distribution
IQ
QT Warehouse
Hotzi
QuikTrip
QT Kitchens
Wally
QT Twister

CONTACTS: Note: Officers with more than one job title may be intentionally listed here more than once.

Chester Cadieux, III, CEO
Chester Cadieux, III, Pres.
Mike Thornbrugh, Mgr.-Public & Gov't Affairs
Troy DeVos, Dir.-Real Estate
Chester Cadieux, III, Chmn.

GROWTH PLANS/SPECIAL FEATURES:

QuikTrip Corporation (QT), a privately held company headquartered in Tulsa, Oklahoma, is a convenience/gasoline retailer. QuikTrip has 705 stores in in Oklahoma, Kansas, Missouri, North Carolina, South Carolina, Iowa, Nebraska, Georgia, Texas and Arizona. The company maintains high detergent levels in its gasoline and offers unique brands of food and beverage products. Because of its IQ detergent additive, QuikTrip gasoline has been named a TOP TIER Detergent Gasoline by a group of major automobile manufacturers. The additive removes engine deposits, thereby increasing efficiency and reducing pollutants. The firm's wholly-owned subsidiary, QT Distribution, is the exclusive distribution center and manufacturing facility for QuikTrip. More than 70% of products sold in QuikTrip stores are shipped via the QT warehouse system. QT Distribution operates warehouses located around Kansas City, Atlanta, Dallas/Ft. Worth and Phoenix. The company's convenience stores feature various food and beverage products including, but not limited to, Hotzi breakfast and QuikTrip sandwiches, QT Kitchens prepared meals, taquitos, egg rolls, hot dogs, Wally drinks, QT Twister frozen treats, Quikshakes and Freezoni frozen drinks, coffee and energy drinks. QuikTrip also sells surplus real estate.

QuikTrip offers its employees medical, dental and vision coverage; life insurance; a 401(k) plan; a profit sharing program; a stock option plan; vacation benefits that increase with the number of years of service; a credit union; a seniority awards program; tuition reimbursement; an employee assistance program; free employee uniform shirts; disability; medical and child care reimbursement accounts; and a scholarship program. Part-time workers receive a more limited benefits package. QuikTrip believes in promotion-from-within, with nearly all executives and managers having risen from the bottom.

FINANCIAL DATA: Note: Data for latest year may not have been available at press time.

In U.S. $	2015	2014	2013	2012	2011	2010
Revenue		11,450,000,000	11,210,000,000	10,770,000,000	8,770,000,000	7,301,400,000
R&D Expense						
Operating Income						
Operating Margin %						
SGA Expense						
Net Income						
Operating Cash Flow						
Capital Expenditure						
EBITDA						
Return on Assets %						
Return on Equity %						
Debt to Equity						

CONTACT INFORMATION:

Phone: 918-615-7700   Fax: 918-615-7377
Toll-Free: 800-848-1966
Address: 4705 S. 129th East Ave., Tulsa, OK 74134 United States

STOCK TICKER/OTHER:

Stock Ticker: Private   Exchange:
Employees: 17,000   Fiscal Year Ends: 04/30
Parent Company:

SALARIES/BONUSES:

Top Exec. Salary: $ Bonus: $
Second Exec. Salary: $ Bonus: $

OTHER THOUGHTS:

Estimated Female Officers or Directors:
Hot Spot for Advancement for Women/Minorities:

QVC Inc

NAIC Code: 454113

www.qvc.com

TYPES OF BUSINESS:

Television Shopping
Internet Shopping
Retail Outlet Stores

BRANDS/DIVISIONS/AFFILIATES:

QVC.com
m.QVC.com
QVC Studio Park
QVC Studio Store
Liberty Interactive Corp
CNR Home Shopping Co Ltd

CONTACTS: Note: Officers with more than one job title may be intentionally listed here more than once.

Michael George, CEO
Meade Rusasill, COO
Michael George, Pres.
Thaddeus Jastrzebsk, CFO
Gregg Bertoni, CEO-QVC Italy
Steve Hofmann, CEO-QVC Europe

GROWTH PLANS/SPECIAL FEATURES:

QVC, Inc., a subsidiary of Liberty Interactive Corp., is a televised shopping network based in West Chester, Pennsylvania. QVC (standing for quality, value and convenience) distributes its television programs, via satellite or optical fiber, to multichannel television distributors for retransmission to subscribers in the U.S, the U.K., Germany, Japan, Italy and other neighboring countries, reaching over 317 million homes worldwide. The network broadcasts themed shopping programming 24 hours a day, 364 days a year, with operators continuously available to take calls and process orders. QVC maintains nine distribution centers and eight call centers worldwide to fulfill orders. The firm markets a wide variety of brand name products in areas such as home furnishing, which accounted for 32% of its 2014 revenue; beauty, 17%; apparel, 16%; jewelry, 12%; accessories, 12% and electronics, 11%. The firm presents 819 products per week. QVC offers products in each of these merchandise groups that are exclusive to QVC as well as popular brand names and other products also available from other retailers. In addition to TV programming, the firm operates QVC.com, which offers the same products marketed on the air, as well as a mobile site at m.QVC.com. Moreover, shoppers can find QVC merchandise in its six outlet stores in Pennsylvania, South Carolina, North Carolina and Delaware, and at the QVC Studio Store located at QVC Studio Park, where the broadcasts originate. In China, the company established CNR Home Shopping Co., Ltd., a joint venture with Beijing-based China National Radio, to operate a multimedia retailing business.

The company offers its employees medical, dental and vision insurance; prescription drug coverage; flexible spending accounts; life and disability insurance; an employee assistance plan; and tuition assistance.

FINANCIAL DATA: Note: Data for latest year may not have been available at press time.

In U.S. $	2015	2014	2013	2012	2011	2010
Revenue		8,801,000,000	8,623,000,000	8,516,000,000	8,268,000,000	7,807,000,000
R&D Expense						
Operating Income						
Operating Margin %						
SGA Expense						
Net Income		1,279,000,000	1,245,000,000	1,268,000,000	1,137,000,000	1,130,000,000
Operating Cash Flow						
Capital Expenditure						
EBITDA						
Return on Assets %						
Return on Equity %						
Debt to Equity						

CONTACT INFORMATION:

Phone: 484-701-1000   Fax: 484-701-8170
Toll-Free:
Address: 1200 Wilson Dr., West Chester, PA 19380 United States

STOCK TICKER/OTHER:

Stock Ticker: Subsidiary
Employees: 17,100
Parent Company: Liberty Interactive Corp

Exchange:
Fiscal Year Ends: 12/31

SALARIES/BONUSES:

Top Exec. Salary: $ Bonus: $
Second Exec. Salary: $ Bonus: $

OTHER THOUGHTS:

Estimated Female Officers or Directors: 1
Hot Spot for Advancement for Women/Minorities:

Sales, profits and employees may be estimates. Financial information, benefits and other data can change quickly and may vary from those stated here.

RaceTrac Petroleum Inc

NAIC Code: 447110

TYPES OF BUSINESS:

Convenience Stores & Travel Centers

BRANDS/DIVISIONS/AFFILIATES:

Raceway
RaceTrac

GROWTH PLANS/SPECIAL FEATURES:

RaceTrac Petroleum, Inc. operates more than 600 gasolin
convenience stores in 12 southeastern states. RaceTra
Petroleum has two distinct operating divisions: RaceTrac an
RaceWay. RaceTrac convenience stores are company owne
and operated. RaceWay stores are leased to third-part
contract operators. A standard RaceTrac/RaceWay locatio
features 18 to 24 fueling positions and a 4,000-square-foo
convenience store, featuring over 4,000 items. The firm'
convenience stores offer food, hot and cold drinks, gift card
money orders, newspapers, health and beauty aid
automotive supplies, maps, air filling and water. Where allowe
by law, many of the company's stations offer lottery tickets. Th
firm also has a RaceTrac-branded credit card that offer
customers the ability to earn rebates on gas purchases.

The company offers summer internships to students enrolled i
a four-year degree program.

CONTACTS: Note: Officers with more than one job title may be intentionally listed here more than once.

Allison Moran, CEO
Max Lenker, Pres.
Carl Bolch, Jr., Chmn.

FINANCIAL DATA: Note: Data for latest year may not have been available at press time.

In U.S. $	2015	2014	2013	2012	2011	2010
Revenue		8,430,000,000	9,100,000,000	9,060,000,000	5,750,000,000	4,701,700,000
R&D Expense						
Operating Income						
Operating Margin %						
SGA Expense						
Net Income						
Operating Cash Flow						
Capital Expenditure						
EBITDA						
Return on Assets %						
Return on Equity %						
Debt to Equity						

CONTACT INFORMATION:

Phone: 770-431-7600   Fax: 770-319-7944
Toll-Free: 888-636-5589
Address: 3225 Cumberland Blvd., Ste. 100, Atlanta, GA 30339 United States

STOCK TICKER/OTHER:

Stock Ticker: Private   Exchange:
Employees: 7,200   Fiscal Year Ends:
Parent Company:

SALARIES/BONUSES:

Top Exec. Salary: $ Bonus: $
Second Exec. Salary: $ Bonus: $

OTHER THOUGHTS:

Estimated Female Officers or Directors: 1
Hot Spot for Advancement for Women/Minorities:

Rack Room Shoes Inc

www.rackroomshoes.com

NAIC Code: 448210

TYPES OF BUSINESS:

Shoes, Retail
Accessories

BRANDS/DIVISIONS/AFFILIATES:

Deichmann Shoe Group
Off Broadway Shoe Warehouse
Rack Room Shoes

CONTACTS: *Note: Officers with more than one job title may be intentionally listed here more than once.*

Mark Lardie, CEO

GROWTH PLANS/SPECIAL FEATURES:

Rack Room Shoes, Inc. (RRS) specializes in shoes, handbags and accessories, operating more than 450 store locations in 34 states. The company is a member of Deichmann Shoe Group, headquartered in Germany and is one of the largest privately owned shoe retailers in the world. Currently, stores are located across the U.S., primarily in the Mid-Atlantic, upper Midwest, Southeast, and Southwestern states. RRS' store selection includes many popular labels, including Anne Klein, Bass, Easy Spirit, Skechers, Nine West, Steve Madden, Dockers, Rockport, Columbia, Nike, Reebok, New Balance and many others. These brands are coupled with RRS' own private brands, which are commissioned from its associate manufacturers. The company seeks to combine style, selection, value and service in its products and appeals to the consumer by striving to sell the top brands at significantly reduced prices compared to manufacturers' retail stores. RRS also operates under the Off Broadway Shoe Warehouse banner in several states. The company plans to expand in the southeastern U.S., with a special focus on Texas and Arizona.

FINANCIAL DATA: *Note: Data for latest year may not have been available at press time.*

In U.S. $	2015	2014	2013	2012	2011	2010
Revenue						
R&D Expense						
Operating Income						
Operating Margin %						
SGA Expense						
Net Income						
Operating Cash Flow						
Capital Expenditure						
EBITDA						
Return on Assets %						
Return on Equity %						
Debt to Equity						

CONTACT INFORMATION:

Phone: 704-547-9200   Fax: 704-547-8159
Toll-Free:
Address: 8310 Technology Dr., Charlotte, NC 28262 United States

SALARIES/BONUSES:

Top Exec. Salary: $ Bonus: $
Second Exec. Salary: $ Bonus: $

STOCK TICKER/OTHER:

Stock Ticker: Private   Exchange:
Employees: Fiscal Year Ends: 12/31
Parent Company:

OTHER THOUGHTS:

Estimated Female Officers or Directors: 1
Hot Spot for Advancement for Women/Minorities:

RaiaDrogasil SA

NAIC Code: 446110

www.raiadrogasil.com.br

TYPES OF BUSINESS:

Drug Stores

BRANDS/DIVISIONS/AFFILIATES:

Droga Raia
Drogasil
Raia SA
Drogasil SA
Pharmaceutical Benefits Program
www.drogaraia.com.br
www.drogasil.combr

CONTACTS: Note: Officers with more than one job title may be intentionally listed here more than once.

Claudio R. Ely, CEO
Claudio R. Ely, Pres.
Ricardo C. de Azevedo, CFO
Marcello De Zagottis, Dir.-Sales, Commercial & Mktg.
Rosangela Maria de Oliveira Lutti, Dir.-Human Resources
Fernando Kozel Varela, Dir.-IT
Antonio Carlos de Freitas, Dir.-Oper. & Retail-Drogasil
Eugenio De Zagottis, Dir.-Investor Rel.
Antonio Carlos Pipponzi, Chmn.
Fernando Kozel Varela, Dir.-Logistics

GROWTH PLANS/SPECIAL FEATURES:

RaiaDrogasil SA, a product of the 2011 merger of Raia SA and Drogasil SA, is a Brazilian retail drugstore chain operator. The firm is a pharmaceutical retailer of generic, branded and over-the-counter (OTC) drugs. RaiaDrogasil also offers non-pharmaceutical items such as personal care, cosmetics and skincare products. The Droga Raia and Drogasil brands are present in 17 Brazilian states, accounting for 89% of the country's pharmaceutical consumer market. The firm operates seven distribution centers located in Sao Paulo, Embu das Artes, Ribeirao Preto, Contagem, Sao Jose dos Pinhais, Aparecida and Barra Mansa. In addition to its pharmaceutical and non-pharmaceutical products, it offers services such as specialized beauty centers that attend to the aesthetic and beauty needs of its customers; associate programs for other companies where purchases from its employees at RaiaDrogasil stores are deducted from their employees' paychecks; an affiliate program aimed at senior citizens; the Pharmaceutical Benefits Program, which offers special discounts for a variety of pharmaceutical products to customers with health care insurance plans; and a customer loyalty program. Purchases can be made over the Internet at www.drogaraia.com.br and www.drogasil.com.br, as well as by telephone. In 2015, the firm announced plans to open another distribution center in the northeastern region of Brazil, scheduled to open in 2016, in order to support its geographical expansion.

FINANCIAL DATA: Note: Data for latest year may not have been available at press time.

In U.S. $	2015	2014	2013	2012	2011	2010
Revenue		1,928,755,000	1,626,417,000	1,404,047,000	712,207,300	523,240,900
R&D Expense						
Operating Income		78,862,300	36,371,630	41,913,210	20,759,600	29,285,020
Operating Margin %		4.08%	2.23%	2.98%	2.91%	5.59%
SGA Expense		418,554,100	356,062,900	306,286,000	121,105,300	96,379,980
Net Income		57,768,440	26,351,020	27,360,850	17,925,530	23,227,560
Operating Cash Flow		93,919,060	79,780,550	27,485,840	7,467,839	13,685,250
Capital Expenditure		71,667,140	62,157,710	67,750,180	21,841,970	26,505,490
EBITDA		127,806,300	77,792,180	74,355,090	41,143,960	41,133,520
Return on Assets %		5.77%	2.90%	3.22%	3.35%	10.76%
Return on Equity %		9.25%	4.39%	4.69%	4.90%	18.04%
Debt to Equity		0.07	0.06	0.05		0.04

CONTACT INFORMATION:

Phone: 55-11-3769-5678   Fax: 55-11-3769-5787
Toll-Free:
Address: 3097 Corifeu de Azevedo Marques Ave., Sao Paulo, SP 5339-900 Brazil

STOCK TICKER/OTHER:

Stock Ticker: RAIDF
Employees: 17,000
Parent Company:

Exchange: GREY
Fiscal Year Ends: 12/31

SALARIES/BONUSES:

Top Exec. Salary: $ Bonus: $
Second Exec. Salary: $ Bonus: $

OTHER THOUGHTS:

Estimated Female Officers or Directors: 3
Hot Spot for Advancement for Women/Minorities: Y

Raise Marketplace Inc

www.raise.com

NAIC Code: 454111

TYPES OF BUSINESS:

Electronic Shopping

BRANDS/DIVISIONS/AFFILIATES:

Raise
www.raise.com

CONTACTS: Note: Officers with more than one job title may be intentionally listed here more than once.

George Bousis, CEO
Bradley Wasz, COO
Milo Todorovich, Chief Technology Officer

GROWTH PLANS/SPECIAL FEATURES:

Raise Marketplace, Inc. operates an online marketplace to buy and sell gift cards. Its platform allows users to turn their unused gift cards into cash by listing them for sale, and also enables them to shop for discounted gift cards by brand, category and value. Before shopping online or in stores, consumers can check out the Raise marketplace to find discounted gift cards to brands such as Target, The Home Depot and Macy's. Via the company's mobile app and www.raise.com web site, applicable card holders can find discounts on brand names, stores, local restaurants and more, and also receive free shipping as well as a 100% money-back guarantee on every order. Raise Marketplace facilitates every transaction so that members can buy and sell gift cards with confidence. Card holders choose their selling price in order to maximize earnings, and after the card has been sold to a buyer, the seller selects the method in which to be paid. Members can also set a preferred price and discount range, and receive notifications when a card becomes available. Whether buying or selling, members can manage orders and listings from their Raise account.

FINANCIAL DATA: Note: Data for latest year may not have been available at press time.

In U.S. $	2015	2014	2013	2012	2011	2010
Revenue						
R&D Expense						
Operating Income						
Operating Margin %						
SGA Expense						
Net Income						
Operating Cash Flow						
Capital Expenditure						
EBITDA						
Return on Assets %						
Return on Equity %						
Debt to Equity						

CONTACT INFORMATION:

Phone: 312-929-4530   Fax: 312-929-4666
Toll-Free: 888-578-8422
Address: 11 E. Madison St., 4th Fl., Chicago, IL 60654-3537 United States

STOCK TICKER/OTHER:

Stock Ticker: Private
Employees:
Parent Company:

Exchange:
Fiscal Year Ends:

SALARIES/BONUSES:

Top Exec. Salary: $ Bonus: $
Second Exec. Salary: $ Bonus: $

OTHER THOUGHTS:

Estimated Female Officers or Directors:
Hot Spot for Advancement for Women/Minorities:

Sales, profits and employees may be estimates. Financial information, benefits and other data can change quickly and may vary from those stated here.

Raley's Family of Fine Stores

NAIC Code: 445110

TYPES OF BUSINESS:

Supermarkets
Discount Warehouse Stores
Pharmacies
Restaurants

BRANDS/DIVISIONS/AFFILIATES:

Bel Air Markets
Nob Hill Foods
Food Source
Raleys Supermarkets and Drug Centers
Something Extra
Aisle 1

CONTACTS: Note: Officers with more than one job title may be intentionally listed here more than once.

Michael J. Teel, CEO
Keith Knopf, COO
Michael J. Teel, Pres.
Ken Mueller, CFO
Mark Foley, Sr.VP-Human Resources & Labor Relations
Joyce Raley Teel, Co-Chmn.
James E. Teel, Co-Chmn.

GROWTH PLANS/SPECIAL FEATURES:

Raley's Family of Fine Stores owns and operates 12
supermarkets located in California and Nevada. Thomas Rale
originally founded the private firm during the Great Depression
and Raley's is still family-owned and based in Wes
Sacramento, California. Stores include Raley's Supermarket:
and Drug Centers, Bel Air Markets, Nob Hill Foods and Food
Source. Raley's Supermarkets stores offer traditiona
supermarket items and an E-cart service that allows shopper:
to buy items online and then pick them up at select locations
Bel Air Markets offers Chinese hot foods, fresh sushi counter:
and sit-down cafes, with stores located throughout the greate
Sacramento area. Nob Hill Foods is a more upscale chain witr
stores located in the East Bay, South Bay and the Centra
Coast regions of California. Food Source currently consists o
eight warehouse-style discount stores in northern Californi<
and Nevada. The firm has five distribution centers specializing
in different products in Sacramento, West Sacramento and
Stockton, California. It also operates Aisle 1 fuel station:
throughout Northern California and Nevada. In addition, the
company offers a customer loyalty program called Something
Extra.

FINANCIAL DATA: Note: Data for latest year may not have been available at press time.

In U.S. $	2015	2014	2013	2012	2011	2010
Revenue		3,420,000,000	3,350,000,000	3,200,000,000	3,100,000,000	3,000,000,000
R&D Expense						
Operating Income						
Operating Margin %						
SGA Expense						
Net Income						
Operating Cash Flow						
Capital Expenditure						
EBITDA						
Return on Assets %						
Return on Equity %						
Debt to Equity						

CONTACT INFORMATION:

Phone: 916-373-3333   Fax: 916-371-1323
Toll-Free:
Address: 500 W. Capitol Ave., West Sacramento, CA 95605 United States

STOCK TICKER/OTHER:

Stock Ticker: Private
Employees: 13,400
Parent Company:

Exchange:
Fiscal Year Ends: 06/30

SALARIES/BONUSES:

Top Exec. Salary: $ Bonus: $
Second Exec. Salary: $ Bonus: $

OTHER THOUGHTS:

Estimated Female Officers or Directors: 1
Hot Spot for Advancement for Women/Minorities: Y

Ralph Lauren Corporation

www.polo.com

NAIC Code: 424300

TYPES OF BUSINESS:

Apparel and Clothing Brands, Designers, Importers and Distributors
Apparel Design & Marketing
Accessories
Fragrances
Home Furnishings
Cosmetics
Retail Stores

BRANDS/DIVISIONS/AFFILIATES:

Polo
Ralph by Ralph Lauren
Club Monaco
Black Label
Purple Label
Blue Label
Denim & Supply Ralph Lauren
Big Pony

CONTACTS: Note: Officers with more than one job title may be intentionally listed here more than once.

Robert Madore, CFO
Ralph Lauren, Chairman of the Board
Stefan Larsson, Director
David Lauren, Director
Avery Fischer, General Counsel
Valerie Hermann, President, Divisional
Christopher Peterson, President, Divisional

GROWTH PLANS/SPECIAL FEATURES:

Ralph Lauren Corporation (Polo) designs, markets and distributes premium lifestyle products. Polo licenses the manufacturing of its products to companies worldwide. Capitalizing on the creative force of its founder, Ralph Lauren, the firm's various brand names have become recognizable cultural symbols across the globe. The firm offers four categories of lifestyle products: apparel products (including extensive collections of men's, women's and children's clothing), home products (including bedding and bath products, furniture, fabric, wallpaper, paints, tabletop and giftware), accessories (including footwear, eyewear, jewelry, leather goods, handbags and luggage) and fragrance products (consisting of fragrances and skin care products). The company markets its products through department, specialty, golf and Ralph Lauren stores as well as via the Internet and mail order catalogs. Polo also offers wholesale products to upscale (and certain mid-tier) department stores, specialty stores and golf/pro shops worldwide. Its brands include Ralph by Ralph Lauren, Romance, Polo, Lauren for Men, Purple Label, Blue Label, Black Label, RRL, RLX Ralph Lauren, Denim & Supply Ralph Lauren, Big Pony, Pink Pony, Chaps and Club Monaco. Ralph Lauren Corporation sells its merchandise through its wholesale distribution channels at approximately 13,000 different retail locations worldwide. It also sells directly to customers through its 466 retail stores, its 536 concession-based shop-within-shops and its 10 e-commerce sites. Additionally, its international licensing partners operate 72 Ralph Lauren stores, 119 Club Monaco stores and 23 Ralph Lauren concession shops.

FINANCIAL DATA: Note: Data for latest year may not have been available at press time.

In U.S. $	2015	2014	2013	2012	2011	2010
Revenue	7,620,000,000	7,450,000,000	6,944,800,000	6,859,500,000	5,660,300,000	4,978,900,000
R&D Expense						
Operating Income	1,035,000,000	1,130,000,000	1,126,700,000	1,039,400,000	845,100,000	706,900,000
Operating Margin %	13.58%	15.16%	16.22%	15.15%	14.93%	14.19%
SGA Expense	3,301,000,000	3,142,000,000	2,971,600,000	2,915,200,000	2,442,700,000	2,157,000,000
Net Income	702,000,000	776,000,000	750,000,000	681,000,000	567,600,000	479,500,000
Operating Cash Flow	894,000,000	907,000,000	1,018,900,000	885,300,000	688,700,000	906,500,000
Capital Expenditure	391,000,000	390,000,000	276,500,000	272,200,000	255,000,000	201,300,000
EBITDA	1,298,000,000	1,374,000,000	1,343,700,000	1,264,800,000	1,037,800,000	892,700,000
Return on Assets %	11.51%	13.48%	13.84%	13.09%	11.78%	10.64%
Return on Equity %	17.71%	19.85%	20.16%	19.57%	17.67%	16.38%
Debt to Equity	0.13	0.13		0.07	0.10	0.10

CONTACT INFORMATION:

Phone: 212 318-7000   Fax:
Toll-Free: 800-377-7656
Address: 650 Madison Ave., New York, NY 10022 United States

SALARIES/BONUSES:

Top Exec. Salary: $882,692   Bonus: $2,000,000
Second Exec. Salary: $1,750,000   Bonus: $

STOCK TICKER/OTHER:

Stock Ticker: RL   Exchange: NYS
Employees: 25,000   Fiscal Year Ends: 03/31
Parent Company:

OTHER THOUGHTS:

Estimated Female Officers or Directors: 2
Hot Spot for Advancement for Women/Minorities: Y

Ratner Companies

NAIC Code: 812110

www.ratnerco.com

TYPES OF BUSINESS:

Salons
Spas
Salon Support Services
Hair Finishing Products

BRANDS/DIVISIONS/AFFILIATES:

Hair Cuttery
Cibu
Bubbles
Salon Cielo and Spa
ColorWorks Salon
Salon Plaza
CibuInternational.com

CONTACTS: Note: Officers with more than one job title may be intentionally listed here more than once.

Dennis Ratner, CEO
Susan Gustafson, Pres.
Ann Ratner, Pres., Upscale Brands

GROWTH PLANS/SPECIAL FEATURES:

Ratner Companies is a salon holding company. With five salon chains, the firm operates nearly 1,000 salons in 16 states, including full-service salons, day spas and exclusive hair color specialty stores. Each chain operates its own web site. Hair Cuttery is a value-priced drop-in unisex salon for the whole family. It is the firm's largest chain, with more than 750 locations on the U.S. East Coast, New England and in the Chicago area. Bubbles is a full-service salon chain with approximately 37 locations in Pennsylvania, Virginia, Maryland and Washington, D.C. The brand targets young professionals and other clients that want the latest hairstyles and colors as well as a variety of hair treatment and texturing processes, facials and facial waxing services. Salon Cielo and Spa is a full-service spa chain that targets a higher income bracket of clients through nine salons and spas in Washington, D.C., Virginia and Florida. Cielo attracts clients by offering a total pampering experience, which it provides by offering massages, waxing, manicures, pedicures and facials. Its hair salon services provide a repertoire of timeless and classic hairstyles and looks. The ColorWorks Salon has one upscale location in Virginia that specializes in hair coloring services. Salon Plaza owns and rents individual salon units to freelance hair stylists, colorists and other salon and spa professionals through more than 20 locations in Maryland and Virginia. Each unit acts as an individual office but is part of a larger salon with its inherent benefits. Bubbles and Salon Cielo and Spa both offer the Cibu brand. Cibu is a line of hair care and styling products that are sulfate and paraben free. Cibu products are also sold through CibuInternational.com.

FINANCIAL DATA: Note: Data for latest year may not have been available at press time.

In U.S. $	2015	2014	2013	2012	2011	2010
Revenue		200,000,000	190,000,000	175,000,000	168,000,000	
R&D Expense						
Operating Income						
Operating Margin %						
SGA Expense						
Net Income						
Operating Cash Flow						
Capital Expenditure						
EBITDA						
Return on Assets %						
Return on Equity %						
Debt to Equity						

CONTACT INFORMATION:

Phone: 703-269-5400   Fax:
Toll-Free:
Address: 1577 Spring Hill Rd., Ste. 500, Vienna, VA 22182 United States

STOCK TICKER/OTHER:

Stock Ticker: Private
Employees: 12,000
Parent Company:

Exchange:
Fiscal Year Ends: 09/30

SALARIES/BONUSES:

Top Exec. Salary: $ Bonus: $
Second Exec. Salary: $ Bonus: $

OTHER THOUGHTS:

Estimated Female Officers or Directors: 2
Hot Spot for Advancement for Women/Minorities: Y

RBC Life Sciences Inc

www.rbclifesciences.com

NAIC Code: 446191

TYPES OF BUSINESS:

Food (Health) Supplement Stores
Personal Care Products
Fitness Products
Herbal Formulas
Vitamins & Minerals
Wound Care Products

BRANDS/DIVISIONS/AFFILIATES:

NeuroBright
OliViva
Microhydrin Plus
MPM Medical Inc
Colo-Vada Plus
Microhydrin
24 Seven

CONTACTS: Note: Officers with more than one job title may be intentionally listed here more than once.

Clinton Howard, CEO
Steven Brown, CFO
Paul Miller, Director
G. Scofield, Vice President, Divisional
Ann Billings, Vice President, Divisional

GROWTH PLANS/SPECIAL FEATURES:

RBC Life Sciences, Inc. (RBCL) markets and distributes nutritional supplements and personal care products. The firm operates in two segments: nutritional products and medical products. The nutritional products segment manufactures and distributes nutritional supplements, natural and organic foods, functional foods, natural and organic personal care and household products. The majority of this segment's net sales are from nutritional supplements. These include Microhydrin and Microhydrin Plus, which are broad-spectrum antioxidants; NeuroBright supplements designed to enhance brain function and energy; OliViva, an antioxidant beverage designed to enhance the immune system and cardiovascular system; Colo-Vada Plus, a colon cleansing program; and 24 Seven, a daily multivitamin and mineral supplement. Its products are distributed by a network of independent distributors in certain markets, primarily the U.S. and Canada, and by licensees in certain other international markets. For the most part, licensees also market the nutritional products in their respective territories through a network of independent associates. These distributors are independent contractors who purchase products for personal use, for resale to retail customers and/or sponsor other individuals as distributors. The medical products segment markets a line of over 35 wound care products in the U.S. under the MPM Medical brand name through its subsidiary MPM Medical, Inc. The wound care products are distributed to hospitals, nursing homes, home health care agencies, clinics and pharmacies through a network of medical/surgical supply dealers and pharmaceutical distributors.

FINANCIAL DATA: Note: Data for latest year may not have been available at press time.

In U.S. $	2015	2014	2013	2012	2011	2010
Revenue		28,270,450	25,470,930	25,160,170	28,447,970	28,157,010
R&D Expense						
Operating Income		-625,266	-624,624	-463,593	-70,885	1,043,771
Operating Margin %		-2.21%	-2.45%	-1.84%	-.24%	3.70%
SGA Expense		15,760,450	12,130,200	13,023,590	13,946,360	12,166,040
Net Income		-602,811	-500,005	-361,436	-71,494	557,746
Operating Cash Flow		-607,732	294,232	445,352	125,297	544,731
Capital Expenditure		1,074,436	267,055	805,385	350,414	163,269
EBITDA		-45,366	-36,337	121,144	435,698	1,583,060
Return on Assets %		-3.59%	-2.81%	-1.96%	-.38%	3.01%
Return on Equity %		-6.91%	-5.39%	-3.73%	-.72%	5.84%
Debt to Equity		0.10	0.12	0.14	0.15	0.17

CONTACT INFORMATION:

Phone: 972 893-4000   Fax: 972 869-4111
Toll-Free: 800-350-9497
Address: 2301 Crown Ct., Irving, TX 75038 United States

STOCK TICKER/OTHER:

Stock Ticker: RBCL
Employees: 89
Parent Company:

Exchange: PINX
Fiscal Year Ends: 12/31

SALARIES/BONUSES:

Top Exec. Salary: $336,200   Bonus: $
Second Exec. Salary: $253,100   Bonus: $

OTHER THOUGHTS:

Estimated Female Officers or Directors: 1
Hot Spot for Advancement for Women/Minorities:

Sales, profits and employees may be estimates. Financial information, benefits and other data can change quickly and may vary from those stated here.

Recreational Equipment Inc (REI)

NAIC Code: 451110

www.rei.com

TYPES OF BUSINESS:

Outdoor Gear & Clothing, Retail
Sporting Equipment Retail & Rental
Adventure Travel Services
Catalog & Online Sales

BRANDS/DIVISIONS/AFFILIATES:

REI
REI Adventures
REI Gear and Apparel
Novara

CONTACTS: Note: Officers with more than one job title may be intentionally listed here more than once.

Jerry Stritzke, CEO
Eric Artz, COO
Jerry Stritzke, Pres.
Eric Artz, CFO
Annie Zipfel, Sr. VP-Mktg.
Michelle Clements, Sr. VP-Human Resources
Julie Averill, VP-IT
Susan Viscon, VP-Merch.
Catherine Walker, General Counsel
Brad Brown, Sr. VP-e-Commerce & Direct Sales
Michael Collins, VP-Public Affairs
Sue Sallee, VP-Finance & Acct.
Tim Spangler, Sr. VP-Retail
Kathleen Peterson, VP-REI Private Brands
John Hamlin, Chmn.
Rick Bingle, VP-Supply Chain

GROWTH PLANS/SPECIAL FEATURES:

Recreational Equipment, Inc. (REI) is one of the larges
consumer cooperatives in the U.S. The firm offers qualit
outdoor gear, clothing and footwear selected for performanc
and durability in outdoor recreation, including hiking, climbing
camping, bicycling, paddling and winter sports. Today, REI ha:
more than 5.1 million active members served by approximatel
135 retail stores in 34 states. Stores include a variety o
facilities for testing equipment, including bike test trails
climbing pinnacles and camp stove demonstration tables
While anyone may shop at the stores, customers who pay :
small fee to become members receive special discounts and :
share in the company's profits through an annual patronage
refund based on their purchases. REI's e-commerce site is one
of the largest outdoor online stores, offering a comprehensiv
library of product information, expert gear advice and outdoo
recreation information. In addition to nationally recognized
brands, the company sells private label apparel and
accessories under the REI Gear and Apparel brand. It also
offers mountain, road and touring bikes under the private
Novara name. Through REI Adventures, the company has
been operating small group tours throughout the world for more
than 20 years, avoiding standard tourist routes and
emphasizing outdoor activities. Each year, REI Adventures
plans domestic and international bicycling, trekking, kayaking
hiking, camping and mountaineering adventures. The firm
invests millions of dollars on an annual basis to build trails
clean up the environment and teach children outdoor ethics.

The firm offers employees health, life and disability plans,
tuition reimbursement; adoption and relocation assistance; an
employee discount program; and a public transit subsidy.

FINANCIAL DATA: Note: Data for latest year may not have been available at press time.

In U.S. $	2015	2014	2013	2012	2011	2010
Revenue		2,217,130,000	2,017,476,000	1,930,635,000	1,798,009,000	1,658,751,000
R&D Expense						
Operating Income						
Operating Margin %						
SGA Expense						
Net Income		44,183,000	19,031,000	29,005,000	30,168,000	30,230,000
Operating Cash Flow						
Capital Expenditure						
EBITDA						
Return on Assets %						
Return on Equity %						
Debt to Equity						

CONTACT INFORMATION:

Phone: 253-891-2500   Fax: 253-891-2523
Toll-Free: 800-426-4840
Address: 6750 S. 228th St., Kent, WA 98032 United States

STOCK TICKER/OTHER:

Stock Ticker: Private
Employees: 11,000
Parent Company:

Exchange:
Fiscal Year Ends: 12/31

SALARIES/BONUSES:

Top Exec. Salary: $ Bonus: $
Second Exec. Salary: $ Bonus: $

OTHER THOUGHTS:

Estimated Female Officers or Directors: 7
Hot Spot for Advancement for Women/Minorities: Y

Red Wing Shoe Company Inc

www.redwingshoe.com

NAIC Code: 424340

TYPES OF BUSINESS:

Footwear Distribution
Retail-Mobile Truck Stores
Leather Tanning Operations

BRANDS/DIVISIONS/AFFILIATES:

Vasque
Irish Setter
Worx
Heritage Collection
Red Wing Europe
Red Wing International
S.B. Foot Tanning Company
Red Wing

CONTACTS: Note: Officers with more than one job title may be intentionally listed here more than once.

David D. Murphy, Pres.
Ralph Balestriere, CFO
Marc Kermisch, CIO

GROWTH PLANS/SPECIAL FEATURES:

Red Wing Shoe Company, Inc. has been hand-making work boots since 1905. Red Wing shoes are used predominately by workmen and laborers in a wide variety of industries, including the military. The company offers shoe styles for different lines of work, including waterproof, insulated, puncture-resistant, static-dissipative, comfort force, steel-toe and tech-toe (plastic) featured footwear. Distributed through retailers all over the U.S., Canada and in several other countries, Red Wing markets shoes under the Red Wing, Worx, Vasque, Irish Setter Work, Setter Hunt and the Heritage Collection brands. The Red Wing brand represents the firm's premium boot line and shoes, while Worx is made as a more affordable, basic work shoe. Vasque specializes in technical boots and shoes for outdoor activities such as hiking and mountaineering. Irish Setter Work and Irish Setter Hunt focus on boots and casual shoes for hunting, fishing/boating and snow activities. The Heritage Collection manufactures classic style 6- and 8-inch boots in the Iron Ranger, Blacksmith, Roughneck, Ice Cutter, Beckman, Classic and Engineer styles. Subsidiaries of the firm include Red Wing Europe, Red Wing International and S.B. Foot Tanning Company. The company operates a manufacturing facility and leather tanning site in Red Wing, Minnesota; footwear factories in Kentucky and Missouri; and other warehouses worldwide. Red Wing maintains a flagship store in Red Wing, Minnesota. The 3-story location houses a shoe museum, retail store and factory outlet center.

FINANCIAL DATA: Note: Data for latest year may not have been available at press time.

In U.S. $	2015	2014	2013	2012	2011	2010
Revenue		700,000,000				
R&D Expense						
Operating Income						
Operating Margin %						
SGA Expense						
Net Income						
Operating Cash Flow						
Capital Expenditure						
EBITDA						
Return on Assets %						
Return on Equity %						
Debt to Equity						

CONTACT INFORMATION:

Phone: 651-388-8211   Fax: 651-388-7415
Toll-Free: 800-733-9464
Address: 315 Main St., Red Wing, MN 55066 United States

SALARIES/BONUSES:

Top Exec. Salary: $ Bonus: $
Second Exec. Salary: $ Bonus: $

STOCK TICKER/OTHER:

Stock Ticker: Private   Exchange:
Employees: Fiscal Year Ends: 11/30
Parent Company:

OTHER THOUGHTS:

Estimated Female Officers or Directors:
Hot Spot for Advancement for Women/Minorities:

Redbox Automated Retail LLC

www.redbox.com

NAIC Code: 532230

TYPES OF BUSINESS:

DVD Rentals

BRANDS/DIVISIONS/AFFILIATES:

Redbox
Outerwall Inc

CONTACTS: Note: Officers with more than one job title may be intentionally listed here more than once.

Mark Horak, Pres.
J. Scott Di Valerio, CEO-Outerwall Inc

GROWTH PLANS/SPECIAL FEATURES:

Redbox Automated Retail LLC is one of the largest DVD rental firms in the U.S. The firm is a wholly-owned subsidiary of Outerwall, Inc. Redbox vends DVDs, Blu-Rays and video games through 12 square foot kiosks in locations such as McDonald's, Walgreens, Albertsons grocery stores and Stop & Shops. The firm has a total of roughly 35,000 units throughout every U.S state. More than 68% of Americans live within a five-minute drive of a Redbox kiosk and up to 118 rental transactions are processed per second. Redbox kiosks can even be found at national landmarks such as the Empire State Building and Willis Tower in Chicago. Movies are priced at roughly $1.20 to $1.50 per day, and video games are priced at $2.00 per day. The kiosks offer up to 200 titles and hold 630 DVDs. Movies can also be rented online and picked up at Redbox locations. Customers can return the movies to any Redbox location. The company has distribution agreements with several major studios, including Universal Studios, Paramount Home Entertainment, Warner Home Video, 20th Century Fox, Lionsgate and Sony Pictures Home Entertainment. Since its inception, Redbox has rented more than 3 billion discs. In October 2014, the firm ended its Redbox Instant business. In March 2015, all Canadian machines were shut off and sent to various U.S. stores, due to low demand.

FINANCIAL DATA: Note: Data for latest year may not have been available at press time.

In U.S. $	2015	2014	2013	2012	2011	2010
Revenue		1,893,135,000	1,974,531,000	1,908,773,000	1,561,598,000	1,159,709,000
R&D Expense						
Operating Income						
Operating Margin %						
SGA Expense						
Net Income		236,769,000	239,043,000	238,685,000	169,502,000	97,405,000
Operating Cash Flow						
Capital Expenditure						
EBITDA						
Return on Assets %						
Return on Equity %						
Debt to Equity						

CONTACT INFORMATION:

Phone: 630-756-8000   Fax: 630-756-8888
Toll-Free:
Address: 1 Tower Ln., Ste. 900, Oakbrook Terrace, IL 60181 United States

STOCK TICKER/OTHER:

Stock Ticker: Subsidiary   Exchange:
Employees: 2,470   Fiscal Year Ends:
Parent Company: OUTERWALL INC

SALARIES/BONUSES:

Top Exec. Salary: $ Bonus: $
Second Exec. Salary: $ Bonus: $

OTHER THOUGHTS:

Estimated Female Officers or Directors: 1
Hot Spot for Advancement for Women/Minorities:

Reebok International Ltd

www.reebok.com

NAIC Code: 424340

TYPES OF BUSINESS:

Footwear Distribution
Apparel
Accessories
Athletic Equipment
Online Sales
Retail Stores

BRANDS/DIVISIONS/AFFILIATES:

Adidas AG
Reebok-CCM Hockey
Sports Licensed Division
Reebok Step
CCM
Rbk
JOFA
KOHO

CONTACTS: Note: Officers with more than one job title may be intentionally listed here more than once.

John Warren, CFO
Bill Holmes, Head-Human Resources
David Mischler, Head-Brand Oper.
David Baxter, Pres., Sports Licensed Div.
John Warren, Gen. Mgr.-Sports Licensed Div.
Chris Froio, Head-Fitness & Training
Charlie Maurath, Head-Latin America

GROWTH PLANS/SPECIAL FEATURES:

Reebok International, Ltd., a subsidiary of Adidas AG, operates under the brand names Reebok, Reebok-CCM Hockey and the Sports Licensed Division. Under the Reebok label, the firm offers a varied mix of athletic apparel, footwear and special collections for men, women and children; accessories such as socks and caps; and exercise equipment such as the Reebok Step. The Reebok-CCM Hockey label specializes in the design and production of professional hockey athletic gear, including skates, apparel, pads and equipment. It brings together a number of individual brands, including CCM, Rbk, JOFA and KOHO. The Sports Licensed Division manufactures performance apparel, uniforms and accessories for professional athletic teams in the National Football League (NFL), Major League Baseball (MLB), National Hockey League (NHL) and the National Lacrosse League (NLL). Additionally, Reebok markets and distributes athletic equipment, including treadmills, heart rate monitors, recumbent bikes, upright bikes and elliptical machines. The company operates retail stores across the U.S. as well as an online store. The firm's online store features a shopping guide, which offers sizing and product information as well as a comprehensive portfolio of products available for direct consumer purchase. Reebok has regional offices in Amsterdam, the Netherlands, Canada, Hong Kong and Mexico. In January 2015, the firm agreed to sell its Rockport business.

The firm offers employees medical, dental and prescription drug coverage; a 401(k) plan; development and training courses; company cafes; sporting event tickets; and fitness facilities.

FINANCIAL DATA: Note: Data for latest year may not have been available at press time.

In U.S. $	2015	2014	2013	2012	2011	2010
Revenue		2,600,000,000	2,601,200,000	2,674,144,000	2,398,041,000	2,154,715,000
R&D Expense						
Operating Income						
Operating Margin %						
SGA Expense						
Net Income		230,000,000	225,588,000	213,152,000	181,903,000	160,852,000
Operating Cash Flow						
Capital Expenditure						
EBITDA						
Return on Assets %						
Return on Equity %						
Debt to Equity						

CONTACT INFORMATION:

Phone: 781-401-5000   Fax: 781-401-7402
Toll-Free:
Address: 1895 J.W. Foster Blvd., Canton, MA 02021 United States

SALARIES/BONUSES:

Top Exec. Salary: $ Bonus: $
Second Exec. Salary: $ Bonus: $

STOCK TICKER/OTHER:

Stock Ticker: Subsidiary
Employees: 9,200
Parent Company: ADIDAS AG

Exchange:
Fiscal Year Ends: 12/31

OTHER THOUGHTS:

Estimated Female Officers or Directors:
Hot Spot for Advancement for Women/Minorities:

Reeds Jewelers Inc

www.reeds.com

NAIC Code: 448310

TYPES OF BUSINESS:

Jewelry, Retail
Online Sales

BRANDS/DIVISIONS/AFFILIATES:

Reeds Jewelers Outlet
Mills Jewelers
Reeds.com
Reeds Jewelers

CONTACTS: *Note: Officers with more than one job title may be intentionally listed here more than once.*

Alan M. Zimmer, CEO
Allan E. Metzner, COO
Alan Zimmer, Pres.
James R. Rouse, CFO
Roberta G. Zimmer, Corp. Sec.
Ed Smith, VP-Oper.
James R. Rouse, Treas.

GROWTH PLANS/SPECIAL FEATURES:

Reeds Jewelers, Inc. operates about 65 specialty retail jewel
stores in enclosed regional malls located in 18 U.S. state
principally in the Southeast and Midwest. The compan
operates stores under the names Reeds Jewelers, Reed
Jewelers Outlet and Mills Jewelers. Reeds Jewelers offers
selection of more than 2,200 items, including diamond ring
and jewelry, gold jewelry and chains, gemstone rings, watche
and other fine jewelry. Gold jewelry is sold primarily in 14- o
18-karat grades, while gemstone rings contain either preciou
stones, such as rubies, sapphires and emeralds, or sem
precious gems, such as opals, blue topaz, amethysts an
garnets. Reeds Jewelers' stores also offer watches in a rang
of prices under many brand names, such as Citizen and Seiko
Moreover, the company buys customers' gold and platinum
jewelry. In addition to its retail stores, the company operates a
e-commerce site that offers consumers the opportunity to bu
jewelry sorted by type, price, material or occasion.

FINANCIAL DATA: *Note: Data for latest year may not have been available at press time.*

In U.S. $	2015	2014	2013	2012	2011	2010
Revenue						
R&D Expense						
Operating Income						
Operating Margin %						
SGA Expense						
Net Income						
Operating Cash Flow						
Capital Expenditure						
EBITDA						
Return on Assets %						
Return on Equity %						
Debt to Equity						

CONTACT INFORMATION:

Phone: 910-350-3100   Fax: 910-350-3353
Toll-Free: 877-406-3266
Address: 2525 S. 17th St., Wilmington, NC 28401 United States

STOCK TICKER/OTHER:

Stock Ticker: Private   Exchange:
Employees: Fiscal Year Ends: 02/28
Parent Company:

SALARIES/BONUSES:

Top Exec. Salary: $ Bonus: $
Second Exec. Salary: $ Bonus: $

OTHER THOUGHTS:

Estimated Female Officers or Directors: 1
Hot Spot for Advancement for Women/Minorities:

Regis Corporation

www.regiscorp.com

NAIC Code: 812110

TYPES OF BUSINESS:

Hair Salons
Hair Care Products
Beauty Schools
Hair Restoration Services

BRANDS/DIVISIONS/AFFILIATES:

Regis Salons
MasterCuts
Cost Cutters
SmartStyle
SuperCuts

GROWTH PLANS/SPECIAL FEATURES:

Regis Corporation is a global owner, operator, franchiser and consolidator of hair and retail product salons. The company owns, franchises or holds ownership interests in 9,564 worldwide locations. Regis' locations consist of 9,349 company-owned and franchised salons and 207 locations in which the company maintains a non-controlling ownership of less than 100%. Salon operations are managed through three operating segments: North American Value, North American Premium and International. The company's North American Value operations are comprised of 5,923 company-owned salons and 2,324 franchised salons in the U.S., Canada and Puerto Rico. The North American Premium salon operations are comprised of 746 company-owned salons, and the International operations, 356. The firm's worldwide salon locations operate primarily under the trade names of Regis Salons, MasterCuts, SmartStyle, Supercuts and Cost Cutters.

CONTACTS: *Note: Officers with more than one job title may be intentionally listed here more than once.*

Daniel Hanrahan, CEO
Steven Spiegel, CFO
Kersten Zupfer, Chief Accounting Officer
Eric Bakken, Chief Administrative Officer
Andrew Dulka, Chief Information Officer
Heather Passe, Chief Marketing Officer
Jim Lain, COO
Carmen Thiede, Other Executive Officer
Annette Miller, Other Executive Officer
Kennith Warfield, Senior VP, Divisional

FINANCIAL DATA: *Note: Data for latest year may not have been available at press time.*

In U.S. $	2015	2014	2013	2012	2011	2010
Revenue	1,837,287,000	1,892,437,000	2,018,713,000	2,273,779,000	2,325,869,000	2,358,434,000
R&D Expense						
Operating Income	3,531,000	-33,990,000	12,326,000	-67,313,000	3,948,000	97,218,000
Operating Margin %	.19%	-1.79%	.61%	-2.96%	.16%	4.12%
SGA Expense	687,618,000	697,257,000	755,368,000	842,102,000	879,865,000	837,572,000
Net Income	-33,842,000	-135,727,000	29,194,000	-114,093,000	-8,905,000	42,740,000
Operating Cash Flow	93,962,000	117,403,000	69,148,000	153,700,000	229,178,000	192,223,000
Capital Expenditure	38,257,000	49,439,000	105,857,000	88,356,000	89,459,000	61,485,000
EBITDA	88,091,000	67,695,000	139,447,000	55,888,000	113,868,000	216,392,000
Return on Assets %	-2.62%	-9.67%	1.97%	-6.75%	-.47%	2.24%
Return on Equity %	-5.02%	-17.20%	3.34%	-11.87%	-.87%	4.70%
Debt to Equity	0.19	0.16		0.29	0.27	0.38

CONTACT INFORMATION:

Phone: 952 947-7777   Fax: 952 947-7700
Toll-Free:
Address: 7201 Metro Blvd., Minneapolis, MN 55439 United States

STOCK TICKER/OTHER:

Stock Ticker: RGS
Employees: 47,000
Parent Company:

Exchange: NYS
Fiscal Year Ends: 06/30

SALARIES/BONUSES:

Top Exec. Salary: $882,000   Bonus: $
Second Exec. Salary: Bonus: $
$482,000

OTHER THOUGHTS:

Estimated Female Officers or Directors: 5
Hot Spot for Advancement for Women/Minorities: Y

Rent-A-Center Inc

www.rentacenter.com

NAIC Code: 532210

TYPES OF BUSINESS:

Assorted Merchandise, Rental
Retail
Financing

BRANDS/DIVISIONS/AFFILIATES:

Get It Now
Rent-A-Center
ColorTyme
Home Choice
RimTyme
Acceptance Now
Rent-A-Center Franchising International Inc

CONTACTS: *Note: Officers with more than one job title may be intentionally listed here more than once.*

Dawn Wolverton, Assistant General Counsel
Robert Davis, CEO
Guy Constant, CFO
Mark Speese, Chairman of the Board
Christopher Korst, Chief Administrative Officer
Charles White, Executive VP, Divisional
Fred Herman, Executive VP, Divisional
Mark Denman, Executive VP, Divisional
Ricardo Cordon, Executive VP, Subsidiary
Joel Mussat, Executive VP
Maureen Short, Senior VP, Divisional

GROWTH PLANS/SPECIAL FEATURES:

Rent-A-Center, Inc. (RAC) is a rent-to-own operator in North America, providing customers the opportunity to obtain ownership of high-quality durable products, such as consumer electronics, appliances, computers, furniture and accessories, under flexible rental purchase agreements with no long-term obligation. Operations are conducted through the company's four segments: Core U.S., Acceptance Now, Mexico and Franchising. The Core U.S. segment, consisting of company-owned stores in the U.S. and Puerto Rco, accounted for 76% of RAC's revenue and 74% of its profit in 2014. Its 2,824 stores derive 77% of its business from repeat customers. Included in this segment are 45 retail installment sales stores under the names Get it Now and Home Choice. The Acceptance Now segment provides an onsite rent-to-own option at a third-party retailer's location by processing customer retail purchase credit applications. These applications are non-formal credit investigations and most customers are approved. Acceptance Now kiosks are located in various retail stores. The Mexico segment consists of 177 company-owned rent-to-own stores in Mexico. The Franchising segment operates its rent-to-own stores through Rent-A-Center Franchising International, Inc. The rent-to-own stores primarily offer high quality products such as consumer electronics, appliances, computers, furniture, wheels and tires. This segment franchises 187 stores in 30 states operating under the Rent-A-Center (106 stores), ColorTyme (50) and RimTyme (31) names.

The firm offers employees 401(k) plan; medical, dental, disability and life insurance; an employee stock purchase plan; access to training; paid sick and personal time; and 10 days paid vacation after one year of employment.

FINANCIAL DATA: *Note: Data for latest year may not have been available at press time.*

In U.S. $	2015	2014	2013	2012	2011	2010
Revenue		3,157,796,000	3,104,183,000	3,082,646,000	2,882,184,000	2,731,632,000
R&D Expense						
Operating Income		193,462,000	246,169,000	318,472,000	293,157,000	303,769,000
Operating Margin %		6.12%	7.93%	10.33%	10.17%	11.12%
SGA Expense		1,891,046,000	1,891,748,000	1,809,556,000	1,730,621,000	126,319,000
Net Income		96,422,000	128,238,000	183,492,000	164,637,000	171,642,000
Operating Cash Flow		19,113,000	134,342,000	217,898,000	286,626,000	216,489,000
Capital Expenditure		83,785,000	108,367,000	102,453,000	132,710,000	93,007,000
EBITDA		957,013,000	982,585,000	1,019,604,000	920,228,000	872,488,000
Return on Assets %		3.06%	4.35%	6.47%	5.99%	6.68%
Return on Equity %		7.05%	9.11%	12.97%	12.13%	13.19%
Debt to Equity		0.75	0.68	0.46	0.54	0.51

CONTACT INFORMATION:

Phone: 972 801-1100   Fax: 866 260-1424
Toll-Free: 800-275-2996
Address: 5501 Headquarters Dr., Plano, TX 75024 United States

STOCK TICKER/OTHER:

Stock Ticker: RCII
Employees: 22,200
Parent Company:

Exchange: NAS
Fiscal Year Ends: 12/31

SALARIES/BONUSES:

Top Exec. Salary: $750,000   Bonus: $
Second Exec. Salary: $642,057   Bonus: $

OTHER THOUGHTS:

Estimated Female Officers or Directors: 1
Hot Spot for Advancement for Women/Minorities: Y

Restoration Hardware Holdings Inc (RH)

www.restorationhardware.com
NAIC Code: 442110

TYPES OF BUSINESS:
Furniture & Housewares, Retail
Online Sales
Catalog Sales

BRANDS/DIVISIONS/AFFILIATES:
RH Atelier
RH Antiques and Artifacts
RH
RH New York, The Gallery
RH Modern

CONTACTS: Note: Officers with more than one job title may be intentionally listed here more than once.
Karen Boone, CFO
Gary Friedman, Chairman of the Board
Kenneth Dunaj, COO
J. Chu, Directorf

GROWTH PLANS/SPECIAL FEATURES:

Restoration Hardware Holdings, Inc. (RH) is a specialty retailer of upscale home furnishings, functional and decorative hardware and related merchandise. The firm rebranded its stores to RH in order to reflect its growing assortment of merchandise that includes lifestyle items and luxury goods. RH Atelier is its line of clothing and jewelry, while RH Antiques and Artifacts is its line of one-of-a-kind items. The firm's store strategy for the mid-term is to replace existing stores with massive, multi-story buildings that are 40,000 square feet and up. They have features such as valet parking, wine bars and staged rooms such as billiard rooms or home cinema rooms. RH operates 67 retail stores, consisting of 57 galleries, seven large format galleries and three Baby & Child Galleries as well as 17 outlet stores throughout the U.S. and Canada. In June 2014, RH opened RH New York, The Gallery in the historic Flatiron district. The 19th-century building houses The Gallery across three floors and 30,000 gross square feet. In October 2015, the firm launched RH Modern, a multi-channel business with a distinctive 540-page source book, a dedicated web site and retail presence, offering curated and fully-integrated assortments of modern furnishings, lighting and dÃ©cor.

Employee benefits include life and disability insurance; health, vision and dental plans; a 401(k) savings plan; an employee assistance program; an employee discount program; and health and dependent care spending accounts.

FINANCIAL DATA: Note: Data for latest year may not have been available at press time.

In U.S. $	2015	2014	2013	2012	2011	2010
Revenue	1,867,422,000	1,550,961,000	1,193,046,000	958,084,000	772,752,000	625,685,000
R&D Expense						
Operating Income	165,726,000	54,851,000	-69,036,000	26,843,000	-4,239,000	-25,833,000
Operating Margin %	8.87%	3.53%	-5.78%	2.80%	-.54%	-4.12%
SGA Expense	525,048,000	502,029,000	505,485,000	329,506,000	275,859,000	238,889,000
Net Income	91,002,000	18,195,000	-12,789,000	20,588,000	-8,074,000	-28,651,000
Operating Cash Flow	82,491,000	87,521,000	-3,864,000	17,121,000	-11,810,000	57,068,000
Capital Expenditure	110,812,000	93,868,000	49,368,000	25,593,000	39,907,000	2,024,000
EBITDA	200,189,000	82,505,000	-42,288,000	56,029,000	27,024,000	17,232,000
Return on Assets %	7.13%	2.00%	-1.85%	3.78%	-1.72%	-6.63%
Return on Equity %	14.58%	3.65%	-3.64%	8.83%	-3.69%	-12.95%
Debt to Equity	0.21	0.22	0.18	0.48	0.51	0.25

CONTACT INFORMATION:
Phone: 415 924-1005   Fax: 415 927-9133
Toll-Free: 800-910-9836
Address: 15 Koch Rd., Ste. J, Corte Madera, CA 94925 United States

STOCK TICKER/OTHER:
Stock Ticker: RH
Employees: 4,000
Parent Company:

Exchange: NYS
Fiscal Year Ends: 01/31

SALARIES/BONUSES:
Top Exec. Salary: Bonus: $
$1,250,000
Second Exec. Salary: Bonus: $
$716,346

OTHER THOUGHTS:
Estimated Female Officers or Directors: 1

Hot Spot for Advancement for Women/Minorities:

Sales, profits and employees may be estimates. Financial information, benefits and other data can change quickly and may vary from those stated here.

REWE Group AG

NAIC Code: 445110

www.rewe-group.com

TYPES OF BUSINESS:

Grocery Stores & Hypermarkets
Discount Stores
Electronics, Audio & Appliance Stores
Home Improvement Centers
Sewing & Fabric Stores
Travel Services
Department Stores

BRANDS/DIVISIONS/AFFILIATES:

Rewe Trading Group
BILLA
REWE
toom
DER Touristik
b1
Oh Angie!
DERPART

CONTACTS: *Note: Officers with more than one job title may be intentionally listed here more than once.*

Alain Caparros, CEO
Christian Mielsch, Dir.-IT
Manfred Esser, Dir.-Prod. & Quality Assurance
Christian Mielsch, Dir.-Finance
Frank Wiemer, Dir.-Real Estate, Logistics & Corp. Security
Christian Mielsch, Dir.-Bus. Admin.
Lionel Souque, Dir.-Full-Range National
Jan Kunath, Head-PENNY National
Heinz-Bert Zander, Chmn.
Manfred Esser, Dir.-Strategic Purchasing

GROWTH PLANS/SPECIAL FEATURES:

REWE Group AG is one of Germany's largest food retailers an
travel and tourism companies. The company's retail subsidiar
REWE Trading Group (RTG), operates more than 15,00
stores in 12 European countries, most of which are i
Germany. Its stores include supermarkets, hypermarket;
home improvement centers, department stores and travel an
tourism under several brand names. Its brand names c
regional supermarkets include BILLA and REWE center;
Hypermarkets encompass six brands, including large-scal
hypermarkets under the brand name toom, which offer 14,00
food and non-food articles, and Penny Market stores, which se
food and non-food items at discounted prices. Outside of it
primary food retailers, REWE operates specialty stores suc
as toom Baumarkt DIY (do-it-yourself) home improvemer
stores, BIPA (a textile store chain) and b1 (a discount DI\
chain). The company's DER Touristik subsidiary owns an
operates travel agencies, cooperation partners an
franchisees under the DER and DERPART banners as well a
tour operator businesses under the DERTOUR, ITS, JAHN
REISEN, Meier's Weltreisen, TJAEREBORG, ADAC Reise
and ITS BILLA REISEN banners. Oh Angie! is the firm'
gastronomy restaurant concept which combines value with
healthy nutrition, and are either located in direct neighborhood
or integrated into REWE supermarkets.

FINANCIAL DATA: *Note: Data for latest year may not have been available at press time.*

In U.S. $	2015	2014	2013	2012	2011	2010
Revenue		58,117,181,000	63,083,220,000	61,324,560,000	63,995,070,000	53,601,691,000
R&D Expense						
Operating Income						
Operating Margin %						
SGA Expense						
Net Income		531,821,670	500,000,000	130,237,053	650,000,000	500,892,000
Operating Cash Flow						
Capital Expenditure						
EBITDA						
Return on Assets %						
Return on Equity %						
Debt to Equity						

CONTACT INFORMATION:

Phone: 49-221-149-0   Fax: 49-221-149-9000
Toll-Free:
Address: Domstrasse 20, Cologne, D-50668 Germany

STOCK TICKER/OTHER:

Stock Ticker: Private   Exchange:
Employees: 327,548   Fiscal Year Ends: 12/31
Parent Company:

SALARIES/BONUSES:

Top Exec. Salary: $ Bonus: $
Second Exec. Salary: $ Bonus: $

OTHER THOUGHTS:

Estimated Female Officers or Directors:
Hot Spot for Advancement for Women/Minorities: Y

Richemont (Compagnie Financiere Richemont SA)

www.richemont.com

NAIC Code: 448310

TYPES OF BUSINESS:

Retailing-Luxury Goods
Jewelry
Leather Accessories
Writing Accessories

BRANDS/DIVISIONS/AFFILIATES:

Net-a-Porter LLC
Alaia
Purdey
Cartier
Van Cleef & Arpels
Montblanc
Jaeger-LeCoultre
Ralph Lauren Watch & Jewelry Co

CONTACTS: *Note: Officers with more than one job title may be intentionally listed here more than once.*

Bernard Fornas, Co-CEO
Richard Lepeu, Co-CEO
Gary Saage, CFO
Thomas Lindemann, Dir.-Human Resources
Frederick Mostert, Chief Legal Counsel
Hans-Peter Bichelmeier, Dir.-Group Oper.
Alan Grieve, Dir.-Corp. Affairs
Sophie Cagnard, Head-Investor Rel.
Richard Lepeu, Co-CEO
Jerome Lambert, CEO-Montblanc
Stanislas de Quercize, CEO-Cartier
Johann Rupert, Chmn.

GROWTH PLANS/SPECIAL FEATURES:

Financiere Richemont SA is an international retailer of luxury goods. The company's business segments include jewelry, watches and timepieces, writing instruments and other businesses. Financiere Richemont's jewelry segment includes Cartier and Van Cleef & Arpels, which sell watches, brooches, necklaces and other items made with gold, diamonds, natural stones and other precious materials. Jewelry accounts for approximately 32% of the group's sales. The firm's watch and timepiece makers and marketers, which account for 50% of group sales, include Piaget, International Watch Co., Baume & Mercier, Roger Dubuis, Officine Panerai, Vacheron Constantin, A. Lange & Sohne, Jaeger-LeCoultre and joint venture Ralph Lauren Watch & Jewelry Co. Financiere Richemont's writing instruments segment, operated by Montblanc, manufactures high-quality pens and accounts for 3% of the firm's sales. The other business segment, accounting for 15% of sales, consists of the firm's Alfred Dunhill, Lancel Paris, Chloe, Alaia, Shanghai Tang and Purdey brands. Alfred Dunhill and Lancel Paris specialize in men's and women's luxury leather goods. Chloe, Alaia and Shanghai Tang produce and market women's clothing, handbags and other accessories, while Purdey is a manufacturer of shotguns and rifles. Regionally, Financiere Richemont derives the bulk of its sales from Asia Pacific and Europe, 39% and 28% respectively, with the rest from the Americas, Japan, the Middle East & Africa and Russia, 15%, 8%, 8% and 2%. The firm operates a retail network of company-owned stores and franchised stores. The company holds a majority stake in online fashion site Net-a-Porter LLC.

FINANCIAL DATA: *Note: Data for latest year may not have been available at press time.*

In U.S. $	2015	2014	2013	2012	2011	2010
Revenue	11,048,140,000	11,301,790,000	10,772,200,000	9,410,554,000	7,314,485,000	5,493,293,000
R&D Expense						
Operating Income	2,833,673,000	2,567,287,000	2,574,715,000	2,165,053,000	1,438,063,000	880,879,600
Operating Margin %	25.64%	22.71%	23.90%	23.00%	19.66%	16.03%
SGA Expense	4,710,053,000	4,574,206,000	4,330,107,000	3,786,721,000	3,193,454,000	2,470,708,000
Net Income	1,415,775,000	2,199,015,000	2,136,398,000	1,638,648,000	1,156,818,000	635,719,200
Operating Cash Flow	1,808,456,000	2,646,884,000	1,664,120,000	1,572,848,000	1,584,522,000	1,462,472,000
Capital Expenditure	751,401,000	716,378,000	649,516,000	612,370,600	369,332,700	208,014,900
EBITDA	2,383,682,000	3,024,707,000	3,094,753,000	2,602,309,000	1,971,897,000	1,164,247,000
Return on Assets %	7.33%	13.62%	15.33%	14.39%	12.51%	7.91%
Return on Equity %	10.11%	18.68%	21.38%	19.80%	17.24%	11.42%
Debt to Equity	0.02	0.02	0.03	0.04	0.03	0.05

CONTACT INFORMATION:

Phone: 41 227213500   Fax: 41 227213550
Toll-Free:
Address: 50 Chemin de la Chenaie, CP30, Bellevue, Geneva, 1293 Switzerland

STOCK TICKER/OTHER:

Stock Ticker: CFRHF
Employees: 28,324
Parent Company:

Exchange: PINX
Fiscal Year Ends: 03/31

SALARIES/BONUSES:

Top Exec. Salary: $ Bonus: $
Second Exec. Salary: $ Bonus: $

OTHER THOUGHTS:

Estimated Female Officers or Directors: 2
Hot Spot for Advancement for Women/Minorities: Y

Rite Aid Corporation

NAIC Code: 446110

TYPES OF BUSINESS:

Drug Stores

BRANDS/DIVISIONS/AFFILIATES:

GNC
Riteaid.com
RediClinic
Health Dialog Services Corporation
Wellness Plus
Plenti
Envision Pharmaceutical Services

CONTACTS: *Note: Officers with more than one job title may be intentionally listed here more than once.*

John Standley, CEO
Darren Karst, CFO
Kenneth Martindale, COO
Dedra Castle, Executive VP, Divisional
Robert Thompson, Executive VP, Divisional
Anthony Montini, Executive VP, Divisional
James Comitale, General Counsel
Marc Strassler, Other Corporate Officer
Frank Vitrano, Other Executive Officer
Douglas Donley, Senior VP

GROWTH PLANS/SPECIAL FEATURES:

Rite Aid Corporation is a U.S.-based retail drugstore company which operates over 4,570 drug stores in 31 states and Washington, D.C. Rite Aid stores primarily markets prescription drugs, which account for approximately 68.8% of its revenues. Other marketed merchandise, which accounts for the remaining 31.2% of revenues, includes non-prescription medications, health and beauty aids, personal care items, cosmetics, household items, beverages, convenience foods, greeting cards and seasonal merchandise. In addition to its marketed products, the firm offers an automated refill option for customers with ongoing prescriptions; and it also makes prescription refill reminder phone calls. Customers can order prescription refills through the company's e-commerce site Riteaid.com. The firm's average store size is approximately 12,600 square feet. Its larger stores are located in the western U.S. Rite Aid offers approximately 3,000 products under the Rite Aid private brand. The company maintains a strategic alliance with GNC, which enables Rite Aid to sell GNC branded and co-branded products. Rite Aid operates 2,276 GNC store-within-Rite Aid-stores. Approximately 62% of Rite Aid's stores are freestanding, 53% include a drive-through pharmacy, and 50% include a GNC store-within-Rite Aid-store. A majority of stores also include one-hour photo shops. In 2014, Rite Aid acquired RediClinic; and Health Dialog Services Corporation. In May 2015, Wellness Plus was integrated into the new American Express-backed Plenti rewards card, which displays both the Wellness Plus and Plenti logos. That June, Rite Aid acquired Envision Pharmaceutical Services from TPG for $2 billion. In October of the same year, the firm announced it would be acquired by Walgreens Boot Alliance, Inc. The transaction is still awaiting regulatory approval.

The company offers its employees health, dental, vision and prescription plans; vision discount plan; basic and supplemental life and AD&D insurances; flexible spending accounts; bereavement leave; employee assistance; 401(k); stock purchase plan; and more.

FINANCIAL DATA: *Note: Data for latest year may not have been available at press time.*

In U.S. $	2015	2014	2013	2012	2011	2010
Revenue	26,528,380,000	25,526,410,000	25,392,260,000	26,121,220,000	25,214,910,000	25,669,120,000
R&D Expense						
Operating Income	839,145,000	721,268,000	646,652,000	161,871,000	23,778,000	12,701,000
Operating Margin %	3.16%	2.82%	2.54%	.61%	.09%	.04%
SGA Expense	6,695,642,000	6,561,162,000	6,600,765,000	6,531,411,000	6,457,833,000	6,603,372,000
Net Income	2,109,173,000	249,414,000	118,105,000	-368,571,000	-555,424,000	-506,676,000
Operating Cash Flow	648,959,000	702,046,000	819,588,000	266,537,000	395,849,000	-325,063,000
Capital Expenditure	539,386,000	421,223,000	382,980,000	250,137,000	186,520,000	193,630,000
EBITDA	1,241,060,000	1,078,550,000	937,037,000	577,580,000	507,545,000	570,083,000
Return on Assets %	26.68%	3.07%	1.48%	-5.07%	-7.23%	-6.29%
Return on Equity %						
Debt to Equity	97.17					

CONTACT INFORMATION:

Phone: 717 761-2633   Fax: 717 975-5905
Toll-Free: 800-748-3243
Address: 30 Hunter Ln., Camp Hill, PA 17011 United States

STOCK TICKER/OTHER:

Stock Ticker: RAD   Exchange: NYS
Employees: 90,000   Fiscal Year Ends: 02/28
Parent Company:

SALARIES/BONUSES:

Top Exec. Salary: Bonus: $
$1,150,000
Second Exec. Salary: Bonus: $
$900,000

OTHER THOUGHTS:

Estimated Female Officers or Directors: 3

Hot Spot for Advancement for Women/Minorities: Y

Rocky Mountain Chocolate Factory Inc

www.rmcf.com

NAIC Code: 311351

TYPES OF BUSINESS:
Candy Manufacturing
Candy Stores
Franchising
Frozen Yogurt

BRANDS/DIVISIONS/AFFILIATES:
U-Swirl Inc
Yogurtini
Josie's Frozen Yogurt
CherryBerry
Yogli Mogli
Fuzzy Peach
Aspen Leaf Yogurt
Let's Yo! LLC

CONTACTS: *Note: Officers with more than one job title may be intentionally listed here more than once.*
Franklin Crail, CEO
Bryan Merryman, CFO
William Jobson, Chief Information Officer
Tracy Wojcik, Secretary
Edward Dudley, Senior VP, Divisional
Gregory Pope, Senior VP, Divisional
Jay Haws, Vice President, Divisional
Donna Coupe, Vice President, Divisional
Jeremy Kinney, Vice President, Divisional

GROWTH PLANS/SPECIAL FEATURES:
Rocky Mountain Chocolate Factory, Inc. (RMCF) is an international franchiser and confectionery manufacturer. As of March 2015, there were four company-owned, 88 licensed-owned and 276 franchised RCMF stores operating in 40 U.S. states, Canada, Japan, South Korea and the UAE. Also, RCMF holds a 42% interest in U-Swirl, Inc., which operates and franchises self-serve frozen yogurt cafes in the U.S. and internationally. U-Swirl operates 10 company-owned stores and 237 franchised U-Swirl, Yogurtini, Josie's Frozen Yogurt, CherryBerry, Yogli Mogli, Fuzzy Peach and Aspen Leaf Yogurt locations in 37 U.S. states. The majority of RCMF stores are franchised, with 55% of its products made onsite. Customers can observe store personnel making products such as fudge and chocolate covered apples from start to finish, including the mixing of ingredients in old-fashioned copper kettles and the cooling of the fudge on large marble tables. Customers are often invited to sample the store's products. This setting is designed to attract foot traffic, assure customers of the freshness of the products and convey an image of homemade quality. Stores offer over 300 different candy products, including numerous varieties of premium fudge, gourmet caramel apples and other products prepared from proprietary company recipes. Typical stores carry about 100 varieties of these and an additional 200 during holiday seasons. The firm's stores are located in factory outlet malls, regional malls and tourist environments. RMCF is currently selling products in a select number of new distribution channel programs, including wholesaling, fundraising, corporate sales, mail-order and Internet sales. In April 2015, the firm, through its subsidiary U-Swirl, Inc. acquired the assets of Let's Yo!, LLC.

FINANCIAL DATA: *Note: Data for latest year may not have been available at press time.*

In U.S. $	2015	2014	2013	2012	2011	2010
Revenue	41,508,380	39,184,810	36,315,200	34,626,890	31,127,970	28,436,550
R&D Expense						
Operating Income	5,964,967	5,235,521	2,539,827	5,852,874	5,950,362	5,643,335
Operating Margin %	14.37%	13.36%	6.99%	16.90%	19.11%	19.84%
SGA Expense	10,815,510	10,460,540	9,157,648	7,917,430	6,703,234	5,684,534
Net Income	3,937,840	4,392,444	1,478,212	3,876,032	3,910,841	3,580,077
Operating Cash Flow	5,871,515	6,863,501	6,370,070	6,147,051	3,795,726	5,535,061
Capital Expenditure	626,744	11,467,850	1,544,559	3,260,638	1,297,761	498,832
EBITDA	7,464,077	6,365,272	3,475,204	6,603,734	6,679,380	6,369,125
Return on Assets %	10.99%	14.33%	6.15%	16.99%	19.38%	20.02%
Return on Equity %	20.04%	23.86%	8.41%	21.90%	24.92%	25.59%
Debt to Equity	0.26	0.30				

CONTACT INFORMATION:
Phone: 970 259-0554 Fax:
Toll-Free: 888-525-2462
Address: 265 Turner Dr., Durango, CO 81303 United States

STOCK TICKER/OTHER:
Stock Ticker: RMCF
Employees: 300
Parent Company:

Exchange: NAS
Fiscal Year Ends: 02/28

SALARIES/BONUSES:
Top Exec. Salary: $355,000 Bonus: $
Second Exec. Salary: $340,000 Bonus: $

OTHER THOUGHTS:
Estimated Female Officers or Directors: 2
Hot Spot for Advancement for Women/Minorities:

Sales, profits and employees may be estimates. Financial information, benefits and other data can change quickly and may vary from those stated here.

RONA Inc

NAIC Code: 444110

TYPES OF BUSINESS:
Merchandising
Department stores

BRANDS/DIVISIONS/AFFILIATES:
RONA Home & Garden
RONA Cashway
RONA Renovateur
RONA Home Center
RONA L'express
RONA Cashway
RONA Lansing
BOTANIX

CONTACTS: *Note: Officers with more than one job title may be intentionally listed here more than once.*
Robert Sawyer, CEO
Dominique Boies, CFO
Robert Chevrier, Chairman of the Board
Luc Rodier, Executive VP, Divisional
Alain Brisebois, Executive VP
Chantal Glenisson, General Manager, Divisional
France Charlebois, Other Executive Officer
Christian Proulx, Senior VP, Divisional

GROWTH PLANS/SPECIAL FEATURES:
RONA, Inc. is one of the largest Canadian distributors an retailers of hardware, home renovation and gardenin products. The company operates a total network of over 50 corporate, franchise and affiliate stores of various sizes an formats, which it supplies from nine distribution centers. Th firm operates in two segments: the retail segment, whic consists of the company's corporate and franchise stores; an the distribution segment. Consumer sales are made throug three ownership models (corporate, affiliates and franchis stores) and three retail formats (big-box, proximity an specialty stores). The big-box stores sell a wide variety c hardware products, tools, building materials, paints an gardening, decoration and seasonal items under the banner RONA L'entrepot, RONA Home & Garden and Reno-Depo The proximity stores are traditional small or medium-size neighborhood hardware stores, including brand names RON Renovateur, RONA Home Center, RONA L'express, RON Hardware and Totem. Specialty stores include RON Cashway and RONA Lansing, which serve contractors BOTANIX garden centers; Curtis Lumber and Dick's Lumbe building materials stores; and Noble Trade, a plumbing an heating supply wholesaler. The company also operates a wel site where customers can shop online. RONA's distributior centers provide a Canada-wide infrastructure allowing merchandise to be distributed effectively to the complete network of stores. In 2014, the company and Ace Hardware International Holdings, Ltd. entered into an agreement fo master licensing of the Ace brand in Canada, allowing RON specific rights to the Ace Hardware brands.

FINANCIAL DATA: *Note: Data for latest year may not have been available at press time.*

In U.S. $	2015	2014	2013	2012	2011	2010
Revenue		3,068,913,000	3,140,713,000	3,659,015,000	3,599,505,000	3,595,970,000
R&D Expense						
Operating Income		90,376,760	-25,952,400	30,937,450	-23,556,510	174,652,900
Operating Margin %		2.94%	-.82%	.84%	-.65%	4.85%
SGA Expense		539,243,600	564,314,900	961,733,300		
Net Income		58,621,200	-115,397,200	12,958,590	-58,722,340	107,298,500
Operating Cash Flow		104,019,400	56,272,520	94,057,490	172,495,300	93,007,890
Capital Expenditure		45,817,690	46,261,960	64,709,800	81,977,690	112,064,100
EBITDA		157,846,500	57,908,730	121,639,400	92,565,120	257,738,700
Return on Assets %		3.34%	-5.98%	.61%	-2.72%	5.00%
Return on Equity %		4.79%	-8.79%	.91%	-4.08%	7.74%
Debt to Equity		0.11	0.09	0.16	0.12	0.23

CONTACT INFORMATION:
Phone: 514 599-5900   Fax: 514 599-5927
Toll-Free:
Address: 220 Chemin du Tremblay, Boucherville, QC J4B 8H7 Canada

STOCK TICKER/OTHER:
Stock Ticker: RON
Employees: 18,000
Parent Company:

Exchange: TSE
Fiscal Year Ends: 12/31

SALARIES/BONUSES:
Top Exec. Salary: $ Bonus: $
Second Exec. Salary: $ Bonus: $

OTHER THOUGHTS:
Estimated Female Officers or Directors: 4
Hot Spot for Advancement for Women/Minorities: Y

Rooms To Go Inc

www.roomstogo.com

NAIC Code: 442110

TYPES OF BUSINESS:

Furniture Stores
Children's Furniture
Online Sales
Delivery Services

BRANDS/DIVISIONS/AFFILIATES:

Rooms to Go Kids
RoomsToGo.com
RoomsToGoKids.com
Cindy Crawford Home Furniture Collection
Cindy Crawford Kids
iSofa
Dunn Super Center and Distribution Center

CONTACTS: *Note: Officers with more than one job title may be intentionally listed here more than once.*

Jeffrey Seaman, CEO
Stephen Buckley, Pres.

GROWTH PLANS/SPECIAL FEATURES:

Rooms To Go, Inc. is one of the top selling furniture retailers in the U.S. The company markets primarily to customers looking for brand name furniture and who have a limited shopping timeframe. The company offers selections of furniture for living rooms, bedrooms and dining rooms that can be delivered quickly. Furniture can be purchased online at RoomsToGo.com and RoomsToGoKids.com. The firm sells low to moderately priced furniture and offers discounts for buying an entire room or set. Furniture prices range from $120 to $2,000 for individual pieces and $500 to $5,000 for rooms and sets. Rooms To Go also sells the Cindy Crawford Home Collection line of furniture sets and the Cindy Crawford Kids collection, as well as the Sofia Vergara furniture collection. Vergara's iSofa brand allows customers to design custom sofas in three easy steps: style, color and pillows. Rooms To Go Kids, a subsidiary of the company, offers bedroom furniture, bedroom sets and other accessories for children. The company has a distribution center in Katy, TX. In October 2015, the firm opened a new super center in North Carolina, featuring 1.45 million square feet on 120 acres, housing a Rooms To Go showroom, a Rooms To Go Kids/Teens showroom, a Rooms To Go Outlet Center and a huge distribution center housing tens of thousands of pieces of furniture. The Dunn Super Center and Distribution Center will create about 400 new jobs for area residents.

FINANCIAL DATA: *Note: Data for latest year may not have been available at press time.*

In U.S. $	2015	2014	2013	2012	2011	2010
Revenue		2,615,000,000	2,300,000,000	2,250,000,000	2,000,000,000	1,600,000,000
R&D Expense						
Operating Income						
Operating Margin %						
SGA Expense						
Net Income						
Operating Cash Flow						
Capital Expenditure						
EBITDA						
Return on Assets %						
Return on Equity %						
Debt to Equity						

CONTACT INFORMATION:

Phone: 813-628-9724   Fax: 813-620-1717
Toll-Free: 888-709-5380
Address: 11540 Hwy. 92 E., Seffner, FL 33584 United States

STOCK TICKER/OTHER:

Stock Ticker: Private
Employees: 13,000
Parent Company:

Exchange:
Fiscal Year Ends: 12/31

SALARIES/BONUSES:

Top Exec. Salary: $ Bonus: $
Second Exec. Salary: $ Bonus: $

OTHER THOUGHTS:

Estimated Female Officers or Directors:
Hot Spot for Advancement for Women/Minorities:

Sales, profits and employees may be estimates. Financial information, benefits and other data can change quickly and may vary from those stated here.

Ross Stores Inc

www.rossstores.com

NAIC Code: 448140

TYPES OF BUSINESS:

Discount Apparel Stores
Home Furnishings

BRANDS/DIVISIONS/AFFILIATES:

dd's DISCOUNTS
Ross Dress for Less

CONTACTS: *Note: Officers with more than one job title may be intentionally listed here more than once.*

Ken Jew, Assistant Secretary
Barbara Rentler, CEO
Michael Hartshorn, CFO
Norman Ferber, Chairman Emeritus
Michael OSullivan, Co- President
James Fassio, Co- President
Michael Balmuth, Director
Bernard Brautigan, Executive VP, Divisional
John Call, Executive VP, Divisional
Brian Morrow, Other Executive Officer
Lisa Panattoni, President, Divisional

GROWTH PLANS/SPECIAL FEATURES:

Ross Stores, Inc. operates 1,254 off-price retail apparel and home accessories stores in 33 states, Washington, D.C. and Guam, most of which operate under the Ross Dress for Less brand. The company also operates 152 dd's DISCOUNTS locations in 15 states. Most of the stores are located in community and neighborhood strip shopping centers in heavily populated urban and suburban areas. The company's chains target value-conscious women and men ages 18-54. Ross offers new, in-season, name-brand and designer apparel, accessories, footwear and home merchandise at savings of 20%-60% off department and specialty store regular prices, while dd's DISCOUNTS, targeting lower-income customers, offers similar merchandise, but at savings of up to 70% off department and specialty store prices. The company's stores are supplied by four distribution processing facilities. Ross has combined a network of approximately 8,200 vendors and manufacturers, purchasing the vast majority of its merchandise directly from the manufacturer. By purchasing later in the merchandise buying cycle than department and specialty stores, Ross takes advantage of imbalances between retailers' demand for products and manufacturers' supply of those products. In addition, the company typically does not require that manufacturers provide promotional and markdown allowances, return privileges, split shipments, drop shipments to stores or delayed deliveries of merchandise, further enabling Ross to provide significant discounts on in-season merchandise. Sales of ladie's products account for approximately 29% of the firm's revenues; home accents/bed and bath, 24%; men's products, 13%; accessories, lingerie, jewelry and fragrances, 13%; shoes, 13%; and children's products, 8%. In fiscal 2014, Ross Stores opened a total of 73 Ross Dress for Less and 22 dd's DISCOUNTS stores.

Ross offers its employees medical, dental, vision and life insurance; sick pay; health care spending accounts; holiday and personal days; a commuter reimbursement account; a 401(k) plan; and an employee stock purchasing plan.

FINANCIAL DATA: *Note: Data for latest year may not have been available at press time.*

In U.S. $	2015	2014	2013	2012	2011	2010
Revenue	11,041,680,000	10,230,350,000	9,721,065,000	8,608,291,000	7,866,100,000	7,184,213,000
R&D Expense						
Operating Income	1,488,350,000	1,343,063,000	1,271,751,000	1,053,144,000	906,590,000	726,122,000
Operating Margin %	13.47%	13.12%	13.08%	12.23%	11.52%	10.10%
SGA Expense	1,615,371,000	1,526,366,000	1,437,886,000	1,304,065,000	1,229,775,000	1,130,813,000
Net Income	924,724,000	837,304,000	786,763,000	657,170,000	554,797,000	442,757,000
Operating Cash Flow	1,372,865,000	1,022,003,000	979,644,000	820,105,000	673,066,000	888,384,000
Capital Expenditure	646,691,000	550,515,000	424,434,000	416,271,000	198,651,000	158,487,000
EBITDA	1,721,720,000	1,549,674,000	1,457,842,000	1,224,036,000	1,068,414,000	886,972,000
Return on Assets %	21.50%	22.12%	22.57%	20.48%	18.85%	17.28%
Return on Equity %	43.14%	44.37%	48.26%	46.51%	44.56%	41.11%
Debt to Equity	0.17	0.07	0.08	0.10	0.11	0.12

CONTACT INFORMATION:

Phone: 925 965-4400   Fax:
Toll-Free:
Address: 5130 Hacienda Drive, Dublin, CA 94568-7579 United States

STOCK TICKER/OTHER:

Stock Ticker: ROST   Exchange: NAS
Employees: 71,400   Fiscal Year Ends: 01/31
Parent Company:

SALARIES/BONUSES:

Top Exec. Salary: Bonus: $
$1,419,156
Second Exec. Salary: Bonus: $
$1,182,723

OTHER THOUGHTS:

Estimated Female Officers or Directors: 4

Hot Spot for Advancement for Women/Minorities: Y

Roundy's Inc

NAIC Code: 445110

www.roundys.com

TYPES OF BUSINESS:

Grocery Stores & Supermarkets
Private Label Merchandise Manufacturing

BRANDS/DIVISIONS/AFFILIATES:

Pick 'n Save
Clear Value
Copps
Roundy's Select
Metro Market
Mariano's

CONTACTS: Note: Officers with more than one job title may be intentionally listed here more than once.

Robert Mariano, CEO
Kurt Kappeler, Chief Accounting Officer
Donald Fitzgerald, Chief Marketing Officer
Donald Rosanova, Executive VP, Divisional
Jessie Terry, Other Executive Officer
Edward Kitz, Secretary
John Boyle, Vice President, Divisional
Patrick Mullarkey, Vice President, Divisional
Timothy Grabar, Vice President, Divisional
James Hyland, Vice President, Divisional
Michael Turzenski, Vice President

GROWTH PLANS/SPECIAL FEATURES:

Roundy's, Inc. is one of the oldest and largest grocers in the Midwestern U.S. Historically, the firm was active in the wholesale distribution of groceries to independent retailers in the upper Midwest. Roundy's operates solely in the retail grocery market and its store network encompasses 151 grocery stores and 101 pharmacies under its Pick -'n Save (88 stores), Copps (25), Metro Market (4) and Mariano's (34) retail banners. In addition to national brands, Roundy's stores stock premium Roundy's Select and mid-tier Roundy's Private Label merchandise as well as its Clear Value line of entry-level items. Product categories offered by stores include grocery, frozen & dairy; produce; meat & seafood; bakery; deli, cheese & prepared foods; floral; general merchandise; alcohol; pharmacy; and health & beauty care. The company operates two distribution centers with an aggregate of approximately 1.3 million square feet of warehouse and administrative space. Distribution operations are carried out by a company-owned fleet of 68 tractors and 336 trailers. In addition, Roundy's maintains a 116,000-square-foot central commissary that produces a wide range of food products, including its private label products. In 2014, the company sold 18 Rainbow stores in the Minneapolis/St. Paul market to a group of local grocery retailers, including SUPERVALU, Inc.

Roundy's offers its employees benefits including health, dental and prescription insurance; disability benefits; retirement savings; an employee assistance plan; and store discounts.

FINANCIAL DATA: Note: Data for latest year may not have been available at press time.

In U.S. $	2015	2014	2013	2012	2011	2010
Revenue		3,855,156,000	3,949,906,000	3,890,537,000	3,841,984,000	3,766,988,000
R&D Expense						
Operating Income		42,543,000	103,470,000	6,052,000	150,413,000	149,097,000
Operating Margin %		1.10%	2.61%	.15%	3.91%	3.95%
SGA Expense		970,691,000	947,651,000	908,300,000	886,862,000	868,972,000
Net Income		-309,867,000	34,538,000	-69,249,000	48,048,000	46,194,000
Operating Cash Flow		47,951,000	104,039,000	105,734,000	182,017,000	40,633,000
Capital Expenditure		91,757,000	67,109,000	62,004,000	66,497,000	62,932,000
EBITDA		-226,059,000	168,453,000	61,297,000	223,362,000	224,334,000
Return on Assets %		-24.01%	2.43%	-4.78%	3.24%	3.15%
Return on Equity %		-442.54%	16.45%	-37.49%	29.32%	27.35%
Debt to Equity			3.25	3.54	4.59	5.40

CONTACT INFORMATION:

Phone: 414 231-5000   Fax:
Toll-Free:
Address: 875 E. Wisconsin Ave., Milwaukee, WI 53202 United States

STOCK TICKER/OTHER:

Stock Ticker: RNDY
Employees: 21,802
Parent Company:

Exchange: NYS
Fiscal Year Ends: 12/31

SALARIES/BONUSES:

Top Exec. Salary:
$1,061,830
Second Exec. Salary:
$552,890

Bonus: $

Bonus: $

OTHER THOUGHTS:

Estimated Female Officers or Directors:

Hot Spot for Advancement for Women/Minorities:

Rue21 Inc

NAIC Code: 448120

TYPES OF BUSINESS:

Fashion Stores
fragrance
women and men's fashion apparel
intimates
accessories

GROWTH PLANS/SPECIAL FEATURES:

Rue21, Inc. is a specialty retailer of women's and men'
apparel and accessories with over 1,100 stores in various stri
centers, regional malls and outlet centers in 48 state
throughout the U.S. Rue21's stores offer a variety c
merchandise including men's and women's appare
accessories, including jewelry, hats, socks and hair items; an
perfumes and colognes. Rue21 brands include tarea girls
lingerie and yoga wear; rue21 etc! girls' shoes and accessories
ruebeaute! girls' fragrance and beauty; rue+ fashion clothing i
plus sizes; CARBON elements guys' shoes and accessories
and its newest line, ruebleu Swim. In select stores the compan
also offers rueGuy, an expanded men's department with
male-inspired layout, design and fashion selection. The
company's target customers are those who are seeking to loo
and feel 21, an age they feel extends fashion that is modern
trendy and affordable. Rue21 is owned by private company
Apax Partners.

BRANDS/DIVISIONS/AFFILIATES:

rue21
rue21 etc!
tarea
CARBON
ruebleu Swim
rueGuy
rue+
Apax Partners

CONTACTS: *Note: Officers with more than one job title may be intentionally listed here more than once.*

Robert N. Fisch, CEO
Robert N. Fisch, Pres.
Keith A. McDonough, CFO
Michael A. Holland, CIO
Kim A. Reynolds, Gen. Mgr.-Merch.
Stacy B. Siegal, Chief Admin. Officer
Stacy B. Siegal, Chief Legal Officer
Mark K.J. Chrystal, Sr. VP-Planning & Allocation
John P. Bugnar, Sr. VP
Robert R. Thomson, Sr. VP-Real Estate
Robert N. Fisch, Chmn.

FINANCIAL DATA: *Note: Data for latest year may not have been available at press time.*

In U.S. $	2015	2014	2013	2012	2011	2010
Revenue		965,000,000	901,886,016	760,302,016	634,728,000	525,600,000
R&D Expense						
Operating Income						
Operating Margin %						
SGA Expense						
Net Income						
Operating Cash Flow						
Capital Expenditure						
EBITDA						
Return on Assets %						
Return on Equity %						
Debt to Equity						

CONTACT INFORMATION:

Phone: 724 776-9780   Fax:
Toll-Free:
Address: 800 Commonwealth Dr., Ste. 100, Warrendale, PA 15086
United States

STOCK TICKER/OTHER:

Stock Ticker: Private
Employees: 11,200
Parent Company: Apax Partners

Exchange:
Fiscal Year Ends: 01/31

SALARIES/BONUSES:

Top Exec. Salary: $ Bonus: $
Second Exec. Salary: $ Bonus: $

OTHER THOUGHTS:

Estimated Female Officers or Directors: 2
Hot Spot for Advancement for Women/Minorities: Y

Ryohin Keikaku Co Ltd (Muji)

ryohin-keikaku.jp

NAIC Code: 442110

TYPES OF BUSINESS:

Home Furnishings Stores
Cafes, Restaurants & Foods
Apparel & Household Goods
Campsites
Trucking
Online Sales
Trucking

BRANDS/DIVISIONS/AFFILIATES:

MUJI
IDEE Co Ltd
Cafe Muji/Meal Muji
MUJI House Co Ltd
RK Trucks Co Ltd

CONTACTS: *Note: Officers with more than one job title may be intentionally listed here more than once.*

Satoru Matsuzaki, Pres.
Takashi Kato, Managing Dir.
Junichi Tokue, Sr. Exec. Officer
Tetsuo Kameya, Exec. Officer
Hiroto Oki, Exec. Officer
Masaaki Kanai, Chmn.

GROWTH PLANS/SPECIAL FEATURES:

Ryohin Keikaku Co., Ltd., commonly known as MUJI, is a Japanese company operating in several divisions, including MUJI Products; Cafe MUJI/Meal MUJI; MUJI Campsite; MUJI House Co., Ltd., a housing business; and IDEE Co., Ltd., a home furnishings business. MUJI offers over 7,000 items, including clothing, household products, foods and other items. The company's strategy is to offer quality goods at low prices through careful materials selection, streamlined production processes and simple packaging. MUJI products are primarily sold in Japan and internationally. In Japan, the company directly operates approximately 284 stores and also supplies its products to 117 other retail outlets. In the U.S. and internationally, MUJI products are sold in 301 stores. These stores are primarily concentrated in Europe and Southeast Asia. The Cafe MUJI/Meal MUJI business operates cafes and restaurants with the aim of offering simple foods at reasonable prices. The company's housing business, MUJI House Co., Ltd., is focused on developing adaptable residential housing which uses various movable and removable partitions to optimize structures for different family needs over time. This design concept is intended to provide maximum flexibility at affordable housing prices. The IDEE division plans, manufactures and sells home furnishings, interiors, antiques, curtains and rugs and other products. The company distributes its products through wholly-owned subsidiary R.K. Trucks Co., Ltd. MUJI's U.S. presence consists of four shops around Manhattan and JFK and five shops in California.

FINANCIAL DATA: *Note: Data for latest year may not have been available at press time.*

In U.S. $	2015	2014	2013	2012	2011	2010
Revenue	2,112,006,000	1,790,361,000	1,528,492,000	1,446,002,000	1,377,534,000	1,333,655,000
R&D Expense						
Operating Income	193,514,400	169,736,900	148,921,500	125,282,000	112,800,900	114,699,800
Operating Margin %	9.16%	9.48%	9.74%	8.66%	8.18%	8.60%
SGA Expense	122,441,700	27,266,970	90,735,720	88,844,890	94,639,120	30,586,080
Net Income	135,060,800	139,645,900	90,070,280	73,093,340	64,621,100	60,092,840
Operating Cash Flow	118,635,700	122,677,000	106,925,500	78,952,500	58,064,040	93,697,760
Capital Expenditure	165,306,000	106,268,200	47,100,450	39,666,950	32,322,720	45,396,260
EBITDA	254,946,200	245,094,400	172,147,100	150,057,600	131,684,900	130,297,200
Return on Assets %	10.16%	13.17%	9.89%	8.86%	7.98%	7.84%
Return on Equity %	14.22%	16.93%	12.47%	11.11%	10.28%	10.29%
Debt to Equity	0.09	0.01				

CONTACT INFORMATION:

Phone: 81 339894403   Fax:
Toll-Free:
Address: 4-26-3, Higashi-Ikebukuro, Toshima-ku, Tokyo, 170-8424 Japan

STOCK TICKER/OTHER:

Stock Ticker: RYKKF
Employees: 4,101
Parent Company:

Exchange: GREY
Fiscal Year Ends: 02/28

SALARIES/BONUSES:

Top Exec. Salary: $ Bonus: $
Second Exec. Salary: $ Bonus: $

OTHER THOUGHTS:

Estimated Female Officers or Directors: 1
Hot Spot for Advancement for Women/Minorities:

Safeway Inc

NAIC Code: 445110

www.safeway.com

TYPES OF BUSINESS:

Grocery Stores
Food Processing & Packaging
Online Grocery Sales & Home Delivery
Pharmacies
Gift Cards & Payment Processing Technology

BRANDS/DIVISIONS/AFFILIATES:

AB Acquisition LLC
Safeway
Carrs
Genuardi's
Pavilions
Tom Thumb
Dominick's
Randall's

CONTACTS: *Note: Officers with more than one job title may be intentionally listed here more than once.*

Robert G. Miller, CEO
Peter Bocian, CFO
Peter J. Bocian, CFO
Larree Renda, Executive VP
Kelly Griffith, Executive VP, Divisional
Diane Dietz, Executive VP
Melissa Plaisance, Senior VP, Divisional
David Stern, Senior VP, Divisional
Donald Wright, Senior VP, Divisional
Jerry Tidwell, Senior VP, Divisional
Russell Jackson, Senior VP, Divisional
Robert Gordon, Senior VP
Robert G. Miller, Chmn.

GROWTH PLANS/SPECIAL FEATURES:

Safeway, Inc. is one of the largest food retailers in the U.S., operating stores in 33 states and the District of Columbia. These stores operate regionally under the names Safeway, Carrs, Genuardi's, Pavilions, Tom Thumb, Dominick's, Randall's and Vons, each of which offer a wide selection of both food and general merchandise and feature a variety of special departments such as bakery, delicatessen, pharmacy and floral departments. In addition, the company offers online grocery shopping and home delivery through its wholly-owned subsidiary GroceryWorks. Safeway has developed a line of Safeway SELECT brand products, ranging from packaged foods to laundry detergent, and offers corporate-branded products under the Safeway labels: O Organics, Eating Right, Bright Green and Open Nature. Beyond these operations, Safeway manages its Blackhawk Network subsidiary, which is one of the largest providers of third-party prepaid gift cards in the country. In December 2014, Safeway sold its real estate subsidiary, Property Development Centers LLC, as well as its 49% stake in Mexico-based food retailer Casa Ley, SA de CV. In June 2015, AB Acquisition LLC (Albertson's) completed a merger with Safeway. The combined companies have a total of 2,230 stores, 27 distribution centers and 19 manufacturing plants, with 250,000 employees nationwide.

Safeway offers its employees medical, prescription drug, vision and dental coverage; an employee assistance plan; flexible spending accounts; life insurance; short- and long-term disability; paid time off; a stock purchase plan; a retirement plan; and a 401(k) plan.

FINANCIAL DATA: *Note: Data for latest year may not have been available at press time.*

In U.S. $	2015	2014	2013	2012	2011	2010
Revenue		36,330,000,000	36,139,098,112	44,206,501,888	43,630,198,784	41,050,001,408
R&D Expense						
Operating Income						
Operating Margin %						
SGA Expense						
Net Income		111,600,000	3,507,500,032	596,499,968	516,700,000	589,800,000
Operating Cash Flow						
Capital Expenditure						
EBITDA						
Return on Assets %						
Return on Equity %						
Debt to Equity						

CONTACT INFORMATION:

Phone: 925 467-3000   Fax: 925 467-3323
Toll-Free: 877-723-3929
Address: 5918 Stoneridge Mall Rd., Pleasanton, CA 94588-3229 United States

STOCK TICKER/OTHER:

Stock Ticker: Private
Employees: 138,000
Parent Company: AB Acquisition LLC

Exchange:
Fiscal Year Ends: 12/31

SALARIES/BONUSES:

Top Exec. Salary: $ Bonus: $
Second Exec. Salary: $ Bonus: $

OTHER THOUGHTS:

Estimated Female Officers or Directors: 4
Hot Spot for Advancement for Women/Minorities: Y

Saker ShopRites Inc

NAIC Code: 445110

TYPES OF BUSINESS:

Grocery Stores
Liquor Stores
Garden Centers
Food Processing
Pharmacies

BRANDS/DIVISIONS/AFFILIATES:

Wakefern Food Corporation
ShopRite

CONTACTS: Note: Officers with more than one job title may be intentionally listed here more than once.

Richard J. Saker, CEO
Richard J. Saker, Pres.
Michael Shapiro, CFO
Carl L. Montanaro, Sr. VP-Sales
Carl L. Montanaro, Sr. VP-Merch.
Joseph J. Saker, Chmn.

GROWTH PLANS/SPECIAL FEATURES:

Saker ShopRites, Inc. is comprised of 45 members who individually own and operate supermarkets under the ShopRite banner. ShopRite stores are located in New Jersey, New York, Connecticut, Pennsylvania, Delaware and Maryland. All ShopRite owners are members of Wakefern Food Corporation, which buys, warehouses and transports products while also providing other support services to ensure customer satisfaction. Headquartered in Keasbey, New Jersey, Wakefern operates over 2.5 million square feet of grocery and non-food warehousing. Its transport fleet consists of 400 tractors and 2,000 trailers, and travels more than 35 million miles annually. ShopRite products include grocery items, baby items, beverage items, cleaning products, home essentials, meat & seafood, canned & packaged foods, fresh & frozen foods, as well as garden & floral products and more. Its web site offers an online grocery list, grocery categories, recipes, coupons and gift cards.

FINANCIAL DATA: Note: Data for latest year may not have been available at press time.

In U.S. $	2015	2014	2013	2012	2011	2010
Revenue		1,780,000,000	1,700,000,000	1,700,000,000	1,600,000,000	1,550,000,000
R&D Expense						
Operating Income						
Operating Margin %						
SGA Expense						
Net Income						
Operating Cash Flow						
Capital Expenditure						
EBITDA						
Return on Assets %						
Return on Equity %						
Debt to Equity						

CONTACT INFORMATION:

Phone: 732-462-4700   Fax: 732-294-2322
Toll-Free: 800-746-7748
Address: P.O. Box 7812, Freehold, NJ 08818 United States

SALARIES/BONUSES:

Top Exec. Salary: $ Bonus: $
Second Exec. Salary: $ Bonus: $

STOCK TICKER/OTHER:

Stock Ticker: Private
Employees: 51,000
Parent Company:

Exchange:
Fiscal Year Ends: 10/31

OTHER THOUGHTS:

Estimated Female Officers or Directors:
Hot Spot for Advancement for Women/Minorities:

Saks Inc

NAIC Code: 452111

www.saksincorporated.com

TYPES OF BUSINESS:

Department Stores, Luxury
Outlet Stores
Online Sales

BRANDS/DIVISIONS/AFFILIATES:

Saks Fifth Avenue
OFF 5TH
Saks.com
Hudson's Bay Company
15-Sep
Saks Fifth Avenue Men's Collection
BLACK Saks Fifth Avenue
BLUE Saks Fifth Avenue

CONTACTS: Note: Officers with more than one job title may be intentionally listed here more than once.

Steve Sadove, CEO
Ronald L. Frasch, Pres.
Kevin Wills, CFO
Denise Incandela, CMO
Ronald L. Frasch, Chief Merch. Officer
Michael Brizel, General Counsel
Michael Burgess, Pres., Saks Direct
Julia Bentley, Dir.-Investor Rel.
Jennifer de Winter, Exec. VP-Stores
Robert T. Wallstrom, Pres., OFF 5TH
Terron Schaefer, Chief Creative Officer
Stephen I. Sadove, Chmn.

GROWTH PLANS/SPECIAL FEATURES:

Saks, Inc. is a luxury fashion retailer with locations across the U.S., including Saks Fifth Avenue (SFA) and OFF 5TH. It is a subsidiary of Hudson's Bay Company. SFA stores are principally free-standing buildings in exclusive shopping destinations or anchor stores in upscale regional malls. They typically offer a wide assortment of distinctive luxury fashion apparel, shoes, accessories, jewelry, cosmetics and gifts. SFA maintains key relationships with many of the leading American and European fashion houses, including Giorgio Armani, Oscar de la Renta, Dolce and Gabbana, Chanel, Gucci, Prada, Louis Vuitton, St. John, Zegna, Theory, Cartier, David Yurman, Hugo Boss, Elie Tahari, Tory Burch, Ralph Lauren, Akris and Burberry, among others. OFF 5TH is intended to be the premier luxury off-price retailer in the U.S. OFF 5TH stores are primarily located in upscale mixed-use and off-price centers and offer luxury apparel, shoes, accessories, cosmetics and decorative home furnishings, targeting the value-conscious customer. Its private-label offerings include, among others, the Saks Fifth Avenue Men's Collection and 9-15 brands sold at SFA stores as well as the BLACK Saks Fifth Avenue, BLUE Saks Fifth Avenue, RED Saks Fifth Avenue and GREY Saks Fifth Avenue. Additionally, Saks maintains an e-commerce site, Saks.com. Distribution centers include a 471,000 square foot facility in Maryland, a 120,000 square foot facility in California and a 564,000 square foot facility in Tennessee.

The firm offers its employees medical, dental and vision insurance; a 401(k); life insurance; disability coverage; a 529 college savings plan; and associate discounts at company stores and online.

FINANCIAL DATA: Note: Data for latest year may not have been available at press time.

In U.S. $	2015	2014	2013	2012	2011	2010
Revenue		3,200,000,000	3,147,554,048	3,013,593,088	2,785,744,896	2,631,532,032
R&D Expense						
Operating Income						
Operating Margin %						
SGA Expense						
Net Income			62,882,000	74,790,000	47,846,000	-57,919,000
Operating Cash Flow						
Capital Expenditure						
EBITDA						
Return on Assets %						
Return on Equity %						
Debt to Equity						

CONTACT INFORMATION:

Phone: 212 940-5305   Fax:
Toll-Free:
Address: 12 E. 49th St., New York, NY 10017 United States

STOCK TICKER/OTHER:

Stock Ticker: Subsidiary
Employees: 13,000
Parent Company: Hudson's Bay Company

Exchange:
Fiscal Year Ends: 01/31

SALARIES/BONUSES:

Top Exec. Salary: $ Bonus: $
Second Exec. Salary: $ Bonus: $

OTHER THOUGHTS:

Estimated Female Officers or Directors:
Hot Spot for Advancement for Women/Minorities: Y

Salvatore Ferragamo SpA

www.ferragamo.com

NAIC Code: 424340

TYPES OF BUSINESS:

Footwear Distribution
Retail Stores
Leather Goods
Leather Apparel
Watches
Ladies' Shoes
Men's Shoes
Fragrance

BRANDS/DIVISIONS/AFFILIATES:

Ferragamo Parfums SpA

CONTACTS: Note: Officers with more than one job title may be intentionally listed here more than once.

Michele Norsa, CEO
Giovanna Gentile Ferragamo, Vice Chmn.
Ferruccio Ferragamo, Chmn.

GROWTH PLANS/SPECIAL FEATURES:

Salvatore Ferragamo SpA is a leading international designer of luxury shoes, leather products, accessories, jewelry, fragrances and apparel for men and women. Founded in 1927, the firm is still controlled by the Ferragamo family and headquartered in Florence, Italy. The company's products are sold in over 373 Ferragamo directly operated stores, 270 third-party operated Ferragamo stores and department stores and boutiques in 90 countries. Ferragamo shoes, which are aimed at fashion-conscious consumers, have a reputation for high quality, conservative styling and comfort. The company has outfitted such celebrities as Judy Garland (supplying the ruby red slippers worn in The Wizard of Oz), Marilyn Monroe (metal-reinforced stilettos) and Madonna. Though the firm initially made its name producing high-end shoes, Ferragamo now designs and creates a vast product line, including men's and women's ready-to-wear clothing collections, footwear, handbags, watches, fragrances and eyewear. Nearly all of the company's merchandise is manufactured in Italy, as the use of fine Italian leather is of critical importance across its entire product line. Annually, shoes, leather goods and handbags account for approximately 78% of its revenue. Ferragamo owns and operates Ferragamo Parfums SpA and partners with Luxottica to produce eyewear sold under the Ferragamo name. The group has regional headquarters in New York and Miami and also has store locations across Europe and in the U.S., Central and South America, Japan, Hong Kong, China, Taiwan, Korea, Singapore, Thailand, Malaysia, Indonesia and Australia. On average, the Asia Pacific region generates 37.2% of the group's revenue per year; Europe, 26.6%; North America, 22.9%; Japan, 8.4%; and Latin America, 4.9%.

FINANCIAL DATA: Note: Data for latest year may not have been available at press time.

In U.S. $	2015	2014	2013	2012	2011	2010
Revenue		1,413,464,000	1,335,153,000	1,223,643,000	1,039,010,000	829,513,700
R&D Expense		46,157,030	47,103,710	41,574,340	36,293,300	29,387,420
Operating Income		260,460,200	232,486,400	206,234,100	166,251,700	91,735,660
Operating Margin %		18.42%	17.41%	16.85%	16.00%	11.05%
SGA Expense		587,945,700	566,901,200	537,893,800	500,761,000	396,167,600
Net Income		166,162,500	159,673,800	112,022,400	109,588,900	51,873,200
Operating Cash Flow		152,588,500	159,179,200	128,566,000	123,069,500	129,041,400
Capital Expenditure		87,951,060	87,303,660	63,033,840	44,919,560	23,091,780
EBITDA		310,891,100	275,913,800	270,617,900	214,816,800	137,906,500
Return on Assets %		17.07%	18.84%	14.67%	12.48%	8.44%
Return on Equity %		35.12%	45.76%	44.10%	40.19%	28.78%
Debt to Equity		0.04				

CONTACT INFORMATION:

Phone: 39 5533601 Fax: 39 553360444
Toll-Free: 866-337-724-266
Address: Palazzo Feroni, Via del Tornabuoni, 2, Florence, 50123 Italy

STOCK TICKER/OTHER:

Stock Ticker: SFRGF Exchange: GREY
Employees: Fiscal Year Ends:
Parent Company:

SALARIES/BONUSES:

Top Exec. Salary: $ Bonus: $
Second Exec. Salary: $ Bonus: $

OTHER THOUGHTS:

Estimated Female Officers or Directors: 4
Hot Spot for Advancement for Women/Minorities: Y

Sam's Club

NAIC Code: 452910

TYPES OF BUSINESS:

Warehouse Clubs, Retail

BRANDS/DIVISIONS/AFFILIATES:

Wal-Mart Stores Inc
Member's Mark
Bakers & Chefs
Business Membership
Advantage Membership
PLUS Membership Card
Sam's Cafe
Sam's Club

CONTACTS: *Note: Officers with more than one job title may be intentionally listed here more than once.*

Rosalind G. Brewer, CEO
Rosalind G. Brewer, Pres.
Charles M. Holley, Jr., VP
Charles Redfield, Exec. VP-Merch.
Whitney Head, General Counsel
P. Todd Harbaugh, Exec. VP-Oper.
Don Frieson, Sr. VP-Planning & Replenishment
John Boswell, Sr. VP-e-Commerce
Bill Durling, Sr. Dir.-Corp. Comm.
Mike Turner, Sr. VP-Sam's Club Membership
Whitney Head, Sr. VP- Asset Protection & Compliance

GROWTH PLANS/SPECIAL FEATURES:

Sam's Club, a subsidiary of Wal-Mart Stores, Inc. is an American chain of membership-only retail warehouse clubs. Additionally, Wal-Mart's international division operates over 125 Sam's Clubs in Mexico, 27 stores in Brazil and 11 in China. Sam's Club offers discounted prices on items, including appliances and electronics, office supplies, food, clothing, optical and pharmacy services, home furnishings, books and auto supplies. It also sells selected private-label items under the Member's Mark, Bakers & Chefs and Sam's Club brands. Most locations also offer photo processing, pharmaceuticals, optical departments, gasoline stations and fresh departments, including bakery, meat, produce, floral and Sam's Cafe. Sam's Club requires a customer to become a member, providing two options for an annual fee: Business Membership or Advantage Membership. In addition, Sam's Club offers a PLUS Membership Card, which offers extra benefits on either level, and a Golden Key membership, which allows business members priority shopping hours. In addition to merchandise discounts, the firm offers its members discounted services that include various types of insurance, a travel club, an auto purchase program, discount credit card processing, mail-order pharmacy services, Internet access and long-distance services. Sam's Club stores, averaging 70,000-190,000 square feet, are designed to resemble a warehouse, with merchandise displayed on shipping pallets or in large freezer/cooler units. The company's merchandise consists of five categories: grocery and consumables; fuel and other categories; technology, office and entertainment; home and apparel; and health and wellness.

Parent company Wal Mart offers employees health reimbursement accounts, health savings accounts, HMO plans, life insurance, AD&D insurance, short- and long-term disability and a 401(k) with company match.

FINANCIAL DATA: *Note: Data for latest year may not have been available at press time.*

In U.S. $	2015	2014	2013	2012	2011	2010
Revenue		57,157,000,000	56,423,000,000	53,795,000,000	49,459,000,000	46,710,000,000
R&D Expense						
Operating Income						
Operating Margin %						
SGA Expense						
Net Income		1,975,000,000	1,960,000,000	1,865,000,000	1,711,000,000	1,512,000,000
Operating Cash Flow						
Capital Expenditure						
EBITDA						
Return on Assets %						
Return on Equity %						
Debt to Equity						

CONTACT INFORMATION:

Phone: 479-277-7000   Fax:
Toll-Free: 888-746-7726
Address: 2101 S. E. Simple Savings Drive, Bentonville, AR 72716 United States

STOCK TICKER/OTHER:

Stock Ticker: Subsidiary   Exchange:
Employees: 110,000   Fiscal Year Ends: 01/31
Parent Company: WAL-MART STORES INC

SALARIES/BONUSES:

Top Exec. Salary: $ Bonus: $
Second Exec. Salary: $ Bonus: $

OTHER THOUGHTS:

Estimated Female Officers or Directors: 3
Hot Spot for Advancement for Women/Minorities: Y

Samsonite International SA

www.samsonite.com

NAIC Code: 316998

TYPES OF BUSINESS:

Luggage Manufacturing
Luggage Stores
Electronic Shopping

BRANDS/DIVISIONS/AFFILIATES:

Samsonite
American Tourister
High Sierra
Chic Accent
Lipault
Speck Products
Gregory Mountain Products
Rolling Luggage

CONTACTS: *Note: Officers with more than one job title may be intentionally listed here more than once.*

Ramesh Dungaramal Tainwala, CEO
Kyle F. Gendreau, CFO
Timothy C. Parker, Chmn.
Arne Borrey, Pres., EMEA

GROWTH PLANS/SPECIAL FEATURES:

Samsonite International SA is one of the most recognized designers, manufacturers and distributors of luggage and travel-related consumer products. The firm's family of brands includes Samsonite, American Tourister, High Sierra, Hartmann, Lipault and Speck. Samsonite and American Tourister are travel luggage brands; High Sierra products target at active lifestyle consumers, as well as the global luggage market; Hartmann products target luxury consumers and also feature high-end leather goods in the U.S. and internationally; Lipault is a chic and youthful French luggage brand known for its fashionable products and vibrant colors; and Speck designs and distributes slim protective cases for personal electronic devices. The company's products are available in over 100 countries at numerous retail locations, department and specialty stores, warehouse clubs, electronic stores, office superstores and bookstores. During 2014, the firm acquired Lipault, Gregory Mountain Products and Speck Products. In 2015, it acquired Rolling Luggage; and Chic Accent, a chain of retail stores in Italy that sells travel luggage, handbags and business products and accessories.

FINANCIAL DATA: *Note: Data for latest year may not have been available at press time.*

In U.S. $	2015	2014	2013	2012	2011	2010
Revenue		2,350,707,000	2,037,812,000	1,771,726,000	1,565,147,000	1,215,307,000
R&D Expense						
Operating Income		299,277,000	281,292,000	241,742,000	209,930,000	543,602,000
Operating Margin %		12.73%	13.80%	13.64%	13.41%	44.72%
SGA Expense		922,170,000	802,872,000	704,814,000	647,324,000	519,170,000
Net Income		186,256,000	176,087,000	148,439,000	103,618,000	366,814,000
Operating Cash Flow		229,914,000	193,033,000	202,992,000	64,502,000	34,441,000
Capital Expenditure		69,636,000	57,239,000	37,941,000	37,172,000	29,575,000
EBITDA		337,834,000	318,449,000	283,190,000	249,668,000	565,993,000
Return on Assets %		9.16%	9.39%	8.84%	5.40%	21.32%
Return on Equity %		15.12%	15.69%	15.07%	10.46%	47.96%
Debt to Equity						0.33

CONTACT INFORMATION:

Phone: 508-851-1400   Fax: 508-851-8715
Toll-Free:
Address: 575 West St., Ste. 110, Mansfield, MA 02048 United States

SALARIES/BONUSES:

Top Exec. Salary: $ Bonus: $
Second Exec. Salary: $ Bonus: $

STOCK TICKER/OTHER:

Stock Ticker: SMSEY
Employees: 8,900
Parent Company:

Exchange: PINX
Fiscal Year Ends: 12/31

OTHER THOUGHTS:

Estimated Female Officers or Directors:
Hot Spot for Advancement for Women/Minorities:

Sales, profits and employees may be estimates. Financial information, benefits and other data can change quickly and may vary from those stated here.

Samuels Jewelers Inc

NAIC Code: 448310

www.samuelsjewelers.com

TYPES OF BUSINESS:

Jewelry, Retail
Online Sales

BRANDS/DIVISIONS/AFFILIATES:

Gitanjali Gems Ltd
Gitanjali Retail USA
Andrews Jewelers
Rogers Jewelers
SamuelsJewelers.com
SamuelsDiamonds.com
Rogers-Jewelers.com
Schubach Jewelers

CONTACTS: *Note: Officers with more than one job title may be intentionally listed here more than once.*

Deepak Gandhi, CEO
Deepak Gandhi, Pres.
Robert J. Herman, Chief Acct. Officer

GROWTH PLANS/SPECIAL FEATURES:

Samuels Jewelers, Inc. operates a national chain of specialt
jewelry stores. The firm sells fine jewelry items in a wide range
of styles and prices, with a principal emphasis on conflict-free
diamond and gemstone jewelry, including necklaces, rings
bracelets, earrings and watches. The company also offers
bridal jewelry, which includes engagement rings, solitaire rings
bridal sets and mountings, wraps and guards, three stone
rings, wedding bands, anniversary bands, men's diamond
bands and alternate metal bands. Other merchandise includes
jewelry boxes, miniature jewelry cases, travel bags, jewelry
wallets and rolls and jewelry cleaners. Samuels Jewelers is a
subsidiary of Gitanjali Gems, Ltd., an Indian diamond and
jewelry specialist, which operates Samuels Jewelers through
its Gitanjali Retail USA division. The firm's stores operate under
the names Samuels Diamonds, Samuels Jewelers, Schubach
Jewelers, Rogers Jewelers and Andrews Jewelers. Located in
several U.S. states, most stores operate out of regional
shopping malls, power centers and strip centers. The company
retails its jewelry online though SamuelsJewelers.com,
SamuelsDiamonds.com and Rogers-Jewelers.com. Besides
its sales activities, the firm buys gold, silver, platinum and
diamond jewelry from customers.

Samuels Jewelers offers employees medical and dental
insurance, flexible spending accounts, a 401(k) and paid time
off.

FINANCIAL DATA: *Note: Data for latest year may not have been available at press time.*

In U.S. $	2015	2014	2013	2012	2011	2010
Revenue		123,362,335	131,443,820	136,200,000	131,158,000	89,590,000
R&D Expense						
Operating Income						
Operating Margin %						
SGA Expense						
Net Income		3,706,619	3,817,944	5,636,000	1,002,000	4,899,150
Operating Cash Flow						
Capital Expenditure						
EBITDA						
Return on Assets %						
Return on Equity %						
Debt to Equity						

CONTACT INFORMATION:

Phone: 512-369-1400   Fax: 512-369-1527
Toll-Free: 877-202-2870
Address: 2914 Montopolis Dr., Ste. 200, Austin, TX 78741 United States

STOCK TICKER/OTHER:

Stock Ticker: Subsidiary   Exchange:
Employees: 860   Fiscal Year Ends: 05/31
Parent Company: GITANJALI GEMS LTD

SALARIES/BONUSES:

Top Exec. Salary: $ Bonus: $
Second Exec. Salary: $ Bonus: $

OTHER THOUGHTS:

Estimated Female Officers or Directors:
Hot Spot for Advancement for Women/Minorities:

Saucony Inc

NAIC Code: 424340

TYPES OF BUSINESS:

Footwear Distribution
Outlet Stores
Athletic Apparel

BRANDS/DIVISIONS/AFFILIATES:

Saucony
PowerGrid
Saucony Originals
PWRGRID+
Sauc-Fit
ComfortLite
ISO-Fit
Total Run System

CONTACTS: *Note: Officers with more than one job title may be intentionally listed here more than once.*

Richie Woodworth, Pres.
Chris Lindner, Chief Mktg. Officer
Sharon Barbano, VP-Public Rel.

GROWTH PLANS/SPECIAL FEATURES:

Saucony, Inc., a subsidiary of Wolverine World Wide, Inc., designs, develops and markets athletic footwear and apparel. Saucony offers five categories of footwear products: technical, natural motion, race, trail and lifestyle, all under the Saucony brand name. The firm targets both elite and casual runners through its award-winning design, innovation and performance technology. It is focused on meeting the biomechanical needs of runners while maximizing comfort and protection through its PowerGrid and PWRGRID+ midsole technologies; Sauc-Fit, ComfortLite, Sock Liner, HydraMAX and ISO-Fit upper technologies; and iBR+ and XT-900 outsole material innovations. Saucony also offers its Total Run System, a complete line of performance running apparel.

FINANCIAL DATA: *Note: Data for latest year may not have been available at press time.*

In U.S. $	2015	2014	2013	2012	2011	2010
Revenue						
R&D Expense						
Operating Income						
Operating Margin %						
SGA Expense						
Net Income						
Operating Cash Flow						
Capital Expenditure						
EBITDA						
Return on Assets %						
Return on Equity %						
Debt to Equity						

CONTACT INFORMATION:

Phone: 617-824-6000   Fax: 617-824-6549
Toll-Free: 800-282-6575
Address: 191 Spring St., Lexington, MA 02420 United States

STOCK TICKER/OTHER:

Stock Ticker: Subsidiary   Exchange:
Employees: Fiscal Year Ends: 12/31
Parent Company: WOLVERINE WORLD WIDE INC

SALARIES/BONUSES:

Top Exec. Salary: $ Bonus: $
Second Exec. Salary: $ Bonus: $

OTHER THOUGHTS:

Estimated Female Officers or Directors: 1
Hot Spot for Advancement for Women/Minorities:

Save Mart Supermarkets

www.savemart.com

NAIC Code: 445110

TYPES OF BUSINESS:

Supermarkets
Refrigerated Transport
Dairy Manufacturing & Distribution

BRANDS/DIVISIONS/AFFILIATES:

Save Mart
S-Mart
Lucky
MaxxValue Foods
FoodMaxx
SMART Refrigerated Transport
Sunny Select
Valu Time

CONTACTS: *Note: Officers with more than one job title may be intentionally listed here more than once.*

Steve Junqueiro, COO
Greg Hill, CFO

GROWTH PLANS/SPECIAL FEATURES:

Save Mart Supermarkets, headquartered in Modesto, California, is a privately held supermarket chain with more than 240 grocery stores in Northern & Central California and Northern Nevada. The firm, founded in 1952, operates under the Save Mart, S-Mart, Lucky, MaxxValue Foods and FoodMaxx brand names and offers groceries, produce, dairy and dry goods. Other brands of the firm include Sunny Select juices & foods, Valu Time packaged food & merchandise, SunnySide Farms dairy & frozen foods, Bayview Farms dairy & frozen foods, Pacific Coast Selectrions fresh & packaged foods, Full Circle organic packaged foods, Mast Cuts meats, Maxx Value meats, Master Catch fish & seafood, Top Care over-the-counter medications and Paws Premium pet food. Many of the stores operate a Pacific Coast Cafe kiosk within the store and feature an expanded offering of ethnic and organic foods. Approximately half of the stores offer in-house pharmacies. The firm also owns SMART Refrigerated Transport, Yosemite Wholesale Warehouse, Vacaville Distribution Center, Roseville Distribution Center, and is a voting partner in Super Store Industries, which owns and operates the Mid Valley Dairy, SunnySide Farms Ice Cream Plant and a dairy distribution center in Lathrop, California.

The firm provides its employees benefits including health and welfare plans, training and developmental opportunities and competitive pay.

FINANCIAL DATA: *Note: Data for latest year may not have been available at press time.*

In U.S. $	2015	2014	2013	2012	2011	2010
Revenue		4,500,000,000	4,800,000,000	4,700,000,000	4,600,000,000	4,800,000,000
R&D Expense						
Operating Income						
Operating Margin %						
SGA Expense						
Net Income						
Operating Cash Flow						
Capital Expenditure						
EBITDA						
Return on Assets %						
Return on Equity %						
Debt to Equity						

CONTACT INFORMATION:

Phone: 209-577-1600   Fax: 209-577-3857
Toll-Free:
Address: 1800 Standiford Ave., Modesto, CA 95350 United States

SALARIES/BONUSES:

Top Exec. Salary: $ Bonus: $
Second Exec. Salary: $ Bonus: $

STOCK TICKER/OTHER:

Stock Ticker: Private
Employees: 19,000
Parent Company:

Exchange:
Fiscal Year Ends: 12/31

OTHER THOUGHTS:

Estimated Female Officers or Directors:
Hot Spot for Advancement for Women/Minorities:

Schnuck Markets Inc

www.schnucks.com

NAIC Code: 445110

TYPES OF BUSINESS:

Grocery Stores
Pharmacies
Florists
Video Rentals
Online Grocery Ordering

BRANDS/DIVISIONS/AFFILIATES:

Schnuck Markets
Logli Stores
Schnucks.com

CONTACTS: Note: Officers with more than one job title may be intentionally listed here more than once.

Todd R. Schnuck, CEO
Anthony T. Hucker, Pres.
David Bell, CFO
Mary Moorkamp, General Counsel

GROWTH PLANS/SPECIAL FEATURES:

Schnuck Markets, Inc., founded in St. Louis in 1939, is a chain of nearly 100 supermarkets, with an average size of 60,000 square feet, under the names Schnuck Markets and Logli Stores. The majority of the firm's stores are located in St. Louis, Missouri, with additional locations in Illinois, Indiana, Wisconsin and one in Iowa. Schnuck is one of the largest family-owned and -operated companies in the nation. Stores offer groceries, video rental boxes, in-store banking, florists, sports and amusement park tickets and party planning. In-house pharmacies are available at 96 locations. Schnuck also offers discounted gift cards for nonprofit group fundraising including schools, churches, athletic teams and youth groups. The firm provides ticket sales, meal planning recipes, floral deliveries, pharmacy refills and grocery ordering and company coupons online at its web site, Schnucks.com. Additionally, Schnuck offers an online Special Order Service, in which customers can find groceries online and have them delivered directly to their homes.

In addition to providing employees with health benefits, paid vacations and flexible schedules, Schnuck promotes mainly from within, giving employees ample opportunities for advancement.

FINANCIAL DATA: Note: Data for latest year may not have been available at press time.

In U.S. $	2015	2014	2013	2012	2011	2010
Revenue		2,675,000,000	2,600,000,000	2,500,000,000	2,750,000,000	2,600,000,000
R&D Expense						
Operating Income						
Operating Margin %						
SGA Expense						
Net Income						
Operating Cash Flow						
Capital Expenditure						
EBITDA						
Return on Assets %						
Return on Equity %						
Debt to Equity						

CONTACT INFORMATION:

Phone: 314-994-9900   Fax: 314-994-4465
Toll-Free: 800-264-4400
Address: 11420 Lackland Rd., St. Louis, MO 63146 United States

STOCK TICKER/OTHER:

Stock Ticker: Private
Employees: 15,000
Parent Company:

Exchange:
Fiscal Year Ends: 10/31

SALARIES/BONUSES:

Top Exec. Salary: $ Bonus: $
Second Exec. Salary: $ Bonus: $

OTHER THOUGHTS:

Estimated Female Officers or Directors: 3
Hot Spot for Advancement for Women/Minorities: Y

Sales, profits and employees may be estimates. Financial information, benefits and other data can change quickly and may vary from those stated here.

Sculptz Inc

NAIC Code: 454113

TYPES OF BUSINESS:

Hosiery Products, Retail
Direct Marketing
Online Sales

BRANDS/DIVISIONS/AFFILIATES:

PainVanish
Silkies.com
EnchantressHosiery.com
Silkies.co.uk
Sheer Renu
Silkies Hosiery
Silkies Enriche
Sculptz

CONTACTS: *Note: Officers with more than one job title may be intentionally listed here more than once.*

Sue Dudek, Sr. Dir.-Global Mktg.

GROWTH PLANS/SPECIAL FEATURES:

Sculptz, Inc. markets, manufactures and distributes women'
hosiery and beauty products as Silkies Hosiery. It markets t
consumers throughout the U.S. via mailings and its e
commerce site, Silkies.com; throughout Canada throug
EnchantressHosiery.com; and the U.K. through Silkies.co.uk
The company's main product line includes hosiery, knee-highs
socks and tights for women and girls. Other products includ
the Silkies Enriche anti-aging brand of skincare products and
the PainVanish brand pain relief cream. Silkies.com retail
slimming shapewear such as waist cinchers and contro
underwear under the Sculptz brand; bras; panties and briefs
therapeutic products, such as Sheer Renu firm-suppor
therapeutic knee-highs, pantyhose and thigh-highs; slips and
camisoles; socks; sleepwear; casualwear; gifts; skincare
products; and accessories. The web site also features a sizing
guide and offers gift certificate purchasing. The firm's Silkie
brand-name hosiery is marketed through a continuous produc
shipment program. The program involves mailing to customer
a specially priced introductory hosiery offer, the acceptance o
which enrolls customers in the program and results ir
additional shipments of hose being mailed on a regular basi
upon payment of a prior shipment. Sculptz relies or
sophisticated statistical, regression, segmentation and othe
financial analyses to accurately target, test and acquire
customers through direct-mail solicitation.

FINANCIAL DATA: *Note: Data for latest year may not have been available at press time.*

In U.S. $	2015	2014	2013	2012	2011	2010
Revenue						
R&D Expense						
Operating Income						
Operating Margin %						
SGA Expense						
Net Income						
Operating Cash Flow						
Capital Expenditure						
EBITDA						
Return on Assets %						
Return on Equity %						
Debt to Equity						

CONTACT INFORMATION:

Phone: 215-494-2900   Fax:
Toll-Free: 877-745-5437
Address: 1150 Northbrook Dr., Ste. 300, Trevose, PA 19053 United States

STOCK TICKER/OTHER:

Stock Ticker: Private   Exchange:
Employees: Fiscal Year Ends: 12/31
Parent Company:

SALARIES/BONUSES:

Top Exec. Salary: $ Bonus: $
Second Exec. Salary: $ Bonus: $

OTHER THOUGHTS:

Estimated Female Officers or Directors: 1
Hot Spot for Advancement for Women/Minorities:

Sears Canada Inc

www.sears.ca

NAIC Code: 452111

TYPES OF BUSINESS:

Department Stores
Travel Agencies
Parts and Service Network
Portrait Studios
Floor Coverings
Appliance Stores

BRANDS/DIVISIONS/AFFILIATES:

Corbeil Electrique Inc
Sears Home
S.L.H. Transport
Searstravel.ca
Sears.ca

CONTACTS: *Note: Officers with more than one job title may be intentionally listed here more than once.*

Klaudio Leshnjani,
Deborah Rosati,
E. Bird, CFO
William Crowley, Chairman of the Board
Ronald Boire, Director
Timothy Flemming, Director
Danita Stevenson, Director
Jeffrey Severts, Other Corporate Officer
Franco Perugini, Secretary
Gail Galea, Senior VP, Divisional
William Harker, Vice Chairman of the Board

GROWTH PLANS/SPECIAL FEATURES:

Sears Canada, Inc. is a multi-channel retail network in Canada. The company operates through two business segments. The merchandising operations segment includes the sales of goods and services through the firm's stores, as well as through its catalogue and Internet operations. This division also comprises its wholly-owned subsidiary Corbeil Electrique, Inc., a retailer of home appliances. Sears Canada operates 172 corporate stores, which include its full-line department stores, Sears Home stores (furniture and appliances), outlet and specialty stores; 201 Hometown stores, a retailer of home appliances, lawn and garden equipment, apparel, mattresses, sporting goods and tools; 35 Corbeil stores; six NLCs (Newcastle, Ontario stores); 96 travel offices, providing flight booking, hotel reservations, car rentals, vacation packages and travel insurance; and 1,335 catalogue merchandise pick-up locations. The company publishes one of the largest general merchandise catalogues in Canada, issued to more than 3 million households, and offers shopping online at Sears.ca. The real estate joint venture operations segment includes income from the company's joint venture interests in shopping centers across Canada. Sears offers many specialty services, including a parts and service network, travel offices, hair care centers, optical services, health food shops, portrait studios, income tax services, carpet upholstery and air duct cleaning and home installed products and services. Sears Travel offers online travel service at Searstravel.ca as well as through the toll-free number 1-866-Fly-Sears. Sears also owns S.L.H. Transport, a trucking fleet operation. The firm offers an online points redemption feature, which allows Sears credit card holders to earn points as they shop. These points can be redeemed for discounts. The company's JPMorgan Chase credit card partnership expired in November 2015, and will not be renewed.

FINANCIAL DATA: *Note: Data for latest year may not have been available at press time.*

In U.S. $	2015	2014	2013	2012	2011	2010
Revenue	2,565,572,000	2,990,583,000	3,222,005,000	3,460,694,000	3,714,292,000	3,896,193,000
R&D Expense						
Operating Income	-305,141,600	-140,696,300	-62,107,150	-48,022,540	162,647,300	258,992,000
Operating Margin %	-11.89%	-4.70%	-1.92%	-1.38%	4.37%	6.64%
SGA Expense	1,141,603,000	1,222,290,000	1,224,462,000	1,311,892,000		
Net Income	-253,822,700	334,509,500	75,817,170	-45,025,810	112,227,400	175,832,900
Operating Cash Flow	-198,233,400	-19,328,880	-59,859,600	63,680,430	73,719,460	371,669,000
Capital Expenditure	40,455,800	53,042,050	73,045,200	63,156,000	46,748,930	49,221,220
EBITDA	-202,054,300	458,648,900	180,402,900	45,550,240	253,148,400	367,248,800
Return on Assets %	-16.26%	18.33%	3.80%	-2.24%	5.06%	7.03%
Return on Equity %	-41.20%	41.53%	7.97%	-4.88%	11.27%	14.82%
Debt to Equity	0.04	0.02	0.02	0.08	0.13	0.02

CONTACT INFORMATION:

Phone: 416 362-1711   Fax: 416 941-2321
Toll-Free: 866-359-7327
Address: 290 Yonge St., Ste. 700, Toronto, ON M5B 2C3 Canada

SALARIES/BONUSES:

Top Exec. Salary: $800,000   Bonus: $
Second Exec. Salary: Bonus: $
$700,000

STOCK TICKER/OTHER:

Stock Ticker: SRSC   Exchange: NAS
Employees: 29,128   Fiscal Year Ends: 01/31
Parent Company:

OTHER THOUGHTS:

Estimated Female Officers or Directors: 1
Hot Spot for Advancement for Women/Minorities: Y

Sales, profits and employees may be estimates. Financial information, benefits and other data can change quickly and may vary from those stated here.

Sears Holdings Corporation

www.sears.com

NAIC Code: 452111

TYPES OF BUSINESS:

Department Stores
Catalog Sales
Online Sales
Automotive Parts & Services
Appliances & Electronics
Health & Beauty Products

BRANDS/DIVISIONS/AFFILIATES:

Sears, Roebuck & Co
Kmart Holding Corporation
Kenmore
Craftsman
Sears Auto Centers
DieHard
Sears Canada Inc

CONTACTS: *Note: Officers with more than one job title may be intentionally listed here more than once.*

Dorian Williams, Assistant Secretary
Alasdair James, CEO, Divisional
Edward Lampert, CEO
Robert Riecker, Chief Accounting Officer
Jeffrey Balagna, Chief Information Officer
Robert Schriesheim, Executive VP
Leena Munjal, Senior VP, Divisional
Kristin Coleman, Senior VP

GROWTH PLANS/SPECIAL FEATURES:

Sears Holdings Corporation is the parent firm of Kmart Holding Corporation and Sears, Roebuck & Co. As a broadline retailer, the company owns 1,980 full-line and specialty retail stores in the U.S. operating through Sears and Kmart; and 449 full-line and specialty retail stores in Canada operating through Sears Canada, Inc., a 51%-owned subsidiary. The firm operates in three segments: Kmart, Sears domestic and Sears Canada. Kmart operates 1,152 stores in 49 states, Puerto Rico, Guam and the U.S. Virgin Islands, including both discount stores and super centers. Most Kmart stores are one-floor, free-standing units that carry a wide assortment of general merchandise and proprietary Sears brand products, including Kenmore, Craftsman and DieHard. Of these stores, 840 operate in-store pharmacies. The super centers generally operate 24-hours-a-day and combine a full-service grocery along with the general merchandise selection of a discount store. There are also 16 Sears Auto Centers operating in Kmart stores. Sears Auto Centers offer a variety of professional automotive repair and maintenance services as well as a full assortment of automotive accessories. Sears domestic operates 778 full-line stores in the U.S. and Puerto Rico that offer products such as home appliances; consumer electronics; tools; fitness, lawn and garden equipment; certain automotive services and products; home fashion products; apparel; footwear; and accessories. The segment also operates 10 Sears essentials/grand stores, offering health and beauty products, pantry goods, household products and toys. Sears' 50 specialty stores include 34 free standing Auto Centers. In 2014, the firm spun off its Lands' End business.

The firm offers employees medical and dental care; a flex spending account; and disability, survivor and retirement benefits.

FINANCIAL DATA: *Note: Data for latest year may not have been available at press time.*

In U.S. $	2015	2014	2013	2012	2011	2010
Revenue	31,198,000,000	36,188,000,000	39,854,000,000	41,567,000,000	43,326,000,000	44,043,000,000
R&D Expense						
Operating Income	-1,508,000,000	-927,000,000	-838,000,000	-1,501,000,000	474,000,000	713,000,000
Operating Margin %	-4.83%	-2.56%	-2.10%	-3.61%	1.09%	1.61%
SGA Expense	8,220,000,000	9,383,999,000	10,660,000,000	10,664,000,000	10,571,000,000	10,654,000,000
Net Income	-1,682,000,000	-1,365,000,000	-930,000,000	-3,140,000,000	133,000,000	235,000,000
Operating Cash Flow	-1,387,000,000	-1,109,000,000	-303,000,000	-275,000,000	130,000,000	1,507,000,000
Capital Expenditure	270,000,000	329,000,000	378,000,000	432,000,000	441,000,000	361,000,000
EBITDA	-791,000,000	-23,000,000	354,000,000	-609,000,000	1,396,000,000	1,611,000,000
Return on Assets %	-10.68%	-7.26%	-4.56%	-13.75%	.54%	.93%
Return on Equity %	-426.90%	-60.74%	-26.43%	-49.09%	1.51%	2.54%
Debt to Equity		1.62	0.70	0.48	0.24	0.18

CONTACT INFORMATION:

Phone: 847 286-2500   Fax:
Toll-Free:
Address: 3333 Beverly Rd., Hoffman Estates, IL 60179 United States

STOCK TICKER/OTHER:

Stock Ticker: SHLD   Exchange: NAS
Employees: 196,000   Fiscal Year Ends: 01/31
Parent Company:

SALARIES/BONUSES:

Top Exec. Salary: $390,151   Bonus: $1,200,000
Second Exec. Salary: Bonus: $600,000
$750,000

OTHER THOUGHTS:

Estimated Female Officers or Directors: 2
Hot Spot for Advancement for Women/Minorities:

Sears Hometown & Outlet Stores Inc   www.searsoutlet.com

NAIC Code: 444110

TYPES OF BUSINESS:

Home Centers

BRANDS/DIVISIONS/AFFILIATES:

Kenmore
Craftsman
DieHard

CONTACTS: Note: Officers with more than one job title may be intentionally listed here more than once.

Charles Hansen, General Counsel
William Powell, President
Ryan Robinson, Senior VP
Becky Iliff, Vice President, Divisional

GROWTH PLANS/SPECIAL FEATURES:

Sears Hometown & Outlet Stores, Inc. is a national retailer primarily focused on selling home appliances, hardware, tools and lawn and garden equipment. The company and its dealers and franchisees operate approximately 1,260 stores across all 50 states and Puerto Rico and Bermuda. In addition to merchandise, it provides its customers with access to a full suite of services, including home delivery and installation and product protection agreements. The firm operates through the Sears Hometown and Hardware segment and the Sears Outlet segment. The Sears Hometown and Hardware segment's stores (1,109) are designed to provide its customers with in-store and online access to a wide selection of home appliances, tools, lawn and garden equipment, sporting goods, consumer electronics and household goods, depending on the particular store. Most of its hometown stores carry proprietary Sears brand products, such as Kenmore, Craftsman, and DieHard, as well as a wide assortment of other national brands. The Sears Outlet stores (151) are designed to provide its customers with in-store and online access to purchase new, one-of-a-kind, out-of-carton, discontinued, obsolete, used, reconditioned, overstocked and scratched and dented products, collectively referred to as outlet-value products, across a broad assortment of merchandise categories, including home appliances, lawn and garden equipment, apparel, mattresses, televisions, sporting goods and tools, and at prices that are significantly lower than manufacturers' suggested retail prices.

FINANCIAL DATA: Note: Data for latest year may not have been available at press time.

In U.S. $	2015	2014	2013	2012	2011	2010
Revenue	2,356,033,000	2,421,562,000	2,453,606,000	2,344,199,000	2,347,387,000	
R&D Expense						
Operating Income	-171,159,000	61,075,000	99,525,000	55,274,000	82,462,000	
Operating Margin %	-7.26%					
SGA Expense	546,636,000	506,630,000	504,400,000	458,635,000	442,296,000	
Net Income	-168,805,000	35,550,000	60,080,000	33,056,000	49,756,000	
Operating Cash Flow	24,400,000	-54,368,000	121,584,000	38,465,000	48,954,000	
Capital Expenditure	12,849,000	10,704,000	8,110,000	9,991,000	5,819,000	
EBITDA	-157,838,000	73,081,000	110,353,000	65,470,000	94,071,000	
Return on Assets %	-22.61%	4.35%	8.35%	5.07%		
Return on Equity %	-33.34%	6.14%	10.88%	6.14%		
Debt to Equity						

CONTACT INFORMATION:

Phone: 847 286-2500   Fax:
Toll-Free:
Address: 5500 Trillium Blvd., Ste. 501, Hoffman Estates, IL 60176 United States

STOCK TICKER/OTHER:

Stock Ticker: SHOS
Employees: 3,634
Parent Company:

Exchange: NAS
Fiscal Year Ends: 01/31

SALARIES/BONUSES:

Top Exec. Salary: Bonus: $623,891
$1,000,000
Second Exec. Salary: Bonus: $232,349
$550,000

OTHER THOUGHTS:

Estimated Female Officers or Directors: 3

Hot Spot for Advancement for Women/Minorities: Y

Seven & I Holdings Co Ltd

NAIC Code: 445120

TYPES OF BUSINESS:

Retail Operations
Insurance-Health, Property & Specialty
IT/Information Services
Convenience Stores
Restaurants
Superstores & Supermarkets
Department Stores
Banking Services & Electronic Cash Cards

BRANDS/DIVISIONS/AFFILIATES:

7-Eleven Inc
Sogo & Seibu Co Ltd
Ito-Yokado Co Ltd
York Mart
York-Benimaru
Poppo
Seven Premium
Seven Financial Service Co Ltd

CONTACTS: *Note: Officers with more than one job title may be intentionally listed here more than once.*

Toshifumi Suzuki, CEO
Noritoshi Murata, COO
Noritoshi Murata, Pres.
Kunio Takahashi, CFO
Yasuhiro Suzuki, CIO
Atsushi Kamei, Pres., Ito-Yokado Co., Ltd.
Zenko Oh taka, Pres., York-Benimaru Co., Ltd.
Ryu Matsumoto, Pres., Sogo & Seibu Co., Ltd.
Toshifumi Suzuki, Chmn.
Joseph M. DePinto, CEO

GROWTH PLANS/SPECIAL FEATURES:

Seven & I Holdings Co., Ltd. is a holding company that plan: manages and operates a large network of companies based Japan. The company owns and operates approximately 55,00 stores in several countries. The firm operates in six primar business areas: convenience stores; department store: superstores; food services; financial services, includin insurance; and others. The convenience store operation include 7-Eleven stores located in Japan, North America an China (Beijing, Tianjin, and Chengdu). U.S.-based subsidiar 7-Eleven, Inc. handles the worldwide licensing and franchis rights to the 7-Eleven brand. Seven & I's department store segment, through subsidiary Sogo & Seibu Co. Ltd., operate stores under brands Sogo and Seibu. The superstore segment consists of a number of retail chains, includin Japanese fashion giant Ito-Yokado and food supermarkets i Japan and Beijing such as York-Benimaru and York Mart. Thi division also includes the company's specialty retail stores including lifestyle merchandise stores under the name Lof music stores under the Tower Records brand, sporting good: outlets under the Oshman's name and maternity and bab stores operated as Akachan Honpo. The food service: segment operates restaurants (including Denny's-branded and other specialty restaurants), cafeterias and fast foo establishments (primarily Poppo-branded stores) in Japan and restaurants in Beijing. The financial services segment include: ATM operations, credit card operations, electronic mone; services, leasing and insurance in Japan, and operates throug subsidiaries Seven Financial Service Co. Ltd.; Seven Carc Service Co. Ltd.; Seven CS Card Service Co. Ltd.; Seven Banl Ltd.; and K.K. York Insurance. The other segmen encompasses real estate, security and manufacturing and processing businesses as well as its Internet-related service: businesses, which include online marketplace and auction wet sites under subsidiary Seven & I Netmedia Co. Ltd. Seven & has a private brand, Seven Premium, touting high quality as it: products' main appeal.

FINANCIAL DATA: *Note: Data for latest year may not have been available at press time.*

In U.S. $	2015	2014	2013	2012	2011	2010
Revenue	49,007,090,000	45,703,180,000	40,508,030,000	38,842,000,000	41,547,550,000	41,479,040,000
R&D Expense						
Operating Income	2,786,190,000	2,756,391,000	2,399,534,000	2,370,117,000	1,974,794,000	1,839,433,000
Operating Margin %	5.68%	6.03%	5.92%	6.10%	4.75%	4.43%
SGA Expense	2,475,541,000	2,091,515,000	1,897,789,000	1,775,786,000	1,696,614,000	1,700,291,000
Net Income	1,481,433,000	1,526,042,000	1,232,557,000	1,140,660,000	908,582,600	364,168,300
Operating Cash Flow	3,381,510,000	3,687,006,000	3,176,326,000	3,754,419,000	2,519,980,000	2,614,724,000
Capital Expenditure	2,490,562,000	2,349,074,000	2,401,344,000	1,791,805,000	2,496,088,000	1,358,057,000
EBITDA	4,144,239,000	3,948,655,000	3,603,420,000	3,170,589,000	3,084,333,000	2,774,090,000
Return on Assets %	3.44%	3.87%	3.38%	3.40%	3.02%	1.21%
Return on Equity %	7.86%	8.80%	7.54%	7.48%	6.53%	2.55%
Debt to Equity	0.29	0.33	0.27	0.25	0.25	0.25

CONTACT INFORMATION:

Phone: 81-3-6238-3000   Fax:
Toll-Free:
Address: 8-8, Nibancho, Chiyoda-ku, Tokyo, 102-8452 Japan

STOCK TICKER/OTHER:

Stock Ticker: SVNDF   Exchange: PINX
Employees: 52,814   Fiscal Year Ends: 02/28
Parent Company:

SALARIES/BONUSES:

Top Exec. Salary: $ Bonus: $
Second Exec. Salary: $ Bonus: $

OTHER THOUGHTS:

Estimated Female Officers or Directors: 2
Hot Spot for Advancement for Women/Minorities:

Sherwin Williams Company (The)

www.sherwin-williams.com

NAIC Code: 325510

TYPES OF BUSINESS:

Paints & Coatings Manufacturing
Retail Paint Stores
Wall Coverings
Automotive Finishing Products
Design Consulting

BRANDS/DIVISIONS/AFFILIATES:

Sherwin-Williams
Sayerlack
Pratt & Lambert
Martin Senour
Dutch Boy
Thompson's
Minwax
Krylon

CONTACTS: *Note: Officers with more than one job title may be intentionally listed here more than once.*

Christopher Connor, CEO
Sean Hennessy, CFO
Allen Mistysyn, Chief Accounting Officer
John Morikis, COO
Catherine Kilbane, General Counsel
Mike Conway, Other Corporate Officer
Robert Davisson, President, Divisional
David Sewell, President, Divisional
Robert Wells, Senior VP, Divisional
Thomas Hopkins, Senior VP, Divisional
Steven Oberfeld, Senior VP, Divisional

GROWTH PLANS/SPECIAL FEATURES:

The Sherwin-Williams Company is one of the largest international manufacturers, distributors and retailers of paint and related products to professional, industrial, commercial and retail customers. The company operates in four segments: paint stores group, consumer group, global finishes group and Latin America coatings group. The paint stores group consists of 4,003 company-operated stores, which sell Sherwin-Williams brand architectural paint, coatings and other associated products and brands. Several subsidiaries operate under this division, including Duron, Inc., a Maryland paint producer. It has operations in the U.S., Canada, Puerto Rico, Jamaica, St. Maarten, Curacao, Trinidad and Tobago and the Virgin Islands. This division also sells industrial products, marine products and finishes for original equipment manufacturers (OEM). The consumer group produces and distributes paint, coatings and related products to third-party customers and to the paint stores group (which represented 66% of the consumer group's sales in 2014). The global finishes group, through 300 branches, manufactures, licenses, distributes and sells paints and coatings, industrial and marine products, automotive finishes, refinish products and OEM coatings throughout Europe, North and South American and Asia. The Latin America coatings group develops, licenses, manufactures and sells architectural paint and coatings, OEM product finishes and protective and marine products in North and South America. The segment maintains 276 company-operated stores. In all segments, the company's varnish, applicators, paint, finishes and coatings are marketed under various name brands, including several private labels such as Sherwin-Williams, Sayerlack, Pratt & Lambert, Martin Senour, Dutch Boy, Thompson's, Minwax and Krylon.

FINANCIAL DATA: *Note: Data for latest year may not have been available at press time.*

In U.S. $	2015	2014	2013	2012	2011	2010
Revenue		11,129,530,000	10,185,530,000	9,534,462,000	8,765,699,000	7,776,424,000
R&D Expense						
Operating Income		1,304,036,000	1,146,366,000	946,578,000	775,525,000	744,669,000
Operating Margin %		11.71%	11.25%	9.92%	8.84%	9.57%
SGA Expense		3,822,966,000	3,467,681,000	3,259,648,000	2,963,545,000	2,728,122,000
Net Income		865,887,000	752,561,000	631,034,000	441,860,000	462,485,000
Operating Cash Flow		1,081,528,000	1,083,766,000	887,886,000	735,812,000	706,590,000
Capital Expenditure		200,545,000	166,680,000	157,112,000	153,801,000	125,162,000
EBITDA		1,521,376,000	1,336,466,000	1,129,299,000	964,949,000	923,690,000
Return on Assets %		14.32%	11.92%	11.00%	8.49%	9.74%
Return on Equity %		63.42%	43.94%	41.41%	32.14%	34.68%
Debt to Equity		1.12	0.64	0.96	0.47	0.46

CONTACT INFORMATION:

Phone: 216 566-2000   Fax:
Toll-Free: 800-474-3794
Address: 101 W. Prospect Ave., Cleveland, OH 44115 United States

SALARIES/BONUSES:

Top Exec. Salary:
$1,221,987

Bonus: $

Second Exec. Salary:
$849,444

Bonus: $

STOCK TICKER/OTHER:

Stock Ticker: SHW
Employees: 39,674
Parent Company:

Exchange: NYS
Fiscal Year Ends: 12/31

OTHER THOUGHTS:

Estimated Female Officers or Directors: 2

Hot Spot for Advancement for Women/Minorities: Y

Shoe Carnival Inc

NAIC Code: 448210

www.shoecarnival.com

TYPES OF BUSINESS:

Shoes, Retail
Accessories
Online Sales

BRANDS/DIVISIONS/AFFILIATES:

UNR8ED
Solanz
Cabrizi
Donna Lawrence
WHEN YOU WANT 2
Laces for Learning
Victoria Spenser
Y-NOT?

CONTACTS: *Note: Officers with more than one job title may be intentionally listed here more than once.*

Clifton Sifford, CEO
W. Jackson, CFO
J. Weaver, Chairman of the Board
Timothy Baker, Executive VP, Divisional
Carl Scibetta, Executive VP
David Kapp, Secretary

GROWTH PLANS/SPECIAL FEATURES:

Shoe Carnival, Inc. is one of the largest family footwear retailers in the U.S. The company operates 400 stores in 34 states and Puerto Rico. These stores are primarily located in strip malls and offer an assortment of both name brand and private label dress, casual and athletic footwear for men, women and children as well as boots, sandals and accessories. On average, each location carries approximately 28,200 pairs of shoes. Athletic merchandise is the highest earning product group, accounting for 50% of sales; women's merchandise, 27%; children's, 14%; men's, 14%; and accessories and miscellaneous items, 4%. Besides footwear from nationally-recognized brands, the company sells merchandise under its owned labels, including: Shoe Carnival, The Carnival, Donna Lawrence, Victoria Spenser, Innocence, Y-NOT?, UNR8ED, Solanz, Cabrizi, Shoe Perks, WHEN YOU WANT 2, JUMP BACK IN, STEP OUT OF BORING and Laces for Learning. The company emphasizes the creation of an exciting, fun retail environment through the use of marketing tactics, such as utilizing bold colors and graphics as well as setting up a stage and microphone at each store front's entry and announcing various games and contests throughout the day, offering prizes to customers, such as on-the-spot discounts on purchases. In conjunction with its extensive in-store promotions, the firm uses television, radio and newspaper ads to announce special sale products. ShoeCarnival.com allows customers the option of shopping online.

FINANCIAL DATA: *Note: Data for latest year may not have been available at press time.*

In U.S. $	2015	2014	2013	2012	2011	2010
Revenue	940,162,000	884,785,000	854,998,000	762,534,000	739,189,000	682,422,000
R&D Expense						
Operating Income	41,853,000	43,667,000	48,494,000	42,137,000	42,385,000	25,130,000
Operating Margin %	4.45%	4.93%	5.67%	5.52%	5.73%	3.68%
SGA Expense	231,826,000	215,650,000	208,983,000	182,716,000	179,154,000	168,476,000
Net Income	25,527,000	26,871,000	29,338,000	26,382,000	26,821,000	15,166,000
Operating Cash Flow	57,654,000	38,620,000	25,850,000	30,875,000	29,423,000	27,897,000
Capital Expenditure	33,543,000	30,966,000	25,977,000	21,260,000	14,412,000	9,794,000
EBITDA	61,930,000	61,107,000	64,481,000	56,666,000	56,285,000	40,151,000
Return on Assets %	5.66%	6.36%	7.39%	7.21%	8.16%	5.01%
Return on Equity %	7.87%	8.82%	10.18%	9.80%	11.26%	7.11%
Debt to Equity						

CONTACT INFORMATION:

Phone: 812 867-6471   Fax: 812 867-4055
Toll-Free: 800-430-7463
Address: 7500 E. Columbia St., Evansville, IN 47715 United States

SALARIES/BONUSES:

Top Exec. Salary: $575,000   Bonus: $
Second Exec. Salary: $520,000   Bonus: $

STOCK TICKER/OTHER:

Stock Ticker: SCVL
Employees: 5,900
Parent Company:

Exchange: NAS
Fiscal Year Ends: 01/31

OTHER THOUGHTS:

Estimated Female Officers or Directors: 4
Hot Spot for Advancement for Women/Minorities: Y

Shopify

NAIC Code: 511210K

TYPES OF BUSINESS:
Computer Software, Sales & Customer Relations

BRANDS/DIVISIONS/AFFILIATES:
Shopify Plus
www.shopify.com/plus

CONTACTS: Note: Officers with more than one job title may be intentionally listed here more than once.
Russell Jones, CFO
Tobias Lutke, Chairman of the Board
Craig Miller, Chief Marketing Officer
Cody Fauser, Chief Technology Officer
Joseph Frasca, General Counsel
Daniel Weinand, Other Executive Officer
Harley Finkelstein, Other Executive Officer
Toby Shannan, Vice President, Divisional
Brittany Forsyth, Vice President, Divisional

GROWTH PLANS/SPECIAL FEATURES:
Shopify is a cloud-based, multi-channel commerce platform designed for small- and medium-sized businesses. Merchants can use the Shopify software to design, set up and manage their stores across multiple sales channels, including web, mobile, social media, brick-and-mortar locations and pop-up shops. The platform also provides merchants with a back-office and single view of their business. Currently, the company powers over 175,000 businesses in approximately 150 countries, including Tesla Motors, Budweiser, Wikipedia, LA Lakers, the New York Stock Exchange and GoldieBlox. Shopify offers a free 14-day trial and provides its packages and rates in four groups: lite, basic, pro and unlimited. Lite is $9 per month, is without a personal online store, but features items on all Shopify points of sale (POS) references and Facebook. Basic is $29 per month, comes with a personal online store, and items can be sold via the online store, POS, Facebook and Pinterest. Pro is $79 per month, comprises all of the Basic package but credit card purchase rates are cheaper, among other incentives. Unlimited is $179 per month, with credit card purchase rates being cheaper than that of Pro, among other incentives. All packages allow an unlimited number of featured products, no transaction fees, discount codes and an unlimited amount of file storage. Shopify Plus is a cloud-based, fully-hosted enterprise e-commerce platform for high-volume merchants. Its website can be found at www.shopify.com/plus.

FINANCIAL DATA: Note: Data for latest year may not have been available at press time.

In U.S. $	2015	2014	2013	2012	2011	2010
Revenue		105,018,000	50,252,000	23,713,000		
R&D Expense		25,915,000	13,682,000	6,452,000		
Operating Income		-21,615,000	-4,269,000	-1,514,000		
Operating Margin %		-20.58%	-8.49%	-6.38%		
SGA Expense		57,495,000	27,326,000	13,999,000		
Net Income		-22,311,000	-4,837,000	-1,232,000		
Operating Cash Flow		-801,000	1,396,000	2,041,000		
Capital Expenditure		22,700,000	4,504,000	2,016,000		
EBITDA		-16,943,000	-2,511,000	-747,000		
Return on Assets %		-23.36%	-5.04%			
Return on Equity %						
Debt to Equity						

CONTACT INFORMATION:
Phone: 1-888-746-7439   Fax:
Toll-Free:
Address: 150 Elgin St., Fl. 8, Ottawa, ON K2P 1L4 Canada

STOCK TICKER/OTHER:
Stock Ticker: SHOP
Employees: 632
Parent Company:

Exchange: NYS
Fiscal Year Ends:

SALARIES/BONUSES:
Top Exec. Salary: $ Bonus: $
Second Exec. Salary: $ Bonus: $

OTHER THOUGHTS:
Estimated Female Officers or Directors:
Hot Spot for Advancement for Women/Minorities:

Sales, profits and employees may be estimates. Financial information, benefits and other data can change quickly and may vary from those stated here.

Shopko Stores Operating Co LLC

www.shopko.com

NAIC Code: 452112

TYPES OF BUSINESS:

Discount Department Stores
Optical Centers
Pharmacies

BRANDS/DIVISIONS/AFFILIATES:

Shopko Express Rx
Sun Capital Partners Inc
Shopko
Shopko Hometown
Bailey's Point
NorthCrest
Energy Zone
Soft Sensations

CONTACTS: *Note: Officers with more than one job title may be intentionally listed here more than once.*

Peter K. McMahon, CEO
Michael J. Bettiga, COO
Brian W. Bender, CFO
Jill A. Soltau, Chief Merch. Officer
Gary Gibson, VP-Treas.
James Ruben, Founder

GROWTH PLANS/SPECIAL FEATURES:

Shopko Stores Operating Co. LLC is a specialty discoun
retailer located primarily in mid-size and larger communitie
Shopko organizes its operations into two divisions: Shopko an
Shopko Express Rx. The company's 344 Shopko store
located in 24 states, are multi-department retail stores, carryin
products in such categories as home, family basics, casua
apparel and seasonal. Name brands available in Shopko store
include Nike, Adidas, Reebok, Kitchen Aid, Fisher-Price an
Sony. Private label brands include Bailey's Point, NorthCres
Energy Zone, Soft Sensations and Green Soda. The Shopk
Express Rx division has five stores. Shopko Express Rx store
have a neighborhood drug store format and provid
professional pharmacy services, health and wellness product
and information, home business solutions, photo processing
food and beverages and traditional drug store merchandise
The company has three distribution centers in DePere
Wisconsin; Boise, Idaho; and Omaha, Nebraska. Shopko is a
affiliate of private investment firm Sun Capital Partners, Inc
The company's 203 Shopko Hometown stores aim to meet th
needs of smaller communities, offering food items, consumable
goods, home products and apparel as well as national an
private brand merchandise.

Shopko offers its employees a 401(k) plan; educationa
assistance; flexible spending accounts; medical, dental an
vision insurance; and service recognition awards.

FINANCIAL DATA: *Note: Data for latest year may not have been available at press time.*

In U.S. $	2015	2014	2013	2012	2011	2010
Revenue		2,860,000,000	2,850,000,000	2,600,000,000	2,000,000,000	2,300,000,000
R&D Expense						
Operating Income						
Operating Margin %						
SGA Expense						
Net Income						
Operating Cash Flow						
Capital Expenditure						
EBITDA						
Return on Assets %						
Return on Equity %						
Debt to Equity						

CONTACT INFORMATION:

Phone: 920-429-2211   Fax: 920-429-4799
Toll-Free: 800-869-5819
Address: 700 Pilgrim Way, Green Bay, WI 54304 United States

STOCK TICKER/OTHER:

Stock Ticker: Private   Exchange:
Employees: 16,000   Fiscal Year Ends: 01/31
Parent Company: SUN CAPITAL PARTNERS INC

SALARIES/BONUSES:

Top Exec. Salary: $ Bonus: $
Second Exec. Salary: $ Bonus: $

OTHER THOUGHTS:

Estimated Female Officers or Directors: 2
Hot Spot for Advancement for Women/Minorities: Y

Shoppers Drug Mart Inc

www.shoppersdrugmart.ca

NAIC Code: 446110

TYPES OF BUSINESS:
Merchandising
Specialty Stores
Pharmaceuticals
Home Health Care Products
Cosmetics

BRANDS/DIVISIONS/AFFILIATES:
Loblaw Companies Limited
Shoppers Drug Mart Corporation
Pharamprix Inc
Shoppers Simply Pharmacy
Shoppers Home Health Care
HealthWATCH
MediSystem Technologies Inc
Shoppers Drug Mart Specialty Health Network Inc

CONTACTS: Note: Officers with more than one job title may be intentionally listed here more than once.
Mike Motz, Pres.
Mary Kelly, Sr. VP-Merch. & Category Mgmt.
Frank Perdinelli, General Counsel
Mike Motz, Exec. VP-Oper.
Geoffrey Martin, Sr. VP-Bus. Dev.
Erik Botines, Sr. VP-Peers Rel.
John Caplice, Sr. VP-Investor Rel. & Corp. Affairs
John Caplice, Treas.
Loreen Paananen, Exec. VP-Retail Dev.
Mark Valesano, Exec. VP-Pharmacy
Terry Landry, Sr. VP-Pharmaprix
Paul Damiani, Sr. VP-Health Care Businesses
Galen G. Weston, Chmn.
Kevin Whibbs, Sr. VP-Supply Chain & Logistics

GROWTH PLANS/SPECIAL FEATURES:
Shoppers Drug Mart, Inc. (also known as Shoppers Drug Mart Corporation) is the licenser of full-service drug stores operating under the name Shoppers Drug Mart (Pharmaprix in Quebec). The firm is a subsidiary of Loblaw Companies Limited. Today, there are more than 1,253 Shoppers Drug Mart and Pharmaprix retail drug stores owned and operated by the company's licensed associates. The firm also licenses or operates over 50 medical clinic pharmacies operating as Shoppers Simply Pharmacy (Pharmaprix Simplement Sante in Quebec); 62 Shoppers Home Health Care stores, a retailer of assisted-living and mobility devices such as wheelchairs, walkers and modified vehicles; and six stand-alone beauty destinations under the Murale brand. The firm's proprietary brands include Life Brand, Quo and SANIS products. Shoppers Drug Mart also offers the HealthWATCH program, which provides patient counseling with respect to medications, disease management and health and wellness. In addition to its retail network, the company also owns MediSystem Technologies, Inc., a provider of pharmaceutical products and services to long-term care facilities in Ontario and Alberta; and Shoppers Drug Mart Specialty Health Network, Inc., a provider of specialty drug distribution, pharmacy and patient support services.

FINANCIAL DATA: Note: Data for latest year may not have been available at press time.

In U.S. $	2015	2014	2013	2012	2011	2010
Revenue		11,057,659,000	11,216,939,008	10,937,154,560	10,519,665,664	10,436,599,808
R&D Expense						
Operating Income						
Operating Margin %						
SGA Expense						
Net Income		601,685,000	610,352,000	617,245,888	617,515,648	594,189,312
Operating Cash Flow						
Capital Expenditure						
EBITDA						
Return on Assets %						
Return on Equity %						
Debt to Equity						

CONTACT INFORMATION:
Phone: 416 493-1220   Fax: 416 490-2700
Toll-Free:
Address: 243 Consumers Rd., Toronto, ON M2J 4W8 Canada

STOCK TICKER/OTHER:
Stock Ticker: Subsidiary   Exchange:
Employees: 1,323   Fiscal Year Ends: 12/31
Parent Company: Loblaw Companies Limited

SALARIES/BONUSES:
Top Exec. Salary: $ Bonus: $
Second Exec. Salary: $ Bonus: $

OTHER THOUGHTS:
Estimated Female Officers or Directors: 6
Hot Spot for Advancement for Women/Minorities: Y

Sales, profits and employees may be estimates. Financial information, benefits and other data can change quickly and may vary from those stated here.

Shoprite Holdings Limited

NAIC Code: 452910

www.shoprite.co.za

TYPES OF BUSINESS:

Warehouse Clubs and Supercenters

BRANDS/DIVISIONS/AFFILIATES:

Shoprite Checkers
Checkers Hypers
Usave
OK Furniture
OK Power Express
House & Home
Hungry Lion
MediRite

CONTACTS: *Note: Officers with more than one job title may be intentionally listed here more than once.*

J. Whitey Basson, CEO
P.C. Engelbrecht, COO
Marius Bosman, Dir.-Finance
Christoffel H. Wiese, Chmn.

GROWTH PLANS/SPECIAL FEATURES:

Shoprite Holdings Ltd. is engaged in the owning and operation of supermarkets and franchise outlets, offering food, clothing, general merchandise, cosmetics, liquor, furniture, household appliances and pharmaceutical products, among others. One of Africa's largest food retailers, the firm operates through 1,751 corporate and 360 franchise outlets in 15 countries across Africa and the Indian Ocean Islands. It operates primarily through the Shoprite Checkers supermarket group, consisting of 541 Shoprite supermarkets, 197 Checkers supermarkets, 33 Checkers Hypers, 333 Usave stores, 374 OK Furniture outlets, 33 OK Power Express stores, 12 OK Furniture Dreams stores, 52 House & Home stores, 176 Hungry Lion fast food outlets, 156 MediRite pharmacies and 293 LiquorShops. The company's ticketing business, Computicket, operates 1,258 counters in its group stores, as well as 40 free-standing outlets. Shoprite's OK Franchise division procures and distributes stock to 49 OK MiniMark convenience stores, 18 OK Foods supermarkets, 86 OK Grocer stores, 28 Megasave wholesale stores, 33 OK Value stores, 26 Enjoy stores, 64 Sentra stores, as well as 47 Friendly supermarkets, three Friendly Liquor stores, one OK Express and one OK Liquor store. Its Checkers, Checkers Hyper and House & Home stores direct their sales toward higher income demographics, while Shoprite and OK Furniture aim for the middle to lower income demographics. Shoprite Usave markets toward the lower demographic. The company has a 72% market share in South Africa.

FINANCIAL DATA: *Note: Data for latest year may not have been available at press time.*

In U.S. $	2015	2014	2013	2012	2011	2010
Revenue	7,923,810,000	7,123,024,000	6,463,949,000	5,765,841,000	5,038,734,000	4,697,558,000
R&D Expense						
Operating Income	430,919,100	397,814,400	373,493,600	318,021,800	272,345,200	236,056,800
Operating Margin %	5.43%	5.58%	5.77%	5.51%	5.40%	5.02%
SGA Expense						
Net Income	287,418,800	259,959,300	250,739,500	210,933,800	176,294,400	159,411,200
Operating Cash Flow	261,771,400	398,650,700	79,982,370	232,416,400	107,583,100	105,220,100
Capital Expenditure	322,753,800	272,574,000			209,446,300	174,888,400
EBITDA	589,821,900	519,221,700	467,644,500	394,009,000	344,005,200	305,880,600
Return on Assets %	9.76%	10.07%	11.17%	11.72%	12.97%	13.05%
Return on Equity %	22.71%	23.02%	25.76%	30.52%	38.64%	41.72%
Debt to Equity	0.22	0.25	0.25	0.31	0.06	0.07

CONTACT INFORMATION:

Phone: 27 219804284   Fax: 27 219804468
Toll-Free:
Address: Cnr William Dabs and Old Paarl Roads, Brackenfell, Western Cape, 7561 South Africa

STOCK TICKER/OTHER:

Stock Ticker: SRHGF   Exchange: PINX
Employees: 123,100   Fiscal Year Ends: 06/30
Parent Company:

SALARIES/BONUSES:

Top Exec. Salary: $ Bonus: $
Second Exec. Salary: $ Bonus: $

OTHER THOUGHTS:

Estimated Female Officers or Directors:
Hot Spot for Advancement for Women/Minorities:

Siam FamilyMart Co Ltd

www.familymart.co.th

NAIC Code: 445120

TYPES OF BUSINESS:

Convenience Stores

BRANDS/DIVISIONS/AFFILIATES:

FamilyMart Co Ltd
FamilyMart

GROWTH PLANS/SPECIAL FEATURES:

Siam FamilyMart Co., Ltd. is the Thai subsidiary of Japanese convenience store operator FamilyMart Co., Ltd., with 1,000 store and 3,000 outlet locations throughout Thailand. The company franchises the FamilyMart stores in Thailand, which sells packaged food products, hot snacks, sandwiches, electronic products and other daily necessities. The firm provides its franchisees with store layouts, managerial strategies, training courses, advertising services, IT assistance and tax and accounting assistance. Siam FamilyMart also provides the systems and software necessary to implement a POS (point of sale) system at each store. Its field counselors visit each franchised store location on a weekly basis for a consultation on the store's operations. FamilyMart stores are open 24 hours a day and are a minimum of 330 square feet in size, including storage space.

CONTACTS: Note: Officers with more than one job title may be intentionally listed here more than once.

Chiranun Phuphat, Pres.
Rutsadanu Meesri, VP-Oper.
Uchida Kazutaka, CFO
Akarin Phureesith, Sr. Exec. VP-Prod. Mgmt. & Purchasing
Phong Sakuntanak, VP-Human Franchise
Sumitra Kammart, Chief Officer-Merch. Support Center
Ratchapa Khampee, Gen. Mgr.-Legal Support Center
Piratpon Gopatta, Chief Officer-Corp. Planning
Pajaree Wongtrangan, Asst. Chief Officer-Acct. & Internal Audit
Phatsakorn Siwaleelawilart, Chief Officer-Store Dev.
Hisatomi Takashi, Asst. Chief Officer-Logistics

FINANCIAL DATA: Note: Data for latest year may not have been available at press time.

In U.S. $	2015	2014	2013	2012	2011	2010
Revenue						
R&D Expense						
Operating Income						
Operating Margin %						
SGA Expense						
Net Income						
Operating Cash Flow						
Capital Expenditure						
EBITDA						
Return on Assets %						
Return on Equity %						
Debt to Equity						

CONTACT INFORMATION:

Phone: 66-2836-5999   Fax: 66-2836-5998
Toll-Free:
Address: 9/99 at Central Plaza Rama, Level 21 Moo 2 Tambon, Bangkok, 11120 Thailand

STOCK TICKER/OTHER:

Stock Ticker: Subsidiary
Employees:
Parent Company: FAMILYMART CO LTD

Exchange:
Fiscal Year Ends:

SALARIES/BONUSES:

Top Exec. Salary: $ Bonus: $
Second Exec. Salary: $ Bonus: $

OTHER THOUGHTS:

Estimated Female Officers or Directors: 5
Hot Spot for Advancement for Women/Minorities: Y

Sales, profits and employees may be estimates. Financial information, benefits and other data can change quickly and may vary from those stated here.

Signet Jewelers Limited (Zale, Kay & Sterling Jewelers)

www.signetjewelers.com

NAIC Code: 448310

TYPES OF BUSINESS:

Jewelry, Retail
Online Sales
Earring Stores

BRANDS/DIVISIONS/AFFILIATES:

Kay Jewelers
Piercing Pagoda Inc
Jared, The Galleria of Jewelry
Zale Jewelers
Gordon's Jewelers
H. Samuel
Ernest Jones
Peoples Jewelers

CONTACTS:
Note: Officers with more than one job title may be intentionally listed here more than once.

Mark Light, CEO
Robert Trabucco, CFO, Divisional
Michele Santana, CFO
Daniel Shull, Chief Information Officer
George Murray, Chief Marketing Officer
Ed Hrabak, COO
Sebastian Hobbs, Managing Director, Geographical
Shaun Carney, Other Corporate Officer
Lynn Dennison, Other Executive Officer
Steven Becker, Other Executive Officer
Mark Jenkins, Other Executive Officer
James Garlish, Senior VP, Divisional

GROWTH PLANS/SPECIAL FEATURES:

Signet Jewelers Limited is one of the largest specialty reta jewelry operators in the world, selling gold, silver, diamond an gemstone jewelry, watches, collectibles and gifts. Signe divides its company's operations into three divisions: the Sterling Jewelers, the Zale and the UK Jewelry division. The Sterling Jewelers division operates 1,504 stores in 50 U.S states in malls and off-mall locations as Kay Jewelers, Jared' The Galleria of Jewelry (Jared's) and regionally under number of well-established mall-based brands. The Zale division consists of two sub-divisions: Zale Jewelry and Piercing Pagoda. Zale Jewelry has 972 jewelry stores locate primarily in shopping malls throughout the US, Canada and Puerto Rico. It includes national brands Zales Jewelers, Zale Outlet and Peoples Jewelers, along with regional brands Gordon's Jewelers and Mappins Jewelers. Piercing Pagoda operates 605 mall-based kiosks at located primarily ir shopping malls throughout the US and Puerto Rico. The UK Jewelry division operates 498 stores, with locations in major regional shopping malls as H. Samuel, Ernest Jones and Leslie Davis.

The company offers its employees medical, dental and vision insurance; prescription drug coverage; tuition assistance; 401(k) plan; a discounted stock purchase plan; and life and disability insurance.

FINANCIAL DATA:
Note: Data for latest year may not have been available at press time.

In U.S. $	2015	2014	2013	2012	2011	2010
Revenue	5,736,300,000	4,209,200,000	3,983,400,000	3,749,200,000	3,437,400,000	3,290,700,000
R&D Expense						
Operating Income	576,600,000	570,500,000	560,500,000	507,400,000	372,500,000	275,800,000
Operating Margin %	10.05%	13.55%	14.07%	13.53%	10.83%	8.38%
SGA Expense	1,712,900,000	1,196,700,000	1,138,300,000	1,056,700,000	980,400,000	916,500,000
Net Income	381,300,000	368,000,000	359,900,000	324,400,000	200,400,000	164,100,000
Operating Cash Flow	283,000,000	235,500,000	312,700,000	325,200,000	323,900,000	515,400,000
Capital Expenditure	220,200,000	152,700,000	134,200,000	97,800,000	57,500,000	43,600,000
EBITDA	726,300,000	680,700,000	659,900,000	599,800,000	471,000,000	385,500,000
Return on Assets %	7.36%	9.50%	9.82%	9.68%	6.66%	5.58%
Return on Equity %	14.19%	15.04%	15.61%	15.38%	10.72%	9.63%
Debt to Equity	0.48					0.15

CONTACT INFORMATION:

Phone: 441 296-5872   Fax:
Toll-Free:
Address: 375 Ghent St., Akron, OH 44333 United States

STOCK TICKER/OTHER:

Stock Ticker: SIG
Employees: 28,949
Parent Company:

Exchange: NYS
Fiscal Year Ends: 01/31

SALARIES/BONUSES:

Top Exec. Salary: $970,500   Bonus: $
Second Exec. Salary: Bonus: $
$858,248

OTHER THOUGHTS:

Estimated Female Officers or Directors: 2
Hot Spot for Advancement for Women/Minorities:

Skechers USA Inc

www.skx.com

NAIC Code: 424340

TYPES OF BUSINESS:

Footwear Distribution
Retail Stores
E-commerce Sites
Factory Outlet Stores
Concept Stores

BRANDS/DIVISIONS/AFFILIATES:

Skechers USA
Skechers Sport
BOBS from Skechers
Sketchers Work
Skechers Kids
GOrun
GOwalk
GObionic

CONTACTS: *Note: Officers with more than one job title may be intentionally listed here more than once.*

Robert Greenberg, CEO
David Weinberg, CFO
Jeffrey Greenberg, Director
Mark Nason, Executive VP, Divisional
Philip Paccione, Executive VP, Divisional
Michael Greenberg, President

GROWTH PLANS/SPECIAL FEATURES:

Skechers U.S.A., Inc. is a manufacturer and marketer of footwear operating 362 domestic and 87 international Skechers retail concept stores, factory outlets and warehouse outlets. The company targets fashion-conscious consumers ages 12-24. It offers an array of styles for men, women and children subdivided into two categories, lifestyle and Skechers performance. The lifestyle brands include Skechers USA, Skechers Sport, Skechers Active, BOBS from Skechers, Skechers Work and Skechers Kids. Skechers performance specialty fitness brands consist of technical footwear designed for specific activities such as GOrun, GOwalk, GOtrain, GOgolf and GObionic. Skechers products are also sold by department and specialty stores, athletic and independent retailers and boutiques as well as catalog and Internet retailers in more than 100 countries and territories throughout the world and on its e-commerce site Skechers.com. Skechers products can be purchased from over 900 retailers internationally. In Europe, the company's direct distribution operations are handled through a warehouse in Liege, Belgium as well a Swiss subsidiary that oversees its international sales, marketing and distribution.

FINANCIAL DATA: *Note: Data for latest year may not have been available at press time.*

In U.S. $	2015	2014	2013	2012	2011	2010
Revenue		2,386,668,000	1,854,095,000	1,567,425,000	1,613,574,000	2,011,436,000
R&D Expense						
Operating Income		209,071,000	93,609,000	22,319,000	-133,793,000	196,740,000
Operating Margin %		8.76%	5.04%	1.42%	-8.29%	9.78%
SGA Expense		871,941,000	732,917,000	668,111,000	765,099,000	719,734,000
Net Income		138,811,000	54,788,000	9,512,000	-67,484,000	136,148,000
Operating Cash Flow		163,882,000	98,977,000	-3,447,000	164,919,000	-47,379,000
Capital Expenditure		56,905,000	41,381,000	52,452,000	122,248,000	82,310,000
EBITDA		252,150,000	137,414,000	66,245,000	-87,962,000	226,015,000
Return on Assets %		9.00%	3.98%	.72%	-5.21%	11.83%
Return on Equity %		13.84%	6.06%	1.10%	-7.66%	16.46%
Debt to Equity		0.01	0.12	0.14	0.08	0.05

CONTACT INFORMATION:

Phone: 310 318-3100   Fax:
Toll-Free:
Address: 228 Manhattan Beach Blvd., Manhattan Beach, CA 90266 United States

STOCK TICKER/OTHER:

Stock Ticker: SKX
Employees: 7,772
Parent Company:

Exchange: NYS
Fiscal Year Ends:

SALARIES/BONUSES:

Top Exec. Salary:
$3,000,000
Second Exec. Salary:
$1,656,153

Bonus: $

Bonus: $1,000,000

OTHER THOUGHTS:

Estimated Female Officers or Directors:

Hot Spot for Advancement for Women/Minorities:

Sleepy's LLC

www.sleepys.com

NAIC Code: 442110

TYPES OF BUSINESS:

Mattress & Bedding Retail
E-commerce & Tele-Sales

BRANDS/DIVISIONS/AFFILIATES:

1-800-MATTRESS
Sleepys.com
1800mattress.com
Mattress Firm Holding Corp.

CONTACTS: *Note: Officers with more than one job title may be intentionally listed here more than once.*

Adam Blank, COO
David Acker, Pres.
Christopher Cucuzza, VP-Tech.
Adam Blank, General Counsel

GROWTH PLANS/SPECIAL FEATURES:

Sleepy's LLC is a leading retailer of mattresses, bedding and sleep furniture. The company operates 1,050 showrooms throughout Illinois, Indiana, Maryland, New York, North Carolina and Pennsylvania. Additionally, the company sells mattresses nationwide through tele-sales (1-800-MATTRESS) and its e-commerce sites, Sleepys.com and 1800mattress.com. The firm delivers its mattresses from seven distribution centers in the Northeastern U.S. as well as one in Florida and another in northern California. Sleepy's sells 13 different brands of mattresses in innerspring, foam, latex, box spring and futon varieties. Mattresses are then categorized into budget subdivisions, ranging from the cheapest end to the most expensive. Mattress sales are complemented by the firm's bedding products, such as mattress protectors, sheets, comforters and pillows. The company's sleep furniture division markets adjustable beds, daybeds, headboards and footboards, frames and futons as well as nightstands, chairs and various home decor furnishings. Sleepy's offers its customers an 8-year comfort guarantee on all of its mattresses. In late 2015, the company agreed to be acquired by Mattress Firm Holding Corp.

Sleepy's offers its employees health insurance, a 401(k) plan, short- and long-term disability, term life insurance, an employee assistance program, flexible spending accounts, direct deposit and employee discounts at various institutions.

FINANCIAL DATA: *Note: Data for latest year may not have been available at press time.*

In U.S. $	2015	2014	2013	2012	2011	2010
Revenue		860,000,000	831,000,000	850,000,000	846,000,000	750,000,000
R&D Expense						
Operating Income						
Operating Margin %						
SGA Expense						
Net Income						
Operating Cash Flow						
Capital Expenditure						
EBITDA						
Return on Assets %						
Return on Equity %						
Debt to Equity						

CONTACT INFORMATION:

Phone: 516-844-8800　　Fax: 516-844-8847
Toll-Free: 866-753-3797
Address: 1000 S. Oyster Bay Rd., Hicksville, NY 11801 United States

SALARIES/BONUSES:

Top Exec. Salary: $　　Bonus: $
Second Exec. Salary: $　　Bonus: $

STOCK TICKER/OTHER:

Stock Ticker: Subsidiary　　　　　Exchange:
Employees: 2,900　　　　　　　　Fiscal Year Ends:
Parent Company: Mattress Firm Holding Corp

OTHER THOUGHTS:

Estimated Female Officers or Directors:
Hot Spot for Advancement for Women/Minorities:

Smart & Final Stores Inc

www.smartandfinal.com

NAIC Code: 452112

TYPES OF BUSINESS:

Food & Related Products, Retail
Warehouse Clubs
Foodservice Distribution
Restaurant Equipment & Supplies
Online Sales

BRANDS/DIVISIONS/AFFILIATES:

Smart & Final Extra!
Smart & Final
Smart Foodservice Cash & Carry
Smart & Final Stores LLC

CONTACTS: Note: Officers with more than one job title may be intentionally listed here more than once.

David Hirz, CEO
Richard Phegley, CFO
David Kaplan, Chairman of the Board
Richard Link, Chief Accounting Officer
Michael Laddon, Chief Information Officer
Scott Drew, Executive VP, Divisional
Martin Trtek, President, Divisional
Michael Mortensen, Senior VP, Divisional
Jeff Whynot, Senior VP, Divisional
Eleanor Hong, Senior VP
Donald Alvarado, Senior VP
Eugene Smith, Vice President

GROWTH PLANS/SPECIAL FEATURES:

Smart & Final Stores, Inc. operates a chain of nearly 270 warehouse grocery stores that offer food, supplies and equipment, primarily in bulk sizes and quantities. Products include frozen and refrigerated foods, delicatessen products, fresh produce, paper products, janitorial supplies, restaurant equipment, candy, beverages and party supplies. Smart & Final stores specialize in providing merchandise and customer services to meet the foodservice needs of restaurants, caterers, clubs, organizations and small and mid-sized businesses. Large chain restaurants and other major foodservice operators also use Smart & Final as a fill-in or backup supplier. In addition, the company attracts value-oriented retail customers who prefer to purchase items in large sizes or quantities. The relatively small size of Smart & Final stores compared to typical warehouse clubs allows it to locate more stores in urban and suburban neighborhoods. While similar to Smart & Final stores, Smart Foodservice Cash & Carry stores focus primarily on restaurant and foodservice customers. The company operates Smart & Final stores in Mexico through a joint venture with the owners of the Calimax store chain. The company also features Smart & Final Extra!, larger stores ranging in size from 25,000 to 40,000 square feet, much larger than the typical 17,000 square foot traditional store. In 2014, the company became a public trading company in the New York Stock Exchange. In October 2015, the firm through its subsidiary, Smart & Final Stores LLC, reached an agreement to acquire 28 store leases and related assets from affiliates of Haggen Holdings, LLC.

Employees of the firm receive a comprehensive benefits package including credit union membership and a 401(k).

FINANCIAL DATA: Note: Data for latest year may not have been available at press time.

In U.S. $	2015	2014	2013	2012	2011	2010
Revenue		3,534,244,000	3,210,293,000		2,840,336,000	
R&D Expense						
Operating Income		88,761,000	86,803,000		46,833,000	
Operating Margin %		2.51%	2.70%		1.64%	
SGA Expense		438,528,000	387,133,000		379,371,000	
Net Income		33,118,000	8,171,000		10,479,000	
Operating Cash Flow		125,337,000	107,517,000		74,653,000	
Capital Expenditure		117,499,000	55,093,000		56,275,000	
EBITDA		152,955,000	147,562,000		100,476,000	
Return on Assets %		1.98%	.51%			
Return on Equity %		7.71%	2.39%			
Debt to Equity		1.13	2.04			

CONTACT INFORMATION:

Phone: 323-869-7500   Fax:
Toll-Free: 800-793-9344
Address: 600 Citadel Dr., Commerce, CA 90040 United States

SALARIES/BONUSES:

Top Exec. Salary: $850,000   Bonus: $
Second Exec. Salary: $330,769   Bonus: $150,000

STOCK TICKER/OTHER:

Stock Ticker: SFS
Employees: 9,370
Parent Company:

Exchange: NYS
Fiscal Year Ends: 12/31

OTHER THOUGHTS:

Estimated Female Officers or Directors:
Hot Spot for Advancement for Women/Minorities: Y

Sales, profits and employees may be estimates. Financial information, benefits and other data can change quickly and may vary from those stated here.

Sotheby's

NAIC Code: 453998A

TYPES OF BUSINESS:

Auction Houses (General Merchandise)
Art, Jewelry, Antiquities & Collectibles
Financial Services
Appraisal Services
Catalogs & Online Sales
Real Estate
Trust & Estate Services

BRANDS/DIVISIONS/AFFILIATES:

Acquavella Modern Art

CONTACTS: Note: Officers with more than one job title may be intentionally listed here more than once.

Kevin Ching, CEO, Subsidiary
Patrick McClymont, CFO
Kevin Delaney, Chief Accounting Officer
David Ulmer, Chief Technology Officer
The Devonshire, Deputy Chairman
Domenico De Sole, Director
Thomas Smith, Director
Mitchell Zuckerman, Executive VP, Divisional
David Goodman, Executive VP, Divisional
Susan Alexander, Executive VP
Maarten Holder, Managing Director, Geographical
Jan Prasens, Managing Director, Subsidiary
Jonathan Olsoff, Senior VP

GROWTH PLANS/SPECIAL FEATURES:

Sotheby's is one of the world's largest auctioneers of fine arts, antiques and collectibles. It operates in three segments: agency, principal and finance. The agency segment accepts property on consignment, stimulates buyer interest through professional marketing techniques and matches sellers (known as consignors) to buyers through auction or private sale processes. Prior to offering a work of art for sale, Sotheby's specialists perform significant due diligence activities to authenticate and determine the ownership of the property being sold. Following a sale, the firm invoices the buyer for the purchase price, collects payment from the buyer and remits to the consignor the net sale proceeds after deducting its commissions, expenses and applicable taxes and royalties. In 2014, auction commission revenues accounted for approximately 81% of Sotheby's consolidated revenues, and the private sale commission revenues accounted for 6%. Payments are due no more than 30 days from the sale date and payments to consignors are due 35 days from the sale date. The principal segment sells artworks that have been purchased opportunistically by Sotheby's, including property acquired for sale at auction. This segment also sells retail wine and the activities of Acquavella Modern Art, an equity investee. The finance segment provides certain collectors and art dealers with financing secured by works of art that Sotheby's either has in its possession or permits borrowers to possess. This segment generally makes two types of loans: advances secured by consigned property where the borrowers are contractually committed through the agency segment, and general purpose loans secured by property not presently intended for sale.

FINANCIAL DATA: Note: Data for latest year may not have been available at press time.

In U.S. $	2015	2014	2013	2012	2011	2010
Revenue		938,053,000	853,678,000	768,492,000	831,836,000	774,309,000
R&D Expense						
Operating Income		226,044,000	222,575,000	214,419,000	271,471,000	273,998,000
Operating Margin %		24.09%	26.07%	27.90%	32.63%	35.38%
SGA Expense		486,296,000	496,767,000	449,350,000	444,686,000	398,044,000
Net Income		117,795,000	130,006,000	108,292,000	171,416,000	160,950,000
Operating Cash Flow		44,265,000	237,427,000	-65,380,000	402,983,000	341,738,000
Capital Expenditure		10,868,000	23,467,000	19,689,000	17,111,000	17,999,000
EBITDA		248,785,000	247,840,000	221,807,000	290,491,000	288,890,000
Return on Assets %		3.87%	4.75%	4.35%	7.48%	8.55%
Return on Equity %		11.57%	12.19%	11.42%	20.46%	23.87%
Debt to Equity		0.84	0.45	0.51	0.51	0.61

CONTACT INFORMATION:

Phone: 212 606-7000   Fax: 212 606-7107
Toll-Free: 800-813-5968
Address: 1334 York Ave., New York, NY 10021 United States

STOCK TICKER/OTHER:

Stock Ticker: BID
Employees: 1,550
Parent Company:

Exchange: NYS
Fiscal Year Ends: 12/31

SALARIES/BONUSES:

Top Exec. Salary: $700,000   Bonus: $
Second Exec. Salary: $689,242   Bonus: $

OTHER THOUGHTS:

Estimated Female Officers or Directors:
Hot Spot for Advancement for Women/Minorities: Y

Southeastern Grocers LLC

www.segrocers.com/

NAIC Code: 445110

TYPES OF BUSINESS:

Grocery Stores
Food Processing
Distribution Services
Liquor Stores
Pharmacies
Fuel Centers

BRANDS/DIVISIONS/AFFILIATES:

BI-LO LLC
J H Harvey Co LLC
Winn-Dixie Stores Inc
BI-LO
Harveys
Winn-Dixie

GROWTH PLANS/SPECIAL FEATURES:

Southeastern Grocers, LLC is a U.S. supermarket chain. It is the parent of BI-LO, LLC, J.H. Harvey Co., LLC and Winn-Dixie Stores, Inc., which are all supermarket chains under the BI-LO, Harveys and Winn-Dixie banners. Together, Southeastern operates more than 750 grocery stores, 145 liquor stores and 500 in-store pharmacies, primarily located in the states of Alabama, Florida, Georgia, Louisiana, Mississippi, North Carolina, South Carolina and Tennessee. The company's stores provide non-perishable products including grocery, dairy, frozen food, general merchandise, alcoholic beverages, tobacco and fuel products; perishable products such as fresh & packaged meat, seafood, deli, bakery, produce and floral items; and pharmaceuticals.

The company offers its employees a 401(k); medical, dental, life, disability and vision coverage; training programs; ID protection; and an employee assistance program.

CONTACTS:
Note: Officers with more than one job title may be intentionally listed here more than once.

Ian MacLeod, CEO
D. Mark Prestidge, COO
Brian P. Carney, CFO
Lawrence A. Stablein, CMO
D. Mark Prestidge, Exec. VP-Oper.

FINANCIAL DATA:
Note: Data for latest year may not have been available at press time.

In U.S. $	2015	2014	2013	2012	2011	2010
Revenue		11,500,000,000	7,744,989,000	8,632,900,000	2,779,200,000	2,641,000,000
R&D Expense						
Operating Income						
Operating Margin %						
SGA Expense						
Net Income			221,750,000	103,100,000	5,700,000	15,000,000
Operating Cash Flow						
Capital Expenditure						
EBITDA						
Return on Assets %						
Return on Equity %						
Debt to Equity						

CONTACT INFORMATION:

Phone: 904-783-5000   Fax: 904-783-5294
Toll-Free:
Address: 5050 Edgewood Ct., Jacksonville, FL 32254 United States

STOCK TICKER/OTHER:

Stock Ticker: Private
Employees: 74,000
Parent Company:

Exchange:
Fiscal Year Ends: 06/30

SALARIES/BONUSES:

Top Exec. Salary: $ Bonus: $
Second Exec. Salary: $ Bonus: $

OTHER THOUGHTS:

Estimated Female Officers or Directors:
Hot Spot for Advancement for Women/Minorities: Y

SpartanNash Company

www.spartanstores.com

NAIC Code: 445110

TYPES OF BUSINESS:

Grocery Wholesale Distribution
Grocery Stores
Discount Food & Drug Stores
Marketing & Management Services
Business & Financial Services
Pharmacies
Gas Stations

BRANDS/DIVISIONS/AFFILIATES:

Family Fresh Markets
Family Fare Supermarkets
Sun Mart
Econo Foods
No Frills
Nash Brothers Trading Company
Full Circle
Family Fare Quick Stop

CONTACTS: *Note: Officers with more than one job title may be intentionally listed here more than once.*

David Staples, CFO
Craig Sturken, Chairman of the Board
Thomas Van Hall, Chief Accounting Officer
Dennis Eidson, Director
Larry Pierce, Executive VP, Divisional
Theodore Adornato, Executive VP, Divisional
Kathleen Mahoney, Executive VP
Edward Brunot, Executive VP
Derek Jones, Executive VP
Jerry Jones, Senior VP, Divisional
Peter ODonnell, Vice President, Divisional
David Couch, Vice President

GROWTH PLANS/SPECIAL FEATURES:

SpartanNash Company, formerly Spartan Stores, Inc., is a wholesale distributor and grocery retailer providing services mainly to military commissaries and exchanges in the U.S. The firm operates in three business segment: military, food distribution and retail. The military segment delivers products to 169 military commissaries and over 442 exchanges located in 37 states across the United States and the District of Columbia, Europe, Puerto Rico, Cuba, Egypt, Bahrain and Honduras. The food distribution segment distributes groceries to independent and corporate owned grocery retailers. The company operates in 42 states with 12 distribution centers supporting approximately 2,100 independently owned supermarkets. The retail segment consists of 165 retail supermarkets operating under the brand names Family Fare Supermarkets, No Frills, Bag -˜N Save, Family Fresh Markets, D&W Fresh Markets, Sun Mart and Econo Foods. Besides popular brand products, the stores offer private brand items, including flagship Spartan, such as Spartan Fresh Selections and Our Family brands; Top Care, a health and beauty care brand and Tippy Toes by Top Care, a baby brand; Full Circle and Nash Brothers Trading Company, both natural and organic brands; World Classics, a premium, unique and worldly brand; Paws, a pet supplies brand; B-leve, a premium bath and beauty brand; and Valu Time and me too!, value brands. Pharmacy services are offered in 79 supermarkets. The firm also operates fuel centers at 29 supermarket locations under the brand name Family Fare Quick Stop, D&W Quick Stop, VG's Quick Stop, Forest Hills Quick Stop, FTC Express Fuel and Sun mart Express Fuel.

Employees of Spartan receive medical, prescription, dental and vision insurance; short- and long-term disability insurance; life insurance; flexible spending accounts; employee assistance programs; wellness and health programs; tuition reimbursement; adoption assistance; a pension plan; and a 401(k) plan.

FINANCIAL DATA: *Note: Data for latest year may not have been available at press time.*

In U.S. $	2015	2014	2013	2012	2011	2010
Revenue		7,916,062,000	2,608,160,000	2,634,226,000	2,533,064,000	2,551,956,000
R&D Expense						
Operating Income		114,846,000	60,968,000	66,483,000	67,966,000	58,664,000
Operating Margin %		1.45%	2.33%	2.52%	2.68%	2.29%
SGA Expense		1,022,387,000	482,987,000	489,650,000	488,017,000	493,832,000
Net Income		58,596,000	27,410,000	31,758,000	32,307,000	25,558,000
Operating Cash Flow		139,073,000	59,341,000	93,658,000	89,756,000	88,557,000
Capital Expenditure		90,012,000	42,012,000	42,518,000	33,029,000	50,472,000
EBITDA		203,338,000	95,531,000	103,360,000	103,336,000	93,697,000
Return on Assets %		3.03%	3.52%	4.19%	4.29%	3.45%
Return on Equity %		7.84%	8.31%	10.09%	11.15%	10.05%
Debt to Equity		0.73	0.43	0.41	0.55	0.75

CONTACT INFORMATION:

Phone: 616 878-2000   Fax: 616 878-8092
Toll-Free: 800-343-4422
Address: 850 76th St. SW, Grand Rapids, MI 49518 United States

SALARIES/BONUSES:

Top Exec. Salary: $891,202   Bonus: $
Second Exec. Salary: $509,138   Bonus: $

STOCK TICKER/OTHER:

Stock Ticker: SPTN   Exchange: NAS
Employees: 8,400   Fiscal Year Ends: 03/31
Parent Company:

OTHER THOUGHTS:

Estimated Female Officers or Directors: 3
Hot Spot for Advancement for Women/Minorities: Y

Spectrum Group International Inc

www.stacksbowers.com

NAIC Code: 453998A

TYPES OF BUSINESS:

Auction Houses (General Merchandise)
Precious Metals Trading
Online Auctions

BRANDS/DIVISIONS/AFFILIATES:

Stack's Bowers Galleries

GROWTH PLANS/SPECIAL FEATURES:

Spectrum Group International, Inc. is an auctioneer of coins, arms, armor and militaria and other memorabilia, targeting both collectors and dealers. Spectrum operates under the name Stack's Bowers Galleries. Stack's Bowers Galleries conducts live, Internet and specialized auctions of rare U.S. and world coins and currency and ancient coins, as well as direct sales through retail and wholesale channels. Stack's Bowers Galleries is an Official Auctioneer for several important numismatic conventions, including American Numismatic Association events; the New York International Numismatic Convention; the Professional Numismatists Guild New York Invitational; the Whitman Coin & Collectibles Spring, Summer and Winter Expos; and its own April, August and December Hong Kong Auctions. The company is headquartered in Irvine, California, with offices in New York, Wolfeboro, Hong Kong, and Paris. In 2014, Spectrum spun off Afinsa Bienes Tangibles, SA En Liquidacion, Auctentia S.L. and A-Mark Precious Metals, Inc.

CONTACTS:

Note: Officers with more than one job title may be intentionally listed here more than once.

Greg Roberts, CEO
Brian Kendrella, Pres., Stack's Bowers Galleries
Greg Roberts, Pres.
Carol Meltzer, General Counsel
John Vong, Corp. Controller
David Madge, Pres., A-Mark Precious Metals
Brian Kendrella, Dir.-Oper.-U.S. Collectibles
Thor Gjerdrum, CFO

FINANCIAL DATA:

Note: Data for latest year may not have been available at press time.

In U.S. $	2015	2014	2013	2012	2011	2010
Revenue		7,304,597,000	7,406,043,136	7,974,830,080	7,202,170,880	6,012,438,016
R&D Expense						
Operating Income						
Operating Margin %						
SGA Expense						
Net Income						
Operating Cash Flow						
Capital Expenditure						
EBITDA						
Return on Assets %						
Return on Equity %						
Debt to Equity						

CONTACT INFORMATION:

Phone: 949 955-1250   Fax:
Toll-Free:
Address: 18061 Fitch, Irvine, CA 92614 United States

SALARIES/BONUSES:

Top Exec. Salary: $ Bonus: $
Second Exec. Salary: $ Bonus: $

STOCK TICKER/OTHER:

Stock Ticker: Private
Employees: 149
Parent Company:

Exchange:
Fiscal Year Ends: 06/30

OTHER THOUGHTS:

Estimated Female Officers or Directors: 1
Hot Spot for Advancement for Women/Minorities:

Spiegel Brands Inc

NAIC Code: 454113

www.spiegel.com

TYPES OF BUSINESS:

Apparel, Direct Selling
Jewelry & Accessories
Home Furnishings
Catalog & Online Sales
Private-Label Credit Cards

BRANDS/DIVISIONS/AFFILIATES:

Spiegel Rewards
Newport News
Shape FX
Spiegel
Patriarch Partners LLC

GROWTH PLANS/SPECIAL FEATURES:

Spiegel Brands, Inc. is a direct marketer of women's apparel.
operates a number of brands, including Spiegel, Newpo
News, and Shape FX. Founded in 1865, it began distributin
apparel catalogs in 1905 and launched its e-commerce site i
1995. The company retails private-label women's clothing
footwear, jewelry, fragrances and accessories as well as ba
and bedroom furnishings via its mail-order catalog and e
commerce web site. The firm's apparel includes sweaters
jackets, t-shirts, blouses, pants, skirts, dresses, suits
coordinated sets, lingerie, bras, other undergarments an
accessories, such as purses, shoes and jewelry. In addition t
retail, the firm's annual Spiegel catalog includes advice fror
designers and stylists. Spiegel has a private label credit car
through which it runs the Spiegel Rewards program. Th
company is owned by New York-based private equity firn
Patriarch Partners LLC.

CONTACTS: Note: Officers with more than one job title may be intentionally listed here more than once.

Lynn Tilton, Managing Dir.
Lynn Tilton, CEO-Patriarch Partners LLC

FINANCIAL DATA: Note: Data for latest year may not have been available at press time.

In U.S. $	2015	2014	2013	2012	2011	2010
Revenue						
R&D Expense						
Operating Income						
Operating Margin %						
SGA Expense						
Net Income						
Operating Cash Flow						
Capital Expenditure						
EBITDA						
Return on Assets %						
Return on Equity %						
Debt to Equity						

CONTACT INFORMATION:

Phone: 212-986-2585   Fax: 212-916-8281
Toll-Free: 800-688-2830
Address: 711 3rd Ave., New York, NY 10017 United States

SALARIES/BONUSES:

Top Exec. Salary: $ Bonus: $
Second Exec. Salary: $ Bonus: $

STOCK TICKER/OTHER:

Stock Ticker: Private   Exchange:
Employees: Fiscal Year Ends: 12/31
Parent Company: PATRIARCH PARTNERS LLC

OTHER THOUGHTS:

Estimated Female Officers or Directors: 1
Hot Spot for Advancement for Women/Minorities: Y

Sport Chalet Inc

www.sportchalet.com

NAIC Code: 451110

TYPES OF BUSINESS:

Sporting Goods Stores
Equipment Repair
Scuba Training
Equipment Rental
Sports-Related Services
Online Sales

BRANDS/DIVISIONS/AFFILIATES:

Vestis Retail Group
Versa Capital Management

CONTACTS: Note: Officers with more than one job title may be intentionally listed here more than once.

Craig L. Levra, CEO
Craig L. Levra, Pres.
Howard K. Kaminsky, CFO
Brad Morton, Sr. VP-Sales
Ted Jackson, CIO
Tom Tennyson, Chief Merch. Officer
Howard K. Kaminsky, Sec.
Tim A. Anderson, Exec. VP-Retail Oper. & Loss Prevention
Dennis D. Trausch, Exec. VP-Growth & Dev.
Howard K. Kaminsky, Exec. VP-Finance
Tim A. Anderson, Exec. VP-Specialty Svcs.
Craig L. Levra, Chmn.

GROWTH PLANS/SPECIAL FEATURES:

Sport Chalet, Inc. is a leading operator of full-service sporting goods superstores in California, Arizona, Utah and Nevada. The company's 50 stores feature a number of specialty sporting goods divisions, offering a large assortment of brand-name merchandise at competitive prices. The stores offer traditional sporting goods merchandise, including footwear, apparel and equipment, as well as specialty products, such as snowboarding, skateboarding, mountaineering and Scuba merchandise. The company purchases its merchandise from over 1,000 vendors, with Nike, Inc. as its largest vendor. A typical Sport Chalet store features multiple specialty shops for beginners to experts in several sports, consisting of products such as traditional and nontraditional sports equipment and athletic footwear for a variety of activities. Additionally, the stores feature custom fitting services, including wet suits, scuba masks and boot mountings. Sport Chalet stores also generally offer more than 50 services for customers, such as backpacking, canyoneering and kayaking instruction; custom golf club fitting; snowboard and ski rental and repair; Scuba training and certification; Scuba boat charters; racquet stringing; and bicycle tune-ups and repair. The stores are designed to feature a natural and outdoor-feeling color scheme, 30-foot clear ceilings, a pool for water sports instruction and demonstrations and a 100-foot shoe wall. To keep its stores stocked, the firm operates a 326,000 square foot distribution center in Ontario, California. The firm's Team Sales division is a full-service team dealer primarily offering in-house silk screen, embroidery, embellishment and custom artwork on footwear, uniforms and equipment. The division's target market includes high schools, universities, youth sport leagues, athletic teams, booster clubs and recreational organizations. In 2014, the company was acquired by Vestis Retail Group, which is owned by Versa Capital Management.

Employees receive discounted Scuba lessons, Scuba scholarships, discounts from vendors, free or discounted ski lift tickets and free equipment rentals.

FINANCIAL DATA: Note: Data for latest year may not have been available at press time.

In U.S. $	2015	2014	2013	2012	2011	2010
Revenue		365,000,000	360,644,992	349,883,008	362,483,008	353,695,008
R&D Expense						
Operating Income						
Operating Margin %						
SGA Expense						
Net Income		-2,900,000	-3,335,000	-5,072,000	-3,015,000	-8,274,000
Operating Cash Flow						
Capital Expenditure						
EBITDA						
Return on Assets %						
Return on Equity %						
Debt to Equity						

CONTACT INFORMATION:

Phone: 818 949-5300   Fax: 818 949-5301
Toll-Free:
Address: 1 Sport Chalet Dr., La Canada, CA 91011 United States

STOCK TICKER/OTHER:

Stock Ticker: Subsidiary   Exchange:
Employees: 2,900   Fiscal Year Ends: 04/30
Parent Company: Vestis Retail Group

SALARIES/BONUSES:

Top Exec. Salary: $ Bonus: $
Second Exec. Salary: $ Bonus: $

OTHER THOUGHTS:

Estimated Female Officers or Directors:
Hot Spot for Advancement for Women/Minorities:

Sports Authority Inc (The)

www.sportsauthority.com

NAIC Code: 451110

TYPES OF BUSINESS:

Sporting Goods Stores
Athletic Apparel & Footwear
Team Sports Equipment

BRANDS/DIVISIONS/AFFILIATES:

SportsAuthority.com
Sports Authority Field at Mile High
Leonard Green & Partners LP
Alpine Design
Sims
SA Gear
Sports Authority

CONTACTS: Note: Officers with more than one job title may be intentionally listed here more than once.

Michael Foss, CEO
Jeremy Aguilar, CFO
Stephen Binkley, CMO
Robert Gordon, Sr. VP-Human Resources
Kathy Persian, CIO
Greg Waters, Exec. VP-Merch.
Paul Gaudet, Exec. VP-Store Oper.
Darrell Webb, Chmn.

GROWTH PLANS/SPECIAL FEATURES:

The Sports Authority, Inc., owned by private equity firm Leonard Green & Partners LP, is a full-line sporting goods dealer. The firm operates more than 450 stores in 41 U.S. states. These stores offer an extensive product selection for sports and leisure activities, such as golf, tennis, skiing, cycling, hunting, fishing and bowling. Merchandise includes men's, women's and children's athletic apparel; athletic footwear; and team sports equipment. Sports Authority stores are located primarily in regional strip or power centers, although some stores are located in malls and stand-alone locations. Sports Authority emphasizes features such as specialty stores within stores, interactive kiosks, in-store customer clinics, demonstrations, small batting cages or basketball courts and a wide array of audiovisual entertainment. The firm's merchandise assortment includes hundreds of brand names, such as Adidas, Champion, Mongoose, Nike, Reebok and Wilson. Additionally, the company markets its own private label brands such as Sims, which offers snowboards and seasonal clothing; SA Gear, which sells fitness equipment and men's sportswear; and Alpine Design, a line of outdoor goods and seasonal clothing. The company tailors merchandise to reflect customer preferences at each store location, which may mean the elimination of items such as stationary bicycles or swimming goods at certain stores. Sports Authority also maintains an e-commerce site, SportsAuthority.com, operated by GSI Commerce, Inc. Through its joint venture with Aeon Co., Ltd. the company has several Sports Authority locations in Japan through a licensing agreement. The company also owns the corporate naming rights to Sports Authority Field at Mile High, home to the NFL's Denver Broncos.

FINANCIAL DATA: Note: Data for latest year may not have been available at press time.

In U.S. $	2015	2014	2013	2012	2011	2010
Revenue		2,865,000,000	2,700,000,000	2,500,000,000	2,450,000,000	
R&D Expense						
Operating Income						
Operating Margin %						
SGA Expense						
Net Income						
Operating Cash Flow						
Capital Expenditure						
EBITDA						
Return on Assets %						
Return on Equity %						
Debt to Equity						

CONTACT INFORMATION:

Phone: 303-200-5050   Fax: 303-832-4738
Toll-Free: 800-360-8721
Address: 1050 W. Hampden Ave., Englewood, CO 80110 United States

STOCK TICKER/OTHER:

Stock Ticker: Private   Exchange:
Employees: 14,000   Fiscal Year Ends: 01/31
Parent Company: LEONARD GREEN & PARTNERS LP

SALARIES/BONUSES:

Top Exec. Salary: $ Bonus: $
Second Exec. Salary: $ Bonus: $

OTHER THOUGHTS:

Estimated Female Officers or Directors:
Hot Spot for Advancement for Women/Minorities:

Sportsman's Guide Inc (The)

www.sportsmansguide.com

NAIC Code: 451110

TYPES OF BUSINESS:

Outdoor & Hunting Products
Online & Catalog Sales
Outdoor Apparel & Footwear
Boating Supplies

BRANDS/DIVISIONS/AFFILIATES:

Northern Tool and Equipment Company Inc
365outdoorwear.com
SportsmansGuide.com
Truckmonkey.com
Buyers' Club (The)
Buyer's Advantage Catalog

CONTACTS: *Note: Officers with more than one job title may be intentionally listed here more than once.*

Gregory Binkley, CEO
Charles B. Lingen, CFO
Tim Arland, Sr. VP-e-commerce

GROWTH PLANS/SPECIAL FEATURES:

The Sportsman's Guide, Inc., a subsidiary of Northern Tool and Equipment Company, Inc., is a multi-channel direct marketer of value-priced outdoor gear and clothing, golf equipment and general merchandise. The company sells its products through main and specialty catalogs and several e-commerce sites, including SportsmansGuide.com, 365outdoorwear.com and TruckMonkey.com. The firm's main catalog is mailed monthly and offers merchandise across a broad range of categories. Additional specialized catalogs are also offered during the course of each year and focus on individual categories such as camping, government surplus, ammunition and shooting supplies, gifts and hunting. The Buyers' Club, which customers can join for an annual fee, offers 10% discounts on most merchandise (5% on ammunition); a monthly Buyer's Advantage Catalog; and exclusive special offers, discounts and coupons. The Sportsman's Guide e-commerce site offers a selection similar to its print catalog in addition to certain specialty categories available exclusively online. An online resource center features a variety of articles, advice columns and information about outdoor lifestyles and pursuits, including a section specifically aimed at female outdoor enthusiasts. In addition, customers can find maps, fish and game forecasts, local guide and outfitter listings, ballistics charts, useful links and other information on the web site. Merchandise orders can be placed 24-hours-a-day by phone or online, and the company ships all orders directly from its 591,000-square-foot warehouse.

FINANCIAL DATA: *Note: Data for latest year may not have been available at press time.*

In U.S. $	2015	2014	2013	2012	2011	2010
Revenue						
R&D Expense						
Operating Income						
Operating Margin %						
SGA Expense						
Net Income						
Operating Cash Flow						
Capital Expenditure						
EBITDA						
Return on Assets %						
Return on Equity %						
Debt to Equity						

CONTACT INFORMATION:

Phone: 651-451-3030   Fax: 651-450-6130
Toll-Free: 888-844-0667
Address: 411 Farwell Ave. S., St. Paul, MN 55075 United States

SALARIES/BONUSES:

Top Exec. Salary: $ Bonus: $
Second Exec. Salary: $ Bonus: $

STOCK TICKER/OTHER:

Stock Ticker: Subsidiary   Exchange:
Employees: Fiscal Year Ends: 12/31
Parent Company: Northern Tool and Equipment Company Inc

OTHER THOUGHTS:

Estimated Female Officers or Directors:
Hot Spot for Advancement for Women/Minorities:

Sales, profits and employees may be estimates. Financial information, benefits and other data can change quickly and may vary from those stated here.

Sprouts Farmers Market LLC

NAIC Code: 445110

www.sprouts.com

TYPES OF BUSINESS:

Supermarkets

BRANDS/DIVISIONS/AFFILIATES:

Apollo Management
Sprouts.com

CONTACTS: *Note: Officers with more than one job title may be intentionally listed here more than once.*

Amin Maredia, CEO
Susannah Livingston, CFO
James Sanders, Chairman of the Board
Donna Berlinski, Chief Accounting Officer
Daniel Bruni, Chief Information Officer
James Nielsen, COO
Shon Boney, Director
Nancy Clark-Lamons, Other Executive Officer
Theodore Frumkin, Other Executive Officer
Brandon Lombardi, Other Executive Officer

GROWTH PLANS/SPECIAL FEATURES:

Sprouts Farmers Market LLC is an Arizona-based independe[
natural foods retailer. The firm operates approximately 19
stores in 12 states, and is one of the largest specialty retaile[
of natural and organic foods in the U.S. Perishable item[
constitute 50.8% of the firm's revenues, and non-perishable
make up the other 49.2%. The firm's products include bake
goods, beer, wine, over 200 bulk food bins (rice and othe
grains, nuts, spices, dried fruit and old fashioned candies
dairy products, meat, poultry, produce, seafood, vitamins an[
supplements. In addition to Sprouts' own private label natur[
and organic foods, the company acquires products primaril[
from U.S. suppliers, emphasizing local buying practice[
However, the company purchases certain seasonal fruits an[
vegetables from growers around the world. The firm's store
host a variety of events, such as cooking classes, healt[
screenings and health information sessions. The company'[
web site (Sprouts.com) offers recipes, gift cards, nutritiona[
information and a health guide. Apollo Management holds [
minority ownership in the company.

The company offers employees benefits including medica[
dental, vision, disability and AD&D insurance; 401(k); a[
employee assistance program; flexible spending accounts
employee discounts; health savings accounts; and scholarshi[
opportunities.

FINANCIAL DATA: *Note: Data for latest year may not have been available at press time.*

In U.S. $	2015	2014	2013	2012	2011	2010
Revenue		2,967,424,000	2,437,911,000	1,794,823,000	1,105,879,000	516,816,000
R&D Expense						
Operating Income		199,711,000	139,504,000	70,685,000	-25,721,000	8,567,000
Operating Margin %		6.73%	5.72%	3.93%	-2.32%	1.65%
SGA Expense		685,492,000	585,763,000	459,624,000	304,493,000	140,435,000
Net Income		107,692,000	51,326,000	19,500,000	-27,445,000	4,861,000
Operating Cash Flow		181,218,000	160,588,000	84,431,000	52,384,000	22,222,000
Capital Expenditure		127,065,000	87,463,000	46,485,000	27,594,000	17,071,000
EBITDA		259,531,000	168,487,000	106,028,000	29,282,000	23,025,000
Return on Assets %		8.47%	4.51%	1.76%		
Return on Equity %		17.96%	11.39%	5.04%		
Debt to Equity		0.54	0.82	1.36		

CONTACT INFORMATION:

Phone: 480-814-8016   Fax: 480-814-8017
Toll-Free: 888-577-7688
Address: 11811 N. Tatum Blvd., Ste. 2400, Phoenix, AZ 85028 United
States

STOCK TICKER/OTHER:

Stock Ticker: SFM
Employees: 17,000
Parent Company: Apollo Management

Exchange: NAS
Fiscal Year Ends:

SALARIES/BONUSES:

Top Exec. Salary: $553,077   Bonus: $
Second Exec. Salary: Bonus: $
$395,644

OTHER THOUGHTS:

Estimated Female Officers or Directors: 1
Hot Spot for Advancement for Women/Minorities:

Sales, profits and employees may be estimates. Financial information, benefits and other data can change quickly and may vary from those stated here.

St John Knits International Inc

www.sjk.com

NAIC Code: 424300

TYPES OF BUSINESS:

Apparel and Clothing Brands, Designers, Importers and Distributors
Women's Knits & Accessories
Boutiques & Outlet Stores
Yarn & Fabric Manufacturing
Footwear

BRANDS/DIVISIONS/AFFILIATES:

Vestar Capital Partners Inc
Santana Knit
Collection
Couture

CONTACTS: *Note: Officers with more than one job title may be intentionally listed here more than once.*

Geoffroy van Raemdonck, CEO
Bruce A. Fetter, COO
Roger G. Ruppert, CFO
Max Weinstein, Exec. VP-Oper.
Roger G. Ruppert, Exec. VP-Finance
Daniel S. O'Connell, CEO-Vestar Capital
James P. Kelley, Pres., Vestar Capital
Bernd Beetz, Chmn.

GROWTH PLANS/SPECIAL FEATURES:

St. John Knits International, Inc., founded in 1962 by fashion model Marie Gray and her husband Robert, is an international designer, manufacturer and distributor of fine women's clothing; accessories, such as eyewear, shoes, belts, handbags, scarves and jewelry; and fragrances. The company offers several product lines including evening wear, jackets, tops, dresses, bottoms, jewelry, belts and a line of caviar colored clothing. Its Collection line consists of ready-to-wear styles, including daytime knit fashions of dresses and suits. Its Couture line consists of day and evening apparel produced in limited quantities. The firm markets its products to wholesale clients, which include high-end department stores in the U.S. such as Neiman Marcus, Nordstrom and Saks Fifth Avenue as well as retailers to more than 205 locations throughout Europe, the Middle East, South America and Asia. Additionally, the company maintains company-operated boutiques and outlets throughout the U.S. and Canada. The company is dedicated to maintaining consistently high product quality, and to that end, controls almost every stage in the design and manufacturing process. St. John has developed a vertically integrated manufacturing process, including twisting and dyeing its own brand of wool and rayon yarns and knitting (including its trademark Santana Knit), constructing, pressing and finishing garments at company-owned facilities. Vestar Capital Partners Inc. owns 78% of the firm.

FINANCIAL DATA: *Note: Data for latest year may not have been available at press time.*

In U.S. $	2015	2014	2013	2012	2011	2010
Revenue		335,000,000	325,000,000	253,900,000	269,500,000	325,000,000
R&D Expense						
Operating Income						
Operating Margin %						
SGA Expense						
Net Income						
Operating Cash Flow						
Capital Expenditure						
EBITDA						
Return on Assets %						
Return on Equity %						
Debt to Equity						

CONTACT INFORMATION:

Phone: 949 863-1171   Fax: 949 223-3390
Toll-Free:
Address: 17622 Armstrong Ave., Irvine, CA 92614 United States

SALARIES/BONUSES:

Top Exec. Salary: $ Bonus: $
Second Exec. Salary: $ Bonus: $

STOCK TICKER/OTHER:

Stock Ticker: Private
Employees: 4,925
Parent Company: VESTAR CAPITAL PARTNERS INC

Exchange:
Fiscal Year Ends: 10/31

OTHER THOUGHTS:

Estimated Female Officers or Directors:
Hot Spot for Advancement for Women/Minorities:

Stage Stores Inc

NAIC Code: 452111

TYPES OF BUSINESS:

Department Stores
Online Sales

BRANDS/DIVISIONS/AFFILIATES:

Stage
Bealls
Goody's
Peebles
Palais Royal

CONTACTS: Note: Officers with more than one job title may be intentionally listed here more than once.

Oded Shein, CFO
Richard Stasyszen, Chief Accounting Officer
Steven Hunter, Chief Information Officer
William Montgoris, Director
Michael Glazer, Director
Russell Lundy, Executive VP, Divisional
William Gentner, Executive VP
Steven Lawrence, Other Executive Officer
Stephen Parsons, Other Executive Officer
Chadwick Reynolds, Other Executive Officer

GROWTH PLANS/SPECIAL FEATURES:

Stage Stores, Inc. is a specialty department store retailer offering moderately priced, nationally recognized brand-name and private-label apparel, accessories, cosmetics and footwear. The company operates approximately 854 department stores located in 40 states, with an average store size being 18,200 square feet. Stage stores operate under the Bealls, Goody's, Palais Royal, Peebles and Stage nameplates and a direct-to-consumer business. Approximately 85% of sales consist of nationally recognized brands, such as Levi Strauss, Nike, Calvin Klein, Chaps, Izod, Dockers, Carters, Jockey, Estee Lauder, Clinique, Nautica, Skechers and New Balance; and the remaining 15% consists of the company's private labels. In targeting small and midsize markets, the company has developed a store format that is smaller than typical department stores yet large enough to offer a carefully chosen but broad selection of merchandise. The firm attempts to locate its stores by, or in the vicinity of, other tenants that it believes will help attract additional foot traffic to the area, such as grocery stores, drug stores or major discount stores. Approximately 66% of the company's stores operate in towns with populations under 50,000 people; 20% of its stores are in mid-sized communities; and 14% are in higher-density markets with populations greater than 150,000. The company's direct-to-consumer business consists of an e-commerce website and in-store Send program, which allows customers to have merchandise shipped directly to their homes from another store if the preferred size or color is not available in their local store. The firm currently distributes all merchandise to its stores through three distribution centers located in Jacksonville, Texas; South Hill, Virginia; and Jeffersonville, Ohio.

The firm offers employees medical, dental, cancer, accident and life insurance; flexible spending accounts; product discounts; a 401(k) plan; and tuition reimbursements.

FINANCIAL DATA: Note: Data for latest year may not have been available at press time.

In U.S. $	2015	2014	2013	2012	2011	2010
Revenue	1,638,569,000	1,633,556,000	1,645,800,000	1,511,919,000	1,470,590,000	1,431,927,000
R&D Expense						
Operating Income	63,702,000	26,805,000	63,391,000	51,096,000	62,767,000	45,827,000
Operating Margin %	3.88%	1.64%	3.85%	3.37%	4.26%	3.20%
SGA Expense	386,104,000	398,294,000	392,727,000	353,834,000	354,057,000	341,592,000
Net Income	30,850,000	16,642,000	38,179,000	30,960,000	37,640,000	28,721,000
Operating Cash Flow	102,214,000	46,527,000	75,981,000	78,055,000	77,875,000	120,936,000
Capital Expenditure	70,580,000	61,263,000	49,489,000	45,731,000	36,990,000	42,707,000
EBITDA	127,149,000	99,474,000	123,817,000	112,800,000	125,272,000	114,290,000
Return on Assets %	3.77%	2.07%	4.98%	4.04%	4.71%	3.66%
Return on Equity %	6.63%	3.62%	8.70%	6.86%	7.79%	6.20%
Debt to Equity	0.09	0.13	0.02	0.08	0.05	0.08

CONTACT INFORMATION:

Phone: 800 579-2302   Fax: 713 660-3330
Toll-Free: 800-324-3244
Address: 10201 Main St., Houston, TX 77025 United States

STOCK TICKER/OTHER:

Stock Ticker: SSI
Employees: 14,300
Parent Company:

Exchange: NYS
Fiscal Year Ends: 01/31

SALARIES/BONUSES:

Top Exec. Salary: $966,077   Bonus: $
Second Exec. Salary: $630,493   Bonus: $

OTHER THOUGHTS:

Estimated Female Officers or Directors: 3
Hot Spot for Advancement for Women/Minorities: Y

Staples Inc

www.staples.com

NAIC Code: 453210

TYPES OF BUSINESS:

Office Supplies, Retail
Contract Stationery Services
Online & Catalog Sales
Catalogs
Office Furniture

BRANDS/DIVISIONS/AFFILIATES:

Quill.com
Staples

CONTACTS: *Note: Officers with more than one job title may be intentionally listed here more than once.*

Ronald Sargent, CEO
Christine Komola, CFO
Michael Williams, General Counsel
John Wilson, President, Divisional
Demos Parneros, President, Divisional
Shira Goodman, President, Divisional
Joseph Doody, Vice Chairman

GROWTH PLANS/SPECIAL FEATURES:

Staples, Inc. markets office supply products through three sales channels: North American stores & online, North American commercial and international operations. North American stores & online consists of 1,364 stores in the U.S. and 315 stores in Canada as well as the firm's web site. The Staples.com operations consist of the combined direct mail catalog and Internet sales both in the U.S. and Canada, and it is tailored primarily to the needs of small and medium-sized businesses. The North American commercial division comprises two business units: Staples Advantage and Quill.com. Staples Advantage, the firm's contract stationery operation, focuses primarily on serving medium to large businesses. Quill.com, a direct mail catalog and Internet distributor, supplies business products to more than 1 million small to medium-sized businesses in the U.S. Its international operations division consists of 284 stores in 16 countries, with the highest concentration being in Scandinavia, Germany, the U.K. and the Netherlands. The office product segment in this division is highly fragmented. It also operates a mail order and Internet-based businesses with a significant concentration of sales in France, Italy and the U.K. A typical superstore carries Staples-brand and brand-name products, including ink and toner, paper, small business machines, computers and peripherals. Typical stores also contain a copy center and a business technology center. In February 2015, Staples announced plans to acquire competitor Office Depot for $6.3 billion. That same year, the firm announced it would close up to 225 stores in North America by year's end.

FINANCIAL DATA: *Note: Data for latest year may not have been available at press time.*

In U.S. $	2015	2014	2013	2012	2011	2010
Revenue	22,492,360,000	23,114,260,000	24,380,510,000	25,022,190,000	24,545,110,000	24,275,450,000
R&D Expense						
Operating Income	309,866,000	1,177,501,000	510,065,000	1,628,434,000	1,573,513,000	1,382,345,000
Operating Margin %	1.37%	5.09%	2.09%	6.50%	6.41%	5.69%
SGA Expense	4,816,433,000	4,735,294,000	4,884,284,000	5,048,492,000	4,913,188,000	4,907,236,000
Net Income	134,526,000	620,069,000	-210,706,000	984,656,000	881,948,000	738,671,000
Operating Cash Flow	1,042,938,000	1,108,286,000	1,219,188,000	1,576,475,000	1,446,491,000	2,084,208,000
Capital Expenditure	360,866,000	371,229,000	349,574,000	383,654,000	408,889,000	313,228,000
EBITDA	784,146,000	1,640,352,000	915,213,000	2,114,948,000	2,070,282,000	1,945,360,000
Return on Assets %	1.25%	5.28%	-1.63%	7.20%	6.38%	5.52%
Return on Equity %	2.35%	10.11%	-3.20%	14.10%	12.86%	11.97%
Debt to Equity	0.19	0.16	0.16	0.22	0.29	0.36

CONTACT INFORMATION:

Phone: 508 253-5000   Fax: 508 370-8955
Toll-Free: 800-782-7537
Address: 500 Staples Dr., Framingham, MA 01702 United States

SALARIES/BONUSES:

Top Exec. Salary: Bonus: $
$1,249,208
Second Exec. Salary: Bonus: $
$693,050

STOCK TICKER/OTHER:

Stock Ticker: SPLS   Exchange: NAS
Employees: 79,075   Fiscal Year Ends: 01/31
Parent Company:

OTHER THOUGHTS:

Estimated Female Officers or Directors: 3

Hot Spot for Advancement for Women/Minorities: Y

Starbucks Corporation

NAIC Code: 722515

www.starbucks.com

TYPES OF BUSINESS:

Coffee Houses & Coffee Stores
Coffee-Related Accessories & Equipment
Wholesale Coffee Distribution
Tea and Accessories

BRANDS/DIVISIONS/AFFILIATES:

Starbucks Coffee Korea Co Ltd
President Starbucks Coffee Corporation (Taiwan)
President Starbucks Coffee (Shanghai) Co Ltd
Tata Starbucks Limited (India).
North American Coffee Partnership (The)
Order and Pay App
Ethos
Teavana

CONTACTS: Note: Officers with more than one job title may be intentionally listed here more than once.

Howard Schultz, CEO
Scott Maw, CFO
Troy Alstead, COO
Kevin Johnson, Director
Lucy Helm, Executive VP
John Culver, President, Divisional
Clifford Burrows, President, Divisional

GROWTH PLANS/SPECIAL FEATURES:

Starbucks Corporation is a roaster, marketer and retailer o
specialty coffee, operating in 65 countries, with more tha
22,500 retail stores. The firm purchases and roasts high-qualit
coffees that it sells, along with handcrafted coffee, tea an
other beverages and a variety of fresh food items, throug
company-operated stores. Starbucks also licenses i
trademarks through other channels such as grocery stores an
national foodservice accounts. In addition to its flagshi
Starbucks brand, the company's portfolio includes goods an
services offered under the following brands: Teavana, Tazo
Seattle's Best Coffee, Starbucks VIA, Starbucks Refreshers
Evolution Fresh, La Boulange and Ethos. The firm has fou
operating segments: Americas (the U.S., Canada and Lati
America), accounting for 73% of total 2014 net revenues
Europe, Middle East and Africa (EMEA), 8%; China/Asia
Pacific (CAP), 7%; and channel development, 9%; with all othe
segments, 3%. The Americas, EMEA and CAP segment
include both company-operated and licensed stores. Th
Americas and EMEA segments include certain food servic
accounts, primarily in Canada and the UK. Additionally, the
Americas includes the company's La Boulange retail stores
Seattle's Best Coffee is reported in a minor other segment, wit
less than 1% of total net revenues. The company owns a 50%
interest in each of the following companies: Starbucks Coffe
Korea Co. Ltd., President Starbucks Coffee Corporatio
(Taiwan), President Starbucks Coffee (Shanghai) Company
Limited and Tata Starbucks Limited (India). It also licenses the
rights to produce and distribute Starbucks-branded products to
its 50% joint venture with Pepsi-Cola Company, The Nort
American Coffee Partnership, which develops and distribute
bottled Starbucks beverages. The company's updated mobile
app labelled Order and Pay App, allows customers to place
pay and pick up orders.

Starbucks offers employee benefits including 401(k), adoptio
assistance, health coverage, employee discounts, educatio
assistance, time off and discount stock purchase plans.

FINANCIAL DATA: Note: Data for latest year may not have been available at press time.

In U.S. $	2015	2014	2013	2012	2011	2010
Revenue	19,162,700,000	16,447,800,000	14,892,200,000	13,299,500,000	11,700,400,000	10,707,400,000
R&D Expense						
Operating Income	3,601,000,000	3,081,100,000	-325,400,000	1,997,400,000	1,728,500,000	1,419,400,000
Operating Margin %	18.79%	18.73%	-2.18%	15.01%	14.77%	13.25%
SGA Expense	6,607,800,000	5,629,500,000	5,224,000,000	4,719,300,000	4,301,200,000	4,120,900,000
Net Income	2,757,400,000	2,068,100,000	8,300,000	1,383,800,000	1,245,700,000	945,600,000
Operating Cash Flow	3,749,100,000	607,800,000	2,908,300,000	1,750,300,000	1,612,400,000	1,704,900,000
Capital Expenditure	1,303,700,000	1,160,900,000	1,151,200,000	856,200,000	531,900,000	440,700,000
EBITDA	4,907,300,000	3,972,200,000	453,800,000	2,672,400,000	2,394,400,000	2,010,500,000
Return on Assets %	23.77%	18.57%	.08%	17.76%	18.12%	15.80%
Return on Equity %	49.72%	42.41%	.17%	29.15%	30.91%	28.14%
Debt to Equity	0.40	0.38	0.29	0.10	0.12	0.14

CONTACT INFORMATION:

Phone: 206 447-1575   Fax: 206 447-0828
Toll-Free: 800-782-7282
Address: 2401 Utah Ave. S., Seattle, WA 98134 United States

STOCK TICKER/OTHER:

Stock Ticker: SBUX   Exchange: NAS
Employees: 191,000   Fiscal Year Ends: 09/30
Parent Company:

SALARIES/BONUSES:

Top Exec. Salary: Bonus: $
$1,500,000
Second Exec. Salary: Bonus: $
$858,329

OTHER THOUGHTS:

Estimated Female Officers or Directors: 5

Hot Spot for Advancement for Women/Minorities: Y

Sales, profits and employees may be estimates. Financial information, benefits and other data can change quickly and may vary from those stated here.

Stater Bros Markets

www.staterbros.com

NAIC Code: 445110

TYPES OF BUSINESS:

Grocery Stores, Retail
Delivery Services
Beverage Processing

GROWTH PLANS/SPECIAL FEATURES:

Stater Bros. Markets operates approximately 168 grocery stores in southern California. Most Stater Bros. stores feature a full-service deli and bakery, butcher, pharmacy and a florist kiosk. The firm's headquarters in San Bernardino, California features an approximately 200-acre campus, which includes corporate offices and a 2.3 million square feet distribution center.

BRANDS/DIVISIONS/AFFILIATES:

CONTACTS: *Note: Officers with more than one job title may be intentionally listed here more than once.*

Jack H. Brown, CEO
Pete Van Helden, COO
Pete Van Helden, Pres.
Dan Meyer, Exec. VP-Retail Oper.
Jack H. Brown, Chmn.

FINANCIAL DATA: *Note: Data for latest year may not have been available at press time.*

In U.S. $	2015	2014	2013	2012	2011	2010
Revenue		3,950,000,000	4,000,000,000	3,900,000,000	3,800,000,000	3,600,000,000
R&D Expense						
Operating Income						
Operating Margin %						
SGA Expense						
Net Income						
Operating Cash Flow						
Capital Expenditure						
EBITDA						
Return on Assets %						
Return on Equity %						
Debt to Equity						

CONTACT INFORMATION:

Phone: 909-733-5000   Fax: 909-733-3930
Toll-Free:
Address: 301 S. Tippecanoe Ave., San Bernardino, CA 92408 United States

STOCK TICKER/OTHER:

Stock Ticker: Private
Employees: 16,300
Parent Company:

Exchange:
Fiscal Year Ends: 09/30

SALARIES/BONUSES:

Top Exec. Salary: $ Bonus: $
Second Exec. Salary: $ Bonus: $

OTHER THOUGHTS:

Estimated Female Officers or Directors:
Hot Spot for Advancement for Women/Minorities:

Stefanel SpA

NAIC Code: 424300

www.stefanel.com/us_en/investors.html

TYPES OF BUSINESS:

Apparel and Clothing Brands, Designers, Importers and Distributors
Casual Apparel
Retail Apparel Stores
Online Sales
Apparel Distribution

BRANDS/DIVISIONS/AFFILIATES:

Marithe
Francoise Girbaud
Stefanel
Interfashion SpA
Girbaud.com

GROWTH PLANS/SPECIAL FEATURES:

Stefanel SpA designs, manufactures and markets brand and licensed knitwear and casualwear for women and men. The firm's knitwear and casual clothes are retailed under the Stefanel brand. Stefanel's knitwear is produced almost entirely in a single factory in Salgareda, Italy. Stefanel also offers a complete line of jeanswear and casualwear for men and women under the Marithe and Francoise Girbaud brand. The company distributes Marithe and Francois Girbaud through subsidiary Interfashion SpA. The firm also retails through several e-commerce sites, including Girbaud.com.

CONTACTS: *Note: Officers with more than one job title may be intentionally listed here more than once.*

Giuseppe Stefanel, CEO
Giuseppe Stefanel, Pres.
Federico Girotto, CFO
Giuseppe Stefanel, Dir.-Admin.
Federico Girotto, Dir.-Investor Rel.
Giuseppe Stefanel, Chmn.

FINANCIAL DATA: *Note: Data for latest year may not have been available at press time.*

In U.S. $	2015	2014	2013	2012	2011	2010
Revenue		176,800,000	233,191,000	247,498,333	254,720,000	251,100,000
R&D Expense						
Operating Income						
Operating Margin %						
SGA Expense						
Net Income		-8,900,000	-32,993,000	-27,957,000	38,633,000	-48,600,000
Operating Cash Flow						
Capital Expenditure						
EBITDA						
Return on Assets %						
Return on Equity %						
Debt to Equity						

CONTACT INFORMATION:

Phone: 39-0422-8191   Fax: 39-0422-819342
Toll-Free:
Address: Via Postojna 85, Ponte di Piave, 31047 Italy

STOCK TICKER/OTHER:

Stock Ticker: STEF
Employees: 1,519
Parent Company:

Exchange: Milan
Fiscal Year Ends: 12/31

SALARIES/BONUSES:

Top Exec. Salary: $ Bonus: $
Second Exec. Salary: $ Bonus: $

OTHER THOUGHTS:

Estimated Female Officers or Directors: 2
Hot Spot for Advancement for Women/Minorities:

Stein Mart Inc

NAIC Code: 452112

www.steinmart.com

TYPES OF BUSINESS:

Discount Department Stores
Apparel
Linens
Accessories
Gifts
Shoes

BRANDS/DIVISIONS/AFFILIATES:

Stein Mart Boutique

CONTACTS: Note: Officers with more than one job title may be intentionally listed here more than once.

Jay Stein, CEO
Gregory Kleffner, CFO
David Hawkins, COO
John Williams, Director
Gary Pierce, Executive VP
Linda Tasseff, Other Corporate Officer

GROWTH PLANS/SPECIAL FEATURES:

Stein Mart, Inc. is a retail chain that offers current-season, fashionable and primarily branded merchandise. The company currently operates 270 stores in 30 states and Washington, D.C., typically in neighborhood shopping centers in metropolitan areas. Target customers are fashion-conscious, value-seeking women ages 35-55 with above-average annual household incomes. The company's focused assortment of merchandise features moderate and designer brand-name apparel for women and men as well as accessories, home decor, gifts, linens and shoes. Stein Mart purchases its products from roughly 1,200 vendors. Ladies' and boutique apparel accounts for 45% of sales; men's, 19%; ladies' accessories, 11%; home, 13%; shoes, 7%; and other, 5%. The company strives to keep prices low through its vendor relationships, tight control over corporate and store expenses and efficient management of inventory. To this end, Stein Mart's shoe department inventory is exclusively supplied and owned by DSW, Inc. A unique store feature is its Stein Mart Boutique, which is designed to be a store within a store. Store employees known as Boutique Ladies provide customers with specific fashion advice and personal service as well as acting as personal shoppers. Other services include the Stein Mart Preferred Customer rewards program, a private label credit card and a co-branded Stein Mart MasterCard.

Stein Mart offers its employees medical, dental, vision and life insurance; flexible spending accounts; a 401(k) plan; a discount stock purchase plan; and an employee assistance program.

FINANCIAL DATA: Note: Data for latest year may not have been available at press time.

In U.S. $	2015	2014	2013	2012	2011	2010
Revenue	1,317,677,000	1,263,571,000	1,232,366,000	1,160,367,000	1,181,510,000	1,219,109,000
R&D Expense						
Operating Income	44,709,000	40,833,000	36,223,000	32,257,000	53,146,000	34,647,000
Operating Margin %	3.39%	3.23%	2.93%	2.77%	4.49%	2.84%
SGA Expense	342,027,000	326,520,000	306,407,000	289,114,000	288,592,000	314,115,000
Net Income	26,906,000	25,555,000	25,027,000	19,828,000	48,753,000	23,553,000
Operating Cash Flow	52,431,000	40,066,000	71,339,000	59,568,000	49,632,000	98,329,000
Capital Expenditure	40,231,000	36,266,000	45,426,000	33,449,000	29,550,000	7,585,000
EBITDA	73,825,000	68,585,000	60,134,000	51,194,000	70,474,000	53,870,000
Return on Assets %	4.89%	5.03%	5.18%	4.35%	11.59%	5.51%
Return on Equity %	9.60%	10.25%	10.14%	7.82%	21.06%	11.71%
Debt to Equity						

CONTACT INFORMATION:

Phone: 904 346-1500   Fax: 904 398-4341
Toll-Free: 888-783-4662
Address: 1200 Riverplace Blvd., Jacksonville, FL 32207 United States

STOCK TICKER/OTHER:

Stock Ticker: SMRT
Employees: 11,300
Parent Company:

Exchange: NAS
Fiscal Year Ends: 01/31

SALARIES/BONUSES:

Top Exec. Salary: $582,139   Bonus: $
Second Exec. Salary: $447,781   Bonus: $

OTHER THOUGHTS:

Estimated Female Officers or Directors: 3
Hot Spot for Advancement for Women/Minorities: Y

Sterling Jewelers Inc

www.sterlingjewelers.com

NAIC Code: 448310

TYPES OF BUSINESS:

Jewelry, Retail
Jewelry Repair
Custom Jewelry Design
Online Sales

BRANDS/DIVISIONS/AFFILIATES:

Signet Jewelers Limited
Kay Jewelers
Jared, The Galleria of Jewelry
Osterman Jewelers
Marks & Morgan Jewelers
Belden Jewelers
Shaw's Jewelers
Rogers Jewelers

CONTACTS: *Note: Officers with more than one job title may be intentionally listed here more than once.*

Mark Light, CEO
William Montalto, Sr., COO
Mark Light, Pres.
Robert Trabucco, CFO

GROWTH PLANS/SPECIAL FEATURES:

Sterling Jewelers, Inc. is a U.S. jewelry retailer. The firm is a wholly-owned subsidiary of Signet Jewelers Limited, which operates in the U.S. and the U.K. Sterling Jewelers maintained over 1,504 jewelry stores nationwide, including Kay Jewelers stores and Jared The Galleria of Jewelry (Jared) as of January 2015. Each store in the U.S. has at least one trained diamontologist. It emphasizes diamond products which include the Leo Diamond brand. Some of the other competitive brands carried by Sterling include Hearts Desire; Artistry Diamonds Charmed Memories; Diamonds in Rhythm; and Open Hearts by Jane Seymour. Kay Jewelers is a nationwide chain targeting the middle-income consumer, operating in mall stores in all 50 states and Washington, D.C. Jared targets the upper end of the middle market as a leading off-mall destination specialty retail jewelry chain. It has a significantly expanded product range and enhanced customer services, including in-store repair and custom design facilities as well as a private viewing room, complimentary refreshments and a children's play area. Other regional chain stores include Marks & Morgan Jewelers, Weisfield Jewelers, JB Robinson Jewelers, Osterman Jewelers, Shaw's Jewelers, Rogers Jewelers, LeRoy's Jewelers, Goodman Jewelers and Belden Jewelers.

The company offers its employees a 401(k) plan; a discounted stock purchase plan; life, disability, medical, vision and prescription drug insurance; paid time off; tuition reimbursement; health and wellness programs; and merchandise discounts.

FINANCIAL DATA: *Note: Data for latest year may not have been available at press time.*

In U.S. $	2015	2014	2013	2012	2011	2010
Revenue						
R&D Expense						
Operating Income						
Operating Margin %						
SGA Expense						
Net Income						
Operating Cash Flow						
Capital Expenditure						
EBITDA						
Return on Assets %						
Return on Equity %						
Debt to Equity						

CONTACT INFORMATION:

Phone: 330-668-5000   Fax: 330-668-5052
Toll-Free:
Address: 375 Ghent Rd., Fairlawn, OH 44333 United States

STOCK TICKER/OTHER:

Stock Ticker: Subsidiary
Employees:
Parent Company: Signet Jewelers Limited

Exchange:
Fiscal Year Ends: 01/31

SALARIES/BONUSES:

Top Exec. Salary: $ Bonus: $
Second Exec. Salary: $ Bonus: $

OTHER THOUGHTS:

Estimated Female Officers or Directors:
Hot Spot for Advancement for Women/Minorities:

Steven Madden Ltd

www.stevemadden.com

NAIC Code: 424340

TYPES OF BUSINESS:

Footwear Distribution
Retail Stores
Online Sales
Women's Jewelry & Accessories
Brand Licensing

BRANDS/DIVISIONS/AFFILIATES:

Steve Madden
Steven
Betseyville
Betsey Johnson
Madden Girl
Big Buddha
Dolce Vita Holdings Inc
Blondo

CONTACTS: Note: Officers with more than one job title may be intentionally listed here more than once.

Arvind Dharia, CFO
Awadhesh Sinha, COO
Edward Rosenfeld, Director
Karla Frieders, Other Executive Officer
Amelia Varela, President

GROWTH PLANS/SPECIAL FEATURES:

Steven Madden, Ltd. designs, sources, markets and sells shoes for men, women and children. Headquartered in New York, it distributes products through its retail stores, its e-commerce web site and department and specialty stores throughout the U.S. and Canada as well as Europe, Latin America and the Asia-Pacific. The company operates in five segments: wholesale footwear, wholesale accessories, retail, first cost and licensing. The wholesale footwear segment is comprised of the Women's, Men's, Madden Girl, Steven, Elizabeth and James and other licensed brands. Madden women's wholesale, the company's largest division, designs, sources and markets the Steve Madden brand to a variety of stores and boutiques. Madden men's wholesale designs and markets men's casual and athletic shoes. Madden Girl markets young women's shoes geared to females ages 13-20. Steven designs, sources and markets footwear under the Steven brand. Through a license agreement with Dualstar Entertainment Group, LLC, the firm produces luxury footwear under the Elizabeth and James brand. The wholesale accessories segment designs, sources and markets name brand and private label fashion handbags and accessories. Its brands include Betsey Johnson, Big Buddha and Betseyville in addition to Steve Madden brands. The retail segment, operating through Steven Madden Retail, Inc., manages over 160 retail stores. The first cost division acts as a buying agent for footwear products sold under private labels for mass merchandisers. The licensing segment is responsible for the licensing of the Steve Madden and Betsey Johnson brands. In 2014, the firm acquired Dolce Vita Holdings, Inc., a designer and marketer of branded and private label footwear. In January 2015, the firm acquired Blondo, a footwear brand specializing in waterproof leather boots.

FINANCIAL DATA: Note: Data for latest year may not have been available at press time.

In U.S. $	2015	2014	2013	2012	2011	2010
Revenue		1,334,951,000	1,314,223,000	1,227,072,000	987,264,000	635,418,000
R&D Expense						
Operating Income		167,642,000	203,768,000	178,976,000	153,770,000	121,624,000
Operating Margin %		12.55%	15.50%	14.58%	15.57%	19.14%
SGA Expense		315,081,000	295,223,000	283,689,000	226,893,000	176,859,000
Net Income		111,880,000	132,007,000	119,626,000	97,319,000	75,725,000
Operating Cash Flow		151,975,000	155,453,000	143,341,000	74,968,000	86,873,000
Capital Expenditure		18,341,000	20,746,000	20,102,000	15,477,000	3,424,000
EBITDA		186,681,000	222,058,000	196,878,000	169,903,000	135,860,000
Return on Assets %		12.49%	15.67%	16.57%	17.89%	19.55%
Return on Equity %		16.60%	20.22%	21.72%	23.38%	24.22%
Debt to Equity						

CONTACT INFORMATION:

Phone: 718 446-1800   Fax: 718 446-5599
Toll-Free:
Address: 52-16 Barnett Ave., Long Island City, NY 11104 United States

STOCK TICKER/OTHER:

Stock Ticker: SHOO
Employees: 3,256
Parent Company:

Exchange: NAS
Fiscal Year Ends: 12/31

SALARIES/BONUSES:

Top Exec. Salary: $725,000   Bonus: $
Second Exec. Salary: $607,754   Bonus: $

OTHER THOUGHTS:

Estimated Female Officers or Directors: 1
Hot Spot for Advancement for Women/Minorities:

Stew Leonard's

NAIC Code: 445110

TYPES OF BUSINESS:

Grocery Stores

BRANDS/DIVISIONS/AFFILIATES:

Stew's University
Stew Leonard's Wines
Stew Leonard's

CONTACTS: *Note: Officers with more than one job title may be intentionally listed here more than once.*

Stew Leonard, Jr., CEO
Stew Leonard, Jr., Pres.
Chaz Fable, Dir.-Kitchen Oper.
Meghan Bell, Dir.-Public Relations
Jill Leonard Tavello, VP-Culture
Beth Leonard Hollis, Exec. VP
Michael Luboff, Exec. Chef-Stew Leonard's Norwalk

GROWTH PLANS/SPECIAL FEATURES:

Stew Leonard's is a family-owned specialty grocery store providing dairy products, meats, fish, produce, bakery items, cheese and wine as well as flowers. The company, founded in 1969, was originally a small dairy store with only seven employees. The business has since grown into a multi-million dollar organization with annual sales of nearly $400 million. Currently, there are four store locations: three in Connecticut (Danbury, Norwalk and Newington) and one in New York (Yonkers). Unlike the majority of grocery stores throughout the U.S., which offer more than 45,000 products, Stew Leonard's offers approximately 2,200. The firm chooses to limit its offerings and focus on the quality and freshness of its food. The company's stores feature petting zoos, animatronics, entertainment programming and costumed characters. The company also operates nine Stew Leonard's Wines stores across Connecticut, New York and New Jersey. Additionally, Stew Leonard's provides services including kid's parties, private catering, gift baskets, photo cakes, gardening workshops and floral design for special events. Stew's University provides a number of customer service seminars that are open to the public. The company maintains a web site that showcases its products and specials, lists recipes and provides children's activities.

The firm offers employees medical, prescription, dental, disability and vision coverage; a 401(k) plan with a company match; tuition assistance; life insurance; and legal services.

FINANCIAL DATA: *Note: Data for latest year may not have been available at press time.*

In U.S. $	2015	2014	2013	2012	2011	2010
Revenue		420,000,000	415,000,000	400,000,000	341,000,000	355,000,000
R&D Expense						
Operating Income						
Operating Margin %						
SGA Expense						
Net Income						
Operating Cash Flow						
Capital Expenditure						
EBITDA						
Return on Assets %						
Return on Equity %						
Debt to Equity						

CONTACT INFORMATION:

Phone: 203-847-7214   Fax: 203-846-3472
Toll-Free:
Address: 100 Westport Ave., Norwalk, CT 06851 United States

STOCK TICKER/OTHER:

Stock Ticker: Private   Exchange:
Employees: 2,300   Fiscal Year Ends:
Parent Company:

SALARIES/BONUSES:

Top Exec. Salary: $ Bonus: $
Second Exec. Salary: $ Bonus: $

OTHER THOUGHTS:

Estimated Female Officers or Directors: 3
Hot Spot for Advancement for Women/Minorities: Y

Stewart's Shops Corp

www.stewartsshops.com

NAIC Code: 447110

TYPES OF BUSINESS:

Convenience Stores
Ice Cream
Packaged Foods
Gasoline Retail
Real Estate Investments

BRANDS/DIVISIONS/AFFILIATES:

GROWTH PLANS/SPECIAL FEATURES:

Stewart's Shops Corp. owns a chain of 331 convenience stores in New York and Vermont, most of which are located within a 150-mile radius of its headquarters in Saratoga Springs, New York. The company, which is approximately one-third owned by its employees, manufactures and distributes about 75% of its products, including coffee, milk, eggs, sandwiches, hot dogs, chili, soups and ice cream. Stewart's focuses on creating ice cream and offers over 50 varieties of ice cream available hand-scooped and in prepackaged pints. Most shops also sell gasoline. Additionally, the firm generates revenues through the sale of real estate investments, including retail and office space and multi-family apartments.

Stewart's employees are automatically enrolled in the company's profit sharing plan. The company also provides its own health insurance, a credit union membership, discounts to local YMCAs and a scholarship program. It also maintains a company condo in Lake Placid, New York that is available on reservation for employee use.

CONTACTS: Note: Officers with more than one job title may be intentionally listed here more than once.

Gary C. Dake, Pres.
William Dake, Chmn.

FINANCIAL DATA: Note: Data for latest year may not have been available at press time.

In U.S. $	2015	2014	2013	2012	2011	2010
Revenue		1,545,000,000	1,525,000,000	1,500,000,000	1,400,000,000	1,400,000,000
R&D Expense						
Operating Income						
Operating Margin %						
SGA Expense						
Net Income						
Operating Cash Flow						
Capital Expenditure						
EBITDA						
Return on Assets %						
Return on Equity %						
Debt to Equity						

CONTACT INFORMATION:

Phone: 518-581-1200   Fax: 518-581-1209
Toll-Free:
Address: P.O. Box 435, Saratoga Springs, NY 12866 United States

STOCK TICKER/OTHER:

Stock Ticker: Private
Employees: 4,500
Parent Company:

Exchange:
Fiscal Year Ends: 12/31

SALARIES/BONUSES:

Top Exec. Salary: $ Bonus: $
Second Exec. Salary: $ Bonus: $

OTHER THOUGHTS:

Estimated Female Officers or Directors:
Hot Spot for Advancement for Women/Minorities:

Sales, profits and employees may be estimates. Financial information, benefits and other data can change quickly and may vary from those stated here.

Stock Building Supply Inc

NAIC Code: 444190

www.stockbuildingsupply.com

TYPES OF BUSINESS:

Building Materials/Hardware Stores
Design & Installation Services
Lending & Insurance

BRANDS/DIVISIONS/AFFILIATES:

Gores Group, LLC (The)
Building Materials Holding Corporation

CONTACTS: *Note: Officers with more than one job title may be intentionally listed here more than once.*

Jeffrey Rea, CEO
James Major, CFO
Andrew Freedman, Director
Lisa Hamblet, Executive VP, Divisional
Bryan Yeazel, Executive VP
Mark Necaise, Other Corporate Officer
Walter Randolph, President, Divisional
Duff Wakefield, President, Divisional
Steven Wilson, President, Divisional
C. Ball, Senior VP
Michael Farmer, Vice President, Divisional

GROWTH PLANS/SPECIAL FEATURES:

Stock Building Supply, Inc. (SBS) is a supplier of buildin materials to professional homebuilders and contractors in th U.S. SBS is a wholly-owned subsidiary of Gores Group, LLC The company serves the single- and multi-family residentia repair, remodeling and light commercial construction industrie through over 69 stores in 13 U.S. states. The firm divides it products into five categories: structural components; millwor and other interior products; lumber and lumber sheet goods windows and other exterior products; and other buildin products and services. In 2013, the company's combined sale of structural components, millwork and other interior products and windows and other exterior products represented 53% o net sales. Structural components are factory-built substitute for job-site framing and include floor trusses, roof trusses, wa panels and engineered wood that are designed and cut fo each home. Millwork and other interior products include interior doors, interior trim, custom millwork, moldings, stairs stair parts, flooring, cabinets, gypsum and other products Lumber and lumber sheet goods include dimensional lumber plywood and oriented strand board products. Windows and other exterior products includes exterior door units, as well as roofing and siding products. Other building products and services consist of hardware, boards, insulation and othe products. The firm also provides professional estimating product advisory and product display services. In June 2015 the firm reached a definitive agreement to merge with Building Materials Holding Corporation.

SBS offers its employees life, disability, medical, dental and vision insurance; a health reimbursement account; a health care flexible spending account; a 401(k) plan; employee discounts from 10%-15%; health and wellness programs; a 24/7 nurse line; and tobacco cessation programs.

FINANCIAL DATA: *Note: Data for latest year may not have been available at press time.*

In U.S. $	2015	2014	2013	2012	2011	2010
Revenue		1,295,716,000	1,197,037,000	942,398,000	759,982,000	751,706,000
R&D Expense						
Operating Income		18,324,000	761,000	-18,907,000	-59,301,000	-122,834,000
Operating Margin %		1.41%	.06%	-2.00%	-7.80%	-16.34%
SGA Expense		279,717,000	254,935,000	221,192,000	213,036,000	246,338,000
Net Income		10,419,000	-4,635,000	-14,533,000	-42,133,000	-69,994,000
Operating Cash Flow		16,941,000	-40,264,000	-12,243,000	-7,001,000	-57,999,000
Capital Expenditure		43,306,000	7,448,000	2,741,000	1,339,000	2,506,000
EBITDA		32,454,000	13,694,000	-6,860,000	-44,707,000	-71,587,000
Return on Assets %		3.02%	-2.14%	-8.88%	-18.19%	
Return on Equity %		7.75%	-7.99%	-56.11%	-90.07%	
Debt to Equity		0.68	0.50	0.16	0.01	

CONTACT INFORMATION:

Phone: 919-431-1000   Fax:
Toll-Free:
Address: 8020 Arco Corporate Dr., Raleigh, NC 27617 United States

STOCK TICKER/OTHER:

Stock Ticker: STCK
Employees: 3,104
Parent Company:

Exchange: NAS
Fiscal Year Ends: 07/31

SALARIES/BONUSES:

Top Exec. Salary: $600,000   Bonus: $
Second Exec. Salary: $310,000   Bonus: $200,000

OTHER THOUGHTS:

Estimated Female Officers or Directors:
Hot Spot for Advancement for Women/Minorities:

Sun Art Retail Group Ltd

www.sunartretail.com

NAIC Code: 452112

TYPES OF BUSINESS:

Hypermarkets

BRANDS/DIVISIONS/AFFILIATES:

RT-Mart
Auchan
www.fieldschina.com
Concord Greater China Limited
Kofu International Limited
Auchanhyper SA
Monicole Exploitatie Maatschappij BV
A-RT Retail Holdings Limited

GROWTH PLANS/SPECIAL FEATURES:

Sun Art Retail Group, Ltd. operates hypermarkets in China. The firm currently operates 388 complexes located in 27 of China's 31 provinces under two 95%-owned brands: RT-Mart and Auchan. These stores all carry food and non-food merchandise. In addition, RT-Mart and Auchan locations include a mix of convenient third-party stores and amenities inside their complexes, including pharmacies, casual dining restaurants, automated teller machines and drycleaners. Sun Art Retail is primarily owned by Ruentex, a conglomerate comprised of Concord Greater China Limited and Kofu International Limited; Auchanhyper SA and its indirect subsidiary Monicole Exploitatie Maatschappij BV, both of which are part of The Auchan Group; and A-RT Retail Holdings Limited, a joint venture that is 51%-owned by Auchan and 49%-owned by Ruentex. In April 2015, the firm acquired online grocery store www.fieldschina.com.

CONTACTS: Note: Officers with more than one job title may be intentionally listed here more than once.

Bruno Mercier, CEO
Jean-Patrick Paufichet, CFO
Ming-Tuan Peter Huang, Exec. Dir.
Jean-Patrick Paufichet, CFO-Auchan China
Yeong-Fang Chiang, CEO-RT-Mart China

FINANCIAL DATA: Note: Data for latest year may not have been available at press time.

In U.S. $	2015	2014	2013	2012	2011	2010
Revenue		14,377,500,000	13,491,580,000	12,185,540,000	10,656,770,000	8,791,635,000
R&D Expense						
Operating Income		662,565,700	649,104,700	550,651,100	454,858,500	387,240,100
Operating Margin %		4.60%	4.81%	4.51%	4.26%	4.40%
SGA Expense		2,728,838,000	2,365,702,000	2,065,490,000	1,778,894,000	1,372,402,000
Net Income		476,145,700	460,493,400	396,475,100	310,700,000	252,629,600
Operating Cash Flow		879,977,500	1,094,728,000	873,873,000	902,203,800	766,654,100
Capital Expenditure		861,664,100	1,070,937,000	803,280,800	838,968,200	596,043,100
EBITDA		1,070,467,000	996,744,300	856,185,900	694,340,000	572,721,000
Return on Assets %		5.68%	5.87%	5.60%	4.49%	3.45%
Return on Equity %		15.13%	15.59%	15.07%	16.37%	23.41%
Debt to Equity						0.04

CONTACT INFORMATION:

Phone: 852 29801888   Fax: 852 28610285
Toll-Free:
Address: Level 54, Hopewell Centre, 183 Queen's Rd. E., Hong Kong, 6808 HK Hong Kong

STOCK TICKER/OTHER:

Stock Ticker: SURRF   Exchange: PINX
Employees: 130,097   Fiscal Year Ends:
Parent Company:

SALARIES/BONUSES:

Top Exec. Salary: $ Bonus: $
Second Exec. Salary: $ Bonus: $

OTHER THOUGHTS:

Estimated Female Officers or Directors:
Hot Spot for Advancement for Women/Minorities:

SuperGroup PLC

NAIC Code: 448140

TYPES OF BUSINESS:

Casual Apparel Stores
Activewear
Ski Apparel
Franchising

BRANDS/DIVISIONS/AFFILIATES:

Superdry

GROWTH PLANS/SPECIAL FEATURES:

SuperGroup PLC is a UK-based designer and retailer of branded premium quality clothing and accessories. It sells through multiple routes to market, including retail, wholesale and online. The company has approximately 350 stores, both owned and franchised, and is the owner of the Superdry brand. The majority of its stores are located in the UK and Europe. In early 2015, the firm announced it would buy up its franchised stores in the U.S., and concentrate on expanding its operations in Asia, Europe and North America. That April, it formed a joint venture with Trendy International Group to invest in approximately 3,000 fashion stores across China.

CONTACTS: Note: Officers with more than one job title may be intentionally listed here more than once.

Peter Bamford, Chmn.

FINANCIAL DATA: Note: Data for latest year may not have been available at press time.

In U.S. $	2015	2014	2013	2012	2011	2010
Revenue	727,419,500	644,153,400	538,762,800	469,100,400	355,637,300	208,389,400
R&D Expense						
Operating Income	89,993,120	66,822,140	76,987,470	76,688,490	70,559,390	33,934,280
Operating Margin %	12.37%	10.37%	14.28%	16.34%	19.84%	16.28%
SGA Expense	356,235,200					
Net Income	67,868,570	40,960,320	53,667,000	53,965,980	44,996,560	107,932,000
Operating Cash Flow	52,321,580	96,122,220	57,254,760	66,224,180	26,908,240	40,362,360
Capital Expenditure	40,810,840	50,527,700	26,609,260	78,332,890	30,645,500	23,619,460
EBITDA	129,907,000	100,158,500	104,194,700	96,421,200	82,369,120	40,212,870
Return on Assets %	11.55%	8.06%	12.27%	14.32%	16.11%	79.51%
Return on Equity %	16.43%	11.34%	17.61%	21.56%	23.95%	124.21%
Debt to Equity						

CONTACT INFORMATION:

Phone: 44 1242588089   Fax:
Toll-Free:
Address: Unit 60 The Runnings, Gloucestershire, GL51 9NW United Kingdom

STOCK TICKER/OTHER:

Stock Ticker: SEPGY
Employees: 2,352
Parent Company:

Exchange: PINX
Fiscal Year Ends: 05/31

SALARIES/BONUSES:

Top Exec. Salary: $ Bonus: $
Second Exec. Salary: $ Bonus: $

OTHER THOUGHTS:

Estimated Female Officers or Directors:
Hot Spot for Advancement for Women/Minorities:

Supervalu Inc

www.supervalu.com

NAIC Code: 445110

TYPES OF BUSINESS:

Grocery Stores
Food Distribution & Logistics

BRANDS/DIVISIONS/AFFILIATES:

Retail Food
Save-A-Lot
Shopper's Value
Culinary Circle
Java Delight
Stockman & Dakota
Wild Harvest
Essential Everyday

CONTACTS: *Note: Officers with more than one job title may be intentionally listed here more than once.*

Gerald Storch, Chairman of the Board
Randy Burdick, Chief Information Officer
Bruce Besanko, COO
Mark Van Buskirk, Executive VP, Divisional
Michele Murphy, Executive VP, Divisional
Susan Grafton, Executive VP
Karla Robertson, Executive VP
Robert Woseth, Executive VP
Janel Haugarth, Executive VP
Ritchie Casteel, President, Subsidiary

GROWTH PLANS/SPECIAL FEATURES:

Supervalu, Inc. is a supermarket retailer and food distributor. Supervalu conducts its operations through three business segments: independent business, Save-A-Lot and retail food. The independent business segment provides wholesale distribution of products to independent retailers and is the largest public company food wholesaler in the nation. This segment's network spans 41 states and serves as primary grocery supplier to approximately 1,825 stores, in addition to its own stores, as well as serving as a secondary grocery supplier to approximately 208 stores of independent retail customers. The Save-A-Lot segment consists of 1,334 stores, including 903 licensed Save-A-Lot stores, located throughout the U.S. This segment's operations are supplied by 17 distribution centers providing wholesale distribution to the company's own stores and to licensed stores. Supervalu owns 431 Save-A-Lot stores. The retail food segment operates its business through 194 company-owned retail food stores throughout the U.S. under five regionally-based retail banners of Cub Foods, Shoppers Food & Pharmacy, Shop 'n Save, Farm Fresh and Hornbacher's and two Rainbow stores. Products include a wide variety of nationally-advertised brand name and private-label products, primarily grocery (both perishable and non-perishable); general merchandise; home, health and beauty care; and pharmacy. Supervalu's private label products include: Culinary Circle, Java Delight, Stockman & Dakota, Wild Harvest, Essential Everyday, equaline, Artic Shores Seafood Company, Baby Basics, Carlita, Farm Stand, Stone Ridge Creamery and SuperChill. The firm's value brand is Shopper's Value. In July 2015, the firm announced that it has begun preparations to allow for a possible spin-off of Save-A-Lot into a stand-alone, publicly traded company.

Supervalu offers its employees medical, dental and life insurance; short- and long-term disability coverage; a 401(k) plan; profit sharing; tuition reimbursement; flexible spending accounts; and an employee assistance program.

FINANCIAL DATA: *Note: Data for latest year may not have been available at press time.*

In U.S. $	2015	2014	2013	2012	2011	2010
Revenue	17,820,000,000	17,155,000,000	17,097,000,000	36,100,000,000	37,534,000,000	40,597,000,000
R&D Expense						
Operating Income	424,000,000	418,000,000	-157,000,000	-519,000,000	-976,000,000	1,201,000,000
Operating Margin %	2.37%	2.43%	-.91%	-1.43%	-2.60%	2.95%
SGA Expense	2,154,000,000	2,114,000,000	2,445,000,000	7,106,000,000	7,516,000,000	7,952,000,000
Net Income	192,000,000	182,000,000	-1,466,000,000	-1,040,000,000	-1,510,000,000	393,000,000
Operating Cash Flow	408,000,000	19,000,000	898,000,000	1,056,000,000	1,163,000,000	1,474,000,000
Capital Expenditure	239,000,000	111,000,000	228,000,000	661,000,000	597,000,000	681,000,000
EBITDA	714,000,000	720,000,000	211,000,000	370,000,000	-44,000,000	2,165,000,000
Return on Assets %	4.33%	2.36%	-12.69%	-8.05%	-10.00%	2.30%
Return on Equity %				-152.82%	-71.44%	14.37%
Debt to Equity				279.42	4.73	2.43

CONTACT INFORMATION:

Phone: 952 828-4000   Fax: 952 828-8998
Toll-Free:
Address: 7075 Flying Cloud Dr., Eden Prairie, MN 55344 United States

STOCK TICKER/OTHER:

Stock Ticker: SVU
Employees: 38,500
Parent Company:

Exchange: NYS
Fiscal Year Ends: 02/28

SALARIES/BONUSES:

Top Exec. Salary: $637,019   Bonus: $925,000
Second Exec. Salary: $1,528,846   Bonus: $

OTHER THOUGHTS:

Estimated Female Officers or Directors: 3
Hot Spot for Advancement for Women/Minorities: Y

Sales, profits and employees may be estimates. Financial information, benefits and other data can change quickly and may vary from those stated here.

Sur La Table

www.surlatable.com

NAIC Code: 442299

TYPES OF BUSINESS:

Culinary Supplies, Retail
Cookware
Cookbooks
Linens
Housewares & Barware
Specialty Foods
Culinary Instruction
Online Sales

BRANDS/DIVISIONS/AFFILIATES:

Art & Soul of Baking (The)
Things Cooks Love
Baking Kids Love
Sur La Table
Investcorp

CONTACTS: Note: Officers with more than one job title may be intentionally listed here more than once.

Diane Neal, CEO
Debbie Brownfield, Corp. Sec.
Kevin Ertell, VP-e-commerce

GROWTH PLANS/SPECIAL FEATURES:

Sur La Table, founded and headquartered in Seattle Washington, operates over 115 culinary stores throughout th U.S. The stores feature specialty cooking tools, cookware foods, kitchen items, housewares and linens. Merchandise designed for upscale consumers who are passionate abou food and cooking. Sur La Table operates one of the larges culinary programs in the U.S. as well as an e-commerce we site which features an expanded selection of products, a gi registry, store event information, recipes and cooking tips. Wit products from vendors worldwide, Sur La Table focuses o attracting new customers through culinary diversity, innovatio and authenticity. Products include a variety of appliances bakeware, barware, coffee/espresso accessories, cookbooks knives, copperware, dishware, glassware, seasona accessories, tabletop accessories and a large assortment o specialty foods. Additionally, the firm features hard to find item including cookie molds, duck presses and truffle shavers. The company also offers Sur La Table exclusive items manufactured specifically for its stores. Through collaboration with several chefs and authors, Sur La Table has publishe several cookbooks including Memorable Recipes: to Share with Family and Friends, Baking Kids Love, Things Cooks Love and The Art & Soul of Baking. The firm is owned by Bahrain based Investcorp, an investment company that formerly hac stakes in Gucci and Tiffany & Co.

FINANCIAL DATA: Note: Data for latest year may not have been available at press time.

In U.S. $	2015	2014	2013	2012	2011	2010
Revenue		1,958,000,000	1,900,000,000	1,800,000,000	1,750,000,000	1,500,000,000
R&D Expense						
Operating Income						
Operating Margin %						
SGA Expense						
Net Income						
Operating Cash Flow						
Capital Expenditure						
EBITDA						
Return on Assets %						
Return on Equity %						
Debt to Equity						

CONTACT INFORMATION:

Phone: 206-613-6000   Fax: 206-613-6137
Toll-Free: 866-328-5412
Address: 6100 4th Ave. S., Ste. 500, Seattle, WA 98108 United States

STOCK TICKER/OTHER:

Stock Ticker: Private   Exchange:
Employees: 2,500   Fiscal Year Ends: 12/31
Parent Company: Investcorp

SALARIES/BONUSES:

Top Exec. Salary: $ Bonus: $
Second Exec. Salary: $ Bonus: $

OTHER THOUGHTS:

Estimated Female Officers or Directors: 2
Hot Spot for Advancement for Women/Minorities: Y

Swank Inc

NAIC Code: 424300

TYPES OF BUSINESS:

Apparel and Clothing Brands, Designers, Importers and Distributors
Men's Jewelry

BRANDS/DIVISIONS/AFFILIATES:

Swank
Randa Accessories Leather Goods LLC

CONTACTS: *Note: Officers with more than one job title may be intentionally listed here more than once.*

Jeffrey Spiegel, CEO-Randa
Arthur T. Gately, III, VP-Admin.

GROWTH PLANS/SPECIAL FEATURES:

Swank, Inc., a subsidiary of Randa Accessories Leather Goods LLC, is engaged in the import, sale and distribution of men's belts, leather accessories, suspenders and men's jewelry. The company's products include belts, wallets and other small leather goods, including billfolds, key cases, card holders and other items; and men's jewelry, including cuff links, tie clips, chains and tacs, bracelets, neck chains, vest chains, collar pins, key rings and money clips. The firm distributes these products under its own brand name, Swank, as well as licensed brands Geoffrey Beene, Kenneth Cole, Chaps, Donald Trump, Tommy Hilfiger, Guess, Buffalo David Bitton and Nautica. Additionally, the company distributes men's costume jewelry under the brands Geoffrey Beene, Claiborne, Kenneth Cole, Chaps, Donald Trump, Guess, Buffalo David Bitton and Nautica; men's suspenders under the Geoffrey Beene brand; and women's leather accessories under the Pierre Cardin and Buffalo David Bitton brands. Swank no longer manufactures the products it sells, which are instead sourced from third-party vendors; it purchases most of its small leather goods, chiefly wallets, from a single supplier in India. Swank sells its products both domestically and internationally, principally through department stores, but also through national chain stores, specialty stores, mass merchandisers, catalog retailers and U.S. military retail exchanges. The company's three largest customers include Macy's, Inc.; Kohl's Department Stores; and The TJX Companies, Inc.

FINANCIAL DATA: *Note: Data for latest year may not have been available at press time.*

In U.S. $	2015	2014	2013	2012	2011	2010
Revenue		155,000,000	145,000,000	140,000,000	138,620,000	132,702,000
R&D Expense						
Operating Income						
Operating Margin %						
SGA Expense						
Net Income						
Operating Cash Flow						
Capital Expenditure						
EBITDA						
Return on Assets %						
Return on Equity %						
Debt to Equity						

CONTACT INFORMATION:

Phone: 212-768-8800   Fax:
Toll-Free:
Address: 417 5th Ave, 11th Fl, New York, NY 10016 United States

STOCK TICKER/OTHER:

Stock Ticker: Subsidiary   Exchange:
Employees: Fiscal Year Ends: 12/31
Parent Company: Randa Accessories Leather Goods LLC

SALARIES/BONUSES:

Top Exec. Salary: $ Bonus: $
Second Exec. Salary: $ Bonus: $

OTHER THOUGHTS:

Estimated Female Officers or Directors:
Hot Spot for Advancement for Women/Minorities:

Takashimaya Company Limited

www.takashimaya.co.jp

NAIC Code: 452111

TYPES OF BUSINESS:

Department Stores
Interior Design
Shopping Centers
Credit Cards
Apparel Manufacturing
Restaurants

BRANDS/DIVISIONS/AFFILIATES:

Takashimaya Card

GROWTH PLANS/SPECIAL FEATURES:

Takashimaya Company Limited is primarily a Japanese owner and operator of department stores. The firm operates in five divisions: department stores, contract & design, real estate, finance and other. The department stores segment operates the firm's 17 domestic and three international department stores in Shanghai, Taipei and Singapore. The contract & design segment carries out a variety of interior decorating for corporate customers. The real estate segment holds the company's physical properties and operates shopping centers. The finance segment operates the firm's Takashimaya Card and provides various financial services to group companies. The other segment comprises the firm's mail-order, online and catalogue businesses as well as clothing manufacture and processing. The company's products include clothing and accessories, personal items, household goods, home furnishings, food items, plants and gardening supplies, sporting goods and groceries. Takashimaya also operates restaurants.

CONTACTS: Note: Officers with more than one job title may be intentionally listed here more than once.

Shigeru Kimoto, CEO
Koji Suzuki, Pres.
Toshiaki Seki, Sr. Managing Dir.-Sales
Yoko Yasuda, Dir.-Personnel Affairs
Yasuhiko Matsumoto, Sr. Managing Dir.-Planning
Masao Yamada, Managing Dir.-Gen. Affairs
Kaoru Omata, Sr. Exec.-Special Mission

FINANCIAL DATA: Note: Data for latest year may not have been available at press time.

In U.S. $	2015	2014	2013	2012	2011	2010
Revenue	7,405,272,000	7,337,567,000	7,062,893,000	6,963,814,000	7,055,938,000	7,123,180,000
R&D Expense						
Operating Income	259,864,000	236,143,300	206,742,100	171,222,000	147,477,000	108,970,500
Operating Margin %	3.50%	3.21%	2.92%	2.45%	2.09%	1.52%
SGA Expense	1,155,682,000	1,147,120,000	1,115,917,000	1,116,899,000	1,141,926,000	1,196,874,000
Net Income	189,959,900	158,172,800	134,224,900	88,414,780	112,387,000	62,559,850
Operating Cash Flow	332,868,100	329,329,900	358,211,700	259,044,400	167,537,700	190,122,200
Capital Expenditure	1,011,718,000	280,346,700	165,752,400	132,764,200	235,023,500	161,427,000
EBITDA	460,430,400	398,008,500	373,736,100	310,770,400	352,474,300	242,805,900
Return on Assets %	2.40%	2.21%	2.07%	1.34%	1.72%	1.00%
Return on Equity %	5.94%	5.44%	5.23%	3.64%	4.74%	2.72%
Debt to Equity	0.31	0.34	0.24	0.29	0.40	0.33

CONTACT INFORMATION:

Phone: 81 666311101   Fax: 81 666319850
Toll-Free:
Address: 1-5, Namba 5-Chome, Chuo-ku, Osaka, 542-8510 Japan

STOCK TICKER/OTHER:

Stock Ticker: TKSHF   Exchange: GREY
Employees: 15,340   Fiscal Year Ends: 02/28
Parent Company:

SALARIES/BONUSES:

Top Exec. Salary: $ Bonus: $
Second Exec. Salary: $ Bonus: $

OTHER THOUGHTS:

Estimated Female Officers or Directors:
Hot Spot for Advancement for Women/Minorities:

Talbots Inc (The)

NAIC Code: 448120

TYPES OF BUSINESS:

Women's Apparel, Retail
Online & Catalog Sales
Footwear
Accessories

BRANDS/DIVISIONS/AFFILIATES:

Talbots Classics National Bank
Sycamore Partners
Talbots.com
Talbots Classics Finance Company Inc

CONTACTS: Note: Officers with more than one job title may be intentionally listed here more than once.

Trudy F. Sullivan, CEO
Michael Scarpa, COO
Trudy F. Sullivan, Pres.
Michael Scarpa, CFO
John Kovac, CIO
Benedetta Casamento, Exec. VP-Finance
Lesli Gilbert, Sr. VP-Stores
Richard T. O'Connell, Jr., Exec. VP-Real Estate, Store Planning & Design
Gary M. Pfeiffer, Chmn.
Greg Poole, Chief Supply Chain Officer

GROWTH PLANS/SPECIAL FEATURES:

The Talbots, Inc., owned by private equity company Sycamore Partners, is a leading international specialty retailer of women's apparel, shoes and accessories. The firm currently operates 500 stores in the U.S. and Canada. These stores include 425 core Talbots stores, 65 Talbots Factory Outlet stores (U.S.) and five Talbots Clearance stores (four in U.S. and one in Canada). The company offers classic sportswear, casual wear, dresses, coats, sweaters, accessories and shoes, consisting almost exclusively of privately branded merchandise in misses, petites, woman and woman petite sizes. The firm's target demographic is women 32 years and older. In addition to brick-and-mortar retail operations, Talbots maintains a significant direct marketing sales division that includes catalogs, red-line phone sales and an e-commerce site, Talbots.com. Through wholly-owned subsidiaries Talbots Classics National Bank and Talbots Classics Finance Company, Inc., the firm manages and administers a Talbots credit card program.

The company offers its employees an associate merchandise discount, health and dental insurance, paid time off, life and disability insurance and tuition assistance.

FINANCIAL DATA: Note: Data for latest year may not have been available at press time.

In U.S. $	2015	2014	2013	2012	2011	2010
Revenue		1,100,000,000	1,050,000,000	1,140,000,000	1,213,060,000	1,235,632,000
R&D Expense						
Operating Income						
Operating Margin %						
SGA Expense						
Net Income						
Operating Cash Flow						
Capital Expenditure						
EBITDA						
Return on Assets %						
Return on Equity %						
Debt to Equity						

CONTACT INFORMATION:

Phone: 781-749-7600   Fax: 781-741-4369
Toll-Free: 800-825-3371
Address: 1 Talbots Dr., Hingham, MA 02043 United States

STOCK TICKER/OTHER:

Stock Ticker: Private
Employees: 9,000
Parent Company: Sycamore Partners

Exchange:
Fiscal Year Ends: 01/31

SALARIES/BONUSES:

Top Exec. Salary: $ Bonus: $
Second Exec. Salary: $ Bonus: $

OTHER THOUGHTS:

Estimated Female Officers or Directors: 3
Hot Spot for Advancement for Women/Minorities: Y

Tamara G Designs

NAIC Code: 448310

www.tamaragdesign.com

TYPES OF BUSINESS:

Faux Jewelry, Retail
Fine Art Galleries
Reproduction Art
Children's & Specialty Jewelry
Fine Jewelry
Online Sales

BRANDS/DIVISIONS/AFFILIATES:

Platinique
TamaraGDesign.com

GROWTH PLANS/SPECIAL FEATURES:

Tamara G. Designs is primarily a retailer of imitation jewelr
from artificial, lab-created gemstones. It also sells fine jewelr
and sterling silver jewelry. The firm currently operates five reta
locations in California. Tamara G. Designs sells copies of fin
jewelry, including rings, pendants, earrings, necklaces
bracelets, pearl enhancers and ear charms. These items are
manufactured in 14-carat gold, sterling silver vermeil and gold
bonded white metal. The company also offers its own
trademarked metal Platinique, which is a mixture of sterling
silver and platinum with a rhodium finish. Since it uses synthetic
and laboratory-grown stones, the company can offer its
imitation jewelry at significantly lower prices than fine jewelry
The firm offers 15 different artificial stones, including cubi
zirconia and artificial sapphires, rubies, emeralds and topaz
Customers can purchase imitation jewelry and precious stones
directly from the firm's web site, TamaraGDesign.com.

CONTACTS: Note: Officers with more than one job title may be intentionally listed here more than once.

James C. Cardinal, CEO
Gavin Gear, Pres.
Tamara Gear, Sec.
Tamara Gear, Treas.

FINANCIAL DATA: Note: Data for latest year may not have been available at press time.

In U.S. $	2015	2014	2013	2012	2011	2010
Revenue						
R&D Expense						
Operating Income						
Operating Margin %						
SGA Expense						
Net Income						
Operating Cash Flow						
Capital Expenditure						
EBITDA						
Return on Assets %						
Return on Equity %						
Debt to Equity						

CONTACT INFORMATION:

Phone: 831-649-1814   Fax: 831-649-1001
Toll-Free:
Address: 542 Lighthouse Ave., Ste. 5, Pacific Grove, CA 93950 United States

STOCK TICKER/OTHER:

Stock Ticker: Private   Exchange:
Employees: Fiscal Year Ends: 12/31
Parent Company:

SALARIES/BONUSES:

Top Exec. Salary: $ Bonus: $
Second Exec. Salary: $ Bonus: $

OTHER THOUGHTS:

Estimated Female Officers or Directors: 1
Hot Spot for Advancement for Women/Minorities:

Target Corporation

www.target.com

NAIC Code: 452910

TYPES OF BUSINESS:

Supercenters
Online Sales
Catalog Sales
Groceries
Credit Cards

BRANDS/DIVISIONS/AFFILIATES:

SuperTarget
Target.com
CityTarget
Archer Farms
Merona
REDcards
Xhilaration
Room Essentials

CONTACTS: *Note: Officers with more than one job title may be intentionally listed here more than once.*

Brian Cornell, CEO
Catherine Smith, CFO
Robert Harrison, Chief Accounting Officer
Jeffrey Jones, Chief Marketing Officer
Jacqueline Rice, Chief Risk Officer
John Mulligan, Executive VP
Timothy Baer, Executive VP
Jodeen Kozlak, Executive VP
Laysha Ward, Executive VP
Tina Tyler, Executive VP
Casey Carl, Other Executive Officer

GROWTH PLANS/SPECIAL FEATURES:

Target Corporation operates large-format general merchandise and food discount stores in the U.S., which include Target and SuperTarget stores. Target operates approximately 1,934 stores in the U.S. SuperTarget stores combine grocery and general merchandise in a single format and feature coffee bars, bakeries, banking areas, pharmacies and photo services. Recently, Target launched eight CityTarget stores which cater to busy consumers living in tighter urban locations such as Chicago, Los Angeles, Seattle and San Francisco. Target carries brands such as Cherokee, Mossimo, Simply Shabby Chic and Sutton & Dodge, among many others. In addition, Target sells merchandise under its own private-label brands including Market Pantry, Archer Farms, Merona, Xhilaration, Circo, Room Essentials, Target and Simply Balanced. Target stores derive the largest percentage of sales from household essentials (approximately 25%); food and pet supplies account for 21%; apparel and accessories for 19%; electronics, music, movies, sporting goods and toys for 18%; and home furniture and decor for 17%. The company's proprietary credit card products, called REDcards, provide discounts in an attempt to gain customer loyalty. REDcards are sold under the Target Visa and Target Card names. Target also sells merchandise via its e-commerce site Target.com. Target has 38 distribution centers in the U.S. In 2014, the firm opened up 16 new stores and closed 19. In June 2015, the firm agreed to sell its pharmacies and clinics to CVS Health Corp. for 1.9 billion. The 1,600 drugstores inside target will be rebranded as CVS/pharmacy, while Target's 80 medical clinics will be rebranded as CVS's MinuteClinic. Also in 2015, the firm exited the Canadian market and Target Canada Co. and other wholly-owned Canadian subsidiaries of Target filed for bankruptcy protection in Canada.

Target offers employees benefits including medical, dental, vision, prescription drug, life and disability insurance; wellness programs; flexible spending accounts; childcare discounts; a 401(k) plan; tuition reimbursement; and 10% team member discount on store merchandise.

FINANCIAL DATA: *Note: Data for latest year may not have been available at press time.*

In U.S. $	2015	2014	2013	2012	2011	2010
Revenue	72,618,000,000	72,596,000,000	73,301,000,000	69,865,000,000	67,390,000,000	65,357,000,000
R&D Expense						
Operating Income	4,535,000,000	4,229,000,000	5,371,000,000	5,322,000,000	5,252,000,000	4,673,000,000
Operating Margin %	6.24%	5.82%	7.32%	7.61%	7.79%	7.15%
SGA Expense	14,676,000,000	15,375,000,000	14,914,000,000	14,106,000,000	13,469,000,000	13,078,000,000
Net Income	-1,636,000,000	1,971,000,000	2,999,000,000	2,929,000,000	2,920,000,000	2,488,000,000
Operating Cash Flow	4,439,000,000	6,520,000,000	5,325,000,000	5,434,000,000	5,271,000,000	5,881,000,000
Capital Expenditure	1,786,000,000	3,453,000,000	3,277,000,000	4,368,000,000	2,129,000,000	1,729,000,000
EBITDA	6,664,000,000	6,452,000,000	7,513,000,000	7,456,000,000	7,339,000,000	6,699,000,000
Return on Assets %	-3.80%	4.25%	6.32%	6.48%	6.61%	5.61%
Return on Equity %	-10.82%	12.02%	18.52%	18.71%	18.94%	17.12%
Debt to Equity	0.90	0.77	0.88	0.84	1.00	0.98

CONTACT INFORMATION:

Phone: 612 304-6073   Fax: 612 370-5502
Toll-Free:
Address: 1000 Nicollet Mall, Minneapolis, MN 55403 United States

STOCK TICKER/OTHER:

Stock Ticker: TGT   Exchange: NYS
Employees: 347,000   Fiscal Year Ends: 01/31
Parent Company:

SALARIES/BONUSES:

Top Exec. Salary: $950,000   Bonus: $380,000
Second Exec. Salary: $919,231   Bonus: $400,000

OTHER THOUGHTS:

Estimated Female Officers or Directors: 9
Hot Spot for Advancement for Women/Minorities: Y

Sales, profits and employees may be estimates. Financial information, benefits and other data can change quickly and may vary from those stated here.

TBC Corporation

www.tbccorp.com

NAIC Code: 441320

TYPES OF BUSINESS:

Tire Stores
Wholesale Tire Distribution

BRANDS/DIVISIONS/AFFILIATES:

Sumitomo Corporation
Sumitomo Corporation of America
Carroll Tire Company
TBC Retail Group Inc
TBC Brands LLC
Big O Tires LIC
Midas Inc
SpeeDee Oil Change & Auto Service

CONTACTS: Note: Officers with more than one job title may be intentionally listed here more than once.

Erik R. Olsen, CEO
J. Glen Gravatt, Pres.
Timothy J. Miller, CFO
Brian Maciak, General Counsel
Timothy J. Miller, Treas.
J. Glen Gravatt, Pres., Purchasing & Dist. Div.

GROWTH PLANS/SPECIAL FEATURES:

TBC Corporation markets and distributes replacement automobile tires through wholesale and retail operations. TBC's wholesale business markets and distributes its proprietary brands of tires, as well as other tires and related products, to regional tire chains and distributors serving independent tire dealers covering the U.S., Canada and Mexico. The company also markets directly to independent tire dealers in the U.S. through its Carroll Tire Company wholesale distribution centers. The company's TBC Retail Group, Inc. operates nearly 800 tire and automotive service centers under the Tire Kingdom, Merchant's Tire & Auto Centers and National Tire & Battery (NTB) brands. Subsidiary TBC Brands, LLC represents 13 proprietary brands of tires throughout North America, including Multi-Mile, Eldorado, Sumitomo, Harvest King, Power King and Towmax. Big O Tires, LLC serves over 400 franchised and company-owned tire stores. Wholly-owned Midas, Inc. provides automotive services such as brake, maintenance, tires, exhaust, steering and suspension services at nearly 2,250 franchised, licensed and company-owned Midas shops in 13 countries. SpeeDee Oil Change & Auto Service provides neighborhood oil change and auto maintenance services. There are approximately 160 SpeeDee service centers in the U.S. and Mexico. TBC Corporation is owned by Sumitomo Corporation of America, which itself is a subsidiary of Sumitomo Corporation.

FINANCIAL DATA: Note: Data for latest year may not have been available at press time.

In U.S. $	2015	2014	2013	2012	2011	2010
Revenue		3,500,000,000	3,000,000,000	2,750,000,000	2,600,000,000	2,450,000,000
R&D Expense						
Operating Income						
Operating Margin %						
SGA Expense						
Net Income						
Operating Cash Flow						
Capital Expenditure						
EBITDA						
Return on Assets %						
Return on Equity %						
Debt to Equity						

CONTACT INFORMATION:

Phone: 561-383-3100   Fax: 531-383-3149
Toll-Free:
Address: 4300 TBC Way, Palm Beach Gardens, FL 33410 United States

SALARIES/BONUSES:

Top Exec. Salary: $ Bonus: $
Second Exec. Salary: $ Bonus: $

STOCK TICKER/OTHER:

Stock Ticker: Subsidiary   Exchange:
Employees: 10,000   Fiscal Year Ends: 12/31
Parent Company: SUMITOMO CORPORATION

OTHER THOUGHTS:

Estimated Female Officers or Directors:
Hot Spot for Advancement for Women/Minorities:

Teavana Holdings Inc

www.teavana.com

NAIC Code: 722515

TYPES OF BUSINESS:

Retail Tea Stores
Tea Bar
Tea Accessories

BRANDS/DIVISIONS/AFFILIATES:

Starbucks Corporation
Teavana.com
Teavana
Teavana Oprah Chai Tea

CONTACTS: Note: Officers with more than one job title may be intentionally listed here more than once.

Cliff Burrows, Pres.
Daniel P. Glennon, CFO

GROWTH PLANS/SPECIAL FEATURES:

Teavana Holdings, Inc., a subsidiary of Starbucks Corporation, is a specialty retailer of premium loose-leaf tea, artisanal teawares and other tea-related merchandise. The company has more than 300 stores operating under the name Teavana in the U.S., Canada and Mexico. Teavana also operates the e-commerce site Teavana.com and has global partners in Kuwait. While the stores were traditionally only found in malls and outlets, after its acquisition by Starbucks, Teavana began expanding locations on to the street and in neighborhoods. The company's goal is to introduce the customer to high-quality, healthy tea as an alternative to other unhealthy beverages. To that end, Teavana offers in both its stores and on its web site over 100 different varieties of loose-leaf tea, ranging from White and Green to Rooibos and Mate. Additionally, the company also offers all the accessories needed for the brewing and storage of tea, such as tea pots and tins. Many of the Teavana stores serve tea as well. In 2014, Starbucks and Teavana collaborated with Oprah Winfrey to develop a tea called Teavana Oprah Chai Tea, along with related tea accessories. For every sale of Oprah Chai Tea products, Starbucks said it would donate to the Oprah Winfrey Leadership Foundation Academy, which supports youth education.

FINANCIAL DATA: Note: Data for latest year may not have been available at press time.

In U.S. $	2015	2014	2013	2012	2011	2010
Revenue		460,000,000	391,024,200	349,289,876	168,100,000	124,701,000
R&D Expense						
Operating Income						
Operating Margin %						
SGA Expense						
Net Income						
Operating Cash Flow						
Capital Expenditure						
EBITDA						
Return on Assets %						
Return on Equity %						
Debt to Equity						

CONTACT INFORMATION:

Phone: 404 995-8200   Fax:
Toll-Free:
Address: 3630 Peachtree Rd., Ste. 1480, Atlanta, GA 30326 United States

STOCK TICKER/OTHER:

Stock Ticker: Subsidiary
Employees: 2,000
Parent Company: Starbucks Corporation

Exchange:
Fiscal Year Ends: 01/31

SALARIES/BONUSES:

Top Exec. Salary: $ Bonus: $
Second Exec. Salary: $ Bonus: $

OTHER THOUGHTS:

Estimated Female Officers or Directors:
Hot Spot for Advancement for Women/Minorities:

Sales, profits and employees may be estimates. Financial information, benefits and other data can change quickly and may vary from those stated here.

Teespring Inc

teespring.com

NAIC Code: 454111

TYPES OF BUSINESS:

Electronic Shopping

BRANDS/DIVISIONS/AFFILIATES:

teespring.com

CONTACTS: *Note: Officers with more than one job title may be intentionally listed here more than once.*

Robert Chatwani, Chief Revenue & Mktg. Officer

GROWTH PLANS/SPECIAL FEATURES:

Teespring, Inc. is an e-commerce platform established to enable anyone to design and sell products. The company was founded in 2011 by two Brown University students which developed a web site in mere hours to sell commemorative shirts in lieu of the closing of their favorite local bar. The site was designed to accept prepaid orders before printing anything so as to bypass heavy upfront production costs. Obtaining hundreds of orders within hours, the concept and site was then launched, allowing anyone to create a crowdfunding campaign for custom apparel. The Teespring platform allows people to take their own designs, print them on clothing and then sell them without the restrictions usually associated with starting an online store. The platform sells the items in campaigns (or limited edition runs) so they can be printed in bulk. Popular categories at the teespring.com site include Nurses, Firefighters, Fishing, Running, Music, Yoga, Camping, Dogs, Cats, Horses, Mechanics and Engineering. Currently Teespring has offices in Providence, Rhode Island, San Francisco, California and Hebron, Kentucky. As of late 2015, the firm had raised $56 million in venture capital and had four offices in San Francisco, California; Providence, RI; Hebron, Kentucky and London, England.

FINANCIAL DATA: *Note: Data for latest year may not have been available at press time.*

In U.S. $	2015	2014	2013	2012	2011	2010
Revenue						
R&D Expense						
Operating Income						
Operating Margin %						
SGA Expense						
Net Income						
Operating Cash Flow						
Capital Expenditure						
EBITDA						
Return on Assets %						
Return on Equity %						
Debt to Equity						

CONTACT INFORMATION:

Phone: 1-855-833-7774   Fax:
Toll-Free: 855-833-7774
Address: 460 Bryant St., Ste. 200, San Francisco, CA 94107 United States

STOCK TICKER/OTHER:

Stock Ticker: Private   Exchange:
Employees: Fiscal Year Ends:
Parent Company:

SALARIES/BONUSES:

Top Exec. Salary: $ Bonus: $
Second Exec. Salary: $ Bonus: $

OTHER THOUGHTS:

Estimated Female Officers or Directors:
Hot Spot for Advancement for Women/Minorities:

Tesco plc

www.tescoplc.com

NAIC Code: 445110

TYPES OF BUSINESS:

Grocery Stores & Superstores
Online Grocery Sales & Home Delivery
Financial Services
Convenience Stores
Gasoline, Retail
Telecommunications Services
Books, CDs & DVDs

BRANDS/DIVISIONS/AFFILIATES:

Tesco Express
Tesco Bank
Dunnhumby
Dunnhumby USA
Spenhill
Homeplus

CONTACTS: Note: Officers with more than one job title may be intentionally listed here more than once.

Philip Clarke, Group Chief Exec.
Laurie McIlwee, CFO
Matt Atkinson, Chief Mktg. Officer
Mike McNamara, CIO
Adrian Morris, General Counsel
Jill Easterbrook, Managing Dir.-Developing Bus.
Ken Towle, Managing Dir.-Central Europe & Turkey
Jonathan Lloyd, Company Sec.
Chris Bush, Managing Dir.-UK
Kevin Grace, Dir.-Commercial
Benny Higgins, CEO-Tesco Bank
Richard Broadbent, Chmn.
Trevor Masters, CEO-Asia
Gordon Fryett, Property Dir.

GROWTH PLANS/SPECIAL FEATURES:

Tesco plc operates approximately 7,817 supermarkets, superstores and convenience stores in 12 countries, including around 3,300 in the U.K. International markets include China, the Czech Republic, Hungary, India, Malaysia, Poland, the Republic of Ireland, Slovakia, South Korea, Thailand and Turkey. Tesco Express locations combine convenience stores and gasoline stations. Tesco Bank offers financial services such as savings accounts, online banking and insurance policies. Additionally, the company owns a majority stake in Dunnhumby, a customer science company based in Cincinnati, Ohio. During 2015, the firm closed each of its Homeplus stores; sold its Blinkbox streaming business, as well as its home telephone and broadband business to TalkTalk for approximately $7.7 million (5 million pounds); and agreed to sell 14 Spenhill mixed-used & residential development sites across London, the South East and Bath. That same year, The Kroger Company offered to purchase a majority stake in Dunnhumby USA.

FINANCIAL DATA: Note: Data for latest year may not have been available at press time.

In U.S. $	2015	2014	2013	2012	2011	2010
Revenue	93,108,500,000	95,011,510,000	96,908,540,000	96,479,500,000	90,374,320,000	85,074,890,000
R&D Expense						
Operating Income	-8,658,475,000	3,933,088,000	3,270,846,000	5,957,186,000	5,855,533,000	5,167,878,000
Operating Margin %	-9.29%	4.13%	3.37%	6.17%	6.47%	6.07%
SGA Expense	4,028,762,000	2,477,053,000				
Net Income	-8,582,235,000	1,456,035,000	185,367,900	4,194,696,000	3,968,966,000	3,478,638,000
Operating Cash Flow	723,532,700	4,761,264,000	4,241,038,000	6,589,530,000	6,378,748,000	7,093,311,000
Capital Expenditure	3,465,184,000	4,306,813,000	4,465,273,000	5,543,098,000	5,308,399,000	4,511,615,000
EBITDA	-6,465,453,000	7,431,159,000	7,129,189,000	8,595,688,000	8,260,831,000	7,610,548,000
Return on Assets %	-12.16%	1.94%	.24%	5.72%	5.69%	5.08%
Return on Equity %	-52.70%	6.21%	.72%	16.35%	17.05%	16.95%
Debt to Equity	1.50	0.63	0.60	0.55	0.58	0.80

CONTACT INFORMATION:

Phone: 44 1992646484   Fax:
Toll-Free: 44-0800-505-555
Address: Tesco House, Delamare Rd., Hertfordshire, EN8 9SL United Kingdom

STOCK TICKER/OTHER:

Stock Ticker: TSCDF
Employees: 506,984
Parent Company:

Exchange: PINX
Fiscal Year Ends: 02/28

SALARIES/BONUSES:

Top Exec. Salary: $ Bonus: $
Second Exec. Salary: $ Bonus: $

OTHER THOUGHTS:

Estimated Female Officers or Directors: 3
Hot Spot for Advancement for Women/Minorities: Y

Thomas Kinkade Company

NAIC Code: 442299

thomaskinkade.com/

TYPES OF BUSINESS:

Art & Collectibles, Retail
Photolithographs
Decorative Accessories
Online Sales

BRANDS/DIVISIONS/AFFILIATES:

Art Brand Studios
Thomas Kinkade
Signature Galleries
Next Point Capital
Zachary Thomas Kinkade

CONTACTS: *Note: Officers with more than one job title may be intentionally listed here more than once.*

John Hasting, CEO

GROWTH PLANS/SPECIAL FEATURES:

Thomas Kinkade Company is a designer, manufacturer, marketer and branded retailer of art-based home decorative accessories, collectibles and gift products based upon the works of the late Thomas Kinkade. The company's products consist primarily of canvas and paper lithographs that feature the artist's unique rendering of light in peaceful and inspiring themes. They also include collectible framed canvas and paper lithographs, books, sculpture, stationery, ceramics, mini-prints on easels, magnets, inspirational prints, decorative tins, gift baskets and picture frames. Kinkade's paintings often focus on gardens, cityscapes, cottages, lighthouses and country villages. Products generally sell at retail price points ranging from $20 for small gift prints to between $150 and $10,000 for paper and canvas lithographs. Thomas Kinkade products are sold through a distribution network of Signature Galleries, retailers and Showcase Galleries in the U.S., the U.K., Canada, Ireland, Russia and Malaysia. The average Kinkade gallery is between 750 and 1,000 square feet. Thomas Kinkade has strategic relationships with many companies, as well as an e-commerce web site. The company utilizes multi-media marketing programs, including print, radio and television to enhance its marketing capabilities to consumers and collectors. In January 2015, the company was acquired by Art Brand Studios, an affiliate of private investment firm, Next Point Capital. That August, the firm announced a new artist, Zachary Thomas Kinkade, the late Thomas Kinkade's nephew, whose art will be published by the company.

FINANCIAL DATA: *Note: Data for latest year may not have been available at press time.*

In U.S. $	2015	2014	2013	2012	2011	2010
Revenue						
R&D Expense						
Operating Income						
Operating Margin %						
SGA Expense						
Net Income						
Operating Cash Flow						
Capital Expenditure						
EBITDA						
Return on Assets %						
Return on Equity %						
Debt to Equity						

CONTACT INFORMATION:

Phone: 408-201-5000   Fax: 408-201-5192
Toll-Free: 800-366-3733
Address: 18635 Sutter Blvd, Morgan Hill, CA 95037 United States

STOCK TICKER/OTHER:

Stock Ticker: Private   Exchange:
Employees: Fiscal Year Ends: 12/31
Parent Company: Art Brand Studios

SALARIES/BONUSES:

Top Exec. Salary: $ Bonus: $
Second Exec. Salary: $ Bonus: $

OTHER THOUGHTS:

Estimated Female Officers or Directors:
Hot Spot for Advancement for Women/Minorities:

Tiffany & Co

www.tiffany.com

NAIC Code: 448310

TYPES OF BUSINESS:

Jewelry & Other Luxury Items, Retail
Catalog & Online Sales
Jewelry
Fragrance
Timepieces
Stationery
Home DÃ©cor

BRANDS/DIVISIONS/AFFILIATES:

Tiffany and Company

CONTACTS: Note: Officers with more than one job title may be intentionally listed here more than once.

Ralph Nicoletti, CFO
Michael Kowalski, Chairman of the Board
John Barresi, Chief Accounting Officer
Caroline Naggiar, Chief Marketing Officer
Frederic Cumenal, Director
Andrew Hart, Senior VP, Divisional
John Petterson, Senior VP, Divisional
Victoria Berger-Gross, Senior VP, Divisional
Pamela Cloud, Senior VP, Divisional
Jean-Marc Bellaiche, Senior VP, Divisional
Jennifer De Winter, Senior VP, Geographical
Leigh Harlan, Senior VP

GROWTH PLANS/SPECIAL FEATURES:

Tiffany & Co. is a holding company operating through its principle subsidiary, Tiffany and Company, a retail firm primarily selling jewelry as well as timepieces, sterling silver goods, china, crystal, stationery, fragrances and personal accessories. Its products are sold through U.S. and international Tiffany & Co. stores as well as through direct marketing, including business-to-business (B2B), mail-order, Internet and wholesale sales. The firm operates 122 branch stores in the Americas, consisting of 95 stores in the U.S., 11 in Canada, 11 in Mexico, five in Brazil; 73 branch stores in the Asia-Pacific, consisting of 26 in China, 14 in Korea, nine in Hong Kong, eight in Taiwan, seven in Australia, five in Singapore, two in Macau and two in Malaysia; 56 branch stores in Japan; 38 branch stores in Europe, consisting of 10 in the U.K., seven in Germany, seven in Italy, five in France, two in Spain, two in Switzerland, and one each in Austria, Belgium, the Czech Republic, Ireland and the Netherlands; and other stores in emerging regions comprise five stores in the United Arab Emirates and one in Russia. Operations in the Americas account for roughly 48% of the firm's sales (88% of which are derived from the U.S.); Asia Pacific activities, 24%; Japan activities, 13%; European operations, 12% (more than 40% derived from the U.K.); and 3% from emerging regions. Approximately 92% of net sales are derived from Tiffany & Co. jewelry, while the remaining 8% of sales come from all other brand products and wholesale sales of diamonds and third-party licensing agreements.

Tiffany & Co. offers its employees benefits including flexible spending accounts; medical, dental and vision insurance; fitness programs; disability coverage; a 401(k); employee discounts; paid time off; tuition reimbursement; employee assistance programs; adoption assistance; and stock shares.

FINANCIAL DATA: Note: Data for latest year may not have been available at press time.

In U.S. $	2015	2014	2013	2012	2011	2010
Revenue	4,249,913,000	4,031,130,000	3,794,249,000	3,642,937,000	3,085,290,000	2,709,704,000
R&D Expense						
Operating Income	891,429,000	304,329,000	697,217,000	708,426,000	594,781,000	440,492,000
Operating Margin %	20.97%	7.54%	18.37%	19.44%	19.27%	16.25%
SGA Expense	1,645,746,000	1,555,903,000	1,466,067,000	1,442,728,000	1,227,497,000	1,089,727,000
Net Income	484,179,000	181,369,000	416,157,000	439,190,000	368,403,000	264,823,000
Operating Cash Flow	615,117,000	154,652,000	328,290,000	210,606,000	298,925,000	681,312,000
Capital Expenditure	247,394,000	221,452,000	302,194,000	239,443,000	127,002,000	75,403,000
EBITDA	994,598,000	498,149,000	866,294,000	859,459,000	749,639,000	584,434,000
Return on Assets %	9.74%	3.86%	9.46%	11.12%	10.19%	8.03%
Return on Equity %	17.43%	6.81%	16.82%	19.40%	18.14%	15.25%
Debt to Equity	0.31	0.27	0.29	0.22	0.27	0.27

CONTACT INFORMATION:

Phone: 212 755-8000   Fax: 212 605-4465
Toll-Free:
Address: 727 Fifth Ave., New York, NY 10022 United States

SALARIES/BONUSES:

Top Exec. Salary: $997,315   Bonus: $
Second Exec. Salary: $896,625   Bonus: $

STOCK TICKER/OTHER:

Stock Ticker: TIF   Exchange: NYS
Employees: 12,000   Fiscal Year Ends: 01/31
Parent Company:

OTHER THOUGHTS:

Estimated Female Officers or Directors: 6
Hot Spot for Advancement for Women/Minorities: Y

Tilly's Inc

NAIC Code: 448140

www.tillys.com

TYPES OF BUSINESS:

Retail Surf and Board Wear Stores
E-commerce

BRANDS/DIVISIONS/AFFILIATES:

Tillys.com
Ambitious
Division 7
Eldon
RSQ
Full Tilt
Blue Crown
Vindicated

CONTACTS: Note: Officers with more than one job title may be intentionally listed here more than once.

Michael Henry, CFO
Hezy Shaked, Chairman of the Board
Debbie Anker-Morris, Other Executive Officer
Edmond Thomas, President
Christopher Lal, Vice President

GROWTH PLANS/SPECIAL FEATURES:

Tilly's, Inc. is a specialty retailer of surf-inspired clothing and accessories based in Irvine, California. Targeting teens and young adults, the company offers apparel, footwear and lifestyle accessories inspired by the West Coast surf, action sport and music culture. The firm currently operates 212 retail stores in 33 states, with an average store size of approximately 7,650 square feet. These stores offer numerous popular third party and emerging brands centered on the youth culture of its target customers, including Billabong, Hurley, Levi's, LRG, Neff, RVCA, UGG and Volcom. Tilly's also sells extensive lines of proprietary merchandise under the Ambitious, Division 7, Eldon, RSQ, Full Tilt, Blue Crown and Vindicated labels. In addition to its bricks-and-mortar stores, the company operates an e-commerce site at Tillys.com. The firm handles merchandise distribution and fulfillment from a 126,000 square-foot distribution facility co-located at its headquarters in Irvine. Tilly's uses its own fleet of trucks to ship merchandise to local (Southern California) stores and third-party distributors to ship merchandise to stores outside this area.

FINANCIAL DATA: Note: Data for latest year may not have been available at press time.

In U.S. $	2015	2014	2013	2012	2011	2010
Revenue	518,294,000	495,837,000	467,291,000	400,624,000	332,604,000	282,764,000
R&D Expense						
Operating Income	23,189,000	29,737,000	31,390,000	34,925,000	24,947,000	21,422,000
Operating Margin %	4.47%	5.99%	6.71%	8.71%	7.50%	7.57%
SGA Expense	132,343,000	122,558,000	118,805,000	94,217,000	77,668,000	65,912,000
Net Income	14,075,000	18,137,000	23,893,000	34,340,000	24,416,000	20,863,000
Operating Cash Flow	48,288,000	43,794,000	41,730,000	52,584,000	41,702,000	35,256,000
Capital Expenditure	23,636,000	42,701,000	33,298,000	20,223,000	15,674,000	17,514,000
EBITDA	44,426,000	49,104,000	48,069,000	50,054,000	39,239,000	35,337,000
Return on Assets %	5.74%	8.28%	13.61%	24.82%	19.81%	18.07%
Return on Equity %	9.39%	14.04%	48.93%	161.82%	40.03%	34.83%
Debt to Equity	0.01	0.01	0.02		0.07	0.08

CONTACT INFORMATION:

Phone: 949 609-5599   Fax:
Toll-Free:
Address: 10 Whatney, Irvine, CA 92618 United States

STOCK TICKER/OTHER:

Stock Ticker: TLYS
Employees: 4,500
Parent Company:

Exchange: NYS
Fiscal Year Ends: 01/31

SALARIES/BONUSES:

Top Exec. Salary: $700,000   Bonus: $
Second Exec. Salary: Bonus: $
$400,000

OTHER THOUGHTS:

Estimated Female Officers or Directors: 9
Hot Spot for Advancement for Women/Minorities: Y

Timberland Co

www.timberland.com

NAIC Code: 424340

TYPES OF BUSINESS:

Footwear Distribution
Apparel & Accessories
Retail Stores
Online Sales

BRANDS/DIVISIONS/AFFILIATES:

Timberland PRO
Timberland Boot Company
SmartWool
Earthkeepers
VF Corp
Timberland

CONTACTS: *Note: Officers with more than one job title may be intentionally listed here more than once.*

Eric C. Wiseman, CEO
Steve Rendle, Pres., Outdoor & Action Sports America-VF Corp.

GROWTH PLANS/SPECIAL FEATURES:

Timberland Co., a subsidiary of VF Corp., designs, develops, engineers, markets and distributes footwear, apparel and accessories products for men, women and children under the Timberland, Timberland PRO, Timberland Boot Company, SmartWool and Earthkeepers brands. The Timberland brand offers outdoor adventure and leisure products that combine performance benefits and versatile styling, including premium quality footwear, apparel and accessories for men, women and children. Timberland brand footwear offerings include boots, hiking boots and shoes, casual shoes, boat shoes, sandals, and custom shoes. The Timberland PRO series is developed to address the distinct footwear needs of skilled tradespeople and working professionals. The Timberland Boot Company is a premium footwear series that pays homage to the turn-of-the-century art of shoemaking in New England. The SmartWool brand includes apparel and accessories such as performance socks, lifestyle socks, cycling jerseys and shorts, sweaters, hats, scarves and technical ski gloves. The Earthkeepers collection utilizes renewable, organic, and recycled materials to reduce environmental impact. The firm's products are sold primarily through independent retailers, better-grade department stores, athletic stores and other national retailers as well as through Timberland specialty stores, Timberland factory outlet stores, Timberland footwear stores and online throughout the U.S., Canada, Europe, Asia, Latin America, Africa and the Middle East.

Timberland Co. offers employees health insurance, an employee assistance plan, disability coverage and retirement savings plans.

FINANCIAL DATA: *Note: Data for latest year may not have been available at press time.*

In U.S. $	2015	2014	2013	2012	2011	2010
Revenue		1,700,000,000	1,655,000,000	1,475,000,000	1,500,000,000	1,429,484,000
R&D Expense						
Operating Income						
Operating Margin %						
SGA Expense						
Net Income			111,861,450	99,651,000	101,385,000	96,622,000
Operating Cash Flow						
Capital Expenditure						
EBITDA						
Return on Assets %						
Return on Equity %						
Debt to Equity						

CONTACT INFORMATION:

Phone: 603-772-9500   Fax: 603-926-9239
Toll-Free: 888-802-9947
Address: 200 Domain Dr., Stratham, NH 03885 United States

STOCK TICKER/OTHER:

Stock Ticker: Subsidiary   Exchange:
Employees: 6,000   Fiscal Year Ends: 12/31
Parent Company: VF CORP

SALARIES/BONUSES:

Top Exec. Salary: $ Bonus: $
Second Exec. Salary: $ Bonus: $

OTHER THOUGHTS:

Estimated Female Officers or Directors:
Hot Spot for Advancement for Women/Minorities: Y

TJX Companies Inc (The)

NAIC Code: 448140

TYPES OF BUSINESS:

Discount Apparel Stores
Domestics
Footwear
Jewelry
Home Furnishings
Accessories

BRANDS/DIVISIONS/AFFILIATES:

T.J. Maxx
Marshalls
HomeGoods
Winners
T.K. Maxx
HomeSense
Sierra Trading Post
SierraTradingPost.com

CONTACTS: Note: Officers with more than one job title may be intentionally listed here more than once.

Carol Meyrowitz, CEO
Scott Goldenberg, CFO
Ann McCauley, Executive VP
Richard Sherr, President, Divisional
Nan Stutz, President, Divisional
Kenneth Canestrari, President, Geographical
Michael MacMillan, President, Geographical
Ernie Herrman, President

GROWTH PLANS/SPECIAL FEATURES:

The TJX Companies, Inc. is a low-price apparel and home fashions retailer, operating over 3,300 stores in the U.S. and worldwide. TJX's stores offer merchandise sold at 20% to 60% below department and specialty store regular prices The firm operates through four major divisions: Marmaxx, made up of T.J. Maxx and Marshalls in the U.S.; HomeGoods, made up of the HomeGoods chain in the U.S.; TJX Canada, comprised of Winners, HomeSense and Marshalls; and TJX Europe, operating T.K. Maxx and HomeSense. The Marmaxx group is the largest off-price retailer in the U.S., with 2,094 stores. T.J. Maxx and Marshalls stores offer brand-name family apparel, including footwear and accessories, and home fashions, including home basics, accent furniture and giftware. The chains are similar, although Marshalls features a full-line shoe department and larger men's and juniors' departments, while T.J. Maxx carries an extended line of jewelry and accessories. The HomeGoods segment offers discounted home fashions in 487 stores throughout the U.S. TJX Canada operates a total of 234 Winners, 96 HomeSense and 38 Marshalls locations. The TJX Europe segment operates 407 T.K. Maxx stores in the U.K., Ireland, Poland, Austria and Germany. Additionally, this segment operates 33 HomeSense locations in the U.K.; and Sierra Trading Post, an off-price Internet retailer (sierratradingpost.com) of brand name and quality outdoor gear, family apparel and footwear, sporting goods and home fashions. Sierra Trading Post also operates six retail stores in the U.S. The company purchases its inventory from over 17,000 vendors worldwide. In July 2015, the firm agreed to acquire the Trade Secret and Home Secret off-price retail businesses from Gazal Corporation Limited.

TJX offers its employees medical, dental, vision, disability and life insurance; a 401(k) plan; a profit sharing plan; group auto and home insurance; a college savings program; store discounts; a mortgage discount program; paid vacation; and adoption assistance. Corporate employees have access to an onsite day care center, tuition assistance, basketball courts, fitness classes and indoor golf driving ranges.

FINANCIAL DATA: Note: Data for latest year may not have been available at press time.

In U.S. $	2015	2014	2013	2012	2011	2010
Revenue	29,078,410,000	27,422,700,000	25,878,370,000	23,191,460,000	21,942,190,000	20,288,440,000
R&D Expense						
Operating Income	3,606,501,000	3,350,570,000	3,106,526,000	2,411,414,000	2,203,229,000	1,951,562,000
Operating Margin %	12.40%	12.21%	12.00%	10.39%	10.04%	9.61%
SGA Expense	4,695,384,000	4,467,089,000	4,250,446,000	3,890,144,000	3,710,053,000	3,328,944,000
Net Income	2,215,128,000	2,137,396,000	1,906,687,000	1,496,090,000	1,343,141,000	1,213,572,000
Operating Cash Flow	3,008,369,000	2,590,329,000	3,045,614,000	1,916,034,000	1,976,481,000	2,271,926,000
Capital Expenditure	911,522,000	946,678,000	978,228,000	803,330,000	707,134,000	429,282,000
EBITDA	4,194,239,000	3,914,403,000	3,627,112,000	2,943,798,000	2,671,158,000	2,436,058,000
Return on Assets %	20.77%	21.68%	21.43%	18.40%	17.40%	17.79%
Return on Equity %	52.15%	54.13%	55.46%	47.42%	44.85%	48.31%
Debt to Equity	0.39	0.30	0.21	0.24	0.25	0.27

CONTACT INFORMATION:

Phone: 508 390-1000   Fax: 508 390-2091
Toll-Free:
Address: 770 Cochituate Rd., Framingham, MA 01701 United States

STOCK TICKER/OTHER:

Stock Ticker: TJX   Exchange: NYS
Employees: 198,000   Fiscal Year Ends: 01/31
Parent Company:

SALARIES/BONUSES:

Top Exec. Salary: $1,575,002   Bonus: $
Second Exec. Salary: $1,327,693   Bonus: $

OTHER THOUGHTS:

Estimated Female Officers or Directors: 4

Hot Spot for Advancement for Women/Minorities: Y

Tommy Bahama Group Inc

www.tommybahama.com

NAIC Code: 448140

TYPES OF BUSINESS:

Family Clothing Stores

BRANDS/DIVISIONS/AFFILIATES:

Oxford Industries Inc
Tommy Bahama
TommyBahama.com

CONTACTS: *Note: Officers with more than one job title may be intentionally listed here more than once.*

Rob Goldberg, Exec. VP-Mktg.
Lisa Atwood, Exec. VP-IT

GROWTH PLANS/SPECIAL FEATURES:

Tommy Bahama Group, Inc., wholly-owned by Oxford Industries, Inc., is a manufacturer of casual, men's and women's sportswear and activewear, denim, swimwear, accessories, footwear and home furnishings. Its Tommy Bahama brand is an island-inspired lifestyle label that defines relaxed, sophisticated style. Home furnishings and decor include indoor and outdoor furniture, indoor and outdoor fabrics, ceiling fans, lighting, rugs, candles and scented items, glassware/barware/dinnerware and table linens, as well as bedding and bath collections. The company owns and operates 160 Tommy Bahama stores worldwide, with a few of those locations offering a Tommy Bahama restaurant and bar. The company's products are also available at retailers such as Nordstrom, Macy's and Neiman Marcus, as well as other specialty retailers. TommyBahama.com ships to over 100 countries.

The company offers its employees medical, dental and vision benefits: employee & travel assistance; a 401(k), employee stock purchase, flexible spending accounts, short- and long-term disability, life/accidental death iplans and insurances and employee discounts and perks.

FINANCIAL DATA: *Note: Data for latest year may not have been available at press time.*

In U.S. $	2015	2014	2013	2012	2011	2010
Revenue						
R&D Expense						
Operating Income						
Operating Margin %						
SGA Expense						
Net Income						
Operating Cash Flow						
Capital Expenditure						
EBITDA						
Return on Assets %						
Return on Equity %						
Debt to Equity						

CONTACT INFORMATION:

Phone: 206-622-8688   Fax:
Toll-Free: 866-986-8282
Address: 400 Fairview Ave. N., Ste. 488, Seattle, WA 98109 United States

STOCK TICKER/OTHER:

Stock Ticker: Subsidiary
Employees:
Parent Company: Oxford Industries Inc

Exchange:
Fiscal Year Ends:

SALARIES/BONUSES:

Top Exec. Salary: $ Bonus: $
Second Exec. Salary: $ Bonus: $

OTHER THOUGHTS:

Estimated Female Officers or Directors:
Hot Spot for Advancement for Women/Minorities:

Tommy Hilfiger Corp

www.tommy.com

NAIC Code: 424300

TYPES OF BUSINESS:

Apparel and Clothing Brands, Designers, Importers and Distributors
Jeans & Sportswear
Children's Apparel
Footwear
Fragrances
Home Goods
Intimate Apparel
Swimwear

BRANDS/DIVISIONS/AFFILIATES:

PVH Corp
Tommy Hilfiger Corporate Foundation
Tommy Hilfiger
Hilfiger Denim

CONTACTS: *Note: Officers with more than one job title may be intentionally listed here more than once.*

Daniel Grieder, CEO
Avery Baker, Exec. VP-Global Comm.
Tommy Hilfiger, Principle Designer
Daniel Grieder, CEO-Tommy Hilfiger Europe
Gary Sheinbaum, CEO-Tommy Hilfiger North America
Fred Gehring, Chmn.

GROWTH PLANS/SPECIAL FEATURES:

Tommy Hilfiger Corp. designs, sources and markets men's an
women's sportswear, jeans and children's wear under th
Tommy Hilfiger trademarks. It is wholly-owned by PVH Cor
Tommy Hilfiger operates over 1,400 retail stores in
distribution network of more than 90 countries. The firm offer
a broad array of apparel, accessories, footwear, fragrance an
home furnishings. Tommy Hilfiger's products are purchased b
department and specialty stores throughout the world an
operate through a number of clothing divisions. The Tomm
Hilfiger division offers casual sportswear and accessorie
targeting men and women ages 24-45. The Hilfiger Denir
division supplies denim separates for men and women an
targets those between the ages of 18-28. In addition, th
Tommy Hilfiger Children's Wear division offers casua
sportswear and denim lines. Tommy Hilfiger remains the firm'
principal designer and overseer of the design process. Th
Tommy Hilfiger Corporate Foundation, established in 1995
serves as the charitable outreach arm of the company
regularly sponsoring a variety of educational and cultura
programs throughout the U.S.

FINANCIAL DATA: *Note: Data for latest year may not have been available at press time.*

In U.S. $	2015	2014	2013	2012	2011	2010
Revenue		3,582,000,000	3,433,262,000	3,216,990,000	3,050,801,000	1,945,230,000
R&D Expense						
Operating Income						
Operating Margin %						
SGA Expense						
Net Income		504,000,000	503,043,000	420,933,000	281,839,000	89,207,000
Operating Cash Flow						
Capital Expenditure						
EBITDA						
Return on Assets %						
Return on Equity %						
Debt to Equity						

CONTACT INFORMATION:

Phone: 852-2216-0668   Fax: 852-2312-1368
Toll-Free:
Address: 850-870 Lai Chi Kok Rd., Novel Industrial Bldg., Hong Kong,
Hong Kong 999077 Hong Kong

STOCK TICKER/OTHER:

Stock Ticker: Subsidiary
Employees: 17,000
Parent Company: PVH CORP

Exchange:
Fiscal Year Ends: 03/31

SALARIES/BONUSES:

Top Exec. Salary: $ Bonus: $
Second Exec. Salary: $ Bonus: $

OTHER THOUGHTS:

Estimated Female Officers or Directors: 8
Hot Spot for Advancement for Women/Minorities: Y

Tory Burch LLC

www.toryburch.com

NAIC Code: 424300

TYPES OF BUSINESS:

Apparel and Clothing Brands, Designers, Importers and Distributors
Women's Shoes
Women's Accessories
Retail Stores
Eyewear
Children's Shoes

BRANDS/DIVISIONS/AFFILIATES:

Reva
Robinson
Tory Sport
ToryBurch.com

CONTACTS: Note: Officers with more than one job title may be intentionally listed here more than once.

Tory Burch, Co-CEO
Roger Farah, Co-CEO
Brigitte Kleine, Pres.
Reepal Shah, CFO
Robert Isen, Chief Legal Officer
Robert Isen, Pres., Bus. Dev.

GROWTH PLANS/SPECIAL FEATURES:

Tory Burch LLC, headquartered in New York and established in 2004, is a lifestyle brand that manufactures and designs apparel and accessories for women. The firm focuses the design of its products on an American classic sportswear concept. The Tory Burch collection consists of a variety of products, such as ready-to-wear clothing, shoes, jewelry and handbags. The Tory Burch Clothing brand designs products such as tunics, tops, dresses, skirts, sweaters, jackets and outerwear, denim, swimwear and pants and shorts for women and children. The Tory Burch shoe line manufactures a variety of heels, wedges, sandals, flip flops, and flats through the Reva brand. Handbags are produced under the Robinson brand and include totes, clutches, top handles and shoulder bags. Additional accessories include belts, hats, scarves, gloves, eye wear, wristlets, wallets, cosmetic cases, dog wear and phone cases. Since its establishment, the company continues to expand its product portfolio through partnerships with other brands, such as the Luxottica Group, which designs and manufacturers an exclusive collection of Tory Burch eyewear. Products can be purchased at 160 Tory Burch boutiques, located across the U.S., Middle East, Europe and Asia; over 3,000 department store chains; and online at ToryBurch.com. The firm sees international expansion as an important part of its strategy, evidenced by its opening of a flagship store in Paris. In another important strategic move, the company announced the launch of a new Tory Sport line in the fall of 2015, featuring clothing for such activities as tennis and golf, with a very traditional look.

Founder and designer, Tory Burch maintains the Tory Burch Foundation, which provides economic support through microfinancing and grants to small business owning women.

FINANCIAL DATA: Note: Data for latest year may not have been available at press time.

In U.S. $	2015	2014	2013	2012	2011	2010
Revenue		1,150,000,000	1,000,000,000	800,000,000	505,000,000	330,000,000
R&D Expense						
Operating Income						
Operating Margin %						
SGA Expense						
Net Income						
Operating Cash Flow						
Capital Expenditure						
EBITDA						
Return on Assets %						
Return on Equity %						
Debt to Equity						

CONTACT INFORMATION:

Phone: 212-683-2323 Fax:
Toll-Free: 866-480-8679
Address: 11 West 19th St. 7th Fl., New York, NY 10011 United States

SALARIES/BONUSES:

Top Exec. Salary: $ Bonus: $
Second Exec. Salary: $ Bonus: $

STOCK TICKER/OTHER:

Stock Ticker: Private Exchange:
Employees: 1,400 Fiscal Year Ends:
Parent Company:

OTHER THOUGHTS:

Estimated Female Officers or Directors: 2
Hot Spot for Advancement for Women/Minorities:

Toys R Us Inc

www.toysrusinc.com

NAIC Code: 451120

TYPES OF BUSINESS:

Toys, Retail
Children's Apparel
Online Retailing
Catalog Sales
Sporting Goods
Personalized Gifts

BRANDS/DIVISIONS/AFFILIATES:

Babies R Us
ToysRUs.com
BabiesRUs.com
KB Toys
FAO Schwarz
Vornado Realty Trust
Kohlberg Kravis Roberts & Co)
Bain Capital LLC

CONTACTS: *Note: Officers with more than one job title may be intentionally listed here more than once.*

David A. Brandon, CEO
Michael J. Short, CFO
Richard Barry, CMO
Richard Barry, Chief Merch. Officer
David J. Schwartz, General Counsel
Troy Rice, Exec. VP-Stores & Svcs.
Deborah Derby, Exec. VP
Ira Hernowitz, Exec. VP-R Us Brands
David A. Brandon, Chmn.
Monica Merz, Pres.-Asia Pacific

GROWTH PLANS/SPECIAL FEATURES:

Toys R Us, Inc. retails toys, games, sporting goods, electronics, software, baby and children's apparel and juvenile furniture. The investment firms Bain Capital LLC, Vornado Realty Trust and Kohlberg, Kravis, Roberts & Co. all own an equal operating share in the company. Toys R Us has approximately 863 stores including both Toys R Us and Babies R Us stores. The company also has over 740 international stores and 245 licensed stores that are located in more than 38 countries. Babies R Us is a subsidiary that offers apparel, furniture and related accessories for infants and toddlers. The company also sells its products through its ToysRUs.com, BabiesRUs.com, eToys.com and Toys.com e-commerce sites. Many of the company's stores sell name brand, designer and private label boys' and girls' clothing. The firm's e-commerce business capacity is expanded by a distribution center in McCarran, Nevada. In addition, the company operates several superstores, each featuring a Toys R Us next door to a Babies R Us. The combined superstores are 30,000 square feet to 70,000 square feet. Moreover, Toys R US owns toy retailers FAO Schwarz and the brand and intellectual property rights for KB Toys.

Toys R Us offers its employees medical, AD&D, life, dental, vision and prescription coverage; discounted merchandise; employee assistance programs; a 529 college savings plan; and a 401(k) plan.

FINANCIAL DATA: *Note: Data for latest year may not have been available at press time.*

In U.S. $	2015	2014	2013	2012	2011	2010
Revenue		11,500,000,000	12,543,000,000	13,543,000,000	13,909,000,000	13,864,000,000
R&D Expense						
Operating Income						
Operating Margin %						
SGA Expense						
Net Income		-292,000,000	-1,036,000,000	39,000,000	151,000,000	167,000,000
Operating Cash Flow						
Capital Expenditure						
EBITDA						
Return on Assets %						
Return on Equity %						
Debt to Equity						

CONTACT INFORMATION:

Phone: 973-617-3500   Fax: 973-617-4006
Toll-Free:
Address: 1 Geoffrey Way, Wayne, NJ 07470 United States

STOCK TICKER/OTHER:

Stock Ticker: Private   Exchange:
Employees: 60,000   Fiscal Year Ends: 02/02
Parent Company: KKR & CO LP (KOHLBERG KRAVIS ROBERTS & CO)

SALARIES/BONUSES:

Top Exec. Salary: $ Bonus: $
Second Exec. Salary: $ Bonus: $

OTHER THOUGHTS:

Estimated Female Officers or Directors: 2
Hot Spot for Advancement for Women/Minorities: Y

Tractor Supply Company

www.tractorsupplyco.com

NAIC Code: 444130

TYPES OF BUSINESS:

Farming Supplies, Retail
Work Apparel
Light Truck Equipment
Footwear
Animal Care Products
Private Label Credit Cards

BRANDS/DIVISIONS/AFFILIATES:

Del'sFeed & Farm Supply Inc
TractorSupply.com
Tractor Supply Company
HomeTown Pet

CONTACTS: Note: Officers with more than one job title may be intentionally listed here more than once.

Gregory Sandfort, CEO
Anthony Crudele, CFO
Cynthia Jamison, Chairman of the Board
Robert Mills, Chief Information Officer
Lee Downing, Executive VP, Divisional
Steve Barbarick, Executive VP, Divisional
Benjamin Parrish, General Counsel
Chad Frazell, Senior VP, Divisional

GROWTH PLANS/SPECIAL FEATURES:

Tractor Supply Company is one of the largest operators of retail farm and ranch stores in the U.S. and is focused on supplying the needs of recreational farmers and ranchers, tradesmen and small businesses. The company operates approximately 1,465 stores in 49 states under the names Tractor Supply Company, HomeTown Pet and Del's Feed & Farm Supply. Del's Feed & Farm Supply, a wholly-owned subsidiary, operates stores located primarily in the Pacific Northwest. The company also operates an e-commerce site, TractorSupply.com. Stores are located in towns on the outskirts of major metropolitan markets and in rural communities. Merchandise selection includes equine, pet and animal products, including items necessary for health, care, growth and containment; maintenance products for agricultural and rural use; hardware and tools; seasonal products, including lawn and garden power equipment; truck and towing products; and work/recreational clothing and footwear. The livestock and pet category accounts for approximately 44% of sales; hardware, tool and truck products account for 22%; seasonal, gift and toy products, 20%; clothing and footwear, 9%; and agriculture supplies, 5%. Average store size ranges from 15,000 to 19,000 square feet combined inside and outdoor selling space. Almost 70% of Tractor Supply Company's products are supplied to stores through seven regional distribution centers, located in Kentucky, Indiana, Georgia, Maryland, Texas, Nebraska and Washington. The remaining 30% is shipped to the stores directly from vendors. The firm offers private label credit cards for individual retail and business customers.

The company offers employees benefits including medical, dental, vision, disability and life insurance; 401(k) for both part- and full-time employees; stock purchase options; and merchandise discounts.

FINANCIAL DATA: Note: Data for latest year may not have been available at press time.

In U.S. $	2015	2014	2013	2012	2011	2010
Revenue		5,711,715,000	5,164,784,000	4,664,120,000	4,232,743,000	3,638,336,000
R&D Expense						
Operating Income		589,472,000	514,650,000	436,792,000	352,703,000	266,224,000
Operating Margin %		10.32%	9.96%	9.36%	8.33%	7.31%
SGA Expense		1,246,308,000	1,138,934,000	1,040,287,000	973,822,000	867,644,000
Net Income		370,885,000	328,234,000	276,457,000	222,740,000	167,972,000
Operating Cash Flow		409,178,000	333,681,000	378,302,000	254,144,000	222,608,000
Capital Expenditure		160,613,000	218,200,000	152,924,000	166,156,000	96,511,000
EBITDA		704,107,000	614,675,000	525,767,000	433,050,000	336,021,000
Return on Assets %		18.83%	18.18%	16.74%	14.56%	12.46%
Return on Equity %		29.19%	28.89%	27.19%	22.94%	20.15%
Debt to Equity						

CONTACT INFORMATION:

Phone: 615 440-4000   Fax:
Toll-Free: 800-872-7721
Address: 200 Powell Pl., Brentwood, TN 37027 United States

STOCK TICKER/OTHER:

Stock Ticker: TSCO   Exchange: NAS
Employees: 21,100   Fiscal Year Ends: 12/31
Parent Company:

SALARIES/BONUSES:

Top Exec. Salary: $934,615   Bonus: $
Second Exec. Salary: Bonus: $
$482,692

OTHER THOUGHTS:

Estimated Female Officers or Directors: 3
Hot Spot for Advancement for Women/Minorities: Y

Sales, profits and employees may be estimates. Financial information, benefits and other data can change quickly and may vary from those stated here.

Trader Joe's Company Inc

NAIC Code: 445110

www.traderjoes.com

TYPES OF BUSINESS:

Grocery Stores
Specialty Groceries
Vitamins & Dietary Supplements
Organic Foods

BRANDS/DIVISIONS/AFFILIATES:

ALDI Group

CONTACTS: Note: Officers with more than one job title may be intentionally listed here more than once.

Dan Bane, CEO
Tara Miller, Dir.-Mktg.
Laurie Mead, VP-Human Resources
Charles Pillitier, Sr. VP-Oper.
Brandt Sharrock, VP-Real Estate
Dan Bane, Chmn.

GROWTH PLANS/SPECIAL FEATURES:

Trader Joe's Company, Inc. operates a chain of approximately 457 company-owned and -operated specialty grocery stores in over 38 states and Washington, D.C., with about half of its stores located in California, where the company was founded. Although the stores sell some brand-name products, the vast majority of the selection comprises more than 3,000 Trader Joe's private-label products, including specialty vegetarian, kosher, organic food and vitamin supplement products as well as regional fare, such as Thai and Mexican foods. Prices tend to be comparable to or lower than traditional groceries, as a result of Trader Joe's efforts to buy many items and ingredients directly from suppliers and the chain's focus on its private label lines. The company also keeps costs down by eliminating service departments and using spaces of 15,000 square feet or less for its stores. Selections and inventory tend to vary from state to state and store to store because of the company's commitment to experimentation, regional and seasonal products and bringing variety to its customers. The firm is owned by a trust created by Theo Albrecht, co-founder of German supermarket chain ALDI.

Trader Joe's offers employees medical, dental and vision insurance; a company-paid retirement plan; a 10% employee discount; and paid time off. Medical, dental and vision coverage is available to both full and part-time employees of the firm.

FINANCIAL DATA: Note: Data for latest year may not have been available at press time.

In U.S. $	2015	2014	2013	2012	2011	2010
Revenue		12,000,000,000	9,725,000,000	9,500,000,000	9,000,000,000	8,500,000,000
R&D Expense						
Operating Income						
Operating Margin %						
SGA Expense						
Net Income						
Operating Cash Flow						
Capital Expenditure						
EBITDA						
Return on Assets %						
Return on Equity %						
Debt to Equity						

CONTACT INFORMATION:

Phone: 626-599-3700　　　Fax: 626-301-4431
Toll-Free:
Address: 800 S. Shamrock Ave., Monrovia, CA 91016 United States

STOCK TICKER/OTHER:

Stock Ticker: Subsidiary
Employees: 12,500
Parent Company: ALDI GROUP

Exchange:
Fiscal Year Ends: 06/30

SALARIES/BONUSES:

Top Exec. Salary: $　　　Bonus: $
Second Exec. Salary: $　　　Bonus: $

OTHER THOUGHTS:

Estimated Female Officers or Directors: 2
Hot Spot for Advancement for Women/Minorities:

Trans World Entertainment Corp

www.twec.com

NAIC Code: 443142

TYPES OF BUSINESS:

Music Stores
CDs, DVDs, Videos & Video Games
Online Sales
Digital Music Content
Used Music & Video Retail

BRANDS/DIVISIONS/AFFILIATES:

Record Town Inc
f.Y.e.
Suncoast Motion Pictures
WhereHouse.com
SecondSpin.com
Fye.com
Second Spin

CONTACTS: *Note: Officers with more than one job title may be intentionally listed here more than once.*

Michael Feurer, CEO
John Anderson, CFO
Robert Higgins, Chairman of the Board
Bruce Eisenberg, Executive VP, Divisional
Edwin Sapienza, Secretary

GROWTH PLANS/SPECIAL FEATURES:

Trans World Entertainment Corp. (TWE) is a retailer of entertainment software, including music, videos and video games and related products in the U.S. The firm operates 310 stores totaling approximately 1.8 million square feet in the U.S., Washington, D.C. and the U.S. Virgin Islands. Mall-based (270) and free-standing (40) stores operate primarily under the f.Y.e. (For Your Entertainment) brand with products including video, music, electronics, trend, video games and related products. Mall-based square footage averages about 5,300 and free-standing stores average about 9,800 square feet. The company operates three retail web sites: Fye.com, WhereHouse.com and.SecondSpin.com, with fye.com being the company's flagship site that carries a broad selection of new and used DVDs, Blu-Ray, CDs and games. TWE owns 100% of Record Town, Inc., through which it conducts most of its operations; and Second Spin, a used CD, video and DVD retailer. The firm has five merchandise category groups: video, which accounts for 43.9% of sales; music, 27%; trend, 15.2%; electronics, 9.6%; and video games, 4.3%. TWE operates nine video-only stores under the Suncoast Motion Pictures brand. The company's distribution center facility is located in Albany, New York, through which it ships approximately 74% of its merchandise inventory. The distribution center consists of nearly 39,800 square feet of office space and 141,500 square feet of storage and distribution space.

The firm offers employees health and dental insurance, life insurance, long-term disability coverage, a 401(k) plan and a store merchandise discount.

FINANCIAL DATA: *Note: Data for latest year may not have been available at press time.*

In U.S. $	2015	2014	2013	2012	2011	2010
Revenue	358,490,000	393,659,000	458,544,000	542,589,000	652,416,000	813,988,000
R&D Expense						
Operating Income	3,775,000	10,375,000	36,300,000	5,501,000	-27,342,000	-52,692,000
Operating Margin %	1.05%	2.63%	7.91%	1.01%	-4.19%	-6.47%
SGA Expense	132,143,000	137,529,000	158,572,000	192,653,000	244,749,000	310,710,000
Net Income	1,778,000	8,277,000	33,734,000	2,162,000	-30,963,000	-42,449,000
Operating Cash Flow	16,808,000	7,308,000	35,633,000	16,771,000	10,464,000	49,789,000
Capital Expenditure	8,774,000	7,828,000	3,351,000	2,105,000	2,944,000	4,586,000
EBITDA	8,233,000	14,759,000	40,803,000	12,371,000	-14,973,000	-36,053,000
Return on Assets %	.60%	2.63%	10.73%	.65%	-8.33%	-9.62%
Return on Equity %	.97%	4.44%	19.69%	1.33%	-17.43%	-19.81%
Debt to Equity			0.01	0.02	0.03	0.03

CONTACT INFORMATION:

Phone: 518 452-1242   Fax: 518 452-3547
Toll-Free:
Address: 38 Corporate Cir., Albany, NY 12203 United States

SALARIES/BONUSES:

Top Exec. Salary: $725,000   Bonus: $
Second Exec. Salary: $400,000   Bonus: $

STOCK TICKER/OTHER:

Stock Ticker: TWMC   Exchange: NAS
Employees: 3,000   Fiscal Year Ends: 01/31
Parent Company:

OTHER THOUGHTS:

Estimated Female Officers or Directors:
Hot Spot for Advancement for Women/Minorities:

Sales, profits and employees may be estimates. Financial information, benefits and other data can change quickly and may vary from those stated here.

Trendy Group International Holding Ltd (TGI)   trendygp.com
NAIC Code: 339910

TYPES OF BUSINESS:
Jewelry and Silverware Manufacturing
Jewelry, Watch, Precious Stone, and Precious Metal Merchant
Wholesalers

GROWTH PLANS/SPECIAL FEATURES:
Trendy Group International Holding Ltd (TGI) is a Hong Kong-based wholesale jewelry company. The firm designs and manufactures its products from a factory in Shatoujiao, Shenzhen. Its products are divided into three selections, Classics Collection, Banquet Collection and Wedding Collection, and use silver, rose gold and platinum with precious and semiprecious stones including diamonds and sapphires.

BRANDS/DIVISIONS/AFFILIATES:
Bouquet Collection
Wedding Collection
Classics Collection

CONTACTS: *Note: Officers with more than one job title may be intentionally listed here more than once.*
Lui So Yuk, General Mgr.

FINANCIAL DATA: *Note: Data for latest year may not have been available at press time.*

In U.S. $	2015	2014	2013	2012	2011	2010
Revenue						
R&D Expense						
Operating Income						
Operating Margin %						
SGA Expense						
Net Income						
Operating Cash Flow						
Capital Expenditure						
EBITDA						
Return on Assets %						
Return on Equity %						
Debt to Equity						

CONTACT INFORMATION:
Phone: 852-2356-0029   Fax: 852-2333-9660
Toll-Free:
Address: 23 Man Lok Street, Hunghom, 999077 Hong Kong

STOCK TICKER/OTHER:
Stock Ticker: Private   Exchange:
Employees: Fiscal Year Ends:
Parent Company:

SALARIES/BONUSES:
Top Exec. Salary: $ Bonus: $
Second Exec. Salary: $ Bonus: $

OTHER THOUGHTS:
Estimated Female Officers or Directors:
Hot Spot for Advancement for Women/Minorities:

True Religion Apparel Inc

www.truereligionbrandjeans.com

NAIC Code: 448140

TYPES OF BUSINESS:

Jeans & Apparel Retail

BRANDS/DIVISIONS/AFFILIATES:

True Religion Brand Jeans
True Religion Japan KK
TrueReligionBrandJeans.com
True Religion Brand Jeans Germany GmbH
Tower Brook Capital Partners LP

CONTACTS: Note: Officers with more than one job title may be intentionally listed here more than once.

John Ermatinger, CEO
Eric P. Bauer, CFO
Peter Collins, VP-Finance & Acct.
Jeffrey Lubell, Chmn.

GROWTH PLANS/SPECIAL FEATURES:

True Religion Apparel, Inc. is a designer, manufacturer and marketer of the True Religion Brand Jeans brand. This brand includes high fashion designer jeans and related sportswear apparel. True Religion products fall into three categories: knits, including hoodies, t-shirts and sweats; denim fabrics, which includes its line of jeans; and non-denim fabrics, such as corduroy and twill. The firm's jeans usually sell between $158 and $398 per pair. True Religion operates in four segments: U.S. wholesale, international, U.S. consumer direct and core services. The U.S. wholesale division markets the firm's products to boutique and specialty stores and major retail chains such as Saks Fifth Avenue, Neiman Marcus, Nordstrom and Bloomingdale's. The international segment distributes products through subsidiary True Religion Japan, K.K., joint venture True Religion Brand Jeans Germany GmbH (40%-owned by UNIFA Premium GmbH) and other distributors/sales agents who sell to upscale boutiques in their respective geographic areas. The company owns full-price retail stores and outlet stores in the countries of Canada, Germany, the U.K. Japan, Austria, The Netherlands and Ireland. The U.S. consumer direct segment includes True Religion Apparel's e-commerce web site TrueReligionBrandJeans.com and its self-branded retail locations. The company's core services division handles its licensing business, including the licensing of the True Religion brand and logo to other companies. True Religion's average branded retail store measures approximately 1,700 square feet, while its outlet stores measure roughly 2,600 square feet. The company is a subsidiary of Tower Brook Capital Partners, LP.

FINANCIAL DATA: Note: Data for latest year may not have been available at press time.

In U.S. $	2015	2014	2013	2012	2011	2010
Revenue		510,000,000	500,000,000	467,284,992	419,798,016	363,713,984
R&D Expense						
Operating Income						
Operating Margin %						
SGA Expense						
Net Income						
Operating Cash Flow						
Capital Expenditure						
EBITDA						
Return on Assets %						
Return on Equity %						
Debt to Equity						

CONTACT INFORMATION:

Phone: 323 266-3072   Fax: 323 266-8060
Toll-Free:
Address: 2263 E. Vernon Ave., Vernon, CA 90058 United States

SALARIES/BONUSES:

Top Exec. Salary: $ Bonus: $
Second Exec. Salary: $ Bonus: $

STOCK TICKER/OTHER:

Stock Ticker: Private   Exchange:
Employees: 3,086   Fiscal Year Ends: 12/31
Parent Company: TowerBrook Capital Partners LP

OTHER THOUGHTS:

Estimated Female Officers or Directors:
Hot Spot for Advancement for Women/Minorities:

True Value Company

www.truevaluecompany.com

NAIC Code: 444130

TYPES OF BUSINESS:

Hardware Stores
Rental Stores
Gardening Stores
Party Supply Stores

BRANDS/DIVISIONS/AFFILIATES:

Master Plumber
Grand Rental Station
Taylor Rental Center
Party Central
Home & Garden Showplace
InduServe Supply
Master Mechanic
Green Thumb

CONTACTS: Note: Officers with more than one job title may be intentionally listed here more than once.

John Hartmann, CEO
John Hartmann, Pres.
Deborah O'Connor, CFO
Blake Fohl, VP-Mktg.
Cathy Anderson, Sr. VP-Human Resources
Rosalee Hermens, CIO
Michael Clark, Chief Merch. Officer
Cathy Anderson, General Counsel
Steve Poplawski, Sr. VP-Retail Oper.
Barbara Wagner, Corp. Treas.
Mark Flowers, VP-Retail Growth
Eric Lane, VP-Specialty Bus.
Blake Fohl, Chief Customer Officer
Don Deegan, VP-Logistics

GROWTH PLANS/SPECIAL FEATURES:

True Value Company is a member-owned wholesaler
hardware and related merchandise. Organized as
cooperative, the company operates over 4,400 stores in 5
countries. True Value stores offer building and home repa
tools and accessories. The firm supplies its stores through 1
regional U.S. distribution centers. In addition to its reta
business, True Value manufactures paint and paint applicators
The company requires members to enter retail membe
agreements and then provides marketing, advertising
merchandising, store location, private-label products an
design services in exchange for exclusive selling rights
Members operate under six trademark names: True Value
Grand Rental Station, Taylor Rental, Party Central, Home
Garden Showplace and InduServe Supply. The firm's Grand
Rental Station and Taylor Rental stores are full-line general
rental locations offering tools, party supplies and contracto
equipment to homeowners and professionals. TruServ's Part
Central stores offer supplies for parties, corporate events and
weddings. Home & Garden Showplace is one of the larges
independent gardening wholesaler centers in the U.S
InduServe Supply is an independent commercial and industria
distributor that offers power/hand tools, paint, janitorial supplies
and material handling items to commercial and industria
customers. Private-label products are sold under the True
Value, Green Thumb, Master Mechanic and Master Plumbe
brands. In total, the cooperative carries over 60,000 products.

True Value offers employees benefits including medical, denta
and vision insurance; prescription drug coverage; flexible
spending accounts; life, AD&D, short- and long-term disability
and business travel accident insurance; a 401(k) savings plan
with company matching; tuition reimbursement; access to the
True Value University; employee assistance and wellness
programs; adoption assistance; and employee discounts.

FINANCIAL DATA: Note: Data for latest year may not have been available at press time.

In U.S. $	2015	2014	2013	2012	2011	2010
Revenue		2,014,840,000	1,900,018,000	1,883,796,000	1,863,991,000	1,804,000,000
R&D Expense						
Operating Income						
Operating Margin %						
SGA Expense						
Net Income		52,515,000	55,318,000	74,920,000	60,287,000	60,700,000
Operating Cash Flow						
Capital Expenditure						
EBITDA						
Return on Assets %						
Return on Equity %						
Debt to Equity						

CONTACT INFORMATION:

Phone: 773-695-5000   Fax: 773-695-6516
Toll-Free:
Address: 8600 W. Bryn Mawr Ave., Chicago, IL 60631 United States

SALARIES/BONUSES:

Top Exec. Salary: $ Bonus: $
Second Exec. Salary: $ Bonus: $

STOCK TICKER/OTHER:

Stock Ticker: Cooperative
Employees: 2,800
Parent Company:

Exchange:
Fiscal Year Ends: 12/31

OTHER THOUGHTS:

Estimated Female Officers or Directors: 5
Hot Spot for Advancement for Women/Minorities: Y

Sales, profits and employees may be estimates. Financial information, benefits and other data can change quickly and may vary from those stated here.

Tuesday Morning Corporation

www.tuesdaymorning.com

NAIC Code: 452112

TYPES OF BUSINESS:

Discount Stores
Housewares
Accessories
Toys
Clothing

BRANDS/DIVISIONS/AFFILIATES:

Tuesday Morning
Tuesday Morning Perks

GROWTH PLANS/SPECIAL FEATURES:

Tuesday Morning Corporation is a leading off-price retailer. It specializes in selling deeply discounted, upscale decorative home accessories, housewares, seasonal goods and famous-maker gifts. Tuesday Morning provides brand name merchandise which are never seconds or irregulars and are generally sold in department and specialty stores, catalogues and through online chains. The company operates 769 stores in 41 U.S. states, averaging 10,900 square feet in size. It specializes in upscale home furnishings, housewares and gifts, but carries an ever-changing assortment of products in categories such as home decor, bed & bath, kitchen, toys, crafts, pets and seasonal goods. High-end brands such as Peacock Alley, Sferra, Lenox, Waterford and Hartmann are offered. Trademarks of the company include Tuesday Morning and Tuesday Morning Perks.

CONTACTS:

Note: Officers with more than one job title may be intentionally listed here more than once.

Steven Becker, CEO
Kelly Munsch, Chief Accounting Officer
Terry Burman, Director
Phillip Hixon, Executive VP, Divisional
Meredith Bjorck, General Counsel
Melissa Phillips, President

FINANCIAL DATA:

Note: Data for latest year may not have been available at press time.

In U.S. $	2015	2014	2013	2012	2011	2010
Revenue	906,365,000	864,844,000	838,314,000	812,782,000	821,150,000	828,265,000
R&D Expense						
Operating Income	12,356,000	-8,053,000	-56,495,000	7,437,000	18,043,000	20,145,000
Operating Margin %	1.36%	-.93%	-6.73%	.91%	2.19%	2.43%
SGA Expense	314,263,000	310,205,000	315,933,000	301,427,000	295,273,000	293,850,000
Net Income	10,385,000	-10,176,000	-56,376,000	3,913,000	9,579,000	10,748,000
Operating Cash Flow	9,685,000	31,198,000	-3,188,000	59,481,000	-62,000	32,071,000
Capital Expenditure	15,541,000	13,434,000	9,608,000	13,765,000	20,600,000	17,432,000
EBITDA	24,287,000	3,553,000	-48,279,000	22,177,000	34,768,000	35,197,000
Return on Assets %	3.08%	-3.11%	-15.68%	1.00%	2.62%	3.20%
Return on Equity %	4.85%	-4.95%	-24.11%	1.50%	3.77%	4.44%
Debt to Equity						

CONTACT INFORMATION:

Phone: 972 387-3562   Fax:
Toll-Free:
Address: 6250 LBJ Fwy., Dallas, TX 75240 United States

STOCK TICKER/OTHER:

Stock Ticker: TUES
Employees: 8,820
Parent Company:

Exchange: NAS
Fiscal Year Ends: 06/30

SALARIES/BONUSES:

Top Exec. Salary: $676,667   Bonus: $
Second Exec. Salary: $360,227   Bonus: $200,000

OTHER THOUGHTS:

Estimated Female Officers or Directors: 3
Hot Spot for Advancement for Women/Minorities: Y

Tupperware Brands Corporation

www.tupperwarebrands.com

NAIC Code: 454390

TYPES OF BUSINESS:

Direct Selling
Food Storage Products
Cosmetics & Beauty Products

BRANDS/DIVISIONS/AFFILIATES:

Nuvo
Avroy Shlain
BeautiControl
Fuller
NaturCare
Nutrimetics

CONTACTS: *Note: Officers with more than one job title may be intentionally listed here more than once.*

E. V. Goings, CEO
William Wright, Senior VP, Divisional
Nicholas Poucher, Chief Accounting Officer
Jose Timmerman, Executive VP, Divisional
Michael Poteshman, Executive VP
Lillian Garcia, Executive VP
Thomas Roehlk, Executive VP
Patricia Stitzel, President, Divisional
Asha Gupta, President, Geographical
Christian Skroder, President, Geographical
Allan Dando, President, Geographical
Simon Hemus, President
Josef Hajek, Senior VP, Divisional

GROWTH PLANS/SPECIAL FEATURES:

Tupperware Brands Corporation is a global direct seller, operating in approximately 100 countries. Product brands and categories include design-centric preparation, storage and serving solutions for the kitchen and home through the Tupperware brand; and cosmetics and personal care products through its Armand Dupree, Avroy Shlain, BeautiControl, Fuller, NaturCare, Nutrimetics and Nuvo brands. The firm relies primarily on the party method of sales, which is designed to demonstrate the features and benefits of Tupperware products to customers prior to purchase. Demonstrations, referred to as Tupperware parties, are led by independent distributors, managers and dealers who have been granted the right to market Tupperware products, and are performed annually by an independent sales force of approximately 2.9 million. Tupperware also promotes its products through brochures, retail access points, Internet selling and television shopping. Additionally, through business-to-business transactions, the company sells products to a partner company that sells to consumers through its distribution channel. In 2014, the firm ceased operating the Armand Dupree business in the U.S.

Employees receive medical, dental, vision and prescription drug coverage; life insurance; wellness programs; domestic partner coverage; access to onsite fitness facilities; tuition assistance; flexible spending accounts; college savings plans; and discounts on Tupperware products.

FINANCIAL DATA: *Note: Data for latest year may not have been available at press time.*

In U.S. $	2015	2014	2013	2012	2011	2010
Revenue		2,606,100,000	2,671,600,000	2,583,800,000	2,585,000,000	2,300,400,000
R&D Expense						
Operating Income		367,700,000	403,500,000	306,500,000	342,300,000	329,400,000
Operating Margin %		14.10%	15.10%	11.86%	13.24%	14.31%
SGA Expense		1,346,100,000	1,369,700,000	1,329,500,000	1,340,000,000	1,193,100,000
Net Income		214,400,000	274,200,000	193,000,000	218,300,000	225,600,000
Operating Cash Flow		282,100,000	323,500,000	298,700,000	274,700,000	299,500,000
Capital Expenditure		69,400,000	69,000,000	75,600,000	73,900,000	56,100,000
EBITDA		408,400,000	455,400,000	357,300,000	394,100,000	378,700,000
Return on Assets %		11.82%	14.96%	10.52%	11.31%	11.83%
Return on Equity %		97.74%	74.91%	39.39%	33.82%	31.60%
Debt to Equity		3.31	2.45	0.86	0.82	0.54

CONTACT INFORMATION:

Phone: 407 826-5050   Fax: 407 826-8849
Toll-Free: 800-366-3800
Address: 14901 S. Orange Blossom Tr., Orlando, FL 32837 United States

STOCK TICKER/OTHER:

Stock Ticker: TUP
Employees: 13,100
Parent Company:

Exchange: NYS
Fiscal Year Ends: 12/31

SALARIES/BONUSES:

Top Exec. Salary:
$1,045,475

Bonus: $

Second Exec. Salary:
$645,363

Bonus: $

OTHER THOUGHTS:

Estimated Female Officers or Directors: 5

Hot Spot for Advancement for Women/Minorities: Y

Tween Brands Inc

NAIC Code: 448130

TYPES OF BUSINESS:

Apparel-Children's, Retail
Footwear
Sportswear
Jewelry
Accessories
Online & Catalog Sales

BRANDS/DIVISIONS/AFFILIATES:

Ascena Retail Group Inc
Justice
ShopJustice.com

CONTACTS: Note: Officers with more than one job title may be intentionally listed here more than once.

Michael W. Rayden, CEO
Rolando de Aguiar, CFO
Brian Rogers, Sr. VP-Human Resources
Lece Lohr, Chief Merch. Officer
Chris Kaighn, Sr. VP-Stores & Store Oper.
Chris Williams, Sr. VP-Planning & Allocation
Alan J. Hochman, Sr. VP-Real Estate & Store Planning
Michael W. Rayden, Chmn.

GROWTH PLANS/SPECIAL FEATURES:

Tween Brands, Inc. is a clothing and accessories retailer that primarily works through its Justice subsidiary, which markets to girls aged 7-12r years old. Justice sell apparel, underwear, sleepwear, swimwear, lifestyle and personal care products as well as non-apparel merchandise, such as candy, electronic toys and games, through over 1,000 retail locations and their respective e-commerce sites, ShopJustice.com. The company operates in both shopping mall locations and non-mall locations such as power centers, which attract customer's intent on apparel shopping. Tween Brands' clothing and other products are developed internally. Tween Brands stores feature furniture, fixtures, lighting and music to create a shopping experience matching the energetic lifestyle of youth culture. To keep store atmosphere fresh, the firm continually reassesses the layout of its stores. The company is a wholly-owned subsidiary of Ascena Retail Group, Inc. In early 2015, the firm discontinued its Brothers brand.

The firm offers its employees medical, prescription, dental and vision coverage; life and disability insurance; health savings accounts and flexible savings accounts; adoption assistance; an employee stock purchase plan; paid time off; a 401(k); and an employee assistance plan.

FINANCIAL DATA: Note: Data for latest year may not have been available at press time.

In U.S. $	2015	2014	2013	2012	2011	2010
Revenue		1,349,000,000	1,330,000,000	1,306,700,000	1,150,000,000	1,050,000,000
R&D Expense						
Operating Income						
Operating Margin %						
SGA Expense						
Net Income			180,000,000	172,500,000	129,300,000	55,000,000
Operating Cash Flow						
Capital Expenditure						
EBITDA						
Return on Assets %						
Return on Equity %						
Debt to Equity						

CONTACT INFORMATION:

Phone: 614-775-3500   Fax:
Toll-Free:
Address: 8323 Walton Pkwy., New Albany, OH 43054 United States

SALARIES/BONUSES:

Top Exec. Salary: $ Bonus: $
Second Exec. Salary: $ Bonus: $

STOCK TICKER/OTHER:

Stock Ticker: Subsidiary   Exchange:
Employees: 3,350   Fiscal Year Ends: 07/31
Parent Company: ASCENA RETAIL GROUP INC

OTHER THOUGHTS:

Estimated Female Officers or Directors: 2
Hot Spot for Advancement for Women/Minorities: Y

Ulta Salon Cosmetics & Fragrance Inc

www.ulta.com

NAIC Code: 446120

TYPES OF BUSINESS:

Cosmetic & Fragrance Retail
Salon Services

BRANDS/DIVISIONS/AFFILIATES:

Ulta
Ulta.com
ULTAmate Rewards

CONTACTS: Note: Officers with more than one job title may be intentionally listed here more than once.

Scott Settersten, Assistant Secretary
Charles Philippin, Chairman of the Board
David Kimbell, Chief Marketing Officer
Mary Dillon, Director
Jodi Caro, General Counsel
Karen May, Other Corporate Officer
Jeffrey Childs, Other Executive Officer
Laurel Lefebvre, Vice President, Divisional

GROWTH PLANS/SPECIAL FEATURES:

Ulta Salon Cosmetics & Fragrance, Inc. (Ulta) is one of th largest one-stop beauty retailers of prestige, mass and sale products and salon services in the U.S. Ulta focuses it business on providing the product breadth, value an convenience of a beauty superstore with the experience an distinctive environment of a specialty retailer. Throughout it 1,200 stores located across the U.S., Ulta stores offer th customer over 20,000 prestige and mass beauty product organized by category and in such a manner that encourage the customer to play with, touch, test, learn about and explor the products. In addition, every Ulta store offers a full-servic salon coupled with a wide range of salon hair care products The firm views itself as a destination retailer, locating its store in high-traffic, off-mall locations, such as power centers an lifestyle centers. With an approximate average size of 10,50 square feet and an open store layout, the company believes is able to respond to consumer trends and changes i merchandising strategy with great flexibility. Ulta offers a loyalt program, ULTAmate Rewards. In addition to its retail stores Ulta maintains the website Ulta.com, which gives the custome access to information beyond that of the stores and access t over 19,000 beauty products from hundreds of brands. The firm operates three distribution facilities, in Romeoville, Illinois Phoenix, Arizona; and Chambersburg, Pennsylvania, with square footage of 317,000 square feet, 437,000 square fee and 373,000 square feet respectively. A fourth distribution center in Greenwood, Indiana is expected to open in 2015, an a fifth in Dallas, Texas in 2016.

FINANCIAL DATA: Note: Data for latest year may not have been available at press time.

In U.S. $	2015	2014	2013	2012	2011	2010
Revenue	3,241,369,000	2,670,573,000	2,220,256,000	1,776,151,000	1,454,838,000	1,222,771,000
R&D Expense						
Operating Income	410,415,000	327,588,000	279,978,000	196,195,000	118,884,000	68,153,000
Operating Margin %	12.66%	12.26%	12.61%	11.04%	8.17%	5.57%
SGA Expense	726,372,000	613,660,000	488,880,000	420,645,000	365,201,000	304,896,000
Net Income	257,135,000	202,849,000	172,549,000	120,264,000	71,030,000	39,356,000
Operating Cash Flow	396,592,000	327,725,000	239,001,000	220,887,000	176,543,000	172,827,000
Capital Expenditure	249,067,000	226,024,000	188,578,000	128,636,000	97,115,000	68,105,000
EBITDA	542,179,000	433,871,000	368,211,000	272,126,000	183,820,000	130,319,000
Return on Assets %	14.34%	14.09%	15.45%	14.25%	11.06%	7.01%
Return on Equity %	22.85%	22.66%	25.15%	24.36%	20.43%	14.64%
Debt to Equity						

CONTACT INFORMATION:

Phone: 630 410-4800   Fax: 630 226-8367
Toll-Free: 866-983-8582
Address: 1000 Remington Blvd., Suite 120, Bolingbrook, IL 60440 United States

STOCK TICKER/OTHER:

Stock Ticker: ULTA
Employees: 22,400
Parent Company:

Exchange: NAS
Fiscal Year Ends: 01/31

SALARIES/BONUSES:

Top Exec. Salary: $971,250   Bonus: $
Second Exec. Salary: $457,000   Bonus: $280,000

OTHER THOUGHTS:

Estimated Female Officers or Directors: 5
Hot Spot for Advancement for Women/Minorities: Y

Uniqlo Co Ltd (Fast Retailing Co Ltd)

www.uniqlo.com

NAIC Code: 448140

TYPES OF BUSINESS:

Apparel, Retail
Men's, Women's & Children's Apparel
Fast Fashion

BRANDS/DIVISIONS/AFFILIATES:

Fast Retailing Co Ltd
Comptoir Des Cotonniers
G.U.
Helmut Lang
J Brand
PLST
Princess Tam Tam
Theory

CONTACTS: Note: Officers with more than one job title may be intentionally listed here more than once.

Tadashi Yanai, CEO
Tadashi Yanai, Pres.
Tadashi Yanai, Chmn.
Nubuo Domae, CEO

GROWTH PLANS/SPECIAL FEATURES:

Uniqlo Co. Ltd., a subsidiary of Fast Retailing Co. Ltd., is a trendy clothing store operator based in Japan. The company specializes in fast fashion, clothing that is fashion-forward, moderately priced and constantly changing in style and color. In total, the company operates over 1,486 stores, with 852 locations in Japan. The firm's group companies include Comptoir Des Cotonniers, a French women's clothier; G.U., a Japanese discount casual wear store; Helmut Lang, an Austrian fashion brand; J Brand, an American jeans manufacturer; PLST, a Japanese original style producer; Princess Tam Tam, an international bathing suit, lingerie and loungewear store; and Theory, an international fashion store. 47% of Uniqlo's sales are generated by women's categories. The firm maintains its ability to sell affordable, quality clothing by controlling every step of the process (R&D, manufacturing, distribution and retail). It partners with factories throughout Asia to create its three main clothing sections: sophisticated minimalism, sophisticated fashion and the preppy student. The firm's approach allows its customers to create their own style with basic pieces, rather than being branded by the company's sense of fashion. Uniqlo operates global flagship stores in New York City, London, Paris and Shanghai. By some counts, the company's founder is the richest person in Japan. Uniqlo sees tremendous potential in China, with an eventual goal of 3,000 stores. By mid-2015, the firm had 374 stores in China and planned to open 100 new stores there yearly.

FINANCIAL DATA: Note: Data for latest year may not have been available at press time.

In U.S. $	2015	2014	2013	2012	2011	2010
Revenue	13,647,940,000	11,222,750,000	9,275,664,000	7,536,307,000	6,657,272,000	6,612,330,000
R&D Expense						
Operating Income	1,334,645,000	1,058,234,000	1,078,668,000	1,026,163,000	944,321,800	1,074,270,000
Operating Margin %	9.77%	9.42%	11.62%	13.61%	14.18%	16.24%
SGA Expense	5,452,283,000	4,456,811,000				
Net Income	892,887,900	643,833,300	756,788,400	603,979,600	456,973,400	500,551,800
Operating Cash Flow	1,094,988,000	897,497,300	806,964,500	1,035,845,000	463,846,900	719,190,700
Capital Expenditure	415,220,800	397,148,300	257,559,300	255,067,900	207,245,200	173,031,700
EBITDA	1,781,889,000	1,308,247,000	1,388,879,000	1,202,628,000	971,905,300	1,112,833,000
Return on Assets %	10.20%	7.93%	12.20%	12.69%	10.44%	12.71%
Return on Equity %	16.07%	12.64%	19.06%	20.39%	18.09%	22.63%
Debt to Equity			0.03	0.02	0.04	0.02

CONTACT INFORMATION:

Phone: 81 362720050   Fax: 81 362720076
Toll-Free:
Address: 717-1 Sayama, Yamaguchi City, Yamaguchi 754-0894 Japan

STOCK TICKER/OTHER:

Stock Ticker: FRCOF   Exchange: GREY
Employees: 23,982   Fiscal Year Ends: 08/31
Parent Company: FAST RETAILING CO LTD

SALARIES/BONUSES:

Top Exec. Salary: $ Bonus: $
Second Exec. Salary: $ Bonus: $

OTHER THOUGHTS:

Estimated Female Officers or Directors: 1
Hot Spot for Advancement for Women/Minorities:

United Natural Foods Inc

www.unfi.com

NAIC Code: 424410

TYPES OF BUSINESS:

Food Distribution
Natural & Organic Foods Distribution
Nutritional Supplements Distribution
Personal Care Products Distribution
Retail Stores

BRANDS/DIVISIONS/AFFILIATES:

United Natural Trading Co
Woodstock Farms
Albert's Organics
Select Nutrition
Earth Origins Market
UNFI Canada Inc
Tony's Fine Foods

CONTACTS: *Note: Officers with more than one job title may be intentionally listed here more than once.*

Steven Spinner, CEO
Mark Shamber, CFO
Eric Dorne, Chief Information Officer
Sean Griffin, COO
Michael Funk, Director
Thomas Dziki, Other Executive Officer
Chirstopher Testa, President, Divisional
Craig Smith, President, Divisional
Donald Mcintyre, President, Divisional
Michael Zechmeister, Senior VP
Joseph Traficanti, Senior VP

GROWTH PLANS/SPECIAL FEATURES:

United Natural Foods, Inc. (UNFI) is a national distributor of natural and organic foods and related products. The company, which is a Certified Organic Distributor, carries more than 80,000 natural and organic products; these are sold under regional brand, national brand, private and master distribution labels. The firm offers six types of products: grocery and general merchandise, personal care items, produce, nutritional supplements and sports nutrition perishables and frozen foods and bulk and food service products. UNFI serves over 40,000 customers, including supernatural chains (large chains of natural foods supermarkets), independently owned natural products retailers and conventional supermarkets located across the U.S. The company also distributes through the food service, international and buying club channels. The company has been the primary distributor to one of the largest natural food chains in the U.S., Whole Foods Market, Inc. for more than 16 years. The firm's operations consist of three principal divisions: wholesale, which includes the operations of its 32 distribution centers; retail, which consists of UNFI's 12 owned and managed retail store through its subsidiary which does business as Earth Origins Market, and one natural products retail store in British Columbia which does business as Drive Organics; and manufacturing, which is comprised of its subsidiaries United Natural Trading Co. (which does business as Woodstock Farms) and UNFI Canada Inc. Woodstock Farms is an importer, processor, packager and wholesale distributor of natural and organic products, trail mixes, nuts, seeds, dried fruit and confections. Distribution members of UNFI include Albert's Organics and Select Nutrition. In 2014, the company acquired Tony's Fine Foods, a leading distributor of perishable food products, including a wide array of specialty protein, cheese, deli, food service and bakery goods, throughout the Western U.S. as well as Alaska and Hawaii.

UNFI offers employees medical, dental, life and disability insurance; an assistance program; and educational assistance.

FINANCIAL DATA: *Note: Data for latest year may not have been available at press time.*

In U.S. $	2015	2014	2013	2012	2011	2010
Revenue	8,184,978,000	6,794,447,000	6,064,355,000	5,236,021,000	4,530,015,000	3,757,139,000
R&D Expense						
Operating Income	241,957,000	210,788,000	185,494,000	155,158,000	129,681,000	114,902,000
Operating Margin %	2.95%	3.10%	3.05%	2.96%	2.86%	3.05%
SGA Expense	1,017,755,000	916,857,000	837,953,000	755,744,000	688,859,000	
Net Income	138,734,000	125,482,000	107,854,000	91,342,000	76,673,000	68,321,000
Operating Cash Flow	48,864,000	62,419,000	44,331,000	66,244,000	49,844,000	66,132,000
Capital Expenditure	129,134,000	147,303,000	66,554,000	31,492,000	40,778,000	55,109,000
EBITDA	308,067,000	263,919,000	222,411,000	195,077,000	166,731,000	145,330,000
Return on Assets %	5.72%	6.23%	6.69%	6.31%	5.78%	5.91%
Return on Equity %	10.55%	10.71%	10.38%	9.88%	10.22%	11.62%
Debt to Equity	0.38	0.36	0.14	0.11		0.07

CONTACT INFORMATION:

Phone: 401 528-8634   Fax:
Toll-Free:
Address: 313 Iron Horse Way, Providence, RI 02908 United States

STOCK TICKER/OTHER:

Stock Ticker: UNFI   Exchange: NAS
Employees: 8,700   Fiscal Year Ends: 07/31
Parent Company:

SALARIES/BONUSES:

Top Exec. Salary: $872,300   Bonus: $
Second Exec. Salary: Bonus: $
$440,300

OTHER THOUGHTS:

Estimated Female Officers or Directors: 3
Hot Spot for Advancement for Women/Minorities: Y

United Supermarkets LLC

www.unitedtexas.com

NAIC Code: 445110

TYPES OF BUSINESS:

Supermarkets
Fuel Stations
Pharmacies
Florists
Culinary Classes

BRANDS/DIVISIONS/AFFILIATES:

Albertsons LLC
United Supermarkets
Market Street
United Express
Albertsons
Amigos
Praters
Food Club

CONTACTS: Note: Officers with more than one job title may be intentionally listed here more than once.

Robert Taylor, CEO
Sidney Hopper, COO
Matt Bumstead, Pres.
Wes Jackson, Chief Merch. Officer

GROWTH PLANS/SPECIAL FEATURES:

United Supermarkets LLC, a subsidiary of Albertsons LLC, is a supermarket chain operating 66 stores across Texas under the United Supermarkets, Market Street, United Express, Albertsons and Amigos brands. The firm's 37 United Supermarkets-brand stores represent the core of the company's operations and offer a variety of products, including deli products, meat and seafood, wine and beer, fresh baked goods, produce, household items and bulk items. Its 14 Market Street stores offer traditional groceries as well as specialty items, whole health products, gourmet products and take-home meals. United Express operates fuel and convenience stores, with 32 locations throughout Texas. Its 12 Albertsons markets offer groceries in west Texas and eastern New Mexico. Its four Amigos stores supplement traditional grocery offerings with international foods and specialty items. Many of the company's stores offer an FTD (Florists' Transword Delivery)-affiliated florist and a pharmacy. In United Supermarkets' Dallas/Ft. Worth locations, the company offers the Dish Event Center culinary school, which features a variety of classes and demonstrations. Its subsidiary Praters produces a line of specially cooked meats and side dishes found in all United stores and grocers throughout the U.S., both in private label and Praters packaging. Brands associated with United Supermarkets include Food Club, Red River Farms, Arriba!, Hearth of Texas Bread Company, Traditions, Top Care, Valu Time, Paws pet food, Smokehouse Ranch, Full Circle, Kristal ice and water and World Classics Trading Company. The company's 200,000-square foot distribution center serves several of the firm's existing stores, including those in the Dallas-Fort Worth, Wichita Falls and Abilene areas.

United Supermarkets offers employees benefits including medical, dental and vision insurance; life and disability coverage; a retirement plan that includes a 401(k) and profit sharing; a Texas College Savings plan; and flexible spending accounts.

FINANCIAL DATA: Note: Data for latest year may not have been available at press time.

In U.S. $	2015	2014	2013	2012	2011	2010
Revenue		1,250,000,000	1,200,000,000	1,100,000,000	1,000,000,000	970,000,000
R&D Expense						
Operating Income						
Operating Margin %						
SGA Expense						
Net Income						
Operating Cash Flow						
Capital Expenditure						
EBITDA						
Return on Assets %						
Return on Equity %						
Debt to Equity						

CONTACT INFORMATION:

Phone: 806-791-7457   Fax: 806-791-7476
Toll-Free: 877-848-6483
Address: 7830 Orlando Ave., Lubbock, TX 79423 United States

STOCK TICKER/OTHER:

Stock Ticker: Subsidiary
Employees: 11,000
Parent Company: ALBERTSONS LLC

Exchange:
Fiscal Year Ends: 01/31

SALARIES/BONUSES:

Top Exec. Salary: $ Bonus: $
Second Exec. Salary: $ Bonus: $

OTHER THOUGHTS:

Estimated Female Officers or Directors: 1
Hot Spot for Advancement for Women/Minorities:

UNY Co Ltd

NAIC Code: 445120

www.uny.co.jp

TYPES OF BUSINESS:

Convenience Stores
DIY Home Repair Stores
Bookstores
General Merchandise Stores
Clothing Stores
Real Estate Investment
Financial Services
Repair Business

BRANDS/DIVISIONS/AFFILIATES:

UNY Group Holdings Co Ltd
U Home
Yume-ya Bookstore
Piago-Kanto
Venga Venga
Apita
Sagami Co Ltd
UNY (Shanghai) Trading Co Ltd

GROWTH PLANS/SPECIAL FEATURES:

UNY Co., Ltd. operates retail stores in Japan. It has three main
operating divisions: U Home, Yume-ya Bookstore and Piago
Kanto. U Home is a home center concept that offers do-it-
yourself (DIY) items, gardening supplies, pet supplies, exterior
housing equipment, furniture, indoor electrical lighting, as well
as grocery and household goods. Brands within this division
include Apita and Piago. Yume-ya Bookstore is a shop that
features books, magazines and DVDs on culture, information
and knowledge. The bookstores also sell stationery items.
Piago Kanto operates the Venga Venga food stores. UNY is a
subsidiary of UNY Group Holdings Co. Ltd., which also owns
Sagami Co. Ltd., Palemo Co. Ltd., Molie Co. Ltd., 991Chiba Co
Ltd., Circle K Sunkus Co. Ltd., Sun Sougou Maintenance Co
Ltd., UNICOM Inc., Sun Reform Co. Ltd., My Support Co. Ltd.
Kanemi Co. Ltd., City Tours Co. Ltd., Tacky Foods Co. Ltd.
UNY (HK Co. Ltd., UNY (Shanghai) Trading Co. Ltd., Unifood
Co. Ltd., Nagai Co. Ltd. and UCS Co. Ltd.

CONTACTS: Note: Officers with more than one job title may be intentionally listed here more than once.

Norio Sako, Pres.
Jun Takahashi, Dir.-Group Strategy

FINANCIAL DATA: Note: Data for latest year may not have been available at press time.

In U.S. $	2015	2014	2013	2012	2011	2010
Revenue	8,269,018,000	8,375,870,000	8,360,720,000	8,757,487,000	9,030,407,000	9,206,068,000
R&D Expense						
Operating Income	164,226,700	205,541,000	284,193,300	357,075,600	284,850,600	171,189,500
Operating Margin %	1.98%	2.45%	3.39%	4.07%	3.15%	1.85%
SGA Expense	40,088,940	78,489,930	92,667,130	107,233,900	104,604,600	94,655,350
Net Income	-28,906,240	53,616,930	250,288,100	100,271,000	78,871,340	-25,132,680
Operating Cash Flow	469,397,700	287,155,300	300,521,000	342,119,300	490,683,800	470,030,700
Capital Expenditure	406,034,400	444,248,800	266,039,600	222,558,500	256,212,200	430,818,200
EBITDA	353,026,100	447,072,900	657,969,900	508,861,800	465,348,200	304,911,300
Return on Assets %	-.25%	.83%	3.39%	.87%	.64%	-.52%
Return on Equity %	-.81%	2.51%	11.33%	3.45%	2.54%	-2.07%
Debt to Equity	0.68	0.47	0.51	0.82	0.93	1.08

CONTACT INFORMATION:

Phone: 81-587-24-8111   Fax:
Toll-Free:
Address: 1 Amaikegotanda-cho, Inazawa, 4928276 Japan

SALARIES/BONUSES:

Top Exec. Salary: $ Bonus: $
Second Exec. Salary: $ Bonus: $

STOCK TICKER/OTHER:

Stock Ticker: UNYAF   Exchange: GREY
Employees: 31,156   Fiscal Year Ends: 02/28
Parent Company: UNY Group Holdings Co Ltd

OTHER THOUGHTS:

Estimated Female Officers or Directors:
Hot Spot for Advancement for Women/Minorities:

Urban Outfitters Inc

www.urbanoutfittersinc.com

NAIC Code: 448140

TYPES OF BUSINESS:

Casual Apparel Stores
Household & Gift Merchandise
Accessories
Wholesale Distribution
Online Sales
Footwear
Catalog Sales
Furniture

BRANDS/DIVISIONS/AFFILIATES:

Urban Outfitters
Anthropologie
Free People
Terrain
Bhldn

CONTACTS: *Note: Officers with more than one job title may be intentionally listed here more than once.*

David McCreight, CEO, Divisional
Richard Hayne, CEO
Frank Conforti, CFO
Calvin Hollinger, Chief Administrative Officer
Scott Belair, Co-Founder
Margaret Hayne, Director
Glen Bodzy, Secretary

GROWTH PLANS/SPECIAL FEATURES:

Urban Outfitters, Inc. is a clothing and accessories company that operates specialty retail stores under the Urban Outfitters, Anthropologie, Terrain, Free People and BHLDN brands, and operates a wholesale division under the Free People brand. Urban Outfitters targets ages 18-28 through a style-conscious merchandise mix and store environment. Urban Outfitters operate 238 stores in North America and Europe, and these stores have 75,000 to 80,000 stock keeping units (SKUs). This includes women's and men's apparel, footwear, accessories, apartment wares and gifts. Anthropologie targets upscale female customers from 28-45 years old. Anthropologie operates approximately 204 stores, comprising both the Anthropologie and Bhldn brands, offering women's casual apparel, accessories, home furnishings, gifts and decorative items and carrying 60,000 to 65,000 SKUs. The Bhldn brand emphasizes elements that contributes to a wedding, including wedding gowns, bridesmaid frocks, party dresses, jewelry, headpieces, footwear, lingerie and decorations. Terrain is targeted to men and women interested in outdoor living and gardening. Currently, there are two Terrain stores. Products include lifestyle home and garden items combined with antiques and live plants and flowers. Additionally, Terrain offers landscape and design service solutions. Free People, targeting contemporary women aged 25-30, designs, develops and markets young women's casual apparel. Free People retail stores average 1,600 square feet and carry between 20,000 and 25,000 SKUs, while operating 102 stores. In 2015, the firm integrated the Bhldn and Anthropologie brands into all Anthropologie stores.

Urban Outfitters offers employees medical, dental and vision coverage; wellness programs (discounted gym memberships, smoking cessation, nutrition counseling and alternative health); a 401(k); short-term and long-term disability, AD&D and life insurance; employee discounts; and paid holidays.

FINANCIAL DATA: *Note: Data for latest year may not have been available at press time.*

In U.S. $	2015	2014	2013	2012	2011	2010
Revenue	3,323,077,000	3,086,608,000	2,794,925,000	2,473,801,000	2,274,102,000	1,937,815,000
R&D Expense						
Operating Income	365,385,000	426,831,000	374,285,000	284,725,000	414,203,000	338,984,000
Operating Margin %	10.99%	13.82%	13.39%	11.50%	18.21%	17.49%
SGA Expense	809,545,000	734,511,000	657,246,000	575,811,000	522,417,000	447,161,000
Net Income	232,428,000	282,360,000	237,314,000	185,251,000	272,958,000	219,893,000
Operating Cash Flow	322,321,000	423,155,000	395,680,000	282,702,000	385,113,000	325,394,000
Capital Expenditure	229,804,000	186,101,000	168,875,000	190,010,000	143,642,000	109,260,000
EBITDA	503,495,000	559,495,000	492,949,000	392,837,000	515,308,000	431,334,000
Return on Assets %	11.31%	14.05%	14.46%	11.30%	15.91%	14.83%
Return on Equity %	15.38%	18.52%	19.60%	14.95%	20.15%	18.70%
Debt to Equity						

CONTACT INFORMATION:

Phone: 215 454-5500   Fax: 215 568-1549
Toll-Free: 800-282-2200
Address: 5000 S. Broad St., Philadelphia, PA 19112 United States

STOCK TICKER/OTHER:

Stock Ticker: URBN
Employees: 24,000
Parent Company:

Exchange: NAS
Fiscal Year Ends: 01/31

SALARIES/BONUSES:

Top Exec. Salary: $929,231   Bonus: $5,000
Second Exec. Salary: $717,692   Bonus: $5,000

OTHER THOUGHTS:

Estimated Female Officers or Directors: 3
Hot Spot for Advancement for Women/Minorities: Y

Sales, profits and employees may be estimates. Financial information, benefits and other data can change quickly and may vary from those stated here.

Valentino Fashion Group SpA

www.valentinofashiongroup.com

NAIC Code: 424300

TYPES OF BUSINESS:

Apparel and Clothing Brands, Designers, Importers and Distributors
Fashion and Luxury Items
Couture Fashion
Perfume
Eyewear
Wedding Gowns
Watches

BRANDS/DIVISIONS/AFFILIATES:

Valentino
Valentino Garavani
Valentino Roma
Mayhoola for Investments
R.E.D. Valentino
Proenza Schouler

CONTACTS: *Note: Officers with more than one job title may be intentionally listed here more than once.*

Stefano Sassi, CEO
Maria Grazia Chiuri, Designer
Pier Paolo Piccioli, Designer
Alessandra Facchinetti, Dir- Women's Collections
Stefano Sassi, Chmn.

GROWTH PLANS/SPECIAL FEATURES:

Valentino Fashion Group SpA is a fashion and luxury company headquartered in Milan, Italy. Maintaining an international presence, the firm specializes in clothing, accessories and footwear for men and women. Valentino's activities are divided between the following two business units: Valentino, which includes the brands Valentino, Valentino Garavani, Valentino Roma and R.E.D. Valentino; and licensed brands, which includes M Missoni. Valentino offers exclusive products in the couture, ready-to-wear, designer, diffusion and bridge segments. Valentino Garavani is a provider of prestigious handbags, footwear, small leather goods, belts and other accessories for men and women. It was created when Marzotto SpA, a firm dedicated to the textile and fashion business, vested its clothing sector to the newly formed Valentino Fashion Group. Marzotto formed a separate firm to operate its textile business, allowing Valentino to be exclusively concerned with fashion and luxury items. Since the fashion group's inception, Valentino has begun an expansion process to include several new product lines, most notably perfume, eyewear and wedding gowns. The firm currently operates in over 90 countries, with more than 150 single-brand boutiques and 98 directly managed shops. Additionally, the company owns an interest in U.S.-based fashion label Proenza Schouler.

FINANCIAL DATA: *Note: Data for latest year may not have been available at press time.*

In U.S. $	2015	2014	2013	2012	2011	2010
Revenue		700,000,000	644,100,000	500,500,000	436,000,000	356,493,700
R&D Expense						
Operating Income						
Operating Margin %						
SGA Expense						
Net Income						
Operating Cash Flow						
Capital Expenditure						
EBITDA						
Return on Assets %						
Return on Equity %						
Debt to Equity						

CONTACT INFORMATION:

Phone: 39-02-624921   Fax: 39-02-62492584
Toll-Free:
Address: Via Turati 16/18, Milan, 20121 Italy

STOCK TICKER/OTHER:

Stock Ticker: Private   Exchange:
Employees: Fiscal Year Ends: 12/31
Parent Company: Mayhoola for Investments

SALARIES/BONUSES:

Top Exec. Salary: $ Bonus: $
Second Exec. Salary: $ Bonus: $

OTHER THOUGHTS:

Estimated Female Officers or Directors: 2
Hot Spot for Advancement for Women/Minorities:

Vans Inc

NAIC Code: 448210

TYPES OF BUSINESS:

Shoes, Retail
Sports Apparel & Accessories
Online Sales
Helmets
Snowboard Bindings
Concert Tours

BRANDS/DIVISIONS/AFFILIATES:

Vans Triple Crown Series
VF Corp
PRO-TEC
Vans Warped Tour
SWITCH

CONTACTS: Note: Officers with more than one job title may be intentionally listed here more than once.

Scott J. Blechman, CFO
Chris D. Strain, VP-Mktg.
Cheryl A. Van Doren, VP-Human Resources
Eric Wiseman, CEO

GROWTH PLANS/SPECIAL FEATURES:

Vans, Inc., a subsidiary of VF Corp., is a sports retailing company that merchandises, designs, sources and distributes Vans-branded footwear, apparel and accessories primarily for skateboarding, snowboarding, surfing, BMX bike riding and motor cross. Vans' products are also sold under the SWITCH brand of step-in snowboard boot bindings and the PRO-TEC line of protective helmets and pads sold through Pro-Tec, Inc. The company distributes its products through Vans retail stores in the U.S., Mexico and Europe as well as on the Internet. Vans was founded in 1966 in Southern California as a domestic manufacturer of vulcanized canvas shoes, many of which appealed to skateboard enthusiasts and the Southern California skate and surf culture. Its primary strategy is to continue to build and reinforce the authenticity and credibility of the Vans brand for a core customer base of 10-24 year-old sports enthusiasts. The company sponsors a skateboarding team, the Vans Triple Crown of Surfing, as well as many skateboarding events. Many of these events are available on videos on its web site and through cell phone downloads. The brand is also a driving force behind the Vans Warped Tour, a music festival that features more than 40 bands traveling to over 40 cities in North America. Vans' sister brands owned by VF Corp. include Timberland, Kipling, lucy, Napapijri, Reef, 7 For All Mankind, Splendid and Ella Moss.

Vans offers its employees medical, dental and vision benefits; a 401(k) program; retirement contributions; flexible spending accounts; an employee assistance program; life and AD&D insurance; short- and long-term disability; onsite gym and lunch vendors; a tobacco cessation program; a scholarship program for employees' children; and education assistance.

FINANCIAL DATA: Note: Data for latest year may not have been available at press time.

In U.S. $	2015	2014	2013	2012	2011	2010
Revenue						
R&D Expense						
Operating Income						
Operating Margin %						
SGA Expense						
Net Income						
Operating Cash Flow						
Capital Expenditure						
EBITDA						
Return on Assets %						
Return on Equity %						
Debt to Equity						

CONTACT INFORMATION:

Phone: 714-889-6100   Fax:
Toll-Free: 888-691-8889
Address: 6550 Katella Ave., Cypress, CA 90630 United States

STOCK TICKER/OTHER:

Stock Ticker: Subsidiary   Exchange:
Employees: Fiscal Year Ends: 05/31
Parent Company: VF CORP

SALARIES/BONUSES:

Top Exec. Salary: $ Bonus: $
Second Exec. Salary: $ Bonus: $

OTHER THOUGHTS:

Estimated Female Officers or Directors:
Hot Spot for Advancement for Women/Minorities:

Vente Privee

us.venteprivee.com

NAIC Code: 454111

TYPES OF BUSINESS:

Electronic Shopping

BRANDS/DIVISIONS/AFFILIATES:

GROWTH PLANS/SPECIAL FEATURES:

Vente Privee is a members-only French online retailer offerin
designer brands for fashion, home, travel, jewelry and lifestyl
products on a limited-time sales basis. Its site was develope
to host sales of designer brands with discounted prices fror
50% to 70% off. Brands on the Vente site each have their ow
dedicated Boutique page featuring their products. The site ha
millions of members across Europe and partners with mor
than 2,500 international brands. Brand names include Kooba
Effy, Mary Katrantzou, Wacoal, Godinger, Hush Puppies
Durance, Victor Mayer and Jacob & Co. In October 2014, the
firm announced that it was closing its U.S. branch and joir
venture with American Express by the end of the year.

CONTACTS: *Note: Officers with more than one job title may be intentionally listed here more than once.*

Jacques-Antoine Granjon, CEO
Timothy Quinn, VP-Finance
Robin Domeniconi, VP-Mktg.
Nicholas Genest, VP-Tech.
Timothy Quinn, VP-Finance
Katherine Wu Brady, CEO-Vente-Privee USA LLC

FINANCIAL DATA: *Note: Data for latest year may not have been available at press time.*

In U.S. $	2015	2014	2013	2012	2011	2010
Revenue		1,945,225,000	1,971,751,385	1,744,125,508	1,429,611,072	1,335,000,000
R&D Expense						
Operating Income						
Operating Margin %						
SGA Expense						
Net Income						
Operating Cash Flow						
Capital Expenditure						
EBITDA						
Return on Assets %						
Return on Equity %						
Debt to Equity						

CONTACT INFORMATION:

Phone: 0800 026 0687   Fax:
Toll-Free: 877-453-3909
Address: 249 avenue du President Wilson, La Plaine Saint Denis, Paris, 93210 France

STOCK TICKER/OTHER:

Stock Ticker: Private
Employees: 2,100
Parent Company:

Exchange:
Fiscal Year Ends: 12/31

SALARIES/BONUSES:

Top Exec. Salary: $ Bonus: $
Second Exec. Salary: $ Bonus: $

OTHER THOUGHTS:

Estimated Female Officers or Directors: 2
Hot Spot for Advancement for Women/Minorities:

VF Corp

www.vfc.com

NAIC Code: 424300

TYPES OF BUSINESS:

Apparel and Clothing Brands, Designers, Importers and Distributors
Swimsuits
Outdoor Gear & Apparel
Image Wear
Outlet Stores
Footwear

BRANDS/DIVISIONS/AFFILIATES:

Vans Inc
lucy
SmartWool
Wrangler
Timberland
North Face
Nautica
Majestic

CONTACTS: *Note: Officers with more than one job title may be intentionally listed here more than once.*

Eric Wiseman, Director
Steven Rendle, Director
Laura Meagher, General Counsel
Craig Hodges, Other Corporate Officer
Karl Salzburger, President, Divisional
Scott Baxter, President, Divisional
Lance Allega, Vice President, Divisional
Scott Roe, Vice President
Bryan McNeill, Vice President

GROWTH PLANS/SPECIAL FEATURES:

VF Corp., organized in 1899, is one of the world's largest brand-name apparel manufacturers and a leading producer of jeanswear, outerwear, footwear, sportswear and occupational apparel. VF products are sold globally throughout the U.S., Canada, Europe, Asia and Latin America. The company divides its brands into five business groups, called coalitions: outdoor & action sports, which includes outerwear, sportswear, footwear, equipment, backpacks, daypacks, luggage and accessories; jeanswear, which consists of jeans as well as shorts, casual pants, knit and woven tops and outerwear; imagewear, which includes occupational apparel, uniforms and owned and licensed sports and lifestyle apparel; sportswear, which includes outerwear, underwear, swimwear, sleepwear, luggage and accessories; and contemporary brands, which focuses on lifestyle brands. The outdoor & action sports coalition includes the firm's largest brand, the North Face, as well as Timberland, SmartWool, Vans, JanSport, Eastpak, Kipling, Napapijri, Reef and lucy. In jeanswear, Lee and Wrangler are its largest brand names. The image business includes the firm's uniforms and career occupational clothing. These brands include Red Kap work clothes; Bulwark flame resistant and protective clothing; and Horace Small apparel for law enforcement and public safety officials. Sportswear brands include Nautica and Kipling. The licensed business consists of VF's owned and licensed high profile athletic apparel, marketed under the Majestic and Harley-Davidson brand names. The company's contemporary brands coalition includes its premium upscale lifestyle brands such as Splendid, Ella Moss and 7 For All Mankind.

FINANCIAL DATA: *Note: Data for latest year may not have been available at press time.*

In U.S. $	2015	2014	2013	2012	2011	2010
Revenue		12,282,160,000	11,419,650,000	10,879,850,000	9,459,232,000	7,702,589,000
R&D Expense						
Operating Income		1,437,724,000	1,647,147,000	1,465,267,000	1,244,791,000	820,860,000
Operating Margin %		11.70%	14.42%	13.46%	13.15%	10.65%
SGA Expense		4,159,885,000	3,841,032,000	3,596,708,000	3,085,839,000	2,574,790,000
Net Income		1,047,505,000	1,210,119,000	1,085,999,000	888,089,000	571,362,000
Operating Cash Flow		1,697,629,000	1,506,041,000	1,275,000,000	1,081,371,000	1,001,282,000
Capital Expenditure		302,020,000	325,142,000	282,830,000	249,128,000	125,250,000
EBITDA		1,713,974,000	1,900,536,000	1,753,436,000	1,441,056,000	1,001,346,000
Return on Assets %		10.32%	12.13%	11.46%	11.26%	8.83%
Return on Equity %		17.89%	21.60%	22.50%	21.17%	14.88%
Debt to Equity		0.25	0.23	0.27	0.40	0.24

CONTACT INFORMATION:

Phone: 336 424-6000   Fax:
Toll-Free:
Address: 105 Corporate Ctr. Blvd., Greensboro, NC 27408 United States

STOCK TICKER/OTHER:

Stock Ticker: VFC   Exchange: NYS
Employees: 59,000   Fiscal Year Ends: 12/31
Parent Company:

SALARIES/BONUSES:

Top Exec. Salary: Bonus: $
$1,300,000
Second Exec. Salary: Bonus: $
$896,738

OTHER THOUGHTS:

Estimated Female Officers or Directors: 5

Hot Spot for Advancement for Women/Minorities: Y

Sales, profits and employees may be estimates. Financial information, benefits and other data can change quickly and may vary from those stated here.

Viavarejo SA

www.viavarejo.com.br

NAIC Code: 452111

TYPES OF BUSINESS:
Retail

BRANDS/DIVISIONS/AFFILIATES:
Ponto Frio
Ponto Frio Digital
Grupo Pao de Acucar
PontoFrio.com.br
Casas Bahia
Bartira

CONTACTS: *Note: Officers with more than one job title may be intentionally listed here more than once.*
Francisco Valim, CEO
Wilma Loures, Mgr.-Press Office
Ronaldo Iabrudi dos Santos Pereira, Chmn.

GROWTH PLANS/SPECIAL FEATURES:

Viavarejo SA is a Brazilian retailer that specializes in home appliances, furniture and electronic goods. The firm is part of Brazilian retail conglomerate Grupo Pao de Acucar. The firm operates stores in Brazil under two primary names: Ponto Frio and Casas Bahia. Ponto Frio's 390 store locations fall under four layouts: Ponto Frio Digital stores, with selling space ranging from 753 to 3,229 square feet, which focus on high-tech products such as digital cameras/camcorders, video equipment, audio equipment and computer equipment and mobile phones; mall stores, with selling space ranging from 1,292 to 21,528 square feet that displays part of the firm's product mix from all categories; street stores located in commercial districts, with selling space ranging from 2,152 to 37,674 square feet that displays part of the company's product mix from all product categories; and megastores, with selling space of over 10,764 square feet that displays the entire product mix and with part of the space used under partnerships with suppliers for product demonstrations. Ponto Frio also markets its products through its e-commerce web site (PontoFrio.com.br), telephone sales from its call centers, corporate sales directly to other firms and wholesale marketing to smaller retailers. Casas Bahia has more than 600 Brazilian stores and specializes in furniture and home appliances. In addition to its stores, the firm also owns Bartira, a furniture manufacturer. Bartira makes furniture for bedrooms, kitchens and living rooms, among other things, with an annual production of more than 3 million pieces of furniture, which are sold exclusively at Casas Bahia and Pontofrio stores.

FINANCIAL DATA: *Note: Data for latest year may not have been available at press time.*

In U.S. $	2015	2014	2013	2012	2011	2010
Revenue		5,916,551,000	5,676,994,000	5,961,498,000	5,484,100,000	2,245,660,000
R&D Expense						
Operating Income		368,447,100	440,114,300	316,881,200	221,857,400	79,042,610
Operating Margin %		6.22%	7.75%	5.31%	4.04%	3.51%
SGA Expense		1,327,662,000	1,293,357,000	1,301,521,000	1,228,999,000	392,597,900
Net Income		244,761,600	302,570,800	83,685,770	23,605,930	-16,480,180
Operating Cash Flow		588,680,400	584,110,800	600,323,800	-132,548,100	-183,739,000
Capital Expenditure		150,301,400	98,163,240	85,627,160	74,593,840	41,558,070
EBITDA		415,155,400	483,684,500	368,645,200	263,380,500	96,398,500
Return on Assets %		6.36%	9.08%	2.69%	.83%	-1.02%
Return on Equity %		21.64%	33.58%	11.47%	3.49%	-3.96%
Debt to Equity		0.06	0.22	0.33	0.56	0.62

CONTACT INFORMATION:
Phone: 55-11-4225-8668   Fax: 55-11-4225-8671
Toll-Free:
Address: Rua Joao Pessoa, 83 - Centro, Rio De Janeiro, RJ 21241460 Brazil

STOCK TICKER/OTHER:
Stock Ticker: GBXPY   Exchange: GREY
Employees: 61,000   Fiscal Year Ends: 12/31
Parent Company:

SALARIES/BONUSES:
Top Exec. Salary: $ Bonus: $
Second Exec. Salary: $ Bonus: $

OTHER THOUGHTS:
Estimated Female Officers or Directors: 1
Hot Spot for Advancement for Women/Minorities:

Victoria's Secret

www.victoriassecret.com

NAIC Code: 448120

TYPES OF BUSINESS:

Intimate Apparel-Women's, Retail
Cosmetics
Fragrances
Personal Care Products
Online Sales
Catalogs
Women's Shoes
General Women's Apparel

BRANDS/DIVISIONS/AFFILIATES:

PINK
Victoria's Secret Direct
Victoria's Secret Beauty
Angels
IPEX
Body by Victoria
La Senza
Limited Brands Inc

CONTACTS: *Note: Officers with more than one job title may be intentionally listed here more than once.*

Sharen Jester Turney, CEO
Brian VanOoyen, VP-Merch. Planning
Bridget Ryan-Berman, CEO-Victoria's Secret Direct
Sharen Jester Turney, CEO

GROWTH PLANS/SPECIAL FEATURES:

Victoria's Secret, a wholly-owned subsidiary of Limited Brands, Inc., purchases, distributes and sells lingerie, personal care products and women's apparel through over 1,000 retail stores, the Internet and direct mail channels. The stores offer branded merchandise such as IPEX, PINK, Very Sexy, Body by Victoria, VS Cotton, Dream Angels, Beauty Rush and Angels. The firm also owns several standalone PINK stores in the U.S. and Canada, which sell intimate apparel, denim, casual apparel and body products targeted to young women ages 13-25, and standalone Victoria's Secret Beauty and Accessories Stores. Victoria's Secret Beauty offers a complete line of fragrance, cosmetics and body products for skin and hair. In addition to its retail stores, the company operates Victoria's Secret Direct, which consists of the famous Victoria's Secret Catalog and an e-commerce site, VictoriasSecret.com. Street apparel such as dresses, pants, skirts, shorts, tops and shoes are available from the catalog and online, but not in stores. Once each year, Victoria's Secret conducts a televised fashion show featuring some of the world's top models and performances by acclaimed musicians such as Maroon 5 or Kanye West. The Victoria's Secret group also includes the operations of La Senza, a Canadian lingerie store chain owned by Limited Brands. Approximately 25% of the firm's sales are made via the catalogs and online.

The company offers employees medical, dental, vision and prescription drug coverage; a 401(k) plan; a discount stock purchase plan; life insurance; discounts on products; tuition reimbursement; a commuter discount program; and an employee assistance program.

FINANCIAL DATA: *Note: Data for latest year may not have been available at press time.*

In U.S. $	2015	2014	2013	2012	2011	2010
Revenue		7,207,600,000	6,884,200,000	6,574,000,000	6,121,000,000	5,520,000,000
R&D Expense						
Operating Income						
Operating Margin %						
SGA Expense						
Net Income		1,042,000,000	903,000,000			
Operating Cash Flow						
Capital Expenditure						
EBITDA						
Return on Assets %						
Return on Equity %						
Debt to Equity						

CONTACT INFORMATION:

Phone: 614-577-7111   Fax:
Toll-Free: 800-411-5116
Address: 4 Limited Pkwy. E, Reynoldsburg, OH 43068 United States

STOCK TICKER/OTHER:

Stock Ticker: Subsidiary   Exchange:
Employees: 65,000   Fiscal Year Ends: 01/31
Parent Company: L Brands Inc

SALARIES/BONUSES:

Top Exec. Salary: $ Bonus: $
Second Exec. Salary: $ Bonus: $

OTHER THOUGHTS:

Estimated Female Officers or Directors: 3
Hot Spot for Advancement for Women/Minorities: Y

Sales, profits and employees may be estimates. Financial information, benefits and other data can change quickly and may vary from those stated here.

Village Super Market Inc

NAIC Code: 445110

www.shoprite.com

TYPES OF BUSINESS:

Grocery Stores
Superstores
Pharmacies

BRANDS/DIVISIONS/AFFILIATES:

ShopRite
Wakefern Food Corp

CONTACTS: Note: Officers with more than one job title may be intentionally listed here more than once.

James Sumas, CEO
John Van Orden, CFO
Luigi Perri, Chief Accounting Officer
Nicholas Sumas, Chief Marketing Officer
John Sumas, COO
John Sumas, Director
William Sumas, Director
Robert Sumas, Director

GROWTH PLANS/SPECIAL FEATURES:

Village Super Market, Inc. operates a chain of 29 ShopRit supermarkets, 18 of which are located in northern New Jersey eight in southern New Jersey, two in Maryland and one i northeastern Pennsylvania. The company is a member c Wakefern Food Corp., one of the nation's largest retailer owned food cooperatives and owner of the ShopRite name This relationship provides Village Super Market with many c the economies of scale in purchasing, distribution, private labe products, advanced retail technology and advertisin associated with chains of greater size and geographi coverage. Village Super Market attempts to utilize its sellin space efficiently and gives continuing attention to the decor an format of its stores, tailoring each store's product mix to the preferences of the local community. Of the company's 2! stores, 14 average more than 60,000 square feet; 8 averag between 50,001 and 60,000; five, between 40,000 and 50,000 and two are less than 40,000. These superstores allow the company to provide a one-stop shopping experience and te feature expanded specialty departments such as home mea replacement, an onsite bakery, an expanded delicatessen including prepared foods, a variety of natural and organic foods, ethnic and international foods and a fresh seafoo section. Superstores also offer an expanded selection of non food items, such as cut flowers, health and beauty aids greeting cards, small appliances, photo processing and pharmacy.

The firm offers employees health, dental and vision insurance life insurance; a pension plan; and a 401(k) plan.

FINANCIAL DATA: Note: Data for latest year may not have been available at press time.

In U.S. $	2015	2014	2013	2012	2011	2010
Revenue	1,583,789,000	1,518,636,000	1,476,457,000	1,422,243,000	1,298,928,000	1,261,825,000
R&D Expense						
Operating Income	43,531,000	29,828,000	44,177,000	55,552,000	38,316,000	45,258,000
Operating Margin %	2.74%	1.96%	2.99%	3.90%	2.94%	3.58%
SGA Expense	366,254,000	356,396,000	333,230,000	313,516,000	293,222,000	280,767,000
Net Income	30,620,000	5,045,000	25,784,000	31,445,000	20,982,000	25,381,000
Operating Cash Flow	17,468,000	52,447,000	51,273,000	43,432,000	64,144,000	35,313,000
Capital Expenditure	23,517,000	50,322,000	21,888,000	16,729,000	13,346,000	20,204,000
EBITDA	69,260,000	54,724,000	68,764,000	77,882,000	59,144,000	64,178,000
Return on Assets %	6.71%	.85%	6.00%	7.90%	5.64%	7.29%
Return on Equity %	12.32%	1.58%	10.58%	14.34%	10.13%	12.91%
Debt to Equity	0.17	0.19	0.17	0.17	0.20	0.20

CONTACT INFORMATION:

Phone: 201-467-2200   Fax:
Toll-Free: 800-746-7748
Address: 733 Mountain Ave., Springfield, NJ 07081 United States

SALARIES/BONUSES:

Top Exec. Salary: $916,851   Bonus: $351,000
Second Exec. Salary: Bonus: $295,000
$740,158

STOCK TICKER/OTHER:

Stock Ticker: VLGEA
Employees: 7,050
Parent Company:

Exchange: NAS
Fiscal Year Ends: 07/31

OTHER THOUGHTS:

Estimated Female Officers or Directors: 1
Hot Spot for Advancement for Women/Minorities:

Vitamin Shoppe Inc

www.vitaminshoppe.com

NAIC Code: 446191

TYPES OF BUSINESS:

Nutritional Supplements, Retail
Catalog & Online Sales

BRANDS/DIVISIONS/AFFILIATES:

Vitamin Shoppe
Super Supplements
Vitapath
Healthy Awards Program
BodyTech
Mytrition
plnt
ProBioCare

CONTACTS: *Note: Officers with more than one job title may be intentionally listed here more than once.*

Brenda Galgano, CFO
Richard Markee, Chairman of the Board
Dan Lamadrid, Chief Accounting Officer
Lou Weiss, Chief Marketing Officer
Colin Watts, Director
Michael Jaffe, General Counsel
Michael Beardall, President, Subsidiary

GROWTH PLANS/SPECIAL FEATURES:

Vitamin Shoppe, Inc. is a national retailer of nutritional supplements and vitamins primarily through The Vitamin Shoppe stores. The stores' offerings include vitamins, minerals, nutritional supplements, herbs, sports nutrition formulas, homeopathic remedies and other health and beauty aids. The company operates in two segments: retail and direct. The Vitamin Shoppe's retail segment operates 717 stores located in 45 states, Washington, D.C., Puerto Rico and Ontario, Canada under the Vitamin Shoppe, Super Supplements and Vitapath retail store formats. Additionally, the firm provides alternative, direct retail channels to its customers through monthly catalogs and comprehensive web sites. The company carries 25,000 SKUs (stock keeping units) from more than 900 brand names, including Solgar, Optimum Nutrition, Cellucor, Garden of Life and Nature's Way, and proprietary brands such as Vitamin Shoppe, BodyTech, Mytrition, plnt, ProBioCare, Next Step, Nutri-Force, Betancourt Sports Nutrition and True Athlete. It offers participation in the free of charge Healthy Awards Program, which has approximately 6.1 million members, allowing them to earn points redeemable for future purchases.

The company offers employees a 401(k); medical, dental and vision coverage (benefits vary based on position); short-term disability coverage; employee stock purchase program; health & fitness programs; onsite fitness centers; global fit program; cell phone plan discounts; and pet insurance.

FINANCIAL DATA: *Note: Data for latest year may not have been available at press time.*

In U.S. $	2015	2014	2013	2012	2011	2010
Revenue		1,213,046,000	1,087,469,000	950,902,000	856,586,000	751,482,000
R&D Expense						
Operating Income		102,656,000	110,292,000	99,372,000	76,834,000	59,662,000
Operating Margin %		8.46%	10.14%	10.45%	8.96%	7.93%
SGA Expense		301,603,000	267,354,000	233,610,000	216,125,000	189,872,000
Net Income		61,241,000	66,546,000	60,825,000	44,864,000	29,246,000
Operating Cash Flow		100,147,000	81,122,000	78,350,000	77,133,000	55,184,000
Capital Expenditure		43,646,000	43,430,000	31,174,000	25,046,000	18,448,000
EBITDA		136,724,000	138,242,000	122,448,000	96,509,000	79,475,000
Return on Assets %		8.72%	10.49%	11.29%	9.19%	6.12%
Return on Equity %		11.33%	13.63%	15.14%	13.73%	10.99%
Debt to Equity						0.18

CONTACT INFORMATION:

Phone: 201 868-5959   Fax:
Toll-Free: 866-293-3367
Address: 2101 91st St., North Bergen, NJ 07047 United States

STOCK TICKER/OTHER:

Stock Ticker: VSI
Employees: 5,583
Parent Company:

Exchange: NYS
Fiscal Year Ends: 12/31

SALARIES/BONUSES:

Top Exec. Salary: $754,000   Bonus: $
Second Exec. Salary: $470,000   Bonus: $

OTHER THOUGHTS:

Estimated Female Officers or Directors: 8
Hot Spot for Advancement for Women/Minorities: Y

Sales, profits and employees may be estimates. Financial information, benefits and other data can change quickly and may vary from those stated here.

Walgreens Boots Alliance, Inc.   www.walgreens.com

NAIC Code: 446110

TYPES OF BUSINESS:

Drug Stores
Mail-Order Pharmacy Services
Pharmacy Benefit Management
Health Care Center Management
Online Pharmacy Services
Photo Printing Services
Specialty Pharmacy Services
Home Infusion Services

BRANDS/DIVISIONS/AFFILIATES:

Take Care Health Systems Inc
Intercom Plus
Drugstore.com Inc
Walgreens.com
Duane Reade
Walgreens Boots Alliance Inc
Alliance Boots
Kerr Drug

CONTACTS: Note: Officers with more than one job title may be intentionally listed here more than once.

Ornella Barra, CEO, Divisional
Bradley Fluegel, Other Executive Officer
Stefano Pessina, CEO
George Fairweather, CFO
James Skinner, Chairman of the Board
Kimberly Scardino, Chief Accounting Officer
Marco Pagni, Chief Administrative Officer
Timothy Theriault, Chief Information Officer
Theodore Heidloff, Controller
Kathleen Wilson-Thompson, Executive VP
Ken Murphy, Executive VP
Simon Roberts, Executive VP
Jeffrey Berkowitz, Executive VP
Alexander Gourlay, Executive VP
Jan Reed, General Counsel
Richard Ashworth, President, Divisional
Mark Wagner, President, Divisional
Sona Chawla, President, Divisional

GROWTH PLANS/SPECIAL FEATURES:

Walgreens Boots Alliance, Inc., a product of the Walgreen Co. and Alliance Boots GmbH merger, operates one of the largest chains of U.S. drug stores. The company has approximately 8,309 locations in all 50 U.S. states, Washington, D.C., U.S. Virgin Islands and Puerto Rico. Stores offer prescription and non-prescription drugs as well as general merchandise. To coordinate its operations, the firm uses Intercom Plus, a proprietary computer system for filling prescriptions, linking all stores into a single network. A large percentage of the company's stores have drive-through pharmacies, and most stores offer one-hour photo processing. The firm also accepts prescription refill orders online through its web site. Prescription sales accounted for approximately 64% of total sales; non-prescription drugs roughly 10%; and general merchandise 26%. The company operates more than 400 care clinics operated by Take Care Health Systems, Inc. within its drugstores. Approximately 6.2 million customers shop at Walgreen's stores each day. In addition, Walgreens.com receives approximately 59.7 million visits each month. Walgreen also owns and operates Drugstore.com as well as the Manhattan drug store chain Duane Reade. In 2014, the company acquired the 55% interest in Alliance Boots. That December, the two companies merged to form a new holding company, Walgreens Boots Alliance Inc., with Walgreens becoming a subsidiary of the new company, which trades on the NASDAQ under the WBA symbol. Also in 2014, the firm sold a controlling interest in Take Care Employer Solutions LLC; and acquired certain assets of Kerr Drug, which include 76 retail drugstore locations as well as a specialty pharmacy business and a distribution center, all based in North Carolina. In October 2015, Walgreens announced that it would acquire Rite Aid Corporation. The purchase would give the firm an additional 4,600 stores in 31 states. The acquisition is still awaiting regulatory approval.

The company offers employees medical, prescription and dental coverage; life and accident insurance; a profit sharing plan; a stock purchase program; employee discounts; a flexible spending account; personal leave; domestic partner coverage; and onsite childcare at the corporate office.

FINANCIAL DATA: Note: Data for latest year may not have been available at press time.

In U.S. $	2015	2014	2013	2012	2011	2010
Revenue	103,444,000,000	76,392,000,000	72,217,000,000	71,633,000,000	72,184,000,000	67,420,000,000
R&D Expense						
Operating Income	4,668,000,000	4,194,000,000	3,940,000,000	3,464,000,000	4,365,000,000	3,458,000,000
Operating Margin %	4.51%	5.49%	5.45%	4.83%	6.04%	5.12%
SGA Expense	22,571,000,000	17,992,000,000	17,543,000,000	16,878,000,000	16,561,000,000	15,518,000,000
Net Income	4,220,000,000	1,932,000,000	2,450,000,000	2,127,000,000	2,714,000,000	2,091,000,000
Operating Cash Flow	5,664,000,000	3,893,000,000	4,301,000,000	4,431,000,000	3,643,000,000	3,744,000,000
Capital Expenditure	1,251,000,000	1,106,000,000	1,212,000,000	1,550,000,000	1,213,000,000	1,014,000,000
EBITDA	6,410,000,000	5,510,000,000	5,223,000,000	4,630,000,000	5,451,000,000	4,488,000,000
Return on Assets %	7.96%	5.31%	7.10%	6.98%	10.10%	8.13%
Return on Equity %	16.44%	9.68%	13.00%	12.85%	18.55%	14.53%
Debt to Equity	0.43	0.18	0.23	0.22	0.16	0.16

CONTACT INFORMATION:

Phone: 847 315-2500   Fax: 847 914-2804
Toll-Free: 800-925-4733
Address: 108 Wilmot Rd., Deerfield, IL 60015 United States

SALARIES/BONUSES:

Top Exec. Salary: Bonus: $
$1,381,667
Second Exec. Salary: Bonus: $
$820,833

STOCK TICKER/OTHER:

Stock Ticker: WBA   Exchange: NAS
Employees: 251,000   Fiscal Year Ends: 08/31
Parent Company:

OTHER THOUGHTS:

Estimated Female Officers or Directors: 7

Hot Spot for Advancement for Women/Minorities: Y

Sales, profits and employees may be estimates. Financial information, benefits and other data can change quickly and may vary from those stated here.

Walking Company Holdings Inc (The)   www.thewalkingcompany.com

NAIC Code: 448210

TYPES OF BUSINESS:

Shoe Stores
Accessories & Gifts
Catalog & Online Sales

BRANDS/DIVISIONS/AFFILIATES:

Walking Company (The)
BigDogs.com
Big Dog USA Inc

GROWTH PLANS/SPECIAL FEATURES:

The Walking Company Holdings, Inc. is the parent company to two retail entities: The Walking Company and Big Dog USA, Inc. The Walking Company, a retailer of comfort footwear and accessories, operates over 200 specialty stores in malls across the country. The chain sells walk-wear and walking accessories from around the world under the ABEO, Ecco, Dansko, Merrell, Ugg, Pikolinos, Mephisto, Keen, Beautifeel, Sofft, Naot, Earth, Born, Olukai, Suzzato, Anhu, Ara, Asics, Birkenstock, Cobb Hill, Haflinger, Klogs, New Balance, Rockport, Trotters and Tommy Bahama brands. Big Dogs USA develops, markets and retails active-wear, casual sportswear, accessories and gifts online at BigDogs.com.

The firm offers its employees a 401(k) savings plan and medical, dental and vision insurance.

CONTACTS: *Note: Officers with more than one job title may be intentionally listed here more than once.*

Andrew D. Feshbach, CEO
Andrew D. Feshbach, Pres.
Roberta J. Morris, CFO
Michael Grenley, Sr. VP-Merch.
Fred Kayne, Chmn.

FINANCIAL DATA: *Note: Data for latest year may not have been available at press time.*

In U.S. $	2015	2014	2013	2012	2011	2010
Revenue						
R&D Expense						
Operating Income						
Operating Margin %						
SGA Expense						
Net Income						
Operating Cash Flow						
Capital Expenditure						
EBITDA						
Return on Assets %						
Return on Equity %						
Debt to Equity						

CONTACT INFORMATION:

Phone: 805-963-8727   Fax: 805-962-9460
Toll-Free: 800-642-9265
Address: 121 Gray Ave., Ste. 300, Santa Barbara, CA 93101 United States

STOCK TICKER/OTHER:

Stock Ticker: WALK   Exchange: PINX
Employees: 2,300   Fiscal Year Ends: 12/31
Parent Company:

SALARIES/BONUSES:

Top Exec. Salary: $ Bonus: $
Second Exec. Salary: $ Bonus: $

OTHER THOUGHTS:

Estimated Female Officers or Directors: 1
Hot Spot for Advancement for Women/Minorities:

Walmart de Mexico Y Centroamerica www.walmartmexicoycam.com

NAIC Code: 452112

TYPES OF BUSINESS:

Discount Department Stores

BRANDS/DIVISIONS/AFFILIATES:

Supertiendas Paiz
La Despensa de Don Juan
La Union
Mas x Menos
Walmart
Maxi Pali
ClubCo
Bodega Aurreras

CONTACTS: *Note: Officers with more than one job title may be intentionally listed here more than once.*

Scot Rank, CEO
Scot Rank, Pres.
Eduardo Solorzano Morales, Chmn.

GROWTH PLANS/SPECIAL FEATURES:

Walmart de Mexico Y Centroamerica is a retailer that operate several Walmart discount stores, supermarkets, wineries hypermarkets, membership warehouse clubs, clothing stores restaurants and banks in Mexico, Costa Rica, El Salvado Guatemala, Honduras and Nicaragua. Walmart Mexico an Central Walmart operated independently until 2010, whe Walmart de Mexico acquired the central branch, expanding it presence into 540 cities. In Mexico, the company operate more than 2,290 retail locations, including Walma Supercenters, Sam's Clubs, Bodega Aurreras, Superamas Surburbias and Factura Electronica. In Central America, th company operates retail locations under several brand including Supertiendas Paiz, La Despensa de Don Juan, L Union, Mas x Menos, Maxi Pali, Maxi Despensa, Walmar Despensa Familiar, Pali and ClubCo. The firm has 2! distribution centers across Central America and purchases it products from over 28,000 suppliers. The real estate divisio rents out commercial space in its existing stores to loca businesses and entrepreneurs.

FINANCIAL DATA: *Note: Data for latest year may not have been available at press time.*

In U.S. $	2015	2014	2013	2012	2011	2010
Revenue		26,628,470,000	25,396,000,000	24,986,280,000	23,000,550,000	20,280,310,000
R&D Expense						
Operating Income		2,096,292,000	1,903,998,000	1,956,374,000	1,816,259,000	1,633,046,000
Operating Margin %		7.87%	7.49%	7.82%	7.89%	8.05%
SGA Expense			3,749,935,000	3,739,348,000	3,237,767,000	2,838,940,000
Net Income		1,837,231,000	1,371,730,000	1,405,441,000	1,343,770,000	1,180,527,000
Operating Cash Flow		2,303,789,000	1,733,184,000	1,789,831,000	1,964,361,000	1,743,032,000
Capital Expenditure		766,327,600	844,587,600	885,198,200	1,108,180,000	792,836,000
EBITDA		2,684,200,000	2,428,713,000	2,470,542,000	2,278,122,000	2,055,300,000
Return on Assets %		12.77%	10.03%	10.40%	10.60%	11.92%
Return on Equity %		20.75%	16.07%	17.07%	17.42%	19.01%
Debt to Equity						

CONTACT INFORMATION:

Phone: 52 53283500   Fax: 52 53283557
Toll-Free:
Address: Nextengo N 78, Mexico DF, 02770 Mexico

STOCK TICKER/OTHER:

Stock Ticker: WMMVF
Employees: 170,014
Parent Company:

Exchange: PINX
Fiscal Year Ends: 12/31

SALARIES/BONUSES:

Top Exec. Salary: $ Bonus: $
Second Exec. Salary: $ Bonus: $

OTHER THOUGHTS:

Estimated Female Officers or Directors:
Hot Spot for Advancement for Women/Minorities:

Wal-Mart Stores Inc

www.walmartstores.com

NAIC Code: 452910

TYPES OF BUSINESS:

Supercenters
Supermarkets
Warehouse Membership Clubs
Online Sales
Pharmacies
Vision Centers
Auto Repair Centers

BRANDS/DIVISIONS/AFFILIATES:

Sam's Club
Wal-Mart Supercenter
Marketside
Neighborhood Markets
Walmart.com
Walmart
Wal-Mart
Plus Members

CONTACTS: *Note: Officers with more than one job title may be intentionally listed here more than once.*

Neil Ashe, CEO, Divisional
M. Chambers, Executive VP, Divisional
Rosalind Brewer, CEO, Divisional
David Cheesewright, CEO, Divisional
Gregory Foran, CEO, Divisional
C. McMillon, CEO
Brett Biggs, CFO, Divisional
Charles Holley, CFO
S. Walton, Chairman of the Board
Steven Whaley, Chief Accounting Officer
Rollin Ford, Chief Administrative Officer
Greg Penner, Director
Daniel Bartlett, Executive VP, Divisional
Jeffrey Gearhart, Executive VP, Divisional
Gordon Allison, General Counsel

GROWTH PLANS/SPECIAL FEATURES:

Wal-Mart Stores, Inc., one of the world's largest retailers, operates through a massive base of Wal-Mart stores, supercenters, Sam's Clubs, Marketside, Neighborhood Markets and Walmart.com. The company operates in three business segments: Walmart U.S., Walmart international and Sam's Club. Walmart U.S. is a mass merchandiser of consumer products, operating under the Walmart or Wal-Mart brands, as well as Walmart.com. This segment operates retail stores in the USA, including all 50 states, Washington D.C. and Puerto Rico, with supercenters in 49 states, Washington D.C. and Puerto Rica, discount stores in 42 states and Puerto Rico and Neighborhood Markets and other small formats in 31 states and Puerto Rico. Walmart international consists of operations in 26 countries outside the USA, and includes numerous formats divided into three major categories: retail, wholesale and other. These categories consist of formats such as supercenters, supermarkets, hypermarkets, warehouse clubs (including Sam's Clubs), cash & carry, home improvement, specialty electronics, restaurants, apparel stores, drug stores and convenience stores. Sam's Club operates membership-only warehouse clubs, as well as samsclub.com in the U.S. All memberships include a spouse/household card at no additional cost and Plus Members are eligible for cash rewards which provides $10 for every $500 in qualifying Sam's Club purchases up to a $500 cash reward annually.

FINANCIAL DATA: *Note: Data for latest year may not have been available at press time.*

In U.S. $	2015	2014	2013	2012	2011	2010
Revenue	485,651,000,000	476,294,000,000	469,162,000,000	446,950,000,000	421,849,000,000	408,214,000,000
R&D Expense						
Operating Income	27,147,000,000	26,872,000,000	27,801,000,000	26,558,000,000	25,542,000,000	23,950,000,000
Operating Margin %	5.58%	5.64%	5.92%	5.94%	6.05%	5.86%
SGA Expense	93,418,000,000	91,353,000,000	88,873,000,000	85,265,000,000	81,020,000,000	79,607,000,000
Net Income	16,363,000,000	16,022,000,000	16,999,000,000	15,699,000,000	16,389,000,000	14,335,000,000
Operating Cash Flow	28,564,000,000	23,257,000,000	25,591,000,000	24,255,000,000	23,643,000,000	26,249,000,000
Capital Expenditure	12,174,000,000	13,115,000,000	12,898,000,000	13,510,000,000	12,699,000,000	12,184,000,000
EBITDA	36,433,000,000	35,861,000,000	36,489,000,000	34,850,000,000	33,384,000,000	31,288,000,000
Return on Assets %	8.01%	7.85%	8.57%	8.39%	9.32%	8.58%
Return on Equity %	20.75%	20.99%	23.02%	22.45%	23.53%	21.07%
Debt to Equity	0.53	0.58	0.54	0.66	0.63	0.51

CONTACT INFORMATION:

Phone: 479 273-4000   Fax: 479 273-1986
Toll-Free: 800-925-6278
Address: 702 SW 8th St., Bentonville, AR 72716 United States

SALARIES/BONUSES:

Top Exec. Salary:
$1,152,850   Bonus: $551,852
Second Exec. Salary:
$846,910   Bonus: $500,000

STOCK TICKER/OTHER:

Stock Ticker: WMT   Exchange: NYS
Employees: 2,200,000   Fiscal Year Ends: 01/31
Parent Company:

OTHER THOUGHTS:

Estimated Female Officers or Directors: 13

Hot Spot for Advancement for Women/Minorities: Y

Sales, profits and employees may be estimates. Financial information, benefits and other data can change quickly and may vary from those stated here.

Warby Parker

NAIC Code: 446130

TYPES OF BUSINESS:

Eyeglasses Sales Online and Retail

BRANDS/DIVISIONS/AFFILIATES:

monacle

GROWTH PLANS/SPECIAL FEATURES:

Warby Parker is a brand of prescription eyeglasses and sunglasses. It sells its products online and has a limited number of showrooms in the U.S., including Philadelphia, Oklahoma City, Chicago, Miami Beach, Charleston, Nashville, Dallas and Richmond. It has retail stores in Atlanta, New York City, Los Angeles, San Francisco and Boston. Warby Parker's frames feature a vintage-inspired style, designs its glasses in-house and sells directly to customers in order to avoid retail markups. A price of $95.00 is possible for a pair of Warby Parker glasses because of its in-house design, the elimination of licensing fees and direct-sell procedure. Customers can order online, choosing either acetate or metal materials, various colors, frame shapes and widths. Select eyewear offers home try-ons, allowing customers to choose five frames from the website, which they receive to try on at home for five days free of charge. Warby Parker's signature offering is a monocle, available with a prescription lens. As of June 2015, the firm had 12 retail outlets. It plans to expand to 20 over the near term.

CONTACTS:
Note: Officers with more than one job title may be intentionally listed here more than once.

David Gilboa, CEO

FINANCIAL DATA:
Note: Data for latest year may not have been available at press time.

In U.S. $	2015	2014	2013	2012	2011	2010
Revenue		40,000,000	35,000,000			
R&D Expense						
Operating Income						
Operating Margin %						
SGA Expense						
Net Income						
Operating Cash Flow						
Capital Expenditure						
EBITDA						
Return on Assets %						
Return on Equity %						
Debt to Equity						

CONTACT INFORMATION:

Phone: 646-517-5223   Fax:

Toll-Free:

Address: 161 Ave. of the Americas, New York, NY 10013 United States

STOCK TICKER/OTHER:

Stock Ticker: Private   Exchange:

Employees: Fiscal Year Ends:

Parent Company:

SALARIES/BONUSES:

Top Exec. Salary: $ Bonus: $

Second Exec. Salary: $ Bonus: $

OTHER THOUGHTS:

Estimated Female Officers or Directors:

Hot Spot for Advancement for Women/Minorities:

Warnaco Swimwear Inc

www.speedousa.com

NAIC Code: 424300

TYPES OF BUSINESS:

Apparel and Clothing Brands, Designers, Importers and Distributors
Online Sales
Aquatic Fitness Equipment
Swim Accessories

BRANDS/DIVISIONS/AFFILIATES:

Warnaco Group Inc (The)
FastSkin FS-Pro
FastSkin LZR Racer
PVH Corp

CONTACTS: Note: Officers with more than one job title may be intentionally listed here more than once.

Martha Olson, Pres.
James Christl, CFO

GROWTH PLANS/SPECIAL FEATURES:

Warnaco Swimwear, Inc., the swimwear marketing arm of Warnaco Group, Inc., which itself is owned by PVH Corp., designs, manufactures and markets swimwear, swim accessories and active fitness apparel. Its products are primarily sold under the Speedo brand name, which the firm has licensed in North America and the Caribbean, from British firm the Pentland Group, whose Speedo International affiliate provides the company with various apparel accessories. Throughout the U.S., Mexico, Canada and the Caribbean, Warnaco distributes Speedo fitness and fashion swimwear, Speedo swimwear for kids, Speedo footwear, Speedo active apparel and aquatic fitness equipment. Speedo is sold in over 11,000 stores in North America and is available in approximately 170 countries worldwide. Other distribution channels include department stores, independent retailers, chain stores, sporting goods stores, team dealers, membership clubs and other retailers as well as the company's SpeedoUSA.com web site. The swimwear accessories line includes a diverse range of products such as swim goggles; swimming fins; swim caps; kickboards; nose clips; earplugs; duffle bags and backpacks; watches; waterproof digital cameras and MP3 players; swimming vests; masks and snorkels; and aquatic exercise gear such as leg trainers, barbells and swimming gloves. The company often forms long-term promotional contracts with Olympic medalists and world-champion swimmers to better market its products. Warnaco products also include FastSkin FS-Pro, a line of high-quality skin-like bodysuits for swim racing; and FastSkin LZR Racer, which was co-developed by Speedo's research and development facility Aqualab and NASA. Warnaco also markets Calvin Klein-brand swimwear, which is distributed in the U.S., Europe, Canada, Mexico and Asia through department stores, high-end specialty stores and boutiques, including Saks, Bloomingdale's, Nordstrom, Macy's and Dillard's.

FINANCIAL DATA: Note: Data for latest year may not have been available at press time.

In U.S. $	2015	2014	2013	2012	2011	2010
Revenue						
R&D Expense						
Operating Income						
Operating Margin %						
SGA Expense						
Net Income						
Operating Cash Flow						
Capital Expenditure						
EBITDA						
Return on Assets %						
Return on Equity %						
Debt to Equity						

CONTACT INFORMATION:

Phone: 213-482-7622   Fax:
Toll-Free: 888-477-3336
Address: 1201 W. 5th St., #1100, Los Angeles, CA 90017 United States

STOCK TICKER/OTHER:

Stock Ticker: Subsidiary
Employees:
Parent Company: PVH Corp

Exchange:
Fiscal Year Ends: 12/31

SALARIES/BONUSES:

Top Exec. Salary: $ Bonus: $
Second Exec. Salary: $ Bonus: $

OTHER THOUGHTS:

Estimated Female Officers or Directors: 1
Hot Spot for Advancement for Women/Minorities:

Wawa Inc

NAIC Code: 447110

www.wawa.com

TYPES OF BUSINESS:

Convenience Stores
Gas Stations
Dairy Operations
Wholesale Distribution

BRANDS/DIVISIONS/AFFILIATES:

Wawa Dairy
Wawa Real Estate
Wawa Foundation Inc (The)

CONTACTS: *Note: Officers with more than one job title may be intentionally listed here more than once.*

Chris Gheysens, CEO
Chris Gheysens, Pres.
Jim Morey, CFO
Kathy Curry, Coordinator-Eng. & Construction
Salvatore J. Mattera, VP-Store Oper.
Susan Bratton, Sr. Mgr.-Real Estate
Patrick Cerrone, Div. Mgr.-Real Estate
Mary Ann Souder, Sr. Property Mgr.
Richard D. Wood Jr., Chmn.

GROWTH PLANS/SPECIAL FEATURES:

Wawa, Inc. owns and operates convenience stores. The fir
has over 645 Wawa convenience stores in Delaware
Maryland, New Jersey, Pennsylvania, Florida and Virginia.
supplies its stores with a large fresh food selection, whic
includes Wawa-brand built-to-order hoagies, fresh coffee an
coffee products, breakfast sandwiches, wraps, soups an
sides, rice bowls, party platters, dairy products, juices and teas
ready-to-go salads and fresh fruit and produce. The company'
Wawa Dairy division supplies artificial growth hormone-fre
dairy products to Wawa stores, producing and distributing th
company's line of milk, ice cream, flavored iced teas, juices an
fruit drinks. Wawa Dairy also oversees the firm's wholesal
operations. It is a major supplier of dairy products t
approximately 1,000 institutional customers, including schoo
districts, colleges, universities, hospitals, nursing homes
restaurants and hotels. The division handles the distribution c
its products at its 82,000-square-foot refrigerated warehous
facility, located in Wawa, Pennsylvania. More than 365 Waw
stores also feature gasoline sales, with 16 dispensers and dail
fuel deliveries. Wawa's Real Estate division handles th
acquisition/building of store locations as well as th
management and maintenance of existing stores. Th
company also maintains an e-commerce site that sells novelt
items, coffee and store gift cards and provides nutritiona
information about its products. In 2014, to celebrate its 50t
anniversary, Wawa launched The Wawa Foundation, Inc. t
donate $50 million to health and hunger initiatives.

Wawa provides employees benefits such as an employee stoc
ownership plan, a 401(k) plan, prescription drug coverage
dental and vision coverage, various life and supplemental lif
insurances, disability coverage, flexible health spendin
accounts, reimbursement for fitness centers and weigh
management programs, educational assistance plans
employee assistance programs and an employee credit union

FINANCIAL DATA: *Note: Data for latest year may not have been available at press time.*

In U.S. $	2015	2014	2013	2012	2011	2010
Revenue		9,330,000,000	7,350,000,000	7,250,000,000	7,000,000,000	5,700,000,000
R&D Expense						
Operating Income						
Operating Margin %						
SGA Expense						
Net Income						
Operating Cash Flow						
Capital Expenditure						
EBITDA						
Return on Assets %						
Return on Equity %						
Debt to Equity						

CONTACT INFORMATION:

Phone: 610-358-8000   Fax: 610-358-8878
Toll-Free: 800-444-9292
Address: 260 W. Baltimore Pike, Wawa, PA 19063 United States

STOCK TICKER/OTHER:

Stock Ticker: Private
Employees: 20,400
Parent Company:

Exchange:
Fiscal Year Ends: 12/31

SALARIES/BONUSES:

Top Exec. Salary: $ Bonus: $
Second Exec. Salary: $ Bonus: $

OTHER THOUGHTS:

Estimated Female Officers or Directors:
Hot Spot for Advancement for Women/Minorities: Y

Wegman's Food Markets Inc

www.wegmans.com

NAIC Code: 445110

TYPES OF BUSINESS:

Grocery Stores/Supermarkets
Home Improvement Stores
Restaurants
Photo Processing
Pharmacies

BRANDS/DIVISIONS/AFFILIATES:

Wegmans Market Cafe
Ultimate Coffee Adventure (The)
WKids Fun Center

CONTACTS: Note: Officers with more than one job title may be intentionally listed here more than once.

Daniel R. Wegman, CEO
Colleen Wegman, Pres.
Colleen Wegman, Pres.
Daniel R. Wegman, Chmn.

GROWTH PLANS/SPECIAL FEATURES:

Wegmans Food Markets, Inc., founded in 1916, is a regional supermarket chain in the northeastern U.S. The company operates 85 stores in New York, New Jersey, Pennsylvania, Virginia, Maryland and Massachusetts. Wegmans supermarkets are larger than average, ranging from 80,000 to 140,000 square feet in size. They offer over 70,000 products as well as amenities such as photo labs, pharmacies, in-store dining and child play centers. Typical selection includes produce, artisan breads and other baked goods, seafood, meat, deli products, international foods and specialty cheeses in addition to standard groceries and household items. Its Market Cafes offer in-store or take-out dining including hot soups and sandwiches, a Chinese buffet, fruit and grain bars, pizza and sushi as well as The Ultimate Coffee Adventure, a cappuccino bar. Other offerings include ready-to-cook meals, European bakeries, French pastries, natural foods and supplements, upscale kitchen cookware, floral shops, gift shops, cosmetics and WKids Fun Centers. Wegmans focuses on serving upscale working couples by featuring depth of selection, cooking demonstrations and a broad range of freshly prepared meals to go.

Wegmans offers employees benefits including medical and dental insurance, life insurance, flexible spending accounts, a 401(k) savings plan, Wegmans retirement plan, adoption assistance, disability benefits, an employee assistance program, scholarship competition and employee discounts.

FINANCIAL DATA: Note: Data for latest year may not have been available at press time.

In U.S. $	2015	2014	2013	2012	2011	2010
Revenue		6,900,000,000	6,850,000,000	5,800,000,000	5,600,000,000	5,200,000,000
R&D Expense						
Operating Income						
Operating Margin %						
SGA Expense						
Net Income						
Operating Cash Flow						
Capital Expenditure						
EBITDA						
Return on Assets %						
Return on Equity %						
Debt to Equity						

CONTACT INFORMATION:

Phone: 585-328-2550   Fax:
Toll-Free: 800-934-6267
Address: 1500 Brooks Ave., Rochester, NY 14603 United States

STOCK TICKER/OTHER:

Stock Ticker: Private
Employees: 44,000
Parent Company:

Exchange:
Fiscal Year Ends: 12/31

SALARIES/BONUSES:

Top Exec. Salary: $ Bonus: $
Second Exec. Salary: $ Bonus: $

OTHER THOUGHTS:

Estimated Female Officers or Directors: 1
Hot Spot for Advancement for Women/Minorities:

Sales, profits and employees may be estimates. Financial information, benefits and other data can change quickly and may vary from those stated here.

Weis Markets Inc

NAIC Code: 445110

www.weismarkets.com

TYPES OF BUSINESS:

Grocery Stores
Ice Manufacturing
Ice Cream Manufacturing
Milk Processing
Meat Processing

BRANDS/DIVISIONS/AFFILIATES:

Weis Markets
Weis Club Preferred Shopper
Weis Gold Card

CONTACTS: *Note: Officers with more than one job title may be intentionally listed here more than once.*

Jonathan Weis, CEO
Scott Frost, CFO
Robert Weis, Chairman Emeritus
Jeanette Rogers, Chief Accounting Officer
Kurt Schertle, COO
Harold Graber, Director
David Gose, Senior VP, Divisional
James Marcil, Senior VP, Divisional

GROWTH PLANS/SPECIAL FEATURES:

Weis Markets, Inc. operates retail supermarkets. Founded in 1912, the company is a grocer in Pennsylvania and surrounding states under the brand name Weis Markets. The firm operates 25 stores in Maryland, five stores in New Jersey, nine stores in New York, 122 stores in Pennsylvania and two stores in West Virginia, for a total of 163 retail food stores operating under the Weis Markets trade name. Its retail food stores offer groceries, dairy products, frozen foods, meats, seafood, fresh produce, floral items, pharmacy services, deli/bakery products, prepared foods, fuel, beer and wine and general merchandise (health, beauty, and household products). In addition, many locations offer services such as in-store banks, laundry services and take-out restaurants. The company also utilizes a loyalty card program, Weis Club Preferred Shopper, which provides members with an opportunity to receive discounts, promotions and rewards. Certain customers, specifically those who spent at least $3,500 in a calendar year, are eligible for the Gold Card. It affords a special value to these loyal customers and gives them exclusive access to personalized offers. Weis Markets also operates an ice cream plant, an ice plant, a meat processing plant and a milk processing plant at its warehouse in Sunbury, Pennsylvania, with a total of 259,000 square feet. This allows Weis Markets to offer private label products. In addtion, the company operates a 1.1 million square-foot distribution center in Milton, Pennsylvania and a 76,000 square-foot distribution center in Northumberland. Moreover, Weis Markets owns and operates a single Save-A-Lot food store. Center store contributions (consisting of groceries, dairy products, frozen foods, alcohol and general merchandise) account for 57.9.0% of net sales; fresh (meats, seafood, produce, floral and bakery products) account for 29%; pharmacy services, 9%; fuel, 3.9%; and other, 0.2%.

FINANCIAL DATA: *Note: Data for latest year may not have been available at press time.*

In U.S. $	2015	2014	2013	2012	2011	2010
Revenue		2,776,683,000	2,692,588,000	2,701,405,000	2,752,504,000	2,620,378,000
R&D Expense						
Operating Income		82,711,000	111,182,000	127,032,000	114,280,000	105,316,000
Operating Margin %		2.97%	4.12%	4.70%	4.15%	4.01%
SGA Expense		670,251,000	634,286,000	615,521,000	621,575,000	608,309,000
Net Income		55,167,000	71,721,000	82,511,000	75,584,000	68,291,000
Operating Cash Flow		123,110,000	142,632,000	123,961,000	152,409,000	146,742,000
Capital Expenditure		80,656,000	128,992,000	110,213,000	110,638,000	69,869,000
EBITDA		149,580,000	169,457,000	177,683,000	173,663,000	160,374,000
Return on Assets %		4.71%	6.40%	7.78%	7.47%	7.15%
Return on Equity %		6.52%	8.80%	10.70%	10.25%	9.62%
Debt to Equity						

CONTACT INFORMATION:

Phone: 570 286-4571   Fax:
Toll-Free: 866-999-9347
Address: 1000 S. 2nd St., Sunbury, PA 17801 United States

STOCK TICKER/OTHER:

Stock Ticker: WMK   Exchange: NYS
Employees: 18,200   Fiscal Year Ends: 12/31
Parent Company:

SALARIES/BONUSES:

Top Exec. Salary: $857,961   Bonus: $
Second Exec. Salary: Bonus: $
$848,678

OTHER THOUGHTS:

Estimated Female Officers or Directors:
Hot Spot for Advancement for Women/Minorities:

West Marine Inc

www.westmarine.com

NAIC Code: 441222

TYPES OF BUSINESS:

Boating Supplies, Retail
Catalog & Online Sales
Wholesale Operations
Marine Insurance
Financing
Boating Services

BRANDS/DIVISIONS/AFFILIATES:

Port Supply
West Advantage Rewards
Third Reef
Black Tip
Pure Oceans
Lifesling
Seafit

CONTACTS: Note: Officers with more than one job title may be intentionally listed here more than once.

Jeff Lasher, Assistant Secretary
Matthew Hyde, CEO
Barbara Rambo, Director
Randolph Repass, Director
Paul Rutenis, Executive VP, Divisional
Barry Kelley, Executive VP, Divisional
Pamela Fields, General Counsel
Deborah Ajeska, Vice President, Divisional

GROWTH PLANS/SPECIAL FEATURES:

West Marine, Inc. is a specialty retailer of recreational and commercial boating supplies in North America. The company operates 279 stores in 38 U.S. states, Puerto Rico and Canada under the brand name West Marine. The firm offers a selection of marine products ranging from boats and engines to clothing, safety products, deck hardware, navigational equipment and electronics. West Marine sells directly through its catalogs and an e-commerce web site as well as through its virtual call center, allowing customers access to technical product advice through trained sales representatives. The firm maintains two distribution centers located in Rock Hill, South Carolina and Hollister, California. West Marine's wholesale division, Port Supply, offers marine equipment at wholesale prices to customers involved in boat sales, boat building and boat commissioning. Additionally, the firm sells private label products under the brand names West Marine, Third Reef, Black Tip, Pure Oceans, Lifesling and Seafit. The firm also operates the West Advantage program, which includes both free and paid memberships that allow customers to earn points on qualifying purchases for future discounts, exclusive offers and invitations to unique shopping events designed to reward customers for their support and loyalty. In early 2015, the firm announced that its franchise agreement in Turkey terminated, causing the franchises to separate from West Marine. The company also announced it would be closing all of its Canadian stores by 2019 as their leases expire.

Employees receive medical, dental, vision and prescription drug coverage; life insurance; tuition reimbursement; flexible spending accounts; and merchandise discounts.

FINANCIAL DATA: Note: Data for latest year may not have been available at press time.

In U.S. $	2015	2014	2013	2012	2011	2010
Revenue		675,751,000	663,174,000	675,251,000	643,443,000	622,802,000
R&D Expense						
Operating Income		4,432,000	15,743,000	25,170,000	22,139,000	14,884,000
Operating Margin %		.65%	2.37%	3.72%	3.44%	2.38%
SGA Expense		188,755,000	175,892,000	172,837,000	162,860,000	160,838,000
Net Income		1,948,000	7,837,000	15,529,000	29,662,000	13,227,000
Operating Cash Flow		23,958,000	13,552,000	26,041,000	37,229,000	24,893,000
Capital Expenditure		24,573,000	28,553,000	17,953,000	17,710,000	14,139,000
EBITDA		22,666,000	30,703,000	40,471,000	36,453,000	29,810,000
Return on Assets %		.51%	2.18%	4.50%	9.20%	4.40%
Return on Equity %		.67%	2.76%	5.81%	12.42%	6.20%
Debt to Equity						

CONTACT INFORMATION:

Phone: 831-728-2700   Fax:
Toll-Free:
Address: 500 Westridge Dr., Watsonville, CA 95076 United States

SALARIES/BONUSES:

Top Exec. Salary: $600,000   Bonus: $
Second Exec. Salary: $358,240   Bonus: $

STOCK TICKER/OTHER:

Stock Ticker: WMAR
Employees: 3,642
Parent Company:

Exchange: NAS
Fiscal Year Ends: 12/31

OTHER THOUGHTS:

Estimated Female Officers or Directors: 6
Hot Spot for Advancement for Women/Minorities: Y

Western Beef Inc

www.westernbeef.com

NAIC Code: 445110

TYPES OF BUSINESS:

Warehouse Grocery Stores
Wholesale Food Distribution
Ethnic & Exotic Foods

GROWTH PLANS/SPECIAL FEATURES:

Western Beef, Inc. operates 28 high-volume, warehouse-typ
supermarkets in New York, New Jersey and Florida. Wester
Beef establishes supermarkets primarily in inner-cit
neighborhoods abandoned by many other supermarket chain:
It carries all major national and private label brands. Th
company also operates a wholesale food business, whic
deals mainly in beef, pork, poultry, provisions and private-lab
groceries to customers in New Jersey and New Yor
Operating its own meat, grocery and produce warehouse
allows the company to cut out the middle man and provid
lower priced products to customers. Western Beef provide
ethnic foods that suit the densely populated, culturally divers
make-up of the areas in which its stores are located. Since
large portion of the firm's customers come from foreig
countries, the supermarkets supply exotic, importe
ingredients. Western Beef performs extensive demographi
research on ethnic backgrounds, income levels, populatio
density and food preferences in order to stock the brands an
sizes of products that its customers prefer. The stores als
include brick-oven bakeries, which bake a variety of old-worl
bread and rolls from basic ingredients. The Western Bee
supermarkets are distinguishable from traditional supermarke
formats by their no-frills approach, including an unusually broa
selection of meat and produce and a very limited selection c
non-food items, such as health and beauty aids.

BRANDS/DIVISIONS/AFFILIATES:

CONTACTS: *Note: Officers with more than one job title may be intentionally listed here more than once.*

Peter Castellana, Jr., CEO
Peter Castellana, Jr., Pres.
Chris Darrow, CFO
Michael Castellana, Sr. VP-Retail Oper.
Peter R. Admirand, Corp. Sec.

FINANCIAL DATA: *Note: Data for latest year may not have been available at press time.*

In U.S. $	2015	2014	2013	2012	2011	2010
Revenue						
R&D Expense						
Operating Income						
Operating Margin %						
SGA Expense						
Net Income						
Operating Cash Flow						
Capital Expenditure						
EBITDA						
Return on Assets %						
Return on Equity %						
Debt to Equity						

CONTACT INFORMATION:

Phone: 718-218-4705   Fax:
Toll-Free:
Address: 47-05 Metropolitan Ave., Ridgewood, NY 11385 United States

STOCK TICKER/OTHER:

Stock Ticker: Private   Exchange:
Employees: Fiscal Year Ends: 12/31
Parent Company:

SALARIES/BONUSES:

Top Exec. Salary: $ Bonus: $
Second Exec. Salary: $ Bonus: $

OTHER THOUGHTS:

Estimated Female Officers or Directors:
Hot Spot for Advancement for Women/Minorities:

Wet Seal LLC (The)

www.wetseal.com

NAIC Code: 448120

TYPES OF BUSINESS:

Casual Apparel-Young Women's, Retail
Accessories
Footwear
Online Retailing

BRANDS/DIVISIONS/AFFILIATES:

Wet Seal
WetSeal.com
Blink by Wet Seal
iRunway
Versa Capital Management LLC
The Wet Seal Inc
Arden B

CONTACTS: Note: Officers with more than one job title may be intentionally listed here more than once.

Thomas Hillebrandt, CFO
Edmond Thomas, Director
Adam Rothstein, Director
John Mills, Director
Christine Lee, Executive VP
Kimberly Bajrech, Other Corporate Officer
Debra Shinn, Other Corporate Officer
Alyson Barker, Secretary

GROWTH PLANS/SPECIAL FEATURES:

The Wet Seal, LLC is a specialty clothing retailer offering moderately priced, fashionable and contemporary apparel and accessories designed for female consumers aged 15-39. The company operates 171 stores in 42 states under the Wet Seal name. All of the company's retail concepts offer a wide range of women's apparel, such as tops, sweaters, bottoms, dresses, outerwear, shoes and accessories. Most of its stores are located in regional, high-traffic shopping malls, which contain at least one anchor department store. The firm's locations target trendy young women by providing an ever-changing array of new apparel and accessories. It also operates an e-commerce site, WetSeal.com. The company's iPhone application, iRunway, offers customers the ability to view, purchase and share outfits created using Wet Seal products. The company does not design any of its apparel in-house, instead it relies on buying teams at each of its divisions to identify emerging fashion trends and work with vendors to develop consistent fashion themes. Wet Seal's most recent store concept, Blink by Wet Seal, focuses on denim products for young women. It also has store-in-store plus-size departments. In January 2015, the firm filed for Chapter 11 bankruptcy protection and closed 66% (338) of its stores, including all of its Arden B stores. That April, private equity company Versa Capital Management, LLC purchased it out of bankruptcy and changed its name from The Wet Seal, Inc. to The Wet Seal, LLC.

FINANCIAL DATA: Note: Data for latest year may not have been available at press time.

In U.S. $	2015	2014	2013	2012	2011	2010
Revenue		530,134,000	580,397,000	620,097,000	581,194,000	560,918,000
R&D Expense						
Operating Income		-37,946,000	-70,289,000	25,000,000	25,247,000	22,852,000
Operating Margin %		-7.15%	-12.11%	4.03%	4.34%	4.07%
SGA Expense		158,311,000	183,790,000	165,933,000	150,432,000	141,633,000
Net Income		-38,383,000	-113,231,000	15,082,000	12,570,000	93,430,000
Operating Cash Flow		-17,589,000	-26,191,000	61,900,000	50,080,000	40,456,000
Capital Expenditure		21,464,000	20,406,000	26,486,000	30,727,000	21,304,000
EBITDA		-24,022,000	-52,650,000	44,612,000	42,397,000	38,440,000
Return on Assets %		-20.29%	-40.65%	4.31%	3.47%	30.58%
Return on Equity %		-39.15%	-61.23%	5.83%	4.63%	42.67%
Debt to Equity						0.01

CONTACT INFORMATION:

Phone: 949 699-3900   Fax: 949 583-0715
Toll-Free:
Address: 26972 Burbank, Foothill Ranch, CA 92610 United States

STOCK TICKER/OTHER:

Stock Ticker: WTSLQ   Exchange: PINX
Employees: 7,413   Fiscal Year Ends: 01/31
Parent Company: Versa Capital Management LLC

SALARIES/BONUSES:

Top Exec. Salary: $800,000   Bonus: $
Second Exec. Salary: $449,858   Bonus: $50,000

OTHER THOUGHTS:

Estimated Female Officers or Directors: 13
Hot Spot for Advancement for Women/Minorities: Y

Weyco Group Inc

NAIC Code: 424340

www.weycogroup.com

TYPES OF BUSINESS:

Footwear Distribution
Men's Footwear, Retail

GROWTH PLANS/SPECIAL FEATURES:

Weyco Group, Inc. is a distributor of men's footwear. The firm sells mid-priced formal and casual men's footwear under the brands Florsheim, Nunn Bush, Stacy Adams, BOGS, Umi and Rafters. Products consist of both mid-priced leather dress shoes and leather casual footwear in addition to all weather boots. All of Weyco Group's shoes are purchased from outside suppliers. The firm operates in two segments: North American wholesale and North American retail. Wholesale distribution sales, which include both wholesale sales and licensing revenues, account for approximately 76% of Weyco Group's total sales. At the wholesale level, shoes are marketed nationwide through over 10,000 shoe, clothing and department stores. The North American retail operation, accounting for 7% of total sales, consists of 16 stores, primarily under the Florsheim banner, and an Internet business. In addition to the sale of the company's brands in these retail stores, other branded footwear and accessories are sold in order to enhance selection. Moreover, the firm provides distribution and retail services in Europe, South Africa, Australia and Asia Pacific, accounting for 17% of total sales. Weyco Group has licensing agreements with third parties who sell its branded shoes overseas and specialty shoe, apparel and accessory manufacturers in the U.S. It maintains a 1,025,000-square-foot office and distribution center in Glendale, Wisconsin as well as office and distribution properties in Canada, Italy, Australia, South Africa, Australia and China.

BRANDS/DIVISIONS/AFFILIATES:

Florsheim
Nunn Bush
Rafters
Bogs
Umi

CONTACTS: Note: Officers with more than one job title may be intentionally listed here more than once.

John Florsheim, Assistant Secretary
Thomas Florsheim, CEO
John Wittkowske, CFO
Thomas Florsheim, Chairman Emeritus
Anderson Judy, Chief Accounting Officer

FINANCIAL DATA: Note: Data for latest year may not have been available at press time.

In U.S. $	2015	2014	2013	2012	2011	2010
Revenue		320,488,000	300,284,000	293,471,000	271,100,000	229,231,000
R&D Expense						
Operating Income		30,657,000	27,755,000	29,797,000	23,197,000	18,781,000
Operating Margin %		9.56%	9.24%	10.15%	8.55%	8.19%
SGA Expense		92,411,000	89,558,000	85,090,000	83,525,000	71,516,000
Net Income		19,020,000	17,601,000	18,957,000	15,251,000	13,668,000
Operating Cash Flow		17,843,000	29,826,000	17,987,000	17,143,000	98,000
Capital Expenditure		2,890,000	2,699,000	9,695,000	8,344,000	1,665,000
EBITDA		35,256,000	32,797,000	35,136,000	28,477,000	24,233,000
Return on Assets %		6.98%	6.36%	6.78%	6.13%	6.34%
Return on Equity %		9.98%	9.66%	11.14%	9.01%	8.11%
Debt to Equity						

CONTACT INFORMATION:

Phone: 414 908-1600   Fax: 414 908-1601
Toll-Free:
Address: 333 W. Estabrook Blvd., Milwaukee, WI 53212 United States

STOCK TICKER/OTHER:

Stock Ticker: WEYS   Exchange: NAS
Employees: 640   Fiscal Year Ends: 12/31
Parent Company:

SALARIES/BONUSES:

Top Exec. Salary: $591,100   Bonus: $
Second Exec. Salary: Bonus: $
$565,200

OTHER THOUGHTS:

Estimated Female Officers or Directors: 5
Hot Spot for Advancement for Women/Minorities: Y

Whole Foods Market Inc

www.wholefoodsmarket.com

NAIC Code: 445110

TYPES OF BUSINESS:

Natural Foods Grocery Stores
Nutritional Supplements
Seafood Processing
Coffee Roasting
Supermarkets
Bakeries
Prepared Meals to Go

BRANDS/DIVISIONS/AFFILIATES:

Whole Catch
365 Everyday Value
Whole Foods Market
Allegro Coffee
Engine 2 Plant-Strong
Whole Paws
365

CONTACTS: Note: Officers with more than one job title may be intentionally listed here more than once.

Glenda Chamberlain, CFO
John Elstrott, Chairman of the Board
Jason Buechel, Chief Information Officer
John Mackey, Co-CEO
Walter Robb, Co-CEO
A.C. Gallo, COO
Kenneth Meyer, Executive VP, Divisional
David Lannon, Executive VP, Divisional
James Sud, Executive VP, Divisional

GROWTH PLANS/SPECIAL FEATURES:

Whole Foods Market, Inc. owns and operates a chain of natural organic food supermarkets in the U.S. and internationally. The firm's stores generally feature foods made from natural ingredients and free of chemical additives. Whole Foods' merchandise items includes organically grown and high-grade commercial produce; grocery products; environmentally safe household items; hormone- and antibiotic-free meats; bulk foods; fresh bakery goods; soups, salads, entrees and sandwiches; vitamins; cosmetics; and miscellaneous items. Merchandise is sold through its private-label brands: 365 Everyday Value, Whole Catch and Whole Foods Market, which are chef quality, all natural foods. Its stores, averaging 38,000 square feet in size, are supplemented by regional distribution centers, bakeries, commissary kitchens, seafood-processing facilities, produce procurement centers and a coffee roasting operation. The company operates a web site that offers features such as online recipes, health information and environmental issue information. Other brands include Allegro Coffee, Engine 2 Plant-Strong and Whole Paws. As part of a renewable energy initiative, the company has converted 17 locations to either use or host solar power to supplement traditional power, four stores with fuel cells, two with a rooftop farm and a commissary kitchen that is using biofuel from internally generated waste cooking oil. The company also installed electric vehicle charging stations at over 45 stores around the U.S. In addition, the firm discontinued the use of plastic bags and refunds at least a nickel per reusable bag at checkout. In May 2015, the firm announced plans to open, beginning in 2016, a smaller, value-focused chain of stores under the name 365. Eventually, the retailer plans to expand to 1,200 stores in the U.S. from 431 currently. The company is focusing on lowering its prices, improving its computer systems and enhancing operating efficiency. For 2015, sales per square foot of retail space per year were running $990. The prepared foods department accounts for about 20% of total sales.

Whole Foods offers employees life, disability, medical, dental and vision insurance; dependent care reimbursement; employee discounts; credit union; 401(k); paid time off; profit sharing and stock options.

FINANCIAL DATA: Note: Data for latest year may not have been available at press time.

In U.S. $	2015	2014	2013	2012	2011	2010
Revenue	15,389,000,000	14,194,000,000	12,917,000,000	11,698,830,000	10,107,790,000	9,005,794,000
R&D Expense						
Operating Income	861,000,000	934,000,000	883,000,000	743,506,000	547,620,000	437,975,000
Operating Margin %	5.59%	6.58%	6.83%	6.35%	5.41%	4.86%
SGA Expense	4,555,000,000	4,110,000,000	3,746,000,000	3,412,268,000	2,988,929,000	2,697,426,000
Net Income	536,000,000	579,000,000	551,000,000	465,573,000	342,612,000	245,833,000
Operating Cash Flow	1,129,000,000	1,088,000,000	1,009,000,000	919,715,000	754,845,000	585,285,000
Capital Expenditure	338,000,000	283,000,000	198,000,000	194,539,000	166,664,000	256,793,000
EBITDA	1,300,000,000	1,311,000,000	1,233,000,000	1,063,948,000	842,703,000	720,418,000
Return on Assets %	9.33%	10.26%	10.17%	9.71%	8.27%	6.18%
Return on Equity %	14.13%	15.05%	14.34%	13.70%	12.77%	12.01%
Debt to Equity	0.01	0.01				0.21

CONTACT INFORMATION:

Phone: 512 477-4455   Fax: 512 477-1069
Toll-Free:
Address: 550 Bowie St., Austin, TX 78703 United States

STOCK TICKER/OTHER:

Stock Ticker: WFM
Employees: 52,500
Parent Company:

Exchange: NAS
Fiscal Year Ends: 09/30

SALARIES/BONUSES:

Top Exec. Salary: $472,350   Bonus: $59,840
Second Exec. Salary: $472,350   Bonus: $59,840

OTHER THOUGHTS:

Estimated Female Officers or Directors: 9
Hot Spot for Advancement for Women/Minorities: Y

Sales, profits and employees may be estimates. Financial information, benefits and other data can change quickly and may vary from those stated here.

Wild Birds Unlimited Inc

www.wbu.com

NAIC Code: 453910

TYPES OF BUSINESS:
Bird Feeders & Accessories, Retail
Bird Watching Products

BRANDS/DIVISIONS/AFFILIATES:
Pathways to Nature Conservation Fund

CONTACTS: Note: Officers with more than one job title may be intentionally listed here more than once.
Jim Carpenter, CEO

GROWTH PLANS/SPECIAL FEATURES:
Wild Birds Unlimited, Inc. is a privately owned retail chain an franchise business based in Carmel, Indiana that provide products and advice to bird watching enthusiasts. The firm ha more than 250 franchised retail stores across the U.S. an Canada that offer an assortment of bird feeders, birdseed species identification books, bird houses, binoculars, spottin scopes and videos. Storeowners encourage communicatio between customers and employees regarding the birds in the backyards, making the storefront a forum for informatio exchange as well as a place for commerce. The firm is als interested in educating the public about the importance c environmental issues affecting birds and their habitats. Th company has many alliances with bird watching and wildlif associations and institutes, including the Cornell Laboratory c Ornithology, the National Fish and Wildlife Foundation, Bir Studies Canada and the Organization for Bat Conservatior Furthermore, the company has a high degree of concern fo threatened wild bird habitats. Due to this concern, Wild Bird Unlimited founded the Pathways to Nature Conservation Fun (PTN), which supports education, conservation and wildlif viewing projects at wildlife refuges, parks, sanctuaries an nature conservancies throughout North America. The fund i managed jointly with the National Fish and Wildlife Foundatio (NFWF).

FINANCIAL DATA: Note: Data for latest year may not have been available at press time.

In U.S. $	2015	2014	2013	2012	2011	2010
Revenue						
R&D Expense						
Operating Income						
Operating Margin %						
SGA Expense						
Net Income						
Operating Cash Flow						
Capital Expenditure						
EBITDA						
Return on Assets %						
Return on Equity %						
Debt to Equity						

CONTACT INFORMATION:
Phone: 317-571-7100   Fax: 317-571-7110
Toll-Free: 800-302-2473
Address: 11711 N. College Ave., Ste. 146, Carmel, IN 46032 United States

STOCK TICKER/OTHER:
Stock Ticker: Private
Employees:
Parent Company:
Exchange:
Fiscal Year Ends: 12/31

SALARIES/BONUSES:
Top Exec. Salary: $ Bonus: $
Second Exec. Salary: $ Bonus: $

OTHER THOUGHTS:
Estimated Female Officers or Directors:
Hot Spot for Advancement for Women/Minorities: Y

Williams Sonoma Inc

www.williams-sonomainc.com

NAIC Code: 442299

TYPES OF BUSINESS:

Housewares, Retail
Garden Supplies & Accessories
Home Furnishings & Accessories
Specialty Foods
Online & Catalog Sales
Outlet Stores
Lighting
Monograms

BRANDS/DIVISIONS/AFFILIATES:

Pottery Barn
Pottery Barn Kids
Pbteen
Rejuvenation
West Elm
Williams-Sonoma
Williams-Sonoma Home
Mark & Graham

CONTACTS: *Note: Officers with more than one job title may be intentionally listed here more than once.*

Laura Alber, CEO
Julie Whalen, CFO
Adrian Bellamy, Chairman of the Board
Patrick Connolly, Director
David King, General Counsel
Janet Hayes, President, Divisional
Sandra Stangl, President, Divisional

GROWTH PLANS/SPECIAL FEATURES:

Williams-Sonoma, Inc. is a national specialty retailer of high-quality cooking/serving equipment, home furnishings and home and garden accessories. The firm markets its products through 601 retail stores in the U.S., Puerto Rico, Australia, the U.K. and Canada; direct-mail catalogs; and e-commerce sites. The company offers home merchandise through eight brands: Williams-Sonoma, Williams-Sonoma Home, Pottery Barn, PBteen, Pottery Barn Kids, West Elm, Rejuvenation and Mark & Graham. Williams-Sonoma stores offer culinary and serving equipment, including cookware, dinnerware, cookbooks, cutlery, glassware and table linens. These stores also carry a variety of quality food, including a line of Williams-Sonoma food products. Williams-Sonoma Home offers an assortment of casually elegant furniture, lighting and decorative accessories. Pottery Barn stores feature casual home furnishings, flatware and table accessories. PB Teen offers home furnishings and decorative accessories that are specifically designed to reflect the personalities of the teenage market. Pottery Barn Kids features child-sized versions of much of the merchandise offered at Pottery Barn. West Elm features home furnishings such as furniture, lighting, tabletop items, textiles and decorative accessories that are designed in a modern style. Rejuvenation offers lighting and home-goods product lines inspired by periods that date back to the 1870's. With manufacturing facilities in Portland, Oregon, Rejuvenation offers a wide assortment of high-quality lights, hardware, furniture and home dÃ©cor. Mark & Graham offers personalized gift-buying items such as women's and men's accessories, small leather goods, jewelry, apparel, paper, home dÃ©cor and seasonal items which can be personalized with over 100 unique monogram and font-type treatments.

Williams-Sonoma offers employees health, life and travel insurance; tax-free commuter benefits; employee assistance programs; 401(k); long-term disability; and dependent care spending accounts.

FINANCIAL DATA: *Note: Data for latest year may not have been available at press time.*

In U.S. $	2015	2014	2013	2012	2011	2010
Revenue	4,698,719,000	4,387,889,000	4,042,870,000	3,720,895,000	3,504,158,000	3,102,704,000
R&D Expense						
Operating Income	502,265,000	452,098,000	409,163,000	381,732,000	323,414,000	121,442,000
Operating Margin %	10.68%	10.30%	10.12%	10.25%	9.22%	3.91%
SGA Expense	1,298,239,000	1,252,118,000	1,183,313,000	1,078,124,000	1,050,445,000	981,795,000
Net Income	308,854,000	278,902,000	256,730,000	236,931,000	200,227,000	77,442,000
Operating Cash Flow	461,697,000	453,769,000	364,127,000	291,334,000	355,989,000	490,718,000
Capital Expenditure	204,800,000	193,953,000	205,404,000	130,353,000	61,906,000	72,263,000
EBITDA	664,538,000	601,893,000	543,616,000	512,285,000	468,044,000	273,473,000
Return on Assets %	13.23%	12.32%	12.08%	11.30%	9.50%	3.85%
Return on Equity %	24.90%	21.74%	20.02%	18.84%	16.20%	6.56%
Debt to Equity						

CONTACT INFORMATION:

Phone: 415 421-7900   Fax: 415 434-0881
Toll-Free: 877-812-6235
Address: 3250 Van Ness Ave., San Francisco, CA 94109 United States

STOCK TICKER/OTHER:

Stock Ticker: WSM   Exchange: NYS
Employees: 26,800   Fiscal Year Ends: 01/31
Parent Company:

SALARIES/BONUSES:

Top Exec. Salary: Bonus: $
$1,409,619
Second Exec. Salary: Bonus: $
$1,160,945

OTHER THOUGHTS:

Estimated Female Officers or Directors: 2

Hot Spot for Advancement for Women/Minorities: Y

Sales, profits and employees may be estimates. Financial information, benefits and other data can change quickly and may vary from those stated here.

Wm Morrison Supermarkets PLC

www.morrisons.co.uk

NAIC Code: 445110

TYPES OF BUSINESS:

Supermarkets and Other Grocery (except Convenience) Stores

BRANDS/DIVISIONS/AFFILIATES:

Match & More
Morrisons

CONTACTS: *Note: Officers with more than one job title may be intentionally listed here more than once.*

Dalton T. Philips, CEO
Trevor Strain, Dir.-Group Finance
Charles McKendrick, Head-Asset Mgmt.
Neil Nugent, Head Chef

GROWTH PLANS/SPECIAL FEATURES:

Wm Morrison Supermarkets PLC operates as a food retailer, mainly grocery distribution. Operating more than 500 stores and an online home delivery service across the U.K., the company focuses on providing healthy, fresh food at an affordable price. Wm Morrison serves 11 million customers through its stores every week, as well as more than 11 million households through its Morrisons.com service. The firm is also involved in the manufacture and distribution of fresh food products, as well as in property development activities. It also operates as a fresh meat processor, produce packer, baby product retailer and grocery retailer. In 2014, the company began Match & More, promising to price match Asda, Tesco and Sainsbury's as well as Aldi and Lidl through a points-based card initiative. In October 2015, Morrison partnered with Motor Fuel Group to supply branded and own-brand food to the forecourt stores. The shops, all above 1,200 square feet, will be branded Morrisons and are expected to commence by year's end.

FINANCIAL DATA: *Note: Data for latest year may not have been available at press time.*

In U.S. $	2015	2014	2013	2012	2011	2010
Revenue	25,138,280,000	26,429,870,000	27,081,650,000	26,404,460,000	24,634,490,000	23,036,440,000
R&D Expense						
Operating Income	-1,040,452,000	-142,015,700	1,418,662,000	1,454,540,000	1,351,392,000	1,355,876,000
Operating Margin %	-4.13%	-.53%	5.23%	5.50%	5.48%	5.88%
SGA Expense	2,496,487,000	1,868,628,000	502,287,200			
Net Income	-1,137,621,000	-355,786,800	967,201,900	1,031,483,000	944,778,300	893,951,600
Operating Cash Flow	1,306,545,000	1,079,320,000	1,650,372,000	1,387,269,000	1,342,422,000	1,113,702,000
Capital Expenditure	777,349,200	1,524,800,000	1,465,004,000	1,189,942,000	884,982,200	1,369,331,000
EBITDA	-463,419,700	1,263,192,000	1,961,312,000	1,982,241,000	1,835,740,000	1,807,337,000
Return on Assets %	-7.64%	-2.23%	6.34%	7.26%	7.05%	7.04%
Return on Equity %	-18.36%	-4.79%	12.17%	12.75%	12.19%	12.63%
Debt to Equity	0.69	0.52	0.45	0.29	0.19	0.20

CONTACT INFORMATION:

Phone: 44 8456115000   Fax:
Toll-Free:
Address: Hilmore House, Gain Lane, Bradford,   BD3 7DL United Kingdom

STOCK TICKER/OTHER:

Stock Ticker: MRWSF
Employees: 119,778
Parent Company:

Exchange: PINX
Fiscal Year Ends: 01/31

SALARIES/BONUSES:

Top Exec. Salary: $ Bonus: $
Second Exec. Salary: $ Bonus: $

OTHER THOUGHTS:

Estimated Female Officers or Directors:
Hot Spot for Advancement for Women/Minorities:

Wolford AG

www.wolford.com

NAIC Code: 424300

TYPES OF BUSINESS:

Apparel and Clothing Brands, Designers, Importers and Distributors
Retail Stores
Intimate Apparel
Men's Socks
Swimwear
Knit Clothing

BRANDS/DIVISIONS/AFFILIATES:

Wolford

CONTACTS: *Note: Officers with more than one job title may be intentionally listed here more than once.*

Ashish Sensarma, CEO
Thomas Melzer, CFO
Axel Dreher, Head-Merch. & Prod. Mgmt.
Anton Mathis, Staff Council
Axel Dreher, Head-e-commerce & Wholesale Distribution
Sabine Labonte, Head-Corp. Comm.
Antonella Mei-Pochtler, Deputy Chmn.
Antonella Mei-Pochtler, Chmn.

GROWTH PLANS/SPECIAL FEATURES:

Wolford AG manufactures and distributes women's lingerie, swimwear, legwear and ready-to-wear collections, which evolved from its bodywear line. The company also offers a men's collection, which comprises socks and knee-highs with a soft band. Wolford sells its products through its own specialty stores, boutiques and department stores under the Wolford brand name. While the company also sells its products in department stores and factory outlets, a significant portion of its revenues come from the company's boutiques situated throughout the world. Around 121 of these boutiques are owned by Wolford, while the remaining 90 are owned and operated by various partners. The firm's international subsidiaries distribute its products in 60 countries. The U.S. is the largest market for Wolford's fashions, Germany is the second largest, and its presence is growing in Asian markets. The company's core focus is its existing products, but the firm also invests in research and development of new products and fabrics. The firm has also produced co-branded, collaborative collections with leading fashion houses such as Vivienne Westwood, Karl Lagerfeld, Missoni, Zac Posen and Valentino. Wolford plans to expand its presence through additional boutiques and shop-in-shops in the U.S., Spain, the Netherlands, Central and Eastern Europe and Asia/Oceania.

FINANCIAL DATA: *Note: Data for latest year may not have been available at press time.*

In U.S. $	2015	2014	2013	2012	2011	2010
Revenue	166,995,700	165,428,100	166,057,500	163,508,200	161,478,000	152,869,800
R&D Expense						
Operating Income	1,280,990	-6,245,755	-961,539	7,424,860	7,776,151	4,777,976
Operating Margin %	.76%	-3.77%	-.57%	4.54%	4.81%	3.12%
SGA Expense						72,226,820
Net Income	1,096,324	-2,986,500	-2,926,006	1,444,430	5,359,569	2,717,991
Operating Cash Flow	3,828,112	6,689,379	6,693,624	7,714,595	15,053,490	23,498,260
Capital Expenditure	11,794,240	7,914,120	6,220,284	8,772,712	6,438,912	8,858,677
EBITDA	11,805,910	3,534,132	8,486,161	16,451,220	16,053,240	12,660,260
Return on Assets %	.72%	-2.00%	-1.91%	.93%	3.48%	1.70%
Return on Equity %	1.38%	-3.68%	-3.40%	1.62%	6.18%	3.21%
Debt to Equity	0.06	0.08		0.21	0.12	0.20

CONTACT INFORMATION:

Phone: 43 55746900   Fax: 43 557479544
Toll-Free:
Address: Wolfordstrasse 1, Bregenz, 6900 Austria

SALARIES/BONUSES:

Top Exec. Salary: $ Bonus: $
Second Exec. Salary: $ Bonus: $

STOCK TICKER/OTHER:

Stock Ticker: WLFDY   Exchange: PINX
Employees: 1,574   Fiscal Year Ends: 04/30
Parent Company:

OTHER THOUGHTS:

Estimated Female Officers or Directors: 3
Hot Spot for Advancement for Women/Minorities: Y

Wolverine World Wide Inc

NAIC Code: 424340

www.wolverineworldwide.com

TYPES OF BUSINESS:

Footwear Distribution
Retail Stores
Work & Industrial Footwear
Slippers & Moccasins
Tanning Operations

BRANDS/DIVISIONS/AFFILIATES:

Hush Puppies
Sebago
Wolverine
HyTest
Merrell
Chaco
Bates
Cat Footwear

CONTACTS: Note: Officers with more than one job title may be intentionally listed here more than once.

Blake Krueger, CEO
Brendan Gibbons, General Counsel
Andrew Simister, President, Divisional
James Gabel, President, Divisional
Ted Gedra, President, Divisional
Michael Jeppesen, President, Divisional
James Zwiers, President, Divisional
Melissa Howell, Senior VP, Divisional
Michael Stornant, Senior VP

GROWTH PLANS/SPECIAL FEATURES:

Wolverine World Wide, Inc. designs, manufactures an markets a broad line of casual shoes and rugged outdoor an work footwear. Its products are marketed under recognize brand names, including Bates, Cat Footwear, Harley-Davidso Footwear, Hush Puppies, HyTest, Merrell, Chaco, Cush Sebago and Wolverine. The company's footwear products ar organized under three operating units. The Performance Grou produces merchandise under the Chaco, Cushe, Merrell an Saucony branded product lines. The Heritage Group consist of Wolverine boots, shoes and branded apparel; Sebag footwear and apparel; and footwear under the Cat, Bates Harley-Davidson, Sebago and HyTest brands. The Lifestyl Group includes Hush Puppies footwear and apparel; Sperr Top-Sider, Stride Rite, Hush Puppies and Keds brande merchandise; and Soft Style footwear. The firm also license its brands for use on non-footwear products including appare eyewear, watches, socks, gloves, handbags and othe accessories. Products are marketed worldwide in roughly 20 countries through company-owned wholesale operation licensees, distributors and retailers, including departmer stores, footwear chains, catalogs, specialty retailers, mas merchants and Internet retailers. Wolverine's consumer-direc operations consist of Wolverine's 417 owned or licensed store in North America and the U.K. and 64 e-commerce sites Additionally, through its Wolverine Leathers division, th company operates a tannery that produces pigskin leather fo the shoe and leather goods industries.

The firm offers employees disability, health, dental and lif insurance; a pension plan; a 401(k); a discount stock purchas plan; tuition reimbursement; wellness programs; and produc discounts.

FINANCIAL DATA: Note: Data for latest year may not have been available at press time.

In U.S. $	2015	2014	2013	2012	2011	2010
Revenue		2,761,100,000	2,691,100,000	1,640,838,000	1,409,068,000	1,248,517,000
R&D Expense						
Operating Income		229,900,000	192,300,000	113,724,000	170,218,000	142,247,000
Operating Margin %		8.32%	7.14%	6.93%	12.08%	11.39%
SGA Expense		815,200,000	872,200,000	514,436,000	386,534,000	347,499,000
Net Income		133,100,000	100,400,000	80,686,000	123,287,000	104,470,000
Operating Cash Flow		314,600,000	202,300,000	91,640,000	78,814,000	67,866,000
Capital Expenditure		30,000,000	41,700,000	14,942,000	19,397,000	16,370,000
EBITDA		280,200,000	235,900,000	141,623,000	186,212,000	159,998,000
Return on Assets %		5.19%	3.83%	4.65%	15.05%	13.98%
Return on Equity %		15.03%	13.56%	13.21%	21.96%	20.36%
Debt to Equity		0.91	1.30	1.89		

CONTACT INFORMATION:

Phone: 616 866-5500   Fax:
Toll-Free: 800-789-8586
Address: 9431 Courtland Dr. NE, Rockford, MI 49351 United States

STOCK TICKER/OTHER:

Stock Ticker: WWW
Employees: 6,600
Parent Company:

Exchange: NYS
Fiscal Year Ends: 12/31

SALARIES/BONUSES:

Top Exec. Salary:
$1,183,654
Second Exec. Salary:
$627,577

Bonus: $440,249

Bonus: $

OTHER THOUGHTS:

Estimated Female Officers or Directors: 4

Hot Spot for Advancement for Women/Minorities: Y

Sales, profits and employees may be estimates. Financial information, benefits and other data can change quickly and may vary from those stated here.

Yamada Denki Co

www.yamada-denki.jp

NAIC Code: 443141

TYPES OF BUSINESS:
Household Appliance Stores

BRANDS/DIVISIONS/AFFILIATES:
Minami-Kyushu Yamada Denki Co Ltd
California Integration Coordinators Inc
Yamada Eco Solution Co Ltd

GROWTH PLANS/SPECIAL FEATURES:
Yamada Denki Co., Ltd. is engaged in the sale and repair of electrical appliances, such as color televisions, videos, audios, refrigerators, washing machines, cooking appliances, air conditioners and other cooling and heating apparatus. It also engages in the collection of industrial wastes, the leasing of real estate properties, the purchase of secondhand personal computers, the credit card business and equipment works. Yamada owns several companies, including Minami-Kyushu Yamada Denki Co. Ltd., which sells household appliances; California Integration Coordinators, Inc., which provides circuit board related products and services; and Yamada Eco Solution Co. Ltd., which provides delivery and installation services of electrical products.

CONTACTS: Note: Officers with more than one job title may be intentionally listed here more than once.
Noboru Yamada, CEO
Tadao Ichimiya, COO
Tadao Ichimiya, Pres.
Noboru Yamada, Chmn.

FINANCIAL DATA: Note: Data for latest year may not have been available at press time.

In U.S. $	2015	2014	2013	2012	2011	2010
Revenue	13,506,650,000	15,369,900,000	13,807,870,000	14,895,020,000	17,474,060,000	16,361,320,000
R&D Expense						
Operating Income	161,638,000	278,066,300	275,347,700	722,071,600	996,250,800	708,478,700
Operating Margin %	1.19%	1.80%	1.99%	4.84%	5.70%	4.33%
SGA Expense						
Net Income	68,832,870	161,986,900	169,826,200	473,130,700	576,704,600	454,587,500
Operating Cash Flow	186,502,800	366,383,700	-103,784,900	278,017,600	755,287,000	1,085,144,000
Capital Expenditure	238,318,200	326,830,400	315,996,600	253,777,600	150,187,500	836,057,300
EBITDA	403,810,900	499,610,500	571,819,300	991,901,100	1,180,757,000	966,662,800
Return on Assets %	.80%	1.59%	2.13%	6.24%	7.73%	6.66%
Return on Equity %	1.84%	3.51%	4.21%	11.78%	16.19%	14.76%
Debt to Equity	0.46	0.26	0.30	0.18	0.42	0.58

CONTACT INFORMATION:
Phone: 81 272335522   Fax:
Toll-Free:
Address: 1-1 Sakae-cho, Tokyo, 371-0841 Japan

STOCK TICKER/OTHER:
Stock Ticker: YMDAF   Exchange: PINX
Employees: Fiscal Year Ends:
Parent Company:

SALARIES/BONUSES:
Top Exec. Salary: $ Bonus: $
Second Exec. Salary: $ Bonus: $

OTHER THOUGHTS:
Estimated Female Officers or Directors:
Hot Spot for Advancement for Women/Minorities:

Yankee Candle Company Inc

www.yankeecandle.com

NAIC Code: 453220

TYPES OF BUSINESS:

Gift/Sundry Stores
Home Decor Products
Retail Stores
Wholesale Sales

BRANDS/DIVISIONS/AFFILIATES:

Samplers
Tarts
Yankee Candle Car Jars
Yankee Candle
Jarden Corporation

CONTACTS: *Note: Officers with more than one job title may be intentionally listed here more than once.*

Hope Margala, CEO
Harlan M. Kent, Pres.
Brad Wolansky, CMO
Jeff Warhover, Dir-IT
Hope Margala Klein, Sr. VP-Brand, Innovation & Merch.
Lisa K. McCarthy, Sr. VP-Finance
Deborah Norris, Sr. VP- Fundraising & Canada
John Fontana, Pres., Int'l

GROWTH PLANS/SPECIAL FEATURES:

Yankee Candle Company, Inc. is a leading designer, manufacturer, retailer and wholesaler of premium scented candles in the giftware industry. The firm's candle products are available in over 150 fragrances as well as various sizes and styles. These include jar candles, Samplers votive candles, Tarts wax potpourri, pillars, tea lights, novelty candles and other candle products, primarily marketed under the Yankee Candle brand. The company also sells a wide range of coordinated candle and home decor accessories and has extended its brand into the premium home fragrance market segment, with products such as electric home air fresheners, potpourri, scented oils and oil warmers, reed diffusers, on-the-go travel sprays, room sprays, car gels and vent sticks and Yankee Candle Car Jars air fresheners as well as candle-related holders and accessories. The firm also offers personalized photo label candles and custom votives, as well as scent delivery systems that deliver consistent fragrance impressions for commercial environments. Yankee Candle products are sold through a wholesale network of approximately 19,100 specialty retailers in North America, primarily in non-mall locations, and 500 company-owned retail stores in the U.S. The company also has an international distribution and a Yankee Candle Fundraising division. Yankee Candle is a subsidiary of the Jarden Corporation.

Yankee Candle offers its full-time employees medical and dental insurance, voluntary vision insurance, a 401(k) plan, company-paid term life insurance, disability coverage, long-term care coverage, medical and dependent care reimbursement plans, discounts on products and an employee assistance program.

FINANCIAL DATA: *Note: Data for latest year may not have been available at press time.*

In U.S. $	2015	2014	2013	2012	2011	2010
Revenue		994,452,000	927,383,220	844,200,000	785,800,000	733,717,000
R&D Expense						
Operating Income						
Operating Margin %						
SGA Expense						
Net Income						
Operating Cash Flow						
Capital Expenditure						
EBITDA						
Return on Assets %						
Return on Equity %						
Debt to Equity						

CONTACT INFORMATION:

Phone: 413-665-8306   Fax: 413-665-4815
Toll-Free:
Address: 16 Yankee Candle Way, South Deerfield, MA 01373 United States

STOCK TICKER/OTHER:

Stock Ticker: Subsidiary   Exchange:
Employees: 1,690   Fiscal Year Ends: 12/31
Parent Company: JARDEN CORPORATION

SALARIES/BONUSES:

Top Exec. Salary: $ Bonus: $
Second Exec. Salary: $ Bonus: $

OTHER THOUGHTS:

Estimated Female Officers or Directors: 3
Hot Spot for Advancement for Women/Minorities: Y

Zara International Inc

NAIC Code: 448140

TYPES OF BUSINESS:

Apparel Manufacturing
Apparel Stores-Men, Women & Children
Household Linens
Teen Women's Clothing
Maternity Clothing
E-commerce

BRANDS/DIVISIONS/AFFILIATES:

Industria De Diseno Textil SA (INDITEX)
Zara Home
Zara
Zara for Mum
Kiddy's Class
Affinity Card
Lefties

CONTACTS: Note: Officers with more than one job title may be intentionally listed here more than once.

Oscar Perez Marcote, Managing Dir.

GROWTH PLANS/SPECIAL FEATURES:

Zara International, Inc. is the primary subsidiary of Inditex (Industria de Diseno Textil SA), one of the largest fashion retail groups in the world. Zara is considered Inditex's flagship brand, with around 2,000 Zara brand stores in 88 markets. Some Zara stores operate as Lefties, a brand for low-cost fashion. Zara sells women's, men's and children's apparel, offering chic, trendy looks for those on a budget. Zara also offers the maternity collection, Zara for Mum. Zara Kids carries children's appeal designed to suit children from toddlers to the pre-teens. In addition, the company has a juniors-focused Zara store, Kiddy's Class, in Spain. Moreover, the company operates Zara Home, an independent store concept at approximately 437 stores in 48 countries. Zara Home offers an exclusive line of textile products for the bed, table and bathroom as well as silverware, household items, small decorative objects and cosmetics. The company makes and markets special edition seasonal fragrances for men and women. Services offered at Zara include alterations, gift cards and the Affinity Card, which is Zara's own credit card and is currently only available in Spain, Greece, Italy, Portugal and Mexico.

FINANCIAL DATA: Note: Data for latest year may not have been available at press time.

In U.S. $	2015	2014	2013	2012	2011	2010
Revenue						
R&D Expense						
Operating Income						
Operating Margin %						
SGA Expense						
Net Income						
Operating Cash Flow						
Capital Expenditure						
EBITDA						
Return on Assets %						
Return on Equity %						
Debt to Equity						

CONTACT INFORMATION:

Phone: 34-981-185-400   Fax: 34-981-185-544
Toll-Free:
Address: Ave. de la Diputacion s/n, Edificio Inditex, Arteixo, 15142 Spain

STOCK TICKER/OTHER:

Stock Ticker: Subsidiary   Exchange:
Employees: Fiscal Year Ends: 01/31
Parent Company: INDITEX (INDUSTRIA DE DISENO TEXTIL SA)

SALARIES/BONUSES:

Top Exec. Salary: $ Bonus: $
Second Exec. Salary: $ Bonus: $

OTHER THOUGHTS:

Estimated Female Officers or Directors:
Hot Spot for Advancement for Women/Minorities:

Zegna (Ermenegildo Zegna Holditalia SpA)   www.zegna.com
NAIC Code: 424300

TYPES OF BUSINESS:
Apparel and Clothing Brands, Designers, Importers and Distributors
Fabric Manufacturing
Accessories
Womenswear

BRANDS/DIVISIONS/AFFILIATES:
Ermenegildo Zegna
Zegna Sport
Z Zegna
Agnona

CONTACTS: Note: Officers with more than one job title may be intentionally listed here more than once.
Ermenegildo Zegna, CEO
Paolo Zegna, Pres.
David Au, CMO
Benedetta Zegna, Mgr.-Talent
Anna Zegna, Dir.-Image
Paolo Zegna, Chmn.

GROWTH PLANS/SPECIAL FEATURES:
Zegna (Ermenegildo Zegna Holditalia SpA) is a world leader i
high-end menswear and sportswear, accessories and fabric
Founded as a textile mill, the company produces its own high
quality fabrics and supplies them to top designers and tailor
including a line of clothing for Gucci. Zegna fabrics are wove
from extra-fine materials like inner Mongolian cashmere, Sout
African kid mohair and superfine fibers from Australian merin
wool. In addition to this exclusive production process, th
company attaches high importance to design. Zegna als
carries a line of prescription eyewear, a sunglass collectio
and, through a partnership with Perofil, a luxury underwear lin
Over four generations of family members have owned an
operated the firm. With production plants in Spain, Switzerland
Mexico and Turkey, Zegna is present in 555 mono-brand store
(311 of which are under direct group ownership) in over 8
countries. These stores include three men's product line
Ermenegildo Zegna, the contemporary style with its exclusiv
luxury materials; Zegna Sport, a balance between a luxuriou
and a sporty look; and Z Zegna, the younger, more urba
brand. The women's clothing line, Agnona, focuses o
contemporary styles. Recently, the firm announced a licensin
agreement with Estee Lauder Companies, Inc., which allow
the exclusive rights for said company to market fragrance
under Zegna's brands. In 2014, the company signed a licensin
agreement with Marcolin Group to produce and distribut
sunglasses and eyeglasses for the brands Ermenegildo Zegn
and Agnona.

FINANCIAL DATA: Note: Data for latest year may not have been available at press time.

In U.S. $	2015	2014	2013	2012	2011	2010
Revenue		1,384,482,000	1,580,351,000	1,743,360,000	1,558,050,000	1,250,000,000
R&D Expense						
Operating Income						
Operating Margin %						
SGA Expense						
Net Income		81,238,200	138,871,791	179,728,000	158,161,000	
Operating Cash Flow						
Capital Expenditure						
EBITDA						
Return on Assets %						
Return on Equity %						
Debt to Equity						

CONTACT INFORMATION:
Phone: 39-01-575911   Fax: 39-015-756139
Toll-Free:
Address: Via Roma 99/100, Trivero, BI, 13835 Italy

STOCK TICKER/OTHER:
Stock Ticker: Private
Employees: 7,000
Parent Company:

Exchange:
Fiscal Year Ends: 12/31

SALARIES/BONUSES:
Top Exec. Salary: $ Bonus: $
Second Exec. Salary: $ Bonus: $

OTHER THOUGHTS:
Estimated Female Officers or Directors: 2
Hot Spot for Advancement for Women/Minorities: